IBM DICTIONARY
OF COMPUTING

IBM DICTIONARY OF COMPUTING

Compiled and edited by
GEORGE McDANIEL

McGRAW-HILL, INC.
New York   San Francisco   Washington, D.C.   Auckland   Bogotá
Caracas   Lisbon   London   Madrid   Mexico City   Milan
Montreal   New Delhi   San Juan   Singapore
Sydney   Tokyo   Toronto

6 7 8 9 0   DOC/DOC   9 9 8 7

ISBN 0-07-031488-8 (HC)
ISBN 0-07-031489-6 (PBK)

The sponsoring editor for this book was Daniel A. Gonneau and the production supervisor was Thomas G. Kowalczyk.

Printed and bound by R. R. Donnelley & Sons Company.

Tenth Edition (August 1993)

This is a major revision of the *IBM Dictionary of Computing,* SC20-1699-8, which is made obsolete by this edition. Changes are made periodically to the information provided herein.

It is possible that this material may contain reference to, or information about, IBM products (machines and programs), programming, or services that are not announced in your country. Such references or information must not be construed to mean that IBM intends to announce such IBM products, programming, or services in your country. Comments may be addressed to IBM Corporation, Department E37/656, P. O. Box 12195, Research Triangle Park, NC 27709.

International Edition

When ordering this title, use ISBN 0-07-113383-6.

This book is printed on acid-free paper.

Special Notice

The following terms are trademarks or registered trademarks of the IBM Corporation in the United States or other countries:

- ACF/VTAM
- Advanced Function Printing
- AFP
- AIXwindows
- AIX
- AIX Enhanced X-Windows
- AML/2
- Application System/400
- APPN
- AS/400
- BookMaster
- Common User Access
- CUA
- DATABASE 2
- DB2
- DFSMS
- ESCON
- Enterprise Systems Connection
- graPHIGS
- IBM
- IBM Operating System/2
- ImagePlus
- InfoExplorer
- InfoWindow
- LinkWay
- Micro Channel
- MVS/DFP
- MVS/ESA
- MVS/SP
- MVS/XA
- NetView
- Operating System/400
- OS/2
- OS/400
- PC Network
- PenPM operating system
- Port-A-Punch
- Presentation Manager
- PROFS
- PS
- PS/2
- RISC System/6000
- SAA
- Selectric
- SNAP/SHOT
- Storyboard
- System/360
- System/370

- Systems Application Architecture
- Ultimedia
- Virtual Machine/Extended Architecture
- VM/ESA
- VM/XA
- VTAM

The following terms are trademarks or registered trademarks of other organizations:

- AT&T (Trademark of American Telephone and Telegraph Co.)
- Beta (Trademark of Sony Corporation)
- Multimedia PC (Trademark of Multimedia PC Marketing Council)
- Mylar (Trademark of E.I. du Pont de Nemours & Co., Inc.)
- UNIX (Trademark of AT&T Bell Laboratories)
- XENIX (Trademark of the Microsoft Corporation with enhancements by the University of California at Berkeley)

Preface

Although this is the tenth edition of the *IBM Dictionary of Computing,* it is the first edition to be made generally available to the public. Beginning as a small manual more than 20 years ago, when it was used primarily as a reference for IBM's technical writers, it has grown steadily in size, scope, and audience. It now contains more than 22,000 entries selected from the full range of IBM's hardware and software products. In addition, it reprints by permission entries from industry standards in both the United States and the international community (see below).

This dictionary provides a comprehensive reference for anyone who uses, maintains, or has an interest in information processing systems, communication products and facilities, personal computers and office systems. Some of these terms may have other meanings in other contexts, or among people not familiar with the use of these terms in information processing, communication, personal computers, and office systems. With the exception of common electrical and metric measures, the dictionary excludes terms that are defined in nontechnical dictionaries and that have no special meaning in information processing.

Sources

This dictionary includes terms and definitions from:

- The *American National Standard Dictionary for Information Systems,* ANSI X3.172-1990, copyright 1990 by the American National Standards Institute (ANSI). Copies may be purchased from the American National Standards Institute, 11 West 42nd Street, New York, New York 10036. Definitions are identified by the symbol (A) after the definition.

- The ANSI/EIA Standard–440-A, *Fiber Optic Terminology.* Copies may be purchased from the Electronic Industries Association, 2001 Pennsylvania Avenue, N.W., Washington, DC 20006. Definitions are identified by the symbol (E) after the definition.

- The *Information Technology Vocabulary,* developed by Subcommittee 1, Joint Technical Committee 1, of the International Organization for Standardization and the International Electrotechnical Commission (ISO/IEC JTC1/SC1). Definitions of published parts of this vocabulary are identified by the symbol (I) after the definition; definitions taken from draft international standards, committee drafts, and working papers being developed by ISO/IEC JTC1/SC1 are identified by the symbol (T) after the definition, indicating that final agreement has not yet been reached among the participating National Bodies of SC1.

- Information for IBM products. Definitions that are specific to IBM products are so labeled, for example, "In SNA," or "In VM."

Sequence and Organization of Entries

This dictionary uses the letter-by-letter method of alphabetizing entries. Only alphabetic and numerical characters are used to determine sequence; special characters and spaces between words are ignored.

Each entry consists of a single-word or multiple-word term or the abbreviation or acronym for a term, followed by a commentary. A commentary includes one or more items (definitions or references) and is organized as follows:

- An item number, if the commentary contains two or more items.

- A usage label, indicating the area of application of the term, for example, "In programming," or "In SNA."

- A descriptive phrase, stating the basic meaning of the term. The descriptive phrase is assumed to be preceded by "the term is defined as ..." The part of speech being defined is indicated by the opening words of the descriptive phrase: "To ..." indicates a verb and "Pertaining to ..." indicates a modifier. Any other wording indicates a noun or noun phrase.

- Annotative sentences, providing additional or explanatory information.

- References, directing the reader to other entries or items in the dictionary.

- A source label, for example, (A), (E), (I), or (T), that follows the definition and identifies the originator of the definition. See "Sources" above. Definitions without source labels are IBM definitions.

References

The following cross-references are used in this dictionary:

Contrast with This refers to a term that has an opposed or substantively different meaning.

Synonym for This indicates that the term has the same meaning as a preferred term, which is defined in its proper place in the dictionary.

Synonymous with This is a backward reference from a defined term to all other terms that have the same meaning.

See This refers the reader to multiple-word terms that have the same last word.

See also This refers the reader to terms that have a related, but not synonymous, meaning.

Deprecated term for This indicates that the term should not be used. It refers to a preferred term, which is defined in its proper place in the dictionary.

Selection of Terms

A term is a word or group of words to be defined. In this dictionary, the singular form of the noun and the infinitive form of the verb are the terms most often selected to be defined. If the term may be abbreviated, the abbreviation is given in parentheses immediately following the term. The abbreviation is also defined in its proper place in the dictionary.

Comments Requested

Terminology in the computer field is constantly evolving. No printed reference can hope to remain current for long. For that reason, we are continually revising the content of this book, adding new terms and definitions as they gain acceptance, discarding old entries as they become obsolete. In order to keep up with these changes, we invite comments from all of our users. Please address them as follows:

IBM Dictionary of Computing
IBM Corporation
Dept. E37, Bldg. 656
Research Triangle Park, NC 27709
Telephone 919-254-0209
Fax 919-254-0343
Internet: ibmterms@vnet.ibm.com

When you send comments to IBM, you grant IBM a nonexclusive right to use or distribute your comments in any way it believes appropriate without incurring any obligation to you.

Acknowledgments

Only someone who has tried to make a large dictionary has any idea of how many people are needed to complete the task. Moreover, not even the dictionary maker himself knows exactly who all those people are. Entries, suggestions, complaints, and queries seem to come from everywhere, and the terms and definitions that eventually result have been touched by many hands, not a few of them unseen. For this reason, any "Acknowledgments" list is likely to be incomplete. This list is no exception.

There are some colleagues, however, both inside and outside IBM, whose assistance and support demand recognition. With apologies to those equally deserving who have been omitted, the editor would like to thank the following, in no particular order:

- The users of earlier editions who took the time to comment and make suggestions

- Gary Violette, contract administrator extraordinary, without whose help this edition would have been impossible

- Lisa Champion, David Heath, Robin Langford, Lori Lathrop, Anita Mannion, Anne Rice, Adrianne Roberts, Carolyn Stephens, H. Ueno, Ian Wright, and all the other IBM terminology coordinators and editors who have provided me and this book with glossaries, comments, and other valuable input.

- Mary Sturgeon, who did the same, but in such generous measure as to warrant special recognition

- The members and consultants of ANSI-approved committee X3K5: Richard Batey, Lionel Difford, Eugene Dwyer, Rex Klopfenstein, Stanley Kurzban, Stefan Langsner, Jimmie Logan, Roy Mullinax, D. F. Stevens, Helmut Thiess, Saul Zaveler

- Past and present members of ISO SC/1 Working Group 7, including: Lars Algotsson, Bernard Bourguignon, Chantal Brochu, Boris Ermolayev, Gunnar Grahn, Evelyn Gray, Hideo Kikuchi, Hanna Kuznicka, Johanne L'Heureux, Francine Pitre

- Bao Pham and Christian Mayer for their translation assistance

- Dan Aitken, Rich Overton, and Mike Payst, for their invaluable help with macros, style files, programs, and other tools, always provided readily and, very often, immediately

- Edie Lessick, who always understood why this book kept shoving all other projects aside

- Daniel Gonneau of McGraw-Hill

- Aleck, Jim, Debbie, Judy, Betty, and Al

- My Production Department buddies, Jean Billings, Steve Joyce, Marie Kolodij, Sandra Raynor, and Carole Lynch, who had to explain repeatedly the arcane details of such topics as BookMaster, PostScript, and the internal distribution of IBM books, and kept inviting me to lunch anyway

- Last and most importantly of all, the creator and for two decades sustainer of this book, John Wood. Through edition after edition, it was he more than anyone else who left his indelible imprint here. I would be dishonest not to recognize that this work is, and will continue to be, "The Book of John."

George McDaniel
Research Triangle Park, N.C.

IBM DICTIONARY
OF COMPUTING

A

A (1) Ampere (2) Angstrom.

ablation A technique for writing data to optical memory in which a laser burns holes (or pits) into thin metal film.

abbreviated address calling Calling that enables a user to employ an address having fewer characters than the full address when initiating a call. (I) (A) Networks may enable a user to designate a given number of abbreviated address codes. The allocation of abbreviated address codes to a destination or group of destinations may be changed as required by means of a suitable procedure.

abbreviated addressing A direct addressing mode that can access only part of storage and can provide a faster means of processing data because of the shortened code. (A)

abbreviated combined relation condition In COBOL, the combined condition that results from the explicit omission of a common subject and a common relational operator in a consecutive sequence of relation conditions.

abbreviated installation In the AS/400 system and System/38, an installation process in which verification and error recovery is done without restoring the saved version of the operating system. Contrast with normal installation.

abbreviation An ordered and shortened representation of data that retains the identity of the data element that is represented. See also data code. (A)

abend Abnormal end of task.

abend code A system code that identifies the system message number and type of error condition causing the abend.

ABIC Adaptive Bilevel Image Compression.

ABM Asynchronous balanced mode.

ABME Asynchronous balanced mode extended.

abnormal end Synonym for abnormal termination.

abnormal end of task (abend) Termination of a task before its completion because of an error condition that cannot be resolved by recovery facilities while the task is executing.

abnormal termination (1) The cessation of processing prior to planned termination. (T) (2) A system failure or operator action that causes a job to end unsuccessfully. (3) In System/38, termination by a means other than the successful execution of the Power Down System command. See normal termination, system termination. See also abnormal end of task (abend).

abort In data communication, a function invoked by a sending primary, secondary, or combined station that causes the recipient to discard and ignore all bit sequences transmitted by the sender since the preceding flag sequences or to discard and ignore all data transmitted by the sender since the previous checkpoint.

aborted connection In computer security, disconnection that does not follow established procedures, possibly enabling other users to gain unauthorized access.

abort sequence A specified bit pattern, occurring anywhere in the bit stream, that is used to terminate transmission of a transmission frame prematurely. (T)

About... (1) In SAA Common User Access architecture, a help action that displays ownership and copyright information about the application. (2) In SAA Common User Access architecture, a help action that displays the logo window of the application.

ABP Actual block processor.

AB roll In multimedia applications, synchronized playback of two recorded video images to perform effects such as dissolves, wipes, or inserts, using both images simultaneously.

absolute address (1) A direct address that identifies a location without reference to a base address. An absolute address may itself be a base address. (T) (2) An address that is permanently assigned by the machine designer to a storage location. (A) (3) Synonymous with explicit address, machine address, specific address. (4) See base address, relative address.

absolute addressing A method of addressing in which the address part of an instruction contains an absolute address. (I) (A)

absolute coding Coding that uses computer instructions with absolute addresses. (A) Synonymous with specific coding.

absolute command In computer graphics, a display command that causes the display device to interpret the data following the command as absolute coordinates. (I) (A) Synonymous with absolute instruction.

absolute coordinate (1) One of a pair of coordinates that identify the position of an addressable point with respect to the origin of a specified coordinate system. (I) (A) Contrast with relative coordinate.

absolute data In computer graphics, the values in a computer program that specify the actual coordinates in a display space or in storage. Contrast with relative data.

absolute device A locating device, such as a tablet, that reports its position to the operating system as a set of numbers on a coordinate system.

absolute error (1) The algebraic result of subtracting a true, specified, or theoretically correct value from the value computed, observed, measured, or achieved. (I) (A) (2) The amount of error expressed in the same units as the quantity containing the error. (A) (3) Loosely, the absolute value of the error, that is, the magnitude of the error without regard for its algebraic sign. (A)

absolute expression An assembly-time expression whose value is not affected by program relocation. An absolute expression can represent an absolute address.

absolute instruction (1) A computer instruction in its final, executable form. (I) (A) (2) Synonym for absolute command.

absolute loader A routine that reads a computer program into main storage, beginning at the assembled origin. (A)

absolute order Deprecated term for absolute command.

absolute positioning Positioning an item of data with respect to an origin.

absolute priority In the OS/2 operating system, pertaining to a priority of a process that is not varied by the operating system. Contrast with dynamic priority.

absolute term A term whose value is not affected by relocation.

absolute value The magnitude of a real number regardless of its algebraic sign.

absolute vector (1) In computer graphics, a vector whose start and end points are specified in absolute coordinates. (I) (A) (2) Contrast with incremental vector. See also relative vector. See Figure 1.

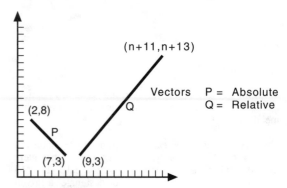

Figure 1. Absolute and Relative Vectors

abstract symbol (1) A symbol whose meaning and use have not been determined by a general agreement but have to be defined for each application of the symbol. (I) (A) (2) In optical character recognition, a symbol whose form does not suggest its meaning and use; these must be defined for each specified set of applications. (A)

AC Alternating current.

Academy Studies The body of work collectively performed by the IBM Academy, which is comprised of IBM Fellows and Senior Technical Staff members. Academy studies, which include analyses of key technical issues, are selected by the Academy members for research, then brought forward to senior management.

ACB (1) Access method control block. (2) Adapter control block. (3) Application control block.

ACB address space In VTAM, the address space in which the ACB is opened. See also associated address space, session address space.

ACB-based macroinstruction In VTAM, a macroinstruction whose parameters are specified by the user in an access method control block.

ACBGEN Application control block generation.

ACB name (1) The name of an ACB macroinstruction. (2) A name specified either on the VTAM APPL definition statement or on the VTAM application program's ACB macroinstruction. Contrast with network name.

ACC (1) Accumulate. (2) Accumulator. (3) Application control code.

acceleration time That part of access time required to bring an auxiliary storage device, typically a tape drive, to the speed at which data can be read or written.

accelerator (1) In the AIXwindows program, a keyboard alternative to a mouse button action; for example, holding the <Shift> and <M> keys on the keyboard can be made to post a menu in the same way that a mouse button action does. Accelerators typically provide increased input speed and greater convenience. (2) In SAA Common User Access architecture, a key or combination of keys that invokes an application-defined function.

accept (1) In a VTAM application program, to establish a session with a logical unit (LU) in response to a CINIT request from a system services control point (SSCP). The session-initiation request may begin when a terminal user logs on, a VTAM application program issues a macroinstruction, or a VTAM operator issues a command. See also acquire. (2) An SMP process that moves distributed code and MVS-type programs to the distribution libraries.

acceptance test A test of a system or functional unit, usually performed by users on their premises after installation, with the participation of the vendor to ensure that contractual requirements are met. (I) (A)

accept-command-key indicator (AC indicator) In the System/36 workstation utility, an indicator that signals the status of any current user-defined command key request.

accepting station In systems with ACF/TCAM, a destination station that accepts a message.

accept-sequence-error indicator (AE indicator) An indicator that allows operators to bypass required displays.

access (1) To obtain the use of a computer resource. (T) (2) The use of an access method. See (A) (3) The manner in which files or data sets are referred to by the computer. (4) To obtain data from or to put data in storage. (5) In computer security, a specific type of interaction between a subject and an object that results in the flow of information from one to the other. See read access, write access. (6) In FORTRAN, the means by which a scoping unit accesses entities in a module subprogram or, in the case of an internal procedure, in its host. Such entities may be explicitly or implicitly accessible. Access is provided by the USE statement. (7) See direct access, direct access storage, dynamic access, immediate

access storage, indexed access, indexed sequential access, random access, remote access, sequential access, serial access.

access arm (1) In a magnetic disk unit, an arm on which magnetic heads are mounted. (T) (2) A part of a magnetic disk storage unit that is used to hold one or more reading and writing heads. (A)

access authority An authority that relates to a request for a type of access to data.

access barred In data communication, a condition in which a data terminal equipment (DTE) cannot call the DTE identified by the selection signals.

access capability (1) In computer security, a "ticket" that allows its holder to gain a specified type of access to a specified object; for example, to erase a specified file. (2) See capability.

access category In computer security, a class to which a user may be assigned, based on the resources that the user is authorized to use.

Note: The access category determines a user's access rights.

access channel control In the IBM Token-Ring Network, the logic and protocols that manage the transfer of data between link stations and medium access control (MAC).

access code (1) In the AS/400 system, a 4-digit number, assigned to documents and folders, that allows authorized users to access the documents and folders. (2) In DPCX, an 8-bit binary code, assigned to a program that determines the terminal operators who are to be allowed to use the program.

access control (1) In computer security, ensuring that the resources of a computer system can be accessed only by authorized users in authorized ways. See discretionary access control, identity-based access control, information flow control, mandatory access control, resource-based access control. (2) A technique used to establish the sequence of data stations that are in temporary control of the transmission medium, but may need to be moved elsewhere. (T)

access control byte In the IBM Token-Ring Network, the byte following the start delimiter of a token or frame that is used to control access to the ring.

access control field (1) A bit pattern that identifies whether a frame is a token, indicates the data stations that may use the token, indicates when the frame should be canceled, and allows stations to request the next token. (T) (2) In 8100, the field of a translation table entry that controls the types of storage access permitted during fetching and execution of an instruction or during a channel I/O operation.

access control key Synonym for privacy key. (A)

access controller In an information resource directory system with entity-level security, a pair of locks, one for read access, the other for write access. Locks may be used for other purposes, such as to permit execution. (A)

access control list (1) In computer security, a collection of all access rights for one object. (2) In computer security, a list associated with an object that identifies all the subjects that can access the object and their access rights; for example, a list associated with a file that identifies users who can access the file and identifies their access rights to that file. See capability list. (3) In the AIX operating system, a file attribute that contains the basic and extended permissions that control access to the file. (4) In the AIX operating system, a list of hosts, maintained by Enhanced X-Windows, that have access to client programs. By default, only programs on the local host and those in this list can use the display. The list can be changed by clients on the local host; some server implementations can also modify the list. The authorization protocol name and data received by the server at connection setup may also affect this list. Synonymous with access list.

access control lock Synonym for privacy lock. (A)

Access Control — Logging and Reporting In VSE, an IBM licensed program used to log access to protected data and to print selected formatted reports on such access.

access environment A description of the current user, including user ID, current connect group, user attributes, and group authorities. An access environment is constructed during user identification and verification.

access key In an information resource directory system with entity-level security, an authorization to perform a set of operations on an entity secured by a lock. (A)

access level (1) In computer security, the level of authority a subject has when using a protected resource; for example, authority to access a particular security level of information. (2) In computer security, the hierarchical portion of the security level used to identify the sensitivity of data and the clearance or authorization of users. (3) In the IBM LinkWay product, the characteristic of a folder that determines how much a user can modify the folder. The access level is determined by the person who creates the folder.

access line A telecommunication line that continuously connects a remote station to a data switching exchange (DSE). A telephone number is associated with the access line.

access list Synonym for access control list. See also standard access list.

access lock Synonym for privacy lock. (A)

access macro A macroinstruction that establishes the linkage between a program requesting execution of a system routine and the system routine requested.

access matrix In computer security, a two-dimensional array, one dimension of which represents objects and the other dimension subjects, where the intersections represent permitted access types.

access mechanism (1) A mechanism responsible for moving an access arm or a comb. Synonymous with actuator. (T) (2) A group of access arms that move together as a unit. See Figure 2.

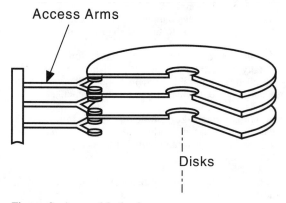

Figure 2. Access Mechanism

access method (1) A technique to obtain the use of data, storage, or the use of an input/output channel to transfer data; for example, random access method, sequential access method. (T) (2) The technique that is used to locate data stored on a physical medium. (A) (3) A technique for moving data between main storage and input/output devices. (4) The way that a system refers to records in files; the reference can be consecutive (records are referred to one after another in the order in which they appear in the file) or it can be random (the individual records are referred to in any order).

access method control block (ACB) A control block that links an application program to VSAM or VTAM programs.

access method interface (AMI) The TCAM function for managing communication on the access method control block (ACB) interface between TCAM and VTAM programs.

access method routines Routines that move data between main storage and input/output devices.

access method services (AMS) The facility used to define and reproduce VSAM key-sequenced data sets (KSDS).

access mode (1) A technique that is used to obtain a particular logical record from, or to place a particular logical record into, a file assigned to a mass storage device. (A) (2) The manner in which files are referred to by a computer. Access can be sequential (records are referred to one after another in the order in which they appear on the file), access can be random (the individual records can be referred to in a nonsequential manner), or access can be dynamic (records can be accessed sequentially or randomly, depending on the form of the input/output request). (3) In COBOL, the manner in which records are to be operated upon within a file. (4) See file access mode. See also random access, sequential access.

access name (1) In a database, a name that identifies an entity. (2) In an information resource dictionary, the name by which an entity is known to the user interfaces. It is the combination of an assigned access name and version identifier that together serve as the primary identifier of each entity. (A)

accessor (1) In computer security, any user of a protected resource. (2) In MSS, the component of the IBM 3851 Mass Storage Facility that transports data cartridges between the cartridge cells, data recording devices, and the cartridge access station.

accessor control In MSS, the component of the IBM 3851 Mass Storage Facility that decodes and sequences messages from the mass storage control and directs the motion of the accessor.

accessor environment element (ACEE) In RACF, a description of the current user including userid, current connect group, user attributes, and group authorities. An ACEE is constructed during user identification and verification.

accessory (1) A basic part, subassembly, or assembly used with another assembly, unit, or set. (2) A separately orderable part that has no type number, is for purchase only, and does not receive normal IBM maintenance.

access path (1) A sequence of data items used by a database management system to access records or other data items stored in a database. There may simultaneously exist more than one access path for one data item. (T) (2) A chain of addresses that leads to the desired data. (A) (3) The procedure used by a database management system to access data stored in a database. (A) (4) The order in which records in a database file are organized for processing by a program. See arrival sequence access path, keyed sequence access path. (5) In SQL, the path used to locate data specified in SQL statements. An access path can be indexed, sequential, or a combination of both.

access path independence The independence of logical data descriptions on access paths. Programs using access path independent logical data descriptions need not be changed when access paths are changed. (T)

access path journaling A method of recording changes to an access path as changes are made to the data in the database file so that the access path can be recovered automatically by the system.

access period In computer security, a period of time during which specified access rights prevail.

access permission (1) All of a user's access rights. (A) (2) All access rights a user has regarding an object. (I) (3) In the AIX operating system, a group of designations that determine who can access a particular file and how the user can access the file. See base permission, extended permission. See also permission code.

access plan In SQL, the control structure produced during compile time that is used to process SQL statements encountered when the program is run.

access priority In the IBM Token-Ring Network, the maximum priority that a token can have for transmission via the token-ring adapter.

access procedure The procedure or protocol used to gain access to a shared resource; for example, in a local area network the shared resource is the transmission medium. The medium access procedures specified by the IEEE 802 standard are CSMA/CD token, bus, and ring.

access right (1) In computer security, permission for a subject to use an access type for a particular object; for example, permission for a process to read a file. (2) The right to use a defined computer resource such as a library or file. (3) Synonymous with permission.

access time (1) The time interval between the instant at which a call for data is initiated and the instant at which the delivery of data is completed. Access time equals latency plus transfer time. (T) (2) Deprecated term for cycle time. (3) See seek time. See also latency. Contrast with response time. See Figure 3.

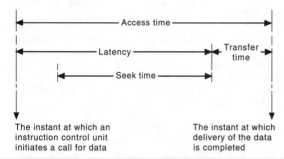

Figure 3. Time Intervals for Accessing Data

access type In computer security, a kind of access to an object; for example, access to read a file, access to write in a file, access to delete a file.

access unit In an IBM Token-Ring Network, a wiring concentrator. See multistation access unit.

account In the AIX operating system, the login directory and other information that gives a user access to the system.

accountability In computer security, the property that enables activities on a system to be traced to individuals who may then be held responsible for their actions.

accountability information An audit trail for security purposes.

account file A direct access file maintained by VSE/POWER to hold the accounting information it generates and the programs that it controls.

accounting check digit See self-check digit.

accounting code In the AS/400 system and System/38, a 15-character field, assigned to a job by the system when it is processed by the system, that is used to collect statistics for the system resources used for that job when job accounting is active.

accounting entry In the AS/400 system and System/38, a journal entry that contains statistics of system resources used for job accounting.

accounting exit routine In VTAM, an optional installation exit routine that collects statistics about session initiation and termination.

accounting level In the AS/400 system and System/38, a system value identifying the type of data to be recorded when job accounting is active.

accounting machine (1) A keyboard-actuated machine that prepares accounting records. (A) (2) A machine that reads data from external storage media, such as cards or tapes, and automatically produces accounting records or tabulations, usually on continuous forms. (A)

accounting segment In the AS/400 system and System/38, the period of time during which statistics are gathered, beginning when the job starts or when the job's accounting code is changed, and ending when the job ends or when the job's accounting code is next changed.

accounting system A part of the AIX operating system for RISC System/6000 that monitors various aspects of system operations; it collects detailed data on each transaction and provides tools for processing the data in order to produce different kinds of reports.

account number (1) In the IBM 3600 Finance Communication System, a number assigned by a financial institution to a particular customer account. See customer identification number. See also personal code, primary account. number. (A)

accreditation In computer security, the authorization that is granted to an information system to process sensitive information in its operational environment.

Note: Accreditation is based on a comprehensive security evaluation of system hardware, firmware, and software security design, its configuration and implementation, and administrative, communications, personnel, physical, and procedural security controls.

accumulate (ACC) (1) To collect, for example, the values in a field. (2) To enter the result of an operation in an accumulator.

accumulating The process of totaling values in a particular field as records are being processed.

accumulator (1) A register in which one operand of an operation can be stored and subsequently replaced by the result of that operation. (T) (2) In the IBM 3800 Printing Subsystem Models 3 and 8, a feature that supplies a separate storage that can hold data in raster form. It can be used either for composing a sheet of data that combines a large amount of variable and constant data, or for storing an electronic overlay in raster form that will be merged with variable data as the sheet is printed.

accuracy (1) A quality of that which is free of error. (A) (2) A qualitative assessment of freedom from error, with a high assessment corresponding to a small error. (I) (A) (3) Contrast with precision.

accuracy control character A control character used to indicate whether the data with which it is associated are in error, or are to be disregarded, or cannot be represented on a particular device. (A) Synonymous with error control character.

ACD Automatic call distribution.

AC/DC ringing A method of telephone ringing that uses alternating current to operate a ringer and direct current to actuate a relay that stops the ringing when the called party answers.

ACD group In telephony, the set of multiple agents assigned to process incoming telephone calls that are directed to the same dialed number. The routing of incoming calls to one of the agents in the ACD group is based on such properties as availability of the agent and the length of time since the agent completed the last incoming call.

ACDI Asynchronous Communications Device Interface.

ACD pilot number In telephony, the common telephone number that calling parties can dial to route calls to one of multiple agents.

ACEE Accessor environment element.

ACF Advanced Communications Function.

ACF/NCP Advanced Communications Function for the Network Control Program. See Network Control Program (NCP).

ACF/SSP Advanced Communications Function for the System Support Programs. See System Support Program Product.

ACF/TAP Advanced Communications Function for the Trace Analysis Program. See Trace Analysis Program (TAP).

ACF/TCAM Advanced Communications Function for the Telecommunications Access Method. See Telecommunications Access Method (TCAM).

ACF/TCAM base system A system in which ACF/TCAM is installed without the Multisystem Networking Facility.

ACF/VTAM product Advanced Communications Function for the Virtual Telecommunications Access Method product. See Virtual Telecommunications Access Method (VTAM) product.

ACF/VTAM application program A program that opens an access method control block (ACB) to iden-

tify itself to ACF/VTAM and can issue ACF/VTAM macroinstructions.

ACF/VTAM definition The process of defining the user application network to ACF/VTAM programs and modifying IBM-defined characteristics to suit the needs of the user.

ACF/VTAM definition library The operating system files or data sets that contain the definition statements and start options filed during ACF/VTAM definition.

ACF/VTAME Advanced Communications Function for the Virtual Telecommunications Access Method Entry. See Virtual Telecommunications Access Method Entry (VTAME).

ACF/VTAM operator A person or program authorized to issue ACF/VTAM operator commands. See domain operator, network operator, program operator.

ACF/VTAM operator command A command issued to monitor or control an ACF/VTAM domain.

"A" Change The correction of an error in transcribing information from approved EC documents to formal documents; the issuing agency releases a new notice page and correcting documents under the same EC number with an alphabetic suffix; for example, 750123A.

ACK The acknowledge character. (A)

acknowledge (1) To answer. To respond to a poll, address, or message. (2) In the X.25 API, to confirm that a data packet with the D-bit set has arrived.

acknowledge character (ACK) A transmission control character transmitted by a station as an affirmative response to the station with which the connection has been set up. (I) (A) See negative-acknowledge character.

acknowledged mail A function that allows a user to request and receive an acknowledgment that the mail item he sent was received.

acknowledged service In communications, the service that provides for the establishment of a data link level connection. Acknowledged service provides for functions such as sequencing, flow control, and error recovery. SNA requires the use of acknowledged services.

acknowledge timeout The number of seconds that a station should wait for an acknowledgment from a remote station after sending data.

acknowledgment (1) The transmission, by a receiver, of acknowledge characters as an affirmative response to a sender. (T)   (2) An indication that an item sent was received.

acknowledgment character Deprecated term for acknowledge character.

ACK0 (1) A transmission control character for even positive acknowledgment.   (2) In BSC, the even-numbered positive acknowledge character.

Note: The ACK0 character indicates that text was received without transmission errors. In BSC text transmission, ACK0 is used alternately with ACK1 to perform sequence validation.

ACK1 (1) A transmission control character for odd positive acknowledgment.   (2) In BSC, the odd-numbered positive acknowledge character.

Note: The ACK1 character indicates that text was received without transmission errors. In BSC text transmission, ACK1 is used alternately with ACK0 to perform sequence validation.

ACM Association for Computing Machinery.

ACO Automated console operations.

acoustic coupler A device that interconnects a communicating unit with a telephone handset by converting sound signals to or from electrical signals. (A)

acoustic delay line A delay line whose operation is based on the time of propagation of sound waves in a given medium. (A) Synonymous with sonic delay line.

acoustic emanations In computer security, sound inadvertently transmitted from information processing equipment that might permit unauthorized access to information. See compromising emanations.

acoustic impulse A brief excursion of the sound pressure level. See also impulsive noise.

acoustic memory Synonym for acoustic storage.

acoustic panel A panel bonded with a material to reduce operating noise from the devices in a rack.

acoustic storage A storage device consisting of acoustic delay lines. (A) Synonymous with acoustic memory.

acquire (1) In MSS, to allocate space on a staging drive and to stage the volume table of contents from a cartridge to the staging drive.   (2) In System/36, to assign a display station or session to a program. (3) In VTAM programs , to take over resources that were formerly controlled by an access method in another domain, or to resume control of resources that were controlled by that domain but released. Contrast with release. See also resource takeover.   (4) In a VTAM application program, to initiate and establish a session with another logical unit (LU). The acquire process begins when the application program issues a macroinstruction. See also accept.

acquired session In System/36, a session that has been started by a program using an acquire operation, or in BASIC, using an OPEN statement. See also remotely started session.

acquire-program-device operation In the AS/400 system and System/38, an operation that makes a program device available for input or output operations. Contrast with release-program-device operation.

ACRE APAR control remote entry.

ACS routing Automatic class selection routing.

action In a conceptual schema language, one or more elementary actions that, as a unit, change a collection of sentences into another one or make known a collection of sentences present in the information base or conceptual schema. (T)   See elementary action, permissible action. (A)

action bar In SAA Common User Access architecture, the area at the top of a window that contains choices that give a user access to actions available in that window.

action bar pull-down In SAA Common User Access architecture, a list of choices associated with a choice on the action bar. A user selects a choice from the action bar and a pull-down menu appears.

action code In SAA Basic Common User Access architecture, a number or letter assigned to an action in an action list.

action description In a conceptual schema language, a linguistic object describing an action or permissible action. (A)

action entity world In a conceptual schema language, a collection of entities of interest that is described in an actual information base and its conceptual schema. (A)

action entry field In SAA Basic Common User Access architecture, the entry field used in action lists. A user can type an action code to apply one of several possible actions against the object. See extendable action entry field.

action list In SAA Basic Common User Access architecture, a set of choices from which a user can select multiple choices and specify that a different action be performed on each choice at the same time.

ActionMedia II (IBM PS/2 ActionMedia II) An IBM MultiMedia solution using Digital Video Interactive (DVI) technology. Capture and playback adapters provide digital video and audio.

action message (1) A message issued because of a condition that requires an operator response. (2) In SAA Common User Access architecture, a message that tells a user that an action requested by the user has been suspended because something unexpected has occurred or because something undesirable could occur. The user can continue the requested action after correcting the situation, continue the requested action without correcting the situation, withdraw the requested action, or get help. See also information message, warning message.

action-object In SAA Basic Common User Access architecture, a process sequence in which a user selects an action and then selects the objects to apply that action to. Contrast with object-action.

Actions In SAA Basic Common User Access architecture, an action that moves the cursor to the action bar. See Switch to action bar.

action statement C language program fragments that define how the generated lexical analyzer reacts to regular expressions that it recognizes.

action table In the AIXwindows Toolkit, a table that specifies the mapping of externally available procedure strings to the corresponding procedure implemented by the widget class. All widget class records contain an action table.

activate (1) To put a device into an operational state. (2) To pass control to a program, procedure, or routine. (3) To make a resource ready to perform its function. Contrast with deactivate. (4) See also initialize.

activating (1) Making a program, system, or device available for use. See also initialization, initial program load (IPL). (2) In a document copying machine, the action of an activator on the exposed sensitized material in some photochemical processes to cause development of the latent image. (T)

activation (1) In programming languages, the representation of a procedure created by the invocation of that procedure. (I) (2) In a network, the process by which a component of a node is made ready to perform the functions for which it was designed. See automatic activation, session activation. See also LU-LU session initiation. Contrast with deactivation.

activation stack In DPPX, a linked list of entries indicating which processes have been invoked and are to be executed for a particular thread. Each activation stack entry keeps a record of the status of a program. There must be at least one activation stack entry per thread.

activator In a document copying machine, a liquid used for developing certain types of sensitized material. (T)

active (1) Operational. (2) Pertaining to a file, page, or program that is in main storage or memory, as opposed to a file, page, or program that must be retrieved from auxiliary storage; for example, an active page in an IBM personal computer. (3) Pertaining to a node or device that is connected or is available for connection to another node or device. (4) The state of a resource when it has been activated and is operational. Contrast with inactive, inoperative. See also pending active session. (5) In the AIX operating system, pertaining to the window pane in which the text cursor is currently positioned. (6) In VTAM programs, pertaining to a major or minor node that has been activated by VTAM. Most resources are activated as part of VTAM start processing or as the result of a VARY ACT command.

active address In the OS/2 Office Configuration utility the address of the adapter card being used by the machine being configured.

active application The application subsystem currently in an extended recovery facility (XRF) session with a terminal user. See alternate application.

active code page The code page to which a device is logically connected at a particular point in time.

active configuration In an ESCON environment, the ESCON Director configuration determined by the status of the current set of connectivity attributes. Contrast with saved configuration.

active device In an ESCON environment, a physical node capable of transmitting and receiving optical data, and serializing, deserializing, and retiming electrical data. Contrast with passive component.

active environment group In the Print Services Facility, an internal object in a composed-text page or an overlay that defines the page environment.

active file (1) A permanent file or a temporary file whose expiration date is later than the job date. (2) A diskette file or tape file whose expiration date is later than the system date.

active gateway A gateway that is treated like a network interface in that it is expected to exchange routing information. If it does not do so for a period of time, the route associated with the gateway is deleted. Contrast with passive gateway. See also exterior gateway, interior gateway, neighbor gateway.

active grab In Enhanced X-Windows, a grab actually owned by the grabbing client. Contrast with passive grab. See also button grabbing, keygrabbing, pointer grabbing, server grabbing.

active group job In the AS/400 system, a group job that was not suspended by the Transfer to Group Job (TFRGRPJOB) command.

active keyboard The character set layout that is available for data or text entry and that is, at most, the set of characters on the active code page.

active line A telecommunication line that is currently available for transmission of data. Contrast with inactive line.

active link (1) A link that is currently available for transmission of data. (2) In RSCS, a data link for which a line driver has been initiated; the RSCS operator uses the RSCS START command to initiate a line driver. The link is active until the line driver is terminated by another operator command. (3) Contrast with inactive link.

active mass storage volume See active volume.

active matrix In multimedia applications, a technology in which every pel (dot) on the screen has a transistor to control it more accurately. This allows for better contrast and less motion smearing.

active monitor In the IBM Token-Ring Network, a function in a single adapter that initiates the transmission of tokens and provides token error recovery facilities. Any active adapter on the ring has the ability to provide the active monitor function if the current active monitor fails. Synonymous with token monitor.

active node A node that is connected to, or is available for connection to, another node. Contrast with inactive node.

active open In TCP/IP, the state of a connection that is providing a service. Contrast with passive open.

active page (1) A page in main storage that can be modified or displayed. (2) In OS/VS and VM, an addressable page currently residing in real storage. (3) In IBM personal computers with the Color/Graphics Monitor Adapter, a page in the screen buffer to which the user can write information while displaying a visual page. See visual page. See also screen buffer.

Note: The user can build an active page in memory while viewing a different visual page on the screen.

active page queue In OS/VS, a queue of pages in real storage currently assigned to tasks. Pages on this queue are eligible for placement on the available page queue. See also available page queue, hold page queue.

active pane In AIX extended curses, the pane in which the text cursor is positioned.

active partition In the IBM 3270 Information Display System, the partition in whose viewpoint the operator is currently working.

active pixel region The area of the screen on which pixel information is displayed.

active program Any program that is loaded and ready to be executed. Contrast with inactive program.

active record (1) A record available for processing. (2) Any record format that is currently displayed. (3) In the AS/400 system and System/38, an active subfile record or any record format that is currently shown on a display. See also active subfile record. Contrast with inactive record.

active sort table In the AS/400 system, a system-supplied double-byte character set (DBCS) sort table that contains the collating sequences for all defined double-byte characters in a double-byte character set. These tables are maintained by the character generator utility function of the AS/400 Application Development Tools licensed program.

active state In SNA, the state in which a component of a node can perform the functions for which it was designed. Contrast with inactive state.

active station A station that is currently eligible for entering or accepting messages. Contrast with inactive station.

active storage See main storage.

active subfile In the AS/400 system and System/38, a subfile in which a write operation was issued to the subfile record format or to the subfile control record format with the DDS keyword SFLINZ in effect.

active subfile record In the AS/400 system and System/38, a record that was added to the subfile by a write operation, or a record that was initialized by the DDS keyword SFLINZ. Contrast with inactive subfile record.

active translation plan The second status in the Translation Planning System (TPS) of a translation plan.

active video lines In video systems, those video lines not occurring in the horizontal and vertical blanking intervals.

active virtual terminal In the AIX operating system, the virtual terminal that is currently visible on the display device and that is capable of receiving input from a keyboard, mouse, tablet or other interactive input device. Interactive input is possible to only one virtual terminal at a time.

active volume (1) A volume that is ready for reading or writing data. (2) In MSS, a mass storage volume residing within the IBM 3851 Mass Storage Facility and available for mounting by the operating system.

active wait In VM/SP HPO, a process in which an idle processor in an attached processor (AP) or multiprocessor (MP) system scans the dispatch request queues and dispatch list looking for work.

active window In SAA Advanced Common User Access architecture, the window that a user is currently interacting with. This is the window that receives keyboard input. Contrast with inactive window.

active wiretapping In computer security, wiretapping through the use of an unauthorized device to generate false signals or alter the communications of legitimate users. Contrast with passive wiretapping.

activity The percentage of records in a file that are processed in a run. See also volatility.

activity content Synonym for activity inventory.

activity inventory In an information processing system, all of the functions and processes and their interdependencies. (T) Synonymous with activity content.

activity level In the AS/400 system and System/38, a characteristic of a subsystem that specifies the maximum number of jobs that can compete at the same time for the processing unit.

activity loading A method of storing records on a file in which the most frequently processed records can be located with the least number of reads.

activity queue In System/36, a list of entries for messages and batch jobs that are to be sent or submitted at a specific date and time.

activity ratio The ratio of the number of records in a file that are in use to the total number of records in that file.

activity trail A record of operations that is used to identify what activities have been done, the order in which they were done, and who performed the activities.

ACTLU Activate logical unit. In SNA, a command used to start a session on a logical unit.

ACTPU (1) Activate physical unit. (2) In SNA, a command used to start a session on a physical unit.

actual address Synonym for absolute address.

actual argument Synonym for actual parameter.

actual block processor (ABP) In OS/VS2, one of several programs that translate I/O requests into the proper format for the I/O supervisor.

actual data transfer rate The average number of bits, characters, or blocks per unit of time transferred from a data source and received by a data sink.

actual decimal point The representation, using the decimal point character (. or ,), of the decimal point position in a data item. The actual decimal point appears in printed reports and requires a position in storage. Contrast with assumed decimal point.

actual information base An information base whose propositions hold during a specific period of time. (T)

actual instruction Deprecated term for effective instruction.

actual parameter (1) In a programming language, a language object that appears in a procedure call and that is associated with the corresponding formal parameter for use in the execution of the procedure. (I) (2) Synonymous with actual argument.

actuator (1) The device in an auxiliary storage device that moves the read/write heads. (2) A device that causes mechanical motion. (3) Synonym for access mechanism. (T)

ACV Address control vector.

Ada A general-purpose high-level procedure-oriented language, originally developed under the aegis of the U.S. Department of Defense to provide a means, independent of proprietary machine languages, for implementing embedded systems; it features structured programming, data structures with strong typing, multitasking, and facilities for object-oriented programming. (A)

Note: Ada is named after Lady Augusta Ada Byron Lovelace, the daughter of Lord Byron, who is said to have been the first programmer.

A/D Analog-to-digital.

Adaptable Process A process designed to maintain effectiveness and efficiency as requirements change. The process is deemed adaptable when there is agreement among the suppliers, owners, and customers that the process will meet requirements through the strategic period.

adapter (1) A mechanism for attaching parts; for example, parts having different diameters. (2) A part that electrically or physically connects a device to a computer or to another device. (3) Hardware used to join different optical fiber connector types. Contrast with coupler. (4) A printed circuit board that modifies the system unit to allow it to operate in a particular way.

adapter blank A machine element of a network controller that is placed in an empty adapter position to maintain proper airflow.

adapter check In the network control program, an error condition detected by the communication scanner or channel adapter and presented to the communication controller by a level 1 interrupt.

adapter code In X.25 communications, the IBM X.25 Interface Co-Processor/2 Protocol Code, which controls the frame-level and packet-level communication processing.

adapter control block (ACB) In NCP, a control block that contains line control information and the states of I/O operations for BSC lines, SS lines, or SDLC links.

Adapter Support Interface In an IBM Token-Ring Network, the software used to operate the token-ring adapter cards in attached IBM personal computers.

Adaptive Bilevel Image Compression (ABIC) A 4-bit image capable of displaying up to 16 shades of gray.

adaptive differential pulse code modulation In multimedia applications, a technique in which pulse code modulation samples are compressed before they are stored on a disc. ADPCM, an extension of the PCM format, is a standard encoding format for storing audio information in a digital format. It reduces storage requirements by storing differences between successive digital samples rather than full values.

adaptive pacing Synonym for adaptive session-level pacing.

adaptive session-level pacing A form of session-level pacing in which session components exchange pacing windows that may vary in size during the course of a session. This allows transmission within a network to adapt dynamically to variations in availability and demand of buffers on a session-by-session basis. Session-level pacing occurs within independent stages along the session path according to local congestion at the intermediate and endpoint nodes. Synonymous with adaptive pacing, adaptive session pacing. See pacing, session-level pacing, virtual route pacing.

adaptive session pacing Synonym for adaptive session-level pacing.

adaptive thresholding A process used in text scanning that increases the contrast between the scanned image (text) and the background to increase legibility.

ADC Analog-to-digital converter.

ADCS IBM Advanced Data Communications for Stores.

AD/Cycle An IBM product that offers an enterprise modeling approach supported by tools that will assist in the creation of an enterprise model to be validated, analyzed, and then used to generate applications. It consists of a framework for, and a set of, application development tools provided by an Application Development (AD) platform, designed to support the integration of tools through a consistent user interface, workstation services, an AD information model, tool services, Repository Services, and Library Services. It provides control for defining and sharing application development data.

add See false add.

add authority In the AS/400 system, a data authority that allows the user to add entries to an object; for example, add job entries to a job queue or add records to a file. Contrast with delete authority. See also read authority, update authority.

addend In an addition operation, a number or quantity added to the augend. (I) (A)

adder A functional unit whose output data is a representation of the sum of the numbers represented by its input data. (T)

adder-subtracter A functional unit that acts as an adder or subtracter, depending upon the control signal received. An adder-subtracter may be constructed so as to yield the sum and the difference at the same time. (T)

add file A file to which records are being added.

addition See parallel addition, serial addition.

addition without carry Deprecated term for non-equivalence operation.

additive attribute (1) In PL/I, a file description characteristic that must be stated explicitly or implied by another explicitly stated characteristic. Contrast with alternative attribute. (2) In data communications, a collection of multipoint addresses. Each address can be associated with an individual communications session. Contrast with alternative attribute.

additive color system In computer graphics, a system that reproduces an image by mixing (adding) appropriate quantities of red, green, and blue light. See also primary color. Contrast with subtractive color system.

add mode In addition and subtraction operations, a mode in which the decimal marker is placed at a predetermined location with respect to the last digit entered. (I) (A)

add operation (1) A disk or diskette operation that adds records to an existing file. (2) An operation caused by an add instruction.

address (1) A character or group of characters that identifies a register, a particular part of storage, or some other data source or destination. (A) (2) To refer to a device or an item of data by its address. (I) (A) (3) In word processing, the location, identified by an address code, of a specific section of the recording medium or storage. (T) (4) A name, label, or number identifying a location in storage, a device in a system or network, or any other data source. (5) In data communication, the unique code assigned to each device or workstation connected to a network.

addressability (1) In computer graphics, the number of addressable points on a display surface or in storage. (2) In micrographics, the number of addressable points, within a specified film frame, computed as follows: the number of addressable horizontal points by the number of addressable vertical points; for example, 4000 by 4000. (A) (3) The ability to locate an item in online storage.

addressability measure On a display screen, the number of addressable points within the display space.

addressable horizontal positions (1) In micrographics, the number of positions, within a specified

film frame, at which a vertical line can be placed. (A) (2) In computer graphics, the number of positions on a display surface at which a full-length display column can be placed.

addressable point In computer graphics, any point of a device that can be addressed. (I) (A) Synonymous with addressable position. See Figure 4.

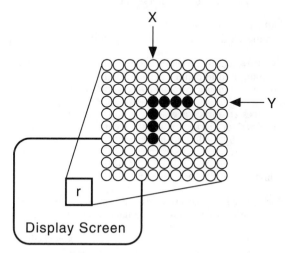

Figure 4. Addressable Point

addressable position Synonym for addressable point.

addressable vertical positions (1) In micrographics, the number of positions, within a specified film frame, at which a horizontal line can be placed. (A) (2) In computer graphics, the number of positions on a display surface at which a full-length display column can be placed. (A)

address administration The assignment of LAN individual addresses locally or on a universal basis. (T)

address aliasing See network address translation.

address base The field of an address control vector that designates the origin of a logical address space in the processor address space. It is concatenated with a logical address during dynamic address relocation.

address book A collection of entries containing information that can be referenced and used to perform OS/2 Office functions. In the OS/2 Office product, there is a Personal address book and a Public address book contained inside each directory.

address book entry An entry of information contained inside a Public or Personal address book for use performing OS/2 Office functions.

Address Book service An OS/2 Office service that maintains a database of address books accessed by the users and other Office services.

address bus The path used for the transmission of address information in a computer.

address code In word processing, a program instruction that identifies an address. (T)

address constant A value, or an expression representing a value, used in calculating storage addresses.

address control vector (ACV) The formatted information used to control dynamic address relocation and the activation of dynamic address translation.

addressed direct access In systems with VSAM, the retrieval or storage of a data record identified by its relative byte address, independent of the location of the record relative to the previously retrieved or stored record. See also addressed sequential access, keyed direct access, keyed sequential access.

addressed sequential access In systems with VSAM, the retrieval or storage of a data record in its entry sequence relative to the previously retrieved or stored record. See also addressed direct access, keyed direct access, keyed sequential access.

addressee (1) The person to whom an item is directed. See also receiver. (2) The intended recipient of a message. (3) A name identifying an individual that is used when distributing documents or mail.

address extension In X.25 communications, the called and calling address extensions are optional CCITT-specified facilities, available on networks that conform to the 1984 version of X.25. Synonymous with extended address.

address family Synonym for protocol family.

address field The part of a packet containing addressing information. See also packet.

address format (1) The arrangement of the address parts of an instruction. The expression "plus-one" is frequently used to indicate that one of the addresses specifies the location of the next instruction to be executed, such as one-plus-one, two-plus-one, three-plus-one, four-plus-one. (A) (2) The arrangement of address parts that allows identification of those parts required to indicate a channel, a device, a cylinder, a read/write head, or a record on a magnetic disk storage device. (A)

addressing (1) The assignment of addresses to the instructions of a program. (2) A means of identifying

storage locations. (3) In data communication, the way in which a station selects the station to which it is to send data. (4) Specifying an address or location within a file.

addressing characters Identifying characters sent by the computer over a line that cause a particular station or component to accept a message sent by the computer.

addressing ID The unique identifying character or characters associated with a station when writing.

addressing mode (AMODE) In MVS and the MVS/XA program, a program attribute that refers to the address length that a program is prepared to handle upon entry. In MVS/370, addresses may be 24 bits in length. In the MVS/XA program, addresses may be 24 bits or 31 bits in length.

address limit The field of an address control vector (ACV) that designates the maximum logical address in a logical address space. It is used to check the validity of a logical address during dynamic address relocation.

address list In the AIX operating system, the list used to associate user's names with network user addresses and other information, for the purpose of making outgoing X.25 calls without the caller having to know the addresses. There is one address list for the system and one for each user. See also system address list, user address list.

address mark A byte of data on a disk or diskette, used to identify the data field and ID field in the record.

address modification Any arithmetic, logic, or syntactic operation performed on an address. (A)

address output file In System/36 RPG, either a record address file or a limits file.

address part The part of a machine instruction or microinstruction that specifies one or more addresses of operands. (T) See operation part.

address pool In System/36 data communication, a collection of multipoint addresses. Each address can be associated with an individual SSCP-ICF session.

address reference Synonym for address.

address register (1) A register in which an address is stored. (A) (2) See base address register, instruction address register.

Address Resolution Protocol (ARP) A protocol that dynamically maps between Internet addresses, baseband adapter addresses, X.25 addresses, and token-ring adapter addresses on a local area network.

address space (1) The range of addresses available to a computer program. (A) (2) The complete range of addresses that are available to a programmer. See also virtual address space. (3) A set of addresses used to uniquely identify network accessible units, sessions, adjacent link stations, and links in a node for each network in which the node participates. An APPN node has one address space for intranode routing and one for each transmission group on which it can send message units. (4) In the AIX operating system, the code, stack, and data that are accessible by a process. (5) In VSE, a subdivision of the total of virtual storage if the computer system operates in 370 mode. (6) In SPPS II, the virtual storage that is assigned to a particular task. No other task may address this space. (7) In the terminal display language (TDL), an area on a display screen or in a buffer in the store controller. (8) The area of virtual storage available for a particular job. (9) See associated address space.

address space control mode The mode, determined by the program status word, that indicates where to find referenced data. Three types of address space control modes are primary, secondary, and access register. VTAM macroinstructions must be invoked in primary address space control mode.

address space identifier (ASID) A unique, system-assigned identifier for an address space.

address space manager (ASM) A component in an APPN or LEN node that assigns and frees session addresses.

address stop A capability to specify at the system console an address that causes a halt in processing when it is encountered. See also breakpoint, instruction address stop.

address substitution A facility for type 2 communication scanners that modifies the scan output to replace certain pairs of interface addresses with another address.

address switches Switches on a device that the user sets to represent the address of that device.

address trace A service aid by which the contents of selected areas of communication controller storage, and selected external registers, can be recorded at each successive interrupt.

address track A track that contains addresses used to locate data on other tracks of the same data medium. (I) (A)

address translation (1) The process of changing the address of an item of data or the address of an instruction to the address in main storage at which it is to be loaded or relocated. (2) In virtual storage systems, the process of changing the address of an item of data or an instruction from its virtual storage address to its real storage address. See dynamic address translation, network address translation.

address translator A functional unit that transforms virtual addresses to real addresses. (I) (A)

ADDR function In DPPX, an integrated function of Programming Language for Distributed System (PL/DS) that is used to obtain the address of data.

add rights In System/38, the authority to add an entry to an object. Contrast with delete rights. See also read rights, update rights.

add time The time required for one addition, not including the time required to get the quantities from storage and return them to storage.

A-disk In CMS, the primary user disk that is allocated to a CMS user. This read/write disk is used to store files created under CMS; such files are retained until deleted by the user. See also B-disk, CMS system disk, D-disk, virtual disk, Y-disk, Z-disk. Synonymous with primary user disk.

adjacency (1) In character recognition, a condition in which the character spacing reference lines of two consecutively-printed characters on the same line are separated by less than a specified distance. (A) (2) In a network, pertaining to devices, nodes, programs, or domains that are directly connected by a data link or that share common control.

adjacent control point A control point (CP) that is directly connected to an APPN, LEN, or composite node by a link.

adjacent domains (1) Two domains interconnected by means of equipment located at adjacent nodes. (T) (2) Domains that share a common subarea node, for example, a communication controller, or two domains connected by a cross-domain subarea link with no intervening domains.

adjacent link station In SNA, a link station directly connected to a given node by a link connection over which network traffic can be carried.

Note: Several secondary link stations that share a link connection do not exchange data with each other and therefore are not adjacent to each other.

adjacent link station image Information within a node about an adjacent link station.

adjacent NCPs Network control programs (NCPs) that are connected by subarea links with no intervening NCPs.

adjacent networks Two SNA networks joined by a common gateway NCP.

adjacent nodes Two nodes connected together by at least one path that connects no other node. (T)

adjacent SSCP table A table that contains lists of the system services control points (SSCPs) that VTAM programs can be in session with or can use to reach destination SSCPs in the same network or in other networks. The table is filed in the VTAM definition library.

adjacent subareas Two subareas connected by one or more links with no intervening subareas. See subarea.

adjunct register A 32-bit register used as storage for an address control vector (ACV); only the low-order 16-bit positions are available to a program.

adjunct register set A set of eight adjunct registers located consecutively in the adjunct register group.

adjust To move text so that it is aligned between the defined left and right margins or between the first and last typing lines. See also justify, left-align, right-align.

adjust (line end) See line-end adjustment.

adjustable-size aggregate In programming languages, an aggregate formal parameter with some or all of its subscript ranges dynamic. (I) See also assumed-size aggregate.

adjusted ring length In a multiple-wiring-closet ring, the sum of all wiring closet-to-wiring closet cables in the main ring path less the length of the shortest of these cables.

adjust text mode (1) A mode in which text can be reformatted to accommodate specified line widths and page lengths. (T) (2) In word processing, a mode in which the operator can adjust text to specified line lengths and page sizes.

ADM (1) Asynchronous disconnected mode. (2) Administrative management.

Administration See telecommunication Administration.

administrative management (ADM) An IBM-supplied OFFICE/38 program that facilitates common office tasks such as the creation and maintenance of document logs, calendar, message-processing, and dictionary functions.

administrative operator See control operator.

administrative operator station See control operator's terminal.

administrative repository A database that contains configuration, problem, change, and inventory information needed to administer the information system. The customer uses the administrative repository to perform the functions of configuration management, problem management, and change management.

administrative security In computer security, the management constraints and supplemental controls established to provide an acceptable level of protection for data. Synonymous with procedural security.

ADO AMPEX Digital Optics; a device for creating digital video effects (DVEs).

adopted authority In the AS/400 system, an authority given to the user by the program for the duration of the job that uses that program. The program must be created with owner authority.

ADP Automatic data processing. (A)

ADPCM Adaptive differential pulse code modulation.

ADP system Synonym for computer system.

ADR (1) Address. (2) Application definition record.

ADU Automatic dialing unit.

Advanced Communications Function (ACF) A group of IBM licensed programs, principally VTAM programs, TCAM, NCP, and SSP, that use the concepts of Systems Network Architecture (SNA), including distribution of function and resource sharing.

Advanced Function Printing (AFP) In the AS/400 system, the ability of programs to print all-points-addressable text and images.

Advanced Function Printing data stream In AS/400 AFP support, the printer data stream used for printing advanced function printing data. The AFPDS includes composed text, page segments, electronic overlays, form definitions, and fonts that are downloaded from the AS/400 system to the printer.

Advanced Peer-to-Peer Networking (APPN) An extension to SNA featuring (a) greater distributed network control that avoids critical hierarchical dependencies, thereby isolating the effects of single points of failure; (b) dynamic exchange of network topology information to foster ease of connection, reconfiguration, and adaptive route selection; (c) dynamic definition of network resources; and (d) automated resource registration and directory lookup. APPN extends the LU 6.2 peer orientation for end-user services to network control and supports multiple LU types, including LU 2, LU 3, and LU 6.2.

Advanced Peer-to-Peer Networking end node   A node that provides a broad range of end-user services and supports sessions between its local control point (CP) and the CP in an adjacent network node. It uses these sessions to dynamically register its resources with the adjacent CP (its network node server), to send and receive directory search requests, and to obtain management services. An APPN end node can also attach to a subarea network as a peripheral node or to other end nodes.

Advanced Peer-to-Peer Networking network   A collection of interconnected network nodes and their client end nodes.

Advanced Peer-to-Peer Networking network node   A node that offers a broad range of end-user services and that can provide the following:

- Distributed directory services, including registration of its domain resources to a central directory server

- Topology database exchanges with other APPN network nodes, enabling network nodes throughout the network to select optimal routes for LU-LU sessions based on requested classes of service

- Session services for its local LUs and client end nodes

- Intermediate routing services within an APPN network

Advanced Peer-to-Peer Networking node   An APPN network node or an APPN end node.

advanced program-to-program communication   The general facility characterizing the LU 6.2 architecture and its various implementations in products.

advisory lock   In the AIX operating system, a type of lock that a process holds on a region of a file preventing any other process from locking the region or an overlapping region. See enforced lock.

advisory system   An expert system that gives advice rather than dictates to the user. (T)

AE indicator   See accept-sequence-error indicator.

aerial cable   A telecommunication cable connected above ground to poles or similar structures.

affinity analysis   A technique for identifying the degree of association between two objects. If two objects (e.g., subject areas) are never used by another object (e.g., function), their affinity will be zero. If the same two objects are always used together by the other object, their affinity will be one. This analysis calculates an affinity factor for two objects, which is used as input for performing a cluster analysis. See also cluster analysis.

affinity-based routing   In ACF/TCAM, message routing in which a temporary relationship, or routing affinity, is established between a source and a destination; all messages from the source station are routed to the destination for the duration of the relationship. See also invariant routing, routing by destination, routing by key, transaction-based routing.

affinity diagramming   A technique for gathering large amounts of subjective data (idea, opinions, etc.) and organizing it into groupings based on the natural relationships among the items. Synonymous with Jiro Kawakita (JK) Method.

AFP   Advanced Function Printing.

AFPDS   Advanced Function Printing data stream.

AFP resources   In the AS/400 system, the form definitions, page definitions, fonts, overlays (electronic forms), and page segments (graphic images). With PrintManager, resources can either exist in a system library, or be placed inline with a print job as the job is written to the spool.

after-image   (1) A copy of a block of a record after a modification. (T)   (2) In the AS/400 system and System/38, the contents of a physical file record after the data is changed by a write or an update operation. Contrast with before-image.

AFTRA   American Federation of TV and Radio Artists.

agenda   A prioritized list of pending activities.

Note: Usually such an activity is the application of a certain piece of knowledge. (T)

aggregate   (1) In programming languages, a structured collection of data objects that form a data type. (I)
(2) A transmitted carrier signal that consists of the 12 single sidebands being sent over the transmission circuit. (3) See data aggregate.

aggregate line speed   The maximum possible speed that data can be transmitted using a communications controller. The speed is determined using the sum of the speeds of the communication lines attached to the communications controller.

aggregate resource In the NetView Graphic Monitor Facility, an object that represents a collection of real resources.

aggregation In computer security, acquisition of sensitive information by collecting and correlating information of lesser sensitivity. See also attack.

aging date In the ImagePlus Folder Application Facility, the date used to calculate the priority of the document.

aging priority number A priority number that is automatically assigned to a document according to its urgency when it first enters the routing queue. This number is increased each day that the document remains in the routing queue.

AI Artificial intelligence.

AID Attention identifier.

AID key Attention identifier key.

aiming circle Synonym for aiming symbol.

aiming field Synonym for aiming symbol.

aiming symbol On a display space, a circle or other pattern of light used to guide the area in which the presence of a light pen can be detected at a given time. (I) (A) Synonymous with aiming circle, aiming field. See also icon. See Figure 5.

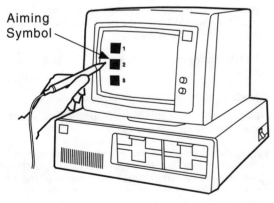

Figure 5. Aiming Symbol

AIP Average instructions per second.

airbrush In multimedia, an application used to create halos, fog, clouds, and similar effects.

air-floating head Synonym for floating head. (I) (A)

airline reservation system An online application in which a computing system is used to keep track of seat inventories, flight schedules, and other related information required to run an airline. The reservation system is designed to maintain up-to-date data files and to respond within seconds or less to inquiries from ticket agents at locations remote from the computing system.

AIX Advanced Interactive Executive.

AIX operating system IBM's implementation of the UNIX (trademark of AT&T Bell Laboratories) operating system. The RISC System/6000 system, among others, runs the AIX operating system. See UNIX operating system.

AIXwindows Desktop An iconic view of the AIX file system providing users with windows, icons, and menus to perform program and file management tasks.

AIXwindows Environment for RISC System/ 6000 A software graphical user interface environment based on OSF/MOTIF, consisting of the AIXwindows toolkit, graphics libraries, window manager, and AIXwindows desktop running on a compatible operating system.

AIXwindows toolkit An object-oriented collection of C language data structure and subroutines that supplement the Enhanced X Windows toolkit and simplify the creation of interactive client application interfaces.

alarm A signal, either audible or visual, at a device such as a display station or printer that is used to get the user's attention.

ALC Annual License Charge.

ALD Automated logic diagram.

ALE Annualized loss expectancy.

alert (1) A message sent to a management services focal point in a network to identify a problem or an impending problem. (2) In the NetView program, a high-priority event that warrants immediate attention. A database record is generated for certain event types that are defined by user-constructed filters.

alert condition A problem or impending problem for which information is collected and possibly forwarded for problem determination, diagnosis, or resolution.

alert controller description A controller description that defines the system to which alerts are to be sent on an alert controller session. See also alert controller session.

alert controller session A type of SSCP-PU session on which alerts can be sent to a system that is designated as an alert focal point.

alert description Information in an alert table that defines the contents of a Systems Network Architecture (SNA) alert for a particular message ID.

alert focal point The system in a network that receives and processes (logs, displays, and optionally forwards) alerts. An alert focal point is a subset of a problem management focal point.

alert ID number A value created from specific fields in the alert using a cyclic redundancy check. A focal point uses this value to refer to a particular alert, for example, to filter out duplicate alerts.

alert table In the AS/400 system, an object consisting of alert descriptions that define the contents of a Systems Network Architecture (SNA) alert for particular error conditions.

alert type A value in an alert that indicates the problem being reported.

algebra See relational algebra.

algebraic expression manipulation statement A statement that specifies the operands and operations that are to be performed on symbols rather than on numeric values. (T)

algebraic language An algorithmic language many of whose statements are structured to resemble the structure of algebraic expressions, for example, ALGOL, FORTRAN. (A)

algebraic manipulation The processing of mathematical expressions without concern for the numeric values of the symbols that represent numbers. (A)

algebraic sign conventions The rules of algebra that determine whether a result is positive or negative when numbers are added, subtracted, multiplied, or divided.

ALGOL Algorithmic language. A language used to express computer programs by algorithms. (A)

ALGOL 60 (algorithmic language 60) A programming language designed for applications requiring numeric computations and some logical processes. (T)

ALGOL 68 (algorithmic language 68) An extensible programming language, more powerful than but not an extension of ALGOL 60, designed for several application areas. (T)

algorithm An ordered set of well-defined rules for the solution of a problem in a finite number of steps.

algorithmic Pertaining to methods of problem solving that involve use of algorithms. Contrast with heuristic.

algorithmic language An artificial language for expressing algorithms. (I)

alias (1) An alternate label; for example, a label and one or more aliases may be used to refer to the same data element or point in a computer program. (A) (2) An alternate name for a member of a partitioned data set. (3) In pulse code modulation, a spurious signal resulting from beats between the signal frequencies and the sampling frequency. (4) In the AIX operating system, an alternative name used for a network. Synonymous with nickname. (5) In IDDU and DDS, an alternative name for a field in a record format description. An alias is used by some high-level programming languages as an alternative name for the field. (6) In FORTRAN, a data object that has a data type, type parameters, and a rank. It may not be referenced or defined unless it is associated with a data object or subobject that may be referenced or defined. If it is an array, it does not have a shape unless it is alias-associated. See parent of an alias.

alias association In FORTRAN, the association of an alias with a nonalias object, following a valid execution of an IDENTIFY statement.

alias file In the Network Carrier Interconnect Manager program, a host file that identifies a resource in the network by providing a cross reference between the 8-character resource name used by the NetView and NETCENTER programs and the object name used by the carrier management system.

aliasing In multimedia applications, the phenomenon of generating a false (alias) frequency, along with the correct one, as an artifact of sampling a signal at discrete points. In imaging, it produces a jagged edge, or stair-step effect. In audio, it produces a "buzz." Contrast with antialiasing. See also moire.

alias name (1) An alternate name. (2) A name that is defined in one network to represent a logical unit name in another interconnected network. The alias name does not have to be the same as the real name; if these names are not the same, translation is required.

alias name translation facility A function, available with the NetView or NCCF licensed programs, for converting logical unit names, logon mode table names, and class-of-service names used in one network into equivalent names to be used in another network.

alias network address An address used by a gateway NCP and a gateway system services control point (SSCP) in one network to represent a logical unit (LU) or SSCP in another network.

align (1) To bring into or be in line with one or more reference points. For example, to align numbers on the decimal point. (2) To arrange in a column in which all values either start in the same position (left-aligned) or end in the same position (right-aligned). See also justify.

Note: This operation can differ for bidirectional and double-byte character set (DBCS) languages.

aligner A device that enables the paper to be correctly lined-up in a machine for typing. (T)

alignment (1) The storing of data in relation to certain machine-dependent boundaries. (2) See boundary alignment.

align text In word processing, to balance irregular line lengths in a document, starting at the point indicated by the position of the cursor. See also justify.

ALL (1) Application load list. (2) In SAA usage, a choice in the View pull-down that a user selects to view all of the items pertaining to an item. See also By..., Some....

all authority In the AS/400 system, an object authority that allows the user to perform all operations on the object except those limited to the owner or controlled by authorization list management authority. The user can control the object's existence, specify the security for the object, and change the object. Contrast with exclude authority.

all object authority In the AS/400 system, a special authority that allows the user to use all system resources without having specific authority to the resources. See also save system authority, job control authority, security administrator authority, service authority, spool control authority.

alliance A business entity in which IBM and other enterprises share interests.

allocatable array In FORTRAN, a named array that has a data type, type parameters, and a rank, but that has a shape and may be referenced or defined only when it has space allocated for it.

allocate (1) To assign a resource, such as a disk or a diskette file, to perform a task. Contrast with deallocate. (2) In the Network Computing System, to create a remote procedure call (RPC) handle that identifies an object. (3) A logical unit (LU) 6.2 application program interface (API) verb used to assign a session to a conversation for the conversation's use. Contrast with deallocate.

allocated variable In PL/I, a variable to which storage is assigned.

allowable resources In System/38, attributes of a process that identify the resources the process is allowed to allocate. Some of these attributes are obtained from the user profile at the time the process is created.

allowance The downward adjustment in the selling price of merchandise because of damage, trade-in, or promotion.

allowed In an ESCON Director, the attribute that, when set, establishes dynamic connectivity capability. Contrast with prohibited.

all points addressable (APA) In computer graphics, pertaining to the ability to address and display or not display each picture element (pel) on a display surface.

all points addressable (APA) graphics Graphics that can be addressed to any point on the screen. Each pixel is identified by its own specific address.

all-stations address Synonym for broadcast address.

alphabet (1) An ordered set of symbols used in a language; for example, the Morse code alphabet. (A) (2) An ordered character set, the order of which has been agreed upon. (T) This definition also covers the alphabets of natural languages, which consist of characters represented by letters, including letters with associated diacritical marks.

alphabetic character (1) A letter or other symbol, excluding digits, used in a language. (2) Any one of the letters A through Z (uppercase and lowercase). Some licensed programs include as alphabet characters the special characters #, $, and @. (3) In COBOL, a letter or a space character. (4) In BASIC, a character that is one of the 26 uppercase or 26 lowercase letters of the alphabet. (5) In DDS and IDDU, any one of the uppercase letters A through Z or one of the characters #, $, or @.

alphabetic character set A character set that contains letters and may contain control characters, special characters, but not digits. (T)

alphabetic character subset A character subset that contains letters and may contain control characters, special characters, and the space character, but not digits. (I) (A)

alphabetic code A code whose application results in a code element set whose elements are formed from an alphabetic character set. (T)

alphabetic coded character set A coded character set that consists of all the letters of an alphabet

alphabetic shift A control for selecting the alphabetic character set in an alphanumeric keyboard printer.

alphabetic string (1) A string consisting solely of letters from the same alphabet. (I) (A) (2) A character string consisting solely of letters and associated special characters from the same alphabet. (A)

alphabetic word (1) A word that consists of letters from the same alphabet. (T) (2) A word consisting of letters and associated special characters, but not digits. (A)

alphabet-name In COBOL, a user-defined word, in the SPECIAL-NAMES paragraph of the Environment Division, that assigns a name to a specific character set, to a collating sequence, or to both.

alphameric Synonym for alphanumeric.

alphanumeric Pertaining to data that consist of letters, digits, and usually other characters, such as punctuation marks. (T), (A) Synonymous with alphameric.

alphanumeric accounting machine An accounting machine that has a means for entering unlimited alphabetic information. (A)

alphanumeric character In COBOL, any character in the character set of a computer.

alphanumeric character set A character set that contains both letters and digits and may contain control characters and special characters. (T)

alphanumeric character subset A character subset that contains both letters and digits and may contain control characters, special characters, and the space character. (I) (A)

alphanumeric code A code whose application results in a code element set whose elements are formed from an alphanumeric character set. (T)

alphanumeric coded character set A coded character set whose character set is an alphanumeric character set. (I) (A)

alphanumeric cursor In GDDM, a physical indicator on a display. The alphanumeric cursor may be moved from one hardware cell to another.

alphanumeric data Data represented by letters and digits, perhaps together with special characters and the space characters. (T)

alphanumeric display device Synonym for character display device.

alphanumeric edited item In COBOL, an alphanumeric data item with a PICTURE character string that contains at least one B, 0, or /.

alphanumeric field A field that can contain any alphabetic, numeric, or special character.

alphanumeric keyboard A keyboard used to enter letters, numbers, and special characters; it is also used to perform special functions such as backspacing and to produce special control signals.

Already-Verified indicator An indication in the Attach function management header that a conversation request on a session between two logical units is being sent with a user ID, but without a password, because the ID-password confirmation has already been verified.

ALS Asian Language Services.

Alt A key on a keyboard that a user presses with one or more other keys to perform an operation, thus extending the function of a standard keyboard.

alteration switch A manual switch on a computer console or a program-simulated switch that can be set on or off to control coded machine instructions.

alter/display In System/370, a feature that enables data in main storage to be displayed and altered at the display/keyboard console.

alternate application The subsystem that is prepared to take over a particular active application's extended recovery facility (XRF) sessions with terminal users, in case the application fails. See active application.

alternate character set A set of characters that includes some special characters, such as mathematical characters and Greek characters, and that is defined for some printers.

alternate code In SNA, a code, frequently ASCII, selected at session activation, to be used to encode end-user data in the request unit (RU) instead of using extended binary-coded decimal interchange code (EBCDIC).

alternate code page In the OS/2 operating system, a code page that replaces a primary code page.

alternate collating sequence Synonym for alternative collating sequence.

alternate cursor In computer graphics, a cursor other than the one that appears on the display surface at power-on time.

alternate extended route In ACF/TCAM, an extended route defined as an additional extended route between two host nodes. The alternate route is taken automatically when no virtual routes to the destination are available. See also extended route, parallel extended routes, primary extended route, route.

alternate function key A key that normally produces a character but that performs a special function when another key is held down simultaneously. See command key, function key, program attention key, program function key.

alternate index (1) A secondary or subordinate index in a hierarchy of indexes. (2) In systems with VSAM, a collection of index entries related to a given base cluster and organized by an alternate key, that is, a key other than the prime key of the associated base cluster data records; it gives an alternate directory for finding records in the data component of a base cluster. See also path.

alternate index cluster In VSAM, the data and index components of an alternate index.

alternate-index entry In VSAM, a catalog entry that contains information about an alternate index. An alternate-index entry points to a data entry and an index entry to describe the components of the alternate index, and to a cluster entry to identify the base cluster of the alternate index. See also cluster entry.

alternate-index record In VSAM, a collection of items used to sequence and locate one or more data records in a base cluster. Each alternate-index record contains an alternate-key value and one or more pointers. When the alternate index supports a key-sequenced data set, the pointer is the prime key value of each data record. When the alternate index supports an entry-sequenced data set, the RBA value of the data record is the pointer. See also alternate index, alternate key, base cluster, key.

alternate index upgrade In systems with VSAM, the process of reflecting changes made to a base cluster in its associated alternate indexes.

alternate installation disk A disk storage unit other than the primary IPL disk on which a DPCX system or another operating system is installed.

alternate key In systems with VSAM, one or more consecutive characters other than the prime key, taken

from each data record of a base cluster and used to build an alternate index for that base cluster. See also key, key field, prime key.

alternate key stroke On a typewriter, actuation of two keys alternately in rapid succession. (T)

alternate library In VSE, an interactively accessible library that can be accessed from a terminal when the user of that terminal issues a connect or switch library request. Synonymous with public library.

alternate name (1) An alternate label; for example, a label and one or more alternate names may be used to refer to the same data element or point in a computer program. (2) In an information resource dictionary, any name by which an entity is known and that may be associated with more than one entity. (3) Synonymous with alias. (A)

alternate path (1) Another channel an operation can use after a failure. See also alternate path retry (APR). (2) In CCP, one of two paths that can be defined for information flowing to and from physical units attached to the network by means of an IBM 3710 Network Controller. See primary path.

alternate path retry (APR) A facility that allows a failed I/O operation to be retried on another channel assigned to the device performing the I/O operation. It also provides the capability to establish other paths to an online or offline device.

alternate record key In COBOL, a key, other than the prime record key, whose contents identify a record within an indexed file.

alternate recovery A facility that attempts system recovery when a processing unit fails by transferring work to another processing unit.

alternate route A secondary or backup route that is used if normal routing is not possible.

alternate screen size (1) An option that permits the size of a display screen to be defined differently from the standard size. (2) In the IBM 3270 Information Display System, the usable area of the display surface in implicit partition state following an Erase/Write Alternate command until the CLEAR key is pressed, the display is powered off, or an Erase/Write command is received.

alternate tape In VSE, a tape drive to which the operating system switches automatically for tape read or write operations if the end of volume has been reached on the originally used tape drive.

alternate track (1) A spare track used in place of a normal track in the event that the latter is damaged or inoperable. Synonymous with alternative track. (T) (2) On a direct access device, a track designated to contain data in place of a defective primary track.

alternating array In RPG, two arrays that are loaded together.

alternating current (AC) An electric current that reverses its direction at regularly recurring intervals.

alternating operating systems In VM/370, multiple operating systems that are loaded consecutively into a virtual machine. Information is passed between the operating systems via CP spooling facilities.

alternating table In RPG, two tables that are loaded together.

alternative analysis Process simplification resulting from the search for alternatives and solutions.

alternative attribute An attribute that may be chosen from a group of two or more alternatives. If none is specified, one of the alternatives is assumed.

alternative collating sequence A user-defined collating sequence that replaces the collating sequence that is normally used. Synonymous with alternate collating sequence.

alternative console A display device assigned by the operating system to function as the console if the console is not working.

alternative cylinder A disk cylinder that is made available by the computer in place of a cylinder that cannot be used.

Alt IMPL Abbr alternative initial microprogram load abbreviated. The process of loading the System/38 microprogramming code from diskettes rather than from auxiliary storage and then activating the code to perform system startup, bypassing certain hardware tests.

Alt IMPL Alternative initial microprogram load. The process of loading the System/38 microprogramming code from diskettes rather than from auxiliary storage and then activating the code.

alternative initial program load (AIPL) In System/38, a process that when combined with the initial program load sequence prepares the system for operation and installs the Control Program Facility (CPF) from a diskette magazine or tape drive.

alternative line A second switched line to which a remote controller can be attached if the first communication line is not available.

alternative sector A disk sector that is made available by the system in place of a sector that cannot be used. See sector.

alternative system console A command display station that can be designated as the system console.

alternative track Synonym for alternate track. (T)

ALTU AIX translation utility.

ALU Arithmetic and logic unit. See arithmetic unit, logic unit.

always-call In MVS, a data management function that calls RACF whenever a data set is accessed, whether the data set is RACF-indicated or not, or when DASD space is allocated for a data set. With always-call in effect, a user can access the data set only if a RACF profile or an entry in the global access checking table exists for that data set.

AM Amplitude modulation.

ambience In audio, the reverberation pattern of a particular concert hall, or listening space.

ambient light In 3D graphics, light that reflects off of one or more surfaces in a scene before arriving at the target surface. Ambient light is assumed to be nondirectional and is reflected uniformly in all directions by the reflecting surface.

ambient noise In acoustics, the noise associated with a particular environment, usually a composite of sounds from many distant or nearby sources. See also background noise, burst noise, impulsive noise.

American National Standard control characters Control characters defined by X3.9-1978 ANSI Programming Language FORTRAN.

American National Standard Labels (ANL) Magnetic tape labels that conform to the conventions established in American National Standards.

American National Standards Institute (ANSI) An organization consisting of producers, consumers, and general interest groups, that establishes the procedures by which accredited organizations create and maintain voluntary industry standards in the United States. (A)

AMH Application message handler.

AMI Access method interface.

AMODE Addressing mode.

ampere (A) A unit of measure for electric current that is equivalent to a flow of one coulomb per second, or to the current produced by one volt applied across a resistance of one ohm.

AM phase shift keying (AM/PSK) A modulation in which a combination of AM and phase shift keying is applied to a single frequency carrier. (T)

amplifier (1) A device that delivers an enlarged reproduction of the essential characteristics of the received wave by enabling the wave to control a local source of power. See operational amplifier. See also repeater.

amplitude The size or magnitude of a voltage or current waveform.

amplitude modulation (AM) Modulation by varying the strength (amplitude) of a fixed-frequency carrier signal in accordance with an information signal. Contrast with frequency modulation (FM). See Figure 6.

Figure 6. Amplitude Modulation

AMS Access method services.

analog Pertaining to data that consists of continuously variable physical quantities. (T)   Contrast with digital, discrete. See network analog. See Figure 7.

Figure 7. Analog Signal

analog adder Synonym for summer.

analog channel A data communication channel on which the information transmitted can take any value between the limits defined by the channel. Voice-grade channels are analog channels.

analog computer (1) A computer whose operations are analogous to the behavior of another system and that accepts, processes, and produces analog data. (T)   (2) A computer that uses analog techniques to process data. (3) See also digital computer, hybrid computer.

analog data Data in the form of a physical quantity that is considered to be continuously variable and

whose magnitude is made directly proportional to the data or to a suitable function of the data. (I)   (A)

analog divider A functional unit whose output analog variable is proportional to the quotient of two input analog variables. (I)   (A)

analog input channel In process control, the analog data path between the connector and the analog-to-digital converter in the analog input subsystem. (T)

Note: This path may include a filter, an analog signal multiplexer, and one or more amplifiers.

analog input channel amplifier An amplifier attached to one or more analog input channels that adapts the analog signal level to the input range of the succeeding analog-to-digital converter. (I)   (A)

analog multiplier A functional unit whose output analog variable is proportional to the product of two input analog variables. This term may also be applied to a device that can perform more than one multiplication; for example, a servo multiplier. (I)   (A)

analog output channel In process control, the analog data path between the connector and the digital-to-analog converter in the analog output subsystem. The path may include a filter, a digital signal multiplexer, and one or more amplifiers. (I)   (A)

analog output channel amplifier An amplifier attached to one or more analog output channels that adapts the output signal range of the digital-to-analog converter to the signal level necessary to control the technical process. (I)   (A)

analog representation A representation of the value of a variable by a physical quantity that is considered to be continuously variable, the magnitude of the physical quantity being made directly proportional to the variable or to a suitable function of the variable. (I)   (A)

analog sound Sound that must be converted to digital form before it can be stored or processed by a computer.

analog-to-digital conversion (A/D) The conversion of an analog signal into a digital bit stream, including the steps of sampling, quantizing, and encoding.

analog-to-digital converter (ADC) (1) A functional unit that converts data from an analog representation to a digital representation. (I)   (A)   (2) A device that senses an analog signal and converts it to a proportional representation in digital form. See Figure 8.

Figure 8. Analog-to-Digital Converter

analog variable A continuously variable signal representing either a mathematical variable or a physical quantity. (A)

analog video Video where the information that represents images is in a continuous-scale electrical signal for amplitude and time. Contrast with digital video.

analysis The methodical investigation of a problem, and the separation of the problem into smaller related units for further detailed study. (A)

analysis routine A routine that analyzes error records, provided by an error handler, to isolate failures to one or more field replaceable units (FRUs).

analyst A person who defines problems and develops algorithms and procedures for their solution. (I) (A)

ancestor widget In AIX Enhanced X Windows, a widget that has inferior widgets. An ancestor is the superior or predecessor of an inferior widget; for example, if W is an inferior of A, then A is an ancestor of W.

anchor Synonym for hot spot.

anchor point In SAA Advanced Common User Access architecture, the position or choice from which selection or deselection is extended.

ancillary equipment Synonym for auxiliary equipment.

AND A logic operator having the property that if P is a statement, Q is a statement, R is a statement...., then the AND of P, Q, R.... is true if all statements are true, false if any statement is false. P AND Q is often represented by P.Q, PQ, PλQ. (I) (A) Synonymous with logical multiply.

AND element Synonym for AND gate.

AND gate (1) A logic element that performs the Boolean operation of conjunction. (T) (2) Synonymous with AND element. See Figure 9.

AND-NOT operation Deprecated term for exclusion.

AND operation Synonym for conjunction.

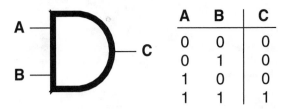

Figure 9. AND Gate

And/Or selection criteria Criteria that can be used when specifying more than one criterion in a search. For example, a user might specify search criteria in two fields. Requesting an "And" search would produce only the address book entries that meet the criteria of both fields. Requesting an "Or" search would produce all the address book entries that meet the criteria of either field.

AND relationship The specification of conditioning indicators so that an operation is performed only when all conditions are met.

angstrom (A) One ten-billionth of a meter.

ANI Automatic number identification.

animate In multimedia applications, to make or design in such a way as to create apparently spontaneous, lifelike movement.

animated screen capture In multimedia applications, recording a computing session for replay on a similar computer with voice annotation; for example, sending a spreadsheet with an accompanying screen recording as an explanation and overview.

animatic In multimedia applications, pertaining to a limited animation consisting of artwork shot on film or videotape and edited to serve as an on-screen storyboard.

anisochronous transmission A transmission process in which there is always an integral number of unit intervals between any two significant instants in the same group; between two significant instants located in different groups, there is not always an integral number of unit intervals. (I) (A) In data transmission the group is a block or a character. See asynchronous transmission.

A/N/K Pertaining to alphabetic, numeric, or Katakana characters.

ANL American National Standard Labels.

annotation (1) An added descriptive comment or explanatory note. (A) (2) In the AS/400 Business

Graphics Utility, the option that allows text to be placed on a chart.

annualized loss expectancy (ALE) In computer security, average loss anticipated per year due to the absence of one or more security measures.

Note: ALE calculation includes analysis of threats and vulnerabilities.

annunciator A visual or audible signaling device, operated by relays, that indicates conditions of associated circuits.

ANSI American National Standards Institute.

answer To respond to a call to complete the connection between data stations.

answerback The response of a terminal to remote control signals. See also handshaking.

answering The process of responding to a calling station to complete the establishment of a connection between data stations. (I) (A) See automatic answering, manual answering.

answer lamp A telephone switchboard lamp that lights when a connecting plug is inserted into a calling jack, goes out when the called telephone answers, and lights when the call is completed.

answer list A list of switched-line station IDs with any required control information. This list is used to ensure that the switched line is connected to an authorized user.

anthropomorphic software agent In multimedia applications, a simulated agent, seemingly living inside the computer, that talks to and listens to the user and acts for the user on command.

antialiasing (1) In computer graphics, techniques used to smooth the "jaggies" otherwise found on lines and polygon edges caused by scan conversion. Common techniques include adjusting pixel positions or setting pixel intensities according to the percentage of pixel area coverage at each point. (2) In imaging, using several intensities of colors (a ramp) between the color of the line and the background color to create the effect of smoother curves and fewer jagged edges on curves and diagonals. (3) In multimedia imaging or audio, removing aliases by eliminating frequencies above half the sample frequencies. (4) Contrast with aliasing.

anticipatory buffering A technique by which data is stored in a buffer before they are needed. (A)

anticipatory paging The transfer of a page from auxiliary storage to real storage prior to the moment of need. (I) (A)

anti-clash key On a typewriter, a control used to restore jammed type bars to their rest positions. (T)

any-mode (1) In VTAM, the form of a RECEIVE request that obtains input from any (unspecified) session. (2) In VTAM, the form of an ACCEPT request that completes the establishment of a session by accepting any one (unspecified) queued CINIT request. Contrast with specific-mode. See continue-any mode. See also accept.

AO (1) Automated office. (2) Automated operator.

AOI Automated operator interface.

AP (1) Attached processor. (2) Alternate printer.

APA All points addressable.

APAR Authorized program analysis report.

APA graphics All points addressable graphics.

aperture (1) One or more adjacent characters in a mask that cause retention of the corresponding characters. (I) (A) (2) An opening in a data medium or device such as a card or magnetic core; for example, the opening in an aperture card combining a microfilm with a punched card, or in a multiple aperture core. (A) (3) A part of a mask that permits retention of the corresponding portions of data. (A) (4) See also multiaperture core.

aperture card A processible card of standard dimensions into which microfilm frames may be inserted. (A)

aperture core See multiaperture core.

APF (1) Authorized program facility. (2) Application processing function.

APG Automatic priority group.

API (1) Application program interface. (2) Application programming interface.

"A" pins Module pins used for interconnecting within the physical circuit of a single substrate.

API verbs A set of programming verbs used to call the PrintManager API functions.

APL A high-level, general-purpose programming language for mathematical applications that simplifies notations and the handling of arrays. (A)

APPC Advanced Program-to-Program Communication.

APPCCB LU 6.2 control block.

APPC/PC Advanced-Program-to-Program Communication / Personal Computers. A protocol that allows systems or devices such as IBM personal computers to be attached to the IBM Token-Ring Network so that they may communicate and process the same programs.

append (1) A function or mode that enables a user to add a new document or character string to the end of previously entered text. (T) (2) In word processing, to attach a file to the end of another file. Contrast with link.

appendage (1) An application program routine provided to assist in handling a specific occurrence. (2) See I/O appendage.

appendage routine Code physically located in a program or subsystem, but logically an extension of a VSE supervisor routine.

appendage task A task assigned the highest-level dispatching priority by the network control program. See also immediate task, nonproductive task, productive task.

APPL Application program.

application (1) The use to which an information processing system is put; for example, a payroll application, an airline reservation application, a network application. (2) A collection of software components used to perform specific types of user-oriented work on a computer. (3) In the AS/400 system, the collection of CSP/AE objects that together can be run on the system. An application consists of a program object, up to five map group objects (depending on how many different devices are supported), and any number of table objects.

application-association In Open Systems Interconnection architecture, a cooperative relationship between two application entities, supported by the exchange of application protocol control information using the services of the presentation services. (T)

application control block (ACB) The control blocks created from the output of DBDGEN and PSBGEN and placed in the ACB library for use during online and DBB region type execution of IMS/VS.

application control block generation (ACBGEN) The process by which the application control blocks are generated.

application control code (ACC) The part of DPCX that handles the execution of program requests and DPCX system services.

application definition record (ADR) An SPPS II record that defines a store controller or terminal application and its corresponding elements such as the program name, subroutine package name, data members, and user files.

application group name In IMS/VS, a name that represents a defined group of resources (program specification blocks, transaction names, and logical terminal names).

application host A data processing system where production applications reside. See also host computer.

application icon In SAA Advanced Common User Access architecture, a unique icon that represents an application when the application is minimized.

application ID In the ImagePlus Folder Application Facility, the ID of the application the user is signed on to.

application ID code In the ImagePlus Folder Application Facility, the identifier of the application the user wants to use. The application ID code is defined during installation of the Folder Application Facility.

application information services In DPCX, the part of application services that gives a program access to certain types of system-maintained information, such as time, date, and operator ID.

application integrity The condition that exists as long as an application remains available and operates according to its specifications. See also data integrity, system integrity.

Application Launch In OfficeVision products, the application that allows the user to add any OS/2 or DOS application that appears in the public or private application list to the Office window.

application layer In the Open Systems Interconnection reference model, the layer that provides means for application processes residing in open systems to exchange information and that contains the application-oriented protocols by which these processes communicate. (T) See open systems interconnection reference model.

application load balancing In IMS/VS, an optional facility that enables an application program to be scheduled into more than one message or batch message region at the same time.

application load list (ALL) In SPPS II, a list of application definition records (ADRs) that are grouped for a particular application load.

application management Functions in the application layer related to the management of Open System Interconnection application processes. (T)

application message handler (AMH) In ACF/TCAM, a user-defined routine that processes messages received by the message control program (MCP) from an application program or sent by the MCP to an application program. See device message handler, internodal message handler, message handler.

application mode In DPPX, the privilege mode that allows processing of all instructions, except supervisor-privileged or I/O-privileged instructions. See also I/O mode, master mode, supervisor mode.

application object In SAA Advanced Common User Access architecture, a form that an application provides for a user; for example, a spreadsheet form. Contrast with user object.

application object name In the IBM ImagePlus system, the name by which the application host knows the object. The name provided by the application host when an object is stored. See also object name.

application option In SAA Common User Access architecture, a choice programmers may implement in their applications. See also user option.

application-oriented language (1) A programming language that has facilities or notations useful for solving problems in one or more specific classes of applications, such as numerical scientific, business data processing, civil engineering, simulation; for example, FORTRAN, COBOL, COGO, SIMSCRIPT. Synonymous with problem-oriented language. (T) (2) A problem-oriented language whose statements contain or resemble the terminology of the occupation or profession of the user. (A)

application plan The control structure produced during the bind process and used by the DB2 program to process SQL statements during application execution.

application problem A problem submitted by an end user and requiring information processing for its solution. (T)

application profile In VSE, a control block in which the system stores the characteristics of one or more application programs.

application program (1) A program that is specific to the solution of an application problem. Synony-

mous with application software. (T) (2) A program written for or by a user that applies to the user's work, such as a program that does inventory control or payroll. (3) A program used to connect and communicate with stations in a network, enabling users to perform application-oriented activities. (4) In SDF/CICS, the program using the physical maps and symbolic description maps generated from a source map set.

application program exit routine In VTAM programs, a user-written exit routine that performs functions for a particular application program and is run as part of the application program; for example, the RPL exit routine, the EXLST exit routine, and the TESTCB exit routine. Contrast with installation exit routine.

application program identification The symbolic name by which an application program is identified to VTAM programs. It is specified in the APPLID parameter of the ACB macroinstruction.

application program image In the IBM 3601 Finance Communication System, an application program that has been processed by the finance image processor and ready to be inserted into a load image or transmitted to the 3601 Finance Communication Controller.

application program interface (API) (1) A functional interface supplied by the operating system or by a separately orderable licensed program that allows an application program written in a high-level language to use specific data or functions of the operating system or the licensed program. (2) The interface through which an application program interacts with an access method. In VTAM programs, it is the language structure used in control blocks so that application programs can reference them and be identified to VTAM.

application program major node In VTAM programs, a group of application program minor nodes. In the VTAM definition library, it is a member, book, or file that contains one or more APPL statements, which represent application programs. In MVS, it is a member of the library; in VSE, it is a book; and in VM, it is a CMS file of filetype VTAMLIST.

application programmer A programmer who designs programming systems and other applications for a user that applies to the user's work.

Application Programming Interface In System/38, the Control Program Facility (CPF) graphics routines that perform basic graphics tasks when called by high-level language application programs.

application program output limits In IMS/VS, an option that allows users to limit the size and number of output segments produced by an application program. This option is intended to minimize the impact of errors in application program operations.

application service element That part of an entity of the application layer that provides a capability within the OSI environment, using underlying service when appropriate. (T)

application services Part of the program service layer of DPCX that assists in such operations as data movement, data conversions, and managing of structured records in system-defined data sets.

application software (1) Software that is specific to the solution of an application problem. (T) (2) Software coded by or for an end user that performs a service or relates to the user's work. See also system software. (3) Software products such as games, spreadsheets, and word processing programs designed for use on a personal computer. See also vendor-logo product. See Figure 10.

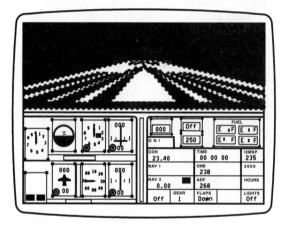

Figure 10. Application (Flight Simulator)

application structure In SDF/CICS, the symbolic names, sequence, and structure of variable fields in a map as required by the application program. The application structure is defined in the map editor function; the items defined are part of the symbolic description map.

application structure definition An alternative for the SDF/CICS application structure specification in which the application structure related aspects of map fields (name, length, sequence number, index, pictures, comment) are displayed and can be edited.

application structure preserving In SDF/CICS, a mode of editing a source map that does not change a symbolic description map generated for the source map.

application structure review A subfunction of the SDF/CICS map editor used to review and edit an application structure.

application structure specification A subfunction of the SDF/CICS map editor that is used to define application structure or full screen naming details of the application structure.

application-to-application services In DPCX, the part of application services that assists a DPCX user program to communicate with other programs executing at 8100/DPCX or at the host.

Application System/400 (AS/400) A family of products designed to offer solutions for commercial data processing, office, and communications environments, as well as to provide simple, consistent programmer and end-user interfaces for businesses of all sizes.

application transaction program A program written for or by a user to process the user's application; in an SNA network, an end user of a type 6.2 logical unit. Contrast with service transaction program.

application window In the AIX operating system, a rectangular area that displays the graphics associated with a specific application. Application windows can be opened, closed, combined with other types of windows, moved, stacked, and otherwise manipulated through user interaction with a window manager.

applicative programming language A programming language whose statements are expressed as functions, either recursively or in combination with other functions. (A)

APPLID Application ID.

APPL-TERMINAL-ID The front-end application terminal identifier indicating association with a document.

APPL-USERID The front-end application user ID of the person making the request for a display, modify, print, or delete of a specific object

apply (1) In journaling, to place after-images of records into a physical file member. The after-images are recorded as entries in a journal. (2) An SMP process that moves distributed code and MVS-type programs to the system libraries.

Apply In SAA Advanced Common User Access architecture, a push button that carries out selected choices in the window that a user is working with; for example the type style or font that a document is to be printed in.

APPN Advanced Peer-to-Peer Networking.

APPN connection A link over which APPN protocols are used.

APPN end node Advanced Peer-to-Peer Networking (APPN) end node.

APPN intermediate routing The capability of an APPN network node to accept traffic from one adjacent node and pass it on to another, with awareness of session affinities in controlling traffic flow and outage notifications.

APPN intermediate routing network The portion of an APPN network consisting of the network nodes and their interconnections.

APPN network Advanced Peer-to-Peer Networking (APPN) network.

APPN network node Advanced Peer-to-Peer Networking (APPN) network node.

APPN node Advanced Peer-to-Peer Networking (APPN) node.

APPN subnetwork In NETDA/2, a group of APPN nodes that are connected through APPN protocols and have the same network ID.

APPN transmission group A transmission group connecting any two APPN nodes.

approach-of-end-of-medium indicator On dictation equipment, a device that gives an audible or visual signal at a precise distance from the end of the recording medium. (I)

APR Alternate path retry.

APT (automatically programmed tools) A programming language for numerically controlled machine tools. (T)

APTO Asia Pacific Technical Operations.

Arabic numerals The 10 numerals used for depicting decimal numbers: the digits 0, 1, 2, 3, 4, 5, 6, 7, 8, and 9. No font is implied. See also Roman numerals.

arbitration A process that determines which device or subsystem gains control of a bus when two or more devices or subsystems simultaneously compete for control.

archival database A backup copy or an historical copy of a database that is saved so that the database can be restored if necessary.

archival quality In a document copying machine, the quality of the copy image that, if it is stored under the stated conditions, guarantees legibility for a specified number of years. (T) See also shelf life.

archive (1) A copy of one or more files or a copy of a database that is saved for future reference or for recovery purposes in case the original data is damaged or lost. (2) In System/36, to store backup copies of folder members or entire folders on tape or diskette. This process may remove an entire member, remove only the data, or leave the member in the system. (3) In System/38, an administrative management function that deletes document log records from a document log after saving all the records that can be saved, thereby ensuring that no records are lost if the save operation terminates abnormally. (4) In NPM, the storage location for historical files, usually grouped by time span.

archived file A file for which an archive file exists. (T)

archived member In System/36, a folder member that has been saved on diskette or tape.

archive file A file out of a collection of files that is set aside for later research or for verification or for security purposes. (T)

archive flag In the OS/2 operating system, a flag of files and directories that the operating system uses to determine which files are new or modified. Files with this flag are included when a backup copy is made or when all the files are restored on a hard disk. See flag.

archiving The storage of backup files and any associated journals, usually for a given period of time. (T)

area (1) In programming languages, a space together with a mechanism for inserting data objects into it, and for accessing and deleting data objects. (I) (2) In the IMS/VS Fast Path feature, a subset of a data entry database (DEDB) that consists of a root-addressable part, an independent-overflow part, and a sequential-dependent part. Areas contain the entire logical structure of a set of root segments and their dependent segments. Each area can have up to seven copies. (3) Synonym for realm. (T)

area code A three-digit number that identifies a geographic area of the USA or Canada to permit direct distance dialing on the telephone system. See also direct distance dialing, numbering plan.

area exchange An area set up for administrative reasons for telephone service covered on a single rate basis, usually a single city or large division, town, or village.

area fill In computer graphics, the filling in of an enclosed area with a pattern.

area-specific help In a program, help information for the area of the screen where the cursor is located when the user presses the Help key.

argument (1) An independent variable. (I) (A) (2) Any value of an independent variable; for example, a search key; a number identifying the location of an item in a table. (I) (A) (3) A parameter passed between a calling program and a called program. (4) See dummy argument.

argument keyword In FORTRAN, a dummy argument name. It may be used in a procedure reference before the equals symbol provided that the procedure has an explicit procedure interface.

argument list A string of arguments.

ARIP Approximate relative index of performance.

arithmetical instruction Synonym for arithmetic instruction.

arithmetic and logic unit A part of a computer that performs arithmetic operations, logic operations, and related operations. (I) (A)

arithmetic check Synonym for mathematical check.

arithmetic comparison In PL/I, a comparison of signed numeric values. See also bit comparison, character comparison.

arithmetic constant In programming languages, a constant of type integer, real, double precision, or complex.

arithmetic conversion The transformation of a value from one arithmetic representation to another.

arithmetic exception An overflow, underflow, or divide check exception.

arithmetic expression (1) An expression that contains arithmetic operations and operands and that can be reduced to a single numeric value. (T) (2) A statement containing any combination of data items joined together by one or more arithmetic operators in such a way that the statement can be evaluated as a single numeric value. (3) In COBOL, an identifier of a numeric elementary item, a numeric literal, such identifiers and literals separated by arithmetic operators, or two arithmetic expressions separated by an arithmetic operator or by another arithmetic expression enclosed in parentheses.

arithmetic function A function that represents one of the basic arithmetic operations such as addition, division, multiplication, and subtraction.

arithmetic instruction An instruction in which the operation part specifies an arithmetic operation. (I) (A) Synonymous with arithmetical instruction.

arithmetic object In the AIX operating system, one or more integral objects having the float, double, or long double type.

arithmetic operation (1) An operation that follows the rules of arithmetic. (I) (A) (2) An operation such as addition, subtraction, multiplication, division, or exponentiation that is performed only on numeric fields. (3) In COBOL, the process caused by the execution of an arithmetic statement, or the evaluation of an arithmetic expression, that results in a mathematically correct solution to the arguments presented. (4) See binary arithmetic operation.

arithmetic operator (1) A symbol used to represent a mathematical operation, such as + or −, used to indicate addition or subtraction. (2) In COBOL and FORTRAN, one of the symbols +, −, *, /, or **, used to indicate, respectively, addition, subtraction, multiplication, division, and exponentiation. (3) See binary operator, unary operator.

arithmetic overflow (1) In an arithmetic operation, a result whose absolute value is too large to be represented within the range of the numeration system in use; for example, the condition that exists either in a fixed-point or floating-point representation system when the result requires more exponent space than is available. (2) Synonymous with overflow. (3) Contrast with arithmetic underflow.

arithmetic register A register that holds operands or the results of arithmetic operations or logic operations. (T)

arithmetic relation Two arithmetic expressions separated by a relational operator.

arithmetic shift A shift, applied to the representation of a number in a fixed-radix numeration system and in a fixed-point representation system, in which only the characters representing the fixed-point of the number are moved. An arithmetic shift is usually equivalent to multiplying the number by a positive or negative integral power of the radix, except for the effect of any rounding; compare the logical shift with the arithmetic shift, especially in the case of floating point representation. (I) (A) See Figure 11.

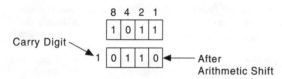

Figure 11. Arithmetic Shift

arithmetic statement In COBOL, a statement that causes an arithmetic operation to be executed.

Note: The arithmetic statements are the ADD, COMPUTE, DIVIDE, MULTIPLY, and SUBTRACT statements.

arithmetic term A term that can be used only in an arithmetic expression.

arithmetic underflow (1) In an arithmetic operation, a result whose absolute value is too small to be represented within the range of the numeration system in use; for example, the condition, existing particularly when a floating-point representation system is used, when the result is smaller than the smallest nonzero quantity that can be represented. The result may underflow because of the generation of a negative exponent that is outside the permissible range. (I) (A) (2) Synonymous with underflow. (3) Contrast with arithmetic overflow.

arithmetic unit A part of a computer that performs arithmetic operations, logic operations, and related operations. (I) (A)

ARM Asynchronous response mode.

ARP Address Resolution Protocol.

ARQ Automatic request for repetition.

array (1) An arrangement of data in one or more dimensions: a list, a table, or a multidimensional arrangement of items. (2) In programming languages, an aggregate that consists of data objects, with identical attributes, each of which may be uniquely referenced by subscripting. (I) (3) See alternating array, programmable logic array.

array declarator The part of a statement that describes an array. The description includes the name of the array, the number of dimensions, and the size of each dimension.

array element A data item in an array.

array expression (1) An expression that represents an array of values. (2) In BASIC, an expression representing an array of values, and used only in a MAT statement. The expression can be numeric, character, or one of several specific forms.

array file An input file containing array elements.

array index The number of an element in an array, or the field containing the number or relative position of an element in an array.

array name The name of an ordered set of data items.

array of structures In PL/I, an array whose elements are structures that have identical names, levels, and characteristics.

array pitch Synonym for row pitch.

array processor (1) A processor capable of executing instructions in which the operands can be arrays of data and not only single elements. In a special case where the array processor works on single elements, such elements are called "scalars." Synonymous with vector processor. (T) (2) A processor that can execute instructions with operands that are arrays of data. Synonymous with vector processor. See also parallel processor architecture.

array section In FORTRAN, an array subobject designated by the symbolic name of an array with a section subscript list, optionally followed by a substring range.

ARRAY type In Pascal, a structured type that consists of an indexed list of elements with each element of the same type.

array variable In PL/I, a variable that represents a collection of data items that must have identical characteristics. Contrast with structure variable.

arrival sequence An order in which records are retrieved that is based on the order in which records are stored in a physical file. See also keyed sequence.

arrival sequence access path An access path that is based on the order in which records are stored in a physical file. See also access path, keyed sequence access path.

arrow button In the AIX operating system, a graphic control that simulates a push button with a directional arrow. The pointer and mouse are used to push the button and start some action that has an associated direction.

artifact A product resulting from human activity; in computer activity, a (usually unwanted) by-product of a process.

artificial intelligence (AI) (1) Simulation by a computer system of functions that are usually associated with human intelligence. (T)   (2) The capability of a device to perform functions that are normally associated with human intelligence, such as reasoning, learning, and self-improvement. (A)   (3) See also expert system, inference engine, knowledge base, knowledge engineering, LISP, machine learning.

artificial language (1) A language whose rules are explicitly established prior to its use. (I) (A) (2) Contrast with natural language.

artificial reality Synonym for virtual reality.

artwork window In the AIX operating system, one of three types of windows available when running the InfoExplorer program with a graphics display. It is available only to graphics displays and contains objects such as syntax diagrams and drawings of devices.   One artwork window is available per InfoExplorer session.   See also navigation window, reading window.

ARU Audio response unit.

ASCAP American Society of Composers, Authors, and Publishers.

ascender The parts of characters;   for example, certain lowercase letters, such as b, d, or f, that rise above the top edge of other lowercase letters such as a, c, and e. Contrast with descender. See Figure 12.

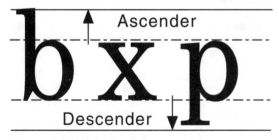

Figure 12. Ascender

ascender height In a font, the distance from the baseline to the top of the character box.   See also maximum ascender.

Note: Ascender height varies for different characters in a font.

ascending key The values by which data are ordered from the lowest value to the highest value of the key according to the rules for comparing data items. Contrast with descending key.

ascending key sequence The arrangement of data in order from the lowest value of the key field to the highest value of the key field.   Contrast with descending key sequence.

ascending sequence The arrangement of data in order from the lowest value to the highest value, according to the rules for comparing data.   Contrast with descending sequence.

ASCII American National Standard Code for Information Interchange. The standard code, using a coded character set consisting of 7-bit coded characters (8 bits including parity check), that is used for information interchange among data processing systems, data communication systems, and associated equipment. The ASCII set consists of control characters and graphic characters. (A)

Note: IBM has defined an extension to ASCII code (characters 128-255).

ASCII control characters Characters listed in the ASCII code table.   See American National Standard control characters.

ASCII line-mode display station A display station that has the characteristics of Teletype equipment or typewriters.   The display station has a one-line input field at the bottom of the screen. The output field is located above the input field and receives data, one line at a time, with the most recent data at the bottom of the output field.

ASCIIZ format A string of ASCII characters ending with a null character.

ASDEC Application Solutions Development Executive Council.

AS/400 Application System/400.

ASI Automated system initialization.

ASID Address space identifier.

ASLOB Application Solutions Line of Business.

ASM (1) Auxiliary storage manager.   (2)   Address space manager.

ASP (1) Attached support processor.   (2) Auxiliary storage pool.

A space In the Print Management Facility, the area in the character box to the left of the first picture element (pel) of the graphic character raster pattern. See also B space, C space.

aspect The qualification of a descriptor. (T)

aspect ratio (1) The ratio of the height of a rectangle to its width.   A rectangle of width 10 inches and height 5 inches has an aspect ratio of 10/5 or 2.

(2) On a display screen, the ratio of the maximum length of a display line to the maximum length of a display column.

ASR Automatic send/receive.

assemble (1) To translate an assembly language program into an object program. (T) (2) In an IBM 3790 Communication System, to convert a set of 3790 programming statements into machine instructions in the host which, after additional processing by the 3790 program validation services, can be transmitted to a 3791 controller and executed in the controller. (3) In a network that has an 8100/DPCX system, to convert at the host computer a set of programming statements into operation codes and operand values which, after additional processing by the program validation services, can be transmitted to an 8100/DPCX system and executed. (4) See also cross assembler.

assemble-and-go An operating technique in which there are no stops between the assembling, loading, and execution of a computer program. (A)

assembled DSCB In the 3790 Communication System and in DPCX, a set of data set definition statements assembled by the host system assembler program, but not yet processed by program validation services.

assembled origin The address of the initial storage location assigned to a computer program by an assembler, a compiler, or a linkage editor. (A)

assembled program In the 3790 Communication System and in DPCX, a set of programming statements assembled at the host system but not yet processed by program validation services.

assemble duration Synonym for assembling time.

assemble editing Putting sequences of video together from a playback VCR to a recording VCR without the use of any feature to ensure smooth edits, such as an edit controller or pre-roll. Synonymous with punch-and-crunch editing. See insert editing.

assembler (1) A translator that can assemble. (T) (2) A computer program that converts assembly language instructions into object code. See also cross assembler.

assembler language A source language that includes symbolic machine language statements in which there is a one-to-one correspondence with the instruction formats and data formats of the computer.

assembler program Deprecated term for assembler.

assembling phase Synonym for assembly phase.

assembling time The elapsed time taken for the execution of an assembler. (I) (A) Synonymous with assemble duration.

assembly language Deprecated term for assembler language.

assembly listing The output of an assembler.

assembly phase (1) The logical subdivision of a run that includes the execution of the assembler. (I) (A) (2) Synonymous with assembling phase.

assembly program Deprecated term for assembler.

assembly time (1) Any instant when the assembler is translating a program. (T) (2) The time at which an assembler translates the symbolic machine language statements into their object code form (machine instructions). See also preassembly time.

assertion A statement that a particular condition holds at a specified point in a program. Assertions may be used for debugging, verification, or as comments. (T)

assessment See risk assessment.

assign To redirect a local device name to a shared resource on a network.

Assign A menu choice that specifies a drive designation to a network directory or specifies a port designation to a network printer.

assigned access name In an information resource dictionary, a name, assigned by a user or by the system, that provides unique access to an entity when it is first added to the information resource dictionary. (A)

assigned descriptive name In an information resource dictionary, a name for an entity that is more descriptive than its assigned access name. (A)

assigned documents In the IBM ImagePlus system, documents currently in a document processing session are referred to as assigned. See document processing session.

assign/free area In System/36, an area of main storage that contains control information for all system activity and for each active job.

assignment (1) A mechanism to give a value to a variable. (I) (2) The process of giving values to variables. (3) A unique setting that can be changed. See also button assignment, gesture assignment.

assignment by name In programming languages, an assignment of a record value to a record variable pertaining only to those components with the same identifier. (I)

assignment compatible In Pascal, pertaining to whether the type of a value allows it to be assigned to a variable. See also compatible types.

assignment conversion In the C and FORTRAN languages, a change to the form of a value where the operand being assigned is converted to the type of the variable receiving the assignment.

assignment expression In XL C, an expression that assigns the value of the right operand expression to the left operand variable and has as its value the value of the right operand.

assignment name In COBOL, a word that associates a file name with a device.

assignment profile A profile of a user that is authorized to use the Folder Application Facility. This profile specifies the types of work that the employee is qualified and authorized to do. See also authorization, user profile.

assignment statement (1) In a high-level language, a statement used to bind variables. (T)   (2) In programming languages, a statement that assigns the value of an expression to a variable. (3) A statement that gives a value to a variable. It always contains the assignment symbol (=); for example, Pascal uses :=.

associated address space In ACF/VTAM programs, the address space in which RPL-based requests are issued that specify an access method control block (ACB) opened in another address space.

associated data On the IBM 3540 Diskette Input/Output Unit, data residing in diskette data sets that are separate from the job stream data and are to be spooled as SYSIN data sets.

association In the Open Systems Interconnection reference model, a cooperative relationship between two peer entities, supported by the exchange of protocol control information using the services of the next lower layer. (T)

association control service element (ACSE) An application service element that provides a single consistent means for establishing and terminating all associations. (T)

associative The mathematical property of addition and multiplication such that $(a + b) + c = a + (b + c)$ and $(a \times b)c = a(b \times c)$.

associative array register A special purpose device used to compensate for inherent delays of segment or page table translation.

associative storage (1) A storage device whose storage locations are identified by their contents, or by part of their contents, rather than by their names or positions. (I) (A) Synonymous with content-addressable storage.   (2) Storage that supplements another storage. (A)

associative storage pool In DPCX, the part of the extended area in processor storage that contains task virtual storage and DPCX indexes. This part is present when DPCX Feature 6001 is installed and the associative storage pool is configured.

assumed decimal point A logical decimal point position that does not occupy a storage position in a data item. It is used by a compiler to align a value properly for calculation or input/output operations. Contrast with actual decimal point.

assumed-size aggregate In programming languages, an aggregate formal parameter that takes some or all of its subscript ranges from a corresponding actual parameter. (I)   See adjustable-size aggregate.

assumed value (1) A value supplied by the system when no value is specified by the move. (2) Synonym for default value.

assurance See quality assurance.

asterisk fill A type of numeric editing that puts asterisks to the left of a number to fill unused positions; for example, "*****476.12."

"A" switchboard A manual telephone switchboard in a local central office, used primarily to receive subscribers' calls and to complete connections either directly or through some other switching equipment.

asymmetric cryptography Synonym for public key cryptography.

asymmetric devices In multiprocessing, devices that have only one path to or from a multiprocessor. They are physically attached to only one processing unit.

asymmetric I/O I/O devices physically attached to only one processing unit, that are available to jobs executing on another processing unit.

asymmetric video compression In multimedia applications, the use of a powerful computer to compress a video for mastering so that a less powerful (less expensive) system is needed to decompress it. Contrast with symmetric video compression.

ASYNC Asynchronous.

asynchronous (ASYNC) (1) Pertaining to two or more processes that do not depend upon the occurrence of specific events such as common timing signals. (T) (2) Without regular time relationship; unexpected or unpredictable with respect to the execution of program instructions.

asynchronous balanced mode (ABM) An operational mode of a balanced data link in which either combined station can send commands at any time and can initiate transmission of response frames without explicit permission from the other combined station. See also asynchronous response mode, normal response mode.

asynchronous balanced mode extended (ABME) In communications, an operational mode in which modulus 128 sequence numbers are used. See also asynchronous balanced mode.

asynchronous communications A method of communications supported by the operating system that allows an exchange of data with a remote device, using either a start-stop line or an X.25 line. Asynchronous communications includes the file transfer support and the interactive terminal facility support.

Asynchronous Communications Dev. Interface An application programming interface or service that is used by application programs. Application programs use the ACDI service to communicate with programs on other systems that use asynchronous communications.

asynchronous controller description A controller description that represents a remote system or device when using asynchronous transmission methods on an asynchronous communication line or when using non-SNA protocols on an X.25 communication line to communicate with the system. See also generic controller description.

asynchronous data transfer A physical transfer of data to or from a device that occurs without a regular or predictable time relationship following execution of an I/O request. Contrast with synchronous data transfer.

asynchronous device A device using data transmission in which transmission of a character or a block of characters can begin at any time, but in which the bits that represent the character or block have equal time duration.

asynchronous disconnected mode (ADM) A nonoperational mode of a balanced or unbalanced data link in which the secondary or combined station is logically disconnected from the data link and therefore cannot transmit or receive information. See also initialization mode, normal disconnected mode.

asynchronous entry point In an application program for an IBM 3601 Finance Communication Controller, the address to which control is passed when data is waiting for an idle station.

asynchronous exit In RSCS, a program call to a task subroutine directly from the RSCS supervisor, not as a result of dispatching.

asynchronous exit routine (1) An exit routine that can be executed at an unpredictable point in the mainline code of a program. (2) In VTAM programs, an RPL exit routine or an EXLST exit routine other than LERAD or SYNAD. (3) Contrast with inline exit routine.

asynchronous flow See expedited flow.

asynchronous I/O A series of input/output operations that are being done separately from the job that requested them.

asynchronous operation (1) An operation that occurs without a regular or predictable time relationship to a specified event; for example, the calling of an error diagnostic routine that may receive control at any time during the execution of a computer program. (A) (2) A sequence of operations that are executed out of time coincidence with any event. (A) (3) Simultaneous operations of software or hardware. In software, an operation, such as a request for session establishment or data transfer, in which the application program is allowed to continue execution while the operation is performed. The access method informs the application program after the operation is completed. (4) Contrast with synchronous operation. (5) Synonymous with synchronous working.

asynchronous procedure In programming languages, a procedure that can be executed concurrently with the calling part of the program. (I)

asynchronous processing A series of operations performed separately from job in which they were requested; for example, submitting a batch job from an interactive job at a workstation. Contrast with synchronous processing.

asynchronous request In VTAM programs, a request for an asynchronous operation. Contrast with synchronous request.

asynchronous response mode (ARM) An operational mode of an unbalanced data link in which a secondary station may initiate transmission without explicit permission from the primary station. See also asynchronous balanced mode, normal response mode.

asynchronous/SDLC A data-link level communications protocol that allows data to be transmitted over an asynchronous line using a control protocol similar to SDLC.

asynchronous terminal A computer terminal that uses asynchronous signals to communicate with a host machine.

asynchronous transmission Data transmission in which transmission of a character or a block of characters can begin at any time but in which the bits that represent the character or block have equal time duration. Contrast with synchronous transmission. See also anisochronous transmission.

asynchronous working Synonym for asynchronous operation.

AS/400 Cryptographic Support The IBM licensed program that provides support for the encryption and decryption of data, according to the Data Encryption Algorithm, and for the management of cryptographic keys and personal identification numbers (PINs).

ATCVT VTAM communication vector table.

at end condition In COBOL, a condition caused:

1. During the execution of a READ statement for a sequentially accessed file, when no next logical record exists in the file, or when the number of significant digits in the relative record number is larger than the size of the relative key data item, or when an optional input file is not present.

2. During the execution of a RETURN statement, when no next logical record exists for the associated sort or merge file.

3. During the execution of a SEARCH statement, when the search operation terminates without satisfying the condition specified in any of the associated WHEN phrases.

atom (1) In the AIX operating system, a unique ID corresponding to a string name. Atoms are used to identify properties, types, and selections. (2) In the AIX operating system, a 32-bit number that represents a string value. (3) See also intern procedure.

atomic In SQL, a characteristic of database data definition functions that allows the function to complete or return to its original state if a power interruption or abnormal end occurs.

atomic operation In the AIX operating system, an operation in which signals cannot occur between the operations of setting masks and waiting for the signal.

attach (1) In programming, to create a task that can be executed asynchronously with the execution of the mainline code. (2) To connect a device logically to a ring network.

attached In System/38, pertaining to a journal receiver that is connected to a journal and is receiving journal entries for that journal. Contrast with detached.

attached message A message that can be sent with an object (such as a note, letter, or memo) to give instructions or additional information to the receiver.

attached processor (1) A processor that has no I/O capability. An attached processor is always linked to a processor that handles I/O. (2) In telephony, a host computer that is attached by a communications line to a telephone switch and that is controlling some, if not all, of the switch functions.

attach header In System/38 Advanced Program-to-Program Communication, control information that identifies the program to be activated at the remote system.

attaching device Any device that is physically connected to a network and can communicate over the network. See ring attaching device.

attaching unit See lobe attaching unit.

attachment A device or feature attached to a processing unit, including required adapters. Contrast with adapter.

attachment feature The circuitry by which a cable from a local terminal or a modem for a remote terminal is attached to a 3792 Auxiliary Control Unit or to a 3791 Controller.

attachment unit interface (AUI) (1) In a local area network, the interface between the medium attachment unit and the data terminal equipment within a data station. (I) (A) (2) See also transceiver cable.

attack (1) In computer security, an attempt to violate data security. (2) See also aggregation, cryptanalysis, exhaustion attack, impersonate, malicious logic, penetration, salami technique, scavenge, spoof, tracker, Trojan horse, wiretapping.

attended mode An operating mode in which an operator is present at the system operator station.

attended operation An application in which human operators are required at both stations to establish the connection and transfer the modems from talk (voice) mode to data mode. Contrast with unattended operation.

attended trail printer In word processing, a trail printer that has no paper handling device and therefore requires operator intervention before and after printing each page. (T)

attention (ATTN) An occurrence external to an operation that could cause an interruption of the operation.

attention field In the 3270 Information Display System, a detectable field in which the designator character is a null, space, or ampersand.

attention identifier (AID) (1) A code in the inbound 3270 data stream that identifies the source or type of data that follow. (2) A character in a data stream indicating that the user has pressed a key, such as the Enter key, that requests an action by the system.

attention identifier character A nondisplayable character, sent to DPCX when the operator takes an action such as using a selector pen or pressing a PF key, that produces a data-entry signal. The character identifies the action or key that generates the condition and is available to programs that use full-screen processing.

attention identifier (AID) key A key that causes an attention identifier (AID) to be sent to the host system when pressed, such as a function key or the Clear, Enter, Page Up, Page Down, Help, Print, and Home keys.

attention interruption (1) An I/O interruption caused by a terminal user pressing an attention key, or its equivalent. See also simulated attention. (2) In MSS, a signal from the mass storage control to the processing unit that a message is waiting. (3) See also signaling attention.

attention key A function key on terminals that, when pressed, causes an I/O interruption in the processing unit.

Attention-key-handling program A user-defined program that is called when the workstation user presses the Attention (Attn) key.

attention symbol On printing terminals under the VM/370 control program, the exclamation point (!) character, used to indicate each time the attention key is pressed.

attenuation (1) The fall-off of light intensity with distance. (2) A decrease in magnitude of current, voltage, or power of a signal in transmission between points. (3) In fiber optics, a decrease in magnitude of average optical power. (E) See Figure 13.

Note: In an optical fiber, attenuation results from absorption, scattering, and other radiation. Attenuation is usually expressed in decibels (dB). However, atten-

uation is often used as a synonym for attenuation coefficient. (E)

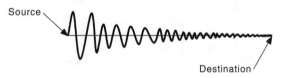

Figure 13. Attenuation

attenuation coefficient In fiber optics, the rate of decrease in magnitude of average optical power with respect to distance along the fiber, usually expressed in decibels per kilometer (dB/km). (E)

attenuator Synonym for pad.

ATTN Attention.

attribute (1) A named property of an entity. (2) A terminal display language or transformation definition language (TDL) keyword that specifies a particular quality for the TDL object with which it is associated. (3) In AIX graphics, a parameter that can affect the "color." If it is set to "RED," it will remain red until it is changed, and everything that is drawn will be drawn in red. Other attributes include linestyle, linewidth, pattern, and font. See also pipeline options. (4) In the AS/400 Business Graphics Utility, a characteristic that determines the chart format. (5) In an SQL database design, a characteristic of an entity; for example, the telephone number of an employee is one of that employee's attributes. (6) In FORTRAN, a property of a data object that may be specified in a type declaration statement, namely data type, type parameters, rank, shape, whether variable or constant, initial value, accessibility (PUBLIC or PRIVATE), intent (IN, OUT, or INOUT), whether allocatable, whether alias, whether optional, whether to be saved, and whether ranged. See value attribute.

attribute byte (1) In 3270 applications, the byte used for data security to indicate whether a field can be or has been changed. (2) In DPCX, a nondisplayable character that defines the location and characteristics of the field that follows. (3) In SAA Basic Common User Access architecture, an undisplayed character that defines the characteristics of the field that follows it. On some terminals, some attribute bytes occupy space on the screen.

attribute character (1) In SDF/CICS, a character used in the field attribute definition subfunction of the map editor, denoting a set of field attributes. The set of field attributes can be associated with the character in the session profile or with an EQUATE command; synonymous with equate character. (2) A character associated with a field in a display file that defines how the field is displayed; for example, underlined, blinking, or intensified.

attribute data element In a database, a data element that describes the properties of another data element.

attribute domain The set of possible values of an attribute. (T)

attribute file In AIX system configuration, a text file that is organized into stanzas, each of which has a stanza name and a set of attribute definitions in the form of Attribute=Value pairs. Configuration files have the attribute file format.

attribute label In the Generalized Markup Language markup, a name of an attribute that is entered in the source document when specifying the value of the attribute.

attribute relationship A perceived association among attributes. (T)

attribute simulation In IMS/VS, a message format service (MFS) option that allows an application program to simulate display (video) attributes such as high intensity on printer devices.

attribute type (1) In a relational database, a set of all possible attribute values, corresponding to the same property, of entity occurrences of an entity type. The name of a column of a relation table can be viewed as the name of an attribute type. (2) In the 3270 data stream, a code that identifies the properties from which an associated set of attribute values can be selected. See also extended color, field validation.

attribute value (1) In a relational database, a specific occurrence of an attribute type. (T)   (2) In the 3270 data stream, a code immediately following the attribute type that specifies a particular property from the set defined by the attribute type.

audible alarm An alarm that is sounded when designated events occur that require operator attention or intervention before continuing system operation.

audible cue A sound generated by a computer to draw a user's attention to, or provide feedback about, an event or state of the computer. Audible cues enhance and reinforce visible cues. See also visible cue.

audio Pertaining to the portion of recorded information that can be heard.

audio clip In multimedia applications, a section of recorded audio material.

audio dithering A technique for creating audio samples of equal size by changing the samples of frames with too much data so that each frame contains an equal number of samples for an equal period of time (1/30th of a second).

audio dubbing In multimedia, recording audio on a videotape without erasing the video.

audio file A file used for audio sounds on a waveform device.

audio frequencies Frequencies that can be heard by the human ear (approximately 15 hertz to 20,000 hertz).

audio inquiry Keying or dialing data into a computer that has an audio response unit attached to provide an audible response.

audio line See audio telecommunication line.

audio mixer A device used to simultaneously combine and blend several sound inputs into one or two outputs.

audio mixing Creating a single audio track from more than one source, through the use of a sound mixing device such as a mike mixer.

audio processing In multimedia applications, manipulating digital audio; for example, by editing or creating special effects.

audio response message An audible response generated by an audio response unit from output accepted from a computer.

audio response unit (ARU) An output device that provides a spoken response to digital inquiries from a telephone or other device. The response is composed from a prerecorded vocabulary of words and can be transmitted over telecommunication lines to the location from which the inquiry originated. See also voice synthesizer.

audio segment In multimedia applications, a contiguous set of recorded data from an audio track. An audio segment might or might not be associated with a video segment.

audio stream Frames of compressed audio.

audio synthesis The conversion of digital data stored in a computer to analog output that simulates sounds such as music or the human voice.

audio telecommunication line A switched telecommunication line attached to an audio response unit.

audio terminal A unit of equipment associated with an audio response unit at which keyed or dialed data is entered for transmission to the computer; an associated audio response unit produces an audible response.

audio track (1) The audio (sound) portion of a program. (2) In multimedia applications, the track on which sound is recorded beside the recording of the image. A system with two audio tracks can have either stereo sound or two independent audio tracks. Synonymous with sound track.

Audio-Video Support System (AVSS) In a Digital Video Interactive (DVI) application, the software that plays motion video and audio.

audiovisual Pertaining to experiences, equipment, and materials used for communication that make use of both hearing and sight.

Audio Visual Authoring (AVA) language A language used by the Audio Visual Connection (AVC) to add logic, arithmetic, file actions, trigger fields, and similar advanced functions to stories.

Audio Visual Connection (AVC) The desktop system used on an IBM PS/2 that enables an author to develop and display audio-visual shows.

Audio Visual Kernel (AVK) The software driver for IBM ActionMedia II. AVK extracts the compressed video from the blocks.

audiovisual computer program A computer program that makes use of both sound and images.

audit To review and examine the activities of a data processing system mainly to test the adequacy and effectiveness of procedures for data security and data accuracy. See computer-system audit. See also audit review file, audit trail.

audit area In the OfficeVision products, a part of the status line in the document window of the Writing Pad function. The audit area provides information about control code characters when selected with the cursor.

audit events In computer security, occurrences on a system that may be security violations. These events cause an audit record to be written.

audit review file A file created by executing statements included in a program for the explicit purpose of providing data for auditing. (I) (A)

audit trail (1) Data, in the form of a logical path linking a sequence of events, used for tracing the transactions that have affected the contents of a record. (T) (2) Information that allows tracing of the history of things such as a customer account or item record.

audit window In System/36, a field in the status line that displays the name of a text instruction when the cursor is under the instruction.

augend In an addition operation, a number or quantity to which numbers or quantities are added. (I) (A)

AUI Attachment unit interface.

authentication (1) In computer security, verification of the identity of a user or the user's eligibility to access an object. (2) In computer security, verification that a message has not been altered or corrupted. (3) In computer security, a process used to verify the user of an information system or protected resources. (4) A process that checks the integrity of an entity. (5) See also identity validation, message authentication code, password.

authentication algorithm An algorithm used to generate a unique value from a contiguous string of bits, characters, or data units.

author (1) To create a computer application, often through the use of an authoring language or authoring system. (2) A person who creates an interactive videodisc or a multimedia control program.

authoring In multimedia applications, a structured approach to combining all media elements within an interactive production, assisted by computer software designed for this purpose.

authoring language A high-level computer application that enables a non-programmer to create courseware. An authoring language usually provides fewer features than an authoring system. See also authoring system.

authoring system A set of tools for users to create an interactive application without implementing formal programming.

authority The right to access objects, resources, or functions.

authority checking A function of the system that looks for and verifies a user's authority to an object.

authority credentials In DPPX, a value assigned to users, commands, data sets, and load modules to establish a scheme for: (a) restricting certain users from accessing certain commands, data sets, and load modules; and (b) restricting certain load modules from requesting execution of certain other load modules.

authority holder In the AS/400 system, an object that specifies and reserves an authority for a program-described database file before the file is created. When the file is created, the authority specified in the holder is linked to the file.

authorization (1) In computer security, the right granted to a user to communicate with or make use of a computer system. (T) (2) An access right. (3) The process of granting a user either complete or restricted access to an object, resource, or function. (4) See also clearance.

authorization checking The action of determining whether a user is permitted access to a RACF-protected resource.

authorization code A code made up of user identification and password, used to protect against unauthorized access to data and system facilities.

authorization credentials The evidence of a user's authority to access DPPX/DTMS resources. Authorization credentials are defined for a user in the user's profile. The authorization credentials required for access to a DPPX/DTMS resource, such as a database, are defined in the profile for the resource.

authorization exit routine In VTAM programs, an optional installation exit routine that approves or disapproves requests for session initiation.

authorization ID In SQL, a user profile. A name identifying a user to whom privileges can be granted.

authorization list In the AS/400 system, a list of two or more user IDs and their authorities for system resources.

authorization list management authority In the AS/400 system, an object authority that allows the user to add users to, remove users from, and change users' authorities on the authorization list.

authorization message An NCCF message that is directed to an authorized operator; for example, a message about the use of NCCF, such as a successful logon, repeated unsuccessful logons, a logon rejected because of an invalid password, a data services manager error message, or logoff.

authorize To permit or give authority to a user to communicate with or make use of an object, resource, or function.

authorized APPN end node In APPN, an end node that is "trusted" by its network node server to supply directory and routing information about its resources that will affect the network directory database. If a node is authorized, all information it sends about itself is accepted. The authorization status of an end node is system-defined in its network node server. Contrast with unauthorized APPN end node.

authorized command In DPPX, a command with a nonzero function authority credential (FAC) in its command profile.

authorized end node Synonym for authorized APPN end node.

authorized environment In DPPX, an active environment whose associated user profile contains a nonzero function authority credential (FAC).

authorized library A library that may contain authorized programs.

authorized operator In the NetView program, an operator who has been authorized to receive undeliverable messages and lost terminal messages.

authorized path In VTAM programs for MVS, a facility that enables an application program to specify that a data transfer or related operation be carried out in a privileged and more efficient manner.

authorized program A system program or user program that is allowed to use restricted functions.

authorized program analysis report (APAR) A report of a problem caused by a suspected defect in a current unaltered release of a program.

authorized program facility A facility that permits identification of programs authorized to use restricted functions.

authorized receiver In the NetView program, an authorized operator who receives all the unsolicited and authorized-receiver messages not assigned to a specific operator.

authorized state A condition in which a problem program has access to resources that would otherwise not be available.

authorized user (1) In DPPX, a user whose user profile contains a nonzero function authority credential (FAC). See also database administrator. See space manager.

auto-abstract (1) Pertaining to the material abstracted from a document by machine methods. (2) To select keywords from a document by machine methods.

auto-answer Synonym for automatic answering.

auto-baud In CCP, a line speed designation by which the IBM 3710 Network Controller determines the line speed.

auto-call Synonym for automatic calling.

auto-call unit A device that allows a system to automatically call a remote location.

autodialer Synonym for automatic dialing unit.

auto-duplication feature A data file utility (DFU) function that duplicates into the current record certain types of information from predetermined fields in a previous record.

autoexec A LinkWay button that is executed as soon as the user accesses the page on which the button resides.

auto-index To prepare an index by a machine method.

auto key In word processing, a control that starts the continuous printout or scanning of selected recorded text. (T)

autolink In System/36, a part of the overlay linkage editor that automatically resolves external references by searching the library for the appropriate object program.

autoloader The part of an IBM 3540 Diskette Input/Output Unit that automatically feeds diskettes to the drive and ejects and stacks diskettes. The stacker and hopper have a capacity of 20 diskettes each.

autologon Synonym for automatic logon.

automate To convert a process or equipment to automatic operation. (I) (A)

automated console operations (ACO) The use of automated procedures to replace or simplify the actions that an operator takes from a console in response to system or network events.

automated data medium Synonym for machine-readable medium.

automated graphics The method of building or drawing geometric figures, for example, lines, circles, rectangles, by way of computers.

automated logic diagram (ALD) A computer generated diagram that represents functioning circuitry in terms of logic blocks, interconnecting conductor networks, and input/output terminals.

automated office (AO) An office in which operations on information, such as word processing and file management, are performed in conjunction with a data processing system.

automated operator (AO) In IMS/VS, an application program that can issue a subset of IMS/VS operator commands and receive status information on the execution of the commands.

automated operator interface (AOI) In IMS/VS, an interface that allows installations to monitor and control IMS/VS activities. The interface enables: (1) an application program, using DL/I calls, to issue a subset of IMS/VS operator commands and receive command responses, (2) a user exit routine to monitor activities and take appropriate action, and (3) operator commands, responses, and asynchronous output destined for the IMS/VS master terminal to be logged to the secondary master terminal.

automated operator user exit routine A user exit routine that is passed a copy of system messages destined for the master terminal, operator-entered commands, and command responses. The user exit routine may examine the commands and command responses and write a message to any terminal or to a queue for processing by an application program.

automated system initialization (ASI) A function of VSE that allows control information for system startup to be cataloged for automatic retrieval during system startup.

automatic Pertaining to a process or device that, under specified conditions, functions without intervention by a human operator. (I) (A)

automatic activation In VTAM, the activation of links and link stations in adjacent subarea nodes as a result of channel device name or RNAME specifications related to an activation command that names a subarea node. See also direct activation.

automatically programmable tools (APT) One of the main software languages used in computer-aided manufacturing to program numerically controlled machine tools. (T)

automatic answer In data communications, a line type that does not require operator action to receive a call over a switched line. Contrast with manual answer.

automatic answering (1) Answering in which the called data terminal equipment (DTE) automatically responds to the calling signal. The call may be established whether or not the called DTE is attended. (I) (A) (2) A machine feature that permits a station to respond without operator action to a call it receives over a switched line. (3) Synonymous with auto-answer. See also manual answering. Contrast with automatic calling.

automatic backup In the Data Facility Hierarchical Storage Manager, the process of automatically copying eligible data sets from primary volumes or migration volumes to backup volumes during a specified backup cycle.

automatic bind In SQL, the bind that automatically takes place when an application program is run and the bound access plan is nullified; that is, without a user issuing a CRTSQLxxx command (where xxx: is C, CBL, FTN, PLI or RPG). See also bind, dynamic bind.

automatic call distribution (ACD) In telephony, a service that allows incoming telephone calls directed to the same dialed number to be routed to one of multiple agents, all of whom can provide the same service to the calling party and all of whom are assigned to the same ACD group.

automatic calling (1) Calling in which the elements of the selection signal are entered into the data network contiguously at the full data signaling rate. The selection signal is generated by the data terminal equipment. A limit may be imposed by the design criteria of the network to prevent more than a permitted number of unsuccessful call attempts to the same address within a specified period. (I) (2) A feature that permits a station to initiate a connection with another station over a switched line without operator action. (3) Synonymous with auto-call. See also direct call, manual calling. Contrast with automatic answering.

automatic calling unit (ACU) A dialing device that permits a computer to automatically dial calls over a network. See also automatic dialing unit.

automatic carriage A control mechanism for a typewriter or other listing device that can automatically control the feeding, spacing, skipping, and ejecting of paper or preprinted forms. (A)

automatic carrier The unit that carries the type element on SELECTRIC devices.

automatic catalog search In DPPX, the process in which the linkage editor searches a catalog for control sections to resolve external references not resolved by primary input processing.

automatic check A check performed by equipment built-in specifically for checking purposes. (A) Synonymous with built-in check, hardware check. Contrast with programmed check.

automatic class selection (ACS) routines A user-supplied routine called by MVS/DFP 3.2 that provides the storage class, storage group, and management class for objects being stored or retrieved.

automatic coding A type of automatic programming in which a computer is used to prepare computer instruction code. (T) Synonym for automatic programming.

automatic configuration In the AS/400 system, a function that names and creates the descriptions of network devices and controllers attached to a preexisting line. The objects are also varied on at a user's request.

automatic constant On a calculator, a number automatically held in the machine for repeated use. (T)

automatic constant function In a calculator, the function that allows a number automatically held to be used repeatedly. (I) (A)

automatic control engineering The branch of science and technology that deals with the design and use of automatic control devices and systems. (I) (A)

automatic data processing (ADP) Data processing by means of one or more devices that use common storage for all or part of a computer program and also for all or part of the data necessary for execution of the program; that execute user-written or user-designated programs; that perform user-designated symbol manipulation, such as arithmetic operations, logic operations, or character-string manipulations; and that can execute programs that can modify themselves during their execution. Automatic data processing may be performed by a stand-alone unit or by several connected units. (A) Synonym for data processing.

automatic data set protection (ADSP) In MVS, a user attribute that causes all permanent data sets created by the user to be automatically defined to RACF with a discrete RACF profile.

automatic deactivation In VTAM programs, the deactivation of links and link stations in adjacent subarea nodes as a result of a deactivation request that names a subarea node. Automatic deactivation occurs only for automatically activated links and link stations that have not also been directly or indirectly activated. See also direct deactivation.

automatic decimal alignment In word processing, a feature that automatically aligns columns of numbers on either side of a decimal marker.

automatic dial A function of the system that allows a system to automatically dial a remote station over a switched line without the assistance of an operator.

automatic dialing unit (ADU) A device capable of automatically generating dialing digits. Synonymous with autodialer. See also automatic calling unit.

automatic document feeder On a document copying machine, a device in which a quantity of originals may be placed so that they are automatically fed onto the platen. (T)

automatic document handler On a document copying machine, an automatic document feeder that incorporates additional facilities to provide for recycling of originals as may be required by the copying program selected. (T)

automatic-feed punch A punch that automatically moves punch cards from a card hopper, along a card track, and to a card stacker. (A)

automatic function (1) On a calculator, a machine function or series of machine functions controlled by the program cycle and carried out without the assistance of the machine operator. (T) (2) Work done by a computer that a user does not explicitly have to request.

automatic gain control A feature of a dictation machine that automatically adjusts the level of input to the recording medium largely independently of the volume of the source. (I)

automatic hyphenation An option available when creating a document that automatically hyphenates words at the end of a line when the lines are adjusted.

automatic key generation In System/36, a data file utility (DFU) feature that assigns five-digit keys to the records of a file.

automatic library call The process in which control sections are processed by the linkage editor or loader to resolve references to members of partitioned data sets.

automatic licensed internal code completion A function of the system that automatically attempts to complete interrupted machine instructions following an abnormal end of the system processing.

automatic line adjust A function that makes text fit between defined left and right margins automatically when characters are inserted or deleted and when the left, right, or temporary left margin is changed.

automatic logon (1) A process by which VTAM automatically creates a session-initiation request to establish a session between two logical units (LUs). The session is between a designated primary logical unit (PLU) and a secondary logical unit (SLU) that is neither queued for nor in session with another PLU. Synonymous with autologon. See also controlling application program, controlling logical unit. (2) In VM, a process by which a virtual machine is initiated by other than the user of that virtual machine; for example, the primary VM operator's virtual machine is activated automatically during VM initialization.

automatic message-switching center A location at which messages are automatically routed according to information they contain.

automatic migration In the Data Facility Hierarchical Storage Manager, the process of automatically moving eligible data sets either from primary volumes to migration level 1 volumes or from migration level 1 volumes to migration level 2 volumes without a specific request for each data set so moved. See general migration, interval migration.

automatic noise suppression A feature of a dictation machine that automatically reduces electrical noise during input to the recording medium or during playback or both. (I)

automatic number identification (ANI) In telephony, a service provided by enhanced switch networks that passes the calling party's telephone number through the network to the called party's telephone number.

automatic page numbering The ability of a text editor to automatically generate page numbers to the successive pages of a document. This function enables the user to enter text without regard for final page endings. The system will create pages of desired length and will number them appropriately. (T)

automatic pagination The automatic arrangement of text according to a preset number of page layout parameters. (T)

automatic paragraph numbering The ability of a text editor to automatically generate paragraph numbers to the successive paragraphs of a document. (T)

automatic polling See auto-poll.

automatic priority group (APG) In OS/VS2, a group of tasks at a single priority level that are dispatched according to an algorithm that attempts to provide optimum use of the processing unit and I/O resources. See also dynamic dispatching.

automatic profile In MVS, a TAPEVOL profile that RACF creates when a RACF-defined user protects a tape data set. The TAPEVOL profile created in this manner is called an automatic profile because, when the last data set on the volume is deleted, RACF automatically deletes the TAPEVOL profile. See also nonautomatic profile.

automatic program control In duplicating machines capable of automatic or semi-automatic operation, a control that initiates the working of the machine in accordance with a predetermined program. (T)

automatic programming The process of using a computer to perform some stages of the work involved in preparing a computer program. (A) Synonymous with automatic coding.

automatic purge/copy/redirect In ACF/TCAM, a collection of message-handler and extended operator control functions that permit messages to be conditionally or unconditionally redirected to another destination, copied to another destination, or purged.

automatic ranging In the AS/400 Business Graphics Utility, the use of system-supplied values to determine the intervals on a chart so that the maximum and minimum data values can be represented on the workstation or plotter.

automatic reactivation In the NetView program, the activation of a node from the inactive state without any action by the network operator.

automatic reconfiguration and retry In tightly coupled multiprocessing and MVS, reconfiguration of the system from multiprocessing to uniprocessing while allowing applications to continue running without interruption.

automatic request for repetition (ARQ) A feature that automatically initiates a request for retransmission when a transmission error is detected.

automatic response severity level See severity level.

automatic restart A restart that takes place during the current run, that is, without resubmitting the job. An automatic restart can occur within a job step or at the beginning of a job step. Contrast with deferred restart.

automatic scrolling In the AIX operating system, the scrolling action that takes place automatically when a cursor is moved to the border of a pane.

automatic search catalog In DPPX, a catalog the linkage editor can search to resolve references left unresolved after it has searched the input catalog.

automatic send/receive (ASR) A teletypewriter unit with keyboard, printer, paper tape, reader/transmitter, and paper tape punch. This combination of units may be used online or offline and, in some cases, online and offline concurrently.

automatic sequential operation Synonym for iterative operation. (I) (A)

Automatic Shape Determination The process that decides which of as many as four shapes should be used for an Arabic character. The decision is based on whether the character is at the beginning, middle, or end of a word, or whether the character is the only character in the word.

automatic skip On an IBM 3270 Display Station, a feature that, after entry of a character into the last character position of an unprotected display field, repositions the cursor to the first character position of the next unprotected display field.

automatic software re-IPL In the VM/XA Migration Aid, the process by which the control program attempts to restart the system after abnormal termination. This process does not involve the hardware IPL process. See also preferred virtual machine recovery.

automatic stop A feature of a dictation machine or of a transcription machine that automatically stops the recording medium when it reaches the end of its travel (forward and backward) and which may also switch off the machine. (I)

automatic storage allocation In programming languages, a mechanism for allocating space to data objects only for the duration of the execution of their scope. (I)

Note: Automatic storage allocation is one form of dynamic storage allocation; another form is program controlled storage allocation.

automatic tax calculation Calculation of tax by a point of sale terminal, added when totals are taken.

automatic teller machine (ATM) Synonym for consumer transaction facility.

automatic toning control In a document copying machine, a built-in metering device that regulates the supply of the toner to the developing system of an electrostatic machine. (T)

automatic upshift On some display terminals, a feature that actuates the SHIFT or NUMERIC key on the keyboard when the cursor enters a display field that can contain only numeric characters.

automatic variable A variable allocated on entry to a routine and deallocated on the return. Contrast with static variable.

automatic vary on An option specified during the creation of configuration objects that allows them to be available when the system is started (IPLed).

automatic volume recognition (AVR) A feature that allows the operator to mount labeled volumes on available I/O devices before the volumes are needed by a job step.

automatic volume switching A facility that provides access to a sequential data set that extends across two or more volumes, and to concatenated data sets stored on different volumes.

automation (1) The conversion of processes to automatic operation or the results of the conversion. (T) (2) The theory, art, or technique of making a process more automatic. (3) The investigation, design, development, and application of methods of rendering processes automatic, self-moving, or self-controlling.

auto-network shutdown An optional network control program procedure that initiates system closedown when the operator requests it through the 370X panel when the channel between the host processor and the communication controller fails or when the data link between the local and the remote communication controller fails.

autonomous system In the AIX operating system, a group of networks and gateways for which one administrative authority has responsibility.

auto-parity In CCP, a method that allows an IBM 3710 Network Controller to decide whether to use odd or even parity when communicating with an SS terminal.

auto-poll A machine feature of a transmission control unit that permits the unit to handle negative responses to polling without interrupting the processing unit.

autoprompting In System/38 control language programs, a function that provides the automatic prompting of a CL command. Contrast with selective prompting.

autoranging In System/38 graphics, the use of system defaults to determine the intervals on a chart so that the maximum and minimum data values can be represented on the graphics display station or plotter.

auto removal On a network, the removal of a device such as an attached IBM personal computer from the data passing activity without human intervention;

accomplished by the adapter. This action is accomplished by the adapter.

autoskip option In System/36, an option of the source entry utility that allows the cursor to skip fields automatically.

autostart (1) In VSE, a facility that starts-up VSE/POWER with little or no operator involvement. (2) In System/38, a facility that automatically initiates a job when a subsystem is started.

autostart job A job that does repetitive work or one-time initialization work associated with a particular subsystem. The autostart jobs associated with a subsystem are automatically started each time the subsystem is started.

autostart job entry In System/38, a work entry in a subsystem description that specifies a job to be initiated automatically each time the subsystem is started.

auto tab In SAA Advanced Common User Access architecture, an application option that automatically moves the text cursor to the next entry field after a user types a character into the last character position of an entry field.

autotask An unattended NetView operator station task that does not require a terminal or a logged-on user. Autotasks can run independent of VTAM programs and are typically used for automated console operations. Contrast with logged-on operator.

autowriter In System/36, a System Support Program Product option that causes the spool writer program to be loaded without operator action whenever output exists in the spool file. See also spool writer.

auxiliary directory In CMS, an extension of the CMS file directory that contains the names and locations of certain CMS modules not included in the CMS file directory.

auxiliary equipment Equipment not under direct control of the processing unit. Synonymous with ancillary equipment.

auxiliary file In CMS, a file that contains a list of filetypes of update files to be applied to a particular source file. See also control file.

auxiliary network address In VTAM programs, any network address, except the main network address, assigned to a logical unit capable of having parallel sessions. Contrast with main network address.

auxiliary operation An offline operation performed by equipment not under control of the processing unit. (A)

auxiliary storage (1) All addressable storage, other than main storage, that can be accessed by means of an input/output channel; for example, storage on magnetic tape or direct access devices. Synonymous with external storage, secondary storage. (2) Contrast with main storage. (3) Synonym for external storage.

auxiliary storage management In OS/VS, a set of routines in the paging supervisor that control transfer of pages between real storage and external page storage.

auxiliary storage pool (ASP) In the AS/400 system, a group of units defined from the disk units that make up auxiliary storage. ASPs provide a means of isolating certain objects on specific disk units to prevent the loss of data due to disk media failures on other disk units. See also unit, system ASP, user ASP.

AVA Audio Visual Authoring language.

availability (1) The ratio of the total time a functional unit is capable of being used to the total time the functional unit is required for use. (A) (2) In computer security, the property of being accessible and usable on demand by an authorized subject. (3) The ability of a functional unit to be in a state to perform a required function under given conditions at a given instant of time or over a given time interval, assuming that the required external resources are provided. See instantaneous availability. (4) The degree to which a system or resource is ready when needed. (T)

available In VTAM programs, pertaining to a logical unit that is active, connected, enabled, and not at its session limit.

available choice In SAA Common User Access architecture, an item that a user can select. Contrast with unavailable choice.

available file space A description in a menu or directory that indicates the number of characters that can be entered before reaching the file size limit.

available frame count In OS/VS2 and VM, a count of page frames that are ready for occupancy by virtual pages.

available light The amount of light ordinarily present in the environment.

available memory In an IBM personal computer, the number of bytes of memory that can be used after active files are created.

available page queue In OS/VS and VM, a list of pages whose real storage is currently available for allocation to any task. See also active page queue, hold page queue.

available state The state of a device is in when it is configured. The device status field in the Customized Devices Object Class reflects whether or not a device is in the available state.

available time From the point of view of a user, the time during which a functional unit can be used. (I) (A) Contrast with maintenance time.

available unit queue In ACF/TCAM, a queue in main storage to which all buffer units are assigned initially; that is, prior to assignment to ACF/TCAM lines and application programs requiring buffers.

AVC Audio Visual Connection.

average access time The average time between the instant of request and the delivery from a storage device.

average conditional information content Synonym for conditional entropy.

average information content Synonym for entropy.

average information rate In information theory, the mean entropy per character per time unit; in mathematical notation, this H* equals the mean entropy per character H' divided by the mathematical expectation τ of the duration τ_i of any one character x_i from the character set $x_i......x_n$:

$$H* = \frac{H'}{\tau} \; where \; \tau = \sum_{i=1}^{n} \tau_i \, p(x_i)$$

The average information rate may be expressed in a unit such as shannon per second. (I) (A)

average transinformation content Synonym for mean transinformation content. (I)

average transinformation rate In information theory, the mean transinformation content per character per time unit; in mathematical notation this T* equals the mean transinformation content per character T' divided by the mathematical expectation, τ of the mean duration τ_{ij} of any compound event $(x_i, \; y_j)$; $x_i, \; y_a$ from sets $x_i......x_b$ and $y_i......y_c$:

$$T* = \frac{T'}{\tau} \; where \; \tau = \sum_{i=1}^{n} \sum_{j=1}^{m} \tau_{ij} \, p(x_i, \; y_j)$$

The average transinformation rate per time may be expressed in a unit such as shannon per second. (I) (A)

AVK Audio Visual Kernel.

AVK API Audio Visual Kernel Application Programming Interface. A group of function calls used to access the functions of ActionMedia II.

AVR Automatic volume recognition.

AVSS Audio-Video Support System.

AVT Address vector table.

awaken (1) To automatically remove the hold status from suspended documents in a folder and place the documents in the routing queue. When a document is placed in a folder that contains suspended documents, the document triggers the wakeup function. The form type of the document determines whether an active document awakens suspended documents in a folder. See also form type, hold status, suspended. (2) Synonym for wakeup.

A-weighted impulse sound pressure level In acoustics, the A-weighted sound pressure level determined with a sound level meter set for the dynamic characteristic "impulse."

A-weighted level In acoustics, the level obtained with a standardized instrumentation system that incorporates A-weighting; for example, an A-weighted sound power level or an A-weighted sound pressure level.

A-weighted peak sound pressure level In acoustics, the maximum instantaneous A-weighted sound pressure level that occurs during a stated time interval.

A-weighting In acoustics, a prescribed frequency response in a sound level meter; a meter with A-weighting is progressively less sensitive than the human ear to sounds of frequencies below 1000 hertz.

axiom In a conceptual schema language, any closed sentence that is asserted to be considered as such by an authorized source. (A)

axis One of the intersecting horizontal and vertical straight reference lines relative to which data values are plotted on a chart. The axes are commonly referred to as the X axis and the Y axis.

axis grid lines In AS/400 and System/38 graphics, straight lines in a chart extending perpendicular to either axis at each major tick.

axis label In the AS/400 Business Graphics Utility, the name of a major tick on a vertical or horizontal axis.

axis range In the AS/400 Business Graphics Utility, the upper and lower limits of the vertical or horizontal lines.

axis title In GDDM, a text string describing what an axis represents.

AZERTY The key layout of keyboards used in some European typewriters. The term describes the sequence of the first six letters in the first row of alphabetic keys. See also Dvorak, QWERTY. See Figure 14.

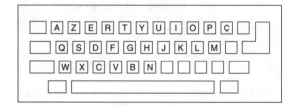

Figure 14. AZERTY Keyboard

azo dye In a document copying machine, dye formed by the reaction between diazo compound and a coupler.

B

B Bel.

b Byte.

Bi Input blocking factor.

Bo Output blocking factor.

Babbage, Charles (1792-1871) English inventor of Difference Engines, the first automatic calculators, and the Analytical Engine, precursor of modern computers.

babble The aggregate crosstalk from a large number of interfering channels.

backbone (1) A set of nodes and their interconnecting links providing the primary data path across a network. (2) In a local area network multiple-bridge ring configuration, a high-speed link to which the rings are connected by means of bridges. A backbone may be configured as a bus or as a ring. (3) In a wide area network, a high-speed link to which nodes or data switching exchanges (DSEs) are connected. (4) A common distribution core that provides all electrical power, gases, chemicals, and other services to the sectors of an automated wafer processing system. See Figure 15.

backbone ring A ring that interconnects ring networks.

back chaining Synonym for backward chaining. (T)

backdoor See trap door.

backend In the AIX operating system, the program that sends output to a particular device. Synonymous with backend program.

backend program Synonym for backend.

backfacing polygon In AIX graphics, a polygon in which vertices appear in clockwise order in screen space and are, therefore, not drawn.

background (1) On a document copying machine, the area of an original, master, or copy that surrounds

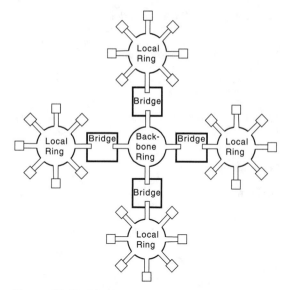

Figure 15. Backbone

the subject matter. (T) (2) In multiprogramming, the conditions under which low-priority programs are executed. (3) In TSO, the conditions under which jobs submitted through the SUBMIT command or SYSIN are executed. A background job executes one job step at a time. It does not execute interactively with the user; processing continues on other jobs in the foreground. (4) Contrast with foreground.

background activity Synonym for background process.

background color (1) The color assigned to a background image. (2) In the AIXwindows program and Enhanced X-Windows, the single electronic color assigned to the graphic field that appears behind the foreground elements inside the border of a displayed widget or gadget. Contrast with foreground color.

background display image See background image.

background image (1) The part of a display image, such as a form overlay, that is not changed during a particular sequence of transactions. (I) (A) (2) Contrast with foreground image. (3) Synonymous with display background, static display image, static image.

background ink In optical character recognition, a type of ink with high reflective characteristics that is not detected by the scan head; it is used to print location guides, logotypes, instructions, and any other desired preprinting in order to prevent interference with reading.

background job (1) A low-priority job, usually a batched or noninteractive job. (2) In TSO, a job entered through the SUBMIT command or through SYSIN. Contrast with foreground job.

background music In videotaping, music that accompanies dialog or action.

background noise In acoustics, total of all interference sources in a system used to produce, detect, measure, or record a signal, excluding noise produced by the signal itself. See also ambient noise, burst noise, impulsive noise.

background partition In VSE, a space of virtual storage in which programs are executed under control of the system. By default, the partition has a processing priority lower than any of the existing foreground partitions.

background picture In the NetView Graphic Monitor Facility, a metafile (such as a world map) placed in the background of a view.

background process (1) A process that does not require operator intervention but can be run by the computer while the workstation is used to do other work. (2) In the AIX operating system, a mode of program execution in which the shell does not wait for program completion before prompting the user for another command. (3) Contrast with foreground process.

background processing (1) The execution of lower-priority computer programs when higher-priority programs are not using the system resources. (I) (A) (2) In word processing, the execution of an operator request, such as printing a document, while the operator is performing other tasks. (3) Contrast with foreground processing.

background program (1) In multiprogramming, program with the lowest priority. Background programs are executed from batched or stacked job input. (2) In TSO, a program executed in a region of main storage not swapped. Contrast with foreground program.

background reader A system task started by the operator to process foreground-initiated background jobs.

background region A region in main storage to which a background job is assigned.

backing sheet In a duplicator, a sheet of material attached to the back of a stencil master to strengthen and support it during the preparation of the image and which is discarded before the duplicating process is started. (T)

backing store (1) In a virtual storage system, auxiliary storage that contains active pages. See also demand paging. (2) In the AIX operating system, the collection of off-screen, saved pixels maintained by the Enhanced X-Windows server. (3) Synonym for backup storage.

back-level Pertaining to an earlier release of an IBM product, which may not support a particular, current function.

back light (1) In multimedia, light that is present behind an image to be photographed. (2) The fluorescent lighting on a device such as a liquid crystal display (LCD).

back margin The margin of a page that is closest to the binding edge. Normally, this is the left margin of the recto page and the right margin of the verso page.

back matter In a book, those sections such as a glossary or an index that are placed after the main chapters or sections.

backout (1) To restore a file to a previous condition by removing changes in the inverse chronological order from which the changes were originally made. (2) In IMS/VS, the process of removing all the database updates performed by an application program that has terminated abnormally. See dynamic backout, resynchronization.

backscrolling (1) Reversing the normal (top-to-bottom) direction of flow of paper through a printer. (2) On a video display unit, moving text through the viewing area from top to bottom.

backspace (1) To move a data medium backwards a specified distance; for example, to move a punched tape backwards by one row, to move a magnetic tape backwards by one block. (I) (A) (2) Escapement that occurs in a direction contrary to that of the writing direction without a character being typed on the paper. (T) (3) In word processing, movement of the writing position in a direction opposite to the writing direction along the writing line. (4) To move a cursor one character position backward. (5) Contrast with space. (6) In SAA Advanced Common User Access architecture, a typing action that deletes the selection if one exists. If there is no selection, backspace deletes the character to the left of the cursor. (7) In SAA Basic Common User Access architecture, a typing action that moves the cursor to the left one space.

Note: This operation can differ for bidirectional and double-byte character set (DBCS) languages.

Backspace A key on a keyboard that a user presses to move the cursor backward one character position. Contrast with Delete.

Note: In some applications, the Backspace function deletes characters.

backspace character (BS) A format effector that causes the print or display position to move one position backward along the line without producing the printing or the display of any graphic. (I) (A) See also numeric backspace character, unit backspace character.

backspace control On dictation equipment, a device that permits return of the recording medium or of the recording head, playback head, or combined head, to a point that may be predetermined. (I)

backspace key A control for effecting the backspace function. (T)

backspace mechanism A device that performs a step-by-step movement between the paper carrier and the typing position contrary to the writing position. (T)

backtab In SAA Advanced Common User Access architecture, to move the cursor to the beginning of the previous entry field or the previous selection field, if no choice is selected. If the previous selection field has a choice selected, the cursor moves to the selected choice. Contrast with tab.

back-to-back gateways Two gateways separated by one intervening network that contains no gateway system services control point (SSCP) function involved with either of the two gateway NCPs.

back tracking A search procedure in which a choice is made at a certain node based on a guess and, when the choice leads to an unacceptable result, the search goes back to the original node to make another choice. (T)

back up To copy information, usually to diskette or tape, for safekeeping.

backup (1) Pertaining to a procedure, technique, or hardware used to recover lost or destroyed data or to keep a system operating. (T) (2) Pertaining to a system, device, file, or facility that can be used in the event of a malfunction or loss of data. (3) The act of saving some or all of the objects on a system on tape or disk. (4) In PSS, a condition in which the store loops in one supermarket are controlled by a store controller in another supermarket. This allows customer checkout to continue at the terminals of a supermarket that has an inoperative store controller. (5) In the Data Facility Hierarchical Storage Manager, the process of copying to a backup volume a data set

residing on a level 0 volume or level 1 volume. (6) Pertaining to an alternative copy used as a substitute if the original is lost or destroyed, such as a backup log. (7) To copy information, usually onto diskette or tape, for safekeeping.

backup control data set A VSAM key-sequenced data set that contains information about backup versions of data sets, backup volumes, and volumes under control of the backup function of the Data Facility Hierarchical Storage Manager.

backup copy A copy of information or data that is kept in case the original is changed or destroyed.

backup cycle In the Data Facility Hierarchical Storage Manager, a period of days for which a pattern is used to specify the days in the cycle on which automatic backup is scheduled to occur.

backup diskette A diskette that contains information copied from another diskette. It is used in case the original information is unintentionally altered or destroyed.

backup file A copy of a file made for possible later reconstruction of the file. (T) Synonymous with job-recovery control file.

backup frequency In the Data Facility Hierarchical Storage Manager, the number of days that must elapse since making the latest backup version of a data set and the time when a changed data set is again eligible for backup.

backup path In the IBM Token-Ring Network, an alternative path for signal flow through access units and their main ring path cabling. The backup path allows recovery of the operable portion of the network while problem determination procedures are being performed.

backup plan See contingency plan.

backup procedures In computer security, the provisions made in a contingency plan for the recovery of data and for restart or replacement of computer equipment after a system failure or disaster; for example, the copying of files or the acquisition of spare equipment.

backup session The session that replaces the failing primary extended recovery facility (XRF) session between a terminal user and the active subsystem.

backup storage A storage device that retains information copied from a recording medium to save the information in case the original information is unintentionally lost or altered; for example, a high-capacity diskette drive, a streaming tape, a virtual disk. Synonymous with backing store.

backup store A supermarket system that provides backup for the supermarket terminals on store loops (a maximum of two) normally supported by the store controller.

backup version See backup copy.

backup volume A volume owned by the Data Facility Hierarchical Storage Manager upon which backup versions of data sets are written.

backup volume cleanup process In the Data Facility Hierarchical Storage Manager, a process that erases data set backup versions that are no longer needed.

Backus Naur form (BNF) A metalanguage used to specify or describe the syntax of a language in which each symbol, by itself, represents a set of strings of symbols. Synonymous with Backus normal form. (A)

Backus normal form (BNF) Synonym for Backus Naur form. (A)

Backward In SAA Basic Common User Access architecture, an action that shows the information that precedes the visible information in a panel.

backward chaining An iterative procedure for solving a problem by which the problem is transformed into an instantiation of an axiom or a proven proposition applied to the conclusion, and another problem to be solved until the conclusion is found to be true or the problem is unsolvable. Synonymous with back chaining. (T)

backward channel A channel associated with the forward channel, used for supervisory or error control signals, but with a direction of transmission opposite to that of the forward channel in which user information is being transferred. Contrast with forward channel. (I)

Note: In case of simultaneous transfer of information in both directions, this definition applies with respect to the data source under consideration.

backward file recovery The reconstruction of an earlier version of a file by using a newer version and data that have been recorded in a journal. (T) Contrast with forward file recovery.

backward LAN channel In a broadband LAN, the channel assigned for uplink data transmission from the data stations to the headend. Synonymous with reverse LAN channel. (T)

backward processing In systems with VSAM, a method of sequential processing in which the previous, rather than the next, record in entry, key, or relative-record sequence is retrieved.

backward recovery See backward file recovery.

backward reference A facility of the job control language that allows the user to copy information or refer to DD statements that appear earlier in the job.

backward supervision The use of supervisory sequences sent from the slave to the master station. Contrast with forward supervision.

badge security In System/36, a System Support Program Product option that helps prevent the unauthorized use of a display station by checking the data from a magnetic stripe on a badge before allowing an operator to sign on.

BAL (1) Branch and link. (2) Branch linkage.

balanced (to ground) The state of impedance on a two-wire line when the impedance to ground as measured from one wire is equal to the impedance to ground as measured from the other wire. Contrast with unbalanced (to ground).

balanced data link In data communication, a data link between two participating combined stations; for transmissions it originates: each station can transmit both command frames and response frames, organize its data flow, and perform error recovery operations at the data link level. Contrast with unbalanced data link.

balanced error A set of errors, the distribution of which has the mean value zero. (I) (A)

balanced merge An external sort that places strings created by an internal sort phase on half of the available storage devices and then merges strings by moving them back and forth between an equal number of devices until merging is complete. (A)

balanced merge sort (1) A merge sort, which is an external sort, such that the sorted subsets created by the internal sorts are equally distributed among half of the available auxiliary storage devices. The subsets are merged onto the other half of the auxiliary storage devices and the process is repeated until all items are in one sorted set. (A) (2) Contrast with unbalanced merge sort.

balanced routing A method of assigning network routes so that all routes are used equally.

balanced station Synonym for combined station.

balanced system An IMS/VS system in a multi-system environment in which some terminals are handled, some messages are routed to other systems for processing, and messages are accepted from other systems for processing.

balancing In multicolumn text formatting, the process of making column depths on a page approximately equal.

balancing network Lumped circuit elements (inductances, capacitances, and resistances) connected so as to simulate the impedance of a uniform cable or open-wire circuit over a band of frequencies.

balun A transformer used to connect balanced cables, such as twisted-pair cables, to unbalanced cables, such as coaxial cables, by matching the electrical characteristics of the cables.

band (1) A group of tracks on a recording medium, all of which are read or written in parallel. (2) In data communication, the frequency spectrum between two defined limits. (A)

band level In acoustics, the sound pressure level or the sound power level within a specified frequency band.

Note: The band may be specified by its lower and upper cut-off frequencies or by its geometric center frequency and bandwidth. The width of the band may be indicated by a modifier; for example, critical band level, octave band level, one-third octave band level.

band printer An impact printer in which the character set available for printing is carried on a flexible band. (T) (A)

bandwidth The difference, expressed in hertz, between the highest and the lowest frequencies of a range of frequencies.

bank (1) An aggregation of similar devices, such as transformers or lamps, connected to each other and used cooperatively. (2) In automatic switching, an assemblage of fixed contacts used to establish electrical connections. (3) See data bank.

banking In optical character recognition (OCR), a misalignment of the first character of a line with respect to the left margin.

bar See type bar.

bar chart In GDDM, a chart consisting of several bars of equal width. The value of the dependent variable is indicated by the height of each bar.

bar code A code representing characters by sets of parallel bars of varying thickness and separation that are read optically by transverse scanning. (I) See Figure 16.

UPC Symbol

Figure 16. Bar Code

bar printer An impact printer in which the type slugs are carried on a type bar. (A)

barrel buttons Buttons on the side of a pen device, used to request or initiate an action.

BARSA Billing, accounts receivable, sales analysis.

bars and tone A video and audio reference used to assure that color, luminance, and audio remain consistent between pieces of production equipment and recorded segments of tape.

base (1) In a numeration system, the number that is raised to the power denoted by the exponent and then multiplied by the mantissa to determine the number represented; for example, the number 5 in the expression: $2.8 \times 5^2 = 70$ (T) (2) A reference value. (A) (3) A number that is multiplied by itself as many times as indicated by an exponent. (A) (4) The number system in terms of which an arithmetic value is represented. (5) In a document copying machine, a supporting material for an emulsion or other sensitizing agent. (T) Synonymous with substrate. (6) Contrast with radix.

base address (1) An address used as the origin in the calculation of addresses. (T) (2) A given address from which an absolute address is derived by combination with a relative address. (A) (3) In the IBM 8100 Information System, either the instruction address or the content of a general register from which a logical address is derived during instruction execution by combination with a displacement.

base address register A register that holds a base address. (I) (A) Synonymous with base register.

baseband (1) A frequency band occupied by a signal, or by a number of multiplexed signals. (T)   (2) A frequency band that uses the complete bandwidth of a transmission.

baseband LAN A local area network in which data are encoded and transmitted without modulation of a carrier. (T)

baseband signaling (1) Synonym for baseband transmission. (T)   (2) In a network, transmission of an encoded signal over a transmission medium as a continuous stream of voltage transitions. One node at a time may send; signals from multiple nodes are multiplexed over the single channel.   Contrast with broadband signaling.

baseband system A data transmission system that encodes, modulates, and impresses information on the transmission medium without shifting or altering the frequency of the information signal.

baseband transmission Transmission of a digital or analog signal in its original form, not changed by modulation.   Synonymous with baseband signaling. (T)

base cluster In systems with VSAM, a key-sequenced or entry-sequenced file over which one or more alternate indexes are built. See also cluster.

base color In the IBM 3270 Information Display System, the colors displayed or printed on a color terminal for all characters in a field by using combinations of the field protection and field intensity bits in the field attribute.

Note: For devices supporting color, when used in the base color mode of the IBM 3279 Display Station, the following colors are used depending on the combination of 3270 field attributes defined for the field:

field attribute:	base color:
unprotected, normal intensity	green
unprotected, intensified	red
protected, normal intensity	blue
protected, intensified	white

BASE disk The virtual disk that contains the text decks and macroinstructions for VTAM programs, the NetView program, and VM/SNA console support (VSCS). It also contains control files and sample files used when running VTAM programs on the VM operating system. See also DELTA disk, MERGE disk, RUN disk, ZAP disk.

based variable In PL/I, a variable that provides attributes for data, such as data located in a buffer, for which the storage address is provided by a pointer. It does not identify a fixed location in storage.

base group A number of carrier channels forming a channel bank to be further modulated to a final frequency band.

baseline (1) The primary horizontal reference line for character alignment and measurement of vertical distances. (T)   (2) In a font, the imaginary line on which the bottom of each successive character is aligned.

baseline angle In System/38 graphics, the angle of a mode-3 graphics symbol or string of such symbols relative to a baseline.

baseline axis The axis on which successive lines of text are placed. Synonymous with B axis.

baseline direction The direction in which successive lines of text are added.

baselined documents Documents that are considered vital to a project's success. After a baselined document is approved, changes to that document may only be made through the designated change control process for the project.

baseline extent In printing, the perpendicular distance between the initial point and the farthest toned picture element (pel) of any character pattern within a font, measured in the direction of the baseline progression. The distance cannot be smaller than the baseline offset. Synonymous with B extent.

baseline increment The distance between successive baselines.

baseline offset The perpendicular distance between the initial point and the sequential baseline.

baseline sequential axis See baseline axis.

base mass storage volume See base volume.

base name (1) In the AIX operating system, the last element to the right of a full path name. (2) In the AIX operating system, a file name specified without its parent directories.

base node Synonym for root record.

base number The part of a self-check field from which the check digit is calculated.

base page In the IBM LinkWay product, a page in a folder on which objects created will appear on all other pages in the folder.

base permission In the AIX operating system, an access mode that is assigned to a file owner, file group, or others who want access to the file. Access modes include read (r) permission, write (w) permission, and execute/search (x) permission. See also access permission, extended permission.

base pool In the AS/400 system, a storage area that contains all unassigned main storage on the system.

base priority number A priority number that is used to calculate the standard priority number.

base RBA In VSAM, the RBA stored in the header of an index record that is used to calculate the RBAs of data or index control intervals governed by the index record.

base register (1) A register that holds a base address. (T) (2) A general-purpose register that a programmer chooses to contain a base address.

base scalar type In XL Pascal, the scalar type from which a set type or subrange type is derived. See also subrange scalar type.

base segment Synonym for RACF segment.

base set The set of functions, including verbs, parameters, return codes, and what-received indications that is supported by all products that implement a particular architecture. See also option set.

base shape The shape of a character such as an Arabic character, which identifies the character but not its presentation shape. See also presentation shape.

base storage pool In System/38, a storage pool that contains all unassigned main storage on the system.

base volume A mass storage volume that can have copies or duplicates.

BASIC (1) Beginner's all-purpose symbolic instruction code. A procedural algebraic language originally designed for ease of learning with a small instruction repertoire. (A) (2) A high-level programming language with a small number of statements and a simple syntax that is designed to be easily learned and used and that is widely used for interactive applications on microcomputers.

basic access method Any access method in which each input/output statement causes a corresponding machine input/output operation to occur. Contrast with queued access method.

basic characters In the AS/400 system, frequently used double-byte characters that are stored in the hardware of a double-byte character set (DBCS) device. The number of double-byte characters that are stored in the device varies with the language supported and the storage size of the device. A DBCS device can display or print basic characters without using the extended character processing function of the operating system. Contrast with extended characters. See also extended character processing.

basic control (BC) mode A mode in which additional System/370 features, such as new machine instructions, are operational. See also extended control (EC) mode.

basic controller The part of a communication controller that performs arithmetic and logic functions.

basic conversation (1) An LU 6.2 conversation type specified by the allocating transaction program. Transaction programs using basic conversation have available to them a wider variety of LU 6.2 functions, but they are responsible for more of their own error recovery and must manage details of the data stream used on the conversation. (2) In the AIX operating system, a connection between two transaction programs that allows them to exchange logical records that contain a 2-byte prefix that specifies the length of the record. LUs 1, 2, and 3 do not use the 2-byte prefix; however, LU 1, 2, and 3 conversations must be basic conversations. This conversation type is used by service transactions and by LU 1, 2, and 3 application transaction programs. (3) See conversation. Contrast with mapped conversation.

basic data exchange A file format for exchanging data on diskettes or tape between systems or devices.

basic device unit (BDU) In ACF/TCAM, a part of a basic transmission unit that is exchanged between the host access method and the network control program. It specifies a request for action by some device in the network. A BDU consists of a command and its modifiers, functional flags, and a data count.

basic direct access method (BDAM) An access method used to directly retrieve or update particular blocks of a data set on a direct access device.

basic DST authority In the AS/400 system, a dedicated service tools (DST) authority used by a service representative or an experienced system user that provides access to DST functions that do not access sensitive data. See also full DST authority.

basic edit In IMS/VS, a facility that performs general editing functions for terminal input and output messages.

basic exchange format A format for exchanging data on diskettes between systems or devices.

basic field attribute A characteristic of a 3270 kanji display field. The basic field attributes of a display field are: protected or unprotected against manual input and copy operations; numeric-only or alphameric input control; displayed, nondisplayed, and display-intensified; selector-pen detectable; and modified or not modified.

basic format Synonym for default format. (T)

basic functions In the 3650 Retail Store System, functions provided by the controller to allow specific operations to be performed. Examples are batch printing and ticketing.

basic ideographic character set A character set defined by IBM that contains 3226 kanji and 481 additional characters. The additional characters include katakana, hiragana, the alphabet (A through Z and a through z), numbers (0 through 9), Roman numerals (I through X), Greek, Cyrillic, and special symbols. Contrast with extended ideographic character set. See also ideographic character set.

basic increment The smallest unit of motion of which a device is capable.

basic indexed sequential access method An access method used in one form to directly retrieve or update particular blocks of a data set on a direct access device, using an index to locate the data set. The index is stored in direct access storage along with the data set. Other forms of this method can be used to store or retrieve blocks of the same data set in a continuous sequence.

basic information unit (BIU) In SNA, the unit of data and control information passed between half-sessions. It consists of a request/response header (RH) followed by a request/response unit (RU).

Basic Input/Output System (BIOS) Code that controls basic hardware operations, such as interactions with diskette drives, hard disk drives, and the keyboard.

basic line space On a typewriter, the basic distance provided on the machine between two consecutive typing lines. (T)

basic link unit (BLU) In SNA, the unit of data and control information transmitted over a link by data link control. Synonymous with frame.

basic mapping support (BMS) An interface between CICS and application programs that formats input and output display data and routes multiple-page output messages without regard for control characters used by various terminals.

basic mode (1) In VTAM Release 1 and in VTAM programs, a mode of data transfer in which the appli-

cation program can communicate with non-SNA terminals without using SNA protocols. Contrast with record mode. (2) In DPCX, a mode of operation in which a terminal operator can select programs, select system services, and issue some commands. See command mode.

basic mode link control Control of data links by use of the control characters of the ISO/CCITT 7-bit character set for information interchange. (I)

Basic Network Utilities (BNU) A group of programs and files that provide basic networking utilities. These utilities include a set of directories, files, programs, and commands that allow the user to communicate with a remote AIX or UNIX (trademark of AT&T Bell Laboratories) system over a dedicated line or a telephone line. See also UNIX-to-UNIX Copy Program.

basic operator command Synonym for basic operator control command.

basic operator control In ACF/TCAM, the function of a system service program that processes a set of basic operator commands. These commands allow the operator to determine the status of the TCAM system and to alter, start, and stop TCAM and its resources by entering appropriate commands from either the system console or a basic operator control station. The basic operator control system service program is required in order to execute a TCAM message control program (MCP).

basic operator control command In ACF/TCAM, an operator command directed to the basic operator control system service program. Synonymous with basic operator command.

basic operator control SSP In ACF/TCAM, a system services program that processes a set of basic operator commands that allow the operator to determine the status of the network and to alter, activate, and deactivate portions of the network by entering appropriate commands from the system console, a remote station, or an application program.

basic operator control station In ACF/TCAM, a station, logical unit (LU), or application program that is authorized to enter operator commands to be executed by the basic operator control system service program (SSP). See also basic primary operator control station, basic secondary operator control station, extended operator control station.

basic operator panel (BOP) In the IBM 8100 Information System, a display control panel that enables the user to enter information, display system status, control powering and IPL, and override normal IPL parameters. With the keylock feature installed, the BOP restricts panel access.

basic operator panel display register In the IBM 8100 Information System, a register whose contents provide the value for the four-character hexadecimal display of the basic operator panel.

basic partitioned access method (BPAM) An access method that can be applied to create program libraries in direct access storage for convenient storage and retrieval of programs.

basic primary operator control station A basic operator control station to which are sent all TCAM error-recovery messages and TCAM reply messages to basic operator commands. See basic secondary operator control station, extended primary operator control station, extended secondary operator control station.

basic real constant A string of decimal digits containing a decimal point and expressing a real value.

basic secondary operator control station A basic operator control station to which are sent only the reply messages to basic operator commands entered from it. See basic primary operator control station, extended primary operator control station, extended secondary operator control station.

basic sequential access method (BSAM) (1) An access method for storing or retrieving data blocks in a continuous sequence, using either a sequential access or a direct access device. (2) In NPM, the method by which all PIUs collected for selected LUs can be logged into a sequential data set as they pass through VTAM programs.

basic services In the Programmable Store System, one of two categories of fixed functions provided by IBM for administrative support devices. See also retail services.

basic status register (BSTAT) In the IBM 8100 Information System, a 1- or 2-byte register that contains control logic status information.

basic telecommunications access method An access method that permits read/write communication with remote devices.

basic timing cycle The time period used as a base for controlling periodic routine execution and incrementing time-of-day clocks. The minimum value is 50 microseconds.

basic transmission unit (BTU) In SNA, the unit of data and control information passed between path control components. A BTU can consist of one or more path information units (PIUs). See also blocking of PIUs.

basic working display In System/38, the display that serves as the base from which a user makes requests at a workstation. It is usually the display received at sign-on.

basis In the AIX Graphics Library, a curve or patch basis is a 4x4 matrix that controls the relationship between control points and the approximating spline. B-splines, Bezier curves, and Cardinal splines all differ in that they have different bases.

basis weight The weight in pounds of a ream (500 sheets) of paper cut to a given standard size for that grade, for example, 25 x 38 inches for book papers, 17 x 22 inches for bond, and other sizes for other grades. The basis weight of continuous forms for computer output is based on the size for bond papers.

batch (1) An accumulation of data to be processed. (2) A group of records or data processing jobs brought together for processing or transmission. (3) Pertaining to activity involving little or no user action. Contrast with interactive. See Figure 17.

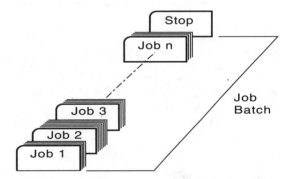

Figure 17. Batch

batch accumulator In System/38, a storage area in which subtotals for a field are stored. Contrast with total accumulator.

batch application In VSE, a set of programs that normally processes data without user interaction; for example, an application to print a company payroll. Such an application uses a device, a data file, or the processor intensively for a longer time than online applications.

batch BSC In System/36, the SSP support that provides data communication with BSC computers and devices via the RPG T specification or the assembler DTFB macroinstruction.

batch checkpoint/restart In IMS/VS, the facility that enables batch processing programs to synchronize checkpoints and to be restarted at a user-specified checkpoint.

batch coding sheets In SDF/CICS, coding sheets used to define objects for the load utility.

batch compilation A method of compiling programs without the continual attention of an operator.

batch data exchange (BDE) In DPCX, the procedure of sending programs and batch data between the host and DPCX, using either tapes or diskettes.

batch data exchange services (BDES) In DPCX, programs that are executed in the host system to send data and programs to the IBM 8100 Information System via diskettes or tapes or to send data from the system to the host via diskettes or tapes.

batch device Any device that can read serial input or write serial output, or both, but cannot communicate interactively with the system.

batched communication The sending of a large body of data from one station to another station in a network, without intervening responses from the receiving unit. Contrast with inquiry/response communication.

batched job (1) A job that is grouped with other jobs as input to a computing system. (2) A job whose job control statements are grouped with job control statements of other jobs as input to a computing system. Synonymous with stacked job.

batch entry Entry of an accumulation of data as opposed to immediate entry of the data as it becomes available. See also remote batch entry.

batch environment (1) An environment in which noninteractive programs are executed. (2) In DPPX, an environment to which batch jobs in command lists are submitted and in which their execution is scheduled, independently of their submitter.

batch execution Execution of programs and data that have been submitted or accumulated as batched input.

batch facility See CMS batch facility.

batch-header document A document that accompanies and identifies a batch of input documents and may be used to validate them, for example, a document that includes balances, control totals, hash totals, or checksums. (T)

batch file A file that contains a series of commands to be processed sequentially.

batch initiation In DPCX, the initiation of a subtask by a host application program using the batch initiator.

batch input processing In the ImagePlus system, the capability to index and route many documents as a batch. See also batch processing.

batch interface file (ITF) A VSAM file containing model job control statements and control information for batch SDF/CICS.

batch interface JCL mask file (ITF) A VSAM file containing model job control statements and control information for batch SDF/CICS.

batch interface log file (ITFB) A VSAM file containing information about the status of jobs that have been submitted for batch SDF/CICS execution.

batch job A job submitted as a predefined series of actions to be performed with little or no interaction between user and system.

batch message processing (BMP) program In IMS/VS, a batch processing program that has access to online databases and message queues. See also batch processing program, message processing program.

batch mode In AS/400 query management, the query mode associated with a query instance that does not allow users to interact with the query commands while a procedure is running.

batch number In the IBM 3881 Optical Mark Reader and the IBM 3886 Optical Character Reader Model 1, a number printed on a document by the serial numbering feature.

batch-oriented BMP program In IMS/VS, a batch message processing (BMP) program that has access to online databases and message queues while it performs batch-type processing. Contrast with transaction-oriented BMP.

Note: A batch-oriented BMP does not access the IMS/VS message queues for input. It can access online databases, GSAM databases, and OS/VS files for both input and output.

batch print function A feature of PSS that prints out reports on the IBM 3284 Model 3 Printer that is attached to the store controller.

batch printing Queueing one or more documents to print in a separate job as a background process.

batch processing (1) The processing of data or the accomplishment of jobs accumulated in advance, in such a manner that the user cannot further influence processing while it is in progress. (I) (A) (2) The processing of data accumulated over a period of time. (A) (3) Loosely, the execution of computer programs serially. (A) (4) Pertaining to the technique of executing a set of computer programs such that each is completed before the next program of the set is started. (A) (5) In realtime systems the processing of related transactions that have been grouped together. (6) Processing in which there is little or no operator action. (7) Contrast with interactive processing. See remote batch processing, sequential batch processing, stacked job processing.

batch processing program In IMS/VS, an application program that has access to databases and OS/VS data management facilities but does not have access to the IMS/VS control region or its message queues. See also batch message processing program, message processing program.

batch processor log In DPPX, a data set in which are recorded any messages generated by the system during execution of command lists submitted by a user to the batch environment.

batch PVS In DPCX, the part of program validation services that executes as a batch program in the host system. The validation, testing, and preparation phases are executed as a batch program. Contrast with interactive PVS.

batch queue In DPPX, a queue in the batch environment.

batch region In a multiprogramming environment, one of several regions controlled by the operating system in which batch processing can be performed. There may be several batch regions, which normally run at lower priority than interactive regions.

batch request In SDF/CICS, a request submitted to batch SDF/CICS by an online user.

batch save/restore An optional facility of a partitioned online batch system. It allows a realtime job to preempt a partition being used for batch processing on the basis of assigned priorities. Upon preemption, the batch program is saved on direct access storage, and when the realtime program is completed, the batch program is loaded into storage and execution resumes.

batch scanner workstation In the ImagePlus system, an ImagePlus Personal System/2 workstation that is equipped with a batch scanner. The batch scanner can be either a high- or low-speed scanner. See scanner.

batch scanning In the ImagePlus system, the process of scanning large volumes or batches of similar types of documents before indexing them.

batch session (1) A session established to transmit batches of records or messages. Contrast with inquiry session. (2) In SDF/CICS a list of object definitions to be interpreted by the load utility, delimited by session header and session trailer cards; the list can use a session profile of default values as in an online session.

batch storage processing In the ImagePlus Folder Application Facility, Version 2 Release 1.1, the capability to index and route many documents as a batch. See also batch processing.

bathtub curve A plot of the rate of defect discovery versus time over the life of a product. Usually this curve starts out high (due to latent defects), then it decreases to a minimum value, and it potentially rises again due to wear-out mechanisms at the end of product life.

batch subsystem (1) A subsystem in which batch jobs are to be processed. (2) In the AS/400 system, a part of main storage where batch jobs are processed.

battery A source of direct current, or the current itself. The source need not be a storage device.

battery-powered calculator A calculator that depends solely for its power upon a chemical, solar, or rechargeable battery. (T) (A)

baud (1) A unit of signaling speed equal to the number of discrete conditions or signal events per second; for example, one baud equals one-half dot cycle per second in Morse code, one bit per second in a train of binary signals, and one 3-bit value per second in a train of signals each of which can assume one of eight different states. (A) (2) In asynchronous transmission, the unit of modulation rate corresponding to one unit interval per second; that is, if the duration of the unit interval is 20 milliseconds, the modulation rate is 50 baud. (A)

baudot code A code for transmission of data in which five equal-length bits represent one character. It is used in some teletypewriter machines where one start element and one stop element are added. Depending on the system, the stop element may be a minimum of 1, 1.42, or 2 unit intervals in duration.

baud rate In remote communications, the transmission rate that is synonymous with signal events. The baud rate is usually expressed in bits per second.

B axis Synonym for baseline axis.

BB Begin bracket indicator.

BCB Block control byte.

BCC Block-check character.

BCD Binary-coded decimal notation.

BCH Block control header.

BC mode Basic control mode.

BCU Block control unit.

BCUG Bilateral closed user group.

BDAM Basic direct access method.

BDE Batch data exchange.

BDES Batch data exchange services.

B-disk In VM/SP, an optional user disk.

BDU Basic device unit.

beacon frame (1) A frame sent by an adapter indicating a serious ring problem, such as a broken cable. An adapter is "beaconing" if it is sending such a frame. (2) Synonym for beacon message.

beaconing Pertaining to repeated transmission of a beacon message when a normal signal is not received because of a serious fault, such as a line break or power failure. The message is repeated until the error is corrected or bypassed.

beaconing station A data station in a local area network that reports hard failures to neighboring stations. (T)

beacon message A frame or message repeatedly transmitted by a station on detection of a line break or outage. Transmission of beacon messages stops when the fault is bypassed or eliminated. See also beacon frame.

beam deflection On a video display unit, the process of changing the direction of the electron beam and thus its position on a display surface.

BEC Bus extension card.

BED Bus extension driver card.

before-image (1) A copy of block of a record before a modification. (T) (2) In the AS/400 system and System/38, the contents of a record in a physical file before the data is changed by a write, an update, or a delete operation. (3) Contrast with after-image.

begin block underline In System/36, a text instruction that indicates the beginning of a block of text to be underlined.

begin bracket In SNA, the value (binary 1) of the begin-bracket indicator in the request header (RH) of the first request in the first chain of a bracket; the value denotes the start of a bracket. Contrast with end bracket. See also bracket.

begin chain In SNA, deprecated term for first-in-chain (FIC).

beginning attribute character In the AS/400 system and System/38, the character in a display file that precedes the first position in a field and that defines how the data in the field is displayed.

beginning-of-chain In SNA, deprecated term for first-in-chain.

beginning of data In SAA Advanced Common User Access architecture, a function that moves the selection cursor to the leftmost position in the current field.

Note: This function can differ for bidirectional and double-byte character set (DBCS) languages.

beginning-of-file label (1) An internal label of a file, that identifies and locates it, and contains data used in file control. (T) (2) Synonymous with header label. See Figure 18.

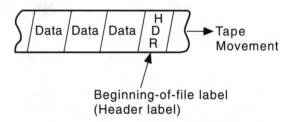

Figure 18. Beginning-of-File Label

beginning of line In SAA Advanced Common User Access architecture, a function that moves the selection cursor to the leftmost choice.

Note: This function can differ for bidirectional and double-byte character set (DBCS) languages.

beginning-of-tape marker (1) A marker on a magnetic tape used to indicate the beginning of the recordable area; for example, a photoreflective strip, a transparent section of tape. (T) (2) Contrast with end-of-tape marker.

beginning-of-volume label An internal label that identifies a volume and indicates the beginning of recorded data. Synonymous with volume header, volume label. (T) (A)

BEL The bell character. (A)

bel (B) (1) A unit that describes the ratio of two power levels. (2) 10 decibels.

bell character (BEL) A control character that is used when there is a need to call for human attention and that may activate alarm or other attention devices. (I) (A)

Bell-LaPadula security model See computer security model.

belt printer An impact printer in which the character set available for printing is carried on a belt. (T) (A)

benchmark A point of reference from which measurements can be made. See also benchmark test.

benchmark problem (1) A problem used to evaluate the performance of hardware or software or both. (A) (2) A problem used to evaluate the performance of several computers relative to each other, or a single computer relative to system specifications. (A)

benchmark test A test that uses a representative set of programs and data designed to evaluate the performance of computer hardware and software in a given configuration. (T)

bend loss See macrobend loss, microbend loss.

benign environment In computer security, a nonhostile environment protected from external threats by physical, human, and procedural security countermeasures.

BER (1) Bit error rate. (2) Bus extension receiver card. (3) Box event record.

Bernoulli Pertaining to a technology used for backup storage devices that applies the Bernoulli principle to prevent destructive physical contact between the read/write head and a rotating disk. See also Winchester. See Figure 19.

best-first search A search that, at each node along the search sequence, evaluates all the possible routes from it to the goal in terms of a predetermined set of criteria and, based on the evaluation results, selects the best route of search. (T)

beta format In multimedia applications, a consumer and industrial 0.5-inch tape format.

between failures See mean time between failures.

between-the-lines entry In computer security, access obtained through active wiretapping by an unauthor-

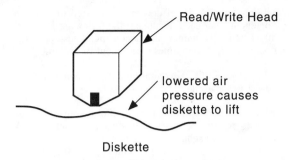

Figure 19. Bernoulli Effect

ized user to a momentarily inactive terminal of a legitimate user assigned to a data communication channel.

BEX Broadband exchange.

B extent Synonym for baseline extent.

bezel buttons Buttons built into the case (bezel) of a pen-based computer or peripheral device, used to request or initiate an action.

Bezier cubic curve In the AIX Graphics Library, a cubic spline approximation to a set of four control points that passes through the first and fourth control points and that has a continuous slope where two spline segments meet.

BFT Boundary function table.

BG Background.

BGU Business graphics utility.

BH Block handler.

BHR Block handling routine.

BHSET Block handler routines.

bias (1) A systematic deviation of a value from a reference value. (I) (A) (2) The amount by which the average of a set of values departs from a reference value. (A) (3) A selection process in which the occurrence of one entity is more likely than the occurrence of another. (4) See ordering bias.

bias distortion See distortion.

bias error An error which is due to bias, for example, the error that is caused by a shrunken measuring tape; in computation, an error that is caused by truncation. (I) (A)

Biba See computer security model.

bibliography A list of documents referred to within a document. For each document, the following is generally listed: the author, the document, notes about the document, and sometimes notes about its author.

BICARSA Billing, inventory control, accounts receivable, sales analysis.

BID (1) In SNA, a data flow control command that is used to request permission to start a bracket. (2) A BSC protocol exchange in preparation for the transmitting and also the receiving data. The transmitting station transmits an ENQ character, and the receiving station acknowledges the receipt of the ENQ character by sending an ACK0 control character.

bid In the contention form of invitation or selection, an attempt by the computer or by a station to gain control of a line in order to transmit data.

bidder Synonym for bidder session.

bidder session The half-session defined at session activation as having to request and receive permission from the other half-session to begin a bracket. Contrast with first-speaker session. See contention-loser session. Synonymous with bidder.

BIDI Bidirectional bus.

bidirectional bus (BIDI) A bus on which data can be sent in either direction.

bidirectional flow Flow in either direction represented on the same flowline in a flowchart. (I) (A)

bidirectional language The ability to write and read a language in two directions, such as from left to right and from right to left.

bidirectional port See shared port.

bidirectional printer A printer that can print left to right and right to left. Synonymous with reverse printer. (T) (A)

bidirectional transmission A transmission that may occur in either direction along a transmission medium. (T)

bilateral closed user group (BCUG) (1) In data communication, two users who have bilaterally agreed to communicate with each other, but not with other users. See also closed user group. (2) In X.25 communications, an optional facility that allows calls to be made only between two designated DTEs. Each user can belong to more than one bilateral closed user group and to more than one closed user group by means of outgoing access.

bilateral closed user group with outgoing access In data communication, two users in a bilateral closed user group who can access users outside the closed group, where appropriate.

bilevel Having black or white pels. See pel.

bilevel image An image in which the pels are either black or white. Contrast with gray image.

bilingual command list In the NetView program, a command list written in a combination of REXX and the NetView command list language.

bin In AFP support, the standard-size paper source on the IBM 3820.

binary (1) Pertaining to a selection, choice, or condition that has two possible different values or states. (I) (A) (2) Pertaining to a fixed radix numeration system having a radix of 2. (I) (A) (3) Pertaining to a system of numbers to the base two; the binary digits are 0 and 1. (A) (4) In the AIX object data manager, a terminal descriptor type used to define a variable as a bit string that is not null-terminated. See also terminal descriptor. (5) In SQL, a data type indicating that the data is a binary number with a precision of 15 (halfword) or 31 (fullword) bits. (6) See Chinese binary, column binary, row binary.

binary arithmetic operation (1) An arithmetic operation in which the operands and the result are represented in the pure binary numeration system. (I) (A) (2) Synonym for dyadic operation.

binary Boolean operation Deprecated term for dyadic Boolean operation.

binary card A card containing data in column binary or row binary form. (A)

binary cell (1) A storage cell that can hold one binary character. (I) (A) (2) A storage cell of one binary digit capacity; for example, a single-bit register. (A)

binary character Either of the characters of a binary character set; for example, T (true) or F (false), Y (yes) or N (no). (T)

binary character set A character set that consists of two characters. (T)

binary code (1) A code whose application results in a code element set whose elements are formed from a binary character set. (T) (2) A code that makes use of exactly two distinct characters, usually 0 and 1. (A) (3) See also gray code.

binary-coded decimal character code A coded character set containing 64 six-bit characters. See also extended binary-coded decimal interchange code.

binary-coded decimal code Synonym for binary-coded decimal notation.

binary-coded decimal interchange code See binary-coded decimal character code, extended binary-coded decimal interchange code.

binary-coded decimal notation (BCD) A binary-coded notation in which each of the decimal digits is represented by a binary numeral; for example, in binary-coded decimal notation that uses the weights 8, 4, 2, 1, the number "twenty-three" is represented by 0010 0011 (compare its representation 10111 in the pure binary numeration system). (I) (A) Synonymous with binary-coded decimal code, binary-coded decimal representation, coded decimal notation.

binary-coded decimal representation Synonym for binary-coded decimal notation. (T) (A)

binary-coded notation A binary notation in which each character is represented by a binary numeral. (T)

binary coded set A coded set whose elements are formed from a binary character set. (T)

binary constant A constant that is made up of one or more binary digits.

binary digit Synonym for bit.

binary digit string A string consisting solely of symbols of binary digits. (T)

binary element The constituent element of data that assumes either of two values or states. The term bit, which is originally the abbreviation for the term binary digit, is misused in the sense of binary element or in the sense of shannon. (I) (A)

binary element string A string consisting solely of binary elements. (I) (A)

binary exponential backoff See truncated binary exponential backoff.

binary file A file that contains codes that are not part of the ASCII character set. Binary files can utilize all 256 possible values for each byte in the file.

binary fixed-point value An integer that consists of binary digits and an optional binary point. Contrast with decimal fixed-point value.

binary floating-point number The conceptual form of a numeric value that contains a significand and a signed exponent. The numeric value of the number is the signed product of the significand of the number and 2 raised to the power of the exponent of the number.

binary floating-point value An approximation of a real number in the form of a significand, which can be considered a binary fraction, and an exponent, which can be considered an integer exponent to the base of 2. Contrast with decimal floating-point value.

binary format Representation of a decimal value in which each field must be 2 or 4 bytes long. The sign (+ or −) is in the far left bit of the field, and the number value is in the remaining bits of the field. Positive numbers have a 0 in the sign bit and are in true form. Negative numbers have a 1 in the sign bit and are in twos complement form.

binary image data A pattern of bits with 0 and 1 values that define the pels in an image; a 1-bit is a toned picture element (pel). See also gray-scale image data, thresholding.

binary-image transfer See bit block transfer.

binary incremental representation Incremental representation in which the value of an increment is rounded to one of the two values of plus or minus one quantum and is represented by one binary digit. (I)

binary item A numeric data item represented in binary notation, that is, as a number in the base 2 numbering system; internally, each bit of the item is a binary digit with the sign as the leftmost bit.

binary notation (1) Any notation that uses two different characters, usually the binary digits 0 and 1; for example, the gray code. The gray code is a binary notation but not a pure binary numeration system. (I) (A) (2) Fixed-radix notation where the radix is two; for example, in binary notation the numeral 110.01 represents the number 1 x 2 squared plus 1 x 2 to the first power plus 1 x 2 to the minus 2 power, that is, six and a quarter. (A)

binary number Loosely, a binary numeral. (A)

binary numeral (1) A numeral in the binary numeration system; for example, "101" is a binary numeral and "V" is the equivalent Roman numeral. (T) (2) A binary representation of a number; for example, 101 is a binary numeral and 5 is the equivalent decimal numeral.

binary (numeration) system The fixed-radix-numeration system that uses the digits "0" and "1" and the radix two; for example, in this numeration system the numeral "110.01" represents the number "6.25": 1 x 2^2 + 1 x 2^1 + 1 x 2^{-2} (T)

binary operation Deprecated term for binary arithmetic operation, Boolean operation, dyadic operation.

binary operator (1) An arithmetic operator having two terms. The binary operators that can be used in absolute or relocatable expressions and in arithmetic expressions are addition (+), subtraction (-), multiplication (*), and division (/). (2) A symbol representing an operation to be performed on two data items, arrays, or expressions. The four types of binary operators are numeric, character, logical, and relational. (3) Synonym for dyadic operator. Contrast with unary operator.

binary search A dichotomizing search in which, at each step of the search, the set of data elements is divided by two; some appropriate action is taken in the case of an odd number. (T)

binary search tree A search structure in which, at each step of the search, the set of data elements is divided by two; some appropriate action is taken in the case of an odd number of data elements.

binary serial signaling rate In two-state serial transmission, the reciprocal of the unit interval measured in seconds and expressed in bits per second. (T)

binary stream In the C and Pascal languages, a sequence of characters that corresponds on a one-to-one basis with the characters in the file. No character translation is performed on binary streams.

binary symmetric channel A channel designed to convey messages consisting of binary characters and that has the property that the conditional probabilities of changing any one character to the other character are equal. (I) (A)

binary synchronous communication (BSC) A form of telecommunication line control that uses a standard set of transmission control characters and control character sequences, for binary synchronous transmission of binary-coded data between stations. Contrast with Synchronous Data Link Control.

BSCEL support (1) binary synchronous communications equivalence link (2) In the AS/400 system, the intersystem communications function (ICF) support that provides an AS/400 system binary synchronous communications with another AS/400 system, System/36, or System/38, and with many other BSC computers and devices. (3) In System/36, the SSP-ICF subsystem that provides BSC communication with another System/36 and with many other BSC computers and devices.

binary synchronous transmission Data transmission in which synchronization of characters is controlled by timing signals generated at the sending and receiving stations. See also start-stop transmission, synchronous data link control.

binary-to-decimal conversion Conversion of a binary number to the equivalent decimal number, that is, a base two number to a base ten number.

bin collection In the AIX operating system, a method of collecting auditing data that writes audit records to a temporary bin file. After the data is processed by the auditbin daemon, records are written to an audit trail file for storage.

bind (1) To relate an identifier to another object in a program; for example, to relate an identifier to a value, an address or another identifier, or to associate formal parameters and actual parameters. (T) (2) To associate a variable with an absolute address, identifier, or virtual address, or with a symbolic address or label in a program. (3) In SNA products, a request to activate a session between two logical units. See also session activation request. (4) In MSS: (a) An attribute of a data set that keeps the data set on one or more staging drives until the data set is released by the user regardless of the length of time or demands for space. (b) An attribute of a mass storage volume that reserves an entire staging pack for the mass storage volume whenever the volume is mounted. (5) In the Object Distribution Manager, to connect the Object Distribution Manager and the Object Access Method together for use with the DB2 program, so that the data can be accessed by both programs. (6) In the ImagePlus program, the process by which the output from the DB2 precompiler is converted to a usable control structure called an application plan. This is the process during which access paths to the data are selected and some authorization checking is performed. (7) In SQL, the process by which the output from the SQL precompiler is converted to a usable structure called an access plan. This process is the one during which access paths to the data are selected and some authorization checking is performed. See also automatic bind, dynamic bind. (8) Synonymous with set.

BIND (1) In SNA, a request to activate a session between two logical units (LUs). See also bind session, session activation request. Contrast with UNBIND.

BIND command In SNA, a command used to start a session and define the characteristics of that session. Contrast with UNBIND command.

binder Deprecated term for linkage editor.

binder-hole card A card that contains one or more holes for binding. (A)

bind image In SNA, the session parameters passed in a Control Initiate request by the system services control point (SSCP) to the primary logical unit (PLU); the parameters specify the proposed protocol options for an LU-LU session.

bind image table In ACF/TCAM, the data area that contains the bind images for all of the sessions possible in the network. Synonymous with mode table.

binding (1) In programming, an association between a variable and a value for that variable that holds within a defined scope. The scope may be that of a rule, a function call or a procedure invocation. (T) (2) In the AIX operating system, a temporary association between a client and both an object and a server that exports an interface to the object. A binding is meaningful only to the program that sets it and is represented by a bound handle.

binding edge The edge of a page to be bound, stapled, or drilled.

BIND pacing A technique by which the address space manager (ASM) at one node controls the rate of transmission of BIND requests of a sending ASM at another node. BIND pacing can be used to prevent BIND standoff, in which each of two nodes has reserved most of its resources for sessions it is attempting to initiate through the other and thus rejects any BINDs received from the other.

BIND password One of the two communication security passwords. In an LU-LU session, it is the password that the system checks against the remote system to verify that the program to which the user is connected is the correct one. See also node verification. See also communications authority password.

bind session (BIND) In SNA products, a request to activate a session between two logical units.

BIOCA Block input/output communication area.

biometric In computer security, pertaining to the use of specific attributes that reflect unique personal characteristics, such as a fingerprint, an eye blood vessel print, or a voice print, to validate the identity of users.

bionics A branch of technology relating the functions, characteristics, and phenomena of living systems to the development of mechanical systems. (A)

BIOS Basic Input/Output System.

bipolar transmission Synonym for polar transmission.

biquinary code A notation in which a decimal digit n is represented by the pair of numerals a, b, where a equals 0 or 1, b equals 0, 1, 2, 3, or 4, and the sum of $5a + b$ is equal to n. (T) (A)

BISAM Basic indexed sequential access method.

BIST Built-in self-test.

bistable Pertaining to a device capable of assuming either of two stable states. (A)

bistable circuit See bistable trigger circuit.

bistable trigger circuit (1) A trigger circuit that has two stable states. (T) (2) Synonymous with flip-flop.

BISYNC Binary synchronous.

bit Either of the digits 0 or 1 when used in the binary numeration system. Synonymous with binary digit. (T) Deprecated term for binary element, shannon.

bit-block transfer (bitblt) (1) Transfer of a rectangular array of bit-map data. (2) In the AIX operating system, the movement of a binary image (a bitmap or pixmap) by specifying the lower-left and upper-right corners of the image and the destination address.

bitblt Bit-block transfer.

bit clocking In an EIA 232 interface, the field that indicates which piece of equipment, either the modem or the computer, provides the clock signal for synchronized data transactions.

bit comparison In PL/I, a left-to-right, bit-by-bit comparison of binary values. See also arithmetic comparison, character comparison.

bit configuration The order for encoding the bits of information that define a character. (T) (A)

bit constant In PL/I, either a series of binary numbers enclosed in apostrophes and followed immediately by B or B1, or a series of hexadecimal numbers enclosed in apostrophes and followed immediately by B4. Contrast with character constant.

bit density A measure of the number of bits recorded per unit of length or area. Synonymous with recording density.

bit error rate (BER) In fiber optics, a comparison of the number of bits received incorrectly to the total number of bits transmitted. The BER relates directly to receiver sensitivity, transmitter power output, pulse dispersion, and total link attenuation.

bit field A member of a structure or union that contains one or more named bits.

bit gravity In AIX Enhanced X-Windows, the attraction of window contents for a location in a window. When a window is resized, its contents can be relocated. The server can be requested to relocate the previous contents to a region of the window.

bit map (1) A representation of an image by an array of bits. (2) A pixmap with a depth of one bit plane. See also stipple. (3) In DPCX, a control record that describes 1432 256-byte blocks of disk storage.

bit map display A display on which characters or images are generated by writing the bit pattern to be displayed into the associated storage, each bit of which is mapped to a pixel on the display surface. (T)

bit-map graphics (1) A form of graphics in which all points on the display are directly addressable. (2) In multimedia applications, a form of graphics in an area of computer memory or storage that can be displayed as an image.

bit-mapped display A display with a display adapter that has a hardware representation of each separately addressable point on the display. The hardware representation can be processor memory or adapter memory. See all points addressable display.

bit plane In computer graphics, one bit of color information per pixel on the display. Thus, an eight bit-plane system allows 2 to the eighth power different colors to be displayed at each pixel. See also overlay planes.

bit position (1) A character position in a word in a binary notation. (T)   (2) A digit position in a binary number.

bit rate The speed at which bits are transmitted, usually expressed in bits per second. See also baud.

bits per character The number of bits in a data character.

bits per pixel In a digitized image, a measure of the color value of a given pixel.

bit stream A binary signal without regard to grouping by character.

bit string A string consisting solely of bits. (I)   (A)

bit value In PL/I, a sequence of binary numbers stored in consecutive bits.

BIU Basic information unit.

BIU segment In SNA, the portion of a basic information unit (BIU) that is contained within a path information unit (PIU). It consists of either a request/response header (RH) followed by all or part of a request/response unit (RU), or of only a part of an RU.

blackboard In artificial intelligence, a common working data storage accessible to several knowledge sources and used to communicate intermediate results. (T)

blackout (1) A dark period or area where light is eliminated or screened out.   (2) In the ImagePlus system, an area where all white pixels are converted to black pixels. See noise filter.

blank (1) A part of a data medium in which no characters are recorded. (A)   (2) In computer graphics, to suppress the display of all or part of a display image.

blank after In RPG, an output specification option that changes the contents of a field so that it contains either zeros (if it is a numeric field) or blanks (if it is a character field) after that field is written to the output record.

blank character (1) A graphic representation of the space character. (A)   (2) A character that represents an empty position in a graphic character string. (T)

blank coil A tape intended for perforation in which only the feed holes are punched.

blank common In XL FORTRAN, an unnamed common block.

blank deleter A device that prevents the receipt of blanks in perforated paper tape.

blanket In a duplicator, a removable sheet of material with a compressible surface covering the blanket cylinder that provides the intermediate surface in the duplicating process. (T)

blanket cleaning control In a duplicator, a device for controlling operation of the blanket cleaning device. (T)

blanket cleaning device In a duplicator, a mechanism for removing the image from the blanket by applying a solvent to it. (T)

blanket clip In a duplicator, a device for fixing a blanket to the blanket cylinder. (T)

blanket cylinder In a duplicator, the cylinder to which a blanket is attached. (T)

blanking (1) The suppression of the display of one or more display elements or segments. (I) (A) (2) The process of electronically interrupting a video signal.

blanking interval In video presentations, the period during which the monitor receives no video signal while the videodisc player searches for the next video segment or frame of play.

blanking level In a video signal, the signal level during the horizontal and vertical blanking intervals, usually representing zero output.

blank line In the IBM 3886 Optical Character Reader, a line on a form that may contain delimiters, but does not contain other characters.

blank medium A data medium in or on which neither marks of reference nor user data have been recorded. Synonymous with virgin medium. (T) (A)

BLDL table A list of the track addresses of frequently used modules in the link library. The purpose of the table is to reduce the time required to access and load the associated modules.

bleeding In computer graphics, an undesirable effect of color appearing outside an object on a background, such as a red smear to the right of a brightly colored object on a dark background.

blend In computer graphics, the smooth transition from one color to another, giving a realistic look to a drawing.

blind To make a device unreceptive to unwanted data, through recognition of field definition characters in the received data. See also lockout, polling, selection.

blind copy recipient A recipient whose identity is not to be disclosed to other recipients of the same message. (T)

blind folio Pertaining to a document in which the pages of the document are counted but not numbered. See folio, dropped folio, expressed folio.

blinking An intentional periodic change in the intensity of one or more display elements or segments. (I) (A)

blip Synonym for document mark.

blip facility See CMS blip facility.

blit See bit block transfer.

blitter Hardware that performs bit-block transfer operations.

block (1) In text processing, a user-defined segment of text on which a text processing operation is to be performed. (T) (2) In programming languages, a compound statement that coincides with the scope of at least one of the declarations contained within it. A block may also specify storage allocation or segment programs for other purposes. (I) (3) A string of data elements recorded or transmitted as a unit. The elements may be characters, words or physical records. (T) (4) A collection of contiguous records recorded as a unit. Blocks are separated by interblock gaps and each block may contain one or more records. (A) (5) In word processing, sequential characters of text that are to be treated as a unit; for example, text to be moved from one point to another in a document. (6) A subdivision of a track on a diskette. (7) To record data in a block. (8) In the AS/400 system, a sequential group of statements, defined using line commands, that are processed as a unit. (9) In PL/I, a sequence of statements, processed as a unit, that specify the scope of names and the allocation of storage for names declared within it. Contrast with DO group. (10) In FORTRAN, a sequence of executable constructs embedded in another executable construct, bounded by statements that are particular to the construct, and treated as an integral unit. (11) In COBOL, a physical unit of data that is normally composed of one or more logical records. Synonymous with physical record.

block cancel character A cancel character used to indicate that the preceding portion of the block, back to the most recently occurring block mark, is to be disregarded. (I) (A) Synonymous with block ignore character.

block character See end-of-transmission-block character.

block check That part of the error control procedure used for determining whether a data block is structured according to given rules. (I)

block-check character (BCC) (1) In longitudinal redundancy checking and cyclic redundancy checking, a character that is transmitted by the sender after each message block and is compared with a block-check character computed by the receiver to determine if the transmission was successful. (2) In BSC, a transmission control character that is used to determine whether all the bits transmitted are also received.

block check procedure That part of the error control procedure used for determining whether a data block is structured according to given rules. (T)

block control byte (BCB) In a multi-leaving telecommunications access method, a control character used for transmission block status and sequence count.

block control unit (BCU) A network control program data area built by the channel manager and other routines such as block handling and control command routines. It is used to request work and contains a buffer prefix, event control block, work area, and basic transmission unit.

block copy (1) A function or mode that enables the user to duplicate a block of text to insert it at another part within the document, or into another document. Synonymous with copy. (T)   (2) To make a duplicate of a block of text in one location in a document and place the duplicate at another location in the document.

block data subprogram In XL FORTRAN, a subprogram headed by a BLOCK DATA statement that is used to initialize variables in named common blocks.

block delete To delete a block of text.

block device file (1) In the AIX operating system, one of the types of files in the file system, described by an i-node.   (2) In the AIX operating system, a device that is accessed by means of an AIX device driver.

block diagram A diagram of a system in which the principal parts or functions are represented by blocks connected by lines that show their relationships. Block diagrams are not restricted to physical devices. (T)   Contrast with flowchart.

blocked In an ESCON Director, the attribute that when set removes the communication capability of a specific port. Contrast with unblocked.

block error rate The ratio of the number of received blocks that contain errors to the total number of blocks transmitted.

block file In the AIX operating system, a file listing the usage of blocks on a disk. See character special file, special file.

block gap Deprecated term for interblock gap.

block group In VSE/POWER, the basic organizational unit for fixed-block architecture (FBA) devices. Each block group consists of a certain number of units of transfer.

block handler (BH) In the network control program, a group of block handling routines that are executed sequentially to process a block control unit at a specified point in its path through the network control program.   See also block handling routine, block control unit.

block handler (BH) set In the network control program, a group of up to three block handlers. A BH set may be associated with one or more devices. See also block handler.

block handling macroinstruction (BH macro) One of the network control program generation macroinstructions that describe optional block processing functions to be included in the network control program.

block handling routine (BHR) A routine that performs a single processing function for a block control unit passing through the network control program; for example, inserting the date and time of day in a block.

block ignore character Synonym for block cancel character.

blocking (1) The process of combining two or more records in one block. (2) The process of combining incoming messages in a single message. See also concentrator. (3) In a telephone switching system, inability to make a connection or obtain a service because the devices needed for connection or service are in use. (4) Synonym for concentration. Contrast with deblocking.

blocking factor The number of records in a block. A blocking factor is calculated by dividing the size of the block by the size of the record. (T)   Synonymous with grouping factor. See also input blocking factor, output blocking factor.

blocking of PIUs In SNA, an optional function of path control that combines multiple path information units (PIUs) in a single basic transmission unit (BTU). When blocking is not done, a BTU consists of one PIU.

block input/output communication area In the AIX operating system, a block of storage in the kernel address space that is used to communicate with a block I/O subsystem.

block I/O Input/output operations on blocks of data stored in random locations. See also character I/O.

block length Synonym for block size.

block level sharing In IMS/VS, a kind of data sharing that enables application programs in different IMS/VS systems to update data concurrently.

block loading Bringing the control sections of a load module into adjoining positions in main storage. Contrast with scatter loading.

block move (1) A function or mode that enables the user to designate a block of text and to move it to another point within a document or into another document. Synonymous with move. (T)   (2) To relocate a block of text from one part of a document to another part of the document.

block movement In word processing, the ability to move a block of information from one point to another in a document or into another document. (T)

block multiplexer channel A multiplexer channel that interleaves blocks of data.   See also byte multiplexer channel. Contrast with selector channel.

block multiplexer mode A data transfer mode that permits interleaving of records in block form. Contrast with byte multiplexer mode.

block paging Paging of multiple pages simultaneously to or from real or external storage.

block prefix An optional, variable length field that may precede unblocked records or blocks of records recorded in ASCII on magnetic tapes.

block processor See actual block processor.

block separator See interblock gap.

block size (1) The number of data elements in a block. (T)   (2) A measure of the size of a block, usually specified in units such as records, words, computer words, or characters. (A)   (3) Synonymous with block length.

block sort A sort that separates a file into segments, using the highest-order portion of the key, orders the segments separately, and then joins them.

block special file (1) In the AIX operating system, a special file that provides access to an input or output device utilizing in-core buffers and is capable of supporting a file system.   (2) In the AIX operating system, a special file for a block device.

block splitting In DPPX, the process by which DPPX gets more space on one level of an index to insert index entries.

block statement In the C language, a group of data definitions, declarations, and statements appearing between a left brace and a right brace that are processed as a unit. The block statement is considered to be a single, C language statement.

block structure A hierarchy of program blocks. (A)

block transfer The process of transferring one or more blocks of data. (T)

blowback Synonym for reenlargement.

BLT Bit block transfer.

BLU Basic link unit.

BMP Batch message processing.

BMP program Batch message processing program.

BMS Basic mapping support.

BNC A connector used with some coaxial cables.

BNF (1) Backus Naur form.   (A)   (2) Backus normal form. (A)

BNN Boundary network node.

BNU Basic Networking Utilities.

board A panel made of insulating material that contains circuits on one or both sides. See bubble board, daughterboard, expansion board. See also short card.

body (1) On a printed page, the portion between the top and bottom margins that contains the text. (2) In a book, the portion between the front matter and the back matter. (3) See page body.

body group In COBOL, the generic name for a report group of TYPE DETAIL, CONTROL HEADING, or CONTROL FOOTING.

BOF Beginning-of-file. (A)

boilerplate (1) A frequently used segment of stored text that may be combined with other text to create a new document. (T)   (2) In word processing and desktop publishing, text that is stored for repeated use in various documents; for example the wording of an edition notice. Synonymous with stored paragraph.

boldface (1) A heavy-faced type.   (2) Printing in heavy-faced type. (3) See also double-strike, emphasized.

bonding See equipotential bonding.

book In programming languages, a group of source statements.

book copying On a document copying machine, the making of a copy or copies from a bound original. (T)

BookManager products A family of IBM licensed programs that allow users to create and display softcopy.   See also BookManager BUILD/MVS, BookManager READ/DOS, BookManager Read/MVS, BookManager READ/2.

BookManager BUILD/MVS An IBM licensed program that lets users create softcopy on an MVS host system from tagged source files (known as data sets).

BookManager READ/2 An IBM licensed program that lets readers display, search, and annotate online books on a programmable workstation running the OS/2 operating system.

BookManager READ/DOS An IBM licensed program that lets readers display, search, organize, and annotate softcopy on a programmable workstation running the DOS operating system.

BookManager READ/MVS An IBM licensed program that lets readers on an MVS host system display, search, organize, and annotate softcopy.

bookmark A marker left in a application or a presentation to which the system will return when next executed.

BookMaster product A document markup language for developing technical publications. BookMaster offers a richer tag vocabulary than the GML Starter Set that is available with DCF. BookMaster is an IBM licensed program. See also Document Composition Facility (DCF) and Generalized Markup Language (GML) Starter Set.

book message Synonym for broadcast message.

Boolean (1) Pertaining to the processes used in the algebra formulated by George Boole. (A) (2) A value of 0 or 1 represented internally in binary notation.

Boolean ADD Synonym for OR.

Boolean complementation Deprecated term for negation.

Boolean data Data that is limited to values of one and zero.

Boolean function A switching function in which the number of possible values of the function and each of its independent variables is two. (I) (A)

Boolean literal In COBOL, a literal composed of a Boolean character enclosed in double quotation marks and preceded by a B; for example, B "1". See also literal.

Boolean operation (1) Any operation in which each of the operands and the result take one of two values. (I) (A) (2) An operation that follows the rules of Boolean algebra. (I) (A) (3) See dyadic Boolean operation, n-adic Boolean operation.

Boolean operation table An operation table in which each of the operands and the result take one of two values. (I) (A)

Boolean operator (1) An operator each of whose operands and whose result take one of two values. (I) (A) (2) See dyadic operator, monadic operator.

boom In multimedia applications, a long, relatively horizontal supporting brace used for holding a microphone or camera.

boot To prepare a computer system for operation by loading an operating system.

boot block In a file system, the first block where the bootstrap program resides. Synonymous with bootstrap block.

bootstrap (1) A sequence of instructions whose execution causes additional instructions to be loaded and executed until the complete computer program is in storage. (T) (2) A technique or device designed to bring itself into a desired state by means of its own action; for example, a machine routine whose first few instructions are sufficient to bring the rest of itself into the computer from an input device. (A) (3) A small program that loads larger programs during system initialization. (4) To execute a bootstrap. The term bootstrapping is also used for translating a compiler by using the compiler or a previous version as the translator. (T) (5) See also bootstrap loader, initial program loader.

bootstrap block Synonym for boot block.

bootstrap loader An input routine in which preset computer operations are used to load a bootstrap. (I) (A) See also bootstrap, initial program loader.

BOP Basic operator panel.

border (1) A visual boundary that separates a displayed object from everything else on a screen. (2) In SAA Common User Access architecture, a visual indicator of a window's boundaries.

border node An APPN network node that interconnects APPN networks having independent topology databases in order to support LU-LU sessions between these networks. See extended border node, peripheral border node.

border region In a video display, the area of the screen surrounding the active pixel region, where many systems allow a separate color to be specified.

borrow An arithmetically negative carry. (A)   See end-around borrow.

borrow digit A digit generated when a difference in a digit place is arithmetically negative and is transferred for processing elsewhere.   In a positional representation system, a borrow digit is transferred to the digit place with the next higher weight for processing there. (I) (A)

BOT Beginning-of-tape. (A)

both field A field that can be used for either input data or output data. See output/input field.

both regular and immediate command In NCCF, a command that may be executed as either a regular or an immediate command, depending on where it is encountered. If the command is received from an operator terminal, it is executed as an immediate command. If it is received in another way; for example, in a command list, it is executed as a regular command.

both-way communication Deprecated   term   for two-way simultaneous communication.

both-way operation Synonym for duplex operation.

BOT marker Beginning-of-tape marker.

bottom margin (1) On a page, the space between the body or the running footing, if any, and the bottom edge of the page. (2) In COBOL, an empty area that follows the page body.

bottom shadow In the AIXwindows program, a narrow band of a dark color across the bottom of a rectangular graphical object (a widget or gadget) that creates a three-dimensional appearance when the object is manipulated. See also top shadow.

bottom-up Pertaining to a method or procedure that starts at the lowest level of abstraction and proceeds toward the highest level. (T)   Contrast with topdown.

bounce The reflection of a transmission on a telecommunication line.

boundary See character boundary, integral boundary.

boundary alignment The positioning in main storage of a fixed-length field, such as a halfword or doubleword, on an integral boundary for that unit of information.

boundary fill In some computer paint applications, the technique of flooding a specified color until a boundary color is encountered.

boundary function (1) In SNA, a capability of a subarea node to provide protocol support for adjacent peripheral nodes, such as: (a) transforming network addresses to local addresses, and vice versa, (b) performing session sequence numbering for low-function peripheral nodes, and   (c) providing session-level pacing support. (2) In SNA, the component that provides these capabilities. See also intermediate routing function, network addressable unit, path control network. (3) In VTAM, the programming component that performs FID2 (format identification type 2) conversion, data link control, pacing, and channel or device error recovery procedures for a locally attached peripheral node. These functions are similar to those performed by a network control program for an NCP-attached station.   See also boundary node, network addressable unit (NAU), peripheral path control, subarea node, subarea path control.

boundary network node (BNN) Deprecated term for boundary node.

boundary node In SNA, a subarea node with boundary function.   A subarea node may be a boundary node, an intermediate routing node, both, or neither, depending on how it is used in the network.

boundary violation An attempt to write beyond the externally defined boundaries of a sequential file.

bounding box (1) In computer graphics, the smallest rectangle that encloses the shape of the character at the same x, y origin.   (2) In AIX graphics, a two-dimensional rectangle that bounds a primitive.   A bounding box is used to determine whether the primitive lies inside a clipping region. See also clipping, fixed box. (3) Synonym for character box. (T)

BOV Beginning-of-volume. (A)

BPAM Basic partitioned access method.

BPCB Buffer pool control block.

BPDTY Buffer pool directory.

bpi Bits per inch.

"B" pins Module pins used only for stacking purposes and located in the top substrate.

bpp Bits per pixel.

Bps Bytes per second.

bps Bits per second. In serial transmission, the instantaneous bit speed with which a device or channel transmits a character.

braces The characters { (left brace) and } (right brace).

bracket In SNA, one or more chains of request units and their responses that are exchanged between two session partners and that represent a transaction between them. A bracket must be completed before another bracket can be started. Examples of brackets are database inquiries/replies, update transactions, and remote job entry output sequences to workstations.

bracket protocol In SNA, a data flow control protocol in which exchanges between two session partners are achieved through the use of brackets, with one partner designated at session activation as the first speaker and the other as the bidder. The bracket protocol involves bracket initiation and termination rules.

brackets The characters [(left bracket) and] (right bracket).

bracket state manager In ACF/TCAM, a routine that enforces the bracket protocol by making proper bracket state changes and detecting bracket errors.

branch (1) In a network, a path that connects two adjacent nodes and that has no intermediate nodes. (T) (2) In the execution of a computer program, to select one from a number of alternative sets of instructions. (I) (A) (3) A set of instructions that are executed between two successive branch instructions. (A) (4) In video presentations, to go directly from one sequence to another. (5) In an interactive video presentation, a video segment selected by a viewer. (6) Loosely, a conditional jump. (A) (7) To select a branch. (A) (8) Deprecated term for jump.

branch cable A cable that diverges from a main cable to reach some secondary point.

branch construct In programming languages, a language construct specifying a choice between different execution sequences using label references. (I)

branch exchange A switching system that provides telephone communication between branch stations and external networks.

branching (1) The technique of bypassing specific instructions to alter the sequential execution of instructions in a program. (2) Performing a statement other than the next one in sequence.

branching point In an interactive video presentation, the location in a program where the viewer may choose between two or more optional paths.

branch instruction (1) An instruction that controls branching. (A) Synonymous with decision instruc-

tion. (2) An instruction that changes the sequence in which the instructions in a computer program are performed. The sequence of instructions continues at the address specified in the branch instruction. (A) (3) Deprecated term for jump instruction. (A)

branch linkage (BAL) In DPPX, a linkage within a load module. Contrast with system-assisted linkage.

branch point (1) A point in a computer program at which branching occurs, in particular the address or the label of an instruction. (I) (A) (2) A place in a routine where a branch is selected. (A)

branch table A table of arguments and related addresses to which control can be passed on the basis of tests.

breach In computer security, the successful circumvention or disablement of a security control, with or without detection, which if carried to completion, could result in a penetration of the system.

breadth-first search A search which proceeds from higher levels to lower levels, checking all the nodes across all the possible alternatives at each level. (T)

break (1) To interrupt the sending end and take control of a circuit at the receiving end. (2) A separation of continuous paper forms, usually at the perforation. (3) To stop operations, as on a personal computer. either by pressing the Control (Ctl) key and Break key or by issuing a command. (4) In the Documentation Composition Facility, an interruption in the formatting of input lines so that the next input line is printed on a new output line. (5) See also interrupt, receive interruption.

Break A key on a keyboard that a user presses with another key to stop an action.

break character In PL/I, the underscore symbol (_), which can be used to improve the readability of identifiers; for example, a variable could be called OLD_INVENTORY_TOTAL instead of OLDINVENTORYTOTAL.

break delivery The method of delivering messages to a message queue in which the job associated with that message queue is interrupted as soon as the message arrives.

breakdown Synonym for cue sheet.

break mode In IBM 3270 emulation, the method of operation in effect when a program is interrupted.

breakpoint (1) A point in a computer program where execution may be halted. A breakpoint is usually at the beginning of an instruction where halts, caused by external intervention, are convenient for resuming execution. (T) (2) An instruction in a program for halting execution. Breakpoints are usually established at positions in a program where halts, caused by external intervention, are convenient for restarting. (T) (3) A place in a program, specified by a command or a condition, where the system halts execution and gives control to the workstation user or to a specified program. (4) See instruction address stop. Synonymous with breakpoint instruction, dynamic stop.

breakpoint halt A closed loop consisting of a single jump instruction that effects a jump to itself; it is often used to achieve a breakpoint. (I) (A) Synonymous with breakpoint instruction, dynamic stop.

breakpoint instruction Synonym for breakpoint halt.

breakpoint program In a batch job, a user program that can be invoked when a breakpoint is reached.

break sequence In start-stop protocol, the transmission of all 0 bits.

break signal A signal sent over a remote connection to interrupt current activity on the remote system.

break statement A C language control statement that contains the keyword "break" and a semicolon.

breakup In video presentations, disruptions in a signal caused by damage to the tape or disc or by loss of sync.

break value In AIX data segment space allocation, the address of the first location beyond the current end of the data segment.

B-register Deprecated term for index register.

bridge (1) A functional unit that interconnects two local area networks that use the same logical link control protocol but may use different medium access control protocols. (T) (2) A functional unit that interconnects multiple LANs (locally or remotely) that use the same logical link control protocol but that can use different medium access control protocols. A bridge forwards a frame to another bridge based on the medium access control (MAC) address. (3) In the connection of local loops, channels, or rings, the equipment and techniques used to match circuits and to facilitate accurate data transmission.

Note: A bridge connects networks or systems of the same or similar architectures, whereas a gateway connects networks or systems of different architectures.

bridge input circuit In process control, an analog input circuit in which the sensing component of the technical process is in one branch of the bridge and the reference components in another. (T)

Note: The reference bridge voltage is usually supplied by the user.

bridge tap An unterminated length of line attached somewhere between the extremities of a telecommunication line. Bridge taps are undesirable. Contrast with terminated line.

bridging In OCR, a combination of peaks and smudges that may close or partially close a loop of a character.

bring-up The process of starting a computer system or a subsystem that is to operate under control of the system.

bring-up test In the IBM 8100 Information System, test modules contained in read-only storage, that verify the capability of selected functions within the system.

broadband (1) A frequency band broad enough to be divided into several narrower bands, each of which can be used for different purposes or be made available to different users. Synonymous with wideband. (T) (2) A frequency band divisible into several narrower bands so that different kinds of transmissions such as voice, video, and data transmission can occur at the same time. Synonymous with wideband. See also baseband. (3) Transmission media and techniques that use a broad frequency range, divided into sub-bands of narrower frequency, so that different kinds of transmission can occur at the same time.

broadband channel A data transmission channel 6MHz wide. (T)

broadband exchange (BEX) A public switched telecommunication system of Western Union, featuring various bandwidth duplex connections.

broadband LAN A local area network in which data are encoded, multiplexed, and transmitted with modulation of carriers.

Note: A broadband LAN consists of more than one channel. (T)

broadband signaling In a network, transmission using analog signals, carrier frequencies, and multiplexing techniques to allow more than one node to transmit at a time. Contrast with baseband signaling.

Note: Multiple channels or frequency bands can be created by using frequency-division multiplexing (FDS).

broadcast (1) Transmission of the same data to all destinations. (T)　(2) Simultaneous transmission of data to more than one destination.

broadcast address In SDLC protocol, a station address (eight 1's) reserved as an address common to all stations on a link. Synonymous with all-stations address.

broadcast data set In TSO, a system data set containing messages and notices from the system operator, administrators, and other users. Unless suppressed by the user, its contents are displayed to all terminal users when they log on to the system.

broadcast Locate search Synonym for broadcast search.

broadcast message (1) A message transmitted to two or more stations on a network. (2) In VM, information that can be sent by the system operator to all terminal users that are enabled to receive messages. The three major classes of messages are:　(a) Log (LOGMSG) messages that are automatically displayed at user terminals when they log on, (b) Optional lower priority log messages, (c) Informational warning messages that alert users to some imminent event or action. (3) Synonymous with book message.

broadcast quality In video programming, a measure of the quality of a video picture; in the U.S., a standard of 525 lines of video picture information at a rate of 60 Hz. See also NTSC.

broadcast search The simultaneous propagation of a search request to all network nodes in an APPN network. This type of search may be used when the location of a resource is unknown to the requester. Contrast with directed search.

broadcast topology The topology in which all stations are connected in parallel with the medium and are capable of concurrently receiving a signal transmitted by any other station connected to the medium.

broadcast videography Synonym for teletext. (T)

broken pipe message In the AIX operating system, a message that occurs if the pipe becomes unsynchronized.

broker In the Network Computing System (NCS), a server that manages information about objects and interfaces to the objects. A program that wishes to become the client of an interface can use a broker to obtain information about servers that export the interface. See Location Broker.

browse (1) To look at records in a file. (2) To look at information without changing it. See also scan and search. (3) To rapidly scan information on a display screen by scrolling or paging. Synonymous with high-speed scan, high-speed scroll. (4) In the AIX operating system, a function available when the user selects the List of Books button at the bottom of a navigation window. The user can move forward and backward through an online book in the same way as through a book in hardcopy. (5) In the NetView Graphic Monitor Facility, to open a view that cannot receive status changes from the NetView program. Contrast with monitor.

browse display In System/38, the source entry utility display for browsing a member. It can be called from the member list display.

browse member In System/38, the member displayed in the lower part of the split-edit display. Records from the browse member can be copied, but no changes can be made to records in the browse member.

browsing In text processing, rapid review of displayed text by scrolling. (T)

brush In a computer paint application, a tool for creating images.

BS The backspace character. (A)

BSAM Basic sequential access method.

BSC Binary synchronous communication.

BSCA Binary Synchronous Communication Adapter.

BSC 3270 device emulation A program that allows a device such as a personal computer or a system such as System/38 to be perceived by a BSC host system as a 3271 control unit.

BSCEL subsystem Binary synchronous communication equivalence link subsystem.

BSCEL support Binary synchronous communications equivalence link support.

BSC file A file created to support binary synchronous communication. Contrast with communication file.

BSC or SS line A line that uses binary synchronous or start-stop protocols.

BSC or SS session In ACF/TCAM, a defined sequence of data exchanges between the host processor and a station attached to a network control program via binary synchronous or start-stop lines; it allows the network control program to interleave transmissions to and from many stations on a multipoint line.

BSC or SS station A station on a binary synchronous or start-stop line.

BSC/SS communication adapter In the IBM 8100 Information System, a hardware feature that is required in order to transfer data and commands between the processor and a device using binary synchronous communication or start-stop transmissions. A BSC/SS communication adapter is available for attachment to a communication port on an 8101 Storage and Input/Output Unit, an 8130 Processor, or an 8140 Processor.

BSC/SS communication control In the IBM 8100 Information System, the logic that allows system connection to a variety of devices using start-stop or binary synchronous communication facilities.

B space In the Print Management Facility, the area in the character box that has a pel defined for any row of the graphic character pattern. See also A space, C space.

B-spline cubic curve In computer graphics, a cubic spline approximation to a set of four control points having the property such that slope and curvature are continuous across sets of control points.

BSTAT Basic status register.

BTAM Basic telecommunications access method.

BTAM-ES Basic telecommunications access method extended storage. An IBM-supplied telecommunication access method that permits read and write communication with remote devices.

BTS Burster-trimmer-stacker.

Btu British thermal unit.

BTU Basic transmission unit.

bubble board In a personal computer, bubble memory in the form of an expansion board that operates as if it were either a hard disk drive or a diskette drive.

bubble memory (1) A magnetic storage that uses cylindrically shaped magnetized areas in thin film that are movable, nonvolatile, and changeable. (T) (2) A storage device in which data are stored by polarizing small areas within a film of magnetizable material.

bubble sort A sort in which the first two items to be sorted are examined and exchanged if necessary to place them in the specified order; the second item is then compared with the third (exchanging them if required), the third is compared with the fourth, and

the process is repeated until all pairs have been examined and all items are in the proper sequence. Synonymous with sifting sort.

bucket One or more fields in which the result of an operation is kept. See also accumulator, buffer.

buckslip A short message that can be sent with a document to give instructions to the receiver.

buffer (1) A routine or storage used to compensate for a difference in rate of flow of data, or time of occurrence of events, when transferring data from one device to another. (A) (2) An isolating circuit used to prevent a driven circuit from influencing the driving circuit. (A) (3) To allocate and schedule the use of buffers. (A) (4) A portion of storage used to hold input or output data temporarily. See Figure 20.

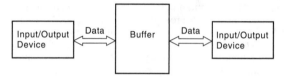

Figure 20. Buffer

buffer delay In ACF/TCAM, a delay specified for a buffered station to allow the hardware buffer to be emptied before it receives another message block.

buffer depletion In the network control program, a condition resulting when all buffers in the pool of available buffers have been allocated, and none is available for holding additional data.

buffered input The ability to enter new items or function instructions into the machine before current operations are completed. (T)

buffered output area In a 3790 program, the area in which the output data stream is accumulated for the terminal device. It is part of a work area shared by the source area and is unrelated to the defined buffers. See also source area.

buffer fields In the creation of a new form, the fields in which the data will be typed.

buffer group In VTAM, a group of buffers associated with one or more contiguous, related entries in a buffer list. The buffers may be located in discontiguous areas of storage and may be combined into one or more request units.

buffer invalidation In a System/370 multiprocessing configuration, communication between processing units to ensure that all real storage references by both processing units access the most recently stored data.

Data placed in the high-speed buffer of one processing unit is sent to the other processing unit; if the data is also being maintained in its high-speed buffer, that obsolete version of the data is marked invalid.

buffer list In VTAM, a contiguous set of control blocks (buffer list entries) that allow an application program to send function management data (FMD) from a number of discontiguous buffers with a single SEND macroinstruction.

buffer list entry A control block within a buffer list that points to a buffer containing function management data (FMD) to be sent.

buffer loop On the 3800 Printing Subsystem, the loop of continuous forms paper formed between the burster and trimmer assemblies.

buffer management (1) In OS/VS, the part of job management that provides a central buffer-handling facility for the job entry subsystem, maintaining unassigned buffers in a buffer pool, assigning them to requestors, and maintaining a table showing the status of each buffer. (2) A portion of the network control program supervisor that controls buffer chains, senses critical storage usage requirements, and initiates recovery procedures.

buffer offset The first field within a physical ASCII record; it precedes the first logical record. For D-format variable-length records, the buffer offset may contain information about the data in the logical records.

buffer pad characters A sequence of characters that the network control program sends to an access method buffer preceding message data, to provide space for the host access method to insert message prefixes.

buffer pool (1) An area of storage in which all buffers of a program are kept. (2) In ACF/TCAM, a group of buffers having the same size. A buffer pool is established at initialization time in the message control program; the buffers are built in extents chained together.

buffer prefix An area within a buffer that contains buffer control information. A user must allow space for the buffer prefix when specifying buffer size.

buffer storage (1) A special-purpose storage or storage area allowing, through temporary storage, the data transfer between two functional units having different transfer characteristics. A buffer storage is used between non-synchronized devices, or where one is serial and the other is parallel or between those having different transfer rates. Synonymous with buffer. (T) (2) In word processing, a temporary storage in which text is held for processing or communication. (T)

buffer store See buffer storage.

buffer unit Smallest block of main storage from which TCAM buffers and main storage message queues can be built. Synonymous with main storage unit.

buffer-unit pool All the buffer units in a particular ACF/TCAM system.

bug An error in a program.

build (1) For OS/2 Office directories, the process of installing a directory table on the server. (2) OS/2 Office Configuration utility, the process of creating a configuration file and a machine profile entry based on selections made using the utility.

built-in (1) In programming languages, pertaining to a language object that is declared by the definition of the programming language; for example, the built-in function SIN in PL/I, the predefined data type INTEGER in FORTRAN. (I) Synonymous with predefined. (2) Synonym for integrated.

built-in adapter Deprecated term for integrated adapter.

built-in check Synonym for automatic check.

built-in function (1) A function that is supplied by a language. See EXEC built-in function. (2) In PL/I and AS/400 control language (CL), a predefined function, such as a commonly used arithmetic function or a function necessary to high-level language compilers; for example, a function for manipulating character strings or converting data. It is automatically called by a built-in function reference.

built-in function reference In PL/I and AS/400 control language (CL), a built-in function name, having an optional, and possibly empty, argument list that holds the value returned by the built-in function.

bulk eraser On dictation equipment, a device for instantaneous and complete removal of recordings from the recording medium. (I)

bulk print In the 8100 Information System, a host-initiated system application that is used to print batch data from the host at a printer attached to the 8100.

bulk storage Deprecated term for mass storage.

bulletin board A graphic object that simulates a real-life bulletin board in that it displays text and graphic information in the form of messages to the user from client applications that are currently running.

bumping up In video applications, the process of transferring recorded video to a higher-quality tape format, such as from a half-inch tape to three-quarter-inch tape.

burned-in address See hard address.

burn in A process of increasing the reliability performance of hardware employing functional operation of every functional unit in a prescribed environment with successive corrective maintenance at every failure during the early failure period. (T)

burnt-in time code In videotaping, the time of day as displayed in a window on a videotape.

burst (1) In data communication, a sequence of signals counted as one unit in accordance with some specific criterion or measure. (A)   (2) To separate continuous-form paper into discrete sheets. (A) (3) See error burst.

burster A device to detach from one another previously-perforated forms or formsets of continuous stationery. (T)

burster-trimmer-stacker (BTS) A printer feature that bursts continuous forms into separate sheets, trims the carrier strip from both edges of the forms, and stacks single sheets. See also job offset.

burst isochronous transmission Synonym for burst transmission.

burst mode A mode in which data is transmitted by means of burst transmission.

burst noise In acoustics, noise characterized by acoustic impulses that significantly exceed the level of ambient noise.

burst pages On continuous-form paper, pages of output that can be separated at the perforations.

burst transmission (1) Data transmission at a specific data signalling rate during controlled intermittent intervals. (I) (A)   (2) Synonymous with burst isochronous transmission, interrupted isochronous transmission.

bus (1) A facility for transferring data between several devices located between two end points, only one device being able to transmit at a given moment. (T)   (2) A computer configuration in which processors are interconnected in series.   See also hypercube.   (3) One or more conductors used for transmitting signals or power. (A)   (4) See

bidirectional bus, control bus, data bus. See also bus network.

bus extension card (BEC) In the AS/400 system, the bus extension driver card or the bus extension receiver card.

bus extension driver (BED) card In the AS/400 system, the card, connected by a cable to a bus extension receiver (BER) card, that is used to route data from one card enclosure to another card enclosure. The direction of data can be from the processing unit to an input/output processor in one of the card enclosures, or from an input/output processor in one of the card enclosures to the processing unit. See also bus extension receiver (BER) card.

bus extension receiver (BER) card In the AS/400 system, the card, connected by a cable to a bus extension driver (BED) card, that is used to route data from one card enclosure to another card enclosure. The direction of data can be from the processing unit to an input/output processor in one of the card enclosures, or from an input/output processor in one of the card enclosures to the processing unit. See also bus extension driver (BED) card.

business area A product area where business is performed.

business graphics See graphics.

business graphics utility (BGU) An IBM-supplied OFFICE/38 utility that provides a menu-driven means of using the System/38 chart functions without knowledge of programming.

business machine (1) A machine designed to facilitate clerical operations in commercial or scientific activities. (2) Customer-provided data terminal equipment (DTE) that connects to telecommunication equipment of a communication common carrier, a Recognized Private Operating Agency, or a telecommunication Administration, for the purpose of data transfer. See also COAM equipment.

business machine clocking A time base oscillator supplied by the business machine for regulating the bit rate of transmission. Synonymous with non-data-set clocking. Contrast with data set clocking.

business partner Any non-IBM organization, with whom IBM has a written contract defining a complementary marketing relationship, that provides end users with information-handling solutions that use or rely upon an IBM offering.

bus master A device or subsystem that controls data transfers between itself and a slave.

bus network (1) A local area network in which there is only one path between any two data stations and in which data transmitted by any station is concurrently available to all other stations on the same transmission medium. (2) A network configuration that provides a bidirectional transmission facility to which all nodes are attached. A sending node transmits in both directions to the ends of the bus. All nodes in the path copy the message as it passes.

Note: A bus network may be a linear network, a star network, or a tree network. In the case of a tree or star network, there is a data station at each endpoint node. There is no data station at an intermediate node; however, one or more devices such as repeaters, connectors, amplifiers, and splitters are located there. (T)   See Figure 21.

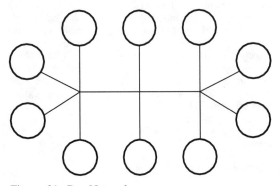

Figure 21. Bus Network

bus quiet signal In a token-bus network, a signal indicating that the transmission medium is inactive. (T)

bussback The connection by a common carrier of the output portion of a circuit back to the input portion of a circuit. See also loopback test.

bust this A phrase used instead of a normal message ending to indicate that the entire message, including heading, is to be disregarded. See also CANTRAN.

busy test A test to determine whether telephone circuits are available for use.

busy token Deprecated term for frame.

button (1) In SAA usage, a mechanism on a pointing device, such as a mouse, used to request or initiate an action. See mouse button. (2) A graphical device that identifies a choice. See radio button, push button. (3) A graphical mechanism in a window that, when selected, results in an action; for example, a list button produces a list of choices. See list button, maximize button, minimize button, and restore button.

(4) In the AIX operating system, a word or picture on the screen that can be selected. Once selected and activated, a button begins an action in the same manner that pressing a key on the keyboard can begin an action. Buttons include those on the keyboard, mouse, lightpen, or buttons on the dial and button box. See arrow button, cascade button, drawn button, toggle button. (5) An object that performs an action. In the IBM LinkWay product, button types include Go, Link, Find, Text Pop-up, Picture Pop-up, Script, Document, and Reference.

button assignment An assignment that defines the action or actions performed as a result of activating a button or combination of buttons.

button grabbing In the AIX operating system, enacting an active grab using a mouse button. See key grabbing, keyboard grabbing, pointer grabbing, server grabbing. See also active grab, passive grab.

buy In multimedia applications, videotape footage that is judged acceptable for use in the final video. Synonymous with keeper.

By... In SAA usage , a choice in the View pull-down that a user selects to change the order in which displayed items appear. See also All, Some....

bypass (1) To eliminate a station or an access unit from a ring network by allowing the data to flow in a path around it. (2) At an 8100 loop wiring concentrator, to manually disconnect a radial cable and the associated device from the loop signal flow path without physically removing the radial cable and the device. See also lobe bypass, wrapping.

bypass plug In the AS/400 system, a plug that allows power to flow through an unused outlet in the power control compartment.

byte (1) A string that consists of a number of bits, treated as a unit, and representing a character. (T) (2) A binary character operated upon as a unit and usually shorter than a computer word. (A)   (3) A group of 8 adjacent binary digits that represent one EBCDIC character. (4) See n-bit byte.

byte boundary addressing Memory addressing based on 8-bit intervals. Each memory location contains an 8-bit value that can range from 0 to 255 in decimal notation.

byte mode Synonym for multiplex mode.

byte multiplexer channel A multiplexer channel that interleaves bytes of data. See also block multiplexer channel. Contrast with selector channel.

byte multiplexer mode A data transfer mode that permits interleaving of bytes of data. Contrast with block multiplexer mode.

byte order In AIX Enhanced X-Windows, the order of bytes as defined by the server for pixmap or bitmap data. Clients with different byte ordering must swap bytes as necessary.

byte-serial transmission Transmission in sequential bytes.

Note: The individual bits of each byte can be transmitted serially (described as serial by bit and byte) or simultaneously (described as parallel by bit, serial by byte).

byte space In VSAM, the ascending set of logical addresses (0 through 2^{32} -1) in which a component exists; a byte space contains only one component, and a component exists in only one byte space.

byte string The resulting digitized image from a scanned document.

C

C (1) Coulomb. (2) Celsius.

c Centi. One hundred or one hundredth part.

CA (1) Computer-aided. (T) (2) Channel adapter. (3) Change accumulation. (4) Channel attachment.

cable The physical medium for transmitting signals; it includes copper conductors and optical fibers.

cable path A series of cables connected in sequence.

cable test A network controller test to verify that data can be sent and received over the length of all attached cables.

cable through feature A special feature that allows multiple workstations to be attached to a single cable path.

cache (1) A special-purpose buffer storage, smaller and faster than main storage, used to hold a copy of instructions and data obtained from main storage and likely to be needed next by the processor. (T) (2) A buffer storage that contains frequently accessed instructions and data; it is used to reduce access time. (3) An optional part of the directory database in network nodes where frequently used directory information may be stored to speed directory searches. (4) To place, hide, or store in a cache. (5) See converter cache, image cache, write-back cache.

cache line In VM/SP HPO, a boundary between blocks of storage that maps to a specific area in the cache or high-speed buffer.

cache memory A special buffer storage, smaller and faster than main storage, that is used to hold a copy of instructions and data in main storage that are likely to be needed next by the processor, and that have been obtained automatically from main storage. (T) (A)

caching (1) Storing instructions and data in a cache. (2) See client-side caching, GC caching.

caching disk On personal computers, a diskette that simulates the operation of cache memory.

CAD/CAM Computer-Aided Design/Computer-Aided Manufacturing. An application in which devices such as personal computers can be used to design and develop products such as circuit boards and other computers. See also schematic capture.

CAF Call attachment facility.

CAI Computer-assisted instruction.

calculated link loss In an ESCON environment, the total optical attenuation (loss) calculated for a specific link, the value of which cannot exceed the maximum loss allowed for that link. See also maximum allowable link loss.

calculating machine A machine that performs the arithmetic functions of a calculator, principally by electromechanical means; the predecessor to the calculator. See nonprinting calculating machine, printing calculating machine. (A)

calculating punch A calculator with a card reader and a card punch that reads the data on a punched card, performs some arithmetic operations or logic operations on the data, and punches the results on the same or another punched card. (I) (A) Synonymous with multiplying punch.

calculation specifications In RPG, a coding form on which a programmer describes the processing to be done by the program.

calculator A device that is especially suitable for performing arithmetic operations, but that requires human intervention to alter its stored program, if any, and to initiate each operation or sequence of operations. A calculator performs some of the functions of a computer but does not usually operate without frequent human intervention. (A)

calculator with algebraic logic A calculator in which the internal circuitry requires that after the input of the first operand, the operating symbol be given before the input of each subsequent operand for addition and subtraction operations. When combining addition and subtraction with multiplication and division, the user is not required to take interim results. (T) (A) See Figure 22.

$$\frac{12 + 3 - 5}{2} = 5$$

Key	Display	Print
12	12	
+	12	12 +
3	3	
−	15	3 −
5	5	
÷	10	5 ÷
2	2	
=	5	2 =
		5 *

Figure 22. Calculator with Algebraic Logic

calculator with arithmetic logic A calculator in which the internal circuitry requires that the operating symbol be given after the input of each operand for addition and subtraction operations. When combining addition and subtraction with multiplication and division, the user must take interim results. (T) (A) See Figure 23.

$$\frac{12 + 3 - 5}{2} = 5$$

Key	Display	Print
12	12	
⬆	12	12 +
3	3	
⬆	15	3 +
5	5	
=	10	5 −
÷	10	10 ◊
2	2	10 ÷
⬆	5	2 =
		5 *

Figure 23. Calculator with Arithmetic Logic

calculator with external program input A calculator that allows a given number of program steps to be entered from an external data medium and to be retained in the calculator for repeated use. (T) (A)

calculator with keyboard and external program input A calculator that allows a given number of program steps to be entered either via the keyboard or from an external data medium and to be retained in the calculator for repeated use. (T) (A)

calculator with keyboard-controlled addressable storage A calculator that allows only keyboard-controlled storage and accumulation of data; the data in storage is changed only by keyboard operations addressed to those devices. (T) (A)

calculator with keyboard program input A calculator that allows a given number of program steps to be entered via the keyboard and retained in the calculator for repeated use. (T) (A)

calculator without addressable storage A calculator in which data cannot be stored without being cleared by subsequent operations, but that may or may not have a facility for storing constants. (T) (A)

calculator with postfix notation A calculator in which the internal circuitry allows the first operand to be entered without operating symbols by means of an Enter key; the subsequent operands are immediately followed by the operating symbols. When combining addition and subtraction with multiplication and division, the user is not required to take interim results; for example, the sequence of operations used in a calculator with postfix notation logic entry to solve the problem. (I) See Figure 24.

calculator with program-controlled addressable storage A calculator that allows only program-controlled storage and accumulation of data; the data in the storage devices are changed only by program operations addressed to those devices. (T)

$$\frac{12 + 3 - 5}{2} = 5$$

Key	Display	Print
12	12	12 #
ENTER	12	
3	3	3 +
+	15	
5	5	5 −
−	10	
2	2	2 ÷
÷	5	
		5 *

Figure 24. Calculator with Postfix Notation

calculator with program-controlled and keyboard-controlled addressable storage A calculator that allows both program-dependent and keyboard-controlled storage and accumulation of data; the data in the storage devices are changed only by subsequent operations addressed to those devices. (T)

calculator with reverse-Polish notation logic A calculator in which the operating rule for a calculation is such that the first item is entered without operating instructions by means of an ENTER key, and the subsequent items are immediately followed by the operating instruction. When combining addition and subtraction with multiplication and division, it is unnecessary to take interim totals. (T)

calculus See relational calculus. (A)

calculus of variations The theory of maxima and minima of definite integrals whose integrand is a function of the dependent variables, the independent variables, and their derivatives. (A)

calendar A displayed list or schedule of appointments, reminders, and jobs. See clock/calendar.

calendar description A field associated with a calendar that identifies its contents.

calendar item An entry in a calendar.

calendar manager In System/36, the user who controls a calendar and who receives any messages sent by the system as notification of an event on the calendar.

calendar view In System/36, one of four ways of showing calendar appointments: for a day, for a week, for weeks combined from several calendars, or by listing the entire calendar, including jobs and reminders in addition to appointments.

calibration The adjustment of a piece of equipment so that it meets normal operational standards; for example, in the IBM InfoWindow system, calibration refers to touching a series of points on the screen so that the system can accurately determine their location for further reference.

call (1) The action of bringing a computer program, a routine, or a subroutine into effect, usually by specifying the entry conditions and jumping to an entry point. (I) (A) (2) In data communication, the actions necessary to make a connection between two stations on a switched line. (3) In communications, a conversation between two users. (4) To transfer control to a procedure, program, routine, or subroutine. (5) To attempt to contact a user, regardless of whether the attempt is successful. (6) Synonymous with cue.

callable interface The name of the interface program, the definition of the arguments passed to the interface program, and the definition of the data structures passed to the interface program.

call-accepted packet A call supervision packet that a called data terminal equipment (DTE) transmits to indicate to the data circuit-terminating equipment (DCE) that it accepts the incoming call.

call-accepted signal A call control signal that is sent by the called data terminal equipment (DTE) to indicate that it accepts the incoming call. (I) (A)

call attachment facility (CAF) A DB2 attachment facility for application programs running in TSO or MVS batch. The CAF is an alternative to the DSN command processor and thus allows greater control over the execution environment.

callback (1) In computer security, a procedure in which a system identifies a calling terminal, disconnects the call, and dials the calling terminal, in order to attempt to ensure the location and eligibility of the calling terminal. Synonymous with dial back. (2) In the AIX operating system: (a) A characteristic of the UUCP file USERFILE that tells a remote system whether the local system it tries to access will call back to check its identity. (b) A procedure that is called if and when certain specified conditions are met. This is accomplished by specifying the procedure in a callback list. Synonymous with callback function.

callback function Synonym for callback.

callback list (1) A list of procedures that are called if and when certain specified conditions are met. (2) In the AIXwindows program, individual widgets can define callback lists as required.

callback reason The conditions that, if met, result in a callback procedure being called.

call collision A condition that occurs when data terminal equipment (DTE) transmits a call request signal and data circuit-terminating equipment (DCE) simultaneously transmits an incoming call signal; neither the DTE nor the DCE receives the expected response. See also carrier-sense multiple-access with collision detection (CSMA/CD), clear collision, reset collision.

call connected packet A call supervision packet that a data circuit-terminating equipment (DCE) transmits to indicate to a calling data terminal equipment (DTE) that the connection for the call has been completely established.

call control That set of telephony functions that includes call establishment, call transfer, and call disconnection (the program control of a telephone call).

call control procedure The implementation of a set of protocols necessary to establish and release a call. (I) (A)

call control signal One of the set of signals necessary to establish, maintain, and release a call. (T)

call detail record (CDR) In telephony, a unit of information containing data about a completed call, such as the time the call began, its duration and date, the originating extension, and the number called.

call directing code An identifying call transmitted to an outlying telegraph receiver that causes it to automatically turn on its printer. See also selective calling, station selection code.

called In X.25 communications, pertaining to the location or user to which a call is made.

called address extension See address extension.

called line address modified notification In X.25 communications, an optional CCITT-specified facility.

called party On a switched line, the location to which a connection is established.

called program (1) A program whose execution is requested by another program (a calling program) or by a command. (2) In COBOL, a program that is the object of a CALL statement combined at object time with the calling program to produce a run unit. Synonymous with subprogram.

called service user In the Open Systems Interconnection reference model, a service user with which a calling service user wishes to establish a connection. (T)

called subaddress See subaddress.

caller The requester of a service.

call establishment The complete sequence of events necessary to establish a data connection.

call identifier A name assigned by a network to a virtual call; when used with the calling data terminal equipment (DTE) address, it uniquely identifies the virtual call.

calligraphic display device A display device in which the display elements of a display image may be generated in any program-controlled sequence. (I) (A) Synonymous with directed-beam display device.

CALLIN The logical channel type on which the data terminal equipment (DTE) can receive a call, but cannot send one.

calling (1) The process of transmitting selection signals in order to establish a connection between data stations. (I) (A) (2) In X.25 communications, pertaining to the location or user that makes a call. (3) See automatic calling.

calling address See network user address.

calling address extension See address extension.

calling conventions Specified ways for routines and subroutines to exchange data with each other.

calling party On a switched line, the location that originates a connection.

calling program (1) A program that requests execution of another program (a called program). (2) In the AS/400 system, a program that starts a CALL to another program.

calling sequence (1) A sequence of instructions together with any associated data necessary to execute a call. (T) (2) A polling list. See also polling.

calling service user In the Open Systems Interconnection reference model, a service user that initiates a request for the establishment of a connection. (T)

CALLIO The logical channel type on which the data terminal equipment (DTE) can send or receive a call.

call level The position of a program in a nest of programs called explicitly by the CALL instruction or implicitly by some event. The first program has a call level of 1. Any program called by a level 1 program has a call level of 2, and so on.

call-not-accepted signal A call control signal sent by the called data terminal equipment to indicate that it does not accept the incoming call. (I) (A)

callout In the AIX operating system, a kernel parameter that establishes the maximum number of scheduled activities that can be pending simultaneously.

CALLOUT The logical channel type on which the data terminal equipment (DTE) can send a call, but cannot receive one.

callout table In the AIX* operating system, a kernel table that keeps track of all sleeping processes and the channel on which each is waiting.

call profile In telephony, a set of characteristics that may be used when establishing or manipulating a program-controlled telephone call.

call progress signal (1) A call control signal transmitted from the data circuit-terminating equipment (DCE) to the calling data terminal equipment (DTE) to indicate the progress of the establishment of a call, the reason why the connection could not be established, or any other network condition. (T) (2) In virtual call service, a control signal that informs the calling and called data terminal equipment (DTEs) why the call has been cleared. (3) In permanent virtual circuit service, a control signal that informs the calling and called data terminal equipment (DTEs) why the permanent virtual circuit has been reset. (4) In datagram service, a control signal that informs the calling data terminal equipment (DTE) whether a particular datagram has been delivered, or describes the operation of services at the interface between the DTE and the data circuit-terminating equipment (DCE).

call redirection notification In X.25 communications, an optional CCITT-specified facility that informs the caller that the call has been redirected to another DTE.

call request (CRQ) A signal sent by a computer to data communications equipment to request that a communications connection be established with another computer in the network.

call request packet (1) A call supervision packet that a data terminal equipment (DTE) transmits to ask that a connection for a call be established throughout the network. (2) In X.25 communications, a call supervision packet transmitted by a DTE to ask for a call establishment through the network.

call request signal During establishment of the connection for a call, a signal that informs the data circuit-terminating equipment (DCE) that a data terminal equipment (DTE) has asked to make a call.

call supervision packet A packet used to establish or clear a call at the interface between the data terminal equipment (DTE) and the data circuit-terminating equipment (DCE).

call user data (CUD) In X.25 communications, data optionally included in the call-request packet by the user application.

CAM Computer-aided manufacturing.

CA mode See continue-any mode.

camp-on A method of holding a call for a line that is in use and of signaling when it becomes free. Synonymous with clamp-on.

CAN The cancel character. (A)

CANCEL An SNA command used to cancel a partially transmitted RU chain in the network.

cancel To end a task before it is completed.

Cancel (1) In SAA Advanced Common User Access architecture, an action that removes the active pop-up window without performing any unentered changes and returns to the window that preceded it. See also Close. Contrast with Exit. (2) In SAA Basic Common User Access architecture, an action that removes the current panel without processing it and returns to the panel displayed before it. Contrast with Exit.

cancel character (CAN) (1) A control character used by some convention to indicate that the data with which it is associated are in error or are to be disregarded. (I) (A) Synonymous with ignore character. (2) An accuracy control character used to indicate that

the data with which it is associated are in error or are to be disregarded. (A) (3) See block cancel character.

cancel closedown A closedown in which the VTAM programs are abnormally terminated either because of an unexpected situation or as the result of an operator command. See also orderly closedown, quick closedown.

cancel indicator In VTAM programs, an indicator that signifies to its receiver that the chain being received should be discarded.

cancel key Synonym for stop key.

canonical processing In the AIX operating system, processing that occurs according to a defined set of rules. This is the style of input that is typically used by the shell and simple commands.

CANTRAN Cancel transmission. See also bust this.

capability In computer security, an architecturally defined representation of the address of an object and a set of authorized types of access to the object. A capability is an embodiment of a ticket. See access capability.

capability list In computer security, a list associated with a subject that identifies all the subject's access types for all objects; for example, a list associated with a process that identifies all its access types for all files and other protected resources. See access control list.

capacitor An electronic part that permits storage of an electrical charge.

capacitor storage A storage device that uses the capacitive properties of certain materials. (I) (A)

capacity See channel capacity, storage capacity.

capital letter matrix The maximum part of the full character matrix that is available to write a capital letter.

caps (1) Capital letters, an uppercase font. (2) A printing style that uses two type sizes of a single uppercase font. The smaller size is used instead of a lowercase font.

Caps Lock A key on a keyboard that a user presses to change the keyboard from lowercase to uppercase or from uppercase to lowercase.

capstan A spindle or shaft used to drive the recording medium at a constant speed. (I) See Figure 25.

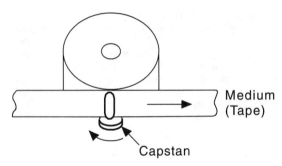

Figure 25. Capstan

caption Text associated with, and describing, a table or figure.

capture (1) In optical character recognition, to gather picture data from a field on an input document, using a special scan.

capture adapter A computer adapter that converts an analog signal to digital representation for either audio or video.

capture file A file used by a communications program to capture, or record, data coming in over a connection to a remote system or device.

capture key A toggle control key that starts or stops the process of saving the data displayed on the screen during an active connection.

CAR Check authorization record.

carbon ribbon On a typewriter, a paper or plastic ribbon that may be designed for multiple or one-time use. (T)

carbon ribbon supply indicator On a typewriter, a device that indicates the amount of carbon ribbon still available for use. (T)

card (1) An electronic circuit board that is plugged into a slot in a system unit. See also adapter, expansion board. (2) A plug-in circuit assembly.

card code The combinations of punched holes that represent characters; for example, letters or digits in a punched card.

card column (1) A line of punch positions parallel to the shorter edge of a punch card. (I) (A) (2) A line of punch positions parallel to the Y-datum line of a punch card. (A)

card deck (1) A group of punched cards. (I) (A) (2) Synonymous with card pack.

card duplicator Synonym for card reproducing punch. (T) (A)

card enclosure A frame that holds logic cards.

card feed The mechanism that moves cards from the card hopper to the card path. (T) (A)

card field A specific combination of punch positions, mark-sensing positions, or both, on a card. (A)

card file A device file created by the user to support a card device.

card form See printed card form.

card holder On a typewriter, a device for holding a card in close contact with the platen so that it follows the curvature of that component. (T)

card hopper (1) The part of a card-processing device that holds the cards to be processed and makes them available to the card feed.(I) (A) (2) Contrast with card stacker.

card image A one-to-one representation of the hole patterns of a punched card; for example, a matrix in which a one represents a punch and a zero represents the absence of a punch. (A)

cardinality In a relational database, the number of tuples in a relation. (T) (A)

cardinal spline cubic curve In computer graphics, a cubic spline in which the end points are the second and third of four control points. A series of cardinal splines has a continuous slope and passes through all but the first and last control points.

card jam A malfunction of a card-processing device in which cards become jammed. (A)

cardless system A system configured without a card reader or card punch.

card-on-board (COB) logic The type of technology that uses pluggable, air-cooled cards.

card pack Synonym for card deck.

card path In a card-processing device, the path along which cards are moved and guided. (I) (A)

card punch An output unit that produces a record of data in the form of hole patterns in punched cards. (T) (A)

card reader (1) An input unit that reads or senses the holes in a punched card, transforming the data from the hole patterns to electric signals. (T) (2) An input device that senses hole patterns in a punched card and translates them into machine language. (A) Synonymous with punched card reader.

card reproducer Synonym for card reproducing punch.

card reproducing punch A punched-card device that prepares one punched card from another punched card, copying all or part of the data from the punched card that is read. (I) (A) Synonymous with card reproducer.

card row (1) A line of punch positions parallel to the longer edges of a punch card. (I) (A) (2) A line of punch positions parallel to the X-datum line of a punch card. (A)

card sorter A device that deposits punched cards in pockets selected according to the hole patterns in the cards. (I) (A)

card stacker (1) The part of a card-processing device that receives the cards after they have been processed. (I) (A) (2) Contrast with card hopper.

card storage See magnetic card storage.

card-to-tape Pertaining to equipment that transfers data directly from punched cards to punched or magnetic tape.

card track The part of a card-processing device that moves and guides the card through the device. (A)

CARR Carrier.

carriage See automatic carriage.

carriage control character The first character of an output record (line) that is to be printed; it determines how many lines should be skipped before the next line is printed.

carriage control data set A data set whose records are preceded by carriage controls.

carriage control tape (1) A tape that is used to control vertical tabulation of printing positions or display positions. (A) (2) A tape that contains line feed control data for a printing device. (A)

carriage lock A control by means of which the paper carrier or type element can be held in a fixed position. (T)

carriage release A control that enables the paper carrier or type element to be moved freely to the right or to the left. (T)

carriage return (CR) (1) The movement of the printing position or display position to the first position on the same line. (T) (2) The operation that prepares for the next character to be printed or displayed at the first position on the same line. (A) (3) An action that indicates to continue printing at the left margin of the next line. A carrier return is equivalent to the carriage return of a typewriter. (4) A keystroke generally indicating the end of a command line.

carriage return character (1) A format effector that causes the print or display position to move to the first position on the same line. (I) (A) (2) Contrast with new-line character.

carrier (1) An electric or electromagnetic wave or pulse train that may be varied by a signal bearing information to be transmitted over a communication system. (T) (2) In data communication, a continuous frequency that can be modulated or impressed with an information carrying signal. (3) In an IBM SELECTRIC device or an ink jet mechanism, the part that carries the type element. (4) See automatic carrier, communication common carrier, data carrier, moving paper carrier, paper carrier, stationary paper carrier, toner carrier, type carrier. (5) See also automatic carriage.

carrier beads Small iron spheres with a layer of triboelectrically positive epoxy that are used to move toner particles. See also toner carrier.

carrier holes The holes in the side margins on continuous forms paper. When placed on the tractor pins, the holes maintain printer alignment and registration and control movement of the paper. Synonymous with tractor holes.

carrier management system A network management product that a communication common carrier provides to a customer; this product monitors and manages the telecommunication equipment that the communication common carrier provides for the customer's network.

carrier return An indication to continue printing at the left margin of the next line.

carrier return character (CRE) A word processing formatting control that moves the printing or display point to the first position of the next line. Carrier return may be ignored during text adjust mode operations. Synonymous with new line character. See required carrier return character.

carrier sense In a local area network, an ongoing activity of a data station to detect whether another station is transmitting. (T)

carrier signal A signal with a constant frequency that can be modulated to carry a data signal.

carrier system In data communication, a means of obtaining a number of channels over a single path by modulating each channel on a different carrier frequency and demodulating at the receiving point to restore the signals to their original form.

carry (1) The action of transferring a carry digit. (I) (A) (2) One or more digits, produced in connection with an arithmetic operation on one digit place of two or more numerals in positional notation, that are forwarded to another digit place for processing there. (A) (3) The number represented by the digit or digits in *(2)*. (A) (4) Most commonly, a digit as defined in *(2)*, that arises when the sum or product of two or more digits equals or exceeds the radix of the number representation system. (A) (5) Less commonly, a borrow. (A) (6) The command directing that a carry be forwarded. (A) (7) To transfer a carry digit. (I) (A) (8) To forward a carry. (A)

carry digit A digit that is generated when a sum or a product in a digit place exceeds the largest number that can be represented in that digit place and that is transferred for processing elsewhere. In a positional representation system, a carry digit is transferred to the digit place with the next higher weight for processing there. (I) (A)

carry-save adder An adder which has, for each digit place, three inputs, one sum output and one carry output and which does not propagate the carry digits by itself within one cycle of operation. (T)

Cartesian coordinate Either of two coordinates that locate a point on a plane and measure its distance from either of two intersecting straight-line axes along a line parallel to the other axis.

cartridge (1) A storage device that consists of magnetic tape, on supply and takeup reels, in a protective housing. (2) Read-only memory (ROM) in a protective housing, used to prevent users from copying application software. (3) See magnetic tape cartridge. See also magnetic tape cassette. See Figure 26.

cartridge access station In MSS, an opening in the 3851 Mass Storage Facility where data cartridges are manually loaded or removed.

cartridge cell In MSS, a hexagonal compartment within the 3851 Mass Storage Facility where a data cartridge is stored.

cartridge label In MSS, an area on the magnetic tape that contains the cartridge identification and other information about the data cartridge.

Figure 26. Cartridge

cartridge serial number In MSS, a unique number that identifies a data cartridge, recorded magnetically and visible on the magnetic tape.

cartridge storage slots A storage area in an optical library where cartridges are stored.

cartridge store In MSS, the part of the 3851 Mass Storage Facility that consists of the cartridge cells, accessors, and accessor controls.

cascade (1) In SAA usage, deprecated term for overlap, or stack. (2) In the AIX operating system, to arrange in a series. See pop-up cascade.

Cascade In SAA Advanced Common User Access architecture, a choice in the Window pull-down of some applications. It arranges the secondary windows and icons so that each window is offset on two sides from the window it overlaps.

cascade button In the AIXwindows program, a rectangular graphic control that can be made to appear from behind another graphic control to provide an additional option or range of options.

cascaded carry In parallel addition, a procedure in which the addition results in a partial sum numeral and a carry numeral which, in turn, are added; this process is repeated until a zero carry is generated. (I) (A) Contrast with high-speed carry.

cascade entry In ACF/TCAM, a terminal-table entry associated with a cascade list. See also group entry, line entry, logtype entry, process entry, single entry.

cascade list In ACF/TCAM, a list of pointers to single entries. When a cascade entry is named as the destination for a message, the message is sent to the valid entry in the list having the fewest messages queued.

cascaded menu In SAA Common User Access architecture, a menu that appears from a selected cascading choice in another menu and contains a set of choices that are related to the cascading choice. See cascading choice.

cascading (1) The connecting of unidirectional devices such as amplifiers in series and in the same direction. (T) (2) The connecting of network controllers to each other in a succession of levels, to concentrate many more lines than a single level permits. See also line concentration.

cascading choice In SAA Common User Access architecture, a choice in a menu that, when selected, produces a cascaded menu containing other choices. An arrow ( ) appears to the right of the cascading choice.

cascading menu In SAA Common User Access architecture, a menu that appears from a selected choice in a pull-down menu or context menu.

cascading pull-down In SAA Advanced Common User Access architecture, a menu that appears from a selected choice in another pull-down.

CASE Computer assisted software engineering. A set of tools or programs to help develop complex applications.

case clause In an XL C compiler switch statement, a CASE label followed by any number of statements.

CASE label In Pascal, a value or range of values that come before a statement in a CASE statement branch. When the selector is evaluated to the value of a CASE label, the statement following the CASE label is processed.

case management The use of a computer program to manage the flow of paper related to a case. For example, the tracking and management of an application for health insurance that results in health checks and examinations before the application is approved.

case-sensitive Pertaining to the ability to distinguish between uppercase and lowercase letters.

cashier mode In PSS, a retail services selectable function that allows a sign-on/sign-off procedure; it is suitable for installations in which the operator may work at different terminals during a day.

cash-like document A document such as a check, gift, or certificate that is used in the same manner as cash, for payment of merchandise. Synonymous with cash-like tender, noncash document.

cash-like tender Synonym for cash-like document.

cash on delivery (COD) A sales transaction in which a customer agrees to pay when merchandise is delivered.

cash receipt An itemized list of merchandise purchased and paid for by the customer with cash or a cash-like document.

cash receipt tape Itemized statements of merchandise sold during a retail sales transaction, including item numbers, amounts, and totals.

cash register A device that usually has means for entering and accumulating and exhibiting or recording financial data at the time of a transaction and which includes means for protection. A cash register has a money receptacle or means for printing a bill, or both. (A)

cash send A sales transaction in which a customer pays for merchandise with cash or a cash-like document and has the merchandise sent or delivered elsewhere. Contrast with cash take.

cash take A sales transaction in which a customer pays for merchandise with cash or a cash-like document and takes the merchandise from the store. Contrast with cash send.

CASS Common address space section.

cassette See magnetic tape cassette.

cast In the C language, an expression that converts the type of the operand to a specified scalar data type (the operator).

cast animation In multimedia applications, a sequence of frames consisting of manipulations of graphical objects. See also frame animation.

casual connection (1) In a subarea network, a connection in which type 5 nodes are attached through the boundary function using low-entry networking (LEN). Therefore, the nodes appear as LEN nodes rather than subarea nodes. (2) In an APPN network, a connection between an end node and a network node with different network identifiers.

CAT Computer-assisted typesetting.

catalog (1) A directory of files and libraries, with reference to their locations. A catalog may contain other information such as the types of devices in which the files are stored, passwords, and blocking factors. (I) (A) (2) To enter information about a file or a library into a catalog. (I) (A) (3) The collection of all data set indexes that are used by the control program to locate a volume containing a specific data set. (4) In DPPX, a data set containing information that describes data sets, other catalogs, and the direct access storage assigned to data sets and catalogs. (5) To include the volume identification of a data set in the catalog. (6) In VSE, to store a library member such as a phase, module, or book in sublibrary. (7) In SQL, tables, maintained by the database manager, that contain descriptions of objects, such as tables, views, and indexes. (8) See integrated catalog facility, VSAM master catalog, VSAM user catalog.

catalog directory A table in a catalog that identifies the items it contains.

cataloged data set A data set that is represented in an index, or hierarchy of indexes, in the system catalog; the indexes provide the means for locating the data set.

cataloged procedure A set of control statements placed in a library and retrievable by name.

catalog record In VSAM, any record in the data component of the catalog.

catalog recovery area (CRA) In systems with VSAM, an entry-sequenced data set that exists on each volume owned by a recoverable catalog, including the catalog volume itself. The CRA contains copies of the catalog records and can be used to recover a damaged or invalid catalog.

catalog views In SQL, a set of views containing information about the objects in a collection, such as tables, views, indexes, and column definitions.

category (1) In computer security, a nonhierarchical designation applied to sensitive information so that access to the data can be controlled more finely than with hierarchical classification alone. See also compartment, security level, security category. (2) In DPCX, a user-defined partition of disk storage created by collecting bit maps into a group.

category of work An indication of the business nature of a user's work assignment, such as processing claims, archiving documents, or scanning documents. Contrast with transaction type. See also line of business.

cathode ray storage An electrostatic storage that uses a cathode ray beam for access to data. (I) (A)

cathode ray tube (CRT) A vacuum tube in which a beam of electrons can be moved to draw lines or to form characters or symbols on its luminescent screen.

cathode ray tube display (CRT display) (1) A device that presents data in visual form by means of controlled electron beams. (A) (2) The data display

produced by such a device. (A) (3) See also visual display unit.

causal analysis A step in defect prevention process that focuses on identifying defects, analyzing the root cause(s), and creating suggested actions leading to defect prevention.

cause code In X.25 communications, a 1-byte code included in clear- and reset-indication packets that indicates the origin of the packet and the reason for sending it. Synonymous with clear cause. See also diagnostic code.

CAV Constant angular velocity.

CAW Channel address word.

CAX Community automatic exchange.

CBC Cipher block chain.

CBEMA (1) Computer and Business Equipment Manufacturers Association. (2) Canadian Business Equipment Manufacturers Association.

CBIPO Custom-Built Installation Process Offering.

CBPDO Custom-Built Product Delivery Offering.

CBT Computer-based training.

CBX Computerized branch exchange.

CCA Common communication adapter.

CCB Command control block.

CCF Controller configuration facility.

CCH Channel-check handler.

CCHS Cylinder-cylinder-head-sector. The representation of the address of a data field on a disk.

CCITT International Telegraph and Telephone Consultative Committee. An organization (one of four permanent organs of the International Telecommunication Union [ITU], headquartered in Geneva, Switzerland) that is concerned with the problems relating to international telephony and telegraphy. The CCITT Plenary Assembly meets at regular intervals to prepare a list of technical questions related to telephone and telegraph services. The Assembly assigns these questions to study groups, which then prepare recommendations to be presented at the next plenary meeting. Approved recommendations are published for the use of engineers, scientists, and manufacturers around the world.

CCITT Group III A compression algorithm widely used for FAX transmission.

CCITT Group IV A compression algorithm used for compressing images for optical disk storage.

CCITT V.35 feature A feature that allows devices using the V.35 interface to be attached to a system.

CCP (1) Communication Control Program. (2) Configuration Control Program.

CCP subsystem In System/36, the SSP-ICF subsystem that provides data communication with a System/3, Model 15D.

CCPT Controller creation parameter table.

CCS (1) Console communication services. (2) Common communications services.

CCSA Common control switching arrangement.

CCU Central control unit.

CCW Channel command word.

ccw Counterclockwise.

CCW translation See channel program translation.

CD Compact disc.

CD-DA Compact disc-digital audio.

CD+G Compact disc + graphics.

CD-I Compact disc-interactive.

cd-name In COBOL, a user-defined word that names a message control system (MCS) interface area described in a control communication description entry within the Communication Section of the Data Division.

CDNM session Cross-domain network manager session.

CDR Call detail record.

CDRM Cross-domain resource manager.

CDRM-CDRM session A cross-domain session between two CDRMs located in different domains.

CD-ROM High-capacity read-only memory in the form of an optically read compact disc.

CD-ROM XA Compact disc-read only memory extended architecture.

CDRSC Cross-domain resource.

CDS (1) Control data set. (2) Central directory server.

CDSTL Connect data set to line.

CDU Coolant distribution unit.

CE (1) IBM Customer Engineer. See IBM service representative. (2) Correctable error. (3) Channel-end.

CE area A reserved area on disk used for analyzing hardware.

CEB Conditional end bracket.

CECP Country extended code page.

CEGL Cause-effect graph language.

ceiling In mathematics, an arithmetic function that rounds up to the nearest integer.

cel In multimedia applications, a single frame of an animation.

Note: The term was derived from cartoon art in which an artist drew each image on a sheet of celluloid film.

cell (1) In a spreadsheet, an area at the intersection of a column and a row that may contain a value computed according to a defined relationship with other cells; for example, a value representing a total of the cell values in a column or row or an average of those values. When a cell value is changed, the values in all affected cells are recalculated automatically. (2) See binary cell, cartridge cell, color cell, data cell, magnetic cell, storage cell. See Figure 27.

cell array In computer graphics, a display element that consists of a rectangular grid of equal-sized rectangular cells, each having a single color and intensity.

Note: The cells do not necessarily map 1 to 1 with pixels.

cell cube In MSS, a block of 32 cartridge cells, four X addresses by four Y addresses by two Z addresses.

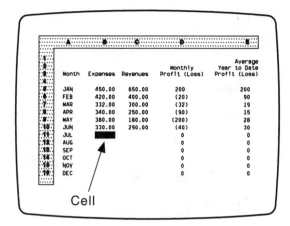

Figure 27. Cell

CEMT The CICS-supplied transaction that allows checking of the status of terminals, connections and other CICS entities from a console or from CICS terminal sessions.

center To arrange text in such a way that it is evenly positioned with respect to reference points on a horizontal line, a vertical line, or both. (T)

center alignment tab A tab that marks the position where text is to be centered.

centering In word processing, the positioning of a text string so that its midpoint is aligned with a given reference point position. (T)

centesimal floating-point format In BASIC, the representation for numbers within the computer.

centi Hundred or one hundredth.

centiliter (cl) One hundredth of a liter; 0.338 fluid ounces.

centimeter (cm) One hundredth of a meter; 0.39 inch.

central computer Deprecated term for host computer.

central control unit (CCU) The communication controller hardware unit that contains the circuits and data flow paths needed to execute instructions and to control controller storage and the attached adapters.

central directory A repository for storing resource location information centrally registered by network nodes or cached as the result of network searches.

central directory server (CDS) A network node that provides a repository for information on network

resource locations; it also reduces the number of network searches by providing a focal point for queries and broadcast searches and by caching the results of network searches to avoid later broadcasts for the same information.

centralized control Control in which all the primary station functions of the data link are centralized in one data station.

centralized dictation system On dictation equipment, a system that enables dictation originating from a number of points to be recorded on any one of a group of centrally located machines so that a written record can be produced. (I)

centralized multipoint facility A multipoint facility that allows a centralized data terminal equipment (DTE) to transmit data simultaneously to two or more remote DTEs and to receive data transmitted by the remote DTEs, one transmission at a time.

Note: Data transmitted by a remote DTE to the centralized DTE are not delivered to the other remote DTEs.

centralized network Synonym for star network.

central location The place at which a computer system's control device, normally the system console in the computer room, is installed.

central message facility In the ESCON Manager, the facility that allows all other ESCM components to build a message used to explain processing status.

central office (1) In the U.S.A., the place where communication common carriers terminate customer lines and locate the equipment that connects customer lines. See also end office, exchange, local central office. (2) In telephony, a switching system that connects customer lines to other customer lines or to trunks. The central office is the point at which local subscriber lines end for switching to other points. A central office-switching system does not reside on a customer's premises.

central processing unit (CPU) (1) Synonym for processing unit. (T) (2) The part of a computer that includes the circuits that control the interpretation and execution of instructions. See central processor, processing unit, processor. See also processor complex.

central processor A processor that contains the sequencing and processing facilities for instruction execution, interruption action, timing functions, initial program loading, and other machine-related functions.

central resource registration A process in which an APPN network node sends information about itself and its client end nodes to a central directory server.

central service One of the types of services described in the IBM licensing agreement that can be specified for a licensed program. If central service is offered, one or more IBM service locations will accept and respond to APARs on the licensed program. See also local assistance, local service.

central site In a network of AS/400 systems, the system that receives program temporary fixes (PTFs) and distribution tapes from IBM. This system is also used to provide problem handling support to other systems in a network. In a distributed data processing network, the central site is usually defined as the focal point in a communications network for alerts, application design, and remote system management tasks such as problem management.

central site control facility (CSCF) A function of the NetView program that allows a network operator to execute the test facilities of the 3174 Establishment Controller remotely from the NetView console.

central station Deprecated term for control station.

central storage Storage that is an integral part of the processor unit. Central storage includes both main storage and the hardware system area.

centrex Central office telephone equipment serving subscribers at one location on a private automatic branch exchange basis. The system allows such services as direct inward dialing, direct distance dialing, and console switchboards.

CE/operator panel See maintenance/operator panel.

CE panel See maintenance panel.

certainty factor A measure of confidence placed in the validity of a proposition, a hypothesis, an inference rule, or a conclusion of an inference. (T)

certification In computer security, a technical evaluation, made as part of and in support of the accreditation process, that establishes the extent to which a particular computer system or network design and implementation meet a prespecified set of requirements. (A)

CESD Composite external symbol dictionary.

CESD record A composite external symbol dictionary record built by the linkage editor or the loader, containing information about a control section name or an entry name.

CFB Cipher feedback.

CFIA Component failure impact analysis.

CF key See command function key.

CFP Creation facilities program.

CFS Continuous forms stacker.

CG (1) Channel grant. (2) See current-group indicator.

CGA Color Graphics Adapter.

CGA Mode A mode of video display that provides 320 x 200 resolution with four colors.

CG-hi Channel grant high, the first priority channel grant.

CG indicator Current-group indicator.

CG-lo Channel grant low, the third priority channel grant.

CG-med Channel grant medium, the second priority channel grant.

CGU Character generator utility.

chad (1) The material separated from a data medium when punching a hole. (I) (A) (2) The residue separated from the carrier holes in continuous forms paper. (3) Synonymous with chip.

chadded Pertaining to the punching of tape in which chad results.

chadless tape Punched tape that has been punched in such a way that chad is not formed. (I) (A)

chain (1) A group of logically linked user data records processed by LU 6.2. (2) A group of request units delimited by begin-chain and end-chain. Responses are always single-unit chains. See RU chain. (3) In the System/38 data file utility (DFU), a method of changing from one display format to another after the user signals that the first display format has been completed. (4) In BASIC, an operation in which a program passes control to another program, then ends. (5) In RPG, an operation code that reads input records identified by specified relative record numbers or keys. (6) See daisy chain, Markov chain, print chain. See also chained list.

chain code An arrangement in a cyclic sequence of some or all of the possible different n-bit words, in which adjacent words are related such that each is derivable from its neighbor by displacing the bits one digit position to the left, or right, dropping the leading bit and inserting a bit at the end. The value of the inserted bit needs only to meet the requirement that a word must not recur before the cycle is complete; for example, 000 001 010 101 011 111 110 100 000 ... (A)

chain delivery mechanism In a duplicator, a delivery system in which a number of chain-mounted gripping devices extract the paper from the machine and forward it into the delivery tray. (T) See also conveyor delivery mechanism.

chained In an ESCON environment, pertaining to the physical attachment of two ESCDs to each other.

chained ESCD configuration An ESCD configuration that requires a dedicated connection in one ESCD to complete the information path.

chained fields In System/36, fields that combine to form a single field that the workstation utility uses as the record key to read or write a record in a master file.

chained file An input, output, or update disk file from which records can be read randomly.

chained list (1) A list in which the data elements may be dispersed but in which each data element contains information for locating the next. (T) (2) Synonymous with linked list. See Figure 28.

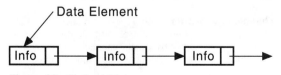

Figure 28. Chained List

chained list search (1) A search that uses a chained list. (T) (2) Synonymous with linked list search.

chained sublibraries In VSE, a facility that allows sublibraries to be chained by specifying the sequence in which these sublibraries are to be searched for a library member of a certain type.

chain error An error condition that relates to the contents of a single RU chain. Examples are an RU with an invalid FM header, and RU containing a request for a function that is not supported at the destination. Recovery from a chain error does not normally require resynchronization of the synchronized unit of work. Contrast with SUW error.

chain field In System/38, when file chaining is specified in query, a field in the primary record format that links the primary record format to the secondary

record format. A chain field corresponds in length and attributes to a key field in the secondary record format.

chaining (1) A method of storing records in which each record belongs to a list or group of records and has a linking field for tracing the chain. (2) In VSE, a logical connection of sublibraries to be searched by the system for members of the same type; for example, phase or object modules.

chaining of RUs See RU chain.

chaining overflow In a direct access storage device, the writing of overflow records on the next higher available track; each track contains a record that provides a link between the home track and the overflow track. Contrast with progressive overflow.

chaining search A search in which each item contains the means for locating the next item to be considered in the search. (I) (A)

chain link record In CMS, a record that contains a series of pointers to the physical blocks, normally not contiguous, currently assigned to a CMS disk file.

chain operation In BASIC, the program operation that passes control to another program, and then ends.

chain printer An impact printer in which the type slugs are carried by the links of a revolving chain. (I) (A)

change A function or mode that enables a user to modify a specified character string in previously entered text. (T) (A)

change accumulation (1) In IMS/VS, the process of creating a compacted version of one or more IMS/VS log data sets by eliminating records that are not related to recovery and by merging multiple changes to a single segment into a single change. (2) The compacted log created in (1).

change authority In the AS/400 system, an object authority that allows a user to perform all operations on the object except those limited to the owner or controlled by object existence authority and object management authority. The user can add, change, and delete entries in an object, or read the contents of an entry in the object. Change authority combines object operational authority and all of the data authorities.

change bar A character used to indicate a change to a line in a document.

change bit In System/370 virtual storage systems, a bit associated with a page in real storage; the change bit is turned ON by hardware whenever the associated page in real storage is modified.

change character See font change character.

change control process A defined process to be followed when a change to a controlled document or procedure is proposed. A typical use is to control changes proposed to baselined documents.

change-direction-command indicator In VTAM programs, an indicator specifying that the sender has finished sending and is prepared to receive.

change-direction protocol In SNA, a data flow control protocol in which the sending logical unit (LU) stops sending normal-flow requests, signals this fact to the receiving LU using the change-direction indicator (in the request header of the last request of the last chain), and prepares to receive requests.

change-direction-request indicator In VTAM programs, an indicator that requests return of a change-direction-command indicator.

changed record In System/38, an active subfile record to which a put or update operation has been issued, or an active subfile record that has been changed by the workstation user.

change dump (1) A dump of those storage locations whose contents have changed during a specified period. (T) (2) See also selective dump.

change management The part of the Communications and System Management feature that allows System/36 to be connected to a Distributed Systems Executive (DSX) network. Synonymous with Distributed Systems Node Executive (DSNX).

change-over system A temporary information processing system used to facilitate the transition from an operational system to its successor. (T) See also cutover.

change sign The reversal of a sign of a number held in the machine. (T)

channel (1) A path along which signals can be sent, for example, data channel, output channel. (A) (2) The portion of a storage medium that is accessible to a given reading or writing station; for example, track, band. (A) (3) In data communication, a means of one-way transmission. See data communication channel. Contrast with circuit. (4) A functional unit, controlled by the processor, that handles the transfer of data between processor storage and local peripheral equipment. See input/output channel. (5) In the AIX operating system, one of 32 bits in a table used to represent which event classes are active

or inactive. The most significant bit is called channel 0 and the least significant bit is called channel 31. See also logical channel.

channel adapter A communication controller hardware unit that is used to attach the communication controller to a host channel.

channel adapter input/output supervisor A portion of network control program code that interacts with the communication controller channel adapter to transfer data across an I/O channel to and from the host processor.

channel address word (CAW) An area in storage that specifies the location in main storage at which a channel program begins.

channel-attached (1) Pertaining to attachment of devices directly by data channels (I/O channels) to a computer. (2) Pertaining to devices attached to a controlling unit by cables, rather than by telecommunication lines. (3) Synonymous with local, locally attached. Contrast with link-attached.

channel-attached network control program A network control program in a channel-attached controller. Synonymous with local NCP. Contrast with link-attached network control program.

channel-attached station A station attached by a data channel to a host node. Synonymous with local station. Contrast with link-attached station.

channel-attached terminal A terminal such as a 3279 Display Station whose control unit is directly connected to a computer by a data channel. Synonymous with local terminal. Contrast with link-attached terminal.

channel-attachment major node (1) A major node that includes an NCP that is channel-attached to a data host. (2) A major node that may include minor nodes that are the line groups and lines that represent a channel attachment to an adjacent (channel-attached) host. (3) In VM or VSE operating systems, a major node that may include minor nodes that are resources (host processors, NCPs, line groups, lines, SNA physical units and logical units, cluster controllers, and terminals) attached through a communication adapter.

channel capacity The measure of the ability of a given channel subject to specific constraints to transmit messages from a specified message source expressed as either the maximum possible mean transinformation content per character or the maximum possible average transinformation rate, which can be achieved with an arbitrary small probability of errors by use of an appropriate code. (I) (A)

channel-check handler (CCH) In the System/370 system, a feature that records information about channel errors and issues appropriate messages to the operator.

channel command An instruction that directs a data channel, control unit, or device to perform an operation or set of operations.

channel command word (CCW) A doubleword at the location in main storage specified by the channel address word. One or more CCWs make up the channel program that directs data channel operations.

channel control character In System/36, a value used by MSRJE to determine which line on a page to skip before printing the next line of output.

channel-control check A category of I/O errors affecting channel controls and sensed by the channel to which a device is attached. See also channel-data check.

channel control vector (CHCV) In the IBM 8100 Information System, the formatted information that specifies the controlling parameters, such as the channel I/O command (write or read) and the channel pointer number; the CHCV is used during a channel I/O operation.

channel-data check A category of I/O errors, indicating a machine error in transferring data to or from storage and sensed by the channel to which a device is attached. See also channel-control check.

channel grant (CG) In the IBM 8100 Information System, a signal from the processor granting the control logic permission to start a previously requested channel I/O operation. The signal can be one of three priorities: channel grant low (CG-lo), channel grant medium (CG-med), and channel grant high (CG-hi).

channel I/O (CHIO) burst operation In the IBM 8100 Information System, that portion of a channel operation during which the channel and an I/O device are logically connected for transferring information.

channel I/O (CHIO) operation In the IBM 8100 Information System, the transfer of data between main storage and an I/O device. It is accomplished in one or more channel I/O burst operations and is initiated by the control logic rather than the processor, and is controlled by processor channel logic. Processor instruction execution is suspended until a CHIO operation concludes.

channel I/O command In the IBM 8100 Information System, the field of a channel control vector that directs a channel and an I/O device to perform a channel I/O burst operation.

channel link A System/370 I/O channel to control unit interface that has an SNA network address. A channel link can be either a subarea link or a peripheral link and is defined in an NCP generation definition using the GROUP, LINE, and PU definition statements. See also link, subarea link.

channel manager Synonym for channel adapter input/output supervisor.

channel mask In the IBM 8100 Information System, a 1-byte mask used to suspend channel operations.

channel number In the AIX operating system, a number that identifies the path by which data are transferred between a particular input or output device and the processor of the computer. The major device number, minor device number, and channel number uniquely identify a hardware device.

channel overload A state in which data transfer to or from the processor and I/O devices reaches a rate that approaches the capacity of the data channel.

channel-path configuration In an ESCON environment, the interconnection between a channel and a control unit or between a channel, an ESCON Director, and one or more control units. See also link, point-to-point channel-path configuration, switched point-to-point channel-path configuration.

channel path identifier (CHPID) In a channel subsystem, a value assigned to each installed channel path of the system that uniquely identifies that path to the system.

channel pointer (CHP) In the IBM 8100 Information System, the principal register, containing the logical address used during a channel I/O (CHIO) operation.

channel pointer number In the IBM 8100 Information System, the field of a channel control vector that designates the pointer to be used during a channel I/O operation.

channel program One or more channel command words that control a specific sequence of data channel operations. Execution of the specific sequence is initiated by a single start I/O instruction.

channel request A request to start a channel I/O (CHIO) operation.

channel scheduler In VSE, the part of the supervisor that controls all input/output operations.

channel service unit (CSU) An American Telephone and Telegraph (AT&T) unit that is part of the AT&T nonswitched digital data system.

channel set A collection of channels that can be addressed concurrently by a processor.

channel status word (CSW) An area in storage that provides information about the termination of input/output operations.

channel subsystem (CSS) A collection of subchannels that directs the flow of information between I/O devices and main storage, relieves the processor of communication tasks, and performs path management functions.

channel-to-channel (CTC) A method of connecting two computing devices.

channel-to-channel adapter A hardware device that can be used to connect two channels on the same computing system or on different systems.

channel-to-channel (CTC) A method of connecting two computing devices.

chapter In a video presentation or computer application, a single, self-contained segment.

chapter cues In video production, a set of nine pulses inserted into the vertical blanking interval on the master videotape to identify a tape frame as the first frame of a new chapter. See picture cues, still cues.

chapter search A function of most videodisc players whereby a specific chapter may be accessed by its chapter number.

chapter stop A code on some videodiscs indicating the break between two chapters, allowing a chapter search function to locate specific chapters.

CHAR Character.

char In the AIX object database manager, a terminal descriptor used to define a variable as a fixed-length, null-terminated string. See also terminal descriptor.

character (1) A member of a set of elements that is used for the representation, organization, or control of data. (T) (2) A letter, digit, or other symbol that is used as part of the organization, control, or representation of data. A character is often in the form of a spatial arrangement of adjacent or connected strokes. (A) (3) In COBOL, the basic indivisible unit of the COBOL language.

character addressing The process of locating a character by using an address.

character arrangement An arrangement composed of graphic characters from one or more modified or unmodified character sets.

character arrangement table In the 3800 Printing Subsystem, a table, including a 256-byte translate table that translates the user's data code to the 3800's control electronics code, and identifiers for up to four character sets and graphic character modification modules to be used.

character array A named list or matrix of character data items.

character assembly The process by which bits are put together to form characters as the bits arrive on a data link. In a communication controller, character assembly is performed either by the control program or by the communication scanner, depending on the type of scanner installed. Contrast with character disassembly.

character-at-a-time printer Synonym for character printer.

character attribute In the 3270 data stream, a code that defines a single property of a character or characters; for example, extended color, character set, or extended highlighting. A character can have more than one defined character attribute.

character average information content Synonym for character mean entropy.

character boundary In character recognition, the largest rectangle, with a side parallel to the document reference edge, each of whose sides is tangential to a given character outline. (A)

character box (1) An imaginary parallelogram on a display surface that contains all parts of one graphic character. Synonymous with bounding box. (T) (2) The maximum area in which a symbol and all associated elements, such as a cursor, an underline, or space surrounding the symbol to separate it from other symbols, can be printed or displayed. Synonymous with character cell. (3) The imaginary parallelogram whose boundaries govern the size, orientation, and spacing of individual characters to be displayed on a graphics display device. See also text box. (4) See also capital letter matrix, character matrix, full character matrix.

See Figure 29.

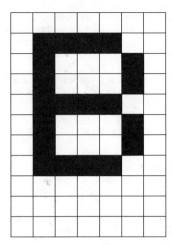

Figure 29. Character Box

character buffer In the 3270 Information Display System, the read/write storage used by a partition for storing alphanumeric data for display or printing on a terminal.

character cell (1) An addressable location on a display surface or printing medium. (2) The physical width and height in pels of a font. See also bounding box. (3) In GDDM, the imaginary box whose boundaries govern the size, orientation, and spacing of individual characters to be displayed on a workstation. (4) Synonym for character box.

character check A check that verifies the observance of rules for the formation of characters. (A)

character-coded Synonym for unformatted.

character-coded request In SNA, a request encoded and transmitted as a character string; the format indicator in the request header (RH) for the request is set to zero. Synonymous with unformatted request. Contrast with field-formatted request.

character comparison In PL/I, a left-to-right, character-by-character comparison according to the collating sequence. See also arithmetic comparison, bit comparison.

character constant (1) A constant with a character value. (2) A string of any of the characters that can be represented, usually enclosed in apostrophes. (3) The actual character value (a symbol, quantity, or constant) in a source program that is itself data, instead of reference to a field that contains the data. Contrast with numeric constant. (4) In some languages, a character enclosed in apostrophes. See also bit constant, hexadecimal constant.

character data Data in the form of letters and special characters such as punctuation marks. See also numeric data.

character definition display For the System/36 character generator utility, the enter and update mode prompt used to enter data that defines ideographic characters.

character delete The action that erases the character at the current cursor location and moves any trailing text one character position to the left.

character-deletion character A character within a line of terminal input specifying that it and the immediately preceding character are to be removed from the line. See also line-deletion character, logical character delete symbol.

character delimiter In the IBM 3886 Optical Character Reader, a user-specified character defining the end of a field within a line.

character density A measure of the horizontal spacing of characters.

character device A device that handles data one character at a time. See also character special file.

character disassembly The process by which characters are broken into bits for transmission over a data link. In the communication controller, character disassembly is performed either by the control program or by the communication scanner, depending on the type of scanner installed. Contrast with character assembly.

character display (1) A display device that provides a representation of data only in the form of graphic characters. (T) (2) A display that uses a character generator to display predefined character boxes of images (characters) on the screen. This kind of display cannot address the screen any less than one character box at a time. Contrast with all points addressable display.

character display device (1) A display device that gives a representation of data only in the form of characters. (I) (A) Synonymous with alphanumeric display device, read-out device.

character error rate In data communication, the ratio of the number of characters incorrectly received to the number of characters transmitted.

character expansion A keyboard function that increases escapement.

character expression A character constant, a simple character variable, a scalar reference to a character array, a character-valued function reference, or a sequence of them separated by the concatenation operator (&) and parentheses.

character field An area reserved for a particular unit of information and that can contain any of the characters in the data character set. Contrast with numeric field.

character fill To insert as often as necessary into a storage medium the representation of a specified character that does not itself convey data but may delete unwanted data. (I)   (A)

character generation The process of placing selected graphic characters and images on an output medium.

character generator (1) A functional unit that converts the coded representation of a character into the graphic representation of the character for display. (I)   (A)   See dot matrix character generator, stroke character generator.   (2) In word processing, the means within equipment for generating visual characters or symbols from coded data. (T)

character generator utility (CGU) In System/36, a program that is used to create, maintain, and display ideographic characters.

character graphic The visual representation of a character, defined by toned or untoned picture elements (pels).

Note: An untoned pel (a reverse character) is visually represented by the toned pels around it.

character graphics Graphics that are composed of symbols printed in a monospace font.   Some symbols are stand-alone, others are intended for assembling larger figures.

character grid In the AS/400 system and System/38, an invisible network of uniformly spaced horizontal and vertical lines covering the chart area.   It is used by the AS/400 Business Graphics Utility to determine the physical dimensions of the chart and the placement of the data on it.

character grid unit In the AS/400 system and System/38, the distance between two adjacent horizontal or vertical lines on a character grid.

character group Any number of character graphics and character properties.

character height On a typewriter, the height of capital letters without descenders and without optical correction. (T)

character identifier (1) A symbol that represents a character.   (2) In the 3800 Printing Subsystem, the

identifier that represents a character, regardless of its style;   for example, all uppercase A's have the same character ID.   Synonymous with graphic character identifier.

character increment The distance the current print position is increased for the particular character printed.   Synonymous with character spacing.

character information rate Synonym for character mean entropy.

character insert In word processing, to place a character between two other characters.   See also line insert.

character I/O Serial input and output of data.   See also block I/O.

characteristic (1) The numeral that represents the exponent in a floating-point representation.   The characteristic often differs from the exponent in a floating-point representation by a constant.   In this case, it is known as a biased exponent;   for example, if this constant was "50," the floating-point representation shown in the example for "mantissa" would be: 0.1234 47. (T)   (2) Distortion caused by transients which, as a result of the modulation, are present in the transmission channel and depend on its transmission qualities. (3) Contrast with mantissa.

characteristic distortion See distortion.

character key (1) In word processing, a control used to process text, one character at a time. (T)   (2) A key that allows the user to enter the character shown on the key.   See also command key, function key.

character literal A symbol, quantity, or constant in a source program that is itself data, rather than a reference to data.   Contrast with numeric literal.

character matrix In computer graphics, the vertical and horizontal pel representation of a character for a terminal.   See capital letter matrix, full character matrix.

character mean entropy In information theory, the mean per character of the entropy for all possible messages from a stationary message source;   in mathematical notation, if H_m is the entropy of the set of all sequences of m characters from the source, then this mean per character H' equals:

$$H^* = \lim_{m \to \infty} \frac{H_m}{m}$$

The mean entropy per character may be expressed in a unit such as a shannon per character.   The limit of H_m/m may not exist if the source is not stationary. (I) (A) Synonymous with character average information content, character information rate, character mean information content.

character mean information content Synonym for character mean entropy.

character mean transinformation content In information theory, the mean per character of the mean transinformation content for all possible messages from a stationary message source; in mathematical notation, if T_m is the mean transinformation content for all pairs of corresponding input and output sequences of m characters, then this mean per character T' equals:

$$T^* = \lim_{m \to \infty} \frac{T_m}{m}$$

The mean transinformation content per character may be expressed in a unit such as shannon per character. (I) (A)

character mode A mode in which input is treated as alphanumeric data, rather than graphic data. See also graphics mode.

character operator A symbol representing an operation to be performed on character data, such as concatenation in BASIC.

character outline The graphic pattern established by the stroke edges of a character. (A)

character pattern See character raster pattern.

character position (1) In COBOL, the amount of physical storage required to store a single standard data format character whose usage is DISPLAY. Further characteristics of the physical storage are defined by the implementor. (2) Synonym for display position.

character printer (1) A device that prints a single character at a time. (T) (A) Synonymous with serial printer. (2) Contrast with line printer, page printer. See Figure 30.

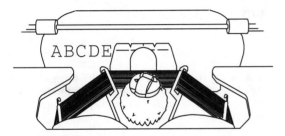

Figure 30. Character Printer

character properties Details about how a character is printed relative to the other characters around it. Character properties are box size, horizontal and vertical character cell size, character ID, center line, baseline, left space, right space, above space, and below space.

character raster pattern The scan patterns for a graphic character of a particular size, weight, and style.

character reader An input unit that performs character recognition. (I) (A)

character recognition (1) The identification of characters by automatic means. (I) (A) (2) The identification of geographic, phonic, or other characters by various means, including magnetic, optical, or mechanical means. (A) (3) See magnetic ink character recognition, optical character recognition, pattern recognition.

character reference point In printing, the point along the baseline within the character box that coincides with the current print position.

character relation Two character strings separated by a relational operator.

character rotation In printing, the alignment of a character with respect to the baseline.

character row Synonym for display line.

character set (1) A finite set of different characters that is complete for a given purpose; for example, the character set in ISO Standard 646, "7-bit Coded Character Set for Information Processing Interchange." (T) (2) An ordered set of unique representations called characters; for example, the 26 letters of the English alphabet, Boolean 0 and 1, the set of symbols in the Morse code, and the 128 ASCII characters. (A) (3) A defined collection of characters. (4) All the valid characters for a programming language or for a computer system. (5) A group of characters used for a specific reason; for example, the set of characters a printer can print.

character skew The angular rotation of a character relative to its intended or ideal placement.

character space The horizontal size of a character; this size depends on the character font and the device on which the character is printed.

character spacing Synonym for character increment.

character spacing reference line In character recognition, a vertical line that is used to evaluate the horizontal spacing of characters. It may be a line that equally divides the distance between the sides of a character boundary or that coincides with the centerline of a vertical stroke. (A)

character special file In the AIX operating system, a special file that provides access to an input or output device. The character interface is used for devices that do not use block I/O. See also block file, block special file, special file.

characters per inch (CPI) The number of characters printed within an inch horizontally across a page.

character string (1) A string consisting solely of characters. (I) (A) (2) A sequence of consecutive characters that are used as a value. (3) In COBOL, a sequence of contiguous character that form a COBOL word, a literal, a PICTURE character string, or a comment-entry. (4) In SQL, a sequence of bytes or characters associated with a single-byte or mixed (single-byte character set (SBCS) and double-byte character set (DBCS) character set.

character subset (1) A selection of characters from a character set, comprising all characters that have a specified common feature; for example, in each of the character sets of ISO Standard 646, "7-bit Coded Character Set for Information Processing Interchange," the digits 0 and 9 may constitute a character subset. (I) (A)

character substring A contiguous portion of a character string.

character table See character arrangement table.

character times In CCP, the maximum number of times the temporary text delay character can be sent to a terminal before the operation stops or that can be sent between the end of a receive and the beginning of a transmit operation.

character translation In international character support, the use of various commands and conversion subroutines that translate between extended characters and ASCII escape strings to preserve unique character information.

character type A data type that consists of alphanumeric characters. See also data type.

character variable The name of a character data item whose value is assigned or changed during program execution.

charge A sales transaction in which a customer has a partial or total value of purchased merchandise added to a charge account, for later payment.

charger unit Synonym for corona unit.

charger unit cleaner Synonym for corona unit cleaner.

charge send A sales transaction in which a customer charges the merchandise to be delivered.

charging In a document copying machine, the process of establishing an electrostatic surface charge on an insulating medium. (T)

charging requesting service In X.25 communications, an optional facility that specifies that charging information (segment count data, monetary unit data, or call duration data) is required.

chart In the AS/400 Business Graphics Utility, displayed, printed, or plotted output used to compare one or more sets of variable data in chart form. The types of charts are bar, line, pie, surface, histogram, Venn diagram, and text.

chart area In GDDM, the part of the picture space in which a business chart is to be drawn.

chart format In the AS/400 system and System/38, an object containing characteristics, such as the chart type, chart heading, legend position, and so on. The chart format does not include the data values to be plotted.

chart layout In the AS/400 system and System/38, the arrangement of the various parts in the chart area and surrounding margins.

CHASE An SNA command used by the host to determine when the secondary logical unit has finished processing all previously sent RUs.

chat message A message transmitted over a network that appears on a display screen but is not stored.

chat script In remote communications, a list of expect-send sequences that a modem uses to establish a communication link with another modem. See also expect-send sequence, handshaking.

CHCV Channel control vector.

check (1) A process for determining accuracy. (A) (2) An error condition. (3) To look for a condition.

check authorization record (CAR) In the 3650 Retail Store System, a record referred to by the store controller when accepting or rejecting a request to cash a customer's check.

check bit (1) A binary check digit; for example, a parity bit. (A) (2) In data communication, a bit used to check for errors in transmitted data. (3) See redundancy check bit.

check box In SAA Advanced Common User Access architecture, a square box with associated text that represents a choice. When a user selects a choice, an X appears in the check box to indicate that the choice is in effect. The user can clear the check box by selecting the choice again.

check card (1) A punched card suitable for use as a bank check. (A) (2) A punch card used for checking. (A)

check character (1) A character used for the purpose of performing a check. (A) (2) A check key consisting of a single character. (T) (3) See cyclic redundancy check character, redundancy check character.

check digit (1) A digit used for the purpose of performing a check. (A) (2) A check key consisting of a single digit. (T) (3) In System/36, the rightmost digit of a self-check field used to check the accuracy of the field.

check disc In multimedia applications, a videodisc produced from the glass master that is used to check the quality of the finished interactive program.

checking program A program that examines other programs or sets of data for mistakes of syntax and semantics. (T) (A)

check key One or more characters derived from and appended to a data item that can be used to detect errors in the data item. (T)

check mark In SAA Advanced Common User Access architecture, a check (√) that shows that a choice is currently in effect.

checkout Synonym for debug.

checkout environment area An arrangement of point-of-sale terminals in which all or most of the terminals are grouped in a single location near the store exit.

checkpoint (1) A sequence of instructions in a computer program for recording the status of execution for restarting. (T) (2) A point at which information about the status of a job and the system can be recorded so that the job step can be later restarted. (3) To record such information. (4) See simple checkpoint, system checkpoint, system scheduled checkpoint.

checkpoint data set (1) A data set that contains checkpoint records. (2) In ACF/TCAM, an optional data set that contains the checkpoint records used to reconstruct the message control program (MCP) environment after closedown or system failure when the ACF/TCAM checkpoint/restart facility is used.

checkpoint dump A dump of the entire contents of main storage and registers, taken at a checkpoint. (A)

checkpoint records Records that contain the status of a job and the system at the time the records are written by the checkpoint routine. These records provide the information necessary for restarting a job without having to return to the beginning of the job. See also checkpoint request record, control record, environment record, incident record.

checkpoint request record In ACF/TCAM, a checkpoint record taken as a result of the execution of a CKREQ macroinstruction in an application program; the record contains the status of a single destination queue for the application program. See also control record, environment record, incident record.

checkpoint restart The process of resuming a job at a checkpoint within the job step that caused abnormal termination. The restart may be automatic or deferred, when deferred restart involves resubmitting the job. See also automatic restart, deferred restart. Contrast with step restart.

checkpoint/restart service facility (1) A facility for restarting execution of a program at some point other than at the beginning, after the program was terminated due to a program or system failure. A restart can begin at a checkpoint or from the beginning of a job step, and uses checkpoint records to reinitialize the system. (2) In ACF/TCAM, a service facility that records the status of the network or the TCAM system at designated intervals or following certain events. After system failure, the TCAM system can be restarted and continue without loss of messages. (3) See extended checkpoint/restart.

checkpoint start In VM/370, a system restart that attempts to recover information about closed spool files that was previously stored on the checkpoint cylinders. The spool file chains are reconstructed, but the original sequence of spool files is lost. Unlike warm start, CP accounting and system message information are also lost. Contrast with cold start, force start, warm start.

check problem A problem with a known solution used to determine whether a functional unit is operating correctly. (T)

checksum (1) The sum of a group of data associated with the group and used for checking purposes. (T) (2) In error detection, a function of all bits in a block. If the written and calculated sums do not agree, an error is indicated. (3) On a diskette, data written in a sector for error detection purposes; a calculated checksum that does not match the checksum of data written in the sector indicates a bad sector. The data are either numeric or other character strings regarded as numeric for the purpose of calculating the checksum.

checksum protection (1) In the AS/400 system, a function that protects data stored in the system auxiliary storage pool from being lost because of the failure of a single disk. When checksum protection is in effect and a disk failure occurs, the system automatically reconstructs the data when the system program is loaded after the device is repaired. (2) In TCP/IP, the sum of a group of data associated with the group and used for error checking purposes.

checksum set In the AS/400 system, units of auxiliary storage defined in groups to provide a way for the system to recover data if a disk failure occurs when checksum protection is in effect.

check symbol On an IBM 2260 or 2265 Display Station, the character displayed for any code entered from the keyboard for which no character or symbol has been assigned. Also, a symbol displayed on the screen to indicate each character position for which a parity error occurred during transfer of data from the device.

check verification record In PSS, the record checked by the store controller to enable the controller to accept or reject a request to cash a customer's check.

chemical transfer process Synonym for diffusion transfer process.

child (1) In the AIX operating system, pertaining to a secured resource, either a file or library, that uses the user list of a parent resource. A child resource can have only one parent resource. In the operating system, a child is a process, started by a parent process, that shares the resources of the parent process. Contrast with parent. (2) In Enhanced X-Windows and the AIXwindows program, a first-level subwindow. A widget managed by another widget is the child of the managing parent widget; for example, composite widgets typically manage the primitive child widgets attached to them. The parent widget typically controls the placement of the child as well as when and how it is mapped. (3) See pop-up child. See also managed children, siblings.

child class See subclass.

child device In the AIX operating system, a hierarchical location term that indicates what can be connected to a parent device; for example, a small computer interface (SCSI) disk can be a child device of an SCSI adapter.

child gadget In the AIX operating system, a windowless child widget. See child widget.

child process In the AIX and OS/2 operating systems, a process, started by a parent process, that shares the resources of the parent process. See also fork.

child resource (1) A secured resource, either a file or library, that uses the user list of a parent resource. A child resource can have only one parent resource. Contrast with parent resource. (2) In the NetView Graphic Monitor Facility, a resource immediately below the parent resource in a hierarchy.

child segment In a hierarchical database, a segment immediately below its parent segment. A child segment has only one parent segment. See also parent segment.

child spacing In the AIXwindows program and Enhanced X-Windows, the physical spacing and placement of child widgets by the parent widget within the border of the parent.

child widget In the AIXwindows program and Enhanced X-Windows, a widget managed by another widget is the child of the managing parent widget; for example, composite widgets typically manage the primitive children widgets attached to them. The parent widget typically controls the placement of the child as well as when and how it is mapped. When a parent widget is deleted, all the children controlled by that parent are automatically deleted as well.

child window A window that appears within the border of its parent window (either a primary window or another child window). When the parent window is resized, moved, or destroyed, the child window also is resized, moved, or destroyed. However, the child window can be moved or resized independently from the parent window, within the boundaries of the parent window. Contrast with parent window.

Chinese binary Synonym for column binary.

CHIO Channel input/output.

chip (1) Synonym for integrated circuit (IC). (T) (2) In micrographics, a piece of microfilm smaller than a microfiche containing microimages and coded identification. (A) (3) Synonym for chad. (4) See microchip.

choice (1) In SAA Common User Access architecture, an item that a user can select. (2) In the AIX operating system, an option in a pop-up or menu used to influence the operation of the system.

choice device (1) An input device that provides one value from a set of alternatives; for example, a function keyboard. (I) (A) (2) See also locator device, pick device, valuator device.

choice entry field In SAA Basic Common User Access architecture, an entry field where a user types numbers, letters, or characters to indicate their selections.

choice list Deprecated term for menu.

chord (1) In graphics, a short line segment whose end points lie on a circle. Chords are a means for producing a circular image from straight lines. The higher the number of chords per circle, the smoother the circular image. (2) To press more than one button at a time on a pointing device.

CHP Channel pointer.

CHPID Channel path identifier.

chroma Synonym for chrominance.

chroma-key color The specified first color in a combined signal. See chroma-keying.

chroma-keying In multimedia applications, combining two video signals that are in sync. The combined signal is the second signal whenever the first is of some specified color, called the chroma-key color, and is the first signal otherwise; for example, if a television weatherman stands in front of a blue background, blue is the chroma-key color. The TV viewer sees the weather map in place of the chroma-key color, with the weatherman standing in front of the map.

chroma signal The portion of image information that provides the color (hue and saturation).

chrominance (1) The difference between a color and a reference white of the same luminous intensity. (2) In an image reproduction system, signals representing the color components of an image, such as hue and saturation. A black-and-white image has a chrominance of zero. In the NTSC television system, the I and Q signals carry the chrominance information. (3) Synonymous with chroma. See also luminance.

cicero In the Didot point system, a unit of 0.1776 inch (4.512 millimeters) used in measuring typographical material.

CICP Communication interrupt control program.

CICS Customer Information Control System.

CICS/DOS/VS Customer Information Control System/Disk Operating System/Virtual Storage. A general-purpose licensed program that controls online communication between terminal users and a database.

CICS region The CICS area of the computer system in which an application is running.

CICS subsystem In System/36, the SSP-ICF subsystem that allows binary synchronous communication with CICS/VS.

CICS/VS Customer Information Control System for Virtual Storage, which operates on a host system such as a System/370 system, or a 30XX or 43XX processor.

CICS/VS BMS generation An SDF/CICS function that builds an OS/VS or VSE batch job that generates the symbolic description map and physical maps from the source map set.

CID (1) Communication identifier. (2) Connection identifier.

CIDA Channel indirect data addressing.

CIDF Control interval definition field.

CIE Commission Internationale de l'Eclairage.

CIL Condition-incident log.

CIM (1) Computer input microfilm. (2) Computer Integrated Manufacturing.

cine-oriented image (1) In micrographics, an image appearing on a roll of microfilm in such a manner that the top edge of the image is perpendicular to the long edge of the film. (A) (2) Contrast with comic-strip oriented image. See Figure 31.

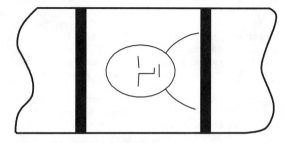

Figure 31. Cine-Oriented Image

CINIT In SNA products, a network services request sent from a system services control point (SSCP) to a logical unit (LU) requesting that LU to establish a session with another LU and to act as the primary half-session.

CIOCS Communications input/output control system.

cipher block chain (CFB) mode A mode of operation that cryptographically connects one block of ciphertext to the next plaintext block.

cipher feedback A cryptographic operation that exclusively ORs the plaintext with the output of a cryptographic algorithm and feeds the result back as input to the cryptographic algorithm. See also output feedback.

cipher system In computer security, any system of communications in which groups of symbols are used to represent plaintext elements of equal length. Contrast with code system. See also cryptographic system.

ciphertext (1) In computer security, text produced by encryption. (2) Synonym for enciphered data.

circuit (1) One or more conductors through which an electric current can flow. See physical circuit, virtual circuit. (2) A logic device.

circuit breaker A switch that automatically interrupts an electric circuit because of an abnormal condition.

circuit grade The information-carrying capability of a circuit, expressed in speed or type of signal. The grades of circuits are broadband, voice, subvoice, and telegraph. For data use, these grades are identified with certain speed ranges.

circuit load Synonym for line load.

circuit noise level The ratio of circuit noise to some arbitrary amount chosen as reference. This ratio is normally indicated in decibels above the reference noise (dbrn) or in adjusted decibels (dba) that signify a noise meter reading adjusted to represent the interfering effect under specified conditions. See also decibel.

circuit-switched connection A connection that is established and maintained on demand between two or more data stations in order to allow the exclusive use of a data circuit until the connection is released. (T)

circuit-switched data transmission service A service using circuit switching to establish and maintain a connection before data can be transferred between data terminal equipment (DTEs). (T) See also packet switched data transmission service.

circuit switching (1) A process that, on demand, connects two or more data terminal equipment (DTEs) and permits the exclusive use of a data circuit between them until the connection is released. (I) (A)

(2) Synonymous with line switching. (3) See also message switching, packet switching.

circular shift Synonym for end-around shift.

circulating register A shift register in which data moved out of one end of the register are reentered into the other end as in a closed loop. (A)

circulating storage Dynamic storage involving a closed loop. (A) Synonymous with cyclic storage.

CKD (1) Count-key-data. (2) Cryptographic key distribution center.

CKDS In the Programmed Cryptographic Facility, cryptographic key data set.

CKT Cryptographic key translation center.

CL Control language.

cl Centiliter.

CLA Communication line adapter.

cladding In an optical cable, the region of low refractive index surrounding the core. See also core, optical fiber.

clamp-on Synonym for camp-on.

C language A language used to develop software applications in compact, efficient code that can be run on different types of computers with minimal change.

Clark-Wilson Integrity model See computer security model.

class (1) In object-oriented design or programming, a group of objects that share a common definition and that therefore share common properties, operations, and behavior. Members of the group are called instances of the class. (2) In RACF, a collection of defined entities (users, groups, and resources) with similar characteristics. The class names are USER, GROUP, DATASET, and the classes that are defined in the class descriptor table. (3) Any category to which things are assigned or defined. (4) In VSE/POWER, a means of grouping jobs that require the same set of resources. (5) In System/38, an object that contains the execution parameters for a routing step. (6) In the AIX Base Operating System, pertaining to the I/O characteristics of a device. System devices are classified as block or character devices. (7) In AIX Enhanced X Windows, a general group to which a specific object belongs. (8) In the AIXwindows program, an object-oriented data structure containing generalized information about a group of similar graphical objects known as widgets or gadgets. Each class of graphical objects inherits some or all of the appearance characteristics and behavior characteristics of the classes that precede it in the object hierarchy.

class any user Any user, regardless of class, who is allowed to use a subset of CP commands to log onto VM/SP, have the terminal logically connected to a multiple-access virtual machine, or send messages to the operator or to other users.

class attributes In the AS/400 system, the values in a class object that control the processing of routing steps in a job. These values include the run priority, time slice, eligibility for purge, default wait time, maximum processing unit time, and maximum temporary storage parameters.

class A user See primary system operator privilege class.

class authority (CLAUTH) In RACF, an authority that allows a user to define RACF profiles in a class defined in the class descriptor table. A user can have class authorities to one or more classes.

class B user See system resource operator privilege class.

class condition In COBOL, the proposition, for which a truth value can be determined, that the contents of an item is wholly alphabetic or is wholly numeric or consists exclusively of those characters listed in the definition of a class-name.

class C user See system programmer privilege class.

class descriptor A RACF-supplied control block for all the classes in the class descriptor table, which are all the classes except the USER, GROUP, and DATASET classes.

class descriptor table (CDT) In RACF, a table consisting of an entry for each class except the USER, GROUP, and DATASET classes. The table is generated by executing the ICHERCDE macro once for each class.

class D user See spooling operator privilege class.

class E user See system analyst privilege class.

class F user See service representative privilege class.

class G user See general user privilege class.

classification (1) In computer security, the determination that information requires a specific degree of protection against unauthorized disclosure.   (2) In computer security, a designation signifying the result of such a determination;   for example, "top secret, secret, confidential." See also category, compartment.

class lock In the IBM 8100 Information System, a set of locks, including sublocks, used to lock a member of a class of resources.

class method In System Object Model, an action that can be performed on a class object. Synonymous with factory method.

class-name In COBOL, a user-defined word defined in the SPECIAL-NAMES paragraph of the Environment Division that assigns a name to the proposition, for which a truth value can be defined, that the contents of a data item consists exclusively of those characters listed in the definition of a class-name.

class object In the AS/400 system, an object that identifies the run attributes of a job.

class (of entities) In a conceptual schema language, all possible entities in the universe of discourse for which a given proposition holds. (A)

class of service (COS) (1) A set of characteristics (such as route security, transmission priority, and bandwidth) used to construct a route between session partners. The class of service is derived from a mode name specified by the initiator of a session. (2) See also user class of service.

class of service database A database maintained independently by each network node, and optionally by APPN end nodes. It contains one entry per class-of-service name; each database entry contains:

- A definition of the acceptable values for transmission group (TG) and node characteristics for routes described by that class-of-service name and the weight function to be used to compute the weights of nodes and TGs that meet the acceptable values

- The transmission priority to be used for traffic that flows on routes described by that class-of-service name.

class-of-service description In the AS/400 system, a system object created for an Advanced Peer-to-Peer Networking (APPN) node that provides the information required to assign relative priority to the transmission groups and intermediate routing nodes for an APPN session.

class transition In the IBM ImagePlus system, a change in an object's management class and/or storage class when an event occurs that brings about a change in an object's service level or management criteria.

Note: Class transition occurs during a storage management cycle.

clause (1) In COBOL, an ordered set of consecutive COBOL character-strings whose purpose is to specify an attribute of an entry. See data clause, environment clause, file clause, report clause. (2) In SQL, a distinct part of a statement in the language structure, such as a SELECT clause or a WHERE clause.

CLAUTH Class authority.

CLB Communication services local block.

cleaning down In a duplicator, the process in which the blanket, inker, and damping system are cleaned to make them ready for further use. (T)

cleaning web On a document copying machine, a device for cleaning a photoreceptor. (T)

cleaning web indicator On a document copying machine, an indicator showing that the cleaning web needs to be replaced. (T)

cleanup (1) In SNA products, a network services request, sent by a system services control point (SSCP) to a logical unit (LU), that causes a particular LU-LU session with that LU to be ended immediately without requiring the participation of either the other LU or its SSCP. (2) See file cleanup.

clear (1) To put one or more storage locations or registers into a prescribed state, usually that denoting zero. (I) (A) (2) In a calculator, the cancellation of data in the working registers of the machine. (T) (3) To cause one or more storage locations to be in a prescribed state, usually that corresponding to zero or that corresponding to the blank character. (T) (4) In X.25 communications, to reject a call, if it has not yet been accepted, or end a call. (5) Deprecated term for set.

CLEAR In SNA, a command used to delete all requests and responses related to the active session.

Clear In SAA Common User Access architecture, a choice that removes a selected object without compressing the space it occupied. Contrast with Delete.

clear all In a calculator, the cancellation of data in the working registers and storage devices. (T)

clearance In computer security, permission granted to an individual to access information at or below a particular security level. See also authorization.

clear area In character recognition, a specified area that is to be kept free of printing or any other markings not related to machine reading.

clear cause Synonym for cause code.

clear collision A condition that occurs when a data terminal equipment (DTE) and a data circuit-terminating equipment (DCE) simultaneously transmit a clear request packet and a clear indication packet over the same logical channel. See also call collision, carrier-sense multiple-access with collision detection (CSMA/CD), reset collision.

clear confirmation packet See DCE clear confirmation packet.

clear cryptographic key In the Programmed Cryptographic Facility, a cryptographic key that is not enciphered.

clear data Data that are not enciphered. Synonymous with plaintext.

clear display The action of deleting all information from a display. (T)

clear entry In a calculator, the cancellation of data entered into the machine but not yet processed. (T)

clear indication packet A call supervision packet that a data circuit-terminating equipment (DCE) transmits to inform a data terminal equipment (DTE) that a call has been cleared.

clearing In computer security, the overwriting of classified information on a recording medium so that the medium may be reused at the same classification level. See also sanitizing.

Note: Clearing does not lower the classification level of the recording medium.

clear key See clear cryptographic key.

clear memory Synonym for clear storage.

clear panel key In the IBM 8100 Information System, a button on the basic operator panel used to clear the four-character digital display area.

clear request packet A call supervision packet transmitted by a data terminal equipment (DTE) to ask that a call be cleared.

clear session A session in which only clear data is transmitted or received. Contrast with cryptographic session.

clear storage In a calculator, the cancellation of data in the storage devices to which the keys refer. (T) Synonymous with clear memory.

Note: There may be other "clear" keys on the machine used to cancel specified functions.

cleartext Synonym for plaintext.

clear user data In X.25 communications, data optionally included in the clear request packet by the user application.

C library A system library that contains common C language subroutines for file access, string operators, character operations, memory allocation, and other functions.

click To press and release a button on a pointing device without moving the pointer off the choice. See double-click. See also drag select.

client (1) A user. (2) A functional unit that receives shared services from a server. (T). (3) In an AIX distributed file system environment, a system that is dependent on a server to provide it with programs or access to programs. (4) In AIX Enhanced X-Windows, an application program that connects to an Enhanced X-Windows server by means of an inter-process communication (IPC) path, such as a Transmission Control Protocol (TCP) connection or a shared memory buffer. The program can be referred to as the client of the server, but it is actually the interprocess communication path itself. Programs with multiple paths open to the server are viewed as multiple clients by the protocol. (5) In AIX Enhanced X-Windows, a Toolkit routine that uses a widget in an application or for composing another widget. (6) In AIXwindows, a software application that fills the role of the client in the traditional client-server model upon which Enhanced X-Windows and AIXwindows are based.

client agent See Location Broker Client Agent.

client area In SAA Advanced Common User Access architecture, the part of the window inside the border that is below the action bar. It is the user's workspace, where a user types information and selects choices from selection fields. In primary windows, it is the area where an application programmer presents the objects that a user works on.

client end node An end node for which the network node provides network services.

client-server In TCP/IP, the model of interaction in distributed data processing in which a program at one site sends a request to a program at another site and awaits a response. The requesting program is called a client; the answering program is called a server.

client-side caching In the AIX operating system, a high-speed buffer storage that contains frequently accessed information associated with a client applica-

tion. The primary purpose of client-side caching is to reduce access time to key information.

client window The window in which the application displays output and receives input. This window is located inside the frame window, under the window title bar and any menu bar, and within any scroll bars.

client workstation In the NetView Graphic Monitor Facility, a workstation that depends on a server workstation to provide it with views and status information. A client workstation receives status information from the server workstation over an LU 6.2 session.

clip (1) In SAA Advanced Common User Access architecture, to truncate information by removing those parts of a displayed image that lie outside a given boundary. (2) In multimedia applications, a section of recorded, filmed, or videotaped material. See also audio clip, video clip.

clip art In personal computer software applications, machine-readable artwork that can be retrieved from a file (a "clipboard file") and used completely or in part to create graphics such as computer-generated foils, slides, and hardcopy or softcopy graphs, charts, or pictures.

clipboard In SAA Common User Access architecture, an area of computer memory, or storage, that temporarily holds data. Data in the clipboard is available to other applications.

clip list In AIX Enhanced X-Windows, a list of rectangles designated for clipping.

clipping (1) In computer graphics, removing those parts of display elements that lie outside of given boundary. (I) (A) (2) In System/38 graphics, the process of cutting off the picture at the edge of the window but allowing the lines to be constructed on world coordinates that extend outside the window. (3) In AIX graphics, removal of parts of a primitive that overlap the boundaries of a window. The part of a primitive that appears in the window is displayed and the rest is ignored. There are several types of clipping that occur in the system. Three-dimensional drawing primitives are clipped to the boundaries of a frustum (for perspective transformations) or to a rhombohedron (for orthographic projections). This three-dimensional clipping applies as well to the origin of character strings, but not to the characters themselves. A two-dimensional clipping is also performed, in which all drawing is clipped to the boundaries of the Enhanced X-Windows window. For character strings, clipping of the individual characters to the screenmask is performed. See fine clipping, gross clipping. See also clipping planes, screenmask, transformation, window. (4) Synonym for scissoring.

clipping plane In AIX graphics, primitive space that is mapped to normalized viewing coordinates in homogeneous coordinates. The clipping planes x=+w, y=+w, or z=+w correspond to the left, right, top, bottom, near, and far planes bounding the viewing frustum.

clipping region In AIX Enhanced X-Windows, a type of graphics output. In a graphics context, the image defined by the bitmap or rectangles used to restrict output to a particular region of a window.

CLK Clock.

clock (CLK) (1) A device that generates periodic, accurately spaced signals used for purposes such as timing, regulation of the operations of a processor or generation of interrupts. (T) (A) (2) In data communication, equipment that provides a time base used in a transmission system to control the timing of certain functions such as sampling, and to control the duration of signal elements. (I) (A) (3) See master clock. (4) See also time-of-day clock.

clock/calendar In personal computers, a function provided by several software applications and multifunction boards that keeps track of the time and date regardless of whether the computer is on or off; it replaces a desktop clock and calendar and allows recording of appointments such as meeting dates and travel arrangements.

clock comparator A System/370 hardware feature that causes an interruption when the time-of-day clock has equaled or exceeded the value specified by a program or virtual machine.

clocking (1) In binary synchronous communication, the use of clock pulses to control synchronization of data and control characters. (2) A method of controlling the number of data bits sent on a telecommunication line in a given time. (3) See bit clocking, external clocking, internal clocking.

clocking bits Magnetically encoded signals, usually zeros, that precede the data and that are used for establishing timing intervals on an identification card. (T) (A)

clock pointer In the OS/2 operating system, a visual cue in the shape of a clock that indicates that the computer is performing operations. The mouse pointer changes to this shape while the computer is processing.

clock pulse (1) A synchronization signal provided by a clock. (A) (2) Synonym for clock signal.

clock register Synonym for timer.

clock signal (1) A periodic signal used for synchronization and for measuring intervals of time. (T) (2) Synonymous with clock pulse.

clock track A track on which a pattern of signals is recorded to provide a timing reference. (I) (A)

close (1) The function that ends the connection between a file and a program, and ends the processing. Contrast with open. (2) A data manipulation function that ends the connection between a file and a program. Contrast with open. (3) To end the processing of a file. (4) In the AIX operating system, to end an activity and remove that window from the display.

Close In SAA Advanced Common User Access architecture, a choice that removes a window and all its associated windows from the screen.

closed circuit In multimedia applications, a system of transmitting television signals from a point of origin to one or many restricted destination points specially equipped to receive the signals.

closed fix package In the IBM 8100 Information System, the last fix package that applies to a given service level. A closed fix package is always numbered 99.

closed loop (1) A loop whose execution can be interrupted only by intervention from outside the program in which the loop is included. (A) (2) Synonym for infinite loop. (T)

close dot In some graphical user interfaces, the small rectangle in the upper left corner of dialog boxes, messages, and selection boxes used to close the message or box.

closedown (1) The deactivation of a device, program, or system. (2) In ACF/TCAM, the orderly deactivation of the message control program (MCP). (3) See also cancel closedown, flush closedown, orderly closedown, quick closedown.

closed security environment In computer security, an environment in which authentications, clearances, and configuration controls provide a sufficient presumption that malicious logic has not been introduced and provide sufficient assurance that malicious logic will not be introduced prior to or during the operation of the system. Contrast with open security environment.

closed shop Pertaining to the operation of a computer facility in which most productive problem programming is performed by a group of programming specialists rather than by the problem originators. The use of the computer itself may also be described as closed shop if full-time trained operators, rather than users or programmers, serve as the operators. (A) Contrast with open shop.

closed subroutine A subroutine that can be called for use at more than one place in a computer program without inserting a copy of the routine wherever it is needed. Contrast with open subroutine.

closed system (1) A system whose characteristics comply with proprietary standards and that therefore cannot readily be connected to other systems. (T) (2) In computer security, a system in which resources not defined to the system are protected. Contrast with open system.

closed user group (CUG) In data communication, a group of users who can communicate with other users in the group, but not with users outside the group. See also bilateral closed user group, preferential closed user group.

Note: Data terminal equipment (DTE) may belong to more than one closed user group.

closed user group with outgoing access (1) A closed user group that has a user-assigned facility which enables that user to communicate with other users of a data network transmission service where appropriate, with users having a data terminal equipment connected to any other switched network to which interworking facilities are available, or both. (T) (A) (2) In data communication, a closed user group in which one or more users can communicate with users outside the closed group, under certain conditions.

close-up In videotaping, a picture obtained when the camera is positioned to show only the head and shoulders of a subject; in the case of an object, the camera is close enough to show details clearly. See also extreme close-up.

closing (a file) Dissociating a file from a data set.

closure line In GDDM, a line added by the system to enclose an area being filled with a pattern, in instances when the routines that precede the GSENDA routine fail to form an enclosed area.

CLP Current line pointer.

CLPA Create link pack area.

CLSDST Close destination.

cluster (1) A station that consists of a control unit (a cluster controller) and the terminals attached to it. (2) In systems with VSAM, a named structure consisting of a group of related components; for example, a data component with its index component. See also alternate index cluster, base cluster. (3) On

an IBM personal computer, a particular measure of space on a diskette that DOS establishes when it formats the diskette; DOS then allocates space to files in cluster increments.

Note: For a single-sided diskette, a cluster is a sector. For dual-sided diskettes, a cluster is two consecutive sectors.

cluster agent A workstation containing the Mail service that allows OS/2 Office nodes to communicate with OS/2 Office nodes at a remote location or with OS/2 Office Release 1 nodes.

cluster analysis A formal technique for analyzing the associations of one object type to another object type based on their commonality of involvement, or affinity factors. See also affinity analysis.

cluster controller A device that can control the input/output operations of more than one device connected to it. A cluster controller may be controlled by a program stored and executed in the unit; for example, the IBM 3601 Finance Communication Controller. Or, it may be entirely controlled by hardware; for example, the IBM 3272 Control Unit. See also cluster, cluster controller node. Synonymous with cluster control unit.

cluster controller node A peripheral node that can control a variety of devices. See also host node, NCP node, terminal node.

cluster control unit Synonym for cluster controller.

cluster entry A catalog entry that contains information about a key-sequenced or entry-sequenced VSAM cluster: ownership, cluster attributes, and the cluster passwords and protection attributes. A key-sequenced cluster entry points to a data entry and an index entry. An entry-sequenced cluster entry points to a data entry.

Cluster feature In the AS/400 system, a feature that provides four cable connections and allows up to four workstations to be attached to a 5251 Model 12 Display Station. See also Dual Cluster feature.

cluster function In the AS/400 system, a function that allows up to four workstations to be attached to a 5294 Control Unit.

CLUT Color look-up table.

CLV Constant linear velocity.

cm Centimeter.

CMC Communication management configuration.

CMND Command.

CMOD A user-written module for a subsystem controller.

CMOS Complementary metal-oxide semiconductor. A technology that combines the electrical properties of n-type semiconductors and p-type semiconductors. See also NMOS, n-type semiconductor, PMOS, p-type semiconductor.

Note: The positive and negative voltage requirements of paired p-type and n-type semiconductors complement each other. A low-power input pulse to a gate of a CMOS device turns one semiconductor on and the other off. There is no current flow except for capacitance charging and discharging and for switching operations. CMOS devices therefore use considerably less power than other types of semiconductor devices. They are ideal for use in microcomputers and battery-powered devices such as calculators and portable computers.

CMS Conversational monitor system.

CMS batch facility A facility that allows a user to run time-consuming or noninteractive CMS jobs in batch mode in another CMS virtual machine dedicated to that purpose, thus freeing the terminal and the virtual machine for other work.

CMS editor The CMS facility that allows the user to create, modify, insert, delete, or rearrange lines of data in a CMS file. See also edit mode, input mode.

CMS file directory A directory on each CMS disk that contains the name, format, size, and location of all the CMS files on the disk. Synonymous with master file directory block.

CMS nucleus The portion of CMS that usually resides in the user's virtual storage when CMS is executing. Each CMS user receives a copy of the CMS nucleus at initial program load (IPL) of CMS. See also saved system, shared segment.

CMS primary disk Synonym for A-disk.

CMS system disk The virtual disk (S-disk) that contains the CMS nucleus and the disk-resident CMS commands. The CMS system disk can have extensions, usually the Y-disk and Z-disk. Synonymous with S-disk.

CMS system file Any file residing on the CMS system disk instead of on a user's disk.

CMS user disk One or more virtual disks that contain CMS or read-only VSE or OS files that may be accessed by the user. If the user has read/write access

to a disk, that user can create programs and data files on the disk. Files are retained until the user deletes them. The user may also link to and access other users' disks, usually on a read-only basis.

CMY Cyan/magenta/yellow

CMYK Cyan/magenta/yellow/black.

CNM Communication network management.

CNM application program A VTAM application program that issues and receives formatted management services request units for physical units; for example, the NetView program.

CNM interface The interface that the access method provides to an application program for handling data and commands associated with communication system management. CNM data and commands are handled across this interface.

CNM processor A program that manages one of the functions of a communications system. A CNM processor is executed under control of the NetView program.

CNP Communications statistical network analysis procedure.

CO Central office.

coalesce (1) To combine two or more sets of items into one set of any form. (I) (2) To combine two or more files into one file.

COAM equipment Customer owned and maintained communication equipment connected to telecommunication lines. See also business machine.

coarse-grain parallel processing Parallel processing in which parts of a job are performed concurrently. Contrast with fine-grain parallel processing.

coated card See edge-coated card.

coated paper Paper to which a layer of material has been added to make it smooth.

coaxial cable A cable consisting of one conductor, usually a small copper tube or wire, within and insulated from another conductor of larger diameter, usually copper tubing or copper braid. See Figure 32.

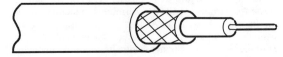

Figure 32. Coaxial Cable

COB Card-on-board logic.

COBOL (common business-oriented language) A high-level programming language, based on English, that is used primarily for business applications.

COBOL character Any of the 51 characters of the COBOL character set.

COBOL character set In COBOL, the character set that consists of the following characters: 0, 1, ... , 9 (digits), A, B, ... , Z (uppercase letters), a, b, ... , z (lowercase letters), (space), + (plus sign), - (minus sign), * (asterisk), / (slant), = (equals sign), $ (currency sign), , (comma), ; (semicolon), . (period), " (quotation mark), ((left parenthesis),) (right parenthesis), > (greater than symbol), < (less than symbol), : (colon).

COBOL word In COBOL, a character-string of not more than 30 characters that forms a user-defined word, a system-name, or a reserved word.

COD Cash on delivery.

Codabar A type of bar code that provides a limited character set with 12 available characters.

CODASYL Conference on Data Systems Languages.

CODASYL model In a database management system, a network model whose pattern of organization is based on set types that specify associations among record types. (A)

code (1) A set of rules that maps the elements of one set onto the elements of another set. The elements may be characters or character strings. The first set is the coded set and the second is the code element set. An element of the code element set may be related to more than one element of the coded set but the reverse is not true. (T)   (2) A set of items, such as abbreviations, representing the members of another set. (A) (3) In computer security, a set of rules in which code groups are substituted for plaintext elements that are primarily words, phrases, or sentences. (4) Loosely, one or more computer programs, or part of a computer program.   (5) Instructions written for a computer. (6) A coded character set.   (7) A representation of a condition, such as an error code.   (8) To represent data or a computer program in a symbolic form that can be accepted by a data processor. (I) (A) (9) To write a routine. (A)   (10) To write instructions for a computer.   Synonymous with program.   (11) Deprecated term for coded character set, code element, code element set, program. (12) Synonymous with coding scheme. (13) Synonym for encode.

code area In computer micrographics, that part of a microform reserved for retrieval keys. (A)   See also work area.

code book encoding In video compression, a technique that uses a table of values to reconstruct the original digital signal from a compressed signal.

code breaking Synonym for cryptanalysis.

code conversion A process for changing the bit grouping for a character in one code into the corresponding bit grouping for a character in a second code.

code converter A functional unit that changes the representation of data by using one code in place of another or one coded character set in place of another. (T) (A)

coded See binary-coded decimal notation.

coded arithmetic data (1) Arithmetic data that are stored in a form that is acceptable, without conversion, for arithmetic calculations.   (2) In PL/I, data items that represent actual numeric values that are characterized by their base (decimal or binary), scale (fixed-point or floating-point), and precision (the accuracy, as in binary or decimal places, with which a number can be represented).

coded character set (1) A coded set whose elements are single characters; for example, all characters of an alphabet. (T)   (2) Loosely, a code. (A)   (3) A set of graphic characters and their code point assignments. The set may contain fewer characters than the total number of possible characters: some code points may be unassigned.

coded data overlay In the IBM ImagePlus system, coded data specifically formatted for use with an image overlay.

coded data storage In the ImagePlus system, this refers to the process of reading objects, including coded data objects, from a batch file and storing them on optical storage or another storage medium.

coded decimal notation Synonym for binary-coded decimal notation.

code-dependent system A mode of data communication that uses a link protocol that depends on the character set or code used by the data source. Synonymous with code-sensitive system.   Contrast with code-independent system.

coded document A document composed of coded data only.

coded font A font library member that associates a code page and font character set. For extended graphics, a coded font associates multiple pairs of code pages and font character sets.

coded font local identifier A one-byte local identifier that the map coded font structured field assigns to each coded font it selects. The identifier is then specified in the text control sequence that precedes the string of text to be printed with the particular font.

coded font section A font character set and code page pair. A single-byte coded font consists of only one coded font section; a double-byte coded font can consist of more than one.

coded graphic character-set ID A 10-digit identifier (two 5-digit identifiers separated by a space) that is the combination of a graphic character-set ID and a code-page ID. See also graphic character-set ID, code-page ID.

coded graphics Deprecated term for coordinate graphics.

coded image In computer graphics, a representation of a display image in a form suitable for storage and processing. (I) (A) Synonymous with encoded image. See also display image.

coded image space In computer graphics, an area in main storage or in a display buffer where one or more coded images are stored.

coded overlay In the 3800 Printing Subsystem, an overlay that is stored in the printing subsystem in a coded (not raster) format.

coded representation Synonym for code element.

coded set A set of elements onto which another set of elements has been mapped according to a code; for example, a list of the names of airports which is mapped into a corresponding set of three letter abbreviations. (T)

code element The result of applying a code to an element of a coded set; for example, "CDG" as the representation of Paris-Charles-De-Gaulle in the code for three-letter representation of airport names, the seven binary digits representing the delete character in ISO Standard 646, 7-bit coded character set for information processing interchange. (T) Synonymous with coded representation, code value.

code element set The result of applying a code to all elements of a coded set; for example, all the three-letter international representations of airport names. (T) Synonymous with code set.

code extension character A control character used to indicate that one or more of the succeeding coded elements are to be interpreted according to a different code. (T)

code group In a computer security code system, an apparently meaningless sequence of letters, digits, or both, that represents a plaintext element, which may be a word, phrase, or sentence.

code-independent data communication A mode of data communication that uses a character-oriented protocol that does not depend on the character set or code used by the data source. (I) (A)

code-independent system A mode of data communication that uses a character-oriented link protocol that does not depend on the character set or code used by the data source. (I) (A) Synonymous with code-insensitive system, code-transparent system. Contrast with code-dependent system.

code-insensitive system Synonym for code-independent system.

code key In word processing, a key, which when operated in conjunction with another key, gives an alternate meaning to the key, such as to initiate a program or execute a function. (T)

code level The number of bits used to represent a character.

code line index In micrographics, a visual index consisting of an optical pattern of clear and opaque bars parallel to the long edge of the roll of microfilm and located between the images. (A)

code page (1) An assignment of graphic characters and control function meanings to all code points; for example, assignment of characters and meanings to 256 code points for an 8-bit code, assignment of characters and meanings to 128 code points for a 7-bit code. (2) In the Print Management Facility, a font library member that associates code points and character identifiers. A code page also identifies invalid code points. (3) A particular assignment of hexadecimal identifiers to graphic characters. (4) In AFP support, a font file that associates code points and graphic character identifiers.

Code Page Global Identifier (CPGID) A five digit-decimal identifier assigned to a code page. The range of values is 00001 to 65534 (hexadecimal 0001 to hexadecimal FFFE).

code-page ID A 5-digit registered identifier used to specify a particular assignment of code points to graphic characters. See also graphic character-set ID.

code page switching In the OS/2 operating system, to replace the matrix of characters that the computer prints or displays with another matrix of characters.

code parameter Deprecated term for parameter.

code point (1) A 1-byte code representing one of 256 potential characters. (2) In the AS/400 system, one of the bit patterns assigned to a character in a character set, represented by a hexadecimal number; for example, in code page 256 (EBCDIC), the letter "e" is assigned a code point of hex 85. (3) An identifier in an alert description that represents a short unit of text. The code point is replaced with the text by an alert display program. (4) In AFP support, an 8-bit binary number representing one of 256 potential characters. (5) For SNA alerts, a 1-or 2-byte hexadecimal code that designates a particular piece of text to be displayed at the focal point. (6) In the NetView/PC program and in the NetView program, a 1- or 2-byte hexadecimal value that indexes a text string stored at an alert receiver and is used by the alert receiver to create displays of alert information.

code position Synonym for punch position.

coder A person who writes but does not usually design computer programs. (I) (A)

code regenerator In multimedia development, a device used while creating an audio score to maintain a stable signal.

code-sensitive system Synonym for code-dependent system.

code set Synonym for code element set.

code system In computer security, any system of communications in which groups of symbols are used to represent plaintext elements of varying length. Contrast with cipher system. See also cryptographic system.

code-transparent data communication A mode of data communication that uses a bit-oriented protocol that does not depend on the bit sequence structure used by the data source. (I) (A)

code-transparent system Synonym for code-independent system.

Code 3 of 9 A type of bar code also known as Code 39. It is the most common type of bar code. This bar code provides the largest number of available characters of any bar code type. Each character is represented by a group of nine elements. Three of these nine elements are wide.

code value Synonym for code element.

code violation In differential Manchester encoding, a bit that does not have a state transition at the mid-bit point. (T)

coding scheme Synonym for code.

coefficient unit A functional unit whose output analog variable is equal to the input analog variable multiplied by a constant. (T) (A) Synonymous with scale multiplier.

coexistence The ability of different types of systems to support a program.

coexistence model In a database, a structure that supports the coexistence of different data models. (T)

coffret A transmission interface used to connect with the French telephone network.

cognitive modeling In artificial intelligence, the simulation of human perception, action, memory, and thinking in terms of information processing. (T)

COGO (coordinate geometry) A programming language designed for coordinate geometry problems in civil engineering. (T)

coincidence error The error caused by a time difference in switching different integrators to the compute mode or to the hold mode. (I)

coincident-current selection In any array of magnetic storage cells, the selective switching of one cell in the array by the simultaneous application of two or more currents such that the resultant magnetomotive force exceeds a threshold value only in the selected cell. (I) (A)

cold restart (1) In ACF/TCAM, startup of a message control program (MCP) following either a flush closedown, a quick closedown, or a system failure. A cold restart ignores the previous environment; that is, the MCP is started as if this were the initial startup. It is the only type of restart possible when no checkpoint/restart facility is used. Contrast with warm restart. (2) Synonym for initial program load. (3) See also checkpoint restart, system restart.

cold site In computer security, an alternative facility with at least the equipment necessary to support the installation and operation of a computer center in the event of a disaster such as flood or fire. Contrast with hot site.

cold start (1) The start of a database management system without preprocessing before-images or after-images. (T) (2) A system start, using an initial program load procedure. (3) In VM, a system restart that ignores previous data areas and accounting information in main storage, and the contents of paging and spool files on CP-owned disks. (4) In the AS/400 system and System/38, a process in which all temporary objects (objects created by the system after the operating system is installed) are deleted and created again as a group. (5) Contrast with checkpoint start, force start, warm start.

collaborative document production In multimedia applications, a system feature that provides the ability for a group of people to manage document production.

collate To alter the arrangement of a set of items from two or more ordered subsets to one or more other subsets each containing a number of items, commonly one, from each of the original subsets in a specified order that is not necessarily the order of any of the original subsets. (I) (A) See also merge.

collating sequence (1) A specified arrangement used in sequencing. (I) (A) (2) An ordering assigned to a set of items, such that any two sets in that assigned order can be collated. (A) (3) In COBOL, the sequence in which the characters that are acceptable to a computer are ordered for the purposes of sorting, merging, comparing, and for processing indexed files sequentially. (4) Deprecated term for order. (5) Synonymous with sequence.

collator A device that collates, merges, or matches sets of punched cards or other documents. (I) (A)

collection (1) In the AS/400 system, an object that consists of, and logically classifies, a set of objects, such as tables, views, and indexes. (2) In SQL, a set of objects created by the SAA Structured Query Language/400 licensed program that consists of, and logically classifies, a set of objects, such as tables, views, and indexes. An SQL collection consists of a library; a data dictionary that contains descriptions and information for all tables, views, indexes, and files created in the library; SQL catalog views; and a journal and journal receiver that are used to record changes on all tables created in the collection.

collection point block (CPB) In NPM, a control block used to coordinate the collection of network and session data.

collection station See data collection station.

collision An unwanted condition that results from concurrent transmissions on a channel. (T)

collision detection In CSMA/CD, a signal indicating that two or more stations are transmitting simultaneously.

collision enforcement In a CSMA/CD network, the transmission of a jam signal by a data station after it has detected a collision, to ensure that all other data stations become aware of the collision. (T)

colon alignment tab A tab that marks where text is to be aligned to the left of a colon.

color (1) In optical character recognition, the spectral appearance of the image dependent upon the spectral reflectance of the image, the spectral response of the observer, and the spectral composition of incident light. (A) (2) A specific hue or tint, including black and white. (3) See background color, direct color, pseudocolor, true color.

color balance In a color video system, the process of matching the amplitudes of the red, green, and blue signals so that the three together combine to make a true white color.

color bars In video presentations, a test pattern composed of eight rectangles of the following colors: white, yellow, cyan, green, magenta, red, blue, black, used as a reference for brightness, contrast, color intensity, and correct color balance.

color cell In AIX Enhanced X-Windows, an entry in a colormap that consists of three values based on red, green, and blue intensities. The values are 16-bit, unsigned numbers. Zero represents the minimum intensity. The values are scaled by the server to match the particular display in use.

color corrector In video presentations, a device used to adjust the color values of a color video signal.

color cycling In multimedia applications, an animation effect in which colors in a series are displayed in rapid succession.

color display A display device that can display more than two colors and the shades produced by combinations of two colors. Contrast with monochrome display.

color expansion operation In the AIX operating system, a graphics programming operation that occurs automatically when the source pixel map data area contains only 1 byte per pixel and the destination pixel map data area is a color display adapter buffer frame defined to have more than 1 bit per pixel.

color graphics adapter (CGA) An adapter that simultaneously provides four colors and is supported on all IBM Personal Computer and Personal System/2 models.

colorization In multimedia applications, the color tinting of a monochrome original.

color lookup table (CLUT) (1) In the AIX operating system, synonym for color map. (2) In multimedia, synonym for color palette.

color map (1) In AIX graphics, a lookup table in which each index is associated with a red, green, and blue value. Synonymous with color lookup table, color palette, color table. (2) In AIX Enhanced X-Windows, a set of color cells. A pixel value indexes the color map to produce RGB-intensities. A color map consists of a set of entries defining color values that, when associated with a window, is used to display the contents of the window. See also direct color, pseudocolor. (3) In AIX graphics, a lookup table that translates color indexes into RGB triplets.

color menu A menu in LinkWay and LinkWay Paint that lets the user select a color for use in drawing or in the fonts used in a text field object. CGA mode has three available colors. EGA and VGA have 16 available colors. MCGA 256 has 256 available colors.

color model A technique for describing a color. See also cyan/magenta/yellow (CYA).

color noise In video systems, random interference in the color portion of an image, caused by reduced color bandwidth or color subsampling and appearing as streaks of incorrect color in the image.

color number In the IBM LinkWay product, the number assigned to a given color in a color palette. The background color is color number 0. The rest of the colors are numbered sequentially, starting with 1.

color palette A set of colors that can be displayed on the screen at one time. This can be a standard set used for all images or a set that can be customized for each image. Synonymous with color lookup table (CLUT). See also standard palette, custom palette.

color ramp A progression of colors in a color map; for example, the full range of colors of the rainbow, loaded into the color map. Most color ramps have only a small number, if any, of discontinuities. See also gamma ramp.

color register An area in computer memory that stores information about color.

color resolution In video systems, a measure of the sharpness of a color image.

color scanner A device used for converting color photographs and art to digital data for use in an audio visual development application.

color separation A negative used for making the plates that print each separate color.

color space All the colors that can be represented by red, green, blue, cyan, magenta, yellow, black, and white.

color subsampling In video systems, the technique of using less resolution for the color difference components of a video signal compared with the brightness component.

color table (1) In System/38 graphics, a compilation of eight entries, each defining a color to be used in System/38 graphics, from which individual colors are selected. Many color tables can be defined, but only one can be current. (2) In AIX graphics, synonym for color map.

color temperature A precise measure of the hue of a given source of light stated as the temperature to which a black body would have to be heated in order to display the same color. Color temperature is expressed in degrees Kelvin (°K).

color value The three numbers specifying a given color. See pixel value.

column (1) One of two or more vertical arrangements of lines, positioned side by side on a page or screen. (T) (2) A vertical arrangement of characters or other expressions. (A) (3) A character position within a print line or on a display. The positions are numbered from 1, by 1, starting at the leftmost character position and extending to the rightmost position. (4) In SQL, the vertical part of a table. A column has a name and a particular data type; for example, character, decimal, or integer. (5) In COBOL, a character position within a print line. Columns are numbered consecutively from 1, starting at the leftmost character position of the print line and extending to the rightmost position of the print line. (6) Contrast with row. (7) See card column, mark-sensing column, punch column.

column balancing The process of redistributing lines of text among a set of columns so that the amount of text in each column is as equal as possible.

column binary (1) Pertaining to the binary representation of data on cards in which the weights of punch positions are assigned along card columns. For example, each column in a 12-row card may be used to represent 12 consecutive bits. (A) Synonymous with Chinese binary. (2) Contrast with row binary.

column function In SQL, a process that calculates a value from a set of values and expresses it as a function name followed by an argument enclosed in parentheses.

column heading One or more words at the top of a column of information that identify the information in that column.

column mark line In an XL compiler error message, the line that contains the | symbol to indicate the column of code where the error was detected.

column separator A symbol on each side of a position of a field on a display. The symbol does not occupy a position on the display.

column split The capability of a card-processing device to read or punch two parts of a card column independently. (I)

COM Computer output microfilming. (A)

comb In a magnetic disk unit, an assembly of access arms that moves as a unit. (T)

combination A given number of different elements selected from a set without regard to the order in which the selected elements are arranged. (I) (A) Contrast with permutation. See forbidden combination.

combinational circuit (1) A logic device whose output values at any given instant depend only upon the input values at that time. (T) (2) Synonymous with combinatorial circuit.

combinational gate A device having at least one output channel and zero or more input channels, all characterized by discrete states, such that at any instant the state of each output channel is completely determined by the states of the input channels at the same instant. (T) (A)

combinational logic element (1) A device having at least one output channel and zero or more input channels, all characterized by discrete states, such that at any instant the state of each output channel is completely determined by the states of the input channels at the same instant. (A) (2) Contrast with sequential logic element.

combination box In SAA Advanced Common User Access architecture, a control that combines the capabilities of an entry field and a list box. The list box contains choices that a user can scroll and select to complete the entry field. See drop-down combination box. See also list box.

combinatorial circuit Synonym for combinational circuit.

combined alert In the NetView program, an alert that includes both a non-generic alert and a generic alert in one network management vector transport (NMVT).

combined condition In COBOL, a condition that is the result of connecting two or more conditions with the AND or the OR logical operator. Contrast with negated combined condition.

combined dictation and transcription machine Dictation equipment designed to record and to reproduce speech so that a written record can be produced. (T)

combined file A data file that is used as both an input file and an output file. The output file contains only those fields described for the output file; that is, the output record does not necessarily contain the same fields as the input record.

combined head On dictation equipment, a device that combines the functions of any two or all three of the following parts: a recording head, a playback head, and an erase head. (I) Synonym for read/write head.

combined station (1) In high level data link control (HDLC), the part of a data station that supports the combined control functions of the data link and that generates commands and responses for transmission and interprets received commands and responses. (I) (2) A data station that generates commands and responses for transmission over a data link and interprets received commands and responses. (3) Synonymous with balanced station. See also primary station, secondary station.

COM device Computer output microfilmer. (A)

comic-strip oriented image (1) In micrographics, an image appearing on roll microfilm in such a manner that the top edge of the image is parallel to the long edge of the film. (A) (2) Contrast with cine-oriented image. See Figure 33.

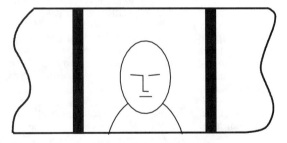

Figure 33. Comic-Strip-Oriented Image

comma alignment tab A tab that marks where text is to be aligned to the left of a comma.

command (1) An order for an action to take place. (A) (2) A control signal. (A) (3) In a conceptual schema language, the order or trigger for an action or permissible action to take place. (A) (4) Loosely, a mathematical or logic operator. (A)　(5) Synonymous with order. (A)　(6) A statement used to request a function of the system. A command consists of the command name abbreviation, which identifies the requested function, and its parameters.　(7) In SDLC, a frame transmitted by a primary station. Asynchronous balanced mode stations send both commands and responses. Contrast with response. (8) A request from a terminal for the performance of an operation or the execution of a particular program. (9) In SNA, any field set in the transmission header (TH), request header (RH), and sometimes portions of a request unit (RU), that initiates an action or that begins a protocol;　for example:　(a) Bind Session (session-control request unit), a command that activates an LU-LU session, (b) The change-direction indicator in the RH of the last RU of a chain, (c) The virtual route reset window indicator in an FID transmission header.　See also VTAM operator command. (10) A request for system action.　(11) A character string from a source external to a system that represents a request for system action. (12) In data communication, an instruction represented in the control field of a frame and transmitted by a primary or combined station.　It causes the addressed secondary/combined station to execute a data link control function.　See also response. (13) Deprecated term for instruction.

Command (1) In SAA Basic Common User Access architecture, an action that displays a pop-up containing the command area.　(2) The typed name and parameters associated with an action that can be performed by an application. A command is one form of action request.

command analyzer In System/38, an IBM-supplied program that processes commands.　Command processing includes validity checking, transferring control to a command processing program (CPP), and returning to the caller of the command analyzer.

command area (1) An area of a display screen in which the user enters commands, for example, on the screen of a 3790 display component, the first of four areas in the system control area, providing system communication and instructions for the operator.　On some devices, the user must change from a working mode to a command mode to place the cursor in the command area.　(2) In SAA Basic Common User Access architecture, the area on a panel that contains the command entry field.　See also command entry field.

command attention (CA) key In DDS, a keyboard key that can be specified with the CA keyword to request the function specified by the keyword. Data is not returned to the system. Contrast with command function (CF) key.

command condition In a conceptual schema language, the precondition, including synchronization aspects, that must be met before a permissible action may take place. (A)

command control block (CCB) In the IBM Token-Ring Network, a specifically formatted information provided from the application program to the adapter support software to request an operation.

command definition In the AS/400 system and System/38, an object that contains the definition of a command, including the command name, parameter descriptions, and validity-checking information, and identifies the program that performs the function requested by the command.

command definition statement In the AS/400 system and System/38, a source statement that defines keywords and parameter values, qualified names, elements in a list, parameter requirements and interrelationships, and prompt text for a command. Command definition statements are used to create a command language (CL) command.

command display In System/36, a display that allows an operator to display and send messages and use control commands and procedure commands to start and control jobs.　Contrast with standby display.　See also console display, subconsole display.

command display station In System/36, a display station from which an operator can start and control jobs.　A command display station can become an alternative system console, can be designated as a subconsole, and can also be used as a data display station.　See also alternative system console, data display station, subconsole.

command entry field In SAA Basic Common User Access architecture, an entry field in which a user types commands.　See also command area.

command facility The component of the NetView program that is a base for command processors that can monitor, control, automate, and improve the operation of a network.

command field (1) On a display screen, a part of a command area.　(2) In DPCX, the first of four areas on the bottom line of a display during field-by-field operations.　See also communication field, message field, mode field.

command field prompt In SAA Basic Common User Access architecture, a field prompt showing the location of the command entry field in a panel (Command ===>).

command file In AS/400 RJE, a remote job input stream that can contain host system commands and job control language (JCL), data, and RJE control statements (READFILE or EOF). Contrast with data file.

command frame (1) A frame transmitted by a primary station. (2) A frame transmitted by a combined station that contains the address of the other combined stations.

command function (CF) key (1) In DDS, a keyboard key that can be specified with the CF keyword to request the function specified by the keyword. Data is returned to the system. Contrast with command attention (CA) key. (2) In System/36, a key that is used with the command (CMD) function control key to request preassigned functions. At the system console, a keyboard key, called a CF key, that is used to request preassigned functions.

command help In the ImagePlus Folder Application Facility, online help about the commands the users enter on the command line.

command interpreter In the AIX operating system, a program that sends instructions to the kernel. See also shell.

command key (1) Any key that causes a device to perform a predefined operation. (2) A key on a display station keyboard used to request a specific programmed action. (3) On the keyboard of an IBM personal computer, a key that causes the PC to perform a particular operation as opposed to a key used to enter data. See also typewriter key. The command keys are the alternate (Alt) key, Caps Lock key, control (Ctrl) key, cursor movement keys, delete (Del) key, End key, enter key, escape (Esc) key, function keys, Home key, insert (Ins) key, Num Lock key, page down (PgDn) key, page up (PgUp) key, print screen (PrtSc) key, Scroll Lock (and Break) key, shift key, and tab key. (4) See alternate function key, character key, function key, program attention key, program function key.

command key indicator In RPG, an indicator defined to correspond with the function keys to tell the program when one of the function keys is pressed.

command language A set of procedural operators with a related syntax, used to indicate the functions to be performed by an operating system. (I) (A) Synonymous with control language.

command level Pertaining to an operation performed for a particular command in a program. Contrast with program level.

command library In TSO, a partitioned data set consisting of command processor programs. A user

command library can be concatenated to the system command library.

command line (1) On a display screen, a display line usually at the bottom of the screen, in which only commands can be entered. See also floating command line. (2) In SAA usage, deprecated term for command area.

command list In the NetView program, a list of commands and statements designed to perform a specific function for the user. Command lists can be written in REXX or in the NetView command list language.

command mode (1) A state of a system or device in which the user can enter commands. (2) In TSO, the entry mode immediately following LOGON, or following completion of a command processor. In command mode, the system is ready to accept any command in the command libraries. (3) In DPCX, a mode of operation in which a terminal operator can do any operation in basic mode, issue additional operator commands, and execute command procedures (PROCs).

command name The first term in a command, usually followed by operands.

command phase In the network control program, the portion of the system response field in a basic transmission unit that identifies the step to which a combination command; for example, Write with Contact, has progressed.

command privilege class See privilege class.

command procedure (PROC) (1) In DPCX, a user-written set of commands that an operator can invoke by name. A command procedure consists of operator commands and PROC commands. See command list. (2) In TSO, a data set or a member of a partitioned data set containing TSO commands to be performed sequentially by the EXEC command. (3) In the NetView program, a command list, a command processor written in a high-level language (HLL), or a NetView pipeline.

command processing The reading, analyzing, and performing of commands issued via a console or through an input stream.

command processing program (CPP) In the AS/400 system and System/38, a program that performs some validity checking and processes a command so that the requested function is performed.

command processor (1) A problem program executed to perform an operation specified by a command. (2) In System/36, the part of the System

Support Program Product that processes control commands and passes procedure commands and operation control language statements to the initiator. (3) In the NetView program, a module designed to perform a specific function for the user. Users can write command processors in assembler language or in a high-level language (HLL); command processors are invoked as commands.

command profile See profile.

command programming language A language that allows programming by the use of commands rather than by writing statements in a conventional programming language.

command prompt A displayed character or string of characters that indicates that a user may enter a command to be processed.

command/response application In the Network Carrier Interconnect Manager and Agent programs, a function that allows a NetView operator to execute commands in a carrier management system.

command retry A channel and control unit procedure that causes a command to be retried without requiring an I/O interruption.

command scan In CMS, a routine that scans the command line entered and converts it to a standard CMS parameter list.

command statement A job control statement that is used to issue commands to the system through the input stream.

command string In AS/400 query management, a character string that contains a query command.

command substitution In the AIX operating system, the ability to capture the output of any command as a value to another command by placing that command line within (grave accents). The shell first runs the command or commands enclosed within the grave accents and then replaces the whole expression, including grave accents, with their output. This feature is often used in assignment statements.

command virtual terminal In the AIX operating system, the virtual terminal that becomes active when the command window hot key is pressed. See also command window hot key.

command window hot key In the AIX operating system, a key combination that activates the command virtual terminal. The command window hot key combination is Alt-Action on the keyboard, the two buttons on a mouse, or button number 4 on a tablet. See also command virtual terminal.

command word In the AIX operating system, the name of the 16-bit units used for storing graphic primitive strings. The first command word determines the primitive type and sets the length of the string. Subsequent command words contain information in multiples of quid, or 4 bits of data.

comment (1) In programming languages, a language construct for the inclusion of text in a program and having no impact on the execution of the program. Comments are used to explain certain aspects of the program. (I)   (2) A statement used to document a program or file. Comments include information that may be helpful in running a job or reviewing an output listing. (3) In the C language, a token that consists of one or more lines, delimited by /* and */. Comments can be written anywhere in the program. (4) In Pascal, a token consisting of characters on one or more lines, delimited by /* */, (* *), or { } . Comments can be written anywhere in the program. (5) In SQL, source program information that is not translated by the compiler. The format of a comment is language specific. (6) Synonymous with computer program annotation, note, remark.

comment-entry In COBOL, an entry in the Identification Division that may be any combination of characters from the character set of a computer.

comment line In COBOL, a source program line represented by an asterisk (*) in the indicator area of the line and any characters from the character set of the computer in area A and area B of that line.

comment statement A source language statement that has no effect other than to be reproduced on an output listing.

commercial instruction set A combination of instructions of the standard instruction set and the decimal feature.

Commission Internationale de l'Eclairage (CIE) An international committee that develops color standards.

commit (1) In DPPX/DTMS, to ensure action on requests made by a program during its current scope of recovery to change resettable or recreatable databases and to execute transactions. (2) To end the current scope of recovery and begin a new one. (3) To make all changes permanent that were made to one or more database files since the last commit or rollback operation, and make the changed records available to other users. (4) In SQL, the process that allows data changed by one application or user to be used by other applications or users. When a commit operation occurs, the locks are released to allow other applications to use the changed data. (5) A service that performs commit actions. (6) In IMS/VS, an indication in an application program that a section of work is done and that the data it has modified or created is consistent and complete.

commit cycle In System/38, the sequence of changes made between commitment boundaries.

commit cycle identifier In System/38, the journal sequence number associated with the start commitment entry that is used to identify the journal entries in a particular commit cycle.

commit identifier In the AS/400 system and System/38, the information that associates a commitment operation with a specific set of database changes. The commit ID is placed in the notify object if a system or routing step failure occurs, or if uncommitted changes exist when a routing step ends normally. See also notify object.

commitment, concurrency, and recovery (CCR) An application service element that controls operations performed by two or more application processes on shared data to ensure that the operations are performed either completely or not at all. (T)

commitment boundary In a commitment controlled environment, a point at which there are no changes to a database file pending within a job.

commitment control In FORTRAN, a means of grouping file operations that allows the processing of a group of database changes as a single unit or the removal of a group of database changes as a single unit.

commitment definition In the AS/400 system, information used by the system to maintain the commitment control environment throughout a routing step and, in the case of a system failure, throughout an initial program load IPL. This information is obtained from the Start Commitment Control command, which establishes the commitment control environment, and the file open information in a routing step.

commitment function In CICS/VS, a synchronization processing function that allows a transaction program involved in a synchronized unit of work to ensure that all restorable resources associated with that unit are brought to a constant state of update. See also preparation function.

commit operation An operation that saves a file in permanent storage.

commit point In SQL, the point in time when data is considered to be consistent.

committed change A database change that will not be backed out during system failure. Changes made by a

logical unit of work are committed when the synchronization point at the end of the logical unit of work is complete.

committed state The state of the resources associated with a synchronized unit of work following successful execution of the commitment function.

common action In SAA Common User Access architecture, one of a set of actions that has common meaning across all applications; for example, exit, cancel, help.

common address space section (CASS) In DPPX, subpools in all address spaces that are associated with the same real storage location. This area is addressable by any process running in any address space. It is made up of the read-only and read-write subpools.

common area (1) A control section used to reserve a main storage area that can be referred to by other modules. (2) In OS/VS2, the area of virtual storage that is addressable by all address spaces. (3) In FORTRAN, a storage area that is used for communication between a main program and one or more subprograms.

common battery central office A central office that supplies transmitter and signal current for its associated stations and for signaling by the central office equipment from a power source located in the central office. See also tip.

common block In XL FORTRAN, a storage area that can be referred to by a calling program and one or more subprograms.

common buffer In DPCX, a block of processor storage made up of four 256-byte blocks that can be used by all active programs.

common carrier See communication common carrier.

common communication adapter (CCA) A general purpose adapter that inserts or removes control information and converts message data into an appropriate form for the terminal in which the data are used.

Common Communications Support Protocols and conventions for connecting systems and software. One of the three SAA architectural areas. See also Common Programming Interface, Common User Access architecture.

common field A field that can be accessed by two or more independent routines. (A)

common key In COBOL, the key fields that are common to all record formats in the file starting with the first key field (the most significant) and ending with the last key field (the least significant).

common language A language in machine-sensible form that is common to a group of computers and associated equipment.

common library In VSE, an interactively accessible library that can be accessed by any user of the system or subsystem that owns the library.

common mode rejection The capability of a differential amplifier to suppress the effects of the common mode voltage. (T)

common mode voltage In a differential amplifier, the unwanted part of the voltage, between each input connection point and ground, that is added to the voltage of each original signal. (T)

common network In SNA, deprecated term for path control (PC) network.

common operations services (COS) The portion of SNA management services that pertains to the major vectors for limited remote operations control.

common program In COBOL, a program that, despite being directly contained within another program, may be called from any program directly or indirectly contained in the other program.

Common Programming Interface Definitions of those application development languages and services that have, or are intended to have, implementations on and a high degree of commonality across the SAA environments. One of the three SAA architectural areas. See also Common Communications Support, Common User Access architecture.

common segment In an overlay structure, an overlay segment on which two exclusive segments depend.

common service area In OS/VS2, a part of the common area that contains data areas addressable by all address spaces. These data areas are protected during use by the key of the requester.

Common User Access (CUA) architecture Guidelines for the dialog between a human and a workstation or terminal. One of the three SAA architectural areas. See also Common Programming Interface, Common Communications Support.

common-use sizes A set of paper form sizes most commonly used throughout the world.

Note: Common-use sizes are used on the 3800 Printing Subsystem.

communicating text processor A functional unit that can transmit and receive information. (T) (A)

communicating word processing equipment Word processing equipment capable of transmission and reception of text, data, or both, using telecommunication techniques. (T)

communication adapter (1) An optional hardware feature, available on certain processors, that permits communication facilities to be attached to the processors. (T) (2) A circuit card with associated software that enables a processor, controller, or other device to be connected to a network. (3) A mechanism that enables communication facilities to be attached to host processors. (4) See EIA communication adapter, V.35 communication adapter, X.21 communication adapter.

communication area On the screen of a 3790 display component, the second of four areas in the system control area; it provides system communication and instructions for the operator and displays error conditions, operator actions, or both, as required for program continuation. See also operator guidance indicator, system control area.

communication authority password In the AIX operating system, one of the two communications security passwords. It controls access to communication configuration menus so that only authorized persons can change the profiles, encrypt a portion of the communication profile database, or control the startup of processes. See also BIND password.

communication card In a personal computer, an expansion board that contains a modem or that allows use of network services. See Figure 34.

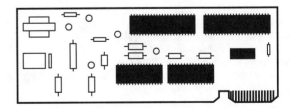

Figure 34. Communication Card

communication channel See data communication channel.

communication common carrier In the USA and Canada, a public data transmission service that provides the general public with transmission service facilities; for example, a telephone or telegraph company. See also Post Telephone and Telegraph Administration, public data network, public data transmission service, Recognized Private Operating Agency, telecommunication administration.

communication control character (1) Synonym for transmission control character. (2) Synonym for data link control character.

communication controller (1) A device that directs the transmission of data over the data links of a network; its operation may be controlled by a program executed in a processor to which the controller is connected or it may be controlled by a program executed within the device. (T) (2) A type of communication control unit whose operations are controlled by one or more programs stored and executed in the unit. It manages the details of line control and the routing of data through a network. (3) See also cluster controller, communication controller node, transmission control unit.

communication controller node A subarea node that does not contain a system services control point (SSCP). See also NCP node.

Communication Control Program (CCP) A portion of the network control program communication interrupt control program (CICP) that initiates and ends I/O line operations, handles first-level line error recovery and recording, and administers commands issued by background programs. See also communication interrupt control program.

communication control unit A communication device that controls transmission of data over lines in a network.

communication coprocessor Synonym for networking coprocessor.

communication description entry In COBOL, an entry in the Communication Section of the Data Division that is composed of the level indicator.

communication device In COBOL, a hardware or software device that can send data to a queue, receive data from a queue, or both.

Note: This mechanism may be a computer or a peripheral device. One or more programs containing communication description entries and residing within the same computer define one or more of these mechanisms.

communication facility See telecommunication facility.

communication field In DPCX, the second of four areas on the bottom line of a display during field-by-field operations. It communicates error conditions and operator actions required for program continuation. See also command field, message field, mode field.

communication file (1) A device file created by the user to support LU1 or advanced program-to-program communication. Contrast with BSC file. (2) In the System/36 interactive data definition utility (IDDU), a file that describes an advanced program-to-program communication (APPC) subsystem session between a System/36 program and a remote device, another program, or another system.

communication file definition The format in the communication file that contains the APPC subsystem session description.

communication identifier (CID) In VTAM programs, a key for locating the control blocks that represent a session. The key is created during session establishment and deleted when the session ends.

communication interface See transmission interface.

communication interrupt control program A portion of the network control program that controls operation of the telecommunication lines and line adapters. It consists primarily of the character service program and the communication control program.

communication line Deprecated term for telecommunication line.

communication line adapter (CLA) A functional unit that converts the serial-by-bit output of a station to a parallel bit form and from a parallel bit form to serial-by-bit input to a station.

communication link See data link.

communication macroinstructions In VTAM programs, the set of RPL-based macroinstructions used to communicate during a session.

communication management configuration (1) In VTAM programs, a technique for configuring a network that allows for the consolidation of many network management functions for the entire network in a single host processor. (2) A multiple-domain network configuration in which one of the hosts, called the communication management configuration host, performs most of the controlling functions for the network, thus allowing the other hosts, called data hosts, to process applications. This is accomplished by configuring the network so that the communication management host owns most of the resources in the network that are not application programs. The resources that are not owned by the communication management host are the resources that are channel-attached stations of data hosts.

communication mgmt configuration host node The type 5 host processor in a communication management configuration that does all network-control functions in the network except for the control of devices channel-attached to data hosts. Synonymous with communication management host. See also data host node.

communication management host Synonym for communication management configuration host node. See also data host node.

communication network See data network, distributed data processing network, path control network, public network, remote access data processing network, SNA network, user application network.

communication network management (CNM) The process of designing, installing, operating, and managing distribution of information and control among users of communication systems.

communication parameter list The means of transferring information between ACF/TCAM operator control and the master scheduler for commands entered from the system console.

communication port (1) An access point for data entry or exit to or from a communication device such as a terminal. (2) On a personal computer, a serial port to which a stand-alone modem can be attached. (3) A physical location on an 8101 Storage and Input/Output Unit, an 8130 Processor, or an 8140 Processor with a specific physical I/O address. Features for attaching terminal devices are assigned to communication ports.

communication queue A list used for mail that keeps track of documents to be sent to independent workstation users, local users, and other systems.

communication region In VSE, an area of the supervisor that is set aside for transfer of information within and between programs.

communication routing table A table that lists the remote locations used for sending and receiving mail.

communications See data communication.

communications and systems management (C & SM) In the AS/400 system, a part of the system that contains the remote management support, also referred to as DHCF, the change management support, referred to as DSNX, and the problem management support, referred to as alerts.

communications area In AS/400 query management, a control block used to communicate between the system code supporting the Common Programming

Interface (CPI) and the application program using the CPI.

communication scanner A communication controller hardware unit that provides the connection between lines and the central control unit. The communication scanner monitors telecommunication lines and data links for service requests.

communication scanner processor (CSP) A processor in the 3725 Communication Controller that contains a microprocessor with control code. The code controls transmission of data over links attached to the CSP.

communications controller See communication controller.

Communication Section In COBOL, the section of the Data Division that describes the interface areas between the message control system (MCS) and the program; it is composed of one or more communication description entries.

communication server In a personal computer, a microprocessor, often on an expansion board, that handles operations between a computer and transmission facilities.

communication services (CS) (1) In DPPX, a level of communication support that is available through the data-stream interface using SEND and RECEIVE macroinstructions. (2) In DPCX, a part of program services that provides methods for programs to exchange data with the host system. (3) See transmission service.

communications feature type In the AS/400 system, the 4-digit number that IBM assigns to identify the different packages of communications cards and cables available on the system.

communications line See telecommunication line.

communications link See data link.

communications management configuration See communication management configuration.

communications management host See communication management host.

Communications Manager A function of the OS/2 Extended Edition program that lets a workstation connect to a host computer and use the host resources as well as the resources of other personal computers to which the workstation is attached, either directly or through a host system. Communications Manager provides application programming interfaces (APIs) so that users can develop their own applications.

communications security (COMSEC) (1) Measures taken to deny unauthorized persons information derived from telecommunications, and to ensure the authenticity of such telecommunications. Communications security consists of cryptosecurity, transmission security, emission security, and physical security. (2) In the AS/400 system, a system option that requires the identity of a remote location to be verified before that location can run programs on the system.

commun. statistical network analysis procedure A procedure that allows service personnel to obtain statistics on telecommunication line activity.

communications subsystem See subsystem.

communications type In the AS/400 system, a method by which application programs communicate on a local system, or between a local system and a remote system, using the intersystem communications function (ICF). Examples of these communications methods include: (a) asynchronous communications, (b) binary synchronous communications (BSC), (c) finance communications, (d) intrasystem communications, (e) retail communications, and (f) Systems Network Architecture (SNA), such as Advanced Program-to-Program Communication (APPC) and SNA upline facility (SNUF).

communication task In OS/VS, the part of job management that handles transfer of messages between the operator console and the system.

communication theory (1) The mathematical discipline dealing with the probabilistic features of the transmission of messages in the presence of noise and any other disturbances. (I) (A) (2) Deprecated term for information theory.

community automatic exchange (CAX) A small dial telephone office serving a community.

commutative Combining mathematical elements or having elements that combine in a way that the result is independent of the order in which they are processed; for example, such that a + b = b + a and a x b = b x a.

compact Synonym for compress. (A)

compact disc (CD) (1) A disc, usually 4.75 inches in diameter, from which data is read optically by means of a laser. (2) A disc with information stored in the form of pits along a spiral track. The information is decoded by a compact-disc player and interpreted as digital audio data, which most computers can process.

compact disc-digital audio (CD-DA) The specification for audio compact discs. See also Redbook audio.

compact disc-interactive (CD-I) An interactive audio/video/computer system, developed by Sony and Philips for the consumer market, the standards for which are known as the "Green Book."

compact disc-read-only memory (CD-ROM) A 4.75-inch optical memory storage medium, capable of storing about 550 megabytes of data. The standards for CD-ROM storage are known as the "Yellow Book."

compact disc-read only memory extended architecture An extension to CD-ROM that supports additional audio levels for compression and interlacing of audio and digital data.

compaction (1) Any method for encoding data to reduce the storage it requires. (2) In SNA, the transformation of data by packing two characters in a byte so as to take advantage of the fact that only a subset of the allowable 256 characters is used; the most frequently sent characters are compacted. See also compaction table, compression, string control byte. (3) In the Data Facility Hierarchical Storage Manager, a method of compressing and encoding data that migrates or is backed up.

compaction table In SNA, a table used by a sending LU-LU half-session to transform data so that fewer bytes are sent to the receiving half-session. The receiving LU-LU half-session uses the same table to reverse the process, restoring the data to its original form. See also compaction.

companding In video systems, a process of nonlinear quantization used to improve signal-to-noise ratio when digitizing with a limited number of bits per sample.

compandor Compressor-expandor. Equipment that compresses the outgoing speech volume range and expands the incoming speech volume range on a long distance telephone circuit. Such equipment makes efficient use of voice telecommunication channels. See also compressor, expandor.

comparator (1) A functional unit that compares two items of data and indicates the result of the comparison. (T) (2) A device for determining the dissimilarity of two items, such as two pulse patterns or words. (A)

compare (1) To examine two items to discover their relative magnitudes, their relative positions in an order or in a sequence, or whether they are identical in given characteristics. (I) (A) (2) To examine two or more items for identity, similarity, equality, relative magnitude, or order in a sequence. (A)   (3) See logical comparison.

comparison The process of examining two or more items for identity, similarity, equality, relative magnitude, or for order in a sequence. See logical comparison. (A)

comparison definition Two operands separated by a comparison operator that appears on an IF statement.

comparison operator An infix operator used in comparison expressions. Comparison operators are ¬< (not less than), <= (less than or equal to), ¬= (not equal to), = (equal to), >= (greater than or equal to), > (greater than), and ¬> (not greater than).

comparison test A test that compares one value with another. A comparison test is performed within a procedure; the next action performed by the procedure usually depends on the result of the test.

compartment (1) In computer security, a particular category of information within a sensitivity level that is identified by a designation such as "nuclear." (2) A nonhierarchical designation applied to sensitive information in one or more categories to denote special handling and access control restrictions. See also category, classification.

compatibility The capability of a hardware or software component to conform with the interface requirements of a given data processing system without adversely affecting its functions. (T)   See object code compatibility, source code compatibility, type compatibility.

compatibility character sets In the Print Services Facility, library character sets supplied for use in compatibility mode.

compatibility feature A feature that allows one IBM system to run programs written for another IBM system.

compatibility mode A mode of operation for running 3800 Model 1 application programs on the 3800 Model 3 with little or no change to the application or job control language. Contrast with page mode.

compatible (1) Pertaining to computers on which the same programs can be run without appreciable alteration. See also upward compatibility. (2) Pertaining to the capability of hardware or software to meet the requirements of a specified interface. See assignment compatible.

compatible types Pertaining to different data types that can be operands for the same operation.

compilable unit (1) In Pascal and FORTRAN, a block of code that can be compiled independently of the remainder of the program.   (2) In Pascal, a program unit or a segment unit.

compilation Translation of a source program into an executable program (an object program).

compilation time (1) Any instant when the compiler is translating a program. (T)   (2) The time during which a source program is translated from a high-level language to a machine language program.

compilation unit (1) A portion of a computer program sufficiently complete to be compiled correctly. (A)   (2) The source file that a compiler accepts. (3) In Pascal, a program or a segment.

compile (1) To translate all or part of a program expressed in a high-level language into a computer program expressed in an intermediate language, an assembly language, or a machine language. (T) (2) To prepare a machine language program from a computer program written in another programming language by making use of the overall logic structure of the program, or generating more than one computer instruction for each symbolic statement, or both, as well as performing the function of an assembler. (A)   (3) To translate a source program into an executable program (an object program). (4) To translate a program written in a high-level programming language into a machine language program.

compile-and-go An operating technique in which there are no stops between compiling, loading, and execution of a computer program. (A)

compiled knowledge In artificial intelligence, knowledge which has been translated from a declarative form into a procedural form so that it can be immediately processed by a computer. (T)

compiled program The set of machine language instructions that is the output of the compilation of a source program.

compiled statement A high-level language statement translated into machine language.

compile duration Synonym for compiling time.

compile phase The logical subdivision of a run that includes execution of the compiler. (I) (A)   Synonymous with compiling phase.

compiler (1) A translator that can compile. (T) (2) A program that translates a source program into an executable program (an object program).   (3) A program that decodes instructions written as pseudo codes and produces a machine language program to be executed at a later time. See also assembler. (4) A program that translates instructions written in a high-level programming language into machine language. (5) Contrast with interpretive routine. Synonymous with compiling program. See also cross compiler, incremental compiler.

compiler-directing statement (1) In COBOL, a statement, beginning with a compiler-directing verb, that causes the compiler to take a specific action during compilation. The compiler-directing statements are the COPY, ENTER, REPLACE, and USE statements. (2) In RPG, an instruction that controls a compilation listing or causes records to be inserted. The four compiler directives are /TITLE, /EJECT, /SPACE, and /COPY. (3) Synonym for compiler directive.

compiler directive (1) A language construction for the purpose of controlling the compilation of a program. (T) (2) A statement that controls what the compiler does rather than what the user program does. Synonymous with compiler directing statement.

compiler generator A translator or an interpreter that is used to construct compilers. (I) (A)

compiler listing A printout produced by compiling a program or creating a file and that optionally includes, for example, a line-by-line source listing, cross-reference list, diagnostic information, and for programs, a description of externally described files. See also source listing.

compiler options Keywords that can be specified to control certain aspects of compilation. Compiler options can control the nature of the load module generated by the compiler, the types of printed output to be produced, the efficient use of the compiler, and the destination of error messages.

compile-time array In RPG, an array that is compiled with the source program and becomes a permanent part of the program. Contrast with run-time array, prerun-time array.

compile-time statement See preprocessor statement.

compile-time table or array A table or array built into a source program that becomes a permanent part of the compiled program. See also execution-time table or array, preexecution-time table or array.

compiling phase Synonym for compile phase.

compiling program Synonym for compiler.

compiling time (1) The elapsed time taken for execution of a compiler. (I) (A) Synonymous with

compile duration. (2) The time during which a source program is translated by a compiler into an executable program (an object program). (A)

complement A number that can be derived from a specified number by subtracting it from a second specified number; for example, in radix notation, the second specified number may be a given power of the radix or one less than a given power of the radix. The negative of a number is often represented by its complement. (A)

complementary metal oxide semiconductor See CMOS.

complementary operation Of a Boolean operation, another Boolean operation whose result, when performed on the same operands as the first Boolean operation, is the negation of the result of the first Boolean operation; for example, disjunction is the complementary operation of nondisjunction. (I) (A)

complementary operator The logic operator whose result is the NOT of a given logic operator. (A)

complement base In a fixed-radix numeration system, the specified number whose digital representation contains the digits from which the corresponding digits of the given number are subtracted in obtaining a complement of the given number. (I) (A)

complementer A device whose output data are a representation of the complements of the numbers represented by its input data. (T) (A)

complement (of a number) The value that can be added to a number to equal a given value.

complement-on-nine Synonym for nines complement.

complement-on-one Synonym for ones complement.

complement-on-ten Synonym for tens complement.

complement-on-two Synonym for twos complement.

complete carry (1) In parallel addition, a procedure in which each of the carries is immediately transferred. (I) (A) (2) Contrast with partial carry.

completeness check A check to determine whether data are present where data are required. (T)

complete packet sequence Either an individual X.25 data packet or a sequence of packets with the M-bit set to 1 and the D-bit set to 0, followed by another data packet with the M-bit set to 0 and the D-bit set as required.

completion code A return code indicating that an operation has ended.

completion message A message that conveys completion status of work.

complex condition In COBOL, a condition in which one or more logical operators act upon one or more conditions. Contrast with simple condition.

complex constant In FORTRAN, an ordered pair of signed or unsigned real or integer constants separated by a comma and enclosed in parentheses. The first constant of the pair is the real part of the complex number; the second is the imaginary part.

complex data Arithmetic data, each item of which consists of a real part and an imaginary part.

complex number A number consisting of an ordered pair of real numbers, expressible in the form a+bi, where a and b are real numbers and i squared equals minus one. (I) (A)

complex type In FORTRAN, an approximation of the value of a complex number, consisting of an ordered pair of real data items separated by a comma and enclosed in parentheses. The first item represents the real part of the complex number; the second represents the imaginary part.

compliance The flexible behavior of a robot or any associated tool in response to external forces exerted on it. When the behavior is independent of sensory feedback, it is passive compliance; if not, it is active compliance. (T)

component (1) Hardware or software that is part of a functional unit. (2) A functional part of an operating system; for example, the scheduler or supervisor. (3) A set of modules that performs a major function within a system; for example, a compiler or a master scheduler. (4) In systems with VSAM, a named, cataloged collection of stored records, such as the data component or index component of a key-sequenced file or alternate index. (5) A part of a structured type or value, such as an array element or a record field. (6) In the AIXwindows program or Enhanced X-Windows, the widget, gadget, or other graphical object that makes up an interactive user interface. (7) In Pascal, the name of each separate value, where a variable has multiple values in a structured type. (8) In System/38 graphics, the representation of a data group on a chart. (9) See solid state component, terminal component.

component address The fixed address of a terminal component, not the address of the terminal itself.

component code A code consisting of three or four alphabetic characters that IBM assigns to system and application licensed programs to ensure uniqueness of filenames and component names and that customers use to ensure uniqueness of their filenames.

Note: IBM component codes use the letters A through I in the first character position. Customers use the letters J through Z in the first position. See also information file prefix code.

component entry In ACF/TCAM, a terminal-table entry associated with a component of a binary synchronous or start-stop station that may be individually addressed.

component failure impact analysis (CFIA) An account management technique that determines the impact of a critical system component failure.

component video In multimedia applications, a video signal using three signals, one of which is luminance, and the other two of which are the color vectors. See also composite video, S-video.

composed page In the 3800 Printing Subsystem, a page that can be printed only on an all-points-addressable output medium. It may contain composed text and raster images. Contrast with formatted page.

composed-text block In the Print Services Facility, an internal object that specifies text and optional text controls defined entirely in structured fields.

composed-text data stream A data stream that contains a composed text format print data set.

composed-text page A page composed entirely of structured fields; this type of page is usually the output of a text formatting program, such as the Document Composition Facility.

composed-text print data set A data set that is the output of a text formatting program such as the Document Composition Facility. It is composed entirely of structured fields.

composed view A view of an object in which relationships of the parts contribute to the overall meaning. Composed views are provided primarily for data objects. See also contents view, help view.

composite In multimedia applications, the combination of two or more film, video, or electronic images into a single frame or display. See also composite video.

composite bar chart In GDDM, a bar chart in which multiple vertical axis values for the same horizontal axis value are stacked one on top of another. Contrast with multiple bar chart.

composite console A console consisting of two different physical devices that are considered as one unit. One device is used for input and the other for output; for example, a reader and printer.

composite data element Synonym for data aggregate. (A)

composited circuit A circuit that can be used simultaneously for telephone and direct-current telegraph or signaling applications; separation between the two is accomplished by frequency discrimination.

composite end node (CEN) A group of nodes made up of a single type 5 node and its subordinate type 4 nodes that together support type 2.1 protocols. To a type 2.1 node, a CEN appears as one end node; for example, NCP and the VTAM programs act as a composite end node.

composite external symbol dictionary Control information associated with a load module that identifies the external symbols in the module.

composite file In the 3600 Finance Communication System, a logical grouping of two or more temporary files or of specified subfiles within a temporary file.

composite key A key for a file or record format composed of more than one key field.

composite LEN node A type 5 node and its subordinate type 4 nodes that support LEN protocols and appear to an attached APPN or LEN node as a single LEN node.

Composite Manager In the AIXwindows program, a manager widget with special knowledge about the handling of one or more of its child widgets. Normally, a manager widget has no knowledge of its children, but a TitleBar widget and a ScrollBar widget can be registered as children of a certain type of Composite Manager widget known as a Panel widget, and the Panel widget will correctly control the positioning of the TitleBar and ScrollBar widgets.

composite monitor A monitor that can decode a color image from a single signal, such as NTSC or PAL signals.

composite network node A type 5 node and its subordinate type 4 nodes that support APPN network node protocols and appear to an attached APPN or LEN node as a single network node.

composite node A composite LEN node or a composite network node.

composite object An object that contains other objects; for example, a document object that contains not only text, but also graphics, audio, image, and video objects, each of which can be manipulated separately as an individual object.

composite operator An operator composed of two operator symbols; for example, ¬>. Synonymous with composite symbol.

composite symbol Synonym for composite operator.

composite video A single signal composed of chroma, luminance, and sync. NTSC is the composite video that is currently the U.S. standard for television. See also component video, S-video.

composite widget In the AIX Enhanced X-Windows program, a widget that is a container for an arbitrary, implementation-defined collection of children. These children may be instantiated by the composite widget itself, by other clients, or by a combination. Composite widgets contain methods for managing the geometry (layout) of any child widget. See also constraint widget.

composite widget class In AIX Enhanced X-Windows, a metaclass that does not instantiate any widgets of its own, but provides the resources and functionality that allow parent widgets to manage the layout and mapping of their child widgets and gadgets.

composite window A window composed of other windows (such as a frame window, frame-control windows, and a client window) that are kept together as a unit and that interact with each other.

composition The act or result of formatting a document.

compound command processor A series of commands that appears to run as a single command. It can have interactions with other tasks or with tasks in other domains.

compound condition In COBOL, a statement that tests two or more relational expressions. The result can be true or false.

compound object In the AIXwindows program, a graphical object made up of several widgets and gadgets collected within a single container widget.

compound statement (1) In programming languages, a statement constructed by sequencing statements. Most often the statements are grouped together by some syntactic device. (I) (2) A statement whose statement body contains one or more other statements.

compound string A type of string designed to simplify national language support by allowing text to be displayed without hard-coding language-dependent attributes such as character sets and text.

compress (1) In a character string, to reduce the space taken on a data medium by repetitive characters. (T) (2) To save storage space by eliminating gaps, empty fields, redundancy, or unnecessary data to shorten the length of records or files. (3) To move files, libraries, or folders together on disk to create a continuous area of unused space.

compressed audio Audio resulting from the process of digitally encoding and decoding up to 40 seconds of voice-quality audio for each individual videodisc, resulting in a potential for over 150 hours of audio per 12-inch videodisc. Synonymous with still-frame audio.

compressed disk file In System/36, a file that contains unprocessed records.

compressed encoding (1) A process in which a contiguous string of bits, characters, or data units is reduced to a shorter string in such a way that a second contiguous string, yielding the same short string, cannot be found and the process cannot be reversed. (2) A process in which variable-length messages are reduced to a shorter, fixed-length message.

compressed pattern storage Storage that holds the extended fonts for the 3800 printer.

compressed video Video resulting from the process of digitally encoding and decoding a video image or segment using a variety of computer techniques to reduce the amount of data required to represent the content accurately.

compression (1) The process of eliminating gaps, empty fields, redundancies, and unnecessary data to shorten the length of records or blocks. (2) In SNA, the replacement of a string of up to 64 repeated characters by an encoded control byte to reduce the length of the data stream sent to the LU-LU session partner. The encoded control byte is followed by the character that was repeated (unless that character is the prime compression character). See also compaction, string control byte. (3) In Data Facility Hierarchical Storage Manager, the process of moving data instead of allocated space during migration and recall in order to release unused space. (4) Contrast with decompression.

compressor An electronic device that compresses the volume range of a signal. See also compandor, expandor.

COM printer A page printer that produces on a photographic film a microimage of each page. Synonymous with computer output microfilm printer. (T) (A)

compromise In computer security, a violation of the security policy of a system in which unauthorized intentional or unintentional disclosure, modification, or destruction, or loss, of an object, may have occurred.

compromise net A network, used in conjunction with a hybrid coil to balance a subscriber's loop, that is adjusted for an average loop length or an average subscriber's set, or both, to secure compromise (not precision) isolation between the two directional paths of the hybrid.

compromising emanations In computer security, unintentional intelligence-bearing signals that may convey data and that, if intercepted and analyzed, may compromise sensitive information being processed or transmitted by a computer system.

COMPUSEC Computer security.

computational stability The degree to which a computational process remains valid when subjected to effects such as errors, mistakes, or malfunctions. (A)

compute mode That operating mode of an analog computer during which the solution is in progress. Synonymous with operate mode. (T)

computer A functional unit that can perform substantial computations, including numerous arithmetic operations and logic operations without human intervention during a run. In information processing, the term computer usually describes a digital computer. A computer may consist of a stand-alone unit or may consist of several interconnected units. (T)

computer abuse In computer security, a willful or negligent unauthorized activity that affects the availability, confidentiality, or integrity of computer resources. Computer abuse includes fraud, embezzlement, theft, malicious damage, unauthorized use, denial of service, and misappropriation. See also information system abuse.

computer-aided (CA) Pertaining to a technique or process in which part of the work is done with the assistance of a data processing system. Synonymous with computer-assisted. (T)

computer-aided design (CAD) The use of a computer to design or change a product, tool, or machine, such as using a computer for drafting or illustrating.

Note: Sometimes, CAD and CAM are used together and expressed as CAD/CAM. (T)

computer-aided engineering (CAE) Analysis of a design to check for basic errors, or to optimize manufacturability, performance or economy; for example, by comparing various possible materials or designs.

Note: Information from the CAD/CAM design database is used to analyze the functional characteristics of a part, product under design, and to simulate its performance under various conditions. (T)

computer-aided industry (CAI) The use of computer systems to assist in the operation of an industry. (T)

computer-aided instruction (CAI) The use of a computer to assist human instruction. (T) Synonymous with computer-assisted instruction.

computer-aided manufacturing (CAM) The use of computer technology to direct and control the manufacturing process. (T)

computer-aided planning (CAP) All activities for preparation of the basic data about production processes by usage of computer technology. (T)

computer-aided publishing Synonym for electronic publishing. (T)

computer-aided quality assurance (CAQ) The use of computer technology to plan, monitor and control processes, parts and products throughout all phases of the product life cycle; this includes an overall quality report system from design to field performance and from shop floor to the management. (T)

computer-aided retrieval (CAR) Systems that combine the document storage capabilities of micrographics with the indexing and retrieval capabilities of a computer database.

computer-aided software engineering (CASE) (1) The automation of well-defined methodologies that are used in the development and maintenance of products. These methodologies apply to nearly every process or activity of a product development cycle, examples of which include project planning and tracking, product designing, coding, and testing. (2) A set of computer-based development tools to automate certain portions of methodologies. Thus, CASE tools work within a methodology rather than compose a methodology themselves. See also CCASE, ICASE.

computer-animated graphics In multimedia applications, graphics animated by means of a computer, rather than videotape or film.

computer architecture (1) The logical structure and functional characteristics of a computer, including the interrelationships among its hardware and software components. (T) (2) The organizational structure of a computer system, including hardware and software. (A) (3) See also hypercube, parallel processor architecture.

computer-assisted Synonym for computer-aided (CA). (T)

computer-assisted instruction (CAI) Synonym for computer-aided instruction.

computer-assisted publishing Synonym for electronic publishing. (T)

computer-based training Synonym for computer-assisted instruction.

computer center A facility that includes people, hardware, and software, organized to provide information processing services. Synonymous with data processing center, installation. (T) (A)

computer conferencing Computerized communication that allows people distant from each another to enter and receive text and graphic messages via interconnected terminals. (T) See also conference call, teleconferencing, videoconferencing.

computer crime (1) In computer security, a crime committed through the use of software or data. (T) (2) A crime committed through the use of software or data residing in a computer. (T) (A)

computer cryptography In computer security, the use of a cryptographic algorithm in a computer to perform encryption and decryption to protect information or to authenticate users, sources, or information.

computer edit system A video editing system, controlled by a computer and connected to machines for recording and playback.

computer-dependent language Synonym for computer-oriented language.

computer fraud (1) In computer security, a computer crime that involves deliberate misrepresentation or alteration of data in order to obtain something of value, usually for monetary gain. (T) (2) Deception by means of a computer, deliberately practiced in order to secure unfair or unlawful gain. (A)

computer generation A category in a historical classification of computers based mainly on the technology used in their manufacture; for example, first generation based on relays or vacuum tubes, the second on transistors, the third on integrated circuits. (T)

computer graphics (1) Methods and techniques for converting data to or from graphic display via computers. (T) (2) That branch of science and technology concerned with methods and techniques for converting data to or from visual presentation, using computers. (A) (3) See also coordinate graphics, fixed-image graphics, interactive graphics, passive graphics, raster graphics.

computer input microfilm (CIM) A reversal of the digital-to-microimage process. Mixed media such as illustrations, graphics, and text can be digitized by a variety of methods and condensed into OCR-font CIM, then entered into the computer through an OCR workstation to update or create a document. See also optical character recognition (OCR).

computer instruction Synonym for machine instruction. (T)

computer instruction code Synonym for instruction code. (T)

computer instruction set A complete set of the operators of the instructions of a computer together with a description of the types of meanings that can be attributed to their operands. (A) Synonymous with machine instruction set.

computer-integrated manufacturing (CIM) The integration of computer operations, communications, and organizational functions for total factory automation.

Note: CIM comprises the information-technological cooperation between CAD, CAP, CAM, CAQ, and PPS. (T)

computerization Automation by means of computers. (T) (A)

computerize To automate by means of computers. (T)

computerized branch exchange (CBX) An exchange in which a central node acts as a high-speed switch to establish direct connections between pairs of attached nodes.

computer language Synonym for machine language.

computer micrographics Methods and techniques for converting data to or from microform with the assistance of a computer. (I) (A)

computer-name In COBOL, a system-name that identifies the computer on which a program is to be compiled or run.

computer network (1) A network of data processing nodes that are interconnected for the purpose of data communication. (T) (2) A complex consisting of two or more connected computing units. (A)

computer numerical control (CNC) A technique in which a machine-tool control uses a computer to store numerical-control instruction which has been generated by CAD/CAM for controlling the machine. (T)

computer operation (1) Synonym for machine operation. (T) (2) One of the elementary operations that a computer is designed to perform. (A) Synonymous with machine operation.

computer-oriented language (1) A programming language that reflects the structure of a given computer or that of a given class of computers. (I) (A) Synonymous with low-level language. (2) A programming language whose words and syntax are designed for use on a specific class of computers. (A) Synonymous with computer-dependent language, machine-oriented language. (3) See also computer language.

computer output microfilm (COM) Microfilm that contains data recorded directly from computer-generated signals. (T)

Note: The abbreviation COM is also used for the technique (computer output microfilming) and for the device (computer output microfilmer).

computer output microfilm (COM) printer A page printer that produces a micro-image of each page on a photographic film. (T)

computer output microfilmer A device for computer output microfilming. (T) (A)

computer output microfilming (COM) A technique for converting and recording data from a computer directly to a microfilmer. (A)

computer program A sequence of instructions suitable for processing by a computer. Processing may include the use of an assembler, a compiler, an interpreter, or a translator to prepare the program for execution, as well as the execution of the program. The sequence of instructions may include statements and necessary declarations. (T) (A)

computer program annotation Synonym for comment.

computer program origin The address assigned to the initial storage location of a computer program in main storage. (A)

computer resource Synonym for resource. (T)

computer science The branch of science and technology that is concerned with methods and techniques relating to data processing performed by automatic means. (T) (A)

computer security (COMPUSEC) (1) Concepts, techniques, technical measures, and administrative measures used to protect the hardware,software, and data of an information processing system from deliberate or inadvertent unauthorized acquisition, damage, destruction, disclosure, manipulation, modification, or use, or loss. (2) Protection resulting from the application of computer security *(1)*.

Note: Technical measures include system mechanisms for protecting programs and data such as access control, information flow control, encryption, and privileged states. Administrative measures include controls outside the system for involving personnel and the physical security of the computing system such as authorization, clearances, privacy protection, and auditing controls. Computer security also involves networks and telecommunication facilities to which computer systems are connected.

computer security incident An adverse event associated with a computer system that: (a) is a failure to comply with security regulations or directives, or (b) results in suspected or actual compromise of information, or (c) results in the misuse, loss, or damage of property or information.

computer security model A mathematical description of the subjects, objects and other entities of a system for the purpose of analyzing the security of the system.

Note: Computer security models include Bell-LaPadula, Biba, Clark-Wilson, lattice, and take-grant.

computer simulator A computer program that translates computer programs prepared for a computer of one model for execution on a computer of a different model. (I) (A)

computer system (1) A functional unit, consisting of one or more computers and associated software, that uses common storage for all or part of a program and also for all or part of the data necessary for the execution of the program; executes user-written or user-designated programs; performs user-designated data manipulation, including arithmetic operations and logic operations; and that can execute programs that modify themselves during their execution. A computer system may be a stand-alone unit or may consist of several interconnected units. Synonymous with ADP system, computing system. (A) (2) Synonym for data processing system.

computer-system audit An examination of the procedures used in a computer system to evaluate their effectiveness and correctness, and to recommend improvements. (T)

computer system fault tolerance The ability of a computer system to continue to operate correctly even though one or more of its component parts are malfunctioning. The speed of performance, the throughput, or both, may be diminished from normal until the faults are corrected. Synonymous with computer system resilience. (I) (A)

computer system resilience Synonym for computer system fault tolerance. (I) (A)

computer system security Synonym for data processing system security.

computer time In simulation, the time required to process the data that represent a process or that represent a part of a process. (A)

computer word (1) A word suitable for processing by a given computer, usually treated as a unit. (T) (2) Synonymous with machine word. (3) See also halfword.

computing system Synonym for data processing system. (T) (A)

computing system catalog In the Data Facility Hierarchical Storage Manager, the master catalog and any associated user catalogs used as sources during the audit process.

computing system RPQ A customer request for a price quotation on alterations or additions to the functional capabilities of a computing system, hardware product, or device. The RPQ may be used in conjunction with programming RPQs to solve unique data processing problems. See also programming RPQ, RPQ.

COMSEC Communications security.

COMWRITE The subtask of the TCAM initiator that formats and writes trace records to the COMWRITE data set.

COMWRITE data set A TCAM data set on a sequential storage device in which trace information is written.

concatenate (1) To link together. (2) To join two character strings.

concatenated data sets A group of logically connected data sets that are treated as one data set for the duration of a job step.

concatenated field Two or more fields from a physical file record format that have been combined to make one field in a logical file record format.

concatenated key In IMS/VS, the key constructed to access a particular segment. It consists of the key fields, including those of the root segment and successive child segments, down to the key fields of the accessed segment.

concatenation (1) An operation that joins two characters or strings in the order specified, forming one string whose length is equal to the sum of the lengths of the two characters or strings. (2) In AIX graphics, combining a series of geometric transformations such as rotations, translations, and scaling. Concatenation of transformations corresponds to matrix multiplication.

concatenation operator A symbol used to join two characters or strings of characters.

concentrated messages Incoming messages from a group of terminals directed to a remote device that combines them into a single physical message for forwarding to the processing unit. Or, conversely, a single physical message made up of a group of messages for a group of terminals that is sent by the processing unit to a remote device for deconcentration.

concentration (1) The process of combining multiple messages into a single message for transmission. Contrast with deconcentration. (2) Synonym for blocking. (3) See line concentration.

concentrator (1) In data transmission, a functional unit that permits a common transmission medium to serve more data sources than there are channels currently available within the transmission medium. (T) (2) Any device that combines incoming messages into a single message (concentration) or extracts individual messages from the data sent in a single transmission sequence (deconcentration). (3) See wiring concentrator. (4) See also blocking, deblocking.

concentrator data ready queue (DRQ) An ACF/TCAM data area used to aid in concentrating messages for output to each concentrator defined in the ACF/TCAM system. It contains a pointer to the element chain, a link address, and a pointer to the STCB chain.

concentrator device ID table (DVCID) An ACF/TCAM work area that defines a concentrator and each terminal attached to it. Each concentrator defined in the ACF/TCAM system has a concentrator device ID table, which consists of a control area containing information about the entire table; an entry for the concentrator; and one entry for each of the attached terminals.

concept statement A description of a proposed product which helps in the market segmentation process. Used primarily in consumer product development.

conceptualization principle In a conceptual schema language, a description of only the conceptually relevant aspects, both static and dynamic, of the universe of discourse, excluding all aspects of external or internal data representation, physical data organization and access procedures, as well as particular user external representation such as message formats and data structures. (T) (A)

conceptual level In a database, all aspects dealing with the interpretation and manipulation of information describing a particular universe of discourse or entity world in an information processing system. (T)

conceptual model In a database, a representation of a universe of discourse, using entities and entity relationships. (T)

conceptual schema (1) In a database, a consistent collection of sentences expressing the necessary propositions that hold for a universe of discourse. (T) (2) In a database, a schema that describes a conceptual model.

conceptual schema language A database language for formulating the sentences in a conceptual schema and an information base and for manipulating them in terms of actions, commands, and command conditions. (T)

conceptual subschema In a database, a part of a conceptual schema for one or more applications. (T)

conceptual system design A system design activity concerned with specifying the logical aspects of the system organization, its processes, and the flow of information through the system. (T)

concurrence In audio visual systems, the simultaneous transmission of audio and video signals.

concurrent (1) Pertaining to processes that take place within a common interval of time during which they may have to alternately share common resources; for example, several programs, when executed by multiprogramming in a computer having a single instruction control unit, are concurrent. (T) (2) Contrast with simultaneous. (3) See also consecutive, sequential.

concurrent control count In SNA, the number of control points concurrently controlling a network resource. See also share limit.

concurrently shared resource In ACF/TCAM, a resource that is defined to more than one host node and can be owned by up to eight host nodes at a time. Concurrently shared resources can be network control programs, SDLC peripheral links, or SDLC subarea links. See also serially shared resources.

concurrent maintenance The capability that allows a service representative to perform a hardware maintenance action while normal operations continue without interruption. See also nondisruptive installation, nondisruptive removal.

concurrent operation A processing mode in which two or more operations are performed within a given interval of time. (I) (A)

concurrent peripheral operations Synonym for spooling.

concur role Provide a mandatory concurrence or non-concurrence position for an organization.

condense In System/36, to move library members together in a library to create one continuous area of unused space in the library.

condition (1) One of a set of specified values that a data item can assume. (2) An expression in a program or procedure that can be evaluated as either true or false when the program or procedure is running. (3) In the C language, a relational expression that can be evaluated to a value of either true or false. (4) In COBOL, the status of a program at object time for which a truth value can be determined. (5) In FORTRAN, a named circumstance in which it is inappropriate to continue the normal execution sequence.

conditional access list In RACF, an access list within a resource profile that associates a condition with a userid or group id and the corresponding access authority. Contrast with standard access list.

Note: The user can access the resource at the specified access authority only while the condition is true. For example, for program access to data sets, the condition is that the user must be executing the program specified in the access list.

conditional assembly An assembler facility for altering at preassembly time the content and sequence of source statements to be assembled.

conditional branching In video systems, an instruction that causes the program to branch if a specified condition is satisfied and otherwise to proceed in the normal sequence.

conditional branch instruction Deprecated term for conditional jump instruction.

conditional capture In the IBM 3886 Optical Character Reader with the picture processing feature, the activation of picture capture because of the discovery of a reject character in a designated field.

conditional compilation statement A preprocessor statement that causes the preprocessor to process specified code in the file depending on how a specified condition evaluates.

conditional construct In programming languages, a statement or part of a statement that specifies several different execution sequences; for example, a CASE statement, an IF statement. (T) (A)

conditional construction In programming languages, a language construct that specifies several different execution sequences; for example, a CASE statement, an IF statement, a conditional expression in ALGOL. (I)

conditional control transfer instruction Deprecated term for conditional jump instruction.

conditional end bracket (CEB) In SNA, the value (binary 1) of the conditional end bracket indicator in the request header (RH) of the last request of the last chain of a bracket; the value denotes the end of the bracket. Contrast with end bracket. See also bracket, begin bracket.

conditional entropy In information theory, the mean of the measure of information conveyed by the occurrence of any one of a finite set of mutually exclusive and jointly exhaustive events of definite conditional probabilities, given the occurrence of events of another set of mutually exclusive events; in mathematical notation, this means H(x|y) for a set of events $x_1......x_n$ which are dependent on the occurrence of events from another set $y_1......y_m$ with joint probabilities $p(x_i, y_j)$ of the occurrence of both events x_i,y_j equals the mathematical expectation of the conditional information content $I(x_i|y_j)$ of all pairs of events. (I) (A) Synonymous with average conditional information content, mean conditional information content.

conditional expression (1) A statement that compares the relationship, such as greater than or equal, of two items. (2) In COBOL, a simple condition or a complex condition specified in an IF, a PERFORM, or a SEARCH statement. See complex condition, simple condition.

conditional external reference An external reference that causes autolink to be performed.

conditional force (1) In System/36 SORT, the replacement of control field characters before the records are sorted if the control field in the input record contains a particular entry. (2) In the System/38 Conversion Reformat Utility, a function that replaces the specified control field character before the record is resequenced only if the control field in the input record contains a particular entry.

conditional implication operation Synonym for implication.

conditional information content (1) In information theory, a measure of information conveyed by the occurrence of an event of a definite conditional probability, given the occurrence of another event; in mathematical notation, this measure $I(x_i|y_j)$ for an event from the set $x_1......x_n$, that is dependent on the occurrence of another event from the set $y_1......y_m$, equals the logarithm of the reciprocal of the conditional probability $p(x_i|y_j)$ of the occurrence of the event x_i given the occurrence of the event y_j

$$I(x_i|y_j) = \log \frac{1}{p(x_i|y_j)}$$

(I) (A) (2) See average conditional information content, mean conditional information content.

conditional jump (1) A jump that takes place only when the instruction that specifies it is executed and specified conditions are satisfied. (I) (A) (2) Contrast with unconditional jump.

conditional jump instruction (1) A jump instruction that specifies a condition for the jump. (T) (2) An instruction that specifies a conditional jump and the conditions that have to be satisfied for the conditional jump to occur. (I) (A) (3) Contrast with unconditional jump instruction.

conditional phrase In COBOL, a phrase that specifies the action to be taken upon determination of the truth value of a condition resulting from the execution of a conditional statement.

conditional prompting Pertaining to prompting that is provided by the system depending on the values selected by the user for other parameters. Contrast with selective prompting.

conditional statement (1) A statement that permits execution of one of a number of possible operations, with or without a transfer of control; for example, a case statement, a computed GOTO in FORTRAN, an IF statement. (T) (2) A statement used to express an assignment or branch based on specified criteria; for example, an IF-THEN statement. (A) (3) In COBOL, a statement specifying that the truth value of a condition is to be determined and that the subse-

quent action of the object program is dependent on that truth value.

conditional transfer Synonym for conditional jump. (A)

conditional transfer instruction Deprecated term for conditional jump instruction, jump instruction.

conditional variable In COBOL, a data item, one or more values of which has a condition-name assigned to it.

condition code A code that reflects the result of a previous input/output, arithmetic, or logical operation.

condition-incident log (CIL) (1) In DPCX, a record of hardware errors or programming events, primarily used for diagnostic and historical purposes and maintained by the operating system. (2) A record kept by the 3791 Controller of unit incidents (such as a malfunction or not-ready condition of a terminal), machine checks in the 3791 and 3792, system incidents (such as logon rejection, abend, initialization, and shutdown), and incidents related to testing the data link to the host system.

condition indicators (1) In the IBM 8100 Information System, the four bits in a program status vector (PSV) that reflect the result of a previous arithmetic, logical, or I/O operation. (2) In System/38, lights numbered 0 through 15 on the operator/service panel that come on to indicate: (a) specific machine conditions during the IMPL process, or (b) an unusual condition that prevents continuation of normal system operation.

conditioning (1) In data communication, the addition of equipment to a nonswitched voice-grade channel to provide minimum values of line characteristics required for data transmission. (2) In RPG, the use of indicators in a program to control when calculations are done; in a file, the use of indicators or condition names to control when certain functions or operations are done.

conditioning indicator An indicator that shows when calculations are done or which attributes apply to a format or format field.

condition name In a display file, a name used to control the selection of keywords and display locations based on the screen size associated with the display file.

condition-name (1) A user-identified name that assigns a name to a subset of values that a conditional variable may assume. (2) A user-defined word assigned to a status of an implementor-defined switch or device.

Note: When condition-name is used in the general formats, it represents a unique data item reference consisting of a syntactically correct combination of a condition-name, together with qualifiers and subscripts, as required for uniqueness of reference.

condition-name-condition In COBOL, the proposition, for which a truth value can be determined, that the value of a conditional variable is a member of the set of values attributed to a condition-name associated with the conditional variable.

conditions See entry conditions.

condition values In the IBM 8100 Information System, the values assigned to various combinations of the condition indicators; they may be used as mask values in conditional branching operations.

conduit A pipe for protecting electric wires or cables.

conference call Teleconferencing in which all participants are connected through telephone circuits that allow for the transmission of voice and possibly FAX messages. (T)   See also computer conferencing.

conference control Synonym for sensitivity control.

conference microphone On dictation equipment, a microphone specially designed to record speech simultaneously from more than one directional source. (I)

confetti In video systems, the undesirable appearance of small, colored spots caused by signal drop-outs or by other forms of video noise. See also noise.

configuration (1) The manner in which the hardware and software of an information processing system are organized and interconnected. (T)   (2) The physical and logical arrangement of devices and programs that make up a data processing system. See also communications configuration, controller configuration, device configuration. (3) The devices and programs that make up a system, subsystem, or network. (4) In CCP, the arrangement of controllers, lines, and terminals attached to an IBM 3710 Network Controller. Also, the collective set of item definitions that describe such a configuration. (5) See also system configuration.

configuration control board Qualified personnel who evaluate, for approval or disapproval, all proposed changes to the current developmental baseline. (T)

Configuration Control Program (CCP) An IBM licensed program used interactively to define, display, and alter configurations that contain network controllers.

Configuration Exchange Utility In the Network Carrier Interconnect Manager and Agent programs, a host utility that converts configuration data from a carrier management system into a format that can be handled by host network management products, specifically, the NetView and NETCENTER programs. This utility also converts configuration data from the VTAM definition library (VTAMLST) and from NETCENTER network definition files into a format that can be handled by a carrier management system.

configuration file (1) A file that specifies the characteristics of a system or subsystem.   (2) In the ImagePlus System, the file that is created by running the Configuring Facility of the ImagePlus Workstation Program, and which contains the features of a specific ImagePlus workstation.   The file is stored on the installation diskette, and is used by the Installation Facility.

configuration image In the 3600 Finance Communication System, a combination of formatted configuration data with selected modules of controller data; when loaded into 3601 control storage, the configuration image determines the operations of the 3601 Finance Communication Controller.   A configuration image is produced by the Finance Image Processor. The completed image is stored in the 3600 and transmitted later to a 3601 controller.

configuration manager A program that supervises device configuration during initial program load (IPL).

configuration matrix In an ESCON environment, an array of connectivity attributes that appear as rows and columns on a display device and can be used to determine or change active and saved configurations.

configuration member In System/36, a member that defines the attributes of a communication subsystem or line.

configuration procedure The multistep process, performed in the host computer, of constructing a configuration image for a 3601 Finance Communication Controller.

configuration report program (CRP) An SSP utility program that creates a configuration report listing network resources and resource attributes for networks with NCP, EP, PEP, or VTAM programs.

configuration report server (CRS) In the AS/400 system, a function that resides on each ring in an environment of multiple token-ring networks in which configuration is being monitored.   This function receives notifications about inserting and removing stations and notifications about active monitor failures.

configuration restart In the VTAM programs, the recovery facility that can be used after a failure or deactivation of a major node, VTAM, or the host processor, to restore the domain to its status at the time of the failure or deactivation.

Configuration Rules Object Class In the AIX operating system, an object class that contains the configuration rules used by the configuration manager during initial program load (IPL).

Configuration Section In COBOL, a section of the Environment Division that describes overall specifications of source programs and object programs.

configuration services One of the types of network services in a control point (SSCP, NNCP, ENCP, or PUCP). Configuration services activates, deactivates, and records the status of physical units, links, and link stations.

configuration tables The DB2 tables containing system-wide parameters, and defining the interfaces to the Object Distribution Manager.

configure To describe to a system the devices, optional features, and programs installed on the system.

configuring facility A facility of the ImagePlus Workstation Program that allows the user to tailor the ImagePlus Workstation Program software to a specific environment. The output of the configuring process is a diskette that can be installed on each workstation.

confirmation A type of response by a receiver that permits a sender to continue.

confirmation of delivery In the AS/400 system, the automatic notification to the sender of a message, note, or document as to when the message, note, or document is received. Confirmation of delivery must be requested by the sender.

confirm primitive A primitive issued by a service provider to indicate that it has completed a procedure previously invoked by a request primitive at the same service access point. (T)

conflict resolution The technique of resolving the problem of multiple matches in a rule-based system. (T)

conformance In FORTRAN, pertaining to an executable program that uses only the forms and relationships described in *Programming Language FORTRAN, ANSI X3.9-1978* or to a program unit that can be included in an executable program in a manner that allows the executable program to comply with that standard. See core conformance.

conformant string In XL Pascal, a string whose declared length does not match that of a formal parameter. See also formal parameter.

conforming In multimedia applications, performing final editing on film or video using an offline edited master as a guide.

CONFT VTAM configuration table.

conjunct One of a number of subproblems or conditions of a conjunction, all of which are required to be satisfied in order for the conjunction as a whole to be satisfied. (T)

conjunction (1) The Boolean operation whose result has the Boolean value 1 if and only if each operand has the Boolean value 1. (I) (A) Synonymous with AND operation, intersection. (2) Contrast with non-conjunction.

connect data set to line (CDSTL) In SNA, an option that determines how the data terminal ready (DTR) signal to the modem operates. It is used if a DTR indicates an unconditional command from the data terminal equipment (DTE) to the attached data circuit-terminating equipment (DCE) to connect to or remove itself from the network.

connected (1) In VTAM programs, pertaining to a physical unit (PU) or logical unit (LU) with an active physical path to the host processor containing the system services control point (SSCP) that controls the PU or LU. (2) In an ESCON Director, the attribute that, when set, establishes a dedicated connection. Contrast with disconnected. (3) In FORTRAN, pertaining to a unit that refers to a file that refers to the unit.

connected unit In XL FORTRAN, a unit that is connected to a file by either an OPEN, READ, or WRITE statement.

connection (1) In data communication, an association established between functional units for conveying information. (I) (A) (2) In programming, a mechanism that enables interaction among modules, particularly procedure calls to asynchronous procedures; for example, in COBOL, an ENABLE statement establishes a communication connection, and an OPEN statement establishes an input/output connection. (I) (3) In Open Systems Interconnection architecture, an association established by a given layer between two or more entities of the next higher layer for the purpose of data transfer. (T) (4) In VTAM programs, synonym for physical connection. (5) In SNA, the network path that links together two logical units (LUs) in different nodes to enable them to establish communications. (6) In X.25 communication, a virtual circuit between two data terminal equipments (DTEs). A switched virtual circuit (SVC) connection lasts for the duration of a call; a permanent virtual circuit (PVC) is a permanent connection between the DTEs. (7) In AIX Enhanced X-Windows, the inter-process communication (IPC) path between the server and a client program. A client program typically, but not necessarily, has one connection to the server over which requests and events are sent. (8) In system communications, a line over which data can be passed between two systems or between a system and a device. (9) In TCP/IP, the path between two protocol applications that provides reliable data stream delivery service. In Internet, a connection extends from a TCP application on one system to a TCP application on another system. (10) In a telephone call, a logical association between a party and a switch. A call consists of two or more connections. A partial call consists of a connection to a real party along with a connection to a virtual party. (11) In an ESCON Director, an association established between two ports that provides a physical communication path between them.

connection identifier (CID) In the IBM 8100 Information System, a value used to identify a resource. It is returned to the connecting program after connect processing has established a session and must be used on subsequent requests to the resource.

connectionless-mode transmission The transmission of a single unit of data from a source service access point to one or more destination service access points without establishing a connection. (T)

connectionless service A network service for which no acknowledgment is returned to the originating source.

connection location In the AIX operating system, the location on an intermediate device where a child device can be connected.

connection-mode transmission The transmission of units of data from a source service access point to one or more destination service access points via a connection.

Note: The connection is established prior to data transfer and released following data transfer. (T)

connection name In DPPX, a name that establishes a tie between the name a program uses for a resource (data set, program, or application program) and the name given to the resource when it was defined. In most cases, the connection name derives from a program's I/O statement and is assigned to a specific resource with an Associate command.

connection network A representation within an APPN network of a shared-access transport facility (SATF), such as a token ring, that allows nodes identifying their connectivity to the SATF by a common virtual routing node to communicate without having individually defined connections to one another.

connection point manager In SNA, a component of the transmission control layer that: (a) performs session-level pacing of normal-flow requests, (b) checks sequence numbers of received request units, (c) verifies that request units do not exceed maximum permissible size, (d) routes incoming request units to their destinations in the half-session, and (e) enciphers and deciphers FMD request units when cryptography is selected. The connection point manager coordinates the normal and expedited flows for one half-session.

Note: The sending connection point manager in a half-session builds the request/response header (RH) for outgoing request/response units (RUs), and the receiving connection point manager interprets the request/response headers that precede incoming request/response units.

connective In COBOL, a word or a punctuation character that associates a data name, paragraph name, condition name, or text name with its qualifier; links two or more values in a series; or forms a conditional expression.

connectivity (1) The capability of a system or device to be attached to other systems or devices without modification. (T) (2) The capability to attach a variety of functional units without modifying them. (3) In ACF/TCAM, the state of two subareas that have an operative explicit route between them.

connectivity attribute In an ESCON Director, the characteristic that determines a particular element of a port's status. See allowed, blocked, connected, disconnected, prohibited, unblocked.

connectivity capability (1) The capability that allows attachment of a device to a system without requiring physical reconfiguration of the device or its interconnections. (2) In an ESCON Director, the capability that allows logical manipulation of link connections to provide physical device attachment. See also configuration matrix, connectivity control, dynamic connection.

connectivity control In an ESCON Director, the method used to alter a port's connectivity attributes, thereby determining the communication capability of the link attached to that port.

connectivity subsystem (CSS) An expansion frame, such as the 3746 Model 900, that extends connectivity and enhances the performance of the IBM 3745 Communication Controller.

connector (1) A flowchart symbol that represents a break in a flowline and indicates where the flowline is continued. (I) (A) See Figure 35. (2) A means of establishing electrical flow. (A) (3) An electrical part used to join two or more other electrical parts. (4) See also inconnector, outconnector. (5) In an AS/400 query management command, the TO word in the EXPORT command, the FROM word in the IMPORT command, or the AS word in the SAVE DATA command. (6) See external file connector, file connector, internal file connector. (7) See optical fiber connector.

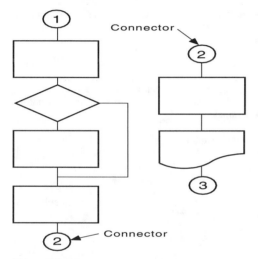

Figure 35. Connectors

connector-induced optical fiber loss In an optical cable, part of the insertion loss, expressed in decibels (dB), caused by termination or handling within the connector, which results in impurities or structural changes to the optical fiber.

connector insertion loss See insertion loss.

connect phase An optional phase of link activation during which initial communication is established. It includes "dialing" and "answering" on switched links and can include modem equalization. The connect phase is followed by the optional prenegotiation phase or by the contact phase.

connect time The length of time that a terminal is connected and able to communicate with a computer. (T) (A)

consecutive In a process, pertaining to two events that follow one another without the occurrence of any

other event between them. (T) Contrast with sequential. See also concurrent, simultaneous.

consecutive operation Synonym for sequential operation.

consecutive organization See consecutive data set organization.

consecutive processing A method of processing in which the records in the file are read, written to, or deleted in the order in which they exist in a file. See also random processing, sequential processing.

consensus processing In the ESCON Manager, the function that informs other hosts of connectivity changes, thereby allowing general agreement for changes to affected resources.

consistency check A check to determine whether specific data items are compatible; for example, a check to determine whether two occurrences of a data item are equal. (T)

console (1) A part of a computer used for communication between the operator or maintenance engineer and the computer. (A) (2) See display console, operator console.

console communication services (CCS) The SNA facility that acts as an interface between the control program and the VSCS component of the VTAM programs for VM.

console display A display at a system console on which an operator can display, send, and reply to messages and use all control commands.

console document copying machine A document copying machine designed to free-stand on the floor. (T)

console function In VM, the subset of CP commands that allows the user to simulate almost all of the functions available to an operator at a real system console. Contrast with CP command.

console input buffer Synonym for console stack.

console spooling See virtual console spooling.

console stack In VM, one or more CMS command or data lines (set up by means of appropriate EXEC or EDIT subcommands) that are passed, one at a time, to CMS when CMS issues a read to the user's terminal. Synonymous with console input buffer, terminal input buffer.

console word processing equipment Word processing equipment incorporated into a larger unit containing other equipment. If it is not integrated word processing equipment, its control unit is usually designed also to fit into the unit. (T)

constant (1) In programming languages, a language object that takes only one specific value. (I) (2) In a calculator, a number entered and held for repeated use. (T) (3) A data item with a value that does not change. (4) In Pascal, a value that is either a literal or an identifier that has been associated with a value in a CONST declaration. (5) In FORTRAN, a symbolic constant, a literal constant, or a subobject of a constant containing no expression in its designator that is not a constant expression. Contrast with variable. (6) Data that have an unchanging, predefined value to be used in processing. A constant does not change during execution of a program, but the contents of a field or variable can. See also literal. (7) Contrast with variable.

constant angular velocity In multimedia applications, a technology in which the angular velocity of a disc is always the same no matter what track is being read, as in a phonograph player. Constant angular velocity (CAV) is the interactive format of videodiscs, allowing freeze-frame and slow-motion. Contrast with constant linear velocity.

constant expression (1) An expression having a value that can be determined during compilation and that does not change during the running of the program. (2) In Pascal, an expression that can be completely evaluated by the compiler at compile time and used as a constant value.

constant field (1) A field defined by a display format to contain a value that does not change. (2) In SDF/CICS, a field defined in a map and not known to the application program. Such a field contains data that cannot be changed by either the application program or its user. (3) In an externally described display or printer file, an unnamed field that contains actual data that are passed to the display or printer but are unknown to the program passing it.

constant field marks User defined characters used in the field definition subfunction of the SDF/CICS map editor to mark the beginning of a constant field.

constant function In a calculator, the function that allows a number to be held in memory for repeated use. (T) (A)

constant linear velocity In multimedia applications, a technology in which the linear velocity of the disc is constant under the laser head; the disc spins more slowly when the outside tracks are being read. Constant linear velocity (CLV) is the format for one-hour (long-play) linear videodiscs. Contrast with constant angular velocity.

constant-pitch spacing mechanism On a printer or typewriter, a device that moves the paper carrier or the print or type element a fixed distance in a regular step-by-step manner, parallel to the printing or typing line. Contrast with proportional spacing mechanism.

constant ratio code A code in which all characters are represented by combinations having a fixed ratio of ones to zeros.

Constraint class In the AIXwindows program, a class of objects from which a unique resource set can be inherited. The reference material associated with each widget specifies those that inherit resources from the Constraint class.

constraint rule A rule limiting a search such that its associated pattern is not permitted to occur in a valid solution. (T)

constraints In NETDA/2, the set of essential requirements specified with the node, connection, or application definitions. A change in a constraint value changes the input to the network design. Contrast with parameters.

constraint widget In AIX Enhanced X-Windows, a widget that is a subclass of a composite widget. It manages the geometry of its children, based on constraints associated with each child.

construct See conditional construct, executable construct, loop construct.

constructing Synonym for blocking.

consumer procedure An asynchronous procedure that uses data provided by other asynchronous procedures. (T)

consumer transaction facility (CTF) A stand-alone finance device used to handle transactions for banking customers. Synonymous with automatic teller machine (ATM).

contact bounce An unwanted making and breaking of the connection while opening or closing a contact. (T)

contact copying In a document copying machine, a method of making a copy in which the sensitized material and the master are brought together. (T) See also transmission copying.

contact input A binary input to a device generated by opening or closing a switch. (T)

Note: The switch can be either mechanical or electronic.

contact interrogation signal A signal whose value indicates whether a contact is open or closed. (T) (A)

contact phase A phase of link activation during which negotiation-proceeding XID3s are exchanged between the connected link stations to establish the primary and secondary roles of the link stations, the TG number to be used, and other characteristics of the link, and during which the mode-setting command is sent and acknowledged after the primary and the secondary roles are established. Link activation may consist only of the contact phase, or it may also have either a connect phase or a prenegotiation phase or both preceding the contact phase.

contact port Synonym for well-known port.

contact protection Protection of a mechanical contact against overcurrent or overvoltage. (T)

container In SAA Common User Access architecture, an object that holds other objects. A folder is an example of a container object. See also folder and object.

containment In the AIX operating system, location of a pointer in the window, and not within an inferior of the window, and location of the cursor hotspot within a visible region of a viewable window or one of its inferiors. The border of the window is considered part of the window.

contamination In computer security, the intermixing of data having different classification levels or need-to-know levels. The lower level data are said to be contaminated by the higher level data with the possible result that the contaminating data do not receive the required level of protection.

content-addressable storage Synonym for associative storage.

contention (1) In a local area network, a situation in which two or more data stations are allowed by the medium access control protocol to start transmitting concurrently and thus risk collision. (T) (2) In a session, a situation in which both network accessible units (NAUs) attempt to initiate the same action at the same time, such as when both attempt to send data in a half-duplex protocol (half-duplex contention), or both attempt to start a bracket (bracket contention). At session initiation, one NAU is defined to be the contention winner; its action will take precedence when contention occurs. The contention loser must get explicit or implicit permission from the contention winner to begin its action. (3) In ACF/TCAM, any point-to-point line configuration in which the station on the line does not use polling and addressing characters. (4) For BSC, the state that exists after the EOT

character has been received or sent and before a BID command is complete.

contention-loser session To a network accessible unit (NAU), a session for which it was defined during session initiation to be the contention loser.

contention mode In data communication, a mode of transmission in which any station may transmit whenever the line is available. If stations transmit simultaneously, protocols determine who wins the contention.

contention polarity The role of each LU when contention occurs for use of a session. One LU is the contention winner and the other LU is the contention loser.

contention state In data communications, a condition of a half-duplex line or data link control in which either user may transmit any time the line or link is available. If both users attempt to transmit at the same time, the protocols or the hardware determines who can transmit first.

contention system A system in which one or more stations compete for use of the line.

contents directory In OS/VS2, a series of queues that indicate the routines either in a particular region or in the link pack area.

contention-winner session To a network accessible unit (NAU), a session for which it was defined during session initiation to be the contention winner.

contents list In word processing, the display or printout of a list of available stored information for selection by the operator. (T)

contents view A view of an object that shows the contents of the object in list form. Contents views are provided for containers, and for any object that has container behavior; for example, a device object such as a printer. See also composed view, help view.

context (1) A stated or implied sense in which a thing has meaning, or a category or scope to which it applies. (2) In System/38, a system object that contains addressability to system objects by name. It is used in system pointer resolution to obtain system pointers to system objects. See also system object.

context editing A method of editing a line without using line numbers. To refer to a particular line, all or part of the contents of that line is specified.

contextual help In SAA Common User Access architecture, help that gives specific information about the item the cursor is on. The help is contextual because it provides information about a specific item as it is currently being used. Contrast with extended help.

contiguous Touching or joining at a common edge or boundary, for example, an unbroken consecutive series of storage locations.

contiguous items In COBOL, items that are described by consecutive entries in the Data Division, and that bear a definite hierarchical relationship to each other.

contingency plan In computer security, a plan for emergency response, backup procedures, and post-disaster recovery. Synonymous with disaster plan, emergency plan.

contingency procedure A procedure that is an alternative to the normal path of a process if an unusual but anticipated situation occurs.

Note: A contingency procedure may be triggered by events such as an overflow or an operator intervention. (T)

continuation line A line of a source statement into which characters are entered when the source statement cannot be contained on the preceding line or lines.

continuation mode In VTAM programs, the state of a conversation or session: either continue-any mode or continue-specific mode.

continue-any mode In VTAM programs, the state of a session or conversation that allows its input to satisfy a RECEIVE request issued in any-mode. While this state exists, input on the session or conversation can also satisfy RECEIVE requests issued in specific-mode. For conversations, continue-any mode is further qualified as either buffer continue-any or logical record continue-any. This specifies whether VTAM is to receive the data in terms of logical records or buffers. Contrast with continue-specific mode.

continue-specific (CS) mode In VTAM programs, the state of a session or conversation that allows its input to satisfy only RECEIVE requests issued in specific-mode. Contrast with continue-any mode.

continue statement A C language control statement that contains the keyword "continue" and a semicolon.

continuity In videotaping, the consistency maintained from shot to shot and throughout the take; for example, a switch that is on in one shot should not be off in the next unless it was shown being turned off.

continuity check A check to verify that an electrical path exists.

continuous branching In interactive video, a feature allowing a user to modify the program at any point rather than at specific branch points.

continuous-form cards Special cards attached together in continuous strips to facilitate printing. They can be separated into individual punched cards. (A)

continuous forms (1) Blank paper or forms fed through a printer continuously. Synonymous with continuous forms paper. (T) (2) A series of connected forms that feed continuously through a printing device. The connection between the forms is perforated to allow the user to tear them apart. Before printing, the forms are folded in a stacked arrangement, with the folds along the perforations. Contrast with cut form.

continuous forms attachment A device that feeds continuous forms into a paper carrier.

continuous forms paper (1) A continuous length of single-ply, fanfolded paper with both edges punched for tractor feeding and with perforation between pages. Paper is available in various sizes and basis weights. (2) Synonym for continuous forms. (T)

continuous forms stacker (CFS) An output assembly that refolds and stacks continuous forms after printing. Synonymous with refolder.

continuous function The continuous repetition of a machine function; for example, the operation of a repeat key or typematic key.

continuous mode In MSS, a method of operation of the system-initiated scratch function. It allows non-VSAM data sets on candidate volumes to be scratched and uncataloged when they become eligible. See also interval mode.

continuous spectrum In acoustics, a wave spectrum with components continuously distributed over a frequency range.

continuous-tone original An original document in which the subject matter consists of areas of actual tonal graduation. (T) Synonymous with full-tone original.

contouring In a digital video system, the undesirable appearance of patterns in a digitized image caused by an insufficient number of quantization levels.

contrast (1) In optical character recognition, the difference between color or shading of the printed material on a document and the background on which it is printed. (A) See print contrast ratio. (2) In a document copying machine, the difference between the densities of two surface elements of an image. (T) (3) In computer graphics, difference in brightness or color between a display image and the area in which it is displayed. (T)

contrast ratio In video systems, the degree of difference between the light and dark areas of a scene.

control (1) The determination of the time and order in which the parts of a data processing system and the devices that contain those parts perform the input, processing, storage, and output functions. (2) See loop control, numerical control, process control, real-time control, sequential control. (3) In SAA Advanced Common User Access architecture, a component of the user interface that allows a user to select choices or type information; for example, a check box, an entry field, a radio button.

control application In the IBM 8100 Information System, a complex application often used to handle access by multiple users to a resource or set of resources.

control area (1) A storage area used by a computer program to hold control information. (I) (A) (2) In systems with VSAM, a group of control intervals used as a unit for formatting a data set before adding records to it. Also, in a key-sequenced data set, the set of control intervals, pointed to by a sequence-set index record, that is used by VSAM for distributing free space and for placing a sequence-set index record adjacent to its data. (3) Synonym for control block.

control-area split In systems with VSAM, the movement of the contents of some of the control intervals in a control area to a newly created control area in order to facilitate insertion or lengthening of a data record when there are no remaining free control intervals in the original control area.

control ball Synonym for trackball.

control block (1) A storage area used by a computer program to hold control information. (I) Synonymous with control area. (2) The circuitry that performs the control functions such as decoding microinstructions and generating the internal control signals that perform the operations requested. (A) (3) In the IBM Token-Ring Network, a specifically formatted block of information provided from the application program to the Adapter Support Interface to request an operation.

control break (1) A suspension of program execution. (2) On an IBM personal computer, simultaneous actuation of the control (Ctrl) key and Break key to stop an operation. (3) An indication that the

end of data pertaining to a particular category or application has been reached. (4) In RPG, a change in the contents of a control field that indicates all records from a particular control group were read and a new control group is starting. (5) In COBOL, a change in the value of a data item that is referenced in the CONTROL clause. A change in the value of a data item that is used to control the hierarchical structure of a report.

control break level In COBOL, the relative position within a control hierarchy at which the most major control break occurred.

control bus A bus carrying signals that regulate system operations. (A)

control bytes Bytes associated with a physical record that serve to identify the record and indicate characteristics such as length and blocking factor.

control card A punched card containing input data or parameters for initializing or modifying a program.

control character (1) A character whose occurrence in a particular context specifies a control function. (T) (2) In Telnet, a character that is used to represent the CTRL key on an ASCII keyboard. (3) Synonymous with nonprinting character. (4) See accuracy control character, device control character, print control character, transmission control character.

Note: A control character may be recorded for use in a subsequent action. A control character is not a graphic character but may have a graphic representation in some circumstances.

control code A code point and its assigned control function meaning; for example, "end of transmission." For 7-bit codes such as ASCII and ISO 646, the first 32 code points are reserved for control purposes. For EBCDIC 8-bit codes, the first 64 code points are reserved.

control code characters In OfficeVision, special characters containing formatting information for a document in the Writing Pad function.

control command (1) In System/36, a command used by an operator to control the system or a workstation. A control command does not run a procedure and cannot be used in a procedure. (2) In the AIX operating system, a command that allows conditional or looping logic flow in shell procedures.

control counter Deprecated term for instruction address register.

control data Deprecated term for control information, control record.

control data item In COBOL, a data item, a change in whose contents may produce a control break.

control data-name In COBOL, a data-name that appears in a control clause and refers to a control data item.

control data set (CDS) In NPM, an SMP data set used in the NPM installation process.

control dictionary The external symbol dictionary together with the relocation dictionary of an object or load module.

control engineering See automatic control engineering.

control field (1) A field that is compared with other fields to determine the record sequence in the output field. (2) A field in a record that identifies the relationship of the record to other records such as a part number in an inventory record. Control fields determine when certain operations are to be performed. (3) In sorting or merging records, a group of contiguous bits in a control word used in determining sequence. (4) In RPG, one or more fields that are compared from record to record to determine when the information in the fields changes. When the information changes, the control level indicator (L1 through L9) assigned to a control field is set on. (5) In data communications, a field within a frame that contains the commands, responses, sequence numbers, and poll or final bit for data link control.

control file In CMS, the file that contains records that identify the updates to be applied and the macrolibraries, if any, needed to assemble that source program. See also auxiliary file.

control flow In programming languages, an abstraction of all possible paths the execution sequence may take through a program. (I)

Note: The control flow can be represented by a control flow graph.

control footing In COBOL, a report group that is presented at the end of the control group of which it is a member.

control frame In the Open Systems Interconnection reference model, a transmission frame sent by a layer or a sublayer to a peer entity of the same layer or sublayer in another system, but not passed to higher layers or sublayers; for example, a MAC frame. (T)

control functions In a data manipulation language, the computer instructions that manage access to system resources so that files and buffers are made available only to authorized users and application programs. (A) See also control operation.

control group In COBOL, a set of body groups that is presented for a given value of a control data item or of FINAL.

Note: Each control group may begin with a control heading, end with a control footing, and contain detail report groups.

control heading In COBOL, a report group that is presented at the beginning of the control group of which it is a member.

control hierarchy In COBOL, a designated sequence of report subdivisions defined by the positional order of FINAL and the data-names within a CONTROL clause.

control hole Synonym for designation hole. See also index hole.

control instruction register Deprecated term for instruction address register.

control interval A fixed-length area of direct access storage in which VSAM stores records and creates distributed free space. Also, in a key-sequenced data set or file, the set of records pointed to by an entry in the sequence-set index record. The control interval is the unit of information that VSAM transmits to or from direct access storage. A control interval always comprises an integral number of physical records.

control interval access In systems with VSAM, the retrieval or storage of the contents of a control interval.

control interval definition field (CIDF) In VSAM, a field located in the four bytes at the end of each control interval; it describes the free space, if any, in the control interval.

control interval split In systems with VSAM, the movement of some of the stored records in a control interval to a free control interval to facilitate insertion or lengthening of a record that does not fit in the original control interval.

control language (CL) The set of all commands with which a user requests functions. Synonym for command language. See job control language.

control language program An executable object that is created from sources consisting entirely of control language commands.

control language variable A program variable declared in a control language program and available only to the program.

controlled cancel In System/36, the system action that ends a job step being run and saves any new data that has been created. The job that is running can continue with the next job entry.

controlled maintenance A method to sustain a desired quality of service by the systematic application of analysis techniques using centralized supervisory facilities and/or sampling to minimize preventive maintenance and to reduce corrective maintenance. (T)

controlled slip A slip in which a fixed number of digits are lost or gained.

controller A device that coordinates and controls the operation of one or more input/output devices, such as workstations, and synchronizes the operation of such devices with the operation of the system as a whole. See communication controller, store controller, subsystem controller. See also input/output control unit.

controller card In the AS/400 system, any of the I/O controller logic cards, such as a magnetic storage device controller, workstation controller, or communications controller.

controller configuration facility (CCF) Set of macrostatements to be coded by a user and modules in Programmable Store System Host Support, used to define and create a 3651 or 7480 Store Controller operational environment.

controller creation parameter table (CCPT) In PSS, a table containing pointers to all tables and data areas used by the controller configuration facility in defining the 3651 or 7480 Store Controller operational environment.

controller data IBM-provided modules, tables, lists, and control blocks that are used at a host system to create an operational environment for a controller.

controller description (CTLD) In the AS/400 system, an object that contains a description of the characteristics of a controller that is either directly attached to the system or attached to a communication line.

controller disk In the 3650 Retail Store System, an integral part of the retail store controller that is used for auxiliary storage of controller data, user files, and application programs.

controller function An action or series of actions built into a controller and taken by the controller in response to a request from a terminal, another controller function, or a host system.

controller information fields In the 3790 Communication System, a set of fields, assigned to each 3790 program and to which the program has access, that contain information the program may need while being executed, such as terminal operator ID, date, and record numbers of print data set and transaction data set records being used by the program.

controller storage In the 3650 Retail Store System, the generic name for auxiliary (disk) storage and active (monolithic) storage in a 3651 store controller.

controller storage save In the 3650 Retail Store System, automatic writing of the critical areas of store controller active storage onto the integrated disk when power is turned off or when a power failure is detected.

control-level indicator In RPG, an indicator used to specify certain fields as control fields and to control the operations that are to be performed at total and detail time in the RPG program cycle.

control lever Synonym for joy stick.

controlling application program In VTAM programs, an application program with which a logical unit other than a secondary application program is automatically put in session whenever the logical unit is available. See also automatic logon.

controlling logical unit In VTAM programs, a logical unit with which a secondary logical unit, other than an application program, is automatically put in session whenever the secondary logical unit is available. A controlling logical unit can be either an application program or a device-type logical unit. See also automatic logon, controlling application program.

controlling subsystem An interactive subsystem that is started automatically when the system is started and through which the system operator controls the system.

control logic In the IBM 8100 Information System, I/O hardware that can decode and perform commands addressed to it by I/O instructions.

control logical unit (CLU) A logical unit that resides in a Transaction Processing Facility (TPF) type 2.1 node and that is used to pass private protocol request units between this TPF type 2.1 node and the logon manager (a VTAM application program). The communication flow between the control logical unit and the logon manager enables a logical unit controlled by VTAM to establish a session with TPF.

control mode (1) The state in which all terminals on a line must be in order for line discipline, line control, or terminal selection to occur. (2) A mode in which a tributary station can be polled or addressed by a control station.

control objectives Criteria that must be met to obtain an acceptable level of integrity required for a data processing system. (T)

control operation An action that affects the recording, processing, transmission, or interpretation of data; for example, starting or stopping a process, carriage return, font change, rewind and end of transmission. (I) (A) See also control functions.

control operator (1) The person who generally performs special administrative, control, and testing functions. (2) For logical unit (LU) 6.2, a service transaction program that describes and controls the availability of certain resources; for example, it describes network resources accessed by the local LU and it controls session limits between the LU and its partners. See also contention.

control operator's terminal The terminal at which the control operator has logged on.

control overrun In the IBM 8100 Information System, an attempted entry into an SDLC receive control block that is already full.

control panel (1) A part of a computer console that contains manual controls. (A) (2) A panel that contains lights and keys used to observe and operate the status of the operations within a system. (3) In the AS/400 system, a panel, located on the processing unit on the front of the rack, that contains lights and switches to operate or service the system. (4) Synonym for plugboard. (5) See operator control panel.

control point (CP) (1) A component of an APPN or LEN node that manages the resources of that node. In an APPN node, the CP is capable of engaging in CP-CP sessions with other APPN nodes. In an APPN network node, the CP also provides services to adjacent end nodes in the APPN network. (2) A component of a node that manages resources of that node and optionally provides services to other nodes in the network. Examples are a system services control point (SSCP) in a type 5 subarea node, a physical unit control point (PUCP) in a type 4 subarea node, a network node control point (NNCP) in an APPN network node, and an end node control point (ENCP) in an APPN or LEN end node. An SSCP and an NNCP can provide services to other nodes. (3) In computer graphics, one of a number of points in real

space that control the shape of an approximation spline curve.

Control Point Profile Name In the AIX operating system, the name of the control point profile that defines the node ID of the physical unit associated with the attachment.

control program (1) A computer program designed to schedule and to supervise the execution of programs of a computer system. (I) (A) (2) The part of the AIX Base Operating System that determines the order in which basic functions should be performed. (3) See VM/370 control program, resident control program, IMS/VS control program, VM/XA Migration Aid control program.

Control Program Facility (CPF) The system support licensed program for System/38. It provides many functions fully integrated in the system such as work management, database data management, job control, message handling, security, programming aids, and service.

control program generation language The set of macroinstructions and associated operands with which a user defines the network configuration for a communication controller.

control program generation procedure A two-stage procedure that creates a control program load module for a communication controller based on parameters specified by a user through the control program generation language.

control program keys In OS/VS2, protection keys (0-7) that are reserved for control program use.

control punch Synonym for designation hole.

control range In VM, a subdivision of a component; each control range consists of an integral number of control areas exclusively occupying the area of one extent not suballocated to another component.

control read-only memory (CROM) A read-only storage in the control block of some microprocessors that has been microprogrammed to decode the control logic. (A)

control record (1) A checkpoint record containing data used to initiate, modify, or stop a control operation or determine the manner in which data are processed. (2) In ACF/TCAM, a record included in a checkpoint data set to keep track of correct environment records, incident records, and checkpoint request records for use in restructuring the message control program environment during restart. See also checkpoint request record, environment record, incident record.

control region In IMS/VS, the OS/VS main storage region that contains the IMS/VS control program.

control register (1) In System/370 computing systems, a register used for operating system control of relocation, priority interruption, program event recording, error recovery, and masking operations. (2) Deprecated term for instruction address register.

control scheme In a network, a method for regulating access among nodes. See carrier sense multiple access with collision detection (CSMA/CD), master node control, register insertion, slotted-ring control, token-access control.

control section (CSECT) The part of a program specified by the programmer to be a relocatable unit, all elements of which are to be loaded into adjoining main storage locations.

control segment (1) Part of an IBM 3663 Supermarket Terminal Model 1P or all of an IBM 3663 Supermarket Terminal Model 3P, either of which operates on the store loop to control the attached checkstand stations. (2) Part of an IBM 3684 Point of Sale Control Unit Model 2 used as a master control unit for the store-loop-attached IBM 3683 Point of Sale Terminals.

control sequence chaining See text control chaining.

control specification (1) In RPG, a coding form on which the programmer provides information that affects the creating and running of programs. (2) In BASIC, any of the specifications POS, CUR, SKIP, or X, used in the FORM statement to format records or to control printing.

control specifications A statement of the rules and regulations to be applied within a data processing system to ensure the required level of integrity. (T)

control standards Control specifications accepted as criteria for preventing, detecting, and correcting errors or omissions. (T)

control statement (1) In programming languages, a statement that is used to alter the continuous sequential execution of statements; a control statement may be a conditional statement, such as IF, or an imperative statement, such as STOP. (T) (2) In the NetView program, a statement in a command list that controls the processing sequence of the command list or allows the command list to send messages to the operator and receive input from the operator. (3) In FORTRAN, any of the several forms of GO TO, IF and DO statements, or the PAUSE, CONTINUE, and STOP statements, used either to change the normally sequential processing of the statements, or to stop the program. (4) See job control statement.

control statement analyzer A component of Subsystem Support Services that edits Subsystem Support Services input command statements and that creates and manages buffers during subsystem definition.

control station (1) In basic mode link control, the data station that nominates the master station and supervises polling, selecting, interrogating, and recovery procedures. (I) (A) (2) A station that can poll or address tributary stations. (3) The primary or controlling station on a multipoint line. The control station controls the sending and receiving of data.

control stick Synonym for joy stick.

control storage (1) A part of storage that contains microcode. (2) Printer storage in which data can be entered, held, and retrieved. Control storage contains microcode instructions and other control information; for example, the print buffer. (3) Computer storage that contains the programs used to control input and output operations and the use of main storage. See also auxiliary storage, main storage. (4) High-speed memory, containing microcode, that can be implemented as read only or direct access.

control storage initial program load The loading of control storage programs from disk or diskette to control storage.

control storage processor The hardware that performs control storage instructions to handle data transfer, main storage, and input/output assignments.

control storage save In PSS, the automatic writing of critical areas of store controller storage onto areas of the integrated disk unit when a power failure is detected or when certain machine errors occur.

control structure Synonym for inference engine. (T)

control supply indicator In System/38, a light on the operator/service panel that comes on when the main line circuit breaker is closed and the control supply power for the power controller is on.

control switching points (CSP) Collectively, the class 1, 2, and 3 offices (regional, sectional, and primary centers) needed for nationwide dialing.

control tape See carriage control tape.

control techniques Procedures, in a particular computer installation, some or all of which may be appropriate to maintain integrity. (T)

control terminal (1) Any active terminal at which the user is authorized to enter commands affecting system operation. (2) In VM, any terminal currently controlling system resources and being used by the primary system operator (privilege class A), the resource operator (privilege class B), or the spooling operator (privilege class D). (3) See control operator's terminal.

control total A sum, resulting from the addition of a specified field from each record in a group of records, that is used for checking machine, program, and data reliability. Synonymous with hash total.

control track In videotaping, a series of electromagnetic pulses recorded as a separate track by a videotape recorder. The control track is used to control the speed of the tape and head during playback to ensure that the heads are properly aligned with the recorded video track.

control track pulses Speed control pulses created by a videotape recorder.

control transfer In the execution of a program, any departure from the implicit or declared sequence in which the instructions are being executed. (A)

control transfer instruction Deprecated term for jump instruction.

control transfer statement A statement that causes the execution of a statement other than the next statement written in the source program. (T)

control unit See device control unit, input/output control unit, instruction control unit, main control unit, transmission control unit. See also communication controller.

control unit description (CUD) In System/38, an object that contains a description of the features of a control unit attached directly to the system or to a telecommunication line.

control unit terminal (CUT) mode An IBM protocol used for communications with an IBM 3174 or 3274 Control Unit or other appropriate interface unit. In this protocol, a program in the workstation emulates a 3278 or 3879 terminal for a user at a virtual terminal, and the interface unit is responsible for enforcing the protocol.

control variable (1) In PL/I, a variable that is used to control the operation of a program, as in a DO statement. (2) See loop control variable.

control vector One of a general class of RU substructures that has variable length, is carried within some enclosing structure, and has a one-byte key used as an identifier.

control volume A volume that contains one or more indexes of the catalog.

control window A window that is used as part of a composite window to perform simple input and output tasks.

control word (1) All control fields used to sort or merge a particular group of records. The major field appears first and other fields follow in descending order of importance. (2) An instruction within a document that identifies its parts or indicates how to format the document. (3) See also macro.

control word line An input line that contains at least one control word.

convenience workstation An ImagePlus workstation equipped with a printer and a scanner. When a request is made to print a document, it may be printed at a printer workstation or a convenience workstation.

conversation (1) A dialog between a user and an interactive data processing system. (2) In IMS/VS, a dialog between a terminal and a message processing program using conversational processing facilities. (3) Interaction between a computer and a user by means of a keyboard. (4) In APPC, the communications between the application program and another application program at the remote system. See also session, transaction. (5) A connection between two transaction programs over an LU-LU session that allows them to communicate with each other while processing a transaction.

Note: A conversation begins when a message unit with the begin bracket set on its RH flows on a session and ends when a subsequent message unit with the end bracket set on in its RH flows on the session.

conversational Pertaining to a program or a system that carries on a dialog with a terminal user, alternately accepting input and then responding to the input quickly enough for the user to maintain a train of thought. See also interactive.

conversational file A binary synchronous communication BSC file that allows data characters instead of acknowledgment characters to be sent as a response.

conversational mode (1) A mode of operation of a computer system in which a sequence of alternating entries and responses between a user and the system takes place in a manner similar to a dialog between two persons. (I) (A) Synonymous with interactive mode. (2) A mode in which the next message received by a station after it enters an inquiry message is a reply to that message.

conversational monitor system (CMS) A virtual machine operating system that provides general interactive time sharing, problem solving, and program development capabilities, and operates only under control of the VM/370 VM control program.

conversational processing In IMS/VS, an optional facility that allows a user's application program to accumulate information acquired through multiple interchanges with a terminal, even though the program terminates between interchanges.

conversational remote job entry (CRJE) Facility for entering job control language statements from a remote terminal, and causing scheduling and execution of jobs described in the statements. The terminal user is prompted for missing operands or corrections.

conversation group ID An identifier of a particular session between two specific LUs or CPs. Specified in a conversation allocation command, the conversation group ID allows the requested conversation to be allocated to the identified session. This then permits a pair of transaction programs (one in each LU) to serially share use of the designated session with a group of related pairs of transaction programs that use the same conversation group ID.

conversation-level security See session-level security. See also end-user verification.

conversion (1) In programming languages, the transformation between values that represent the same data item but belong to different data types. Information may be lost due to conversion since accuracy of data representation varies among different data types. (I) (2) The process of changing from one method of data processing to another or from one data processing system to another. (3) The process of changing from one form of representation to another; for example, to change from decimal representation to binary representation.

Conversion Reformat Utility A System/38 licensed program that allows a user to run System/3-style sort programs on System/38.

convert (1) To change the representation of data from one form to another, without changing the information they convey; for example, radix conversion, code conversion, analog to digital conversion, media conversion. (T) (2) See also copy, duplicate.

converted command An intermediate form of a character-coded command produced by the VTAM programs through use of an unformatted system services definition table. The format of a converted command is fixed; the unformatted system services definition table must be constructed in such a manner that the character-coded command, as entered by a logical unit, is converted into the predefined converted command format. See also unformatted.

converted journal entry In the AS/400 system and System/38, the version of a journal entry that can be displayed, printed, or written to a database output file.

converter A device that can convert impulses from one form to another, such as analog to digital, parallel to serial, one code to another, or one protocol to another. See code converter, data converter.

converter cache In the AIX operating system, a high-speed buffer storage that contains frequently accessed information associated with a client application. The primary purpose of a converter cache is to reduce access time to key information.

convertible drive In MSS, a drive that can be designated to be either a staging drive or a nonstaging drive.

convex programming In operations research, a particular case of nonlinear programming in which the function to be maximized or minimized and the constraints are appropriately convex or concave functions of the controllable variables. (I) (A) See dynamic programming, integer programming, linear programming, mathematical programming, nonlinear programming, quadratic programming.

conveying roller Synonym for moistening pressure roller.

conveyor delivery mechanism In a duplicator, a delivery system in which the paper is transported into the delivery tray by means of an endless belt system. (T)

coolant distribution unit (CDU) A unit providing liquid cooling to the processor unit. A coolant distribution unit has pumps, a heat exchanger, and its own logic control and power supply.

cooperative application In SAA usage, a type of distributed application, in which the user interface portion of the application runs on a programmable workstation while some or all of the remaining code runs on one or more linked systems.

cooperative processing In SAA usage, the coordinated use of a programmable workstation with one or more linked systems to accomplish a single goal.

coordinate Any of a set of numbers used to specify the location of a point on a line, on a surface, or in space. See absolute coordinate, device coordinate, incremental coordinate, normalized device coordinates, relative coordinate, user coordinate, world coordinate.

coordinate data (1) Data that specify a location in a display space or an image space. (2) The series of data bytes following a display order that contain the information needed to perform the specified operation. (3) See also absolute data, relative data.

coordinate graphics Computer graphics in which display images are generated from display commands and coordinate data. (I) (A) Contrast with raster graphics. Synonymous with line graphics.

coordinate system In the AIXwindows program, a convention for locating pixels on a given display or window, where X is the horizontal axis and Y is the vertical axis. The origin is [0,0] at the upper left or lower left corner, depending on the convention in use. For a window, the origin is at the upper left or lower left, depending on the convention in use, inside the border. Coordinates are discrete and specified in pixels. Each window and pixmap has its own coordinate system.

COPR Control operator control block.

coprocessor (1) A supplementary processor that performs operations in conjunction with another processor. (2) In personal computers, a microprocessor on an expansion board that extends the address range of the processor in the system unit or adds specialized instructions to handle a particular category of operations; for example, an I/O coprocessor, math coprocessor, or networking coprocessor.

copy (1) A product of a document copying process. (T) Synonymous with print. (2) Synonym for block copy. (T) (3) See hardcopy, softcopy. See Figure 36.

Copy In SAA Common User Access* architecture, a choice that places onto the clipboard a copy of what the user has selected.

copy control In the 3800 Printing Subsystem, the functions that determine the number of copies to be printed for each data set, and which copies will be printed with a forms overlay or have copy modification.

copy counter In a document copying machine, a device that indicates the number of copies that have been produced or the number of copies to be produced in relation to the setting made on the copy selector. (T)

copy cycle A complete process of a document copying machine in producing one copy. (T)

copy function In VM, the function initiated via a program function key to copy the contents of a display screen onto an associated hard copy printer. A remote

	Source			
	External Storage or Input	Internal Storage	A Register	
To read	To load	To load	A Register	
To read	To move	To store	Internal Storage	Destination
To transmit or to read or to write	To write	To write	External Storage or Output	

Figure 36. Copy

display terminal copies the entire contents of the screen onto a printer attached to the same control unit. A local display terminal copies all information from the screen, except the screen status information, onto any printer attached to any local display control unit.

copy group In Print Services Facility, one or more copies of a sheet of paper; each copy can have changes like text suppression, form flash, and overlays.

copy guide On a typewriter, a device to prevent the inadvertent reentrance of paper into the paper feed aperture as the typing operation progresses. (T)

copying See book copying, contact copying, document copying, double-sided copying, projection copying, reflex copying, single-sided copying, transmission copying. See also copying speed.

copying machine See document copying machine.

copying speed In a document copying machine, the rate of delivery of successive copies from the same original after production of the first copy. (T)

copy length selector On roll-fed document copying machines, a means of preselecting the length of copy material to be cut from the roll. (T)

copy mass storage volume See copy volume.

copy modification (1) In the 3800 Printing Subsystem, a feature that allows the printing of predefined data on all pages of specified copies of a data set. (2) The process of adding, deleting, or replacing data on selected copies of certain pages of a data set.

copy modification segment In the 3800 Printing Subsystem, the portion of copy change that has the six control bytes and a maximum of 204 text bytes. When transferred to a printer, these bytes alter specific copies of a data set.

copy-on-write In the AIX operating system, an option that creates a mapped file with changes that are saved in the system paging space, instead of saving the changes in a copy of the file on a disk.

copy operation (1) In DPPX, a method of reproducing as many as seven sources into one target. (2) In the 3270 Information Display System, an operation that copies all or a part of the contents of the character buffer from one terminal to another terminal.

copy recipient A recipient for whom a message is not primarily intended but who is included in the distribution list to be kept informed. Synonymous with secondary recipient. (T)

copy screen mode In the 3270 Information Display System, the mode of operation in which the user can divide the display area into a user active area and one or more user reference areas.

copy selector On a document copying machine, a control for selecting the number of copies to be produced from one original. (T)

copy separation In the 3800 Printing Subsystem, the alternate placing of one or two vertical bars in the left carrier strip between pages by the End of Transmission command. In the continuous forms stacker, these marks distinguish between successive copies in a single data set. The marks are trimmed off by the burster-trimmer-stacker, which separates copies by offset stacking.

copy stand In video production, a device for holding and adjusting a video camera during the shooting of flat art or still objects.

copy volume In MSS, an inactive mass storage volume that is an exact reproduction of another mass storage volume. Both volumes have the same volume identification.

Core In the AIXwindows program, the top-level superclass from which all widgets and gadgets are derived. Core consists of three subclasses that collectively provide the appearance resources and behavioral resources required by all widgets and gadgets in the AIXwindows Toolkit.

core (1) In an optical cable, the central region of an optical fiber through which light is transmitted. See also cladding, optical fiber. (2) In FORTRAN, the set of language facilities that are not identified as deprecated features. It is a complete language. (3) Deprecated term for main storage, memory, tape spool. (4) See magnetic core, multiaperture core, paper core.

core conformance In FORTRAN, pertaining to a standard-conforming program that contains no deprecated features.

core image Deprecated term for storage image.

co-resident Pertaining to the condition in which two or more modules are located in main storage at the same time.

core storage (1) Magnetic storage where the magnetic medium consists of magnetic cores. (A) (2) Deprecated term for main storage. (3) See magnetic core storage.

Note: Core storage is an obsolete technology.

core widget In AIX Enhanced X-Windows, the widget that contains the definitions of fields common to all widgets. All widgets are subclasses of the core widget.

corner cut A corner removed from a card as a means of orienting the card.

corner separator On a document copying machine or duplicator, a device that rests on the leading corners of the paper in the paper stack to facilitate separation of successive sheets. (T)

corona The effect of ionizing air by means of a high voltage, creating a charge that can be used to perform various functions during printing or copying.

corona unit In a document copying machine, a unit containing elements energized from a high voltage source to produce an ionized atmosphere for electrically charging or discharging elements in the copying process. (T) Synonymous with charger unit.

corona unit cleaner A device incorporated in a document copying machine for cleaning the corona unit. (T) Synonymous with charger unit cleaner.

coroutine A subroutine that, when called again after an execution, resumes at the return point of its previous execution. (T)

correcting feature On a typewriter or word processor, a feature used to remove or block out typed characters.

correction code check A noncomparative data validity check performed by the 2835 Storage Control to provide the 2305 Fixed Head Storage with correction capabilities.

correction key On a typewriter or word processor, a control used to obliterate incorrectly typed characters before correcting them. (T)

corrective maintenance (1) Maintenance performed specifically to overcome existing faults. (T) (2) Contrast with preventive maintenance.

corrective maintenance time Time, scheduled or unscheduled, used to perform corrective maintenance. (A)

corrective service In VSE, the installation of a PTF or an APAR fix that corrects a specific problem.

Corrective Service Diskette A diskette provided by IBM to registered service coordinators for resolving user-identified problems with previously installed software. This diskette includes program updates designed to resolve problems.

correlated subquery In SQL, a subquery, part of a WHERE or HAVING clause, applied to a row or group of rows of the table or view named in the outer SELECT statement.

correlation name In SQL, an identifier that designates a table, a view, or an individual row of a table or view within a single SQL statement. The name can be defined in any FROM clause or in the first clause of an UPDATE or DELETE statement.

correspondent entities In Open Systems Interconnection architecture, entities in the same layer that have a connection between them at the next lower layer. (T)

COS (1) Class of service. (2) Common operations services.

COS table In ACF/TCAM, a list of classes of service for a network. See class of service.

coulomb The amount of electricity transferred in one second by a one-ampere current.

count See message count.

counter (1) A functional unit with a finite number of states each of which represents a number that can be, upon receipt of an appropriate signal, increased by unity or by a given constant. This device is usually capable of bringing the represented number to a specified value; for example, zero. (T) (2) In COBOL, a data item used for storing numbers or number representations in a manner that permits these numbers to be increased or decreased by the value of another number, or to be changed or reset to zero or to an arbitrary positive or negative value. See linage counter, sum counter. (3) A register or storage location to accumulate number of event occurrences. (4) See instruction counter, modulo-n counter, preselector counter, reversible counter, total counter.

countermeasure In computer security, any action, device, procedure, technique, or other measure that reduces the vulnerability of or threat to a system. See also exposure, risk.

counter-pressure cylinder In a duplicator, a cylinder that brings the paper into contact with the master or blanket under pressure to effect the transfer of the image. (T)

count-key-data (CKD) device A disk storage device that stores data in a format consisting of a count field, usually followed by a key field, followed by the actual data of a record. The count field contains, among others, the address of the record in the format CCHHR (CC = cylinder number, HH = head number, R = record number) and the length of the data; the key field contains the record's key (search argument). Contrast with fixed-block-architecture (FBA) device.

country code In X.25 communications, the 3-digit number that precedes the national terminal number in the network user address for public networks.

country extended code page (CECP) An 8-bit code page that has a 93-character set on its nationally standardized code points but is extended to the multilingual character set for the national languages of some European countries.

coupler (1) In a document copying machine, a chemical compound that reacts with another compound to form a dye. (T) (2) A device that connects a modem to a telephone network. See acoustic coupler. (3) In an ESCON environment, link hardware used to join identical optical fiber connector types. Contrast with adapter.

coupling loss In fiber optics, the power loss suffered when coupling light from one optical device to another. (E) See also gap loss.

courseware In computer-assisted education, a complete set of materials necessary to take a course, such as videodiscs, computer software, and any other materials, including workbooks, charts, diskettes, etc.

covert channel In computer security, a channel that allows a process to transfer information in a manner that violates the security policy of a system.

CP (1) VM/370 control program. (2) VM/XA migration aid control program. (3) Control point.

CPAR Customer problem analysis and resolution. A process by which a customer identifies the cause of a problem and the maintenance necessary to fix the problem. A CPAR can result in an APAR.

CPB Collection point block.

CP capabilities The level of network services provided by the control point (CP) in an APPN end node or network node. CP capabilities information is exchanged during the activation of CP-CP sessions between two nodes. A node's CP capabilities are encoded in the CP capabilities (X'12C1') GDS variable.

CP command In VM, a command by which a terminal user controls his virtual machine. The VM/370 control program commands are called CP commands. The CP commands that perform console simulation are called console functions.

CP-CP session-capable connection A link over which a node permits CP-CP sessions to be established.

CP-CP sessions The parallel sessions between two control points, using LU 6.2 protocols and a mode name of CPSVCMG, on which network services requests and replies are exchanged. Each CP of a given pair has one contention-winner session and one contention-loser session with the other.

CPF Control Program Facility.

cpi Characters per inch.

"C" pins Module exit pins used for circuit-board connections. These are usually located around the periphery of the substrate.

CP/M Control Program/Monitor. A disk operating system designed for single-task single-user applications on a variety of computers.

Notes:

1. *Trademark of Digital Research Corporation.*
2. *Another version, Concurrent CP/M, allows multi-tasking.*

CP manager Connection point manager.

CP name A network-qualified name of a control point (CP), consisting of a network ID qualifier identifying the network (or name space) to which the CP's node belongs, and a unique name within the scope of that network ID identifying the CP. Each APPN or LEN node has one CP name, assigned to it at system-definition time.

CP-owned disk In VM, any disk designated as owned by CP during system generation; for example, the CP residence volume or any disk that contains CP paging, spooling, or temporary disk space.

CPP Command processing program.

CP privilege class See privilege class.

CP read In VM/370, the mode in which the control program (CP) waits for a response or request for work

from the user. On a typewriter terminal, the keyboard is unlocked; on a display terminal, the screen status area indicates CP READ.

CP READ screen status For a display terminal used as a virtual console under VM, an indicator located in the lower right of the screen displaying that CP is waiting for a response or request for work from the user.

CP receive session The contention-loser CP-CP session. On this session, directory services in a CP receives a Locate search or registration request from a partner CP.

cps Characters per second.

CP send session The contention-winner CP-CP session. On this session, directory services in a CP sends a Locate search or registration request to a partner CP.

CP system disks In VM, any disk space used by CP other than the CP paging, spooling, and temporary disk space; for example, virtual disks.

CP trace table A table used for debugging VM; its size is a multiple of 4096 bytes and is dependent on the size of real storage available at IPL time. This table contains the chronological occurrences of events that take place in the real machine, recorded in a wraparound fashion within the trace table. System programmers use it to determine the event that preceded a CP system failure.

CPU Central processing unit. See processing unit, processor. See also processing and control element (PCE).

CPU timer See processor timer.

CR (1) An abbreviation denoting a credit symbol in the account field. (A) (2) The carriage return character. (A)

CRA (1) Catalog recovery area. (2) Component recovery area.

cradle The part of a telephone that holds the handset.

crane In video production, a platform on a large boom on which a camera is mounted and on which the camera operator and possibly another person can be seated. A crane is used to get high-angle shots during which the camera is raised or lowered.

crash (1) An unexpected interruption of computer service, usually due to a serious hardware or software malfunction. (2) See failure, head crash, malfunction.

crawl (1) In video presentations, alphanumeric text that moves across a video screen, either horizontally or vertically; for example, the display of credits at the end of a program. (2) In video systems, the undesirable shimmer on the borders of bright colors on a poorly recorded tape.

CRC The cyclic redundancy check character. (A)

CRE Carrier return character.

create To bring an object into existence in a system.

create link pack area (CLPA) An option used during IPL to initialize the link pack pageable area.

creation date The date at the time a file is created. See also program date, session date, system date.

creation facilities program (CFP) The 3650 Retail Store System component that allocates controller storage and builds an image of the data transmitted to the controller.

credit card An identification card that allows deferred payment for a financial transaction. (A)

CR-hi Channel request high priority, the first level of priority.

critical band See fletcher critical band.

critical field In the IBM 3886 Optical Character Reader, any user-specified field that initiates machine action.

critical resource In the NetView Graphic Monitor Facility, a resource that is considered important to the operation of the network.

critical section In programming languages, a part of an asynchronous procedure that cannot be executed simultaneously with a certain part of another asynchronous procedure. (I)

critical situation notification In System/370 multiprocessing, the ability of one processing unit to signal the other that it is having trouble and request help.

CRJE Conversational remote job entry.

CRLF Carriage return linefeed.

CR-lo Channel request low priority, the third level of priority.

CR-med Channel request medium priority, the second level of priority.

CROM Control read-only memory. (A)

crop In multimedia applications, to cut off or trim.

cross-assembler An assembler run on a computer to produce machine-language output that is to be executed on a computer of different architecture.

crossbar switch A relay-operated device that makes a connection between a line in a set of lines and a line in another set. The two sets are physically arranged along adjacent sides of a matrix of contacts or switch points. See also line switching, step-by-step system.

crossbar system A type of line-switching system that uses crossbar switches. See also step-by-step switch.

cross compiler A compiler that assembles a program that is to be executed on a type of computer different from the computer on which the cross compiler is executed. See also cross assembler.

cross-configuration See processor configuration.

cross-domain In SNA, pertaining to control or resources involving more than one domain.

cross-domain communication Synonym for networking.

cross-domain keys In SNA, a pair of cryptographic keys used by a system services control point (SSCP) to encipher a session cryptography key sent to another SSCP and decipher a session cryptography key received from the other SSCP in start of cross-domain LU-LU sessions using session-level cryptography. Synonymous with cross keys.

cross-domain link (1) A subarea link connecting two subareas that are in different domains. (2) A link physically connecting two domains.

cross-domain LU-LU session In SNA, a session between logical units (LUs) in different domains. Contrast with same-domain LU-LU session.

cross-domain network manager session A session between two network managers (the NetView program or NCCF) in separate domains.

cross-domain resource (1) Deprecated term for other-domain resource. (2) In VTAM programs, synonym for other-domain resource.

cross-domain resource manager (CDRM) The functions of the system services control point (SSCP) that control initiation and termination of cross-domain sessions.

cross-domain simulation In TPNS, the performance of the role of one or more entire SNA domains in communication with the domain of the system under test.

cross-domain subarea link A link between two subarea nodes in different domains.

crossfade Synonym for dissolve.

crossfire Interfering current in one telegraph or signaling channel resulting from telegraph or signaling currents in another channel.

crossfooting Checking in which individual columns are totaled and the sum of these totals is compared with the sum of the totals of the individual rows. (T)

crossfooting test A check based on the comparison of two totals obtained by adding the same set of numbers in different sequences. (T)

cross keys (1) See cross key 1, cross key 2. (2) Synonym for cross-domain keys.

cross key 1 In the Programmed Cryptographic Facility, a cryptographic key used at a host processor to encipher the operational key used to encipher data sent to another host processor.

cross key 2 In the Programmed Cryptographic Facility, a cryptographic key used at a host processor to decipher the operational key used to encipher data received from another host processor.

cross memory services lock In OS/VS2 and MVS, a global suspend lock used for services that apply to more than one private address space.

cross-network In SNA, pertaining to control or resources involving more than one SNA network.

cross-network LU-LU session In SNA, a session between logical units (LUs) in different networks.

cross-network session An LU-LU or SSCP-SSCP session whose path traverses more than one SNA network.

cross-partition communication control A facility that enables VSE subsystems and user programs to communicate with each other; for example, with VSE/POWER.

cross-platform Pertaining to applications that are operable with more than one operating system.

cross-platform transmission Electronic transmission of information, such as mail, between incompatible operating systems.

cross-reference listing The portion of the compiler listing that contains information on where files, fields, and indicators are defined, referenced, and modified in a program.

cross-subarea In SNA, pertaining to control or resources involving more than one subarea node.

cross-subarea link Synonym for subarea link. See also cross-domain link.

Cross System Product A set of licensed programs designed to permit the user to develop and run applications using independently defined maps (display and printer formats), data items (records, working storage, files, and single items), and processes (logic). The Cross System Product set consists of two parts: Cross System Product/Application Development (CSP/AD) and Cross System Product/Application Execution (CSP/AE).

crosstalk (1) The disturbance caused in a circuit by an unwanted transfer of energy from another circuit. (T) (2) The unwanted energy transferred from one circuit, called the disturbing circuit, to another circuit, called the disturbed circuit. (A)

crowding In OCR, the insufficient horizontal spacing between characters.

CRP (1) Channel request priority. (2) Configuration report program.

CRR Component recovery record.

CRS Configuration report server.

CRT display (1) Cathode ray tube display. (A) (2) A display device that uses a cathode ray tube.

CRT display device A display device in which display images are produced on a cathode ray tube.

CRU Customer replaceable unit.

CRV Cryptography Verification request.

cryogenics The study and use of devices utilizing properties of materials near absolute zero in temperature. (A)

cryogenic storage (1) A storage device that uses the superconductive and magnetic properties of certain materials at very low temperatures. (I) (A) (2) Synonymous with cryogenic store.

cryogenic store Synonym for cryogenic storage.

cryotron A device that makes use of the effects of low temperatures on conductive materials such that small magnetic field changes can control large current changes. (A)

cryptanalysis In computer security, the steps and operations performed in converting encrypted messages into plaintext without initial knowledge of the key used in the encryption algorithm. Synonymous with code breaking. See also attack, cryptology, threat analysis.

cryptographic Pertaining to transformation of data to conceal its meaning. See also decipher, encipher.

cryptographic algorithm (1) In AS/400 Cryptographic Support, a set of rules that specify the mathematical steps required to encrypt and decrypt data. See also algorithm. (2) A set of rules that specify the mathematical steps required to encipher and decipher data.

cryptographic communication The transmission of enciphered data between devices or programs.

cryptographic data unit A finite length of plaintext or ciphertext processed in one cryptographic operation.

cryptographic key (1) A parameter that determines cryptographic transformations between plaintext and ciphertext. See DEA key. (2) See also cross-domain keys, host master key, secondary logical unit key, session cryptography key.

cryptographic key data set (CKDS) (1) A data set that contains the encrypting keys used by an installation. (2) A test value cryptographically related to a specific key and used to ensure that the key has not changed since the test value was generated.

cryptographic key distribution center (CKD) A facility that generates cryptographic keys that can be used by two parties that do not share a common key.

cryptographic key test pattern In the Programmed Cryptographic Facility, a 64-bit value stored with each cryptographic key in the CKDS.

cryptographic key translation center (CKT) A facility transforming cryptographic keys created by one party to a form that can be used by a second party not sharing a common key.

cryptographic master key The highest key encrypting key in a key hierarchy used to protect other keys.

cryptographic security Synonym for cryptosecurity.

cryptographic service message A message used to transport keys or related information used to control a cryptographic relationship.

cryptographic session In SNA products, an LU-LU session in which a function management data (FMD) request may be enciphered before it is transmitted and deciphered after it is received. Contrast with clear session. See also mandatory cryptographic session, selective cryptographic session.

cryptographic session key Deprecated term for session cryptography key.

Cryptographic Support See AS/400 Cryptographic Support.

cryptographic system In computer security, either a cipher system or a code system. Synonymous with cryptosystem.

cryptography (1) The transformation of data to conceal its meaning. (2) In computer security, the principles, means, and methods for encrypting plaintext and decrypting ciphertext. See also cryptology.

cryptography session key Deprecated term for session cryptography key.

cryptography verification (CRV) request A request unit sent by the primary logical unit (PLU) to the secondary logical unit (SLU) as part of cryptographic session establishment, to allow the SLU to verify that the PLU is using the correct session cryptography key and initialization vector (IV).

cryptology In computer security, the field of learning dealing with cryptography and cryptanalysis.

cryptosecurity In computer security, the use of cryptography for security. Synonymous with cryptographic security.

cryptosystem Synonym for cryptographic system.

crystal lattice A regular, three-dimensional arrangement of atoms, ions, or molecules bound by electrical bonds.

CS (1) Communication services. (2) Current state.

CSA Common service area.

CSCF Central site control facility.

CSECT Control section.

C and SM Communications and System Management.

CSMA/CA Carrier sense multiple access with collision avoidance. A network protocol in which the transmitting workstation resends the data if the receiving workstation does not confirm receipt of the data within a given period of time.

CSMA/CD Carrier sense multiple access with collision detection. A network protocol in which the transmitting workstation detects data collisions and waits a random length of time before retrying the transmission.

CSMA/CD network A bus network in which the medium access control protocol requires carrier sense and where a station always starts transmission by sending a jam signal. If there is no collision with jam signals from other stations, it begins sending data; otherwise, it stops transmission and then tries again later. (T)

CS mode Continue-specific mode.

CSNAP Communications statistical network analysis procedure.

CSP (1) Communication scanner processor. (2) Control switching points.

C space In the Print Management Facility, area in character box to right of rightmost picture element for the graphic character pattern. See also A space, B space.

CSR IBM Customer Service Representative.

CSS (1) Channel subsystem. (2) Connectivity subsystem.

CST CMS subtasking; an interface program that enables CMS to execute programs written to run in an OS/VS environment.

CSU (1) Customer setup. (2) Channel service unit.

CSW Channel status word.

CT Control terminal.

CTC Channel-to-channel.

CTCA Channel-to-channel adapter.

CTF Consumer transaction facility.

CTLD Controller description.

Ctrl A key on a keyboard that is pressed and held together with another key to perform another function, thus extending the function of a standard keyboard.

CTS (1) Conversational Terminal System. (2) Clear to send.

CU Close-up.

CUA architecture Common User Access architecture.

CUD (1) Call user data. (2) Control unit description.

cue (1) In video production, a pulse entered onto a line of the vertical blanking interval resulting in such elements as frame numbers, picture codes, chapter codes, closed captions, full-frame IDs, on the master tape or videodisc. (2) Synonym for call.

cueing See depth cueing.

cue inserter In video production, the device that plays cues on lines of the vertical blanking interval of the master tape to indicate to the disc-mastering equipment in which field to put the frame ID code on the disc.

cue sheet In video production, a record of timing points, used to sync audio and video. Synonymous with breakdown.

CUG Closed user group.

culling In AIX graphics, not interpreting commands for operations on a primitive when the primitive is smaller than the minimum size specified in the command. See also clipping, pruning.

cumulative service tape A tape sent with a new function order, containing all current PTFs for that function.

currency sign Synonym for currency symbol.

currency symbol (1) Character like dollar sign ($) to identify monetary values. Synonymous with currency sign. (2) In BASIC, the character defined by the PIC$ function. (3) In COBOL, the character defined by the CURRENCY SIGN clause in the SPECIAL-NAMES paragraph.

Note: If no CURRENCY SIGN clause is present in a COBOL source program, the currency symbol is identical to the currency sign.

current backup version The latest backup copy of a data set or file.

current beam position On a CRT display device, coordinates on display surface where electron beam is aimed. Synonymous with starting point.

current connect group In RACF, the group with which a user is associated, for access checking purposes, during a terminal session or batch job.

current cursor position In the 3270 Information Display System, the position of the cursor in a partition's presentation space.

current device In System/38 graphics, the current output device for the application program, usually a display screen.

current directory (1) In DOS, the directory that is searched when a filename is entered with no indication of the directory that lists that filename. DOS assumes that the current directory is the root directory unless a path to another directory is specified. (2) In the OS/2 operating system, the first directory in which the operating system looks for programs and files and stores temporary files and output. Contrast with working directory. (3) In the AIX operating system, a directory that is active and that can be displayed. Relative path name resolution begins in the current directory. Synonymous with current working directory, working directory.

current directory path A DOS search sequence, consisting of a series of directory names starting with the current directory or root directory and leading to the directory that names a desired file.

current document A document that is being processed.

current drive Synonym for default drive.

current file disk address A file address that consists of disk sector and cylinder (track) numbers.

current files library In the OS/400 operating system, the files library to search for database files to be used by the System/36 environment for the current job.

current form In AS/400 query management, the form being applied against the data to produce the report being displayed or printed.

current graphics window In the AIX Graphics Library (GL), the window to which the system directs the output from graphics routines.

current-group indicator (CG) An indicator that signals whether a displayed record is from the same order set as the previously entered record.

current heap In XL Pascal, the area of storage where dynamic variables allocated by calls to NEW reside. Other heaps can exist at the same time, but only one is current.

current host Synonym for local host.

current left margin In the Document Composition Facility, the left limit of a column in effect for formatting.

current library (1) In System/36, the first library searched for any required members. The current library can be specified during sign-on or while running programs and procedures. (2) In the OS/400 operating system, the library that is specified to be the first user library searched for objects requested by a user.

current line (1) The line in a source document at which a computer program such as an editor or a formatter is positioned for processing. (2) The line on which the cursor is located.

current line pointer In systems with time sharing, a pointer that indicates the display line on which operations are being performed.

current mode In GDDM, the characteristics of the controlling session. For example, when a color is defined, everything the program draws uses that color until the color is changed.

current page In OfficeVision, a part of the status line in the document window of the Writing Pad function. The current page feature displays the page number of the document the user is currently viewing.

current pointer In programming, a pointer that is updated at each execution of a data manipulation language statement to identify the location of the current record of the data manipulation. (T)

current position (1) In the SDF/CICS map editor, the logical cursor position. (2) In computer graphics, the position, in user coordinates, that becomes the starting point for the next graphics routine, if that routine does not explicitly specify a starting point.

current print position In the Print Services Facility, the picture element that defines the character reference point or the upper left hand corner of an image.

current priority level In the IBM 8100 Information System, the number of the active or controlling priority level.

current record (1) The record pointed to by the current line pointer. (2) The record that is currently available to a program. (3) In COBOL file processing, the record that is available in the record area associated with a file.

current record pointer In COBOL, a method of identifying a record that is used in the sequential processing of the next record.

current release The latest available release of the system that replaced the licensed internal code, the operating system. or both.

current security label In RACF: (1) For interactive users, the security label specified when the user logged on, or, if no security label was specified, the default security label in the user's user profile. (2) For batch jobs on MVS, the security label specified in the SECLABEL parameter of the JOB statement, or, if no security label was specified, the default security label in the user profile associated with the job.

current state In SAA Advanced Common User Access architecture, the condition, active or inactive, of a choice. Current state emphasis shows a user that a choice is active. See current state emphasis.

current state emphasis In SAA Advanced Common User Access architecture, a visual cue that shows a user that a specific choice is active. An example is the check mark that is used in action bar pull-downs.

current transformation matrix In AIX graphics, the transformation matrix on top of the matrix stack. All points passed through the graphics pipeline are multiplied by the current transformation matrix before being passed on.

current volume pointer In COBOL, a conceptual entity that points to the current volume of a sequential file.

current working directory Synonym for current directory.

cursor (1) A pointer to an element of a set of results. (T) (2) A movable, visible mark used to indicate a position of interest on a display surface. (A) (3) In SAA Common User Access architecture, a visual cue that shows a user where keyboard input will appear on the screen. See selection cursor, text cursor. (4) In AIX Enhanced X-Windows, the visible shape of the pointer on a screen. A cursor consists of a hotspot, a source bitmap, and a pair of colors. (5) A primitive, such as an arrowhead, that can be moved about the screen by means of an input device, typically a mouse. (6) In SQL, a named control structure used by an application program to point to a row of data. The position of the row is within a table or view, and the cursor is used interactively to select rows from the columns.

cursor control keys Synonym for cursor movement keys.

cursor-dependent scrolling In SAA Basic Common User Access* architecture, a method of scrolling panel areas that scrolls through the information based on

where the cursor is positioned when a user requests the scrolling action.

cursored and selected emphasis In SAA Advanced Common User Access architecture, a visual cue in the form of a dotted outline box and inverse color that shows a user that a choice is currently selected and that the cursor is still on the selected choice. See cursored emphasis, selected emphasis.

cursored emphasis In SAA Advanced Common User Access architecture, a visual cue in the form of a dotted outline box that shows a user that the cursor is on a choice that can be selected.

cursor glyph In AIX graphics, a raster pattern that determines the shape of the cursor. A GL cursor glyph can be 1 or 2 bits deep; therefore, a GL cursor can use up to three colors.

cursor ID In AIX Enhanced X-Windows, a unique identification number that is associated with each unique type of cursor.

cursor-independent scrolling In SAA Basic Common User Access architecture, a method of scrolling panel areas that scrolls the information in fixed increments regardless of where the cursor is positioned when a user requests the scrolling action. The scrolling actions are backward, forward, left, and right.

cursor movement keys Keys that a user presses to move a cursor or a displayed image, labeled with a down arrow, a left arrow, a right arrow, and an up arrow.

curtate (1) A group of adjacent card rows. (A) (2) See lower curtate, upper curtate.

curvature loss Synonym for macrobend loss. (E)

curve fitting (1) The connection of plotted points in a continuous curve. (2) In the System/370 computing system, synonym for smoothness of curve.

curve follower An input unit that reads data represented by a curve. (I) (A)

curve generator A functional unit that converts a coded representation of a curve into the graphic representation of the shape of a curve for display. (I) (A)

curves and arcs In computer graphics, basic shapes of various types; for example, spline curves and three-point curves. See also spline curve, three-point curve.

cushion A contiguous address space in dynamic storage held in reserve and not normally used to satisfy a request for storage until such requests cannot be satisfied from other areas of dynamic storage.

Custom-Built Installation Process Offering A product that simplifies the ordering, installation, and service of MVS system control programs and licensed programs by providing them with current updates and corrections to the software that is already integrated.

customer Anyone who buys the products or services provided by IBM. Contrast with end user, user.

customer access area A designated area of a machine or system to which the customer has access to connect, install and maintain signals, control, power, or other utilities.

Customer Engineer (CE) See IBM service representative.

customer engineer user profile In System/38, the user profile supplied by the Control Program Facility (CPF) that has the authority necessary for a service representative to perform diagnostics and service the machine, and the special authority of job control rights.

customer ID In the Folder Application Facility, an identifier consisting of up to 15 alphanumeric characters. Customer IDs are stored in the customer database. See also customer identification number.

customer identification number A unique number assigned by a financial institution to each customer. The number is usually encoded on a magnetic stripe on a customer identification card that is used with a 3614 Consumer Transaction Facility. See also account number. Contrast with personal code.

Customer Information Control System (CICS) An IBM licensed program that enables transactions entered at remote terminals to be processed concurrently by user-written application programs. It includes facilities for building, using, and maintaining databases.

Cust. Info. Control System for Virtual Storage (CICS/VS) An IBM licensed program that can be used in a communications network.

customer location code Code that is used by the Folder Application Facility to determine proper routing destination for a document.

customer meter A device that records the machine running time accumulated by customer usage.

customer receipt tape In PSS an itemized transaction listing between customer and supermarket or record of administrative information obtained by an operator,

using store support procedures. Contrast with retail sales receipt tape.

customer-replaceable Designed to be removed and replaced by the customer, according to instructions provided by IBM, without the use of tools or help of IBM personnel.

customer replaceable unit (CRU) An assembly or part that a customer can replace in its entirety when any of its components fail. See also field replaceable unit.

Customer Service Representative (CSR) See IBM service representative.

customer setup (CSU) The unpacking, setup, and checkout of IBM CSU-designated machines by user personnel, according to a sequence of instructions provided by IBM, without the use of tools or help of IBM personnel.

customer set-up (CSU) products IBM products such as the 3767 Communication Terminal and 3770 Data Communication System that can be installed by the customer.

customer station equipment Communication common carrier transmitting and receiving equipment used in connection with private line services and located on the customer's premises.

customization (1) The process of designing a data processing installation or network to meet the requirements of particular users. (2) In DPPX, the process of defining and activating a configuration and changing system parameters to meet user requirements. (3) See system customization.

customization procedure The multistep process, performed in the host computer, of constructing a customized image for a 3614 Consumer Transaction Facility.

customization profile (1) A file that contains descriptions of optional changes to the default settings of a device or program. (2) A file containing the flags that specify the devices and parameters for an AIX PC Simulator/6000 session. See also customize.

customized database In the AIX operating system, a database that contains configuration data for defined or available devices in the system. See device configuration database, predefined database.

Customized Devices Object Class In the AIX operating system, an object class that represents each device instance by a unique logical name. The Customized Devices Object Class contains basic information about the device such as device status and how to access the information contained in other object classes.

customized image A combination of formatted customization data with selected modules of controller data which, when loaded into a 3614 Consumer Transaction Facility, determines the operation of the terminal. A customized image is produced by the Finance Image Processor.

custom palette In multimedia applications, a set of colors that is unique to one image or one application. See also color palette, standard palette.

cut (1) In multimedia applications, the process of instantly replacing a picture from one source with a picture from another. This is the most common form of editing scene to scene. (2) The act of copying a page, object, or picture to a separate file for later use. (3) In word processing, to identify a block that is to be deleted or moved to another place in the same or a different document.

CUT Control unit terminal mode.

Cut In SAA Common User Access architecture, a choice that removes a selected object, or a part of an object, to the clipboard, usually compressing the space it occupied in a window.

cut and paste (1) To move or copy artwork or text from a document to a clipboard so that it can be used in other documents. (T) (2) In word processing, to assemble a document by adding, deleting, and relocating artwork or text, or by inserting blocks from other documents.

cut form A single form not connected to other forms. The form may have an original and one or more copies. Contrast with continuous forms.

Note: Cut forms are fed separately into a printer.

cut-forms mode A mode in which a printer produces one form at a time.

cut object In the IBM LinkWay product, an object that has been copied to a file with the Object Cut function.

cutoff The point of degradation, due to attenuation or distortion, at which a signal becomes unusable.

cut-off Synonym for pruning. (T)

cutout A part of a form that has been eliminated or perforated for subsequent removal.

cutover The transfer of functions of a system to its successor at a given moment. (T) See also change-over system.

cut page In the IBM LinkWay product, a page that has been copied to a file with the Page Cut function.

cut picture In the IBM LinkWay product, a picture segment that has been copied to a file with the LinkWay Picture Cut function.

cut-to-tie ratio The ratio of the length of the cut and the length of the tie in the perforations between continuous forms. See also perforation, tie.

cw Clockwise.

CWALL An NCP threshold of buffer availability, below which the NCP will accept only high-priority path information units (PIUs).

cyan (1) The color obtained by mixing equal intensities of green and blue light. (2) The correct name for the subtractive primary color usually called "blue."

cyan/magenta/yellow (CMY) A color model used by the printing industry based on mixing cyan, magenta, and yellow. See also cyan/magenta/yellow/black (CMYK).

cyan/magenta/yellow/black (CMYK) A color model used by the printing industry based on mixing cyan, magenta, yellow, and black. CMYK is an enhancement of the cyan/magenta/yellow (CMY) model, created after printers discovered they could obtain a darker black using special black colorants rather than by combining cyan, magenta, and yellow alone.

cybernetics The branch of learning that brings together theories and studies on communication and control in living organisms and in machines. (I) (A)

cycle (1) An interval of space or time in which one set of events or phenomena is completed. (A) (2) Any set of operations repeated regularly in the same sequence. The operations may be subject to variations on each repetition. (A) (3) A complete vibration, electric oscillation, or alternation of current. (4) See display cycle, machine cycle, search cycle.

cycle sharing (1) The process by which a device uses machine cycles of another device or processing unit. (2) The process by which a channel adapter acquires machine cycles from the network control program for data transfer. Synonymous with cycle stealing.

cycles per second (cps) Synonym for hertz.

cycle steal A hardware function that allows I/O devices to access storage directly.

cycle stealing Synonym for cycle sharing.

cycle time (1) The minimum time interval between starts of successive read-write cycles of a storage device. (I) (A) (2) See access time, display cycle time, read cycle time, write cycle time. See Figure 37.

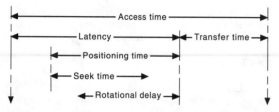

Figure 37. Cycle Time

cycle time reduction Reducing the total time between determining customer wants and needs and fulfilling them to the customer's total satisfaction. The cycle starts with a customer's expression of need, proceeds through the development, production and delivery of solutions, and the final payment of the bill.

cyclic redundancy check (CRC) (1) A redundancy check in which the check key is generated by a cyclic algorithm. (T) (2) A system of error checking performed at both the sending and receiving station after a block check character has been accumulated. See also longitudinal redundancy check, vertical redundancy check.

cyclic redundancy-check character (CRC) A character used in a modified cyclic code for error detection and correction. (A)

cyclic shift Synonym for end-around shift.

cyclic storage Synonym for circulating storage.

cylinder (1) In an assembly of magnetic disks, the set of all tracks that can be accessed by all the magnetic heads of a comb in a given position. (2) The tracks of a disk storage device that can be accessed without repositioning the access mechanism. (3) In a duplicator, a cylindrical rotating component that carries on its peripheral surface various components essential to the duplicating process such as the master, the blanket, the paper, and the ink screen. (T) See blanket cylinder, counter pressure cylinder, delivery cylinder, line-selection machine master cylinder, master cylinder. See Figure 38.

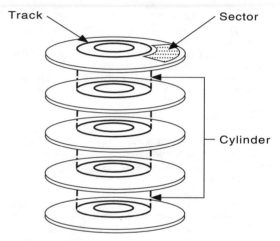

Figure 38. Cylinder

cylinder fault In MSS, a condition that occurs when the operating system requires data that has not been staged. The cylinder fault causes a cylinder of data to be staged.

cylinder gripper In a duplicator, a device built into a cylinder to hold the paper. (T)

cylinder pressure adjuster In a duplicator, a control for varying the pressure between the printing cylinders. (T)

D

d Deci. Ten or tenth part.

da Deka. Ten.

D/A (digital-to-analog) The conversion of data or signal storage from one format or method to the other.

DAA Data access arrangement.

DAC Digital-to-analog converter. (A)

DACTLINK Deactivate link.

DACTLU (1) Deactivate logical unit. (2) In SNA, a command used to end a session on a logical unit.

DACTPU (1) Deactivate physical unit. (2) In SNA, a command used to end a session on a physical unit.

daemon In the AIX operating system, a program that runs unattended to perform a standard service. Some daemons are triggered automatically to perform their task; others operate periodically. Synonymous with demon. See also qdaemon.

daemon process In the AIX operating system, a process begun by the root user or by the root shell that can be stopped only by the root user. Daemon processes generally provide services that must be available at all times, such as sending data to a printer.

DAF Destination address field.

DAF' Destination address field prime.

daily backup volume In the Data Facility Hierarchical Storage Manager, a volume associated with a particular day in the backup cycle and assigned to contain backup versions created on that day.

daily initialization diskette The diskette used to initialize the 3791 Controller. Synonymous with operating diskette.

daily space management In the Data Facility Hierarchical Storage Manager, the automatic space management of data sets that occurs once every 24 hours.

daisy chain A method of device interconnection for determining interrupt priority by connecting the interrupt sources serially.

daisy-chained cable In an IBM personal computer, a cable that has two or more connectors attached in series.

Note: A daisy-chained cable is used in the system unit to attach the 5-1/4 inch diskette drive adapter to one or two diskette drives.

daisy wheel printer An impact printer in which the type elements are mounted at the ends of arms that extend from a center point in the manner of the spokes of a wheel or the petals of a daisy. See Figure 39.

damage assessment routines (DAR) In OS/VS, routines that attempt recovery from system failures caused by software.

Figure 39. Daisy Wheel

damper applicator roller In a duplicator, a roller that applies damping fluid to the master. (T)

damper vibrator roller In a duplicator, a roller that alternately contacts the trough roller and a distributor roller. (T)

damping (1) A characteristic built into electrical circuits and mechanical systems to prevent unwanted oscillatory conditions. (2) In a duplicator, a process by which moistening fluid is conveyed from a reservoir to the master or copy paper. (T)

damping control In a duplicator, a control that governs the amount of fluid entering the damping system. (T)

damping pad In a duplicator, an absorbent pad that, when moistened, is used to dampen the surface of the copy paper either directly or via the moistening roller. (T)

damping pad holder In a duplicator, a case or tray that supports the damping pad. (T)

damping pressure roller In a duplicator, a roller that applies pressure to the trough roller to regulate the amount of fluid fed into the damping system. (T)

damping width selector In a duplicator, a device that determines the width of the damping pad that is moistened. (T)

DAN Direct attachment node.

dangling else A condition arising as a result of nesting an IF statement in the IF part of an IF-ELSE statement. The ELSE statement is associated with the closest IF statement, in this case, the inner one. Placing an empty ELSE statement in the nested statement prevents misinterpretation by forcing the outer ELSE statement to associate with the outer IF statement.

DAR Damage assessment routines.

dark trace tube In computer graphics, a type of cathode ray tube whose electron beam causes the phosphorescent surface of the tube to darken rather than to brighten. (T)

DARPA Defense Advanced Research Projects Agency

DASD Direct access storage device.

DASD conservation option A NetView installation option, available on the VM operating system, that allows the NetView program to be installed without the online help facility and hardware monitor data presentation panels.

DASD dump restore (DDR) program In VM, a service program used to copy all or part of a minidisk onto tape, load the contents of a tape onto a minidisk, or send data from a direct access storage device (DASD) or from tape to the virtual printer.

DASDERASE In MSS, an attribute of a mass storage volume that causes binary zeros to be written on the staging drive after data from the mass storage volume have been destaged.

DASD queue A queue that resides on a direct access storage device.

DASD sharing See shared DASD option.

DAT (1) Dynamic address translation. (2) Disk allocation table.

data (1) A re-interpretable representation of information in a formalized manner suitable for communication, interpretation, or processing. Operations can be performed upon data by humans or by automatic means. (T) (2) Any representations such as characters or analog quantities to which meaning is or might be assigned. (A) (3) A representation of facts or instructions in a form suitable for communication, interpretation, or processing by human or automatic means. Data include constants, variables, arrays, and character strings. (4) See absolute data, alphanumeric data, analog data, digital data, discrete data, input data, numeric data, output data, relative data, test data. (5) See also information.

Note: Programmers make a distinction between instructions and the data they operate on; however, in the usual sense of the word, data includes programs and program instructions.

data access arrangement (DAA) (1) Equipment that permits attachment of privately owned data terminal equipment and telecommunication equipment to a network. (2) Circuitry that allows communications equipment to be connected to the public switched telephone network.

data acquisition The process of identifying, isolating, and gathering source data to be centrally processed. See also data collection.

data administration The performance of functions of specifying, acquiring, providing, and maintaining the data of an organization. (T)

data administrator The person who defines, organizes, manages, controls, and protects data. (A)

data aggregate (1) In a database, a named collection of data items. (T) (2) A logical collection of two or more data items that can be referred to either collectively or individually; for example, in PL/I, an array or a structure.

data analysis A systematic investigation of the data and their flow in a real or planned system. (T)

data area (1) A storage area used by a program or device to hold information. (2) In the AIX operating system, an area of memory that contains specific control variables that are normally predefined in structures or vectors. (3) In the OS/400 operating system and System/38, a system object used to communicate data, such as values of control language variables, between the programs within and between jobs.

data area data structure A data structure used to retrieve data from a data area.

data attribute A characteristic of a unit of data such as length, value, or method of representation. (A)

data authority In the AS/400 system, a specific authority to read, add, update, or delete data. See also add authority, delete authority, read authority, update authority.

data bank (1) A set of data related to a given subject and organized in such a way that it can be consulted by subscribers. (T) (2) A comprehensive collection of libraries of data; for example, one line of an invoice may form an item, a complete invoice may form a record, a complete set of such records may form a file, the collection of inventory control files may form a library, and the libraries used by an organization are known as its data bank.

database (1) A collection of data with a given structure for accepting, storing, and providing, on demand, data for multiple users. (T) (2) A collection of interrelated data organized according to a database schema to serve one or more applications. (T) (3) A collection of data fundamental to a system. (A) (4) A collection of data fundamental to an enterprise. (A)

data base See database.

database administration The performance of the functions of defining, organizing, controlling, and protecting data in a database. (T)

database administration language (DAL) A language for database administration. (T)

database administrator (DBA) (1) An individual responsible for the design, development, operation, safeguarding, maintenance, and use of a database. (T) (2) The person who defines, organizes, manages, controls, and protects a database. (A) (3) A person who is responsible for a database system, particularly for defining the rules by which data are accessed and stored. The database administrator is usually responsible also for database integrity, security, performance, and recovery. (4) In systems with the Hierarchical Storage Manager, the person authorized to issue system programmer and operator commands and responsible for managing auxiliary storage space.

Data Base and Transaction Management System A DPPX licensed program that handles both transaction processing and database requests.

database call In DL/I, a method of identifying specific data within a DB/DC database.

database component In DPPX/DTMS, the component that provides services for databases. This and the transaction processing component are the two major components of DPPX/DTMS.

database description (DBD) In IMS/VS, the collection of macroparameter statements that describes an IMS/VS database. These statements describe the hierarchical structure, IMS/VS organization, device type, segment length, sequence fields, and alternate search fields. The statements are assembled to produce database description blocks.

database description generation (DBDGEN) The process by which a database description is created.

database design aid (DBDA) A design tool that performs a comprehensive analysis of application data requirements for OS/VS and VSE users.

database directory A DL/1 directory of all physical databases to be used by the CICS system.

database facility (DBF) (1) A set of commands in Programmable Store System Host Support used to create and maintain data in the host processor. (2) The group of modules in Programmable Store System Host Support that interpret, control, and execute the user-coded database facility (DBF) commands.

database file (1) An object that contains descriptions of how input data are to be presented to a program from internal storage and how output data are to be presented to internal storage from a program. See also logical file, physical file. (2) In the OS/400 operating system, one of several types of the system object type FILE kept in the system that contains descriptions of how input data is to be presented to a program from internal storage and how output data is to be presented to internal storage from a program. See also physical file, logical file.

database handler The component of a database management system that interprets the database calls, and that coordinates and executes the corresponding database access. (T)

database integrity In IMS/VS, the protection of data items in a database while they are available to any application program. This includes the isolation of effects of concurrent updates to a database by two or more application programs.

database key (1) A key, assigned by the database management system, that unambiguously identifies a record in a database. (T) (2) A unique value that serves as a pointer that identifies a record in the database to a run unit, and that may be used by the run unit to reselect the same record. (A)

database key translation table A table that maps database keys of record to addresses of the blocks containing these records. (T)

database language A language that is specific to databases; for example, a data manipulation language, a data definition language. (T)

database level In a hierarchical database, the successive vertical dependencies of records or segments.

database logging A method of database recovery in which changes to records in a database file are also written to a database log file.

database machine A computer specially designed for database applications. (T)

database management system (DBMS) (1) A computer-based system for defining, creating, manipulating, controlling, managing, and using databases. The software for using a database may be part of the database management system or may be a stand-alone database system. (T) (2) An integrated set of computer programs that collectively provide all of the capabilities required for centralized management, organization, and control of access to a database that is shared by many users. (A) (3) A computer-based system used to establish, make available, and maintain the integrity of a database, that may be invoked by nonprogrammers or by application programs to define, create, revise, retire, interrogate, and process transactions; and to update, back up, recover, validate, secure, and monitor the database. (A)

database position In IMS/VS, the location of a program in database after a DL/I request.

database record In IMS/VS, a collection of segments that contains one occurrence of the root segment type and all of its dependents arranged in a hierarchical sequence. It may be smaller than, equal to, or larger than the access method logical record.

database recovery control (DBRC) A part of IMS/VS that maintains information required for database recoveries and logging control. It also generates recovery jobs, verifies recovery input, maintains a separate change log for database data sets, and supports sharing of IMS/VS databases by multiple IMS/VS subsystems.

database reorganization In IMS/VS, the process of unloading and reloading a database to optimize physical segment adjacency or to modify the database description.

database schema (1) A formal specification of the representation forms and structure of a database; for collections of sentences from the conceptual schema and the information base. (T) (2) In a conceptual schema language, the definition of the representation forms and structure of a database for the possible collection of all sentences that are in the conceptual schema and in the information base, including manipulation aspects of these forms. (A)

database segment In IMS/VS, the unit of access to a database; for the database system, the smallest amount of data that can be transferred by one DL/I operation.

database specification A document that provides the basic design data necessary for the construction of system files, tables, and dictionaries, along with a description of storage allocation and database organization. (T)

database subschema A part of a database schema for one or more applications. (T)

Data Base Surveyor utility feature A utility that scans an IMS/VS database and provides reports that help determine the need to reorganize that database.

Data Base System In IMS/VS, the basic product that supports implementation of multiple applications using a common database. It is a prerequisite for all IMS/VS features.

database system Synonym for database management system (DBMS). (T)

database utility A program for installing, exploiting, or maintaining a database as a whole; for example, programs for loading, unloading, reconstructing, restructuring, consistency checking, statistics. (T)

DATABASE 2 (DB2) An IBM relational database management system.

DATABASE 2 Interactive An interactive relational database management program.

data block (DBLK) In VSE/POWER, the unit of transfer for spooling job input and job output. See block.

data bus (1) A bus used to communicate data internally and externally to and from a processing unit, storage, and peripheral devices. (A) (2) See bus.

data card See source data card.

data carrier Material that serves as a data medium or to which a data medium is applied, and that is designed to facilitate the transport of data; for example, a punch card or paper tape; a disk, drum, tape, or employee badge with a magnetizable surface that serves as the data medium. See also data medium.

data cartridge See magnetic tape cartridge. See also magnetic tape cassette.

data cell A direct access storage volume containing strips of tape on which data are stored.

data chain Synonym for data aggregate. (A)

data chaining In SDLC data transmission, the chaining together of scattered segments of storage data to assemble a complete SDLC frame.

data channel Synonym for input/output channel.

data character set (1) The 256 EBCDIC characters. (2) See character set.

data check (1) An operation used to verify data quality or data integrity. (T) (2) A synchronous or asynchronous indication of a condition caused by invalid data or incorrect positioning of data. Some data checks can be suppressed.

data circuit (1) A pair of associated transmit and receive channels that provide a means of two-way data communication. (I) (2) In SNA, synonym for link connection. (3) See tandem data circuit. See also physical circuit, virtual circuit. See figure at data link.

data circuit-terminating equipment (DCE) In a data station, the equipment that provides the signal conversion and coding between the data terminal equipment (DTE) and the line. (I) See figure at data link.

data circuit transparency The capability of a data circuit to transmit all data without changing the data content or structure. (I) (A)

data clause In COBOL, a clause in a data description entry in the Data Division that describes a particular characteristic of a data item.

data code (1) In data communication, a set of rules and conventions according to which the signals representing data should be formed, transmitted, received, and processed. (I) (A) (2) A structured set of characters used to represent the data items; for example, the codes 01, 02,..., 12 may be used to represent the months January, February,..., December of the data element months of the year. (A) (3) Deprecated term for code set, code element set. (4) See numeric code.

data code set Deprecated term for code element set.

data collection The process of bringing data together from one or more sources. See also data acquisition.

data collection station Synonym for data input station.

data communication (1) Transfer of data among functional units by means of data transmission according to a protocol. (T) (2) The transmission, reception, and validation of data. (A) See also transmission.

data communication adapter (1) An optional hardware feature, available on certain processors, that permits communications facilities to be attached to the processors. (T) (2) See communication adapter.

data communication channel A means of one-way transmission. (I) (A) Synonymous with data transmission channel. Contrast with input/output channel. See also logical channel.

data communication facility (DCF) (1) The group of modules in Programmable Store System Host Support that interpret, control, and execute the communication commands to transfer data between the host processor and one or more store controllers. DCF can use BSC or SDLC line protocol, as selected by the user. (2) Deprecated term for telecommunication facility.

data communication feature In IMS/VS, a feature that provides terminal communication and automatic scheduling of programs based on terminal input.

data communication interface See transmission interface.

data communication line See telecommunication line.

data communication network See network, path control network, public network, SNA network, user application network.

data communications See data communication.

data communication service See data transmission service.

data compaction See compaction.

data component The part of a VSAM data set, alternate index, or catalog that contains the data records of an object.

data compression See compression.

data concentrator (1) A functional unit that permits connection of several input communication lines to one output line of higher speed. (T) (2) See concentrator.

data connection The interconnection of two data terminal equipment (DTEs) by means of switched tandem data circuits to enable data transmission to take place between DTEs. (I)

data constant See figurative constant.

data contamination Synonym for data corruption.

data content Synonym for data inventory.

data control block (DCB) A control block used by access method routines in storing and retrieving data.

data conversion The process of changing data from one form of representation to another.

data converter A functional unit that transforms data from one representation to an equivalent representation. (T) (A)

data corruption (1) A violation of data integrity. (T) (2) Synonymous with data contamination.

data count field (DCF) In SNA, a binary count of the number of bytes in the basic information unit (BIU) or BIU segment associated with the transmission header (TH).

data country code (DCC) In X.25 communications, a 3-digit code, unique to each country, that specifies the X.21 call format used by a network in its International Data Number to call another station.

data declaration A nonexecutable statement that describes the characteristics of the data to be operated upon; for example, PICTURE clause, DIMENSION. (T) Synonymous with data declaration statement.

data declaration statement Synonym for data declaration.

data definition (1) A program statement that describes the features of, specifies relationships of, or establishes context of, data. (A) (2) Information that describes the contents and characteristics of a field, record, or file. A data definition can include such things as field names, lengths, locations, and data types. See field definition, file definition; format definition. (3) In the C language, a definition that describes a data object, reserves storage for a data object, and can provide an initial value for a data object. A data definition appears outside a function or at the beginning of a block statement.

data definition (DD) statement A job control statement describing a data set associated with a specific job step.

data definition language (DDL) A language for describing data and their relationships in a database. Synonymous with data description language. (T)

data definition name (ddname) The name of a data definition (DD) statement that corresponds to a data control block that contains the same name.

data density (1) The number of data characters stored per unit of length, area, or volume. (T) (2) The number of bytes per unit of measure on a recording medium; for example, bytes per inch.

data description For data objects that are not self-describing, components of the data object that describe the data so that it may be processed.

data description entry In COBOL, an entry in the Data Division of a COBOL program that is composed of a level-number followed by a data-name, if required, and then followed by a set of data clauses, as required.

data description language Synonym for data definition language. (T)

data description specifications (DDS) In the AS/400 system and System/38, a description of the user's database or device files that is entered into the system in a fixed form. The description is then used to create files.

data dictionary (1) A database that; for data of a certain set of applications, contains metadata that deal with individual data objects and their various occurrences in data structures. (T) (2) A centralized repository of information about data such as meaning, relationships to other data, origin, usage, and format. It assists management, database administrators, system analysts, and application programmers in planning, controlling, and evaluating the collection, storage, and use of data. (3) In the System/36 interactive data definition utility, a folder that contains field; format, and file definitions. (4) In IDDU, an object for storing field, record format, and file definitions.

data dictionary/directory (DD/D) (1) A database that combines the functions of a data dictionary and a data directory. (A) (2) An inventory of data resources that controls the totality of data elements within an application and that serves as the repository of all descriptive information about each data element, including location information. (A) (3) Loosely, a data dictionary/directory system. (A) (4) Loosely, synonym for information resource dictionary. (A)

data dictionary/directory system (DD/DS) (1) A computer software system that maintains and manages a data dictionary/directory. (A) (2) Loosely, synonym for information resource dictionary system. (A)

data dictionary system A software system for creating, maintaining, processing, and using database dictionaries. (T)

data directory (1) An inventory that specifies the source, location, ownership, usage, and destination of all of the data elements that are stored in a database. (A)   (2) A subset of a data dictionary/directory that has the functions of *(1)*. (A)   (3) Deprecated term for data dictionary. (T)

data directory system The computer software system that manages and maintains a data directory. (A)

data display station In System/36, a display station at which an operator can enter data but not commands. A data display station is acquired and controlled by a program. Contrast with command display station.

Data Division One of the four main parts of a COBOL program. The Data Division describes the files to be used in the program and the records contained within the files. It also describes any internal working-storage records that are needed.

data dump In COBOL, the contents of the data areas used by a program that has failed.

data element A unit of data that, in a certain context, is considered indivisible;   for example, the data element "age of a person" with values consisting of all three-decimal digit combinations. (T)

data element dictionary Synonym for data dictionary. (A)

data-encrypting key A key used to encipher, decipher, or authenticate data.   See also session cryptography key. Contrast with key-encrypting key.

data encryption algorithm (DEA) In computer security, a 64-bit block cipher that uses a 64-bit key, of which 56 bits are used to control the cryptographic process and 8 bits are used for parity checking to ensure that the key is transmitted properly.

Data Encryption Algorithm (DEA) Standard In computer security, the American National Standard ANSI X3.92-1981, which allows hardware and software implementations of the data encryption algorithm.

Data Encryption Standard (DES) In computer security, the National Institute of Standards and Technology (NIST) Data Encryption Standard, adopted by the U.S. government as Federal Information Processing Standard (FIPS) Publication 46, which allows only hardware implementations of the data encryption algorithm.

data encryption subroutine A subroutine that codes and decodes data for security purposes.

data entry (1) The process of putting data onto a machine-readable medium; for example, to enter data into a payroll file on a flexible disk from a terminal. (T)   (2) The entry of data into a computer from a device, usually a terminal. (3) In FORTRAN, an entity that has or may have a data value. (4) In VSAM, a catalog entry that describes a data component of a cluster or catalog. A data entry contains the attributes of the data component, allocation and extent information, and statistics. A data entry for a cluster or catalog data component can also contain the passwords and protection attributes of the data component.

data entry database (DEDB) In IMS/VS, a direct access database used for the Fast Path feature that consists of one or more areas that contain segments and dependent segments. The database is accessed using VSAM improved control interval processing (ICIP). See also sequential dependent segment.

data entry panel A panel in which the user communicates with the system by filling in one or more fields. See also menu, panel.

data exchange The use of data by more than one program or system. Data recorded or transmitted in a format is referred to as exchange data. See also data interchange.

data extent block (DEB) An extension of the data control block that contains information about the physical status of the data set being processed.

Data Facility Data Set Services (DFDSS) A backup and restore program product.

Data Facility Product (DFP) A program that isolates applications from storage devices, storage management, and storage device hierarchy management.

Data Facility Storage Management Subsystem An operating environment that helps automate and centralize the management of storage.   To manage storage, SMS provides the storage administrator with control over data class, storage class, management class, storage group, and automatic class selection routine definitions.

data field (1) A component of a record corresponding to an attribute. (T)   (2) In IMS/VS, any designated portion of a database segment.   A segment may contain one or more data fields.   (3) In SAA Advanced Common User Access, the Dialog Manager term for an area in which a user types information.

data file (1) A collection of related data records organized in a specific manner; for example, a payroll file (one record for each employee, showing such information as rate of pay and deductions) or an inventory file (one record for each inventory item, showing such information as cost, selling price, and number in stock). See also data set, file, logical file. (2) In BASIC, the table containing the values from the DATA statements of a program. (3) In RJE, a remote job input stream that can contain host system commands and job control language as well as data. Contrast with command file. (4) In the OS/400 operating system, a group of related data records organized in a specific order. A data file can be created by the specification FILETYPE(*DATA) on the create commands. Contrast with source file. (5) In System/38, any file that is not a source file. (6) In System/38 RJEF, a remote job input stream that can contain host system commands and job control language (JCL) as well as data. Contrast with command file. (7) In the System/36 MSRJE utility, a disk file, procedure member, or source member that can contain only records to be transmitted to the host system. Contrast with command file. (8) A direct access file maintained by VSE/POWER to hold the input and output data records required and generated by VSE programs under VSE/POWER control. The file may occupy from one to five extents of direct access storage according to the user's requirements. The total space provided by the user is divided into units called track groups for count-key-data (CKD) devices, or block groups for fixed-block architecture (FBA) devices.

data-file object In the OS/2 operating system and the PenPM operating system extension, an object that represents a file in the file system. Its primary purpose is to convey information, such as text, graphics, audio, or video. A document or spreadsheet is an example of a data-file object. Contrast with program-file object.

data file pointer In BASIC, an indicator that moves through the DATA file, consecutively pointing to each value as it is assigned to a corresponding variable in a READ statement.

data file utility (DFU) (1) In System/36, a part of the Utilities Program Product used to create a file, enter new information into a record, add new records, and display or print the records in a file. (2) In System/38, the utility of the Interactive Data Base Utilities licensed program used to maintain and display records in a database file.

data flow (1) In programming languages, the transfer of data between constants, variables, and files accomplished by the execution of statements, procedures, modules, or programs. (I) (2) In ACF/TCAM, the type of route or extended route that a message takes from the originating station or application program to its destination, including the host nodes that process the message while it is en route to its destination. See also level 1 data flow, level 2 data flow, level 2 + data flow, level 3 data flow.

data flow control (DFC) In SNA, a request/response unit (RU) category used for requests and responses exchanged between the data flow control layer in one half-session and the data flow control layer in the session partner.

data flow control (DFC) layer (1) In SNA, the layer within a half-session that controls whether the half-session can send, receive, or concurrently send and receive, request units (RUs); groups related RUs into RU chains; delimits transactions via the bracket protocol; controls the interlocking of requests and responses in accordance with control modes specified at session activation; generates sequence numbers; and correlates requests and responses. (2) See Systems Network Architecture (SNA).

data flow control (DFC) protocol In SNA, the sequencing rules for requests and responses by which network addressable units (NAUs) in a session coordinate and control data transfer and other operations; for example, bracket protocol.

data flow synchronous (DFSYN) response In VTAM programs, a normal-flow response that is treated as a normal-flow request so that it may be received in sequence with normal-flow requests.

data frame Synonym for packet.

data function keyboard In DPPX, the keyboard on the operator panel used to submit data or commands to the operating system.

data gathering See data acquisition, data collection.

data generator A data set utility program that creates multiple data sets within a job for the sequential and partitioned access methods.

data glossary A reference document that lists all of the data elements stored in a database and provides for each element a definition of its meaning and a specification of its uses in that database; the glossary may be included in a data dictionary, or it may be published separately for easy reference. (A)

datagram (1) In packet switching, a self-contained packet, independent of other packets, that carries information sufficient for routing from the originating data terminal equipment (DTE) to the destination DTE without relying on earlier exchanges between the DTEs and the network. (I) (2) In TCP/IP, the basic unit of information passed across the Internet environment. A datagram contains a source and destination address along with the data. An Internet Protocol (IP) datagram consists of an IP header followed by the transport layer data. See also packet, segment.

datagram delivery confirmation A facility that sends a call progress signal to inform the source data terminal equipment (DTE) that a datagram has been accepted by the destination DTE.

datagram nondelivery indication A facility that sends a call progress signal to inform the source data terminal equipment (DTE) that a datagram cannot be delivered to the destination DTE.

datagram service In packet switching, a service that routes a datagram to the destination identified in its address field without reference to datagrams previously sent or datagrams to be sent.

Notes:

1. *Datagrams may be delivered to a destination address in a different order than that in which they were entered into the network.*

2. *It may be necessary for users to provide DTE-to-DTE procedures; for example, to ensure delivery of datagrams to the destination address.*

3. *For a DTE/DCE interface operating in the packet mode, a datagram is conveyed as a single packet.*

data group (1) In the AS/400 Business Graphics Utility and System/38, a collection of values that identify the comparisons in a chart; for example, the relative size of the slices in a pie chart or the relative height of the bars in a bar chart. See also paired data. Contrast with data value. (2) In GDDM, a collection of data values displayed; for example, as a pie chart or as the plotted points on a line of a line chart. More than one data group may be displayed on a chart.

data hierarchy (1) A data structure consisting of sets and subsets such that every subset of a set is of lower rank than the data of the set. (A) (2) In COBOL, the relationship between a group item or record and the group data items and elementary data items that make it up.

data host (1) In an ACF/TCAM communication management configuration, a host that is dedicated to processing applications and does not control network resources, except for its locally attached devices. See also communication management host. (2) In the NetView program, synonym for data host node.

data host node In a communication management configuration, a type 5 host node that is dedicated to processing applications and does not control network resources, except for its channel-attached or communication adapter-attached devices. Synonymous with

data host. See also communication management configuration host node.

data independence (1) The property of a database management system that allows for application programs to be independent of changes in the data structure. (T) (2) The property of a database management system that enables data to be processed independently of access mode, storage method, or arrangement of data. (T) (3) In IMS/VS, the concept defining logical and physical data so that application programs do not depend on where physical units of data are stored; data independence reduces the need to modify application programs when data storage and access methods are modified.

data input station A user terminal primarily designed for entering data into a computer. Synonymous with data collection station. (T)

data integrity (1) The condition that exists as long as accidental or intentional destruction, alteration, or loss of data does not occur. (T) (2) Preservation of data for its intended use. (3) See also application integrity, system integrity.

data interchange The use of data by systems of different manufacture. See also data exchange.

data inventory In an information processing system, all of the data and their characteristics, including interdependencies. (T) Synonymous with data content.

data item (1) The smallest unit of named data that has meaning in the schema or subschema. (T) Synonymous with data element. (2) A unit of data, either a constant or a variable, to be processed. (3) In the AIX operating system, a unit of data to be processed that includes constants, variables, array elements, and character substrings. (4) In COBOL, a unit of data, excluding literals, defined by a COBOL program. See external data item, index data item, internal data item, variable occurrence data item. (5) In FORTRAN, a constant, variable, or array element. (6) Synonymous with host variable.

data-item separator Two characters used to indicate the end of a dummy data item to the testing phase of program validation services (PVS).

data key In cryptography, a key used to encipher, decipher, or authenticate data. Synonymous with cryptographic data key (KD). See data encrypting key.

data label In the AS/400 Business Graphics Utility and in GDDM, a text string that describes a set of data values. Data labels are used with bar charts, pie charts, and Venn diagrams.

Data language 1 (DL/I) (1) In IMS/VS, the data manipulation language that provides a common high-level interface between a user application and IMS/VS. (2) A database access language used under VSE and CICS/VS. (3) See parallel DL/I.

data library A set of related files; for example, in stock control a set of inventory control files may form a library of data. (I) (A)

data line (1) In the AS/400 Business Graphics Utility, a straight line drawn from either axis that shows the exact data values on a chart. (2) In GDDM, a line drawn parallel to a chart axis, through a specified value along the other axis.

data link (1) The assembly of parts of two data terminal equipment that are controlled by a link protocol, and the interconnecting data circuit, that enable data to be transferred from a data source to a data sink. (I) (2) The interconnecting data circuit and the link protocol between two or more equipments; it does not include the data source or the data sink. (3) In SNA, synonym for link. (4) Contrast with telecommunication line. (5) See also multiplex link.

Note: A telecommunication line is only the physical medium of transmission; for example, a telephone wire, a microwave beam. A data link includes the physical medium of transmission, the protocol, and associated devices and programs — it is both logical and physical. See Figure 40.

data link adapter (DLA) In DPCX, an adapter that performs the function common to the synchronous data link control (SDLC) protocol and allows for connection of displays and printers to the DPCX system by means of telecommunication facilities.

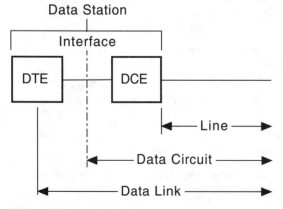

Figure 40. Data Link

data link attached loop In the IBM 8100 Information System, a transmission loop that is used to attach I/O

devices to the system through a data link facility rather than directly by means of cables. Contrast with directly attached loop.

data link connection identifier (DLCI) A numeric identifier that is used in a frame-relay network to identify the next segment of a permanent virtual circuit over which a frame is to be relayed.

data link control (DLC) A set of rules used by nodes on a data link (such as an SDLC link or a token ring) to accomplish an orderly exchange of information.

data link control character A control character intended to control or facilitate transmission of data over a network. Synonymous with communication control character.

data link control (DLC) layer (1) In SNA, the layer that consists of the link stations that schedule data transfer over a link between two nodes and perform error control for the link. Examples of data link control are SDLC for serial-by-bit link connection and data link control for the System/370 channel. (2) See Systems Network Architecture (SNA). (3) See also logical link control (LLC) sublayer, medium-access control (MAC) sublayer.

Note: The DLC layer is usually independent of the physical transport mechanism and ensures the integrity of data that reach the higher layers.

data link escape character (DLE) (1) A transmission control character that changes the meaning of a limited number of contiguously following characters or coded representations. (I) (A) (2) In BSC, a transmission control character used usually in transparent mode to indicate that the next character is a transmission control character.

data link layer (1) In the Open Systems Interconnection reference model, the layer that provides services to transfer data between entities in the network layer over a communication link. The data link layer detects and possibly corrects errors that may occur in the physical layer. (T) (2) See Open Systems Interconnection architecture reference model.

data link level (1) In the hierarchical structure of a data station, the conceptual level of control or processing logic between high level logic and the data link that maintains control of the data link. The data link level performs such functions as inserting transmit bits and deleting receive bits; interpreting address and control fields; generating, transmitting, and interpreting commands and responses; and computing and interpreting frame check sequences. See also higher level, packet level, physical level. (2) In X.25 communications, synonym for frame level.

data lock In the AIX operating system: (a) The ensurance of data availability to a single application program as a protection against conflicting updates to a data record. (b) The system lock that locks data segment into memory.

data locking In DPPX, the insurance of data availability to a single application program as a protection against conflicting updates to a data record. See also locked record.

data logging The recording of data about events that occur in time sequence. (A)

data loop transceiver (DLT) A station arrangement (data set) for Western Union's Class D leased data channels. See also data set (2), station arrangement.

data maintenance In PSS, the process of adding to, changing, or deleting information in store controller files.

data management (1) In a data processing system, the function that provides access to data, performs or monitors the storage of data, and controls input/output operations. (T) (2) The function of controlling the acquisition, analysis, storage, retrieval, and distribution of data. (A) (3) In an operating system, the computer programs that provide access to data, perform or monitor storage of data, and control input/output devices. (A) (4) In VSE, a major function of the operating system. It involves organizing, storing, locating, and retrieving data. (5) In System/36, the System Support Program Product support that processes a request to read or write data.

data manipulation language (DML) A programming language, supported by a database management system, used to access a database for operations such as creating, refunding, reading, writing, and deleting data.

Note: These operations may be specified in the form of procedures (procedural data manipulation language) or in the form of logical expressions (descriptive data manipulation language). (T)

data map In the 3800 Print Services Facility, an internal object in a page definition that specifies fonts, page segments, fixed text, page size, and placement and orientation of text.

data map transmission subcase In the 3800 Print Services Facility, an internal object that specifies the information for printing line data. One data map transmission subcase must appear in each data map of a page definition.

data medium (1) A material in or on which data can be recorded and from which data can be retrieved. (T) (2) See also data carrier, recording medium.

data medium protection device A movable or removable device that allows only reading of a data medium. (T)

data migration The moving of data from an online device to an offline or low-priority device, as determined by the system or as requested by the user. Contrast with staging.

data mode (1) A time at which BSC is transmitting or receiving characters on the line. (2) In the OS/400 operating system, System/36, and System/38 BASIC, the entry mode in which a user can enter BASIC statements and commands from a display station into the system without having the data checked. Contrast with program mode.

data model (1) A logical view of the organization of data in a database. (T) (2) In a database, the user's logical view of the data in contrast to the physically stored data, or storage structure. (A) (3) A description of the organization of data in a manner that reflects the information structure of an enterprise. (A) (4) See entity-relationship data model. (A)

data modeling A structured set of techniques for defining and recording business information requirements. It is a depiction of the end user's view of the data needs of the organization in a consistent and rigorous fashion. The data model eventually serves as the basis for translation to computer system databases.

data module (1) A removable and hermetically sealed disk pack that incorporates a read/write assembly and disks. (T) (2) A sealed, portable assembly that contains magnetic disks and an access mechanism.

data multiplexer See multiplexer.

data name (1) A character or group of characters used to identify an item of data. (I) (A) (2) In COBOL, a user-defined word that names a data item described in a data description entry. See control data-name, subscripted data-name. (3) See also identifier.

data network (1) An arrangement of data circuits and switching facilities for establishing connections between data terminal equipment. (I) (2) See also synchronous data network.

data network identification code (DNIC) A 4-digit code that specifies the X.21 call format used by a network in its International Data Number to call another station. The first three numbers are the data country code, and the last number is the country network identifier. See also data country code (DCC).

data object (1) A collection of data referred to by a single name. (2) In a program, an element of data structure, such as a file, array, or operand, that is needed for the execution of a program and that is named or otherwise specified by the allowable character set of the language in which the program is coded. (3) A program variable that provides operational and possibly representational characteristics to byte strings in spaces. Contrast with machine object. (4) In FORTRAN, a named datum or a set of data of the same type and type parameters that has a symbolic name and may be referenced as a whole. It may be a named variable or a symbolic constant. See definition of a data object.

data organization See data set organization.

data packet In X.25 communications, a packet used for the transmission of user data on a virtual circuit at the DTE/DCE interface.

data phase See data transfer phase.

Dataphone digital service (DDS) The AT&T** line service that allows the customer to transmit data on the line in a digital format.

data pointer A pointer that provides addressability and scalar representational attributes to a byte string in a space.

data portability The ability to use data sets or files with different operating systems. Volumes whose data sets or files are cataloged in a user catalog can be demounted from storage devices of one system, moved to another system, and mounted on storage devices of that system.

data processing The systematic performance of operations upon data; for example, arithmetic or logic operations upon data, merging or sorting of data, assembling or compiling of programs. Synonymous with automatic data processing. (T) See distributed data processing, integrated data processing, remote access data processing. See also information processing.

data processing center Synonym for computer center. (T)

data processing node In a computer network, a node at which data processing equipment is located. (T)

data processing station (1) At a data processing node, data processing equipment and associated software. (T) (2) See also workstation.

data processing system One or more computers, peripheral equipment, and software that perform data processing. Synonymous with computer system, computing system. (T) See also computer, computer system, information processing system.

data processing system security The technological and administrative safeguards established and applied to a data processing system to protect hardware, software, and data from accidental or malicious modifications, destruction, or disclosure. Synonymous with computer system security. (I) (A)

data processor See processor.

data protection (1) The implementation of appropriate administrative, technical or physical means to guard against unauthorized access to data. (T) (2) A safeguard against the unauthorized modification or destruction of data. See also integrity, security.

data purging The purging by a transaction processing system of a logical record that has been received and buffered but not yet retrieved by a transaction program. Data purging occurs when a receiving transaction program terminates abnormally or encounters an error before it has retrieved all of the buffered data associated with the logical record. Contrast with data truncation.

data quality The correctness, timeliness, accuracy, completeness, relevance, and accessibility that make data appropriate for their use. (T)

data queue In the AS/400 system, an object that is used to communicate and store data used by several programs in a job or between jobs.

data rate The speed of a data transfer process, normally expressed in bits per second or bytes per second. For example, the data rate of a CD-ROM is 150,000 bytes per second.

data receiver A device that converts data from analog representation as transmitted on telecommunication facilities to digital representation for use in digital computers.

data record (1) In VSAM, a collection of items of information from the standpoint of its use in an application, as the user supplies it; VSAM stores the data record, physically separate from its associated control information, in a control interval. (2) In the IBM 3886 Optical Character Reader, the standard or image mode data (1 to 30 bytes) that the 3886 provides to the user along with a header record.

data recording control In MSS, the component of the 3851 Mass Storage Facility that starts and stops data recording devices, encodes and decodes data, and assists in error recovery.

data recording device (DRD) In MSS, the unit in the 3851 Mass Storage Facility that reads and writes data on the data cartridge magnetic tape.

data reduction The transformation of raw data into a more useful form; for example, smoothing to reduce noise. (A)

data reference line In GDDM, a data line that also acts as a shading boundary for the first data group of a surface chart, histogram, or composite bar chart, or for all the data groups of a multiple bar chart. If no data reference line is present, such data groups are shaded from the horizontal axis.

data resource Any data created manually or by automatic means, used by a system or enterprise to represent its information. (A)

data resource management The responsibility for planning, organizing, and controlling data resources consistent with the overall goals and objectives of an enterprise. See also information resource management. (A)

data rights In System/38, the authority to read, add, update (modify), or delete data contained in an object. See also add rights, delete rights, read rights, update rights.

data scaling See scaling.

data security The protection of data from accidental or intentional modification or destruction and from accidental or intentional disclosure to unauthorized personnel. See also data integrity. (A) See also data processing system security.

data security monitor (DSMON) A RACF auditing tool that produces reports that enable an installation to verify its basic system integrity and data security controls.

data sensitive fault A fault that is revealed as a result of the processing of a particular pattern of data. (T) Contrast with pattern-sensitive fault.

data services In DPCX, the part of program services that provides methods of access to data sets residing on disk, diskette, and tape.

data services command processor (DSCP) In the NetView program, a component that structures a request for recording and retrieving data in the application program's database and for soliciting data from a device in the network.

data services manager (DSM) A function in the NetView program that provides VSAM services for data storage and retrieval.

data services request block (DSRB) The control block in the NetView program that contains information that a data services command processor (DSCP) needs to communicate with the data services task (DST).

data services task (DST) The NetView program subtask that gathers, records, and manages data in a VSAM file or a network device that contains network management information.

data service unit (DSU) A device that provides a digital data service interface directly to the data terminal equipment. The DSU provides loop equalization, remote and local testing capabilities, and a standard EIA/CCITT interface.

data set (1) The major unit of data storage and retrieval, consisting of a collection of data in one of several prescribed arrangements and described by control information to which the system has access. See consecutive data set, direct data set, partitioned data set, relative sequential data set, reset information data set, sequential data set. (2) Deprecated term for modem. (3) See also file.

data set access methods In the IBM 3471 Data Station, the methods available in the application control language program to access data sets for online processing.

data set authority credential (DSAC) In DPPX, a value assigned to each user and to each data set for the purpose of establishing a user's rights to access the data sets.

data set clocking A time base oscillator supplied by the data set for regulating the bit rate of transmission. Contrast with business machine clocking.

data set control block (DSCB) (1) A data set label for a data set in direct access storage. (2) Control information used to create a data set that meets defined specifications.

data set definition (DSD) A description of the characteristics of a data set.

data set deletion In the Data Facility Hierarchical Storage Manager, the space management technique for deleting data sets that have not been referred to for a specified number of days.

data set extension (DSE) In TSO, a control block containing control information for each of a terminal user's data sets.

data set group (1) In IMS/VS, an operating system data set that contains a subset of a database with one or more unique segment types. A database always consists of at least one data set group. See also primary data set group, secondary data set group. (2) In the Data Facility Hierarchical Storage Manager, data sets that have the same high level qualifier in their data set names.

data set header A page in printed output that separates copies of a data set. When more than one copy of a data set is printed, a data set header precedes each copy.

data set ID In the 3790 Communication System, a number assigned to a relative or indexed data set when the data set is defined at the host system. The number is later used in 3790 programs to identify the data set.

data set key In the 3790 Communication System, the part of an indexed data set record that uniquely identifies that record within the data set. Each record may have one or two keys (primary and secondary), and they may be binary, decimal, or alphanumeric data. The key or keys are in fixed positions within the first 240 bytes of each record. See also primary key, secondary key.

data set label (DSL) (1) A collection of information that describes the attributes of a data set and is normally stored on the same volume as the data set. (2) Data set control blocks and tape data set labels.

data set members Members of partitioned data sets that are individually named elements of a larger file that can be retrieved by name.

data set name The term or phrase used to identify a data set. See also qualified name.

data set organization The arrangement of information in a data set; for example, sequential organization, partitioned organization.

data set profile (1) In RACF, a profile that provides protection for one or more data sets. The information in the profile can include the data set profile name, profile owner, universal access authority, access list, and other data. See discrete profile, generic profile. (2) In DPPX, an area of a data set that describes characteristics of the data set such as record size, block size, and authorization requirements.

data set retirement In the Data Facility Hierarchical Storage Manager, the space management technique for deleting data sets that have not been referred to for a specified number of days, have a current backup version, and have not been referred to since the backup version was made.

data set security See data security.

data set utility programs Programs that can be used to update, maintain, edit, and transcribe data sets.

data signal A signal that represents a set of digits used to convey information, service functions, or both, and which may include check digits.

data signaling rate (1) The aggregate of the number of binary digits (bits) per second in the transmission path of a data transmission system. (I) (2) In data communication, the data transmission capacity of a set of parallel channels. The data signaling rate is expressed in bits per second. (A)

Notes:

1. *The data signaling rate is given by:*

$$\sum_{i=0}^{m} \frac{1}{T_i} \log_2 n_i$$

   where m is the number of parallel channels; T_i is the minimum interval for the i-th channel expressed in seconds; n_i is the number of significant conditions of the modulation in the i-th channel.

2. *For a single channel (serial transmission) the rate is $(1/T) \log_2 n$; with a two-condition modulation (n=2), it is $1/T$.*

3. *For parallel channels with equal minimum intervals and equal number of significant conditions on each channel, it is $(m/T) \log_2 n$; with a two-condition modulation, it is m/T.*

data sink (1) The functional unit that accepts transmitted data. (I) (2) The part of a data terminal equipment (DTE) that receives data from a data link. (3) Contrast with data source.

data source (1) The functional unit that originates data for transmission. (I) (2) The part of a data terminal equipment (DTE) that enters data into a data link. (3) Contrast with data sink.

data space In VSAM and DPPX, a storage area defined in the volume table of contents of a direct-access volume to store files, indexes, and catalogs.

data staging In ACF/TCAM, an extended networking technique in which high-volume, low-priority message traffic is moved from one host node to another, progressively approaching the destination host. Data staging allows such traffic to be moved at a convenient time to avoid overloading the network and to protect response times for high-priority inquiries. See staging.

data station The data terminal equipment (DTE), the data circuit-terminating equipment (DCE), and any intermediate equipment. (I) (A) Synonymous with data terminal installation. See Figure 40.

data storage definition language Synonym for data storage description language. (T)

data storage description language A language for defining the representation of stored data in terms that are independent of any particular storage device or operating system. (T)

data stream (1) All information (data and control commands) sent over a data link usually in a single read or write operation. (2) A continuous stream of data elements being transmitted, or intended for transmission, in character or binary-digit form, using a defined format. See also data stream format. (3) In the AIX operating system, all information sent to the high function terminal (HFT) device driver with a write subroutine. Synonymous with stream. (4) In DPCX, data that is being transmitted, or intended for transmission to or from a program or system services. A data stream is identified by its direction and its intended source or destination. (5) See input stream, output stream.

data stream format In SNA, the format of the data elements (end-user data) in the request unit (RU). See also 3270 data stream, SNA character string (SCS).

data streaming The uninterrupted transfer of information over an interface in order to achieve high data transfer rates. (A)

data-stream interface (DSI) In DPPX, an intermediate level of communication support accessed through SEND and RECEIVE macros. At this level, the user is responsible for handling the format of data sent to devices.

data structure (1) The syntactic structure of symbolic expressions and their storage allocation characteristics. (T) (2) In the AS/400 system and System/38 RPG, an area in storage that defines the layout of the fields, called subfields, within the area. A data structure can be either program described or externally described. (3) See logical data structure, physical data structure. (4) Synonymous with host structure.

data sublanguage A set of statements for using a database, added to a conventional programming language; for example, embedded SQL. (T)

data switching exchange (DSE) (1) The equipment installed at a single location to provide switching functions, such as circuit switching, message switching,

and packet switching. (I) (2) See also digital data switching.

data terminal equipment (DTE) That part of a data station that serves as a data source, data sink, or both. (I) (A)

data terminal installation Synonym for data station.

data terminal ready (DTR) A signal to the modem used with the EIA 232 protocol.

data traffic In data communication, the quantity of data transmitted past a particular point in a path. See also throughput.

data traffic reset state The state a session usually enters before the start data traffic state, and after Clear or Bind Session, if cryptography verification (CRV) is used. While a session is in this state, requests and responses for data and data flow control cannot be sent. Only certain session control requests can be sent. See also command.

data transfer The movement, or copying, of data from one location and the storage of the data at another location.

data transfer mode Synonym for data transfer phase.

data transfer phase The phase of a data call during which data signals can be transferred between data terminal equipments (DTEs) connected via the network. Synonymous with data transfer mode. See also network control phase.

data transfer rate The average number of bits, characters, or blocks, per unit time passing between corresponding equipment in a data transmission system. (I) See actual data transfer rate, effective data transfer rate.

data transfer state See data transfer phase.

data transformation In System/38, changing the form of data according to specific rules as data are moved by means of a logical file between the database and the using program. Data transformation includes changing data type and length.

data transmission The conveying of data from one place for reception elsewhere by telecommunication means. (I)

data transmission channel Synonym for data communication channel.

data transmission facility See telecommunication facility.

data transmission interface (1) A shared boundary defined by functional characteristics, common physical interconnection characteristics, signal characteristics, and other characteristics as appropriate. The concept involves the specification of the connection of two devices having different functions. (I) (A) (2) See transmission interface.

data transmission line Synonym for telecommunication line.

data transmission service See transmission service.

data truncation Truncation of a logical record by the sending transaction processing system. Data truncation occurs when the sending transaction program terminates abnormally or encounters an error while sending the record; as a result, when the record arrives at the receiving transaction processing system, the value in the length field is greater than the actual length of the record. Contrast with data purging.

data type (1) In programming languages, a set of values together with a set of permitted operations. (I) (2) The mathematical properties and internal representation of data and functions. The four basic types are integer, real, complex, and logical. (3) An attribute used for defining data as numeric or character. (4) A category that identifies the mathematical qualities and internal representation of data. (5) In FORTRAN, a set of data values, together with a way to denote these values and a collection of operations that interrupt and manipulate the values. A type may be parameterized, in which case the set of data values depends on the values of the parameters. (6) In C language and Pascal, a set of values, together with a set of permitted operations. A data type determines the kind of values that a variable can assume, or that a function can return. (7) In SQL, an attribute of columns, constants, and host variables. (8) See enumeration data type.

data types In the NetView program, a description of the organization of panels. Data types are alerts, events, and statistics. Data types are combined with resource types and display types to describe the NetView program's display organization. See also display types, resource types.

data validation (1) A process used to determine if data are inaccurate, incomplete, or unreasonable; the process may include format checks, completeness checks, check key tests, reasonableness checks and limit checks. (T) (A) (2) The checking of data for correctness or compliance with applicable standards, rules, and conventions. (A)

data value (1) In a database, an item of data viewed as a member of a data type. (T) (2) In the AS/400 Business Graphics Utility, a single, numeric data item

entered as a value for a horizontal line or vertical line. Contrast with data group.

data volatility Pertaining to the rate of change in the values of stored data over a period of time. (A)

date field In the System/38 source entry utility, a field in a source record that contains the date of the last change.

datum line In System/38 graphics, a straight reference line drawn from either axis that helps the user see the exact data values on the chart. See X-datum line, Y-datum line.

daughterboard In a personal computer, a board or card, containing circuits on microchips, that can be plugged into a motherboard.

DB Database.

dB Decibel.

DBA Database administrator.

dBa Adjusted decibels.

DBCS Double-byte character set.

DBCS code The hexadecimal code, 2 bytes in length, that identifies a double-byte character.

DBCS conversion In the OS/400 operating system, a function that allows a DBCS display station user to enter alphanumeric data and request that the alphanumeric data be converted to double-byte data.

DBCS conversion dictionary In the OS/400 operating system, a collection of alphanumeric entries with the double-byte entries that correspond to the alphanumeric entries. It is used by the DBCS conversion function.

DBCS font file In the OS/400 operating system, a system-supplied file that holds the 24x24 character images of one of the following groups of commonly used characters: (a) Japanese non-Kanji and basic-Kanji, (b) Korean non-Hangeul/non-Hanja, Hangeul, and a subset of Hanja, (c) Traditional Chinese non-Chinese and a subset of primary Chinese characters, or (d) all IBM-defined Simplified Chinese characters.

DBCS font table In the OS/400 operating system, a system-supplied table that holds either 24x24 or 32x32 pel character images of a double-byte character set. A Japanese 24x24 DBCS font table holds Japanese extended Kanji and user-defined characters. A Korean 24x24 DBCS font table holds a subset of Hanja and user-defined characters. A Traditional Chinese 24x24 DBCS font table holds a subset of primary Traditional

Chinese, all secondary Chinese, and user-defined characters. A Simplified 24x24 DBCS font table holds IBM-supplied Simplified Chinese characters as well as user-defined characters. A 32x32 DBCS font table holds 32x32 pel character images of a double-byte character set, including its user-defined characters.

DBCS number In the OS/400 operating system, the decimal value, 5 digits in length, that identifies a double-byte character.

DBCS-only field In the OS/400 operating system, a field that must contain only double-byte characters. See also either field, open field.

DBCS sort table In the OS/400 operating system, a system-supplied object that contains sequencing information to sort double-byte characters. See active sort table, master sort table.

DBD Database description.

DBDA Database design aid.

DB (database) monitor In IMS/VS, an optional facility that traces the internal activities of an IMS/VS database system.

DB/DC Database/data communication.

DBDGEN Database description generation.

DBF Database facility.

D-bit In X.25 communications, the bit in a data packet or call-request packet that is set to 1 if end-to-end acknowledgment (delivery confirmation) is required from the recipient. See also M-bit, Q-bit.

DBLK Data block.

dBm Decibel based on one milliwatt.

dB meter A meter having a scale calibrated to read directly in decibel values at a reference level that must be specified. Usually one milliwatt equals zero dB. It is used to indicate volume level in audio-frequency amplifier circuits of broadcast stations, public address systems, and receiver output circuits.

DBMS Database management system.

dBrn Decibels above reference noise.

DB2 Data Base 2.

DC (1) Data communication. (2) Direct current. (3) Data chaining.

DCB (1) Data control block. (2) Device control block.

DCC Data country code.

DC (data communication) monitor In IMS/VS, an optional facility that records activity within the control region and dependent regions.

DCE Data circuit-terminating equipment.

DCE clear confirmation packet A call supervision packet that a data circuit-terminating equipment (DCE) transmits to confirm that a call has been cleared.

DCE/DTE interface See DTE/DCE interface.

DCF (1) Data communication facility. (2) Data count field. (3) Document Composition Facility, an IBM licensed program used to format input to a printer.

DCM Diagnostic control manager.

DC1, DC2, DC3, DC4 Device control characters. (A)

DD Device driver.

DDA Digital differential analyzer. (A)

DDD Direct distance dialing.

DDDEF DD definition.

DD definition Definition of the libraries and data sets to be used by SMP/E during installation.

DD/DS Data dictionary/directory system. (A)

DDIR Database directory.

D-disk In CMS, the disk that becomes a user disk with a mode letter of D if the user logs on and a virtual disk at address 192 is defined in the virtual machine configuration.

DDL Data description language.

DDM Distributed Data Management.

DDM file In the OS/400 operating system, a system object with type *FILE, created by a user on the local (source) system, that identifies a data file that is kept on a remote (target) system. The DDM file provides the information needed for a local system to locate a remote system and to access the data in the remote data file.

DDN Defense Data Network.

ddname Data definition name.

DDP Distributed data processing.

DDR (1) DASD dump restore. (2) Dynamic device reconfiguration.

DDS (1) Dataphone digital service. (2) Data description specifications.

DDSA Digital data service adapter.

DD statement Data definition statement.

DDX Digital data exchange.

DE Device-end.

DEA Data encryption algorithm.

deactivate To take a resource of a node out of service, rendering it inoperable, or to place it in a state in which it cannot perform the functions for which it was designed. Contrast with activate.

deactivation The process of taking any element out of service, rendering it inoperable, or placing it in a state in which it cannot perform the functions for which it was designed.

DEA device The electronic part or subassembly that implements only the Data Encryption Algorithm (DEA) , as specified in ANSI X3.92-1981.

dead key Deprecated term for nonescaping key.

dead-letter file A file containing mail messages that could not be sent to a proper destination file.

dead-letter queue In ACF/TCAM, a queue with messages that couldn't be placed in a proper destination queue for a station or application program.

deadlock (1) A situation in which two or more activations of asynchronous procedures are incapable of proceeding because of their mutual dependencies. (T) (2) Unresolved contention for use of a resource. (3) An error condition in which processing cannot continue because each of two elements of the process is waiting for an action by or a response from the other. (4) An impasse that occurs when multiple processes are waiting for the availability of a resource that will not become available because it is being held by another process that is in a similar wait state. (5) See also starvation.

deadly embrace Deprecated term for deadlock. (A)

dead position The last position of a 3270 Kanji display field that ends at an even-address location; that is, the next field starts at the next odd-address location. When the cursor is located at this location, depression of any graphic key causes an input-inhibit condition.

dead zone An area of a tablet from which no input reports are generated. Each virtual terminal can set its own dead zones. Synonymous with no-input zone.

dead zone unit A functional unit whose output analog variable is constant over a particular range of the input analog variable. (I) (A)

DEA input block A block entered into the Data Encryption Algorithm (DEA) for encryption or decryption. The input block is designated (I1, I2,..., I64), where I1, I2,..., I64 represent bits.

deallocate (1) To release a resource assigned to a task. Contrast with allocate. (2) A logical unit (LU) 6.2 application program interface (API) verb that terminates a conversation, thereby freeing the session for a future conversation. Contrast with allocate.

deallocation See memory deallocation.

DEA output block A block that is the final result of an encryption or decryption operation. The output block is designated (O1, O2,..., O64), where O1, O2,..., O64 represent bits.

DEB Data extent block.

debit card An identification card that may be used to transfer funds from one account to another. (A)

deblock To separate the parts of blocks; for example, to select records from a block. (A)

deblocking (1) The process of making each logical record of a block available for processing. Contrast with blocking. (2) See also deconcentration.

debossed character A character that is depressed in relief into the surface of a medium such as a credit card. Contrast with embossed character. (A)

debug (1) To detect, to locate, and to eliminate errors in computer programs. (T) (2) To detect, diagnose, and eliminate errors in programs. (T) (3) Synonymous with checkout, troubleshoot.

debugger A program or programs used to detect, trace, and eliminate errors in computer programs or other software.

debugging Acting to detect and correct errors in software or system configuration.

debugging line (1) In COBOL, a COBOL statement run only when the WITH DEBUGGING MODE clause is specified. Debugging lines can help determine the cause of an error. (2) In COBOL, any line with a D in the indicator area of the line.

debugging mode A mode in which a program provides detailed output about its activities in order to aid a user in detecting and correcting errors in the program itself or in the configuration of the program or system.

Debugging Section (1) In COBOL, a declaratives section that receives control when an identifier, file-name, or procedure-name is encountered in the Procedure Division. (2) In COBOL, a section that contains a USE FOR DEBUGGING statement.

debug mode (1) In the Data Facility Hierarchical Storage Manager, a mode used by a system programmer during testing to determine the changes that would occur in normal volume processing without moving user data. (2) An environment in which programs can be tested.

deca (da) Ten.

decaliter (dal) (1) Ten liters. (2) 2.64 gallons.

decameter (dam) (1) Ten meters. (2) 32.81 feet.

decay constant In TSO, a weighting factor used in calculating the duration of a job's next time slice based on its use of previous time slices. Recent time slices are more heavily weighted than earlier time slices.

deceleration time The time required to stop a tape after reading or recording the last piece of information from a record on that tape.

deci Tenth part.

decibel (dB) (1) One tenth of a bel. (2) A unit that expresses the ratio of two power levels on a logarithmic scale. (3) A unit for measuring relative power. The number of decibels is ten times the logarithm (base 10) of the ratio of the measured power levels; if the measured levels are voltages (across the same or equal resistance), the number of decibels is 20 times the log of the ratio. See also circuit noise level, neper, power level.

deciliter (dl) (1) One tenth of a liter. (2) 0.21 pints.

decimal (1) Characterized by a selection, choice, or condition that has 10 possible different values or states. (I) (A) (2) Pertaining to a system of numbers to the base ten. Decimal digits range from 0 through 9. (3) Synonymous with denary. (4) See binary-coded decimal notation.

decimal alignment See automatic decimal alignment.

decimal arithmetic operation A type of arithmetic operation in which data enter and leave a system as zoned decimal and are processed as packed decimal.

decimal constant A number containing any of the digits 0 through 9.

decimal digit A digit used in the decimal numeration system; for example, the "Arabic" digits 0 through 9. (T)

decimal feature In the System/370 computing system, a feature that permits storage-to-storage decimal arithmetic operation.

decimal fixed-point constant A constant consisting of one or more decimal digits with an optional decimal point.

decimal fixed-point value A rational number consisting of a sequence of decimal digits with an assumed position of the decimal point. Contrast with binary fixed-point value.

decimal floating-point constant A value made up a significand that consists of a decimal fixed-point constant, and an exponent that consists of the letter E, followed by an optionally signed integer constant not exceeding three digits.

decimal floating-point value An approximation of a real number, in the form of a significand, which can be considered as a decimal fraction, and an exponent, which can be considered as an integer exponent to the base ten. Contrast with binary floating-point value.

decimal marker A visual indication of the position of the decimal point or decimal comma in a number. (T)

decimal mode See fixed decimal mode, floating decimal mode. (A)

decimal notation (1) A notation that uses ten different characters, usually the decimal digits; for example, the character string 196912312359, construed to represent the date and time one minute before the start of the year 1970; the representation used in the Universal Decimal Classification (UDC). (I) (A) (2) Contrast with decimal numeration system.

decimal numeral A numeral in the decimal numeration system. (A)

decimal numeration system The fixed radix numeration system that uses the decimal digits and the radix 10 and in which the lowest integral weight is 1; for example, in this numeration system, the numeral 576.2 represents the number $5 \times 10^2 + 7 \times 10^1 + 6 \times 10^0 + 2 \times 0^{-1}$ (I) (A) Contrast with decimal notation.

decimal point (1) The radix point in the decimal numeration system. The decimal point may be represented, according to various conventions, by a comma, by a period, or by a point at the mid-height of the digits. (I) (A) (2) A graphic symbol, usually a period or comma, used to separate the fractional part of a decimal number from the whole part of a decimal number. Synonymous with decimal symbol. (3) See actual decimal point, assumed decimal point.

decimal symbol Synonym for decimal point.

decimal tabulation In word processing, automatic vertical alignment of decimal symbols such as commas or periods in a list of figures.

decimal tabulator keys On a typewriter, a row of nine keys by means of which the starting points for typing figures in columns are automatically located in advance of the decimal marker according to the number of digits selected. (T)

decimeter (dm) (1) One tenth of a meter. (2) 3.94 inches.

decipher (1) To convert enciphered data in order to restore the original data. (T) (2) In computer security, to convert ciphertext into plaintext by means of a cipher system. (3) To convert enciphered data into clear data. Contrast with encipher. Synonymous with decrypt.

decision See leading decision, trailing decision.

decision content In information theory, a logarithmic measure of the number of decisions needed to select a given event among a finite number of mutually exclusive events; in mathematical notation, this measure is:

$$H_0 = \log n,$$

where n is the number of events. The base of the logarithm determines the unit used. The decision content is independent of the probabilities of the occurrence of the events. However, in some applications, it is assumed that these probabilities are equal. (I) (A)

decision instruction (1) Deprecated term for discrimination instruction. (2) Synonym for branch instruction.

decision support services (DSS) Services that assist humans in decision-making.

Note: The decision support services can make use of spreadsheets, artificial intelligence, computer graphics, and online corporate data. (T)

decision support system (DSS) A system which assists humans in decision making.

Note: The decision support system can make use of spreadsheets, artificial intelligence, computer graphics, and online corporate data. (T)

decision table (1) A table of conditions that are to be considered in the analysis of a problem, together with the actions to be taken for each condition. (T) (2) Presentation in either matrix or tabular form of a set of conditions and their corresponding actions. (A)

deck See card deck.

declaration (1) In programming languages, the mechanism for establishing a language object. A declaration normally involves attaching an identifier and allocating attributes to the language object concerned. (I) (2) In a programming language, a meaningful expression that affects the interpretation of other expressions in that language. (A) Synonymous with directive. (3) Synonymous with declarative statement. (4) In the AIX operating system, a description that makes a defined object available to a function or a block. (5) In the C language, a description that makes an external object or function available to a function or a block statement. (6) See explicit declaration, implicit declaration, type declaration.

declarative Deprecated term for declaration.

declarative knowledge The representation of assertions and facts about objects, events, and situations. (T)

declarative language A programming language for expressing declarations; for example, a data description language. (T)

declaratives In COBOL, a set of one or more special purpose sections written at the beginning of the Procedure Division, the first of which is preceded by the keyword DECLARATIVES and the last of which is followed by the keywords END DECLARATIVES.

Note: A declarative is composed of a section header, followed by a USE compiler directing sentence, followed by a set of zero, one, or more than one associated paragraphs.

declarative sentence In COBOL, a compiler-directing statement that specifies when a debugging section or an exception/error procedure is to be run. It consists of a single USE statement terminated by the operator period.

declarative statement Synonym for declaration.

declarator In the AIX operating system, an identifier and optional symbols that describe the data type. See array declarator, function declarator.

declare To identify the variable symbols to be used at preassembly time.

decode (1) To convert data by reversing the effect of some previous encoding. (I) (A) (2) To interpret a code. (A) (3) In computer security, to convert encoded text into plaintext by means of a code system. (4) Contrast with encode.

decoder (1) A functional unit that has a number of input lines such that any number may carry signals and a number of output lines such that not more than one at a time may carry a signal and such that the combination of input signals serves as a code to indicate which output line carries the signal. (T) (2) A device that has a number of input lines of which any number may carry signals and a number of output lines of which not more than one may carry a signal, there being a one-to-one correspondence between the outputs and the combinations of the input signals. (I) (A) (3) Contrast with encoder. (4) See operation decoder.

decollate To separate the plies of a multipart form or paper stock. (A) Synonymous with deleave.

decompaction In the Data Facility Hierarchical Storage Manager, the process of decoding and expanding data that were compacted during migration or backup.

decompression A function that expands data to the length that preceded data compression. See also compression.

deconcentration The process of extracting individual messages from data sent in a single transmission sequence. Contrast with concentration. See also concentrator. See also deblocking.

deconcentrator Any device that extracts individual messages from data sent in a single transmission sequence.

decrement (1) The quantity by which a variable is decreased. (2) In some computers, a specific part of an instruction word.

decrypt (1) In computer security, to decipher or decode. (2) Synonym for decipher. (T)

decryption In computer security, transforming encoded text or ciphertext into plaintext.

decurl In a printer, to remove abnormal curving of the paper. In the 3800 Printing Subsystem, this operation is associated with the burster-trimmer-stacker where excessive paper curl may be troublesome during stacking.

DEDB Data entry database.

dedicate When running the AIX PC Simulator/6000, assigning a resource to the AIX PC Simulator/6000 in such a way that it cannot be used by AIX for RISC System/6000 or other PC Simulator sessions. Contrast with share.

dedicated channel (1) A channel that is not switched. (2) In VM, a channel that is attached to a virtual machine for its sole use, so that the VM control program can bypass translating the addresses of virtual devices.

dedicated circuit A circuit that is not switched.

dedicated connection (1) In an ESCON Director, a connection between two ports that is not affected by information contained in the transmission frames. This connection, which restricts those ports from communicating with any other port, can be established or removed only as a result of actions performed by a host control program or at the ESCD console. The two links having a dedicated connection appear as one continuous link. Contrast with dynamic connection. (2) Deprecated term for nonswitched connection.

dedicated data set In OS/VS, a data set assigned to an initiator that is allocated space when the initiator is started; every job step running under the initiator can use the dedicated data set as a temporary data set.

dedicated device A device that cannot be shared among users.

dedicated line Deprecated term for nonswitched line.

dedicated node An OS/2 Office node dedicated to mail processing. The only user enrolled on this node is the administrator.

dedicated service tools (DST) The part of the service function used to service the system when the operating system is not working.

dedication Pertaining to the assignment of a system resource; for example, an I/O device, a program, or a whole system, to one application or purpose.

de-edit In COBOL, the logical removal of all editing characters from a numeric edited data item in order to determine the unedited numeric value of the item.

default (1) Pertaining to an attribute, condition, value, or option that is assumed when none is explicitly specified. (I) (2) See also default value.

default accelerator See accelerator.

default button labels In the AIXwindows program, XmLabel widgets or gadgets that are used when no other button label has been specified.

default choice In SAA Basic Common User Access, a selected choice that an application provides for the initial appearance of a group of selection choices. See also initial value.

default clause In an XL C compiler switch statement, the keyword default followed by a colon and one or more XL C statements. When the conditions of the specified case labels in the switch statement do not hold, the default clause is chosen.

default code point In alerts, a 2-byte code point in which the first byte indexes text providing a high-level description of a type of condition. The second byte is zero. See replacement code point.

default delivery The method of delivering messages to a message queue in which messages are placed in the queue without interrupting the job, and the default reply is sent for any messages requiring a reply.

default department number In PSS, a department number entered automatically in certain retail sales transactions when the operator has not entered a department number.

default device In the AIX operating system, the device, such as a printer or disk drive, attached to a computer, that is used when no alternative is specified by the operator.

default directory In the AIX operating system, the directory name supplied by the operating system if none is specified.

default drive The drive name supplied by the operating system if none is specified. Synonymous with current drive.

default file In the AIX operating system, a data file in which resource default values are stored in ASCII form to permit the assignment of alternative resource values at run time without need for rewriting or recompiling source code.

default file attributes In CMS, certain reserved file type names that cause the CMS editor to assume certain values for record length, tab settings, upper/lowercase setting, record sequence numbering, verification mode, record type, fixed or variable length record type, truncation column, and other related record characteristics.

default focal point A network node that receives alerts from nodes that do not have defined focal points. Contrast with primary focal point.

default form In the OS/400 operating system, a temporary object that contains the description of the format of a printed or displayed report that was built without explicitly specifying a form to be applied against it.

default format A preset format that is automatically implemented unless the user specifies otherwise. Synonymous with basic format. (T)

default group (1) The group to which a user is associated when a group name is not specified on the TSO LOGON command or batch JOB statement. (2) In RACF, the group specified in a user profile that is the default current connect group.

default initialization In the AIX operating system, the initial value assigned to a data object by the compiler if no initial value is specified by the programmer. In the XL C compiler, external and static variables receive a default initialization of zero, while the default initialization for auto and register variables is undefined. See also default value.

default label See label.

default literal In IMS/VS message format services (MFS), a literal field that MFS inserts into an input message when no data for the field are received from the terminal. See also explicit literal, system literal.

default mass storage volume group In MSS, the collection of mass storage volumes that belong to a mass storage volume group defined by the Mass Storage System Communicator program. The name of the group is always SYSGROUP.

default network message queue In the OS/400 operating system, a message queue to which messages related to network activity are sent when either the user profile does not have a message queue specified or the message queue named in the user profile cannot be used.

default network output queue In the OS/400 operating system, an output queue to which spooled files are sent when either the user does not have an output queue specified or the output queue name in the user profile cannot be used.

default option The implicit option assumed when no option is explicitly stated. (A)

default printer A printer that accepts all the printed output from a display station assigned to it, unless another is specified.

default program A user-specified program assumed when no other program is specifically named on a debug command, or a special program defined for handling error messages.

default prompt In System/36, a field name from a D-specification used to prompt for the contents of the field.

default record A record that consists entirely of default values.

default reply A system-assigned reply to an inquiry or notify message that is used when the message queue at which the message arrives is in default delivery mode.

default routing entry In SNADS, the routing table entry specifying the route to be used when the table contains no explicit routing entry.

default screen size In the 3270 Information Display System, the usable display area when the display device is in the implicit partition state and the alternate screen size is not in effect.

defaults file See default files.

default SSCP list A list of system services control points (SSCPs), either in a VTAM network or another network, that can be used when no predefined cross-domain resource (CDRSC) or name translation function is provided, specifying an LU's owning cross-domain resource manager (CDRM). This list is filed as a part of an adjacent SSCP table in the VTAM definition library.

default SSCP selection A VTAM function that selects a set of one or more system services control points (SSCPs) to which a session request can be routed when there is no predefined cross-domain resource (CDRSC) or name translation function provided that specifies an LU's owning cross-domain resource manager (CDRM). See also default SSCP list.

default system control area (DSCA) In IMS/VS, the part of the device output format block that, when present, causes specific terminal functions to be per-formed if the destination terminal has the required features. See also system control area.

default user name In System/38, a name provided by the Control Program Facility (CPF) for user identification for an installation that does not require separate user identifications.

default value A value assumed when no value has been specified. Synonymous with assumed value.

defect Any failure to meet customer requirements (expectations).

defect elimination (1) One of IBM's five key Market-Driven Quality initiatives, the focus of which is on identifying and preventing defects.

Defense Advanced Research Projects Agency (DARPA) The United States Department of Defense agency responsible for creating ARPANET, a large TCP/IP network.

Defense Data Network (DDN) The MILNET, ARPANET, and TCP/IP networks and protocols.

deference (1) A process by which a data station delays its transmission when the transmission medium is busy to avoid collision with ongoing transmission. (T) (2) See also carrier sense multiple access with collision avoidance (CSMA/CA) network.

deferred addressing A method of addressing in which one indirect address is replaced by another to which it refers for a predetermined number of times or until the process is terminated by an indicator. (I) (A)

deferred entry An entry into a subroutine that occurs as a result of a deferred exit from the program that passed control to it.

deferred exit The passing of control to a subroutine at a time determined by an asynchronous event instead of at a predictable time.

deferred I/O In DPCX, automatic postponement of individual I/O operations during field-by-field processing until a combination of several I/O operations can be done together, or until an I/O operation must be done to complete the execution of an instruction.

deferred maintenance Maintenance specifically intended to eliminate an existing fault, which did not prevent continued successful operation of the device or computer program. (A)

deferred maintenance time Time, usually unscheduled, used to perform deferred maintenance. (A)

deferred restart A restart performed by a system on resubmission of a job by the programmer. The operator submits the restart deck to the subsystem through a system input reader. Contrast with automatic restart.

deferred-shape array In FORTRAN, an allocatable array or an alias array.

deferred update In IMS/VS, a Fast Path capability that keeps updates to databases in main storage buffers until a synchronization point is reached. Synchronization point processing schedules VSAM writes and response messages to terminals after physically logging the changed data.

defer status A condition specifying whether spooled output can begin printing before a job has ended.

definable In FORTRAN, a variable whose value may be changed as a whole. Constants, allocatable arrays that have not been allocated, many-to-one alias arrays, and aliases for which an IDENTIFY statement has not been executed are examples of data objects that are not definable. Many-to-one vector-valued array sections are examples of data subobjects that are not definable.

define (1) In the AIX operating system, to create an entry in the Customized Devices Database and establish the parent device and connection location. (2) In DPPX, to create a profile for a resource with the DEFINE command.

defined assignment statement In FORTRAN, an assignment statement that is not an intrinsic assignment statement and is defined by a subroutine subprogram whose interface is explicit.

defined operation In FORTRAN, an operation that is not an intrinsic operation and is defined by a function subprogram whose interface is explicit.

define method In the AIX operating system, a method used to create a device instance in the Customized Database. It takes a device from the undefined or nonexistent state to the defined state.

define statement A preprocessor statement that causes the preprocessor to replace an identifier or macro call with specified code.

definite response (DR) In SNA, a protocol requested in the form-of-response-requested field of the request header that directs the receiver of the request to return a response unconditionally, whether positive or negative, to that request chain. Contrast with exception response, no response.

definition (1) In a document copying machine, a qualitative evaluation of the clarity of a copy. (T)

(2) The degree of detail or sharpness in a TV picture. (3) See data definition, macrodefinition. (4) See also resolution.

definition of a data object In FORTRAN, the assignment of a valid value to a valid variable during program execution. Under certain other circumstances, the variable ceases to have a valid value and becomes undefined.

definition of a procedure or type In FORTRAN, the definition of a procedure by a subprogram or the definition of a derived type by a sequence of statements commencing with a TYPE statement and terminating with an END TYPE statement.

definition statement (1) In VTAM, the statement that describes an element of the network. (2) In NCP, a type of instruction that defines a resource to the NCP. See also macroinstruction.

definition statement identifier A specific character string that identifies the purpose of a definition statement.

degradation factor A measure of the loss in performance that results from reconfiguration of a data processing system; for example, a slow-down in run time due to a reduction in the number of processing units.

degree In NETDA/2, the maximum number of attachments (such as links, Ethernet connections, or token-ring connections) that a node can have. For example, if a node can have six attachments, that node has a degree of 6.

deka (da) See deca.

dekaliter (dal) See decaliter.

dekameter (dam) See decameter.

DEL The delete character. (A)

delay The amount of time by which an event is retarded. (A)

delay characteristics The average amount of time taken for operations such as call setup, call clearing, and data transfer to be performed on a packet switching network.

delay compensation In CCP, a responding arrangement by which the IBM 3710 Network Controller answers for a receiving station.

delay distortion See distortion.

delayed maintenance In the OS/400 operating system, a method of logging changes to an access path for database files and applying the changes the next time the file is opened instead of rebuilding the access path completely or maintaining it immediately. Contrast with rebuild maintenance, immediate maintenance.

delayed port In the AIX operating system, a port that is enabled like a shared port except that the login herald is not displayed until the user types 1 or more characters (usually carriage returns). A port directly connected to a remote system or intelligent modem is usually enabled as a delayed port.

delayed-request mode In SNA, an operational mode in which the sender may continue sending request units on the normal flow after sending a definite-response request chain on that flow, without waiting to receive the response to that chain. See also delayed-response mode. Contrast with immediate-request mode.

delayed response In MSS, an indication from the mass storage control that a mass storage control I/O operation is finished.

delayed-response mode In SNA, an operational mode in which the receiver of request units can return responses to the sender in a sequence different from that in which the corresponding request units were sent. An exception is the response to a CHASE request, which is returned only after all responses to requests sent before the CHASE have been returned. Contrast with immediate-response mode.

delay element A device that yields, after a given time interval, an output signal essentially similar to a previously introduced input signal. (I) (A)

delay line (1) A line or network designed to introduce a desired delay in the transmission of a signal. (I) (A) (2) A sequential logic element with one input channel and in which an output channel state at any one instant T is the same as the input channel state at the instant T-N, where N is a constant interval of time for a given output channel; for example, an element in which the input sequence undergoes a delay of N time units. (A) (3) See acoustic delay line, electromagnetic delay line, magnetic delay line.

delay line storage A storage device that uses delay lines. (I) (A)

delay maintenance In System/38, a method of maintaining keyed access paths for database files. This method does not update an access path when the file is closed, but it retains updates in a delayed form so that they can be quickly applied at the next open,

avoiding a complete rebuild. Contrast with immediate maintenance, rebuild maintenance.

delay programming See minimum delay programming.

delay unit A device that yields, after a given time interval, an output signal essentially similar to a previously introduced input signal. (I) (A)

deleave Synonym for decollate.

delegate A user who is authorized to work for another user.

delegation In RACF, the act of giving other users or groups authorities to perform RACF operations.

delete (1) A function that enables a user to remove all or part of a previously entered text. (T) (2) In SAA usage, to remove something and close up the space it occupied; for example, to remove the character at the cursor position and shift the characters that are to the right of the cursor one position to the left. Contrast with erase. (3) To remove an object or a unit of data, such as a character, field, or record.

Delete (Del) A key that a user presses to remove characters at the current cursor position. Contrast with Backspace.

Delete In SAA Common User Access, a choice that removes a selected object and compresses the space it occupied. Contrast with Clear.

delete authority In the OS/400 operating system, a data authority that allows the user to remove entries from an object; for example, delete messages from a message queue or delete records from a file. Contrast with add authority. See also read authority, update authority.

delete-capable file A file from which records can be logically removed without compressing the file.

delete character (DEL) (1) A control character used primarily to obliterate an erroneous or unwanted character; on perforated tape this character consists of a code hole in each punch position. (I) (A) (2) A character that identifies a record to be removed from a file.

deleted record A record that has been initialized or removed so that it is not eligible for access. A deleted record holds a place in a physical file member and can be replaced with a data record by an update operation.

delete key In word processing, a control that enables deletion of text already recorded on the recording medium or in storage. (T) (A)

delete-mode indicator (DL) An indicator that signals that the transaction file record selected by the operator for review is to be deleted logically when the processing cycle ends.

delete rights The authority to delete an entry from an object or to delete the object itself. Contrast with add rights, read rights, update rights.

deletion (1) The removal of data from storage. (2) In a conceptual schema language, the removal of a previously inserted sentence from the information base or conceptual schema.

deletion record A new record that replaces or removes an existing record.

delimited identifier In SQL, a sequence of one or more characters of the standard character set enclosed within SQL escape characters that are used to form a name.

delimited scope statement In COBOL, any statement that includes its explicit scope terminator.

delimiter (1) A character used to indicate the beginning and end of a character string. (T) (2) A flag that separates and organizes items of data. (A) Synonymous with punctuation symbol, separator. (3) A character that groups or separates words or values in a line of input. (4) In COBOL, a character or a sequence of contiguous characters that identify the end of a string of characters and separates that string of characters from the following string of characters. See pseudo-text delimiter. (5) See ending frame delimiter, starting frame delimiter.

Note: A delimiter is not part of the string of characters that it delimits.

delimiter line In the IBM 3886 Optical Character Reader, a line on a form that may contain delimiters but does not contain other characters.

delimiter macroinstruction A TCAM message-handler macroinstruction that classifies and identifies sequences of functional message-handler macroinstructions and directs control to the appropriate sequence of functional macroinstructions. Contrast with functional macroinstruction.

delimiter statement A job control statement used to mark the end of data.

delimiter token In SQL, a string constant, a delimited identifier, a symbol; for example, ||, /, *, +, or -, or other special characters. See also token, ordinary token.

delivery See master delivery, paper delivery.

delivery-confirmation bit See D-bit.

delivery cylinder In a duplicator, a cylinder that extracts the paper from the printing medium and transports it to the delivery tray. (T)

delivery end stop In a document copying machine or duplicator, a device that arrests the copies in the delivery tray. (T)

delivery mechanism See chain delivery mechanism, conveyor delivery mechanism, tray delivery mechanism.

delivery paper deflector In a document copying machine or duplicator, a device that guides the copies to the delivery end stop. (T)

delivery platform Synonym for delivery tray.

delivery rollers (1) In a document copying machine or duplicator, components that transport the finished copies to the delivery tray. (T) (2) Synonymous with delivery wheels.

delivery side guides In a document copying machine or duplicator, devices that prevent sideways movement of the copies in the delivery tray. (T)

delivery tray In a document copying machine or duplicator, the tray or platform that supports the finished copies. (T) Synonymous with delivery platform, receiving tray. See also swinging delivery tray.

delivery wheels Synonym for delivery rollers.

DELTA disk The virtual disk in a VM operating system that contains program temporary fixes (PTFs) that have been installed but not merged. See BASE disk, MERGE disk, RUN disk, ZAP disk.

delta-YUV (DYUV) In multimedia, an efficient color-coding scheme for natural pictures. Since the human eye is less sensitive to chrominance (color) variations than to luminance (intensity) variations, DYUV encodes luminance (Y) information at full bandwidth and chrominance (UV) information at half bandwidth or less, storing only the differences (deltas) between each value and the one following it.

demand paging (1) The transfer of a page from auxiliary storage to real storage at the moment of need. (I) (A) (2) In System/370 virtual storage systems, transfer of a page from external page storage to real storage at the time it is needed for execution.

demarcation strip Usually a terminal board acting as a physical interface between a business machine and a common carrier. See also interface.

demodulate To return a modulated signal to its original state.

demodulation (1) The process of retrieving intelligence (data) from a modulated carrier wave. (2) The reverse of modulation.

demodulator (1) A functional unit that converts a modulated signal into the original signal. (I) (A) (2) Contrast with modulator.

demon Synonym for daemon.

demo session editor In SDF/CICS, an editor that allows sequences of maps and pages to be defined and displayed.

demount To remove a volume from a tape unit or a direct access device.

demultiplexer A device that recovers as output signals, each of the signals combined by a preceding multiplexer. (T)

denary Synonym for decimal.

denial of service In computer security, the act of impeding or denying a user the use of system resources. Synonymous with interdiction.

density (1) In a document copying machine, the degree of resistance in a material to the passage of light or other radiation. (T)   (2) In printing, the number of characters per inch, horizontally. (3) See data density, packing density, recording density.

dependability The collective term used to describe the availability performance and its influencing factors: reliability performance, maintainability performance and maintenance support performance.

Note: Dependability is used only for general descriptions in non-quantitative terms. (T)

dependency (1) An entity attribute relationship which denotes that the existence of one entity attribute is of interest only if another entity attribute exists. (T) (2) In a database, a relationship between entities in which an entity has meaning only if the other entity exists.

dependency line In the AIX operating system, the first line of an entry in a description file. It contains a list of target files, followed by an optional list of prerequisite files or dependencies.

dependent code A code that has segments that are dependent upon other segments in order to provide unique identification of a coded item. (A)

dependent compilation (1) The compilation of a compilation unit using all the necessary interface and context information from related compilation units. Interface and context information is used by the compiler to check validity and to resolve references. (T) (2) Synonym for separate compilation.

dependent LU See SSCP-dependent LU.

dependent segment (1) In a tree structure, a segment that relies on at least the root segment and possibly on other dependent segments for its full meaning. (2) In a database, a segment that relies on a higher level segment for its full hierarchical meaning.

dependent workstation In the AIX operating system, a workstation having little or no stand-alone capability that must be connected to a host or server in order to provide any meaningful capability to the user. Contrast with stand-alone workstation.

deprecated Pertaining to terms that should not be used. In this dictionary, the reference "Deprecated term for..." refers the reader to the preferred term, which is defined.

deprecated feature In FORTRAN, an element of a language that is intended to be removed from the next version of the standard.

depth (1) In a three-dimensional context, the second dimension. (2) In the AIX Enhanced X-Windows program, the number of bits per pixel for a window or pixmap.

depth of field In photography, the area of a picture between the closest and the farthest objects in focus; depth of field varies with the F Stop.

depth cueing In 3D computer graphics, varying the intensity of a line with depth. Typically, the points on the line further from the eye are darker, so the line seems to fade into the distance.

depth-first search A search that first picks up one of the possible branches of the search tree, proceeds along the chosen branch until the goal or a predetermined depth is reached, and, if the goal has not been reached, goes back to the start point and picks up another branch. (T)

dequeue To remove items from a queue. Contrast with enqueue.

dereferenced pointer In XL Pascal, an expression using the -> or @ operator used to locate a dynamic variable from a pointer.

derivative action A series of processes required to derive a conclusion from a given set of premises. (T)

derived data Data values that are derived from the values of other data by a specified algorithm. (A)

derived data element A data element that has a domain identical to that of a specified general data element; for example, country of citizenship is derived from the element, countries of the world. (A)

derived type In FORTRAN, a type whose data have components of intrinsic types and other derived types.

DES Data Encryption Standard.

DES algorithm See Data Encryption Algorithm (DEA).

descendant See child.

descender In a font, the distance from the baseline to the bottom of the character box. This value may differ for different characters in a given font.

descending key The values by which data are ordered from the highest value to the lowest value of the key, in accordance with the rules for comparing data items. Contrast with ascending key.

descending key sequence The arrangement of data in order from the highest value of the key field to the lowest value of the key field.

descending sequence The arrangement of data in an order from high to low based on the contents of a specific field. Contrast with ascending sequence.

description See problem description.

descriptive name In an information resource dictionary, the combination of assigned descriptive name and version identifier that provides a unique and more descriptive name for the access name. (A)

descriptive text In SAA Basic Common User Access architecture, text used in addition to a field prompt to give additional information about a field.

descriptor (1) A word or phrase used to categorize or index information. Synonymous with keyword. (T) (2) In the AIX object data manager (ODM), a named and typed variable that defines a single characteristic of an object. See link descriptor, method descriptor, terminal descriptor. (3) See parameter descriptor.

descriptor code Under Multiple Console Support, a code that indicates the means of message presentation and message deletion on display devices.

deselect To cancel the selection of a button.

deserialize To change from serial-by-bit to parallel-by-byte. Contrast with serialize.

deserializer Synonym for staticizer.

design See conceptual system design, functional design, logic design, system design.

designated gateway SSCP A gateway system services control point (SSCP) designated to perform all the gateway control functions during LU-LU session setup.

designation hole A hole punched in a punch card to indicate the nature of the data on the card or the functions that a machine is to perform. (I) (A) Synonymous with control hole, control punch, function hole.

designator In FORTRAN, a symbolic name, followed by any number of component selectors, array section selectors, array element selectors, and substring selectors.

design verification In computer security, the use of formal proofs to demonstrate consistency between a formal specification of a system and a formal security policy model. See also implementation verification.

desk application An application program that can be run directly from a workstation to obtain office automation services. (T)

desk checking The manual simulation of program execution to detect faults through step-by-step examination of a source program for errors in function or syntax. (T) (A)

desk-mounted word processing equipment Word processing equipment that is mounted into a specially designed or adapted desk or table. If it is not integrated word processing equipment, its control unit may also be mounted into, or stand on, a desk, a table, or elsewhere. (T)

desktop (1) A folder that fills the entire screen and holds all the objects with which the user can interact to perform operations on the system. (2) See AIXwindows desktop.

desktop calculator A calculator designed primarily for use on a desk or table. (T)

desktop computer A microcomputer such as the IBM Personal Computer AT, or the IBM PC/XT, that is designed to be placed together with optional units on the top of a desk or table. Portable computers such as the IBM PC Convertible can be used for both desktop and laptop operations. See also laptop computer, personal computer, portable computer.

desktop document copying machine A document copying machine designed to stand on a desk or similar supporting platform. (T)

desktop organizers Personal computer application software and multifunction boards that replace desktop items such as appointment books, calculators, calendars, clocks, notepads, and telephone listings.

desktop publishing (1) Electronic publishing using a microcomputer small enough to fit on a desk. (T) (2) The use of personal computer application software to integrate text, charts, and pictures and to design, display, and print high-quality documents comparable to typeset documents printed by professional publishers.

desktop video (DTV) In video production, a presentation produced with low-cost video equipment and desktop computers.

destage In MSS, to move data from a staging drive to a mass storage volume.

destaging error In MSS, the result of a permanent reading error when data are being transferred from a staging pack to a data cartridge.

destination (1) Any point or location, such as a node, station, or a particular terminal, to which information is to be sent. (2) In ACF/TCAM, the place to which a message being handled by a message handler is to be sent. (3) An external logical unit (LU) or application program to which messages or other data are directed. (4) In IMS/VS with the data communication (DC) feature, an application program, a logical terminal, or an operator command that is associated with the control region. (5) In COBOL, the symbolic identification of the receiver of a transmission from a queue. Contrast with source.

destination address A code that identifies the location to which information is to be sent. Contrast with origin address, source address.

destination address field (DAF) In SNA, a field in a format identification 0 or format identification 1 transmission header that contains the network address of the destination. In a format identification 2 header, the field is called destination address field prime (DAF'). Contrast with origin address field (OAF).

destination code A code that represents a destination address.

Destination Control table (DCT) In CICS, a table containing an entry for each extrapartition, intrapartition, and indirect destination. Extrapartition entries address data sets external to the CICS region. Indirect destination entries redirect data to a destination controlled by another DCT entry. Intrapartition destination entries contain the information required to locate the queue in the intrapartition data set.

destination field A field in a message header that contains the destination code.

destination logical unit (DLU) The logical unit to which data is to be sent. Contrast with origin logical unit (OLU).

destination parent In IMS/VS, the physical or logical parent in a database that can be reached by the logical child path.

destination queue In ACF/TCAM, a queue in which messages bound for a particular destination are placed after being processed by the incoming group of the message handler. See also process queue.

destination service access point (DSAP) In SNA and TCP/IP, a logical address that allows a system to route data from a remote device to the appropriate communications support.

destination station A station to which a message is directed.

destination subarea field (DSAF) In SNA, a field in a FID4 transmission header that contains a subarea address, which combined with the element address in the destination element field, gives the complete network address of the destination network addressable unit (NAU). Contrast with origin subarea field.

destination system (1) In an IMS/VS multisystem environment, the system in which the logical destination resides. (2) In SNADS, a system that can receive messages, documents or objects.

destructive cursor On a CRT display device, a cursor that erases any character through which it passes as it is advanced, backspaced, or otherwise moved. Contrast with nondestructive cursor.

destructive read A read that erases the data in the source location. (T) (A)

DET Device entry table.

detached In System/38, pertaining to a journal receiver that is not connected to a journal and not receiving entries for that journal. Contrast with attached.

detail calculation In RPG, specified calculation operations that are performed for every record read.

detail card Synonym for trailer card.

detail file Synonym for transaction file.

detail line In RPG, a detail record in an output file.

detail record A record that contains the daily activities or transactions of a business; for example, the items on a customer order. Contrast with header record.

detail time In System/36 and System/38, the part of the RPG program cycle in which calculation and output operations are performed for each record read. Contrast with total time.

detectable element A display element that can be detected by a pick device. (I) (A)

detectable segment A display group that can be detected by a pick device. (I) (A)

detector In fiber optics, a device that converts optical power to other forms. (E).

detent In the 3800 Printing Subsystem, a depression or groove at specific intervals that determines exact placement of the tractor, trimming assembly, steering assembly, or paper width lever.

determinant A value given by a mathematical operation on an array.

DEV Device address field.

DEVD Device description.

developed image An image that has been exposed onto a photoconductor and covered with toner by a developer.

developer (1) In a document copying machine, a solution or material used to make the latent image visible. (T) (2) In the 3800 Printing Subsystem, the unit that provides a flow of developer mix over the photoconductor to develop a latent image.

developer mix A combination of carrier beads and toner in which the beads electrically charge the toner.

developer reservoir In a document copying machine, a receptacle in which liquid developer is stored within the machine. (T)

developing In a document copying machine, the process of making visible the latent image. (T)

developing trough In a document copying machine, a shallow tray supplied with liquid developer through which the copy material is passed during the developing process. (T)

developmental baseline The specifications that are in effect at a given time for a system under development. (T)

development time (1) The part of operating time used for debugging new routines or hardware. (A) (2) Contrast with makeup time. (3) See program development time.

device (1) A mechanical, electrical, or electronic contrivance with a specific purpose. (2) In the AIX operating system, a valuator, button, or the keyboard. Buttons have values of 0 or 1 (up or down); valuators return values in a range, and the keyboard returns ASCII values.

device address (1) The identification of an input/output device by its channel and unit number. See logical device address, physical device address. (2) In data communication, the identification of any device to which data can be sent or from which data can be received.

device backup Pertaining to assignment of alternate devices. See automatic device backup, manual device backup.

device characteristics list Deprecated term for device parameter list.

device class The generic name for a group of device types; for example, all display stations belong to the same device class. Contrast with device type.

device code A two-character code used during system configuration to identify the models of display stations and printers.

device configuration In the OS/400 operating system, the physical placement of equipment such as display stations and printers and the description to the system of the configuration and how it will be used. See also controller configuration.

device configuration database In the AIX operating system, a database that stores all relevant information to support the device configuration process. It consists of a predefined database and a customized database.

device control block (DCB) In the PenPM operating system extension, a data structure that contains data and addresses for indirect calls for a logical device.

device control character A control character used to specify a control function for peripheral devices associated with a system. (T)

device control panel In multimedia applications, an integrated set of controls that is used to manage a device or media object (such as by playing, rewinding, increasing volume, and so on).

device control unit A hardware device that controls the reading, writing, or displaying of data at one or more input/output devices or terminals. See also transmission control unit.

device coordinate (1) In computer graphics, a coordinate specified in a coordinate system that is device dependent. (I) (A) (2) See normalized device coordinates.

device definition In the AIX operating system, information about a device that is in the Customized Database, including attributes and connection locations.

device dependence Reliance on the characteristics of particular types of devices in writing and executing programs or in performing functions. Contrast with device independence.

device-dependent (1) Pertaining to a function that can be accomplished only if particular types of devices are available. (2) Pertaining to a program that can be executed successfully only if particular types of devices are available. (3) Contrast with device-independent.

device description (1) In the OS/400 operating system, an object that contains information describing a particular device or logical unit that is attached to the system. (2) In System/38, an object that contains information describing a particular device that is attached to the system.

device driver (1) A file that contains the code needed to use an attached device. (2) A program that enables a computer to communicate with a specific peripheral device; for example, a printer, a videodisc player, or a CD drive. (3) A collection of subroutines that control the interface between I/O device adapters and the processor.

device emulation The programming that allows one device to appear to the user or to a system as another device. See also display emulation, 3270 emulation, printer emulation.

device-end (DE) In channel operations, a signal from an I/O device that denotes the end of an operation.

device error log A record that contains information about problems that have occurred with devices on the system.

device field (DFLD) In IMS/VS message format service, the smallest area in a device input or output format block whose content and structure are defined by the user.

device file In the AS/400 system and System/38, one of several types of the system object type *FILE. A device file contains a description of how data is to be presented to a program from a device or how data is to be presented to the device from the program.

device font A font particular to a device, such as a video display or printer, and loaded in the memory of the device. Some device fonts have size and language-support restrictions.

device handler In the AIX operating system, the component of a device driver that communicates directly with the hardware. Synonymous with virtual device driver.

device head In the AIX operating system, the component of a device driver that implements the application program interface to a device.

device helper (DevHlp) functions Kernel services (memory, hardware interrupts, software interrupts, queuing, semaphores, and so forth) available to physical device drivers.

device ID A unique identification number assigned to a logical device. A device ID is unique across an entire system.

device independence The capability to write and execute programs or perform functions without regard for the physical characteristics of devices. Contrast with device dependence.

device-independent (1) Pertaining to a function that can be accomplished without regard for the characteristics of particular types of devices. (2) Pertaining to a program that can be executed successfully without regard for the characteristics of particular types of devices. See also symbolic I/O assignment. (3) Contrast with device-dependent. (4) See also symbolic I/O assignment.

device input queue In the network control program, a queue of block control units (BCUs) directed to a device but not yet validated.

device instance In the AIX operating system, a Customized Devices Object Class entry, created when a device is defined. There is a device instance for each device defined in the system.

device-level addressing In an I/O interface, one of two levels of addressing, this level pertaining to an I/O device and identifying that device to the channel or control unit once the control unit has been determined through link-level addressing. Contrast with link-level addressing.

device location In the AIX operating system, a field in the Customized Devices Object Class that indicates the location path of a device.

device manager In the AIX operating system, a collection of routines for complex interfaces that acts as an intermediary between drivers and virtual machines; for example, supervisor calls from a virtual machine are examined by a device manager and routed to the appropriate subordinate device drivers.

device media control language (DMCL) In a database management system, a language for mapping the data onto physical storage and for describing the physical location and organization of the data. (T)

device message handler (DMH) In ACF/TCAM, a user-written routine that processes messages being received from or sent to an external logical unit (LU). See also application message handler, internodal message handler, message handler.

device name The logical or symbolic name assigned to a device.

device number (1) The reference number assigned to any external device. (2) A part of an external page address that refers to a particular paging device. In OS/VS2, the device number together with a group number and slot number identify the location of a page in storage. In VM, the device number together with a cylinder number and page number identify the location of a page in auxiliary storage.

device object A device that provides a means of communication between a computer and the outside world. A printer is an example of a device object.

device page (DPAGE) In IMS/VS message format service (MFS), a user-defined group of device field definitions that make up one or more physical pages to be presented to or received from the device.

device parameter list In the 3600 Finance Communication System, one to five bytes of information that indicate the operational characteristics an application program is to assume to exist for the device associated with a particular logical device address.

device pool management Under System/370 Model 158 or 168 Multiprocessing with MVS, control of all I/O on both processors by a single MVS control program.

device processor The part of DPCX that handles communication between DPCX and specific devices. There is one device processor for each specific group of devices.

device selection character In BSC, the control character sent to a receiving system or device to select the BSC device that is to receive the subsequent output.

device space In computer graphics, a space defined by the complete set of addressable points of a display device. (A)

device spanning In systems with VSAM, the storage of a key-sequenced data set on a volume or volumes of one type of device and the storage of its index on a volume or volumes of another type of device.

device stanza In the AIX operating system, the definition of a device attached to a queue in the print spooling system.

device state In the AIX operating system, a field in the Customized Devices Object Class that indicates the current configuration status of a device instance. Possible values are defined, available, and stopped.

device subclass In the AIX operating system, a subclass that distinguishes devices within the same functional class. It is used to indicate different interfaces; for example, the printer class has three subclasses: EIA-232, EIA-422, and parallel.

Device Support Facilities (DSF) An IBM-supplied system control program for performing operations on disk volumes so that they can be accessed by IBM and user programs.

Note: Examples of these operations are initializing a disk volume and assigning an alternate track.

device support station (DSS) In a processor, a station that communicates with power/thermal controls, sensors, switches, and valves; regulates power; senses circuit breaker (CB) trips, voltage, waterflow, temperature, water mixer valve; and turns pumps or valves off or on as needed. In the central processor, a DSS monitors current and voltage and detects regulator failures.

device switch table In the AIX operating system: (1) A table that is used as an interface to the device drivers. (2) A table that contains a pointer to the entry points for each device head.

device token In GDDM, an 8-byte code, required to set the devices to a predefined set of hardware characteristics.

device type (1) The name for a kind of device sharing the same model number; for example, 2311, 2400, 2400-1. Contrast with device class. (2) The generic name for a group of devices; for example, 5219 for IBM 5219 Printers. Contrast with device class.

device type code The four- or five-digit code to be used for defining an I/O device to a computer system.

device-type logical unit In VTAM, a logical unit that has a session limit of 1 and usually acts as the secondary end of a session. It is typically a logical unit (LU) in an SNA terminal, such as a 3270. It can be the primary end of a session; for example, the logical unit representing the Network Routing Facility (NRF) logical unit.

device work queue In the network control program, a queue of block control units (BCUs) that have been validated and are waiting to be executed on the line.

dewet An electrode area that has interacted with solder in such a way as to cause the solder to draw back, forming a phase or intermetallic compound that does not readily form a metallurgical bond.

DFC Data flow control.

DFDSS Data Facility Data Set Services.

DFLD Device field.

D format A data set format in which ASCII records are variable in length.

DFP Data Facility Product.

DFP segment The portion of a RACF profile containing information relating to the users and resources that are managed by the data facility product (DFP).

DFSYN response Data flow synchronous response.

DFT (1) Diagnostic function test. (2) Distributed function terminal.

DFU Data file utility.

DFU application See application.

DHCF Distributed host command facility.

diacritic A mark added to a letter to indicate a special phonetic value.

DIA document distribution services The set of services that allows office users to send and receive electronic mail.

diagnosed-source file A library member containing source statements and associated error messages.

diagnosed-source member See diagnosed-source file.

diagnose interface In VM/370, a programming mechanism that allows any virtual machine, including CMS, to communicate directly with CP via the System/370 DIAGNOSE instruction. Specific DIAGNOSE codes allow a virtual machine to more efficiently request specific CP services.

diagnostic Pertaining to the detection and isolation of errors in programs and faults in equipment.

diagnostic aid A tool, such as a program, or reference manual, used to detect and isolate a device or program malfunction or error.

diagnostic code In X.25 communications, a 1-byte code included in clear and reset indication packets that gives information about the reason for sending the packet. See also cause code.

diagnostic control manager (DCM) Microcode that sets up programs and information to handle error analysis.

diagnostic diskette A diskette used by service personnel to diagnose hardware problems in a device.

diagnostic function The capability of a functional unit to detect problems and identify the type of error. (T)

diagnostic function test (DFT) A program to test overall system reliability.

diagnostic message A message that contains information about errors in the execution of an application program or a system function.

diagnostic microcode Microcode that isolates and identifies a malfunctioning field replaceable unit (FRU).

diagnostic program A computer program that is designed to detect, locate and describe faults in equipment or errors in computer programs. (T)

diagnostics The process of investigating the cause or the nature of a condition or problem in a product or system.

diagnostic control program In the AIX operating system, the top-level control program and configuration manager for diagnostics. It traverses the configuration database, testing resources and their interdependencies, analyzes conclusions from diagnostic applications, and generates a problem report.

diagram [196] **dichotomizing search**

diagram See block diagram, functional diagram, logic diagram, setup diagram, Veitch diagram, Venn diagram.

dial (1) A computer input device that allows a user to set parameter values. A dial is a type of valuator. See also valuator. (2) An I/O device used to input variables by means of thumbwheels. (3) To use a dial or push button telephone to initiate a telephone call. In telecommunication, this action is taken to attempt to establish a connection between a terminal and a telecommunication device over a switched line.

dial and switch box In the AIX operating system, an I/O device with eight dials (valuators) and 32 switches.

dial back Synonym for callback.

dial-code In Basic Network Facilities (BNU), a code representing a telephone number or portion of a telephone number.

dialed line Synonym for switched connection.

dialed number identification service (DNIS) In telephony, a number supplied by the public telephone network to identify a logical called party; for example, two 800 numbers might be translated to the same telephone number. The DNIS is sent when the real telephone number is called to allow end users to distinguish which service is being called when a call arrives to the real number.

dial exchange An exchange in which all subscribers can originate calls by dialing.

dial-in Pertaining to the direction in which a switched connection is requested by any node or terminal other than the receiving host or an NCP.

dialing Deprecated term for calling.

dialing directory In Asynchronous Terminal Emulator (ATE), a list of telephone numbers that can be called with ATE. It is similar to a page in a telephone directory.

dial line Synonym for switched connection.

dialog (1) The interaction between a user and a computer. (2) In an interactive system, a series of related inquiries and responses similar to a conversation between two people. (3) In the AIXwindows program, a two-way text interface between an application and its user. The interface takes the form of a collection of widgets and gadgets, including a DialogShell widget, a BulletinBoard widget (or a subclass of a BulletinBoard widget or some other container widget), plus various children, including Label,

PushButton, and Text widgets. (4) In VSE/SP, a set of panels that can be used to complete a specific data processing task; for example, defining a file. (5) See modal dialog, modeless dialog.

dialog box In SAA Advanced Common User Access architecture, a movable window, fixed in size, containing controls that a user uses to provide information required by an application so that it can continue to process a user request. See also message box, primary window, secondary window.

Note: In CUA architecture, this is a programmer term. The end user term is pop-up window.

dialog pop-up In SAA Basic Common User Access architecture, a bordered area of the screen that is directly associated with a panel in a primary window. Through a dialog pop-up, a user provides information needed to complete a dialog in the underlying panel.

dial-out Pertaining to the direction in which a switched connection is requested by a host or an NCP.

dial pulse An interruption in the DC loop of a calling telephone. The interruption is produced by the breaking and making of the dial pulse contacts of a calling telephone when a digit is dialed. The loop current is interrupted once for each unit of value of the digit.

dial set A user-specified combination of switched, point-to-point lines from which the network control program selects a line for communicating with a station.

dial tone An audible signal indicating that a device is ready to be dialed.

dial-up The use of a dial or push button telephone to initiate a station-to-station telephone call.

dial-up terminal A terminal on a switched line.

diazo document copying machine A document copying machine that uses the diazo process. (T)

diazo process In a document copying machine, a process in which a copy results from the effect of radiation, particularly ultra-violet light, on diazonium-sensitive material. (T) See also pressure diazo.

dibit A group of two bits. In four-phase modulation, each possible dibit is encoded as one of four unique carrier phase shifts. The four possible states for a dibit are 00, 01, 10, and 11.

dichotomizing search (1) A search in which an ordered set of data elements is partitioned into two mutually exclusive parts, one of which is rejected; the process is repeated on the accepted part until the search is completed. (T)   (2) See also binary search.

dictionary (1) A database of specifications of data and information processing resources. (A)   (2) In the Document Composition Facility, a collection of word stems that is used with the spelling verification and automatic hyphenation functions.

dictionary administrator The person who defines, organizes, manages, controls, and protects a dictionary. (A)

dictionary/directory See data dictionary/directory. (A)

Didot point system A standard printer's measurement system on which type sizes are based. A Didot point is 0.0148 inch (0.376 millimeter). There are 12 Didot points to a cicero. See also cicero, point.

difference In a subtraction operation, the number or quantity that is the result of subtracting the subtrahend from the minuend. (I)   (A)

differential amplifier An amplifier that has two input circuits and amplifies the difference between the two input signals. (T)

differential analyzer (1)   An analog computer using connected integrators to solve differential equations. (I)   (A)   (2) See digital differential analyzer.

differential gear In analog computers, a mechanism that relates the angles of rotation of three shafts, usually designed so that the algebraic sum of the rotation of two shafts is equal to twice the rotation of the third. A differential gear can be used for addition or subtraction. (A)

differential Manchester encoding A digital encoding technique in which each bit period is divided into two complementary halves: a transition at the beginning of the bit period represents one of the two binary digits, "0" and "1," according to an established convention, while an absence of transition at the beginning of the bit period represents the other binary digit.   See Figure 41.

Notes:

1. *Transition may occur between two states of a physical variable such as voltage, magnetic polarity, light intensity.*

2. *If the physical variable is electrical, this type of encoding is polarity independent and helps to prevent DC drift.*

(T)

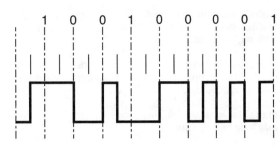

Figure 41. Differential Manchester Encoding

differential PCM (DPCM) In computer graphics, a digital system where the data transmitted or stored represents the difference between data elements (for example, pixels), rather than the data elements themselves.

differentiator A device whose output function is proportional to the derivative of the input function with respect to one or more variables;   for example, a resistance-capacitance network used to select the leading and trailing edges of a pulse signal. (A)

Diffie-Hellman cryptosystem In computer security, a system for public key cryptography.

diffuser In video and film production, a piece of a cellular diffusing substance placed in front of studio lamps to soften the light.   Synonymous with jelly. See also scrim.

diffusion transfer process In a document copying machine, a variation of the silver process in which the diffusion or transfer of chemicals from a specially prepared negative master to sensitized material produces a positive copy. (T)   Synonymous with chemical transfer process.

digest In the AIX operating system, data that has been organized into a format that provides for quick access to each piece of data.

digit (1) A character that represents a nonnegative integer;   for example, one of the characters 0 through F in the hexadecimal numeration system.   Synonymous with numeric character. (T)   (2) A symbol that represents one of the nonnegative integers smaller than the radix;   for example, in decimal notation, a digit is one of the characters from 0 to 9. (3) Any of the numerals from 0 through 9. (4) Synonymous with numeric character. (5) See binary digit, borrow digit, carry digit, check digit, decimal digit, equivalent binary-digit factor, sign digit, significant digit.

digital (1) Pertaining to data that consist of digits. (T)   (2) Pertaining to data in the form of digits. (A)   (3) Contrast with analog.

digital audio In multimedia applications, audio data that has been converted to digital form. Synonymous with digitized audio.

digital audio tape (DAT) player In video systems, a device that records and plays back digital audio on small magnetic tape cassettes.

digital cassette See magnetic tape cassette. See also magnetic tape cartridge.

digital computer (1) A programmable functional unit that is controlled by internally stored programs and that uses common storage for all or part of a program and also for all or part of the data necessary for the execution of the programs; executes user-written or user-designated programs; performs user-designated data manipulation, including arithmetic operations and logic operations; and that can execute programs that modify themselves during their execution. A digital computer operates on discrete data represented as strings of binary digits. (T) (2) See also analog computer, hybrid computer.

Note: A computer may be a stand-alone unit or may consist of several connected units.

digital data Data represented by digits, perhaps with special characters and the space character. (T) (A)

digital data service adapter (DDSA) In data communication, a modem used when transmitting data using the digital data service.

digital differential analyzer (DDA) A differential analyzer that uses digital representations for the analog quantities; for example, an incremental computer in which the principal type of computing unit is a digital integrator whose operation is similar to the operation of an integrating mechanism. (A)

digital display area In DPPX, a four-character display screen that is part of the operator panel and is used for communication between the system and the system operator during installation.

digital envelope In computer security, a digital signature used to verify the integrity of a message.

digital optical disc Synonym for optical disc. (T)

digital representation A discrete representation of a quantized value of a variable, that is, the representation of a number by digits, perhaps together with special characters and the space character. (T)

digital signal (1) A variable signal used by almost all computer systems. Digital signals can be represented as a series of numeric values, which can be represented by binary numbers that are used by computers.

(2) A discrete or discontinuous signal; a signal whose various states are discrete intervals apart. See Figure 42.

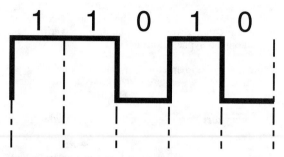

Figure 42. Digital Signal

digital signal processor (DSP) A high-speed coprocessor designed to do real-time manipulation of signals.

digital signature In computer security, encrypted data, appended to or part of a message, that enables a recipient to prove the identity of the sender.

digital-to-analog converter (DAC) (1) A functional unit that converts data from a digital representation to an analog representation. (I) (A) (2) A specialized integrated circuit that converts digital data into analog voltages. DACs are used in video, audio, telecommunications, and networking hardware. (3) In the AIX operating system, that portion of the display subsystem that converts pixels into colors or grayscale. (4) A device that converts a digital value to a proportional analog signal.

digital video In multimedia applications, material that can be seen and that has been converted to digital form. Synonymous with digitized video.

digital video effects (DVE) In multimedia applications, an online editing technique that manipulates on screen a full video image to create sophisticated transitions and special effects. Digital video effects can involve moving, enlarging, or overlaying pictures.

Digital Video Interactive (DVI) An integrated video, audio, and graphics technology allowing all forms of data—full motion video, still images, graphics and text—to be displayed from any digital source. DVI allows real-time compression and decompression as well as display of digital graphics and full-motion video with audio.

digit arithmetic See significant digit arithmetic.

digitize (1) To express or represent in a digital form data that are not discrete data; for example, to obtain a digital representation of the magnitude of a physical quantity from an analog representation of that magnitude. (I) (A) (2) To convert an analog signal into digital format. An analog signal during conversion must be sampled at discrete points and quantized to discrete numbers. See also analog-to-digital conversion, scanning.

digitized audio Synonym for digital audio.

digitized video Synonym for digital video.

digitizer (1) A device that converts to digital format any image captured by the camera. (2) An electronic device that transmits coordinate data to software running on a computer.

digit place In a positional representation system, each site that may be occupied by a character and that may be identified by an ordinal number or by an equivalent identifier. (I) (A) Synonymous with digit position.

digit position (1) The location in physical storage where a single digit is stored. (2) In COBOL, the amount of physical storage required to store a single digit. This amount can vary depending on the usage specified in the data description entry that defines the data item. If the data description entry specifies that the USAGE IS DISPLAY, then a digit position is synonymous with a character position. (3) Synonym for digit place.

digit punch (1) A punch in rows 1, 2,..., 9 of a punched card. (A) (2) Contrast with zone punch. (3) See also eleven punch, twelve punch.

dimension (1) The attribute of size given to arrays and tables. (2) To specify the size of a table or array and the arrangement of its elements.

dimension attribute In PL/I, an attribute that specifies the number of dimensions of an array and indicates the bounds of each dimension.

dimension specification In BASIC, the specification of the size of an array and the arrangement of its elements. Up to seven dimensions can be specified.

diminished radix complement In a fixed radix numeration system, a complement that can be derived from a given number by subtracting it from one less than a specified power of the radix. A diminished radix complement may be obtained by subtracting each digit of the given number from a digit that is one less than the radix. Synonymous with radix-minus-one complement. (T)

dimmed In SAA Common User Access architecture, pertaining to the visible indication that a choice or object cannot be selected or directly manipulated. For example, when a menu choice cannot be selected because the current state of the selected object makes the choice inactive, the choice is dimmed. See graying.

diode An electronic device used to permit current flow in one direction and to inhibit current flow in the other.

DIP Dual in-line package.

dipole modulation Synonym for nonpolarized return-to-zero recording.

dipping In manufacturing, the process of impregnating or coating insulating materials or windings by the method of immersion in liquid insulating material.

DIP switch In an IBM personal computer, a two-position switch on a circuit board that is preset to control certain functions; the user can change the position of a DIP switch to satisfy special requirements.

direct access (1) The capability to obtain data from a storage device, or to enter data into a storage device, in a sequence independent from their relative position, by means of addresses indicating the physical position of the data. (T) (2) Contrast with serial access.

direct access storage (1) A storage device that provides direct access to data. (I) (A) (2) See also immediate access storage, random access memory.

direct access storage device (DASD) A device in which access time is effectively independent of the location of the data.

direct access volume initialization In OS/VS, the use of utility programs for writing a home address, a volume label, and a volume table of contents on a direct access volume for checking for defective tracks and assigning alternate tracks for those that are defective, and for writing the IPL program on a new system volume.

direct activation In VTAM, the activation of a resource as a result of an activation command specifically naming the resource. See also automatic activation. Contrast with indirect activation.

direct address (1) An address that identifies a location without reference to a storage location containing another address. (T) (2) Synonymous with one-level address. (3) Contrast with indirect address.

direct addressing (1) A method of addressing in which the address part of an instruction contains a direct address. (I) (A) (2) An addressing method that uses an expression as an operand entry to represent an instruction address. (3) Contrast with indirect addressing.

direct attach The environment in which an application program directly allocates the 3800 printing subsystem.

direct attachment Synonym for display/printer adapter.

direct call facility A facility that permits calling without requiring the user to provide address selection signals; the network interprets the call request signal as an instruction to establish a connection to one or more predetermined data stations. (I)

Note: This facility may permit call setup faster than usual. No special priority is implied over other users of the network establishing a connection. The designated addresses are assigned for an agreed period of time.

direct-call feature A machine feature of a communication controller that allows outgoing calls to be established on X.21 switched lines without sending a selection sequence into the network. See also automatic calling.

direct color In AIX Enhanced X-Windows, a class of color map in which a pixel value is decomposed into three separate subfields for indexing. One subfield indexes an array to produce red intensity values, the second indexes another array for blue intensity values, and the third for green intensity values. The RGB values can be changed dynamically. See also pseudocolor.

direct connect In the IBM 8100 Information System, the attachment of another 8100 system, a terminal, or other I/O device through a selected communication interface and a limited-length cable. No modem is required.

direct connection The attachment of a system, workstation, or other I/O device through a selected communication interface and a limited-length cable. No modem is required.

direct-control In VTAM, pertaining to an application program and a terminal that must both be active and connected to each other before communication is possible.

direct control feature An optional feature of the System/370 computing system that provides a means of exchanging control signals between one computing system and another under program control.

direct data set A data set whose records are in random order on a direct access volume. Each record is stored or retrieved according to its actual address or its address relative to the beginning of the data set. Contrast with sequential data set.

direct deactivation In VTAM, the deactivation of a resource as a result of a deactivation command specifically naming the resource. See also automatic deactivation. Contrast with indirect deactivation.

direct dependent segment In an IMS/VS data entry database, a segment chained off a root segment. A direct dependent segment is stored in the root-addressable or the overflow portion of a data entry database area.

direct distance dialing A telephone exchange service that enables telephone users to call subscribers outside of their local area without operator assistance. See also area code, numbering plan.

directed-beam display device Synonym for calligraphic display device.

directed beam scan (1) In computer graphics, a technique of generating or recording the display elements of a display image in any sequence. (T) (2) Synonymous with directed scan, random scan. See also raster scan.

Note: The sequence of elements must be determined by a program.

directed Locate search A search request sent to a specific destination node known to contain a resource, such as a logical unit, to verify the continued presence of the resource at the destination node and to obtain the node's connectivity information for route calculation. Contrast with broadcast search.

directed scan Synonym for directed beam scan.

directed search Synonym for directed Locate search.

direct electrostatic process In a document copying machine, an electrostatic process in which photoconductive copying material is used; the copy results from the transfer of the image directly onto the copy material. (T) Contrast with indirect electrostatic process.

direct file In System/36, a disk file in which records are referenced by the relative record number. Contrast with indexed file, sequential file.

direct insert subroutine Synonym for open subroutine.

direct instruction (1) An instruction that contains only direct addresses of operands, or immediate operands. (T)　(2) Contrast with indirect instruction.

direct inward dialing A facility that allows an external telephone caller to call an extension without going through an operator.

direction (1) In System/38 graphics, the orientation of a string of mode-2 or mode-3 graphics symbols. Direction can dictate that the string reads left to right, right to left, top to bottom, or bottom to top. (2) See flow direction.

directional keys Deprecated term for cursor movement keys.

directive (1) In PL/I, a statement that directs the operation of the compiler. (2) Synonym for declaration.

direct line attachment (DLA) A protective device that is installed between the data terminal equipment (DTE) cable and the telecommunication line.

direct litho duplicating In a duplicator, a process in which the image is transferred directly from the master to the copy paper. The printing and nonprinting areas of the master are generally on the same plane; the former accepts the ink and the latter rejects it. (T)　Contrast with offset litho duplicating.　See also spirit duplicating, stencil duplicating.

direct litho duplicator A duplicator that uses the direct litho duplicating process to produce multiple copies from a master. (T)

directly attached loop In the IBM 8100 Information System, a loop that connects to the loop adapter by cables, rather than through a data link, and allows attachment of a variety of I/O devices. Contrast with data link attached loop.

direct manipulation In SAA Advanced Common User Access architecture, the use of a pointing device to work with objects, rather than through menus; for example, changing the size of a window by dragging one of its edges.　See also click, double-click, drag, drag and drop.

direct memory access (DMA) (1) A technique for moving data directly between main storage and peripheral equipment without requiring processing of the data by the processing unit. (T)　(2) The transfer of data between memory and input/output units without processor intervention.　(3) The system facility that allows a device on the Micro Channel bus to get direct access to the system or bus memory without the intervention of the system processor.

direct numerical control (DNC) A system in which sets of numerically controlled machines are connected to a computer.

Note: The machine tools are directly controlled by the computer without use of tape. (T)

direct operation In an 8100 channel I/O (CHIO) operation, the transfer of information from the SDLC control logic to a channel pointer.　Contrast with indirect operation.

director Equipment in communication common carrier telegraph message switching systems, used to make cross-office selection and connection from input line to output line equipment in accordance with addresses in the message.

directory (1) A table of identifiers and references to the corresponding items of data. (I) (A)　(2) A database in an APPN node that lists names of resources (in particular, logical units) and records the CP name of the node where each resource is located. See distributed directory database, local directory database.　(3) A type of file containing the names and controlling information for other files or other directories.　(4) An index that is used by a control program to locate one or more blocks of data that are stored in separate areas of a data set in direct access storage. (5) A listing of the files stored on a diskette.　(6) A listing of related files arranged in a useful hierarchy. (7) In VSE, an index that is used by the system to locate one or more sequential blocks of program information that are stored on direct access storage.　See also library directory, sublibrary directory.　(8) In VM/SP, a CP disk file that defines each virtual machine's normal configuration:　the user ID, password, normal and maximum allowable virtual storage, CP command privilege classes allowed, dispatching priority, logical editing symbols to be used, account number, and CP options desired. (9) A file containing such information as a name, address, and telephone number for each user of OFFICE/36.　Other people may also have entries in the directory.

directory file (1) A file of names, addresses, telephone numbers, and other identifying information, used as the source for distribution lists and telephone directories.　(2) In VM, a disk file that defines the virtual machine configuration of each user.

directory key In the 3790 Communication System, a combination of the file ID, industry code, module ID, and the version and level numbers (if any) for a program or DSCB stored in the 3790 library.

directory mask A pattern of characters that controls which portions of a directory will be retained and which portions will not be retained.

directory profile A description of a RACF-defined directory, including directory name, owner, universal access authority, security level, and other data.

directory service (DS) An application service element that translates the symbolic names used by application processes into the complete network addresses used in an OSI environment. (T)

directory services (DS) A control point component of an APPN node that maintains knowledge of the location of network resources.

directory tree An outline of all the directories and subdirectories on the current drive.

direct outward dialing A facility that allows an internal caller at an extension to dial an external number without going through an operator.

direct percentage On a calculator, the calculation directly of a percentage mark-up or discount value by the implied use of multiplication and division functions. (T)

direct-point repeater A telegraph function in which the receiving relay controlled by the signals received over a line repeats corresponding signals directly into another line or lines without the interposition of any other repeating or transmitting apparatus.

direct positive process In a document copying machine, a variation of the silver process in which a positive copy is produced by direct exposure and subsequent processing. (T)

direct-read-after-write (DRAW) disc In multimedia applications, a videodisc produced directly from a videotape, one copy at a time. A DRAW disc usually is used to check program material and author applications before replicated discs are available.

direct storage access A method of inserting input-output data into storage or obtaining input-output data from storage directly, without involving the usual flow of data through the processor. (A)

direct system output (DSO) writer In OS/VS, a job scheduler function that controls the writing of a job's output data sets directly to an output device during execution of the job.

disable (1) To make nonfunctional. In interactive communications, to disconnect or stop a subsystem. Contrast with enable. (2) To bring a queue or a device attached to a queue off line so that no print jobs are sent to it.

disabled (1) Pertaining to a state of a processing unit that prevents the occurrence of certain types of inter-

ruptions. Synonymous with masked. (2) Pertaining to the state in which a transmission control unit or audio response unit cannot accept incoming calls on a line. (3) Not selectable. (4) In VTAM, pertaining to a logical unit (LU) that has indicated to its system services control point (SSCP) that it is temporarily not ready to establish LU-LU sessions. An initiate request for a session with a disabled logical unit (LU) can specify that the session be queued by the SSCP until the LU becomes enabled. The LU can separately indicate whether this applies to its ability to act as a primary logical unit (PLU) or a secondary logical unit (SLU). See also enabled, inhibited.

disabled module A module that cannot be interrupted during its execution. It must be executed from beginning to end once it has gained control. Contrast with enabled module.

disabled page fault In OS/VS and VM, a page fault that occurs when I/O and external interruptions are disallowed by the processing unit.

disabled port In asynchronous terminal emulation (ATE), a port configuration indicating that a port is ready to call out.

disable state A state of a functional unit characterized by its inability to perform a required function, for any reason. Synonymous with outage. (T)

disable switch A switch in the Subsystem Support Services system parameter table that, when on, indicates that a serious error has occurred (such as inability to obtain access to the subsystem library or another type of I/O error), and that Subsystem Support Services is being shut down.

disaster dump A dump made when a nonrecoverable computer program error occurs. (A)

disaster plan Synonym for contingency plan.

DISC (1) Disconnect. (2) The BSC transmission control sequence for disconnect on a switched line. (3) See disconnect character.

disc (1) Preferred spelling for compact disc. See compact disc. (2) Variant spelling for disk. See magnetic disk.

Discard In SAA Common User Access architecture, a choice in the File pull-down that removes an item.

discarded packet A packet that is intentionally destroyed.

discipline In the AIX operating system, the ordering method used to line up jobs for printing, FCFS (first-come-first-served) or SJN (shortest-job-next). See also first-come-first-served, shortest-job-next.

disclosure In computer security, the acquisition of information without authorization.

disconnect (1) To disengage apparatus used in a connection and restore it to its ready condition when not in use. Synonymous with release. (2) To break a connection, physically or electrically. (3) In X.25 communications, to disconnect a port from the X.25 network.

disconnect (DISC) character In data communication, the part of the BSC transmission control sequence for ending the connection on a switched line.

disconnected In an ESCON Director, the attribute that, when set, removes a dedicated connection. Contrast with connected.

disconnected mode (DM) (1) In SDLC, a response from a secondary station indicating that it is disconnected and wants to be online. (2) Synonym for disconnected phase.

disconnected phase A phase entered by a data circuit-terminating equipment (DCE) when it detects error conditions, recovers from a temporary internal malfunction, or receives a DISC command from a data terminal equipment (DTE). In the disconnected phase, the DCE may initiate link setup but can transmit only DM responses to received frames. See also information transfer phase.

disconnection In VTAM, the termination of a physical connection.

disconnect mode (DM) In VM, the mode of operation in which a virtual machine is executing without a physical line or terminal connected as an operator console. Any attempt to issue a read to the console causes the virtual machine to be logged off after 15 minutes have elapsed, unless the user logs on again within the 15-minute interval.

disconnect signal A signal transmitted from one end of a subscriber line or trunk to indicate at the other end that the established connection is to be disconnected.

disconnect time-out (1) An indication that a station has gone on-hook. (2) A time-out that indicates a loss of communication with a BSC device or workstation.

discontiguous segment In VM/370, a 64K-byte segment of storage that was previously loaded and saved and assigned a unique name. The segment (or segments) can be shared among virtual machines if it

contains reentrant code. Discontiguous segments used with CMS must be loaded into storage at locations above a user's CMS virtual machine, and are attached when needed and detached when no longer needed.

discontiguous shared segment An area of virtual storage outside the address range of a virtual machine. It can contain read-only data or reentrant code. It connects discontiguous segments to a virtual machine's address space so programs can be fetched.

discrete (1) Pertaining to data that consists of distinct elements such as characters, or to physical quantities having a finite number of distinctly recognizable values. (T) (A) (2) Contrast with analog.

discrete cosine transformation (DCT) A video compression algorithm similar to Fast Fourier Transform (FFT) but easier to compute. See also Fourier transforms.

discrete data Data represented by characters.

discrete logarithm In computer security, a basis for a set of schemes for public key cryptography.

discrete profile (1) A description of a single RACF-defined resource that belongs to either the DATASET class or to one of the general resource classes. This description can include authorized users, access authority of each user, location of the data set (device type and volume serial number), number of accesses to the data set, and other information. (2) In RACF, a resource profile that can provide protection for only a single resource. For example, a discrete profile can protect only a single data set or minidisk.

discrete programming Synonym for integer programming.

discrete representation A representation of data by characters, or a group of characters designating one of a number of alternatives. (T) (A)

discrete tone In acoustics, a sound wave whose sound pressure varies as a sinusoidal function of time. See also prominent discrete tone.

discretionary access control (1) In computer security, a means of optionally restricting access to objects, based on the identity of subjects, the groups to which they belong, or based on both of these criteria. Access controls are discretionary in the sense that a subject with a particular access right can pass that access right to any other subject. Contrast with mandatory access control. See also need-to-know. (2) In the AIX operating system, a security mechanism that protects information from unauthorized disclosure or modification through owner-controlled access to files.

See also access control list, access permission, base permission, extended permission.

discretionary hyphen Synonym for soft hyphen. (T)

discriminated union A C-language union that holds several data types, with one arm of the union being an enumeration value, or discriminant, which holds a specific object to be processed over the system first.

discrimination instruction An instruction of the class of instructions that comprises branch instructions and conditional jump instructions. (I) (A)

disjoint network In a network, two or more subnetworks with the same network identifier that are not directly connected, but are indirectly connected, for example, through SNA network interconnection. See also disjoint SSCP.

disjoint SSCP In VTAM, an SSCP that does not have a direct SSCP-SSCP session with every other SSCP in its network-ID subnetwork.

disjunction (1) The Boolean operation whose result has the Boolean value 0 if and only if each operand has the Boolean value 0. (I) (A) Synonymous with inclusive-OR operation, logical add, OR operation. (2) Contrast with nondisjunction.

disk (1) A round, flat, data medium that is rotated in order to read or write data. (T) (2) Loosely, a magnetic disk unit. (3) Synonym for magnetic disk. (4) See integrated disk. (5) See also compact disc, diskette, optical disc.

disk adapter In the IBM 8100 Information System, a hardware feature that is required to transfer data and commands between the processor and a disk unit in an 8101 Storage and Input/Output Unit, an 8130 Processor, or an 8140 Processor.

disk allocation table (DAT) In the 3650 Retail Store System, a data area, built by the creation facilities program (CFP), that contains an entry for each file needing space to be allocated on the store controller's disk storage.

disk array Two or more hard disks interconnected to increase security, performance, or reliability.

Disk BASIC The version of BASIC supplied on the IBM Personal Computer DOS Diskette that, in addition to the features provided by Cassette BASIC, allows reading and writing of data on diskettes and provides a clock that keeps track of the date and time, asynchronous communication support, and support for two additional printers. See also Advanced BASIC, Cassette BASIC.

disk cartridge An assembly of one or more disks that can be removed as a whole from a disk drive, together with the associated container from which the disk cannot be separated. (T) (A)

disk device See compact disc (CD), direct access storage device (DASD), diskette drive, hard disk.

disk drive (1) A device for controlling the rotation of magnetic disks. (T) (2) In an IBM personal computer, a diskette drive or a hard disk drive. (3) The mechanism used to seek, read, and write information on a disk. (4) Deprecated term for magnetic disk unit.

disk duplexing A method of storing data whereby the data from one hard disk is duplicated on another, with each using its own hard-disk controller. Contrast with disk mirroring.

disk enclosure (1) A sealed container that holds the read/write head and disk assembly within a disk unit. (2) A physical enclosure containing one or more disk drives.

diskette (1) A small magnetic disk enclosed in a jacket. (T) (2) A thin, flexible magnetic disk and a semi-rigid protective jacket, in which the disk is permanently enclosed. (3) See daily initialization diskette, diagnostic diskette, DOS diskette, formatted diskette, installation diskette, unformatted diskette, virtual diskette. See also hard disk.

diskette drive (1) The mechanism used to seek, read, and write data on a diskette. See also diskette magazine drive. (2) See diskette storage drive.

diskette file A device file created by the user to support a diskette device.

diskette-formatted tape A tape that is formatted so that it can be read by a data converter unit, which transfers the data written on it to a diskette.

diskette formatting Establishing and identifying the number and size of sectors on a diskette and preparing it for use with a particular computer. See also fixed disk formatting.

Note: Formatting destroys any information that has been previously recorded on a diskette.

diskette location The slot into which the diskette is inserted before being read or written.

diskette magazine drive In System/36 and System/38, a diskette drive that can hold two magazines, each containing 10 diskettes, plus individual diskettes in three separate slots. It is used to transfer information between system internal storage and removable diskettes.

diskette-only feature A special feature or a specify feature that, through macroinstructions or microinstructions on diskette, either activates, suppresses, or adapts product application functions or simulates functions to enhance the capability, storage capacity, or performance of the product; for example, a feature on diskette that enables a processor to execute the instructions of some other machine.

diskette slot In a personal computer, an opening in the system unit through which the user can insert a diskette into the diskette drive.

diskette storage device A direct access storage device that uses diskettes as the storage medium.

diskette storage drive (1) A device that rotates diskette disks in a diskette storage device. (2) Deprecated term for diskette storage device.

diskette unit A physical enclosure containing one or more diskette drives.

diskette writer In the AS/400 system, a system program that writes spooled files to a diskette unit. See also printer writer, spooling writer.

disk file A set of related records on disk that are treated as a unit. See also record file, stream file.

disk mirroring A method of storing data whereby the data from one hard disk is duplicated on another, with both hard disks sharing a single hard-disk controller. Contrast with disk duplexing.

disk operating system An operating system for computer systems that use disks and diskettes for auxiliary storage of programs and data.

Disk Operating System/Virtual Storage See VSE.

disk pack (1) An assembly of magnetic disks that can be removed as a whole from a disk unit, together with the container from which it must be separated when operating. (T) (2) A portable set of flat, circular recording surfaces used in a disk storage device. (A)

disk request word See I/O request word.

disk sector See sector.

disk server A high-capacity disk storage device that each personal computer on a network can access and use as if it were its own hard disk. See also file server.

Note: The computer's operating system controls access to the disk server; files are not shared by other computers on the network.

disk sharing See shared DASD option.

disk storage See magnetic disk storage.

disk storage device See magnetic disk unit.

disk storage drive See disk drive.

disk storage module A nonremovable assembly of magnetic disks serviced by two access mechanisms.

disk unit See magnetic disk unit.

disk-usage accounting In the AIX operating system, the recording of the number of disk blocks occupied by a user's files.

disk volume (1) A disk pack or part of a disk storage module. (2) In DPCX, disk storage on a nonremovable storage medium.

dismount Deprecated term for demount.

DISOSS Distributed Office Support System.

dispatch To allocate time on a processor to jobs or tasks that are ready for execution. (I) (A)

dispatcher (1) The program in an operating system that places jobs or tasks into execution. (2) The routing or controlling routine of Subsystem Support Services. This routine provides multitasking and control support, on a priority basis, for all Subsystem Support Services functions.

dispatcher/scheduler favoring scheme In VM/SP HPO, a set of criteria used by the dispatcher and scheduler to create a bias in favor of queue 1 users, who are usually highly interactive users.

dispatching cycle The process used by the 3601 Finance Communication Controller to check logical workstations for work to be done. When each logical workstation has been given the opportunity to process, a dispatching cycle has occurred.

dispatching priority A number assigned to tasks, used to determine the order in which they use the processing unit in a multitasking situation. See also limit priority.

dispatch list In VM/SP HPO, a subset of the run list that comprises those virtual machines that are currently runnable; that is, not in a short wait state. Synonymous with true run list. See also run list.

dispersant In a document copying machine, a nonconductive liquid used in some electrostatic processes to hold in suspension the toner particles and to act as a dilutant for the toner concentrate. (T)

displacement (1) The distance from the beginning of a record, block, or segment to the beginning of a particular field. (2) Synonym for relative address.

displacement byte A 1-byte value in an indexed instruction that is added to an index register value to obtain a real address or to change the contents of an index register.

display (1) A visual presentation of data. (I) (A) (2) To present data visually. (I) (A) (3) In Enhanced X-Windows, a set of one or more screens and input devices that are driven by a single X server. See bit-mapped display, character display, color display, monochrome display. (4) Deprecated term for panel.

display adapter An adapter within a computer to drive a display monitor. See capture adapter.

display and printer attachment feature In the IBM 8100 Information System, control logic that allows the connection of various I/O devices to the 8101 Storage and Input/Output Unit.

display and printing calculator A calculator that provides the data output facilities of a display calculator and, if selected by the user, a printing calculator. (T) (A)

display area (1) In System/36 ideographic support, an 18-by-18 matrix on the character definition display that is used to display the character currently being defined or updated. (2) Synonym for display space.

Note: Part of a display surface may not be available for presentation of images; for example, on cathode ray tube displays, part of the display surface, bordering the display area, is not scanned by the electron beam.

display attribute In computer graphics, a property that is assigned to a display element, to a display segment, or to the complete display image; for example, a bright intensity or a particular color.

display background Synonym for background image.

display-based word processing equipment Word processing equipment that can electronically display text and other graphics; using for example, a cathode ray tube (CRT) , light emitting diode (LED), or gas plasma display. (T) Contrast with non-display-based word processing equipment.

display calculator A machine in which the data output is shown in the form of illuminated characters. (T)

display character generator On a visual display device, a hardware unit that converts the digital code for a character into signals that cause the electron beam to create the character on the screen.

display column In computer graphics, all display positions that constitute a full-length vertical line on the display surface. Synonymous with addressable vertical positions. Contrast with display line.

display command A command that controls the state or action of a display device. (I) (A) Synonymous with display instruction.

display component A terminal component capable of displaying information on a viewing surface; for example, a cathode ray tube or a gas panel.

display console A console that must include at least one display surface and may also include one or more input devices. (I) (A)

display cycle In computer graphics, the sequence of events needed to generate a display image once.

display cycle time In computer graphics, the minimum time interval between the starts of successive display cycles.

display device (1) An output unit that gives a visual representation of data. Usually the data are displayed temporarily; however, arrangements may be made for making a permanent record. (I) (A) (2) In computer graphics, a device capable of presenting display elements on a display surface; for example, a cathode ray tube, plotter, microfilm viewer, or printer. (3) See calligraphic display device, character display device, directed beam display device, raster display device. (4) See also display, plasma panel, visual display unit.

display element (1) A basic graphic element that can be used to construct a display image; for example, a dot, a line segment, a character string. (I) (A) Synonymous with graphic primitive, output primitive. (2) See also input primitive.

display emulation The part of 3270 emulation support that converts 3270 data streams into 5250 data streams and 5250 data streams into 3270 data streams, thereby allowing a 52xx display station to appear to the host as a 3277 display device.

display entity See display element, display segment, input primitive.

display field In computer graphics, an area in a display buffer or on a display screen that contains a set of characters that can be manipulated or operated upon as a unit.

display file (1) A device file created by the user to support a display workstation or console. (2) In the AS/400 system, a device file that supports a display station. (3) In BASIC, any file that has the keyword DISPLAY specified in the OPEN statement for the file.

display foreground Synonym for foreground image.

display format (1) The name of the device file and the name of the record format to be used when the subsystem obtains routing data from the user. (2) Data that defines or describes a display.

display frame (1) In computer graphics, an area in storage in which a display image can be recorded. (2) In computer micrographics, an area on a microform in which a display image can be recorded.

display function The action of reproducing an image of a document or object on a workstation, using a front-end application.

display group Synonym for display segment.

display image (1) A collection of display elements or segments that are represented together at any one time on a display surface. (I) (A) (2) In 3270 emulation, the 1920-character block that contains data in the sequence in which it would appear on the display screen or the printer. The user can specify the screen image with or without field definitions, such as position, length, and other attributes, when creating the BSC file. (3) See background image, coded image, foreground image, screen image.

display instruction Synonym for display command.

Display keys In SAA Basic Common User Access, an action that gives a user the option of alternately turning off and on the display of the function key area.

display layout sheet A form used to plan the location of data on the display.

display levels Synonym for display types.

display line In computer graphics, all display positions that constitute a full-length horizontal line on the display surface. Synonymous with addressable horizontal positions. Contrast with display column.

display list In AIX graphics, a sequence of drawing commands that have been compiled into a unit. Con-

ceptually, a display list is like a macro; it can be called multiple times simply by referring to its name. The object can be instantiated at different locations, sizes, and orientations by appropriate use of the transformation matrices; for example, series of polygons arranged in the shape of a bolt can be compiled into an object. The bolt can then be drawn multiple times by calling its display list. Synonymous with object.

display mode In the IBM LinkWay product, a screen setting that determines the screen resolution and number of colors that can be used in a folder or picture.

display monitor The display screen of a visual display unit, such as a cathode ray tube (CRT) display, a liquid crystal display (LCD), a light-emitting diode (LED) display.

display order Synonym for display command.

display paging In VM, a technique, used by the CMS Editor for a display terminal in display mode, for scanning through a CMS file up to 20 lines at a time.

display panel In computer graphics, a predefined display image that defines the locations and characteristics of display fields on a display surface.

Display panel IDs In SAA Basic Common User Access, an action that gives a user the option of displaying panel IDs. The default is "off."

display point In GDDM, the smallest addressable area on the screen that defines the resolution of the characters or images. Synonymous with pel.

display position In computer graphics, any position in a display space that can be occupied by a picture element. See also print position.

display/printer adapter (DPA) An 8100 Information System attachment for display and printer devices that can be connected, via hardware, directly to the 8100/DPCX system. Synonymous with direct attachment.

display recall control On a battery-powered calculator, a control for recalling a display that has been blanked out by battery-saving circuitry. (T)

display screen (1) A display surface on which display images are presented. (2) The part of a display station or workstation on which information is displayed.

display segment In computer graphics, a collection of display elements that can be manipulated as a unit. (I) Synonymous with display group.

Note: A display segment may consist of several display elements such as dots, arcs, or line segments.

display space (1) The portion of a display surface that is available for displaying images. (2) Synonymous with display area, operating space. (3) See also coded image space.

display station An input/output device containing a display screen and an attached keyboard that allows a user to send information to or receive information from the system. See also terminal, workstation.

display station field In System/36, a field that each display station uses and modifies independently.

display station indicator In System/36, an indicator that each display station uses and modifies independently.

display station pass-through (1) An APPC function that allows a user's display station at a System/38 to become logically connected to another System/38, enabling the user to sign on at the other system as if his display station were locally attached to it. (2) See passthrough.

display surface In a display device, that medium on which display images may appear; for example, the screen of a cathode ray tube, the paper in a plotter. (I) (A) See Figure 43.

display symbol In the AIX operating system, a predefined printable graphics symbol, such as a character, number, math symbol, or Greek letter, that can be displayed on a high function terminal (HFT) display in keyboard send-receive (KSR) mode.

display symbol set In the AIX operating system, a set of display symbols placed in a table. There are up to 1024 display symbols. Display symbols 0 through 31 represent control functions and have no graphic representation.

display tube A tube, usually a cathode ray tube, used to display data. (A)

display types In the NetView program, a concept to describe the organization of panels. Display types are defined as total, most recent, user action, and detail. Display types are combined with resource types and data types to describe NetView program's panel organization. See also data types, resource types. Synonymous with display levels.

display workstation An ImagePlus workstation equipped with a display monitor.

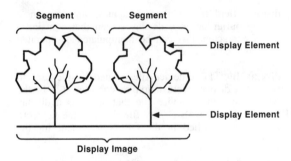

Figure 43. Display Surface

Displaywriter A programmable workstation that uses the Electronic Document Distribution licensed program to communicate with other office products.

Displaywriter user See independent workstation user.

disposition In file processing, the process of specifying whether a file is new, old, or shared, and how the file is to be shared.

disposition processing In OS/VS, a function performed by the initiator at the end of a job step to keep, delete, catalog, or uncatalog data sets, or pass them to a subsequent job step, depending on the data set status or the disposition specified in the DISP parameter of the DD statement.

dissolve In multimedia applications, to fade down a picture as the next fades up. Synonymous with crossfade. See also wipe.

dissuasion tone In telephony, an audible signal indicating that the requested extension is out of order or does not exist, or that the type of call requested is not allowed with a particular class of service.

distinctive ringing A ringing cadence indicating whether a call is internal or external.

distortion An unwanted change in waveform that may occur between two points in a transmission system. The six major forms of distortion are:

bias
A type of telegraph distortion resulting when the significant intervals of the modulation do not all have their exact theoretical durations.

characteristic
Distortion caused by transients that, as a result of the modulation, are present in the transmission channel and depend on its transmission qualities.

delay
Distortion occurring when the envelope delay of a circuit or system is not constant over the frequency range required for transmission.

end

Distortion of start-stop teletypewriter signals. The shifting of the end of all marking pulses from their proper positions in relation to the beginning of the start pulse.

fortuitous (jitter)

A type of telegraph distortion that results in the intermittent shortening or lengthening of the signals. This distortion is entirely random in nature and can be caused by such things as battery fluctuations, hits on the line, and power induction.

harmonic

The resultant presence of harmonic frequencies, due to nonlinear characteristics of a transmission line, in the response when a sinusoidal stimulus is applied.

distributed application (1) An application for which the component application programs are distributed between two or more interconnected processors. (2) In SAA usage, an application that is designed to have its parts split across and run on two or more linked systems.

distributed data In SAA usage, data that is split across two or more linked systems but which can be accessed and processed as if it resided on one.

distributed database (1) A database that is physically decentralized and handled by a database management system in a way that provides a logically centralized view of the database to the user. (T) (2) A database that is controlled by a single database management system but is dispersed over a network.

Distributed Data Management (DDM) A feature of the System Support Program Product that allows an application program to work on files that reside in a remote system.

distributed data processing (DDP) Synonym for distributed processing.

distributed directory database The complete listing of all the resources in the network as maintained in the individual directories scattered throughout an APPN network. Each node has a piece of the complete directory, but it is not necessary for any one node to have the entire list. Entries are created, modified, and deleted through system definition, operator action, automatic registration, and ongoing network search procedures. Synonymous with distributed network directory, network directory database.

distributed file system A file system composed of files or directories that physically reside on more than one computer in a communication network.

distributed free space Space reserved within the control intervals of a key-sequenced data set or file for inserting new records into the data set or file in key sequence; also, whole control intervals reserved in a control area for the same purpose.

distributed function (1) The use of programmable terminals, controllers, and other devices to perform operations previously accomplished by the processing unit, such as managing data links, controlling devices, and formatting data. (2) Functions such as network management processing, and error recovery operations, that are dispersed among the nodes of a network, as opposed to functions that are concentrated at a central location.

distributed function terminal (DFT) In the AIX operating system, a workstation that performs operations previously accomplished by the processing unit, such as managing data links, controlling devices, and formatting data.

distributed host command facility (DHCF) (1) In the OS/400 operating system, a function that supports the data link between a System/370 terminal using an AS/400 application in a Host Command Facility (HCF) environment. (2) The part of an 8100 Information System that helps create the link between a System/370 terminal and an 8100 application.

distributed indexed access method (DXAM) In DPPX, a method that provides keyed access through an index data set to records in a target data set.

distributed intelligence Deprecated term for distributed data processing, distributed function.

distributed network directory Synonym for distributed directory database.

distributed presentation management (DPM) In IMS/VS, a message format service (MFS) option that allows programs to communicate with device independence by sharing message formatting functions between MFS and a user-written remote program. The user-written remote program performs device-dependent formatting.

Distributed Presentation Services (DPS) In DPPX systems, an IBM licensed program that provides the COBOL and assembler language application programmer with support for formatting and modifying the layout of data on displays and printers.

distributed processing (1) Data processing in which some or all of the processing, storage, and control functions, in addition to input/output functions, are dispersed among data processing stations. (T) (2) Processing that takes place across two or more linked systems. (3) Data processing in which application transaction programs distributed among interconnected processors cooperate to perform distributed applications for end users of a network. Two types of distributed data processing are job networking and distributed transaction processing. (4) See also remote access data processing. (5) Synonymous with distributed data processing.

Distributed Processing Control Executive DPCX. An IBM licensed program designed to control the IBM 8100 Information System. DPCX manages the 8100 system resources (devices, storage, and processing time) in such a way as to provide central control of a distributed processing system and application programming capability.

distributed processing network (1) A network in which some or all of the processing, storage, and control functions, in addition to input/output functions, are dispersed among its nodes. See also remote access network. (2) In DPCX, a host system and all connected 8100/DPCX systems. (3) See distributed data processing network.

Distributed Processing Programming Executive (DPPX) A comprehensive collection of licensed programs that make up an operating system for 8100 Information System hardware. DPPX includes the DPPX Base and other licensed programs that provide programming languages, application support, and System/370 network access.

distributed system See distributed data processing, distributed function.

Distributed Systems Executive (DSX) (1) An IBM licensed program that provides central library support and batch transmission control for a system with DPPX. (2) An IBM licensed program available for IBM host systems (System/370, 43xx, and 30xx) that allows the host system to get, send, and remove files, programs, formats, and procedures in a network of computers.

Distributed Systems License Option (DSLO) A license option available to IBM customers with a basic license that permits them to copy certain IBM-licensed materials for the purpose of installing multiple systems.

distributed systems node executive (DSNX) (1) In the OS/400 operating system, a function that receives and analyzes requests from the NetView Distribution Manager licensed program on a host system. If the request is directed to the system that receives it, the request is processed on that system or on a personal computer directly attached to that system. If the request is intended for a different system, it is routed toward its destination. (2) Synonym for change management.

distributed transaction processing In CICS/VS, a type of distributed data processing in which transactions entered by terminal operators are processed by multiple transaction programs under the control of several cooperating transaction processing systems.

distributing frame A structure for terminating permanent wires of a telephone central office, private branch exchange, or private exchange and for permitting the easy change of connections between them by means of crossconnecting wires.

distribution cable A branch off a feeder cable.

distribution document In the OS/400 operating system, an internal document that contains the document content and document details for distribution.

distribution entry In ACF/TCAM, a terminal-table entry associated with a distribution list. See also distribution list, terminal entry.

distribution libraries IBM-supplied partitioned data sets on tape containing one or more components that the user restores to disk for subsequent inclusion in a new system.

distribution list (1) A list of intended recipients defined and named by the originator. (T) (2) In ACF/TCAM, a list of pointers to single or cascade entries. When the distribution entry is named as the destination for a message, the message is sent as separate transmissions to all items in the list. (3) In the OS/400 operating system, a list of system distribution directory entries that allows users to send messages, notes, and documents to a group of users in one step.

distribution medium The medium on which the operating system software, a licensed program, or an application program is distributed to the user. The distribution medium can be any of several different media supported by the hardware, such as streaming cartridge tape, 9-track tape, or 3.5-inch diskette.

distribution panel (1) In an ESCON environment, a panel that provides a central location for the attachment of trunk and jumper cables and can be mounted in a rack, wiring closet, or on a wall. Synonymous with patch panel. (2) In the IBM Token-Ring Network, a wiring board that has a patch panel function and mounts in a rack.

distribution processing A process in which application programs and processing are distributed among interconnected processors to users on a network.

distribution queue In SNADS, a list of documents or mail waiting to be sent to users or libraries on remote systems.

distribution recipient queue In the OS/400 operating system, an internal object that contains entries for incoming object distributions, incoming document distributions, outgoing document distributions, and error distributions.

distribution request A request to OFFICE/36 to send a document or documents to an individual or to a distribution list.

distribution service level In SNADS, the combination of priority, capacity, and protection requirements that must be satisfied to receive or send a distribution. SNADS has service levels of fast, status, data high, and data low. Items with a service level of fast, status, or data high are put on the priority queue. Items with a service level of data low are put on the normal queue.

distribution services In the OS/400 operating system, the support provided by the operating system to receive, forward, and send electronic mail in an SNA network.

distribution tape A magnetic tape that contains; for example, a preconfigured operating system such as VSE/SP. This tape is shipped to the customer for program installation.

distribution tape reel (DTR) A reel of magnetic tape on which IBM sends programs or data to a customer.

distribution tracking object In the OS/400 operating system, an internal object that is used to control office distributions.

distribution zone In SMP/E, a group of VSAM records that describe the SYSMODs and elements in the distribution libraries.

dithering In computer graphics, a technique of interleaving dark and light pixels so that the resulting image looks smoothly shaded when viewed from a distance.

DITTO Data interfile transfer, testing, and operations utility. See VSE/DITTO.

diversion In AIX test formatting, a command used to save text for printing later in a document, such as for footnotes.

divide check exception A condition caused by an attempt to divide by zero.

dividend In a division operation, the number or quantity to be divided. (I) (A)

division In COBOL, a collection of zero, one, or more than one section or paragraph, called the division body, that are formed and combined in accordance with a specific set of rules. Each division consists of the division header and the related division body.

Note: There are four divisions in a COBOL program: Identification, Environment, Data, and Procedure.

division header In COBOL, a combination of words, followed by a separator period, that indicates the beginning of a division. The division headers in a COBOL program are:

    IDENTIFICATION DIVISION
    ENVIRONMENT DIVISION
    DATA DIVISION
    PROCEDURE DIVISION [USING data-name-1 ...]

divisor In a division operation, the number or quantity by which the dividend is divided. (I) (A)

dl Deciliter.

DLA (1) Data link adapter. (2) Direct line attachment.

DLA terminal A terminal attached to an 8100 Information System by a data link.

DLC Data link control.

DLCI Data link connection identifier.

DLE The data link escape character. (A)

DLFDATA segment The portion of a RACF profile containing data for the data lookaside facility.

DL/I Data language 1.

DLIB Distribution library.

DL indicator Delete-mode indicator.

DL/I service program A service program that gives a transaction processing system, and therefore its transaction program, access to a DL/I database located at a different transaction processing system.

DLO Document library object.

DLRPL Dump/load/restart parameter list.

DLT Data loop transceiver.

DLU Destination logical unit.

dm Decimeter.

DM (1) Disconnected mode. (2) Disconnect mode.

DMA Direct memory access.

DMA slave A device on the Micro Channel bus that uses the system-provided direct memory access (DMA) facilities instead of having a built-in controller. See also Bus Master.

DMH Device message handler.

DML Data manipulating language.

DNC Dynamic network collection.

DNIC Data network identification code.

DNIS Dialed number identification service.

DOC Documentation.

DOCID Document Identification. See also object name.

document (1) A named, structural unit of text that can be stored, retrieved, and exchanged among systems and users as a separate unit. (T) (2) Information and the medium on which it is recorded that generally have permanence and can be read by humans or by machine. (3) In word processing, a collection of information that pertains to a particular subject or related subjects. Synonymous with file. (4) In System/36, a collection of one or more lines of text that can be named and stored as a member in a folder.

document administrator The person who defines, organizes, manages, controls, and protects documents. (T) (A)

document architecture A complete set of interrelated rules defining the possible structures of documents taken into consideration in a specific text processing environment. (T)

document area In OfficeVision, the area of the Writing Pad window in which text is entered.

document assembly Synonym for document merge. (T)

documentation (1) The management of documents, which may include the actions of identifying, acquiring, processing, storing, and disseminating them. (I) (A) (2) A collection of documents on a given subject. (I) (A) (3) The aids provided for understanding the structure and intended uses of an information system or its components, such as flowcharts, textual material, and end-user manuals. (A) (4) See system documentation.

document authority Permission granted to one user to work with documents that are owned by another user.

document body The contents of a document, including text and layout information, but excluding the document profile. (T)

Document button A LinkWay button object that lets the user display a document from a specified file.

document class In the OS/400 operating system, a user-defined character string, 1 through 16 characters long, that characterizes a document. It can be used to search for a filed document. For example, a document that is a memo could have a document class of MEMO; a document that is a report, REPORT.

document conversion processor A computer program that processes a machine-readable document, including formatting controls written in one formatter language, to produce a machine-readable document including formatting controls appropriate for another formatter language.

document copying The making of one or more true copies of an original on the same or a different scale by means of a document copying machine. (T)

document copying machine (1) A machine that uses the diazo process, electrostatic process, silver process, or thermographic process primarily to produce copies of an original without affecting the original. (T) (2) See console document copying machine, desk-top document copying machine, diazo document copying machine, electrostatic document copying machine, feed-past document copying machine, feed-through document copying machine, moving-platen document copying machine, photographic document copying machine, stationary-platen document copying machine, thermographic document copying machine.

document delivery The transfer of a document into the recipient's environment. (T)

document description Data that describe the characteristics of a document, such as document type, subject, author, and date created.

document details Data that describes the characteristics of a document; for example, document type, subject, author, and date created.

document drawer A drawer underneath a network controller for storing the operator's guide, the key that locks and unlocks machine elements, and spare lights and fuses.

document environment group In the 3800 Print Services Facility, an internal object that is a required part of every form definition, identifies suppression usage, identifies overlays to be used, and defines the placement of one or more pages on the form.

document folder A folder that contains documents.

document format The selected arrangement of text for a specific document.

document formatter A computer program that allows the user to layout and obtain a printable copy for a document. A document formatter may perform other functions such as page and paragraph numbering. (T)

document formatting In word processing, the arrangement or layout of text on a recording medium.

document image In the IBM ImagePlus system, the electronic representation of a document consisting of one or more page images. See also document image composition.

document image composition In the IBM ImagePlus system, the arrangement and number of individual page images within a document image.

document index In System/36, a list of documents stored in a folder.

document indexing In the IBM ImagePlus system, the process of entering document information that uniquely identifies it for processing, filing, and retrieval.

Document Interchange Architecture (DIA) The rules and structure for the exchange of information between office applications. Document Interchange Architecture includes document library services and document distribution services.

document interchange format The rules for representing documents for the purpose of interchange. (T)

document library (1) A set of VSAM data sets, accessible in a batch environment, that contain documents and related files. (2) In the OS/400 operating system, the system library, named QDOC, that contains all documents and folders.

document library object (DLO) In the OS/400 operating system, any system object that can reside in a document library, such as revisable-form text (RFT) and final-form text (FFT) documents, folders, and PC files.

document library services The service defined by the Document Interchange Architecture (DIA) to work with objects filed in the DIA document library. On the AS/400 system, it is the support that lets office users work with the contents of the document library.

document machine In OfficeVision, a LAN server that stores all documents shared within the OS/2 Office node.

document mark In micrographics, an optical mark within the recording area and outside the image on a roll of microfilm that is used for counting images or film frames automatically. (A) Synonymous with blip.

document merge The ability of a system to create a document from previously recorded texts; for example, the merging of a form letter with the name and address of a recipient recorded in a list. Synonymous with document assembly. (T)

document name In the AS/400 system, the 1- through 12-character name for documents in folders, assigned by the user when creating the document. Contrast with library-assigned document name, document object name.

document number In the AS/400 system, the number assigned to a printed document when a user files that document. The first two digits of the document number are the year, and the last five are in sequence, with the most recent documents having the highest number; for example, the fifth printed document filed in 1991 would have the number 91-00005.

document object name The 10-character name of a document assigned by the system when a user files the document. Contrast with document name, library-assigned document name.

document overlength In the IBM 3881 Optical Mark Reader, two attached documents that overlap and exceed the batch document measurement.

document processing In word processing, performing operations on one or more documents, such as entering, rearranging, sorting, merging, storing, retrieving, displaying, and printing text.

document profile A set of attributes that specifies the characteristics of an entire document such as its type and format. (T)

document reader A character reader whose input is text from specific areas on a given type of form. (T) (A)

document received date A system-generated date indicating when a document is first received into the Folder Application Facility.

document reference edge In character recognition, a specified document edge with respect to which the alignment of characters is defined. (A)

document routing The assignment of documents to departments, units, organizations, or to individuals for processing.

document skew In the IBM 3881 Optical Mark Reader, misalignment of a document at the read station.

document spelling check function An automatic proofreading function that allows a user to check and correct spelling and to replace words with preferred synonyms.

DO group (1) In programming languages, a sequence of statements headed by a DO statement and ended by a corresponding END statement that is used for control purposes. (2) In the OS/400 operating system, a set of commands in a control language program defined by a DO command and an ENDDO command that is conditionally processed as a group. (3) In RPG, a group of calculations done one or more times based on the results of comparing factor 1 and factor 2 of certain calculation operations; for example, DOUxx. A DO operation and an END operation are the delimiters for a DO group. (4) In PL/I, a sequence of statements, run as a unit, that may be processed several times, once, or not at all. Contrast with block.

dolly (1) A wheeled platform for a camera. (2) A camera movement in which the tripod on which the camera is mounted physically moves toward or away from the subject.

DO loop A range of statements run repetitively by a DO statement.

domain (1) That part of a computer network in which the data processing resources are under common control. (T) (2) In SNA, see end node domain, network node domain, system services control point domain. (3) In a database, all the possible values of an attribute or a data element. (4) In computer security, all of the objects that a subject can access. See also shared control. (5) In TCP/IP, the naming system used in hierarchical networks. The domain naming system uses the DOMAIN protocol and the named daemon. In a domain system, groups of hosts are administered separately within a tree-structured hierarchy of domains and subdomains.

domain controller In OfficeVision, an OS/2 LAN server within the domain that manages the LAN domain.

domain model A model of a problem area of an expert system. (T)

domain name In TCP/IP, a name of a host system in a network. A domain name consists of a sequence of subnames separated by a delimiter character.

domain name server In TCP/IP, a server program that supplies name-to-address translation by mapping domain names to internet addresses. Synonymous with name server.

domain name system (DNS) The online distributed database system used to map domain names to internet addresses.

domain operator In a multiple-domain network, the person or program that controls operation of resources controlled by one system services control point (SSCP). See also network operator, node operator.

domain search A search initiated by a network node to all its authorized client APPN end nodes (that allow themselves to be searched) when it receives a search request for which it has no entry in its database.

do-nothing operation Synonym for no-operation instruction.

door swing In video production, the rotation of a video image along any axis with a digital effects generator.

doping Adding a substance such as boron or phosphorus to a semiconductor to increase the predominance of positive charge carriers (holes), or of negative charge carriers (free electrons).

dormant state In OS/VS and VM/370, a state in which the active pages of a job or virtual machine have been paged out.

DOS Disk Operating System. See IBM Disk Operating System.

DOS diskette In IBM personal computers, the diskette that contains IBM PC-DOS and Disk BASIC.

DOS mode A method of operation for running programs and applications that are designed to use the DOS operating system.

DOS partition In the NetView/PC program, a separate area of memory in which NetView/PC programs and other DOS programs can be serially executed.

DOS requester A DOS workstation using the DOS LAN Requester function of OS/2 Extended Edition Version 1.3 to access OS/2 Office resources.

DO statement (1) A statement used to group a number of statements in a procedure. (2) In the XL C compiler, a looping statement that contains the keyword "do," followed by a statement (the action), the keyword "while," and an expression in parentheses (the condition).

DOS/VS Disk Operating System/Virtual Storage. See VSE.

dot cycle One cycle of a periodic alternation between two signaling conditions, each condition having unit duration. In teletypewriter applications, one dot cycle is a successive mark and a space. Telegraph transmission is sometimes considered in terms of dot cycles per second or dot speed, which is half the speed of transmission as expressed in bauds.

dot leader A set of periods that fills in the space between two pieces of split text such as a chapter title and its page number in a table of contents.

dot matrix (1) In computer graphics, a two-dimensional pattern of dots used for constructing a display image. This type of matrix can be used to represent characters by dots. (T) (2) In word processing, a pattern of dots used to form characters. This term normally refers to a small section of the set of addressable points; for example, a representation of characters by dots. (T) See Figure 44.

Figure 44. Dot Matrix

dot-matrix character generator A character generator that produces character images composed of line segments. (T) (A)

dot matrix printer A printer that prints characters or images represented by dots. See Figure 45.

Note: When a dot printer is used for graphics only, it may be called a dot plotter. Synonymous with matrix printer. (T)

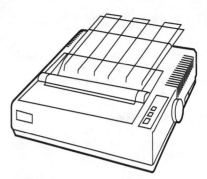

Figure 45. Dot Matrix Printer

dot pitch A measure of display resolution on a color display, expressed as the distance between phosphor dots of the same color.

dots per inch (dpi) A measurement of recording density. See also bpi and ppi.

double buffering In computer animation, displaying an image while keeping the next image to be displayed in memory (thus employing two memory buffers for image information).

double buffer mode In AIX graphics, a mode in which two buffers are alternately displayed and updated. A new image can be drawn into the back buffer while the front buffer, which contains the previous image, is displayed. In double buffer mode, colors are taken from the color map. See single buffer mode.

double-byte character An entity that requires two character bytes.

double-byte character session A display station operating session that uses double-byte character data for the system to communicate with the operator.

double-byte character set (DBCS) A set of characters in which each character is represented by 2 bytes. Languages such as Japanese, Chinese, and Korean, which contain more symbols than can be represented by 256 code points, require double-byte character sets. Because each character requires 2 bytes, the typing, display, and printing of DBCS characters requires hardware and programs that support DBCS. Contrast with single-byte character set.

double-byte coded font In AS/400 Advanced Function Printing (AFP) support, a font in which the characters are defined by 2 bytes: the first defines a coded font section, the second defines a code point. Synonymous with double-byte font. Contrast with single-byte coded font.

double-byte font Synonym for double-byte coded font.

double card A special card that is approximately twice the length of a general-purpose paper card. A double card usually consists of two separable general-purpose paper cards. (A)

double-click In SAA Advanced Common User Access, to press and release a mouse button twice within a time frame defined by the user, without moving the pointer off the choice. See click. See also drag select.

double-dense recording Synonym for modified frequency modulation.

double-density recording Synonym for modified frequency recording.

double-dot image In printing, an image that is enlarged by doubling the pel pattern in the horizontal and vertical directions.

double-ended queue A list of variable length whose content may be changed by adding or removing items at either end. (A) See Figure 46.

Figure 46. Double-Ended Queue

double-length register (1) Two registers that function as a single register. (I) (A) (2) Synonymous with double register.

Note: A double-length register may be used in multiplication for storing the product, in division for storing the partial quotient and the remainder, and in character manipulation for shifting character strings and for accessing the left-hand or the right-hand portion.

double-precision (1) Pertaining to the use of two computer words to represent a number in accordance with the required precision. (I) (A) (2) A specification that causes a floating-point value to be stored internally in the long format. See also precision. Contrast with single precision. (3) In BASIC, synonym for long precision.

double-pulse recording Phase modulation recording with unmagnetized regions on each side of the magnetized regions. (I) (A)

double punch More than one numeric punch in any one column of a punched card.

double rail logic Pertaining to self-timing asynchronous circuits in which each logic variable is represented by two electrical lines that together can take on three meaningful states: zero, one, and undecided. (A)

double recording In the NetView program, pertaining to the recording of certain individual events under two resource levels.

double register Synonym for double-length register.

double sheet detector In a duplicator, a device that senses the presence of two or more superimposed sheets during the feeding process. (T)

double sheet detector control In a duplicator, a means of adjusting the double sheet detector. (T)

double sheet ejector In a duplicator, a mechanism that, when triggered by the double sheet detector, diverts the double sheets away from the normal path of the paper through the machine. (T)

double-sided copying In a document copying machine, making one or more copies, on both sides of the copy paper, not necessarily in a single pass but without manual handling of the paper. (T) Contrast with single-sided copying. Synonymous with duplex copying.

double-strike A process of printing a character twice to create the appearance of bold type, used frequently with impact printers. A more flexible form of double-strike is emphasized printing. See also boldface, emphasized.

double-tap To touch a touch-sensitive surface with a pointing device twice in rapid succession within a small area.

doublet A byte composed of two binary elements. Synonymous with 2-bit byte.

double-wide print A print format in which characters are twice as wide as they normally are.

doubleword A contiguous sequence of bits or characters that comprises two computer words and is capable of being addressed as a unit. (A)

DO variable In XL FORTRAN, a variable, specified in a DO statement, that is incremented or decremented on each iteration of the relative DO loop and controls the number of iterations of the loop.

down Pertaining to a device that is inoperative.

Note: A device may be down because of an internal fault or because of an external condition such as a network problem.

downline Pertaining to the direction of transmission. Contrast with upline.

downlink Pertaining to data transmission from the headend to a data station. (T)   Contrast with uplink.

download (1) To transfer programs or data from a computer to a connected device, typically a personal computer. (T)   (2) To transfer data from a computer to a connected device, such as a workstation or micro-computer.   Contrast with upload.   See also terminal emulation.

downloaded font A soft font copied (downloaded) to the memory of a printer.

downstream (1) In the direction of data flow or toward the destination of transmission. (2) From the processor toward an attached unit or end user. (3) In the direction from a host computer or from a host system. Contrast with upstream.

downstream device For the IBM 3710 Network Controller, a device located in a network so that the 3710 is positioned between the device and a host.   A display terminal downstream from the 3710 is an example of a downstream device.   Contrast with upstream device.

Downstream Load Utility (DSLU) A licensed program that uses the communication network management (CNM) interface to support the load requirements of certain type 2 physical units, such as the IBM 3644 Automatic Data Unit and the IBM 8775 Display Terminal.

down time The time during which a functional unit cannot be used because of a fault within the functional unit or within the environment. (T)   (A)

downward reference In an overlay structure, a reference made from a segment to a segment lower in the path; that is, farther from the root segment.

DP Data processing.

DPA Display/printer adapter.

DPAGE Device page.

DPCX Distributed Processing Control Executive.

DPCX host support In the 8100 Information System, a set of programs and data at the host system that serve as the system control program.   Program validation services (PVS), batch data exchange services

(BDES), interactive program validation services, and the subsystem information retrieval facility are part of host support.

DPCX instruction An expression that can be interpretively executed by DPCX, resulting from the assembly of a DPCX/3790 programming statement.

DPCX/3790 image file See image file.

DPCX/3790 programming statement A statement, actually a macroinstruction, that a programmer at a host system uses to code user programs for DPCX.

dpi Dots per inch.

DPM Distributed presentation management.

DPN Destination program name.

DPPX Distributed Processing Programming Executive.

DPPX/Base An IBM licensed program that schedules and supervises execution of programs written for 8100 Information System processing. DPPX Base provides I/O control, storage management, data management, execution scheduling, application development tools, and related services.

DPPX Distributed Presentation Services An IBM licensed program that provides services for full-screen formatting of display terminals.

DPPX/DPS DPPX Distributed Presentation Services.

DPPX/DTMS DPPX Data Base and Transaction Management System. An IBM licensed program that provides database and transaction processing services in an IBM 8100 Information System processor. DPPX/DTMS operates in its own environment under control of the Distributed Processing Programming Executive (DPPX/Base) licensed program.

DPPX/DTMS system data set A data set used by DPPX/DTMS to manage and control transactions and databases. The DPPX/DTMS system data sets are the recovery data set, reset information data set, pending request outboard data set, audit file, transaction profile library, and database profile library.

DPPX FORTRAN Compiler An IBM licensed program that compiles DPPX FORTRAN programs.

DPPX FORTRAN Library An IBM licensed program that makes intrinsic function routines; service subroutines; internal services for arithmetic, input/output, and other operations;   and software floating-point routines that simulate hardware floating-point available to a DPPX FORTRAN program.

DPS Distributed Presentation Services.

DPSK Differential phase-shift keying.

DR (1) In NCP and CCP, dynamic reconfiguration. (2) In SNA, definite response.

draft copy A version of a document prepared for review, approval, or editing. (T)

draft quality Print quality of text that is not suitable for business correspondence, but good enough for most internal documents. (T)

drag In SAA Common User Access, to use a pointing device to move an object; for example, clicking on a window border, and dragging it to make the window larger.

dragging In computer graphics, moving one or more segments on a display surface by translating. (I) (A)

drag select In SAA Advanced Common User Access, to press a mouse button and hold it down while moving the pointer so that the pointer travels to a different location on the screen. Dragging ends when the mouse button is released. All items between the button-down and button-up points are selected. See also click, double-click.

drain To honor pending allocation requests before deactivating sessions with a partner logical unit 6.2.

DRAM Dynamic random-access memory.

drawable In AIX Enhanced X-Windows, a collective term for both windows and pixmaps when used as destinations in graphics operations. However, an InputOnly window cannot be used as a source or destination drawable in a graphics operation.

DRAW disc Direct-read-after-write disc.

drawn button In the AIXwindows program a graphic object that simulates a real-world button with a symbol or other image drawn on its face.

DRC Data recording control.

DRD Data recording device.

DRDS Dynamic reconfiguration data set.

drift (1) The unwanted change of the value of an output signal of a device over a specified period of time when the values of all input signals of the device are kept constant. (T) (2) The maximum deviation of the statistical mean within a specified time at a constant temperature.

drifting characters See currency symbol, sign character.

drip feed valve In a duplicator, an adjustable device for regulating the flow of the activator in a gravity feed system. (T)

drive See diskette storage drive, disk storage drive, media drive, tape drive.

drive designation A letter, from A to Z, assigned to a physical disk, a partition, or a network directory so that the system has a unique way to refer to the resource.

driver (1) A program (and possibly data files) that contain information needed to run a particular unit, such as a plotter, printer, port, or mouse. See also device driver, printer driver, and queue driver. (2) A system or device that enables a functional unit to operate. (3) A circuit that increases the signal current for sending data over long cables or to many other circuits. (4) A circuit that sends small electronic signals to a device.

drop (1) In the IBM Cabling System, a cable that runs from a faceplate to the distribution panel in a wiring closet. When the IBM Cabling System is used with the IBM Token-Ring Network, a drop may form part of a lobe. Cables between wiring closets are not classified as drops. See subscriber's drop. (2) To fix the position of an object that is being dragged by releasing the select button on the pointing device. See also drag.

drop cable The cable that connects a data station to a trunk coupling unit. Synonymous with stub cable. (T)

drop-down combination box In SAA Advanced Common User Access, a variation of a combination box in which a list box is hidden until a user takes explicitly acts to make it visible. See combination box, list box. See also drop-down list.

drop-down list In SAA Advanced Common User Access, a single selection field in which only the current choice is visible. Other choices are hidden until a user explicitly acts to display the list box that contains the other choices. See also list box, drop-down combination box.

drop-frame time code A nonsequential time code used to keep tape time code matched to real time. It must not be used in tapes intended for videodisc mastering.

drop-in An error detected by the reading of a binary character not previously recorded, in storing or retrieving data from a magnetic storage device.

Note: Drop-ins are usually caused by defects in or the presence of particles on the magnetic surface layer. (T)

drop-out An error caused by the failure to read a binary character, in storing or retrieving data from a magnetic storage device.

Note: Drop-outs are usually caused by defects in or the presence of particles on the magnetic surface layer. (T)

drop-out ink A special ink that is visible to the eye but not to a scanner. When used on forms or documents, this ink causes a form, or the information that is printed using this ink, to be invisible to the scanner during scanning. Only the variable information that is visible to the scanner is picked up.

dropped folio A page numbering style in which the page number is printed at the foot of the page. See blind folio, folio, expressed folio.

DrP See RISC System/6000 7016 POWERstation 730 Graphics Processor Subsystem Drawing Processor.

DRQ Concentrator data ready queue.

drum (1) In a drum printer, a cylinder on which the types are mounted. (2) In the 3800 Printing Subsystem, a hollow cylinder around which the photoconductor is wrapped; the drum continuously rotates during printing and carries the photoconductor past the various stations in the printing process. The drum also contains the photoconductor supply and takeup spools. (3) See magnetic drum.

drum drive A mechanism for moving a magnetic drum and controlling its movement. (I) (A)

drum plotter (1) A plotter that draws a display image on a display surface mounted on a rotating drum. (I) (A) (2) See also flatbed plotter. See Figure 47.

drum printer (1) An impact printer in which a full character set placed on a rotating drum is made available for each printing position. (T) (2) A line printer in which the type are mounted on a rotating drum that contains a full character set for each printing position. (A)

drum storage See magnetic drum storage.

drum unit See magnetic drum unit.

dry contact That part of a circuit containing only contact points and resistive components.

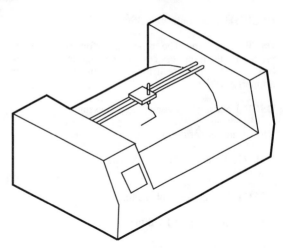

Figure 47. Drum Plotter

dryer In a document copying machine, that part of the machine using wet process development in which residual liquids are removed from the imaged material by such means as ducted air or radiation. (T)

dry pair In a data loop, a pair of wires on which no voltage, current, or signaling is applied when the loop is in an idle state.

dry process In a document copying machine, a method of processing diazonium-sensitized material in which the coupler is contained in the sensitized material and ammonia gas is used to develop the image. (T)

dry process development In a document copying machine, a developing process that uses a nonliquid developer such as gas, powder, or radiation. (T) Contrast with wet process development.

dry reed contact An encapsulated switch consisting of two metal wires that act as the contact points for a relay.

DS (1) Desired state. (2) Directory services.

DSAC Data set authority credential.

DSAF Destination subarea field.

DSAP Destination service access point.

DSB Dispatcher/scheduler block.

DSC 3270 Information Display System data-stream compatibility.

DSCA Default system control area.

DSCB Data set control block.

DSCB processing The process, performed by 3790 program validation services, of segmenting an assembled DSCB to prepare it for processing by Subsystem Support Services.

DSCP Data services command processor.

DSD Data set definition.

DSE (1) Data switching exchange. (2) Data set extension.

DSECT Dummy control section.

DSF Device Support Facilities.

DSI Data-stream interface.

DSID Data set identification.

DSL Data set label.

DSLO Distributed Systems License Option.

DSM Data services manager.

dsname Data set name.

DSN command processor The DB2 component that processes DB2 subcommands (such as BIND, RUN, and so on).

DSNX Distributed Systems Node Executive.

DSO Direct system output.

DSP Digital signal processor.

DSR Data set ready.

DSRLST Direct search list. A message unit that contains a search request that is sent throughout subarea networks to obtain information about a network resource (such as its name, routing information, and status information).

DSS (1) Dynamic support system. (2) Device support station.

DST (1) Data services task. (2) Dedicated service tools.

DST-restricted state In the AS/400 system, the status of the system before an initial program load (IPL) is performed. Only dedicated service tools functions are allowed when the system is in the DST-restricted state.

DSU Data service unit.

DSU/CSU Data service unit/channel service unit.

DSX Distributed Systems Executive.

DTE Data terminal equipment. (A)

DTE clear confirmation packet A call supervision packet that a data terminal equipment (DTE) transmits in order to confirm that a call has been cleared.

DTE/DCE interface The physical interface and link access procedures between a data terminal equipment (DTE) and a data circuit-terminating equipment (DCE).

DTF Define-the-file.

DTITHDR VSCS trace table header record.

DTMF Dual-tone modulation frequency.

DTMS Data Base and Transaction Management System.

DTR (1) Distribution tape reel. (2) Data terminal ready.

DTV Desktop video.

dual cable broadband LAN A broadband LAN that uses separate cables for the forward LAN channel and the backward LAN channel. (T)

dual-channel audio In multimedia development, the capability to reproduce two audio channels, playing them either simultaneously or independently. All optical videodisc systems have this capability.

Dual Cluster feature In the AS/400 system and System/36, a feature that provides eight cable connections and allows the attachment of up to eight workstations to a 5251 Model 12 Display Station. See Cluster feature.

dual density A feature that allows a program to use a tape unit in either of two densities such as 800- or 1600-byte-per-inch recording.

dual-headed configuration A hardware configuration where two display monitors are connected to a single system unit. Contrast with single-headed configuration.

dual in-line package (DIP) In IBM personal computers, an integrated circuit module with two rows of connector pins, ranging from 14-pin to 40-pin configurations. See Figure 48.

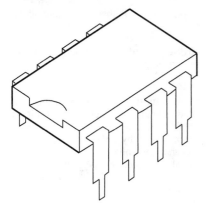

Figure 48. Dual In-Line Package

dual logging In IMS/VS, an optional facility that produces a duplicate copy of log data.

dual-media typewriter (1) A typewriter that uses two different recording materials for recording, manipulating, storing, and printing out information. (A) (2) See electric typewriter. (A)

dual operation A Boolean operation whose result, when performed on operands that are the negation of the operands of another Boolean operation, is the negation of the result of the other Boolean operation. For example, disjunction is the dual operation of conjunction.

dual-pitch printer A printer that can print two or more type sizes using different character spacing. (A)

dual program status vectors In the IBM 8100 Information System, the association of two program status vectors (PSVs) with each priority level to facilitate definition of both an application program and a supervisory program on a single priority level.

dual registration An interface that allows the security administrator of a VM system to add a user to the CP system directory and the RACF data base simultaneously.

dual spectrum process In a document copying machine, a variation of the thermographic process in which an intermediate copy is first made using visible light before the final copy is prepared. (T)

dual-tone modulation frequency (DTMF) Push-button phone tones.

dub (1) To copy a tape. (2) In multimedia applications, to add sound effects or dialog to a film. (3) To provide a new audio track of dialog in a different language.

dumb Deprecated term for nonprogrammable.

dumb terminal Deprecated term for fixed-function terminal, nonprogrammable terminal (NPT).

dumb workstation Deprecated term for nonprogrammable workstation (NWS).

dummy Pertaining to the characteristic of having the appearance of a specified thing but not having the capacity to function as such; for example, a dummy character, dummy plug, or dummy statement. (A)

dummy argument (1) In XL FORTRAN, a variable within a subprogram or statement function definition with which actual arguments from the calling program or function reference are positionally associated. See also formal parameter. (2) In FORTRAN, an entity whose name appears in a dummy argument list in a FUNCTION or SUBROUTINE statement. (3) Synonym for formal parameter.

dummy control section (DSECT) A control section that an assembler can use to format an area of storage without producing any object code. Synonymous with dummy section.

dummy data set (1) A data set for which operations such as disposition processing, input/output operations, and allocation are bypassed. (2) Data sets, created by the programmer and used during the testing phase of program validation services, that represent the data sets the program would use during normal execution.

dummy device (1) A device that is not specified but is allocated by a computer system at the time it is needed. (2) In GDDM, an imaginary output device for which the program does all the normal processing but for which no actual output is received.

dummy device assignment In VSE, the assignment of a logical unit to an unused device address, primarily for the purpose of spooling job input and job output.

dummy host system input In the 3790 Communication System, test data that represent the input the 3790 program would use during normal execution in a 3791 Controller. The test data are supplied by the programmer during the testing phase of program validation services.

dummy instruction An item of data, in the form of an instruction, that requires modification before being executed. (T)

dummy message queue input In the 3790 Communication System, test data that represent the input the 3790 program would receive from the message queue during normal execution in a 3791 Controller. The test data are supplied by the programmer during the testing phase of program validation services.

dummy section Synonym for dummy control section.

dummy terminal input In the 3790 Communication System, test data that represent the input the 3790 program would receive from the terminal operator during normal execution in a 3791 Controller. The test data are supplied by the programmer during the testing phase of program validation services.

dummy variable In BASIC, a scalar variable enclosed in parentheses and placed after the name of a user-written function in a DEF statement. The dummy variable is exchanged for the value in a specified expression when the program is running.

dump (1) To record, at a particular instant, the contents of all or part of one storage device in another storage device. Dumping is usually for the purpose of debugging. (T)   (2) Data that has been dumped. (T)   (3) To copy data in a readable format from main or auxiliary storage onto an external medium such as tape, diskette, or printer.   (4) To copy the contents of all or part of virtual storage for the purpose of collecting error information.   (5) In video systems, the process by which digital program code is transferred from a videodisc to the videodisc player's microprocessor. It is usually read from the second video channel.   (6) In video systems, a unit of program code loaded into the videodisc player's microprocessor at one time. A single videodisc may contain multiple program dumps. See also Levels of Interactive Systems.

dump data In the AIX operating system, the data collected by the kernel dump program. It is obtained from memory locations used by kernel components.

dump diskette In the OS/2 operating system, a diskette, created using the CREATEDD command, that contains the contents of storage at a specified time.

dump file A file that contains the data areas used by a program that has failed.

dump routine A utility routine that dumps. (I) (A)

dump table entry In the AIX operating system, a record in the master dump table that identifies the location of a component dump table. All kernel components that need to have special data collected by the dump program must generate a dump table entry.

dump viewing facility A VM/XA Migration Aid component that allows users to display, format, and

print data interactively from CP abend and stand-alone dumps.

duobinary AM/PSK modulation Modulation in which duobinary encoding is used together with AM/PSK modulation. (T)

duobinary signaling Data transmission by means of a pseudo-binary-coded signal in which a zero bit is represented by either a zero-level current or voltage, and a one bit is represented by either a positive-level or negative-level current or voltage, and in which the polarity of the signal representing "1" is the same as that of the previous "1" if and only if the quantity of intervening zero bits is even.

Notes:

1. *Duobinary signaling requires a smaller bandwidth than NRZ.*

2. *Duobinary signaling permits detection of some errors without the addition of error-checking bits.*

(T)

duodecimal (1) Characterized by a selection, choice, or condition that has twelve possible different values or states. (I) (A)   (2) Pertaining to fixed-radix numeration system, having a radix of twelve. (I) (A)

duplex (1) Pertaining to communication in which data can be sent and received at the same time. Synonymous with full duplex. (2) A mode of copying or printing on both sides of a sheet. (3) See also double-sided copying, duplexed system, duplex operation, duplex transmission. (4) Contrast with half duplex.

duplex circuit A two-way circuit.

duplex connector In an ESCON environment, an optical fiber component that terminates both jumper cable fibers in one housing and provides physical keying for attachment to a duplex receptacle.

duplex copying Synonym for double-sided copying.

duplexed system A system with two sets of facilities, each of which can assume the system function while the other assumes a standby status. Usually, the sets are identical.

duplex operation A mode of operation of a data link in which data may be transmitted simultaneously in both directions over two channels. Synonymous with both-way operation, full-duplex operation, two-way simultaneous communication.

duplex receptacle In an ESCON environment, a fixed or stationary optical fiber component that provides a keyed attachment method for a duplex connector.

duplex scanning The scanning of both the front and back sides of a page.

duplex transmission (1) Data transmission in both directions at the same time. (I) (A) (2) See also half-duplex transmission, simplex transmission.

duplicate To copy from a source to a destination that has the same physical form as the source; for example, to punch new punched cards with the same pattern of holes as an original punched card. (I) (A) Synonymous with reproduce.

duplicate key In word processing, a control that initiates the duplication process. (T)

duplicate key value The occurrence of the same value in a key field or in a composite key in more than one record in a file.

duplicate mass storage volume See duplicate volume.

duplicate volume In MSS, an inactive mass storage volume that has the same identification as another mass storage volume and is not a copy.

duplication In word processing, the reproduction of the entire recorded text from one element of a recording medium to another. (T)

duplication check A check based on the consistency of two independent performances of the same task. (A)

duplicator A machine that uses direct litho duplicating, offset litho duplicating, spirit (or other fluid) duplicating, or stencil duplicating to produce multiple copies from a master. (T) See direct litho duplicator, electrically driven duplicator, manually driven duplicator, offset litho duplicator, spirit duplicator, stencil duplicator. See also duplicator with automatic feed, duplicator with hand feed, duplicator with manual master change, duplicator with semi-automatic master change.

duplicator with automatic feed A duplicator into which copy paper is fed automatically by mechanical means. (T)

duplicator with hand feed A duplicator into which the copy paper is fed manually sheet by sheet. (T)

duplicator with manual master change A duplicator in which the master is introduced manually to the attachment device and is removed either by hand or automatically. (T)

duplicator with semi-automatic master change A duplicator in which masters are fed individually by hand into a loading device, are then introduced automatically to the attachment device, and are finally removed, automatically or by hand. (T)

durability The ability of a functional unit to perform a required function under given conditions of use and maintenance, until a limiting state is reached.

Note: A limiting state of an item may be characterized by the end of the useful life, unsuitability for any economic or technological reasons or other relevant factors. (T)

duration See assemble duration, compile duration, response duration, run duration, translate duration.

DVE Digital video effects.

DVI Digital Video Interactive.

Dvorak A keyboard layout that is an alternative to standard keyboard layouts. It is intended to increase typing speed by placing keys in more natural positions than those used on other keyboards. See also AZERTY, QWERTY.

Note: Standard keyboard layouts were originally designed to limit typing speed in order to prevent mechanical jams. See Figure 49.

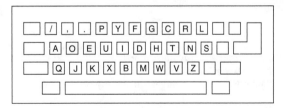

Figure 49. Dvorak Keyboard

DVT Destination vector table.

DXAM Distributed indexed access method.

DXF (Drawing Interchange Format) A platform-independent graphics file format for computer-aided design (CAD) programming.

dyadic Boolean operation (1) A Boolean operation on two and only two operands. (I) (A) (2) Synonymous with binary Boolean operation.

dyadic operation An operation on two and only two operands. (I) (A)

dyadic operator An operator that represents an operation on two and only two operands. (I) (A) Synonymous with binary operator.

dynamic (1) In programming languages, pertaining to properties that can only be established during the execution of a program; for example, the length of a variable-length data object is dynamic. (I) (2) Pertaining to an operation that occurs at the time it is needed rather than at a predetermined or fixed time. (3) Pertaining to events occurring at run time, or during processing. (4) Contrast with static.

dynamic access In COBOL, an access mode in which specific logical records can be obtained from or placed into a mass storage file in a nonsequential manner and obtained from a file in a sequential manner during the scope of the same OPEN statement.

dynamic accounting facility In ACF/TCAM, a service facility that gathers resource utilization data for processing by user-supplied applications.

dynamic address relocation In the IBM 8100 Information System, the mapping of logical storage addresses to relocated storage addresses.

dynamic address translation (DAT) (1) In System/370 virtual storage systems, the change of a virtual storage address to a real storage address during execution of an instruction. See address translation. (2) In the IBM 8100 Information System, the mapping of relocated storage addresses to real storage addresses.

dynamic allocation (1) An allocation technique in which resources assigned for the execution of computer programs are determined by criteria applied at the moment of need. (2) Assignment of system resources to a program when the program is executed rather than when it is loaded into main storage. See also dynamic storage allocation.

dynamic allocation/deallocation In IMS/VS, a function that removes the requirement to allocate DL/I databases, area data sets, and certain system data sets through job control language. A data set is allocated during IMS/VS initialization or when it is first used and is deallocated when it is no longer used; that is, when closed or stopped.

dynamically modified channel program In VM/370, a channel program that is altered by the computer or by data being read in from a channel during the interval between the execution of the START I/O (SIO) instruction and the channel end interruption.

dynamic area In OS/VS, the portion of virtual storage divided into regions or partitions that are assigned to job steps and system tasks. See also nonpageable dynamic area, pageable dynamic area.

dynamic backout In IMS/VS, a process that automatically cancels all activities performed by an application program that terminates abnormally.

dynamic block header In the AIX operating system, a data structure used by a compiler to link dynamic variables that are in the same heap.

dynamic buffer allocation Synonym for dynamic buffering.

dynamic buffering (1) A dynamic allocation of buffer storage. (I) (A) (2) Allocating storage for buffers as needed for incoming data during program execution.

dynamic characteristics In acoustics, characteristics provided for the output circuit of a sound level meter: impulse, fast, and slow.

dynamic connection In an ESCON Director, a connection between two ports, established or removed by the ESCD and that, when active, appears as one continuous link. The duration of the connection depends on the protocol defined for the frames transmitted through the ports and on the state of the ports. Contrast with dedicated connection.

dynamic connectivity In an ESCON Director, the capability that allows connections to be established and removed at any time.

dynamic control function One of the network control program functions initiated by a control command from the host access method. Dynamic control functions include activating and deactivating telecommunication lines, requesting the status of a telecommunication line, and switching channel adapters.

dynamic data exchange The exchange of data between programs or between a program and a data-file object. Any change made to information in one program or session is applied to the identical data created by the other program.

dynamic data set definition The process of defining a data set and allocating auxiliary storage space for it during rather than before job step execution.

dynamic device reconfiguration (DDR) A facility that allows a demountable volume to be moved and repositioned if necessary without abnormally terminating the job or repeating the initial program load procedure.

dynamic dispatching In OS/VS2 and VM/370, a facility that assigns priorities to tasks within an automatic priority group to provide optimum use of the processing unit and I/O resources.

dynamic display image Synonym for foreground image.

dynamic dump Dumping performed during execution of a computer program, usually under control of the computer program. (I) (A)

dynamic image Synonym for foreground image.

dynamic indirect addressing Deprecated term for segment addressing.

dynamicizer Synonym for serializer.

dynamic linking In the OS/2 operating system, the delayed connection of a program to a routine until load time or run time.

dynamic link library (DLL) A file containing executable code and data bound to a program at load time or run time, rather than during linking. The code and data in a dynamic link library can be shared by several applications simultaneously.

dynamic link module In the OS/2 operating system, a module that is linked at load time or run time.

dynamic loading The loading of routines into main storage as needed by an executing program. Dynamically loaded routines are not part of the load module of an executing program.

dynamic LPDA A function that enables a NetView application to set or query the Link Problem Determination Aid (LPDA) status for a link or station.

dynamic network collection (DNC) The NPM subsystem that collects, monitors, and displays data from within the network control program and has an automatic start and stop.

dynamic parameter Synonym for program-generated parameter.

dynamic partition balancing A VSE facility that allows the user to specify that two or more or all partitions of the system should receive about the same amount of time on the processing unit.

dynamic path update The process of changing the network path for sending information without regenerating complete configuration tables.

dynamic print management The use of Print-Manager to make changes to a print operation without interrupting system functions.

dynamic priority In the OS/2 operating system, pertaining to the order of execution of a process that is varied by the operating system. Contrast with absolute priority.

dynamic programming (1) In operations research, a procedure for optimization of a multistage problem solution wherein a number of decisions are available at each stage of the process. (I) (A) (2) Contrast with convex programming, integer programming, linear programming, mathematical programming, nonlinear programming, quadratic programming.

dynamic reconfiguration (DR) The process of changing the network configuration (peripheral PUs and LUs) without regenerating complete configuration tables or deactivating the affected major node.

dynamic reconfiguration data set (DRDS) In VTAM, a data set used for storing definition data that can be applied to a generated communication controller configuration at the operator's request, or can be used to accomplish dynamic reconfiguration of NCP, local SNA, and packet major nodes. A dynamic reconfiguration data set can be used to dynamically add PUs and LUs, delete PUs and LUs, and move PUs. It is activated with the VARY DRDS operator command. See also dynamic reconfiguration.

dynamic region area See dynamic area.

dynamic relocation A process that assigns new absolute addresses to a computer program during execution so that the program may be executed from a different area of main storage. (I) (A)

dynamic resource allocation An allocation technique in which the resources assigned for execution of computer programs are determined by criteria applied at the moment of need. (I) (A)

dynamic routing In the AIX operating system, a method of setting paths between hosts, networks, or both by using daemons that update the routing table, as needed. See also routing table, static routing.

dynamic select/omit In the AS/400 system, selection and omission of logical file records performed during processing, instead of when the access path, if any, is maintained. Dynamic select/omit may also be used when no keyed access path exists.

dynamic space reclamation In VSE, a librarian function that provides for space freed by the deletion of a library member to become reusable automatically.

dynamic SQL Pertaining to the preparation and processing of SQL source statements within a program while the program is running. The SQL source statements are contained in host-language variables rather than being coded directly into the application program.

The SQL statement may change several times while the program is running. Contrast with static SQL.

dynamic stop Synonym for breakpoint halt.

dynamic storage (1) A device that stores data in a manner that permits the data to move or vary with time such that the specified data are not always available for recovery. Magnetic drum and disk storage are dynamic nonvolatile storage. An acoustic delay line is a dynamic volatile storage. (A)   (2) A storage in which the cells require repetitive application of control signals in order to retain stored data. Such repetitive application of the control signals is normally called a refresh operation. A dynamic storage may use static addressing or sensing circuits. (A)

dynamic storage allocation A storage allocation technique in which the storage areas assigned to computer programs and data are determined by criteria applied at the moment of need. (I)   (A)

dynamic subroutine A subroutine in skeletal form with regard to certain features, such as the number of repetitions, decimal point position, or item size, that are selected or adjusted in accordance with data processing requirements. (A)

dynamic support system (DSS) An interactive debugging facility that allows authorized maintenance personnel to monitor and analyze events and alter data.

dynamic threshold alteration The process that allows a network operator to dynamically change the traffic count and temporary error threshold values associated with SDLC and BSC devices in communication controllers and network controllers.

dynamic threshold query The process that allows a network operator to query the current settings of a traffic count or temporary error threshold value associated with an SDLC or BSC device in a communication controller or network controller.

dynamic tool display A CAD/CAM feature that graphically displays a figure representing a numerically controlled cutting tool. The figure is moved along a tool path displayed on the monitor to verify and simulate the cutting procedure. (T)

dynamic variable In Pascal, a variable that is allocated under programmer control. Specifically requested allocations and deallocations are required; the predefined procedures NEW and DISPOSE are provided for this purpose.

DYUV Delta-YUV.

E

EAM Electrical accounting machine. (A)

EAN European article number.

early token release A function, supported by token-ring adapter types 2 and 3, that allows a transmitting station to release the token after transmitting the ending delimiter.

EAROM Electrically alterable read-only memory. See reprogrammable read-only memory.

EAU Erase All Unprotected.

eavesdropping In computer security, the unauthorized interception of information-bearing emanations through the use of methods other than wiretapping.

EAX Electronic automatic exchange.

EB End bracket.

EBCDIC Extended binary-coded decimal interchange code. A coded character set of 256 8-bit characters. See Figure 50.

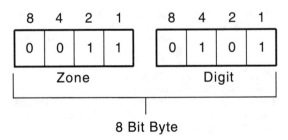

8 Bit Byte

Figure 50. EBCDIC

EBCDIC character Any one of the symbols included in the 8-bit EBCDIC set.

EBCDIC/DP (1) A subset of EBCDIC reserved for assignment of data processing national use graphics. (2) In OCL, one of the possible control character translations between MCC and EBCDIC for data processing applications.

EBCDIC/WP (1) A subset of EBCDIC reserved for assignment of word processing national use graphics. (2) In OCL, one of the possible control character translations between MCC and EBCDIC for word processing applications.

E beam Electron beam.

E beam bonding Formation of interconnection bonds by electron beam welding.

EBR Electron beam recording. (A)

EC Engineering change.

ECB (1) Event control block. (2) Event control bit. (3) Electronic codebook.

ECC (1) Error checking and correction. (2) Error correcting code.

ECDS In the Object Distribution Manager, the Coded Data Storage Exception Report file.

echo (1) In computer graphics, the immediate notification of the current values provided by an input device to the operator at the display console. (I) (A) (2) In word processing, to print or display each character or line as it is keyed in. (3) In data communication, a reflected signal on a communications channel. On a communications terminal, each signal is displayed twice, once when entered at the local terminal and again when returned over the communications link. This allows the signals to be checked for accuracy.

echo check (1) A check to determine the correctness of the transmission of data in which the received data are returned to the source for comparison with the originally transmitted data. (T) (2) A method of checking the accuracy of transmission of data in which the received data are returned to the sending end for comparison with the original data. (A) (3) Synonymous with echo test, loop check.

echoplex mode In data communication, a mode in which characters are automatically returned to the transmitting data terminal equipment (DTE).

echo suppressor A line device used to prevent energy from being reflected back, or echoed, to the transmitter. It attenuates the other direction.

echo test Synonym for echo check.

ECL Electronic cabling link.

EC log Engineering change log.

ECMA European Computer Manufacturer's Association.

EC mode Extended control mode.

EC pads The plated areas around a chip site that are in series with I/O circuits of the chips. Each pad provides a wiring function for bonding two discrete wires, plus a delete area for repairs, ECs, and test probing.

ECPS/VSE Extended control program support for VSE.

ECSA Extended Character Set Adapter.

ECT Environment control table.

ECU Extreme close-up.

ED Enciphered data.

EDA Error data analysis.

EDAC Error detection and correction.

edge See document reference edge, reference edge, stroke edge.

edge-coated card A card strengthened by treating one or more edges. (A)

edge-notched card (1) A card into which notches representing data are punched around the edges. (I) (A) (2) See also edge-punched card.

edge-punched card (1) A card punched with hole patterns in tracks along the edges. (I) (A) (2) See also edge-notched card. (3) Synonymous with verge-punched card.

edge quantization In computer graphics, a digital effect in which contouring errors are greater near high-contrast edges in the image.

EDI Electronic data interchange. (T)

edit (1) To add, change, delete, or rearrange data and to perform operations such as code conversion and zero suppression. (2) To enter, modify, or delete data. (3) To modify a numeric field for output by suppressing zeros and inserting commas, periods, currency symbols, the sign status, or other constant information. (4) To alter or refine information, especially text and illustrations, for publication or display. (5) In System/38, the process of using the source entry utility to key in new source records and update existing source records in a source member. (6) See logical edit, textual edit.

Edit In SAA Common User Access architecture, a choice in the action bar that a user selects to modify original documents and create new documents.

edit check For the IBM 3790 Data Entry Configuration, a check performed by the controller on data entered by the key-entry operator to determine whether the data conforms to the attributes and specifications previously stored for the data.

edit code A letter or number indicating that editing should be done according to a defined pattern before a field is displayed or printed. Contrast with edit word.

edit controller In video production, a device used to coordinate two or more video devices for purposes of editing.

edit decision list (EDL) In video production, a computer program that allows a user to re-create or modify a video presentation. See edit list.

edit description In the AS/400 system and System/38, a description of a user-defined edit code.

edit display A display from which frequently performed operations, such as delete, copy, and insert, are requested.

edited copy In word processing, a draft copy marked with corrections or amendments. (T) See also final copy.

edited master In video production, the first copy of a presentation produced in postproduction for audio or video, by the process of editing together the original material.

editing (1) In programming languages, transforming values to the representations specified by a given format. (I) (2) Synonym for text editing. (3) See also linkage editor, link edit. (T)

editing area In SDF/CICS, the complete area of a source map that can be edited with the map editor. The editing area may be larger than the part displayable in the user area of an SDF/CICS screen and can be accessed by scrolling functions.

editing character In COBOL, a single character or a fixed two-character combination belonging to the following set:

Character	Meaning
B	space
0	zero
+	plus
–	minus
CR	credit
DB	debit

Z	zero suppress
*	check protect
$	currency sign
,	comma (decimal point)
.	period (decimal point)
/	slant (solidus)

editing session A period of time beginning when the editor is invoked and ending when the editor has completed processing.

editing statement A statement that specifies syntactic and formatting operations to be performed on data. (T)

editing symbols In micrographics, symbols on microfilm that are readable without magnification and that provide cutting, loading, and other preparation instructions. (A)

edit list In multimedia applications, a list of the video footage, with time-code numbers, that is to be edited to form a program. It is completed during the offline edit and used during the online edit. See edit decision list.

edit master In multimedia applications, the final videotape from which all copies are made. See also glass master.

edit mode (1) An entry mode in which a user may issue subcommands to enter, modify, delete, or rearrange data. (2) In DPPX, the state of a terminal session after the EDIT command has been issued. In edit mode, interactive editor subcommands may be issued to enter, modify, or delete data.

editor (1) See linkage editor. (2) See editor program.

editor program (1) A computer program designed to perform such functions as rearrangement, modification, and deletion of data in accordance with prescribed rules. (A) (2) Contrast with linkage editor.

edit word A user-defined word with a specific format that indicates how editing should be done. Contrast with edit code.

EDL Edit decision list.

EE Execution element.

EEPROM Electrically erasable programmable read-only memory. An EPROM that can be reprogrammed while it is in the computer. See erasable programmable read-only memory (EPROM).

EEROM Electrically erasable read-only memory. See erasable programmable read-only memory (EPROM).

EFA Extended field attribute.

effective address (1) The contents of the address part of an effective instruction. (I) (A) (2) The address derived by applying indexing or indirect addressing rules to the specified address and that is actually used to identify the current operand. (A) (3) A real storage address that is computed at runtime. The effective address consists of contents of a base register, a displacement, and the contents of an index register if one is present.

effective data transfer rate (1) The average number of bits, characters, or blocks per unit time transferred from a data source to a data sink and accepted as valid. (I) (2) See also staging effective data rate.

Note: The rate is expressed in bits, characters, or blocks, per second, minute or hour.

effective instruction An instruction that may be executed without modification. (I) (A)

effective root directory In the AIX operating system, the point where a system starts when searching for a file.

effective sound pressure In acoustics, the root-mean-square (rms) value of the instantaneous sound pressure, over a time interval at a point in a medium. See also instantaneous sound pressure, static pressure.

effective speed Transmission speed that can be sustained over a significant span of time and that reflects slowing effects, such as those caused by control codes, timing codes, error detection, retransmission, tabbing, or hand keying.

Note: Effective speed is less than the rated speed of a device.

effective transfer rate The actual number of characters of user's data that are transferred per unit of time. (T)

effective user ID In the AIX operating system: (a) The user ID associated with the last authenticated user or the last setuid program. It is equal to either the real or the saved user ID. (b) The current user ID, but not necessarily the user's login ID; for example, a user logged in under a login ID may change to another user's ID. The ID to which the user changes becomes the effective user ID until the user switches back to the original login ID. All discretionary access decisions are based on the effective user ID. See also discretionary access control.

E-format Floating-point format, consisting of a number in scientific notation.

EFP (1) Electronic field production.   (2) Expanded function operator panel.

EFS Extended Function Store.

EFTS Electronic funds transfer system.

EGA Enhanced graphics adapter.

EGA mode A mode of a video display that provides 640 x 350 resolution with 16 colors; supported on EGA and VGA systems. See also enhanced graphics adapter (EGA), video graphics adapter (VGA).

E/GCR Extended group coded recording.

EGCS Extended graphic character set.

EGCS attribute In SDF/CICS, a programmed symbol set attribute with the code X'F8'.

EGCS map In SDF/CICS, a map containing at least one field defined with the EGCS attribute.

EH Error handler.

EIA Electronic Industries Association.

EIA/CCITT Electronic Industries Association / International Telegraph and Telephone Consultative Committee.

EIA/CCITT V.24 feature A feature that allows devices using the EIA/CCITT V.24 interface to be attached to a system.

EIA communication adapter A communication adapter conforming to EIA standards that can combine and send information on two lines at speeds up to 19.2 kbps.

EIA unit A unit of measure, established by the Electronic Industries Association, equal to 44.45 millimeters (1.75 inches).

EIA 232 In data communications, a specification of the Electronic Industries Association (EIA) that defines the interface between data terminal equipment (DTE) and data circuit-terminating equipment (DCE), using serial binary data interchange.

EIA 232D An EIA interface standard that defines the physical, electronic, and functional characteristics of an interface line that connects a communication device and associated workstation. It uses a 25-pin connector and an unbalanced line voltage.

EIA 422A An EIA interface standard that defines the physical, electronic, and functional characteristics of an interface line connecting a computer to communications equipment. It uses a 40-pin connector and balanced line voltage for noise reduction and long distance capability.

EIB External interrupt block.

EID Event identifier.

eight-bit byte Synonym for octet.

eight-millimeter (8mm) videotape A relatively new videotape format for consumers, commonly used in hand-held camera-recorders (camcorders).

EIRV Error interrupt request vector.

EIS External interrupt support.

either field In the AS/400 system, a field that can contain either double-byte data or alphanumeric data. See also only field, open field.

either-or operation Deprecated term for disjunction.

either-way communication Synonym for two-way alternate communication.

either-way operation Synonym for half-duplex operation.

eject (1) In MSS, to move a data cartridge from a 3851 Mass Storage Facility to a cartridge access station.   (2) In formatting, a skip to the next column or page.

eject key In word processing, a control that releases or moves the recording medium to a position for easy removal from the equipment. (T)

ejector control On dictation equipment, a device that releases or moves the recording medium to a position for easy removal from the machine. (I)

EJ indicator See end-of-job indicator.

EL Error loop.

electrically driven duplicator A duplicator in which power required to drive the machine is provided by an electric motor. (T)

electric typewriter A typewriter whose machine functions are initiated by energy input by the operator but completed in many cases with the assistance of electrical components. (T)

electroluminescent (EL) screen A display screen that emits light at each pixel by electrical activation of phosphors or by passing an electrical current through a semiconductor material such as gallium arsenide.

electromagnetic delay line A delay line whose operation is based on the time of propagation of electromagnetic waves through distributed or lumped capacitance and inductance. (A)

electron beam recording (EBR) In micrographics, a specific method of computer output microfilming in which a beam of electrons is directed onto an energy-sensitive microfilm. (A)

electronic archive A collection of documents in storage for historical or backup purposes; for example, a stored collection of various versions of a document. (T)

electronic automatic exchange (EAX) Electronic telephone exchange equipment.

electronic codebook operation A mode of operation used with block cipher cryptographic algorithms in which plaintext or ciphertext is placed in the input to the algorithm and the result is contained in the output of the algorithm.

electronic customer support In the AS/400 system, a part of the operating system that allows a customer to access: the question-and-answer (Q & A) function; problem analysis, reporting, and management; IBM product information; and technical information exchange.

electronic data interchange (EDI) The exchange of data and documents between different users according to standardized rules.

electronic directory An organized list of the users or services that can be addressed on a network. (T)

electronic document A document that is stored on a computer, instead of printed on paper.

electronic field production (EFP) In video production, the use of portable video equipment on location.

electronic filing Creating, storing, processing, and retrieving files on a recording medium such as magnetic tape, magnetic disks, or diskettes.

electronic funds transfer system (EFTS) A computerized payment and withdrawal system used to transfer funds from one account to another and to obtain related financial data.

electronic mail (1) Correspondence in the form of messages transmitted between user terminals over a computer network. (T)   (2) Correspondence in the form of messages transmitted between workstations over a network. See also chat message, voice mail.

Note: The term usually excludes the exchange of messages between offices that handle local mail distribution. It normally pertains to direct user-to-user transmissions of information.

electronic mailbox Synonym for mailbox. (T)

electronic messaging The creation, transfer, storage, and retrieval of text, graphics, images, or voice data by electronic means. (T)

electronic overlay (1) In the 3800 Print Services Facility, a collection of constant data that are electronically composed in the host processor and can be merged with variable data on a sheet during printing. Contrast with page segment. See also forms overlay, preprinted form.   (2) In the AS/400 system, an Advanced Function Printing (AFP) resource object that is a collection of predefined data, such as lines, shading, text, boxes, or logos, that can be merged with variable data on a page while printing.

electronic publishing The production of typeset-quality documents including text, graphics, and pictures with the assistance of a data processing system. Synonymous with computer-aided publishing, computer-assisted publishing. (T)

Electronic Industries Association (EIA) An organization of electronics manufacturers that advances the technological growth of the industry, represents the views of its members, and develops industry standards.

electronic stencil In a duplicator, a specially coated tissue or plastic-based master possessing certain electrical properties designed for creation of an image by means of an electronic stencil cutting machine. (T) See also pressure stencil, thermal stencil.

electronic worksheet In a personal computer spreadsheet application, the complete coded layout of the spreadsheet in memory, portions of which can be viewed on a display screen by scrolling. See Figure 51.

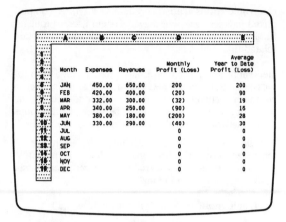

Figure 51. Electronic Worksheet

electro-optical Synonym for opto-electronic.

electrophotographic process The creation of an image on paper by uniformly charging the photoconductor, creating an electrostatic image on the photoconductor, attracting negatively charged toner to the discharged areas of the photoconductor, and transferring and fusing the toner to paper.

electrostatic charge A surge of static electricity.

electrostatic discharge (ESD) An undesirable discharge of static electricity that can damage equipment and degrade electrical circuitry.

electrostatic document copying machine A document copying machine that uses the electrostatic process. (T)

electrostatic image The invisible image consisting of discharged areas of a photoconductor because of exposure by laser raster scans of digital data or forms overlay.

electrostatic plotter A raster plotter that uses a row of electrodes to fix ink electrostatically on paper. (I) (A)

electrostatic printer A nonimpact printer that creates an electrostatic latent image, which is then made visible by a toner and transferred and fixed on paper.

Note: An electrostatic printer may be used in some instances as a plotter. (T)

electrostatic process In a document copying machine, a process in which the copy results directly or indirectly from the effect of light on electrically charged material. (T)   See direct electrostatic process, indirect electrostatic process.

electrostatic storage (1) A storage device that uses electrically charged areas on a dielectric surface layer. (I) (A)   (2) Contrast with storage tube.

electrostatic charge A surge of static electricity.

element (1) In a set, an object, entity, or concept having the properties that define a set. (I) (A) Synonymous with member. (2) In SNA, the particular resource within a subarea that is identified by an element address. (3) A parameter value in a list of parameter values. (4) The smallest unit of data in a table or array. (5) In the AIXwindows program, an object or similar data structure having the properties that define a class. (6) In FORTRAN, see array element. (7) See AND element, binary element, combinational logic element, detectable element, display element, exclusive-OR element, identity element, IF-AND-ONLY-IF element, IF-THEN element, inclusive-OR element, logic element, majority element, NAND element, NOR element, NOT element, NOT-IF-THEN element, obsolete element, picture element, sequential logic element, table element, threshold element.

element address In SNA, a value in the element address field of the network address identifying a particular resource within a subarea.   See also subarea address.

elemental In FORTRAN, pertaining to an operation, function, or assignment that is applied independently to the elements of an array or to corresponding elements of a set of conformable arrays and scalars.

elementary action In a conceptual schema language, the insertion, deletion, or retrieval of a sentence. (T)

elementary command In a conceptual schema language, the order or trigger for an elementary action to take place. (A)

elementary item In COBOL, a data item that is described as not being further logically subdivided.

element ID In SNA, deprecated term for element address.

element string See binary element string.

eleven-punch A punch in the second row from the top of a Hollerith card. (A) Synonymous with x-punch.

ELIAS skeleton maps In SDF/CICS, a set of skeleton maps for various device dimensions that can be used as a skeleton in the definition of a new map.

These maps contain the standard fields of ELIAS maps.

eligible list In VM, a list of virtual machines that are potentially executable, but are not placed on the run list to compete for processing unit resources because of the current load on the system. See also run list.

ELLC Enhanced logical link control.

ELM Error log manager.

EL screen Electroluminescent screen.

else See dangling else.

ELSE clause The part of an IF statement that contains the keyword ELSE, followed by a statement. The else clause provides an action that is started when the if condition evaluates to a value of 0 (false).

EM The end-of-medium character. (A)

em In printing, a unit of measure equal to the width or the height of the character "m" in a particular font. See Figure 52.

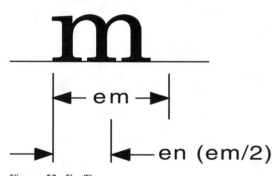

Figure 52. Em/En

embed To insert or merge.

embedded blank (1) A space between characters within a unit of data. (2) A blank that is surrounded by other characters.

embedded command (1) A text processing instruction entered as part of the text that causes a change to the document being processed at the time of a print preview or at the time it is printed. (T) (2) A command specified as a value in a parameter of another command. (3) In word processing, a command that is entered as part of the text that performs an operation such as underscoring or italicizing

words at the time the document is printed or displayed. Contrast with nonimbedded command.

embedded hyphen Synonym for hard hyphen. (T) (A)

embedded SQL SQL statements that are embedded within a program and are prepared in the program preparation process before the program is run. After it is prepared, the statement itself does not change, although values of host variables specified within the statement might change.

embedded system A system that is a part of a larger system whose primary purpose is not computational; for example, a computer system in a satellite or process control system. (A)

embedded text control One or more bytes of control information, preceded by an escape character, contained within a set of text. The text control controls certain operations on following text, but it is not itself to be printed.

emboldening In word processing, the process of intensifying the image of selected characters when displayed or printed. (T)

embossed character A character raised in relief from the surface of a medium such as a credit card. Contrast with debossed character. (A)

embossment (1) A distortion of the surface of a document. (A) (2) In character recognition, the distance between the undistorted surface of a document and a specified part of a printed character. (A)

EMEA Europe, Middle East, Africa. An organization with headquarters in Paris, France which markets products in the above areas. A World Trade Operating Unit.

emergency maintenance Maintenance intended to eliminate an existing fault that makes continued production work unachievable. (A)

emergency maintenance time Time, usually unscheduled, used to perform emergency maintenance. (A)

emergency mode In the Data Facility Hierarchical Storage Manager, the method of operation that prevents data set movement and deletion in space management, backup, and recovery processes.

emergency plan Synonym for contingency plan.

emergency restart A restart of IMS/VS following an IMS/VS or OS/VS failure.

EMH Expedited message handling.

EMI Electromagnetic interference.

emission security In computer security, protection against compromising emanations.

emitter In fiber optics, the source of optical power. (E)

emphasis In SAA Common User Access architecture, highlighting, color change, or other visible indication of conditions relative to an object or choice that affect a user's ability to interact with that object or choice. Emphasis can also give a user additional information about the state of a choice or object.

emphasized Pertaining to a form of double-strike printing in which characters are printed in multiple passes (usually two) with a slight offset creating an artificial bold type. Emphasized printing is used to fill gaps and rough appearance in dot-matrix character forms. It also prints a bold font without changing the mounted character set. See also boldface, double-strike.

empty medium A data medium that contains only marks of reference and no user data. (I)   (A)

empty set A set that has no elements. (I) (A) Synonymous with null set.

emulate (1) To imitate one system with another, primarily by hardware, so that the imitating system accepts the same data, executes the same programs, and achieves the same results as the imitated system. (A)   Contrast with simulate.

emulation (1) The use of a data processing system to imitate another data processing system, so that the imitating system accepts the same data, executes the same programs, and achieves the same results as the imitated system.   Emulation is usually achieved by means of hardware or firmware. (T)   (2) The use of programming techniques and special machine features to permit a computing system to execute programs written for another system.   (3) Imitation;   for example, imitation of a computer or device. (4) See terminal emulation. (5) Contrast with simulation.

emulation mode The function of a network control program that enables it to emulate a transmission control unit. Contrast with network control mode.

emulation program (EP) (1) A program that enables a system or a device to operate as if it were a different system or device. See also terminal emulator. (2) An IBM control program that allows a channel-attached 3705 or 3725 communication controller to emulate the functions of an IBM 2701 Data Adapter Unit, an IBM 2702 Transmission Control, or an IBM 2703 Transmission Control. See also network control program.

emulator (1) A combination of programming techniques and special machine features that permits a computing system to execute programs written for a different system. See also integrated emulator, terminal emulator. (2) A program that causes a computer to act as a workstation attached to another system. See also terminal emulation.

emulator generation The process of assembling and link-editing an emulator program into an operating system during system generation.

emulsion In a document copying machine, a suspension of light-sensitive compounds that, if stored under stated conditions, guarantees legibility for a specified number of years. (T)

en In printing, a unit of measure equal to one-half the width of an em. For many typefaces, lower case characters tend to average the width of an en. See Figure 52.

EN End node.

enable (1) To make functional.   (2) In interactive communications, to load and start a subsystem. Contrast with disable. (3) To design a product in such a way as to facilitate the inclusion of national language functions.

enabled (1) Pertaining to a state of the processing unit that allows the occurrence of certain types of interruptions. Synonymous with interruptible.   (2) Pertaining to the state in which a transmission control unit or an audio response unit can accept incoming calls on a line. (3) Pertaining to a product that is designed to facilitate the inclusion of national language functions without inhibiting the inclusion and usability of national language functions in other products. (4) In VTAM, pertaining to a logical unit (LU) that has indicated to its system services control point (SSCP) that it is now ready to establish LU-LU sessions. The LU can indicate whether it can act as a primary logical unit (PLU) or a secondary logical unit (SLU). See also disabled, inhibited.

enabled CP A control point's view of a partner control point (CP) when both parallel CP-CP sessions between the pair are active and ready for exchange of network services requests and replies.

enabled module A module that can be interrupted at any time during its execution. When the interruption occurs, the enabled module waits for the external routine that interrupted it to complete processing and then continues. Contrast with disabled module.

enabled page fault A page fault that occurs when I/O and external interruptions are allowed by the processing unit.

enabling signal A signal that permits occurrence of an event. (I) (A)

encapsulated type In programming languages, a module representing an abstract data type; for example, a stack processing module. (I)

Note: An encapsulated type hides the representation of its values but permits operations on the values by other modules.

encipher (1) To scramble data or to convert data to a secret code that masks the meaning of the data to any unauthorized recipient. Synonymous with encrypt *(1)*. (2) In computer security, to convert plaintext into an unintelligible form by means of a cipher system. Synonymous with cipher. (3) Contrast with decipher. See also encode.

enciphered data Data whose meaning is concealed from unauthorized users or observers. Synonymous with encode.

encode (1) To convert data by the use of a code in such a manner that reconversion to the original form is possible. (T) (2) In computer security, to convert plaintext into an unintelligible form by means of a code system. (3) In PSS, to magnetically record information on a merchandise ticket, credit card, or employee badge. This information can be read by the point of sale terminal wand reader or the ticket unit reader.

encoding (1) The conversion of data to machine-readable format; the final step in the process of converting an analog signal into a digital signal. The three steps are: sampling, quantizing, and encoding. See also quantizing, sampling. (2) See also encipher. (3) Synonymous with code. (4) Contrast with decode.

encoded format In AS/400 query management, the format of the data in an externalized form file.

encoded image (1) In the IBM 3800 Printing Subsystem, an image in which toned and untoned pels are grouped together and not represented in the overlay definition by a 1 or 0. (2) Synonym for coded image.

encoder (1) A functional unit that has a number of input lines such that not more than one at a time may carry a signal and a number of output lines such that any number may carry signals, and such that the combination of output signals serves as a code to indicate which input line carries the signal. (I) (A) (2) Contrast with decoder.

encoding The conversion of data to machine-readable format; the final step in the process of converting an analog signal into a digital signal. The three steps are: sampling, quantizing, and encoding. See also quantizing, sampling.

ENCP End-node control point.

encrypt (1) In computer security, to encode or encipher. (2) Synonym for encipher *(1)*. (T)

encryption In computer security, the process of transforming data into an unintelligible form in such a way that the original data either cannot be obtained or can be obtained only by using a decryption process.

encryption key In the AIX operating system, a key generated by the makekey command to use with programs that perform encryption. Its input and output are usually pipes.

End A key that a user presses to move the cursor to the last position in the current line.

Note: This operation can differ for bidirectional and double-byte character-set (DBCS) keyboards.

end-around borrow The action of transferring a borrow digit from the most significant digit place to the least significant digit place. (I) (A)

end-around carry The action of transferring a carry digit from the most significant digit place to the least significant digit place. An end-around carry may be necessary when adding two negative numbers that are represented by their diminished radix complements. (I) (A)

end-around shift A logical shift in which the characters moved out of one end of a computer word or register are re-entered into the other end. (I) (A) Synonymous with circular shift, cyclic shift.

end block underline A text instruction that indicates the end of a block of text to be underlined.

end bracket In SNA, the value (binary 1) of the end bracket indicator in the request header of the first request of the last chain of a bracket; the value denotes the end of the bracket. Contrast with begin bracket. See also bracket.

end distortion See distortion.

end frame The last frame, and associated frame number, of a video or audio segment. Synonymous with tail frame.

end frame delimiter Synonym for ending-frame delimiter. (T)

ending attribute character For a display file, the character following the last position in a field.

ending-frame delimiter (1) A specified bit pattern or a specified signal that indicates the end of a transmission frame. Synonymous with end frame delimiter, frame end delimiter. (T)   (2) A specified bit pattern that indicates the end of a transmission frame. (T) (3) Contrast with starting frame delimiter.   (4) See figure at transmission frame.

ending message In PSS, a short message selected by a store and printed at the bottom of a cash receipt given to a customer, such as "We appreciate your business."

end node (EN)   See Advanced Peer-to-Peer Networking (APPN) end node and low-entry networking (LEN) end node.

end of address (EOA) (1) One or more control characters transmitted on a line to indicate the end of non-text characters;   for example, addressing characters. (2) In ACF/TCAM, a character that must be placed in a message if the system is to route the message to several destinations.   The character must immediately follow the last destination code in the message header and be specified in the EOA operand of the FORWARD macroinstruction for the message.

end of block (EOB) A code that marks the end of a block of data. See Figure 53.

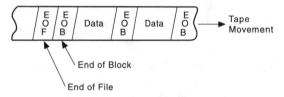

Figure 53. End of Block/End of File

end of chain (EOC) (1) In the IBM 8100 Information System, a signal sent by control logic during a channel I/O operation to indicate that the control is finished with the I/O bus. (2) In SNA, deprecated term for last-in-chain (LIC).

end of data In SAA Advanced Common User Access architecture, a function that moves the selection cursor to the rightmost position in the current field.

Note: This function can differ for bidirectional and double-byte character set (DBCS) languages.

end-of-data indicator A code signaling that the last record of a consecutive data set has been read.

end of extent (EOE) The end of the area on a disk or diskette reserved for a file.

end office A class 5 office of a local telephone exchange in which a subscriber's loop terminates. See also central office, exchange, exchange classes, local central office.

end of file (EOF) A coded character recorded on a data medium to indicate the end of the medium. See also end-of-file label. See Figure 53.

end-of-file delay An interval during which the system holds a file open after the normal end of the file is reached until one or more records are updated or added to the end of the file.

end-of-file label (1) An internal label indicating the end of a file and possibly containing data for file control. (T)   (2) Synonymous with trailer label.

Note: An end-of-file label may include control totals for comparison with counts accumulated during processing.

end-of-job indicator (EJ) In System/36, an indicator signaling that the last operator has specified the end of the work session on the workstation utility display. Synonymous with end-of-work-session indicator.

end-of-job processing level In System/36, the processing level that occurs once per job after the end-of-work session for the last display station or when the program sets the EJ indicator on. Synonymous with end-of-work-session processing level.

end-of-letter marker control On dictation equipment, a device for indicating on an index slip or on the recording medium the position at which a particular passage of dictation is concluded. (I)

end-of-life carrier A carrier bead that attracts fewer toner particles because its surface has a layer of fused-on toner.

end of line (1) The predetermined position on the paper carrier at which the typing line ends. (T) (2) In SAA Advanced Common User Access architecture, a function that moves the selection cursor to the rightmost choice.

Note: This function can differ for bidirectional and double-byte character set (DBCS) languages.

end-of-line indicator On a typewriter, a device providing an acoustic signal when only a few spaces remain before the right-hand margin stop. (T)

end-of-list (EOL) control block A control block used in an SDLC transmit operation.

end-of-medium character (EM) A control character that can be used to identify the physical end of the data medium, end of the used portion of the medium, or end of the wanted portion of the data recorded on the medium. (I) (A)

end-of-medium indicator (1) On dictation equipment, a device that gives an audible or visible signal at the end of the recording medium. (I) (2) The last character position in a display line or in a printed line.

end-of-message code (EOM) The character or sequence of characters that indicates the end of a message or record.

end-of-number character A character that indicates the end of the telephone number to the autocall unit.

end-of-page indicator On a typewriter, a device warning of the approach of the end of a page during operation. (T)

end of Procedure Division In COBOL, the physical position of a COBOL source program after which no further procedures appear.

end-of-sequence-set indicator In System/36, an indicator signaling that the last display in the primary sequence has been processed.

end-of-sequence-set processing level In System/36, the processing level that occurs after the last display in the primary sequence has been processed.

end-of-tape marker (EOT) (1) A marker on a magnetic tape used to indicate the end of the permissible recording area; for example, a photo reflective strip, a transparent section of tape. (I) (A) (2) Contrast with beginning-of-tape marker. See Figure 54.

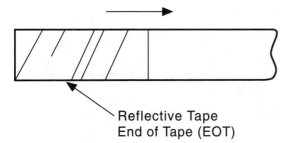

Figure 54. End of Tape

end-of-text character (ETX) (1) A transmission control character used to terminate text. (A) (2) In binary synchronous communication, the transmission control character used to end a logical set of records that began with the start-of-text character. Contrast with end-of-transmission-block character.

end-of-transmission-block character (1) A transmission control character used to indicate the end of a transmission block of data when data are divided into such blocks for transmission purposes. (I) (A) (2) In binary synchronous communication, the transmission control character used to end a block of records that began with the start-of-text character. Contrast with end-of-text character.

end-of-transmission character (EOT) (1) A transmission control character used to indicate conclusion of a transmission that may have included one or more texts and associated message headings. (I) (A) (2) In binary synchronous communication, the transmission control character usually used to end communication.

end-of-transmission code The character or sequence of characters that indicates termination of sending.

end-of-volume (EOV) label An internal label that indicates the end of the data contained in a volume. (T)

end-of-work-session indicator (EW) In System/36, the indicator that signals that an operator has specified end-of-work-session on the workstation utility display. Synonymous with end-of-job indicator.

end-of-work-session processing level In System/36, the processing level that occurs each time an operator specifies the end of the work session on the workstation utility display or when the program sets the EW or EJ indicator ON. Synonymous with end-of-job processing level.

endpoint (1) On a display device, the coordinates on the display surface to which a display writer is to be moved. (2) The system that is the origin or destination of a session.

endpoint node A node that is at the end of only one branch. Synonymous with peripheral node. (T)

endpoint TG vector A pair of control vectors representing a transmission group (TG) available at an end node for use by sessions that terminate in the node. Such a TG is not in the network topology database, and one of the purposes of the Locate/CD-Initiate search is to obtain the endpoint TG vectors for the nodes containing the origin and destination LUs (when one or both resides at an end node) of a particular session. Endpoint TG vectors are carried in the CD-Initiate GDS variables sent to the origin LU's network node server, which combines these endpoint TG vectors with the node and TG data in the topology database to compute a preferred session route between the origin and destination LUs.

end program header In COBOL, a combination of words, followed by a separator period, that indicates the end of a COBOL source program. The end program header is: END PROGRAM program-name

end signal In an online conference, a mutually agreed upon character that indicates the end of a comment by a participant. Common end signals are o and oo.

end-to-end encryption In computer security, the protection of information passed in a communication system by cryptographic means, from point of origin to point of destination.

end-to-end session In TCAM, a logical connection in which an affinity-based routing relationship has been established between a source and a destination, each of which can be either a logical unit (LU) or an application program. End-to-end sessions require routing by key.

end-to-end transit delay In X.25 communications, an optional CCITT-specified facility.

end-use device A device, such as a printer, that provides the final output of an operation without further processing.

end user (1) A person, device, program, or computer system that utilizes a computer network for the purpose of data processing and information exchange. (T) (2) The ultimate source or destination of application data flowing through an SNA network. An end user can be an application program or a workstation operator. (3) Contrast with customer.

end-user language A language intended for purposes of information processing by end users. (A)

end user-to-end user session Synonym for LU-LU session.

end-user to SSCP echo check Synonym for LU connection test.

end-user verification For logical unit (LU) 6.2, checking the identification of end-users by means of identifiers and passwords on attach function-management headers (FMHs). See partner-LU verification. See also conversation-level security.

energy level diagram A line drawing that illustrates both the increases and the decreases of electrical power along a channel.

enforced lock In the AIX operating system, a type of lock that a process holds on a region of a file preventing any other process from accessing that region with read or write system calls. In addition, the create

and open commands are prevented from truncating the files. See advisory lock.

engineering change (EC) log A list of engineering changes that have been installed in a machine; the list is useful for preparing APARs.

enhanced graphics adapter (EGA) An adapter, such as the IBM Enhanced Graphics Adapter, that provides high-resolution graphics, allowing the use of a color display for text processing as well as graphics applications.

enhanced logical link control (ELLC) An X.25 protocol that allows the transfer of data link control information between two adjoining SNA nodes that are connected through X.25 packet-switching data network. ELLC enhances error detection and recovery. Contrast with physical services header (PSH), qualified logical link control (QLLC).

Enhanced X-Windows Toolkit In the AIX operating system, a collection of basic functions for developing a variety of application environments. Toolkit functions manage Toolkit initialization, widgets, memory, events, geometry, input focus, selections, resources, translation of events, graphics contexts, pixmaps, and errors.

Enhanced 5250 Emulation A program that allows a personal computer and a printer to be attached to an AS/400 system and to perform the functions of one or two 5250 workstations on one twinaxial cable. The workstations can be one display station, two display stations, or one display station and one printer.

enlargement In a document copying machine, a copy on a scale larger than 1:1 to the original. (T) Contrast with reduction. See also same size.

ENQ The enquiry character. (A)

enqueue (1) To place items in a queue. Contrast with dequeue. (2) In the OS/400 operating system, applications programming interfaces, an operation that places items, such as messages, on a queue. Contrast with dequeue.

enquiry character (ENQ) (1) A transmission control character used as a request for a response from the station with which the connection has been set up; the response may include station identification, type of equipment in service, and status of the remote station. (I) (A) (2) In binary synchronous communication, the transmission control character used to indicate control of transmission on a point-to-point channel and to indicate a request for a station to repeat its response.

enter (1) To place on the line a message to be transmitted from a terminal to the computer. Contrast with accept. See also receive, send. (2) In the 3790 Communication System, to store the data or commands that have been keyed in by pressing the Enter/Return key. (3) To press the Enter/Rec Adv key (on a workstation keyboard) or the Enter key (on the system console) or a command function key to transfer keyed-in information to the system for processing. See also key in. (4) To type in information on a keyboard and press the Enter key to send the information to the computer. (5) In SAA usage, to submit all selected choices and entry-field information to the computer for processing; for example, to type information on a keyboard and press the Enter key.

Enter (1) In SAA Common User Access architecture, an action that submits information to the computer for processing. Enter tells the computer to perform actions on whatever has been selected. (2) A key that a user presses to submit information to a computer for processing.

Note: This key is sometimes labeled with a bent-arrow symbol.

enter action In the 3270 Information Display System, any terminal action that causes an inbound data stream to be initiated.

enter inhibit In the 3270 Information Display System, a condition that prevents the operator from transmitting data inbound until the terminal receives acknowledgment of successful receipt of previously transmitted data. Contrast with input inhibit.

enter/inquiry mode A mode in which a user can enter data at a terminal and obtain a display or printout of information.

enter mode In System/36, a mode in which an operator can add records to a transaction file.

enterprise model A representation of the goals, organizational structure, business processes, and information resources and requirements of an enterprise.

enterprise number A unique telephone exchange number that permits the called party to be automatically billed for incoming calls. Synonymous with toll-free number.

Enterprise Systems Connection (ESCON) A set of IBM products and services that provide a dynamically connected environment within an enterprise.

enter/update mode In System/36, the mode used to enter new statements into a source or procedure member, or to change statements that already exist in a source or procedure member.

entity (1) Any concrete or abstract thing of interest, including associations among things; for example, a person, object, event, or process that is of interest in the context under consideration, and about which data may be stored in a database. (T) (2) In Open Systems Interconnection architecture, an active element within a subsystem. Cooperation between entities in a layer is controlled by one or more protocols. (T) (3) In RACF, a user, group, or resource that is defined to RACF; for example, a DASD data set or VM minidisk. (4) In FORTRAN, a program unit, a procedure, an operator, an interface block, a common block, an input-output unit, a statement function, a type, a named variable, an expression, a component of a type, a symbolic constant, a statement label, a construct, an exponent letter, a range list, or a condition. See data entity, global entity, local entity, statement entity.

entity identifier In a database, a set of one or more attributes whose attribute values uniquely identify each entity within a given set of entities. (T)

entity instance Synonym for entity occurrence. (T)

entity-integrity property In a relation, the property that precludes a null value for any primary key or component of a primary key. (A)

entity occurrence In a database, a specific entity of a given entity type. (T)

entity relationship In a database, a perceived association among entities or among attributes of the same entity. In certain contexts, an entity relationship may be considered to be an entity. (T)

entity-relationship data model A data model based on the concept of entities and relationships among entities, and of the attributes of entities and relationships. (A)

entity set In a database, a group of entities that have the same attributes.

entity type (1) In a conceptual schema language, the proposition that establishes that an entity is a member of a particular class of entities, implying as well that there is such a class of entities. See also attribute type, relationship type. (A) (2) In a database, a class of entities with common properties, which is of interest within a specific context. (T)

entity world In a database, a collection of entities that are related to a particular aspect of a universe of discourse; for example, "payroll" and "sales accounts" could be perceived as entity worlds in the universe of discourse: "all financial aspects of an organization." (T)

entrance Synonym for entry point.

entrapment In computer security, the deliberate planting of apparent flaws in a system for the purpose of detecting attempted penetrations or confusing an intruder about which flaws to exploit.

entropy (1) In information theory, the mean value of the measure of information conveyed by the occurrence of any one of a finite number of mutually exclusive and jointly exhaustive events of definite probabilities; in the mathematical notation, this means $H(x)$ for a set of events $x_1...x_n$ with the probabilities $p(x_1)...p(x_n)$ equals the mathematical expectation, or mean value, of the information content $I(x_i)$ of the individual events. (I) (A) (2) Synonymous with average information content, mean information content, negentropy. (3) See character mean entropy, conditional entropy, relative entropy.

entry (1) In programming languages, a language construct within a procedure, designating the start of the execution sequences of the procedure. A procedure may have more than one entry; each entry usually includes an identifier, called the entry name, and may include formal parameters. (I) (2) An element of information in a table, list, queue, or other organized structure of data or control information. (3) A single input operation on a terminal. (4) In SAA usage, an input operation on a workstation. (5) In XL FORTRAN, a language construct within a procedure, designating the start of the execution sequences of the procedure. (6) A single input operation on a workstation. (7) In COBOL, any descriptive set of consecutive clauses terminated by a separator period and written in the Identification Division, Environment Division, or Data Division of a COBOL program. See comment-entry, communication description entry, data description entry, file control entry, file description entry, I-O control entry, 77-level-description-entry, object computer entry, object of entry, program name entry, record description entry, report description entry, report group description entry, sort-merge file description entry, source computer entry, special names entry, subject of entry. (8) Synonym for entry point. (9) See remote batch entry, remote job entry.

entry conditions (1) The conditions to be specified on entering a computer program, routine, or subroutine; for example, the address of those locations from which the program, routine, or subroutine will take its operands and of those locations with which its entry points and exits will be linked. (I) (A) (2) The initial data and control conditions to be satisfied for successful execution of a given routine. (A)

entry constant In PL/I, the label of a PROCEDURE statement.

entry data item In PL/I, a data item that represents an entry point to a procedure.

entry field In SAA Common User Access architecture, an area where a user types information. Its boundaries are usually indicated. See also selection field.

entry format A set of fields that can be displayed and modified (entered) on a display.

entry name (1) A name within a control section that defines an entry point and can be referred to by any control section. (2) A programmer-specified name that establishes an entry point. (3) In VSAM, a unique name for a component or object as it is identified in a catalog.

entry point (EP) (1) In a database, the record that is first accessed upon entry into a database, caused by a user's command. (T) (2) The address or label of the first instruction executed on entering a computer program, routine, or subroutine. A computer program, routine, or subroutine may have a number of different entry points, each perhaps corresponding to a different function or purpose. (I) (A) Synonymous with entrance, entry. (3) In a routine, any place to which control can be passed. (A) (4) In SNA, a type 2.0, type 2.1, type 4, or type 5 node that provides distributed network management support. It sends network management data about itself and the resources it controls to a focal point for centralized processing, and it receives and executes focal-point initiated commands to manage and control its resources.

entry point vector (EPV) In the AIX operating system, a record in which fields are pointers to procedures that implement the operations defined by an interface.

entry reference In PL/I, an entry constant, an entry variable, or a function reference that returns value.

entry sequence (1) In MVS/370, MVS/XA programs, and VSE with VSAM, the order in which data records are physically arranged in auxiliary storage, without respect to their contents. (2) Contrast with key sequence.

entry-sequenced data set In MVS/370 and MVS/XA programs with VSAM, a data set whose records are loaded without respect to their contents, and whose relative byte addresses cannot change. Records are retrieved and stored by addressed access, and new records are added at the end of the data set. See Figure 55.

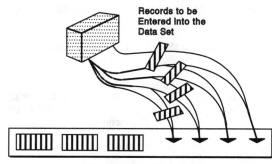

Records to be Entered Into the Data Set

Entry-Sequenced Data Set

Figure 55. Entry-Sequenced Data Set

entry-sequenced file A VSAM file whose records are loaded without respect to their contents and whose relative byte addresses cannot change. Records are retrieved and stored by addressed access, and new records are added at the end of the file.

entry symbol (1) A symbol that represents an entry name or control section name. (2) See also external symbol.

entry variable In PL/I, a variable to which a beginning value can be assigned.

enumerated scalar type (1) In Pascal, a data type defined by listing, in order, the set of distinct values that a variable of that type can assume. (2) In the AIX operating system, a scalar defined by enumerating the elements of the type. Each element is represented by an identifier.

enumeration constant In C language, an identifier, with an associated integer value, defined in an enumerator. An enumeration constant may be used anywhere an integer constant is allowed.

enumeration data type In the C and FORTRAN languages, a data type that represents a set values that a user defines.

enumeration tag In C language, the identifier that names an enumeration data type.

enumerator In C language, an enumeration constant and its associated value.

envelope (1) That part of a message containing information used in the submission, sending, or delivery of the message. (T) (2) A named collection of logical and physical resources used to support the performance of a function. (3) In the AIX operating system, the settings for shell variables and paths set when the user logs in. The user can modify these variables later. See run-time environment. (4) See batch envi-

ronment, home environment, interactive environment, master environment, parent environment, subenvironment.

environmental condition Any of the physical conditions required for the protection and proper operation of a functional unit; for example, temperature, humidity, vibration, dust, and radiation. (T)

Notes:

1. *An environmental condition is usually specified as a nominal value and a tolerance range.*

2. *For a device, there may be more than one set of environmental conditions; for example, one set for transport, another for storage, and another for operation.*

environmental loss time Synonym for external loss time. (T)

Environmental Record Editing and Printing In the Object Access Method, the program that formats and prepares reports from the data contained in the Error Recording Data Set (ERDS).

environmental requirement Any of the physical conditions required for the protection and proper operation of a functional unit; the requirement is usually specified as a nominal value and a tolerance range. For a device, there may be more than one set of environmental requirements; for example, one set for transport, another for storage, and another for operation. (T) (A)

environment clause In COBOL, a clause that appears as part of an Environment Division entry.

environment description In programming languages, a language construct for describing features that are not part of a program but are relevant to its execution; for example, machine characteristics, special properties of files, interfaces with other programs. (I)

Environment Division One of the four main parts of a COBOL program. The Environment Division describes the computers on which the source program is compiled and those on which the object program is run; it also provides a connection between the logical concept of files and their records, and the physical characteristics of the devices on which files are stored.

environment record In ACF/TCAM, a checkpoint record of the total network environment at a single point in time. See also checkpoint request record, control record, incident record.

environment variable Any of a number of variables that describe the way an operating system is going to run and the devices it is going to recognize.

EOA End of address.

EOB End of block.

EOC End of chain.

EOD End of data.

EOE End of extent.

EOF End of file.

EOL (1) End of list. (2) A key on a keyboard that a user presses to move the cursor to the last position in the current line.

Note: This operation can differ for bidirectional and double-byte character-set (DBCS) keyboards.

EOM End of message code.

EOT (1) The end-of-transmission character. (A) (2) End-of-tape marker. (A)

EOV End of volume.

EP Emulation program.

EPCF Extended primary control field.

epifile In the Document Composition Facility, the second portion of a profile that is processed after a main document has been processed.

EPOW Emergency power off warning.

EPROM Erasable programmable read-only memory.

EPS (Encapsulated Postscript) A graphic file format designed for the display of Postscript images in applications for the Apple Macintosh line of computers.

EPV Entry point vector.

equalization Compensation for differences in attenuation (reduction or loss of signal) or time delay at different frequencies.

equals On a calculator, completion of a series of operations and provision of the result. (T)

equals function In a calculator, the function that completes a series of operations and provides the result. (T) (A)

equate character See attribute character.

equipment See data terminal equipment.

equipment rack A metal stand for mounting components.

equipotential bonding A means of limiting differences in ground potential within a building.

equivalence A logic operator having the property that if P is a statement, Q is a statement, R is a statement, the equivalence of P,Q,R,... is true if and only if all statements are true or all statements are false. (A)

equivalence class In the AIX operating system, a grouping of characters or character strings that are considered equal for purposes of collation; for example, many languages place an uppercase character in the same equivalence class as its lowercase form, but some languages distinguish between accented and unaccented character forms for the purpose of collation.

equivalence operation (1) The dyadic Boolean operation whose result has the Boolean value 1 if and only if the operands have the same Boolean value. (I) (A) Synonymous with IF-AND-ONLY-IF operation. (2) Contrast with nonequivalence operation.

equivalent-binary-digit factor The average number of binary digits required to express one radix digit in a non-binary numeration system; for example, approximately 3.33 times as many digits are required to express a binary numeral as to express the equivalent decimal numeral. (A)

equivalent four-wire system A transmission system using frequency division to obtain full-duplex operation over a pair of wires.

equivocation In information theory, the conditional entropy of the occurrence of specific messages at the message source given the occurrence of specific messages at a message sink connected to the message source by a specified channel. If x_i is the input message at the message source and y_j the output message at the message sink, the equivocation is the conditional entropy $H(x|y)$. The equivocation is the mean additional information content that must be supplied per message at the message sink to correct the received messages affected by a noisy channel. (I) (A)

ER (1) Explicit route. (2) Exception response.

ERACT Error action.

erasable optical disc An optical disc that can be erased and written on repeatedly.

erasable programmable read-only memory (EPROM) A PROM that can be erased by a special process and reused. (T)

erasable storage (1) A storage device in which different data can be written successively at the same storage location. (T)　(2) In an IBM personal computer, storage such as user memory or diskette storage in which data can be changed or deleted. (3) Contrast with fixed storage, permanent storage, read-only memory, read-only storage.

erase (1) To remove data from a data medium. Erasing is usually accomplished by overwriting the data or deleting the references. (T)　(2) On dictation equipment, the process of removing the recording from a recording medium. (I)　(3) In SAA usage, to remove something and leave the space it occupied. Contrast with delete.

Erase All Unprotected (EAU) A 3270 data stream command that erases all unprotected fields and inserts nulls.

erase character Deprecated term for delete character.

Erase EOF A key that a user presses to delete information beginning at the cursor position and ending at a field or at the end of a line.

Note: This operation can differ for bidirectional and double-byte character-set (DBCS) keyboards.

erase head (1) A magnetic head capable of erasing only that data on a magnetic data medium. Synonymous with erasing head. (T)　(2) A device on a magnetic tape drive whose function is to erase previous information before new information is written. (3) On dictation equipment, a device for use on a machine using a magnetic recording medium which, when brought into contact or near contact with the recording medium, removes the recording from the magnetic tracks covered by the head as the medium is moved past it. (I)　See Figure 56.

erase-on-scratch The physical overwriting of data on a DASD data set when the data set is deleted (scratched).

eraser On dictation equipment, a device for removing a recording from the recording medium. (I)

erase to end of field In SAA usage, a typing action that deletes text from the current cursor position to the end of the field.

Note: This operation can differ for bidirectional and double-byte character-set (DBCS) languages.

Erase/Write A 3270 data stream command that clears the entire character buffer to nulls, positions the cursor to position 0, resets the buffer address to 0, sets character attributes to their default values, and then performs a write operation. It also returns screen size to the default size if the WCC reset bit is set to 1.

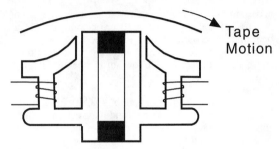

Figure 56. Erase Head

Erase/Write Alternate (EWA) A 3270 data stream command that causes an Erase/Write operation and switches the size of a display screen to the default size if the WCC reset bit is set to 1.

erasing head Synonym for erase head. (T)

erasure current The write current necessary to reduce previously recorded data on a magnetic surface to 1 per cent or less of its maximum amplitude. (A)

ERCOD Error code.

ERDS Error Recording Data Set.

EREP Environmental Record Editing and Printing Program. A program that makes the data contained in the system recorder file available for further analysis.

ergonomics The application of biological and engineering data to the design of systems, programs, and devices in order to adapt them to human requirements, to the tasks they are to perform, and to the environments in which they are to be used. See also human factors, usability, utility.

erlang A unit of telephone traffic specifying the percentage of use of a telephone line or circuit.

ERM Error recovery manager.

ERP Error recovery procedures.

ERR Error.

error (1) A discrepancy between a computed, observed, or measured value or condition and the true, specified, or theoretically correct value or condition. (I)　(A)　(2) Deprecated term for mistake. (T)　(3) Contrast with failure, fault, malfunction, mistake.

error analysis facility In the AIX operating system, a program that provides information about the probable cause of errors.

error burst In data communication, a sequence of signals containing one or more errors but counted as one unit in accordance with a specific criterion or measure. An example of a criterion is that if three consecutive correct bits follow an erroneous bit, then an error burst is terminated. (A)

error-checking and correction (ECC) In a processing unit, the detection and correction of all single-bit errors, plus the detection of double-bit and some multiple-bit errors.

error class In the AIX operating system, a class that identifies whether an error log entry is for a hardware or software failure.

error code See system reference code.

error condition (1) The state that results from an attempt to execute instructions in a computer program that are invalid or that operate on invalid data. (2) On a calculator, the situation in which the operator attempts to carry out an impossible function on the machine. (T)

error condition statement An executable statement that specifies action to be taken upon the occurrence of an event in the execution of a computer program that the programmer has chosen to call an error. (T)

error control The part of a protocol controlling the detection, and possibly the correction, of errors. (I) (A)

error control character Synonym for accuracy control character.

error control software Software that monitors a computer system to detect, record, and possibly correct errors. (T)

error correcting code An error-detecting code designed to allow for automatic correction of certain types of errors. (T)

error correcting system A system in which errors identified by an error detecting code are automatically corrected at the receiving terminal.

error correction A method used to correct erroneous data produced during data transmission, transfer, or storage. (T)

error-correction save point (1) In the 3790 Communication System, a point in a 3790 program to which control is transferred when a terminal operator presses the error-correction (ERR CORR) key during data entry. In enter/inquiry mode, the 3790 program returns to the most recent save point and disregards all data it received after that point. In rerun mode, the 3790 program returns to the most recent save point but retains all data received after that point, thus enabling the operator to correct the information. (2) In the 8100/DPCX system, a point in a program to which control is passed when a terminal operator presses the error-correction (ERR CORR) key during entry of data, or when a program issues a statement that has the same effect.

error-correction submode A mode of operation that provides the ability to go back in a program to a point where the environment was saved, thereby permitting correction of a previously entered field. See also error-correction save point.

error counter In the AIX operating system, a type of error entry generated by device driver components. Certain device drivers can generate retry operations if an operation is not successful on the first attempt. They use counters to monitor the number and cause of retry operations, and they contain algorithms that decide when these counters should be sent to the error log.

error data analysis (EDA) A diagnostic process that localized hardware failures to a field replaceable unit (FRU) or FRU group.

error-detecting code A code in which each coded representation conforms to specific rules of construction so that violation of the rules indicates presence of errors. (T) Synonymous with self-checking code.

error detection A method of determining whether data has been transmitted or transferred incorrectly. (T)

error detection and correction (EDAC) In video production, an encoding technique that detects and corrects errors in digital data.

error device driver In the AIX operating system, a special file driver used by the error logging facilities.

error emphasis In SAA Basic Common User Access architecture, a visual cue to users that the information they have typed into an entry field is incorrect.

error handler (EH) A component that responds to unsolicited interruptions; it analyzes error conditions and takes recovery steps.

error ID Error identifier.

error identifier (error ID) In the AIX operating system, an 8-character code used to identify a particular failure. There is a unique error identifier for each error record template.

error indication On a calculator, a visual indication that the user has attempted to carry out a function that the calculator cannot perform. (I) (A)

error interrupt request vector (EIRV) In the 8100/DPCX system, a code that defines a machine or program check.

error lock In the network control program, for BSC and start-stop devices, the condition of a device following an error. No further commands can be processed for the device until a Control command with a reset modifier is issued.

error log (1) A data set or file in a product or system where error information is stored for later access. (2) A form in a maintenance library that is used to record error information about a product or system. (3) In DPPX, a data set used in the 8100 processor to record information about certain hardware and programming events. (4) A record of machine checks, device errors, and volume statistical data.

error log manager (ELM) In DPPX, a manager scheduling error records to be logged into the system error log data set.

error log table In System/7, a group of storage locations in which errors in processing data and I/O device errors are recorded on a device and module basis.

error message An indication that an error has been detected. (A)

error range (1) The set of values that an error may take. (I) (A) (2) Deprecated term for error span.

error rate (1) The ratio of the total number of errors detected to the total amount of data transmitted or transferred. (T) (2) A measure of the quality of a circuit or system; it is expressed as the number of erroneous bits or characters in a sample, frequently taken per 100,000 characters.

error ratio (1) The ratio of the number of data units in error to the total number of data units. (A) (2) See residual error ratio.

error record (1) A record that indicates the occurrence of errors. (2) In ACF/TCAM, five bytes assigned to each message processed by a message handler. These bytes indicate physical or logical errors that have occurred during transmission or during subsequent processing or queuing of the message. *Note:* A message error record may also be created when a session cannot be established. Error records are checked by error-handling macros in the in-message and out-message subgroups of a message handler. Synonymous with message error record.

error recording analysis procedure An IBM-supplied program that processes and presents recorded errors related to system devices such as disk devices.

error record template In the AIX operating system, a template that describes the error class, error type, error description, probable causes, recommended actions, and failure data for an error log entry.

error recovery The process of correcting or bypassing the effects of a fault to restore a computer system to a prescribed condition. (T)

error recovery manager (ERM) In DPPX, a manager invoked in the event of a system check or process exception on a process. The ERM invokes the appropriate specified process check exit routine for the failing process.

error recovery procedures (ERP) (1) Procedures designed to help isolate and, where possible, to recover from errors in equipment. The procedures are often used in conjunction with programs that record information on machine malfunctions. (2) In ACF/TCAM, a set of routines that attempt to recover from transmission errors.

error span The difference between the highest and the lowest error values. (I) (A)

error statistics by tape volume (ESTV) One of the two options of VSE volume statistics. With this option, a system collects data on tape errors by volume for any volumes used by the system. See also error volume analysis.

error statistics by volume (ESV) In OS/VS, an optional facility that causes a system to collect information about errors that occur on tape volumes when the volumes are open.

error-to-traffic (E/T) The number of temporary errors compared to the traffic associated with a resource.

error type In the AIX operating system, a type that identifies whether an error log entry is for a permanent failure, temporary failure, performance degradation, impending loss of availability, or undetermined failure.

error volume analysis (EVA) One of the two options of VSE volume statistics. With this option, a system issues a message to the operator when a certain number of temporary read or write errors has been exceeded on a currently accessed tape volume. See also error statistics by tape volume.

ERTE Explicit route table entry.

ES Expert system. (T)

ESA Enterprise Systems Architecture.

ESC (1) The escape character. (A) (2) Execution sequence control.

escape To return to the original level of a user interface.

Escape, Esc A key on a keyboard that a user presses to remove the current window without processing the information, or that a user presses with another key to perform a special keyboard function. See also Cancel.

escape character (ESC) (1) A code extension character used, in some cases with one or more succeeding characters, to indicate by some convention or agreement that the coded representations following the character or the group of characters are to be interpreted according to a different code or according to a different coded character set. (I) (A) (2) The control character in a text-control sequence that indicates the beginning of a sequence and the end of any preceding text. (3) In SQL, the symbol used to enclose a delimited identifier. The symbol is the quotation mark ("), except in COBOL programs where the symbol can be specified by the user as either a quotation mark or an apostrophe. (4) See data link escape character. (5) See also logical escape symbol.

escapement (1) Movement of one character space between the paper carrier and typing or printing position, parallel with the typing or printing line. See expand escapement, line escapement. See also unit of escapement. (2) The unit of vertical or horizontal movement that is built into a device; for example, the 1403 Printer with a 10-pitch train has a horizontal escapement unit of 1/10th of an inch.

escape message In the AS/400 system, a message that reports a condition that caused the program to end before the requested function was complete. See also diagnostic message.

escape sequence (1) In the AIX operating system: (a) A character that is preceded by a backslash character and is interpreted to have a special meaning to the operating system. (b) A sequence sent to a terminal to perform actions such as moving the cursor, changing from normal to reverse video, and clearing the screen. Synonymous with multibyte control. (2) In the C language, a sequence made up of an escape character, followed by one or more characters that indicate the following characters are to be interpreted by a different code or according to a different coded character set.

escape to CP In VM, a transfer of control to CP when either a terminal user or the machine stops virtual machine operation. This can be accomplished by a CP command (such as #CP), by invoking a DIAGNOSE function, or by signaling attention. See also attention interrupt, diagnose interface, signaling attention.

escaping key A key that when pressed causes the imprint position to move. Contrast with nonescaping key.

ESCD (1) ESCON Director. (2) Enterprise Systems Connection Director. (3) Extended system contents directory.

ESCD console The ESCON Director input/output device used to perform operator and service tasks at the ESCD.

ESCD console adapter Hardware in the ESCON Director console that provides the attachment capability between the ESCD and the ESCD console.

ESCM (1) ESCON Manager. (2) Enterprise Systems Connection Manager.

ESCON Enterprise Systems Connection.

ESCON channel A channel having an Enterprise Systems Connection channel-to-control-unit I/O interface that uses optical cables as a transmission medium. Contrast with parallel channel.

ESCON Director A device that provides connectivity capability and control for attaching any two links to each other.

ESCON environment The data processing environment having an Enterprise Systems Connection channel-to-control-unit I/O interface that uses optical cables as a transmission medium.

ESCON Manager A licensed program that provides host control and intersystem communication capability for ESCON Director connectivity operations.

ESD (1) Electrostatic discharge. (2) External symbol dictionary.

ES indicator See end-of-sequence-set indicator.

esoteric unit names The names a user assigns to tape drives that have the same device type. When the user specifies the assigned unit name to Data Facility Hierarchical Storage Manager, Data Facility Hierarchical Storage Manager associates the unit name with its device type.

establishing shot In multimedia applications, a long shot used in videotaping the beginning of a program or segment to establish where the action is taking place and to give the sense of an environment.

establishment (1) Deprecated term for session activation, LU-LU session initiation. (2) See call establishment.

ESTAE Extended specify task abnormal exit.

ESTV Error statistics by tape volume.

ESV Error statistics by volume.

E/T Error-to-traffic.

ETB The end-of-transmission-block character. (A)

Ethernet (1) A 10-megabit baseband local area network that allows multiple stations to access the transmission medium at will without prior coordination, avoids contention by using carrier sense and deference, and resolves contention by using collision detection and transmission. Ethernet uses carrier sense multiple access with collision detection (CSMA/CD). (2) In the AS/400 system, a type of local area network that is supported by the Operating System/400 licensed program. OS/400 Ethernet provides support for Digital Equipment Corporation and Intel Corporation standards , for the Xerox standard (Ethernet Version 2), and for the IEEE 802.3 standards.

Ethernet-type LAN A local area network that uses either the Ethernet Version 2 or IEEE 802.3 protocol.

E-time Execution time.

ETX The end-of-text character. (A)

EUI End User Interface.

European article number (EAN) A number that can be assigned to and encoded on an article of merchandise for wanding or scanning in certain countries. The OEM/EAN Wand Attachment RPQ feature is available for IBM point of sale terminals.

EVA Error volume analysis.

evaluation report A system follow-up report that describes how the system objectives have been met, identifies the remaining problems, and is intended to assist future development. (T)

even field All of the even-numbered scan lines on a video screen. See field, odd field.

even positive acknowledgment See ACK0.

event (1) An occurrence or happening. (2) An occurrence of significance to a task; for example, the completion of an asynchronous operation, such as an input/output operation. (3) A data link control command and response passed between adjacent nodes that allows the two nodes to exchange identification and other information necessary for operation over the data link. (4) In the NetView program, a record indicating irregularities of operation in physical elements of a network.

event class In the AIX operating system, a number assigned to a group of trace points that relate to a specific subject or system component. The defined event classes are listed in the trace profile.

event control bit (ECB) In the AIX operating system, a bit assigned to each queue to signal the arrival or departure of an element.

event control block (ECB) A control block used to represent the status of an event.

event manager In the NetView Graphic Monitor Facility, the component of the host subsystem that receives alert and resolution major vectors from the NetView program, translates these major vectors into generic event records, and applies the event status to the resource defined in the Resource Object Data Manager (RODM) cache.

event mask In computer graphics, the set of event types that a client requests relative to a window.

event posting The saving of a computer program and data context of a task and establishing the program and data of another task to which control is to be passed, based on an event such as completion of loading of data into main storage. (A)

event queue In computer graphics, a queue that records changes in input devices such as buttons, valuators, and the keyboard. The event queue provides a time-ordered list of input events.

event trace The process of recording the events that occur on the ImagePlus workstation in a file. An event can be the pressing of a function key, the displaying of a document, and so forth. Event trace is an option that can be specified when running the Installation Facility, and is used for problem determination.

event trapping In an IBM personal computer with Advanced BASIC, a feature that allows a program to branch to a specified line when a certain event occurs such as a light pen detection or activation of a function key or joy stick.

evoke In SSP-ICF, to start a program or procedure so that it can communicate with a program.

EWA Erase/Write Alternate.

EW indicator See end-of-work-session indicator.

EX Exception response.

exact end position An entry in output specifications that indicates where the end position of a field or constant is to be placed in the output record. Contrast with relative end position.

exact-name format In the AS/400 system, Advanced Function Printing (AFP) support, a print descriptor naming convention that uses system-specific group names instead of group alias names.

EXCEPT group name In RPG, a name used in the place of indicators to identify a record or group of records written at exception output time.

exception (1) In programming languages, an abnormal situation that may arise during execution, that may cause a deviation from the normal execution sequence, and for which facilities exist in a programming language to define, raise, recognize, ignore, and handle it; for example, (ON-) condition in PL/I, exception in Ada. (I) (2) An abnormal condition such as an I/O error encountered in processing a data set or a file. See overflow exception, underflow exception. (3) Contrast with interrupt, signal.

exception handler A set of routines used to detect deadlock conditions or to process abnormal condition processing. An exception handler allows the normal running of processes to be interrupted and resumed.

exception message In communicating with a logical unit, a message that indicates an unusual condition such as skipping a sequence number. When such a condition is detected, the VTAM application program is notified. VTAM provides sense information that is included in the response sent to the logical unit.

exception request (EXR) In SNA, a request that replaces another message unit in which an error has been detected and that carries sense data identifying the error.

exception response (ER) In SNA, a protocol requested in the form-of-response-requested field of a request header that directs the receiver to return a response only if the request is unacceptable as received or cannot be processed; that is, a negative response, but not a positive response, can be returned. Contrast with definite response, no response.

except operation Deprecated term for exclusion.

excess-three code The binary-coded decimal notation in which a decimal digit "n" is represented by the binary numeral that represents the number (n+3), in the binary numeration system. (T)

exchange A place where telecommunication lines are interconnected with switching equipment. See data switching exchange, private automatic branch exchange, private automatic exchange, private branch exchange, trunk exchange.

exchange buffering A technique using data chaining to avoid moving data in main storage, in which control of buffer segments and user program work areas is passed between data management and the user program.

exchange classes Class 1 (see regional center), class 2 (see sectional center), class 3 (see primary center), class 4 (see toll center), class 5 (see end office).

exchange file A file format for exchanging data on diskette or tape between systems or devices that use those media. See also basic data exchange.

exchange identification (XID) A specific type of basic link unit that is used to convey node and link characteristics between adjacent nodes. XIDs are exchanged between link stations before and during link activation to establish and negotiate link and node characteristics, and after link activation to communicate changes in these characteristics.

exchange identification (XID) frame In a logical link control (LLC) header, the frame that conveys the characteristics of the sending host.

exchange processing In credit card processing, the rules that govern the transmission of information between a sending and a receiving machine. (T) (A)

exchange service A service permitting connection of any two customers' stations.

exchange sort A sort in which succeeding pairs of items in a set are examined; if the items in a pair are out of sequence according to the specified criteria, the positions of the items are exchanged; for example, as in a bubble sort. This process is repeated until all items are sorted. (A)

exchange station I In communications, a data link command or response for recognizing the primary station and a secondary station.

exchange station ID In SDLC, a control field command and response for passing station IDs between the primary station and a secondary station.

exchange text string In word processing, a function that enables a text string to be changed for another text string at one or a number of points throughout the text. (T)

exclude authority In the AS/400 system, an object authority that prevents the user from using the object or its contents. Contrast with all authority.

exclusion (1) The dyadic Boolean operation whose result has the Boolean value 1 if and only if the first operand has the Boolean value 1 and the second has the Boolean value 0. (I) (A) (2) A logic operator having the property that if P is a statement and Q is a statement, then P exclusion Q is true if P is true and Q is false, false if P is false, and false if both statements are true. P exclusion Q is often represented by a combination of AND and NOT symbols, such as $P \sim \wedge Q$. (A) (3) Synonymous with NOT-IF-THEN, NOT-IF-THEN operation. See Figure 57.

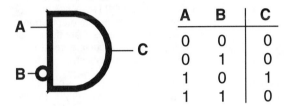

A	B	C
0	0	0
0	1	0
1	0	1
1	1	0

Figure 57. Exclusion

exclusive In MSS, an attribute of a mass storage volume that allows only one processing unit at a time to access the mass storage volume.

exclusive allow-read lock state In the AS/400 system and System/38, the lock on an object that allows only one job to use the object, but allows other jobs to read the object.

exclusive intent In IMS/VS, the type of processing intent defined for an application program to process a database. At scheduling, IMS/VS prevents the application program from being scheduled concurrently with another application program.

exclusive lock In DPPX, an instance of data locking, requested when a program connects to a database, that allows the database to be accessed by the requesting program and makes the database unavailable to other programs as a protection against conflicting access to the database. Contrast with shared lock.

exclusive lock state In the AS/400 system and System/38, the lock on an object that allows only one job to use the object; no other job can use the object.

exclusive mode In IMS/VS, an optional mode of terminal operation in which a terminal may receive no output other than a response to an input. Any output

excluded from being sent is held for transmission until the terminal is removed from exclusive mode.

exclusive-NOR A logic operator having the property that if P is a statement and Q is a statement, then P exclusive-NOR Q is false if either but not both statements are true, and true if both are true or both are false. Contrast with OR.

exclusive-NOR element Synonym for exclusive-NOR gate.

exclusive-NOR gate A logic element that performs the Boolean operation equivalence. (T) Synonymous with exclusive-NOR element. See Figure 58.

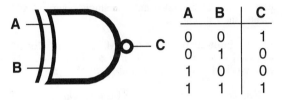

A	B	C
0	0	1
0	1	0
1	0	0
1	1	1

Figure 58. Exclusive-NOR Gate

exclusive-OR (1) A logic operator having the property that if P is a statement and Q is a statement, then P exclusive-OR Q is true if either but not both statements are true, false if both are true or both are false. P exclusive-OR Q is often represented by $P Q$, $P \forall Q$ (A) (2) Contrast with OR.

exclusive-OR element Synonym for exclusive-OR gate.

exclusive-OR gate A logic element that performs the Boolean operation nonequivalence. (T) (A) Synonymous with exclusive-OR element. See Figure 59.

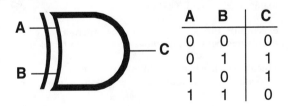

A	B	C
0	0	0
0	1	1
1	0	1
1	1	0

Figure 59. Exclusive-OR Gate

exclusive-OR operation Synonym for nonequivalence operation.

exclusive reference A reference from a segment in storage to an external symbol in a segment; the reference causes overlaying of the calling segment.

exclusive segments Segments in the same region of an overlay program, neither of which is in the path of the other. Exclusive segments cannot be in main storage simultaneously.

EXCP Execute channel program.

EXCP interface In DPPX, a low level of communication support accessed through the EXCP macroinstruction. At this level, the user must manage communication protocols.

exec In the AIX operating system, to overlay the current process with another executable program. See also fork.

EXEC In a VM operating system, a user-written command file that contains CMS commands, other user-written commands, and execution control statements, such as branches.

EXEC built-in function In VM, a special EXEC keyword function that can be invoked to provide specific types of information to a user's EXEC procedure.

EXEC control statement In VM, a special statement that determines what is to be done within an EXEC procedure. It can be used to control logic flow; to communicate with a terminal, a user program, or the VM/SP system; or to create output files via the user's virtual punch.

EXEC procedure In VM, a CMS function that allows users to create new commands by setting up frequently used sequences of CP commands, CMS commands, or both, together with conditional branching facilities, into special procedures to eliminate the repetitious re-keying of those command sequences.

EXEC user-defined variable In VM, a special EXEC keyword variable that can be defined by a user and manipulated in an EXEC procedure.

executable file A file that contains programs or commands that perform operations or actions to be taken.

executable program (1) A program that has been link-edited and therefore can be run in a processor.

(2) The set of machine language instructions that constitute the output from the compilation of a source program. (3) In the AIX operating system, a program that can be run as a self-contained procedure. It consists of a main program and, optionally, one or more subprograms. (4) In FORTRAN, one main program and any number (including zero) of subprograms.

executable segment In the OS/2 operating system, an area of storage that contains processing instructions.

executable statement (1) A statement that specifies one or more actions to be taken by a computer program at execution time, for example, instructions for calculations to be performed, conditions to be tested, flow of control to be altered. (T) (2) In a VM/370 EXEC procedure, any statement processed by the EXEC interpreter: (a) an EXEC control statement or assignment statement, (b) a CMS or CP command line, or (c) a null line. (3) In FORTRAN, an instruction to perform or control one or more computational actions. The executable statements are all those that make up the syntactic class of executable constructs. (4) Contrast with nonexecutable statement.

execute (1) To perform the actions specified by a program or a portion of a program. (T) (2) To carry out an instruction.

execute (EXEC) statement A job control language (JCL) statement that marks the beginning of a job step and identifies the program to be executed or the cataloged or in-stream procedure to be used.

execute phase In a run, the logical subdivision that includes the execution of the target program. (I) (A) Synonymous with executing phase.

executing phase Synonym for execute phase.

execution The process of carrying out an instruction or instructions of a computer program by a computer. (I) (A)

execution element (EE) An element in a central processor that performs all floating-point, fixed-point multiply, fixed-point divide, and convert operations.

execution level In the IBM 8100 Information System, a number ranging from 0 to 7 that designates a relative precedence among interrupt requests so that processing on one level may be suspended temporarily when an interrupt request is generated for a level of higher priority.

execution profile A representation of the absolute or relative execution frequencies or execution times of the instructions of a computer program. (T)

execution sequence In programming languages, the order of execution of statements and parts of statements of a program. (I)

execution time (1) Any instant at which the execution of a particular computer program takes place. (T) (2) The amount of time needed for the execution of a particular computer program. (T) (3) The time during which an instruction in an instruction register is decoded and performed. See also instruction time. (4) Synonymous with run time. (5) Synonym for object time.

execution-time table or array A table or array that is loaded or created in storage after execution of the associated program begins. Contrast with preexecution-time table or array.

executive program Synonym for supervisory program.

executive routine Synonym for supervisory routine.

exerciser In PSS, a set of programs in the terminal that checks the terminal for proper operation.

exhaustion attack In computer security: (1) An attempt to discover plaintext by applying all possible decryption keys to available ciphertext. (2) Encryption of chosen plaintext with a chosen key to discover a value protected by one-way encryption. (3) See also attack.

exit (1) To execute an instruction within a portion of a computer program in order to terminate the execution of that portion. Such portions of computer programs include loops, subroutines, modules, and so on. (T) (2) See installation exit, user exit.

Exit (1) In SAA Advanced Common User Access architecture, an action that ends the active application and removes all windows associated with it. (2) In SAA Basic Common User Access architecture, an action that ends a function or application and removes from the screen all windows associated with that function or application. Contrast with Cancel.

exit program Synonym for exit routine.

exit routine (1) Either of two types of routines: installation exit routines or user exit routines. Synonymous with exit program. See installation exit routine, user exit routine. (2) See accounting exit routine, authorization exit routine, EXLST exit routine, logon-interpret routine, RPL exit routine, virtual route selection exit routine.

exit value In the AIX operating system: (a) A code sent to either standard output or standard error on completion of the command. (b) A numeric value that a command returns to indicate whether it completed successfully. Some commands return exit values that give other information such as whether a file exists. Shell programs can test exit values to control branching and looping.

expand To return compressed data to their original form. (T)

expanded communications buffer A feature of the 3741 device that allows multiple records to be transmitted or received in one block of data.

expanded function operator panel (EFP) In the IBM 8100 Information System, a panel that permits the user to alter, display, and control various areas of the processor and storage.

expanded memory On most computers, additional memory accessed through an adapter or feature card along with a device driver program. On 386 machines, the system memory is the expanded memory, in which case only the device driver program is needed to access the additional memory.

expanded storage On an IBM 3090 processor complex, an extension of processor storage. See also extended storage.

expand escapement To increase escapement by a predetermined unit of escapement. See also line escapement.

expandor A transducer that, for a given amplitude range of input voltages, produces a larger range of output voltages. One important type of expandor employs the information from the envelope of speech signals to expand their volume range. See also compandor, compressor.

expansion board In an IBM personal computer, a panel containing microchips that a user can install in an expansion slot to add memory or special features. Synonymous with expansion card. See bubble board, daughterboard, motherboard, multifunction board. See also hard card, memory expansion option, short card. See Figure 60.

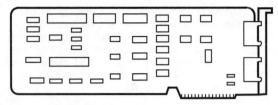

Figure 60. Expansion Board

expansion bus An extension of the Micro Channel bus that has connectors for attaching adapters to the bus.

expansion card Synonym for expansion board.

expansion option See memory expansion option.

expansion slot In personal-computer systems, one of several receptacles in the rear panel of the system unit into which a user can install an adapter.

expansion unit In an IBM personal computer, a unit that can be connected to a system unit to provide additional storage and processing capability.

expect-send sequence In remote communications, a list of characters or signals a program or modem should expect to receive from a remote system, followed by the characters or signals the program or modem should send to the remote system after it receives the expected input. The sequence can also include a subsequence that tells the program or modem what to send if it does not receive the expected input. See also handshaking.

expedited data negotiation In X.25 communications, an optional CCITT-specified facility.

expedited data transfer In X.25 communications, an optional CCITT-specified facility.

expedited data unit In Open Systems Interconnection architecture, a short service data unit whose delivery to a peer entity in the destination open system is ensured before the delivery of any subsequent service data units sent on that connection. (T)

expedited flow In SNA, a data flow designated in the transmission header (TH) that is used to carry network control, session control, and various data flow control request/response units (RUs); the expedited flow is separate from the normal flow, which primarily carries end-user data, and can be used for commands that affect the normal flow. Contrast with normal flow. See also isolated pacing response.

Note: The normal and expedited flows move in both the primary-to-secondary and secondary-to-primary directions. Requests and responses on a given flow, whether normal or expedited, usually are processed sequentially within the path, but the expedited flow traffic may be moved ahead of the normal-flow traffic within the path at queuing points in the half-sessions and for half-session support in boundary functions.

expedited message handling (EMH) In IMS/VS, a Fast Path facility that processes single-segment input and output messages. It bypasses the normal IMS/VS transaction message queuing and application scheduling.

expert system (ES) (1) A system that provides for solving problems in a particular application area by drawing inferences from a knowledge base acquired by human expertise. (T) (2) In artificial intelligence, a system that processes information pertaining to a particular application and performs functions in a manner similar to that of a human who is expert in that field; an expert system can solve problems by drawing inferences from a collection of information that is based on human experience and problems the system has previously encountered. (3) Synonymous with knowledge-based system. See also inference engine, knowledge base, knowledge engineering.

expert system shell Synonym for shell. (T)

expiration check (1) A comparison of a given date with an expiration date; for example, an expiration check for a record or a file. (T) (2) Synonymous with retention period check.

expiration date The date at which a file is no longer protected against automatic deletion by the system.

explanation facility The portion of an expert system that explains how solutions were arrived at and justifies the steps used in reaching them. (T)

explicit address Synonym for absolute address.

explicit command In the NetView program, a direct command used to start an operation or to request information instead of stepping through the panel hierarchy to do so.

explicit declaration (1) A declaration in which the attributes of an identifier are specified. (2) In PL/I, a DECLARE statement that specifies the attributes of a name. (3) Contrast with implicit declaration.

explicit dimensioning In BASIC, the use of a DIM statement to specify the number of elements in an array, the number of dimensions in an array, or the length of a character variable.

explicit literal In IMS/VS message format service, a literal field defined by the user for inclusion in an input or output message. See also default literal, system literal.

explicit partition In the 3270 Information Display System, a partition that has been defined by the create partition structured field and assigned a partition identifier to differentiate it from other partitions. Contrast with implicit partition 0.

explicit partitioned state In the 3270 Information Display System, a device state that has at least one partition explicitly defined using the create partition structured field.

explicit route (ER) In SNA, a series of one or more transmission groups that connect two subarea nodes. An explicit route is identified by an origin subarea address, a destination subarea address, an explicit route number, and a reverse explicit route number. Contrast with virtual route (VR).

explicit route length In SNA, the number of transmission groups in an explicit route.

explicit scope terminator In COBOL, a reserved word that terminates the scope of a particular Procedure Division statement. Contrast with implicit scope terminator.

explicit selection (1) In SAA Advanced Common User Access architecture, a selection technique whereby a user moves the cursor to a choice and presses the Spacebar to select that choice. See also implicit selection. (2) In SAA Basic Common User Access architecture, a selection technique whereby a user moves the cursor to a choice and types a selection character to select that choice. See also implicit selection.

exploitable channel In computer security, a channel that is usable or detectable by subjects external to the trusted computing base.

explosion proof Pertaining to equipment that will neither explode nor cause explosion. (T)

exponent (1) In a floating-point representation, the numeral that denotes the power to which the implicit floating-point base is raised before being multiplied by the mantissa to determine the real number represented. (T) (2) A number, indicating the power to which another number (the base) is to be raised. (3) In floating-point format, an integer constant specifying the power of ten by which the base of the decimal floating-point number is to be multiplied. (4) In inventory control, a sales forecasting technique that uses a weighted moving average; the heaviest weight is given to the most recent data, and older data are geometrically discounted according to age. See also moving average, weighted moving average.

exponentiation The operation in which a value is raised to a power.

exponent (of an E-format number) In BASIC, an integer constant specifying the power of ten by which the base of the decimal floating-point number is to be multiplied.

export (1) To copy data onto removable media. (2) In the AIX operating system, to provide the operations defined by an interface. A server exports an interface to a client. (3) Contrast with import. See also import/export.

exported form In AS/400 query management, the source file member that results from running an EXPORT FORM command.

exported query In AS/400 query management, the source file member that results from running an EXPORT QUERY command.

export/import See import/export.

exposing In a document copying machine, the action of submitting any sensitized material to radiation, normal light, or heat that will act on it to form an image or latent image. (T)

exposure (1) The product of the value assigned to the possible consequence of a riskbearing situation times the probability of its occurrence. This product is usually expressed in monetary terms. (T) (2) In computer security, an instance of vulnerability in which losses may result from the occurrence of one or more attacks. See also compromise, countermeasure.

exposure area In a document copying machine, the part of the machine in which the copy material is exposed to receive an image of the original. (T)

exposure control On a document copying machine, a control for regulating the amount of radiation applied to the sensitized material in order to lighten or darken the image. (T)

exposure event In AIX Enhanced X-Windows, an event sent to clients to inform them when contents have been lost, as when windows are obscured or reconfigured. Servers do not guarantee the preservation of window contents when they are obscured or reconfigured.

expressed folio A page numbering style in which each page, possibly excluding the first page, is numbered. See blind folio, dropped folio.

expression (1) In programming languages, a language construct for computing a value from one or more operands; for example, literals, identifiers, array references, and function calls. (I) (2) A configuration of signs. (A) (3) A group of constants or variables separated by operators that yields a single value. An expression can be arithmetic, relational, logical, or a character string. (4) A representation of a value; for example, variables and constants that appear alone or in combination with operators. See assignment expression, character expression, conditional expression, constant expression, guard expression, integer expression, primary expression, unary expression. (5) In DDS, a pair of values that represents a single parameter value. (6) In PL/I and Pascal, a variable or constant, specified alone or in a combination with arithmetic or comparison operators, that supplies a single value to the program after it is calculated. (7) In SQL, a variable or constant specified alone or in combination with functions and either arithmetic operators or concatenation operators that supply a single value, after being calculated, to the program. (8) In COBOL, an arithmetic expression or a conditional expression. (9) In FORTRAN, a construct formed from operands, operators and parentheses that may be a variable, a constant, a function reference, or that may represent a computation. (10) See absolute expression, arithmetic expression, character expression, complex relocatable expression, relocatable expression.

expression statement In the XL C compiler, an expression that ends with a semicolon (;). An expression statement can be used to assign the value of an expression to a variable or to call a function.

EXR Exception request.

EXT (1) Exterior. (2) External trace file.

extendable action entry field In SAA Basic Common User Access architecture, an entry field in an action list that allows a user to type beyond the visible end of the field. Any subsequent text on the same line as the extendable action entry field is typed over.

extendable disk file A file whose size can be increased whenever more space is needed.

extended address Synonym for address extension.

extended addressing A direct-addressing mode that can access any area in storage.

extended architecture An extension to System/370 architecture that takes advantage of continuing high performance enhancements to computer system hardware. See also computer architecture.

extended area In the 8100/DPCX system, the area of processor storage that contains resident program storage and the associative storage pool.

extended area service A telephone exchange service without toll charges that extends over an area where there is a community of interest in return for a somewhat higher exchange service rate.

extended attribute Additional information, such as comments, history, or author's name, that a system or program associates with a file. The system or program then uses this information to recognize the file.

extended attribute buffer The buffer in which the extended field attribute for the 3270 kanji display field is stored.

extended bind A bind request that includes the Fully Qualified Procedure Correlation Identifier (FQPCID) control vector.

extended border node A border node that interconnects (a) APPN networks having different network identifiers or (b) separate partitions of the same APPN network, where the partitioning is to allow isolated topology subnetworks (or clusters). An extended border node supports intermediate network routing, allowing it to support LU-LU sessions that do not terminate in its native network. Contrast with peripheral border node.

extended character A character other than a 7-bit ASCII character. An extended character can be a 1-byte code point with the eighth bit set (ordinal 128 through 255). See also code page, code point.

extended character file In System/36, an area on disk that contains the extended ideographic character set.

extended character processing In the OS/400 operating system, a function that is required to make characters stored in a double-byte character set (DBCS) font file available to a DBCS device. Basic characters, which are stored in the device, do not require extended character processing. Extended characters, which are stored in a DBCS font table, require extended character processing before they can be displayed or printed. See also basic characters and extended characters.

extended characters In the OS/400 operating system, double-byte characters that are stored in a DBCS font file, not in a DBCS device. When displaying or printing extended characters, the device receives them from the DBCS font table under control of the extended character processing function of the operating system. Contrast with basic characters. See also extended character processing.

Extended Character Set Adapter (ECSA) In the 3270 Information Display System, the storage that provides additional control and buffering for the extended character set in the APL/TEXT feature and for the field and character attributes for extended color, programmed symbols, and extended highlighting.

extended checkpoint/restart In IMS/VS, a facility that allows batch processing programs to establish database positioning and initiate user-specified areas with a DL/I call in place of an OS CHKPT macroinstruction.

extended color In the 3270 Information Display System: (a) The capability to have color terminals display or print fields or characters in colors by using extended field and character attributes, (b) An extended attribute type, (c) An attribute passed between session partners in the Start Field Extended, Modify Field, and Set Attributes orders.

extended color attributes For devices used in extended color mode, attributes defining the colors blue, red, green, pink (or magenta), turquoise (or cyan), yellow, and white (or neutral).

extended common object file format (XCOFF) The object file format for AIX operating system, Version 3. XCOFF combines the standard common object file format (COFF) with the IBM TOC module format concept, which provides for dynamic linking and replacement of units within an object file.

extended control (EC) mode A mode in which all features of a System/370 computing system, including dynamic address translation, are operational. See also basic control (BC) mode.

extended control program support (ECPS:VSE) In VSE, an implementation of the virtual storage concept that does not require software participation in the translation of virtual addresses into real addresses.

extended count-key-data device A disk storage device that has a data transfer rate faster than some processors can utilize and that is connected to the processor through use of a speed matching buffer. A specialized channel program is needed to communicate with such a device. See count-key-data (CKD) device.

extended curses In the AIX operating system, the system library that contains the control functions for writing data to and getting data from the terminal screen. It supports color, multiple windows, and an enhanced character set.

extended DOS partition In the OS/2 operating system, an additional area on a hard disk that DOS uses for storing information.

extended field attribute (EFA) (1) An extended characteristic of a 3270 kanji display field. The extended field attributes of a display field include kanji or EBCDIC. (2) An attribute that defines physical representation characteristics in addition to those defined by the field attributes. (3) A code in the 3270 data stream that defines properties of a field in addition to those defined by the field attribute.

Note: An extended field attribute defines properties such as extended color, character set, extended highlighting, and field validation.

extended floating-point numbers Floating point operand fractions extended for greater precision.

extended font A font in which the characters are wider than its corresponding normal font.

extended fonts In the OS/2 operating system, a character set containing characters that are not included in the Presentation Manager character set.

extended function In a PSS application IBM licensed program, an IBM function other than a basic application function that may be selected by a user to tailor the system to the user's needs. See also fixed function.

extended graphic character set (EGCS) (1) A graphic character set, such as a kanji character set, that requires two bytes to identify each graphic character. (2) In SDF/CICS, a programmed symbol set supported exclusively by the IBM 3278 Model 52 and IBM 3283 Model 52 devices, in which two character positions are combined to represent one graphic symbol. Synonymous with kanji character set.

extended group coded recording (E/GCR) In MSS, the technique used to encode data on a data cartridge. This technique includes error-correction code.

extended help In SAA Common User Access architecture, a help action that provides information about the contents of the application window from which a user requested help. Contrast with contextual help.

extended ideographic character set An ideographic character set, residing in auxiliary storage, that contains 3483 IBM-supplied ideographic characters and up to 4370 user-defined ideographic characters. Contrast with basic ideographic character set. See also ideographic character set.

extended interface (1) In OS/400 query management, the set of language-specific interfaces that allows commands requiring access to program variables to run. The extended interface includes:

Communications area

Command length
Command string
Number of keywords or variables
Array of keyword or variable name lengths
Array of keyword or variable names
Array of keyword or variable value lengths
Array of keyword or variable values
Value type

(2) In the AIX operating system, a set of full function system calls used to communicate with SNA services. These calls contain an extra parameter that points to a structure containing extra function requests. See interface, limited interface.

extended lock mode In ACF/TCAM, a type of lock mode in which an external logical unit (LU) remains in lock mode for the duration of several inquiry/reply cycles. Contrast with message lock mode. See also line lock, lock mode, station lock.

extended MCS console In MVS, a console other than a multiple console support (MCS) console from which operators or programs can issue MVS commands and receive messages. An extended MCS console is defined through an OPERPARM segment.

extended memory In the OS/2 operating system, memory greater than 1MB.

extended mnemonic An operation code that is an extension to an instruction.

extended network A network that includes two or more TCAM systems using extended networking facilities.

extended network addressing The network addressing system that splits the address into an 8-bit subarea and a 15-bit element portion. The subarea portion of the address is used to address host processors or communication controllers. The element portion is used to permit processors or controllers to address resources.

extended networking A TCAM function that uses a collection of TCAM macroinstructions, system service programs, and message-handler facilities to simplify TCAM system definition, management, and error recovery in a network with two or more TCAM systems.

extended operator command In ACF/TCAM, an operator command directed to the extended operator control system service program. Synonymous with extended operator control command.

extended operator control The function of a particular system service program that processes a set of extended operator commands. These commands are not required in order to control a TCAM system, but are useful in some environments. The extended operator control system service program is required if the message control program (MCP) uses one or more of the following functions: (a) extended networking, (b) online retrieval system service program, or (c) automatic purge/copy/redirect.

extended operator control command Synonym for extended operator command.

extended operator control SSP In ACF/TCAM, a system service program that supports a set of extended operator commands that are not required to control a network with ACF/TCAM, but are useful in some network environments. The extended operator control SSP is required if the extended networking capability, online retrieval SSP, or automatic purge/copy/redirect capability is used by the message control program.

extended operator control station (1) A system console, external logical unit (LU), or application program that is authorized to enter extended operator commands. (2) See also basic operator control station, extended primary operator control station, extended secondary operator control station.

extended parameter list In OS/400 query management, the arguments of the extended interface that are not defined on the short interface.

extended permission In the AIX operating system, an access mode that modifies the base permissions to a file for specified individuals or groups. An extended permission can deny or permit an access mode. See access permission, base permission.

extended-precision floating point A feature that permits floating point operand fractions to be 112 bits long in order to achieve greater precision than is possible with short or long floating-point arithmetic.

extended price The total price of a group of items; for example, a group composed of three items priced at $0.21 each have the extended price of $0.63 (tax not included).

extended primary operator control station In ACF/TCAM, an extended operator control station that receives the extended operator control startup and closedown messages; responses to extended operator commands entered from it; responses to extended operator that successfully modify the network; and, optionally, the online retrieval system service program startup and closedown messages (if the online retrieval SSP is part of the network). See also extended secondary operator control station.

extended recovery facility (XRF) A facility that minimizes the effect of failures in MVS, VTAM, the host processor, or high availability applications during sessions between high availability applications and designated terminals. This facility provides an alternate subsystem to take over sessions from the failing subsystem.

extended response byte In the network control program, the portion of the basic transmission unit (BTU) containing line status at I/O completion.

extended response field In the network control program, the portion of the basic transmission unit containing line status information at I/O completion.

extended result output On a calculator, the facility for displaying or printing the result of a calculation in successive operations where the number of digits in the result exceeds the output capacity of the machine to the right of the decimal marker. (T)

extended route In an ACF/TCAM extended network, a series of one or more routes that involves an intermediate TCAM node. See also alternate extended route, parallel extended routes, primary extended route, route.

extended secondary operator control station In ACF/TCAM, an extended operator control station that enters extended operator commands and receives responses to the commands.

extended selection In SAA Advanced Common User Access architecture, a selection technique that allows a user to select one or more choices. See also single selection.

extended services In the AIX operating system, a group of optionally installed operating system functions and programs.

extended specify task abnormal exit (ESTAE) An MVS macroinstruction that provides recovery capability and gives control to the user-specified exit routine for processing, diagnosing an abend, or specifying a retry address. See also STAE.

extended storage (1) In VM/SP HPO, storage above the 16 megabyte line. (2) On 3090 processor complexes with MVS/XA System Product 2.1.3 and later, a high-speed, high volume, electronic extension of real storage that is accessed synchronously in 4K byte increments. See also expanded storage.

extended subarea addressing A network addressing system that is used in a network with more than 255 subareas.

extended symbol processing In the Document Composition Facility, processing a symbol whose value

causes the rest of the line to be stacked and later processed as a new input line.

extended system contents directory (ESCD) In IMS/VS, an extension for Fast Path.

extended time scale (1) The time scale used in data processing when the time scale factor is greater than one. (A) Synonymous with slow time scale. (2) Contrast with fast time scale.

extender card See expansion board.

extend mode In COBOL: (1) A method of adding records to the end of a sequential file when the file is opened. (2) In COBOL, the state of a file after execution of an OPEN statement, with the EXTEND phrase specified, for that file and before the execution of a CLOSE statement without the REEL or UNIT phrase for that file.

extensible language A programming language that permits the user to define new elements such as data types, new operators, types of statements, or control structures in terms of existing elements of the language; for example, ALGOL68. (T)

extension (1) Additional equipment on the same line and on the same premises, but at a location other than the main station. (2) Each telephone served by a private branch exchange. (3) In the AIX Enhanced X-Windows programs, to extend the system, the named extensions can be defined for the Core protocol, including extensions to output requests, resources, and event types.

extension and line counter specifications In RPG, a coding form on which the programmer provides information about record address files, arrays, tables, and their associated files, and the number of lines to be printed on the printer forms.

extension character See code extension character.

extension hunting Calling a group of extensions using one directory number.

extension station An extra telephone set associated with a main telephone station by means of an extension on the same subscriber line and having the same call number designation as the associated main station. See also main station.

extent (1) Continuous space on a disk or diskette that is occupied by or reserved for a particular data set, data space, or file. (2) In DPCX, one of two parts of a relative data set that does not have to be stored contiguously with the other extent, but must contain contiguously stored records. (3) In PL/I, the number of integers between and including the lower and upper bounds of an array. (4) In FORTRAN, the size of one dimension of an array. (5) See also primary space allocation, secondary space allocation.

exterior (EXT) In video or film production, a scene or shot located outdoors or in a studio set up to resemble an outdoor location.

exterior gateway In the AIX operating system, a gateway on one autonomous system that communicates with another autonomous system. Contrast with interior gateway. See also access gateway, neighbor gateway, passive gateway.

external In programming languages, pertaining to a language object that has a scope that extends beyond one module; for example, the entry names of a module. (I)

external call A call involving a public exchange or tie line.

external clocking In data communication, the ability of a modem to provide data clocking. Contrast with internal clocking.

external communication adapter (XCA) A communication adapter that is part of a device (such as the IBM 3172 Interconnect Controller) other than the host processor. Contrast with integrated communication adapter.

external data In COBOL, the data described in a program as external data items. Contrast with internal data.

external data definition A description of a variable appearing outside a function. It causes the system to allocate storage for that variable and makes that variable accessible to all functions that follow the definition and are located in the same file as the definition.

external data item In COBOL, a data item that is described as part of an external record in one or more programs of a run unit and which itself may be referenced from any program in which it is described. Contrast with internal data item.

external data record In COBOL, a logical record that is described in one or more programs of a run unit and whose constituent data items may be referenced from any program in which they are described.

external decimal item See zoned decimal item.

external delay Time lost due to circumstances beyond the control of the operator or maintenance engineer;

for example, failure of an external power source. (A)

external domain In VTAM, the part of the network controlled by a system services control point (SSCP) other than the SSCP that controls that part.

external event In a conceptual schema language, an event that occurs in the environment or in the universe of discourse. Contrast with internal event. (A)

external file connector In COBOL, a file connector that is accessible to one or more object programs in a run unit. Contrast with internal file connector.

external function A function supplied by the compiler when the function is referred to by name in a program. Contrast with intrinsic function.

external indicators Indicators that can be set by another program before a program is run or can be changed while a program is running.

external interruption An interruption caused by a signal from the interruption key on the system console panel, from the timer, or from another computing system.

externalized form In AS/400 query management, the name of the file resulting from running an EXPORT command against a form.

externalized query In AS/400 query management, the name of the form resulting from running an EXPORT command against a query.

external label (1) A label, usually not machine-readable, attached to a data medium container; for example, a paper sticker attached to the outside of a magnetic tape reel. (T) (A) (2) Contrast with internal label. information visible at the outer interfaces of an information system. (A)

external level In a database, all aspects dealing with the user-oriented representation of information visible at the outer interfaces of an information processing system. (T) Contrast with internal level.

external library member Output of the 3800 Print Management Facility that can be used by other program products while running print jobs; for example, coded fonts, code pages, font character sets, form definitions, page definitions, and page segments. Synonym for resource object.

external line A trunk or tie line.

external loss time Down time due to a fault outside the functional unit. Synonymous with environmental loss time. (T)

external LU A logical unit (LU) that communicates with a TCAM message control program (MCP) through VTAM. Each external LU is defined to the MCP with a TERMINAL macroinstruction.

externally described data In System/38, data contained in fields that are described to the Control Program Facility in data description specifications when the file is created. The field descriptions can be used by the program when the file is processed. Contrast with program-described data.

externally described file In the AS/400 system and System/38, a file in which the records and fields are described to the system when the file is created, and used by the program when the file is processed. Contrast with program-described file.

external merge A sorting technique that reduces sequences of records or keys to one sequence, usually after one or more internal sorts.

external message queue In the AS/400 system and System/38, the part of the job message queue that sends messages between an interactive job and the workstation user. For batch jobs, messages sent to the external message queue appear only in the job log.

external model In a database, a collection of entities and their relationships representing a specific application or a type of application in an enterprise or organization. (T)

external modem Synonym for stand-alone modem. Contrast with integrated modem. See Figure 61.

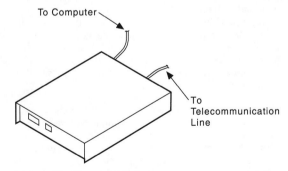

Figure 61. External Modem

external name (1) A name that can be referred to by any control section or separately assembled or compiled module; that is, a control section name or an entry name in another module. (2) In a program, a name whose scope is not necessarily confined to one block and its contained blocks.

external number A number by which a party is called through an external line.

external numbering plan A numbering system for tie lines and trunks.

external number repetition A facility that enables a caller or an operator to store an external number in order to call it later by dialing only two digits.

external object (1) In the AS/400 system, an object that has a defined object type, such as *FILE or *PGM. In general, external objects can be displayed by a user. See also object. Contrast with internal object. (2) Synonym for resource object.

external page address An address that identifies the location of a page in a page data set.

Note: In OS/VS1 and VSE, this address is computed from the page number each time a page is to be transferred between real storage and auxiliary storage. In OS/VS2, the address consists of a relative device number, relative group number, and relative slot number. In VM/370, the address consists of a cylinder number, device number, and page number.

external page storage In System/370 virtual storage systems, the portion of auxiliary storage used to contain pages.

external page storage management In VM/370, the routines in the paging supervisor that control transfer of pages between real storage and external page storage.

external page table (XPT) In OS/VS2 and VM/370, an extension of a page table that identifies the location in external page storage of each page in the table.

external procedure (1) A procedure that is not contained in a block. Contrast with internal procedure. (2) In FORTRAN, a nonintrinsic procedure that is defined by an external program unit. Contrast with internal procedure (3) In the AIX operating system, synonym for external routine.

external program parameter In a computer program, a parameter that must be bound during the calling of the computer program. (I) (A)

external reference (EXTRN) (1) A reference to a symbol defined as an external name in another program or module. (2) See also weak external reference.

external routine (1) In Pascal, a procedure or function that may be called from outside the program in which the routine is defined. (2) In REXX, a program external to the user's program, language processor, or both. These routines can be written in any language, including REXX that supports the system-dependent interfaces used by REXX to start it. (3) In the AIX operating system, a procedure or function called from outside the program in which the routine is defined. Synonymous with external procedure.

external schema (1) A database subschema that pertains to the scope of a particular user's view of the database. (T) (2) In a database, a conceptual schema that has been modified to logically describe an enterprise.

external sort (1) A sort requiring use of auxiliary storage because the set of items to be sorted cannot be held in available internal storage at one time. (A) (2) A sort program, or a sort phase of a multipass sort, that merges strings of items, using auxiliary storage, until one string is formed. (A) (3) When building an alternate index, the sorting of alternate keys into ascending sequence by using work files. (4) See also internal sort.

external storage (1) Storage that is accessible to a processor only through input-output channels. An external storage may sometimes be considered as peripheral equipment. Synonymous with auxiliary storage. (T) (2) See also external page storage.

external switch In COBOL, a hardware or software device, defined and named by the implementor, that is used to indicate that one or more of two alternate states exist.

external symbol (1) A control section name, entry point name, or external reference that is defined or referred to in a particular module. (2) A symbol in the external symbol dictionary. (3) A symbol that is defined in a file other than the file in which the symbol occurs. (4) An ordinary symbol that represents an external reference. (5) In the C, FORTRAN, and Pascal languages, an entry-point name or external variable that is defined or referred to in a particular module or program. (6) Control information associated with an object or load module that identifies the external symbols in the module. (7) See also entry symbol.

external variable (1) A variable accessible to another compilation unit. See also compilation unit. (2) In Pascal, a variable that is outside the lexical scope of the function, procedure, or program that is calling it.

external writer (1) An MVS routine that directs system output to unsupported devices, such as unit record printers and punches, magnetic tape devices, DASD, and plotters.

Note: External writers must be started by the operator when required. Once started, an external writer requests output data sets from the JES3 output service via the subsystem interface. (2) In OS/VS2, a program that supports the ability to write SYSOUT data in ways and to devices not supported by the job entry subsystem.

external program unit In FORTRAN, a program unit that is not contained within another program unit. Contrast with internal program unit.

extract (1) To select and remove from a group of items those items that meet a specific criteria. (T) (2) To separate specific parts of a word from the whole word. (3) To remove specific items from a file. (4) To obtain; for example, information from a file.

extract instruction An instruction that requests formation of a new expression from selected parts of given expressions. (A)

extralingual character In PL/I, any EBCDIC code that is not an alphabetic character, a special character, or a number.

extrapartition destination In CICS, a queue residing on any sequential device that is accessible by programs outside (or within) the CICS region. Logging data, statistics, and transaction error messages are examples of data that can be written to extrapartition destinations. Contrast with intrapartition destination.

extrapartition transient data The CICS support for standard sequential data sets. It is the least efficient of sequential support because CICS issues some operating system waits in processing these data sets. In addition, extrapartition transient data sets are not recoverable.

extra-pulse An inadmissible additional pulse that occurs during recording or reading.

extreme close-up In multimedia applications, a shot obtained when the camera is positioned to show only the face or a single feature of the subject; in the case of an object, the camera is close enough to reveal an individual part of the object clearly. See also close-up.

extreme long shot In video and film production, a camera angle in which the subject is viewed as if from a long distance.

extrinsic semiconductor A semiconductor to which either acceptor impurities or donor impurities have been added so that when it is energized it generates a predominance of either free electrons or holes. Contrast with intrinsic semiconductor. See also doping,

NMOS, n-type semiconductor, PMOS, p-type semiconductor.

EXTRN External reference.

extrusion In computer graphics, the process of creating a three-dimensional shape by stretching a two-dimensional shape along a third axis.

eye coordinates In AIX graphics, the coordinate system in which the viewer's "eye" is located at the origin, and thus all distances are measured with respect to the eye. Viewing transformations map from world coordinates into eye coordinates, and projection transformations map from eye coordinates to normalized device coordinates. Synonymous with eye space, viewer coordinates, viewing coordinates. See also modeling coordinates, primitive coordinates, screen coordinates, transformation, world coordinates.

eye space Synonym for eye coordinates.

EZVU II Runtime Facility An IBM program used to install and configure the ImagePlus Workstation Program/DOS.

F

F (1) Fahrenheit. (2) Farad.

fabric ribbon On a typewriter, a ribbon of woven material; for example, cotton, natural silk, synthetic yarn. (T)

FAC (1) Function authority credential. (2) Features for attaching communications.

face change character Synonym for font change character.

faceplate A wall-mounted or floor-mounted plate for connecting data and voice connectors to a cabling system.

facilities See optional facilities.

facilities extension In the X.25 application program interface (API), an extension to the optional facilities field in a packet that allows further, non-CCITT-specified, optional facility information to be added.

facility (1) An operational capability, or the means for providing such a capability. (T) (2) In Open Systems Interconnection architecture, a part of a service provided by specific layer. (T) (3) A service provided by an operating system for a particular purpose; for example, the checkpoint/restart facility. (4) A measure of how easy it is to use a data processing system. See also system performance. (5) See also telecommunication facility.

facsimile Synonym for FAX.

facsimile (FAX) system A system for transmission of images. The image is scanned at the transmitter, reconstructed at the receiving station, and duplicated on paper.

facsimile machine A functional unit that converts images to signals for transmission over a telephone system or that converts received signals back to images. (T) Synonymous with FAX machine, telecopier.

facsimile-signal level An expression of the maximum signal power or voltage created by scanning the subject copy as measured at any point in a facsimile system. According to whether the system employs positive or negative modulation, this will correspond to picture white or black respectively. The level may be expressed in decibels with respect to some standard value, such as 1 milliwatt or 1 volt.

factor (1) In a multiplication operation, any of the numbers or quantities that are the operands. (I) (A) (2) A dimensionless scalar value used to form a product with another value. Factors can also be expressed as percentages. (3) In RPG, an entry; for example, a field name, file name, literal, or data structure that identifies the data to be used in an operation. (4) An entry such as a field name, literal, or data structure used in an operation. (5) See equivalent-binary-digit factor, multiplier factor, relocation factor, scale factor, time scale factor.

factorial The product of the positive integers 1, 2, 3, up to and including a given integer. (I) (A)

factorial function In a calculator, the function that computes factorials. (T) (A)

factor total On a calculator, the facility for accumulating factors. (T)

fade (1) In multimedia applications, to change the strength or loudness of a video or audio signal, as in "fade up" or "fade down." (2) A tool in LinkWay Paint that operates only in MCGA 256 mode and automatically creates a color range in an area of the screen, from light to dark, or from one color value to another. A fade range is 16 colors in one row of the LinkWay palette.

fail safe A design property of a functional unit which prevents its failures from resulting in critical faults. (T)

failsafe In computer security, pertaining to avoidance of compromise in the event of failure.

failsafe operation The operation of a computer system so that in case of failure of a component the probability of loss or damage of equipment and harm to personnel is kept low. (T)

failsoft Pertaining to a computer system that continues to function because of its resilience. (T)

failure (1) The termination of the ability of a functional unit to perform its required function. (I) (A) Synonymous with malfunction. (2) Contrast with error, fault, mistake. (3) See mean time between failures.

failure access In computer security, an unauthorized and usually inadvertent access to data resulting from a hardware or software failure in an information system.

failure control In computer security, the methodology used to detect and provide failsafe or failsoft recovery from hardware or software failures in an information system.

failure rate The limit, if it exists, of the ratio of the conditional probability that the instant of time, T, of a failure of a functional unit falls within a given time interval, $(t, t + t)$, and the length of this interval, t, when t tends to zero, given that the functional unit is in an up state at the beginning of the time interval.

Note: In this definition T may also denote the time to failure or the time to first failure, as the case may be. (T)

fallback In an IBM 3745 Communication Controller with twin central control units (CCUs) in standby or backup mode, the process by which buses are switched from the failing CCU to the active CCU (backup mode) or the idle CCU (standby mode) to recover the path of communication flow in the failed CCU. See also switchback.

false add To form a partial sum; that is, to add without carries. (A)

false retrievals Library references that are not pertinent to, but are vaguely related to, the subject of a library search and are sometimes obtained by automatic search methods.

family-of-part programming A method of creating new parts on a CAD/CAM system by slight changes in the design of existing parts, or uses identical parts, subassemblies or structures designed earlier. (T)

fanfold paper Continuous forms previously folded as a fan and usually fed by means of feed holes on each side. Synonymous with zig-zag fold paper, z-fold paper. (T) (A)

fanout (1) A feature that allows several data terminal equipments (DTEs) to share the same modem. Only one DTE can transmit at a time. (2) A single output that becomes input to multiple branches. (3) In communications, the process of creating copies of a distribution to be delivered locally or to be sent through the network.

far-end crosstalk Crosstalk that travels along the disturbed circuit in the same direction as the signals in that circuit. To determine the far-end crosstalk between two pairs, 1 and 2, signals are transmitted on pair 1 at station A, and the crosstalk level is measured on pair 2 at station B.

fast copy data set program See VSE/FCOPY.

fast forward control On dictation equipment, a device to provide rapid forward movement of the recording medium or of the recording head, playback head, or combined head. (I)

Fast Fourier Transform (FFT) See Fourier Transforms.

fast path (1) In SAA Basic Common User Access architecture, a method of doing something more directly and quickly that the usual way; for example, pressing a function key is a faster path than typing a command. (2) In IMS/VS, functions for applications that require good response characteristics and that may have large transaction volumes. Programs have rapid access to main-storage databases to the field level and to direct-access data entry databases. Message processing is grouped for load-balancing and synchronized for database integrity and recovery. (3) See also data entry database, load-balancing group, main storage database.

Fast Path dependent region See IMS/VS Fast Path region.

Fast Path exclusive transaction In IMS/VS, a transaction type whose messages are routed to expedited message handling for processing. See also Fast Path potential transaction.

Fast Path potential transaction In IMS/VS, a transaction type that can be routed to either expedited message handling or data communication monitor processing. See also Fast Path exclusive transaction.

fast return control Synonym for fast rewind control.

fast rewind control On dictation equipment, a device used to reverse rapidly the normal forward direction of the recording medium or of the recording head, playback head, or combined head. (I) Synonymous with fast return control.

FASTRUN One of several options available with the NCP/EP definition facility (NDF) that indicates that only the syntax is to be checked in generation definition statements.

fast select (1) An option of a virtual call facility that allows inclusion of data in call-setup and call-clearing packets. (I) (2) In X.25 communications, an optional facility that allows inclusion of data in call-request and clear-request packets.

fast time scale (1) The time scale used in data processing when the time scale factor is less than one. (A) (2) Contrast with extended time scale.

fast turnaround (FTA) An SDLC control bit that reduces the time required to change a station from transmit mode to receive mode.

FAT File allocation table.

fatal error An error that causes further execution to be meaningless. (T)

fatbits In computer graphics, the technique of magnifying individual pixels to allow easy editing of images, one pixel at a time. See also zoom.

fat link Deprecated term for multilink transmission group.

fault (1) An accidental condition that causes a functional unit to fail to perform its required function. (I) (A) (2) Contrast with error, failure, mistake. (3) See data sensitive fault, page fault, pattern sensitive fault, program sensitive fault. (4) See also fault-rate threshold, fault threshold, fault trace.

fault domain In IBM Token-Ring Network problem determination, the portion of a ring that is involved with an indicated error.

fault isolation analysis routine (FIAR) Structured sets of routines and diagnostic tests that dynamically control their own execution, based on available error data and the state of related portions of the processor complex.

fault locator In the IBM 3881 Optical Mark Reader, a diagnostic program that the microprocessing unit uses to isolate machine failures to a field replaceable unit.

fault-rate threshold A fault threshold expressed in terms of the number of faults in a prescribed period of time. (T)

fault threshold A prescribed limit to the number of faults in a specified category which, if exceeded, requires a remedial action. (T)

Note: The remedial action may include notifying the operators, running diagnostic programs, or reconfiguring to exclude a faulty unit.

fault tolerance (1) The ability of a computer system to continue to operate correctly even though one or more of its component parts are malfunctioning. (T) (2) Synonymous with resilience.

Note: The speed of performance, the throughput, or both, of the computer system may be diminished until the faults are corrected.

fault trace A record of faults, obtained by a monitor, reflecting the sequence of states that immediately preceded the occurrence of the faults. (T)

favored execution option In VM, a virtual machine performance option that allows an installation to allocate more of its resource to a given virtual machine than would normally be the case.

fax (1) Hard copy received from a facsimile machine. (T) Synonymous with telecopy. (2) To transmit an image, using a telephone system and facsimile machines. (T)

FAX The use of a telephone system for the electronic transmission and receipt of hard copy images. (T) Synonymous with facsimile, telefax.

fax adapter Synonym for fax board.

fax board An integrated circuit board in a workstation, used to transmit or receive images over a telephone system. (T) Synonymous with fax adapter.

FAX machine Synonym for facsimile machine.

FBA Fixed-block-architecture.

FBA disk drive Contrast with CKD disk drive.

FC A font change character. (A)

FCB (1) Forms control buffer. (2) File control block.

FCC Federal Communications Commission.

FCFC First-character forms control.

FCFS First-come-first-served.

FCOPY See VSE/FCOPY.

FCS (1) Frame check sequence. (2) Frame checking sequence. (3) Function control sequence.

FCT Forms control table.

FD Full duplex. See duplex.

FDC Frame-dependent control mode.

FDDI Fiber Distributed Data Interface.

FD entry File description entry.

FDM Frequency-division multiplexing.

FDP Field-developed program.

FDX Full duplex. See duplex.

FE (1) A format effector character. (A)   (2) Field engineering.

FEALDs Field engineering automated logic diagrams.

feasibility study A study to identify and analyze a problem and its potential solutions in order to determine their viability, costs, and benefits. (T)

feature A part of an IBM product that may be ordered separately by the customer. A feature is designated as either special or specify and may be designated also as diskette-only. See also deprecated feature, diskette-only feature, special feature, specify feature.

feature code A code used by IBM to process hardware and software orders.

features for attaching communications A type of communication capability that is available on the 8100 Information System. Each type of communication capability, including directly attached loops, is identified by a two-digit FAC number.

Federal Communications Commission (FCC) A board of commissioners appointed by the President under the Communications Act of 1934, having the power to regulate all interstate and foreign communications by wire and radio originating in the United States.

feedback The return of part of the output of a machine, process, or system as input to the computer, especially for self-correcting or control purposes.

feedback information In VTAM, information placed in certain RPL fields when an RPL-based macroinstruction is completed.

feedback loop The components and processes involved in correcting or controlling a system by using part of the output as input. (A)

feedback system See information feedback system.

feedboard Synonym for paper platform.

feedboard raising and lowering control In a duplicator, a device for controlling the mechanism that raises and lowers the feedboard. (T)

feed control In a duplicator, a control for starting and stopping the feed mechanism of the machine. (T)

feeder See automatic document feeder, friction feeder, suction feeder.

feeder cable The principal cable from a central office.

feed hole (1) A hole punched in a data medium to enable it to be positioned. (I) (A) (2) A hole that is punched in a data carrier to enable it to be positioned. (3) Synonymous with sprocket hole.

feed-past document copying machine A document copying machine in which the original, essentially a single sheet, is transported externally to the machine past an exposing source. (T) Contrast with feed-through document copying machine.

feed pitch The distance between corresponding points of adjacent feed holes along the feed track. (T) (A)

feed punch See automatic-feed punch.

feed-through document copying machine A document copying machine in which the original, essentially a single sheet, is transported within the machine past an exposing source. (T) Contrast with feed-past document copying machine.

feed track A track in a data medium that contains feed holes. Synonymous with sprocket track. (T) (A)

feed tray See paper feed tray.

FEFO First ended, first out.

fence A separation of one or more components or elements from the remainder of a processor complex. The separation is by logical boundaries rather than power boundaries. This separation allows simultaneous user operations and maintenance procedures.

ferrite An iron compound used in magnetic recording materials.

ferrule In fiber optics, a mechanical fixture, generally a rigid tube, used to confine the stripped end of a fiber bundle or a fiber. (E)

FET Field-effect transistor.

fetch (1) To locate and load a quantity of data from storage. (A)   (2) To obtain load modules from auxiliary storage and load them into main storage. (3) In virtual storage systems, to bring load modules or program phases from auxiliary storage into virtual storage. (4) In VSE, to bring a program phase into virtual storage from a sublibrary and pass control to this phase. (5) A control program routine that accomplishes *(1), (2), (3),* or *(4)*. (6) The name of the macroinstruction (FETCH) used to accomplish *(1), (2), (3),* or *(4)*. (7) See also loader.

fetch protection A storage protection feature that determines right of access to main storage by matching a protection key that is associated with a fetch reference to main storage, with a storage key that is associated with each block of main storage. See also store protection.

fetch routine A routine that loads data from auxiliary storage into main storage.

FF The form feed character. (A)

FFT (Fast Fourier Transform) See Fourier Transforms.

F format A data set format in which logical records are of the same length.

FH Frame handler.

FHP Fixed header prefix.

FHSP Frame handler subport.

FI Failing item.

FIAR Fault isolation analysis routine.

fiber See optical fiber.

fiber buffer Material used to protect an optical fiber from physical damage, thereby providing mechanical isolation or protection, or both.
Note: Cable fabrication techniques vary. Some result in firm contact between fiber and protective buffering (tight buffer), while others result in a loose fit (loose buffer), permitting the fiber to slide in the buffer tube. Multiple buffer layers can be used for added fiber protection.

Fiber Distributed Data Interface (FDDI) An American National Standards Institute (ANSI) standard for a 100-megabit-per-second LAN using optical fiber cables.

fiber optic cable See optical cable.

fiber optics The branch of optical technology concerned with the transmission of radiant power through fibers made of transparent materials such as glass, fused silica, and plastic. (E)
Note: Telecommunication applications of fiber optics use optical fibers. Either a single discrete fiber or a nonspatially aligned fiber bundle can be used for each information channel. Such fibers are often called optical fibers to differentiate them from fibers used in noncommunication applications.

fiber optic subassembly An optical component that contains a serializer, deserializer, transmitter, and receiver. See also transmitter-receiver subassembly (TRS).

Fibonacci number An integer in the Fibonacci series. (A)

Fibonacci search A dichotomizing search in which the number of data elements in the set is equal to a Fibonacci number or is assumed to be equal to the next higher Fibonacci number and then at each step in the search the set of elements is partitioned in accordance with the Fibonacci series. (T)
Note: The Fibonacci series is the series 0, 1, 1, 2, 3, 5, 8,..., each term being the sum of the two preceding terms.

Fibonacci series A series of integers in which each integer is equal to the sum of the two preceding integers in the series. The series is formulated mathematically by $X_i = X_{i-1} + X_{i-2}$, where $X_0 = 0$ and $X_1 = 1$; that is, 0, 1, 1, 2, 3, 5, 8, 13, 21.... (A)

FIC First-in-chain.

fiche See microfiche.

FID Format identification.

fidelity In AS/400 AFP support, the degree of exactness required when processing the input data stream for printing a file. Different levels of fidelity can be specified, which determine how errors are handled, such as substituting fonts when a font named in the data stream cannot be found.

FID field Format identification field.

field (1) On a data medium or a storage, a specified area used for a particular class of data; for example, a group of character positions used to enter or display wage rates on a screen. (T) See also data field, key field. (2) The smallest identifiable part of a record. (3) In SDF/CICS, a defined data area in a map that contains a set of characters defined, manipulated, or operated on as a unit; the data area is associated with a field attribute. (4) In SAA usage, an identifiable area on a screen. See entry field, command entry field, selection field. (5) In a video system, one-half of a complete television scanning cycle: in the NTSC format, 1/60th of a second; in the PAL and SECAM formats, 1/50th of a second. When interlaced, two fields combine to make one video frame. (6) In a video system, all of the scan lines from top to bottom. Two fields, one an even field and the other an odd field, create one frame. See also scan line, interlaced video, NTSC format, PAL format, SECAM formats. (7) See card field, common field, display field.

field analysis standard patterns See print-quality standards patterns.

field area In System/36, an area in main storage that contains all of the fields defined in a workstation utility program.

field attribute A defined characteristic of a field, such as protected or unprotected, alphanumeric or numeric, detectable or nondetectable, displayable or nondisplayable, or intensity.

field attribute definition A subfunction of the SDF/CICS map editor in which maps are displayed in such a way that the 3270 field and extended field attributes are made visible by properly defined attribute characters. Attribute changes are made by overtyping or by redefining the attribute characters by means of the EQUATE command.

field-by-field form In DPCX, a method for addressing data sent to an operator terminal during field-by-field processing or for addressing data sent to the print data set.

field-by-field panel A predefined screen image for an IBM 3277 Display Station display screen that can be displayed by programs that use field-by-field processing. See also panel, panel number.

field-by-field processing In DPCX, a method of communicating with an operator terminal in which only one field of data can be sent and received at a time. Field-by-field processing can be used with either free-form operations or fixed-form operations.

field data code A standardized military data transmission code consisting of 7 data bits plus 1 parity bit.

field definition (1) A subfunction of the SDF/CICS map editor in which the general layout (presentation) of a map is defined and displayed. Field marks are used to define the positions of constant and variable fields, including groups; and two formatting characters (length indicator and spacer) facilitate the setting up of fields in blank lines. (2) In IDDU, information that describes the characteristics of data in a field, such as its name, length, and data type. A field definition resides in a data dictionary. See also file definition, record format definition.

field-developed program An IBM licensed program that performs a function for the user. It may interact with IBM licensed programs, system control programming, or currently available type 1, type 2, or type 3 programs, or it may be a stand-alone program.

field-effect transistor (FET) A semiconductor device in which current between a source terminal and a drain terminal is controlled by voltage applied between the source terminal and a gate terminal that changes the conductance of a channel between the source and drain.

field engineering automated logic diagrams Diagrams used by the customer engineer to analyze card-on-board logic.

field-formatted Pertaining to a request or response that is encoded into fields, each having a specified format such as binary codes, bit-significant flags, and symbolic names. Contrast with character-coded.

field-formatted request In SNA, a request that is encoded into fields, each having a specified format such as binary codes, binary counts, bit-significant flags, and symbolic names; a format indicator in the request/response header (RH) for the request is set to zero. Synonymous with formatted request. Contrast with character-coded request.

field frequency In video systems, the rate at which a complete field is scanned or displayed, normally 59.94 times a second in the NTSC format. See also NTSC format.

field indicator In RPG, an indicator that shows whether a given field in an input record is plus, minus, zero, or blank.

field initialization A subfunction of the SDF/CICS map editor in which fields with programmed symbol set attributes and group subfields can be initialized with data.

field level access checking The RACF facility by which a security administrator can control access to fields or segments in a RACF profile.

field-level help In SAA usage, deprecated term for contextual help.

field level sensitivity In IMS/VS, the ability of an application program to access data at the field level.

field level specifications In DDS, specifications coded on the same line as a field name or on lines immediately following a field name. See also file level specifications, help level specifications, join level specifications, key field level specifications, record level specifications, select/omit level specification.

field macro diagrams (FMDs) Documentation used by the customer engineer to analyze card-on-board logic.

field mark In SDF/CICS, characters used in the field definition function of the map editor to indicate where a constant or variable field starts.

field object In the IBM LinkWay product, an object on the page that displays text and in which users can enter text. Field objects can be multiple lines long and as wide as the page area.

field of view In AIX graphics, the extent of the area that is under view. The field of view is defined by the viewing primitive in use.

field-programmable read-only storage A read-only storage that, after manufacture, can have the data content of each storage cell altered. (A)

field prompt (1) In SAA Advanced Common User Access architecture, descriptive, static text that identifies a selection field or entry field. (2) In SAA Basic Common User Access architecture, descriptive, static text that identifies selection fields, entry fields, and variable output information. See command field prompt.

field record relation indicator In RPG, an indicator that associates fields in an input record with a particular record type. The field record relation indicator is normally used when the record type is one of several in an OR relationship.

field reference file (1) In the AS/400 AFP program, a physical file that contains no data, only descriptions of fields. (2) A physical file that contains no members and whose record format describes the fields used by a group of files.

field replaceable unit (FRU) An assembly that is replaced in its entirety when any one of its components fails. In some cases a field replaceable unit may contain other field replaceable units; for example, a brush and a brush block that can be replaced individually or as a single unit. See also customer replaceable unit.

field return In the AIX operating system, the action that moves a data cursor from field to field in a reverse direction, as determined by the panel layout.

field search argument (FSA) In IMS/VS Fast Path, the I/O area constructed by an application program to identify a field within a segment that is to be processed with a main storage database FLD call.

field selection (1) In the AS/400 AFP program, a function that uses the state of the option indicators to display or print data when a record format is written. (2) In the AS/400 Business Graphics Facility, the selection of fields from a database file for use as data values and data labels. (3) In GDDM, the selection of fields from a database file for use as data values.

field tab (FTAB) In IMS/VS message format service, a character defined for operator use in separating input

fields if the length of the entered data is less than the defined field length, or if there is no data for a field.

field validation (1) In the 3270 Information Display System, a function that provides mandatory field, mandatory fill, and trigger field capability for checking data when the data are entered by the operator from a terminal. (2) An extended field attribute type. (3) An attribute passed between session partners in the Start Field Extended, Modify Field, and Set Attribute orders.

FI-FMD layer Function interpreter for function management data. Deprecated term for presentation services layer.

FIFO First-in-first-out. (A)

fifteen 1's A transmission of fifteen or more consecutive 1's received and detected by an SDLC station, indicating that the sending station is in the idle state.

fifth generation computer A computer that can solve difficult problems using limited knowledge and reasoning capability, that approaches problems in a manner similar to the way in which humans approach them, and that allows humans to communicate with it by means of simple languages.

Note: Earlier generations of computers were characterized by the technology used to implement them: first generation - vacuum tubes, second generation - transistors, third generation - integrated circuits, and fourth generation - very large scale integrated (VLSI) circuits.

FIGS Figures shift.

figurative constant (1) A data name that is reserved for a specified constant in a specified programming language. (I) (A) (2) In COBOL, a compiler generated value referenced through the use of certain reserved words. (3) In RPG, an implied literal that is specified in the calculation specifications without a length definition because the implied length and decimal positions are the same as those of the receiver field. (4) Deprecated term for literal.

figure space (1) A unit of measure equal to the width of the "en" space in a particular font. (2) In the Document Composition Facility, the width of the figure zero (0).

figures shift (FIGS) A physical shift in a teletypewriter that enables printing of images such as numbers, symbols, and uppercase characters. See also letters shift.

file (1) A named set of records stored or processed as a unit. (T) (2) In System/38, a generic term for the object type that refers to a database file, device file, or set of related records treated as a unit. See also logical file, physical file. (3) A collection of information treated as a unit. (4) In word processing, synonym for document. (5) A collection of related data that is stored and retrieved by an assigned name. (6) In the AS/400 AFP program, a generic term for the object type that refers to a database file, a device file, or a save file. (7) In COBOL, a collection of logical records.

File In SAA Common User Access architecture, a choice in the action bar that a user selects to work with items on the computer or on disks or diskettes.

file access mode In VM, a mode that determines whether the file can be used as read-only or read/write.

file allocation table (FAT) In IBM personal computers, a table used by DOS to allocate space on a disk for a file and to locate and chain together parts of the file that may be scattered on different sectors so that the file can be used in a random or sequential manner.

file attribute Any of the attributes that describe the characteristics of a file.

file attribute conflict condition In COBOL, a condition caused when an unsuccessful attempt is made to execute an input-output operation on a file and the file attributes, as specified for that file in the program, do not match the fixed file attributes for the file.

file chaining In System/38 query, a function that allows a query application to use data from two database files.

file clause In COBOL, a clause that appears as part of any of the following Data Division entries: file description (FD) entry and sort-merge file description (SD) entry.

file cleanup (1) The removal of superfluous or obsolete data from a file. (T) (2) Synonymous with file tidying.

file connector In COBOL, a storage area that contains information about a file and is used as the linkage between a file-name and a physical file and between a file-name and its associated record area. See external file connector, internal file connector.

file constant In PL/I, a file for which a complete set of file description attributes exists during the time that the file is open and with which each file must be associated.

FILE-CONTROL In COBOL, the name of an Environment Division paragraph in which the data files for a given source program are declared.

File control block (FCB) A record that contains all of the information about a file, such as its structure, length, and name.

file control entry In COBOL, a SELECT clause and all of its subordinate clauses that declare the relevant physical attributes of a file.

file control table (FCT) A table containing the characteristics of files processed by CICS file management.

file definition (1) Information that describes the contents and characteristics of a file. (2) In VM, equating a CMS file identifier (file name, file type, file mode) with an OS data set name via the FILEDEF command, or equating a VSE file-id with a CMS file identifier via the DLBL command. (3) In VM, identifying the input or output files to be used during execution of a program (via either the FILEDEF or DLBL commands). (4) In RPG, file description and input specifications that describe the records and fields in a file. (5) In IDDU, information that describes the contents and characteristics of a file. A file definition resides in a data dictionary. See also field definition, record format definition.

file description A part of a file where file and field attributes are described.

file description attribute In PL/I, a keyword that describes the characteristics of a file. See also alternative attribute, additive attribute.

file description (FD) entry In COBOL, an entry in the File Section of the Data Division that is composed of the level indicator FD, followed by a file-name, and then followed by a set of file clauses as required.

file description specifications In RPG, a coding form on which the programmer identifies and describes all files used in a program.

file description statement A nonexecutable statement used to specify the characteristics of a file, usually including such information as the names of logical records, header and trailer formats, and the type of device on which the file is stored. (T)

file descriptor In the AIX operating system, a small positive integer that the system uses instead of the file name to identify an open file.

file exception/error subroutine In RPG, a user-written program that may be called following file exceptions or program errors.

file gap An area on a data medium intended to be used to indicate the end of a file and, possibly, the start of another. A file gap is frequently used for other purposes, in particular, as a flag to indicate the end or beginning of some other group of data. (A)

file ID In Subsystem Support Services, two alphanumeric characters that identify the kind of record a data set entry contains.

file index Synonym for i-node.

file key In RPG, all the key fields defined for a file.

file layout The arrangement and structure of data or words in a file, including the order and size of the components of the file. (I) (A)

file level specifications In the AS/400 system and System/38, specifications coded on the lines before the first record format name. See also field level specifications, key field level specifications, help level specifications, join level specifications, record level specifications, select/omit level specifications.

file lock In the AIX operating system, a means to limit or deny access to a file by other users. A file lock can be a read lock or a write lock.

file maintenance (1) The activity of updating or reorganizing a file. (T) (2) Adding, changing, or deleting records in a file to keep the information in the file current.

file management (1) Creation and maintenance of files by means of a computer. (2) In personal computers, the use of application software to access, create, modify, store, and retrieve files and to obtain documents such as reports and mailing lists.

file name (1) A name assigned or declared for a file. (2) The name used by a program to identify a file. See also label.

file-name In COBOL, a user-defined word that names a file connector described in a file description entry or a sort-merge file description entry within the File Section of the Data Division.

file name substitution In the AIX operating system, the process in which the shell recognizing a word (character string) that contains any of the *, ?, [, or { characters, or begins with the ˜ character, and replaces it with an alphabetically sorted list of file names that match the pattern of the word. Synonymous with globbing.

file operation code In RPG, an operation code, such as CHAIN, that lets the user control the input/output operations to a file.

file organization (1) The physical order of the stored records that comprise the contents of a particular file and that determines the access method that must be implemented in order to provide for entry into a database. (T) (2) In COBOL, the permanent logical file structure established at the time that a file is created. See indexed organization, relative organization, sequential organization.

file overrides The file attributes specified at execution time that will override the attributes specified in the file description or in the program.

file owner In the AIX operating system, the user who has the highest level of access authority to a file, as defined by the file.

file pointer (1) In the AIX operating system, an identifier that indicates a structure containing the file name. (2) In Pascal, an identifier that indicates the location of an item of data in an input/output buffer.

file position indicator In COBOL, a conceptual entity that contains the value of the current key within the key of reference for an indexed file, or the record number of the current record for a sequential file, or the relative record number of the current record for a relative file, or that indicates that no next logical record exists, or that the number of significant digits in the relative record number is larger than the size of the relative key data item, or that an optional input file is not present, or that the at end condition already exists, or that no valid next record has been established.

file profile In RACF, a description of a RACF-defined file, including file name, owner, universal access authority, security level, and other data.

file protected Pertaining to a tape reel with the write-enable ring removed.

file protection In computer security, the processes and procedures established in an information system that are designed to inhibit unauthorized access to, contamination of, or deletion of a file.

file-protection ring A removable plastic or metal ring on a magnetic tape reel, the presence or absence of which prevents writing on the magnetic tape and thereby prevents the accidental erasure of a file. Synonymous with safety ring, file protect ring. (T)

file protect ring Synonym for file-protection ring. (T) (A)

file recovery See backward file recovery, forward file recovery.

file reference In BASIC, a numeric expression preceded by a pound sign (#) that is used to specify the file in an input/output statement.

file reference function In the AS/400 AFP system and System/38, a function of the system that lets the user track file use on the system.

File Section In COBOL, the section of the Data Division that contains file description entries together with their associated record descriptions.

file selection box A box that enables the user to choose a file to work with by selecting a file name from the ones listed or by typing a file name into the space provided.

file separator The pages or cards produced at the beginning of each output file to separate the file from the other files being spooled to an output device.

file separator character (FS) The information separator intended to identify a logical boundary between files. (I) (A)

file server A high-capacity disk storage device or a computer that each computer on a network can use to access and retrieve files that can be shared among the attached computers; for example, an IBM 5170 Personal Computer AT used to serve files on a network. See also disk server. See Figure 62.

Note: Access to a file is usually controlled by the file server's software rather than by the operating system of the computer that accesses the file.

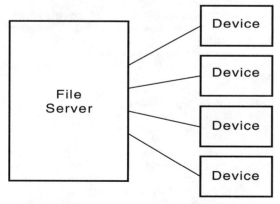

Figure 62. File Server

files library In the AS/400 AFP program, the library that contains database files for System/36 environment jobs.

file spec File specification.

file specification (filespec) In the AIX operating system, the name and location of a file. A file specification consists of a drive specifier, a path name, and a file name.

file standard A standard for access of file-oriented data objects on a storage medium. For example, for CD-ROM, the file standard is specified by ISO 9660.

file system In the AIX operating system, the collection of files and file management structures on a physical or logical mass storage device, such as a diskette or minidisk. See distributed file system, virtual file system.

filetab An AIX kernel parameter establishing the maximum number of files that can be open simultaneously.

file tidying Synonym for file cleanup.

file transfer In remote communications, the transfer of one or more files from one system to another over a communications link.

file transfer, access, and management (FTAM) An application service element that enables user application processes to manage and access a file system, which may be distributed. (T)

File Transfer Protocol (FTP) In TCP/IP, an application protocol used for transferring files to and from host computers. FTP requires a user ID and possibly a password to allow access to files on a remote host system. FTP assumes that the Transmission Control Protocol is the underlying protocol.

file transfer support (FTS) A function of the operating system that moves file members from one system to another by using asynchronous, APPC, or BSCEL communications support.

file translation In RPG, a function that can change any of the 256 EBCDIC characters into another EBCDIC character.

file tree In the AIX operating system, the complete directory and file structure of a particular node, starting at the root directory. A file tree contains all local and remote mounts performed on directories and files.

file type In the AIX operating system, one of the five possible types of files: ordinary file, directory, block device, character device, and first-in-first-out (FIFO or named pipe).

FILE type A data type that allows the program to read input and write output in AS/400 Pascal.

file updating In a file, the activity of adding, changing, or deleting data. (T)

filing The storage of a document either by electronic or optical means or as a hard copy. (T)

fill (1) In a token-ring network, a specified bit pattern that a transmitting data station sends before or after transmission frames, tokens, or abort sequences to avoid what would otherwise be interpreted as an inactive or indeterminate transmitter state. (T)   (2) In computer graphics, a designated area of the screen that is flooded with a particular color.   See seed fill, boundary fill.   (3) See character fill, zerofill.

fill character (1) A character used to occupy an area on a human-readable medium; for example, in a business form or a legal document, dashes or asterisks used to fill out a field to ensure that nothing is added to the field once the form or document has been issued. (2) A character used to fill a field in storage. (3) In IMS/VS message format service, a character used to pad input message fields or output device fields when the length of the received data is less than the length defined for the field or when no data is received for the field.

filler One or more characters adjacent to an item of data that serves to bring the representation of the item up to a specified size. (I)   (A)

filler character A specific character or bit combination used to fill the remainder of a field after justification. (A)

fill light In video and film production, the use of one or more lighting sources to provide even illumination over the entire field of view or subject. Fill light is usually more diffuse and less intense than key light. See key light.

fill pattern In the AS/400 Business Graphics Utility, the shading used inside a bar and pie slice on a chart and below the lines of a chart.

fill validation In the 3270 Information Display System, checking a field to determine whether it is filled with data. Fill validation is performed when the field validation attribute specifies mandatory fill.

film See magnetic thin film, microfilm.

film chain In video or film production, the equipment—usually consisting of film or slide projectors, a multiplexer, and a television camera—used to transfer slide or movie film picture frames to electronic picture frames. Synonymous with telecine.

film storage See magnetic thin film storage.

filter (1) In a document copying machine, material used to modify selectively the transmitted radiation; a color filter modifies the color of the light it transmits. (T)   (2) A device or program that separates data, signals, or material in accordance with specified criteria. (A)   (3) In IBM personal computers, a program that reads output data from the keyboard (the standard input device), modifies the data, and writes output data to the display screen (the standard output device).   (4) In the AIX operating system, a command that reads standard input data, modifies the data, and sends it to the display screen.   (5) In the NetView program, a function that limits the data that is to be recorded on the database and displayed at the terminal. See recording filter, viewing filter.

filtering In the ImagePlus system, the process of augmenting the desired density of the image data in order to reduce other frequencies. Filtering can be used in conjunction with adaptive or fixed thresholding or screening to enhance image quality.

filter primitive In the AIX operating system, a program that separates data in accordance with specified criteria.

FINAC Fast Interline Nonactivate Automatic Control. A leased automatic teletypewriter system provided by the AT&T corporation.

final copy In word processing, the final version of the text. See also draft copy, edited copy. (T)

Final-Form Text: Document Content Architecture In the AS/400 AFP program, the architecture that specifies the structure of the data stream used for the interchange of text documents formatted for presentation.   A Final-Form Text: Document Content Architecture document consists of text and formatting information that controls the presentation of the text.

final script In multimedia applications, the finished script that will be used as a basis for shooting the video. Synonymous with shooting script.

finance communications In the AS/400 AFP program, the data communications support that allows programs on the system to communicate with programs on finance controllers, using the SNA LU session type 0 protocol.

finance device A device, such as the 4700 Finance Communications System devices and the 3694 Document Processor, that performs functions specifically related to the finance industry. The 3180, 3270, and 5250 workstations are not finance devices.

finance image processor (FIP) A function-level routine of Subsystem Support Services that creates the configuration image for a finance industry system.

finance I/O manager (FIOM) In the AS/400 AFP program, a set of routines that can be used by an application program to do I/O operations on a finance device that is configured as a non-intersystem communications function (non-ICF) device.

Finance subsystem The SSP-ICF subsystem that allows System/36 to communicate with the 3601 and 4701 Finance Controllers and the 3694 Document Processor.

finance support In the AS/400 system, a part of the system support that uses an AS/400 system as a host system to which finance devices can be attached.

find Synonym for search. (T)

find and replace Synonym for search and replace. (T)

Find button In the IBM LinkWay product, a type of button object that searches for a text string in the folder and the field the user specifies.

findnext In the IBM LinkWay product, to find the next occurrence of a text string defined by the Find operation.

find text string In word processing, a function that enables a point to be found within the text by entering a set of unique characters identifying the desired point. (T)

fine clipping In the AIX Graphics Library (GL), masking all drawing commands to a rectangular region of the screen. Contrast with gross clipping.

fine-grain parallel processing Parallel processing in which parts of an operation are performed concurrently. Contrast with coarse-grain parallel processing.

finite element analysis (FEA) In computer-aided design, the determination of the structural integrity of a mechanical part or physical construction under design by mathematical simulation of the part and its loading conditions. (T)

finite state machine A computer in which a set of inputs determine not only the set of outputs but also the internal state of the computer, such as the locations of data and instructions in main storage, in order to optimize processing. See also Turing machine, universal Turing machine.

FIOM Finance I/O manager.

FIP Finance image processor.

fire To initiate the action specified by a rule when the condition stated by the rule is satisfied. (T)

firmware (1) An ordered set of instructions and data stored in a way that is functionally independent of main storage; for example, microprograms stored in a ROM. (T) (2) Deprecated term for microcode.

Note: The term "firmware" describes microcode in read-only memory (ROM). At the time they are coded, microinstructions are software. When they are put into ROM they become part of the hardware (microcode), or a combination of hardware and software (microprograms). Usually, microcode is permanent and cannot be modified by the user but there are exceptions: See EPROM, PROM.

first-character forms control (FCFC) A method for controlling the format of printed output. The first character of each record determines the format.

first-come-first-served (FCFS) A queuing technique in which the next item to be retrieved is the item that has been in the queue for the longest time. Contrast with shortest-job-next.

first copy-out time In a document copying machine, the time required between starting the copying process and completely receiving the first copy in the delivery tray. (T)

first draft In multimedia applications, a rough draft of a complete script.

first element of chain Deprecated term for first RU of chain.

first ended, first out (FEFO) A queuing scheme whereby messages in a destination queue are sent to the destination on a first ended, first out basis within priority groups. That is, higher-priority messages are sent before lower-priority messages; when two messages in a queue have equal priority, the one whose final segment arrives at the queue earliest is sent first. See Figure 63.

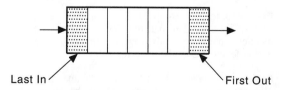

Figure 63. First Ended, First Out

first failure data capture A VTAM problem diagnosis aid that enables VTAM to identify certain

VTAM errors, to gather information about the errors, and to present this information for problem resolution.

first generation In multimedia applications, the original or master videotape; not a copy.

first-generation computer A computer using vacuum tube components.

first-in-chain (FIC) A request unit (RU) whose request header (RH) begin chain indicator is on and whose RH end chain indicator is off. See also RU chain.

first-in-first-out (FIFO) A queuing technique in which the next item to be retrieved is the item that has been in the queue for the longest time. (A)

first-in-first-out (FIFO) pipe In the AIX operating system, a named permanent pipe. A FIFO pipe allows two unrelated processes to exchange information through a pipe connection.

first-level interrupt handler (FLIH) In the AIX operating system, a routine that receives control of the system as a result of a hardware interrupt. One FLIH is assigned to each of the six interrupt levels.

first-level message (1) The initial message presented to the user. The initial message contains general information or designates an error. Contrast with second-level message. (2) In TSO, a diagnostic message that identifies a general condition; more specific information is issued in a second-level message if the text is followed by a "+."

first-level statement In DPCX, a 3790 application programming statement that assembles into only one instruction.

first-level storage In VM, real storage. See also second-level storage, third-level storage.

first line find The capability of a device to advance to a predetermined writing line on the next sheet of continuous forms where printing is to begin. Synonymous with vertical form skip control.

first loop feature (loop 1) The loop feature that is supplied as a standard part of a 3601 Finance Communication Controller. Only a local loop can be attached to this feature. See also loop feature.

first-page indicator In RPG, an indicator, coded as 1P, that specifies the lines, such as headings, that should be printed only on the first page.

first speaker See first-speaker session.

first-speaker session The half-session defined at session activation as: (a) able to begin a bracket without requesting permission from the other half-session to do so, and (b) winning contention if both half-sessions attempt to begin a bracket simultaneously. Synonym for contention-winner session. Contrast with bidder session.

fitness-for-use test Synonym for usability test. (T)

five-bit byte Synonym for quintet.

five-level code A telegraph code that uses five impulses for describing a character. Start and stop elements may be added for asynchronous transmission. A common five-level code is Baudot code.

fix A correction of an error in a program, usually a temporary correction or bypass of defective code. See also fixed, fixing.

fixed (1) In System/370 virtual storage systems, not capable of being paged-out. (2) Synonym for resident. (3) Synonym for read-only.

fixed area The area of main storage occupied by the resident portion of the control program, the nucleus.

fixed aspect ratio In computer graphics, the width (x) to height (y) ratio that keeps an image in correct proportion during sizing maneuvers.

fixed BLDL table In OS/VS, a BLDL table the user has specified to be fixed in the lower portion of real storage.

fixed-block-architecture (FBA) device A disk storage device that stores data in blocks of fixed size; these blocks are addressed by block number relative to the beginning of the particular file. Contrast with count-key-data (CKD) device.

fixed box In the AIX operating system, a type of bounding box that has a fixed number of children created by the parent. These managed children do not make geometry manager requests.

fixed currency symbol A currency symbol that appears in the leftmost position of an edited field. Contrast with floating currency symbol.

fixed-cycle operation An operation completed in a specified number of regularly timed execution cycles. (A)

fixed data In word processing, data or text that is entered and saved for subsequent use; for example, a paragraph that is to be inserted in several documents.

fixed decimal On a calculator, the preselection of the number of decimal places to be shown in the result of a calculation. (T)

fixed-decimal mode In calculators, a mode in which the number of decimal places to be shown in the result of a calculation is shown. (T) (A)

fixed disk Synonym for hard disk.

fixed disk drive Synonym for hard disk drive.

fixed disk formatting Synonym for hard disk formatting.

fixed field (1) In word processing, preset information or an area that may be reserved by the operator for a particular purpose until no longer required. (T) Contrast with variable field. (2) In a 3601 Finance Communication Controller, a field fully identified by providing the segment number, displacement, and field length in a 3600 instruction that refers to the field.

fixed-field addressing In a 3600 Assembler Language instruction, a method of addressing a field by specifying the segment number, displacement, and field length in an instruction. See also segment addressing.

fixed file attributes In COBOL, information about a file that is established when the file is created and cannot subsequently be changed during the existence of the file. These attributes include the organization of the file (sequential, relative, or indexed), the prime record key, the alternate record keys, the code set, the minimum and maximum record size, the record type (fixed or variable), the collating sequence of the keys for indexed files, the blocking factor, the padding character, and the record delimiter.

fixed-form Pertaining to entry of data or the coding of statements in a predefined format. Contrast with free-form.

fixed-format menu In System/36, a menu formatted as two 12-item columns. Contrast with free-format menu.

fixed-format messages Messages in which line control characters have to be inserted on departure from a terminal and deleted on arrival at a terminal; fixed-format messages are intended for terminals that have dissimilar characteristics. Contrast with variable-format messages.

fixed-form operation Communication between a DPCX application program and a terminal that is based on a form defined within the program. The program displays portions of the defined form at the terminal to provide the operator with information or to guide the operator in keying data. Contrast with free-form operation.

fixed function In PSS, an IBM-provided function that cannot be modified. Fixed functions can be performed by programmable point of sale terminals operating only in fixed mode. See also extended function.

fixed-function generator A function generator in which the function it generates is set by construction and cannot be altered by the user. (I) (A)

fixed-function terminal Synonym for nonprogrammable terminal.

fixed-function workstation Synonym for nonprogrammable workstation.

fixed header prefix (FHP) In ACF/TCAM, an optional control block that provides a place to keep message-related information needed by certain optional TCAM functions.

fixed-image graphics (1) In computer graphics, a technique that involves the projection and positioning of selectable fixed images; for example, form flash. (T) (2) Synonymous with image graphics, noncoded graphics.

fixed length A specified length for a record or field that cannot be changed.

fixed-length record (1) A record having the same length as all other records with which it is logically or physically associated. Contrast with variable-length record. See also F format. (2) In COBOL, a record associated with a file whose file description entry or sort-merge description entry requires that all records contain the same number of character positions.

fixed-length string In SQL, a character string whose length is specified and cannot be changed. Contrast with varying-length string.

fixed-line number The line number assigned to a text record and associated with that text record for the duration of the editing work session, unless specifically altered by the user.

fixed link pack area In OS/VS2, an extension of the link pack area that occupies fixed pages in the lower portion of real storage.

fixed memory See read-only memory (ROM).

fixed page In System/370 virtual storage systems, a page in real storage that is not to be paged out.

fixed pane In AIX extended curses, a pane on the screen with fixed horizontal and vertical dimensions.

fixed part In XL Pascal, the part of a record that is common to all instances of a particular record type.

fixed partition A partition having a predefined beginning and ending storage address.

fixed part (of a record) In Pascal, that part of a record that exists in all instances of a particular record type.

fixed pitch Synonym for monospacing. (A)

fixed-point constant A numeric constant shown as an optional sign followed by one or more digits and a decimal point.

fixed-point format (1) The external representation of a decimal value, consisting of an optional sign followed by one or more digits, a decimal point, and zero or more digits. (2) The internal storage format used to represent a fixed-point value that can be stored either in zoned or packed decimal format. (3) The form used to express a fixed-point constant.

fixed-point number A value in fixed-point format.

fixed-point part Synonym for mantissa.

fixed-point register A register used to manipulate data in a fixed-point representation system. (T)

fixed-point representation system (1) A radix numeration system in which the radix point is implicitly fixed in the series of digit places by some convention upon which agreement has been reached. (T) (A) (2) A numeration system in which a real number is represented by a single series of digits and in which the radix point is implicitly fixed in the series. Contrast with variable-point representation system. See also floating-point representation system.

fixed-program read-only storage A read-only storage in which the data content of each cell is determined during manufacture and is thereafter unalterable. (A)

fixed radix notation Synonym for fixed radix numeration system. (T)

fixed-radix numeration system A radix numeration system in which all the digit places, except perhaps the one with the highest weight, have the same radix. The weights of successive digit places are successive integral powers of a single radix, each multiplied by the same factor. Negative integral powers of the radix are used in the representation of fractions. A fixed-radix numeration system is a particular case of a mixed-radix numeration system. Synonymous with fixed-radix notation. (T) (A)

fixed-space font Synonym for uniformly spaced font.

fixed storage Synonym for permanent storage, read-only storage.

fixed thresholding The process of setting the point of demarcation between black and white. This option, typically found on low-end scanners, limits your ability to achieve the broadest range of gray tones. The lower the value, the lighter the page.

fixed word length computer A computer in which data are treated in units of a fixed number of characters or bits.

fixing The action in the document copying process that makes the image permanent. (T) Synonymous with fusing. See heat fixing, pressure fixing. See also fixing level.

fixing level In the document copying process, the degree to which the image adheres to the copy material. (T) Synonymous with fusing level.

fix level An indication of the temporary fixes to a program that are to be included in a modification level or release at a later time. See also modification, release, version.

fix package In DPPX, a package of material that is shipped to customers by IBM to update an IBM licensed program. The package can contain documentation, optional items, and diskettes containing the actual fixes.

flag (1) A variable indicating that a certain condition holds. (T) (2) Any of various types of indicators used for identification; for example, a wordmark (A) (3) A character that signals the occurrence of some condition, such as the end of a word. (A) (4) Deprecated term for mark. (5) Synonymous with sentinel, switch indicator.

flag (F) sequence A unique sequence of eight bits (01111110) used to delimit the opening and closing of a frame.

flag register A special-purpose register in which bits are set according to specified conditions that may occur during the execution of instructions. (T) (A)

flash See form flash.

flashback In multimedia applications, interruption of chronological sequence by interjection of events that occurred earlier.

flash card In micrographics, a target printed with distinctive markings that is photographed to facilitate indexing of microfilm. (I)

flashing (1) In the 3800 Printing Subsystem, turning on and off a light directed toward the forms overlay to create an electrostatic image on the photoconductor. See form flash. (2) Synonym for blinking.

flash item An advertised special or promoted item. A PSS user can create a flash item file for a flash item. When a flash item is sold or returned, the flash item sales function updates the quantity of the item and the amount collected from the sale of that item.

flatbed plotter (1) A plotter that draws a display image on a display of that data and draws the image while the data medium is stationary. (I) (A) (2) See also drum plotter.

flat file (1) A one-dimensional or two-dimensional array: a list or table of items. (2) In a relational database, synonym for relation. (3) A file that has no hierarchical structure.

flat register A special-purpose register in which bits are set according to specified conditions that may occur during the execution of instructions. (T)

flattened character An ASCII character created by translating an extended character to the ASCII character most like it. The code point information is lost and the character cannot be retranslated to an extended character; for example, a cedilla "ç" character would be flattened to a plain "c."

flaw In computer security, an error of commission, omission, or oversight that allows protection mechanisms to be bypassed or disabled.

fletcher critical band In acoustics, a frequency band centered at the frequency of a discrete tone; the tone is just audible in the presence of wide-band noise when the sound pressure level of the tone equals the sound pressure level of the noise in the fletcher critical band.

flexible disk (1) A flexible magnetic disk enclosed in a protective container. Synonymous with floppy disk. (T) (2) Contrast with hard disk. See also diskette.

flicker (1) An undesirable pulsation of a display image on a cathode ray tube. Flicker occurs when the regeneration rate is too low with respect to the phosphor characteristics. (I) (A) (2) Perceptible modulation of luminance.

FLIH First-level interrupt handler.

flip-flop (1) A circuit or device containing active elements capable of assuming either one of two stable states at a given time. (A) (2) Synonym for bistable trigger circuit, toggle.

float In the Document Composition Facility: (a) A keep whose location in the source file can vary in location within the printed document, (b) To format a keep in a location different from its location in the source file.

float constant A number containing a decimal point, an exponent, or both a decimal point and an exponent. The exponent contains an "e" or "E," an optional sign (+ or -), and one or more digits (0 through 9). See also floating point constant.

floating channels In System/370 Model 169 Multiprocessing, channels that are configured so they can be switched between processing units.

floating command line In word processing, any line on which the cursor is located. A floating command line allows the user to enter a command without moving the cursor from the place at which it is currently positioned.

floating currency symbol A currency symbol that appears immediately to the left of the leftmost position in an edited field. Contrast with fixed currency symbol.

floating decimal On a calculator, the automatic positioning of the decimal marker in the result of a calculation irrespective of the mode of entry of the input data. (T)

floating decimal mode A mode in which the decimal marker is automatically positioned in the result of a calculation irrespective of the mode in which the input data are entered. (T) (A)

floating head A magnetic head floating on a layer of air away from the recording surface. Synonymous with air-floating head, flying head. (T) (A)

floating-point Pertaining to a method of encoding real numbers within the limits of finite precision available on computers.

floating-point base In a floating-point representation system, the implicit fixed positive integer base, greater than unity, that is raised to the power explicitly denoted by the exponent or represented by the characteristic and then multiplied by the mantissa part to determine the real number represented; for example, in the floating-point representation of the number 0.0001234, namely 0.1234-3, the implicit floating-point base is 10. Synonymous with floating-point radix.

floating-point constant A numeric constant consisting of an optional sign followed by one or more digits and a decimal point, which may be at the end. See arithmetic constant. See also floating-point format.

floating-point feature A processing unit feature that provides four 64-bit floating-point registers to perform floating-point arithmetic calculations.

floating-point format (1) In binary floating-point representation, the storage format used to represent a binary floating-point value. See also long format, short format. (2) The form used to express a floating-point constant; for example, the representation of a number that consists of an optional sign followed by an integer or fixed-point constant, followed by a decimal point, followed by the letter E, followed by an integer constant with up to 3 significant digits: 3.0E-2 is 3 times 10 to the -2 power or 0.03.

floating-point literal A numeric literal whose value is expressed in floating-point notation; that is, as a decimal number followed by an exponent that indicates the actual placement of the decimal point.

floating-point number A value in floating-point format.

floating-point radix Synonym for floating-point base.

floating-point register A register used to manipulate data in a floating-point representation system. (I) (A)

floating-point representation A representation of a real number in a floating-point representation system.

Example: A floating-point representation of the number 0.0001234 is: 0.1234 -3 where: 0.1234 is the mantissa -3 is the exponent. The numerals are expressed in the variable-point decimal numeration system. (T)

floating-point representation system A numeration system in which a real number is represented by a pair of distinct numerals, the real number being the product of the fixed-point part, one of the numerals, and a value obtained by raising the implicit floating-point base to a power denoted by the exponent in the floating-point representation, indicated by the second numeral. (T) (A)

floating-point status vector (FSV) In the IBM 8100 Information System, the formatted information used to allocate floating-point registers, control exception masking, control precision, and hold and indicate floating-point check and program-exception conditions related to floating-point operations.

flooding In computer security, insertion of data resulting in denial of service. See also attack.

floppy disk Synonym for flexible disk. (T) (A)

FLOPS Floating-point operations per second. See gigaflops, megaflops, supercomputer.

flow In NETDA/2, the amount of traffic that can pass through a node, connection, or route in both directions during a given period of time. See bidirectional flow, normal direction flow, reverse direction flow.

flow analysis (1) In compilers, a technique used to determine the specific interdependencies of elements of a computer program. (A) (2) The detection and recording of the sequencing of instructions in computer programs; for example, as used in monitors and debugging routines. (A)

flowchart (1) A graphical representation of a process or the step-by-step solution of a problem, using suitably annotated geometric figures connected by flowlines for the purpose of designing or documenting a process or program. Synonymous with flow diagram. (T) (2) Contrast with block diagram. (3) See data flowchart, programming flowchart.

flowchart symbol A symbol used to represent operations, data, flow, or equipment in a flowchart. (I) (A)

flowchart text The descriptive information associated with flowchart symbols. (A)

flow control (1) In data communication, control of the data transfer rate. (I) (2) In SNA, the process of managing the rate at which data traffic passes between components of the network. The purpose of flow control is to optimize the rate of flow of message units with minimum congestion in the network, that is, to neither overflow the buffers at the receiver or at intermediate routing nodes, nor leave the receiver waiting for more message units. (3) The methods used to control the flow of information across a network.

flow diagram Synonym for flowchart. (T) (A)

flow direction On a flowchart, the antecedent-to-successor relationship between symbols. (I) (A)

flowline A line representing a connecting path between symbols in a flowchart to indicate transfer of data or control. (I) (A)

flow of control Sequence of execution.

fluerics The branch of the science of fluidics concerning components and systems that perform functions such as sensing, logic, amplification, and control without use of mechanical parts. (A)

fluid container In a duplicator, a tank that may or may not be an integral part of the machine, providing a reservoir of fluid for the damping system. (T)

fluidic Pertaining to the sensing, control, information processing, and actuation functions performed through the use of fluid dynamic phenomena. (A)

fluidics The branch of science and technology concerned with sensing, control, information processing, and actuation functions performed through use of fluid dynamic phenomena. (A)

fluid pump In a duplicator, a device used to supply fluid from the fluid container to the damping system. (T)

flush Having no indentation.

flush closedown A closedown of ACF/TCAM during which incoming message traffic is suspended and queued outgoing messages are sent to their destinations (flushed from the message queues) before closedown is complete. Contrast with quick closedown.

flushing In logical unit (LU 6.2), the process of sending through the network all remaining buffered data generated by a transaction program. The transaction program issues the flush verb to begin the process. It also occurs if the network operator issues the command.

flush left Synonym for left-aligned. (T)

flush right Synonym for right-aligned. (T)

flutter In multimedia applications, a phenomenon that occurs in a videodisc freeze-frame when both video fields are not identically matched, thus creating two different pictures alternating every 1/60th of a second.

fly-by In multimedia applications, animation simulating a birds-eye view of a three-dimensional environment.

fly-in In multimedia applications, a digital video effect in which one picture "flies" into another.

flying erase head In video systems, an additional head on a videotape machine that erases the previously recorded video trace by following the helical scan on the videotape. In doing so, it eliminates the rainbow pattern caused by recording over partially erased tape.

flying head Synonym for floating head. (T) (A)

flying height The distance between a magnetic head and the surface of the recording medium. Synonymous with head gap. (T)

flying-spot scan In computer graphics, a scan in which the intensity of reflected or transmitted light is measured at any point reached on a display space. (T)

flying-spot scanner In optical character recognition, a device employing a moving spot of light to scan a sample space, the intensity of the transmitted or reflected light being sensed by a photoelectric transducer. (A)

FM (1) Frequency modulation. (2) Function management.

FMCB Function management control block.

FMCBE FMCB extensions.

FMCBEXT Function management control block extension.

FMD (1) Function management data. (2) Field macro diagram.

FMD services layer In SNA, former name for presentation services layer.

FME response Deprecated term for definite response.

FMH Function management header.

FMID Function modification identifier.

FNA Free network address.

focus See input focus.

focus window In the AIX operating system, synonym for input focus.

fold (1) To compact data by combining parts of the data; for example, to transform a two-word alphabetic key into a one-word numeric key by adding the numeric equivalents of the letters. (A) (2) To translate the lowercase characters of a character string into uppercase. (3) To place on the next line a portion of a line that does not fit on the line. Contrast with truncate (3).

folder (1) A file used to store and organize documents or electronic mail. (T) (2) In the IBM LinkWay product, the basis of a LinkWay application. The folder contains pages where objects and information are located. (3) In System/36, a type of library on disk containing documents, profiles, office support information, or data definitions. A folder cannot contain load, procedure, source, or subroutine members. (4) In the AS/400 AFP program, a directory for documents. A folder is used to group related documents and to find documents by name. See also document library object, library. (5) In the Folder Application Facility of the IBM ImagePlus system, a device used for storing documents, collections of records, or statements. A folder can be indexed by a date, a department name, an account number, student number, part number, claim number, or document type. Folders can be subdivided by using folder tabs such as "Admission Application," "Medical Records," or "Student Transcripts." See file tab and folder type.

Folder Application Facility An IBM ImagePlus MVS/ESA application provided for the Information Management System (IMS) and the Customer Information Control System (CICS) environments. The Folder Application Facility is responsible for Folder Management and Workflow Management.

Folder Management A feature of the Folder Application Facility. The Folder Management feature organizes document images into electronic file folders, for convenient access and retrieval.

folder member In System/36, a named collection of records or statements in a folder. A document is an example of a folder member.

folder path In the AS/400 AFP program, a folder name, followed by one or more additional folder names, where each preceding folder is found.

folding The substitution of a character set for another character set, usually to map a large character set into a smaller set; for example, to allow the printing of uppercase graphic characters when lowercase are not available in the character array on the print chain.

folding ratio In virtual storage systems, the ratio of the size of real storage to the size of virtual storage.

folio See blind folio, dropped folio, expressed folio.

follower See curve follower.

font (1) A family of characters of a given size and style; for example, 9-point Helvetica. (T) (2) In AIX Enhanced X-Windows, a set of glyphs, usually characters. A font contains additional metric information to determine interglyph and interline spacing. See extended font, primitive font, raster font. (3) See type font. (4) See also font data set.

font change character (FC) A control character that selects and makes effective a change in the specific shape, or size, or shape and size, of the graphics for a set of graphemes; the character set remains unchanged. (I) (A) Synonymous with face change character.

font character set In AS/400 AFP support, a font file that contains the raster patterns, identifiers, and descriptions of characters.

font data set A data set used to generate a set of characters in a particular type style.

font ID A number that identifies the character style and size for certain printers.

font object (1) A member of a font library. (2) In CMS, a file whose filetype matches the name of the font library. (3) In MVS, a member of a partitioned data set (PDS).

font resource In the AS/400 AFP program, a resource object that is required to print Advanced Function Printing data stream (AFP) documents on a printer. The three types of font resources are coded fonts, character sets, and code pages.

font section A portion of an extended graphics coded font where the first byte of each double-byte character has the same value. Each section consists of a font character set and a code page. Synonym for coded font section.

font set The set of fonts to be used in formatting a source document.

footage In multimedia applications, the total number of running feet of film used, as for a scene.

footer (1) A block of text printed consistently at the bottom of one or more pages in a multipage document. A footer may contain variable information, such as a page number. Synonymous with running foot. (T) (2) Text that appears at the bottom of every page of a document, for example, a page number.

footing (1) Words located at the bottom of a text area. See also running foot. (2) See control footing, page footing, report footing.

footing area In COBOL, the position of the page body adjacent to the bottom margin.

footnote (1) A block of text appearing at the bottom of the page where extension or clarification of a topic is required. (T) (2) A note of reference, explanation, or comment, placed below the text of a column or page, but within the body of the page above the running footing.

forbidden combination (1) A combination of bits or other representations that is not valid according to some criteria. (A) (2) Contrast with illegal character.

force-all In System/36 SORT, a specification that tests whether the control field in the input record contains a particular entry; if it does not, the control field character is replaced before the record is sorted.

forced licensed internal code completion In the AS/400 AFP program, a function of the system that allows the user to force a deadlocked system to complete interrupted machine instructions by turning the power switch on the control panel to the Delayed Off position.

forced new page Synonym for required page break. (T)

force of impression In printing, the force with which a type carrier impacts the paper when it types a character.

force start A VM system restart that attempts to recover information about closed spool files that was previously stored on the checkpoint cylinders. All unreadable or invalid spool file information is ignored. Contrast with checkpoint start, cold start, warm start.

force time In the AS/400 AFP program, the time when all items on a distribution queue are sent regardless of how many items are on the queue. See also send depth, send time.

foreground (1) In multiprogramming, the environment in which high-priority programs are executed. (2) In TSO, the environment in which programs are swapped in and out of main storage to allow terminal users to share processing time. Contrast with background. (3) The environment in which interactive programs are executed. Interactive processors reside in the foreground. (4) In the AIX operating system, a mode of running a program in which the shell waits for the program specified on the command line to complete before responding to user input. (5) See foreground image, foreground process.

foreground (Fg) color The color of objects placed on the screen.

foreground display image See foreground image.

foreground image (1) The part of a display image that can be changed for every transaction. (I) (A) (2) Contrast with background image. (3) Synonymous with display foreground, dynamic display image, dynamic image.

foreground-initiated background job In TSO, a job submitted from a remote terminal for scheduling and execution in the background.

foreground job (1) A high-priority job, usually a real-time job. (2) An interactive or graphic display job that has an indefinite running time during which communication is established with one or more users at local or remote terminals. (3) In TSO, any job executing in a swapped region of main storage, such as a

command processor or a terminal user's program. Contrast with background job.

foreground message processing program In TSO, a problem program run in the foreground using ACF/TCAM to handle messages for one or more terminals.

foreground partition In VSE, a space in virtual storage in which programs are executed under control of the system. By default, a foreground partition has a higher processing priority than the background partition.

foreground process In the AIX operating system, a process that must run to completion before another command is issued to the shell. The foreground process is in the foreground process group, which is the group that receives the signals generated by a terminal. Contrast with background process.

foreground processing (1) The execution of a computer program that preempts the use of computer facilities. (I) (A) (2) In word processing, a type of system operation perceived by the operator to execute immediately at the workstation. (3) Contrast with background processing.

foreground program (1) In multiprogramming, a high-priority program. (2) In TSO, a program executed in a main storage region that has been swapped in.

foreground region A region to which a foreground job is assigned.

foreign exchange service A service that connects a customer's telephone to a telephone company central office that does not normally serve the customer's location.

foreign host Synonym for remote host.

foreign key In a relation, a column whose data values correspond to the values of a key column in another relation. (A)

fork In the AIX operating system, to create and start a child process.

form (1) In an IBM 3790 or DPCX application program, a set of programming statements that defines the contents and structure of a data unit by specifying pages, lines in pages, fields within lines, and items within fields. (2) The paper on which output data are printed by a line printer or character printer. (3) The area between perforations on continuous printer paper. (4) In AS/400 AFP support, a physical sheet of paper on which data is printed. Synonymous with medium, physical page, sheet. (5) In AS/400 AFP query management, an object that describes how to format the data for printing or displaying a report. (6) In FORTRAN, any of the three types of records: formatted, unformatted, and endfile. (7) See Backus Naur form, continuous forms, normalized form, precoded form, preprinted form, printed card form.

FORMAC Formula manipulation compiler. An extension of PL/I designed for nonnumeric manipulation of mathematical expressions. (T)

formal logic The study of the structure and form of a valid argument without regard to the meaning of the terms in the argument. (I) (A)

formal parameter (1) In programming languages, a language object, whose identifier appears in an entry of a procedure, that is associated with the corresponding actual parameter specified by the procedure call for use in the execution of the procedure. (I) (2) In Pascal, a language object, declared in the heading of a routine, that is associated with a corresponding actual parameter specified in a call to the routine. A formal parameter is used to specify what can be passed to a routine. Contrast with actual parameter. (3) Synonymous with dummy argument. (4) See also actual parameter.

formal security policy model A mathematically precise statement of a security policy. See computer security model, security policy model.

formal specification A specification that is used to prove mathematically the validity of an implementation or to derive mathematically the implementation. (T)

formal verification In computer security, the use of formal proofs for design verification or implementation verification.

format (1) In programming languages, a language construct that specifies the representation, in character form, of data objects in a file. (I) (2) In text processing, the predetermined arrangement or layout of text in printed or displayed form or on a data medium. (T) (3) A specified arrangement of such things as characters, fields, and lines, usually used for displays, printouts, or files. (4) To arrange such things as characters, fields, and lines. (5) To arrange information on a page, in a file, or on a display screen. (6) See address format, instruction format, record format.

format character set A character set (available in 10-, 12-, and 15-pitch) that provides graphics such as lines, corners, and intersections, that can be used; for example, to print column lines or boxes around data.

format check A check to determine whether data conform to a specified layout. (T)

format definition In the System/36 interactive data definition utility, information that describes the contents and characteristics of data within a group of related fields, such as a record in a file. A format definition is contained in a data dictionary.

format description statement A statement used to specify the format of output data on a medium external to the computer system, for example, payroll checks, order forms. (T)

format effector (FE) (1) A control character used to position printed, displayed, or recorded data. (T) (2) Synonymous with layout character.

format identification (FID) field In SNA, a field in each transmission header (TH) that indicates the format of the transmission header; that is, the presence or absence of certain fields. Transmission header formats differ in accordance with the types of nodes between which they pass. There are six FID types:

FID0
  Used for traffic involving non-SNA devices between adjacent subarea nodes when either or both nodes do not support explicit route and virtual route protocols.

FID1
  Used for traffic involving SNA devices between adjacent subarea nodes when either or both nodes do not support explicit route and virtual route protocols.

FID2
  Used for traffic between a subarea node and an adjacent PU type 2 peripheral node.

FID3
  Used for traffic between a subarea node and an adjacent PU type 1 peripheral node.

FID4
  Used for traffic between adjacent subarea nodes when both nodes support explicit route and virtual route protocols.

FIDF
  Used for certain commands; for example, for transmission group control, sent between adjacent subarea nodes when both nodes support explicit route and virtual route protocols.

format line In the System/38 source entry utility, the abbreviated names of the fields in the source line that are displayed directly above the source line. The format line is displayed when the F (format) line command is executed.

format list In PL/I stream-mode data transmission, a list specifying the format of the data item on the external medium. Contrast with data list.

format member In System/36, a load member that contains display formats generated from S and D specifications in a program.

format record In the IBM 3886 Optical Character Reader, the record loaded into the 3886 to provide specific document, line, and field information and output record specifications.

format selection In word processing, selection of a program for formatting purposes. (T)

format selector In AS/400 and System/38, a user-defined program, either a control language or a high-level language program, that determines where a record should be placed in the database when an application program does not pass a record format name for a record being added to a logical file.

format service program In the 3600 Finance Communication System, one of the host service programs that are used to segment and format application program object modules, configuration data, and customized data before further processing by the Finance Image Processor.

format set In IMS/VS message format service, a format definition, all message definitions that refer to the format definition, and any table referred to by the format.

format sheet In the IBM 3881 Optical Mark Reader, a form used to select the reading parameters that the read control microprogram uses during document processing.

formatted data In FORTRAN, data that is transferred between main storage and an input/output device according to codes specified in a FORMAT statement. See also list-directed data, unformatted data.

formatted diskette A diskette on which track and sector control information has been written and which may or may not contain data. Contrast with unformatted diskette.

Note: A diskette must be formatted before it can receive data.

formatted display A display in which the attributes of one or more display fields have been defined by the user. Contrast with unformatted display.

formatted DSCB In 3790 and 8100/DPCX, a set of data set definition statements that has been assembled, passed through program validation services, and stored in the image file to await processing by subsystem support services.

formatted dump A dump in which certain data areas are isolated and identified.

formatted image In DPCX, a display image in which fields are defined by the presence of attribute bytes. Contrast with unformatted image.

formatted information An arrangement of information into discrete units and structures in a manner that facilitates its access and processing. Contrast with narrative information. (A)

formatted input/output In DPPX, the sequential or direct transfer of data from or to a formatted record; the formatting of the data is controlled by a FORMAT statement or by the input/output list of a list-directed input/output statement.

formatted LOGON In AS/400 RJE, the correctly formatted logon specified in the CRTRJECFG command for the Systems Network Architecture (SNA) environment. No formatting is done at the host for this LOGON.

formatted message In System/36, a two-line display in which the first line (format line) provides information about the message, and the second line (message text line) contains the message itself.

formatted program (1) In the 3790 Communication System, a program that has been assembled, passed through program validation services, and stored in the image file to await processing by subsystem support services. (2) In DPCX, a program that has been assembled and passed through the preparation phase of program validation services and is ready to be processed for transmission to subsystem support services, batch data exchange services, or the Distributed Systems Executive.

formatted program interface The part of 3270 emulation support that converts 3270 data streams into a 1920-character image format that is presented to user-written programs. Contrast with unformatted program interface.

formatted record In DPPX, a record that contains data coded in a form that satisfies the needs of machine representation and that can be read by a programmer when it is printed.

formatted request Synonym for field-formatted request.

formatted system services A facility that provides certain system services as a result of receiving a field-formatted command, such as an INITIATE or TERMINATE command. Contrast with unformatted system services. See also field-formatted request.

formatter (1) A computer program that prepares a source document for printing. (2) The part of a text processor that formats input lines for printing or display on a particular type of device.

formatting (1) The initialization of a data medium so that a particular computer system can store data in and subsequently retrieve data from the medium. (T) (2) In text processing, the capability of a text editor that allows the preparation of the layout of text according to criteria specified by the user. (T)

formatting mode In document formatting, the state in which input lines are concatenated and the resulting output lines are justified.

format translate In the 3881 Optical Mark Reader, that part of read-only storage that interprets and assembles data from a format load sheet into control information to be used by format control.

FORMDEF Form definition.

form definition In AS/400 AFP and the 3800 Print Services Facility, a resource object that defines the characteristics of the printed media; for example, overlays to be used, text suppression, position of page data on the form, and number and modifications of a page.

form environment group (FEG) In the 3800 Print Services Facility, an internal object, located in a medium map, that identifies overlays to be used and defines the characteristics of the form and placement of pages.

form feed (1) Paper throw used to bring an assigned part of a form to the printing position. (I) (A) (2) In word processing, a function that advances the typing position to the same character position on a predetermined line of the next form or page. (T)

form feed character (FF) (1) A format effector that causes the print or display position to move to the next predetermined first line on the next form, next page, or equivalent. (I) (A) (2) In word processing, synonym for page end character.

form flash (1) The display of a form overlay. (I) (A) (2) In computer graphics, the projection of a pattern such as a report form, grid, or map, used as the display image. (T)

form flash negative The photographic plate used to flash an overlay on a form.

form flash unit The unit containing a xenon flash lamp, power supply, and optical path that sends a flash of light through the forms overlay to the photoconductor.

form letter A standard letter addressed to a variety of recipients and having the same or much the same body. (T)

form map Synonym for form definition.

form overlay A pattern such as a report form, grid, or map used as background for a display image. (I) (A)

forms control buffer (FCB) In the 3800 Printing Subsystem, a buffer for controlling the vertical format of printed output. The FCB is similar to the punched-paper, carriage-control tape used on IBM 1403 Printers.

forms control table (FCT) In the AS/400 system, an object that contains the special processing requirements for output data streams received from a host system by a remote job entry (RJE) session.

forms design The process of creating a constant-data design that can be used for preprinted forms, forms overlays, or electronic overlays.

forms flash In AS/400 AFP support on the 3800 Printing Subsystem, a means of printing an overlay using a negative plate projected on a form.

forms number A unique number, assigned by a user to identify each type of paper or form for printed output.

forms overlay (1) In the 3800 Printing Subsystem, the function of the printer that allows user-prepared images to be printed with variable page data. An operator must insert the desired image holder when forms overlay printing is desired. (2) The photographic negative of a predefined design to be exposed to the photoconductor by a flash of light. The forms overlay can be merged with variable data during printing. See also electronic overlay.

form type In the AS/400 system, a 10-character identifier, assigned by the user, that identifies each type of form used for printed output.

formula manipulation Algebraic manipulation of mathematical formulae. (A)

FOR statement In programming languages, a statement that executes one or more statements for each of a set of values assigned to one or more variables.

FORTH A high-level programming language that uses postfix notation and that was designed primarily for process control applications and now is used also for microprocessor applications. FORTH allows compile-time error checking. Programs written in

FORTH can be run on various types of computers with little or no modification.

FORTRAN control characters See American National Standard control characters.

FORTRAN (formula translation) (1) A programming language primarily used to express computer programs by arithmetic formulas. (A) (2) A programming language primarily designed for applications involving numeric computations. (T)

Note: FORTRAN is used primarily for scientific, engineering, and mathematical applications.

fortuitous distortion ("jitter") A type of telegraph distortion that results in the intermittent shortening or lengthening of the signals. This distortion is entirely random in nature and can be caused, for example, by battery fluctuations, hits on the line, and power induction. See also distortion.

forward To send information, such as received mail, to someone else.

Forward In SAA Basic Common User Access architecture, an action that shows the information that follows the visible information in a panel.

forward chaining An iterative procedure for solving a problem by which the problem is transformed into an instantiation of an axiom or a proven proposition applied to the premises, and another problem to be solved until a conclusion is reached or no further inferences can be made. (T)

forward channel (1) A channel in which the direction of transmission is the direction in which user information is being transferred. (I) (2) Contrast with backward channel.

forward difference matrix In AIX graphics, a 4x4 matrix that is interacted by adding each row to the next row; the bottom row is output as the next point. Points so generated generally fall on a rational cubic curve.

forward file recovery The reconstruction of a file by updating an earlier version with data recorded in a journal. (T) Contrast with backward file recovery.

forward LAN channel In a broadband LAN, the channel assigned for downlink data transmission from the headend to the data stations. (T)

forward recovery (1) The reconstruction of a file by updating an earlier version with data recorded in a journal. (T) (2) The process of reconstructing a file from a particular point by restoring a saved version of

the file and then applying changes to that file in the same order in which they were originally made.

forward supervision The use of supervisory sequences sent from the master to the slave station. Contrast with backward supervision.

four-bit byte Synonym for quartet.

four-plus-one address Pertaining to an instruction that contains four address parts. The plus-one address is the address of the next instruction to be executed unless otherwise specified. (A)

Fourier transforms A complex digital video compression technique in which an image is transformed from the spatial domain to the frequency domain.

four-wire circuit A path in which four wires, two for each direction of transmission, are presented to the station equipment.

four-wire repeater A telephone repeater for use in a four-wire circuit consisting of two amplifiers, one servicing one side or transmission direction of the four-wire circuit and the other servicing the second side of the four-wire circuit.

four-wire terminating set An arrangement by which four-wire circuits are terminated on a two-wire basis for interconnection with two-wire circuits.

FQPCID Fully qualified procedure correlator identifier.

FRACHECK request In RACF, the issuing of the FRACHECK macro or the RACROUTE macro with REQUEST=FASTAUTH specified. The primary function of a FRACHECK request is to check a user's authorization to a RACF-protected resource or function. A FRACHECK request uses only in-storage profiles for faster performance.

fractals In computer graphics, irregular, lifelike landscapes and branching forms produced through simple mathematical formulas.

fractional digit A digit to the right of a decimal point.

fragmentation See storage fragmentation.

fragmentation index The qualitative measure of the scattered free space on a volume.

frame (1) In Open Systems Interconnection architecture, a data structure pertaining to a particular area of knowledge and consisting of slots that can accept the values of specific attributes and from which inferences can be drawn by appropriate procedural attachments.

Synonymous with schema. (T) (2) A data structure that consists of fields, predetermined by a protocol, for the transmission of user data and control data. The composition of a frame, especially the number and types of fields, may vary according to the type of protocol. Synonymous with transmission frame. (T) (3) In multimedia applications, a complete television picture that is composed of two scanned fields, one of the even lines and one of the odd lines. In the NTSC system, a frame has 525 horizontal lines and is scanned in 1/30th of a second. (4) A housing for machine elements. (5) The hardware support structure, covers, and all electrical parts mounted therein that are packaged as one entity for shipping. (6) The unit of transmission in some local area networks, including the IBM Token-Ring Network; it includes delimiters, control characters, information, and checking characters. (7) In SDLC, the vehicle for every command, every response, and all information that is transmitted using SDLC procedures. (8) A formatted display. See display frame. (9) Any of two types of distributing frames: (a)type A: a distributing frame carrying on one side (horizontal) all outside lines, and on the other side (vertical) the terminations of the central office equipment and protective devices for them; (b)type B: a distributing frame carrying on one side (vertical) all outside lines and protective devices for those lines, and on the other side (horizontal) all connections of the outside lines toward the central office equipment.

frame address In videotape and optical videodiscs, a number assigned to each frame. The addresses are held collectively in a frame address table.

frame address code A code located in the vertical blanking interval of a video frame.

frame animation In multimedia applications, a process in which still images are shown at a constant rate. See also cast animation.

frame buffer (1) In video systems, a device that can store all the 525 lines (in the NTSC format) of a television frame and function as a time base corrector. See also time base corrector. (2) In video systems, a device in which the contents of an image are stored, pixel by pixel and which is used to refresh a raster image. (3) In the AIX operating system, a part of specialized random access memory that stores color information, pixel by pixel, that is seen on the display monitor.

frame chaining In SDLC, the chaining together of two or more message frames in a single data transmission.

frame checking sequence (FCS) See frame check sequence.

frame check sequence (FCS) (1) A character determined by the data present within the transmission frame and appended to the transmission frame to allow detection of transmission errors. (T) (2) A field immediately preceding the closing flag sequence of a frame that contains a bit sequence checked by the receiver to detect transmission errors. (3) In SDLC, 16 bits in a frame that contain transmission-checking information. See also frame, sequenced frames.

frame control field A specified bit pattern that defines the type of transmission frame and certain control functions. (T)

frame-control window A control window, owned by the frame window, that accepts simple input from the user and notifies the frame window or client window when it receives input.

frame-dependent control (FDC) mode A mode of operation for the processor complex consoles in which commands entered at the console act on the data displayed on the screen.

frame differencing In computer graphics, a technique combining temporal encoding and region encoding so that only those regions of a frame that are different from other frames are recorded; used by production level video (PLV). See also production level video (PLV).

frame end delimiter Synonym for ending-frame delimiter. (T)

frame grabber In multimedia applications, a device that digitizes video images.

frame handler (FH) Synonym for frame-relay frame handler (FRFH).

frame handler subport (FHSP) A subport that serves as an intermediate point on a virtual circuit. Contrast with terminal equipment subport (TESP).

frame level See link level.

frame level interface In packet mode operation, the level of the interface between a data terminal equipment (DTE) and a data circuit-terminating equipment (DCE) associated with the exchange of packets contained in frames for local error control. See also packet level interface.

frame number (1) In System/370 virtual storage systems, the part of a real storage address needed to refer to a frame. See also page number, segment number. (2) In multimedia applications, the number used to identify a frame. On videodisc, frames are numbered sequentially from 1 to 54,000 on each side and can be accessed individually; on videotape, the numbers are assigned by means of the SMPTE time code.

frame pitch In computer graphics, the distance between corresponding points on two successive frames. (T) Synonymous with pulldown.

frame rate In multimedia applications, the speed at which the frames are scanned: 30 frames a second in NTSC video, 25 frames a second in PAL video, and 24 frames a second in most film.

frame-relay frame The frame-relay frame structure defined by American National Standards Institute (ANSI) Standard T1.618.

frame-relay frame handler (FRFH) A router function that uses the address field in a frame-relay frame. Synonymous with frame handler (FH). See also frame-relay switching equipment (FRSE) support and frame-relay terminal equipment (FRTE).

frame-relay network A network that consists of frame-relay frame handlers (FRFH) and in which frames are passed from one frame-relay terminal equipment (FRTE) station to another through a series of one or more FRFHs.

frame-relay segment set The set of subports defining the primary and substitute permanent virtual circuit (PVC) paths in an NCP with frame-relay switching equipment (FRSE) support.

frame-relay switch Synonym for frame-relay switching equipment (FRSE) support.

frame-relay switching equipment (FRSE) See frame-relay switching equipment (FRSE) support.

frame-relay switching equipment subport set The set of primary and, optionally, substitute subports within an NCP that comprise those used for a given frame-relay segment set.

frame-relay switching equipment support A set of NCP frame-relay functions that include the frame-relay frame handler (FRFH) function, which is defined by American National Standards Institute (ANSI) Standards T1.617 and T1.618. Other functions, which are not part of the ANSI Standards, include performance measurement and enhanced reliability. Synonymous with frame-relay switch.

frame-relay terminal equipment (FRTE) A device capable of connecting to a frame-relay network. An FRTE adds a frame header when sending data to the frame-relay network and removes the frame header when receiving data from the frame-relay network.

See also frame-relay frame handler (FRFH) and frame-relay switching equipment (FRSE) support.

frame start delimiter Synonym for starting-frame delimiter. (T)

frame store A device that stores one complete video frame.

frame table See page frame table.

frame table entry (FTE) In System/370 virtual storage systems, an entry in the page frame table that describes how a frame is being used.

frame window (1) The window used as a base when constructing a primary window or composite window. The frame window coordinates the action of frame controls and the client window, enabling them to act as a single unit. (2) In X.25 communications, the number of frames that can be outstanding without acknowledgment. See also packet window.

framing The process of selecting the bit groupings representing one or more characters from a continuous stream of bits.

framing bits Noninformation-carrying bits used to make possible the separation of characters in a bit stream. Synonymous with sync bits.

framing error An asynchronous transmission error usually caused by the number of bits per character not being set the same on the sending and receiving workstations.

franking (1) Pertaining to devices that stamp or print postage. (2) In PSS, printing an indication on a document that the document has been processed. The franking may be a store header line; a "total" line; or a transaction number that is printed when a document such as a check, a discount coupon, or a gift certificate, is inserted in the document insert station of the point of sale terminal during certain types of transactions.

free-block list Synonym for free list.

free control interval In VSAM, a control interval that is formatted, addressable, and available for assignment, but contains no stored records.

free electron A negative charge carrier created when sufficient energy is applied to a crystal lattice to cause an electron to break from its electrical bond, causing a negative current flow. See also hole.

free-form Pertaining to entry of data or the coding of statements without regard for predefined formats. Contrast with fixed-form.

free-format menu In System/36, a menu for which the programmer defines the format of lines 3 through 20. Contrast with fixed-format menu.

free-form format The System/36 source entry utility display format designed for entering and updating statements, such as OCL statements and utility control statements, that do not have a constant format.

free-form operation In DPCX, communication between an application program and a terminal during which the operator enters data without regard for any predefined form or field. Contrast with fixed-form operation.

free list In the AIX operating system, a list of available blocks on each file system. Synonymous with free block list.

freely programmable word processing equipment Word processing equipment on which the programs can be altered within the limits of available controls without exchanging or changing other features of the machine. (T)

free routing A method of traffic handling in which messages are forwarded toward their destination over any available channel without depending on a predetermined routing plan.

free space See distributed free space.

free space administration The use of methods or programs to manage available space in a database. (T)

free storage Storage that is not allocated.

free text method In text processing, a method of obtaining descriptors by recording each text word, except stop words, and its occurrence and relative position in a unit of text.

free token See token.

free toner Toner with little or no electrostatic charge that may become charged and therefore attracted to the hardware or the output paper.

freeze-frame In multimedia applications, a frame of a motion-picture film that is repeated so as to give the illusion of a still picture.

frequency The rate of signal oscillation, expressed in hertz.

frequency analysis In acoustics, use of an instrumentation system for measuring the band pressure level of a sound as a function of frequency.

frequency band A continuous range of frequencies between two limiting frequencies. See also octave band.

frequency-division multiplexing (FDM) Division of a transmission facility into two or more channels by splitting the frequency band transmitted by the channel into narrower bands, each of which constitutes a distinct channel. See also time-division multiplexing.

frequency interleaving In the NTSC or PAL television formats, the technique of choosing the color subcarrier frequency so that the chrominance frequency components of the signal fall between the luminance frequency components of the signal.

frequency modulation (FM) Modulation by varying the frequency of a fixed-amplitude carrier signal in accordance with an information signal. Contrast with amplitude modulation (AM). See Figure 64.

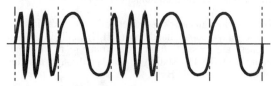

Figure 64. Frequency Modulation

frequency modulation recording Non-return-to-reference recording in which there is a change in the condition of magnetization at each cell boundary, and a further change in the center of the cell to represent a one. (T)

frequency shift keying (FSK) (1) A form of frequency modulation of a carrier by a digital signal such that each frequency, or group of frequencies, is used to represent a character. (T) (2) Frequency modulation of a carrier by a digital modulating signal. (3) See phase coherent FSK, phase continuous FSK.

FRFH Frame-relay frame handler.

friction feeder In a document copying machine or duplicator, a device that separates by friction successive sheets of paper from the paper stack and feeds them into the machine. (T)

friction pressure control In a duplicator, a control for adjusting the amount of friction in the paper feed device. (T)

fringing In a color display, the undesirable effect of incorrect colors appearing at the edges of objects in an image. Fringing is caused by incorrect superimposition of the red, green, and blue images.

front and back buffers In AIX graphics double buffer mode, two bit planes into which bits are separated. Bits in the front buffer planes are visible and those in the back buffer are not. Typically, an application draws into the back buffer and views the front buffer for dynamic graphics.

front compression In VSAM, the elimination, from the front of a key, of characters that are the same as the characters in the front of the preceding key.

front end In the 3660 Supermarket Store System, pertaining to the area at the front of a supermarket where customers check out their purchases. Customer checkout in a supermarket is referred to as a front-end operation.

front-end application In the ImagePlus system, the application that makes requests for actions concerning objects and processes documents before they are entered into the ImagePlus system. The application uses an LU 6.1 or LU6.2 VTAM connection to the Object Distribution Manager through the ImagePlus Application Program Interface.

front-end computer Synonym for front-end processor.

front end processor (1) In a computer network, a processor that relieves a host computer of processing tasks such as line control, message handling, code conversion, and error control. (T)   (2) Synonymous with front-end computer.

front-end system An IMS/VS system in a multi-system environment in which all terminals are handled, messages are routed to the proper processing system, and all replies are routed to the terminals. See also balanced system, pseudo-front-end system, transaction processing system.

front lay In a duplicator, stops against which the leading edge of the paper is positioned before the impression cycle is started. (T)   See also side lay.

front matter In a book, those sections such as preface, abstract, table of contents, and list of illustrations that are placed before the main chapters or sections.

FRR Functional recovery routine.

FRSE Frame-relay switching equipment.

FRTE Frame-relay terminal equipment.

FRU Field replaceable unit.

frustum In AIX graphics, a truncated, four-sided pyramid. In a perspective projection, the shape of the clipping volume is a frustum. The bottom of the frustum is referred to the far clipping plane, the top of the frustum is the near clipping plane, and the sides are respectively the top, left, bottom, and right clipping planes. In an orthographic projection, the clipping volume is a parallelepiped.

FS The file separator character. (A)

FSA Field search argument.

F sequence Flag sequence.

FSK Frequency-shift keying.

FSP Full-screen processing.

F-Stop In photography, the calibration on a lens showing the width of the opening of the lens iris.

FSV Floating-point status vector.

FTA Fast turnaround.

FTAB Field tab.

FTE Frame table entry.

FTP File Transfer Protocol.

FTS (1) Federal Telecommunications System. (2) File transfer support.

FULIST A type of selection panel that allows a user to request a certain file from a set of files or a function from a set of functions to be performed for one or more of the resources listed on the panel.

full-adder A combinational circuit that has three inputs that are an augend, D, an addend, E, and a carry digit transferred from another digit place, F; and two outputs that are a sum without carry, T, and a new carry digit, R, and in which the outputs are related to the inputs according to the following table. (I) (A) Synonymous with three-input adder. See Figure 65.

Input D augend	0	0	1	1	0	0	1	1
Input E addend	0	1	0	1	0	1	0	1
Input F carry digit	0	0	0	0	1	1	1	1
Output T sum without carry	0	1	1	0	1	0	0	1
Output R carry digit	0	0	0	1	0	1	1	1

Full-adder block diagram

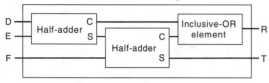

Figure 65. Full-Adder

full backup The process of copying all the files on a system. Contrast with incremental backup.

full character matrix The part of a character box reserved for a symbol, including its diacritical mark and descender, if any. See also capital letter matrix.

Note: The full character matrix can never be smaller than the capital letter matrix, because it must contain space for diacritical marks and descenders.

full data set authority In DPPX, permission through authority credentials to access restricted data sets and, thus, restricted databases.

full DST authority In the AS/400 system, a dedicated service tools (DST) authority used by a service representative or an experienced system user that provides access to all DST functions except changing DST passwords. See also basic DST authority.

full-duplex Synonym for duplex.

full-duplex operation Synonym for duplex operation.

full-frame ID In video production, a code on videotape identifying a new full frame. Synonymous with white flag.

full-frame time code A standardized method, established by the Society of Motion Picture and Television Engineers (SMPTE), of address coding a videotape. It gives an accurate frame count rather than an accurate clock time. Synonymous with nondrop time code.

full install The creation of a new DPCX operating system in the 8100 Information System hardware. Contrast with update install.

full-line mode A form of screen presentation in NCCF in which the message area of the terminal screen consists of 80-byte messages. Full-line mode is used by Network Problem Determination Application (NPDA) . Contrast with standard NCCF mode.

full-motion video A standard of quality for the reproduction of television signals. For signals originally in the NTSC format, full-motion is achieved when reproduced at 30 frames per second (fps); for signals originally in the PAL format, full-motion occurs at 25 fps.

full-page display The display of as many lines of text at a time as can be printed on a page. (T)

full path name In the AIX operating system, the name of any directory or file expressed as a string of directories and files beginning with the root directory. See also path name, relative path name.

full procedural file (1) In RPG, a disk file that can be processed randomly and sequentially. (2) In System/38 RPG, a file for which the input operations are controlled by programmer-specified operation codes instead of by the program cycle. Contrast with primary file.

full recording mode In VM, a mode of operation in which transient processing unit and main storage errors that are corrected or circumvented by hardware retry or error correction code logic are recorded on the VM error recording cylinders.

full-screen editing A type of editing at a display terminal in which an entire screen of data is displayed at once and in which the user can modify data. Contrast with line editing.

full-screen editor A program that allows users to edit an entire screen of data or text at one time.

full-screen field naming In SDF/CICS, an alternative of the application structure specification in which field names can be defined in a full-screen mode.

full-screen form In a DPCX program, a type of form used to address data sent to the output full-screen processing buffer.

full-screen mode (1) A form of screen presentation in which the contents of an entire terminal screen can be displayed at once. Full-screen mode is often used for fill-in-the-blanks prompting. (2) In the VM/XA Migration Aid, a mechanism to allow a virtual machine to have control over a 3270 display screen. Contrast with line mode.

full screen naming In SDF/CICS, an alternative in the application structure specification where field names can be defined in a full screen mode.

full-screen panel In DPCX, a predefined screen image stored in the panel data set that can be retrieved for display by programs that use full-screen processing or for printing. See also panel, panel number.

full-screen processing (FSP) A method of operating a display station that allows the terminal operator to type data into some or all unprotected fields on the display screen before entering the data.

fullselect In SQL, that form of the SELECT statement that includes ORDER BY or UNION operators.

full speed The top-rated speed of transmission equipment, in transoceanic telegraph, 50 baud or 66+ wpm.

full-subtracter A combinational circuit that has three inputs that are a minuend, I, a subtrahend, J, and a borrow digit, K, transferred from another operation; and two outputs that are a difference without carry, W, between the first digit and the sum of the second digit and the borrow digit and a new borrow digit, X, and in which the outputs are related to the inputs according to the table below. (I) (A) See Figure 66.

Input I minuend	0	0	1	1	0	0	1	1
Input J subtrahend	0	1	0	1	0	1	0	1
Input K borrow digit	0	0	0	0	1	1	1	1
Output W difference without carry	0	1	1	1	1	0	0	1
Output X borrow digit	0	1	0	0	1	1	0	1

Full-subtracter block diagram

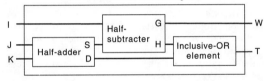

Figure 66. Full-Subtracter

full-tone original Synonym for continuous-tone original.

fullword Synonym for computer word.

fullword binary In SQL, a binary number with a precision of 31 bits. See also integer.

fully connected network A network in which there is a branch between any two nodes. (T) See Figure 67.

fully perforated tape Perforated paper tape in which the perforations are complete, that is, in which the punch makes a complete hole in the tape.

Note: In chadless tape, the hole is not completely punched out.

fully qualified generic profile In RACF, a generic profile that has a name with no generic characters. A fully qualified generic profile protects only resources whose names match the name of the profile.

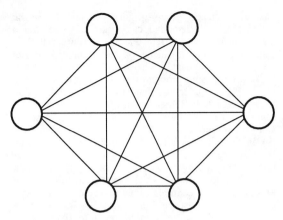

Figure 67. Fully Connected Network

fully qualified name A qualified name that is complete; that is, one that includes all names in the hierarchical sequence above the structure member to which the name refers, as well as the name of the member itself.

fully qualified procedure correlator id. A network-unique identifier that is used for the following:

• Correlating messages sent between nodes, such as correlating a Locate search request with its replies

• Identifying a session for problem determination and resolution

• Identifying a session for accounting, auditing, and performance monitoring purposes

This identifier is normally assigned at the node that contains the LU for which a procedure or session is initiated, except when that node is an end node, in which case its network node server may assign it. The FQPCID consists of a fixed-length correlator concatenated with the network-qualified name of the control point that generated the correlator.

function (1) A mathematical entity whose value, that is, the value of the dependent variable, depends in a specified manner on the values of one or more independent variables, not more than one value of the dependent variable corresponding to each permissible combination of values from the respective ranges of the independent variables. (I) (A) (2) In Open System Interconnection architecture, a part of the activity of entities in the same layer. (T) (3) A specific purpose of an entity, or its characteristic action. (A) (4) A machine action such as a carriage return or a line feed. (A) (5) A subroutine that returns the value of a single variable and that usually has a single exit; for example, subroutines that compute mathematical functions, such as sine, cosine, logarithm, or that compute the maximum of a set of numbers. (T) (6) In the C and FORTRAN languages, a named group of statements that can be called and evaluated, and can return a value to the calling statement. (7) In Pascal, a routine that is called by coding its name on the right side of an assignment statement. The routine passes a result back to the calling program through the routine name. (8) In PL/I, a procedure that has a RETURNS option in the PROCEDURE statement. A function ends by running a RETURNS statement and returning a scalar value to the point of call. Contrast with subroutine. (9) In SQL, an operation that supplies a single value from another value or from a set of values. A function obtains a single value by applying the function name; for example AVG, to the result of the expression, for example, column-name. See also column function, scalar function. (10) In SMP/E, a system component or licensed program that can be optionally installed in a user's system. Functions are defined to SMP/E by the ++FUNCTION statement. Each function must have a unique function modification identifier (FMID).

functional analysis A systematic investigation of the functions of a real or planned system. (T)

functional design The specification of the functions of the components of a system and of the working relationships among them. (T)

functional diagram A diagram that represents the working relationships among the parts of a system. (A)

functional enhancement package A diskette containing enhancements to DPPX/Base.

functionality Synonym for utility.

functional language A programming language in which computations are expressed in terms of function procedure calls; for example, LISP. (T)

functional macroinstruction A TCAM macroinstruction that performs the operations which are required for messages that are directed to the message handler. Contrast with delimiter macroinstruction.

functional performance Synonym for utility.

functional programming A method for structuring programs mainly as sequences of possibly nested function procedure calls. (T)

functional recovery routine (FRR) In OS/VS, a recovery routine that is used by the locked programs, the service request blocks, and the supervisor control routines.

functional subsystem application (FSA) An area within the Print Services Facility functional subsystem that represents a single printing subsystem and from which the printing subsystem is managed.

functional subsystem (FSS) The Print Services Facility address space created by the job entry subsystem.

functional subsystem interface (FSI) A set of services that allow communication between the JES address space or direct printer services subsystem (DPSS) and the Print Services Facility functional subsystem.

functional test In the 3881 Optical Mark Reader, a diagnostic microprogram used by the microprocessing unit to test overall system reliability.

functional unit An entity of hardware or software, or both, capable of accomplishing a specified purpose. (I) (A)

function authority credential (FAC) In DPPX, a value assigned to each user, each command, and each load module to allow: (a) a user to request that a load module be executed, (b) a user to issue a command, and (c) a load module to request that another load module be executed.

function call An expression that moves the path of execution from the current function to a specified function and evaluates to the return value provided by the called function. A function call contains the name of the function to which control moves and a parenthesized list of values.

function check A notification that an unexpected condition has stopped the execution of a program.

function check machine A notification of the malfunction of a machine instruction.

function control sequence (FCS) In the AS/400 system and System/38, a multiple-leaving telecommunications access method (MTAM), control character that controls the flow of individual function streams.

function declaration statement A declaration used to assign a name to a function. (T)

function declarator The part of a function definition that names the function, provides additional information about the return value of the function, and lists the function parameters.

function definition module (1) In DPPX, the programs that control functions performed by an adapter. (2) A module used by DPPX communication programs to access hardware.

function generator A functional unit whose output analog variable is equal to some function of its input analog variables. (I) (A)

function hole Synonym for designation hole.

function identifier Any combination of letters, symbols, or numbers used to identify function keys.

function key (1) In computer graphics, a button or switch that may be operated to send a signal to the computer program controlling the display. (T) (2) A key that performs a specified set of operations when it is pressed. (3) See programmed function key. (4) See also command function key.

function key area In SAA Basic Common User Access architecture, the area at the bottom of a panel that contains the function key assignments.

function keyboard A set of function keys on an input device such as a terminal.

function key indicator In RPG, an indicator that is set on when a valid corresponding function key is pressed. Valid function key indicators are KA through KN and KP through KY.

function management data (FMD) An RU category used for end-user data exchanged between logical units (LUs) and for requests and responses exchanged between network services components of LUs, PUs, and control points.

function management header (FMH) One or more headers, optionally present in the leading request units (RUs) of an RU chain, that allow one LU to (a) select a transaction program or device at the session partner and control the way in which the end-user data it sends is handled at the destination, (b) change the destination or the characteristics of the data during the session, and (c) transmit between session partners status or user information about the destination (for example, a program or device). Function management headers can be used with LU type 1, 4, and 6.2 protocols.

function management (FM) profile In SNA, a specification of various data flow control protocols (such as RU chains and data flow control requests) and FMD options (such as use of FM headers, compression, and alternate codes) supported for a particular session. Each function management profile is identified by a number.

function name In COBOL, an IBM-defined name that identifies system logical units, system-supplied information, printer control characters, and program switches.

function part Synonym for operation part.

function preselection (1) On a typewriter, the determination of a functional cycle by setting one or more control elements prior to the start of the operation. (T) (2) On a calculator, the ability to assign more than one function to a control or key. (T)

function procedure In programming languages, a procedure that, when executed, yields a value and whose procedure call may be used as an operand in an expression; for example, the function SIN yields the value SIN X when called with SIN(X). (I)

function reference (1) The appearance of an intrinsic function name or a user function name in an expression. (2) In PL/I, an entry constant or an entry variable, either of which must represent a function, followed by a possibly empty argument list. Contrast with subroutine call.

function request shipping In CICS/VS, the SNA remote resource access capability.

function subprogram A user-written subprogram defined by FORTRAN statements, the first of which is a FUNCTION statement. See also statement function, subroutine.

function table (1) Two or more sets of data so arranged that an entry in one set selects one or more entries in the remaining sets; for example, a tabulation of the values of a function for a set of values of the variable, a dictionary. (A) (2) A functional unit that can either decode multiple inputs into a single output or encode a single input into multiple outputs. (A)

functor In a conceptual schema language, a linguistic object that refers to a function on other linguistic objects such as terms and sentences and yields corresponding terms and sentences as output values. (A)

fuse In the 3800 Printing Subsystem, to blend, through application of heat and pressure, toner into paper to form a permanent bond.

fused-on toner Toner that is heated enough to attach to a process material such as carrier bead or photoconductor or to hardware.

fuser In the 3800 Printing Subsystem, the assembly that fuses a toned image into paper through the use of heat and pressure.

fuser station The assembly that bonds the toned image to the paper by heat and pressure.

fusing (1) Permanently bonding toner to paper by means of heat and pressure. (2) Synonym for fixing.

fusion splice In fiber optics, a splice accomplished by the application of localized heat sufficient to fuse or melt the ends of two lengths of optical fiber, forming a continuous, single fiber. (E)   Contrast with mechanical splice.

fuzzy logic In artificial intelligence, a technique using approximate rules of inference in which truth values and quantifiers are defined as possibility distributions that carry linguistic labels. (T)

fuzzy set In set theory, a generalization allowing for various degrees of set membership, instead of all or none. (T)

G

G Giga; ten to the ninth power, or 1,000,000,000 in decimal notation. When referring to storage capacity, two to the thirtieth power, 1,073,741,824 in decimal notation.

g Gram.

GA Go-ahead sequence.

GADDR Group address.

gadget In the AIXwindows program, a windowless graphical object that looks like its equivalent like-named widget but does not support the translations, actions, or pop-up widget children supplied by that widget.

gadget ID In the AIXwindows program, a unique identification number assigned to each instance of a gadget used within a given graphical interface.

gaffer In video and film production, a member of a production crew, typically involved in building and striking sets, and in providing general assistance to the director.

gain The strength of an analog signal.

GAM Graphics access method.

game port On a personal computer, a port used to connect devices such as joysticks and paddles.

gamma correction In AIX graphics, a logarithmic assignment of intensities to lookup table entries for shading applications. This is required because the human eye perceives intensities logarithmically rather than linearly.

gamma ramp In AIX graphics, a set of three lookup tables, one for each of the colors red, green, and blue, attached to the electron guns of the monitor. See also color ramp, gamma correction.

gang punch To punch identical hole patterns into each punch card of a card deck. (I) (A)

Gantt Chart A graphical representation of a project schedule that depicts the time relationship between activities.

gap See file gap, interblock gap, interrecord gap.

gap character A character included in a computer word for technical reasons that does not represent data. (I) (A)

gap loss (1) In fiber optics, that optical power loss caused by a space between axially aligned fibers. (E) See also coupling loss. (2) In waveguide-to-waveguide coupling, synonymous with longitudinal offset loss.

gap seal In the 3800, a plastic material that seals the photoconductor gap in the drum. The seal can be released or removed to permit the photoconductor to be advanced or replaced.

gap width The dimension of the air gap between a read/write head and the surface of the recording medium.

garage In MSS, an area at each end of a 3851 Mass Storage Facility in which an accessor is stored when not in use.

garbage Meaningless data.

garbage collection The process of identifying unused areas of main storage. (A)

gas panel Synonym for plasma panel.

gate (1) A combinational circuit that performs an elementary logic operation and usually involves one output. (T) (2) A combinational logic element having at least one input channel. (A) (3) See AND gate, EXCLUSIVE-OR gate, identity gate, IF-AND-ONLY-IF gate, IF-THEN gate, INCLUSIVE-OR gate, majority gate, NAND gate, NOR gate, NOT gate, NOT-IF-THEN gate, OR gate, threshold gate. (4) Synonymous with logic element.

Note: A gate usually involves one output.

gateway (1) A functional unit that interconnects two computer networks with different network architectures. A gateway connects networks or systems of different architectures. A bridge interconnects networks or systems with the same or similar architectures. (T) (2) In the AIX operating system, an entity that operates above the link layer and translates, when required, the interface and protocol used by one network into those used by another distinct network. (3) A network that connects hosts. See active gateway, exterior gateway, interior gateway, neighbor gateway, passive gateway. (4) In TCP/IP, a device used to connect two systems that use either the same or different communications protocols. (5) The combination of machines and programs that provide address translation, name translation, and system services control point (SSCP) rerouting between independent SNA networks to allow those networks to communicate. A gateway consists of one gateway NCP and at least one gateway VTAM. (6) In the IBM Token-Ring Network, a device and its associated software that connect a local area network to another local area network or a host that uses different logical link protocols. (7) See also bridge, LAN gateway, relay, SNA network interconnect.

gateway-capable host A host node that has a defined NETID and SSCPNAME, but does not perform gateway control functions, such as cross-network session initiation and termination.

gateway control functions Functions performed by a gateway system services control point (SSCP) in conjunction with the gateway NCP to assign alias network address pairs for LU-LU sessions, assign virtual routes for the LU-LU sessions in adjacent networks, and translate network names within BIND RUs.

gateway host (1) In the AIX operating system, a host that connects independent networks. It has multiple interfaces, each with a different name and address. (2) In the NetView program, a host node that contains a gateway system services control point (SSCP). See gateway-capable host.

gateway NCP In the NetView program, a network control program (NCP) that performs address translation to allow cross-network session traffic. The gateway NCP connects two or more independent SNA networks. Synonymous with gateway node.

gateway node (1) A node that is an interface between networks. (2) Synonym for gateway NCP.

gateway SSCP Synonym for gateway VTAM.

Gateway-to-Gateway Protocol (GGP) In the AIX operating system, the protocol with which a gateway determines connectivity to networks and neighbor gateways and implements the shortest-path routing algorithm.

gateway VTAM An SSCP that is capable of cross-network session initiation, termination, takedown, and session outage notification. A gateway VTAM is in session with the gateway NCP; it provides network name translation and assists the gateway NCP in setting up alias network addresses for cross-network sessions. Synonymous with gateway SSCP.

gather In input/output operations, to read data from noncontiguous memory locations to write to a device. Contrast with scatter.

GB Gigabyte.

GC Graphics context.

GC caching In the AIX Enhanced X-Windows program, a process that allows independent change requests to be merged into one protocol request.

GContext Graphics context.

GCP (1) RISC System/6000 7016 POWERstation 730 Graphics Processor Subsystem Graphics Control Processor. (2) Graphics Control Processor.

GCR Group code recording, a magnetic tape recording format with a density of 6250 bpi.

GCS Group control system.

GDDM Graphical data display manager.

GDF Graphics data file.

GDF file Graphics data format file.

GDG Generation data group.

GDS General data stream.

GE Greater than or equal to. See relational operator.

General Availability (GA) The time when the product and all ship group material may be ordered by all customers.

general data stream (GDS) The data stream used for conversations in LU 6.2 sessions.

general data stream (GDS) variable A type of RU substructure that is preceded by an identifier and a length field and includes either application data, user control data, or SNA-defined control data.

General help In SAA Advanced Common User Access architecture, a choice that gives a user a brief overview of each action or task, or both, that a user can perform within a window.

generalized interactive executive (GIX) A function of the NetView Distribution Manager licensed program that provides the host system user with interactive use of NetView Distribution Manager.

Generalized Markup Language (GML) (1) A high level formatting expression that, when processed by the DOCUMENT command, expands into one or more

SCRIPT control words. (2) A language that can be used to identify the parts of a source document without respect to a particular processing system.

generalized path information unit trace A record of the flow of path information units (PIUs) exchanged between the network control program and its attached resources. PIU trace records consist of up to 44 bytes of transmission header (TH), request/response header (RH), and request/response unit (RU) data.

generalized sequential access method (GSAM) In IMS/VS, a database access method that provides accessing support for simple physical sequential data sets, such as tape files, SYSIN, SYSOUT, and other files that are not hierarchical in nature.

generalized sort/merge program A program designed to sort or merge a wide variety of records in a variety of formats.

generalized trace facility (GTF) An optional OS/VS service program that records significant system events, such as supervisor calls and start I/O operations, for the purpose of problem determination.

general migration In the Hierarchical Storage Manager, automatic migration that occurs at a specific time of day. See also interval migration.

general poll (1) A technique in which special invitation characters are sent to solicit transmission of data from all attached remote devices that are ready to send. (2) See polling list.

general pool In a Data Facility/ Hierarchical Storage Manager (DF/HSM) environment with JES3, the collection of all Data Facility/Hierarchical Storage Manager primary volumes added to that processor that have a mount status or are permanently resident or reserved, have the automatic recall attribute specified, and can be further restricted by a mount attribute of storage or private.

general-purpose computer A computer designed to operate on a wide variety of problems. (I) (A)

general-purpose interface bus An adapter that controls the interface between the PC, Personal Computer XT, or Personal Computer AT and, for example, the InfoWindow display; it is also known as the IBM IEEE 488.

general-purpose library In the AS/400 system and System/38, the library shipped with the system that contains IBM-provided objects required for many system functions and user-created objects that are not explicitly placed in a different library when they are created.

general-purpose operating system An operating system designed to handle a wide variety of computer system applications.

general-purpose paper card A card that meets specifications in applicable ISO standards, except for the printed card form. (A)

general-purpose register A register, usually explicitly addressable, within a set of registers that can be used for different purposes; for example, as an accumulator, index register, or special handler of data. (I) (A)

general register A register used for operations such as binary addition, subtraction, multiplication, and division. General registers are used primarily to compute and modify addresses in a program.

general resource Any system resource, other than an MVS data set, that is defined in the class descriptor table (CDT). In MVS, general resources include DASD volumes, tape volumes, load modules, terminals, IMS and CICS transactions, and installation-defined resource classes.

Note: VM, general resources include terminals, minidisks, virtual unit record devices, and RSCS nodes.

general resource profile In RACF, a profile that provides protection for one or more general resources. The information in the profile can include the general resource profile name, profile owner, universal access authority, access list, and other data.

general-use interface All programming interfaces that do not meet the definition of a product-sensitive programming interface.

general-use mass storage volume See general-use volume.

general user In System/36, a person, such as a manager, secretary, or clerk, who signs on to and uses OFFICE/36. Contrast with indirect user.

general user privilege class In VM, the subset of CP commands that allow the Class G programmer or problem solver to manipulate and control the virtual machine. A general user cannot display or modify real storage.

general-use volume In MSS, a mass storage volume assigned to a mass storage volume group that can be used for nonspecific requests for a mass storage volume.

general warning indicator On dictation equipment, a device giving an audible or visible signal that recording is impossible, or possible only under certain restrictions; for example, it may signal that there is no recording medium in the machine or no recording facility available in a centralized dictation system. (I)

generate (1) To produce a computer program by selecting subsets from skeletal code under the control of parameters. (A) (2) To produce assembler language statements from the model statements of a macrodefinition when the definition is called by a macroinstruction. (3) In CSP/AD, to produce a representation of an application program, map group, or table that can be interpreted by Cross System Product/Application Execution. (4) See also assemble.

generated address An address formed as a result during execution of a computer program. (I) (A) Synonymous with synthetic address.

generating function In a series of functions or constants, a mathematical function that, when represented by an infinite series, has those functions or constants as coefficients in the series. (I) (A)

generation (1) In micrographics, a measure of the remoteness of the copy from the original material; the first microfilm representation is the first generation microfilm. (I) (A) (2) A means of referencing items with respect to time and ancestry so that an item without antecedents is designated as the first or n-th generation, and subsequent derivations are designated as n+1, n+2, and so on. (A) (3) For some remote systems, the translation of configuration information into machine language. (A) (4) In the NetView program, the process of assembling and link editing definition statements so that resources can be identified to all the necessary programs in a network.

generational loss The reduction in picture quality caused by the copying of video programs.

generation data group (GDG) A collection of data sets with the same base name, such as PAYROLL, that are kept in chronological order. Each data set is called a generation data set.

generation data set One generation of a generation data group.

generation definition The definition statement of a resource used in generating a program.

generation feature An IBM licensed program order option to be used if the object code of a program is to be tailored to user requirements.

generation input stream The part of the sort program that translates the sequence specifications into machine language.

generator See character generator, compiler generator, curve generator, dot matrix character generator, fixed function generator, function generator, macrogenerator, stroke character generator, variable function generator, vector generator.

generic Relating to, or characteristic of, a whole group or class.

generic alert A product-independent method of encoding alert data by means of both (a) code points indexing short units of stored text and (b) textual data.

generic BIND Synonym for session activation request.

generic controller description An asynchronous controller description that is reserved for incoming calls on an X.25 packet-switching data network from a remote system or device that does not use SNA transmission protocols and whose location name and identifier are defined in configuration list QASYNCLOC library QSYS. See also asynchronous controller description.

generic key (1) In a search, an identifier used to find all items that pertain to a particular category. (2) In BASIC, a value specified in the SEARCH clause of a record input/output statement that is less than the full key field length defined for a corresponding file. (3) In systems with VSAM, a leading portion of a key, containing characters that identify those records significant for a certain application; for example, it may be necessary to retrieve all records whose keys begin with the generic key AB.

generic name (1) The name of a category of names. (2) In the AS/400 system, the characters common to object names that can be used to identify a group of objects. A generic name ends with an asterisk (*); for example, ORD* identifies all objects whose names begin with the characters ORD.

generic profile In RACF, a resource profile that can provide protection for one or more resources. The resources protected by a generic profile have similar names and identical security requirements. For example, a generic data set profile can protect one or more data sets. See fully qualified generic profile.

generic unbind Synonym for session deactivation request.

generic unit A possibly parameterized model of a language construct from which, at translation time, a language construct proper is derived.

Note: There is some analogy between generic units and macro-definitions: the language construct derived from the generic unit corresponds to the statement sequence replacing a macro call and is referred to as a "generic instantiation." (T)

genlocking In video systems, the process of synchronizing one video signal to another.

geometric modeling A system that represents three-dimensional shapes in a computer and renders it transportable. (T)

geometric text Text whose character fonts are defined by mathematical descriptions of the strokes required to draw the characters, rather than by raster images. Synonymous with programmable character set, stroke text.

geometry In AIX Enhanced X-Windows, synonym for layout.

gesture A hand-drawn symbol or uppercase letter that, when recognized by the system, invokes an action or a series of actions. A gesture denotes an action and a target for the action.

gesture assignment An assignment that defines the action or actions performed as a result of a gesture.

gesture mode In the PenPM operating system extension, an input mode in which the system interprets pen input as gestures.

get (1) To obtain a record from an input file. (2) In word processing, to retrieve a defined block of text from a document and insert it into the document being created or revised.

get operation An input operation that obtains a record from an input file and passes it to a program.

GETVIS space In VSE, storage space within a partition or the shared virtual area that is available for dynamic allocation to programs.

GFT Grant functional transmission.

GGP Gateway-to-Gateway Protocol.

GID Group ID.

gigabyte (**GB**) (1) One billion (10^9) bytes. (2) When referring to memory capacity, 1 073 741 824 in decimal notation.

gigaflops One billion basic floating-point operations per second.

giga (**G**) Ten to the ninth power; 1,000,000,000 in decimal notation. When referring to storage capacity, two to the thirtieth power; 1,073,741,824 in decimal notation.

giveback The process by which an alternate subsystem releases itself from its extended recovery facility (XRF) sessions with terminal users and is replaced by the primary subsystem. See also takeover.

GIX Generalized interactive executive.

GJP Graphic job processor.

GL Graphics library.

glass master In multimedia applications, the final videodisc format from which copies are made. See also edit master.

GLB Global Location Broker.

glitch Deprecated term for failure, fault.

global (1) In programming languages, pertaining to the relationship between a language object and a block in which the language object has a scope extending beyond that block but contained within an encompassing block. (I) (2) Pertaining to that which is defined in one subdivision of a computer program and used in at least one other subdivision of the computer program. (A) (3) Pertaining to all places in a document or file. (4) Pertaining to information available to more than one program or subroutine. (5) Contrast with local. (6) See also global code, global lock, global processor, global service, global variable symbol.

global access checking In RACF, the ability to allow an installation to establish an in-storage table of default values for authorization levels for selected resources. RACF refers to this table prior to performing normal RACHECK processing, and grants the request without performing a RACHECK if the requested access authority does not exceed the global value. Global access checking can grant the user access to the resource, but it cannot deny access.

global administration Synonym for universal administration. (T)

global area A storage area used for communication between two or more main programs.

global change In word processing, simultaneous modification or deletion of one or more characters or words wherever they appear in a document.

global character Synonym for pattern-matching character.

global code The part of a program that includes the body of any macrodefinition called from a source module and the open code portion of the source module.

global data In the AIX operating system, data that can be addressed by any process while in kernel mode. It contains such tables as the open file table and process table, and other data such as buffer pointers, maintained by the kernel.

global entity In FORTRAN, an entity identified by a lexical token whose scope is a executable program. It may be an external program unit, a common block, or an external procedure.

global file name character Either a question mark (?) or an asterisk (*) used as a variable in a file name or file name extension when referring to a particular file or group of files.

global find and replace Synonym for global search and replace. (T)

Global Location Broker (GLB) In the AIX NCS Location Broker, a server that maintains global information about objects on a network or an internet.

global lock (1) A lock that protects serially reusable resources related to more than one private address space. (2) In DPPX, a one-of-a-kind lock within the system.

global lock management In IMS/VS, lock management that controls access to resources shared among IMS/VS systems participating in block level sharing.

global name In COBOL, a name that is declared in only one program but that may be referenced from that program and from any program contained within that program. Condition-names, data-names, file-names, record-names, report names, and some special registers may be global names.

global processor In JES, the processor that controls job scheduling and device allocation for a complex of processors. See also local processor.

global search In word processing, to find automatically a character or group of characters wherever they appear in a document with a single instruction. A global search may provide the option to change for another character or group of characters at each occurrence; for instance, change "International Organization for Standardization" to "ISO." (T)

global search and replace A function that enables the user to search for repeated occurrences of a character string within a document and to automatically replace all occurrences of one character string with another character string. Synonymous with global find and replace. (T)

global service A service that applies to more than one private address space.

global shared resources (GSR) In MVS/370 and MVS/XA, an option for sharing I/O buffers, I/O-related control blocks, and the channel programs among VSAM data sets in a resource pool that serves all of the address spaces in the system.

global storage In the 3600 Finance Communication System, segments of programmable storage that are associated with and available to all logical workstations defined for a 3601 Finance Communication Controller.

global variable (1) A variable defined in one portion of a computer program and used in at least one other portion of the computer program. (T) (2) In the AS/400 system, a named entity within query management that can be assigned a value used for communications between an application program and Query Management/400.

global variable pool In the AS/400 system, query management, the set of all user- and query-defined variables associated with a query instance.

global zone A group of VSAM records that contains information defining a common area that SMP/E uses to represent data not applicable to a target zone or distribution zone.

globbing Deprecated term for file name substitution.

glossary See data glossary. (A)

glyph (1) An image, usually of a character, in a font. See cursor glyph. (2) A graphic symbol whose appearance conveys information; for example, the vertical and horizontal arrows on cursor keys that indicate the directions in which they control cursor movement, the sunburst symbol on the screen illumination control of a display device.

GM Group mark.

GMFHS Graphic Monitor Facility host subsystem.

GML Generalized Markup Language.

go-ahead sequence (GA) In an 8100 loop, a sequence of bits (01111111) used to minimize the possibility that changing states by secondary stations can affect loop operation. This includes the change of state that occurs when a secondary station begins transmitting.

go-ahead tone An audible signal indicating that the system is ready to accept a message.

gobo In photography, a screen, painted black and placed so that it diverts light from one or more studio lamps, thus preventing the light from entering the camera lens; may also be used to create shadow effects. See also diffuser, scrim.

GOCA Graphic Object Content Architecture.

Gothic character set A character set (available in 10-, 12-, and 15-pitch) with 63 sans serif graphic characters.

GOTO statement In programming languages, a statement that transfers control to another point in a program.

Gouraud shading A method of shading polygons smoothly based on the intensities at their vertices. The color index is uniformly interpolated along each edge, and then the edge values are uniformly interpolated along each scan line. For realistic shading, the colors associated with the color indexes should be gamma-corrected.

GPS Graphic programming services.

GPSS (general purpose systems simulator) A programming language based on block diagrams and used for discrete simulation. (T)

GPT Generalized path information unit trace.

grab In the AIX operating system: (1) The act of selecting keyboard keys, the keyboard, pointer buttons, the pointer, and the server for exclusive use by a client. See active grab, passive grab. See also button grabbing, key grabbing, keyboard grabbing, pointer grabbing, server grabbing. (2) A procedure by which a window acts upon a key or button event that occurs for it or any of its descendants. This precludes the necessity of setting up translations for all windows.

gradation In a document copying machine, the tone scale or contrast range of the subject matter on the original or its image. (T)

graded-index fiber An optical fiber with a refractive index that varies with the radial distance from the fiber axis. Contrast with step-index fiber. (E)

grade of service In data communication, the traffic handling capacity of a network.

gradient fill In computer graphics, a fill composed of a smooth blend from a starting color to an ending color.

gram (g) 0.035 ounces.

grammar rules The structure rules in a parser program. See also parser.

grandfathered equipment Under the FCC Registration Program, customer premises equipment that was legally attached by telephone companies directly to the public switched network, other than party line and coin service, prior to a specified date. New equipment was sold and installed during a transitional period, but equipment produced after that period for direct attachment to the public switched network must be registered with the FCC.

grant A DB2 process that authorizes users to access data.

grant functional transmission (GFT) In the AS/400 system and System/38 multiple-leaving telecommunications access method (MTAM), a control character indicating that the host system gives permission to the AS/400 system to send data or that the system gives permission to the host system to send data. Contrast with request functional transmission.

granularity (1) The extent to which a larger entity is subdivided. For example, a yard divided into inches has finer granularity than a yard divided into feet. (2) In computer security, an expression of the relative size of a data object; for example, protection at the file level is considered to be coarse granularity, whereas protection at the field level is considered to be of finer granularity.

graphic A symbol produced by a process such as handwriting, drawing, or printing. (I) (A) Synonymous with graphic symbol.

graphical data display manager (GDDM) (1) A group of routines that allows pictures to be defined and displayed procedurally through function routines that correspond to graphic primitives. Contrast with presentation graphics routines. (2) In the NetView Performance Monitor (NPM), an IBM licensed program used in conjunction with the Presentation Graphics Feature (PGF) to generate online graphs in the NPM Graphic Subsystem. (3) In the OS/400 operating system, a function that processes both text and graphics for output on a display, printer, or plotter. Contrast with presentation graphics routines (PGR).

graphical user interface (GUI) A type of computer interface consisting of a visual metaphor of a real-world scene, often of a desktop. Within that scene are icons, representing actual objects, that the user can access and manipulate with a pointing device.

graphic character (1) A visual representation of a character, other than a control character, that is normally produced by writing, printing, or displaying. (T) (2) A character that can be displayed or printed.

graphic character identifier Synonym for character identifier.

graphic character modification In the 3800 Printing Subsystem, a feature that allows the substitution or extension of the graphic characters in a previously defined character arrangement.

graphic character set A set of graphic characters in a code page.

graphic communication server The part of the NetView Graphic Monitor Facility that uses LU 6.2 to transport data between the NetView program and the server workstation and between the server workstation and its client workstations.

graphic data server The part of the NetView Graphic Monitor Facility that maintains, on a programmable workstation, the network management data that it receives from the NetView program and that correlates this data with views.

graphic display A display device that provides a representation of data in any graphic form. (T)

graphic display program A program designed to display information in graphic or alphanumeric form on the face of a TV-like display screen.

graphic escape character In the 3270 data stream, a control code (hex 80) used to introduce a graphic character (hex 40 through hex FE) from an alternate character set.

graphic file format Any of several formats for storing computer graphics. See DXF (Drawing Interchange Format), EPS (Encapsulated Postscript), IGES (Initial Graphics Exchange Specification), TIFF (Tag Image File Format).

graphic job processing An optional feature of MFT and MVT that enables users at display units to quickly and conveniently define and start jobs to be processed under the operating system. The feature also allows interactive use of graphic display programs.

graphic job processor (GJP) A program that elicits job control information from a user performing job control operations at a display station. It interprets the information entered by the user and converts it into job control language. See also satellite graphic job processor.

graphic language See graphics language.

graphic monitor The graphical user interface of the NetView Graphic Monitor Facility.

Graphic Monitor Facility host subsystem A NetView feature that manages configuration and status updates for non-SNA resources.

Graphic Object Content Architecture (GOCA) An architecture that provides a collection of graphics values and control structures used to interchange and present graphics data.

graphic overlay Synonym for overlay.

graphic primitive (1) In computer graphics, a basic element, such as an arc or a line, that is not made up of smaller parts and that is used to create diagrams and pictures. (2) Synonym for display element. (3) See also input primitive. See Figure 68.

Figure 68. Graphic Primitives

graphic programming services (GPS) In OS/VS, a number of services provided for use in designing and executing programs that communicate with a user at a display station.

graphics (1) The making of charts and pictures. (2) Pertaining to charts, tables, and their creation. (3) See computer graphics, coordinate graphics, fixed-image graphics, interactive graphics, passive graphics, raster graphics. (4) See also computer micrographics.

graphics access method (GAM) A facility that supports IBM display devices through use of graphic programming services (GPS) and the graphic subroutine package (GSP).

graphics adapter On a personal computer, an expansion board that adds computer graphics features such as color. Synonymous with video board.

graphics context (GC, Gcontext) In AIX Enhanced X-Windows, the storage area for various kinds of graphics output, such as foreground pixels, background pixels, line widths, and clipping regions. A graphics context can be used only with drawables that have the same root and the same depth as the graphics context.

graphics data file A picture definition in a coded format used internally by GDDM that optionally provides the user with a lower level programming interface than GDDM API.

graphics data format (GDF) file A picture definition in a coded order format used internally by GDDM and, optionally, providing the user with a lower-level programming interface than the GDDM application programming interface.

graphic service facility A GraphicsView/2 facility that logs trace and error data.

graphics field In GDDM, that part of the display or the paper that is used for pictures and graphics text.

graphics hierarchy An ordered division of parts of a graphics program, of which the device is the highest level and parts of the picture are lowest.

graphics language A programming language for the processing and visible presentation of graphic data by means of a computer. (T)

graphics mode One of several states of a display. The mode determines the resolution and color content of the screen.

graphics pipeline In AIX graphics, a sequence of steps that does geometric transformations, clipping, lighting, and scaling.

graphics primitive See graphic primitive.

graphics segment In GDDM, a group of graphics primitives (lines, arcs, and text) that are operated as a common set. The graphics primitives inside a graphics segment share characteristics, such as visibility and angle of rotation, but keep their individual characteristics, such as color and line width.

Graphics Support Library (XGSL) A two-dimensional graphics application programming interface to various output devices supported on the AIX PS/2 and RISC System/6000 systems.

graphics symbol set In GDDM, an object that can contain either lines or images. See also vector symbol set (VSS), image symbol set (ISS).

graphics tablet A sensitive board on which computer-generated graphics can be designed using a handheld input device, such as a graphics pen, to draw freehand, create shapes and transmit instructions.

graphics text In GDDM, text displayed by an application program using a graphics symbol set.

GraphicsView/2 An IBM licensed program that is an interface between an application program and a person using a programmable workstation. It enables the user

to display the graphical and topographical information that the application program provides.

graphics window In GDDM, the view of the graphics picture that is defined by the range of the world coordinates specified by the user.

graphic symbol Synonym for graphic.

graPHIGS An implementation of PHIGS used by IBM and based on the American National Standards Institute (ANSI) proposed standard, Programmer's Hierarchical Interactive Graphics System (PHIGS).

GRAPHMOD Graphic character modification module.

gravity In AIX Enhanced X-Windows, the attraction of the contents of windows or subwindows to a location within the window. See bit gravity, window gravity.

gray bar An unwanted, gray-colored, narrow, horizontal stripe of background. See also spot.

gray code A binary code in which sequential numbers are represented by binary expressions, each of which differs from the preceding expression in one place only. (A) Synonymous with reflected binary code.

gray image An image composed of the full spectrum of gray shades ranging from black to white. A gray image can have up to 256 shades of gray pels. See pel. Contrast with bilevel image.

graying In SAA Advanced Common User Access architecture, an indication that a choice in a pull-down is unavailable. For choices that are black when available, graying is accomplished by reducing the contrast between the choice and its background. See unavailable emphasis.

gray level In GDDM, a digitally coded shade of gray that is in a range of 0 through 7. See also gray-scale image.

gray scale (1) A scale that indicates the shades of gray between black and white that can be presented on a display device. (2) In AIX Enhanced X-Windows, a type of degenerate pseudocolor in which the red, green, and blue values in any given colormap entry are equal, thus producing shades of gray. The gray values can be changed dynamically. (3) In a grayscale adapter, the different levels of intensity corresponding to the shades of gray produced.

gray-scale image (1) In GDDM, an image in which the degrees of shading between black and white are represented by different gray levels. Each picture element of the image has a value in the range from 0 through 7. (2) An image whose image data elements are represented by multiple bits and whose image data element values are mapped to more than one level of brightness through an image data element structure parameter or a look-up table.

gray-scale image data A pattern of bits that represents, for each pixel of an image, several levels of luminescence ranging from black to white; for example, an 8-bit byte associated with a pixel can represent black, white, and 254 shades of gray. See also binary image data, thresholding.

Green Book standards See CD-I.

grid (1) In optical character recognition, two mutually orthogonal sets of parallel lines used for specifying or measuring character images. (A) (2) Uniformly spaced horizontal and vertical lines on a chart. See also axis grid lines.

grid lines In System/38 graphics, uniformly spaced horizontal and vertical reference lines on a chart. See also axis grid lines.

grip In video and film production, a person who moves cables, sets, and so forth.

gripper edge In a duplicator, the edge of the copy paper that enables the gripper mechanism to carry the paper through the machine. (T)

gripper mechanism In a duplicator, a delivery system in which a gripping device extracts paper from the machine and forwards it into the delivery tray. (T)

gross clipping In AIX graphics, clipping done by the viewport. Typically, it is the same as fine clipping except in the case of character strings. Contrast with fine clipping.

gross minus The accumulation, during a sales period of all negative amounts such as refunds, allowances, and discounts entered or calculated in sales transactions at the point of sale terminal. Contrast with gross plus.

gross plus The accumulation during a sales period of all positive amounts such as merchandise prices, taxes, and deposits entered or calculated in sales transactions at the point of sale terminal. Contrast with gross minus.

group (1) A set of related records that have the same value for a particular field in all records. (2) A series of records logically joined together. See also print data set, transaction data set. (3) A series of lines repeated consecutively as a set on a full-screen form or full-screen panel. (4) A list of names that are known together by a single name. (5) In RACF, a collection of users who can share access authorities for protected resources. (6) In the NetView/PC program, to identify a set of application programs that are to run concurrently. (7) See body group, control group, default mass storage volume group, display group, mass storage volume group, printable group, record group, report group, slot group, staging drive group.

group address (GADDR) (1) In communications, a multidestination address associated with one or more stations on a network. Contrast with individual address. (2) In SDLC, an address in addition to a specific address that is common to two or more secondary stations.

group addressing The capability by which all stations on a multipoint line recognize addressing characters, but only one of the stations responds.

group authority In the AS/400 system, the authority to use objects, resources, or functions from a group profile.

group box In SAA Advanced Common User Access architecture, a rectangular frame with a title. It is used to group related choices.

group calendar A display that shows the events for up to seven users at one time.

group control system (GCS) A component of VM that provides multiprogramming and shared memory support to virtual machines. It is a saved system intended for use with SNA products.

group control system group A group of virtual machines that share common storage and load the same saved-VM system through a control program (CP) command or directory entry.

group data area In the OS/400 operating system, a data area that is automatically created when an interactive job becomes a group job. This data area is shared by all jobs in the group but cannot be used by jobs outside the group.

group data set In MVS, a RACF-protected data set in which either the high-level qualifier of the data set name or the qualifier supplied by an installation exit routine is a RACF group name.

grouped records Records combined into a unit to conserve storage space or reduce access time.

group entry In ACF/TCAM, a terminal-table entry associated with a group of logical units (LUs). See also cascade entry, line entry, logtype entry, process entry, single entry.

group heading In SAA Common User Access architecture, a word or words that identify a group of related fields.

group ID (GID) (1) In RACF, a string of one to eight characters that identifies a group. The first character must be A through Z, #, $, or @. The rest can be A through Z, #, $, @, or 0 through 9. (2) In the AIX operating system, a number that corresponds to a specific group name. The group ID can often be substituted in commands that take a group name as a value. Synonymous with group number.

group indication In RPG, the printing of control information for only the first record of a group of records containing identical control information.

grouping factor Synonym for blocking factor.

grouping isolation Electrical separation between groups of electrical circuits. (T)

Note: Within a group, there is an electrical connection, as there is within a power supply.

group item (1) In COBOL, a data item that is composed of subordinate data items. (2) Synonymous with host structure.

group job In the OS/400 operating system, one to sixteen interactive jobs that are associated in a group with the same workstation device and user.

group job name In the OS/400 operating system, the name that identifies a given job within a group.

group job transfer In the OS/400 operating system, an operation performed by the Transfer to Group Job (TFRGRPJOB) command that will either start a new group job or resume an existing group job.

group list print descriptor In the AS/400 system, a special type of print descriptor used to define print descriptor groups, and the search order used when a print descriptor is referred to.

group mark (1) A mark that identifies the beginning or end of a set of data, which may include blocks, characters, or other items. (I) (A) (2) A user-defined character that is used in the field definition function of the SDF/CICS map editor to mark the beginning of the group.

group message queue In the AS/400 system, a message queue associated with a group of jobs. When the message queue is set to break or notify mode in the active group job, it is set to the same mode in any job in the group that is transferred to or to any job that gains control when the active group job is canceled.

group name (1) A generic name for a collection of I/O devices; for example, DISK or TAPE. See also device type, unit address. (2) In the AIX operating system, a name that uniquely identifies a group of users to the system and that contains one to eight alphanumeric characters, beginning with an alphabetic, #, $, or > character. (3) In RACF, one to eight alphanumeric characters beginning with an alphabetic, #, $, or > character that identify a group. (4) In SDF/CICS, a major identification of an object in the map specification library. Group names may be map set names, +PROFILE or &PAGE.

group number (1) In OS/VS2 and VM, a part of an external page address that refers to a slot group; together with a device number and a slot number, it identifies the location of a page in external page storage. (2) In 3790 and DPCX, a number that identifies a logical group of records in a print data set or transaction data set. (3) Synonym for group ID.

group of logical units (LUs) In TCAM, a set of external LU definitions associated with the same group entry. See also group entry.

group polling A process whereby a single poll is sent to a collection point for a group of stations, inviting a response from any station in the group that has data to send.

group profile (1) In the AS/400 system, a user profile that provides the same authority to a group of users. See resource group profile. (2) In RACF, a profile that defines a group. The information in the profile includes the group name, profile owner, and users in the group.

group-related user attribute In RACF, a user attribute assigned at the group level that allows the user to control the resource, group, and user profiles associated with the group and its subgroups. Some of the group-related user attributes are group-SPECIAL, group-AUDITOR, and group-OPERATIONS.

group resource record In System/36, a record in the resource security file that secures a group of files or libraries.

group separator character (GS) The information separator intended to identify a logical boundary between groups. (I) (A)

group technology A coding and classification system used in computer-aided design for combining similar, often-used parts into families.

Note: This makes it easier to locate an existing part with specified characteristics and helps to standardize the fabrication of similar parts. (T)

group terminal option In RACF, a function that allows users within a group to log on only from those terminals for which they have been specifically authorized.

Group 4 compression A standard defined by the CCITT for compression of the format data of an image object.

GS The group separator character. (A)

GSAM Generalized sequential access method.

GSBIC RISC System/6000 7016 POWERstation 730 Graphics Processor Subsystem System Bus Interface Card.

GSR Global shared resources.

GSS Graphics symbol set.

GSVC trace Generalized supervisor calls trace.

gt Greater than. See also relational operator.

GTD Global timer data block.

GTF Generalized trace facility.

guard In computer security, a processor that provides a security filter between two systems operating at different security levels or between a user terminal and a database to filter out data that the user is not authorized to access.

guard expression An expression placed at the beginning of Boolean expressions to check that other operations can be done.

guest real storage In the VM/XA Migration Aid, the storage that appears real to the operating system running in a virtual machine. Contrast with guest virtual storage.

guest virtual storage In the VM/XA Migration Aid, the storage that appears virtual to the operating system running in a virtual machine. Contrast with guest real storage.

GUI Graphical user interface.

guidance code See operator guidance code.

guide edge Synonym for reference edge.

guide-in window In System/38, an opening through which a diskette is moved to the read/write position in the diskette magazine drive.

guillotine In a document copying machine, a device that cuts a predetermined length of copy material from a roll. (T)

gutter In multicolumn formatting, the space between columns.

GVM Guest virtual machine.

H

hacker (1) A computer enthusiast. (2) A computer enthusiast who uses his or her knowledge and means to gain unauthorized access to protected resources. (T) (A)

half-adder (1) A combinational circuit that has two inputs, A and B, and two outputs, one a sum without carry, S, and the other a carry, C, and in which the outputs are related to the inputs according to the following table: (I) (A)

Input A	0	0	1	1
Input B	0	1	0	1
Output S sum without carry	0	1	1	0
Output C carry	0	0	0	1

(2) Synonymous with two-input adder.

half-adjust (1) On a calculator, to round by one-half the maximum value of the number base of the counter. (T) (2) A method of rounding off a number by adjusting the last digit to be retained. When the number to the right of the last digit to be retained is 5 or greater, 1 is added to the last retained digit; for example, 2.475 half-adjusted to two decimal places becomes 2.48, but 2.474 becomes 2.47.

half-duplex (HD, HDX) In data communication, pertaining to transmission in only one direction at a time. Contrast with duplex. See also half-duplex operation, half-duplex transmission.

half-duplex operation A mode of operation of a data link in which data can be transmitted in both directions, one way at a time. (T) Synonymous with either-way operation.

half-duplex transmission Data transmission in either direction, one direction at a time. (I) (A)

half path A connection established between a telephone and a junctor in the switching network.

half-inch videotape A videotape format primarily intended for home use; sold in cassettes one-half inch thick. VHS and Beta (trademark of Sony Corporation) are examples of half-inch videotape.

half-session A session-layer component consisting of the combination of data flow control and transmission control components comprising one end of a session. See also session connector.

half-space On a typewriter, the relative movement between the paper carrier and typing position by half a character space parallel to the typing line. (T)

half-space key On a typewriter, a control for effecting the half-space function. (T)

half speed Half the top-rated speed of the associated equipment.

half-subtracter A combinational circuit that has two inputs that are a minuend G and a subtrahend H, and two outputs that are a difference without carry U and a borrow digit V, and in which the outputs are related to the inputs according to the following table: (I) (A)

Input G minuend	0	0	1	1
Input H subtrahend	0	1	0	1
Output U difference	0	1	1	0
Output V borrow digit	0	0	0	1

halftone original In a document copying machine, an original in which the subject matter is divided by screening to give the illusion of tonal gradation. (T)

halftoning The method of representing a gray image as a cluster of bilevel pels.

halfword A contiguous sequence of bits or characters that constitutes half a computer word and can be addressed as a unit. (A)

halfword binary In SQL, a binary number with a precision of 15 bits.

Halogen-Metal-Iodine (HMI) In video or film production, a substitute for daylight.

halt See breakpoint halt.

halt indicators In RPG, an indicator that stops the program when an unacceptable condition occurs. Valid halt indicators are H1 through H9.

halt instruction (1) A machine instruction that stops execution of a program. (2) Synonym for pause instruction.

hamming code A data code that can be corrected automatically. (A)

hamming distance Synonym for signal distance.

hand-feed punch A keypunch into which cards are manually entered and removed one at a time. (I) (A)

hand-held calculator A calculator capable of operating independently of main electric power that is light and small enough to be operated in the hand. (T)

handle (1) In the Advanced DOS and OS/2 operating systems, a binary value created by the system that identifies a drive, directory, and file so that the file can be found and opened. (2) In the AIX operating system, a data structure that is a temporary local identifier for an object. Allocating a handle creates it. Binding a handle makes it identify an object at a specific location. (3) In OS/400 application programming interfaces, a variable that represents an object.

handler (1) A routine that controls a program's reaction to specific external events; for example, an interrupt handler. (2) In FORTRAN, a sequence of statements commencing with a HANDLE statement and ending with the statement before the next HANDLE or END ENABLE, whichever comes first. A handler is executed when a condition specified for it is signaled.

handset A telephone mouthpiece and receiver in a single unit that can be held in one hand.

handshaking (1) In computer security, an exchange of data for the purpose of authenticating the identity of one or both parties. (2) The exchange of predetermined signals when a connection is established between two modems. See also answerback, VM/VS handshaking feature. (3) A method by which two pieces of hardware, such as a personal computer and a plotter, can communicate. Depending upon the devices communicating, handshaking occurs either as a hardware function or through software, such as a device driver.

Hangeul A written language of Korea. Each Hangeul character is composed of two to six Jamo characters.

hanging indent The indention of all lines of a block of text following the first line; the first line is not indented the same number of spaces. See left-hand indent, right-hand indent.

hang-up An undesirable repetition of an audio/video sequence caused by a problem in either the hardware, control software, or media.

Hanja Chinese characters used in Korean written language.

hard address The address of a LAN adapter card, burned into the card and unique to the card.

hard card In a personal computer, an expansion board that contains a hard disk drive and that can be installed in an expansion slot.

hardcopy (1) A permanent copy of a display image generated on an output device such as printer or plotter, and which can be carried away. (T) (2) A printed copy of machine output in a visually readable form; for example, printed reports, listings, documents, and summaries. See also display (1). (3) Contrast with softcopy.

hardcopy log (1) In systems with multiple console support or a graphic console, a permanent record of system activity. (2) In NCCF, a file written on a hardcopy device, such as a printer, that contains a record of all messages passing through NCCF that are associated with one or several operators.

hardcopy task (HCT) The NCCF subtask that controls passage of data between NCCF and the hardcopy log device.

hard disk (1) A rigid magnetic disk such as the internal disks used in the system units of personal computers and in external hard disk drives. Synonymous with fixed disk, nonremovable disk. See also Winchester. Contrast with flexible disk. (2) A rigid disk used in a hard disk drive.

Note: The term hard disk is also used loosely in the industry for boards and cartridges containing microchips or bubble memory that simulate the operations of a hard disk drive.

hard disk drive A stand-alone disk drive that reads and writes data on rigid disks and can be attached to a port on the system unit. Synonymous with fixed disk drive, hard drive.

hard drive Synonym for hard disk drive.

hard error (1) An error condition on a network that requires that the network be reconfigured or that the source of the error be removed before the network can resume reliable operation. Contrast with soft error. (2) Synonym for hard failure. (T)

hard failure An error condition on a network that requires that the network be reconfigured or that the source of the error be removed before the network can resume reliable operation. Synonymous with hard error. (T)

hard fault A complete disruption of transmission at a point in a network; for example, a fault caused by failure of a transmitter or receiver or by a break in wiring. Contrast with soft fault. See also beacon frame, beaconing node.

hard hyphen A hyphen required by the spelling of a word or an expression regardless of its position in a line. Synonymous with embedded hyphen, required hyphen. Contrast with soft hyphen. (T) (A)

hard sector A sector that is established physically on a disk; for example, an index hole at the beginning of the first sector on a diskette or a sector that is written at a predetermined location on a diskette. See also soft sector.

hard sectoring (1) The physical marking of sector boundaries on a magnetic disk. (T) (A) (2) Contrast with soft sectoring. (T) (A)

hard space A space represented by a special character in a string of characters at which a text processor will not break the string. A hard space can also be accomplished by an embedded command. Synonymous with nonbreak space. (T)

hard stop An immediate termination of operation or execution.

hard wait See waiting time.

hardware (1) All or part of the physical components of an information processing system, such as computers or peripheral devices. (T) (A) (2) The equipment, as opposed to the programming, of a system. (3) Contrast with software.

hardware cell In GDDM, the default character box associated with a particular display.

hardware character In GDDM and System/38, an alphanumeric character provided by the display station, usually from a display file. See also mode-2 character, mode-3 character.

hardware check (1) A failure in a hardware unit that halts operation. See also machine check interruption. (2) Synonym for automatic check.

hardware error recovery management system A facility that attempts recovery from hardware malfunctions. It consists of the machine check handler (MCH) and the channel check handler (CCH).

hardware language A representation of a reference language using symbols that are particularly suitable for direct input to a computer; for example, X A in a reference language may become X=A, and X 2 may become X**2 in a hardware language. (T)

hardware logic diagrams (HLDs) A combination of card-on-board logic, power logic, and schematic diagrams for power/thermal subsystems.

hardware monitor The component of the NetView program that helps identify network problems, such as hardware, software, and microcode, from a central control point using interactive display techniques.

hardwired Pertaining to a physical connection; for example, a plug-to-plug wired connection, cable connection, or connection to an auxiliary device via a fixed address.

harmonic The presence of harmonic frequencies, which may be caused by nonlinear characteristics of a transmission line, in a response when a sinusoidal stimulus is applied.

harmonic distortion See distortion.

harmonic telephone ringer A telephone ringer that responds only to alternating current within a very narrow frequency band. A number of such ringers, each responding to a different frequency, are used in one type of selective ringing where there are several parties on a subscriber's line.

hartley In information theory, a unit of logarithmic measure of information equal to the decision content of a set of ten mutually exclusive events expressed by the logarithm to base ten; for example, the decision content of a character set of eight characters equals 0.903 hartley ($\log_{10} 8 = 0.903$). (I) (A) Synonymous with information content decimal unit.

hashing (1) A method of transforming a search key into an address for the purpose of storing and retrieving items of data. The method is often designed to minimize the search time. (T) (2) The application of an algorithm to the records in a data set to obtain a symmetric grouping of the records. Synonymous with key folding. (3) In an indexed data set, the process of transforming a record key into an index value for storing and retrieving a record.

hash table A table of information that is accessed by way of a shortened search key (the hash value). Using a hash table minimizes average search time.

hash total The result obtained by applying an algorithm to a set of heterogeneous data for checking purposes; for example, a summation obtained by treating data items as numbers. (T) Synonym for control total.

HASP Houston automatic spooling priority system. A computer program that provides supplementary job management, data management, and task management functions such as control of job flow, ordering of tasks, and spooling. See also JES2.

HCF Host Command Facility.

HCON 3270 Host Connection Program/6000.

HCON MRI 3270 Host Connection Program/6000 Message Catalog.

HCON user A user who has been given the special permissions necessary to use the 3270 Host Connection Program/6000 (HCON). See 3270 Host Connection Program/6000.

HCP Host command processor.

HCT Hardcopy task.

HD (1) Half duplex. (2) Hierarchic direct.

HDA Head/disk assembly. (A)

HDAM Hierarchic direct access method.

HDLC High-level data link control.

HDR Header.

HDX Half duplex.

head (1) A device that reads, writes, or erases data on a storage medium; for example, a small electromagnet used to read, write, or erase data on a magnetic drum or magnetic tape, or the set of perforating, reading, or marking devices used for punching, reading, or printing on perforated tape. (I) (A) (2) See magnetic head, plotting head, preread head, read head, read/write head, write head.

head crash (1) An accidental contact of a magnetic head with the surface of a rotating data medium. (T) (2) Contact between a read/write head and a rotating disk or diskette that causes damage and loss of recorded data.

Note: A head crash may be caused by shock or damage to the drive mechanism, by contamination of the disk, or by a slowdown in rotational speed that results in a loss of the air cushion that normally separates the head from the surface of the disk.

head/disk assembly (HDA) In a magnetic disk unit, an assembly that includes magnetic disks, magnetic heads, and an access mechanism all enclosed in a container. (T) (A)

headend In a broadband LAN, a device that receives signals from each data station and retransmits them to all data stations. (T)

Note: Retransmission may require a shift of carrier frequencies.

header (1) A block of text printed consistently at the top of one or more pages in a multipage document. A header may contain variable information, such as a page number. Synonymous with page header, running head. (T) (2) System-defined control information that precedes user data. (3) The portion of a message that contains control information for the message such as one or more destination fields, name of the originating station, input sequence number, character string indicating the type of message, and priority level for the message. See block control header, message header, transmission header. (4) Text that appears at the top of the printed pages of a document; for example, the subject of the document. (5) See division header, end program header, paragraph header, section header.

header buffer In ACF/TCAM, a buffer that contains all or the first part of a message header. Contrast with text buffer.

header card A card that contains information related to the data in cards that follow. (A)

header file Synonym for include file.

header label (HDR) (1) A file label or data set label that precedes the data records on a unit of recording media. (2) Synonym for beginning-of-file label.

header message In the 3650 Retail Store System, a message printed at the top of a cash receipt or sales check, containing salesperson number, transaction type, transaction number, terminal number, and date.

header record A record containing common, constant, or identifying information for a group of records that follows. Synonymous with header table, heading record. Contrast with detail record.

header segment A part of a message that contains any portion of the message header.

header table Synonym for header record.

head gap (1) The clearance between a read/write head and the surface of a rotating diskette or hard disk when the head is at its normal operating position. (2) Synonym for flying height. (T)

heading (1) In ASCII and data communication, a sequence of characters preceded by the start-of-heading character used as machine sensible address or routing information. (A) (2) Words placed above information to identify that information. (3) A constant, or field, usually at the top of a page or display, that identifies the information on the page or display.

(4) Words located at the beginning of a chapter or section or at the top of a page, above the first line of text on the page. See also control heading, head-level, page heading, report heading, running heading. (5) Contrast with text.

heading character See start-of-heading character.

heading record (1) In RPG, output records that are printed at the top of a report and include report titles, column headings, or any other data needed to identify the information in the report. (2) Synonym for header record.

head landing zone See landing zone.

head-level The typeface and character size associated with the words standing at the beginning of a chapter or chapter topic.

head loading zone (1) A peripheral area on each disk surface where heads are positioned to the proper flying height for reading and writing data. (T)   (2) See loading zone.

head of form Synonym for first-line find.

headphone On dictation equipment, a device that enables telephone conversations to be recorded on a dictation machine. (I)

head slot An opening in the protective jacket of a diskette that allows the read/write head to read data from and write data on the flexible magnetic disk. Synonymous with read/write slot.

head support arm On dictation equipment, a device that carries a recording head, playback head, erase head, or combined head allowing it to move freely over the surface of the recording medium. (I)

head switching Changing from one read/write head to another to read from or write on another magnetic data medium or on another part of the same medium. (T)   (A)

heap In XL Pascal, a collection of dynamically allocated variables. See also current heap, subheap.

heat fixing In a document copying machine, the action in the copying process of causing the image to be retained on the copy material by heat. (T)   Synonymous with heat fusing.

heat fusing Synonym for heat fixing.

hecto (h) Hundred.

hectometer (hm) One hundred meters. 109.36 yards.

held alert An alert that an alert sender was unable to send to a control point at the time the alert condition was discovered by the sender. The sending of a held alert implies nothing about whether the alert condition it reports is still affecting availability. See delayed alert.

held terminal Synonym for intercepted terminal.

helical scan In video systems, a method of achieving the high tape speeds necessary for video recording by moving both the tape and the video heads. Helical scan uses two video heads mounted on opposite sides of a revolving drum. The video head drum spins at one frame per revolution so that each head scans one field per revolution. As the tape winds around the drum of the video head, it assumes a helical shape, thus giving the process its name.

hello screen The first display image shown on a display screen when a user accesses an application software product. See also LOGO screen.

Help (1) In SAA Advanced Common User Access architecture: (a) Information about the item the cursor is on or about the entire window. (b) A standard push button that provides information about the item the cursor is on or about the entire dialog box. (2) In SAA Basic Common User Access architecture: (a) An action that gives information about the item the cursor is on, an application panel, or the help facility. (b) An action bar choice that has an associated pull-down. Its pull-down contains choices that can be requested to invoke help actions.

help desk operator A person who receives questions or problem reports from network users.

Help for help In SAA Common User Access architecture, a help action that provides information about how the help facility works.

help function One or more display images that describe how to use application software or how to do a system operation.

Help index In SAA Common User Access architecture, a help action that provides an index of the help information available for an application.

Help key A function key that displays help text when it is pressed.

help level specifications In an AS/400 display file, data description specifications coded between the record and field level that define areas on the screen and associate help information with those areas. See also field level specifications, file level specifications, join level specifications, key field level specifications, record level specifications, select/omit level specifications.

help menu A menu that describes alternative actions when a user encounters a problem with a system or application.

help panel Information displayed by a system in response to a help request from a user.

help pop-up In SAA Basic Common User Access architecture, a pop-up containing information to assist a user.

help screen A display screen that gives a condensed description of how to use application software, usually including a description of the operation performed by each function key.

help support See system help support.

help view A view of an object that provides information to assist users in working with that object. See also composed view, contents view.

help text (1) Information associated with an information display, menu, or prompt that explains options or values displayed. (2) Information displayed when a user at a keyboard presses a Help key.

help window In SAA Advanced Common User Access architecture: a window that contains information to assist a user.

Helsinki principle In a conceptual schema language, any meaningful exchange of utterances that depends upon the prior existence of an agreed-upon set of semantic and syntactic rules. (A)

hertz (Hz) A unit of frequency equal to one cycle per second.

Note: In the United States, line frequency is 60 Hz or a change in voltage polarity 120 times per second; in Europe, line frequency is 50 Hz or a change in voltage polarity 100 times per second.

heterogeneous computer network A computer network in which computers have dissimilar architecture, but nevertheless, are able to communicate. (T) Contrast with homogeneous computer network.

heuristic Pertaining to exploratory methods of problem solving in which solutions are discovered by evaluation of the progress made toward the final result. Contrast with algorithmic.

heuristic method A method of solving problems that consists of a sequence of trials yielding approximate results, with control of the progression toward an

acceptable final result; for example, the method of successive approximations. (A)

heuristic rules Rules written to capture the heuristics an expert uses to solve a problem. (T)

hex See hexadecimal.

hexadecimal (1) Pertaining to a selection, choice, or condition that has 16 possible different values or states. (I) (2) Pertaining to a fixed-radix numeration system, with radix of 16. (I) (3) Pertaining to a system of numbers to the base 16; hexadecimal digits range from 0 through 9 and A through F, where A represents 10 and F represents 15. Synonymous with sexadecimal. See Figure 69.

Decimal	Binary	Hexadecimal
0	0000	0
1	0001	1
2	0010	2
3	0011	3
4	0100	4
5	0101	5
6	0110	6
7	0111	7
8	1000	8
9	1001	9
10	1010	A
11	1011	B
12	1100	C
13	1101	D
14	1110	E
15	1111	F

Figure 69. Hexadecimal

hexadecimal constant In PL/I, a series of hexadecimal numbers enclosed in apostrophes that keep the value of the string. See also bit constant, character constant.

hexadecimal number The 1-byte hexadecimal equivalent of an EBCDIC character. See Figure 70.

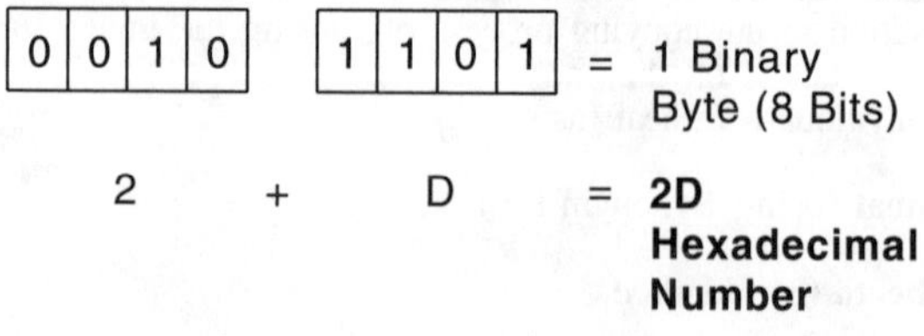

Figure 70. Hexadecimal Number

hexadecimal numeration system The fixed-radix-numeration system that uses the 16 digits 0, 1, 2, 3, 4, 5, 6, 7, 8, 9, A, B, C, D, E, and F, where the characters A, B, C, D, E and F correspond to the numbers 10, 11, 12, 13, 14 and 15, and the radix sixteen in which the lowest integral weight is 1. For example, in the hexadecimal numeration system, the numeral 3EB represents the number one thousand, that is $3 \times 16^2 + 8 \times 16^0$. (T)

HFT High function terminal.

HIDAM Hierarchic indexed direct access method.

hidden character A character that is not normally printed or displayed; for example, an embedded control character. (T)

hidden field A field in a display file that is passed from and to a program but not sent to the display.

hidden file An operating system file that is not displayed by a directory listing.

hidden line In computer graphics, a line segment that represents an edge obscured from view in a two-dimensional projection of a three-dimensional object. (I) (A)

Note: Hidden lines are used to show the shape of an object and are usually represented differently from the lines that represent the visible edges of the object. (A)   See Figure 71.

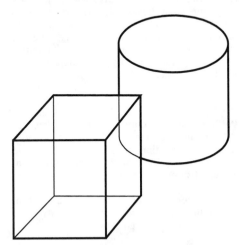

Figure 71. Hidden Lines

hidden line removal In computer graphics, the suppression of hidden lines.

hidden surface A surface that is not visible because it is obscured by other surfaces. See also z-buffer.

hide To remove a window and all its associated windows from the desktop.

hierarchical computer network A computer network in which the control functions are organized in a hierarchical manner and may be distributed among data processing stations. (T)

hierarchical database A database that is organized in the form of a tree structure in which each record or sector has only one owner, that represents how the records or segments are interrelated, and that predetermines the access paths to data stored in the base. See also network database, relational database.

hierarchical model A data model whose data are nodes of a tree structure. (T)

hierarchical network A network in which processing and control functions are performed at several levels by computers specially suited for the functions performed; for example, in factory or laboratory automation. (T)

hierarchical structure A structure of data aggregates or record types having several levels arranged in a tree-like structure, based on one-to-many relationships. (T)

hierarchic direct access method (HDAM) In IMS/VS, a database access method using algorithmic addressability to records in a hierarchic direct organization. The overflow sequential access method (OSAM) and VSAM ESDS are available as a base for HDAM. See also hierarchic indexed direct access method (HIDAM), hierarchic indexed sequential access method (HISAM), hierarchic sequential access method (HSAM), simple HISAM.

hierarchic direct (HD) organization In IMS/VS, the physical storage organization in which database segments that represent a physical database record are related by direct address pointers in the segment's prefix. See also hierarchic sequential (HS) organization.

hierarchic indexed direct access method In IMS/VS, a database access method used for indexed access to records in a hierarchic direct organization. It provides indexed access to the root segments and pointer access to subordinate segments. A HIDAM index can be constructed with ISAM and OSAM or VSAM. See also hierarchic direct access method (HDAM), hierarchic indexed sequential access method (HISAM), hierarchic sequential access method (HSAM), simple HISAM.

hierarchic indexed sequential access method In IMS/VS, a database access method used for indexed access to records in a hierarchic sequential organization. A HISAM index can be constructed with ISAM or VSAM. See also hierarchic direct access method (HDAM), hierarchic indexed direct access method (HIDAM), sequential access method (HSAM), simple HISAM.

hierarchic sequence In an IMS/VS database, the sequence of segment occurrences in a database record defined by traversing the tree, from top to bottom, front to back, and left to right.

hierarchic sequential access method (HSAM) In IMS/VS, a database access method used for sequential storage and access of segments on tape or direct access storage. BSAM and QSAM are used as the basis for HSAM. See also hierarchic direct access method (HDAM), hierarchic indexed direct access method (HIDAM), hierarchic indexed sequential access method (HISAM), simple HISAM.

hierarchic sequential (HS) organization In IMS/VS, the physical organization in which database segments that represent a physical database record are related by adjacency. See also hierarchic direct (HD) organization.

hierarchy (1) In an IMS/VS database, a tree of segments beginning with the root segment and proceeding downward to dependent segment types. As many as 15 levels may be defined. No segment type can be dependent on more than one segment type. (2) See data hierarchy. (3) In COBOL, a set of entries that includes all subordinate entries to the next equal- or higher-level number. (4) In the NetView program, the resource types, display types, and data types that make up the organization, or levels, in a network.

hierarchy of operations Relative priority assigned to arithmetic or logical operations that must be performed.

high-definition television (HDTV) Any one of a variety of television formats offering higher resolution than current NTSC, PAL, or SECAM broadcast standards.

higher level In the hierarchical structure of a data station, the conceptual level of control or processing logic above the data link level that determines the performance of data link level functions such as device control, buffer allocation, and station management. See also data link level, packet level, physical level.

high function terminal (HFT) In the AIX operating system, a virtual terminal that, in addition to displays and keyboards, supports locations, valuations, lighted programmable keys, and sound generators.

high-level data link control (HDLC) In data communication, the use of a specified series of bits to control

data links in accordance with the International Standards for HDLC: ISO 3309 Frame Structure and ISO 4335 Elements of Procedures.

high-level language (HLL) (1) A programming language whose concepts and structures are convenient for human reasoning; for example, Pascal. High-level languages are independent of the structures of computers and operating systems. (T) (2) A programming language that does not reflect the structure of any particular computer or operating system. For the NetView program, the high-level languages are PL/I and C.

high-level language (HLL) pointer A source pointer that the programmer declares in the user program.

high-level message In System/38, a message sent to the program message queue of the program receiving the request. The message is displayed or provided for the user who entered the request. Contrast with low-level message.

highlighting Emphasizing a display element or segment by modifying its visual attributes. (I) (A)

high order end In COBOL, the leftmost character of a string of characters.

high-order position The leftmost position in a string of characters.

high-performance file system (HPFS) In the OS/2 operating system, an installable file system that uses high-speed buffer storage, known as a cache, to provide fast access to large disk volumes. The file system also supports the coexistence of multiple, active file systems on a single personal computer, with the capability of multiple and different storage devices. File names used with the HPFS can have as many as 254 characters.

High Performance Option (HPO) A licensed program that is an extension of VM/SP. It provides performance and operation enhancements for large system environments. See Virtual Machine/System Product High Performance Option.

high-priority record queue In DPCX, a first-in, first-out queue that indicates the programs ready to be dispatched for execution at high priority.

High Sierra format A standard format, developed by the High Sierra Group, for placing files and directories on CD-ROMs.

High Sierra Group A committee of computer vendors, software developers, and CD-ROM system integrators, originally meeting at the High Sierra Hotel in Lake Tahoe, Nevada.

high-speed buffer A cache or a set of logically partitioned blocks that provides significantly faster access to instructions and data than provided by central storage.

high-speed capture In the IBM ImagePlus system, a facility that provides users who have high-speed scanners equipped with a stack feeder with the capability of scanning a large stack of pages into the ImagePlus system.

high-speed carry (1) In parallel addition, any procedure for speeding up the processing of carries; for example, standing-on-nines carry. (I) (A) (2) Contrast with cascaded carry.

high-speed line (1) A communication line that transmits at speeds greater than 19,200 bits per second. (2) A feature that allows a System/38 to communicate at speeds of up to 56,000 bits per second.

high-speed scan Synonym for browse.

high-speed scanner workstation An ImagePlus workstation equipped with a high-speed scanner that can scan large stacks of similar sized paper into the ImagePlus system.

high-speed scroll Synonym for browse.

high threshold of occupancy In the Data Facility Hierarchical Storage Manager, the upper limit of space to be occupied on a primary volume managed by the Data Facility Hierarchical Storage Manager. Contrast with low threshold of occupancy.

highway In a process computer system, the means for connection between the computer system and process interface system. (T)

Note: A bus may be used as a highway.

HIO Halt I/O.

HIPO (hierarchy: input, process, output) A graphics tool for designing, developing, and documenting program function.

hiragana A graphic character set that consists of symbols used in one of the two common Japanese phonetic alphabets. Each character is represented by 1 byte. See also kanji, katakana.

HISAM Hierarchic indexed sequential access method.

histogram In GDDM, a chart in which each value of the dependent variable corresponds to a range of values of the independent variable, represented by the width of the associated bar; for example, such a chart

might display the number of people in various age ranges.

history In the Folder Application Facility, a list of actions performed on a document.

history file (1) A file in which a record is kept of system activities such as jobs run, transactions, and operator actions. (2) Synonymous with history log.

history log (1) In the AS/400 system, a summary of the system activities, such as system and job information, device status, system operator messages, and a record of program temporary fix (PTF) activity on the system. (2) Synonym for history file.

hit (1) A comparison of two items of data that satisfies specified conditions. (A) Contrast with match. (2) A transient disturbance to a communication medium. (A) (3) See light-pen hit. (4) In AIX graphics, drawing within the picking or selecting region by a drawing primitive. A hit is reported back to the user only if the name stack has changed since the last hit.

hit-on-the-fly printer Synonym for on-the-fly printer.

hit point In video or film presentations, a dramatic moment that requires musical emphasis or change. See also scoring.

hit ratio The ratio of the number of successful references to main storage to the total number of references.

Hi8 High-band 8mm videotape format.

HLD Hardware logic diagram.

HLL High-level language.

HLL pointer In System/38, a pointer declared by the programmer in the source of a high-level language (HLL) program.

hm Hectometer.

HMI (1) Halogen-Metal-Iodine. (2) Horizontal motion index.

HMOS High-speed n-channel metal-oxide semiconductor.

hold delivery A method of delivering messages to a message queue that holds the messages until the user requests them. The user is not notified when a message arrives at a message queue that is in hold delivery.

hold-down tabulator key On a typewriter, a tabulator key that effects the tabulation required only if it is kept depressed until the tabulator stop position has been reached. (T)

HOLDING screen status For a display terminal used as a virtual console under VM, an indicator located in the lower right of the screen that displays that the current contents of the screen remains on the screen until the user requests that the screen be erased. This status occurs either by pressing the Enter key, or is triggered by a message or warning displayed on the screen.

hold mode The operating mode of an analog computer during which integration is stopped and all variables are held at the value they had when this mode was entered. (I) (A)

hold page queue In OS/VS and VSE, a queue to which pages in real storage are initially assigned through operations such as page-in or page reclamation. See also active page queue, available page queue.

hold queue (1) In OS/VS, a waiting list for jobs whose initiation is to be delayed until the operator releases them from the queue. (2) In ACF/TCAM, a FEFO-ordered queue that is a part of the priority-level QCB for each destination QCB. If a terminal is intercepted (held), its messages are placed in the hold queue while messages for other terminals on this destination QCB are sent. See also intercepted station, intercepted terminal.

hold time Indicates the time of day until which a document is held, or "suspended," from the routing queue before reentering the routing queue.

hole A positive charge carrier that is created when sufficient energy is applied to a crystal lattice to cause an electron to vacate its position in the lattice structure of a semiconductive material.

Note: When an electron breaks away from its electrical bond, it creates a hole that can be filled by an adjacent electron. The adjacent electron, moving in a negative direction, creates another hole that, in turn, can be filled by another electron. Holes are created in a sequence opposite to the flow of free electrons, thereby establishing a conductive path for positive current flow.

hole in a file In the AIX operating system, empty space in a sparse file that is left open for future additions of data. See sparse file.

hole pattern (1) An array of holes that implements the coded representation of data on a data medium; for example, a punching configuration that implements

the representation of a single character. (T) (2) A punching configuration within a card column that represents a single character of a character set. (A)

Hollerith Pertaining to a particular type of code or punched card utilizing 12 rows per column and usually 80 columns per card. (A) See Figure 72.

Figure 72. Hollerith

Hollerith card A punch card characterized by 80 columns and 12 rows of punch positions. (A)

Note: Hollerith cards conform to American National Standard X3.26-1980: Hollerith Punched Card Code.

Hollerith constant In FORTRAN, a string of any characters capable of representation in the processor and preceded by wH, where w is the number of characters in the string.

Hollerith, Herman (1860 - 1929) American inventor who developed the punched card tabulating machine for the U.S. Census of 1890. In 1911, his Tabulating Machine Company merged with several others to become the Computing-Tabulating-Recording Company, which in 1924 was renamed the International Business Machines Company.

holostore A system of storing data as a holographic (three-dimensional) image using light-sensitive crystals that remember light patterns passing through them.

HOME See $HOME.

Home A key on a keyboard that a user presses to move the cursor to the home position.

$HOME In the AIX operating system, an environment variable, set by the system, that designates a user's home directory. Many programs use this variable to designate a directory where they store temporary work files.

home address (1) The information written on each track of a magnetic disk, that identifies the track number on the face of the disk. (T) (2) An address written on a direct access volume, denoting the address of a track relative to the beginning of the volume.

home address space The address space in which MVS initially dispatches a work unit. When MVS initially dispatches a work unit, the home address space, the primary address space, and the secondary address space are the same. During execution of the work unit, the home address space remains the same, but the primary and secondary address spaces can change.

home directory In the AIX operating system: (a) A directory associated with an individual user. (b) The user's current directory after login or after issuing the cd command with no argument. (c) A parameter that supplies the full path name of the home directory for the transaction program.

home environment In DPPX, the environment into which a thread is attached. A thread may run in different environments, but its home environment remains the same.

home loop An operation involving only the input and output units associated with the local terminal.

home position (1) In SAA usage, the first position of displayed information on a screen or in an active window. (2) A location defined by the user. (3) The beginning of a file or display. (4) The position to which a cursor normally returns.

home record The first record in a chain of records.

home window In the AIX operating system, a window that completely displays the contents of the display buffer.

homogeneous computer network (1) A computer network in which all computers have the same or similar architecture. (T) Contrast with heterogeneous computer network. (2) A network of similar computers. (A)

homogeneous coordinates A four-dimensional method of representing three-dimensional space. A point (x, y, z, w) in homogeneous coordinates is used to represent a point (X, Y, Z) in three-dimensional space by taking X=x/w, Y=y/w, Z=z/w.

homonym In a conceptual schema language, one of two or more identical terms that refer to different entities. (T) (A)

hook ID (1) A location in a program where a compiler inserts an instruction that allows a user to later interrupt the program, by setting breakpoints, for debugging purposes. (2) In the AIX operating system, a unique number assigned to a specific trace point. All trace entries include the hook ID of the originating trace point in the trace entry header. Predefined trace points use assigned hook IDs ranging from 0 to 299.

User-defined trace points can choose hook IDs ranging from 300 to 399.

hooking routine In the AIX operating system, synonym for stub.

hop In APPN, a portion of a route that has no intermediate nodes. It consists of only a single transmission group connecting adjacent nodes.

hop count In the IBM Token-Ring Network, the number of bridges through which a frame passes on the way to its destination.

hop count limit In the IBM Token-Ring Network, the maximum number of bridges through which a frame may pass on the way to its destination.

hop count metric (1) In a gateway, an indication that the next string represents the hop count to the destination host or network. (2) The number of host-to-host connections in a route.

hopper See card hopper.

Hopper, Grace Murray (1907 - 1992) Pioneer computer scientist who co-invented the COBOL programming language. In 1986, she retired from the U. S. Navy as a Rear Admiral and the Navy's oldest serving officer.

horizontal advance Movement between the paper carrier and the typing or printing position in the typing or printing direction, parallel to the typing or printing line.

horizontal blanking interval In video systems, the period of time when a scanning process is moving from the end of one horizontal line to the start of the next line. See vertical blanking interval.

horizontal feed Pertaining to the entry of a punch card into a card feed with a long edge first. (A)

horizontal format Synonymous with landscape. (T)

horizontal formatting In word processing, automatic control of the number of characters per line. See also vertical formatting.

horizontal justification The redistribution of horizontal white space at the end of a line of text to the spaces between the words and letters of the line in order to exactly fill the width of the column with text.

horizontally displayed records In System/38, subfile records that are grouped in a display so that more than one record of the same record format is displayed on each display line. See also vertically displayed records.

horizontal motion index (HMI) On the display screen of an IBM personal computer, a counter below the command area that indicates the position (1 to 80) of the cursor on the writing line.

horizontal pointer In VSAM, a pointer in a sequence-set index record that gives the location of the next sequence-set index record in the sequence set; it is used for keyed sequential access.

horizontal return Movement between the paper carrier and the typing or printing position in a direction opposite to the typing or printing direction, parallel to the typing or printing line.

horizontal tabulation (1) On a printer or a typewriter, movement of the imprint position a predetermined number of character spaces along the writing line. (2) On a display device, movement of the cursor a predetermined number of display positions along a display line. (3) See also vertical tabulation.

horizontal tabulation character (HT) A format effector character that causes the print or display position to move forward to the next of a series of predetermined positions along the same line. (I) (A)

horizontal tabulator key On a typewriter, a control that effects horizontal tabulation. (T)

horizontal wraparound On a display device, the continuation of cursor movement from the last character position in a horizontal row to the first character position in the next row, or from the first position in a row to the last position in the preceding row. Contrast with vertical wraparound.

host (1) In TCP/IP, any system that has at least one Internet address associated with it. A host with multiple network interfaces may have multiple Internet addresses associated with it. (2) In FORTRAN, a program unit that immediately contains an internal procedure. In the case of nested internal procedures, the host is the program unit that immediately contains the internal procedure; for example, if A contains B and B contains C, A is the host of B and B is the host of C, but A is not the host of C.

host access method The access method that controls communication with a domain.

host application program An application program executed in the host computer.

Host Command Facility (HCF) A feature available on a System/370, 43xx, and 30xx host system that enables a user on the host system to use applications on other systems as if they were using remotely attached 5250-type display stations. See also distributed host command facility (DHCF).

host command processor (HCP) The SNA logical unit of the programmable store system store controller.

host computer (1) In a computer network, a computer that usually performs network control functions and provides end users with services such as computation and database access. (T) (2) The primary or controlling computer in a multiple computer installation. (3) A computer used to prepare programs for use on another computer or on another data processing system; for example, a computer used to compile, link edit, or test programs to be used on another system. (4) Synonym for host processor.

host conversational function In PSS, a retail services function that allows an IBM 3653 Point of Sale Terminal or a basic services function for an IBM 3275 Display Station Model 3 to communicate with the host processor.

host ID In TCP/IP, that part of the Internet address that defines the host on the network. The length of the host ID depends on the type of network or network class (A, B, or C). See also Internet address, network ID.

host-initiated program In DPCX, a program executed as a subtask that can be initiated at the request of the host system.

host interface Interface between a network and host computer. (T)

host IOCS In PSS, the input/output control system that handles communication with the host.

host language (1) In a database, a programming language in which a data sublanguage is embedded. (T) (2) In a database management system, pertaining to a programming language, such as COBOL, PL/I, or assembly language, in which the data manipulation capabilities of the database management system are embedded. (A) (3) In SQL, any programming language, such as C, COBOL, FORTRAN, PL/I, and RPG, in which SQL statements can be embedded.

host language system A database management system that is built upon the facilities of a programming language and depends on the application programmer for logical and physical file manipulations. (A)

host logical unit (LU) An SNA logical unit (LU) located in a host processor; for example, an VTAM application program. See TCAM host logical unit (LU).

host LU An SNA logical unit located in a host processor; for example, a VTAM application program. Contrast with peripheral LU.

host master key In SNA, deprecated term for master cryptography key.

host master key variant In the Programmed Cryptographic Facility and the Cryptographic Unit Support System, a cryptographic key derived from the host master key and used to encipher operational keys at the host processor.

host mode The operating mode of a HASP main processor communicating with a HASP workstation.

host node (1) A node at which a host computer is located. (T) (2) A node that provides an application program interface (API) and a common application interface. See also boundary function, boundary node, node type, peripheral node, subarea host node, subarea node. (3) In SNA, a subarea node that contains a system services control point (SSCP); for example, a System/370 computer with OS/VS2 and ACF/TCAM.

host processor (1) A processor that controls all or part of a user application network. (T) (2) In a network, the processing unit in which resides the access method for the network. (3) In an SNA network, the processing unit that contains a system services control point (SSCP). (4) A processing unit that executes the access method for attached communication controllers. (5) The processing unit required to create and maintain PSS. (6) Synonymous with host computer.

host real storage In the VM/XA Migration Aid, the storage that appears real to the control program. If the VM/XA Migration Aid is running stand-alone, it is real storage; if VM/XA is running in a virtual machine, it is virtual storage. Contrast with host virtual storage.

host structure (1) In an SQL application program, a structure referred to by embedded SQL statements. (2) In RPG, synonym for data structure. (3) In C language and PL/I, synonym for structure. (4) In COBOL, synonym for group item.

host subarea A subarea that contains a host node.

host support The facilities a host processor makes available to attached terminals, processors, and other devices, such as problem determination aids and database facilities.

host system (1) A data processing system used to prepare programs and operating environments for use on another computer or controller. (2) The data processing system to which a network is connected and with which the system can communicate. (3) The controlling or highest level system in a data communication configuration; for example, a System/38 is the host system for the workstations connected to it. (4) In TCP/IP, a computer that is a peer system in a network.

host system message blocks In the 3790 Communication System, blocks of data sent by the host system to a 3790 program.

host system responses In the 3790 Communication System, communication control information sent to a 3791 Controller by the host system, some of which is passed on to the 3790 program by means of registers and logical indicators.

host transfer file In VSE with attached programmable workstations, a VSAM data set managed by VSE/SP on the host system. The data set contains files owned by the users of programmable workstations.

host transit time In NPM, average time (in seconds) that all transactions spend in the host. It includes both VTAM and application time. It is also reported as an average for the transactions originating at the logical unit for which data collection is occurring.

host variable (1) In an SQL application program, a variable referred to by embedded SQL statements. (2) In RPG, synonym for field name. (3) In C language, FORTRAN, and PL/I, synonym for variable. (4) In COBOL, synonym for data item.

host virtual storage In the VM/XA Migration Aid, storage that appears virtual to the control program. Contrast with host real storage.

hot I/O A serious error condition caused by an I/O interruption that disrupts system operation.

hot key (1) The key combination used to change from one session to another on the workstation. (2) In the AIX operating system, a key sequence the user presses to switch between two or more virtual terminals. See command window hot key. (3) To jump, or hot key, from a host session to an application on the workstation, or from the workstation to the host session.

hot site In computer security, a fully equipped computer center that provides an alternative computing capability for use in the event of a disaster, such as flood or fire. Contrast with cold site.

hot spot The area of a display screen that is activated to accept user input. Synonymous with touch area, trigger.

hot standby In computer security, pertaining to the immediate readiness of a functional unit to which operations can be readily switched; or, to the unit itself.

hot zone Synonym for line-end zone.

hourglass pointer In SAA Advanced Common User Access architecture, a visual cue in the shape of an hourglass that indicates to a user that the computer is performing simple operations. The pointer changes to this shape while the computer is processing.

housekeeping Operations or routines that do not contribute directly to the solution of a problem but contribute directly to the operation of the computer.

housekeeping operation An operation that facilitates execution of a computer program without making a direct contribution; for example, initialization of storage areas, execution of a calling sequence. (I) (A) Synonymous with overhead operation.

Houston Automatic Spooling Program (HASP) A computer program that provides supplementary job management, data management, and task management functions, such as control of job flow, ordering of tasks, and spooling.

HPO High Performance Option.

HPFS High performance file system

HS Hierarchic sequential.

HSAM Hierarchic sequential access method.

HSCIB Half-session information control block.

HSG High Sierra Group.

HSI Hue saturation intensity.

HT The horizontal tabulation character. (A)

hub Synonym for tape spool.

hub go-ahead In SDLC, a polling technique in which the primary station issues a poll on a duplex channel to the farthest secondary station, then sequentially to each of the other stations until all have been invited to send data. The primary station can send data while the polling sequence is in progress.

hue A particular color as distinct from other colors. See also saturation.

hue component A single color identified by the angle it occupies on a color axis.

hue saturation intensity (HSI) A method of describing color in three-dimensional color space.

huffman coding A character coding technique used to compress data.

human factors The characteristics, limitations, physical requirements, and psychological needs of people that must be considered in designing and developing systems, programs, and devices that can be used easily and are appropriate for the tasks and working environments for which they are intended. See also ergonomics, usability, utility.

human-oriented language A programming language that is considered to be more like a human language than a machine language.

hung Pertaining to the state in which a system appears to stop processing and does not respond to input from the keyboard.

hung terminal A terminal to which a session is disrupted and that cannot send or receive commands.

hunting See trunk hunting.

HWID Hardware identifier.

hybrid coil An arrangement using one or more transformers wired as a balanced bridge to provide two-to-four wire conversion for long distance telecommunication circuits.

hybrid computer (1) A computer that integrates analog computer components and digital computer components by interconnection of digital-to-analog converters and analog-to-digital converters. A hybrid computer may use or produce analog data and digital data. (T) (2) See also analog computer, digital computer.

hybrid integrated circuit A class of integrated circuits in which the substrate is a passive material such as ceramic, and the active chips are attached to its surface.

HYP Required hyphen character.

hypercube A computer architecture in which processors are arranged as nodes in multiple dimensions with direct channel communication among neighboring nodes. See also bus (2), parallel processor architecture.

Note: An n-dimensional hypercube has 2^n nodes.

hypermedia A method of presenting information in discrete units, or nodes, that are connected by links. The information may be presented using a variety of media such as text, graphics, audio, video, animation, image or executable documentation.

hypermedia application An information processing application that has hypertext and/or multimedia capabilities.

hypertext A way of presenting information online with connections between one piece of information and another, called hypertext links. See also hypertext link.

hypertext link A connection between one piece of information and another.

hyphenate To separate a word by inserting a hyphen after a syllable to end a line and moving the remainder of the word to the start of the next line.

hyphen drop The function that ensures that a soft hyphen does not appear in the presentation of a word when it is not necessary to divide the word. (T) (A)

hysteresis loop See magnetic hysteresis loop.

HyTime Hypermedia/Time-based Structuring Language. A standardized hyperdocument structuring language for representing hypertext linking, time scheduling, and synchronization. HyTime provides basic identification and addressing mechanisms and is independent of object data content notations, link types, processing and presentation functions, and semantics.

Hz Hertz.

I

I In phase.

IAC INTERPRET AS command.

IAP Industry applications programs.

IAR Instruction address register.

IATSE International Association of Theatrical and Stage Employees.

IBM Advanced Data Communications for Stores The IBM licensed program that functions on the System/host processor for host system to point-of-sale system communications.

IBM Customer Engineer (CE) An IBM service representative who performs maintenance services for IBM hardware. See also IBM Program Support Representative, IBM Systems Engineering Operations Specialist.

IBM Disk Operating System (DOS) A disk operating system based on MS-DOS (trademark of Microsoft Corporation) that operates with all IBM personal computers.

IBM LinkWay product An application development tool that enables a user to create, present, and modify applications containing text, pictures, video images, and sound without requiring a background in programming or other computer skills.

IBM NetView Distribution Manager An IBM licensed program available for IBM host systems (System/370, 43xx, and 30xx computers) that allows the host system to use, send, and delete files and programs in a network of computers.

IBM Network Control Program (NCP) An IBM licensed program that provides communications controller support for single domain, multiple domain, and interconnected network capability.

IBM OfficeVision/VM An IBM licensed program that allows users to create, change, and send notes and documents; make appointments and maintain calendars; create and maintain schedules; create and main-tain distribution lists; and control electronic mail and personal files. Formerly known as the PROFS licensed program. See also Remote Spooling Communications Subsystem (RSCS), VM/MVS bridge.

IBM Operating System/2 (OS/2) Pertaining to the IBM licensed program that can be used as the operating system for personal computers. The OS/2 licensed program can perform multiple tasks at the same time.

IBM OS/2 Presentation Manager The front-end data manager and user interface for the IBM OS/2 operating system; an example of a graphical user interface.

IBM PC Network See PC Network.

IBM Program Support Representative (PSR) An IBM service representative who performs maintenance services for IBM software at a centralized IBM location. See also IBM Customer Engineer, IBM Systems Engineering Operations Specialist.

IBM PS/2 TouchSelect An add-on panel that can be attached to an existing IBM display to convert it to a touch-sensitive screen.

IBM PS/2 TV A unit that combines a standard PS/2 color display with a television capable of receiving full-motion National Television Systems Committee (NTSC) analog video from a variety of sources, including cable TV, an external TV antenna, video cassette recorder (VCR), or video disc player.

IBM Remote Spooling Communications Subsystem A licensed program that operates on a host system (such as a System/370, 30xx, or 43xx computer) transferring spooled files, commands, and messages between OfficeVision/VM users, remote workstations, and remote and local batch systems through communications programs. See also OfficeVision/VM, VM/MVS bridge.

IBM service representative An individual in IBM who performs maintenance services for IBM products or systems. See also IBM Program Support Representative.

IBM software distribution (ISD) The IBM department responsible for software distribution.

IBM Systems Engineering Operations Specialist An IBM service representative who performs maintenance services for IBM software in the field. See also IBM Customer Engineer, IBM Program Support Representative.

IBM Ultimedia products All of IBM's multimedia products and services.

IC Integrated circuit.

ICA (1) International Communication Association, formerly called Industrial Communication Association. (2) Integrated communication adapter.

ICB Interrupt control block.

ICCF Interactive computing and control facility. See VSE/ICCF.

ICF Intersystem communications function.

ICF file A device file that allows a program on one system to communicate with a program on another system. There can be one or more sessions with the same or different communications devices at the same time.

IC memory Integrated circuit memory. (A)

ICMP Internet Control Message Protocol.

ICNCB Intelligent controller node control block.

icon (1) A graphic symbol, displayed on a screen, that a user can point to with a device such as a mouse in order to select a particular function or software application. Synonymous with pictogram. (T) (2) In SAA Advanced Common User Access architecture, a graphical representation of an object, consisting of an image, image background, and a label.

icon box In the AIXwindows program, a window used as a visual storage area for icons representing minimized windows.

icon layout policy In the AIXwindows program, a specification that determines whether icons representing minimized windows are placed on the root window or within an icon box.

ICR Independent component release.

ICU Interactive chart utility.

ICV Initial chaining value.

ICW (1) Initial control word. (2) Interface control word.

ID (1) Identifier. (2) Identification.

IDDU Interactive data definition utility.

idea processor Personal computer application software that allows a user to organize thoughts in outline form and modify, expand, compress, and reorganize topics as required.

identification In computer security, the process that allows a system to recognize an entity by means of personal, equipment, or organizational characteristics or codes.

identification card In the 3600 Finance Communication System, a card similar to a credit card that contains a customer's identification number written on a magnetic stripe. Customers insert the identification card in the 3614 Consumer Transaction Facility to identify themselves. See also personal code.

identification card reader In the 3614 Consumer Transaction Facility, a component that reads precoded information from the magnetic stripe on a customer's identification card.

Identification Division One of the four main parts of a COBOL program. In addition to identifying the source program and the object program, this part may also describe the author's name, the location where written, and the date written.

identification (ID) characters Characters sent by a station on a switched line to identify the station. TWX, BSC, and SDLC stations use ID characters.

identification number See customer identification number.

identifier (1) One or more characters used to identify or name a data element and possibly to indicate certain properties of that data element. (A) (2) In programming languages, a token that names a data object such as a variable, an array, a record, a subprogram, or a function. (A) (3) In the C language, a sequence of letters, digits, and underscores used to identify a data object or function. (4) In COBOL, a syntactically correct combination of a data name, with its qualifiers, subscripts, and reference modifiers, as required for uniqueness of reference, that names a data item. The rules for an identifier associated with the general formats may, however, specifically prohibit qualification, subscripting, or reference modification. See resultant identifier. (5) In FORTRAN, a lexical unit that names a language object; for example, the names of variables, arrays, and program units. The name of a declared unit. (6) In Pascal, a lexical unit that names a language object; for example, the names of variables, arrays, records, labels, and procedures. The name of a declared item. (7) In PL/I, a single alphabetic character or a string of alphabetic characters, digits, and break characters that starts with an alphabetic character. identifier, ordinary identifier. (8) A sequence of bits or characters that identifies a program, device, or system to another program, device, or system. (9) In the AIX Enhanced X-Windows program, a unique value associated with a resource that a client program uses to name the resource. An identifier can be used over any connection to name the resource. (10) See version identifier.

identity-based access control In computer security, access control based on the identities of subjects and the object that are being accessed. Contrast with resource-based access control.

identity element Synonym for identity gate.

identity gate A logic element that performs an identity operation. (T) Synonymous with identity element.

identity operation (1) The Boolean operation whose result has the Boolean value 1 if and only if all the operands have the same Boolean value. An identity operation on two operands is an equivalence operation. (I) (A) (2) Contrast with nonidentity operation.

identity token In computer security, a device such as a smart card, a metal key, or some other physical token carried by a systems user that allows user identity validation.

identity unit A unit that has several input signals and produces a specified output signal only when all the input signals are alike.

identity validation In computer security, the performance of tests, such as the checking of a password, that enables an information system to recognize users or resources as being identical to those previously described to the system. See also authentication, design verification, implementation verification.

ideogram (1) In a natural language, a graphic character that represents an object or a concept and associated sounds; for example, a Chinese ideogram or a Japanese kanji ideogram. (T) (2) Synonymous with ideographic character.

ideogram entry A text entry method for ideograms that combines multistroke character entry, based on phonograms, with conversion to ideograms, with conversion to ideograms by means of a dictionary and syntax rules; for example, Kana-Kanji conversion entry for Japanese text, Pinyin-Hanji conversion entry for Chinese characters. (T)

ideographic Pertaining to 2-byte characters consisting of pictograms, symbolic characters, and other types of symbols.

ideographic character Synonym for ideogram.

ideographic character set The combination of the basic and extended ideographic character sets. See also basic ideographic character set, extended ideographic character set.

ideographic session A display station operating session during which ideographic data are used for system communication with the operator.

ideographic sort utility A program that sorts ideographic data.

ideographic support The hardware and programming elements that allow processing of ideographic data.

idle character (1) A character transmitted on a telecommunication line that is not intended to represent data and does not result in an output operation at the accepting terminal. (2) See synchronous idle character.

idle line Synonym for inactive line.

idle link Synonym for inactive link.

idle list A list of secondary stations on a network that are polled less often by the primary station due to their inactivity.

idle state In the 3800 Printing Subsystem, the time during which the equipment is not in use. In the idle state, some components are cycled down automatically to extend component life.

idle time (1) The part of operable time during which a functional unit is not operated. (I) (A) (2) Contrast with operating time.

IDN Integrated digital network.

IDU Interactive Data Base Utilities.

IE Instruction element.

IEC International Electrotechnical Commission.

IEEE Institute of Electrical and Electronics Engineers.

I extent Inline extent.

IF-AND-ONLY-IF element Synonym for IF-AND-ONLY-IF gate.

IF-AND-ONLY-IF gate A logic element that performs the Boolean operation of equivalence. (T) Synonymous with IF-AND-ONLY-IF element.

IF-AND-ONLY-IF operation Synonym for equivalence operation.

IF expression An expression in a procedure used to test for a condition. The action performed by the procedure depends on the result of the test.

I-field bytes Data within the information field of a transmit or receive sequenced data frame.

I format Information format.

IFP IMS/VS Fast Path.

I frame Information frame.

IF statement (1) A conditional statement that specifies a condition to be tested and the action to be taken if the condition is satisfied. (T)   (2) A statement used for conditional statement execution. IF is always followed by a THEN clause and optionally, an ELSE clause. (3) In C language, a conditional statement that contains the keyword IF, followed by an expression in parentheses (the condition), a statement (the action), and an optional else clause (the alternative action).

IF-THEN element Synonym for IF-THEN gate.

IF-THEN gate A logic element that performs the Boolean operation of implication. (T)   Synonymous with IF-THEN element.

IF-THEN operation Synonym for implication.

if-then rule A formulated rule which specifies a logical relationship among a set of facts and which consists of an "if" part representing the premise or condition and a "then" part representing the goal or action to be taken when the "if" part is true. (T)

if-then statement Synonym for if-then rule. (T)

IGC See ideographic.

IGES (Initial Graphics Exchange Specification) An industry-standard graphic file format for computer-assisted design (CAD) programming, defined by the American National Standards Institute (ANSI).

ignore character (1) Synonym for cancel character. (2) See block ignore character.

IGS Interchange group separator.

ILBT Interrupt level branch table.

i-list In an AIX Base Operating System file system, blocks 2 through n, containing structures (i-nodes) that relate a file to the data blocks or disk. The size of the i-list depends on the size of the mounted file system. See also i-node, superblock.

illegal character (1) A character or combination of bits that is not valid according to some criteria; for example, with respect to a specified alphabet, a character that is not a member. (A)   (2) Contrast with forbidden combination.

ILU Initiating logical unit.

image (1) An electronic representation of a picture produced by means of sensing light, sound, electron radiation, or other emanations coming from the picture or reflected by the picture. An image can also be generated directly by software without reference to an existing picture. See also page image. (2) An electronic representation of an original document recorded by a scanning device. (3) In a document copying machine, a faithful likeness of the subject matter of the original. (T)   (4) In multimedia applications, a still picture or one frame. (5) In the IBM ImagePlus system, a single page of information; the result of scanning, or digitizing, a single sheet of paper.

image area (1) In micrographics, the part of the film frame reserved for an image. (A)   (2) In computer graphics, synonym for display space.

image block A structure that contains the raster pattern and instructions for placing the pattern on a page.

image cache In the AIXwindows program, a means of associating an image with a name. Once this association is in place, the appropriate AIXwindows subroutines can generate pixmaps through references to an .Xdefaults file, by name, and through an argument list, by pixmap.

image cell A portion of an image that can be replicated to fill a defined area.

image content Image data and its associated image data parameters.

image copy (1) An exact reproduction of all or part of an image. (2) In the DB2 program, the exact reproduction of all or part of a table space. DB2 provides utilities to make full image copies or incremental image copies.

image data (1) Digital data derived from electrical signals that represent a visual image. See binary image data, gray-scale image data, thresholding. (2) In the ImagePlus program, rectangular arrays of raster information that define an image.

image dissector In optical character recognition, a mechanical or electronic transducer that sequentially detects the level of light intensity in different areas of a completely illuminated sample space. (A)

image file A data file containing an image.

image graphics Synonym for fixed-image graphics.

image head adjuster In a duplicator, a control for adjusting the position of the image relative to the leading edge of the paper. (T)

image input area The bottom left area of the image display where numbers appear when entered using the keyboard.

image mode In the IBM 3886 Optical Character Reader, one of two data formats the user selects for a data record. Image mode does not allow blank or character editing, field justification, or blank and zero filling of fields; data validation and the field lengths are not fixed. The resulting output record contains 2-byte fields indicating the length of each field read, followed by the data.

image object (1) An object that contains image data. See also object. (2) A named bit string; for example, in the context of optical programming support, an image object refers to a scanned paper document. IBM format descriptive headers and trailers surround the image object in the system.

Image Object Content Architecture (IOCA) An architected collection of constructs used to interchange and present images.

image overlay See overlay image.

ImagePlus workstation A PS/2 computer with an Image Adapter/A card using the IBM PS/2 ImagePlus Workstation Program. An ImagePlus workstation provides for capture, display, and printing of coded data, voice, and image objects.

image plane In video systems using more than one memory array, a single memory array contributing to a displayed image. See bit plane.

image processing (1) The use of a data processing system to create, scan, analyze, enhance, interpret, or display images. Synonymous with picture processing. (T) (2) Computer graphics in which digital image data are stored, processed, retrieved, and displayed for applications such as processing satellite data, geology, microbiology, petrology, robotics, and textile design. See also binary image data, gray-scale image data, image data, machine vision.

image processing software Software that resides in the ImagePlus workstation. It provides services for the Folder Application Facility and ImagePlus system for the display and printing of page images and coded data. The image processing software also provides for page capture, document image composition, image

page working set interpretation and display, and document image transfer to the ImagePlus host.

image regeneration See regeneration.

image retention In some video cameras, the undesirable tendency to retain an image, causing streaking of moving bright spots. Synonymous with lag.

image server A high-capacity optical storage device or a computer that each computer and image workstation on a network can use to access and retrieve image objects that can be shared among the attached computers and image workstations. See also file server.

image space See coded image space, display space.

image symbol set (ISS) In GDDM, a graphics symbol set in which each character is treated as a small image and is described by a rectangular array of display points. Characters in an image symbol set are always drawn in a fixed size. Contrast with vector symbol set. See also graphics symbol set.

image transfer In a duplicator, the process in which the image is transferred directly or indirectly from the master onto the paper. (T)

image workstation A programmable workstation that can perform image functions by using the Object Distribution Manager and the ImagePlus workstation interface.

imbedded blank See embedded blank.

IMH Internodal message handler.

IML (1) Initial microcode load. (2) Initial microprogram load. (3) Initial machine load.

immediate access storage A storage device whose access time is negligible in comparison with other operating times. (A)

immediate address The contents of an address part that contains the value of an operand rather than an address. (I) (A) Synonymous with zero-level address.

immediate addressing A method of addressing in which the address part of an instruction contains an immediate address. (I) (A)

immediate checkpoint In IMS/VS, the facility that writes simple checkpoint information without requiring termination of message processing programs.

immediate command (1) In VM, a CMS command that, when issued after an attention interruption, causes any program execution currently in progress to be suspended until the immediate command is processed. The immediate commands are HB (halt the execution of the CMS batch virtual machine at the end of current job), HO (halt SVC tracing), HT (halt typing or displaying), HX (halt execution), RO (resume tracing), RT (resume typing or displaying), and SO (suspend tracing temporarily). (2) In the NetView program, a command, such as GO, CANCEL, or RESET, that can be executed while a regular command is being processed.

immediate data (1) Data contained in an instruction rather than in a separate storage location. (2) Data transferred during instruction execution time. (3) In Assembler language, actual data appearing in an instruction, as opposed to the symbolic name of some data. The data is immediately available from the instruction and therefore does not have to be read from memory.

immediate environment termination In DPPX, an emergency termination of environment. There is no resource recovery.

immediate instruction An instruction that contains the value of an operand rather than its address. The operand is then called an immediate operand. (T)

immediate maintenance In the AS/400 system and System/38, a method of maintaining keyed access paths for database files. This method updates the access path whenever changes are made to the database file associated with the access path. Contrast with rebuild maintenance, delayed maintenance.

immediate message In the AS/400 system, a message that is created when it is sent. Contrast with predefined message.

immediate mode In AIX graphics, a mode in which graphics commands are run immediately rather than being compiled into a primitive or display list.

immediate operand The value of an operand contained within an instruction rather than the address of the operand. (T)

immediate-request mode In SNA, an operational mode in which the sender stops sending request units (RUs) on a normal or expedited flow after sending a definite-response request chain on that flow until a response is made to the chain. Contrast with delayed-request mode. See also immediate-response mode.

immediate-response mode In SNA, an operational mode in which the receiver responds to request units (RUs) on a given normal flow in the order it receives them, that is, in a first-in, first-out sequence. Contrast

with delayed-response mode. See also immediate-response mode.

immediate task A task assigned the second highest level dispatching priority by the network control program. It initiates I/O operations on lines that are idle. See also appendage task, nonproductive task, productive task.

impact paper A coated paper used to obtain one or more copies of printed, typed, or handwritten information without need for a ribbon or other inking device. Each sheet is coated on the front side. Pressure on the top sheet in a stack causes the character to appear on the front of that sheet and on the front of sheets beneath the top sheet, thus requiring no carbon paper between sheets.

impact printer (1) A printer in which printing is the result of mechanically striking the printing medium. (T)   (2) Contrast with nonimpact printer. See Figure 73.

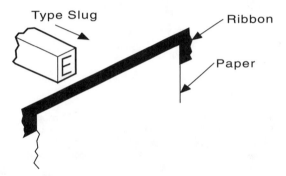

Type Slug   Ribbon

E   Paper

Figure 73. Impact Printer

impedance The combined effect of resistance, inductance, and capacitance on a signal at a given frequency.

imperative statement (1) A statement that specifies an action to be taken unconditionally. (T)   (2) In COBOL, a statement that either begins with an imperative verb and specifies an unconditional action to be taken or is a conditional statement that is delimited by its explicit scope terminator (a delimited scope statement). An imperative statement can consist of a sequence of imperative statements. (3) Synonym for instruction.

impersonate In computer security, to pose as an authorized user to gain access to a system. Synonymous with masquerade, mimic. See also attack.

implementation The system development phase at the end of which the hardware, software and procedures of the system considered become operational. (T)

implementation verification In computer security, the use of verification techniques, usually computer-assisted, to demonstrate a mathematical correspondence between a formal specification of a system and its implementation. See also design verification.

implementer name In COBOL, an IBM-defined name that includes assignment names, computer names, function names, and language names.

implication The dyadic Boolean operation whose result has the Boolean value 0 if and only if the first operand has the Boolean value 1 and the second has the Boolean value 0. Contrast with exclusion. Synonymous with conditional implication operation, IF-THEN operation, inclusion. See Figure 74.

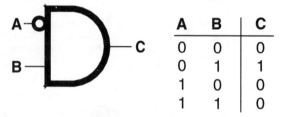

A	B	C
0	0	0
0	1	1
1	0	0
1	1	0

Figure 74. Implication

implication operation See conditional implication operation.

implicit action In PL/I, an action that is described for a condition when the program is started and that remains throughout the program unless overridden by an ON statement for the same condition. Contrast with ON-statement action.

implicit declaration (1) In programming languages, a declaration caused by the occurrence of an identifier and in which the attributes are determined by default. (I) (2) Contrast with explicit declaration.

implicit dimensioning (1) In BASIC, using either context or reference to an array member to specify the number of elements or dimensions in an array. (2) In BASIC, specifying the length of a character variable by context, without explicitly defining the variable in a DIM statement.

implicit partition state In the 3270 Information Display System, the mode of the display when powered on, that is, when it is a single implicitly created partition with the default screen size and has a partition identifier of zero.

implicit partition 0 In the 3270 Information Display System, a partition automatically created and assigned the partition identifier 0 at power-on or session-establishment time, or created when all explicitly created partitions are destroyed. Contrast with explicit partition.

implicit scope terminator In COBOL, a separator period that terminates the scope of any preceding unterminated statement, or a phrase of a statement that by its occurrence indicates the end of the scope of any statement contained within the preceding phrase. Contrast with explicit scope terminator.

implicit selection In SAA Common User Access architecture, a selection technique whereby a user moves the cursor to a choice and that choice becomes automatically selected. See also explicit selection.

implied addressing (1) A method of addressing in which the operation part of an instruction implicitly addresses operands. (I) (A) (2) See also one-ahead addressing.

implied CP command In CMS, a CP command invoked without preceding the command line with CP.

implied DO In FORTRAN, an indexing specification that is similar to a DO statement, but does not specify the word DO and uses lists of data, rather than a set of statements, as its range.

implied EXEC A CMS EXEC procedure invoked as though it were a CMS command without specifying the command name EXEC.

import (1) To bring in data from another system. (2) In the AIX operating system, to request the operations defined by an interface. A client imports an interface from a server. (3) Contrast with export. See also import/export.

import/export The sending of information from one system, application, or information resource dictionary (export) and the acceptance of information by another system, application, or information resource dictionary (import). (T)

imprinter Any device used to produce or impress marks or patterns on a surface; for example, a printing press, typewriter, pen, cash register, bookkeeping machine, or a pressure device such as that used with credit cards and address plates. (A)

imprinting (1) The act of using an imprinter. (A) (2) The output of any imprinter. (A)

imprint position The location on a printing medium in which a character is to be printed or typed.

impromptu message A message that is created when it is sent. Contrast with predefined message.

improved spool file recovery In VM, the process of recovering from the disk the checkpoint data that was previously recorded for closed spool files. If warm start is not possible, the VM system operator may attempt a checkpoint start or force start. See also checkpoint start, force start.

impulse Synonym for pulse.

impulsive noise In acoustics, noise of an impulsive nature whose level is determined with a sound level meter set for the dynamic characteristic "impulse."

impulsive noise correction (Ki) In acoustics, the difference, expressed in decibels, between the sound pressure level measured with the dynamic characteristic "impulse" and the sound pressure level measured with the dynamic characteristic "slow."

IMR (1) Interruption mask register. (2) Intensive mode recording.

IMS Information Management System. Synonym for IMS/VS.

IMS/VS Information Management System/Virtual Storage.

IMS/VS Fast Path (IFP) region In IMS/VS Fast Path, an online environment in which message-driven programs and data entry database online utilities operate. Synonymous with Fast Path dependent region.

IMS/VS subsystem In IMS/VS, an individual batch or online IMS/VS control program executing in an OS/VS address space.

inactive (1) Not operational. (2) Pertaining to a node or device not connected or not available for connection to another node or device. (3) In the AIX operating system, pertaining to a window that does not have an input focus. (4) In VTAM, the state of a resource or a major or minor node that has not been activated or for which the VARY INACT command has been issued. Contrast with active. See also inoperative.

inactive age In the Data Facility Hierarchical Storage Manager, the number of days since the data set was last referred to.

inactive character A filler character, transmitted in the data transfer phase, that does not represent information.

inactive line A telecommunication line currently unavailable for transmitting data. Contrast with active line. Synonymous with idle line.

inactive link A link currently unavailable for transmitting data. Contrast with active link. Synonymous with idle link.

inactive mass storage volume See inactive volume.

inactive node In a network, a node neither connected to nor available for connection to another node. Contrast with active node.

inactive page In OS/VS and VM, a page in real storage that has not been referred to during a preset time period.

inactive program (1) A program that is not loaded or that is loaded but not ready to be executed. (2) In the OS/2 operating system, a program that was started but is suspended and no longer running. Contrast with active program.

inactive record In the AS/400 system and System/38, an inactive subfile record or any record format that is not currently shown on a display. See also inactive subfile record. Contrast with active record.

inactive state In an SNA network, the state in which a component of a node is unable to perform the function for which it was designed. Contrast with active state.

inactive station A station currently ineligible for entering or accepting messages. Contrast with active station.

inactive subfile record In the AS/400 system, a subfile record that either was not added to a subfile by a write operation or was described as inactive by the data description specification (DDS) keywords SFLINZ and SFLRNA. Contrast with active subfile record.

inactive volume In MSS, a mass storage volume not available for mounting by the operating system.

inactive window In SAA Advanced Common User Access architecture, a window that a user is not currently interacting with. The window cannot receive input from the keyboard. Contrast with active window.

inadvertent disclosure In computer security, accidental exposure of sensitive information to an unauthorized user, which may result in a compromise or a need-to-know violation.

in-basket A mailbox that contains only received messages. (T)

inblock subgroup The part of a message handler (MH) incoming group that precedes the inheader subgroup and blocks several physical messages into a longer, logical message or deblocks a physical message into a shorter, logical message.

inbound (1) In SNA, deprecated term for incoming, receiving. (2) In the 3270 data stream, a transmission from the terminal to the application program.

inbound pacing (1) In PSS, a process for controlling the flow of data from store controller to host. (2) In SNA, deprecated term for receive pacing.

inbuffer subgroup The part of a message handler (MH) incoming group that operates on each segment of an incoming message.

inches per second (IPS) A measure of tape speed.

incident See computer security incident.

incidental time Synonym for miscellaneous time. (T)

incident record (1) In ACF/TCAM, a checkpoint record that logs a change in external logical unit (LU) or application program status, and in the contents of an option field that occurred since the last environment record was taken. It is used to update the information contained in environment records at restart after a closedown or system failure. See also checkpoint request record, control record, environment record. (2) In DPPX, a user-defined record, including a 14-byte header, placed in the system log data set in which the user may include information dealing with incidents other than errors.

include file A text file that contains declarations used by a group of functions, programs, or users. Synonymous with header file.

include function In VSE, a function that retrieves a library member for inclusion in program input.

include set In System/36 SORT, specification statements that identify one or more record types to be sorted.

include statement (1) A computer language preprocessor statement that directs the processor to retrieve a specific file that contains instructions and data the program may need. See also include file. (2) In the C language, a preprocessor statement that causes the preprocessor to replace the statement with the contents of a specified file. (3) In FORTRAN, a compiler statement that causes the compiler to replace the statement with the contents of a specified file. (4) In OS/400 application programming interfaces, a statement that causes the compiler to replace the include statement with the contents of the specified header or file.

inclusion Synonym for implication.

inclusive-OR element Synonym for OR gate.

inclusive-OR gate Synonym for OR gate.

inclusive-OR operation Synonym for disjunction.

inclusive reference A reference from a segment in main storage to an external symbol in a segment that does not cause overlay of the calling segment.

inclusive segments Segments in the same region of an overlay program that are in the same path; the segments can be in main storage simultaneously.

incoming call A call arriving at a data terminal equipment (DTE). Contrast with outgoing call.

incoming call packet A call supervision packet transmitted by a data circuit-terminating equipment (DCE) to inform a called data terminal equipment (DTE) that another DTE has requested a call.

incoming group In ACF/TCAM, the portion of a message handler designed to handle incoming messages for the message control program (MCP). Contrast with outgoing group.

incoming message (1) A message transmitted from a station to the computer. Contrast with outgoing record. (2) A message sent from an external logical unit (LU) or application program to the message control program (MCP).

incoming trunk A trunk coming into a central office.

incomplete parameter checking In computer security, a system fault that exists when not all parameters have been checked for accuracy and consistency by the operating system, thus making the system vulnerable to penetration.

inconnector (1) In flowcharting, a connector that indicates a continuation of a broken flowline. (A) (2) Contrast with outconnector.

increment (1) A value used to alter a counter or register. (2) To move a document forward in the read station from one timing mark to the next so that a new line of characters is visible to the scan head. (3) To move a card from column to column in the punch station so that each column presents itself for punching. (4) To move a hopper or stacker upward or downward.

incremental backup (1) In the Data Facility Hierarchical Storage Manager, the process of copying data sets that have been opened for reasons other than read-only access since the last backup version was created and that meet the backup frequency criteria. (2) Contrast with full backup.

incremental compiler A compiler that completes as much of a translation as possible on the input or scanning of each complete source statement. Typically used for online computer program development and checkout. (A)

incremental computer A special-purpose computer designed to process changes in the variables as well as the absolute values of the variables. (A)

incremental coordinate A relative coordinate where the previously addressed point is the reference point. (A)

incremental execution Execution of statements or sections of a program without submission of a complete program.

incremental integrator A digital integrator modified so that the output signal is maximum negative, zero, or maximum positive when the value of the input is negative, zero, or positive. (A)

incremental representation (1) A method of representing variables in which changes in the values of the variable are represented, rather than the values themselves. (I) (A) (2) See ternary incremental representation.

incremental size The distance between adjacent addressable points on the display surface. (I) (A)

incremental tape unit A magnetic tape unit capable of recording one character at a time, creating record gaps only when explicitly directed. (A)

incremental vector (1) A vector whose end point is specified as a displacement from its start point. (I) (A) (2) Synonymous with relative vector. (3) Contrast with absolute vector.

increment size The distance between adjacent addressable points on the display surface. (T) (A)

indent (1) To begin a line farther in from the margin than the other lines. (T) (2) To set typographical material to the right of the left margin.

indentation (1) The action of indenting. (2) The condition of being indented. (3) The blank space produced by indenting. (4) See also hanging indent.

indent tab character (IT) A word processing formatting mode control that requires a device to execute a horizontal tab function after each appearance of a carrier return character. The number of automatic hor-

izontal tabs performed after each carrier return character is equal to the number of indent tab characters keyed since the latest resetting of indent tab mode. Contrast with horizontal tabulation character.

independent compilation The compilation of a compilation unit not using the interface and context information from related compilation units. When independently compiled units are eventually combined, it may be necessary to check interface and context information for validity. (T)

independent data communication See code-independent data communication.

independent data item In COBOL, a data item in the Working-Storage Section that has no relationship to other data items.

independent LU See SSCP-independent LU.

independent utility programs Utility programs that support but are not part of an operating system; they are used by the system programmer to initialize and prepare direct access storage devices for use under operating system control.

independent workstation See programmable workstation, stand-alone workstation.

index (1) A list of the contents of a file or of a document, together with keys or references for locating the contents. (I) (A) (2) In word processing, to move the paper or display pointer in the direction used during normal printout. (T) (3) In programming, an integer that identifies the position of a data item in a sequence of data items. (T) (4) A symbol or a numeral used to identify a particular quantity in an array of similar quantities; for example, the terms of an array represented by X1, X2,..., X100 have the indexes 1, 2,..., 100, respectively. (A) (5) In micrographics, a guide for locating information on a roll of microform, using targets, flash cards, lines, bars, or other optical codes. (A) (6) To prepare a list as in *(1)*. (A) (7) To move a machine part to a predetermined position, or by a predetermined amount, on a quantized scale. (A) (8) A table used to locate records in an indexed sequential data set or an indexed file. (9) In VSAM, an ordered collection of pairs, each consisting of a key and a pointer, used by VSAM to sequence and locate the records of a key-sequenced data set or file; it is organized in levels of index records. See also alternate index, index level, index set, sequence set. (10) In OFFICE/36, a list of document names. (11) In COBOL, a computer storage area or register, the contents of which represents the identification of a particular element in a table. (12) In SQL, pointers that are logically arranged by the values of a key. Indexes provide quick access and can enforce uniqueness on the rows in a table.

(13) In Pascal, a value used to access an element of an array. (14) In the Folder Application Facility, a document's index contains specific information about the document used for Folder Management and routing information used for Workflow Management. (15) See code line index.

index build The automatic process of creating an alternate index through the use of access method services.

index character (INX) A word processing formatting control that moves the printing or display point down to the next line with no horizontal motion. Synonymous with line feed character.

index component In VSAM, the part of a key-sequenced data set, catalog, or alternate index that establishes the sequence of the data records within the object it indexes. The index is used to locate each record in the data component of the object, based on the key value of the record.

index data item In COBOL, a data item in which the values associated with an index-name can be stored in a form specified by the implementor.

indexed access Pertaining to the organization and accessing of the records of a storage structure through a separate index to the locations of the stored records. (A)

indexed address (1) An address that is to be modified by the content of an index register. (T) (2) An address that is changed by the contents of an index register before or while an instruction is performed.

indexed data name In COBOL, a data name identifier that is subscripted with one or more index names.

indexed data set A data set in which records are stored and retrieved on the basis of keys within each record that are part of the data record itself.

indexed file (1) In a database, a file whose access path is built on key values. Each record in the file is identified by a key field. (2) In COBOL, a file with indexed organization. See Figure 75.

indexed instruction An instruction that uses an indexed address.

indexed organization In COBOL, a permanent logical file structure in which each record is identified by the value of one or more keys within that record. Contrast with relative organization, sequential organization.

indexed segment Synonym for index target segment.

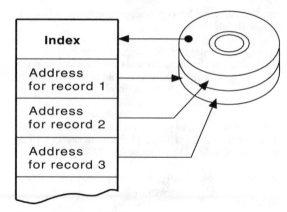

Figure 75. Indexed File

indexed sequential access Pertaining to the organization and accessing of records through an index of the keys that are stored in arbitrarily partitioned sequential files. (A)

indexed sequential access method (ISAM) See basic indexed sequential access method, queued indexed sequential access method.

indexed sequential data set A data set in which each record contains a key that determines its location. The location of each record is computed through the use of an index.

indexed sequential organization A file organization in which records are arranged in logical sequence by key. Indexes to these keys permit direct access to individual records.

index entry In VSAM, a catalog entry that describes the index component of a catalog or key-sequenced cluster's index component. An index entry contains the attributes, passwords and protection attributes, allocation and extent information, and statistics of the index component.

index hole (1) A hole punched in a flexible disk to indicate the beginning of the first sectors of the disk. (T) (2) A hole in a diskette that indicates the beginning of the first sector and that is used to check the speed of rotation.

indexing (1) The association of descriptors with their corresponding documents. (T) (2) In word processing, a feature that causes the typing position or display pointer to be moved to the corresponding character position of the following typing line. (T) See also reverse indexing. (3) A technique of address modification by means of index registers. (4) In the ImagePlus system, the process of assigning a document a unique identifier for eventual storage and retrieval in the system.

indexing segment In an IMS/VS index database, the segment (the index pointer segment) that contains a pointer to a segment containing data (the indexed segment).

index key (1) The field within a record that identifies the record in an indexed file. (2) In SQL, the set of columns in a table used to determine the order of indexed entries.

index level In VSAM, a set of index records that give the location of the index records in the next lower index level or, at the sequence-set level, the control intervals in the file or data set it controls.

index name In COBOL, a user-defined word that names an index associated with a specific table.

index of reference The index specified by a program to DPPX/DTMS for subsequent access to a database.

index pointer segment In an IMS/VS database, the segment that contains the data and pointers used to index the index target segments.

index record In VSAM, a collection of index entries retrieved and stored as a group. See also data record.

index-record header In a VSAM index record, the 24-byte field at the beginning of the record that contains control information about the record.

index register (1) A register whose contents can be used to modify an operand address during the execution of computer instructions. An index register may also be used as a counter to control the execution of a loop, to control the use of an array, for table look-up, as a switch, or as a pointer. (T) (2) A register whose contents are added to the operand or absolute address derived from a combination of a base address with a displacement.

index replication In VSAM, the use of an entire track of direct access storage to contain as many copies of a single index record as possible; replication reduces rotational delay.

index return character (IRT) A word processing multifunction control used as a formatting control and a device control. As a formatting control, it produces the same effect as a required carrier return in printed or displayed text. As a device control, it delimits a line without ending recording on the current magnetic card track when recording multiple lines on the same track. Contrast with required carrier return character.

index search information In the AS/400 system, a searchable part of the online help information that pro-

vides "how-to" and explanatory topics to supplement the help for specific displays.

index set In VSAM, the set of index levels above the sequence set. Together, the index set and the sequence set make up the index.

index slip On dictation equipment, a removable paper slip on which visible marks are made by the marking mechanism of the machine and on which written notes can be made concerning the dictation. (I)

index source segment In an IMS/VS database, the segment containing the data from which the indexing segment is built. It can be the same as the indexed segment or one of its dependents.

index target segment In an IMS/VS database, the segment pointed to by a secondary index entry, that is, from an index pointer segment. Synonymous with indexed segment.

index target set In DPPX, the combination of a target data set and one or more indexes that point to it.

index track A track that contains information required to locate data on other tracks of the same data medium. (T) (A)

index upgrade In VSAM, the process of updating an alternate index to reflect changes made in the contents of its base cluster.

index word An index modifier applied to the address part of a computer instruction. (I) (A)

indicated resource The SNA or non-SNA entity most closely associated with the alert condition.

indication primitive In Open Systems Interconnection architecture, a primitive issued by a service provider either to invoke a procedure or to indicate that a procedure has been invoked by the service user at the peer service access point. (T)

indicator (1) A device that gives a visual or other indication of the existence of a defined state. (T) (2) An internal switch used by a program to remember when a certain event occurs and what to do when the event occurs. (3) See file position indicator, level indicator, message indicator, switch indicator.

indicator light A light that signals a change in status or the presence of a certain predefined condition. See also light-emitting diode (LED).

indicator variable In SQL, a variable used to represent the null value in an application program; for example, if the value for the results column is null, the value in the indicator variable is be negative.

indirect activation In VTAM, the activation of a lower-level resource of the resource hierarchy as a result of SCOPE or ISTATUS specifications related to an activation command naming a higher-level resource. Contrast with direct activation.

indirect address (1) An address of a storage location that contains an address identifying the ultimate location. The storage location may be the first address field of a chained list of address fields, the last of which identifies the ultimate location. (T) (2) Synonymous with multilevel address. (3) Contrast with direct address.

indirect addressing (1) A method of addressing in which the address part of an instruction contains an indirect address. (A) (2) Contrast with direct addressing.

indirect deactivation In VTAM, the deactivation of a lower-level resource of the resource hierarchy as a result of a deactivation command naming a higher-level resource. Contrast with direct deactivation.

indirect electrostatic process In a document copying machine, an electrostatic process in which the image is formed within the machine and subsequently transferred to unsensitized copying material. (T) Contrast with direct electrostatic process.

indirect instruction (1) An instruction that contains at least one indirect address of an operand. (T) (2) Contrast with direct instruction.

indirect operation In an 8100 channel I/O (CHIO) operation, the transfer of information between the SDLC control logic and the storage location whose address is in a channel pointer.

indirect referencing In programming languages, a mechanism for referencing via a data object whose value points to the referenced language object. (I)

indirect user A person who is not enrolled as an OFFICE/36 general user or independent workstation user, but can receive a printed copy of OFFICE/36 mail. Contrast with general user.

individual accountability In computer security, the ability to positively associate the identity of a user with the time, method, and degree of access to a system.

individual address In communications, an address associated with a particular station on the network. Contrast with group address.

individual VM event profile A resource profile that can be used to define the settings for audit and control of VM events for a specific user. Contrast with system VM event profile.

Note: In VM/SP, the profile is in the VMEVENT class. In VM/XA programs, the profile is in the VMXEVENT class.

in-doubt work unit In IMS/VS, a piece of work that is pending during commit processing; if commit processing fails between the polling of subsystems the decision to execute the commit, recovery processing must resolve the status of any work unit that is in doubt.

induced jitter Jitter caused by a magnetic field that is external to the display device.

induction See mathematical induction.

induction coil An apparatus for transforming a direct current by induction into an alternating current.

industry code In Subsystems Support Services, a two-character alphabetic code used in a control statement or terminal-entered command to identify an industry subsystem; for example, the 3790 Communication System.

inference engine In artificial intelligence, the components of an expert system, that apply principles of reasoning to draw conclusions from the information stored in a knowledge base. Synonymous with control structure, rule interpreter. (T)

inferiors In AIX Enhanced X-Windows, all the subwindows nested below a window.

infinite loop (1) A loop whose execution can be interrupted only by intervention from outside the computer program in which the loop is included. (T) (2) Synonymous with closed loop.

infinite pad method In optical character recognition, a method of measuring reflectance of a paper stock such that doubling the number of backing sheets of the same stock will not change the measured reflectance. (A)

infinity (1) In binary floating-point concepts, a value with an associated sign that is mathematically greater in magnitude than any binary floating-point number. (2) A name for the upper boundary of the set of numbers.

infix notation (1) A method of forming mathematical expressions, governed by rules of operator precedence and using paired delimiters such as parentheses, in which the operators are dispersed among the operands, each operator indicating the operation to be performed on the operands or the intermediate results adjacent to it. If it is desired to distinguish the case in which there are more than two operands for an operation, the term distributed infix notation may be used; for example, A added to B and the sum multiplied by C is represented by the expression (A + B) x C, P AND the result of Q AND R is represented by the expression P & (Q & R). (I) (A) (2) Contrast with parentheses-free notation, postfix notation, prefix notation.

infix operator An operator that appears between two operands.

information (1) In information processing, knowledge concerning such things as facts, concepts, objects, events, ideas, and processes, that within a certain context has a particular meaning. (T) (2) See integrated information, measure of information, mutual information, state information, transferred information, transmitted information.

informational message (1) A message that is not the result of an error condition; for example, a message that gives the status of a job or operation. (2) A message that provides information but does not require a response. (3) In the AS/400 system, a message that provides information to the user about the system. See also completion message. (4) In the AIX operating system, a message that provides information to the operator but does not require a response. (5) In the AIX operating system, a message that is not the result of an error condition.

information analysis A systematic investigation of information and its flow in a real or planned system. (T)

information area A part of a window in which information about the object or choice that the cursor is on is displayed. The information area can also contain a message about the normal completion of a process.

information base In a database, a collection of sentences, consistent with each other and with the conceptual schema, expressing propositions that hold for a specific set of entities. (T)

information bearer channel A data communication channel that carries all the information necessary to transmit user data, such as control and synchronizing signals.

information bit In telecommunication, any bit generated by the data source and not used for error control by the data transmission system. (A)

information channel See data channel, data communication channel, information bearer channel.

information content (1) In information theory, a measure of information conveyed by the occurrence of an event of definite probability; in mathematical notation, the measure $I(x_i)$ for the event x_i is expressed as the logarithm of the reciprocal of the probability $p(x_i)$ that the particular event will occur; that is,

$$I(x_i) = \log \frac{1}{p(x_i)} = -\log p(x_i)$$

(I) (A) (2) See average conditional information content, average information content, character average information content, character mean information content, conditional information content, joint information content.

information content binary unit Synonym for shannon.

information content decimal unit Synonym for hartley.

information content natural unit (NAT) In information theory, a unit of logarithmic measure of information expressed by the Napierian logarithm; for example, the decision content of a character set of eight characters equals $\log_e 8 = 2.079 = 3 \log_e 2$ natural units of information content. Let a, b, c be the characters of a character set consisting of three elements, and let the probabilities of their occurrence within any message, from a given message source, be specified as follows. (I) (A)

$$p(a) = \frac{1}{2}$$

$$p(b) = p(c) = \frac{1}{4}$$

1. The decision content of this character set is:

$$H_o = \left\{ \begin{array}{ll} log_2 & 3 = 1.580 \;\; shannons \\ log_{10} & 3 = 0.477 \;\; hartley \\ log_e & 3 = 1.098 \;\; natural\;units \end{array} \right\}$$

2. The information content of these characters is:

$$I(a) = \left\{ \begin{array}{ll} log_2 & 2 = 1.000 \;\; shannons \\ log_{10} & 2 = 0.301 \;\; hartley \\ log_e & 2 = 0.693 \;\; natural\;units \end{array} \right\}$$

$$I(b) = I(c) = \left\{ \begin{array}{ll} log_2 & 4 = 2.000 \;\; shannons \\ log_{10} & 4 = 0.602 \;\; hartley \\ log_e & 4 = 1.386 \;\; natural \end{array} \right\}$$

3. If the occurrences of the three characters within any message are mutually independent, then the entropy of the message source is:

$$H = \frac{1}{2} \, log\, 2 + \frac{1}{4} \, log\, 4 + \frac{1}{4} \, log\, 4$$

$$H = \left\{ \begin{array}{lll} 1.500 & & shannons \\ 1.5 \ X \ 0.301 & = \ 0.452 & hartley \\ 1.5 \ X \ 0.693 & = \ 1.040 & natural \end{array} \right\}$$

4. The redundancy of the message source is:

$$H_o - H = \left\{ \begin{array}{ll} 0.080 & shannons \\ 0.025 & hartley \\ 0.058 & natural \ units \end{array} \right\}$$

information display A display that presents information such as the status of the system to a user, but rarely requests a response.

information environment The working environment of an organization in which users interact with an information processing system.

information feedback system A data transmission system that uses an echo check to verify the accuracy of the transmission. (A)

Information file prefix code A three-character code used in the leading positions of the names of information files that do not support a system or application. It consists of one of the letters A through I in the first character position, followed by one of the letters A though Z or one of the digits 0 through 9 in the second and third character positions; however, either the second, third, or both positions must contain a digit to avoid duplication of component codes. See also component code.

information flow control In computer security, a procedure used to ensure that information transfers within and from a system are made in accordance with security policy. See also access control.

Note: Information flow control is more restrictive than access control.

information (I) format A format used for information transfer.

information (I) frame A frame in I format used for numbered information transfer. See also supervisory frame, unnumbered frame.

information interchange The sending and receiving of data in such a manner that the information content or meaning assigned to the data is not altered during transmission. (A)

Note: The term information interchange is used with respect to ANSI standards for the sending and receiving of data. The terms exchange and data interchange are used with respect to IBM systems and devices.

Information/Management A feature of the Information/System licensed program that provides interactive systems management applications for problem, change, and configuration management.

information management In an information processing system, the functions of controlling the acquisition, analysis, retention, retrieval, and distribution of information. (T)

information management database A system management tool that helps collect, organize, and keep track of problems and their resolutions.

Information Management System / Virtual Storage A database/data communication (DB/DC) system that can manage complex databases and networks. Synonymous with IMS.

information measure (1) In information theory, a suitable function of the frequency of occurrence of a specified event from a set of possible events conventionally taken as a measure of the relative value of the intelligence conveyed by the occurrence. In information theory, the term event is to be understood as used in the theory of probability; for example, the presence of a given element of a set, the occurrence of a specified character or of a specified word in a message. (I) (2) See measure of information.

information message In SAA Common User Access architecture, a message that tells a user that an action requested by the user has ended unexpectedly and cannot continue. The user can acknowledge that the requested action has stopped or get help. See also action message, warning message.

information processing (1) The systematic performance of operations upon information that includes data processing and that may include operations such as data communication and office automation. (T) (2) The systematic performance of operations on information in conjunction with a computer system to obtain, manipulate, duplicate, exchange, or communicate its meaning; for example, file management, word processing, document interchange, facsimile, videotex. See also data processing.

information processing system A system that performs data processing, integrated with processes such as office automation and data communication. See also data processing system. (A)

information processor In a conceptual schema language, the mechanism that, in response to a command, executes an action on the conceptual schema, or on the information base. (A)

information rate See average information rate, character information rate.

information resource All Information created manually or by automated means that an enterprise treats as a resource for decision making and problem solving. (A)

information resource dictionary (IRD) In a database, a collection of entities, attributes, and relationships, that are used by an organization to model its information environment. (T)

information resource dictionary schema The model of the logical structure of the information resource dictionary that consists of descriptors such as entity types, relationship types, and attribute types. (A)

information resource management The policy, action, and procedures concerning information, both automated and nonautomated, that management establishes to serve the overall current and future needs of an enterprise. See also data resource management. (A)

information retrieval (IR) Actions, methods, and procedures for recovering information on a given subject from stored data. (T)

information retrieval system A computing system application designed to recover specific information from a mass of data.

information security (1) In computer security, the concepts, techniques, technical measures, and administrative measures used to protect information assets from deliberate or inadvertent unauthorized acquisition, damage, disclosure, manipulation, modification, loss, or use. See also computer security, data security, password security. (2) See security.

information separator (IS) Any control character used to delimit like units of data in a hierarchic arrangement of data. The name of the separator does not necessarily indicate the units of data it separates. (I) (A) Synonymous with separating character.

information sink See data sink.

information source (1) Synonym for message source. (2) See data source.

information system (1) An information processing system, together with associated organizational resources such as human, technical, and financial resources, that provides and distributes information. (T) (2) A system that consists of people, machines, and methods organization to accomplish specified operations on data that represent information. An information system may include data processing equipment, such as computers and storage devices; office machines, such as word processors and copiers; com-

munication equipment, such as communication controllers and switching devices; peripheral equipment; and related data media and accessories. (A)

Information/System In the NetView program, an interactive retrieval program with related utilities designed to provide systems programmers with keyword access to selected technical information contained in either of its companion products, Information/MVS or Information/VM-VSE.

information system abuse In computer security, willful or negligent activity that affects the availability, confidentiality, or integrity of information systems resources. See also computer abuse.

information theory The branch of learning concerned with the study of measures of information and its properties. (I) (A)

information transfer phase A phase in which a data circuit-terminating equipment (DCE) can accept and transmit information (I) frames and supervisory (S) frames. See also disconnected phase.

Infowindow display An IBM touch-screen monitor that incorporates overlay and videodisc control functions in the monitor itself.

in-frame Pertaining to a subject that is included within a frame. See also frame.

infrared Invisible radiation having a wavelength longer than 700 nm. (T) See also ultra-violet.

inheader subgroup The part of a message handler (MH) incoming group that operates on all or part of an incoming message header.

inherent transparency Data transmission in which there is no need for special control characters.

inherit In the AIX operating system, to copy resources or attributes from a parent to a child.

inheritance The passing of class resources or attributes from a parent class downstream in the class hierarchy to a child class.

inherited error An error carried forward from a previous step in a sequential process. (A)

inhibited (1) Pertaining to a state of a processing unit in which certain types of interruptions are not allowed to occur. (2) Pertaining to the state in which a transmission control unit or an audio response unit cannot accept incoming calls on a line. (3) In VTAM, pertaining to a logical unit (LU) that has indicated to its system services control point (SSCP) that it is temporarily not ready to establish LU-LU sessions. An initiate request for a session with an inhibited LU will be rejected by the SSCP. The LU can separately indicate whether this applies to its ability to act as a primary logical unit (PLU) or a secondary logical unit (SLU). See also disabled, enabled.

inhibiting signal A signal that prevents occurrence of an event. (I) (A)

in-house system Synonym for in-plant system.

IN indicator See insert-mode indicator.

initial alias file In the IBM Network Carrier Interconnect Manager program, the file that is created by the Configuration Exchange Utility when it receives new configuration data from the carrier management system.

initial cap (1) A capital letter occurring as the first letter of a word in a phrase. (2) To set a phrase in initial caps.

initial chaining value (ICV) An 8-byte pseudo-random number used to verify that both ends of a session with cryptography have the same session cryptography key. The initial chaining value is also used as input to the Data Encryption Standard (DES) algorithm to encipher or decipher data in a session with cryptography. Synonymous with session seed. See also session cryptography seed.

Note: A new initial chaining value is selected for each session.

initial condition mode The operating mode of an analog computer during which the integrators are inoperative and the initial conditions are set. (I) (A) Synonymous with reset mode.

initial control word (ICW) The first microcode control word in the central processor used to start execution of an instruction.

initialization (1) The operations required for setting a device to a starting state, before the use of a data medium, or before implementation of a process. (T) (2) Preparation of a system, device, or program for operation. (3) The process of resetting or starting the 3791 Controller or 3792 Auxiliary Control Unit, performed by setting the Data/Function Select switch to a designated position and then pressing the RESET or POWER ON button. (4) See default initialization, loop initialization. (5) See also initial machine load, initial microcode load, initial microprogram load, initial program load.

initialization mode A nonoperational mode of a balanced or unbalanced data link in which a remote sec-ondary or combined station data link control program can be initialized or regenerated by the local primary or combined station, or in which other parameters to be used in the operational mode can be exchanged. See also asynchronous disconnected mode, normal disconnected mode.

initialization vector (IV) In cryptography, a binary vector used in the initial input block in the cipher feedback (CFB) and output feedback (OFB) modes of operation and as the randomizing block for the first data block in the cipher block chain (CBC) mode of operation.

initialize (1) In programming languages, to give a value to a data object at the beginning of its lifetime. (I) (2) To set counters, switches, addresses, or contents of storage to zero or other starting values at the beginning of, or at prescribed points in, the operation of a computer routine. (A) (3) To prepare for use; for example, to initialize a diskette. (4) In the AIX operating system, to prepare the system for operation. After loading the kernel into memory, the system runs internal checks, initializes all memory and some devices, and analyzes the root file system. (5) Contrast with prestore. (6) See also initial program load.

initialize graphics In System/38 graphics, to enter the graphics environment. The graphics environment is the state in which calls to GDDM and PGR routines can occur. Contrast with terminate graphics.

initializer The assignment operator followed by an expression or multiple expressions for aggregate variables.

initial machine load (IML) (1) A procedure that prepares a device for use. (2) In PSS: (a) an initialization procedure that prepares the store controller or the terminal for operation, (b) a portion of the data representing the operational environment loaded into the active storage of the store controller to control its operations, and (c) the procedure for starting the subsystem store controller with a particular supervisor configuration.

initial microprogram load (IML) The action of loading microprograms into computer storage.

initial point The upper left corner of a character box.

initial procedure In the AS/400 system, an external procedure, started by a calling program, that starts a PL/Iprogram.

initial process name In DPPX/DTMS, a field in a user's environment profile that indicates the process to be invoked in the user's session.

initial program (1) A program, specified in a user profile, that is to be executed when the user signs on. (2) In the AS/400 system, a user-profile program that runs when the user signs on and after the command processor program QCMD is started. (3) In COBOL, a program that is placed into an initial state every time the program is called in a run unit.

initial program load (IPL) (1) The initialization procedure that causes an operating system to commence operation. (2) The process by which a configuration image is loaded into storage at the beginning of a work day or after a system malfunction. (3) The process of loading system programs and preparing a system to run jobs. (4) Synonymous with system restart, system startup.

initial program load device (IPL device) The input/output device, usually a hard disk or diskette, from which system software is loaded when the machine is turned on.

initial program loader (IPL) (1) A bootstrap loader used in a computer to load the part of an operating system needed to load the remainder of the operating system. (I) (A) (2) See also bootstrap, bootstrap loader.

initial state In COBOL, the state of a program when it is first called in a run unit.

initial value (1) A value assumed until explicitly changed. (2) In SAA Common User Access architecture, information in an entry field that is provided by an application when an entry field is first displayed. An initial field value can be a partial entry, such as the first few digits of a purchase order number, or a complete entry, such as a person's full name. (3) In SDF/CICS, initial data defined as contents of constant or variable fields by entering the data in place with the full screen editor functions of the map editor. (4) See also default value.

INITIATE A network services request sent from a logical unit (LU) to a system services control point (SSCP) requesting that an LU-LU session be established.

initiate mode In ACF/TCAM, a mode of an incoming message handler in which ACF/TCAM sends the segments of a message from a destination queue to the destination as soon as possible after the segments are placed in the queue, regardless of whether the entire message has arrived at the destination queue.

initiate-transaction-sequence indicator (IS) An indicator that signals the start of a new function request.

initiating LU (ILU) The logical unit (LU) that first requests a session be set up. The ILU may be one of the LUs that will participate in the session, or it may be a third-party LU. If it is one of the session participants, the ILU is also called the origin LU (OLU).

initiating task The job management task that controls job selection and preparation of job steps for execution.

initiation See LU-LU session initiation. See also session-initiation request.

initiator (1) In ACF/TCAM, the component executed as the job-step task. The initiator starts, monitors, and restarts the message control program (MCP), ACF/TCAM system service programs, and user-supplied system service programs. It can also display status information at the system console. (2) The part of the System Support Program Product that reads and processes operation control language statements from the system input device.

initiator procedure The cataloged procedure that controls an initiator.

initiator/terminator The job scheduler function that selects jobs and job steps to be executed, allocates input/output devices for them, places them under task control, and at completion of the job, supplies control information for writing job output on a system output unit.

ink In pen environments, the trail resulting from writing with the pen.

ink distributor roller In a duplicator, a roller that transfers ink. (T)

ink duct In a duplicator, an ink reservoir incorporating a means of supplying a metered quantity of ink to the inking rollers. (T)

ink duct blade In a duplicator, a flexible blade that can be adjusted against the ink duct roller in order to regulate the thickness of the film of ink on an inking roller. (T)

ink duct regulating screws In a duplicator, screws along the length of the ink duct that adjust the thickness of the film of ink on the ink duct roller. (T)

ink duct roller In a duplicator, a roller in the ink duct that, in conjunction with a metering device, supplies ink to the ink rollers. (T)

inked ribbon A continuous inked ribbon used on output units. (T)

inking (1) In computer graphics, creating a line by moving a locator over the display surface, leaving a trail behind the locator in the manner of a pen drawing a line on paper. (I) (A) (2) In a duplicator, the process by which the ink or other substance used for making an image is transferred from the master to the copy paper either directly or indirectly. (T)

inking up In a duplicator, the operation of supplying the master or ink-carrying elements in the machine with ink. (T)

ink jet printer A nonimpact printer in which the characters are formed by projecting particles or droplets of ink onto paper. (T) See Figure 76.

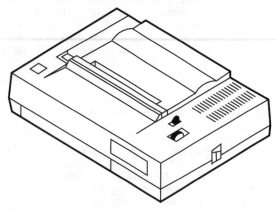

Figure 76. Ink Jet Printer

ink lever In a duplicator, a lever that moves the inking system rollers into and out of their operating positions. (T)

ink metering control In a duplicator, a device that regulates the supply of ink to the master. (T)

ink oscillating roller In a duplicator, an ink distributor roller that has a lateral oscillating motion in addition to rotation to assist in the distribution of ink over the width of the ink rollers. (T)

ink roller cleaning device In a duplicator, a mechanism for cleaning the ink rollers by applying solvent to them. (T)

ink screen In a duplicator, material adjacent to the periphery of the printing cylinder that supports a stencil master and allows a controlled quantity of ink to pass through the perforations in the master. (T)

ink selector In a duplicator, a control for determining the position across the width of the master to which ink is to be applied. (T)

ink vibrator interrupter In a duplicator, a device that interrupts the movement of the ink vibrator roller

during paper feed stoppages to avoid excessive build-up of ink on the master. (T)

ink vibrator roller In a duplicator, a roller that alternately contacts the ink duct roller and an ink distributor roller. (T)

inline (1) In printing, the direction of successive characters in a line of text. Synonymous with inline direction. (2) In the AS/400 system, pertaining to spooled input data that is read into a job by a reader.

inline code In a program, instructions that are executed sequentially, without branching to routines, subroutines, or other programs.

inline data file In the AS/400 system and System/38, a file created by a Data (//DATA) command that is included as part of a job when the job is read from an input device or a database file. The file is deleted when the job ends.

inline direction Synonym for inline.

inline exit routine (1) An exit routine executed at a predetermined point in the mainline code of a program. Contrast with asynchronous exit routine. (2) In VTAM, a SYNAD or LERAD exit routine. Contrast with asynchronous exit routine.

inline (I) extent A measurement of an object in the inline direction.

inline margin The place where the first character appears in each line of text.

inline recovery Error recovery in which an affected process is resumed from a point preceding occurrence of the error. (T)

inmessage subgroup The part of a message handler (MH) incoming group that specifies actions to be taken after a complete message has arrived at the message control program (MCP).

i-node In the AIX operating system, the internal structure that describes the individual files in the operating system; there is one i-node for each file. An i-node contains the node, type, owner, and location of a file. A table of i-nodes is stored near the beginning of a file system. Synonymous with file index. See also i-list, intermediate node, system node, v-node.

i-node number In the AIX operating system, a number specifying a particular i-node file in the file system.

i-nodetab An AIX kernel parameter that establishes a table in memory for storing copies of i-nodes for all active files.

inoperable time The part of down time with all environmental conditions satisfied, during which a functional unit would not yield correct results if it were operated. (I) (A)

inoperative The condition of a resource that has been active, but is not. The resource may have failed, received an INOP request, or is suspended while a reactivate command is being processed. See also inactive.

in-phase (I) In NTSC video, the state of a color difference signal being at 0 degrees with respect to the color subcarrier. See also quadrature (Q).

in-plant system A system whose parts, including terminals, are situated at one location. Synonymous with in-house system.

input (1) Pertaining to a device, process, or channel involved in an input process, or to the associated data or states. The word "input" may be used in place of "input data," "input signal," "input process," when such a usage is clear in a given context. (T) (2) Pertaining to a functional unit or channel involved in an input process or to the data involved in such a process. (3) On a calculator, information entered into the machine for processing or storage. (T) (4) One, or a sequence of, input states. (A) (5) Loosely, input data, input process. (A) (6) Information or data to be processed. (7) In XL Pascal, a predefined standard file definition. (8) See manual input, real-time input. (9) See also input channel, input unit. (10) Contrast with output.

Note: The word input may be used in place of input data, input signal, and input process when such usage is clear in context.

input area An area of storage reserved for input. (A) Synonymous with input block.

input block (1) A block of data received as input. (2) Synonym for input area.

input blocking factor (Bi) In a tape sort, the number of data records in each record of the input file.

input-capable field Any field in a display file that can receive input from a user.

input channel A channel for impressing a state on a device or logic element. (A)

input data (1) Data that are entered into a data processing system or any of its parts for storage or processing. (T) (2) Data received or to be received by a functional unit or by any part of a functional unit. (3) Data to be processed. (A)

input data set (1) A data set that contains data to be processed. (2) In ACF/TCAM, a data set that contains all messages or records sent to an application program from a single process queue. Contrast with output data set.

input data validation A process used to detect input data in order to determine whether they are inaccurate, incomplete, or unreasonable. (T)

Note: Input validation may include format checks, completeness checks, check key tests, reasonableness checks, and limit checks.

input device Synonym for input unit.

input field (1) In computer graphics, an unprotected field on a display surface in which data can be entered, modified, or erased. (2) A field in a display file into which a user can key in data. An input field is passed from the device to the program when the program reads the record containing that field.

input file (1) A file that has been opened in order to allow records to be read. Contrast with output file. (2) In COBOL, a file that is opened in the input mode. Contrast with output file. (3) In RPG, a database or device file that has been opened to allow records to be read. Contrast with output file.

input focus (1) In SAA Advanced Common User Access architecture, the area of a window where user interaction is possible from either the keyboard or the mouse. (2) In an AIX graphics environment, a window defining the scope for processing keyboard input. By default, keyboard events are sent to the client using the window the pointer is in. It is also possible to attach the keyboard input to a specific window. Events are then sent to the appropriate client regardless of the pointer position. Synonymous with focus window.

input inhibit In the 3270 Information Display System, a condition in which operator input from the keyboard or other input devices is not accepted. Contrast with enter inhibit.

input job queue Synonym for input stream, input work queue.

input manager In an AIX graphics environment, a client that controls keyboard input and is usually part of a window manager.

input message (1) Any message entered into a system, terminal, or workstation by an end user. (2) In IMS/VS, valid commands, transactions, and message switches.

input mode (1) A mode in which records can be read from a file. (2) In the CMS Editor, the mode that allows the user to key in new lines of data. Contrast with edit mode. (3) In COBOL, the state of a file after execution of an OPEN statement, with the INPUT phrase specified for that file and before the execution of a CLOSE statement without the REEL or UNIT phrase for that file. Contrast with output mode. (4) In TSO, an entry mode that accepts successive lines of input under the EDIT command for a line data set. The lines are not checked for the presence of subcommands. (5) In IMS/VS, the way in which input fields from certain devices are defined by the user to be scanned by the message format service (MFS). (6) In DPPX, the state of a terminal session in which data may be entered into a data set.

InputOnly window In an AIX graphics environment, an invisible window that can be used to control such things as cursors, input event generation, and grabbing. This window cannot be used for graphics requests.

input/output (I/O) (1) Pertaining to input, output, or both. (A) (2) Pertaining to a device, process, or channel involved in data input, data output, or both.

input/output adapter (IOA) (1) A functional unit or a part of an I/O controller that connects devices to an I/O processor. (2) The electrical circuits on a logic card that connect one device to another.

input/output channel (1) In a data processing system, a functional unit that handles transfer of data between internal and peripheral equipment. (I) (A) (2) In a computing system, a functional unit, controlled by a processor, that handles transfer of data between processor storage and local peripheral devices. In data processing terminology, a channel, that is, an I/O channel or data channel, provides two-way transfers, or moves, of data between processor storage and peripheral devices. In data communication terminology, a channel (that is, a data communication channel), provides one-way (simplex) transmission; data circuits and logical channels provide two-way (duplex) transmission. (3) Synonymous with data channel, I/O channel. (4) Contrast with data communication channel.

input/output controller (IOC) (1) A functional unit that controls one or more input/output channels. (T) (2) In the AS/400 system, a functional unit that combines an I/O processor and one or more I/O adapters, and directly connects and controls one or more input or output devices.

input/output control system (IOCS) In VSE, a group of routines provided by IBM for handling transfer of data between main storage and auxiliary storage devices. See also logical IOCS, physical IOCS.

input/output device Synonym for input/output unit.

input-output file In COBOL, a file that is opened in the I-O mode.

input/output interruption See I/O interruption.

input/output (I/O) (1) Pertaining to a device whose parts can perform an input process and an output process at the same time. (I) (2) Pertaining to a functional unit or channel involved in an input process, output process, or both, concurrently or not, and to the data involved in such a process.

Note: The phrase input/output may be used in place of input/output data, input/output signals, and input/output process when such a usage is clear in context. (3) Pertaining to input, output, or both. (4) See also radial transfer.

input/output list In DPPX FORTRAN, a list of variables in an input/output statement that specifies the storage locations into which data are to be written or from which data are to be read.

input/output processor (IOP) A functional unit or the part of an I/O controller that processes programmed instructions and controls one or more input/output devices or adapters.

Input-Output section In COBOL, the section of the Environment Division that names the files and the external media required by an object program and that provides information required for transmission and handling of data during execution of the object program.

input/output statement (1) Any statement that transfers data between main storage and input/output devices. (2) In COBOL, a statement that causes files to be processed by performing operations upon individual records or upon the file as a unit.

Note: The input-output statements are: ACCEPT (with the identifier phrase), CLOSE, DELETE, DISABLE, DISPLAY, ENABLE, OPEN, PURGE, READ, RECEIVE, REWRITE, SEND, SET (with the TO ON or TO OFF phrase), START and WRITE.

input/output unit A device in a data processing system by means of which data can be entered into the system, received from the system, or both. (I) (A) Synonymous with input/output device.

InputOutput window In an AIX graphics environment, a kind of opaque window used for input and output. InputOutput windows can have both InputOutput and InputOnly windows as inferiors.

input panel Deprecated term for menu.

input primitive (1) In computer graphics, an item of data obtained from an input device such as a keyboard, choice device, locator, pick device, or valuator. (A)   (2) See also display element.

input procedure In COBOL, a set of statements, to which control is given during the execution of a SORT statement, for the purpose of controlling the release of specified records to be sorted.   Contrast with output procedure.

input process (1) The process of entering data into a data processing system or any of its parts for storage or processing. (T)   (2) The reception of data into a functional unit or into any part of a functional unit. (3) The process of transmitting data from peripheral equipment, or external storage, to internal storage. (A)   (4) In data processing, the entry of information by an end user into a computer system, including the conversion of information from human language into language the system can understand. (5) Contrast with output process.

input program A utility program that organizes the input process of a computer. (I)   (A)

input protection For analog input channels, the protection against transient and steady-state overvoltages that can be applied between any two input connectors and also between any input connector and ground. (T)

input queue Synonym for input work queue.

input ramp In the 3800 Printing Subsystem, a support on the continuous forms input stacker that puts paper in position as it is pulled into the printer by the transfer station carriage tractor.

input reader See reader *(4)* and *(5)*.

input redirection In the AIX operating system, the specification of an input source other than the standard one.

input register See manual input register.

input request In an 8100 BSC/SS receive operation, a request by control logic for the processor to read a received byte that has been deserialized.   Contrast with output request.

input routine A utility routine that organizes the input process of a computer. (I)   (A)

input semantics In the AIX operating system, the specified order and format in which user input must be entered.

input specifications In RPG, the means by which the programmer describes the input records and their fields, adds RPG functions to an externally described file, or defines a data structure and its subfields.

input state The state occurring on a specified input channel. (A)

input station See data input station.

input stream (1) A sequence of control statements and data submitted to a system from an input unit. Synonymous with input job stream, job input stream. (2) In the AS/400 system, a group of records submitted as a batch job that contains control language commands for one or more jobs and data from one or more inline data files.   (3) In RJE, data sent to the host system.   (4) Synonym for job stream.   (5) Contrast with output stream.

input stream control Synonym for JES reader.

input subsystem The part of a process interface system that transfers data from the technical process to the process computer system. (T)

input system In an IMS/VS multisystem environment, the system to which the input terminal is attached. Synonymous with origin system.

input terminal In an IMS/VS multisystem environment, the terminal from which a primary request originated.

input-to-process indicator (IP) In System/36, an indicator that signals whenever input data have been received from the previous display.

input unit A device in a data processing system by means of which data can be entered into the system. (I)   (A)   Synonymous with input device.

input validation See input data validation.

input work queue In OS/VS, a queue of job definitions in direct access storage assigned to a job class and arranged in order of assigned priority.   Synonymous with input job queue, input queue, job queue.

inquiry (1) A request for information from storage; for example, a request for the number of available airline seats, or a search for information from a file. (2) A request for information from another system.

inquiry and transaction processing An application in which inquiries and records of transactions received from a number of terminals are used to interrogate or update one or more master files.

inquiry logical terminal In IMS/VS, a type of logical terminal created automatically by IMS/VS and restricted to nonupdate transactions. Inquiry logical terminals are created for non-VTAM switched lines. See also logical terminal.

inquiry message A message that conveys information and that requests a reply.

inquiry mode A mode during which a job currently running from a display station is interrupted so that other work can be done. The operator puts the display station in inquiry mode by pressing the Attn key.

inquiry program (1) A program that allows an operator to obtain requested information. (2) A program that runs while a system is in inquiry mode.

inquiry/reply In ACF/TCAM, an application in which a device message handler receives a message from an external logical unit (LU) and then routes it to an application program that processes the message and generates a reply. The reply is routed back to the inquiring external LU.

inquiry/response communication In a network, the exchange of messages and responses, with one exchange usually involving a request for information and a response that provides the information. Contrast with batched communication.

inquiry/response operation In a network, an operation in which a terminal operator enters a request for information and the information is sent back and displayed at the terminal.

inquiry session A session established between a 3790 program and the host system for inquiry/response operations, that is, for the purpose of transmitting inquiries to the host system and receiving responses from the host system. Contrast with batch session. See also session, work session.

inquiry station (1) A user terminal primarily for the interrogation of a computer. (T) (2) Data terminal equipment used for inquiry into a data processing system.

inquiry transaction A transaction that does not update a database. See also recoverable transaction, unrecoverable transaction.

insert (1) A function or mode that enables the introduction of additional characters within previously entered text. (T) (2) To introduce data between previously stored items of data. (A) (3) In text processing, to introduce new characters or text within previously recorded text. The text is automatically rearranged to accommodate the addition. (A) (4) The source entry utility operation during which

source statements are keyed in and added as new records in a source member. (5) In the IBM Token-Ring Network, to make an attaching device an active part of a ring.

Insert, Ins A key on a keyboard that a user presses to add characters between existing characters.

insert editing In video or audio production, editing in which new video or audio material is inserted into any point of a material already recorded. It replaces previously recorded video or audio with new video or audio, leaving the already-recorded control track intact. See assemble editing.

inserted mode In an 8100 loop, a secondary station operating mode in which the secondary station monitors loop traffic and regenerates the loop signals it receives before placing them back on the loop. See also monitor mode.

insertion (1) The introduction of data or text within previously stored data or text. (A) (2) In a conceptual schema language, the addition of a sentence to the information base or to the conceptual schema. (A)

insertion characters Characters that are inserted in the value of a field when it is displayed or printed, in order to make the value easier to read.

insertion loss In fiber optics, the total optical power loss caused by insertion of an optical component such as a connector, splice, or coupler. (E) Synonymous with splice loss.

insertion sort A sort in which each item in a set is inserted into its proper position in the sorted set according to specified criteria. (A)

insert mode (1) A keyboard mode in which new text is entered within existing text at the cursor position. (2) The source entry utility operation during which source statements are keyed in and added as new records in a source member. (3) In SAA Common User Access architecture, a text-entry mode obtained by pressing the Insert key. Characters are inserted where the cursor is positioned. Text to the right is shifted to the right. Contrast with replace mode. (4) In the IBM Token-Ring Network, to make an attaching device an active part of a ring. (5) In System/36, the workstation utility mode during which operators can insert records in the transaction file.

Note: This function can differ for bidirectional and double-byte character set (DBCS) languages.

install (1) To add a program, program option, or software to a system in such a manner that it is runnable and interacts properly with all affected programs in the system. (2) To connect hardware to a system. (3) In

SMP and SMP/E, to incorporate a system modification (SYSMOD) into the target system libraries or to accept a SYSMOD into the distribution libraries.

installation (1) In system development, preparing and placing a functional unit in position for use. (T) (2) A particular computing system, including the work it does and the people who manage it, operate it, apply it to problems, service it, and use the results it produces. (3) See task set installation.

installation diskette An IBM-supplied diskette that contains a system or part of a system and that usually contains other data needed for installation purposes.

installation exit The means specifically described in an IBM software product's documentation by which an IBM software product may be modified by a customer's system programmers to change or extend the functions of the IBM software product. Such modifications consist of exit routines written to replace one or more existing modules of an IBM software product, or to add one or more modules or subroutines to an IBM software product, for the purpose of modifying or extending the functions of the IBM software product. See user exit.

installation exit routine A routine written by a user to take control at an installation exit of an IBM software product.

Installation Facility A facility that assists the user in installing the output of the configuring process on an ImagePlus workstation and tailoring the ImagePlus Workstation Program software where it may be unique to each workstation.

installation news In SDF/CICS, a set of tutorial topics that can be defined by installations and are selectable from the NEWS topic. This topic is accessible from the initial function selection or with the NEWS tutorial commands.

installation performance specification (IPS) In MVS, a set of installation-supplied control information used by the system workload manager. An IPS includes performance group definitions, performance objectives, and coefficients used to establish the service rate. See also service rate.

installation profile An object that can be tailored and used to control the automatic installation of a system.

installation script In the AIX operating system, a shell procedure or executable file created by the developer of an application program to install the program. The script file must follow specific guidelines in order to be compatible with the program installation tools that are provided in the operating system.

installation time Time spent in installing and testing hardware or software. (A)

installation verification procedure (IVP) A procedure distributed with a system that tests the newly generated system to verify that the basic facilities of the system are functioning correctly.

installation-wide exit The means specifically described in an IBM software product's documentation by which an IBM software product may be modified by a customer's system programmers to change or extend the functions of the IBM software product. Such modifications consist of exit routines written to replace an existing module of an IBM software product, or to add one or more modules or subroutines to an IBM software product for the purpose of modifying (including extending) the functions of the IBM software product. Contrast with user exit routine.

instance In the AIX operating system, a concrete realization of an abstract object class. An instance of a widget or gadget is a specific data structure that contains detailed appearance and behavioral information that is used to generate a specific graphical object on-screen at run time. See widget instance.

instance ID In the AS/400 system query management, an identifier in the communications area. An instance ID is used to identify a particular query instance being used by an application program. See also query instance.

instance (of an entity type) occurrence In a conceptual schema language, an individual entity, for which a particular type of proposition holds, that is, an entity that belongs to a particular class of entities. (A)

instance of a subprogram In FORTRAN, a subprogram created when a function or subroutine defined by a procedure subprogram is invoked.

instantaneous availability The probability that a functional unit is in state to perform a required function under given conditions at a given instant of time, assuming that the required external resources are provided. (T)

instantaneous sound pressure In acoustics, the difference between the sound pressure that exists at a point in a medium at a particular instant and the static pressure. See also effective sound pressure, static pressure.

instantiate (1) To make an instance of; to replicate. (2) In object-oriented programming, to represent a class abstraction with a concrete instance of the class. (3) In the AIXwindows program, to create a specific concrete instance of that general class.

instantiation A formula or pattern rule having its variables replaced by constants. (T)

instant jump A feature of some videodisc players that permits branching between frames within certain minimum distances, usually one to 200 frames away. The branch occurs during the vertical blanking interval between images.

in-stream procedure A set of job control statements placed in the input stream that can be used any number of times during a job by naming the procedure in an execute (EXEC) statement.

instruction (1) A language construct that specifies an operation and identifies its operands, if any. (T) (2) A statement that specifies an operation to be performed by a system and that identifies data involved in the operation. (3) In COBOL and Pascal, one or more clauses, the first of which starts with a keyword that identifies the instruction. Instructions affect the flow of control, provide services to the programmer, or both.

instruction address (1) The address of an instruction word. (I) (A) (2) The address that must be used to fetch an instruction. (A) (3) Contrast with address part.

instruction address register (IAR) (1) A special-purpose register used to hold the address of the next instruction to be executed. Synonymous with program register, instruction pointer register. (T) (2) A register in a processor that contains the address of the next instruction to be performed. (3) See also instruction counter, program counter.

instruction address stop An instruction address that, when fetched, causes execution to stop.

instructional design The field of education that studies the methodology of creating tools, such as computer programs, for enhancing the learning process.

instruction code (1) A code for representing the machine instructions of a computer. (T) (2) See computer instruction code. (A)

instruction control unit In a processing unit, the part that retrieves instructions in proper sequence, interprets each instruction, and applies the proper signals to the arithmetic and logic unit and other parts in accordance with this interpretation. (I) (A)

instruction counter (1) A counter that indicates the location of the next computer instruction to be interpreted. (A) (2) See also instruction address register, program counter.

instruction element (IE) A part of a processor that executes some instructions and generates operand addresses and instruction requests. It also controls the sequencing of instructions through the machine and is usually controlled by microcode.

instruction fetch The act of getting an instruction from storage and loading it into the correct registers.

instruction format The layout of the constituent parts of an instruction. (T)

instruction marker control In dictation equipment, a device used to indicate on an index slip or on the recording medium the position at which an instruction is given. (I)

instruction modifier A word or part of a word that is used to alter an instruction. (I) (A)

instruction pointer In System/38, a pointer that provides addressability for a machine interface instruction in a program.

instruction pointer register Synonym for instruction address register. (T)

instruction register (1) A register used to hold an instruction for interpretation. (I) (A) (2) See control instruction register.

instruction repertoire (1) A complete set of the operators of the statements of a computer programming language, together with a description of the types and meanings that can be attributed to their operands. (A) (2) Loosely, an instruction set. (A)

instructions In SAA Basic Common User Access architecture, text on a panel that tells a user how to interact with a panel and how to continue with the application.

instruction set (1) The set of instructions of a computer, of a programming language, or of the programming languages in a programming system. (I) (A) (2) See computer instruction set.

instruction statement See instruction *(1)*.

instruction time (I-time) The time during which an instruction is fetched from the main storage of a computer into an instruction register. See also execution time.

instruction word A word that represents an instruction. (I) (A)

INT (1) Interior. (2) Internal trace table.

intake rollers In a duplicator, paired rollers that transport paper from the paper feed mechanism to the cylinders. (T)

integer (1) One of the numbers zero, +1, -1, +2, -2... (I) (A) Synonymous with integral number. (2) A positive or negative whole number, that is, an optional sign followed by a number that does not contain a decimal place or zero. (3) In COBOL, a numeric literal or a numeric data item that does not include any digit position to the right of the assumed decimal point When the term "integer" appears in general formats, the integer must not be a numeric data item, and must not be signed, nor zero unless explicitly allowed by the rules of that format.

integer constant A string of decimal digits containing no decimal point.

integer expression An arithmetic expression with only integer type values.

integer programming (1) In operations research, a class of procedures for locating the maximum or minimum of a function subject to constraints, where some or all variables must have integer values. (I) (A) Synonymous with discrete programming. (2) Contrast with convex programming, dynamic programming, linear programming, mathematical programming, nonlinear programming, quadratic programming.

integer type An arithmetic data type that consists of integer values.

integral boundary (1) A location in main storage at which a fixed-length field, such as a halfword or doubleword, must be positioned. The address of an integral boundary is a multiple of the length of the field, expressed in bytes. See also boundary alignment. (2) In PL/I, the multiple of any 8-bit unit of information on which data can be aligned.

integral number Synonym for integer.

integral object In the C language, a character object, an object having an enumeration type, or an object having the type short, int, long, unsigned short, unsignedint, or unsigned long.

integrated Pertaining to a feature that is part of a device. Synonymous with built-in.

integrated adapter An integral part of a processing unit that provides for direct connection of a device and uses neither a control unit nor the standard I/O interface. See also integrated communication adapter, integrated file adapter.

integrated attachment An attachment that is an integral part of the basic hardware.

integrated catalog facility In the Data Facility Product (DFP), a facility that provides for integrated catalog facility catalogs.

integrated catalog facility catalog In the Data Facility Product (DFP), a catalog that consists of a basic catalog structure, which contains information about VSAM and non-VSAM data sets, and at least one VSAM volume data set, which contains information about VSAM data sets only.

integrated circuit (IC) (1) A small piece of semiconductive material that contains interconnected miniaturized electronic circuits. Synonymous with microchip, chip. (T) (2) A combination of connected circuit elements inseparably associated on or within a continuous substrate. See hybrid integrated circuit, monolithic integrated circuit.

integrated circuit memory (IC memory) A storage device composed of transistors, diodes, and other circuit elements, all fabricated on a chip of crystalline material. (T)

integrated communication adapter (ICA) A communication adapter that is an integral part of the host processor. Contrast with external communication adapter.

integrated computing The concurrent use of two or more software applications that share data; for example, word processing and computer graphics, spreadsheets and file management.

integrated database A database that has been consolidated to eliminate redundant data.

integrated digital network (IDN) A public digital end-to-end telecommunication network that is the digital backbone for the telephone network and provides multiple services, including data and leased-line transparent services. See also integrated services digital network (ISDN).

integrated disk In the programmable store system, an integral part of the store controller that is used for magnetically storing files, application programs, controller storage contents, and diagnostics.

integrated emulator An emulator program whose execution is controlled by an operating system in a multiprogramming environment. Contrast with stand-alone emulator.

integrated file adapter An integrated adapter that allows connection of multiple disk storage devices to a processing unit.

integrated information Information that is stored in, and displayable by, a product.

integrated modem A modem that is an integral part of the device with which it operates. Contrast with stand-alone modem.

integrated open hypermedia (IOH) The model of hypermedia linking that allows links to anything, anywhere, at any time.

integrated services digital network (ISDN) A digital end-to-end telecommunication network that supports multiple services including, but not limited to, voice and data. See also integrated digital network (IDN).

Note: ISDNs are used in public and private network architectures.

integrated software (1) Application software such as spreadsheets, word processing programs, and database management programs that can be used interchangeably to exchange and operate on the same data. (2) Personal computer application software that allows the use of two or more applications concurrently. See also windowing.

Integrated Storage Control (ISC) A feature on the IBM System/370 Models 158 and 168 Processing Units that controls the 3330 Disk Storage and Control units and their associated 3330 disk drives.

integrated word processing equipment Word processing equipment that has its associated control unit contained within the body of the machine. (T)

integrating motor A motor designed to give a constant ratio of output shaft rotational speed to input signal. Thus, the angle of rotation of the shaft with respect to a datum is proportional to the time integral of the applied signal. (A)

integration test The progressive linking and testing of programs or modules in order to assure their proper functioning in the complete system. (T)

integrator (1) A functional unit whose output analog variable is the integral of the input analog variable with respect to time. For some integrators, the variable of integration may be a parameter other than time. (I) (A) (2) See incremental integrator.

integrity (1) The protection of systems, programs, and data from inadvertent or malicious destruction or alteration. See application integrity, data integrity, system integrity.

intelligence See artificial intelligence.

intelligent Deprecated term for programmable.

intelligent assistant In artificial intelligence, an expert system for aiding a person to perform a task. (T)

intelligent copier Deprecated term for programmable copier.

intelligent printer data stream (IPDS) (1) An all-points-addressable data stream that allows users to position text, images, and graphics at any defined point on a printed page. (2) In GDDM, a structured-field data stream for managing and controlling printer processes, allowing both data and controls to be sent to the printer.

intelligent remote station support (IRSS) In IMS/VS, the facility that supports System/3 and System/7.

intelligent terminal Deprecated term for programmable workstation (PWS).

intelligent videodisc player A videodisc player that has built-in processing power and memory capability. Synonymous with level two player. See also Levels of Interactive Systems.

intelligent workstation (IWS) Deprecated term for programmable workstation (PWS).

intensified field On a display screen, data in a field displayed at a brighter level than other data.

intensify To increase the level of brightness of all or part of a display image.

intensity In computer graphics, the amount of light emitted at a display point.

intensive mode recording (IMR) An NCP function that forces recording of temporary errors for a specified resource.

intensive recording mode In VM, a special error recording mode that can be invoked by an IBM service representative for only one I/O device at a time. On the first through tenth unit check or other error condition specified by the service representative, an I/O error record is constructed, formatted, and written out onto the VM I/O error recording cylinder, after which no further errors are recorded.

intent propagation In IMS/VS, a condition by which processing intent for one segment can propagate to related segments, depending on the type of processing and the kind of relationship. It determines the compatibility of scheduling processing applications in parallel or serially.

interaction (1) A basic unit used to record system activity, consisting of the acceptance of a line of terminal input, processing of the line, and a response, if any. See also interaction time. (2) The exchange of information between a user and a computer.

interaction time In systems with time sharing, the time between acceptance by the system of a line of input from a terminal and the point at which the system can accept the next line from the terminal. Contrast with response time.

interactive (1) Pertaining to a program or system that alternately accepts input and then responds. An interactive system is conversational, that is, a continuous dialog exists between user and system. Contrast with batch. (2) Pertaining to the exchange of information between a user and a computer.

interactive chart utility Utility provided by graphical data display manager (GDDM) to allow basic graphic handling capability and a menu-driven generation of different forms of graphs. ICU is a part of presentation graphics feature.

Interactive Communications Feature (SSP-ICF) In System/36, a feature of the System Support Program Product that allows a program to interactively communicate with another program or system.

Interactive Computing and Control Facility See VSE/ICCF.

Interactive Data Base Utilities (IDU) A System/38 licensed program that consists of the data file utility (DFU), source entry utility (SEU), query, and screen design aid (SDA) .

interactive data definition utility (IDDU) In the OS/400 operating system and System/36, a function that can be used to externally define the characteristics of data and the contents of files.

interactive debug In DPPX, a mode of operation in which program execution can be monitored through the use of the DEBUG, PGM command and its subcommands.

interactive editor In DPPX, a means of rearranging, modifying, and deleting data through use of an EDIT command and its subcommands at a keyboard-display or keyboard-printer.

interactive environment In DPPX, an environment in which a terminal user interacts with the system.

interactive graphics Computer graphics in which a display device is used in the conversational mode. Contrast with passive graphics.

interactive job A job in which processing actions are performed in response to input provided by a workstation user. During a job, a dialog is maintained between the user and the system.

interactive-keyboard printer In word processing, a printer used in conjunction with a keyboard to print each character as it is keyed. (T)

interactive media (1) Media that derives input from the viewer to determine the content and duration of a message, thus making possible individualized program material. (2) A type of media production that takes maximum advantage of random access, computer-controlled videotape, and videodisc players. (3) Synonymous with interactive multimedia.

interactive mode (1) In AS/400 query management, the query mode associated with a query instance that allows users to interact with the query commands while a procedure is running. (2) Synonym for conversational mode.

interactive multimedia Synonym for interactive media.

interactive partition In VSE, an area of virtual storage dynamically allocated for the purpose of processing a job that was submitted interactively from a terminal.

Interactive Problem Control System (IPCS) A component of VM that permits online problem management, interactive problem diagnosis, online debugging for disk-resident CP abend dumps, problem tracking, and problem reporting.

interactive processing (1) Pertaining to a program or procedure that alternately accepts input and responds to the input. (2) A processing method in which each user action causes a response from the program or the system. (3) Contrast with batch processing.

interactive program A running program that can receive input from the keyboard or another input device. Contrast with noninteractive program.

interactive PVS In DPCX, an extension of the testing phase of batch PVS that allows a programmer to use a terminal to stop PVS testing, enter and view data, enter transactions and receive immediate responses, and request printouts. Contrast with batch PVS.

interactive subsystem A subsystem in which interactive jobs are processed.

Interactive System Productivity Facility An IBM licensed program that serves as a full-screen editor and dialogue manager. Used for writing application programs, it provides a means of generating standard screen panels and interactive dialogues between the application programmer and terminal user.

interactive terminal facility (ITF) In the AS/400 system, an asynchronous communications function that allows the system to communicate with applications that can send and receive data, such as electronic mail, memos, library members, and data files.

interactive user profile In the AS/400 Business Graphics Utility, an area used by some IBM licensed programs to store information between successive calls of those programs, such as the file and library last used, or the setup last used.

interactive video The process of combining video and computer technology so that the user's actions, choices, and decisions affect the way in which the program unfolds.

interactive videodisc system (IVS) A system in which a user can interact with a videodisc display image by entering commands to the computer through a device such as a keyboard or keypad, or directly by touching a touch-sensitive screen at specific points on the display surface.

interactive videography Synonym for videotex. (T)

interactivity The ability of a user (or a computer) to control a multimedia presentation, not only in selecting the material presented but also in affecting the way in which the material is presented.

interblock gap (1) The space between two consecutive blocks on a data medium. (I)　(2) See also interrecord gap. See Figure 77.

intercept In a GDDM chart, a method of describing the position of one axis relative to another; for example, the horizontal axis can be specified so that it intercepts (crosses) the vertical axis at the bottom, middle, or top of the plotting area of a chart.

intercepted resource (1) An external logical unit (LU) to which no messages can be sent for a specified time interval or until an operator command or an application-program macroinstruction is issued to release messages. An intercepted resource can enter messages, but messages destined for it are not sent. (2) In ACF/TCAM, a network resource that can enter but not receive messages.

intercepted station In ACF/TCAM, a station to which no messages can be sent for a specified time interval or until an operator command or an application-program macroinstruction is issued to release messages held for the intercepted station. An intercepted station can enter messages, but messages sent to that station are stopped.

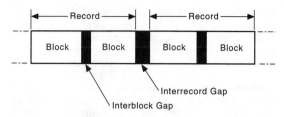

Figure 77. Interblock Gap

intercepted terminal A terminal that cannot accept messages.

intercepting The routing of a call or message that is placed for a disconnected or nonexistent telephone number or terminal address to an operator position or to a specially designated terminal.

intercepting trunk A trunk to which a call for a vacant number or changed number or a line out of order is connected for action by an operator.

intercept operator In intercepting, the operator who requests the number called, determines the reason for the intercept, and relays the information to the calling party.

interchange See information interchange.

interchange code See binary-coded decimal interchange code. See also ASCII, EBCDIC.

interchange format (1) A print descriptor naming convention required to send a print descriptor from one system to another. (2) See document interchange format.

interchange group separator (IGS) A character used to indicate that blanks were removed from a string of data and are to be reinserted.

interchange node A VTAM node that acts as both an APPN network node and a type 5 subarea node to transform APPN protocols to subarea protocols and vice versa. Contrast with migration data host.

interchange record separator (IRS) Synonym for record separator.

interchange transmission group (TG) The logical connection between an interchange node and a node (of any type) that includes at least one hop requiring SSCP-SSCP sessions for session setup. The physical connection underlying an interchange TG can traverse multiple subarea and APPN subnetworks.

intercharacter increment In printing, the space between character boxes.

intercharacter space Horizontal space between two adjacent capital letter matrices. See also interline space.

Note: Intercharacter space can be occupied by portions of oversized symbols.

intercommunicating system A privately owned system without a switchboard, capable of two-way communication, normally limited to a single unit, building, or plant. Stations may or may not be equipped for originating a call, but they can answer any call.

interconnected networks SNA networks connected by gateways.

interconnection See SNA network interconnection.

interconnect panel Synonym for distribution panel.

interdiction Synonym for denial of service.

interexchange channel A channel connecting two different exchange areas.

interface (1) A shared boundary between two functional units, defined by functional characteristics, signal characteristics, or other characteristics, as appropriate. The concept includes the specification of the connection of two devices having different functions. (T) (2) Hardware, software, or both, that links systems, programs, or devices. (3) See data transmission interface, EXCP interface, physical interface, user interface. (4) See procedure interface.

interface of a procedure In FORTRAN, see procedure interface.

interface processor A processor that acts as the interface between another processor or terminal and a network, or a processor that controls data flow in a network. (T)

interfield frame A product of the 3:2 pull-down process for transferring film to video, capable of producing flicker when a single frame is frozen on a videodisc. See also 3:2 pulldown.

interframe coding In video signal transmission, a method of video compression that concentrates on coding areas of high detail at the expense of the less-detailed areas.

interframe time-fill In data communication, the sequence of flag sequences transmitted between frames.

interior/exterior box A cable termination and lightning protection device used in loop installations that have outdoor cabling.

interior gateway In the AIX operating system, a gateway that communicates only with its own autonomous system. Contrast with exterior gateway. See also active gateway, passive gateway, neighbor gateway.

interlaced video A type of video signal in which a complete frame is composed of two fields, each of which carries half the lines of the frame. The lines of the second field fall exactly in between the lines of the first field. See also field, scan line.

interlace flicker In multimedia applications, the apparent flicker that occurs when one field of an interlaced image contains more light than the other field due to the placement of image details with respect to the separate fields. Two methods are used to avoid interlace flicker: (1) limit the vertical resolution on natural images (as opposed to text or graphics), and (2) design characters so that each character has an equal number of pels in each field.

interlacing In multimedia applications, a characteristic of video image display that results in greater image clarity. In effect, the video image is traced across the screen twice. (The time delay between the two tracings makes this effect undesirable for normal computer-generated graphics.) Synonymous with interleaving.

interleave To arrange parts of one sequence of things or events so that they alternate with parts of one or more other sequences of the same nature and so that each sequence retains its identity. (I) (A)

interleaved subscripts A subscript notation, used with subscripted qualified names, in which not all of the necessary subscripts immediately follow the same component name.

interleaving (1) The simultaneous accessing of two or more bytes or streams of data from distinct storage units. (2) The alternating of two or more operations or functions through the overlapped use of a computer facility. (3) In a duplicator, the process of inserting absorbent sheets between successive sheets of the copy paper to prevent set-off. (T) (4) Synonym for interlacing.

interline space On a display screen, the space between the lower print line of a row of capital letter matrices and the upper print line of the next lower row of capital letter matrices. See also intercharacter space.

Note: Interline space can be occupied by cursors, descenders, diacritical marks, intercharacter space, portions of oversized symbols, and underlines.

interlock To prevent a machine or device from initiating further operations until an operation in process is completed. See also deadlock.

intermediate In document copying, synonym for master. (T)

intermediate block check In binary synchronous communication, a check of each record in a block, rather than the contents of the complete buffer, when large blocks of text are received.

intermediate-block-check character (ITB) See intermediate-text-block character (ITB).

intermediate distributing frame (IDF) In a local central office, a distributing frame that connects subscriber lines to the subscriber line circuit. In a private branch exchange, its purpose is similar.

intermediate equipment Auxiliary equipment that may be inserted between data terminal equipment and signal conversion equipment to perform certain additional functions before modulation or after demodulation. (I) (A)

intermediate host node In ACF/TCAM, a host node on an extended route that processes messages flowing along the extended route but does not itself own the originating or destination resources for those messages. In an ACF/TCAM extended network, processing by an intermediate host node includes processing by the incoming group of an internodal message handler (IMH), enqueuing of each message on the internodal destination queue for the next host node on its extended route, and processing by the outgoing group of the IMH. See also host node.

intermediate language A language into which a source program or statement is translated before it is further translated or interpreted. (T)

intermediate materials In video production, all the media selected for assembly onto the premaster disc or tape: for example, 16mm film, video tape, 35mm slides.

intermediate network node In APPN, a node that is part of a route between an origin LU (OLU) and a destination LU (DLU) but neither contains the OLU or the DLU nor serves as the network server for either the OLU or DLU.

intermediate node (1) A node that is at the end of more than one branch. (T) (2) On an AIX widget tree, a widget with one or more children.

intermediate routing function (IRF) A capability within a node that allows it to receive and route path information units (PIUs) that neither originate from, nor are destined for, network accessible units (NAUs) in that node.

intermediate routing network See APPN intermediate routing network.

intermediate routing node (IRN) A node containing intermediate routing function.

intermediate session routing (ISR) A type of routing function within an APPN network node that provides session-level flow control and outage reporting for all sessions that pass through the node but whose end points are elsewhere.

intermediate SSCP An SSCP along a session initiation path that owns neither of the LUs involved in a cross-network LU-LU session.

intermediate storage Any storage device used to hold data temporarily before it is processed. See also buffer storage.

intermediate system In an IMS/VS multisystem environment, a system through which a message passes on its way from an input system to a destination system. It performs no processing other than routing.

intermediate TCAM node In TCAM extended networking, a TCAM node that processes messages flowing along the extended route but does not provide queuing for the originating or destination resources for the messages. Processing by an intermediate TCAM node includes processing by the incoming group of the internodal message handler, queuing of each message on the internodal destination queue for the next TCAM node on its extended route, and processing by the outgoing group of the internodal message handler (MH). See TCAM node.

intermediate-text-block (ITB) character (1) A character used to terminate an intermediate block of characters. The block check character is sent immediately following ITB, but no line turnaround occurs. The response following ETB or ETX also applies to all of the ITB checks immediately preceding the block terminated by ETB or ETX. (2) In binary synchronous communication, a transmission control character used to divide a block of text into smaller groups of text for an intermediate block check.

intermediate total In telegraph usage, the result obtained when a summation is terminated by a change of group that is neither the most nor the least significant.

intermessage delay The elapsed time between receipt of a system response at a terminal and the time when a new transaction is entered. Synonymous with think time.

internal block A block contained in another block. See also nest.

internal clocking In data communications, data clocking provided by an adapter. Contrast with external clocking.

internal data In COBOL, the data described in a program excluding all external data items and external file connectors. Items described in the Linkage Section of a program are treated as internal data. Contrast with external data.

internal data definition A description of a variable appearing at the beginning of a block that directs the system to allocate storage for that variable and makes that variable accessible to the current block.

internal DATA file In BASIC, a file containing the table that contains values from the DATA statements of a program.

internal data item In COBOL, a data item that is described in one program in a run unit. An internal data item may have a global name.

internal decimal item See packed decimal item.

internal event In a conceptual schema language, an event that occurs because of the termination of some permissible action in the information system. Contrast with external event. (A)

internal file connector In COBOL, a file connector that is accessible to only one object program in the run unit. Contrast with external file connector.

internal file ID In the OS/2 operating system, a two-byte value, supplied by the operating system, that refers to a file or device.

internal label (1) A machine-readable label, recorded on a data medium, that provides information about data recorded on the medium. (T) (2) Contrast with external label.

internal level In a database, all aspects dealing with the user-transparent representation of information in an information processing system. (T)

internal library definition A body of data, such as a character group definition, code page definition, or page format definition, that can be accessed or edited only through the 3800 Print Management Facility. Internal library definitions can be used by other licensed programs after they are built into external library members by the Print Management Facility.

internal memory (1) In an IBM personal computer, all of the memory that the processor can access directly without using an I/O channel. Contrast with auxiliary storage. (2) Synonym for internal storage. (T)

Note: Internal memory consists of read-only memory (ROM) and the user memory in the system unit and any attached expansion units that together provide the total addressable memory in which instructions can be executed.

internal model A collection of entities that represent the conceptual model and the external model of a database that can be stored in a data processing system. (T)

internal name A name contained within a program or module or within a part of a program such as a program block or a control section.

internal object (1) In the AS/400 system, an object that the system program uses to store the information needed to perform some system functions. Internal objects cannot be displayed by a user. Contrast with external object. (2) In the 3800 Print Service Utility, groups of structured fields that can be included as part of a resource or a print data set. They cannot be accessed apart from the resource or print data set of which they are a part

internal procedure (1) A procedure contained within a block. (2) In FORTRAN, a procedure that is defined by an internal program unit.

internal program unit In FORTRAN, a program unit that is contained within another program unit.

internal reader A facility that transfers jobs to the job entry subsystem (JES2 or JES3).

internal record Synonym for stored record. (T)

internal routine (1) A routine available only within the lexical scope in which it was declared. (2) In Pascal, a routine that can be used only within the lexical scope in which it was declared.

internal schema (1) A part of a database schema that pertains to the internal level. (T) (2) In a database, a schema that describes the database environment and how data in the database are physically stored.

internal sort (1) A sort performed within internal storage. (A) (2) A sort program or sort phase that sorts two or more items within main storage. (A) (3) A sorting technique that creates sequences of records or keys. Usually, it precedes a merge phase in which the sequences created are reduced to one by an external merge. (4) In VSAM, when building an alternate index, the sorting of the alternate keys into ascending sequence by using virtual storage obtained through a GETVIS. See also external sort.

internal storage (1) Storage that is accessible by a processor without the use of input/output channels. Internal storage may include other kinds of storage such as cache memory and registers. Synonymous with internal memory. (T) (2) Deprecated term for main storage. (3) Synonym for processor storage.

Notes:

1. *Internal storage usually refers to one or more storage devices that together provide the total program-addressable execution space of main storage.*

2. *Internal storage includes processor storage and may include other kinds of storage accessed by a processor, such as cache storage and special registers.*

internal trace table Synonym for CP trace table.

internal writer A facility in the job entry subsystem (JES2 or JES3) that allows user-written output writers to write data on devices not directly supported by the job control manager.

international standard A standards document that is given final approval by the International Organization for Standardization.

International Telecommunication Union (ITU) The specialized telecommunication agency of the United Nations, established to provide standardized communication procedures and practices, including frequency allocation and radio regulations worldwide.

internet A collection of packet-switching networks that are physically interconnected by Internet Protocol (IP) gateways. These networks use protocols that allow them to function as a large, composite network.

Internet A wide area network connecting thousands of disparate networks in industry, education, government, and research. The Internet network uses TCP/IP as the standard for transmitting information.

Internet address The numbering system used in TCP/IP Internetwork communications to specify a particular network or a particular host on that network with which to communicate. Internet addresses are commonly denoted in dotted decimal form.

Internet Control Message Protocol (ICMP) A protocol used by a gateway to communicate with a source host, for example, to report an error in a datagram. It is an integral part of the Internet Protocol (IP).

Internet Protocol (IP) A protocol used to route data from its source to its destination in an Internet environment.

Internet router A device that enables an Internet Protocol host to act as a gateway for routing data between separate networks that use a specific adapter.

internetwork Any wide area network connecting more than one network.

internetworking Communication between two or more networks.

internodal awareness In an ACF/TCAM extended networking, a function used by TCAM systems to share information. This information includes the status of TCAM systems, the status of application programs in TCAM systems, and the contents of selected key-table entries. This function is provided by node path system service programs in the various TCAM systems that communicate with each other.

internodal destination queue In an ACF/TCAM extended networking, a destination queue for an external logical unit (LU) that is a partner in a utility session.

internodal message handler (IMH) In an ACF/TCAM extended networking, a message handler that processes messages flowing on utility sessions.

internodal sequence number synchronization In an ACF/TCAM extended networking, the function of a particular system service program that operates in conjunction with the internodal message handler. Internodal sequence number synchronization is used to request retransmission from any TCAM node of sequence-numbered messages not received in a utility session and to retransmit sequence-numbered messages flowing in a utility session when requested to do so by another TCAM node or an extended operator command.

internodal sequence prefix In an ACF/TCAM extended network, a control block that contains sequence-number information for messages flowing in utility sessions.

internode routing The capability of path control to route PIUs from half-sessions to data link control and from data link control to half-sessions for sessions between NAUs that reside in different nodes.

intern procedure In the AIX operating system, the procedure of defining an atom.

interoffice trunk A direct trunk between local central offices in the same exchange.

interoperability (1) The capability to communicate, execute programs, or transfer data among various functional units in a way that requires the user to have little or no knowledge of the unique characteristics of those units. (T) (2) In SAA usage, the ability to link SAA and non-SAA environments and use the combination for distributed processing.

interpret To analyze and execute each statement in a source program before translating and executing the next statement. (T)

INTERPRET AS Command (IAC) In Telnet, a character that identifies the character or characters following it as a command for Telnet to process.

interpreter (1) A computer program that can interpret. (T) (2) A program that translates and executes each instruction of a high-level programming language before it translates and executes the next instruction. (3) A device that prints on a punched card the characters corresponding to hole patterns punched in the card. (T) (4) Synonymous with interpretive program.

interpreting Translating and executing each source language statement of a computer program before translating and executing the next statement.

interpretive code The instruction repertoire for the source language input to an interpreter. (A)

interpretive execution (1) Execution of an instruction before the next instruction is interpreted and executed. (2) In DPCX, the execution of instructions by application function routines (AFRs).

interpretive program Synonym for interpreter. (T)

interpretive routine A routine that decodes instructions written as pseudocodes and immediately executes the instructions. Contrast with compile.

interpret table In VTAM, an installation-defined correlation list that translates an argument into a string of eight characters. Interpret tables can be used to translate logon data into the name of an application program for which the logon is intended.

interprocess communication (1) In the OS/2 operating system, the exchange of information between processes or threads through semaphores, queues, and shared memory. (2) In the AIX operating system, the process by which programs communicate data to each other and to synchronize their activities. Semaphores, signals, and internal message queues are common methods of inter-process communication. (3) In AIX

Enhanced X-Windows, a communication path. See also client.

interrecord gap (1) The space between two consecutive records on a data medium. (I) (A) (2) Deprecated term for interblock gap.

interrecord-separator character (IRS) In BSC, a transmission control character used to separate records within a block of data.

interrogation The process whereby a master station requests a slave station to indicate its identity or its status. (T) (A)

interrupt (1) A suspension of a process, such as execution of a computer program caused by an external event, and performed in such a way that the process can be resumed. (A) (2) An instruction that directs the microprocessor to suspend what it is doing and run a specified routine. When the routine is complete, the microprocessor resumes its original work. See also routine. (3) To stop a process in such a way that it can be resumed. (4) In data communication, to take an action at a receiving station that causes the sending station to end a transmission. (5) To temporarily stop a process. (6) Synonymous with interruption. (7) See vectored interrupt. (8) Contrast with exception, signal.

interrupt confirmation packet In X.25 communications, a packet used to acknowledge the receipt of an interrupt packet.

interrupted isochronous transmission Synonym for burst transmission.

interrupt handler See first-level interrupt handler, second-level interrupt handler.

interruptible Synonym for enabled.

interruption Synonym for interrupt *(1)*. See also external interruption, I/O interruption, machine check interruption, program-controlled interruption, SVC interruption.

interruption network A network of circuits in a computing system that continuously monitors system operation. The network detects events that normally require intervention and direction by the supervisor, and it initiates interruptions.

interrupt packet In X.25 communications, an expedited packet that is allowed to overtake normal data packets, which are delivered in sequence.

interrupt register A special purpose register that holds data necessary for handling interrupts. (T)

interrupt request (IR) In the IBM 8100 Information System, a request for processing on a particular priority level. It may be generated by the active program, the processing unit, or an I/O device.

intersection Synonym for conjunction.

interstage punching A mode of card punching such that the odd- or even-numbered card columns are used. (A)

intersystem communication (1) Transfer of data between systems by means of data exchange or data interchange. (2) In CICS/VS, a subset of SNA formats and protocols that governs the interactions of transaction processing systems. By defining how transaction programs communicate, even when they are under control of different transaction processing systems, intersystem communication allows construction of a distributed transaction processing application using individual transaction programs as building blocks. (3) In a system environment containing multiple ESCON managers, communication that occurs between ESCON manager hosts connected to the same ESCON Director. (4) An extension of IMS/VS Multiple Systems Coupling that permits the connection of IMS/VS to another IMS/VS subsystem, to CICS/OS/VS, or to a user-written subsystem, provided both subsystems use ISC.

intersystem communications function (ICF) In the OS/400 operating system, a function that allows a program to communicate interactively with another program or system.

intertoll trunk A trunk between toll offices in different telephone exchanges.

inter-user communication vehicle (IUCV) A VM facility for passing data between virtual machines and VM components.

interval migration In the Hierarchical Storage Manager, automatic migration that occurs when the high threshold of occupancy is reached or exceeded on a primary volume during a specified time interval. Data sets are moved from the volume, oldest first, until the low threshold of occupancy is reached.

interval mode In MSS, a method of operation of the system-initiated scratch function. It allows non-VSAM data sets on candidate volumes to be scratched and uncataloged at user-defined intervals. See also continuous mode.

interval service value In the system resources manager, a category of information contained in a period definition that specifies the minimum amount of service an associated job will receive during any interval.

interval timer (1) A device that upon the lapse of a specified length of time, generates an interrupt signal. (T) (2) A timer that provides program interruptions on a program-controlled basis. (3) An electronic counter that counts intervals of time under program control.

intervention-required check In 3800, an unexpected asynchronous condition that requires external intervention to clear it; for example, out-of-forms, out-of-toner.

interword blank Synonym for word space.

interword space Synonym for word space.

intraframe coding In video signal transmission, a method of video compression in which half the picture information is eliminated by discarding every other frame as it comes from the camera. During playback, each frame remains on the screen twice the normal duration to simulate the (NTSC) standard 30 frames-per-second video rate.

intranode routing The capability of path control to route PIUs for sessions between NAUs that reside in the same node.

intrapartition destination A queue of transient data used subsequently as input data to another task within the CICS region. Contrast with extrapartition destination.

intrarecord data structure In COBOL, the entire collection of groups and elementary items from a logical record that is defined by a contiguous subset of the data description entries which describe that record. These data description entries include all entries whose level number is greater than the level number of the first data description entry describing the intrarecord data structure.

intra subsystem In System/36, an SSP-ICF subsystem that enables programs to communicate with other programs on the same system without the use of telecommunication lines.

intrasystem communications A function that allows two programs that are running in two different jobs on the same system to communicate with each other through an ICF file.

intrinsic In FORTRAN, pertaining to types, operators, procedures, and conditions, defined in the ANSI FORTRAN Standard, that may be used in any scoping unit without further definition or specification.

intrinsic function (1) A function supplied by a program, such as a BASIC or FORTRAN program, as opposed to a function supplied by the compiler. Contrast with external function. (2) In the AS/400 system, a function supplied by the AS/400 BASIC licensed program. Contrast with user-defined function. (3) In XL FORTRAN, a function that is supplied with the run time environment that performs math, character, logical, or bit-manipulation operations.

intrinsics In AIX Enhanced X-Windows, a set of management mechanisms that provides for constructing and interfacing between composite widgets, their children, and other clients. Also, intrinsics provide the ability to organize a collection of widgets into an application.

intrinsic semiconductor A semiconductor that has a balance of positive charge carriers (holes) and negative charge carriers (free electrons). Synonymous with i-type semiconductor.

intrusion tone An audible signal superimposed on a conversation, when a third party takes part in a call.

int specifier In the XL C compiler, one of the words int, short, shortint, long, long int, unsigned, unsignedint, unsigned short, unsigned short, int, unsignedlong, or unsigned long int, that describe the type of data a variable represents.

invalid character Deprecated term for illegal character.

invalid exclusive reference An exclusive reference in which a common segment does not contain a reference to the symbol used in the exclusive reference.

invalid key condition In COBOL, a condition, at object time, caused when a specific value of the key associated with an indexed file or relative file is determined to be invalid.

invalid page In System/370 virtual storage systems, a page that cannot be directly addressed by the dynamic address translation feature of the processing unit.

invariant routing In ACF/TCAM, message routing in which messages from the same source are always sent to the same destination. See also affinity-based routing, transaction-based routing.

inventory See mass storage volume inventory.

inverse A matrix that results from a mathematical operation on another matrix such that the two matrices can be multiplied together to obtain the unit matrix.

inverse color highlighting In SAA Advanced Common User Access architecture, a screen emphasis feature that changes both the foreground and background colors of an item. This highlighting is often used as selected emphasis for choice text. See also marquee select.

inverse transpose The inverse of a matrix after it has been transposed.

inverse video Synonym for reverse video.

inversion Deprecated term for negation.

invert To change a physical or logical state to its opposite state. (A)

inverted Pertaining to a file, a set of records, or a relation with respect to a secondary key, such that an index exists for this secondary key and this file, set of records, or relation. (T)

inverted access Pertaining to the organization and access method of a storage structure that maintains a separate index whose entries are ordered by the search keys of the stored records. (A)

inverted file (1) A file whose sequence has been reversed. (A) (2) In information retrieval, a method of organizing a cross-index file in which a keyword identifies a record; the items, numbers, or documents pertinent to that keyword are indicated. (A)

inverter A functional unit whose output analog variable is equal in magnitude to its input analog variable but is of opposite algebraic sign. (I) (A)

invitation The process in which a processor contacts a station in order to allow the station to transmit a message if it has one ready. See also enabling, polling.

invitation delay In ACF/TCAM, a specified period of time, during which the host processor can send outgoing messages to nonswitched polled stations for which host receiving has priority over host sending. This delay is observed for all such stations on a line when the end of the invitation list for that line is reached. The delay in polling is observed for such stations whether or not the host processor has any messages to send them. If no invitation delay is specified for such stations, no messages can be sent to them.

invitation list A series of sets of polling characters or identification sequences associated with the stations on a line; the order in which sets of polling characters are specified determines the order in which polled stations are invited to enter messages on the line.

invitation to send (ITS) A Western Union term for a character sequence sent to an outlying teletypewriter terminal that polls its tape transmitter. See also polling, transmitter start code.

invite To ask for input data from either a display station or an SSP-ICF session.

invite program device operation An input/output operation that invites an acquired program device to send input to a program and returns control to the program without waiting for the input to arrive.

invocation (1) The activation of a program or procedure. (2) An execution of a program.

invocation stack A list of programs linked together as a result of programs calling other programs within the same job. Synonymous with program stack.

invoke (1) To start a command, procedure, or program. (2) In FORTRAN, to call a subroutine by means of a CALL statement or by a defined assignment. (3) In FORTRAN, to call a function by a reference to it during the evaluation of an expression.

inward WATS A telephone service similar to WATS but applicable to incoming calls. See also WATS.

INX Index character.

I/O Input/output.

IOA Input/output adapter.

I/O adapter See input/output adapter.

I/O appendage A user-written routine that provides additional control over I/O operations during channel program operations.

I/O area An area of storage that contains data which is used in input/output operations; for example, an I/O buffer.

IOC Input/output controller. (A)

I/O card licensed internal code The licensed internal code in a controller or adapter card.

I/O Configuration Program (IOCP) A program that defines to a system all available I/O devices and channel paths.

Note: The configuration program is available in three versions: stand-alone, VM/370, and MVS.

I-O-CONTROL In COBOL, the name of an Environment Division paragraph in which object program requirements for rerun points, sharing of the same areas by several data files, and multiple file storage on a single input/output device are specified.

I-O-CONTROL entry In COBOL, an entry in the I-O-CONTROL paragraph of the Environment Divi-

sion that contains clauses which provide information required for the transmission and handling of data on named files during the execution of a program.

I/O controller See input/output controller.

I/O coprocessor In a personal computer, a microprocessor on an expansion board that supplements the operations of the processor in the system unit; for example by handling I/O interrupts and performing input/output operations in parallel with other operations. See also math coprocessor, networking coprocessor.

Note: An I/O coprocessor in a personal computer performs functions similar to those performed by an I/O controller in a large computer system.

IOCP I/O Configuration Program.

IOCS Input/output control system.

I/O device See input/output unit.

I/O diskette slot See slot.

IOH Integrated open hypermedia.

I/O indicator A light on the operator/service panel that comes on when any input/output device other than the SCA (system control adapter) is operating.

I/O interruption An interruption caused by termination of an I/O operation or by operator intervention at the I/O device.

I/O interrupt request vector (IOIRV) In the IBM 8100 Information System, the formatted information used to generate an interrupt request for an I/O device.

IOIRV I/O interrupt request vector.

I/O list A list of variables in an I/O statement, specifying the storage locations into which data are to be read or from which data are to be written.

I/O mode In DPPX, the privilege mode that allows processing of all instructions except those that are supervisor-privileged. See also application mode, master mode, supervisor mode.

I-O mode In COBOL, the state of a file after execution of an OPEN statement, with the I-O phrase specified, for that file and before the execution of a CLOSE statement without the REEL or UNIT phrase for that file.

ionization Loss or gain of electrons in a gas that creates positively or negatively charged particles.

IOP Input/output processor.

IOPD Input/output problem determination.

I/O port System hardware that enables attachment of I/O devices. Master modes but not in application mode.

I/O processor See input/output processor.

IOS I/O Supervisor.

I/O slot In System/38, one of three locations in a diskette magazine drive where individual diskettes can be inserted for input/output operations. Same as manual slot.

I-O status In COBOL, a conceptual entity that contains the two-character value indicating the resulting status of an input/output operation. This value is made available to the program through the use of the FILE STATUS clause in the file control entry for the file.

IOTA I/O transaction area.

I/O tag In the IBM 8100 Information System, a signal that notifies the system and I/O control logic that a channel I/O operation or programmed I/O operation is beginning.

IP Internet Protocol.

I/PAR Incidents/parts activity report.

IPC (1) Illustrated parts catalog. (2) Integrated protective circuits. (3) Interprocess communication.

IPCS Interactive problem control system.

IPDS Intelligent printer data stream.

IP indicator See input-to-process indicator.

IPL (1) Initial program loader. (A) (2) Initial program load.

IPL mode switch A switch located on the operator panel of an IBM 8100 Information System processor that is set to identify the type of initial program load (primary or manual) desired. The primary position indicates that the user does not wish to control the IPL procedure and accepts the IBM-assigned options. The manual position indicates that the user wishes to control the IPL procedure to make changes.

IPM Isolated pacing message.

IPO Installation productivity option.

IPR Isolated pacing response.

IPS (1) Inches per second. (2) Installation performance specification.

IQL Incoming quality level.

IR (1) Information retrieval. (2) Interrupt request.

IRD Information resource dictionary.

IRD schema extensibility Information resource dictionary schema extensibility. The capability to create new functionality in an information resource dictionary system. (A)

IRDS Information resource dictionary system. A software system for creating, maintaining, processing, and using information resource dictionaries. (T)

IRD system extensibility Information resource dictionary system extensibility. The capability to create new functionality in an information resource dictionary system. (A)

IRF Intermediate routing function.

iris (1) In photography, the adjustable opening on a camera lens that controls the amount of light entering the camera. (2) In multimedia, a spiral wipe that simulates the action of a camera iris.

IRM Information resource management. (A)

IRN Intermediate routing node.

irrecoverable error (1) An error for which recovery is impossible without use of recovery techniques external to the computer program or run. (T) (2) Synonymous with unrecoverable error.

irrelevance In information theory, the conditional entropy of the occurrence of specific messages at a message sink, given the occurrences of specific messages at the message source connected to the message sink by a specified channel. (I) (A) Synonymous with spread.

IRS (1) Interrecord-separator character. (2) Interchange record separator. Synonymous with record separator.

IRSS Intelligent remote station support.

IRT Index return character.

IS An information separator character. (A)

ISA Industry Standard Architecture.

ISAM Indexed sequential access method.

ISAM interface program A set of routines that allow a processing program coded to use ISAM (indexed sequential access method) to gain access to a VSAM key-sequenced file or data set.

ISC Integrated Storage Control.

ISD IBM software distribution.

ISDN Integrated services digital network.

IS indicator See initiate-transaction-sequence indicator.

ISMF Interactive Storage Management Facility.

ISO International Organization for Standardization. An organization of national standards bodies from various countries established to promote development of standards to facilitate international exchange of goods and services, and develop cooperation in intellectual, scientific, technological, and economic activity.

isochronous transmission (1) A data transmission process in which there is always an integral number of unit intervals between any two significant instants. (I) (2) See also anisochronous transmission, synchronous transmission.

ISO forms See ISO sizes.

isolated amplifier An amplifier without an electrical connection between the signal circuit and all other circuits including ground. (T)

isolated pacing response (IPR) In SNA, a response to a session-level pacing request sent independently of any particular request without correlation of sequence numbers, and that signals readiness of the receiver to receive an additional pacing group.

Note: An IPR may be sent on either the expedited or normal flow and is particularly useful when no other response is available; for example, when operating under no-response protocols.

isolation (1) In computer security, the containment of subjects and objects in a system in such a way that they are separated from one another, as well as from the protection controls of the operating system. (2) In video production, a technique of recording one camera on one videotape recorder and another camera on a second recorder, then editing the two tapes together.

ISO sizes Pertaining to a set of paper sizes selected from those standardized by the International Organization for Standardization for use in data processing.

ISPF Interactive System Productivity Facility.

ISR Intermediate session routing.

ISS Image symbol set.

ISTATUS In VTAM and NCP, a definition specification method for indicating the initial status of resources. See also indirect activation.

ISTRACTR Internal trace recording routine.

IT Indent tab character.

italic A type style with characters that slant to the right.

ITB (1) Intermediate text block. (2) Intermediate-block-check character. (3) Intermediate-text-block character.

item (1) An element of a set of data; for example, a file may consist of a number of items such as records which in turn may consist of other items. (I) (A) (2) One unit of a commodity such as one box, one bag, or one can. Usually, an item is the smallest unit of a commodity to be sold. (3) In CCP, any of the components, such as communication controllers, lines, cluster controllers, and terminals, that comprise an IBM 3710 Network Controller configuration. (4) See data item, elementary item, external data item, group item, index data item, internal data item, noncontiguous item, nonnumeric item, numeric item, printable item, source item, variable occurrence data item.

item code (1) In PSS, the number assigned to an item that can indicate the manufacturer as well as the specific item in that manufacturer's line of goods. (2) In PSS, the number assigned to an item for indexing into the user's files.

item count On a calculator, the counting of the number of items processed by the machine. (T)

iteration The process of repeatedly running a set of computer instructions until some condition is satisfied.

iterative operation The repetition of the solution of a set of equations with successive combinations of initial conditions or other parameters; each successive combination is selected by a subsidiary computation based on a predetermined set of iteration rules.

Note: Iterative operation is usually used to permit solution of boundary value problems or for automatic optimization of system parameters. Synonymous with automatic sequential operation.

ITF (1) Interactive terminal facility. (2) Batch interface file. (3) Batch interface JCL mask file.

ITF: BASIC A simple language resembling algebra and designed for ease of use at a terminal.

ITF: PL/I A conversational subset of PL/I designed for ease of use at the terminal.

ITFB Batch interface log file.

I-time Instruction time.

ITS Invitation to send.

ITTRC Internal trace table.

ITU International Telecommunication Union.

i-type semiconductor Synonym for intrinsic semiconductor.

IUCV Inter-user communication vehicle.

IUP Installed user program.

IVP Installation verification procedure.

IVS Interactive videodisc system.

IW indicator See work-session-initiation indicator.

J

jabber Transmission by a data station beyond the time interval allowed by the protocol. (T)

jabber control In local area networks, the ability of a medium attachment unit to automatically interrupt transmission in order to inhibit an abnormally long output data stream. (T) (A)

jack A connecting device to which a wire or wires of a circuit can be attached and that is arranged for insertion of a plug. See Figure 78.

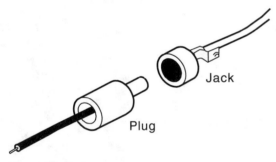

Figure 78. Jack

jacket (1) In an optical cable, the outermost layers of protective covering. Synonymous with sheathing. (2) See protective jacket.

jaggies In computer graphics, distortions of a display image that cause the stair-step-like effects of aliasing. See also aliasing.

jamming In computer security, deliberate insertion of signals or noise to prevent normal operation of a system.

Jamo Elements of the Korean written language. The Korean alphabet.

jam signal (1) The signal sent by a data station to inform the other data stations that they must not transmit. In CSMA/CD networks, the jam signal indicates that a collision has occurred. In CSMD/CD networks, the jam signal indicates that the sending data station intends to transmit. (T) (2) A signal that carries a bit pattern sent by a data station to inform the other stations that they must not transmit. In CSMA/CD networks, the jam signal indicates that a collision has occurred; in CSMA/CA networks, the signal indicates that the sending station intends to transmit. (A)

Japanese basic-Kanji character set A subset of the Japanese double-byte character set (DBCS), consisting of commonly used Kanji characters. There are 3226 Kanji characters in this set.

Japanese dictionary See DBCS conversion dictionary.

Japanese double-byte character set An IBM-defined double-byte character set (DBCS) for Japanese, consisting of the Japanese non-Kanji set, basic Kanji set, extended Kanji set, and up to 4370 user-definable characters.

Japanese extended-Kanji character set A subset of the Japanese double-byte character set DBCS, consisting of less commonly used Kanji characters. There are 3487 characters in this set.

Japanese non-Kanji character set A subset of the Japanese double-byte character set (DBCS), consisting of non-Kanji characters, such as Greek, Russian, Roman numeric, alphanumeric and related symbols, Katakana, Hiragana, and special symbols. There are 550 characters in this set.

JCL Job control language.

JCL mask A mask of JCL statements used by online requests for batch execution of functions. JCL masks, distributed with SDF/CICS, can be modified for an installation by the master operator and can be defined for individual users.

JECS Job entry central services.

jelly Synonym for diffuser.

JEPS Job entry peripheral services.

JES Job entry subsystem.

JES reader The part of the job entry subsystem that receives job input and records it in the job queue and spool data set. Synonymous with input stream control.

JES writer The part of the job entry subsystem that receives job output and writes it to end-use devices. Synonymous with output stream control.

JES2 An MVS subsystem that receives jobs into the system, converts them to internal format, selects them for execution, processes their output, and purges them from the system. In an installation with more than one processor, each JES2 processor independently controls its job input, scheduling, and output processing. See also JES3.

JES3 An MVS subsystem that receives jobs into the system, converts them to internal format, selects them for execution, processes their output, and purges them from the system. In complexes that have several loosely coupled processing units, the JES3 program manages processors so that the global processor exercises centralized control over the local processors and distributes jobs to them via a common job queue. See also JES2.

JES3-managed device A device that JES3 allocates to jobs. See also jointly managed device, MVS-managed device, shared device.

jitter (1) Short-term non-cumulative variations of the significant instants of a digital signal from their ideal positions in time; for example, phase jitter, pulse duration jitter. (T) (2) Undesirable variations of a transmitted digital signal. (3) In computer graphics, synonym for flicker. (4) See induced jitter.

JK method Jiro Kawakita method. Synonym for affinity diagramming.

job (1) A unit of work defined by a user that is to be accomplished by a computer. Loosely, the term job is sometimes used to refer to a representation of a job. This representation may include a set of computer programs, files, and control statements to the operating system. (I) (A) (2) A collection of related programs, identified by appropriate job control statements. (3) See also background job, batched job, foreground job, terminal job.

job accounting A function that collects information pertaining to how a job uses system resources.

job accounting interface In VSE, a function that accumulates accounting information for each job step that can be used for charging usage of the system, planning new applications, and supervising system operation more efficiently.

job accounting table In VSE, an area in the supervisor where accounting information is accumulated for the user.

job action In the AS/400 system, a network attribute that controls the handling of a job submitted from remote locations through either an SNA distribution services (SNADS) network or through the Remote Spooling Communications Subsystem (RSCS).

job batch A succession of job definitions that are placed one behind another to form a batch. Each job batch is placed on an input device and processed with a minimum of delay between one job or job step and another.

job catalog (1) In OS/VS, a catalog made available for a job by means of a JOBCAT DD statement, or for a job step by means of a STEPCAT DD statement. (2) In VSE, a catalog made available for a job by means of the filename IJSYSUC in the respective DLBL job statement.

job class Any one of a number of job categories that can be defined. By classifying jobs and directing initiator/terminators to initiate specific classes of jobs, it is possible to control a mixture of jobs that can be performed concurrently.

job control In VSE, a program called into storage to prepare each job or job step to be run. Some of its functions are to assign I/O devices to symbolic names, set switches for program use, log (or print) job control statements, and fetch the first phase of each job step.

job control authority In the AS/400 system, a special authority that allows a user to: change, delete, display, hold, and release all files on output queues; hold, release, and clear job queues and output queues; start writers to output queues; hold, release, change, and end other users' jobs; change the class attributes of a job; end subsystems; and start (do an IPL of) the system. See also all object authority, save system authority, security administrator authority, service authority, spool control authority.

job control language (JCL) A control language used to identify a job to an operating system and to describe the job's requirements.

job control record In the System/36 workstation utility, the first record in the transaction file.

job control rights In System/38, the authority to change, cancel, display, hold, and release all jobs and, optionally, job and output queues and entries in them.

job control statement A statement in a job that is used in identifying the job or describing its requirements to the operating system. (A)

job cylinder map (JCM) In RTAM, a description of the spool allocation space for each job. One JCM is maintained for each active job.

job date A date, associated with a job, that is usually the system date, but can be changed by the user. See also creation date, system date.

job definition A series of job control statements that define a job. Synonymous with job description.

job description (1) In the AS/400 system and System/38, a system object that defines how a job is to be processed. (2) Synonym for job definition.

job entry See remote job entry.

job entry central services (JECS) The part of the job entry subsystem that provides centralized storage and retrieval of: (1) System input and output data for each job, (2) Control tables representing jobs, thus forming a queue of work, and (3) Job tables used during job execution.

job entry peripheral services (JEPS) The part of the job entry subsystem that schedules and performs reader and writer operations.

Job Entry Subsystem (JES) In the AS/400 system, a System/370-type licensed program that receives jobs into the system and processes all output data produced by the jobs.

job file A file that exists until the end of the job that uses it.

job header A page in printed output that indicates the beginning of a user job.

job-initiation processing level In System/36, the processing level that occurs only once per job when the first operator signs on.

job input device A device assigned by the operator to read job definitions and any accompanying input data.

job input file A data file or data set consisting of a series of job definitions and accompanying data.

job input stream Synonym for input stream.

job (JOB) statement The job control statement that identifies the beginning of a job. It contains such information as the name of the job, account number, and class and priority assigned to the job.

job-level field In the System/36 workstation utility (WSU), a field that remains in the field area in main storage. This field is available to any active display station using the WSU program. Contrast with mode-level field, session-level field.

job library A set of user-identified, partitioned data sets used as the primary source of load modules for a job.

job log (1) A record of jobs submitted to a system over a specified period of time. (2) In the AS/400 system and System/38, a record of requests submitted to the system by a job, the messages related to the requests, and the actions performed by the system on the job. The job log is maintained by the system program.

job management The collective functions of job scheduling and command processing.

job message queue A message queue that is created for each job. A job message queue is used for receiving requests such as commands to be processed and for sending messages that result from processing the requests. A job message queue and a set of program message queues. See also external message queue, program message queue.

job name (1) The name of a job as identified to a system. (2) The name assigned to a JOB statement; it identifies the job to the system. (3) Contrast with qualified job name.

Note: For an interactive job, the job name can be the name of the workstation at which the job was initiated. For a batch job, the job name is specified in the command used to submit the job.

job networking A type of distributed data processing in which batch jobs submitted at one processor may be sent to another processor for execution; results may be returned to the originating processor. This may be done to balance processor utilization in a network, or to access a program or file located at another processor.

job number A number assigned to a job as it enters the system to distinguish the job from other jobs.

job offset In the 3800 Printing Subsystem, the stacking of paper in a sawtooth manner so that individual jobs or copies run on the burster-trimmer-stacker are easy to identify.

job-oriented terminal A terminal designed for a particular application.

job output device A device assigned by the operator for common use in recording output data for a series of jobs.

job output file A data file or data set consisting of output data produced by a series of jobs.

job output stream Synonym for output stream.

job pack area (JPA) An area that contains modules not in the link pack area but needed for execution of jobs.

job priority (1) A value assigned to a job that, together with an assigned job class, determines the priority to be used in scheduling the job and allocating resources to it. (2) In System/38, the order in which batch jobs on a job queue are selected for execution by the Control Program Facility. More than one job may have the same priority.

job processing The reading of job control statements and data from an input stream, the initiating of job steps defined in the statements, and the writing of system output messages.

job queue (1) A list of jobs waiting to be processed by the system. (2) In System/38, an object that contains a list of batch jobs submitted to the system for execution and from which the batch jobs are selected for execution by the Control Program Facility.

job queue entry In System/38, a work entry in a subsystem description that specifies the job queue from which the subsystem can accept batch jobs and transferred jobs.

job queue management In the job entry subsystem, the part of job entry central services responsible for the maintaining and the managing of the SYS1.SYSJOBQE data set and the scheduler work area data sets.

job-recovery control file Synonym for backup file.

job region In System/36, the main storage space reserved by the System Support Program Product for use by a job.

job run The performance of one or more runs. (T) (A)

job scheduler The part of a control program that reads and interprets job definitions, schedules the jobs for processing, initiates and terminates the processing of jobs and job steps, and records job output data.

job step (1) The execution of a computer program explicitly identified by a job control statement. A job may specify that several job steps be executed. (A) (2) A unit of work represented by a single program or a procedure that contains a single program. A job consists of one or more job steps.

job step initiation The process of selecting a job step for execution and allocating input/output devices for it.

job step restart Synonym for step restart.

job step task A task initiated by an initiator / terminator in the job scheduler in accordance with specifications in an execute (EXEC) statement. In an MVT control program configuration, a job step task can initiate any number of other tasks.

job stream (1) The sequence of representation of jobs or parts of jobs to be performed, as submitted to

an operating system. (I) (A) Synonymous with input stream, run stream. (2) In System/36, one or more library source members or procedure members saved on diskette or tape. (3) See also input stream, output stream.

job support task A task that reads and interprets job definitions or converts job input and output data from one input/output medium to another.

job trailer A page in the printed output that indicates the end of a user job.

job transfer and manipulation (JTM) An application service element that enables user application processes to transfer and manipulate documents relating to processing tasks. (T)

joggle To align a card deck, usually before placing it in a card hopper. (I) (A)

join (1) An operation of relational algebra that forms a new relation from two or more relations having common domains for one or more attributes of each relation. The operation proceeds by combining rows from the original relations, having identical values from that attribute domain. (T) (2) An operation that combines data from two or more files using specified fields. (3) In SQL, a relational operation that allows the program to retrieve data from two or more tables based on matching column values.

join field A comparison field that identifies records from two files to be combined into one record.

join level specifications In the AS/400 system, data description specifications for a join logical file, coded between the record and field level that define how to join two physical files. See also field level specifications, file level specifications, help level specifications, key field level specifications, record level specifications, select/omit level specifications.

join logical file In the AS/400 system, a logical file that combines, in one record format, fields from two or more physical files. See also logical file.

join test In the AS/400 system, a condition that determines how files and record formats are joined for use in a query.

joint information content In information theory, a measure of information conveyed by the occurrence of two events of definite joint probability; in mathematical notation, this measure $l(x_i, y_j)$ for two particular events x_i, y_j from the sets $x_1 . . . x_n$ and $y_1 ... y_m$ equals the logarithm of the reciprocal of the joint probability $p(x_i , y_j)$ of the occurrence of both events:

$$I(x_i, y_j) = \log \frac{1}{p(x_i, y_j)}$$

(I)   (A)

jointly managed device In MVS, a device managed by both JES3 and MVS. Only direct access devices with volumes that cannot be physically removed can be jointly managed. See also JES3-managed device, MVS-managed device, shared device.

Joint Photographic Experts Group (JPEG) (1) A group that is working to establish a standard for compressing and storing still images in digital form. (2) The standard under development by this group.

journal (1) A chronological record of changes made in a set of data; the record may be used to reconstruct a previous version of the set. (T)   Synonymous with log. (2) A special-purpose file or data set that can be used to provide an audit trail of operator and system actions, or as a means of recovering superseded data. See also system error log. (3) In the AS/400 system, a system object used to record entries in a journal receiver when a change is made to the database files associated with the journal. See also journal entry, journal receiver. (4) In CICS, a set of one or more data sets to which records are written sequentially during a CICS run. (5) In the AS/400 system, to place entries in a journal and its associated journal receivers. (6) See mass storage volume control journal.

journal code In the AS/400 system, a 1-character code in a journal entry that identifies the category of the journal entry; for example, F identifies an operation on a file; R identifies an operation on a record. See also journal entry.

Journal Control table (JCT) The journal control table describes the system log and user journals and their characteristics for access through journal management.

journal entry (1) A record of changes in a file made at a particular time. (2) In the AS/400 system and System/38, a record in a journal receiver that contains information about database files. See also journal code, journal entry identifier, journal entry qualifier, journal entry type.

journal entry identifier In the AS/400 system, the fields in a journal entry that identifies the journal code, the journal entry type, the date and time of the entry, the job name, the user name, and the program name.

journal entry qualifier In the AS/400 system, the part of a journal entry that identifies the name of the object for which the journal entry was created.

journal entry type In the AS/400 system, a 2-character field in a journal entry that identifies the type of operation of a system-generated journal entry or the type of journal entry of a user-generated journal entry; for example, PT is the entry type for a write operation. See also journal code, journal entry identifier.

journaling (1) The process of recording changes made in a physical file member in a journal. Journaling allows the programmer to reconstruct a physical member by applying the changes in the journal to a saved version of the physical file member. (2) The process of recording information sequentially in a database.

journal receiver In the AS/400 system and System/38, a system object that contains journal entries recorded when changes are made to the data in database files or the access paths associated with the database files. See also journal.

JOVIAL Jules' own version of international algorithmic language. A multipurpose programming language used primarily for command and control applications. (T)

joy stick (1) In computer graphics, a lever that can pivot in all directions and that is used as a locator device. (T)   (2) Synonymous with control lever, control stick. See Figure 79.

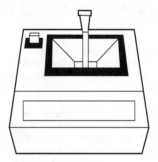

Figure 79. Joy Stick

JPA Job pack area.

JPEG Joint Photographic Experts Group.

jukebox In multimedia systems, a device, analogous to a coin-operated phonograph, that can hold and play several videodiscs or compact discs.

Julian date A date format that contains the year in positions 1 and 2, and the day in positions 3 through 5. The day is represented as 1 through 366, right-

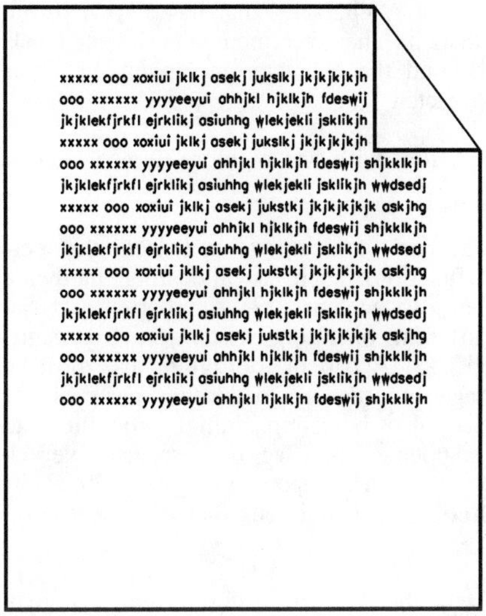

Figure 80. Justified Text

adjusted, with zeros in the unused high-order positions.

jump (1) A departure from the sequential execution of instructions. (T)   (2) See conditional jump, unconditional jump.

jumper Synonym for jumper cable.

jumper cable A metallic wire or optical cable that provides physical attachment between two devices or between a device and a distribution panel. Synonymous with jumper. Contrast with trunk cable.

jump cut In video or film production, an unnatural or jarring edit that may be deliberately created for effect but more often results from unintentional shifts in camera angle, frame size, or movement of a subject.

jump instruction (1) An instruction that specifies a jump. (I) (A)   (2) See conditional jump instruction, unconditional jump instruction.

junctor A device that links two halfpaths in a switching network.

justification (1) Synonym for flush. (T)   (2) The act of adjusting, arranging, or shifting characters to the left or right to fit a prescribed pattern. (3) See horizontal justification, vertical justification.   See Figure 80.

justify (1) In text processing, to align text horizontally so that the first and last character of every line are aligned with their corresponding margins or to align text vertically so that the first and last line of the text are aligned with their corresponding margins. The last line of a paragraph is often not justified. (T)   (2) To shift the contents of a register or field so that the significant character at the specified end of the data is at a specific position. (T) (3) To align characters horizontally or vertically to fit the positioning constraints of a required format. (A) (4) To align text or graphics at both margins.   See also left-align, right-align.

justify to the left Deprecated term for left-align.

justify to the right Deprecated term for right-align.

K

K (1) When referring to storage capacity, two to the tenth power, 1024 in decimal notation. (A) (2) Kelvin.

k An abbreviation for the prefix kilo; 1000 in decimal notation. (A)

Ki. Impulsive noise correction.

kanji (1) A graphic character set consisting of symbols used in Japanese ideographic alphabets. Each character is represented by 2 bytes. (2) See also extended graphic character set, hiragana, katakana.

kanji character A single character in the kanji ideographic character set.

kanji character set Synonym for extended graphic character set (EGCS).

Karnaugh map A rectangular diagram of a logic function of variables drawn with overlapping sub-rectangles such that each intersection of overlapping rectangles represents a unique combination of the logic variables and an intersection is shown for all combinations. (I) (A)

katakana A character set of symbols used in one of the two common Japanese phonetic alphabets, which is used primarily to write foreign words phonetically. See also hiragana, kanji.

Kb Kilobit; 1024 bits.

KB Kilobyte; 1024 bytes.

KD Cryptographic data key. Synonym for data key.

keep In a source document, a collection of lines of text to be printed in the same column. When the vertical space remaining in the current column is insufficient for the block of text, the text is printed in the next column. In the case of single-column format, the next column is on the next page.

keeper Synonym for buy.

kerned character A character that has a total image size greater than its character increment. Toned pels can extend beyond the character increment on either side of the character.

kerned font A font with one or more kerned characters.

kernel (1) The part of an operating system that performs basic functions such as allocating hardware resources. See also nucleus. (2) A program that can run under different operating system environments. See also shell. (3) A part of a program that must be in main storage in order to load other parts of the program. See also bootstrap, initial program load (IPL), root segment. (4) See also security kernel. (5) The part of the AIX operating system for RISC System/6000 containing functions that are needed frequently.

kernel dump In the AIX operating system, synonym for system dump.

kernel mode In the AIX operating system, the state in which a process runs in kernel mode. Contrast with user mode.

kernel parameter In the AIX operating system, a variable that specifies how the kernel allocates certain system resources. Synonymous with system parameter.

kerning (1) Reduction of the space between two adjacent characters; for example, overlapping character boxes to print or display cursive writing. (T) (2) The design of graphic characters so that their character boxes overlap. The toned picture elements (pels) of the character appear outside the character cell.

Note: Kerning allows character boxes to overlap and characters to run together, so that characters can be designed for cursive languages, ligatures, or any other kind of character that requires more than one character box. It also allows for design of proportional-spaced fonts. By overlapping character boxes, characters can be placed closer together, or they can be placed farther apart by using overlapped blank character boxes. See Figure 81.

Without Kerning   With Kerning

Figure 81. Kerning

key (1) An identifier within a set of data elements. (T) (2) One or more characters used to identify the record and establish the order of the record within an indexed file. (3) In VSAM, one or more consecutive characters taken from a data record, used to identify the record and establish its order with respect to other records. See also alternate key, key field. (4) In ACF/TCAM, a character string that matches a definition in the key table. This key identifies the destination of a message or special processing to be done on that message. See also key table. (5) To enter information from a keyboard. (6) In sorting, synonym for control word. (7) In computer security, a sequence of symbols used with a cryptographic algorithm for encrypting or decrypting data. See key-encrypting key, key-exchange key, master key, private key, public key. (8) The value used to identify a record in a keyed sequence file. (9) In SQL, a column or an ordered collection of columns identified in the description of an index. (10) In COBOL, a data item that identifies the location of a record, or a set of data items that serve to identify the ordering of data.

key authentication code A key test pattern.

keyboard (1) An arrangement of typing and function keys laid out in a specified manner. (T) (2) A systematic arrangement of keys by which a machine is operated or by which data are entered. (3) A device used to encode data by key depression, which causes generation of the selected code element. (4) A group of numeric keys, alphabetic keys, or function keys used for entering information into a terminal and into the system. (5) See also AZERTY, DVORAK, QWERTY. See Figure 82.

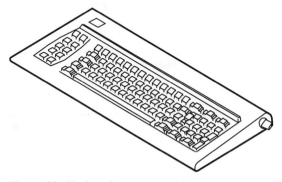

Figure 82. Keyboard

keyboard grabbing In the AIX Enhanced X-Windows program, the process by which a client can actively take control of the keyboard; key events are sent to that client, rather than the client to which the events would normally be sent. See also active grab, button grabbing, key grabbing, passive grab, pointer grabbing, server grabbing.

keyboard mapping A list, usually in a profile, that established correspondence between each key on the keyboard and the character displayed on a display screen, or an action taken by a program, when that key is pressed.

keyboard number An identification number that appears on certain keyboards that are used outside of the United States to help the user identify the keyboard layout.

keyboard overlay A template placed on a keyboard to explain the function of each key for a particular application program or for a keyboard program.

keyboard program Personal computer application software that changes key functions; for example, from a QWERTY layout to an AZERTY layout.

keyboard punch Synonym for keypunch.

keyboard send/receive (KSR) A combination teletypewriter transmitter and receiver with transmission capability from keyboard only.

keyboard send-receive (KSR) mode In the AIX operating system, a mode in which a virtual terminal emulates a standard ASCII terminal during input and output operations.

keyboard shift In AS/400 Data Description Specifications (DDS), a characteristic that can be specified for a field in a display file that automatically shifts the display station keyboard to control what the display station user can enter into the field. In the interactive data definition utility (IDDU) and (DDS) the keyboard shift can also be specified in database files, but only applies when these fields are referred to in a display file.

keyboard type The physical key arrangement and assignments for a keyboard.

key click Transient pulses or surges on a transmission line set up by the opening or closing of keying circuit contacts.

key-click filter A filter that attenuates key clicks.

key component (1) In cryptography, one of at least two characters having the format of a cryptographic key that is exclusive-ORed with one or more like parameters to form a cryptographic key. (2) In cryptography, any one of a combination of elements that make up a cryptographic key.

key compression The elimination of characters from the front and back of a key that VSAM does not need to distinguish the key from the preceding or following key in an index record. Key compression reduces storage space for an index.

keyed access In FORTRAN, a file access method allowing reading and writing of records in an arbitrary order by key. Contrast with direct access, sequential access.

keyed direct access In VSAM, retrieval or storage of a data record by use of either an index that relates the record's key to its relative location in the file, or data set, or a relative-record number, independent of the record's location relative to the previously retrieved or stored record. See also addressed direct access, addressed sequential access, keyed sequential access.

keyed file In PSS, an indirectly addressable file, designed to provide rapid access to logical records that reside on a direct access storage device. See also randomizing.

keyed sequence The order in which records appear in an access path. The access path is based on the contents of one or more key fields contained in the records.

keyed sequence access path An access path to a database file that is ordered according to the contents of key fields contained in the individual records. See also access path, arrival sequence access path.

keyed sequential access In VSAM, the retrieval or storage of a data record in its key or relative-record sequence, relative to the previously retrieved or stored record as defined by the sequence set of an index. See also addressed direct access, addressed sequential access, keyed direct access.

key-encrypting key In computer security, a key used for encryption and decryption of other keys.

key-entry (1) Pertaining to the input of data manually by means of a keyboard. (2) The process of loading cryptographic keys.

key-exchange key In computer security, a key used for encrypted transmission of keys.

key field (1) In VSAM, a field, located in the same position in each record of a file or data set, whose content is used for the key of a record. (2) In IMS/VS, the field in a database segment used to store segment occurrences in sequential ascending order. A key field is also a search field. Synonymous with sequence field. (3) A field in a record whose contents are used to sequence records of a particular type within a file member. See Figure 83.

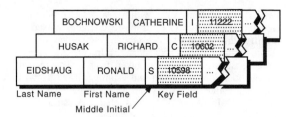

Figure 83. Key Field

key field level specifications In the AS/400 system and System/38, data description specifications coded on the lines following the last field specification. Key field level specifications are permitted only for physical files or logical files. See also field level specifications, file level specifications, help level specifications, join level specifications, record level specifications, select/omit level specifications.

key folding Synonym for hashing *(1)*.

key frames In multimedia applications, the start and end frames of a single movement in an animation sequence; the term also refers to the periodic full-frame image interspersed in the stream to allow random starts from these full-frame images (key frames).

key generator A device that generates cryptographic keys and, where needed, initialization vectors.

key grabbing In the AIX Enhanced X-Windows program, passive grabbing of keys on a keyboard by a client. See button grabbing, keyboard grabbing, pointer grabbing, server grabbing. See also active grab, passive grab.

key in To enter information by means of a keyboard.

keying The forming of signals, such as those employed in telegraph transmission, by the interruption of a direct current or modulation of a carrier between discrete values of some characteristics.

keying chirps Sounds accompanying code signals when a transmitter is unstable and shifts slightly in frequency each time the sending key is closed.

keying relationship In cryptography security, the state that exists between a communicating pair during which they share at least one data key or key encrypting key.

keying wave In telegraph communication, an emission that occurs while the information portions of the code characters are being transmitted. Synonymous with marking wave.

key light In video or film production, a source of light used to provide the primary illumination of a subject or area, usually with greater intensity than that provided with fill light.

key loader In cryptography, a self-contained electronic unit that can store at least one key and transfer that key into cryptographic equipment.

key lock On a keyboard, a device that prevents keys from being actuated. (T)

keylock feature (1) A security feature consisting of a lock and key that can be used to restrict the use of a workstation. (2) In the IBM 8100 Information System, a processor feature that prevents unauthorized system access by means of a three-position, key-operated switch.

keylock switch A switch on a control panel that can be set to one of four different positions to establish the allowable power-on and power-off modes for the system.

key management The generation, storage, secure distribution, and application, of keys in accordance with a security policy.

key management facility A physically protected enclosure such as a device or a room where cryptographic elements such as cryptographic hardware and software reside and where key management processes take place.

keymat A prepunched plastic, user-labeled sheet that fits over a keyboard for key identification.

key matching The technique of comparing the keys of two or more records to select items for a particular stage of processing or to reject invalid records. (T)

key of reference In COBOL, the key, either a prime record key or an alternate record key, currently being used to access records within an indexed file.

key pad A grouping of keys on a keyboard, such as a numeric key pad and a cursor key pad.

keypad (1) A 50-key device used in place of a keyboard to interact with the ImagePlus Workstation Program in the MVS/ESA environment. (2) A small, often hand-held, keyboard.

key pulse Synonym for push button dialing.

keypunch A keyboard-actuated punch that punches holes in a data medium. (I) Synonymous with keyboard punch.

key range In VSAM, a particular key range, such as A-F, that is specifically associated with one or more control ranges of a data set.

key row On a typewriter, a row of keys on a keyboard. (T)

key sequence In VSAM, the collating sequence of data records as determined by the value of the key field in each of the data records. The key entry may be the same as, or different from, the entry sequence of the records.

key-sequenced data set (KSDS) A VSAM file or data set whose records are loaded in key sequence and controlled by an index. The NetView Performance Monitor (NPM) uses this type of file for the session statistics file and the network review file. See Figure 84.

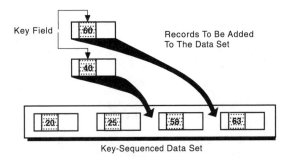

Figure 84. Key-Sequenced Data Set

key-set tabulator On a typewriter, a tabulator stop that is set and released in the required position by means of a tabulator set key usually on the keyboard. (T)

Keys help In SAA Common User Access architecture, a help action that provides a listing of the application keys and their assigned functions.

key stroke Actuation of a key to perform or release a machine function. (T) See alternate key stroke, repeat key stroke, single key stroke, typematic key stroke.

keystroke counter In text processing, a device that counts the number of key actuations. (A)

key stroke verification The verification of the accuracy of a data entry by the reentry of the same data through a keyboard. (T)

key system In telephony, the type of telephone system that provides telephones with more than one line for users. Outside lines appear directly on the telephones instead of being routed through an operator and transferred, as in private branch exchange (PBX) systems.

key table (1) A table of keys and their definitions, which contain information on routing and special processing to be performed on a message. See also key. (2) In ACF/TCAM extended networking, a main storage table that associates each key defined for a message control program with a resource defined in its host node or with a node identifier and a transmission category for a resource defined in another host node. Key table entries for stations, logical units (LUs), and applications located in another host node are dynamically filled in by means of the internodal awareness SSP in the other host node when the host node is available to the extended network.

key touch selector On a typewriter, a control for varying the force required to depress the keys on the keyboard. (T)

key transformation A function that maps a set of keys into a set of integers, which can be handled arithmetically to determine the location of the corresponding data elements. (A)

keyword (1) In programming languages, a lexical unit that, in certain contexts, characterizes some language construct; for example, in some contexts, IF characterizes an if-statement. A keyword normally has the form of an identifier. (I) (2) One of the predefined words of an artificial language. (A) (3) A significant and informative word in a title or document that describes the content of that document. (4) A name or symbol that identifies a parameter. (5) Part of a command operand that consists of a specific character string, such as DSNAME=. (6) In AS/400 Data Description Specifications (DDS) a name that identifies a function. (7) In AS/400 query management, one of the predefined words associated with a query command. (8) In PL/I, an identifier used with related material that takes on a specific meaning, such as an action to be taken or the characteristics of data. (9) In SQL, a name that identifies a parameter used in an SQL statement or SQL precompiler command. See also parameter. (10) In COBOL, a reserved word whose presence is required when the format in which the word appears is used in a source program. (11) In FORTRAN, a statement keyword or an argument keyword. (12) Deprecated term for reserved word. (13) Synonym for password. (14) Synonym for descriptor.

keyword functions In AS/400 Data Description Specifications (DDS), the result of processing DDS keywords in a record format specified for an operation.

keyword operand An operand that consists of a keyword followed by one or more values, such as DSNAME=HELLO. Contrast with positional operand. See also definition statement.

keyword parameter A parameter that consists of a keyword, followed by one or more values. See also positional parameter.

keyword statement In PL/I, a simple statement that begins with a keyword indicating the function of the statement.

kg Kilogram.

KG-KL and KQ-KY indicators See command key indicator *(2)*.

kilobyte (KB) 1024 bytes.

kilogram (kg) One thousand grams; 2.2046 pounds.

kilo (k) (1) Thousand. (2) Kilogram.

kilometer (km) One thousand meters; 0.62 mile.

kiosk A stand-alone information delivery system often used for shopping directories and to provide other interactive information and sales presentations.

KK Key encrypting key.

km Kilometer.

knapsack See public-key cryptography.

knowledge In artificial intelligence, the facts, events, inference rules and heuristics needed by a computer program in order to operate intelligently. (T)

knowledge base In artificial intelligence, a database that contains information about human experience in a particular field of knowledge and data resulting from solution of problems that have been previously encountered. See also expert system. (T) (A)

knowledge-based system Synonym for expert system.

knowledge engineer In artificial intelligence, a person who extracts knowledge from a domain expert and organizes it as a knowledge base for an expert system. (T)

knowledge engineering The branch of computer science that pertains to the design and development of expert systems.

knowledge source In artificial intelligence, the source of information from which a knowledge base has been created for a specific type of problem. (T)

knowledge system Synonym for expert system. (T)

Korean double-byte character set An IBM-defined double-byte character set (DBCS) for Korean, consisting of Korean non-Hangeul/non-Hanja set, Hangeul set, Hanja set and up to 1880 user-definable characters.

Korean Hangeul character set A subset of the Korean DBCS, consisting of 2672 Hangeul characters and 52 Jamo characters.

Korean Hanja character set A subset of the Korean double-byte character set (DBCS), consisting of 5265 Hanja characters.

Korean non-Hangeul/non-Hanja character set A subset of the Korean double-byte characters set (DBCS), consisting of non-Hangeul/non-Hanja characters, such as Greek, Russian, Roman numeric, alphanumeric and related symbols, Katakana, Hiragana, and special symbols. There are 940 characters in this set.

KSDS Key-sequenced data set.

KSR Keyboard send/receive.

kVA Kilovolt ampere. A unit of power.

KWIC Keyword in context.

KWOC Keyword out of context.

L

L Liter.

label (1) In programming languages, a language construction naming a statement and including an identifier. (I)   (2) An identifier within or attached to a set of data elements. (T)   (3) A record that identifies a volume on tape, disk, or diskette or that identifies a file on the volume. (4) An identifier of a command generally used for branching. (5) In BASIC, a name that identifies a BASIC program line. (6) In PL/I, an identifier that names a statement so that it can be referred to at some other point in the program. (7) In RPG, a symbolic name that represents a specific location in a program. A label can serve as the destination point for one or more branching operations. (8) In SQL, a way of describing columns instead of, or in addition to, the table or column name. (9) See beginning-of-volume label, end-of-file label, end-of-volume label, external label, header label, internal label. (10) See also entry name, file name, magnetic tape label, name, symbol. (11) See sensitivity label. (12) Synonymous with tag.

label area Synonym for label information area.

label constant In PL/I, a name written as the label of any statement other than PROCEDURE. Contrast with label variable.

label format record In PSS, a record that defines the size of a shelf label, position and length of each field on the label, and font of each character to be printed in each field.

label information area In VSE, an area on a direct access storage device that stores label information read from job control statements or commands. Synonymous with label area.

label prefix See label.

label variable In PL/I, an identifier that contains the label of a statement so that the statement can be referred to at some other point in the program.

laced card A card punched accidentally or intentionally with holes in excess of the hole patterns of the character set used. (A)

LADN Library-assigned document name.

lag Synonym for image retention.

lag (1) The delay between two events. (A) (2) Synonym for image retention.

LAN Local area network.

LAN broadcast Sending of a transmission frame that is intended to be accepted by all other data stations on the same local area network. (T)

LAN broadcast address An address that identifies the set of data stations on a local area network. Synonymous with LAN global address. (T)

land In optical recording, an area between two pits, typically not touched by the recording laser beam during mastering. See also pit.

landing pad In videodisc systems, a range of frames within which a player can locate a frame or frame sequence from other parts of the disc.

landing zone An area on a disk where the read/write head comes to rest when the disk stops rotating. Synonymous with takeoff zone. See also loading zone, Winchester.

Note: The landing zone is used to prevent damage to the magnetizable surface of the disk and loss of data that could result from contact between the head and an area of the disk where data is recorded (a head crash).

landline facilities Facilities of communication common carriers that are within the continental United States.

landscape (1) The arrangement of text on a page so that it is oriented for normal reading when its width is greater than its length. Synonym for landscape format, horizontal format. (T)   (2) Pertaining to a display or hard copy with greater width than height. Contrast with portrait.

landscape format Synonymous with landscape. (T)

landscape left A page orientation such that the left side of the printed image is at the trailing edge of the paper as it emerges from the printer.

landscape page In desktop publishing, a page that is designed and printed in such a way that it must be turned 90 degrees in order to be read. Contrast with portrait page. Synonymous with turn page.

landscape right A page orientation such that the right side of the printed image is at the trailing edge of the paper as it emerges from the printer.

LAN gateway (1) A functional unit that interconnects a local area network with another network using different protocols. The network may be another local area network, a public data network, or another network. (T)   (2) See also bridge, gateway, relay, SNA network interconnect. (3) See figure at backbone.

LAN global address Synonym for LAN broadcast address. (T)

LAN group address An address that identifies a group of data stations on a local area network. (T)

language A set of characters, conventions, and rules that is used for conveying information. (I)   (A)

language construct In a programming language, a syntactically allowable program or subroutine that may be constructed in accordance with the set of rules that make up the grammar of the language.

language-name In COBOL, a system-name that specifies a particular programming language.

language preprocessor A functional unit that effects preparatory processing of computer programs;   for example, a macrogenerator may function as a preprocessor of a translator. (T)

language processor A functional unit for translating and executing computer programs written in a specified programming language;   for example, a LISP machine. (T)

language shift In a multishift keyboard, a shift that takes the user from one language to another.   For example, the language shift is used to switch between Hebrew and English when entering mixed text.

language statement A statement coded by a programmer, operator, or other user of a computing system to convey information to a processing program, such as a language translator or service program, or to the control program.   A language statement may request that an operation be performed or may contain data to be passed to the processing program.

language subset A part of a language that can be used independently of the rest of the language.

language translation feature See National Requirements feature.

language translator A general term for any assembler, compiler, or other routine that accepts statements in one language and produces equivalent statements in another language.

LAN individual address An address that identifies a particular data station on a local area network. (T)

LAN multicast Sending of a transmission frame that is intended to be accepted by a group of selected data stations on the same local area network. (T)

LAN server A data station that provides services to other data stations on a local area network;   for example, file server, print server, mail server. (T)

LAP Link access procedure.

LAPB Link access protocol-balanced.

lapel mike Synonym for lavalier.

laptop computer (1) A portable computer small enough to be operated on a desk top or in one's lap. (T)   (2) A portable personal computer, usually weighing 15 pounds or less, that can run on battery power and that can be used in such places as hotel rooms and airliners. Laptop computers are equipped with a keyboard and a display such as a liquid crystal display (LCD).

large scale integration (LSI) The process of integrating large numbers of circuits on a single chip of semiconductor material.

laser Light amplification by stimulated emission of radiation.   In the 3800 Printing Subsystem, a device that emits a beam of coherent light that forms the image on the photoconductor that is subsequently transferred to the paper.

laser beam printer Synonym for laser printer. (T)

laser beam sweep In a laser printer, the action of a laser beam moving from left to right across a photoconductor.

laser printer (1) A nonimpact printer that creates, by means of a laser beam directed on a photosensitive surface, a latent image which is then made visible by a toner and transferred and fixed on paper. Synonymous with laser beam printer. (T)   (2) A nonimpact printer that creates latent images by directing a laser beam onto a photoconductive printing medium. Toner particles, attracted to the energized latent image, make the image visible.

laser print head In a laser printer, a subassembly that emits a modulated beam of coherent light that is scanned across the photoconductor to form an electrostatic image.

laser scanning power In a laser printer, the level of power of a laser beam, expressed in milliwatts.

last-in-chain (LIC) A request unit (RU) whose request header (RH) end chain indicator is on and whose RH begin chain indicator is off. See also RU chain.

last-in-first-out (LIFO) A queuing technique in which the next item to be retrieved is the item most recently placed in the queue. (A)

last priority level In the IBM 8100 Information System, the number of the most recent priority level that was active before dispatching the current program status vector.

last record indicator In RPG, an indicator that signals when the last record (LR) is processed. This indicator can then be used to condition calculation and output operations that are to be done at the end of the program.

latch (1) A bistable circuit that is set and reset by appropriate input signals. (T) See Figure 85. (2) In IMS/VS, a programming device that provides short-term serialization for IMS/VS tasks running in the online IMS/VS system. An IMS/VS latch is similar in function to an OS/VS lock. (3) An electronic circuit that records the status of a signal until it is reset.

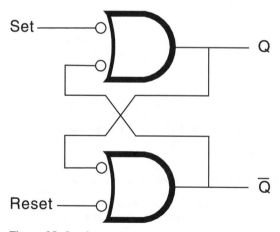

Figure 85. Latch

latch-down key On a typewriter, a control that, when operated, is maintained in its position until it is released. (T)

latch-out tabulator key On a typewriter, a tabulator key that can be released before the tabulator stop position has been reached without affecting operation of the stop. (T) Synonymous with touch tabulator key.

latency (1) The time interval between the instant at which an instruction control unit initiates a call for data and the instant at which the actual transfer of the data starts. Synonymous with waiting time. See Figure 3. (T) (2) The time required for the light emitted from the phosphor on a display screen to decay after the excitation is removed. Long-persistence phosphors create less flicker of still images, but more blurring of moving images. (3) See also ring latency.

latent image In a document copying machine, the invisible image that exists in the sensitized material after exposure but before development. (T)

lateral redundancy check Synonym for transverse redundancy check.

Latin font Synonym for single-byte coded font.

lattice See computer security model.

lavalier A small microphone usually worn on the lapel. Synonymous with lapel mike.

layback In video production, the process used by a production facility of combining dialog or sound with a score.

layer (1) In network architecture, a group of services that is complete from a conceptual point of view, that is one out of a set of hierarchically arranged groups, and that extends across all systems that conform to the network architecture. (T) See application layer, data link layer, network layer, physical layer, presentation layer, session layer, transport layer. (2) In the Open Systems Interconnection reference model, one of seven conceptually complete, hierarchically arranged groups of services, functions, and protocols, that extend across all open systems. (T) (3) In SNA, a grouping of related functions that are logically separate from the functions in other layers. Implementation of the functions in one layer can be changed without affecting functions in other layers. See data flow control layer, data link control layer, path control layer, physical control layer, presentation services layer, transaction services layer, transmission control layer. (4) For local area networks, see logical link control (LLC) sublayer, medium access control (MAC) sublayer. (5) In DPPX, a predefined subset of modules or programs having related functions that can be replaced or modified without affecting other layers.

layering In music or sound production, the technique of combining many sound generators to create a richer sound.

layer management Functions, such as activation and error control, related to the management of a specific layer partly performed in the layer itself, according to the protocol of that layer, and partly performed as a subset of systems management. (T)

layout (1) The arrangement of matter to be printed or displayed. See also format. (2) In the AIX Enhanced X-Windows program, the size and position of a window on the screen. The size of a widget is changed by using geometry management routines. Synonymous with geometry. (3) See file layout, record layout.

layout character Synonym for format effector.

LBG Load balancing group.

LCB Local block common.

LCC Link connection component.

LCCM Link connection component manager.

LCD (1) Liquid crystal display. (2) Line control definer.

LCH Logical channel queue.

LCID Local character set identifier.

LCS Link connection subsystem.

LCSM Link connection subsystem manager.

LCT Level control table.

LCU The IBM 3842 or 3843 Loop Control Unit.

LDA Logical device address.

LDNCB Local device node control block.

LDO Logical device order.

LE Less than or equal to. See also relational operator.

leader (1) The portion of magnetic tape that precedes the beginning-of-tape marker that is used to thread the tape. (T) (2) The blank section of tape at the beginning of a reel of tape. (A) (3) In text formatting: (a) Dots or hyphens used to lead the eye horizontally, as in a table of contents. (b) The divider between text and footnotes on a page, usually a short line of dashes.

leading decision (1) A loop control executed before the loop body. (A) (2) Contrast with trailing decision.

leading edge The edge of a character box closest to the graphic character that appears to precede it on a sequential baseline.

leading end The end of a perforated tape that first enters a perforated-tape reader. (A)

leading graphics From one to seven graphic characters that may accompany an acknowledgment sent to or from a BSC terminal in response to receipt of a block of data.

leading zero (1) In positional notation, a zero in a more significant digit place than the digit place of the most significant nonzero digit of a numeral. (A) (2) A zero, used as a fill character, that appears as the leftmost significant digit in a numeric value displayed on a human readable medium.

lead-in tape On a videodisc, the 40 seconds of video black that precede a program.

lead-out tape On a videodisc, the minimum of 30 seconds of video black that follow a program.

leaf A blank or printed sheet of paper in a document, each side of which is a page.

leapfrog test A check routine that copies itself through storage. (A)

learning See machine learning.

leased line Synonym for nonswitched line.

least privilege In computer security, the principle that requires that each subject be granted the most restrictive set of privileges needed for the performance of authorized functions.

Note: Restriction of privilege limits damage due to accident, error, or malice.

least recently used In MSS, an algorithm that determines the order in which active staged pages must be destaged. The algorithm ensures that the staging drive group always has the amount of allocatable space defined by the space manager.

least significant digit (LSD) In a positional representation system, a digit place having the smallest weight used. (T)

least-weight route In APPN, the one route calculated by topology and routing services (TRS) to have the lowest total weight after TRS compares the node characteristics and TG characteristics of each intermediate node and intermediate TG of each possible route for the class-of-service requested, and computes the total combined weight for nodes and TGs in each route.

After a least-weight route is calculated between two given nodes, the result may be stored to prevent repetition of this calculation in future route selections.

leaves In the AIX operating system, widgets on a widget tree that have no children.

LED Light-emitting diode. See Figure 86.

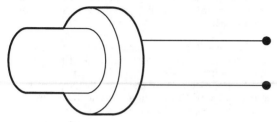

Figure 86. LED

Left In SAA Basic Common User Access architecture, an action that shows the information that precedes the visible information in a panel.

left-adjust Synonym for left-align. (A)

left-adjusted Synonym for left-aligned. (T)

left-align (1) To control the display or printing position of characters on a page so that the left-hand margin of the printing or display is regular. (A) (2) To move the leftmost character of one or more items to a given position. Synonymous with left-adjust. Contrast with right-align. See also justify.

left-aligned Pertaining to text that is aligned to the left margin but need not be aligned to the right margin. (T) Synonymous with left-adjusted, flush left. Contrast with right-aligned.

left-hand margin indent In word processing, a feature that enables blocks of recorded text to be indented with different left-hand margins, irrespective of amendments made to the text and while still retaining the original, fixed, left-hand margin settings. (T)

left-hand margin stop A device limiting the length of the writing line on the left side of the paper. (T) See also right-hand margin stop.

left-hand side The set of facts or statements in the "if" part of an if-then rule. (T) Contrast with right-hand side.

left-justified Deprecated term for left-aligned. (T)

left-justify Deprecated term for left-align.

left margin The area between the left edge of the display or paper and the leftmost character position.

legend In computer graphics, an explanatory list of the symbols, lines, and other components of a display image.

LEN Low-entry networking.

LEN connection A link over which LEN protocols are used.

LEN end node See low-entry networking (LEN) end node.

length (1) In FORTRAN, the number of characters in a character string. (2) See block length, page length, record length, word length.

LEN node A node that supports independent LU protocols but does not support CP-CP sessions. It may be a peripheral node attached to a boundary node in a subarea network, an end node attached to an APPN network node in an APPN network, or a peer-connected node directly attached to another LEN node or APPN end node. See also low-entry networking (LEN) end node.

LERAD exit routine A synchronous EXLST exit routine that is entered automatically when a logic error is detected.

letter (1) A graphic character that, when used alone or combined with others, primarily represents, in a written language, one or more concepts or sound elements of a spoken language. (T) Letters do not include diacritical marks used alone or punctuation marks. (2) A graphic character that, when used alone or combined with others, primarily represents one or more concepts of a written language or one or more sound elements of a spoken language. Diacritical marks used alone and punctuation marks are not considered to be letters. (A) (3) An uppercase or lowercase character from the set A through Z. (4) In COBOL, a character belonging to one of the following two sets: (a) uppercase letters: A, B, C, D, E, F, G, H, I, J, K, L, M, N, O, P, Q, R, S, T, U, V, W, X, Y, Z. (b) lowercase letters: a, b, c, d, e, f, g, h, i, j, k, l, m, n, o, p, q, r, s, t, u, v, w, x, y, z.

letter quality Print quality of text that is suitable for business correspondence and that matches the quality of an office electric typewriter. (T)

letter-quality printer A printer that produces text that cannot be distinguished from text produced by an electric typewriter. (A)

letter row On a keyboard, a row that contains mainly letter keys in a specified sequence. See lower letter row, middle letter row, upper letter row. See also numeral row.

letters shift (LTRS) (1) A physical shift in a teletypewriter that enables the printing of alphabetic characters. (2) The name of the character that causes this shift. (3) See also figures shift.

level (1) The degree of subordination of an item in a hierarchic arrangement. (I) (A) (2) In a hierarchical database, the successive vertical dependencies of records or segments. (3) The version of a program. (4) In acoustics, the logarithm of the ratio of a given quantity to a reference quantity of the same kind. The base of the logarithm, usually 10, the reference quantity, and the kind of level must be indicated. See A-weighted impulse sound pressure level, A-weighted level, A-weighted peak sound pressure level, band level, noise level, noise power emission level, sound power level, sound pressure level, spectrum level. See also sound level meter. (5) See control break level, link level, packet level, physical level. (6) See modification level. (7) See security level.

level checking A function that compares the record level identifiers of a file to be opened with the file description that is part of a compiled program to determine if the record format for the file changed since the program was compiled.

level compensator An automatic gain control device used in the receiving equipment of a telegraph circuit.

level control table (LCT) In DPPX, a control block that contains information about the priority level to which it is assigned. There is an LCT for each priority level. All threads associated with a priority level are chained from that level's LCT.

level indicator (1) In COBOL, two alphabetic characters that identify a specific type of file or a position in a hierarchy. The level indicators in the Data Division are: CD, FD, RD, and SD. (2) In RPG, two characters (L0 through L9 and LR) that control calculation and output processing during total time.

level-number (1) A reference number that indicates the position of an item in a hierarchic arrangement. (I) (A) Synonymous with rank. (2) In the index of a VSAM key-sequenced data set, a binary number in the header of an index record that indicates the index level to which the record belongs. (3) In COBOL, a user-defined word, expressed as a one or two-digit number, that indicates the hierarchical position of a data item or the special properties of a data description entry.

Note: Level-numbers in the range 1 through 9 may be written either as a single digit or as a zero followed

by a significant digit. Level-numbers 66, 77, and 88 identify special properties of a data description entry.

level of access See access level, logical access level.

level one videodisc applications Interactive multimedia applications based on manual keypad functions, picture stops, and chapter stops.

level-sensitive scan design (LSSD) A technology that uses trigger-latch combinations that operate: (1) as logical devices in data flow or control circuitry, for example, a register or a control latch, and (2) as shift register latches that enable the hardware to be initialized or read by a serial scanning technique.

Levels of Interactive Systems Three degrees of videodisc system interactivity proposed by the Nebraska Videodisc Design/Production Group in 1980:

Level One system Usually a consumer-model videodisc player with still/freeze frame, picture stop, chapter stop, frame address, and dual-channel audio, but with limited memory and limited processing power.

Level Two system An industrial-model videodisc player with the capabilities of Level One, plus on-board programmable memory and improved access time.

Level Three system Level One or Two players interfaced to an external computer and/or other peripheral processing devices.

level three videodisc applications Interactive multimedia applications controlled by an external computer that uses the videodisc player as a peripheral device.

level two videodisc applications Interactive multimedia applications controlled by the keypad and the internal computer of a videodisc player. The control program is recorded on the videodisc itself.

level-zero entry In RPG, a calculation specifications entry that indicates the operations to be done during total time for each program cycle when no control break occurs.

level 0 volume A primary volume or a volume not managed by the Data Facility Hierarchical Storage Manager.

level 1 data flow In ACF/TCAM, a data flow within a single-domain network in which the origin and destination logical units (LUs) of each message reside in the same domain.

level 1 volume A volume owned by the Data Facility Hierarchical Storage Manager containing data sets that migrated from a level 0 volume.

level 2 data flow In ACF/TCAM, a data flow on an extended route in which each message enters the TCAM node that provides queuing for the originating resource, another TCAM node that provides queuing for the destination resource, and one or more intermediate TCAM nodes.

level 2+ data flow In ACF/TCAM, a data flow on an extended route in which each message enters both the TCAM node that provides queuing for the originating resource and another TCAM node that provides queuing for the destination resource, but does not pass through any intermediate TCAM nodes.

level 2 volume A volume under control of the Data Facility Hierarchical Storage Manager, containing data sets that migrated from a level 0 or level 1 volume.

level 3 data flow In ACF/TCAM, a data flow within a multiple-domain network in which the origin and destination logical units of each message (LUs) reside in different domains.

lexical analyzer A program that analyzes input and breaks it into categories, such as numbers, letters, or operators.

lexical level The depth to which routines are nested within one another, which determines the scope of the identifiers declared within those routines.

lexical object In a conceptual schema language, a simple linguistic object that expresses an elemental unit of meaning. (A)

lexical scope In Pascal, the portion of a program or segment unit in which a declaration applies. An identifier declared in a routine is known within that routine and within all nested routines. If a nested routine declares an item with the same name, the outer item is not available in the nested routine.

lexical token Synonym for lexical unit.

lexical unit (1) In programming languages, a language construct that by convention represents an elemental unit of meaning; for example, a literal such as "2G5," a keyword such as PRINT, a separator such as a semicolon. (I) (2) Synonymous with lexical token.

LF The line feed character. (A)

LFSID Local-form session identifier.

LFSM Link function state machine.

LGN Logical group number.

libname Library name.

librarian In VSE, the set of programs that maintains, services, and organizes the system and private libraries.

library (1) A file or a set of related files; for example, in stock control, a set of inventory control files. (A) (2) A repository for demountable recorded media, such as magnetic disk packs and magnetic tapes. (A) (3) A collection of functions, calls, subroutines, or other data. (4) A data file that contains files and control information that allows them to be accessed individually. (5) A named area on disk that can contain programs and related information (not files). A library consists of different sections, called library members. (6) In VSE, a collection of data stored in sublibraries on disk. A library consists of at least one sublibrary in which data is stored as members of various types such as phase, object module, or source book. (7) In OS/VS, any partitioned data set. (8) In the AS/400 system and System/38, a system object that serves as a directory to other objects. A library groups related objects, and allows the user to find objects by name. Compare with document library, folder. (9) The set of publications for a product. (10) See C library, data library, Graphics Support Library. job library, link library, private library, production library, program library, test library.

library-assigned document name (LADN) In the AS/400 system, a unique name, which includes a time stamp and a system name, that is assigned by a system in the office network to a document when it is filed in the document library. The time-stamp part of the library-assigned document name is included in a 10-character name that becomes the document object name. See also document name, document object name.

library block In VSE, a block of data stored in a sublibrary.

library character set A named graphic character set stored in a host system library that can be specified for printing.

library control sector In a library directory, the first sector, which contains a record of used and available space in the library.

Library Control System In the Object Access Method, a component that writes and reads objects on optical disc storage, and manipulates the optical volumes on which the objects reside.

library descriptions file In the AS/400 system, a file that lists keywords, document classes, and access codes associated with different document libraries.

library directory (1) In a library, an area that contains information about each member in the library; for example, the member name and the location. (2) In VSE, an index that enables the system to locate a certain sublibrary of the accessed library.

library list (1) An ordered list of library names used to find an object. The library list indicates which libraries are to be searched and the order in which they are to be searched. (2) In the AS/400 system, a list that indicates the libraries that are to be searched and the order in which they are to be searched.

library macrodefinition A macrodefinition stored in a program library; for example, the IBM-supplied supervisor and data management macrodefinitions. See also source macrodefinition.

library member (1) A named collection of records or statements in a library. (2) In VSE, the smallest unit of data that can be stored into and retrieved from a sublibrary.

library member subtype In System/36, a classification of a library member type; for example, a source member can be identified as a COBOL source member or a data file utility source member.

library migration table In VSE, a user-defined control block in virtual storage, used by the system as an aid to migrate from Version 1 of VSE.

library-name In COBOL, a user-defined word that names a COBOL library that is to be used by the compiler for a given source program compilation.

library object A named resource stored in a host library system.

library program A program in a program library. (T)

library routine A proven routine maintained in a program library. (A)

library text In COBOL, a sequence of text words, comment lines, the separator space, or the separator pseudo-text delimiter in a COBOL library.

library work area In DPPX, an area of storage used by FORTRAN library routines for temporary data and for communication among the routines.

LIC (1) Last-in-chain. (2) Licensed internal code (LIC). (3) Line interface coupler.

licensed application program A set of licensed programs used to perform a particular data processing task, such as distribution management or construction management.

licensed documentation See licensed publication.

Licensed Internal Code (LIC) (1) Microcode that IBM does not sell as part of a machine but licenses to the customer, as designated in the Supplement to Agreement for Purchase of IBM Machines. (2) Licensed Internal Code is implemented in a part of storage that is not addressable by user programs. It is used in a product to implement functions as an alternative to hard-wired circuitry. LIC is provided in accordance with the terms and conditions of the applicable written agreement between a customer and IBM. (3) See also model-unique licensed internal code, vertical licensed internal code.

Licensed Internal Code fix A temporary solution to, or bypass of, a defect in a current release of the licensed internal code. Contrast with program temporary fix (PTF).

licensed material The materials that IBM designates as being part of a license program offering and governed by the terms of the licensing agreement. Licensed material can include both basic and optional materials.

licensed optional materials Any licensed machine-readable or printed materials that IBM designates as being available to licensees of the program on request. These materials may or may not involve an additional fee.

licensed program (LP) A separately priced program and its associated materials that bear an IBM copyright and are offered to customers under the terms and conditions of either the Agreement for IBM Licensed Programs (ALP) or the IBM Program License Agreement (PLA). See also programming request for price quotation (PRPQ), program offering.

licensed publication A publication for a licensed program that contains licensed information and therefore is itself licensed.

life cycle See system life cycle.

life cycle phase A portion of the system life cycle of an information resource dictionary that is used as a basis for a logical partition of the information resource dictionary entities. (A)

lifetime In programming languages, the portion of execution time during which a language object exists. (I)

LIFO Last-in-first-out. A queuing technique in which the next item to be retrieved is the item most recently placed in the queue. (A)

lift-off point Location, plotted by a digitizer, where a pointing device is removed from a touch-sensitive surface.

ligature Two or more characters printed together so that they are connected.

light button Synonym for virtual push button.

lighted programmable function keyboard An input device, used primarily in graphic applications, that has lighted keys under control of an application program.

light-emitting diode (LED) A semiconductor chip that gives off visible or infrared light when activated. See also indicator light.

light-emitting diode display (1) A display in which characters are formed from a dot matrix of light-emitting diodes. (T) (2) A display device that creates characters by means of a dot matrix of light-emitting diodes. (A)

light gun Deprecated term for light pen.

light level In video or film production, the intensity of the light measured in footcandles.

light pen A light-sensitive pick device that is used by pointing it at the display surface. (I) (A) See Figure 87.

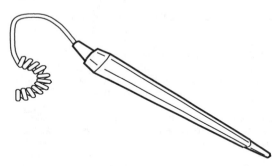

Figure 87. Light Pen

light-pen attention In computer graphics, an interruption generated by a light-pen detect that occurs on a display field that has a null or space designator character. The attention concludes the light-pen operation. Synonymous with selector pen attention.

light-pen detection (1) The sensing by a light pen of light generated by a display element on a display surface. (I) (A) (2) Synonymous with light-pen hit, light-pen strike.

Note: Light-pen detection can provide an interrupt.

light-pen hit Synonym for light-pen detection.

light-pen strike Synonym for light-pen detection.

light-pen tracking The process of tracing the movement of a light pen across the screen of a display device.

light stability In optical character recognition, the resistance to change of the color of the image when exposed to radiant energy. (A)

limit check A check to determine whether a value lies above, below, or at a stipulated limit. (T)

limit count In IMS/VS, the number that determines whether the normal or limit priority value is assigned to a transaction during the scheduling process. See also limit priority, normal priority.

limited broadcast In the IBM Token-Ring Network, the forwarding of specially designated broadcast frames only by bridges that are enabled to forward them. See also LAN multicast.

limited interface In the AIX operating system, a set of system calls that provides a limited function interface. See extended interface.

limited-resource link A link defined by the node operator to be a limited resource, that is, a resource to remain active only when being used. Limited-resource links are deactivated if no session activity has been detected for a specified period of time. See also limited resource session.

limited-resource session A session that traverses a limited-resource link. This session is terminated if no session activity is detected for a specified period of time.

limiter In analog computing, a functional unit used to prevent an analog variable from exceeding specified limits. (I) (A)

limit priority (1) In OS/VS2 and MVT, and in MFT with subtasking, a priority specification associated with every task in a multitask operation, representing the highest dispatching priority that the task may assign to itself or to any of its subtasks. (2) In IMS/VS, the priority to which a transaction is raised when the number of transactions enqueued and waiting to be processed is equal to or greater than the limit count value. See also limit count, normal priority.

limits file In RPG, a file that contains the upper and lower values of the record keys used to read from an indexed file.

limits record In RPG, a record that contains the lowest record key and the highest record key of the records that are to be read in the keyed file.

linage-counter In COBOL, a special register whose value points to the current position within the page body.

line (1) In text, a horizontal, linear arrangement of graphic characters. (T)   (2) The portion of a data circuit external to data circuit-terminating equipment (DCE), that connects the DCE to a data switching exchange (DSE), that connects a DCE to one or more other DCEs, or that connects a DSE to another DSE. (I)   (3) In word processing, a predetermined number of escapement units, including character spaces, forming one line of typing. (T)   (4) On a terminal, one or more characters entered before a return to the first printing or display position. (5) In video scanning, a single pass of the sensor from left to right across the image. (6) In COBOL, a division of a page representing one row of horizontal character positions.   Synonymous with report line.   See comment line, debugging line, report line.   (7) A string of characters accepted by a system as a single block of input from a terminal; for example, all characters entered before a carriage return, all characters entered before the terminal user hits the attention key. (8) Synonymous with channel, circuit.   (9) See acoustic delay line, character spacing reference line, delay line, dependency line, display line, electromagnetic delay line, flowline, hidden line, magnetic delay line, multipoint line, nonswitched line, offline, online, point-to-point line, switched line, telecommunication line, X-datum line, Y-datum line.

line adapter See communication line adapter.

linear audio In multimedia applications, the analog audio on the linear track of a videotape that can be recorded without erasing existing video; it is used for audio dubbing after the video is edited.

linear language A language customarily expressed as a linear representation; for example, FORTRAN is a linear language; a flowchart is not. (A)

linear list A linearly ordered set of data elements that have the same structure and whose order is preserved in storage by using sequential allocation. (T)

linear matrix transformation In video systems, the process of converting a group of video signals from one type to another by combining the signals through addition or subtraction; used, for example, to convert RGB to YUV.

linear network A network in which there are exactly two endpoint nodes, any number of intermediate nodes, and only one path between any two nodes. (T)

linear optimization Synonym for linear programming.

linear play Playback of a recorded sequence from start to finish without branching or other forms of interactivity.

linear programming (LP) (1) In operations research, a procedure for locating the maximum or minimum of a linear function of variables that are subject to linear constraints. (I) (A)   (2) Contrast with convex programming, dynamic programming, integer programming, mathematical programming, nonlinear programming, quadratic programming.   (3) Synonymous with linear optimization.

linear representation An arrangement of graphics in a one-dimensional space. (A)

linear search A search in which a set of data is scanned in a sequential search. (T) (A)

linear video In multimedia applications, a sequence of motion footage played from start to finish without stops or branching, like a movie.

line-at-a-time printer Synonym for line printer.

line/battery-powered calculator A calculator that draws its power from a battery or from the main electrical power supply. (T) (A)

line character See new-line character.

line chart In GDDM, a chart in which the plotted points (each optionally represented by a marker) are joined by straight or curved lines.   See also scatter plot.

line code A code that results from converting terminal output signals to pulses sent over a transmission medium.

line command (1) In text processing, a command used to request a function for a specific line or lines from the command area to the left of the line or lines affected; for example, C for Copy or M for Move. (2) In the System/38 source entry utility, a command, such as D for deleted, I for insert, or C for copy, that is keyed in the sequence number field of displayed records to request an operation on source records.

line concentration The combining of data from many lines or devices into fewer lines.   See also cascading.

line control characters See transmission control characters.

line control discipline Synonym for link protocol.

line counter (1) In text processing, a function of the system that allows for counting and possibly controlling the number of lines printed on each page of text. (T)   (2) In text processing, a device that counts the number of lines processed. (A)

line counter specifications In RPG, a coding sheet on which the programmer indicates or overrides the system defaults for the form length and for the number of lines to print on a page. Line counter specifications can be used for each printer file in a program.

line data Data prepared for printing on a line printer, such as a 3800 Model 1 or 2.

line data set In systems with time sharing, a data set with logical records that are printable lines.

line delete symbol Synonym for logical line delete symbol.

line-deletion character A character that specifies that all characters are to be deleted from a line of terminal input. See also logical line delete symbol.

line description In the AS/400 system and System/38, an object that contains information describing a particular communications line that is attached to the system.

line descriptor Specifications that describe how input data records are formatted into individual print lines. Line descriptors are interpreted by the Print Services Facility (PSF) when formatting printed output.

line device Any of a class of printers that accept one line of text at a time.

line discipline Synonym for link protocol.

line driver An RSCS task that permits communication between RSCS and a specific type of remote station.

line editing Editing in which data is displayed at a terminal one line at a time and in which the user can access data only through commands. Contrast with full-screen editing.

line editor A text editor in which the user has to specify lines in order to access elements of text to be edited within a line or within a group of contiguous lines. Synonymous with line-oriented editor. (T)

line-end adjustment In word processing, an automatic operation that ends each printed line of text within the line-end zone.

line-end control key In word processing, a control by means of which the line-end adjustment feature can be activated or deactivated. (T)

line-ending zone Synonym for line-end zone.

line-end lock On a typewriter, a device preventing further type impressions after engagement of the right-hand margin stop. (T)

line-end symbol Synonym for logical line-end symbol.

line-end zone In word processing, a specified number of character positions before the right margin at which a line is automatically ended. Synonymous with hot zone, line-ending zone. See also adjust text mode.

line entry In ACF/TCAM, a terminal-table entry that defines a switched link used for input/output operations. See also cascade entry, group entry, logtype entry, process entry, single entry.

line escapement (1) Movement of paper perpendicular to the typing line over a predetermined distance. (T)   (2) See also expand escapement.

line feed (1) The movement of the print or display position to the corresponding position on the next line. (T)   (2) The incremental relative movement between the paper carrier and the type carrier in a direction perpendicular to the writing line.

line feed character (LF) (1) A format effector that causes the print or display position to move to the corresponding position on the next line. (I) (A) (2) In word processing, synonym for index character.

line format page In the 3800 Printing Subsystem Models 3 and 8, a page composed of line data and optional structured fields.

line format print data set In the 3800 Printing Subsystem Models 3 and 8, a data set that consists of line data optionally supplemented by a limited set of structured fields.

line graphics Synonym for coordinate graphics.

line group One or more telecommunication lines of the same type that can be activated and deactivated as a unit.

line group data set In ACF/TCAM, a message control program data set that contains the messages transmitted on all the lines in a line group.

line height The vertical measurement of a line of text, measured from the baseline of one line to the baseline of the next line. Line height is usually expressed in points.

line hit An electrical interference causing the introduction of spurious signals on a circuit.

line impedance Impedance of a telecommunication line. Line impedance is a function of resistance, inductance, conductance, and capacitance of the line, and signal frequency. Synonymous with characteristic impedance.

line index See code line index.

line interface base (LIB) A communication controller hardware unit for the attachment of up to 16 telecommunication lines to the controller.

line key In word processing, a control used to process text one line at a time. (T)

line level The signal level in decibels (or nepers) at a particular position on a telecommunication line.

line load Usually a percentage of maximum circuit capability to reflect actual use during a span of time; for example, peak hour line load. Synonymous with circuit load.

line lock In ACF/TCAM, a facility that maintains a connection between a station and an application program for the duration of transmission of an inquiry message and the reception of a reply. During line lock, the line is not available to other stations. See also extended lock mode, lock mode, message lock mode, station lock.

line loop An operation performed over a telecommunication line from an input unit at one terminal to output units at a remote terminal.

line loop resistance The metallic resistance of the local loop. Synonymous with loop resistance.

line merging (1) In compatibility mode, the combination of line data into one print line, or the printing of different columns of data across a sheet, each in different character styles or sizes. (2) In all-point addressability, the ORing of the picture elements (pels) on the same line. This is similar to overstriking on an impact printer.

line mode (1) In VM, when using the System Product Editor or the CMS Editor, the mode of operation of a display terminal that is equivalent to using a typewriter terminal; that is, the terminal displays a chronological log of the XEDIT or EDIT subcommands entered, the lines affected by the editing (unless it is suppressed), and the system responses. Contrast with display mode. (2) A form of screen presentation in which the information is presented a line at a time in the message area of the terminal screen. Contrast with full-screen mode.

line mode switching An optional feature of partitioned emulation programming that allows a designated line to operate as either a network control program line or an emulation program line. The line is switched from one mode to the other by control commands.

line noise Noise originating in a telecommunication line.

line number (1) A number associated with a line in a printout or display. (2) In systems with time sharing, a number associated with a line in a line data set. (3) The number that precedes a line of information in a printout or on a display. (4) In COBOL, an integer that denotes the vertical position of a report line on a page.

line number access In word processing, an automatic capability to find a particular line in a document by indicating an identifying number or the position of the line relative to another line.

line number editing In systems with time sharing, a mode of operation under the EDIT command in which lines or records to be entered, modified, or deleted, are referred to by line or record numbers.

line-oriented editor Synonym for line editor. (T)

line original In a document copying machine, an original without tonal gradation, consisting only of lines or solids. (T)

line overrun In the 3800 Print Management Facility compatibility mode, a condition showing that either the number of graphic characters sent to print a line is more than permitted for the normal print line, or that the copy-modification operation was not completed in time to print the line.

line pacing The sending of a line followed by a waiting interval before continuing transmission.

line pairing In multimedia applications, a faulty interlace pattern in which the lines of the second field begin to pair with the lines of the first field rather than fit exactly within them.

line-powered calculator A calculator that depends solely for its power upon connection to the main electrical power supply. (T) (A)

line printer (1) A device that prints a line of characters as a unit. (I) (A) Synonymous with line-at-a-time printer. (2) Contrast with character printer, page printer.

line printing The printing of a line of characters as a unit.

line probe A generic term for the IBM 3867 Link Diagnostic Unit, a device that provides the NetView user with line quality data and other link information.

line reference A label or line number that specifies where control should be transferred if certain conditions exist when the line is executed.

line relay A relay activated by the signals on a line. Deprecated term for modulation rate.

line response mode In IMS/VS, a variation of response mode in which all operations on the telecommunication line are suspended while the application program output message is being generated. See also response mode, terminal response mode.

line ruler On a typewriter, a device that enables lines to be drawn on the paper while in the machine parallel or perpendicular to the typing line, using manual writing equipment. (T)

line-scan pickup device A type of video pickup device that electronically scans in one direction only. Scanning in the other direction is done mechanically by relative motion between the pickup device and the image.

line-selection machine master cylinder In a duplicator, a cylinder in a line-selection machine to which a heading, master, and masks are attached by means of clips or clamps, some of which may be moving, so that predetermined sections of the master may be reproduced with a common heading. (T)

line space (1) The distance between two consecutive typing lines used for a particular operation, the distance being made up of a whole or split multiple of the basic line space. (T) See basic line space. (2) The vertical distance between the baseline of the current line and the baseline of the preceding line.

line space mechanism On a typewriter, an arrangement of components for controlling the line space set by the operator. (T)

line space ratchet On a typewriter, a ratchet in the line space mechanism for incrementally rotating and latching the platen. (T)

line space selector On a typewriter, a control for varying line space. (T)

line spacing (1) The distance between two adjacent baselines of text, usually expressed as the number of blank lines between them. (2) The number of lines vertically to the inch. (T)

line speed (1) The rate at which data are transmitted from one point to another over a telecommunication line. (2) The number of binary digits that can be sent over a telecommunication line in one second, expressed in bits per second (bps).

lines per inch (LPI) On a printer, a measure of the number of lines per vertical inch of paper; for example, the IBM 3800 Printing Subsystem can print at 6, 8, or 12 lines per inch.

line stretcher An impedance matching device for coaxial transmission lines.

line switching Synonym for circuit switching.

line trace (1) In the network control program, an optional function that logs online diagnostic information. Tracing is limited to only one line at a time. (2) In ACF/TCAM, a table that provides a sequential record in main storage of the I/O interruptions occurring on a specified line.

line traffic The number of transmissions and the amount of data sent and received on a telecommunication line.

line turnaround To change the direction of transmission from send to receive or from receive to send on a half-duplex circuit.

linguistic object In a conceptual schema language, a syntactically allowable construct in a language. See also lexical object. (A)

link (1) In computer programming, the part of a program, in some cases a single instruction or an address, that passes control and parameters between separate portions of the computer program. (I) (A) Synonymous with linkage. (2) The combination of the link connection (the transmission medium) and two link stations, one at each end of the link connection. A link connection can be shared among multiple links in a multipoint or token-ring configuration. (3) In an IMS/VS multisystem environment, the connection between two systems. (4) In hypertext, an author-defined association between two information nodes. See hypertext link. (5) In the AIX file system, a connection between an i-node and one or more file names associated with it. (6) In TCP/IP, a communications line. A TCP/IP link may share the use of a communications line with SNA. (7) In an ESCON environment, the physical connection and transmission medium used between an optical transmitter and an optical receiver. A link consists of two conductors, one used for sending and the other for receiving, thereby providing a duplex communication path. (8) In an ESCON I/O interface, the physical connection and transmission medium used between a channel and a control unit, a channel and an ESCD, a control unit and an ESCD, or, at times, between two ESCDs. (9) To interconnect items of data or portions of one or more computer programs: for example, the linking of object programs by a linkage editor, linking of data items by pointers. (T) (10) In the System/36 interactive data definition utility, to associate a file on disk with a file definition in a data dictionary. This association allows a program or utility to access a file as it is defined by the file definition. (11) In IDDU, to connect a database file on disk with a file definition in a data dictionary. Contrast with unlink. (12) See data link, logical link, multiplex link, physical link. (13) See also link level.

link access procedures (LAP) The link level elements used for data interchange between data circuit-terminating equipment (DCE) and data terminal equipment (DTE) operating in user classes of service 8 to 11, as specified in CCITT Recommendation X.1.

link access protocol-balanced (LAPB) A protocol used for accessing an X.25 network at the link level. LAPB is a duplex, asynchronous, symmetric protocol, used in point-to-point communication.

link address An address assigned at initialization that identifies a channel or control unit and allows it to send and receive transmission frames and perform I/O operations. See also port address.

linkage (1) In computer security, the combination of data or information from one information system with data or information from another system in the hope of deriving additional information; for example, the combination of computer files from two or more sources. (2) Synonym for link.

linkage editor (1) A computer program for creating load modules from one or more object modules or load modules by resolving cross references among the modules and, if necessary, adjusting addresses. (T) (2) In VSE, a program used to create a phase (executable code) from one or more independently translated object modules, from one or more existing phases, or from both. In creating the phase, the linkage editor resolves cross references among the modules and phases available as input. (3) Synonymous with linker. (4) Contrast with editor program. (5) See overlay linkage editor.

linkage instruction In DPPX FORTRAN, an instruction that passes control and parameters between portions of a computer program.

Linkage Section In COBOL, the section in the Data Division of the called program that describes the data items available from the calling program. These data items may be referred to by both the calling and the called program.

link-attached Pertaining to devices that are connected to a controlling unit by a data link. Contrast with channel-attached. Synonymous with remote.

link-attached network control program A network control program in a link-attached controller. Synonymous with remote NCP. Contrast with channel-attached network control program.

link-attached station A station whose control unit is connected to a computer by a data link. Synonymous with remote station. Contrast with channel-attached station.

link-attached terminal A terminal whose control unit is connected to a computer by a data link. Synonymous with remote terminal. Contrast with channel-attached terminal.

link attribute In RSCS, a characteristic of a data link, such as its line address, its linkid, or the type of line driver it requires.

Link button In the IBM LinkWay product, a type of LinkWay button object that brings up any existing folder page the user specifies.

link connection In SNA, the physical equipment providing two-way communication between one link station and one or more other link stations; for example, a telecommunication line and data circuit-terminating equipment (DCE). Synonymous with data circuit.

link connection component manager (LCCM) The transaction program that manages the configuration of the link connection.

link connection network Synonym for connection network.

link connection segment A portion of the configuration that is located between two resources listed consecutively in the service point command service (SPCS) query link configuration request list.

link connection subsystem (LCS) The sequence of link connection components (LCCs) that belong to a link connection and are managed by one LCSM.

link connection subsystem manager (LCSM) The transaction program that manages the sequence of link connection components (LCCs) that belong to a link connection.

link control See basic mode link control.

link-edit To create a loadable computer program by means of a linkage editor.

link integrity verification tests (LIVT) A set of operational procedures and messages that is defined by American National Standards Institute (ANSI) Standard T1.617 Annex D and International Telegraph and Telephone Consultative Committee (CCITT) Standard Q.933 Annex A and that is transferred over DLCI 0. This set of operational procedures and messages provides status and outage notification for frame-relay frame handler (FRFH) and frame-relay terminal equipment (FRTE) connections.

linked list Synonym for chained list.

linked list search Synonym for chained list search.

link encryption (1) In computer security, the use of online crypto-operations on a data link of a data communication system so that all information transmitted over the link is completely encrypted. (2) In cryptography, data encryption and decryption between any two stations on a data link.

linker Synonym for linkage editor. (A)

link escape character See data link escape character.

link header In SNA, control information for data link control at the beginning of a basic link unit (BLU).

linking (to a disk) In VM, sharing of a disk owned by another user. A user can share the disk on a temporary or permanent basis. The sharing is normally read-only and may require a password to access the data.

link level (1) A part of Recommendation X.25 that defines the link protocol used to get data into and out of the network across the full-duplex link connecting the subscriber's machine to the network node. LAP and LAPB are the link access protocols recommended by the CCITT. See data link level. (2) In SNA, the combination of the transmission connection, protocol, devices, and programming joining network nodes.

link-level addressing In an I/O interface, one of two levels of addressing; it pertains to link-level functions and identifies the channel path between the channel and a control unit. Contrast with device-level addressing.

link level 2 test See link test.

link library A partitioned data set from which load modules are fetched when they are referred to in execute (EXEC) statements and in ATTACH, LINK, LOAD, and transfer control (XCTL) macroinstructions.

link loss budget See maximum allowable link loss.

link pack area (LPA) (1) In MVT, an area of main storage containing reenterable routines from system libraries. Their presence in main storage saves loading time. (2) In OS/VS2, an area of virtual storage that contains reenterable routines that are loaded at IPL time and can be used concurrently by all tasks in the system.

link pack area directory In OS/VS2, a directory that contains an entry for each entry point in link pack area modules.

link pack area extension In TSO, an extension of the link pack area containing system routines used only when TSO is operating. It is loaded when the operator starts TSO.

link pack area library In OS/VS2, a partitioned data set that contains the modules that reside in the link pack area.

link pack area queue In OS/VS2, a queue that contains a contents directory entry for each link pack area module currently in use, for each module in the link pack update area, and for each module in the fixed link pack area.

link pack update area In OS/VS2, an area in virtual storage containing modules that are additions to or replacements for link pack area modules for the current IPL.

link problem determination aid (LPDA) A series of procedures that are used to test the status of and to control DCEs, the communications line, and the remote device interface. These procedures, or a subset of them, are implemented by host programs (such as the NetView program and VTAM), communication controller programs (such as NCP), and IBM LPDA DCEs. See Link Problem Determination Aid-1, Link Problem Determination Aid-2.

Link Problem Determination Aid-1 (LPDA-1) The first version of the LPDA command set. LPDA-1 is not compatible with LPDA-2. See link problem determination aid (LPDA), Link Problem Determination Aid-2.

Link Problem Determination Aid-2 (LPDA-2) The second version of the LPDA command set. LPDA-2 provides all of the functions of LPDA-1; it also supports commands such as the following:

- DCE configuration
- Dial

- Set transmit speed
- Commands to operate a contact that can control external devices.

See link problem determination aid (LPDA), Link Problem Determination Aid-1.

link protocol (1) The rules for sending and receiving data at the link level. (2) See protocol. (3) See also link level.

link protocol converter (LPC) A device that changes one type of link-level protocol information to another type of link-level protocol information for processing; for example, 5208 Link Protocol Converter, 5209 Link Protocol Converter, or ROLMbridge 5250 Link Protocol Converter. See also protocol converter.

link segment In an ESCON environment, any portion of an optical cable between connectors, including passive components.

link station (1) The hardware and software components within a node representing a connection to an adjacent node over a specific link. For example, if node A is the primary end of a multipoint line that connects to three adjacent nodes, node A will have three link stations representing the connections to the adjacent nodes. See also adjacent link station. (2) In VTAM, a named resource within an APPN or a subarea node that represents the connection to another APPN or subarea node that is attached by an APPN or a subarea link. In the resource hierarchy in a subarea network, the link station is subordinate to the subarea link.

link status (LS) Information maintained by local and remote modems.

link test In SNA, a test of the operation of a link in which one link station returns data received from another link station without changing the data.

Note: Three tests can be made. They differ in the resources that are dedicated during the test. A link test, level 0, requires a dedicated subarea node, link, and secondary link station. A link test, level 1, requires a dedicated link and secondary link station. A link test, level 2, requires only the dedicated link station.

link trace A sequential log of events that occur on a link. This log can help determine the source of a recurring error.

link trailer In SNA, control information for data link control at the end of a basic link unit (BLU).

LIOCS Logical IOCS.

lip sync The process by which the movements of a person's lips are made to match a recorded voice, either his own or someone else's.

liquid crystal display (LCD) A display device that creates characters by means of the action of reflected light on patterns formed by a liquid that becomes opaque when it is energized. (A)

LISP (1) List processing. A programming language designed for list processing and used extensively for artificial intelligence problems. (T) (2) An applicative programming language oriented to list processing, recursion, and character string manipulation and logic; it is widely used for artificial intelligence applications and is based on the lambda calculus of mathematical logic. (A)

list (1) An ordered set of data. (T) (2) A data object consisting of a collection of related records. See access control list, access list, address list, free list, idle list, i-list, pop-up list, property list, required list, routing list, system address list, user address list. (3) To print or otherwise display items of data that meet specified criteria. (A) (4) Deprecated term for chained list. (5) See pushdown list, pushup list.

list-based access control In computer security, access control in which all of the access rights of a subject occur in the subject's access control lists. See also ticket-based access control.

list box In SAA Advanced Common User Access architecture, a control that contains scrollable choices from which a user can select one choice. See also combination box, drop-down combination box.

Note: In CUA architecture, this is a programmer term. The end user term is selection list.

list-directed In XL FORTRAN, an input/output specification that uses a data list instead of a FORMAT specification.

list-directed data In FORTRAN, data that is transferred between main storage and an input/output device according to the length and type of variables in the input/output list. See also formatted data, unformatted data.

list element One of several values specified in a list parameter.

listen In the X.25 application program interface, to be prepared to receive incoming calls that satisfy criteria specified in an entry in the routing list, through a specified X.25 port.

listening mode A mode in which a station can monitor messages on the line but cannot send or receive messages.

list file In the System/36 data file utility, a file from which information is used to print a report.

list handling statement An executable statement, usually in a list processing language, that specifies operations to be performed on lists of data; for example, statements used to insert data into the middle of a list, add data to the beginning or end of a list, or create common sublists. (T)

listing A printout that lists the source language statements and the output resulting from execution of a program. See also compiler listing.

list-of-groups checking In RACF, an option that allows a user to access all resources available to all groups of which the user is a member, regardless of the user's current connect group. For any particular resource, RACF allows access based on the highest access among the groups of which the user is a member.

list parameter A parameter defined to accept a list of multiple like values or unlike values.

list processing (1) A method of processing data in the form of lists. (T) (2) See also LISP.

Note: Chained lists are usually used so that the order of the data elements can be changed without altering their physical locations.

LIT Load initial table.

literal (1) In programming languages, a lexical unit that directly represents a value; for example, 14 represents the integer fourteen, "APRIL" represents the string of characters APRIL, 3.0005E2 represents the number 300.05. (I) (2) A symbol or a quantity in a source program that is itself data, rather than a reference to data. (3) A character string whose value is given by the characters themselves; for example, the numeric literal 7 has the value 7, and the character literal "CHARACTERS" has the value CHARAC-TERS. (4) In COBOL, a character-string whose value is implied by the ordered set of characters comprising the string. See nonnumeric literal, numeric literal. (5) See character literal, default literal, explicit literal, numeric literal, system literal.

literal constant In FORTRAN, a lexical token that directly represents a scalar value of intrinsic type.

literal pool An area of storage into which an assembler assembles the values of the literals specified in a source program.

literal string A string that does not contain pattern-matching characters and can therefore be interpreted just as it is. Contrast with regular expression.

liter (L) A metric unit of capacity equal to 61.02 cubic inches or 1.06 liquid quarts.

litho master In a duplicator, a sheet of material that carries the image and nonimage areas generally on the same plane; the former accepts the ink, and the latter rejects it. (T)

litre See liter.

LIVT Link integrity verification tests.

LLB Local Location Broker.

LLC (1) Logical link control. (2) Low level code.

LLC/CC Low level code/continuity check.

LLC protocol See logical link control protocol.

LLC sublayer See logical link control sublayer.

LLG Logical line group.

LL2 Link level 2.

LMI Local management interface.

LMPEO Large message performance enhancement outbound. In VTAM, a facility in which VTAM reformats function management data (FMD) that exceed the maximum request unit (RU) size, as specified in the BIND, into a chain or partial chain of RUs.

LM table Logical unit mode table.

LNS LU network services component.

load (1) To feed data into a database. (T) (2) To bring all or part of a computer program into memory from auxiliary storage so that the computer can run the program. (3) To place a diskette into a diskette drive or a magazine into a diskette magazine drive. (4) To insert paper into a printer.

loadable character set In the 3270 Information Display System, a character set stored temporarily in the device. Contrast with nonloadable character set.

load-and-go An operating technique in which there are no stops between the loading and execution phases of a computer program, and which may include assembling or compiling. (A)

load balancing (1) In ACF/TCAM extended networking, a technique for balancing the message flow between any pair of TCAM nodes by assigning different paths to different messages flowing between them. (2) See application load balancing, transaction load balancing.

load balancing group (LBG) In IMS/VS, the grouping of Fast Path input messages for balancing processing by one or more copies of a Fast Path program. There is one LBG for each unique Fast Path message-driven application program.

loaded origin The address of the initial storage location of a computer program in main storage at the time the computer program is loaded. (A)

loader (1) A routine, commonly a computer program, that reads data into main storage. (A)   (2) In the AIX operating system, a program that reads run files into main storage so that the files can be run. (3) See absolute loader, bootstrap loader, initial program loader, relocating loader.

load file generator A Network Configuration Application/MVS function that converts Network Configuration Application configuration data to RODM load utility statements. These statements, when run through the RODM load utility, can create, update, and delete RODM objects that can be viewed through the NetView Graphic Monitor Facility (NGMF).

load image An image, ready for transmission to a communication controller, that contains multiple images; for example, a combination of a configuration image with one or more application program images, or a combination of a configuration image with one or more customized images. See also application program image, configuration image, customized image.

loading (1) Adding inductance (load coils) to a transmission line to minimize amplitude distortion. See lumped loading. (2) See downloading, uploading.

loading control On dictation equipment, a device that enables the recording medium to be inserted into a dictation machine. (I)

loading pattern In MSS, the order in which cartridge cells are filled with data cartridges entered through the cartridge access station.

loading zone On a disk or diskette, a band of unused tracks over which the read/write head rises to the proper head gap at which it can read and write data. See also landing zone.

load initial table (LIT) A table used by the 3651 or 7480 Store Controller to determine which IBM-supplied modules and applications are to be loaded into a programmable 3653 or 3663 terminal.

load leveling The balancing of work between processing units, channels, or devices.

load lever A lever on the front of a diskette unit that holds the diskette in place.

load map A map containing the storage addresses of control sections and entry points of a program loaded into storage.

load member (1) In System/32, a collection of instructions stored in the library that the system can execute to perform a particular function, whether requested by the operator or specified in an operation control language statement.   (2) In System/36, a library member that contains information in machine language, a form the system can use directly. Contrast with source member.

load mode (1) In some variable-word-length computers, data transmission in which certain delimiters are moved with the data. (A)   (2) Contrast with move mode.

load module (1) All or part of a computer program in a form suitable for loading into main storage for execution. A load module is usually the output of a linkage editor. (T)   (2) In the AIX operating system, synonym for run file. (3) See also absolute load module.

load module library A partitioned data set used to store and retrieve load modules. See also object module library, source module library.

load-on-call A function of a linkage editor that allows selected segments of the module to be disk resident while other segments are executing. Disk resident segments are loaded for execution and given control when any entry point they contain is called.

load point (1) The beginning of the recordable area on a magnetic tape.

Note: Some magnetic tape drives use a BOT marker to indicate the position of the load point. (T)
(2) The position on a magnetic tape that is indicated by the beginning-of-tape marker. (A)

lobe (1) A pair of channels between a data station and a lobe attaching unit, one channel for sending and one for receiving, as seen from the point of view of the attached data station. (T)   (2) In a star/ring network configuration, two pairs of conductors that provide separate send and receive paths between a wiring concentrator and a network port, such as a wall outlet. (3) In the IBM Token-Ring Network, the section of cable that attaches a device to an access unit. The cable may consist of several segments. (4) In 8100 directly attached loops, one of two segments of the loop.

lobe attaching unit (1) A functional unit used to connect data stations to and disconnect data stations from a ring network without disrupting network operations. (T) (2) See also access unit.

lobe bypass (1) The capability of a lobe attaching unit to disconnect a lobe, and all attached data stations from a ring network for replacement, relocation, or repair, without disrupting network operations. (T) (2) In a star/ring network configuration, removal of a wiring concentrator and an attached lobe from the network when a fault is detected or when an attached lobe must be disconnected for servicing.

lobe receptacle In the IBM Token-Ring Network, an outlet on an access unit for connecting a lobe.

local (1) In programming languages, pertaining to the relationship between a language object and a block such that the language object has a scope contained in that block. (I) (2) Pertaining to that which is defined and used only in one subdivision of a computer program. (A) (3) Pertaining to a device accessed directly without use of a telecommunication line. (4) Synonym for channel-attached. (5) See local central office, local channel, local code, local lock, local loop, local processor, local service, local service area, local system queue area. (6) Contrast with global, remote.

local address (1) In SNA, an address used in a peripheral node in place of a network address and transformed to or from a network address by the boundary function in a subarea node. (2) In DPPX, an address relative to the origin of a nested address space.

local administration Address administration in which all LAN individual addresses are unique within the same local area network. (T)

local area network (LAN) (1) A computer network located on a user's premises within a limited geographical area. Communication within a local area network is not subject to external regulations; however, communication across the LAN boundary may be subject to some form of regulation. (T) See also wide area network. See Figure 88.

Note: A LAN does not use store and forward techniques. (2) A network in which a set of devices are connected to one another for communication and that can be connected to a larger network. See also token ring.

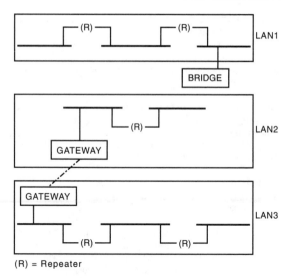

(R) = Repeater

LAN1, LAN2, LAN3 are three local area networks

Figure 88. Local Area Networks

local area network broadcast The transmission of a transmission frame that is intended to be accepted by all other data stations on the same local area network. (T) (A)

local area network multicast The transmission of a transmission frame that is intended to be accepted by a group of selected data stations on the same local area network. (T) (A)

local assistance One of the types of service described in the licensing agreement that may be specified for a licensed program. When local assistance is specified, IBM personnel, on request and as available, will assist the customer in diagnosing problems, checking for the availability of a fix from central service, preparing APARs and, if the program is inoperable, attempting a local fix or bypass. Local assistance is provided by IBM Systems Engineering. See also central service, local service.

local-attached Deprecated term for channel-attached.

local central office A central office arranged for terminating subscriber lines and provided with trunks for establishing connections to and from other central offices. See also central office, end office.

local channel (1) In private line services, the portion of a channel within an exchange that is provided to connect the main station with an interexchange channel. (2) The hardware adapter on a 3791 Controller that allows direct attachment to the multiplexer channel of a central processor without need for modems or telecommunication lines.

local character set identifier (LCID) In the 3270 data stream, a value between hex 40 and hex FE used by an application program or an operator to identify a character set in the device and to select a character set for displaying or printing data.

local controller A functional unit within a system that controls the operation of one or more directly attached input/output devices or communication lines. Contrast with remote controller.

local copy operation In the 3270 Information Display System, the copying of the contents of a display buffer to a printer when the action is initiated by the print key or from the application program.

local data area An area on disk that can be used to pass information between jobs and routing steps during a session. A separate local data area exists for each command display station.

local destination (1) Any location to which data can be transferred without the use of telecommunication lines. (2) In an IMS/VS multisystem environment, a destination that is in the local system. See also remote destination.

local device controller (LDC) line In the 5520 Administrative System, the twinaxial cable to which printers or another IBM 5520 can be connected.

local directory database That set of resources (LUs) in the network known at a particular node. The resources included are all those in the node's domain as well as any cache entries.

local domain name The primary TCP/IP name associated with the local system. A system can have more than one system name, but only one local domain name. The local domain name consists of two parts, the domain and the host.

local entity In FORTRAN, an entity defined by a lexical token whose scope is a scoping unit.

local-form session identifier (LFSID) A dynamically assigned value used at a type 2.1 node to identify traffic for a particular session using a given transmission group (TG). The LFSID is encoded in the ODAI, OAF', and DAF' fields of the transmission headers that accompany session messages exchanged over the TG.

local host In Transmission Control Protocol/Internet Protocol, the host on the network at which a particular operator is working. Synonymous with current host.

local identifier In the 3800 Print Services Facility, a 1-byte identifier assigned to parts of the data stream to facilitate processing.

local key In the Programmed Cryptographic Facility, a cryptographic key used at the host processor to encipher an operational key before the operational key is sent to a terminal. It is also used at the terminal to decipher the operational key.

local-local link (1) In VSE, a connection between two local communication controllers controlled by the same system services control point. (2) In VTAM, an SDLC link connecting two local network control programs.

local location address In SNA, the address of the logical unit.

Local Location Broker (LLB) In the AIX Network Computing System (NCS) Location Broker, a server that maintains information about objects on the local host and provides the Location Broker forwarding facility.

local location name The name by which a system is known to other systems in an SNA network. A local location name is equivalent to an SNA local logical unit name. Contrast with remote location name.

local lock A suspend lock that protects resources assigned to a particular private address space.

local lock management In an IMS/VS multisystem environment, lock management that controls access to database records used by application programs in the same online IMS/VS system. See also global lock management.

local loop A channel connecting a subscriber's equipment to line-terminating equipment in the central office exchange.

locally administered address In a local area network, an adapter address that the user can assign to override the universally administered address. Contrast with universally administered address.

locally attached Synonym for channel-attached.

locally attached station Deprecated term for channel-attached station.

locally attached terminal Deprecated term for channel-attached terminal.

local mode In the 3790 Communication System, operation of a terminal without interacting with a 3790 program. A 3793 Keyboard-Printer operating in this mode remains connected to the 3791 Controller, but allows the terminal printer to function as a typewriter.

local NCP Synonym for channel-attached NCP.

local network control program In ACF/TCAM, a network control program in a controller that is attached directly to the host processor via a channel attachment. Synonym for channel-attached network control program. Contrast with remote network control program.

local non-SNA major node In VTAM, a major node whose minor nodes are channel-attached, non-SNA terminals.

local PC In the NetView/PC program, the PC that has its keyboard locked by the remote control function. Contrast with remote PC.

local processor In a complex of processors under control of JES3, a processor connected to the global processor, for which JES3 performs centralized job input, job scheduling, and job output services via the global processor.

local-remote link In ACF/TCAM, an SDLC link connecting a local network control program with a remote network control program.

local service (1) One of the types of software repair support described in the licensing agreement that may be specified for a licensed program. When local service is specified, IBM personnel will diagnose problems, check to see if there is a fix available from central service, prepare APARs and, if the program is inoperable, attempt a local fix or bypass. See also central service, local assistance. (2) In MVS, a supervisory service that applies to one private address space.

local service area In telecommunication, the area containing the telephone stations that a flat rate customer may call without incurring toll charges.

local session identification (LSID) In SNA, a field in an FID3 transmission header that contains an indication of the type of session and the local address of the peripheral logical unit (LU) or physical unit (PU).

local shared resources An option for sharing I/O buffers, I/O-related control blocks, and channel programs among VSAM data sets in a resource pool that serves one partition or address space.

local SNA major node In VTAM, a major node whose minor nodes are channel-attached peripheral nodes.

local station Synonym for channel-attached station.

local system queue area (LSQA) (1) In TSO, a portion of the foreground (swapped) region used for control blocks that are to be swapped out along with a terminal job. (2) In OS/VS2, one or more segments associated with each virtual storage region; the segments contain job-related system control blocks.

local terminal Synonym for channel-attached terminal.

local topology database A database in an APPN or LEN node containing an entry for each transmission group (TG) having at least one end node for an endpoint. In an end node, the database has one entry for each TG connecting to the node. In a network node, the database has an entry for each TG connecting the network node to an end node. Each entry describes the current characteristics of the TG that it represents. A network node has both a local and a network topology database while an end node has only a local topology database.

local transaction In an IMS/VS multisystem environment, a transaction processed totally by the system in which it is defined. Contrast with remote transaction.

local transaction program The transaction program at the local end of a conversation. Contrast with remote transaction program.

local update procedure The process by which a customer can add his own modifications or enhancements to VM modules or source code during the generation of the CP system, CMS system, or both.

local variable A variable that is defined and used only in one specified portion of a computer program. (T)

local workstation A workstation connected directly to a system without need for data transmission facilities. Contrast with remote workstation.

local 3270 major node See local non-SNA major node.

Locate Synonym for Locate/CD-Initiate.

Locate/CD-Initiate An abbreviated term for a message exchanged between APPN nodes that contains one of the following sets of general data stream (GDS) variables:

- A Locate, a Find Resource, and a Cross-Domain Initiate GDS variable used for a network search request

- A Locate, a Found Resource, and a Cross-Domain Initiate GDS variable used for a search reply when a network resource has been located

These message structures correspond to the CP components that perform the search of the distributed network directory and establish the session. The Locate GDS variable contains information used to control the delivery of the search messages in the network. The Find and Found GDS variables contain information used in the directories: origin cache data (control point information) and search arguments (destination LU name), and located resource information, respectively. The Cross-Domain Initiate GDS variable contains endpoint TG vector information to be used in selecting the route for the session. The length of the Locate/CD-Initiate message is limited to 1024 bytes.

Locate chain A temporary logical connection, spanning a series of CP-CP sessions, between the control point at a search initiator and the control point at the search destination. It is set up when a search is initiated, and ends on completion of the search. It is used to transport directory search control traffic and allows route-outage reporting to the search endpoints if an outage occurs during the search.

locate mode A means of providing data by pointing to its location instead of moving it. See also move mode, substitute mode.

Locate search The means directory services in a node uses to find a resource that is not in that node. The Locate search enables directory services to ask the directory services components in other APPN nodes for information on the target resource. See also broadcast search and directed Locate search.

Locate search message Synonym for Locate/CD-Initiate.

Locate search reply A Locate, a Found Resource, and a Cross-Domain Initiate GDS variable used when a network resource has been located.

Locate search request A Locate, a Find Resource, and a Cross-Domain Initiate GDS variable used to search for a network resource.

location (1) Any place in which data can be stored. (A) (2) See protected location, storage location. (3) Contrast with address.

Location Broker In the AIX Network Computing System, software that includes the Local Location Broker, the Global Location Broker, and the Location Broker Client Agent.

Location Broker Client Agent A part of the AIX Location Broker that programs use to communicate with Global Location Brokers and with remote Local Location Brokers.

location counter (1) A counter whose value indicates the address of data assembled from a machine instruction or a constant, or the address of an area of reserved storage, relative to the beginning of a control section. (2) A counter used to assign storage addresses.

location name In communication, the name identifying a system or device.

locator An input unit that provides coordinates of a position; for example, a mouse, a tablet. (T) (A)

locator device In computer graphics, an input device that provides coordinate data; for example, a mouse, tablet, thumbwheel. (T) See also choice device, pick device, valuator device.

locator sample rate The rate of input from a locator device. Synonymous with sample rate.

lock (1) A serialization mechanism by means of which a resource is restricted for use by the holder of the lock. See exclusive lock, shared lock. (2) The means by which integrity of data is ensured by preventing more than one user from accessing or changing the same data or object at the same time. (3) See advisory lock, data lock, enforced lock, file lock, process lock, read lock, record lock, text lock, write lock.

lock-and-key protection system In computer security, a security system in which a key or password is matched with a specific access requirement.

locked documents In the IBM ImagePlus system, documents undergoing a maintenance function. Documents may also be locked if an error occurred during processing.

locked field A field that cannot be modified by the user.

locked keyboard A keyboard that cannot accept input.

locked page In virtual storage systems, a page that is not to be paged out.

locked record (1) In the 3790 Communication System, a record in an indexed or relative data set that is currently available for updating by a 3790 program and has been marked as unavailable to prevent a conflicting update by another program. (2) In DPCX, a record in a user data set that is unavailable for access or restricted from access by other programs.

locked resource In CICS/VS, a protected resource that is currently associated with a transaction program as part of a synchronized unit of work. As long as this association exists, the resource can be modified only by the transaction program with which it is associated. See also unlocked resource.

lock file (1) In a shared DASD environment under VSE, a system file on disk used by the sharing systems to control their access to shared data. (2) In AIX multiprocess applications, a system file on a disk that the sharing processes use to control their access to shared data or devices.

lock hierarchy In DPPX, a protective measure to prevent deadlocks between threads requesting locks. The locks are granted in lowest to highest order, based on their location in the hierarchy.

locking (1) A characteristic of code extension characters that applies any change in interpretation to all coded representations following, or to all coded representations of a given class, until the next appropriate code extension character occurs. (2) In DPPX, a method of ensuring uninterrupted use of a data area or code by one thread. (3) Contrast with nonlocking.

locking device On dictation equipment, a device used to fix in position a head support arm, playback head, or other critical component during transport of the equipment. (I)

lock management In IMS/VS, the reservation of a segment by a program to prevent other programs from using the segment until the program using it is done. See global lock management, local lock management.

lock mode In ACF/TCAM, a mode in which the next message received by an external logical unit (LU) entering an inquiry message for an application program is a reply from the application program to that inquiry. See also conversational mode, extended lock mode, line lock, message lock mode, station lock.

lockout (1) In a telephone circuit controlled by an echo-suppressor, the inability of one or both subscribers to get through either because of excessive local circuit noise or continuous speech from one subscriber. (2) On a calculator, the facility that inhibits entry of data when the machine is in overflow or error condition. (T) (3) In multiprocessing, a programming technique used to prevent access to critical data by both processing units at the same time. (4) To place unaddressed terminals on a multipoint line in control state so that they will not receive transmitted data. See also blind, polling, selection. (5) Synonym for protection.

lock-out facility The facility that inhibits the entry of data into a calculator when the calculator is in overflow or in error condition. (T) (A)

lock state In the AS/400 system and System/38, a condition defined for an object that determines how it is locked, how it is used (read or write), and whether the object can be shared (used by more than one job).

lock/unlock facility In OS/VS2, a supervisor facility that controls the execution of instruction strings when a disabled page fault occurs.

log (1) In ACF/TCAM, a collection of messages or message segments placed in an auxiliary storage device for accounting or data collection purposes. (2) To record; for example, to log all messages on the system printer. (3) In video production, a record of each take, shot, and scene produced; used as a guide for the editing of the tape. (4) Synonym for journal.

logarithmic axis In GDDM, an axis on which ascending powers of 10 are equally spaced.

log data set A data set consisting of the messages or message segments recorded on auxiliary storage by the ACF/TCAM logging facility.

logged-on operator A NetView operator station task that requires a terminal and a logged-on user. Contrast with autotask.

logger (1) A functional unit that records events and physical conditions, usually with respect to time. (I) (A) (2) A device that enables a user entity to log in; for example, to identify itself, its purpose, and time of entry, and to log out with the corresponding data so that the appropriate accounting procedures can be carried out in accordance with the operating system. (A)

logger task In NCCF, a subtask that records errors from EP mode and local mode devices to the EP database and transmits errors from network control program mode devices supported by VTAM and ACF/TCAM to the network control program database.

logging (1) The recording of data about specific events. (2) See data logging.

logging service facility In ACF/TCAM, a service facility that selectively causes incoming or outgoing messages or message segments to be copied onto tape or disk. The log produced by the logging service facility provides a record of message traffic through the message control program.

logic (1) The systematized interconnection of digital switching functions, circuits, or devices. (2) See double rail logic, formal logic, symbolic logic.

logical (1) Pertaining to content or meaning as opposed to location or actual implementation. (A) (2) Pertaining to a view or description of data that does not depend on the characteristics of the computer system or of the physical storage. (A) (3) Contrast with physical. (A)

logical access control In computer security, the use of information-related mechanisms, such as passwords, rather than physical mechanisms to provide access control. Contrast with physical access control.

logical add Synonym for disjunction.

logical address (1) In the 3790 Communication System, an address associated with each device at the time of manufacture and converted to a physical address by the appropriate device processor. (2) In the IBM 8100 Information System, a storage address that is either supplied to or supplied by a program during fetching and execution of an instruction or that is used as a pointer during an I/O operation.

logical block In DPPX, logically linked, but not necessarily contiguous, areas of storage for logical records. A logical block is the unit of a data set that is transferred between main storage and auxiliary storage when an I/O operation occurs.

logical channel In packet mode operation, a sending channel and a receiving channel that together are used to send and receive data over a data link at the same time. Several logical channels can be established on the same data link by interleaving the transmission of packets.

logical channel identifier A bit string in the header of a packet that associates the packet with a specific switched virtual circuit or permanent virtual circuit.

logical character delete symbol In VM, a special editing symbol, normally the AT (@) sign, that causes CP to delete it and the immediately preceding character from the input line. If many delete symbols are keyed in consecutively, that same number of preceding characters are deleted from the input line. The value may be redefined or unassigned by the installation or user. Synonymous with character delete symbol.

logical child In an IMS/VS database, a pointer segment that establishes an access path between its physical parent segment and its logical parent segment.

Note: A logical child segment is a physical child of its physical parent and a logical child of its logical parent.

logical circuit Deprecated term for logical channel.

logical comparison The examination of two strings to discover whether they are identical. (I) (A)

logical connection terminal In VTAM, for a network control program in network control mode, a description of a terminal (provided by a TERMINAL statement) to be used for a dial-in terminal that cannot be identified.

logical constant A constant with a value of true or false.

logical database In IMS/VS, a set of logical database record occurrences. It is composed of one or more physical databases and represents hierarchic, structured relationships between data segments that can be different from the physical structure in which the segments were loaded. See also physical database.

logical database record In an IMS/VS database, a set of hierarchically related segments of one or more segment types.

Note: As viewed by an application program, the logical database record is always a hierarchic tree structure of segments. The logical database record consists of a given root segment and all of the segments that are hierarchically dependent on it.

logical data structure (1) In a database, the relationships among data elements from the point of view of an end user. (2) In a hierarchical database, a hierarchic structure of segments. (3) Contrast with physical data structure.

Note: Application programs that are written to use IMS/VS deal only with logical data structures.

logical destination See destination, local destination, remote destination.

logical device (1) A file for conducting input or output with a physical device. (2) A file for mapping user I/O between virtual and real devices.

logical device address (LDA) A number used to represent a terminal or terminal component within a workstation. See also physical device address.

logical device order (LDO) In VTAM, a set of parameters that specify a data-transfer or data-control operation to local 3270 Information Display Systems and certain kinds of start/stop or BSC terminals.

logical edit In the 3660 Supermarket Store System, the verification of parameters coded in subsystem definition statements. This edit checks whether the values coded are within the limits allowed. Contrast with textual edit. See also subsystem definition statement.

logical editing symbols In VM, symbols allowing the user to correct keying errors, combine multiple lines of input on one physical line, and key in logical editing symbols as data. Logical editing symbols may be defined, reassigned, or unassigned by customer or user. See also logical character delete symbol, logical escape symbol, logical line delete symbol, logical line end symbol.

logical escape symbol In VM, a special editing symbol, normally the double quote character, that causes CP to consider the immediately following character as a data character instead of as a logical editing symbol.

logical expression (1) An expression that contains logical operators and operands and that can be reduced to a value that is true or false. (T)   (2) An expression composed of logical operators, relational operators, or both, that can be reduced to a value of either true or false. See Figure 89.

A or B and (C<=5)

Figure 89. Logical Expression

logical file In the AS/400 system and System/38, a description of how data is to be presented to or received from a program. This type of file contains no data, but it defines record formats for one or more physical files. See also join logical file, database file. Contrast with physical file.

logical file member In the AS/400 system and System/38, a named logical grouping of data records from one or more physical file members. See also member.

logical group In MVS, a collection of related pages. An address space can consist of multiple groups: one for the link pack area, one for the scheduler work area, and one for the private address space.

logical group number (LGN) In MVS, an identifier of a logical group. It is the base value that the real storage manager and the auxiliary storage manager use to compute a logical page identifier (LPID); for example, all pages of a virtual I/O data set may be represented by a single LGN.

logical indicator One of 40 1-bit switches assigned to each 3790 program and maintained in the 3791 Controller. The first 32 indicators can be set and tested by the 3790 program. The last eight indicators are manipulated by the controller and can be tested only by the 3790 program.

logical IOCS (LIOCS) A comprehensive set of macroinstruction routines that create, retrieve, and modify data files.

logical level (1) All aspects dealing with a database and its architecture, consistent with a conceptual level, but abstract from its physical implementation. (T)

(2) In a conceptual schema language, the level that is, or that describes, an aspect of an information system that is independent of, but related to, the realization of the information system. Contrast with physical level. (A)   See also physical level.

logical line In VM, a command or data line that can be separated from one or more additional command or data lines on the same input line by a logical line end symbol.

logical line delete symbol In VM, a special editing symbol, normally the cent (¢) sign, that causes CP to delete the previous logical line in the input line back to (and including) the previous logical line end symbol. Synonymous with line delete symbol. See also logical line.

logical line end symbol In VM, a special editing symbol, normally the pound (#) sign, that allows the user to key-in several command or data lines in the same physical line; that is, each logical line except the last line is terminated with the logical line end symbol. Synonymous with line end symbol.

logical line group (LLG) Any collection of data links specified by a user as a group at generation of the network control program.

logical link In an IMS/VS multisystem environment, the means by which a physical link is related to the transactions and terminals that can use the physical link.

logical link control (LLC) protocol In a local area network, the protocol that governs the exchange of transmission frames between data stations independently of how the transmission medium is shared. (T)   The LLC protocol was developed by the IEEE 802 committee and is common to all LAN standards. See also enhanced logical link control (ELLC), qualified logical link control (QLLC), physical services header (PSH).

logical link control (LLC) sublayer (1) In a local area network, that part of the data link layer that supports medium-independent data link functions. (T)

Note: The LLC sublayer uses the services of the medium access control sublayer to provide services to the network layer. (2) One of two sublayers of the ISO Open Systems Interconnection data link layer (which corresponds to the SNA data link control layer), proposed for local area networks by the IEEE Project 802 Committee on Local Area Networks and the European Computer Manufacturers Association (ECMA) . It includes those functions unique to the particular link control procedures that are associated with the attached node and are independent of the medium; this allows different logical link protocols to coexist on the same network without interfering with each other. The LLC sublayer uses services provided by the medium access control (MAC) sublayer and provides services to the network layer.

logical link control type 1 (LLC type 1) An unacknowledged connectionless mode of operation within the logical link control sublayer. (T)

logical link control type 2 (LLC type 2) A connection-oriented mode of operation within the logical link control sublayer. (T)

logical link control type 3 (LLC type 3) An acknowledged connectionless mode of operation within the logical link control sublayer. (T)

logical link path In an IMS/VS multisystem environment, the path between any two systems. One or more logical link paths must be defined for each logical link.

logical logging In IMS/VS, the process of moving log records into the log buffers. Contrast with physical logging.

logically connected terminal In VM, a terminal that is connected by means of switched or nonswitched lines or by local attachment to a multiple-access virtual machine via the CP DIAL command. See also multiple-access virtual machine.

logical message (1) In ACF/TCAM, a user-defined message, consisting of one or more related units of data in a transmission, ending with an end-of-message code. Contrast with physical message. (2) In IMS/VS, an input or output message that is in a queue associated with a logical rather than a physical terminal. The message queue can be moved, independently of an application, from device to device.

logical multiply Synonym for AND.

logical name See device name.

logical network A subnetwork of machines set up to function as a whole and separate network. A logical network usually functions as a subnetwork of a larger physical network.

logical operation Synonym for logic operation.

logical operator (1) A logical expression such as AND, OR, NOT, AND NOT, and OR NOT. (2) In COBOL, one of the reserved words AND, OR, or NOT. In the formation of a condition, either AND, or OR, or both, can be used as logical connectives. NOT can be used for logical negation. (3) A word or symbol that defines the logical connection between conditions or that makes opposite a condition. (4) In

FORTRAN, a set of operators used in logical expressions. The operators are: NOT (logical negation), AND (logical conjunction), and OR (logical union).

logical order In COBOL, the order in which records are sequentially read from a file. For sequential and relative files, the logical order corresponds to the physical order of the records in the file. For indexed files, the logical order is based on the order of the keys in the index of the file.

logical output device For line devices, the combination of a physical output device and such logical variables as page size and number of lines per vertical inch.

logical page (LPAGE) (1) The boundary for determining the limits of printing. (2) In the IMS/VS message format service, a user-defined group of related message segment and field definitions. See also physical page. (3) In COBOL, a conceptual entity consisting of the top margin, the page body, and the bottom margin. Contrast with physical page.

logical page identifier (LPID) The unique identifier of a specific page.

logical page number (LPN) The relative page number within a logical group. It is added to the logical group number to create a unique LPID.

logical paging In the IMS/VS message format service, the means by which logical message segments are grouped for formatting. See also operator logical paging.

logical parent In an IMS/VS database, a segment containing common reference data to which a logical child segment points, using a direct or symbolic pointer. A logical child can also point to a physical parent segment.

logical partition In AIX programs, one to three physical partitions. The number of logical partitions within a logical volume is variable.

logical primary A primary that can have a value of true or false.

logical product Deprecated term for conjunction.

logical record (1) A set of related data or words considered to be a record from a logical viewpoint. (T) (2) A record from the standpoint of its content, function, and use rather than its physical attributes, that is, a record defined in terms of the information it contains. (3) In CICS/VS, a data record sent by one transaction program to another. The length of the record is contained in a two-byte field immediately preceding the record. (4) In VSAM, a unit of information normally pertaining to a single subject; a logical record is the user record requested of or given to the data management function. (5) In COBOL, the most inclusive data item. Synonymous with record. See report writer logical record.

logical relation Two expressions separated by a relational operator; for example, EQ, GE, gt, LE, LT, and NE. See also arithmetic relation, character relation.

logical relationship In an IMS/VS database, a path between two independent segments in which the relationship is user defined.

logical ring In a token-bus network, the passing of a token from data station to data station in a manner that simulates the passing of control in a ring network. (T)

logical schema (1) A part of a database schema that pertains to the logical level. (T)   (2) In a database, a schema that describes a data model.   (3) See also physical schema.

logical shift A shift that equally affects all characters of a computer word. (I) (A)   Synonymous with logic shift. See Figure 90.

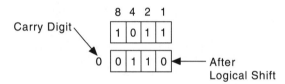

Figure 90. Logical Shift

logical storage In DPPX, the concept of storage space that can be regarded as addressable main storage by an application program, and in which logical addresses are mapped into real addresses through control blocks.

logical structure The relationships among data in a database as perceived by users of the database. (T)

Note: These relationships may differ from the physical relationships of stored data.

logical sum Deprecated term for disjunction.

logical swapping In VM/SP HPO, the process of validating or invalidating virtual machine page table entries and of unchaining or chaining the corresponding entries in the table (the CORTABLE) used to control and allocate real storage. Contrast with physical swapping.

logical term A term that can be used only in a logical expression.

logical terminal (LTERM) In IMS/VS, a destination with a name related to one or more physical terminals.

logical terminal pool In IMS/VS, a user-defined group of logical terminals to be associated with non-VTAM switched telecommunication lines. Each logical terminal pool consists of one or more logical terminal subpools.

logical terminal subpool In IMS/VS, a user-defined group of logical terminals within a logical terminal pool.

logical timer A software logic element representing use of a hardware timer.

logical-to-physical coordination In the ESCON Manager, the coordination of a physical connectivity change in an ESCON Director with an equivalent logical change in any associated host.

logical twins In an IMS/VS database, all occurrences of one type of logical child with a common logical parent. See also physical twins, twin segments.

logical type A data type that contains the values of true and false.

logical unit (LU) A type of network accessible unit that enables end users to gain access to network resources and communicate with each other.

logical unit (LU) 6.2 A type of logical unit that supports general communication between programs in a distributed processing environment. LU 6.2 is characterized by (a) a peer relationship between session partners, (b) efficient utilization of a session for multiple transactions, (c) comprehensive end-to-end error processing, and (d) a generic application program interface (API) consisting of structured verbs that are mapped into a product implementation.

logical unit (LU) services In SNA, the capability of a logical unit to: (1) receive requests from an end user and, in turn, issue requests to the system services control point (SSCP) in order to perform the requested functions, typically for session initiation; (2) receive requests from the SSCP to activate LU-LU sessions via BIND SESSION requests; and (3) provide session presentation and other services for LU-LU sessions. See also physical unit (PU) services, SSCP services.

logical unit name In programming, a name used to represent the address of an input/output unit.

logical unit of work In IMS/VS, the processing that a program performs between synchronization points.

logical volume (1) A portion of a physical volume viewed by the system as a volume. (2) In the AIX operating system, a collection of physical partitions organized into logical partitions all contained in a single volume group. Logical volumes are expandable and can span several physical volumes in a volume group.

Logical Volume Manager In the AIX operating system, a program that manages disk space at a logical level. It controls fixed-disk resources by mapping data between logical and physical storage, allowing data to be discontiguous, span multiple disks, replicated, and dynamically expanded.

logical workstation The combination of storage and a 3601 application program treated as a unit by the 3601 Finance Communication Controller.

logic bomb In computer security, a resident computer program that triggers the perpetration of an unauthorized act when particular states of the system are realized.

logic design A functional design that uses formal methods of description, such as symbolic logic. (T) (A)

logic device A device that performs logic operations. (T) (A)

logic diagram A graphic representation of a logic design. (T) (A)

logic element (1) Synonym for gate. (2) See combinational logic element, sequential logic element.

logic error In VTAM, an error condition that results from an invalid request (a program logic error).

logic function Deprecated term for switching function.

logic instruction An instruction in which the operation part specifies a logic operation. (I) (A)

logic operation (1) An operation that follows the rules of symbolic logic. (I) (A) (2) An operation in which each character of the result depends only on the corresponding character of each operand. (I) (A) (3) Synonymous with logical operation.

logic programming A method for structuring programs as sets of logical rules with predefined algorithms for the processing of input data to a program according to the rules of that program. (T)

logic shift Synonym for logical shift.

logic short fault A fault in logic circuitry in which a short circuit exists between logic blocks and that operates as if it were an additional logic block.

Note: The additional logic block can function either as a logic AND or a logic OR.

logic symbol A symbol that represents an operator, function, or functional relationship. (T) (A)

logic test In TPNS, a conditional test on an input or output message, a counter, or other item using the TPNS IF statement. The IF actions can be used to control the message generation process.

logic unit (1) A part of a computer that performs logic operations and related operations. (I) (A) (2) See arithmetic and logic unit.

logic variable Deprecated term for switching variable.

log in (1) To begin a session at a display station. (2) To begin a session with a remote resource. (3) The act of identifying oneself as authorized to use a resource. Often the system requires a user ID and password to check authorization to use the resource. (4) See also log on.

login In the AIX operating system, the act of gaining access to a computer system by entering identification and authentication information at the workstation.

login directory In the AIX operating system, the directory accessed when a user first logs in to the system.

login domain The location for the resources accessed when a user first logs in to a network.

log-initiated checkpoint See simple checkpoint, system scheduled checkpoint.

login name In the AIX operating system, string of characters that uniquely identifies a user to the system.

login session In the AIX operating system, the period of time during which a user of a workstation can communicate with an interactive system, usually the elapsed time between log in and log off.

login shell In the AIX operating system, the shell that is started when a user logs into the computer system. See also shell.

logmode table Synonym for logon mode table.

logo A letter, combination of letters, or symbol that identifies a product or company.

log off (1) To end a session. Synonymous with log out. (T) (2) To request that a session be terminated. (3) See also sign-off.

logoff (1) The procedure by which a user ends a terminal session. (2) In VTAM, an unformatted session-termination request.

log on (1) To initiate a session. Synonymous with log in. (T) (2) In SNA products, to initiate a session between an application program and a logical unit (LU). (3) See also log in, sign-on.

logon (1) The procedure by which a user begins a terminal session. (2) In VTAM, an unformatted session-initiation request for a session between two logical units.

logon data (1) In VTAM, the user data portion of a field-formatted or unformatted session-initiation request. (2) In VTAM, the entire logon sequence or message from an LU. Synonymous with logon message.

logon-interpret routine In VTAM, an installation exit routine, associated with an interpret table entry, that translates logon information. It may also verify the logon.

logon message Synonym for logon data.

logon mode In VTAM, a subset of session parameters specified in a logon mode table for communication with a logical unit. See also session parameters.

logon mode table (1) In VTAM, a set of entries for one or more logon modes. Each logon mode is identified by a logon mode name. (2) In DPPX, a table in which each entry defines the characteristics of a session between two logical units.

logon request See logon.

logo screen On a personal computer, a hello screen that identifies the name and owner of an application software product.

log out Synonym for log off. (T)

logo window In SAA Advanced Common User Access architecture, a modal dialog box containing the application copyright notice and other information that identifies the application.

log tape write ahead (LTWA) In IMS/VS, an option that ensures that a database log record for a data change is written to the system log before the changed data are written to the database.

logtype entry In ACF/TCAM, a terminal-table entry associated with a queue on which complete messages reside while awaiting transfer to the logging medium. A logtype entry is not needed if message segments are only to be logged. See also cascade entry, group entry, line entry, process entry, single entry.

log write-ahead (LWA) In IMS/VS, the process of writing records of completed operations to the write-ahead data set before entering them in the online log data set.

long (1) In the AIX object data manager, a terminal descriptor type used to define a variable as a signed 4-byte number. See also terminal descriptor. (2) A signed 4-byte number.

long comment In the AS/400 system, up to a full-screen description of a field, record format, or file. Long comments are typed when the field, record format, or file is created or changed, and displayed either from IDDU or Query.

long constant In the AIX operating system, a 4-byte integer constant followed by the letter "l" or "L."

long format In binary floating-point storage formats, the 64-bit representation of a binary floating-point number, not-a-number, or infinity. Contrast with short format.

longitudinal magnetic recording A technique of magnetic recording in which magnetic polarities representing data is aligned along the length of the recording track. (T)

longitudinal offset loss In waveguide-to-waveguide coupling, synonym for gap loss. (E)

longitudinal parity check (1) A parity check on a row of binary digits that are members of a set forming a matrix; for example, a parity check on the bits of a track in a block on a magnetic tape. (T) (2) A system of error checking performed at the receiving station after a block check character has been accumulated. (3) See also transverse parity check. (4) Synonymous with longitudinal redundancy check.

longitudinal redundancy check (LRC) Synonym for longitudinal parity check.

longitudinal redundancy check character On a magnetic tape where each character is represented in a lateral row of bits, a character used for checking the parity of each track in the longitudinal direction. Such a character is usually the last character recorded in each block and is used in some magnetic recording systems to reestablish the initial recording status. (A)

long lens In photography, a telephoto lens.

long precision In BASIC, the level of precision in which values printed in fixed-point format have a maximum of 14 significant digits, and values printed in floating-point format have a maximum of 15 significant digits. Contrast with single precision.

long queue status Synonym for long status.

long shot In multimedia applications, a camera angle that reveals the subject and the subject's surroundings; it is often used as an establishing shot. Synonymous with wide shot.

long status In the AIX operating system, a detailed, multiline status that contains more information about each job than the normal short status. Synonymous with long queue status.

long string In SQL, a string whose actual length, or a varying-length string whose maximum length, is greater than 254 bytes or 127 double-byte characters.

long term fix area In MVS, the space taken by the system queue area, link pack area, and master scheduler.

lookahead field In RPG, a field that allows the program to look at information in a field on the next record in an input file.

loop (1) A sequence of instructions that is to be executed iteratively. (T)   (2) A closed unidirectional signal path connecting input/output devices to a system. (3) In the IBM 8100 Information System, an arrangement of 8100 Information System control units and displays connected directly or by data links to the processor. (4) See closed loop, feedback loop, loop network, magnetic hysteresis loop. (5) Synonym for ring network. (6) See also lobe.

loop adapter (1) In the IBM 8100 Information System, circuitry that allows devices using a directly attached loop to communicate with the system. (2) A feature of the IBM 4300 Processor family that allows the attachment of a variety of SNA and non-SNA devices. To VTAM, these devices appear as channel-attached type 2 physical units (PUs). (3) Synonym for loop feature.

loopback test A test in which signals are looped from a test center through a data set or loopback switch and back to the test center for measurement. See also bussback.

loop body (1) Part of the loop that achieves its primary purpose. (A)   (2) In a counter, a part of the loop control. (A)   (3) Contrast with loop control.

loop check Synonym for echo check.

loop construct In programming languages, a construct that specifies an iteration in the execution sequence; for example, DO loops in FORTRAN, FOR loops in ALGOL, PERFORM loops in COBOL, DO WHILE loops in PL/I. (I)

loop control (1) The parts of a loop that modify the loop control variables and determine whether to execute the loop body or exit from the loop. (A)   (2) Contrast with loop body.

loop-control statement An executable statement used to specify the statements to be executed under control of a loop, the parameters used in executing the loop, the conditions for terminating the loop, and the location to which control is to be passed when the loop is terminated;   for example, FORTRAN DO, ALGOL FOR, COBOL PERFORM. (T)

loop-control variable A variable that affects the execution of instructions in the loop body and is modified by a loop control. (A)

loop counter A counter used to stop execution of a loop when a specified value is reached.

loop feature The circuitry that attaches a loop to a 3601 Finance Communication Controller and handles loop transmissions to and from the controller. Synonymous with loop adapter.

loophole In computer security, an error of omission or oversight in hardware or software that permits circumvention or disablement of access controls.

looping Repetitive execution of the same statement or statements, usually controlled by a DO statement.

looping statement A statement that runs any number of times, depending on the value of a specified expression.

loop initialization The parts of a loop that set its starting values. (A)

loop invariant In programming languages, an assertion that holds throughout a loop construct. (T)

loop jack switchboard A patch panel with rows of jacks for physical access to local loops (maximum capacity of 90 channels). Each column of four jacks accesses one local loop and consists of looping jacks, a set jack, and a miscellaneous jack.

loop network A network configuration in which there is a single path between all nodes and in which the path is a closed circuit. (T)   See Figure 91.

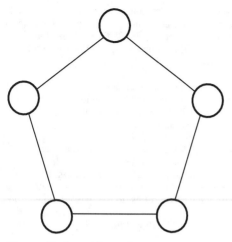

Figure 91. Loop Network

loop splice plate (LSP) In the IBM 8100 Information System, loop hardware that splices two segments of indoor cable or provides a connection point for future expansion of a loop.

loop station connector (LSC) (1) A loop accessory for attaching a controlling unit or an input/output device to the loop. (2) In the IBM 8100 Information System, loop hardware used to attach an 8100 unit, an I/O unit, or an IBM 3842 or 3843 Loop Control Unit to a loop.

loop surge suppressor (LSS) In the IBM 8100 Information System, loop hardware that provides grounding and termination for the attachment of two indoor cables to two outdoor cables, thus enabling the loop to be run outdoors.

looptest mode In IMS/VS, the test mode that permits the establishment of an output write loop, with which continuous attempts are made to transmit a user-entered message to the test terminal.

loop transmission A mode of multipoint operation in which a network is configured as a closed loop of individual point-to-point data links connected by stations that serve as regenerative repeaters. Data transmitted around the loop are regenerated and retransmitted at each station until the data arrive at the destination station. Any station can introduce data into the loop.

loop transmission frame A collection of data sent around a loop as an entity.

loop wiring concentrator (LWC) In the IBM 8100 Information System, loop hardware for attachment of a cluster of I/O units to a loop without a large number of drops on the main loop cable.

loosely coupled multiprocessing In the System/370 computing system, multiprocessing in which two or more processors share access to direct access storage and are coupled by channel-to-channel adapters for passing control information. See also tightly coupled multiprocessing.

loss In computer security, a quantitative measure of harm or deprivation due to a threat acting upon a vulnerable system resource. See annualized loss expectancy.

loss of significance In a register, loss of one or more of the rightmost fractional digits because the result of an operation produced more than seven fractional digits or more than a total of 10 whole-number and fractional digits. See also overflow.

loss time See environmental loss time, external loss time.

loudspeaker control On dictation equipment, a device to switch on or off the equipment's loudspeaker. (I)

low-entry networking (LEN) A capability of nodes to attach directly to one another using basic peer-to-peer protocols to support multiple and parallel sessions between logical units.

low-entry networking (LEN) end node A LEN node receiving network services from an adjacent APPN network node.

low-entry networking (LEN) node A node that provides a range of end-user services, attaches directly to other nodes using peer protocols, and derives network services implicitly from an adjacent APPN network node, that is, without the direct use of CP-CP sessions.

lower curtate The adjacent card rows at the bottom of a punch card. (A)

lower letter row On a keyboard, the bottom letter row. Synonymous with row B. See middle letter row, upper letter row. See also numeral row.

lower print line On a display screen, the line through the lower 50-percent luminance contour of the lowest row of pels of the uppercase character matrix. Contrast with upper print line.

lower window edge In data communication, the sequence number of the last data packet in a window.

low-level code/continuity check (LLC/CC) An IMS/VS application support program that can generate and update low-level codes in a database.

low-level language Synonym for computer-oriented language.

low-level message In System/38, a message sent to the program message queue of the lower-level program invocation. A low-level message is normally not displayed. Contrast with high-level message.

low order end In COBOL, the rightmost character of a string of characters.

low-order position The rightmost position in a string of characters.

low paper indicator On a document copying machine, an indicator showing that the supply of copy material needs to be replenished. (T)

low-priority ready queue In DPCX, a first-in, first-out queue used to indicate the programs ready to be dispatched for execution at a low priority.

low speed transmission Usually, data transmission speed of 600 bps or less.

low tape An indication that the supply of paper tape in a perforator is nearly depleted.

low threshold of occupancy The lower limit of space to be occupied on a primary volume managed by the Data Facility Hierarchical Storage Manager. Contrast with high threshold of occupancy.

low toner indicator On a document copying machine, an indicator showing that the supply of toner needs to be replenished. (T)

LP (1) Linear programming. (A)   (2) Licensed program.

Lp Sound pressure level.

LPA Link pack area.

LPAGE Logical page.

LPBUF Large pageable buffer pool.

LPC Link protocol converter.

LPDA Link Problem Determination Aid.

LPDA-1 Link Problem Determination Aid-1.

LPDA-2 Link Problem Determination Aid-2.

LPFK Lighted programmable function keyboard.

lpi Lines-per-inch.

LPID Logical page identifier.

lpm Lines per minute.

LPN Logical page number.

LQAB Lock queue anchor block.

LRC (1) A longitudinal redundancy check character. (A)   (2) Longitudinal redundancy check.

LRS Local resource sharing.

LS (1) Link status. (2) Long shot.

LSC Loop station connector.

LSI Large scale integration.

LSID Local session identification.

LSP Loop splice plate.

LSQA Local system queue area.

LSR Local shared resources.

LSS Loop surge suppressor.

LSSD Level-sensitive scan design.

LT Less than. See relational operator.

LTERM Logical terminal.

LTRS Letters shift.

LTWA Log tape write ahead.

LU Logical unit.

LUCB Logical unit control block.

LU connection test In SNA products, a diagnostic aid that permits a terminal operator to check whether the path between a system services control point (SSCP) and a logical unit (LU) is operational. Synonymous with end-user to SSCP echo check.

LUD Logical unit description.

LU group In NPM, a file containing a list of related or unrelated logical units. The LU group is used to help simplify data collection and analysis.

Lukasiewicz notation Synonym for prefix notation.

LU-LU session A logical connection between two logical units (LUs) in an SNA network that typically provides communication between two end users.

LU-LU session initiation In SNA, the process beginning with a session initiation request from a logical unit (LU) to a system services control point (SSCP) and culminating in activation of an LU-LU session. See also session activation.

LU-LU session termination In SNA, the process beginning with a session termination request from a logical unit (LU) to a system services control point (SSCP) and culminating in deactivation of an LU-LU session.

LU-LU session type In SNA, the classification of an LU-LU session in terms of the specific subset of SNA protocols and options supported by the logical units (LUs) for that session, namely: (1) mandatory and optional values allowed in the session activation request; (2) usage of data stream controls, FM headers, RU parameters, and sense codes; and (3) presentation services protocols such as those associated with FM header usage. LU-LU session types 0, 1, 2, 3, 4, 6, and 7 are defined.

Note: At session activation, one LU-LU half-session selects the session type and includes or excludes optional protocols of that session type by sending the session activation request, and the other half-session concurs with the selection by sending a positive response or rejects the selection by sending a negative response. In LU-LU session types 4 and 6, the half-sessions may negotiate the optional parameters to be used. For the other session types, the primary half-session selects the optional protocols without negotiating with the secondary half-session.

LU-LU session type 0 In SNA, a type of session between two LU-LU half-sessions using SNA-defined protocols for transmission control and data flow control, but using end-user or product-defined protocols to augment or replace FMD services protocols; for example, a session that involves an application program using IMS/VS and an IBM 3600 Finance Communication System, in which the operator of the 3600 terminal is updating the passbook balance for a customer's savings account.

LU-LU session type 1 In SNA, a type of session between an application program and single- or multiple-device data processing terminals in an interactive, batch data transfer, or distributed processing environment; for example, a session involving an application program using IMS/VS and an IBM 3767 Communication Terminal, in which the 3767 operator is correcting a database that is maintained using the application program. The data stream is the SNA character string (SCS).

LU-LU session type 2 In SNA, a type of session between an application program and a single display terminal in an interactive environment, using the SNA 3270 data stream; for example, an application program using IMS/VS and an IBM 3277 Display Station, in which the 3277 operator is creating data and sending the data to the application program.

LU-LU session type 3 In SNA, a type of session between an application program and a single printer, using the SNA 3270 data stream; for example, an application program using CICS/VS to send data to an IBM 3284 Printer attached to an IBM 3791 Controller.

LU-LU session type 4 In SNA, a type of session between: (1) an application program and a single-device or multiple-device data processing or word processing terminal in an interactive, batch data transfer, or distributed processing environment; for example, a session between an application program using CICS/VS and an IBM 6670 Information Distributor; or (2) logical units (LUs) in peripheral nodes; for example, two 6670s. The data stream is the SNA character string (SCS).

LU-LU session type 6 In SNA, a type of session between two application programs in a distributed processing environment, using the SNA character string (SCS) or a structured-field data stream; for example, an application program using CICS/VS communicating with an application program using IMS/VS.

LU-LU session type 6.2 In SNA, a type of session for communication between peer systems. Synonymous with APPC protocol.

LU-LU session type 7 In SNA, a type of session between an application program and a single display terminal in an interactive environment.

luminance (1) In computer graphics, the amount of light, measured in lumens, that is emitted by a picture element (a pixel) or by a particular area of a display screen. (2) Brightness. See also chrominance.

luminance signal The portion of image information that provides brightness. Alone, luminance provides a monochrome image.

LU-mode pair In the VTAM implementation of the LU 6.2 architecture, the coupling of an LU name entry and a mode name entry. This coupling allows a pool of sessions with the same characteristics to be established. See also LU-mode table.

LU-mode table In the VTAM implementation of the LU 6.2 architecture, a data structure composed of LU-mode pairs that VTAM maintains for the application program.

lumped loading Inserting uniformly spaced inductance coils along a line, since continuous loading is impractical. See also loading.

LU-name entry The entry in an LU-mode pair that contains information about the partner logical unit.

LUS Logical unit services.

LU services manager An SNA component that provides a logical unit (LU) with network services and end-user to end-user services. The LU services manager provides services for all half-sessions within the LU.

LUST Logical unit status table.

LUSTAT An SNA command used to send logical unit status information.

LU type The classification of an LU in terms of the specific subset of SNA protocols and options it supports for a given session, namely:

- The mandatory and optional values allowed in the session activation request
- The usage of data stream controls, function management headers (FMHs), request unit parameters, and sense data values
- Presentation services protocols such as those associated with FMH usage

LU types 0, 1, 2, 3, 4, 6.1, 6.2, and 7 are defined.

LU type 6.2 (LU 6.2) A type of logical unit that supports general communication between programs in a distributed processing environment. LU 6.2 is characterized by (a) a peer relationship between session partners, (b) efficient utilization of a session for multiple transactions, (c) comprehensive end-to-end error processing, and (d) a generic application program interface consisting of structured verbs that are mapped into a product implementation.

LU 6.2 Logical unit 6.2.

LU 6.2 session A session that is initiated by VTAM on behalf of a logical unit (LU) 6.2 application program, or a session initiated by a remote LU in which the application program specifies that the VTAM programs are to control the session by using the APPCCMD macroinstruction.

LU 6.2 verb A syntactical unit in the LU 6.2 application program interface representing an operation.

LUC session Communication, using LU type 0 protocols, between the LUC tasks of two NetView programs. This communication is similar to an LU 6.2 conversation.

LUC task A NetView task, denoted by the NetView domain ID concatenated with the literal "LUC" (for example, CNM01LUC), that serves as the endpoint of an LUC session.

lvalue In the C language, an expression that represents a data object that can be viewed, tested, and changed.

Lw Sound power level.

LWC Loop wiring concentrator.

LWCapture In the IBM LinkWay product, the LinkWay function that lets the user use pictures from other sources.

LWEdit In the IBM LinkWay product, the LinkWay text editor that lets the user create or change documents.

LWFonted In the IBM LinkWay product, the LinkWay font and icon editor that lets the user change or create fonts and icons.

LWPaint In the IBM LinkWay product, the LinkWay picture editor that lets the user create or change pictures.

LWPalette In the IBM LinkWay product, the LinkWay function that lets the user change the colors in imported pictures.

LWRemove In the IBM LinkWay product, the LinkWay function that lets the user remove LWCapture from memory when he has completed work.

M

M Mega; 1,000,000 in decimal notation. When referring to storage capacity, 2 to the twentieth power; 1,048,576 in decimal notation.

m (1) Milli; one thousandth part. (2) Merge order. (3) Meter.

MAC (1) Medium access control. (2) Message authentication code. (3) Mandatory access control.

MAC frame A transmission frame that controls the operation of the IBM Token-Ring Network and any ring station operations that affect the ring.

machine See accounting machine, electrical accounting machine, Turing machine, universal Turing machine.

machine address Deprecated term for absolute address *(1)*.

machine characteristic A value defined in the computer.

machine check An error condition that is caused by an equipment malfunction.

machine check analysis and recording In VSE, a feature that records machine check error information and then attempts to recover from the error.

machine check handler (MCH) A feature that analyzes errors and attempts recovery by retrying the failing instruction. If retry is unsuccessful, it attempts to correct the malfunction or to isolate the affected task.

machine check interruption (MCI) An interruption that occurs as a result of an equipment malfunction or error.

machine code Synonym for instruction code. (T)

machine configuration record In System/38, a series of data fields, modifiable only by the customer service representative, that describes the hardware.

machine cycle The shortest period of time required to execute an instruction.

machine execution priority In System/38, the priority of a routing step when competing with other routing steps for machine resources.

machine handle In a duplicator, a control for manually cycling the machine. (T) Synonymous with machine handwheel.

machine handwheel Synonym for machine handle.

machine-independent Pertaining to procedures or programs created without regard for the actual devices that are used to process them.

machine information code See system reference code.

machine instruction (1) An instruction that can be directly executed by a processor of a computer. A machine instruction is an element of a machine language. (T) (2) An instruction of a machine language. (3) Synonymous with computer instruction.

machine instruction set Synonym for computer instruction set.

machine interface (MI) (1) The means by which a device, program, user, or system interacts with a computer; for example, commands, instructions, display pointers, menus, keyboards. (2) In System/38, the instruction set and interface to the machine.

machine language (1) An artificial language composed of the machine instructions of a computer. (T) (2) A language that can be used directly by a computer without intermediate processing. (3) Synonymous with computer language.

machine learning The ability of a device to improve its performance based on its past performance. (I) (A)

machine object In the AS/400 system, a program object that has no defined storage form; the object is defined internally to the machine. The machine object is not available to the user. Contrast with data object.

machine operation An elementary function that a computer performs in response to a machine instruction. Synonymous with computer operation. (T)

machine-oriented language Synonym for computer-oriented language.

machine-readable Pertaining to data a machine can acquire or interpret (read) from a storage device, a data medium, or other source.

machine-readable information (MRI) All textual information contained in a program, such as a system control program, an application program, or microcode. MRI includes all information that is presented to or received from a user interacting with a system. This includes menus, prompts, messages, report headings, commands, and responses. MRI may appear on printers or on display panels.

machine-readable medium A medium that can convey data to a sensing device. (A) Synonymous with automated data medium.

machine-readable passport A passport that is intended to be read and verified by a machine in accordance with an ISO standard. (T) (A)

machine run The execution of one or more routines that are linked to form one operating unit.

machine-sensible information Synonym for soft copy.

machine space point Synonym for space pointer machine object.

machine storage pool In the AS/400 system and System/38, a storage pool used by the machine and certain highly shared programs.

machine vision In robotics, use of video cameras to obtain visual images that are converted to analog electrical signals and then to digital or gray-scale image data for processing. Two-dimensional and three-dimensional machine vision is used for applications such as robot guidance and automated inspection and quality control.

machine word Synonym for computer word.

MACLIB library A library that contains macros, copy files, or source program statements for use under CMS.

MAC protocol See medium access control protocol.

macro (1) In photography, a magnifying camera lens that can focus down to a few inches. (2) See macrodefinition, macro prototype statement. (3) Synonym for macroinstruction.

macro assembler A program that converts and assembles macroinstructions into machine code.

macrobending In an optical fiber, optical attenuation caused by macroscopic deviations of the axis from a straight line. (E) Contrast with microbending.

macrobend loss In an optical fiber, that loss attributable to macrobending. (E) Synonymous with curvature loss. Contrast with microbend loss.

macro call (1) A statement, embedded in a source language, that is to be replaced by a defined statement sequence in the same source language. The macro call will also specify the actual parameters for any formal parameters in the macrodefinition. (T) (2) Synonym for macroinstruction.

macrodeclaration Synonym for macrodefinition.

macrodefinition (1) A possibly parameterized specification for a statement sequence to replace a macro call. A macrodefinition may be considered as a procedure to be executed by a macrogenerator yielding the statement sequence. (T) (2) A set of statements defining the name of, format of, and conditions for generating a sequence of assembler statements from a single source statement. (3) See also library macrodefinition, source macrodefinition.

macroexpansion (1) The sequence of statements that result from a macrogeneration operation. (2) Synonym for macrogeneration.

macrogenerating program Synonym for macrogenerator.

macrogeneration An operation in which an assembler produces a sequence of assembler language statements by processing a macrodefinition called by a macroinstruction. Macrogeneration takes place at preassembly time. Synonymous with macroexpansion.

macrogenerator A program for replacing macro calls with defined statement sequences according to macrodefinitions. A macrogenerator may be an independent computer program or it may be integrated as a subprogram in a compiler or assembler to generate the source program. (T) Synonymous with macroprocessor, macrogenerating program.

macroinstruction (1) An instruction in a source language that is to be replaced by a defined sequence of instructions in the same source language and that may also specify values for parameters in the replaced instructions. Synonymous with macro, macro statement. (T) (2) In assembler programming, an assembler language statement that causes the assembler to process a predefined set of statements called a macro definition. The statements normally produced from the macro definition replace the macroinstruction in the program. See also definition statement. (3) Synonymous with macro call, macrostatement.

macrolanguage The representations and rules for writing macroinstructions and macrodefinitions.

macrolibrary A library of macrodefinitions used during macroexpansion.

macroprocessing instruction An assembler instruction used in macrodefinitions and processed at preassembly time.

macroprocessor (1) A program that converts macro instructions into specified values. (2) Synonym for macrogenerator. (T)

macroprogramming Computer programming with macroinstructions. (A)

macro prototype Synonym for macro prototype statement.

macrostatement Synonym for macroinstruction.

macrosubstitution During formatting, the substitution of control words, symbols, and text for a macro.

MAC sublayer Medium access control sublayer.

MACSYMA A programming language designed for nonnumeric manipulation of mathematical expressions in conversational mode. (T)

magazine In System/36 and System/38, a container that holds up to 10 diskettes and is inserted into a diskette magazine drive.

magazine slot See slot.

magic number In the AIX operating system, a numeric or string constant in a file that indicates the file type.

magnetic card (1) A card with a magnetizable layer on which data can be stored. (T) (2) In word processing, a recording medium in the form of a paper or plastic card on which recordings can be made on only one side. (T)

magnetic card storage A magnetic storage in which data are stored by magnetic recording on the surface of thin flexible cards. (I) (A)

magnetic cell A storage cell in which different patterns of magnetization are used to represent characters. (I) (A) Synonymous with static magnetic cell.

magnetic core (1) A piece of magnetic material, usually torus-shaped, used for storage. (T) (2) A configuration of magnetic material that is or is intended to be placed in a spatial relationship to current-carrying conductors and whose magnetic properties are essential to its use. It may be used to concentrate an induced magnetic field, as in a transformer

induction coil or an armature, to retain a magnetic polarization for the purpose of storing data, or for its nonlinear properties, as in a logic element. It can be made of materials such as iron, iron oxide, or ferrite and can be in the form of wire, tape, toroid, rod, or thin film. (A)   See Figure 92.

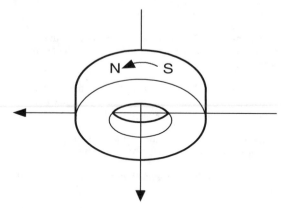

Figure 92. Magnetic Core

magnetic core storage (1) A magnetic storage in which data are stored by the selective polarization of magnetic cores. (I) (A) (2) Deprecated term for main storage.

Note: Magnetic core storage has been replaced by other storage technologies.

magnetic delay line A delay line whose operation is based on time of propagation of electromagnetic waves. (A)

magnetic disk (1) A flat circular plate with a magnetizable surface layer on one or both sides of which data can be stored. (T) (2) In word processing, a recording medium in the form of a flat circular plate on which magnetic recordings can be made on either or both sides. (T) (3) See also diskette. (4) Synonymous with disk.

magnetic disk storage A magnetic storage in which data is stored by magnetic recording on the flat surfaces of one or more disks, which in use rotates around a common spindle. (T)

magnetic disk unit A device that contains magnetic disks, a disk drive, one or more magnetic heads, and associated controls. (T)

magnetic drum A right circular cylinder with a magnetizable layer on which data can be stored. (T) (A)

magnetic drum storage A magnetic storage in which data is stored by magnetic recording on the surface of a magnetic drum which, in use, rotates on its axis. (T)

magnetic drum unit A device that contains a magnetic drum, along with the mechanism for moving it, magnetic heads, and associated controls. (T)

magnetic hand scanner A hand-held device that reads precoded information from a magnetic stripe. See also magnetic stripe reader.

magnetic head (1) An electromagnet that can perform one or more functions of reading, writing, and erasing data on a magnetic data medium. (I) (A) (2) See also preread head, read head, read/write head, write head.

magnetic hysteresis loop A closed curve showing the relation between the magnetization force and the induction of magnetization in a magnetic substance when the magnetized field (force) is carried through a complete cycle. (A)

magnetic ink (1) A special ink that contains particles of magnetic material suitable for recording of data. (T) (2) An ink that contains particles of a magnetic substance whose presence can be detected by magnetic sensors. (A)

magnetic ink character A character whose pattern of magnetic ink is sensed to enable automatic identification. (T)

magnetic ink character reader An input unit which reads characters by magnetic ink character recognition. (T)

magnetic ink character recognition (1) MICR. Character recognition of magnetic ink characters. (T) (2) The identification of characters through the use of magnetic ink. (3) Contrast with optical character recognition.

magnetic recording A technique of storing data by selectively magnetizing portions of a magnetizable material. (I) (A)

magnetic sheet In word processing, a recording medium in the form of a broad rectangular strip on which magnetic recordings can be made on either or both sides. (T)

magnetic slot reader A device that reads coded information from a magnetic stripe as it passes through a slot in the reader. See also magnetic stripe reader.

magnetic storage A storage device that uses the magnetic properties of certain materials. (I) (A)

magnetic storage device controller The I/O controller card in the card enclosure that controls the operation of the disk, diskette, and tape devices.

magnetic stripe (1) A strip of magnetic material on which data, usually identification information, can be recorded and from which the data can be read. (2) In PSS, the magnetic material, similar to recording tape, used on merchandise tickets, credit cards, and employee badges. Information is recorded on the stripe for later reading by the wand attached to the point of sale terminal.

magnetic stripe reader A device that reads precoded information from a magnetic stripe. The device can be hand-held or fixed. See also magnetic hand scanner, magnetic slot reader.

magnetic stripe reference card An identification card that is equipped with a certified magnetic reference tape for use in standardizing encoders and readers. (A)

magnetic tape (1) A tape with a magnetizable layer on which data can be stored. (T) (2) In word processing, a recording medium in the form of a ribbon that has one or more tracks along its length on which magnetic recordings can be made on either one side or both sides. (T)

magnetic tape adapter A hardware feature required to transfer data and commands between a processor and one or more magnetic tape units.

magnetic tape cartridge (1) A container holding magnetic tape, driven by friction, that can be processed without separating it from the container. When the driving mechanisms are not of concern, cassette and cartridge are sometimes used interchangeably. (T) (2) A removable storage device that consists of a housing containing a belt-driven magnetic tape wound on a supply reel and, in some cartridges, a take-up reel.

magnetic tape cassette (1) A container holding magnetic tape, driven on axes, that can be processed without separating it from the container. (T) (2) A removable storage device, usually smaller than a magnetic tape cartridge, that consists of a housing containing magnetic tape, usually wound on supply and take-up reels that are rotated by a drive mechanism.

magnetic tape deck Synonym for magnetic tape drive.

magnetic tape drive A mechanism for controlling the movement of magnetic tape, commonly used to move magnetic tape past a read head or write head, or to allow automatic rewinding. (I) (A) Synonymous with magnetic tape deck, magnetic tape transport mechanism.

magnetic tape label One or more records at the beginning of a magnetic tape that identify and describe the data recorded on the tape.

magnetic tape leader The portion of magnetic tape that precedes the beginning-of-tape marker and is used to thread the tape. (I) (A)

magnetic tape storage A magnetic storage in which data are stored by magnetic recording on the surface of a tape that moves longitudinally in use. (I) (A)

magnetic tape subsystem A tape unit that includes the logic interface hardware necessary to operate with a system unit.

magnetic tape trailer The portion of magnetic tape that follows the end-of-tape marker. (I) (A)

magnetic tape transport Synonym for magnetic tape drive. (A)

magnetic tape transport mechanism Synonym for magnetic tape drive.

magnetic tape unit (1) A device containing a tape drive, magnetic heads, and associated controls. (I) (A) (2) A device for reading or writing data from or on magnetic tape.

magnetic thin film A layer of magnetic material, usually less than one micron thick, often used for logic elements or storage elements. (A)

magnetic thin film storage A magnetic storage in which data are stored by magnetic recording in a film of molecular thickness, coated on a substrate. (I) (A)

magnetic track A track on the surface layer of a magnetic storage. (I) (A)

magnetic wire storage Deprecated term for plated wire storage.

magnetographic printer A nonimpact printer that creates, by means of magnetic heads operating on a metallic drum, a latent image which is then made visible by a toner and transferred and fixed on paper. (T)

magneto-optics A medium for storing information, magnetically sensitive only at high temperatures, while stable at normal temperatures. A laser is used to heat a small spot on the medium for recording; the ability to focus the laser tightly greatly increases the data density over standard magnetic media.

magnify In computer graphics, to increase by a common factor the dimensions of a display image.

mail See electronic mail.

mailbox A file that holds the electronic mail. Synonymous with electronic mailbox. (T)

mail drop The file into which messages are first received.

mailer A program that does the actual delivery of electronic mail.

mail folder In System/36, a folder used to store documents sent and received by users.

mail log A record of all the mail that has been sent or received.

mail queue See communication queue.

main In XL FORTRAN, the default name given to a main program if one was not supplied by the programmer.

main control unit In a processor with more than one instruction control unit, that instruction control unit to which, for a given interval of time, the other instruction control units are subordinated. In an operating system, an instruction control unit may be designated as the main control unit by hardware, by software, or by both. (A) (T) (A)

main distributing frame (MDF) A distributing frame used for associating an outside line with a desired terminal. On one part of the frame, the permanent outside lines entering the central office building terminate and on another part, cabling such as the subscriber line multiple cabling or trunk multiple cabling terminates.

Note: A distributing frame usually carries the central office protective devices and functions as a test point between line and office. In a private exchange, the main distributing frame is used for similar purposes.

main file Synonym for master file.

mainframe (1) A computer, usually in a computer center, with extensive capabilities and resources to which other computers may be connected so that they can share facilities. (T) (2) A large computer, in particular one to which other computers can be connected so that they can share facilities the mainframe provides; for example, a System/370 computing system to which personal computers are attached so that they can upload and download programs and data. See also microcomputer, minicomputer, personal computer, supercomputer. See Figure 93.

Note: The term usually refers to hardware only: main storage, execution circuitry, and peripheral units.

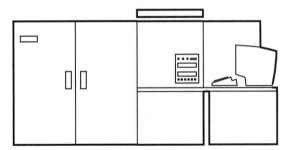

Figure 93. Mainframe

mainframe interactive (MFI) In SAA usage, pertaining to systems in which nonprogrammable terminals are connected to a mainframe.

main folder In the IBM LinkWay product, the folder that is automatically opened when LinkWay is started, unless the user specifies otherwise.

main function In the C language, a function that has the identifier "main." Each program must have only one function named main. The main function is the first user function that gets control when a program starts to run.

mainline code See inline code.

mainline module In the AS/400 system, a sequence of instructions called by a program in the main path after it is compiled.

mainline program (1) A program that performs primary functions, passing control to routines and subroutines for the performance of more specific functions. (2) In VTAM, that part of the application program that issues OPEN and CLOSE macroinstructions.

main loop cabling In the IBM 8100 Information System, the cabling that connects all loop wiring concentrators and wrap loop station connectors.

main memory Synonym for main storage. (T)

main network address In VTAM, the logical unit (LU) network address used for the SSCP-LU session and certain LU-LU sessions with the LU. Contrast with auxiliary network address.

main program (1) A program that performs primary functions, passing control to routines and subroutines for the performance of more specific functions. (2) In a hierarchy of programs and subprograms, the first

program to receive control when the programs are run. (3) In FORTRAN, a program unit that is not a subprogram. (4) Contrast with subprogram.

main ring path In the IBM Token-Ring Network, the part of the ring made up of access units and the cables that connect them.

mains/battery-powered calculator See line/battery-powered calculator. (A)

mains-powered calculator See line-powered calculator. (A)

main station A telephone station with a unique call number designation and that is directly connected to a central office. In dedicated connections for customer equipment, the main point at which such equipment is connected to the local loop. See also extension station.

main storage (1) Program-addressable storage from which instructions and other data can be loaded directly into registers for subsequent execution or processing. (I) (A)   (2) That part of internal storage into which instructions and other data must be loaded for subsequent execution or processing. Synonymous with main memory. (T)   (3) The part of a processing unit where programs are run. Contrast with control storage. (4) Synonymous with memory. (5) Contrast with auxiliary storage. (6) See also cache storage, processor storage, real storage, virtual storage. (7) Deprecated term for internal storage.

Notes:

1. *Main storage refers to the total program-addressable execution space which may include one or more storage devices.*

2. *The term main storage is generally used in large and intermediate computers. The term memory is primarily used in microcomputers, calculators, and some minicomputers.*

main storage database (MSDB) In IMS/VS, a root-segment database residing in main storage that can be accessed to a field level.

main storage dump space In the AS/400 system, a section of storage reserved on the disk unit that is used as a place to save main storage for recovery and debugging.

main storage partition In MFT, a fixed-size subdivision of the dynamic area that is allocated to a job step or a system task.

main storage pool In the AS/400 system, a division of main storage that allows the user to reserve main storage for processing a job or group of jobs, or to use the pools defined by the system. Contrast with auxiliary storage pool.

main storage processor Hardware that performs the machine language instructions in main storage.

main storage region In MVT, a variable-size subdivision of the dynamic area that is allocated to a job step or a system task.

main storage unit Synonym for buffer unit.

main switch (1) A device that makes and breaks the contact between equipment and the main electricity supply. (T)   (2) In a duplicator, a device that makes and breaks the contact between a machine and main electricity supply. (T)

maintainability The ease with which maintenance of a functional unit can be performed in accordance with prescribed requirements. (I)   (A)

maintain system history program (MSHP) In VSE, a program used for automating and controlling various installation, tailoring, and service activities for a VSE system.

main task In VSE, the main program within a partition in a multiprogramming environment.

maintenance (1) Any activity intended to retain a functional unit in, or to restore it to, a state in which it can perform its required function.   Maintenance includes keeping a functional unit in a specified state by performing activities such as tests, measurements, replacements, adjustments, and repairs. (I) (A) (2) The activities intended to keep a machine in, or restore a machine to, good working order.   (3) See corrective maintenance, deferred maintenance, emergency maintenance, file maintenance, preventive maintenance, scheduled maintenance.   (4) See also programming redesign.

maintenance analysis procedure (MAP) A maintenance document that gives an IBM service representative a step-by-step procedure for tracing a symptom to the cause of a failure.

maintenance and operator subsystem (MOSS) A subsystem of an IBM communication controller, such as the 3725 or the 3720, that contains a processor and operates independently of the rest of the controller. It loads and supervises the controller, runs problem determination procedures, and assists in maintaining both hardware and software.

maintenance and operator subsystem extended A subsystem of the IBM 3745 Communication Controller that operates independently of the rest of the controller. It loads and supervises the controller, runs

problem determination procedures, and assists in maintaining both hardware and software.

maintenance hook In computer security, a trap door in software that allows easy maintenance and development of additional features and that may allow entry into the code at unusual points or without the usual checks.

maintenance mode Synonym for service mode.

maintenance mode switch Synonym for service mode switch

maintenance/operator panel Synonym for service / operator panel.

maintenance panel (1) A part of a unit of equipment that is used for interaction between the unit of equipment and a maintenance engineer.   (T) (2) Synonym for service panel.

maintenance services In SNA, one of the types of network services in system services control points (SSCPs) and physical units (PUs).   Maintenance services provide facilities for testing links and nodes and for collecting and recording error information.   See also configuration services, management services, network services, session services.

maintenance support performance The ability of a maintenance organization, under given conditions, to provide upon demand, the resources required to maintain a functional unit, under a given maintenance policy.

Note: The given conditions are related to the functional unit itself and to the conditions under which the functional unit is used and maintained. (T)

maintenance system In the AIX operating system, a special version of the operating system that is loaded from diskette and used to perform system management tasks.

maintenance time (1) Time used for hardware maintenance. It includes preventive maintenance time and corrective maintenance time. (A)   (2) Contrast with available time. (3) See corrective maintenance time, deferred maintenance time, emergency maintenance time, preventive maintenance time.

maintenance tree A logic diagram showing the pertinent alternative sequences of elementary maintenance activities to be performed on a functional unit and the conditions for their choice. (T)

major class field In the System/38 query utility, the field whose contents determine the major, or only, record class in which the query utility processes a record during preparation of a table. Contrast with minor class field.

major control field The most significant control field in a record, the field on which sorting according to the collating sequence is first attempted.

major device number In the AIX operating system, a system identification number for each device or type of device. The major device, minor device, and channel numbers uniquely identify a hardware device. See also minor device number.

major event code In the OS/2 operating system, a code assigned to major operating system events, such as opening or writing to a file. Major event code values range from 0 to 255.

major industry identifier On a credit card, the first digit of the primary account number; it serves as an identifier of the industry group of the card issuer. (A)

majority A logic operator having the property that if P is a statement, Q is a statement, R is a statement, ..., then the majority of P, Q, R, ..., is true if more than half the statements are true, false if half or less are true. (A)

majority element Synonym for majority gate.

majority gate (1) A logic element that performs a majority operation. (T) (2) Synonymous with majority element.

majority operation A threshold operation in which each of the operands may take only the values 0 and 1, and that takes the value 1 if and only if the number of operands having the value 1 is greater than the number of operands that have the value zero. (I) (A)

major node In VTAM, a set of resources that can be activated and deactivated as a group. See NCP major node, packet major node. See also minor node.

major task The task that has control at the outset of execution of a program. It exists throughout execution of the program.

major tick In the AS/400 Business Graphics Utility, a mark on an axis that denotes character grid units on a chart. See also minor tick.

major time slice In systems with the time sharing option (TSO), the period of time during which a terminal job is in main storage. See also minor time slice.

major total The result obtained when a summation is terminated by the most significant change of group.

makeup time (1) The part of available time used for reruns due to faults or mistakes in operating. (I) (A) (2) Contrast with development time.

malfunction (1) Synonym for failure. (2) Contrast with error, fault, mistake.

malfunction alert In System/370 Model 159/168 multiprocessing, an interruption generated by a processing unit in order to attempt recovery when the other processing unit enters a checkstop state because machine error handling has failed, or because power has been lost.

malicious logic In computer security, hardware, software, or firmware that is intentionally included in a system for the purpose of causing harm, loss, or unauthorized use of resources; for example, a Trojan horse. See also attack.

MAN Metropolitan area network.

managed children In the AIX Enhanced X-Windows, children in which the managed field has a value of True. Managed children can have their layout (geometry) changed so that they can be repositioned and resized. Synonymous with managed windows.

managed windows Synonym for managed children.

management See computer-assisted management, data management.

management class A named collection of management attributes describing the retention, backup, and class transition characteristics for a group of objects in a storage hierarchy.

management information system (MIS) (1) An information system designed to aid in the performance of management functions. (A) (2) An information processing system that supports decision-making by the management of an organization. (T)

management services (MS) One of the types of network services in control points (CPs) and physical units (PUs). Management services are the services provided to assist in the management of SNA networks, such as problem management, performance and accounting management, configuration management, and change management.

management services focal point (MSFP) For any given management services discipline (for example, problem determination or response time monitoring), the control point that is responsible for that type of network management data for a sphere of control. This responsibility may include collecting, storing or displaying the data or all of these. (For example, a problem determination focal point is a control point that collects, stores, and displays problem determination data.)

management work element A control block containing the information necessary to direct Data Facility Hierarchical Storage Manager functions.

Manager class In the AIXwindows program, a metaclass that provides the resources and functionality to implement certain features, such as a keyboard interface and traversal mechanism. It is built from the Core, Composite, and Constraint classes.

Manchester code See differential Manchester encoding.

Manchester encoding A digital encoding technique in which each bit period is divided into two complementary halves : a transition in the middle of the bit period represents the binary digit "1," while the opposite transition represents the binary digit "0." (T)

Notes:

1. *Transition may occur between two states of a physical variable such as voltage, magnetic polarity, light intensity.*

2. *If the physical variable is electrical, this type of encoding is polarity dependent and helps to prevent DC drift.*

mandatory access control (MAC) In computer security, a means of restricting access to objects, based on the sensitivity, as represented by a sensitivity label, of the information contained in the objects and the formal authorization or clearance of subjects to access information of that classification level, and enforced by the trusted computing base. Contrast with discretionary access control.

mandatory cryptographic session Synonym for required cryptographic session.

mandatory entry field A field in which a user must enter at least one character.

mandatory-fill field (1) A field a user must fill in completely or leave blank. (2) In the 3270 data stream, a field that must be completely filled with data, or a field that requires the DUP (duplicate) or SUB key to be pressed before the cursor can be moved from this field.

manipulating industrial robot An automatically controlled, reprogrammable, multipurpose, manipulative machine with several degrees of freedom, which may be either fixed in place or mobile for use in industrial automation applications.

manipulation See algebraic manipulation, formula manipulation, symbol manipulation.

mantissa (1) The nonnegative fractional part of the representation of a logarithm. (I) (A) (2) In a floating-point representation, the numeral that is multiplied by the exponentiated implicit floating-point base to determine the real number represented; for example, a floating-point representation of the number 0.0001234 is 0.1234-3, where .1234 is the fixed-point part and -3 is the exponent. (I) Synonymous with fixed-point part. (3) In floating-point format, the number that precedes the E. The value represented is the product of the mantissa and the power of 10 specified by the exponent. (4) Synonym for fixed-point part. (5) Contrast with characteristic.

manual answering (1) Answering in which a call is established only if the called user signals a readiness to receive the call by means of a manual operation. (I) (2) Operator actions to prepare a station to receive a call on a switched line. Contrast with autoanswer.

manual calling (1) Calling that permits the entry of selection signals from a calling data station at an undefined character rate. (I) (2) Operator actions to place a call over a switched line. Contrast with autocall.

Note: The characters may be generated at the data terminal equipment or at the data circuit-terminating equipment.

manual exchange An exchange in which calls are completed by an operator.

manual function A function initiated or accomplished by the machine operator. (T)

manual indicator In System/36, a light on the operator/service panel that comes on when processing has been stopped.

manual inking control In a duplicator, a device for supplying ink manually from an ink container. (T)

manual input (1) The entry of data by hand into a device. (A) (2) The data entered as in *(1)*. (A)

manual input register A register into which data can be entered by hand. (I) (A)

manually driven duplicator A duplicator in which power required to drive the machine is provided by hand. (T)

manual operation Processing of data in a system by direct manual techniques.

manual slot See I/O slot.

manual tax A tax that is keyed in by an operator during a sales transaction at a point of sale terminal.

manual toning control A device that enables the operator to add toner manually to the developing system of an electrostatic document copying machine. (T)

manual typewriter A typewriter whose machine functions are carried out entirely as a result of input by the operator. (T)

manufacturing message service (MMS) An application service element that enables supervisory computer to control the operation of a distributed community of computer-based devices in a network used for manufacturing or process control. (T)

many-to-one alias array In FORTRAN, an alias array that has more than one of its elements associated with the same datum.

many-to-one vector subscript In FORTRAN, a vector subscript that has two or more elements with the same value.

MAP Maintenance analysis procedure.

map (1) A set of values having defined correspondence with the quantities or values of another set. (I) (A) (2) To establish a set of values having a defined correspondence with the quantities or values of another set; for example, to evaluate a mathematical function, that is, to establish the values of the dependent variable for values of the independent variable or variables of immediate concern. (I) (A) (3) In CICS/VS Basic Mapping Support, a defined correspondence between names of program variables and the position in which their values will appear on a display device. The map also contains other formatting information. (4) In CSP/AD, a layout of a display or a printer format that has been defined using the Cross System Product/Application Development licensed program. (5) See bitmap, color map, Karnaugh map, pixel map, pix map.

map editor The major online function of SDF/CICS, used to create, display, and edit BMS maps.

map group In CSP/AD, a collection of maps that have the same type of device characteristics. Maps in a map group can be shared between CSP/AE applications.

mapped In AIX Enhanced X-Windows, pertaining to a window on which a map call has been performed.

mapped buffer A display buffer in which each character position has a corresponding character position on the display surface.

mapped conversation An LU 6.2 conversation type specified by the allocating transaction program. Transaction programs using a mapped conversation can exchange messages of arbitrary format regardless of the underlying data stream. System-defined or user-defined mappers can perform data transformation for the transaction programs. See conversation. Contrast with basic conversation.

mapped file (1) A file that can be accessed through direct memory operations instead of being read from disk each time it is accessed. (2) A file on the hard disk that is accessed as if it is in memory.

mapped physical storage Synonym for addressable storage.

mapper A NetView program function that records errors from resources attached to a communication controller or from certain channel-attached devices.

mapping (1) A list, usually in a profile, that establishes a correspondence between items in two groups; for example, a keyboard mapping can establish what character is displayed when a certain key is pressed. See also keyboard mapping. (2) In a database, the establishing of correspondences between a given logical structure and a given physical structure. (T) (3) In AIX Enhanced X-Windows, pertaining to a window on which a map call has been performed. Mapping makes a window visible if there are no obscuring or occluding windows. (4) See keyboard mapping.

map set editor One of the online functions of SDF/CICS used to create, display, and edit BMS map sets.

map specification library (MSL) A VSAM file in which user-defined objects and system objects are kept; this file also contains status and protection information on all its objects. An SDF/CICS installation can have multiple MSLs.

margin (1) A generally unprinted area that lies between the text area of a page or screen and the edge of the page or screen. Margins may contain small illustrations, notes, and page numbers. A rectangular page or screen therefore has four margins. (T) (2) The space above, below, and on either side of the body of a page. (3) The left or right limit of a column. See Figure 94. (4) See back margin, bottom margin, top margin.

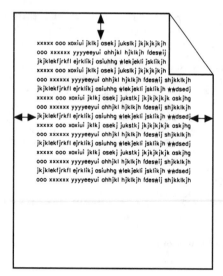

Figure 94. Margin

margin A The margin between the 7th and 8th character positions of a reference format for a COBOL source program line.

margin-adjust zone In text processing, an area generally five to seven characters, in which the right margin is set through hyphenation or carry-over to the next line. Synonymous with hot zone, line-end zone, line-ending zone. (T) (A)

marginal check Synonym for marginal test. (T)

marginal test (1) A technique in which certain operating conditions, such as voltage or frequency supplied, are varied about their nominal values in order to detect and locate components with incipient faults. (I) (A) (2) Synonymous with marginal check.

margin B The margin between the 11th and 12th character positions of a reference format for a COBOL source program line.

margin C The margin between the 6th and 7th character positions of a reference format for a COBOL source program line.

margin control (1) In word processing, automatic control of the right or left margin position. (2) Synonym for range finder.

margin indent In text processing, the temporary displacement of one or more lines with respect to the original margin. (T) (A)

margin L The margin immediately to the left of the leftmost character position of a reference format for a COBOL source program line.

margin-punched card A card punched only on the border, with holes to represent data, thereby leaving the center free for written or printed information.

margin R The margin immediately to the right of the rightmost character position of a reference format for a COBOL source program line.

margin-release control In word processing, a manual control used to override the left and right margin controls to allow printing beyond predefined limits.

margin release key On a typewriter, a control used to override left-hand and right-hand margin stops to allow typing beyond these set limits. (T)

margin release mechanism On a typewriter, a device for temporarily overriding the left-hand margin stop, right-hand margin stop, and line-end lock. (T)

margin scale On a typewriter, a scale corresponding to the pitch of the machine for indicating the position of the margin stops. (T)

margin stop indicator On a typewriter, a pointer indicating the position of a margin stop. (T)

margin stop mechanism On a typewriter, a device limiting the relative movement between the paper carrier and the type carrier parallel to the typing line at the beginning and the end of the writing line. (T)

margin stop setting control On a typewriter, a device for positioning the left-hand and right-hand margin stops. (T)

margin text Notes written in the margins on the top, bottom, left, or right of a document.

mark (1) A symbol or symbols that indicate the beginning or the end of a field, a word, an item of data or a set of data such as a file, record, or block. (I) (A) (2) In computer security, to place a sensitivity designator such as a label with data. (3) See document mark, group mark.

Mark In SAA Basic Common User Access architecture, a choice in the Edit pull-down that users select to highlight text or graphics that they want to perform clipboard operations on. The clipboard operations are: cut, copy, paste, clear, and delete.

mark block In XL Pascal, a dynamic block header that designates a subheap within a heap.

marker (1) In computer graphics, a glyph with a specified appearance that is used to identify a particular location. (I) (A) (2) In the AIX operating system, a visual symbol within a noninteractive pane indicating the location of the cursor when the pane was last interactive. (3) In GDDM, a symbol centered on a point. Line charts may use markers to indicate the plotted points. (4) In hardware, reflective material placed on magnetic tape to indicate the beginning or ending of the recording area. (5) See end-of-tape marker.

mark form sequence In the 3800 Printing Subsystem, a function that prints identifying marks on the perforations between jobs to make it easy to see the end of a job run. The sequence is controlled by the printer when it detects a mark form command.

mark function A function available for a 3790 program to indicate that an index record in a user data set has some update or action pending or completed (defined by the user).

mark-hold The normal no-traffic line condition in which a steady mark is transmitted. This may be a customer-selectable option.

marking In telephony, establishing a path in a network through a series of cross points.

marking wave Synonym for keying wave.

Markov chain A probabilistic model of events in which the probability of an event depends only on the event that precedes it. (A)

mark scanning The automatic optical sensing of marks recorded on a data medium. Synonymous with optical mark reading. (T)

mark-sense To mark a position on a punched card with an electrically conductive pencil for later conversion to machine punching.

mark sensing The electrical sensing of conductive marks, usually recorded manually on a nonconductive data medium. (I) (A)

mark-sensing card A card on which mark-sensible fields have been printed. (A)

mark-sensing column A line of mark-sensible positions parallel to the Y-datum line of a card. (A)

mark-sensing row A line of mark-sensible positions parallel to the X-datum line of a card. (A)

mark-to-space transition The transition, or switching, from a marking impulse to a spacing impulse.

markup (1) Information added to a document to enable a person or system to process it. Markup information can describe the document's characteristics, or it can specify the actual processing to be performed; for example, in SCRIPT/VS, markup consists of Generalized Markup Language tags, attribute labels and values, and control words. (2) To determine the markup for a document. (3) To insert markup into a source document.

markup language A language used to define information to be added to the content of a document as an aid to processing it. (T)

marquee select In SAA Advanced Common User Access architecture, a form of emphasis used to indicate selected icons and bit maps when they are used as choices. See also inverse color highlighting.

married documents In the IBM ImagePlus system, separate documents indexed under the same customer ID and routed through the system together. One document may contain information needed as input for the others.

marshall In the AIX Network Computing System, to copy data into a remote procedure call (RPC) packet. Stubs perform marshalling. Contrast with unmarshall. See also stub.

mask (1) A pattern of characters used to control retention or elimination of portions of another pattern of characters. (I) (A) (2) To use a pattern of characters to control retention or elimination of portions of another pattern of characters. (I) (A) (3) In computer security, to add data to a transmission to make interpretation of the signal more difficult for an unauthorized user. (4) In printing, horizontal and vertical lines printed on an overlay to help in design of the overlay. (5) A pattern of characters that controls the keeping, deleting, or testing of portions of another pattern of characters. (6) In multimedia development, the electronic equivalent of placing transparent tape over selected regions of an image to prevent those regions from being changed in subsequent operations. (7) See directory mask, event mask, plane mask, screenmask, signal mask, subnet address mask, write mask. See also umask.

masked Synonym for disabled.

masking In a document copying machine, a means by which part of the image of the original is obscured so that it is not reproduced on the copy material. (T)

mask-program read-only memory A fixed-program read-only storage in which the data content of each cell is determined during manufacture by the use of a mask. (A)

masquerade Synonym for impersonate.

mass sequential insertion In VSAM, a technique for keyed sequential insertion of two or more records in sequence into a collating position in a file, or data set. Mass sequential insertion is more efficient than insertion of each record individually.

mass storage (1) Storage having a very large storage capacity. (I) (A) (2) The storage of a large amount of data that are readily accessible to the processing unit of a computer. See also 3850 Mass Storage System. (3) In a personal computer, large-capacity backup storage such as a hard disk, external hard disk, cartridge, or streaming tape. (4) In COBOL, a storage medium in which data may be organized and maintained in both a sequential and nonsequential manner. (5) Synonymous with bulk storage.

mass storage control (MSC) In MSS, a micropro-grammed portion of the 3851 Mass Storage Facility that passes information to the accessor control and that controls data and space on staging drives.

mass storage control system (MSCS) In COBOL, an input-output control system that directs or controls the processing of mass storage files.

mass storage control table create In MSS, a program that builds the mass storage control tables.

mass storage control tables pack In MSS, the direct access storage pack that contains the mass storage control tables.

mass storage control twin port In MSS, the feature of a mass storage control that allows it to address up to two 3851 Mass Storage Facilities, and up to four-teen 3830 Model-3 Storage Controls, or Integrated Storage Controls that have the addition of a Staging Adapter.

mass storage device A device having a large storage capacity; for example, magnetic disk, magnetic drum. (A) See Figure 95.

mass storage file A collection of records assigned to a mass storage device.

mass storage file segment A part of a mass storage file whose beginning and end are defined by the file limit clause in the environment division.

mass storage system communicator (MSSC) In MSS, a program that handles communication between system control programs and the mass storage control. The mass storage volume control functions are an integral part of the Mass Storage System Communicator program.

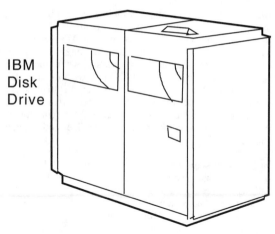

IBM Disk Drive

Figure 95. Mass Storage Device

mass storage volume In MSS, a virtual volume that corresponds to a direct access volume permanently associated with two associated data cartridges.

mass storage volume control (MSVC) In MSS, a collection of functions that reside in the Mass Storage System Communicator program and are designed to assist the space manager in managing mass storage volumes and mass storage volume groups.

mass storage volume control journal In MSS, a data set that contains messages to the space manager and information used to rebuild the mass storage volume inventory data set.

mass storage volume group In MSS, a collection of mass storage volumes. The space manager can define a group, and the Mass Storage System Communicator program can define a default mass storage volume group.

mass storage volume inventory A data set that describes mass storage volumes and mass storage volume groups.

master (1) A document suitable to the document copying process being used. In some cases it is the original, but in others it may need to be specially pre-pared. (T) Synonymous with intermediate. (2) In a duplicator, a sheet of material that carries an image of the text or other material to be copied. See litho master, perforated litho master, pressure type spirit master, spirit master, stencil master. (3) An original audio tape, videotape, or film, used for broadcast or for copying.

master address In DPPX, an address relative to the origin of the master address space. Contrast with local address. Synonymous with universal address.

master address space (1) In MVS, the virtual storage used by the master scheduler task. (2) In DPPX, the entire logical addressing range. All address spaces are nested within the master address space.

master alignment control In a duplicator, a device for lateral adjustment of the position of the master on a machine. (T)

master attachment control In a duplicator, a control for opening and closing the clips or clamps on the master cylinder. (T)

master catalog (1) In DPPX, a relative sequential data set that resides on the system residence volume and contains extensive data set, data space, and volume information. The DPPX Base uses the information to locate data sets and to verify the authority of a user to gain access to data sets in the data space controlled by the master catalog. (2) See VSAM master catalog.

master clamp In a duplicator, a device for clamping an unpunched master to the master cylinder. (T)

master clip In a duplicator, a device for fixing a punched master to the master cylinder. (T)

master clock (1) A clock whose main function is to control other clocks. (I) (A) (2) The primary source of timing signals used to control the timing of pulses.

master configuration record In System/36, information, stored on disk, that describes system characteristics; for example, system date format, disk capacity, and main storage capacity.

master console In a system with multiple consoles, the basic console used for communication between the operator and the system.

master control code (MCC) In DPCX, the code that handles task management, storage management, and other supervisor services.

master cryptography key In SNA products, a key used to encipher operational keys that are to be used at a node.

master cylinder In a duplicator, the cylinder to which the master is attached. (T)

master deck In an video editing system, the video recorder on which a selected signal is recorded to assemble an edited master.

master delivery In a duplicator, the process in which the ejected master is put into a tray. (T)

master dump table In the AIX operating system, a structure containing dump table entries generated by kernel components. The dump program uses this table to locate data structures that should be included in a dump.

master ejection In a duplicator, the process in which the master is removed from the master cylinder by hand or automatically. (T)

master environment In DPPX, the ultimate source of all DPPX resources that are allocated on an environment basis.

master file (1) A file that is used as an authority in a given job and that is relatively permanent, even though its contents may change. (I) (A) Synonymous with main file. (2) A collection of permanent information, such as a customer address file.

master file directory block Synonym for CMS file directory.

master heading In a duplicator, the means by which a master is attached to the machine. (T)

master import file In the Network Carrier Interconnect Manager program, a host file that contains the configuration data that has been imported from a carrier management system.

mastering In optical recording, the original optical recording process.

master key In computer security, the top-level key In a hierarchy of key-encrypting keys.

master key concept In the Programmed Cryptographic Facility, a concept in which only a limited number of clear (unenciphered) cryptographic keys exist within the cryptographic facility.

master key variant key data set (MKDS) In the Programmed Cryptographic Facility, a non-VSAM data set that contains host master key variant 1, host master key variant 2, and the system authentication key.

master loading In a duplicator, the process in which the master is moved into the duplicator by hand or automatically. (T)

master mask In DPPX, the most general type of enable or disable. It affects all levels other than the one on which the requestor is running.

master mode In the IBM 8100 Information System, the privilege mode that allows processing of all instructions and permits overriding of store-protection and execution-protection access control. See also application mode, I/O mode, supervisor mode.

master node In certain ring network or loop control schemes, a node that initiates all data transfers.

master node control In a loop or a ring network configuration, a control scheme in which a single master node initiates all data transmissions. See also register insertion, slotted-ring control, token-access control.

Note: An example is IBM 8100 Communication Loop, in which the master node polls the other nodes around the loop, allowing each of them to transmit data.

master priming In a duplicator, a process of treating the master to make it suitable for inking. (T)

master priming control In a duplicator, a means of operating the master priming device. (T)

master priming device In a duplicator, a mechanism for making the master suitable for inking-up. (T)

master scheduler A control program routine that responds to operator commands and initiates the requested actions.

master scheduler address space (1) In MVS, the virtual storage used by the master scheduler task. (2) In DPPX, the entire logical addressing range. All address spaces are nested within the master address space.

master scheduler task In OS/VS, the command processing task that controls the searching of a queue of pending commands and the attaching of tasks for executing these commands.

master shot In video or film production, a camera angle, usually a medium shot or a wide shot, that includes all the significant action in a scene and into which several close-ups may be inserted.

master slewing device In a duplicator, a device for adjusting the alignment of the master on the master cylinder. (T)

master sort table In the AS/400 system, a system-supplied table that contains sort information required for sorting double-byte characters. This table is maintained by the character generator utility function of the AS/400 Application Development Tools licensed program.

master station (1) In basic mode link control, the data station that has accepted an invitation to ensure a data transfer to one or more slave stations. (I) (A)

(2) A station that can select and transmit a message to a slave station.

Note: At a given instant, there can be only one master station on a data link.

master tape In video production, the edited and final version of a videotape that can be used to create a master videodisc.

master terminal (1) The IMS/VS logical terminal that has complete control of IMS/VS resources during online operations. (2) The terminal or window that has complete control of CICS resources during online operations.

master terminal formatting options An IMS/VS message format service option that provides a format for a 3270 master terminal.

Master Terminal Operator (MTO) The console operator for CICS. See also console, terminal.

master trace A centralized data tracing facility of the master scheduler, used in servicing the message-processing portions of MVS. See also trace.

master/transfer sheet set In a duplicator, a master sheet and a transfer sheet fastened together along one edge. (T)

master tray In a duplicator, the platform supporting the master during the process of clipping or clamping it to the master cylinder. (T)

master user An SDF/CICS user with the master user privilege who starts up and shuts down SDF/CICS.

master videodisc In video production, the disc created from the master tape and used in the first stage of videodisc manufacture.

match (1) A comparison to determine identity of items. (A) (2) Contrast with hit *(1)*.

match fields In RPG primary or secondary multifile processing, fields within a record type that are to be used for checking the order of a single file, or for matching records of one file with those of another file.

matching The technique of comparing the keys of two or more records to select items for a particular stage of processing or to reject invalid records. (T)

matching record (MR) indicator In the AS/400 system, an indicator used in calculation or output specifications to indicate operations that are to be performed only when records match in primary and secondary files.

match level In RPG, the value (M1 through M9) assigned to the match field. The match level identifies fields by which records are matched during primary or secondary multifile processing.

math coprocessor In a personal computer, a microprocessor on an expansion board that supplements the operations of the processor in the system unit, enabling a personal computer to perform complex mathematical operations in parallel with other operations. See also I/O coprocessor, networking coprocessor.

mathematical check A programmed check that uses mathematical relationships. (A) Synonymous with arithmetic check.

mathematical function A mathematical expression describing a relationship between two or more variables.

mathematical induction A method of proving a statement concerning terms based on natural numbers not less than N by showing that the statement is valid for the term based on N and that, if it is valid for an arbitrary value of n that is greater than N, it is also valid for the term based on (n + 1). (I) (A)

mathematical logic Synonym for symbolic logic.

mathematical model A mathematical representation of a process, device, or concept. (A)

mathematical programming (1) In operations research, a procedure for locating the maximum or minimum of a function subject to constraints. (I) (A) (2) Contrast with convex programming, dynamic programming, integer programming, linear programming, nonlinear programming, quadratic programming.

matrix (1) A rectangular array of elements, in rows and columns, that can be manipulated based on matrix algebra rules. (I) (A) (2) In computers, a logic network in the form of an array of input and output leads with logic elements joined at some of their intersections. (A) (3) By extension, an array of any number of dimensions. (A) (4) A two-dimensional array. (5) See dot matrix.

matrix printer Synonym for dot matrix printer. (T)

matrix stack In AIX graphics, a stack of matrices with hardware and software support. The top matrix on the stack is the active matrix, and all points passed through the graphics pipeline are multiplied by that matrix.

matrix storage Storage whose elements are arranged so that access to any location requires use of two or more coordinates; for example, cathode ray storage. (A)

matrix transformation In analog color video, the process of converting color signals from one tristimulus format to another; for example, from RGB to YUV. See also tri-stimulus.

matte In film, an opaque piece of art or a model that leaves a selected area unexposed to be filled on a subsequent pass or in composite.

maximize To enlarge a window to its largest possible size, the size of the screen.

Maximize In SAA Advanced Common User Access architecture, a choice in the system menu pull-down that enlarges the window to the largest possible size, the size of the screen.

maximize icon In SAA usage, a symbol, located to the right of the window title, that a user can select to make the window fill the entire screen. Contrast with minimize icon. See also restore icon.

maximum allowable common mode overvoltage The highest value for the common mode voltage that can be applied to an input subsystem without causing circuit damage, but with possibility of temporary loss of function. (T)

Notes:

1. *If it is clear from the context, this term may be shortened to "maximum allowable overvoltage."*

2. *The maximum common mode voltage is lower than maximum operating common mode voltage, which is lower than the "maximum allowable common mode overvoltage."*

maximum allowable link loss In an ESCON environment, the maximum amount of link attenuation (loss), expressed in decibels, that can exist without causing a potential failure condition. Contrast with calculated link loss.

maximum allowable normal mode overvoltage The highest value for the normal mode voltage that can be applied to an input subsystem without causing circuit damage, but with possibility of a temporary loss of function. (T)

Notes:

1. *If it is clear from the context, this term may be shortened to "maximum allowable overvoltage."*

2. *The following relationship exists: maximum normal mode voltage is lower than maximum operating normal mode voltage, which is lower than "maximum allowable normal mode voltage."*

maximum ascender The maximum height from the baseline of sequential characters to the top mark of the tallest character in a font character set.

maximum common mode voltage Highest value for common mode voltage at which a subsystem will still operate according to specifications. (T)

maximum descender The maximum depth from the baseline of sequential characters to the bottom mark of any character in the font character set.

maximum line length On a typewriter, the maximum width of the paper carrier that can be used for typing. (T)

maximum normal mode voltage Highest value for the normal mode voltage at which the subsystem will still operate according to its specifications. (T)

Note: "Maximum normal mode voltage" is lower than maximum operating normal mode voltage, which is lower than maximum allowable normal mode over-voltage.

maximum operating common mode voltage The highest value for the common mode voltage that can be applied to an input subsystem and at which the subsystem will still operate, but at reduced performance. (T)

Notes:

1. *If clear from context, term may be shortened to "maximum operating voltage."*

2. *The maximum common mode voltage is lower than the "maximum operating common mode voltage," which is lower than the maximum allowable common mode overvoltage.*

maximum operating normal mode voltage The highest value for the normal mode voltage that can be applied to an input subsystem, and at which the subsystem will continue to operate, but at reduced performance. The maximum normal mode voltage is lower than the maximum operating normal mode voltage, which is lower than the maximum allowable normal mode overvoltage. The term may be shortened to maximum operating voltage, if the context is clear. (T) (A)

maximum SSCP rerouting count The maximum number of times a session initiation request will be rerouted to intermediate system services control points (SSCPs) before the request reaches the destination SSCP. This count is used to prevent endless rerouting of session initiation requests.

maximum transfer unit (MTU) The maximum number of bytes that an Internet Protocol (IP) datagram can contain.

Mb Megabit; 1 048 576 bits.

MB Megabyte; 1 048 576 bytes.

mb Millibyte; 1024 bytes.

M-bit (more data bit) In X.25 communications, the bit in a data packet that indicates that there is more data to follow in another data packet, when a message is too large for one packet. See also D-bit, Q-bit.

Mbps One million bits per second.

MC Monitor call instruction.

MCAR Machine check analysis and recording.

MCC (1) Magnetic card code. (2) Master control code.

MCGA mono mode In the IBM LinkWay product, one of the five graphics modes available. MCGA mono mode has high resolution, provides two colors, and is supported on all PS/2 models.

MCGA 256 color mode One of five graphics modes available in the IBM LinkWay product. MCGA 256 color mode provides 256 colors and is supported on all PS/2 models.

MCH Machine check handler.

MCI Machine check interruption.

MCP Message control program.

MCP definition The collection of macrolanguage statements by which a network is defined to TCAM in the resource-definition section of the message control program (MCP).

MCRR Machine check recording and recovery.

MCS (1) Multiple console support. (2) Message control system.

MCS console A non-SNA device defined to MVS that is locally attached to an MVS system and is used to enter commands and receive messages.

MCT Monitoring Control table.

MDC Modification detection code

MDF Main distributing frame.

MDI Medium dependent interface.

MDR Miscellaneous data record.

MDT Modified data tag.

mean access time An average access time resulting from normal operation of a device. (T)

mean accuracy The difference between the true value and the arithmetic mean, or average, of a statistically significant number of readings under specified environmental conditions. It does not include the effect of repeatability.

mean conditional information content Synonym for conditional entropy.

mean down time (MDT) The expectation of the down time. (T)

mean entropy See character mean entropy.

mean information content Synonym for entropy.

mean repair time Deprecated term for mean time to recovery.

mean time between failures (MTBF) For a stated period in the life of a functional unit, the mean value of the lengths of time between consecutive failures under stated conditions. (I) (A)

mean time to failure (MTTF) The expectation of the time to failure. (T)

mean time to recovery (MTTR) For a stated period in the life of a functional unit, the average time required for corrective maintenance. Synonymous with mean time to repair. (T)

mean time to repair Synonym for mean time to recovery. (T)

mean transinformation content (1) In information theory, the mean of the transinformation content conveyed by the occurrence of any one of a finite number of mutually exclusive and jointly exhaustive events, given the occurrence of another set of mutually exclusive events. The mean transinformation content also is equal to the difference between the entropy of one of the two sets of events and the conditional entropy of this set, relative to the other. For instance, in transmitting one message, the difference between the entropy and conditional entropy at the message source and the difference between the entropy and conditional entropy at the message sink and the irrelevance are equal. Synonymous with average transinformation content. (2) See character mean transinformation content.

measure of information A suitable function of the probability of occurrence of an event or of a sequence of events from a set of possible events. In informa-

tion theory, the term "event" is to be understood as used in the theory of probability. For instance, an event may be the presence of a given element of a set or the occurrence of a specified character or of a specified word in a given position of a message. (I) (A)

mechanicals Graphic art materials in camera ready form.

mechanical splice In fiber optics, a splice accomplished by fixtures or materials rather than thermal fusion. Index matching material can be applied between two fiber ends. (E) Contrast with fusion splice.

media access method In the AS/400 system, the method for determining the device that has access to the transmission medium at any time. See also transmission medium.

media drive In word processing, the device used for recording on or reading from a recording medium. (T)

media drive selector A control for selecting a particular element of recording medium on equipment that has more than one media drive. (T)

medialess Pertaining to a computer that has no direct access storage, is used as a workstation in a network, and relies on one or more other computers in the network to supply it with data and instructions.

medium (1) A physical carrier of electrical energy. (2) A physical material in or on which data may be represented. (3) See data medium, empty medium, machine readable medium, transmission medium, virgin medium.

medium access control (MAC) For local area networks, the method of determining which device has access to the transmission medium at any time.

medium access control (MAC) frame (1) In a star/ring network, an address resolution request frame that has the unique part of a destination address and an "all rings" address. A sender issues this request to determine the ring where the destination node is located and whether the node is active. (2) In a star/ring network, a response from an active destination node to the requesting source node that has its complete address and ring number.

medium access control (MAC) protocol In a local area network, the protocol that governs access to the transmission medium, taking into account the topological aspects of the network, in order to enable the exchange of data between data stations. (T) See also logical link control protocol.

medium access control (MAC) sublayer (1) In a local area network, the part of the data link layer that applies a medium access method. The MAC sublayer supports topology-dependent functions and uses the services of the physical layer to provide services to the logical link control sublayer. (T)   (2) One of two sublayers of the ISO Open Systems Interconnection data link layer proposed for local area networks by the IEEE Project 802 Committee on Local Area Networks and the European Computer Manufacturers Association (ECMA). It provides functions that depend on the topology of the network and uses services of the physical layer to provide services to the logical link control (LLC) sublayer. The OSI data link layer corresponds to the SNA data link control layer.

medium attachment unit (1) In a data station on a local area network, a device used to couple the data terminal equipment to the transmission medium. (T)   (2) See figure at attachment unit interface. (3) See also transceiver.

medium close-up (MCU) In video and film production, a camera shot closer than a medium shot but not as close as a standard close-up.

medium dependent interface In a local area network, the material and electrical interface between the transmission medium and a medium attachment unit. (T)   (A)

medium map In the Print Services Facility, an internal object in a form definition that identifies the overlays to be used and defines page placement and modifications to the form.

medium overlay Synonym for overlay.

medium shot In multimedia applications, a camera angle that reveals more of the subject than a close-up but less than a wide shot, usually from face to waistline. Synonymous with mid-shot.

medium speed Usually, data transmission rate between 600 bps and the limit of a voice-grade facility.

megabyte (1) For processor storage and real and virtual memory, 2^{20} or 1 048 576 bytes. (2) For disk storage capacity and transmission rates, 1 000 000 bytes.

megacycle See megahertz.

megaflops (1) Synonym for MFLOPS.   (T) (2) One million basic floating-point operations per second.

megahertz (MHz) A unit of measure of frequency. 1 megahertz = 1,000,000 hertz.

mega (M) Ten to the sixth power;   1,000,000 in decimal notation. When referring to storage capacity, two to the twentieth power;   1,048,576 in decimal notation.

member (1) A partition of a partitioned data set. (2) In VSE, the smallest unit of data that can be stored in and retrieved from a sublibrary. See also library member. (3) A data object in a structure, a union, or a library. (4) In the AS/400 system and System/38, one of several different sets of data, each with the same format, within a database file. See also source member. (5) Synonym for element. (6) See library member.

member list display In System/38, a display that lists the names of the members in a file that can be selected for processing.

member name (1) In SDF/CICS, a minor identification of an object in the map specification library. Member names can be map names, profile names, and page names. (2) In the Data Facility Hierarchical Storage Manager, the name under which a file is stored in a library;   for example, X1BITR is the member name of a font in the font library.

member record A record which is subordinate to the owner record in a set. (T)

membrane keyboard A touch-sensitive keyboard.

memory (1) All of the addressable storage space in a processing unit and other internal storages that is used to execute instructions. (T)   (2) Synonymous with main storage.

memory address register A register in a processing unit that contains the address of the storage location being accessed. (A)

memory deallocation The freeing of memory that has been previously allocated for a specific purpose.

memory dump The means by which a computer system records its state at the time of a failure.

memory expansion option In an IBM personal computer, additional storage space in the form of an expansion board containing memory modules and switch blocks that a user can install in an expansion slot in the system unit.

memory indicator On a calculator, a visual indication that a number is being held in memory. Synonymous with storage indicator, store indicator. (T)   (A)

memory partitioning In calculators, the subdividing of storage into independent sections. Synonymous with storage partitioning. (T) (A)

memory protection Synonym for storage protection.

menu (1) A list of options displayed to the user by a data processing system, from which the user can select an action to be initiated. (T) (2) In text processing, a list of choices displayed to the user by a text processor from which the user can select an action to be initiated. (T) (3) In SQL, a displayed list of available, logically grouped functions for selection by the operator. (4) In SAA Advanced Common User Access architecture, an extension of the menu bar that displays a list of choices available for a selected choice in the menu bar. After a user selects a choice in the menu bar, the corresponding menu appears. Additional pop-up windows can appear from menu choices. (5) See pop-up menu, pull-down menu, submenu, system menu. (6) See also data entry panel.

Note: In CUA architecture, this is a programmer term. The end user term is action bar pull-down.

menu area In a split SDF/CICS screen, the part of the screen that contains the menu. See also user area.

menu bar (1) In the AIX operating system, a rectangular area at the top of the client area of a window that contains the titles of the standard pull-down menus for that application. See also scroll bar. (2) In SAA Advanced Common User Access architecture, the area near the top of a window, below the title bar and above the rest of the window, that contains choices that provide access to other menus.

menu-driven Concerning application software allowing user to select operations from one or more menus without entering keyboard commands.

menu parameter A parameter for an SDF/CICS screen that can be entered in a parameter field on the screen. Usually, it is given a default value from a profile.

menu security (1) A function of the operating system that controls which system resources are available to users. Menu security restricts a user to a single menu or a sequence of menus that are defined in the user profile. (2) In System/36, a System Support Program Product option that restricts an operator to selecting items from a particular menu.

menu system In the AIX operating system, an interactive interface that lists related software options in a manner that expedites review and selection by the user.

mercury storage A storage device that utilizes the acoustic properties of mercury to store data. (A)

mercury-wetted relay A device that uses mercury as the relay contact closure substance.

merge (1) To combine the items of two or more sets that are each in the same given order into one set in that order. (I) (A) (2) In word processing, the automatic recording, printing, or sending onto one element of recording medium of selected recorded text, in correct order, from at least two other elements of recording media. (T) (3) In the AS/400 system, to combine overrides for a file from the first call level up to and including a greater call level, producing the override to be applied when the file is used. (4) See balanced merge. (5) See also collate.

MERGE disk The virtual disk in the VM operating system that contains program temporary fixes (PTFs) after the VMFMERGE EXEC is invoked. See BASE disk, DELTA disk, RUN disk, ZAP disk.

merge file (1) A temporary file that contains all records to be combined. (2) In COBOL, a collection of records to be merged by a MERGE statement. The merge file is created and can be used only by the merge function.

merge order The number of strings that can be merged into one string by a merge program during a pass. (A)

merge pass In sorting, the processing of records to reduce the number of sequences by a factor equal to the specified merge order.

merge sort (1) A sort program in which the items in a set are divided into subsets, the items in each subset are sorted, and the resulting sorted subsets are merged. (A) (2) See balanced merge sort, unbalanced merge sort.

merging (1) In the 3800 Printing Subsystem, the combining of print lines to highlight or subordinate data within a print line, or the printing of different columns of data across a page in different character styles or sizes. (2) See order-by-merging, sequence-by-merging.

mesh network A network in which there are at least two nodes with two or more paths between them. (T) See Figure 96.

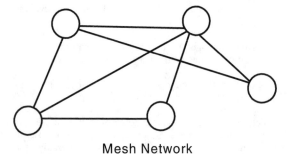

Mesh Network

Figure 96. Mesh Network

message (1) In information theory, an ordered series of characters intended to convey information. (I) (A) (2) An assembly of characters and sometimes control codes that is transferred as an entity from an originator to one or more recipients. A message consists of two parts: envelope and content. (T) (3) A communication sent from a person or program to another person or program. (4) A unit of data sent over a telecommunication line. (5) For BSC devices, the data unit from the beginning of a transmission to the first ETX character, or between two ETX characters. For start/stop, message and transmission have the same meaning. (6) One or more message segments transmitted among terminals, application programs, and systems. (7) In SAA Common User Access architecture, information not requested by a user but displayed by an application in response to an unexpected event, or when something undesirable could occur. (8) In COBOL, data associated with an end of message indicator or an end of group indicator. (9) In SNA, deprecated term for message unit. (10) In VTAM, the amount of function management data (FMD) transferred to VTAM by the application program with one SEND request.

message authentication code (1) In computer security, a value, part of or accompanying a message, used to determine that the contents, origin, author, or other attributes of all or part of the message are as they appear to be. See also authentication. (2) In cryptography: (a) a number or value derived by processing data with an authentication algorithm, (b) the cryptographic result of block cipher operations on text or data using a cipher block chain (CBC) mode of operation, (c) a digital signature code.

message box In SAA Advanced Common User Access architecture, a type of window that shows messages to users. See also dialog box, primary window, secondary window.

message buffering A method of spooling text messages to disk for output with device independence.

message circuit A long-distance telephone circuit used in furnishing regular long-distance or toll service to the general public. The term is used to differentiate these circuits from circuits used for private line service.

message class In IMS/VS, the class the user assigns to a transaction code that determines the message region within which an application program is to process the transaction. See also region class.

message control program In ACF/TCAM, any implementation of TCAM, including initialization and termination routines, resource management routines, message handling routines, and service facilities.

message control system (MCS) In COBOL, a communication control system that supports the processing of messages.

message count In COBOL, the count of the number of complete messages that exist in the designated queue of messages.

message data set A data set on disk storage that contains queues of messages awaiting transmission to particular terminal operators or to the host system.

message delete option In IMS/VS, an option that may be defined to prevent nonessential messages from being sent to a specific terminal. This option helps protect printers that use special forms or depend on forms alignment.

message description The information describing a particular message. A message description is stored in a message field.

message-driven program In IMS/VS, a program designed to operate with expedited message handling (EMH) transactions in a Fast Path region.

message editing In IMS/VS, the process by which messages are formatted for presentation to an application program or terminal. Additional message editing routines may be written by the user. See also basic edit, message format service.

message error record Synonym for error record.

message field (MFLD) (1) An area on the screen of a display device in which messages are displayed. (2) In the IMS/VS message format service, the smallest area in a message input or output descriptor whose content and structure are defined by the user. (3) In DPCX, the third of four areas on the bottom line of a display screen during field-by-field processing. This field informs the operator that a message is waiting.

message file In the AS/400 system, an object that contains message descriptions.

message format service (MFS) In IMS/VS, an editing facility that allows application programs to deal with simple logical messages instead of device-dependent data, thus simplifying the application development process.

message generation In TPNS, the process of executing TPNS MSgtXT statements that generate messages from the resources being simulated by TPNS.

message handler (MH) In ACF/TCAM, a sequence of user-specified macroinstructions and basic assembler language instructions that invoke routines that examine and process control information in message headers and perform functions necessary to prepare messages for forwarding to their destinations. See application message handler, device message handler, internodal message handler. See also delimiter macro, functional macro.

message handling service (MHS) An application service element that provides generalized facility for exchanging electronic messages between systems. (T)

message header The leading part of a message that contains information such as the source or destination code of the message, the message priority, and the type of message. See also message text.

message help Additional information about a message, such as the message type, severity, and date and time sent.

message identification A field in the display or printout of a message that directs the user to the description of the message in a message guide or reference manual. This field consists of up to four alphabetic characters, followed by a dash, followed by the message identification code.

message identifier In the AS/400 system, a seven-character code that identifies a predefined message, and that is used to get the message description from a message file. See also predefined message.

message indicator In COBOL, any of the conceptual indicators EGI (end of group indicator), EMI (end of message indicator), and ESI (end of segment indicator) that serve to notify the message control system that a specific condition exists (end of group, end of message, or end of segment). Within the hierarchy of EGI, EMI, and ESI, an EGI is conceptually equivalent to an ESI, EMI, and EGI. An EMI is conceptually equivalent to an ESI or EMI. Thus, a segment may be terminated by an ESI, EMI, or EGI. A message may be terminated by an EMI or EGI.

message intercept table In MSS, a list of specified message identifications and related actions for the message journaling function.

message journaling function In MSS, the providing of a single data set in which the Mass Storage System Communicator program, running on one or more loosely coupled processing units, can record OS/VS messages. The message journaling function maintains, updates, and retrieves information from the message-record-log data set.

message line In the AS/400 system, an area on a display where messages are displayed.

message lock mode In ACF/TCAM, a type of lock mode in which an external logical unit (LU) remains in lock mode for the duration of a single inquiry and reply. Contrast with extended lock mode. See also line lock, lock mode, station lock.

message member In System/36, a library member that defines the text of each message and its associated message identification code.

message (MSG) mode (1) A manner of operating a data network by means of message switching. (T) (2) A mode of operation in which data entered on a display console are sent to another console as a message. (3) In IMS/VS, a transaction attribute that describes how the transaction is handled by the application program. See also multiple message mode, single message mode.

message number The three-digit number in the message code that identifies the Folder Application Facility message.

message pending In the 3790 Communication System, a condition or indication (communication) that an operator's message queue is not empty. An additional message queue exists for the control operator that provides the same message-pending indication for control operator messages (program abends).

message pop-up In SAA Basic Common User Access architecture, a bordered area of the screen used to display one of the defined message types. See action message, information message, warning message.

Note: In CUA architecture, this is a programmer term. The end user term is message.

message priority In ACF/TCAM, the order in which messages in a destination queue are transmitted to a destination. Higher-priority messages are forwarded before lower-priority messages. See also route transmission priority, station transmission priority.

message processing facility (MPF) An MVS facility that controls message display and message processing.

message processing program (MPP) (1) A program that processes or otherwise responds to messages received from terminals. (2) In IMS/VS, an application program that is driven by transactions and has access to online IMS/VS databases and message queues. See also batch message processing program, batch processing program.

message queue (1) A list of messages awaiting processing or waiting to be sent to a terminal. (2) A queue of messages within a message data set waiting to be transmitted to the host system or to a particular terminal operator. (3) In IMS/VS, the data set on which messages are queued before being processed by an application program or sent to a terminal. (4) In System/38, an object on which messages are placed when they are sent to a person or program.

message queue data set In ACF/TCAM, a data set that contains one or more destination queues. A message queue data set contains messages that have been processed by the incoming group of a message handler and are waiting for ACF/TCAM to dequeue them, route them through an outgoing group of a message handler, and send them to their destinations. Up to three message queue data sets (one in main storage, one on reusable disk, and one on nonreusable disk) may be specified for an ACF/TCAM message control program.

message-record-log data set In MSS, a data set defined on direct access storage devices that is shared among loosely coupled processors that also share a 3850 Mass Storage System containing selected OS/VS messages written during MSS operation.

message recovery point In IMS/VS, the last incoming message for which IMS/VS returned a definite response or the last outgoing message for which IMS/VS requested a definite response.

message reference key In the AS/400 system and System/38, a key assigned to every message on a message waiting line. This key is used to remove a message from a message waiting line, to receive a message, and to reply to a message.

message resynchronization In IMS/VS, a facility that detects and corrects a lost message condition when a network failure occurs.

message retrieval The process of obtaining a message from a messaging system. (T)

message routing (1) The process of selecting the correct path for a message. (2) In ACF/TCAM, a message control program (MCP) function that deter-

mines the correct destination for each message received by the MCP and places each message on the appropriate destination queue. See affinity-based routing, invariant routing, transaction-based routing. See also routing by destination, routing by key.

message segment (1) In COBOL, data that forms a logical subdivision of a message, normally associated with an end of segment indicator. (2) In ACF/TCAM, the portion of a message contained within a single request unit (RU). (3) In IMS/VS, the unit of access when referring to a message to or from a terminal. (4) In SDLC transmission, the portion of a message identified and controlled by two consecutive entries in the transmit control block.

message sink (1) The part of a communication system in which messages are received. (I) (A) (2) See data sink.

message source (1) The part of a communication system from which messages are considered to originate. (I) (A) (2) Synonymous with information source. (3) See data source.

message subfile In the AS/400 system, a subfile in which the records are messages from a program message queue.

message switch In IMS/VS, a terminal input message directed to another terminal without being processed by a message processing program. See also program-to-program message switch.

message switching The process of receiving a message, storing it, and forwarding it to its destination unaltered. (T)

message text The part of a message of concern to the party ultimately receiving the message, that is, the message exclusive of the header or control information. See also message header.

message transfer state In BSC, a state in which a bid exchange has been completed and data can be transmitted.

message unit In SNA, the unit of data processed by any layer; for example, a basic information unit (BIU), path information unit (PIU), request/response unit (RU).

messaging system A system that manages electronic messaging. (T)

metaclass (1) A class of a class. (2) In the AIXwindows program and Enhanced X-Windows, an object class that does not instantiate widgets or gadgets but is capable of passing a unique set of inheritable resources to the subclasses beneath it in the class hierarchy. Each instance of a widget subclass has the features common to that widget class and exports these features to child widgets of that class. Included in this class are Button, Composite, Constraint, Core, Primitive, Manager, MenuMgr, and MenuPane.

meta-data In databases, data that describe data objects. (T)

metafile A file containing a series of attributes that set color, shape, and size, usually of a picture or a drawing. Using a program that can interpret these attributes, a user can view the assembled image. See also background picture.

meta-implementation In SNA, an architectural or design description in a form similar to actual implementations of an architecture; for example, one that uses a programming language to specify a human- or machine-executable model that follows the architectural rules, thereby defining those rules.

metalanguage A language used to specify another language.

metal oxide semiconductor See MOS.

meta-rule A rule that prescribes the conditions, sequence and manner in which a given set of rules should be applied. (T)

metastable state Synonym for unstable state.

metering pulses In telephony, periodic pulses sent by a public exchange over a line to determine the cost of outgoing calls.

meter (m) 1.0936 yards; 3.2808 feet; 39.3696 inches.

method (1) In AIX Enhanced X-Windows, the functions or procedures that a widget itself implements. (2) In the AIX object data manager, executable code associated with an object and defined as the value of a method descriptor for the object. The method can be a command, program, or shell script. See also method descriptor. (3) In System Object Model, an action that can be performed on an object. (4) In the NetView program, the code that runs within the Resource Object Data Manager (RODM) address space. Methods are used to implement behavior specified by an operation. (5) See heuristic method. (A)

method descriptor In the AIX object data manager, a named variable of type method used to define a method or operation to associate with an object. The method can be any executable code such as a command, program, or shell script.

metre See meter.

metropolitan area network (MAN) A network formed by the interconnection of two or more networks which may operate at higher speed than those networks, may cross administrative boundaries, and may use multiple access methods. (T)

MF Modify Field.

MFI Mainframe interactive.

MFI terminal Deprecated term for nonprogrammable terminal (NPT).

MFLD Message field.

MFLOPS Millions of floating point operations per second. A unit of measure of processing performance equal to one million floating point operations per second. Synonymous with megaflops. (T)

MFM Modified frequency recording.

MFR Multifrequency receiver.

MFS Message format service.

MFS dynamic directory In IMS/VS, a directory used by the online IMS/VS control program when operating under OS/VS MVS/XA to manage the format control blocks stored in extended the private storage.

MFSTEST In IMS/VS, an optional message format service (MFS) facility that allows MFS control blocks to be created and tested online without disrupting production activity.

MF/1 System activity measurement facility.

MH Message handler.

MHz Megahertz.

MI (1) Machine interface. (2) Manual intervention.

MIC (1) Middle-in-chain. (2) Message identification code.

MICR Magnetic ink character recognition. (A)

microbending In an optical fiber, sharp curvatures involving local axial displacements of a few micrometers and spatial wavelengths of a few millimeters. Such bends can result; for example, from fiber coating, cabling, packaging, or installation. (E)

Note: Microbending can cause significant radiative losses and mode coupling.

Micro Channel architecture The rules that define how subsystems and adapters use the Micro Channel bus in a computer. The architecture defines the services that each subsystem can or must provide.

microchip (1) Synonymous with integrated circuit (IC). (T) (2) A small piece of semiconductive material, usually silicon, that contains miniaturized electronic circuits. See also microprocessor.

microcircuit A combination of connected elements that are inseparably associated on or within a single continuous substrate to perform an electronic circuit function.

microcode (1) One or more microinstructions. (2) A code, representing the instructions of an instruction set, that is implemented in a part of storage that is not program-addressable. (3) To design, write, and also to test one or more microinstructions. (4) See also microprogram.

Note: The term microcode represents microinstructions used in a product as an alternative to hardwired circuitry to implement functions of a processor or other system component. The term microprogram means a dynamic arrangement of one or more groups of microinstructions for execution to perform a certain function. (5) See also licensed internal code.

microcoding Coding with the use of microinstructions.

microcomputer (1) A digital computer whose processing unit consists of one or more microprocessors, and includes storage and input/output facilities. (T) (2) A small computer that includes one or more input/output units and sufficient memory to execute instructions; for example, a personal computer. The essential components of a microcomputer are often contained within a single enclosure. See also laptop computer, mainframe, minicomputer, personal computer, supermini.

Notes:

1. *Microcomputers are usually desk-top or portable devices with a display, a keyboard, and tape, disk, and diskette storage; they are designed primarily for stand-alone operation but can be used as workstations in terminal emulation mode.*

2. *In terms of size and processing power, the hierarchy of computers consists of supercomputers, mainframes (usually called processing units or processors), superminis, minicomputers, and microcomputers. As the computing power and storage capability of microcomputers grow and the size of minicomputers decreases to table-top dimensions, the distinctions between micros and minis will become less distinct and may eventually disappear.*

microdiagnostic utility In the Data Facility Hierarchical Storage Manager, a program run by a service representative to test a machine.

microfiche (1) A sheet of microfilm capable of containing microimages in a grid pattern, usually containing a title that can be read without magnification. (A) (2) See also ultrafiche.

microfilm (1) A high resolution film for recording microimages. (A) (2) To record microimages on film. (A) (3) Microform whose medium is film, in the form of rolls, that contains microimages arranged sequentially. (4) See computer output microfilm.

microfilmer See computer output microfilmer.

microfilming See computer output microfilming. (A)

microform A medium that contains microimages; for example, microfiche, microfilm. (T) (A)

microform reader A device that enlarges microimages for viewing.

microform reader-copier A device that performs the functions of a reader and a printer to produce hard copy enlargements of selected microimages. Synonymous with microform reader-printer.

microform reader-printer Synonym for microform reader-copier.

microfreeze A machine state in which a central processor is stopped. Microfreeze is initiated by setting the microfreeze bit on in a selected control word. Thereafter, when that control word is sensed, the central processor stops in the microfreeze state.

micrographics (1) The branch of science and technology concerned with techniques for converting any form of information to or from microform. (A) (2) See computer micrographics.

microimage An image too small to be read without magnification. (A)

microinstruction An instruction for operations at a level lower than machine instructions. (T)

micrometer One millionth part of a meter. Synonymous with micron.

micron Synonym for micrometer.

micro order A part of a microcoded control word that controls specific machine operations.

microprocessor (1) A processor whose elements have been miniaturized into one or a few integrated circuits. (T) (2) A microchip containing integrated circuits that executes instructions. See also microcomputer.

microprogram (1) A sequence of microinstructions. Microprograms are mainly used to implement machine instructions. (T) (2) A group of microinstructions that when executed performs a preplanned function.

Note: The term microprogram represents a dynamic arrangement or selection of one or more groups of microinstructions for execution in order to perform a particular function. The term microcode represents microinstructions used in a product as an alternative to hard-wired circuitry to implement certain functions of a processor or other system component.

microprogram load See initial microprogram load.

microprogramming (1) The preparation of microprograms. (2) The technique used in the design of hardware that is to be controlled by microprograms. (T)

microsecond One-millionth of a second.

microwave Any electromagnetic wave in the radio frequency spectrum above 890 megahertz.

MID Machine identifier.

mid-batch recovery In ACF/TCAM, the ability to recover from permanent text errors encountered in any block of data following the first block in a multiple-block message.

middle-in-chain (MIC) A request unit (RU) whose request header (RH) begin chain indicator and RH end chain indicator are both off. See also RU chain.

middle letter row On a keyboard, the center letter row. Synonymous with row C. See lower letter row, upper letter row. See also numeric row.

MIDI Musical Instrument Digital Interface.

mid-shot Synonym for medium shot.

migrate (1) To move data from one hierarchy of storage to another. (2) To move to a changed operating environment, usually to a new release or version of a system.

migration (1) The process of moving data from one computer system to another without converting the data. (2) Installation of a new version or release of a program to replace an earlier version or release. (3) See data migration, general migration, interval migration, page migration.

migration cleanup In the Data Facility Hierarchical Storage Manager, the first phase of daily space management. This process deletes unnecessary records and migration copies.

migration control data set In the Data Facility Hierarchical Storage Manager, a VSAM key-sequenced data set that contains statistics records, control records, user records, records for data sets that have migrated, and records for volumes under migration control of the Data Facility Hierarchical Storage Manager.

migration data host A VTAM node that acts as both an APPN end node and a type 5 subarea node. Contrast with interchange node.

migration volume A volume under control of the Data Facility Hierarchical Storage Manager that contains migrated data sets.

MIH Missing-interrupt handler.

mike mixer In audio and video production, a device for combining input from two or more microphones or other audio sources for recording.

milli (m) One thousandth.

millibyte (mb) Deprecated term for kilobyte (Kb).

milliliter (ml) One thousandth of a liter; 0.27 fluid drams.

millimeter (mm) One thousandth of a meter; 0.04 inch.

Millions of instructions per second (MIPS) A measure of processing performance. (T)

millisecond One thousandth of a second.

mimic Synonym for impersonate.

minicomputer (1) A digital computer that is functionally intermediate between a microcomputer and a mainframe. (T) (2) An intermediate-size computer that can perform the same kinds of applications as a mainframe but has less storage capacity, processing power, and speed than a mainframe. See also mainframe, microcomputer, personal computer, supercomputer, supermini.

Note: Minicomputers are floor-standing or desktop devices, frequently connected to a mainframe to perform subsidiary operations. They are priced for purchase by smaller businesses and are sufficiently compact to be located in a typical office environment.

MINIDASD function Synonym for virtual disk initialization function.

minidisk (1) A disk smaller in diameter than conventional disks or diskettes. (T) Synonymous with minifloppy. (2) Synonym for virtual disk *(2)*.

minidisk directory Synonym for CMS file directory.

minifloppy Synonym for minidisk.

mini-icon In SAA Advanced Common User Access architecture, a smaller version of an icon. Icons and mini-icons represent objects. See icon. See also object.

minimize To remove from the screen all windows associated with an application and replace them with an icon that represents the application.

Minimize In SAA Advanced Common User Access architecture, a choice in the system menu pull-down that a user selects to remove all windows associated with an application from the screen and replace them with an icon that represents the application.

minimize icon In SAA usage, a symbol, located to the right of the window title, that a user can select to change the window to an icon, which is moved to the bottom of the screen. Contrast with maximize icon. See also restore icon.

minimum acceptable receive level In an ESCON environment, the calculated level, expressed in decibels, received at a specific point in the link. This value is used as a rejection criterion when measuring the actual level received at the same point.

minimum delay programming A method of programming in which storage locations for instructions and data are chosen so that access time is reduced and minimized. (I) (A)

minimum distance code A binary code in which the signal distance does not fall below a specified minimum value. (A)

minimum truncation In VM, the shortest form of a command name, operand, or option that can be keyed in that can still be recognized by VM; for example, AC is the minimum truncation for the ACCESS command and the letter A is the minimum truncation for ASSEMBLE. See also truncation.

minor class field In the System/38 query utility, the field whose contents determine the minor record class in which the query utility processes a record during preparation of a table. Contrast with major class field.

minor control field In a sorting operation, any control field that is of less significance than the major control field.

minor device number In the AIX operating system, a number that specifies various types of information about a particular device; for example, a number that distinguishes between several printers of same type. See major device number.

minor node In VTAM, a uniquely defined resource within a major node. See also major node.

minor tick In the AS/400 Business Graphics Utility, one of the marks located between major ticks on an axis of a chart. See also major tick.

minor time slice In TSO, the time within a major time slice when a terminal job has the highest priority for execution. See also major time slice.

minor total The result obtained when a summation is terminated by the least significant change of group.

minuend In subtraction, the number or quantity from which another number or quantity is subtracted. (I) (A)

Note: Minuend – subtrahend = result.

MIOCB Master I/O control block.

MIPS Millions of instructions per second. A unit of measure of processing performance equal to one million instructions per second. (T)

mirrored pair Two units that contain the same data and are referred to by the system as one entity.

mirrored protection In the AS/400 system, a function that protects data by duplicating all disk data in an auxiliary storage pool (ASP) to another disk unit (mirrored unit) in the same ASP. If a disk failure occurs, the system keeps running, using the mirrored unit of the mirrored pair until the disk unit is repaired or replaced. See also mirrored pair, mirrored unit.

mirrored unit In the AS/400 system, one of the units of a mirrored pair of units.

mirror image In a document copying machine, an image that has its parts positioned as if the original were viewed in a mirror. (T) Contrast with right-reading image.

mirroring (1) In computer graphics, turning all or part of a display image 180 degrees about an axis in the plane of the display surface. (T) See Figure 97. (2) In the AS/400 system, the process of writing the same data to two disk units within the same auxiliary storage pool at the same time. The two disk units become a mirrored pair, allowing the system to continue when one of the mirrored units fails. See also mirrored pair, mirrored unit.

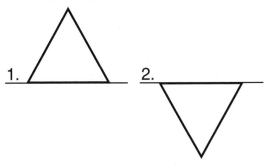

Figure 97. Mirroring

mirror transaction In CICS/VS, a transaction program that executes a request sent to it from another transaction processing system, and returns to the originating transaction processing system a response code and any control fields and data associated with the request. The mirror transaction enables CICS/VS transaction processing systems to perform remote resource access.

MIS Management information system. (A)

miscellaneous data record (MDR) A record of a network hardware error recorded by the NCP and sent to the VTAM host that owns the failing component. Then the VTAM program writes the error on the operating system error data set.

miscellaneous intercept In Bell System leased telegraph message-switching systems, the act of intercepting single-address messages containing a nonvalid call directing code or intercepting multiple-address messages without a proper multiple-address code. See also willful intercept.

miscellaneous time That part of operating time that is not system production time, system test time, or rerun time. Miscellaneous time is typically used for demonstrations, operator training, or other such purposes. Synonymous with incidental time. (T)

missing-interrupt handler (MIH) An MVS and MVS/XA facility that keeps track of I/O interrupts, informing the operator and creating a record whenever an expected interrupt fails to occur in a preset time interval.

missing page interruption Synonym for page fault.

missing pulse A pulse whose level cannot be read or recorded. (T) (A)

mistake (1) A human action that produces an unintended result. (T) (2) Contrast with error, failure, fault.

mix In multimedia applications, the combination of audio or video sources during postproduction.

mix and match Pertaining to different kinds of items that may be grouped and purchased, often for a discount price; for example, $0.50 items that may be purchased in a mixture at 3 for $1.39.

mixed-base notation Synonym for mixed-base numeration system.

mixed-base numeration system A numeration system in which a number is represented as the sum of a series of terms each of which consists of a mantissa and a base, the base of a given term being constant for a given application but the bases being such that there are not necessarily integral ratios between the bases of all the terms; for example, with bases b_3, b_2, and b_1 and b_1 and mantissas 6, 5, and 4, the number represented is given by $6b_3 + 5b_2 + 4b_1$. A mixed-radix numeration system is the particular case of a mixed-base numeration system in which, when the terms are ordered so that their bases are in descending magnitudes, there is an integral ratio between the bases of adjacent terms, but not the same ratio in each case; thus, if the smallest base is b and if x and y represent integers, the numeral 654 in such a numeration system represents the number given by $6 xyb + 5 xb + 4 b$. A fixed-radix numeration system is the particular case of a mixed-base numeration system in which, when the terms are ordered so that their bases are in descending magnitudes, there is the same integral ratio between bases of all pairs of adjacent terms; thus if b is the smallest base and if x represents an integer, the numeral 654 in such a numeration system represents the number given by $6x^2b + 5xb + 4b$. (I) (A) Synonymous with mixed-base notation.

mixed chart In GDDM, the combination of more than one type of chart in a business chart; for example, the overlaying of a line chart on a bar chart.

mixed data set In DPCX, a data set predefined by DPCX whose indexes are contained in system space and whose records are contained in user space. The mixed data sets are the print data set, program data set, transaction data set, transmit data set, panel data set, message data set, RJE data set, and abend dump data set.

mixed data string In SQL, a character string that can contain both single-byte and double-byte characters.

mixed environment A system in which ACF/TCAM and TSO tasks concurrently share all necessary system resources.

mixed file In System/38, a device file created by the user to support one or more display stations, communication devices, or BSC devices.

mixed format print data set In the 3800 Print Services Facility, a data set that consists of line-data pages and composed-text pages.

mixed list A series of unlike values for a parameter that accepts a set of separately defined values. Contrast with simple list.

mixed-media multilink transmission group A multilink transmission group that contains links of different medium types. A mixed-media multilink transmission group may contain token-ring, switched and nonswitched SDLC, and frame-relay links.

mixed-media system Synonym for multimedia system.

mixed-mode expression Synonym for mixed-type expression.

mixed-radix notation Synonym for mixed-radix numeration system.

mixed-radix numeration system A radix numeration system in which the digit places do not all necessarily have the same radix; for example, a numeration system in which three successive digits represent hours, tens of minutes, and minutes; taking one minute as the unit, the weights of the three digit places are 60, 10, and 1 respectively; the radices of the second and third digit places are 6 and 10, respectively. A comparable numeration system that used one or more digits to represent days and two digits to represent hours would not satisfy the definition of any radix numeration system, since there is no integral ratio of the weights of the digit places representing days and hours. (I) (A) Synonymous with mixed-radix notation.

mixed string A string that consists of a mixture of double-byte character set (DBCS) characters and single-byte characters.

mixed-type expression An arithmetic expression that contains both integer and real arithmetic primaries.

mixing (1) In computer graphics, the result of the intersection of two or more colors. (2) In multimedia filming, the combining of audio and video sources that is accomplished during postproduction at the mix.

(3) In multimedia recording, the combining of audio sources.

MKDS In the Programmed Cryptographic Facility, a cryptographic key used to encipher or decipher data.

ml Milliliter.

MLCA Multiline communications adapter/attachment.

MLTG Multilink transmission group.

mm Millimeter.

MMMLTG Mixed-media multilink transmission group.

M65MP Model 65 Multiprocessing System.

MMR Modified modified read.

MMS Manufacturing Monitoring System.

mnemonic (1) A symbol chosen to help the user remember the significance of the symbol. (2) The field of an assembler instruction that contains the acronym or abbreviation for a machine instruction. Using mnemonics frees the programmer from having to remember the numeric operator codes of the computer. (3) In SAA Advanced Common User Access architecture, usually a single character, within the text of a choice, identified by an underscore beneath the character. If all characters in a choice already serve as mnemonics for other choices, another character, placed in parentheses immediately following the choice, can be used. When a user types the mnemonic for a choice, the choice is either selected or the cursor is moved to that choice. See mnemonic selection.

mnemonic-name In COBOL, a user-defined word that is associated in the Environment Division with a specific implementor name.

mnemonic operation code An operation code consisting of mnemonic symbols that indicate the nature of the operation to be performed, type of data used, or format of the instruction that performs the operation.

mnemonic selection In SAA Advanced Common User Access architecture, a selection technique whereby a user selects a choice by typing the mnemonic for that choice.

mnemonic symbol A symbol chosen to assist the human memory; for example, an abbreviation such as mpy for multiply. (I) (A)

modal dialog In the AIXwindows program, a Dialog widget that interrupts the work session to solicit input from the user.

modal dialog box In SAA Advanced Common User Access architecture, a type of movable window, fixed in size, that requires a user to enter information before continuing to work in the application window from which it was displayed. Contrast with modeless dialog box.

Note: In CUA architecture, this is a programmer term. The end user term is pop-up window.

modal pop-up In AIX Enhanced X-Windows, a window that normally is not visible to the window manager and available only after the manager is turned off. This pop-up disables user-event processing except for events that occur in the dialog box.

MO:DCA Mixed Object Document Content Architecture. An architecture developed to allow the interchange of object data among applications within the interchange environment and among environments.

MO:DCA—P Mixed Object Document Content Architecture—Presentation In the ImagePlus program, a subset architecture of MO:DCA that is used as an envelope to contain documents that are sent to the ImagePlus workstation for displaying or printing.

mod/demod Modulator-demodulator unit. See also data set, modem.

mode (1) A method of operation; for an example, see enter/update mode. (2) See access mode, conversational mode, current mode, extend mode, hold mode, initial condition mode, I-O mode, input mode, kernel mode, load mode, move mode, open mode, output mode, potentiometer set mode, static test mode, user mode. See also mode name.

mode description In the AS/400 system, a system object created for advanced-program-to-program communications (APPC) devices that describes the session limits and the characteristics of the session, such as the maximum number of sessions allowed, maximum number of conversations allowed, the pacing value for incoming and outgoing request or response units, and other controlling information for the session.

mode field In DPCX, the fourth of four fields on a display screen during field-by-field processing that notifies the operator about the status of the terminal.

mode indicator In System/36, an indicator that changes when the operating mode changes. Contrast with job indicator, session indicator.

model (1) The conceptual and operational understanding that a person has about something. See mathematical model.

model-based system In artificial intelligence, an expert system that is based on the knowledge of the structure and function of the object the system is designed for. (T)

model driven In artificial intelligence, pertaining to a method of inference that uses a domain model. (T)

modeless dialog In the AIXwindows program, a Dialog widget that solicits input from the user but does not interrupt the work session.

modeless dialog box In SAA Advanced Common User Access architecture, a type of movable window, fixed in size, that allows users to continue their dialog with the application without entering information in the dialog box. Contrast with modal dialog box.

Note: In CUA architecture, this is a programmer term. The end user term is pop-up window.

modeless pop-up In AIX Enhanced X-Windows, a window that is normally visible and is controlled by the window manager.

mode-level field In a System/36 program, a field that has its value saved and is then cleared when the operating mode changes. Contrast with job-level field, session-level field.

modeling (1) In RACF, the ability of a user or an installation to define a sample "model" profile that RACF uses when defining a new profile. Each profile model can contain defaults for fields such as the universal access authority, level, owner, auditing flags, access list, erase indicator, security classification information, and installation-defined data. (2) In computer-assisted instruction, a process whereby a computer-based learning system is made to represent another system or process. The learner can change values and observe the effects of the change on the operation of the system.

modeling coordinates In AIX graphics, the coordinate system in which all drawing primitives do their drawing. The user can select the position and orientation of the modeling space with regard to the world space by means of translations, rotations, scales, or generalized transformations. See also eye coordinates, primitive coordinates, screen coordinates, transformation, world coordinates.

modeling transformation In AIX graphics, transformation that maps modeling coordinates into world coordinates, in which all drawing primitives specify positions that are presumed to be positions in modeling coordinates. Modeling transformation can be used to move the object being drawn.

Model 65 Multiprocessing System (M65MP) A computing system in which two connected 2065 processing units share the same main storage and most I/O devices. The activities of the two processing units are directed by a single control program.

model statement A statement in the body of a macro-definition or in open code from which an assembler language statement can be generated at preassembly time. Values can be substituted at one or more points in a model statement; one or more identical or different statements can be generated from the same model statement under control of a conditional assembly loop.

model-unique licensed internal code The licensed internal code, shipped with system hardware, that provides support for that model. See also licensed internal code.

modem (modulator/demodulator) (1) A functional unit that modulates and demodulates signals. One of the functions of a modem is to enable digital data to be transmitted over analog transmission facilities. (T) (A)   (2) A device that converts digital data from a computer to an analog signal that can be transmitted on a telecommunication line, and converts the analog signal received to data for the computer. (3) See also communication line adapter, modulation.

modem eliminator A device that connects a work-station directly to a computer port through a wired connector with a specific pin arrangement. When two devices both function as data terminal equipment (DTE), the cable that connects them must transmit send and receive signals using a modem eliminator. Synonymous with null modem.

mode name The name used by the initiator of a session to designate the characteristics desired for the session, such as traffic pacing values, message-length limits, sync point and cryptography options, and the class of service within the transport network.

mode-name entry The entry in an LU-mode pair that contains information about the mode associated with the partner logical unit.

mode table Synonym for bind image table.

mode word In the AIX file system, an i-node field that describes the type and state of the i-node.

mode-2 character In GDDM, a graphics character (a symbol), characterized by an unchanging size, constructed from picture elements. Contrast with mode-3 character. See also hardware character.

mode-3 character In GDDM, a graphics character (a symbol), characterized by a variable size and shape, constructed from lines and curves. Contrast with mode-2 character. See also hardware character.

modification (1) An addition or change to stored data or a deletion of stored data. (A)   (2) In a conceptual schema language, the replacement of a sentence in the information base or conceptual schema by another one, thus potentially changing the collection of sentences that are deducible. (A)   (3) The change or customization of a system, subsystem, or application to work more effectively at a given installation. (4) In SMP/E, an alteration or correction to a system control program, licensed program, or user program. Synonymous with system modification (SYSMOD).

modification command In a data manipulation language, one of a set of statements that allows an application program or a database administrator to insert, update, and delete information stored in a database. (A)

modification detection code (MDC) In cryptography, a number or value that interrelates all bits of a data stream so that when enciphered, the modification of any bit in the data stream results in a new MDC.

modification level A distribution of all temporary fixes issued since the previous modification level. A change in modification level does not add new functions or change the programming support category of the release to which it applies. See also release, version.

Note: Whenever a new release of a program is shipped, the modification level is set to 0. When the release is reshipped with the accumulated service changes incorporated, the modification level is incremented by 1.

modified data tag (MDT) (1) In the AS/400 system, an indicator, associated with each input or output/input field in a displayed record, that is set ON when data are keyed into the field. The modified data tag is maintained by the display device and can be used by the program using the file. (2) In 3270, a bit in each input field that, when set, causes that field to be transferred to the host system.

modified frequency modulation (MFM) The process of varying the amplitude and frequency of a write signal. MFM pertains to the number of bytes of storage that can be stored on the recording media. The number of bytes is twice the number contained on the same unit area of recording media at single density. Synonymous with double-dense recording, double-density recording.

modified frequency modulation recording Non-return-to-reference recording in which there is a change in the condition of magnetization in the center of a cell containing a one and a change in the boundary between two cells, each of which contain a zero. (T)

modified modified read (MMR) A compression algorithm.

modified subfile record In System/38, a subfile record into which a workstation user has entered data or a subfile record for which a put or update operation has been issued with the DDS keyword SFLNXTCHG or DSPATR(MDT) in effect.

modifier keys In AIX Enhanced X-Windows, keys such as Shift, Shift Lock, Control, Alt, Caps Lock, and Meta.

modifier register Deprecated term for index register.

Modify Field (MF) A 3270 data stream order that specifies the field and extended field attributes to be modified without having to respecify all attributes of the field.

modify ticket A function at a point of sale terminal that enables an operator to key in a change to the quantity, price, or both, of an item. This function is required only in certain sales transactions, and then only when the wand reader is being used to read merchandise tickets.

modularity The extent to which a system is composed of modules. (A)

modular programming Programming in which discrete program units are coded to perform particular functions.

modular system A system that consists of connected and separately removable parts that allows for alteration of capacity or functions and provides for ease of maintenance. (T)

modulate (1) To vary the amplitude, frequency, or phase of a signal. (2) To vary the angle of a laser beam.

modulation The process by which a characteristic of a carrier is varied in accordance with a characteristic of an information-bearing signal. (T)

modulation rate The reciprocal of the measure of the shortest nominal time interval between successive significant instants of the modulated signal. (I)

Note: If the measure is expressed in seconds, the modulation rate is expressed in bauds.

modulator (1) A functional unit that converts a signal into a modulated signal suitable for transmission. (I) (A) (2) In a laser printer, a device that uses a modulator crystal to deflect a beam of light and effectively turn it on or off. (3) Contrast with demodulator.

modulator crystal A man-made transparent material that can deflect light when high-frequency pulses cause the crystal to oscillate.

modulator-demodulator See modem.

module (1) In programming languages, a language construct that consists of procedures or data declarations and that can interact with other such constructs; for example, in Ada, a package; in FORTRAN, a program unit; in PL/I, an external procedure. (I) (2) A program unit that is discrete and identifiable with respect to compiling, combining with other units, and loading; for example, the input to or output from an assembler, compiler, linkage editor, or executive routine. (A) (3) A packaged functional hardware unit designed for use with other components. (A) (4) A part of a program that usually performs a particular function or related functions. (5) In FORTRAN, an external program unit that contains or accesses definitions to be accessed by other program units. See standard module. (6) See bound control module, control module, disk storage module, load module, object module, programming module, source module, unbound control module. (7) Synonymous with program unit. (8) See also encapsulated type, run file.

modulo (1) Pertaining to a modulus; for example, 9 is equivalent to 4 modulo 5. (2) See also modulus.

modulo check A calculation performed on values entered into a system by an operator. This calculation is designed to detect most common keying errors.

modulo level The maximum number of path information units (PIUs) a device can send before stopping to wait for a response.

modulo-n check (1) A check in which a value is divided by a number n to generate a remainder that is compared with the remainder previously calculated. (T) (2) Synonymous with residue check.

modulo-n counter A counter in which the number represented reverts to zero in the sequence of counting after reaching a maximum value of n-1. (I) (A)

modulo-two sum Deprecated term for nonequivalence operation.

modulus (1) In a modulo check, the number by which the summed digits are divided. See also modulo check. (2) A number, such as a positive integer, in a relationship that divides the difference between two related numbers without leaving a remainder; for example, 9 and 4 have a modulus of 5 (9 - 4 = 5; 4 - 9 = -5; and 5 divides both 5 and -5 without leaving a remainder).

modulus 10 checking/modulus 11 checking (1) A technique for validity checking that involves the association of digits with data. It is used in entering or updating fields in a data record. (2) Formulas used to calculate the check digit for a self-check field.

moire In multimedia applications, an independent, usually shimmering pattern seen when two geometrically regular patterns, such as a sampling frequency and a correct frequency, are superimposed. The moire pattern is an alias frequency. See also aliasing.

moistening pressure roller In a duplicator, a roller that applies pressure to the surface of the moistening roller to transfer the paper through the damping system. (T) Synonymous with conveying roller.

moistening roller In a duplicator, a roller that transfers moisture from the damping pad to the surface of the copy paper. (T)

MOM Monitor mode.

monadic Boolean operator A Boolean operator having only one operand; for example, NOT. (A)

monadic operation An operation with one and only one operand. (I) (A) Synonymous with unary operation.

monadic operator An operator that represents an operation on one and only one operand. (I) (A) Synonymous with unary operator.

monitor (1) A device that observes and records selected activities within a data processing system for analysis. Possible uses are to indicate significant departure from the norm, or to determine levels of utilization of particular functional units. (T) (2) Software or hardware that observes, supervises, controls, or verifies operations of a system. (A) (3) Synonym for video display terminal. (4) The function required to initiate the transmission of a token on the ring and to provide soft-error recovery in case of lost tokens, circulating frames, or other difficulties. The capability is present in all ring stations. (5) In the NetView Graphic Monitor Facility, to open a view that can receive status changes from the NetView program. Problem determination and correction can be performed directly from the view. Contrast with browse. (6) See video monitor.

monitoring program Synonym for monitor program.

monitor mode (1) A mode of the network control program in which the host is immediately notified when an attention, disconnect, or unusual status occurs on a designated line. (2) In an 8100 loop, a secondary station operating mode in which the station is receiving and analyzing loop traffic, but is not inserted into the loop. See also inserted mode. (3) In System/38, the mode during which a communication adapter searches for BSC synchronization characters. (4) In the AIX operating system, a mode in which an application program can directly access the display adapter.

monitor printer A device that prints all messages transmitted over the circuit to which it is connected.

monitor program A computer program that observes, regulates, controls, or verifies the operations of a data processing system. (I) (A) Synonymous with monitoring program.

monitor task In DPCX with the program execution monitor, the task in which the system debugging function is used to monitor a program or subtask.

monitor terminal In DPCX with the program execution monitor, the terminal from which the system debugging function is selected and from which a task or subtask is initiated for monitoring. The monitor terminal is used to enter commands that control the execution of the test task.

monochrome Consisting of a single color.

monochrome display A display device that presents display images in only one color. Contrast with color display. See also gray scale.

monolithic integrated circuit A type of integrated circuit whose substrate is an active material, such as the semiconductor silicon.

monolithic storage Storage made up of monolithic integrated circuits.

monolithic technology A technology in which all electronic components of a circuit, such as transistors, diodes, resistors, and capacitors, are integrated into one chip; for example, MST.

monomode optical fiber Synonym for single-mode optical fiber.

monospacing A method of spacing in which the space between characters does not vary. Contrast with proportional spacing.

monostable Pertaining to a device that has one stable state. (A)

monostable circuit Synonym for monostable trigger circuit.

monostable trigger circuit A trigger circuit that has one stable state and one unstable state. (I) (A) Synonymous with monostable circuit.

montage In multimedia, a series of shots edited in sequence to create a specific impression, such as the passage of time.

Monte Carlo method A method of obtaining an approximate solution to a numerical problem by the use of random numbers; for example, the random walk method, or a procedure using a random number sequence to calculate an integral. (I) (A)

More In SAA Basic Common User Access architecture, scrolling information that indicates to a user that more information is available by scrolling. See scrolling arrows.

more-data bit See M-bit.

MORE screen status For a display terminal used as a virtual console under VM, an indicator located in the lower right of the screen that notifies the user that the display screen is full, but that there is more data to be displayed. After 60 seconds, the screen is automatically erased and the next image is displayed.

MOS Metal oxide semiconductor. A type of semiconductor used in devices such as field-effect transistors. See also CMOS, HMOS, NMOS, PMOS.

mosaic Deprecated term for aggregation.

MOSFET Metal oxide semiconductor field-effect transistor.

MOSS Maintenance and operator subsystem.

MOSS-E Maintenance and operator subsystem extended.

most significant digit (MSD) In a positional representation system, a digit having the largest weight used. (T)

motion-control photography In multimedia applications, a system for using computers to precisely control camera movements so that the different elements of a shot, such as models and backgrounds, can later be composited with a natural and believable unity.

motion video In multimedia, video that displays real motion.

motion video capture adapter In multimedia applications, an adapter that, when attached to a computer, allows an ordinary television picture to be displayed on all or part of the screen, mixing high-resolution computer graphics with video. It also enables a video camera to be used as an input device. See also still video capture adapter.

motor See integrating motor.

mount (1) To place a data medium in a position to operate. (T) (2) To make recording media accessible.

mount attribute The attribute assigned to a volume that controls when the volume can be demounted. The mount attributes are permanently resident, reserved, and removable.

mouse (1) In computer graphics, a hand-held locator operated by moving it on a flat surface. A mouse generally contains a control ball or a pair of wheels. (I) (A) (2) In SAA usage, a device that a user moves on a flat surface to position a pointer on the screen. It allows a user to select a choice or function to be performed or to perform operations on the screen, such as dragging or drawing lines from one position to another. See Figure 98.

Figure 98. Mouse

mouse button In SAA Advanced Common User Access architecture, a mechanism on a mouse that a user presses to select choices or initiate actions.

mouse scaling The distance the cursor moves relative to the mouse movement. The scaling factor is either 1:1 or 2:1.

mouse threshold An operating system parameter that determines the amount of horizontal or vertical mouse movements required to move the cursor on the screen.

move (1) An operation that transfers records from one location in storage to another location in storage. Synonym for block move, transfer. (2) In the OS/2 operating system, to change the location of an object. After the move action, the original exists in its new location and no longer exists in its original location.

Move In SAA Advanced Common User Access architecture, a choice in the system menu pull-down that a user selects to position a window on the screen.

move mode (1) In some variable-word-length computers, data transmission in which certain delimiters are not moved with the data. (A) (2) A transmittal mode in which the record to be processed is moved into a user work area. See locate mode, substitute mode. (3) Contrast with load mode.

moving average An arithmetic mean or an average of a quantity of data gathered over a period of time. See also weighted moving average.

moving cursor In VM/SP HPO, a cylinder selection algorithm that selects the next nonfull cylinder when a cylinder being used for page-slot allocation is fully allocated.

moving paper carrier On a typewriter, a paper carrier that moves the paper in a direction parallel to the typing line and also perpendicular to it. (T)

Moving Pictures Experts Group (MPEG) (1) A group that is working to establish a standard for compressing and storing motion video and animation in digital form. (2) The standard under development by this group

moving platen document copying machine A document copying machine in which the original is laid flat on the platen, which moves during exposure. (T) Contrast with stationary platen document copying machine.

MPC (1) Multimedia PC (trademark of Multimedia PC Marketing Council). (2) Multipath channel.

MPEG Moving Pictures Experts Group.

MPF Message processing facility.

MPP Message processing program.

MP recovery In System/370 Model 158/168 Multiprocessing with MVS, recovery from a failure by switching automatically to an alternate component, and retrying the failed operation.

MPS (1) Multiprogramming system. (2) Multiple partition support. (3) Multiple port sharing.

MPST Memory process scheduling table.

M response Synonym for V response.

MRI Machine-readable information.

MR indicator Matching record (MR) indicator.

MRJE Multileaving remote job entry.

MRO Multiregion operation.

MRT procedure See multiple requester terminal procedure.

MRT program See multiple requester terminal program.

MS (1) Medium shot. (2) Management services.

MSC (1) Multiple Systems Coupling. (2) Mass storage control.

MSCS Mass storage control system.

MSDB Main storage database.

MSF 3851 Mass Storage Facility.

MSG Console messages.

MSHP Maintain system history program

MSL Map specification library.

MSNF Multisystem Networking Facility.

MSRJE Multiple session remote job entry.

MSS 3850 Mass Storage System.

MSS Extensions Mass Storage System Extensions. An IBM licensed program that provides programming enhancements to space management, data management, and problem determination for the 3850 Mass Storage System.

MSSC Mass Storage System Communicator.

MST Monolithic system technology.

MSVC Mass storage volume control.

MTA Multiple terminal access.

MTAM Multileaving telecommunications access method.

MTBF Mean time between failures. (I) (A)

MTO console The system operator's master terminal operator console for CICS.

MT/ST Magnetic tape SELECTRIC typewriter.

MTTR Mean time to repair. (I)   (A)

multiaddress Pertaining to an instruction format containing more than one address part. (A)

MTU Maximum transfer unit.

MU Message unit.

multiaddress calling A process that permits a user to call more than one data station. (T)

multiaddress instruction (1) An instruction that contains more than one address;   for example, two-address instruction, three-address instruction, n address instruction. (T)   (2) Synonymous with multiple address instruction.

multiaperture core A magnetic core, usually used for nondestructive reading, with two or more holes through which wires can be passed in order to create more than one magnetic path. (I)   (A)   Synonymous with multiple aperture core.

Note: Multiple-aperture core is an obsolete technology.

multibyte control Synonym for escape sequence.

multicast (1) Transmission of the same data to a selected group of destinations. (T)   (2) See LAN multicast.

multicast address See group address.

multicolored symbol In the 3270 Information Display System, a programmed symbol of more than one color defined in a triple plane symbol set.

multidimensional language (1) A language whose expressions are assembled in more than one dimension;   for example, flowcharts, logic diagrams, block diagrams, and decision tables. (A)   (2) Contrast with one-dimensional language.

multidomain network Synonym for multiple-domain network.

multidrop (network) A network configuration in which there are one or more intermediate nodes on the path between a central node and an endpoint node. (T)

multidrop line Synonym for multipoint line.

multidrop station One of several stations connected to a multipoint channel at one location.

multidrop topology A network topology that allows multiple control units to share a common channel path, thereby reducing the number of paths between channels and control units.   Contrast with switched point-to-point topology.   See also point-to-point topology.

multifiber cable An optical cable that contains two or more fibers. (E) See jumper cable, trunk cable.   See also optical cable assembly.

multifrequency push button set A telephone using push button dialing and multifrequency signaling.

multifrequency receiver (MFR) A demodulator that decodes multifrequency signals from telephone sets or data terminals.

multifrequency signal A signal made up of several superimposed audio frequency tones.

multifrequency terminal A terminal that transmits data characters as multifrequency signals.

multifunction board In a personal computer, a card or panel containing semiconductor devices that provides a number of options, such as parallel ports and serial ports, for attaching peripheral devices, special features such as a clock/calendar, and additional memory.

multifunction rotary switches In System/38, two switches on the operator/service panel that can be set to one of 16 different positions by rotating them in either a clockwise or counterclockwise direction.

multijob operation Concurrent execution of job steps from two or more jobs.

multilanguage code page An 8-bit code page with the international graphic characters on the code points for the 93-character graphic character set, and the national use graphic characters of other countries on the remaining code points.

multileaving A variation of BSC communication that allows several devices to communicate concurrently over a link without using station addresses.

multileaving remote job entry Fully synchronized, two-directional transmission of a variable number of data streams between two computers using BSC facilities.

multileaving support Fully synchronized two-directional transmission of a variable number of data streams between terminals and a computer using BSC facilities.

multileaving telecomm. access method In the AS/400 system and System/38, the programming support that allows the system to use MRJE functions.

multilevel address Synonym for indirect address.

multilevel device In computer security, a device that can simultaneously process data of two or more security levels without risk of compromising security. Contrast with single-level device.

multilevel duobinary amplitude modulation PSK Duobinary AM/PSK modulation in which additional levels are used for digital encoding. (T)

multilevel encoding Encoding of digital data in such a manner that, at any given instant, the signal can assume any one of three or more possible amplitude levels. (T)

multilevel secure system In computer security, a system containing information with different classification levels that permits simultaneous access by users with different security clearances and needs-to-know, but prevents users from obtaining access to information for which they lack authorization.

multiline communications adapter/attachment A feature that allows up to four telecommunication lines to be connected to System/36.

multilingual code page The code page containing alphanumeric and special symbols that are used by many of the languages of European, North American, and South American countries.

multilink Two or more data links, each with its own link protocol. A multilink may be a multiplexed link.

multilink transmission group (MLTG) A transmission group containing two or more links.

multimedia Material presented in a combination of text, graphics, video, animation, and sound.

multimedia navigation system A tool that gives the information product designer the freedom to link various kinds and pieces of data in a variety of ways so that users can move through it nonsequentially.

Multimedia PC A standard, originally developed by the Tandy and Microsoft corporations, for defining the minimum hardware platform capable of running multimedia software. The Multimedia PC logo (MPC) indicates compatibility between multimedia hardware and software. (Trademark of Multimedia PC Marketing Council)

multimedia system A system capable of presenting multimedia material in its entirety. Synonymous with mixed-media system.

multimode optical fiber A graded-index or step-index optical fiber that allows more than one bound mode to propagate. (E) Contrast with single-mode optical fiber.

multinational character set An option that makes an expanded set of 188 characters available to countries with supported language groups.

multipass sort A sort program designed to sort more items than can be in main storage at one time. (A)

multipath channel (MPC) A channel protocol that uses multiple unidirectional subchannels for VTAM-to-VTAM bidirectional communication.

multiple-access virtual machine A virtual machine running under VM that supports data communication terminals.

multiple address instruction Synonym for multiaddress instruction.

multiple-address message A message to be delivered to more than one destination.

multiple-address space In MVS, a feature that provides each user with a private address space.

multiple aperture core Synonym for multiaperture core.

multiple-attachment support In ACF/TCAM, a facility that allows concurrent sharing of a local network control program node and the resources attached to it by more than one host node.

multiple axis chart In GDDM, a chart in which more than one horizontal or vertical axis, or both, are used. See also secondary axis.

multiple bar chart In GDDM, a form of bar chart in which the bars at a given horizontal axis value are placed side by side.

multiple chart In GDDM, two or more charts that appear together on the workstation or page. Multiple charts can be of the same type or different types. They can be constructed from one or more sets of data.

multiple-choice selection field In SAA Basic Common User Access architecture, a type of field from which a user can select one or more choices or select none. See selection field, single-choice selection field.

multiple-choice selection list In SAA Basic Common User Access architecture, a type of list from which a user can select one or more choices or select none. See selection list. See also single-choice selection list.

multiple console support (MCS) The operator interface in an MVS system.

multiple copy control On a typewriter, a control for varying the rebound distance to accommodate a different thickness of paper. (T)

multiple device file A device file in which the maximum number of program devices is greater than one. It can be either a display file or a mixed file. Contrast with single device file.

multiple-document interface In SAA Advanced Common User Access architecture, a style of user interface in which a user can view many objects at the same time, or the same object many times, within one primary window.

multiple-domain network (1) A network with more than one host node. (T) Synonymous with multidomain network. (2) A network with more than one system services control point. (3) An APPN network with more than one network node.

multiple explicit routes In SNA, two or more explicit routes between subarea nodes used to accommodate changes in network conditions such as route failures or variations in traffic loads and to offer different classes of service.

multiple gateways More than one gateway serving to connect the same two SNA networks for cross-network sessions.

multiple-job processing The control of the performance of more than one data processing job at a time.

multiple-line entry field In SAA Advanced Common User Access architecture, a control into which a user types more than one line of information. See also single-line entry field.

multiple message mode In IMS/VS, a processing mode in which synchronization points occur only at DL/I CHKP calls or application termination. See also single message mode, synchronization point.

multiple occurrence data structure In RPG, a data structure that appears more than once in a program.

multiple partition support (MPS) A DL/I facility that allows several application programs running in different partitions to access the same databases concurrently with full database integrity.

multiple port sharing (MPS) (1) An arrangement for short-hold mode operation in which both the first call and a reconnection call (recall) for a population of data terminal equipment (DTEs) are directed to any available port within a port group. (2) In TCP/IP, a server application that associates domain names with Internet addresses. Usually, all name servers are arranged in a tree structure corresponding to the domain naming hierarchy, and at each domain one or more machines will assume this naming task.

multiple-precision Pertaining to use of two or more computer words to represent a number in order to enhance precision. (I) (A)

multiple pricing A function of a point of sale terminal that enables an operator to key in the quantity and price of one or more units of merchandise when the listed price is given only as a group price, such as five for $1.99.

multiple punching Punching more than one hole in the same card column by several keystrokes, usually to extend the character set of the punch. (I) (A)

multiple requester terminal (MRT) procedure In System/36, a procedure that calls a multiple requester terminal program.

multiple requester terminal (MRT) program In System/36, a program that can process requests from more than one display station or SSP-ICF session at the same time using a single copy of the program. Contrast with single requester terminal (SRT) program.

multiple routing A method of sending a message in which more than one destination is specified in the header of the message.

multiple selection A selection technique in which a user can select any number of objects, or not select any.

multiple session remote job entry (MSRJE) A feature of the System Support Program Product that allows one or more remote job entry sessions to be active at the same time.

multiple-string processing In VSAM, access to a data set or file with two or more concurrent sequential or direct requests, or both, from a processing program or its subtasks, using a single control block to define the data set or file and with a single opening of the data set or file.

Multiple Systems Coupling (MSC) An IMS/VS feature that permits geographically dispersed IMS/VS systems to communicate with each other.

multiple terminal access (MTA) A feature of the network control program that permits it to communicate with a variety of dissimilar, commonly used start-stop stations over the same switched network connection.

Multiple Virtual Storage (MVS) See MVS.

Multiple Virtual Storage / Extended Architecture See MVS/XA product.

multiplex To interleave or simultaneously transmit two or more messages on a single channel. (A)

multiplexed device (1) A device that takes several input signals and combines them into a single output signal in such a manner that each of the input signals can be recovered. (2) A device capable of interleaving events of two or more activities or capable of distributing events of an interleaved sequence to the respective activities.

multiplexer (1) A device that takes several input signals and combines them into a single output signal in such a manner that each of the input signals can be recovered. (T) (2) A device capable of interleaving the events of two or more activities or capable of distributing the events of an interleaved sequence to the respective activities. (A) See Figure 99.

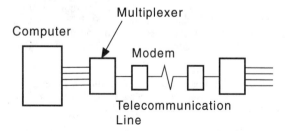

Figure 99. Multiplexer

multiplexer channel A channel designed to operate with a number of I/O devices simultaneously. Several I/O devices can transfer records at the same time by interleaving items of data. See also byte multiplexer, block multiplexer.

multiplexing (1) In data transmission, a function that permits two or more data sources to share a common transmission medium so that each data source has its own channel. (I) (A) (2) See frequency-division multiplexing, time-division multiplexing.

multiplex interface An interface between a data terminal equipment (DTE) and a data-circuit terminating equipment (DCE) that handles several channels by means of time-division multiplexing.

multiplex link A means of enabling a data terminal equipment (DTE) to have several access channels to the data network over a single circuit. (I) (A)

Note: Three methods have been identified: packet interleaving, byte interleaving, and bit interleaving.

multiplex mode A means of transferring records to or from low-speed I/O devices on the multiplexer channel, by interleaving bytes of data. The multiplexer channel sustains simultaneous I/O operations on several subchannels. Bytes of data are interleaved and then routed to or from the selected I/O devices, or to and from the desired locations in main storage. Synonymous with byte mode.

multiplex operation A mode of operation in which the events of two or more activities are interleaved and when required, the events in the interleaved sequence are distributed to the respective activities. (A)

multiplexor See multiplexer.

multiplicand In a multiplication operation, the factor that is multiplied by another number or quantity. (I) (A)

Note: Multiplicand x multiplier = result.

multiplier (1) In multiplication, the number or quantity by which the multiplicand is multiplied. (I) (A) (2) Synonym for multiplier factor. (3) See quarter-squares multiplier.

multiplier factor In a multiplication operation, the factor by which the multiplicand is multiplied. (I) (A) Synonymous with multiplier.

multiplying punch Synonym for calculating punch.

multipoint Pertaining to communication among more than two stations over a single telecommunication line.

multipoint connection A connection established for data transmission among more than two data stations. (I) (A)

Note: The connection may include switching facilities.

multipoint line A telecommunication line or circuit connecting two or more stations. Synonymous with multidrop line. Contrast with point-to-point line.

multipoint network (1) A network in which there are precisely two endpoint nodes, any number of intermediate nodes, and only one path between any two nodes. (T) (2) In data communication, a configuration in which more than two terminal installations are connected. The network may include switching facilities.

multiprocessing (1) A mode of operation for parallel processing by two or more processors of a multiprocessor. (I) (A) (2) Pertaining to the simultaneous execution of two or more computer programs or sequences of instructions by a computer. (A) (3) Loosely, parallel processing. (A) (4) Simultaneous execution of two or more sequences of instructions by a multiprocessor.

multiprocessing system (MPS) A computing system employing two or more connected processing units to execute programs simultaneously.

multiprocessor (1) A computer including two or more processors that have common access to a main storage. (2) A system of two or more processing units, ALUs, or processors that can communicate without manual intervention.

multiprogramming (1) A mode of operation that provides for interleaved execution of two or more computer programs by a single processor. (I) (A) (2) Pertaining to concurrent execution of two or more computer programs by a computer. (A) (3) The processing of two or more programs at the same time.

multiprogramming system A system that can process two or more programs concurrently by interleaving their execution.

multirange amplifier An amplifier that has a switchable, programmable, or automatically set amplification factor in order to adapt different analog signal ranges to a specified output range. (T)

multiregion operation (MRO) Communication between CICS systems in the same processor without the use of SNA network facilities.

multispecification source map In SDF/CICS, a source map associated with more than one specification.

multispeed clock feature In the IBM 8100 Information System, a speed-variable feature that allows up to 16 telecommunication lines to be connected to the 8100 system.

multistation access unit In the IBM Token-Ring Network, a wiring concentrator that can connect up to eight lobes to a ring.

multistreaming Concurrent transmission of parts of several files so that small files are not held up waiting for transmission of large files.

multistroke character entry A text entry method for languages that require multiple keystrokes for certain characters. (T)

multisystem environment The environment in which two or more IMS/VS systems run on any supported combination of OS/VS1 and OS/VS2 systems in one or more System/370 processing units; the environment in which the Multiple Systems Coupling feature runs.

multisystem mode An operating mode of the Model 65 Multiprocessing System in which all of main storage and most auxiliary storage devices are shared by both processing units. See also partitioned mode.

Multisystem Networking Facility (MSNF) An optional feature of TCAM and VTAM Version 1 that permits these access methods, together with NCP, to control a multiple-domain network.

multitail connection Multiple simultaneous connections to the subarea network through one or more boundary nodes using independent LU protocols.

multitailed Pertaining to a communication controller with an NCP attached to more than one host processor. See fanout, tailing, twin-tailed.

multitasking A mode of operation that provides for concurrent performance, or interleaved execution of two or more tasks. (I) (A)

multitask operation Multiprogramming with concurrent execution of a reenterable program used by many tasks.

multithread application program A VTAM application program that processes requests for more than one session concurrently. Contrast with single-thread application program.

multithreading Pertaining to concurrent operation of more than one path of execution within a computer.

multiuser Pertaining to two or more people who use the services of a processor within a given period of time; usage is normally serial unless otherwise specified.

multivolume file (1) A file contained on more than one storage medium. (2) A diskette file that occupies more than one diskette.

MUMPS Massachusetts General Hospital Utility Multiprogramming System. A high-level interactive computer programming language for use in the development and implementation of interactive information systems with shared databases. (A)

Musical Instrument Digital Interface (MIDI) A protocol that allows a synthesizer to send signals to another synthesizer or to a computer, or a computer to a musical instrument, or a computer to another computer.

mute In multimedia applications, to temporarily turn off the audio for the associated medium.

mutual exclusion In programming languages, a principle requiring that, at a given time, only one asynchronous procedure may access the same shared variable or execute members of a group of critical sections. (T)

mutual information Synonym for transinformation content.

mutual suspicion In computer security, the state of two processes that must exchange some data while protecting all other data they have received from each other.

mV millivolt.

MVS (1) Multiple virtual storage. Implies MVS/370, the MVS/XA product, and the MVS/ESA product. (2) Multiple Virtual Storage, consisting of MVS/System Product Version 1 and the MVS/370

Data Facility Product operating on a System/370 processor. See also MVS/XA product.

MVS/ESA product Multiple Virtual Storage / Enterprise Systems Architecture.

MVS-managed device A device that MVS allocates to jobs.

MVS/OCCF Multiple Virtual Storage/Operator Communication Control Facility. A facility that intercepts messages from the MVS supervisor. The NetView program and MVS/OCCF help a network operator control multiple MVS systems from a central site.

MVS/XA product Multiple Virtual Storage/Extended Architecture product, consisting of MVS/System Product Version 2 and the MVS/XA Data Facility Product, operating on a System/370 processor in the System/370 extended architecture mode. MVS/XA allows virtual storage addressing to 2 gigabytes. See also MVS.

MVS/370 MVS/System Product Version 1. See MVS.

Mylar Polyester film, often used as a base for magnetically coated or perforated information media. (Trademark of E. I. du Pont de Nemours & Co., Inc.)

N

N (1) Newton. (2) In sorting, file size; the number of records to be processed by the sort.

NAB Network address block.

n-address instruction An instruction that contains n address parts. N may be any positive integer. (I) (A)

n-adic Boolean operation A Boolean operation on n and only n operands. (I) (A)

n-adic operation An operation on n and only n operands. (I) (A)

NAK The negative acknowledge character. (A)

name (1) An alphanumeric term that identifies a data set, statement, program, or cataloged procedure. The first character of the name must be alphabetic. See also label. (2) See alphabet-name, cd-name, class-name, computer-name, condition-name, control data-name, data name, entry name, external name, file-name, global name, implementor-name, index-name, language-name, library-name, mnemonic-name, paragraph-name, procedure-name, program-name, qualified name, qualified data-name, queue name, record-name, report-name, routine-name, section-name, subscripted data-name, symbolic name, system-name, text-name.

named common In XL FORTRAN, a separate common block consisting of variables and arrays and given a name.

named constant In RPG, a name representing a specific value that does not change during the running of the program.

named system In VM, a system that has an entry in the CP system name table. The entry includes the system name and other pertinent data so that the system can later be saved. See also saved system.

name qualification (1) In programming languages, a mechanism for referencing a component of a language object by means of a reference to the object and an identifier declared for the component; for example,

for referencing record components (B OF A in COBOL), members of a library, or language objects in a module. (I) (2) See also uniform referencing.

name resolution In the AIX operating system, the process of translating a symbolic name into its Internet address.

name server (1) In the AIX operating system, a host that provides name resolution for a network. Name servers translate symbolic names assigned to networks and hosts into the Internet addresses used by machines. See also zone of authority. (2) In TCP/IP, synonym for domain name server.

name stack In AIX graphics, a stack of 16-bit integers, controllable by the user, used to establish the drawing primitive that causes a pick or select event.

name translation In SNA network interconnection, converting logical unit names, logon mode table names, and class-of-service names used in one network into equivalent names to be used in another network. This function can be provided through the NetView program and invoked by a gateway system services control point (SSCP) when necessary. See also alias name.

NaN Not-a-number.

NAND A logic operator having the property that if P is a statement, Q is a statement, R is a statement, ..., then the NAND of P, Q, R, ... is true if at least one statement is false, false if all statements are true. (A) Synonymous with NOT-AND, Sheffer stroke.

NAND element Synonym for NAND gate.

NAND gate A logic element that performs the Boolean operation of nonconjunction. (T) Synonymous with NAND element, NOT-AND element.

NAND operation Synonym for nonconjunction.

nanosecond One thousand millionth of a second.

NAPLPS North American Presentation Level Protocol Syntax. A protocol used for display and communications of text and graphics in a videotex system; a form of vector graphics.

narrative information Information that is presented according to the syntax of a natural language. Contrast with formatted information. (A)

narrowband (1) A relatively restricted frequency band, normally used for a single purpose, or made available to a single user. (T) (2) A range of frequencies that is contained within a broadband.

Note: The term usually pertains to a bandwidth less than 4kHz but its meaning is relative to the application in which it is used.

n-ary (1) Pertaining to a selection, choice, or condition that has n possible different values or states. (I) (A) (2) Pertaining to a fixed-radix numeration system having a radix of n. (I) (A)

n-ary Boolean operation Deprecated term for n-adic Boolean operation.

n-ary operation Deprecated term for n-adic operation.

NAT Information content natural unit. (I) (A)

national language character set The letters, numbers, and special symbols that comprise the language of a particular country or area.

national language support (NLS) The modification or conversion of a United States English product to conform to the requirements of another language or country. This can include the enabling or retrofitting of a product and the translation of nomenclature, MRI, or documentation of a product.

national requirements Translation requirements affecting parts of devices and licensed programs; for example, rules for modification of decals on keys and switches, for translation of message text, and for conversion of symbols such as the US dollar sign to the UK pound sign.

National Requirements feature In DPPX, a program feature available with some DPPX licensed programs to replace US English with another language. This feature is provided on a National Requirements diskette.

National Television Standard Committee (NTSC) (1) A committee that sets the standard for color television broadcasting and video in the United States (currently in use also in Japan). (2) The standard set by the NTSC committee (the NTSC standard).

national terminal number (NTN) In X.25 communications, the 1- to 12-digit number that follows the country code in the network user address.

national use graphic character A graphic character used by one or more nations, such as an alphabetic character with a diacritical mark. In 93-character EBCDIC codes, 13 code points are assigned for national use graphic characters.

native Deprecated term for IBM-supplied, basic, required, or stand-alone.

native attachment Deprecated term for integrated attachment.

native character set In COBOL, the default character set associated with the computer specified in the OBJECT-COMPUTER paragraph.

native collating sequence In COBOL, the default collating sequence associated with the computer specified in the OBJECT-COMPUTER paragraph.

native mode In VTAM, a mode in which VTAM runs directly on the VM operating system rather than on a guest operating system.

native network The subnetwork whose network identifier a node uses for its own network-qualified resource names.

natural language (1) A language whose rules are based on current usage without being specifically prescribed. (I) (A) (2) Contrast with artificial language.

natural number (1) One of the numbers zero, one, two, ... (I) (A) (2) Synonymous with nonnegative number.

NAU (1) Network accessible unit. (2) Network addressable unit.

NAUN Nearest active upstream neighbor.

NAU services In SNA, the functions provided by the transaction services layer and the presentation services layer.

NAU services manager layer In SNA, former name for transaction services layer.

navigate In the IBM NetView Graphic Monitor Facility, to move between levels in the view hierarchy.

navigation In SAA Common User Access architecture, The movement of the cursor around the screen using a pointing device or the keyboard. The user interface defines the mouse and key assignments for navigation.

navigation screen In the AIX operating system, one of two types of screens available when running the InfoExplorer program with an ASCII display. It contains information designed to help the user find desired documentation. One navigation screen is available per InfoExplorer session. See also reading screen.

navigation window In the AIX operating system, one of three types of windows available when running the

InfoExplorer program with a graphics display. It contains information that helps the user find desired documentation. One navigation window is available per InfoExplorer session. See also artwork window, reading window.

N-bit byte A string that consists of n bits. (T)

NBS (1) Numeric backspace character. (2) National Bureau of Standards.

NC (1) Numerical control. (I) (2) Network control.

NCB Node control block.

NCCF (1) Network Communications Control Facility. (2) A command that starts the NetView command facility. NCCF also identifies various panels and functions as part of the command facility.

NCI Noncoded information.

NCK Network Computing Kernel.

NCON Name constant.

n-core-per-bit storage A storage device in which each storage cell uses n magnetic cores per binary character. N may be any positive integer. (I) (A)

NCP (1) Network Control Program. See Advanced Communications Function for the Network Control Function. (2) Network control program.

NCP connectionless SNA transport (NCST) An NCP function that allows a communication controller to transfer data across the SNA subarea routing network using TCP/IP protocols. The NCST function causes LU 0 sessions to be established between NCST logical units in the NCP and between an NCST logical unit in the NCP and SNA network link (SNALINK) logical units in the host processors.

NCP/EP definition facility (NDF) A program that is part of System Support Programs (SSP) and is used to generate a partitioned emulation program (PEP) load module or a load module for a Network Control Program (NCP) or for an Emulation Program (EP).

NCP major node In VTAM, a set of minor nodes representing resources, such as lines and peripheral nodes, controlled by a network control program.

NCP/Token-Ring interconnection (NTRI) An NCP function that allows a communication controller to attach to the IBM Token-Ring Network and that provides both subarea and peripheral node DLC services in the SNA network.

NCP V4 Subset Advanced Communications Function for Network Control Program (NCP) V4 Subset. An IBM licensed program that is a subset of NCP. It operates only on IBM 3720 Communication Controllers with certain capacity limitations such as number of scanners, lines, and channel adapters supported.

NCS Network Computing System.

NCSPL Network configuration services parameter list.

NCST NCP connectionless SNA transport.

NDC Normalized device coordinates.

NDF (1) NCP/EP definition facility. (2) No defect found.

NDM Normal disconnected mode.

NDR Nondestructive read. (I) (A)

NDRO Nondestructive readout. (I) (A)

NE Not equal to. See relational operator.

near-end crosstalk Crosstalk propagated in a disturbed channel in the direction opposite to the direction of propagation of the current in the disturbing channel. Ordinarily, the terminal of the disturbed channel at which the near-end crosstalk is present, is near, or coincides with, the energized terminal of the disturbing channel.

nearest active upstream neighbor (NAUN) In the IBM Token-Ring Network, the station sending data directly to a given station on the ring.

near letter quality Print quality of text that is not as good as that of an office electric typewriter, but good enough for internal letters and bulk external mailings. (T)

necessary proposition In a conceptual schema language, a proposition asserted to hold for all entity worlds and to be a necessary part of all possible proposition worlds. (A)

needle In an information retrieval operation, a probe that may be passed through holes or notches to assist in sorting or selecting cards. (A)

need-to-know In computer security, a determination that a prospective recipient of sensitive information has a legitimate requirement to access, to have knowledge of, or to possess that information. See also clearance, discretionary access control.

negate To perform the operation of negation. (I) (A)

negated combined condition In COBOL, the "NOT" logical operator immediately followed by a parenthesized combined condition. Contrast with combined condition.

negated condition A condition made opposite, either true or false, by the NOT logical operator.

negated simple condition In COBOL, the "NOT" logical operator immediately followed by a simple condition. Contrast with simple condition.

negation The monadic Boolean operation whose result has the Boolean value opposite to that of the operand. (I) (A) Synonymous with NOT operation.

negative In a document copying machine, a copy having tonal arrangements opposite to those on the original. Contrast with positive.

negative-acknowledge character (NAK) (1) A transmission control character transmitted by a station as a negative response to the station with which the connection has been set up. In binary synchronous communication, a transmission control character that indicates a not-ready condition, indicates that an error occurred, or that is sent as a negative response to enquiry. (I) (2) A transmission control character sent by a station as a negative response to the station with which the connection has been set up. (A)

negative-channel metal oxide semiconductor See NMOS.

negative entry On a calculator, the assignment of a negative sign to a number entered in the machine. (T)

negative indication On a calculator, a visual indication that the number shown has a negative value. (T) (A)

negative polling limit For a start-stop or BSC terminal, the maximum number of consecutive negative responses to polling that the communication controller accepts before suspending polling operations.

negative-positive process In a document copying machine, a variation of the silver process in which a positive image is obtained by primary development of a latent image made by printing from a negative. (T)

negative response (NR) (1) In data communication, a reply indicating that data was not received correctly or that a command was incorrect or unacceptable. (2) In SNA, a response indicating that a request did not arrive successfully or was not processed successfully by the receiver. Contrast with positive response.

negentropy Deprecated term for entropy.

negotiable BIND In SNA, a capability that allows two half-sessions to negotiate the parameters of a session when the session is being activated.

negotiable link station The capability of a link station to assume either a primary link-station or secondary link-station role and to negotiate with a partner link station during link activation which role it will assume.

negotiation (1) In X.25 communications, the process by which two data terminal equipments (DTEs) establish the packet size, packet window size, and throughput class to be used during a call procedure. Contrast with validation. (2) The process of deciding what packet size to transmit between a network and a 3710 Network Controller.

neighbor gateway In the AIX operating system, one of the peers acquired by an exterior gateway. All exterior gateways do not communicate with all other exterior gateways. Instead, they acquire neighbors through which they communicate. See also exterior gateway, interior gateway.

neighborhood effect In computer graphics, an apparent variation in the brightness of a picture element (pixel) because of variations in the brightness of neighboring pixels.

neighbor notification In a token-ring network, the process by which each data station identifies the next active station so that all stations that are affected by a hard failure can be informed that a failure has occurred. (T)

NEITHER-NOR operation Synonym for nondisjunction.

neper A unit for measuring power. The number of nepers is the logarithm (base e) of the ratio of the measured power levels. See also decibel.

nest (1) To incorporate one or more structures of one kind into a structure of the same kind; for example, to nest one loop (the nested or inner loop) within another loop (the nesting or outer loop); to nest one subroutine within another subroutine. (T) (2) To place subroutines or data in other subroutines or data at a different hierarchical level so that the subroutines can be executed as recursive subroutines or so that the data can be accessed recursively. (A) (3) See also nested command.

nested address space In DPPX, an address space created in an area of the master address space.

nested command A command or group of commands whose execution is conditional, based on the evaluation of a preceding or associated command. Nesting is a structured form of branching.

nested command list A command list called by another command list.

nested do group A do group contained within another do group.

nested DO statement In XL FORTRAN, a DO loop or DO statement in which the range is entirely contained within the range of another DO loop.

nested procedure A procedure called by another procedure. See also procedure level.

nested sign-on In the IBM 3660 Supermarket Store System, an abbreviated sign-on to another store support procedure or to customer checkout, at a station that is already signed on to store support or customer checkout, without signing the terminal off and then back on.

NetBIOS Network Basic Input/Output System. An operating system interface for application programs used on IBM personal computers that are attached to the IBM Token-Ring Network. See also BIOS, ROM BIOS.

net cash The total of all cash sales, deposits, and payments. Contrast with net noncash.

NETCENTER A software product that assists the network operator and other technical personnel at a network control center in managing the network.

NETDA/2 An IBM licensed program that is a workstation-based tool for designing network topology and routing. NETDA/2 assists the network designer with capacity planning and performance management, network management, configuration management, and business management.

NETID Network identifier.

NETID subnetwork In NETDA/2, a group of nodes that have the same network ID. The NETID subnetwork includes all subarea and APPN subnetworks that have the same network ID.

net noncash The sum of the net balance due on all COD, layaway, and charge transactions. Contrast with net cash.

NETPARS Network performance analysis and reporting system.

net structure In a database, a structure of data aggregates or record types arranged in many-to-many relationships. (T)

NetView Bridge A set of application program interfaces that allow the NetView program to interact with various types of databases in the MVS environment.

NetView Bridge Adapter A feature of the Information/Management licensed program.

NetView command list language An interpretive language that is unique to the NetView program and that is used to write NetView command lists in environments where REXX is not supported.

NetView Graphic Monitor Facility (NGMF) A function of the NetView program that provides the network operator with a graphic topological presentation of a network controlled by the NetView program and that allows the operator to manage the network interactively.

NetView program An IBM licensed program used to monitor a network, manage it, and diagnose network problems.

NetView command list language An interpretive language unique to the NetView program that is used to write command lists.

NetView DM IBM NetView Distribution Manager.

NetView help desk In the NetView program, an online information facility that guides the help desk operator through problem management procedures.

NetView-NetView task (NNT) The task under which a cross-domain NetView operator session runs. See also operator station task.

NetView/PC A PC-based IBM licensed program through which application programs can be used to monitor, manage, and diagnose problems in IBM Token-Ring networks, non-SNA communication devices, and voice networks.

NetView/PC application record In the NetView/PC program, information that defines the communication path between the NetView/PC program and the host.

NetView Performance Monitor (NPM) An IBM licensed program that collects, monitors, analyzes, and displays data relevant to the performance of a VTAM telecommunication network. It runs as an online VTAM application program.

network (1) An arrangement of nodes and connecting branches. (T)   (2) A configuration of data processing devices and software connected for information interchange.   (3) A group of nodes and the links interconnecting them.

network accessible unit (NAU) A logical unit (LU), physical unit (PU), control point (CP), or system services control point (SSCP). It is the origin or the destination of information transmitted by the path control network. Synonymous with network addressable unit.

network adapter A functional unit that allows devices to communicate with other devices on the network.

network address (1) An identifier for a node, station, or unit of equipment in a network. (2) In a subarea network, an address, consisting of subarea and element fields, that identifies a link, link station, physical unit, logical unit, or system services control point. Subarea nodes use network addresses; peripheral nodes use local addresses or local-form session identifiers (LFSIDs). The boundary function in the subarea node to which a peripheral node is attached transforms local addresses or LFSIDs to network addresses and vice versa. Contrast with network name.

network addressable unit (NAU) Synonym for network accessible unit.

network address translation In SNA network interconnection, conversion of the network address assigned to a logical unit in one network into an address in an adjacent network. This function is provided by the gateway NCP that joins the two networks. See also alias network address, real network address.

network administrator A person who manages the use and maintenance of a network.

network analog The expression and solution of mathematical relationships between variables using a circuit or circuits to represent these variables. (A)

network analyzer A device that simulates a network, such as an electrical supply network. (A)

network application The use to which a network is put, such as data collection or inquiry/update.

network application program In the IBM Token-Ring Network, a program used to connect and communicate with adapters on a network, enabling users to perform application-oriented activities and to run other application programs.

network architecture The logical structure and operating principles of a computer network. (T)   See

systems network architecture. See also open systems architecture.

Note: The operating principles of a network include those of services, functions, and protocols.

Network Carrier Interconnect Agent An IBM licensed program that enables the NetView and NETCENTER programs to receive and process configuration and status data from one or more carrier management systems.

Network Carrier Interconnect Manager An IBM licensed program that enables the NETCENTER program to send configuration and status data to one or more carrier management systems.

network chart (1) A directed graph used for describing and scheduling events, activities, and their relationships in project control. (T)   (2) In data communications, a diagram describing the topographical layout of a network. (3) See also network planning.

network class The type of TCP/IP network, such as Class A, Class B, or Class C.

network common carrier Any organization that offers packet-switched data networks to the general public. See also communication common carrier.

Network Communications Control Facility (NCCF) An IBM licensed program consisting of a base for command processors that can monitor, control, and improve the operation of a network.

Network Computing Architecture A set of protocols and architectures that support distributed computing.

Network Computing Kernel (NCK) In the AIX Network Computing System (NCS), the combination of the remote procedure call (RPC) runtime library and the Location Broker, which provide the function necessary required to run distributed applications.

Network Computing System (NCS) In the AIX operating system, a set of software tools, developed by Apollo Computer Inc., that conform to the Network Computing Architecture. These tools include the remote procedure call runtime library, the Location Broker, and the NIDL compiler.

Network Configuration Application/MVS An IBM program offering that allows users to define and store information about network and system resources. This information is then converted to Resource Object Data Manager (RODM) load utility statements. Network Configuration Application/MVS runs in conjunction with Information/Management. See also load file generator.

network configuration tables In ACF/TCAM and VTAM, the tables through which the system services control point (SSCP) interprets the network configuration.

network congestion An undesirable overload condition caused by traffic in excess of what a network can handle.

network control (NC) In SNA, a request/response unit (RU) category used for requests and responses exchanged between physical units (PUs) for such purposes as activating and deactivating explicit and virtual routes and sending load modules to adjust peripheral nodes. See also data flow control, function management data, session control.

network controller A concentrator and protocol converter used with SDLC links. By converting protocols, which manage the way data is sent and received, the IBM 3710 Network Controller allows the use of non-SNA devices with an SNA host processor.

network control mode The mode in which a network control program can direct a communication controller to perform such activities as polling, device addressing, dialing, and answering. See also emulation mode.

network control phase A mode in the data transfer phase during which a user can reestablish a link to obtain network services. See network control mode. See also data transfer phase.

network control program A program, generated by the user from a library of IBM-supplied modules, that controls the operation of a communication controller.

Network Control Program (NCP) (1) An IBM licensed program that provides communication controller support for single-domain, multiple-domain, and interconnected network capability. (2) In System/38, a program transmitted to and stored in a communication controller to control the operation of the controller.

network control program BSC or SS session In ACF/TCAM, a defined sequence of command and data exchanges between the host processor and a start-stop or BSC device attached via a network control program. The primary purpose of the network control program session is to allow the network control program to interleave transmissions to and from many BSC or start-stop stations.

network control program generation The process, performed in a host processor, of validating, assembling, and link-editing network definition statements to produce a network control program.

network control program station In ACF/TCAM, a binary synchronous, start-stop, or SNA station attached to a controller, under control of a network control program.

network database A database that is organized according to ownership of records; each record except the root record may have several owners and there may be several access paths to each record. See also hierarchical database, relational database.

network definition (1) In VTAM, the process of defining the identities and characteristics of each node in the network and the arrangement of the nodes in that system. (2) In ACF/TCAM, MCP definition and network control program definition.

network directory database Synonym for distributed directory database.

network failure In a network, any condition that makes a service unavailable because the network or one of its essential components is not functioning correctly.

network file In AS/400 object distribution, a file, either a physical file or a save file, sent by one user to one or more other users. A network file is placed on the recipient's message queue when it arrives at the destination system.

network gateway accounting (NGA) The NPM subsystem that receives traffic information from the gateway NCP for sessions that flow throughout a network.

network identifier (ID) (1) In TCP/IP, that part of the Internet address that defines a network. The length of the network ID depends on the type of network class (A, B, or C). See also host ID, Internet address. (2) A 1- to 8-byte customer-selected name or an 8-byte IBM-registered name that uniquely identifies a specific subnetwork.

networking (1) In a multiple-domain network, communication between domains. Synonymous with cross-domain communication. See extended networking. (2) Loosely, making use of the services of a network. (3) See also internetworking.

networking coprocessor In a personal computer, a microprocessor on an expansion board that supplements the operations of the processor in the system unit, enabling a personal computer to interact with personal computers and other devices on a network, share the resources of a mainframe, and use communication services in parallel with other operations. Synonymous with communication coprocessor. See also I/O coprocessor, math coprocessor.

network interconnect See SNA network interconnect.

Network Interface Definition Language (NIDL) A declarative language for the definition of interfaces that has two forms, a Pascal-like syntax and a C-like syntax. NIDL is a component of the Network Computing Architecture.

network job In object distribution, a batch input stream sent by one user to one or more users in the network as defined in the system distribution directory.

network job entry In object distribution, an entry in the network job table that specifies the system action required for incoming network jobs sent by a particular user or group of users. Each entry is identified by the user ID of the originating user or group.

network job table In AS/400 object distribution, a table containing entries that control the system action required for incoming network jobs.

network layer In the Open Systems Interconnection reference model, the layer that provides for the entities in the transport layer the means for routing and switching blocks of data through the network between the open systems in which those entities reside. (T)

network log A file containing messages, commands, and command procedures that have been processed by the NetView program. In addition, output resulting from command procedure traces, command echoes, and other activity occurring within the NetView program appears in the network log.

network management The process of planning, organizing, and controlling a communications-oriented system.

network management gateway (NMG) A gateway between the NetView program, which is the SNA network management system, and the network management function of one or more non-SNA networks.

network management vector transport (NMVT) A management services request/response unit (RU) that flows over an active session between physical unit management services and control point management services (SSCP-PU session).

network manager A program or group of programs that is used to monitor, manage, and diagnose the problems of a network.

network model A data model that consists of a modified tree structure that permits all but the root record to have multiple owner records. (A)

network name (1) The symbolic identifier by which end users refer to a network accessible unit, a link, or a link station within a given subnetwork. In APPN networks, network names are also used for routing purposes. Contrast with network address. (2) In a multiple-domain network, the name of the APPL statement defining a VTAM application program. The network name must be unique across domains. Contrast with ACB name. See uninterpreted name.

network node (NN) Synonym for Advanced Peer-to-Peer Networking (APPN) network node.

network-node domain An APPN network-node control point, its attached links, the network resources for which it answers directory search requests (namely, its local LUs and adjacent LEN end nodes), the adjacent APPN end nodes with which it exchanges directory search requests and replies, and other resources (such as a local storage device) associated with its own node or an adjacent end node for which it provides management services.

network node server An APPN network node that provides network services for its local LUs and client end nodes.

network operator (1) A person who controls the operation of all or part of a network. See also domain operator, node operator. (2) In a multiple-domain network, a person or program responsible for controlling all domains. Contrast with domain operator.

network operator/administrator In SNA, the person representing customer installation management who is responsible for controlling the operation of the network via network operator services.

network operator console A system console or terminal in the network from which an operator controls the network.

network operator logon A logon request issued in behalf of a terminal from the network operator console by using a network operator command.

network path See path.

network performance analyzer (NPA) A function of NCP that collects performance data about devices. The data is recorded by NPM.

network planning (1) A technique that uses network charts for planning, scheduling and controlling a project. (T) (2) In data communications, determination of the topographical layout and functional characteristics of a network.

network port See port.

Network Problem Determination Application An IBM licensed program that helps the user identify network problems from a central control point using interactive display techniques.

network product support (NPS) The component of NCCF that provides operations control for the IBM 3710 Network Controller and for NCP. NPS provides operator commands used to run diagnostics for link problem determination and to change product operating parameters.

network provider In X.25 communications, the organization, often a Post, Telephone, and Telegraph authority (PTT) that provides a public network.

network-qualified name A name that uniquely identifies a specific resource within a specific network. It consists of a network identifier and a resource name, each of which is a 1- to 8-byte symbol string.

network resource In ACF/TCAM, a network component such as a local network control program, SDLC data link, or peripheral node. In multiple-domain networking, cross-domain resource managers (CDRMs) and logical units (LUs) in other domains are also network resources.

network resource directory In System/36, an area on disk that lists the files on remote systems that can be accessed using Distributed Data Management (DDM).

Network Routing Facility (NRF) An IBM licensed program that resides in the NCP, which provides a path for messages between terminals, and routes messages over this path without going through the host processor.

network services (1) The services within network accessible units that control network operation through SSCP-SSCP, SSCP-PU, SSCP-LU, and CP-CP sessions. (2) The session services (directory and route-selection functions) and management services provided by an APPN network-node control point to its domain.

network services (NS) header In SNA, a 3-byte field in an FMD request/response unit (RU) flowing in an SSCP-LU, SSCP-PU, or SSCP-SSCP session. The network services header is used primarily to identify the network services category of the RU; for example, configuration services, session services, and the particular request code within a category.

network services procedure error (NSPE) A request unit that is sent by a system services control point (SSCP) to a logical unit (LU) when a procedure requested by that LU has failed.

network session accounting (NSA) The NPM subsystem that receives session accounting information

from the NCP for sessions that flow throughout a network.

network slowdown Synonym for system slowdown.

network structure A data structure that represents entities in nodes and that, in contrast to a tree structure, permits all but the root nodes to have multiple parent nodes. (T)

Network Terminal Option (NTO) An IBM licensed program, used in conjunction with NCP, that allows certain non-SNA devices to participate in sessions with SNA application programs in the host processor. When data is sent from a non-SNA device to the host processor, NTO converts non-SNA protocol to SNA protocol; and when data is sent from the host processor to the non-SNA device, NTO converts SNA protocol to non-SNA protocol.

network terminating unit (NTU) In X.25 communications, the point of access to a network.

network topology The schematic arrangement of the links and nodes of a network. (T)

network topology database The representation of the current connectivity between the network nodes within an APPN network. It includes (a) entries for all network nodes and the transmission groups interconnecting them and (b) entries for all virtual routing nodes to which network nodes are attached.

network user address (NUA) In X.25 communications, the X.121 address containing up to 15 binary code digits.

network user identification (NUI) In X.25, the facility that enables the transmitting data terminal equipment (DTE) to provide billing, security, or management information on a per-call basis to the data circuit-terminating equipment (DCE). The NUI can identify a network user independently of the port being used.

network weaving In computer security, a penetration technique in which different communication networks are used to gain access to a system without detection.

neutral transmission A method of transmitting teletypewriter signals, in which a mark is represented by current on the line, and space is represented by the absence of current. By extension to tone signaling, neutral transmission is a method of signaling employing two signaling states, one representing both a space condition and the absence of any signaling. Synonymous with unipolar. See also polar transmission.

New In SAA Common User Access architecture, a choice in the File pull-down that a user selects to create an object; for example, a file.

new line In SAA Basic Common User Access architecture, a cursor-movement function that moves the cursor to the first entry field on the next line that contains an entry field.

new-line character (NL) (1) A format effector that causes the print or display position to move to the first position on the next line. (I) (A) (2) Contrast with carriage return character. (3) In word processing, synonym for carrier return character.

new page break Synonym for page break. (T)

news information In SDF/CICS, information on new functions in SDF/CICS release 3.0 and, where provided, on installation topics. News can be selected in the initial function selection and with the NEWS tutorial command.

newton (N) The force that when applied to a body having a mass of one kilogram (1 kg) gives it an acceleration of one meter per second per second ($1 m/s^2$)

next In the AIX operating system, the dialog management action for dependent workstations that causes the next portion of a data object to be presented.

next executable sentence In COBOL, the next sentence to which control will be transferred after execution of the current statement is complete.

next operable sentence In COBOL, the next sentence to which control will be transferred after the running of the current statement is complete.

next record In COBOL, the record that logically follows the current record of a file.

next system In SNA distribution services (SNADS), a node that is physically connected to the local system, and through which distribution items can be routed.

next system queue In SNA distribution services (SNADS), a queue that is used to hold distribution items that are being routed to a next system. See also normal queue, priority queue.

next system table In SNA distribution services (SNADS), a table identifying all the systems physically connected to the local system.

NFF No fault found.

NFY Notify.

NGA Network gateway accounting.

NGMF NetView Graphic Monitor Facility.

NIB Node initialization block.

nibble Deprecated term for a part of a byte, usually a halfbyte.

NIB list A series of contiguous node initialization blocks.

nickname Synonym for alias.

NIDL Network Interface Definition Language.

NIDL compiler In the AIX operating system, a Network Computing System (NCS) tool that converts an interface definition, written in Network Interface Definition Language (NIDL), into several program modules, including source code for client and server stubs. The NIDL compiler accepts interface definitions written in either syntax of NIDL and generates C language source code and C or Pascal header files.

nines complement The diminished radix complement in the decimal numeration system. (I) (A) Synonymous with complement-on-nine.

nine-track compatibility A feature that allows the reading and writing of nine-track magnetic tape at 800 bytes per inch as well as 1600 bytes per inch.

NIP Nucleus initialization program.

NL The new-line character. (A)

NLDM (1) Network logical data manager. (2) A command that starts the NetView session monitor. NLDM also identifies various panels and functions as part of the session monitor.

n-level address An indirect address that specifies n levels of addressing. (A)

NLS National language support.

NLSCHAR In AIX extended curses, a data type that represents a character from code page P0, P1, or P2. A single NLSCHAR variable can contain either a 1-byte or a 2-byte character.

NMG Network management gateway.

NMOS Negative-channel metal oxide semiconductor. A technology used in the manufacture of field-effect transistors that utilizes the properties of an n-type semiconductor material, usually doped silicon, and that when energized, produces a flow of negative charge carriers.

NMVT Network management vector transport.

NN Network node.

NNCP Network node control point.

NNT NetView-NetView task.

No In SAA Advanced Common User Access architecture, a push button that is used in messages to provide a negative response to a question.

no-buffer queue In ACF/TCAM, the chain of CPBs for read operations when no buffers are in the buffer pool.

no-consoles condition In systems with multiple console support, a condition in which the system is unable to access any full-capability console device.

no-CPB queue In ACF/TCAM, the chain of elements to be processed by the CPB initialization routine.

node (1) In a network, a point at which one or more functional units connect channels or data circuits. (I)   (2) In network topology, the point at an end of a branch. (T)   (3) The representation of a state or an event by means of a point on a diagram. (A)   (4) In a tree structure, a point at which subordinate items of data originate. (A)   (5) An endpoint of a link or a junction common to two or more links in a network. Nodes can be processors, communication controllers, cluster controllers, or terminals. Nodes can vary in routing and other functional capabilities.   (6) In VTAM, a point in a network defined by a symbolic name. See major node, minor node. (7) In the IBM 8100 Information System, a junction point in a network represented by one or more physical units. (8) In NETDA/2, a combination of hardware, software, and microcode that can generate message traffic, receive and process message traffic, or receive and relay message traffic. (9) See Figure 100.

node identification A unique string of characters that identifies a node.

node identifier In ACF/TCAM, the portion of the network address of a resource that indicates which TCAM node provides message queuing for that resource. See resource identifier.

node initialization block (NIB) In VTAM, a control block associated with a particular node or session that contains information used by the application program to identify the node or session and to indicate how communication requests on a session are to be handled by VTAM.

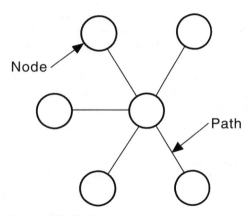

Figure 100. Node

node name In VTAM, the symbolic name assigned to a specific major or minor node during network definition.

node operator In SNA, a person or program responsible for controlling the operation of a node via the physical unit control point (PUCP). See also domain operator, network operator.

node table For ACF/TCAM extended networking, a main storage table that associates each node identifier with internodal destination queues.

node type A designation of a node according to the protocols it supports or the role it plays in a network. Node type was originally denoted numerically (as 1, 2.0, 2.1, 4, and 5) but is now characterized more specifically by protocol type (APPN network node, LEN node, subarea node, and interchange node, for example) because type 2.1 nodes and type 5 nodes support multiple protocol types and roles.

node verification An additional level of security beyond that provided by the network addressing scheme. Node verification helps to ensure that a connection reaches the correct remote station. It is available on LU-LU 6.2 connections only. See also BIND password.

no-input zone Synonym for dead zone.

noise (1) A disturbance that affects a signal and that can distort the information carried by the signal. (T)
(2) Random variations of one or more characteristics of any entity such as voltage, current, or data. (A)
(3) A random signal of known statistical properties of amplitude, distribution, and spectral density. (A)
(4) Loosely, any disturbance tending to interfere with normal operation of a device or system. (A)   (5) In acoustics, any undesired sound. See ambient noise, background noise, burst noise, impulsive noise.
(6) See reference noise.

noise burst signal In a token-bus network, a signal indicating that there is activity on the transmission medium that did not result in a valid transmission frame. (T)

noise emission In acoustics, noise emitted by a sound source. Contrast with noise immission. See noise power emission level.

Note: Noise emission is expressed in terms of the sound power of the source.

noise immission In acoustics, noise received at the ear of an observer. It may be emitted by one or more nearby or distant sources. Contrast with noise emission.

Note: Noise immission is expressed in terms of the sound pressure at the observer's ear.

noise killer An electrical network inserted in a telegraph circuit, usually at the sending end, for the purpose of reducing interference with other telecommunication circuits.

noise level Synonym for sound pressure level.

noise power emission level (NPEL) In acoustics, the A-weighted sound power level in bels. The reference sound power is one picowatt.

nomenclature A set of terms and or symbols such as those that appear on keys, switches, and labels.

nominal page A part of text contained in a usually rectangular area with dimensions equal to the page length.

Note: Paper size tolerances, skew, etc., are not considered in the concept of nominal page. (T)

nominal paper size Synonym for page length. (T)

nominal (rated) speed Maximum speed or data rate of a device or facility. Nominal speed makes no allowance for necessary delaying functions, such as checking or tabbing.

nominal transfer rate The designated or theoretical number of binary characters that can be transferred per unit of time. (T)

non-add On a calculator with a printing mechanism, the printing of characters without affecting calculations. (T)

nonautomatic profile In MVS, a TAPEVOL profile that RACF creates in response to an RDEFINE command or when tape data set protection is not active. A TAPEVOL profile created in this manner is called a nonautomatic profile because RACF never deletes the profile except in response to the RDELETE command. See also automatic profile.

nonbreak space Synonym for hard space. (T)

noncash Money owed as a result of certain sales transactions, but not yet paid in cash or cash-like documents; for example, money owed in charge, COD, or layaway transactions.

noncash document Synonym for cash-like document.

noncoded graphics Synonym for fixed-image graphics.

nonconjunction (1) The dyadic Boolean operation whose result has the Boolean value 0 if and only if each operand has the Boolean value 1. (I) (A) Synonymous with NAND operation, NOT BOTH operation. (2) Contrast with conjunction.

noncontiguous item In COBOL, elementary items, in the Working Storage and Linkage Sections, that bear no hierarchical relationship to other data items.

non-data-set clocking Synonym for business machine clocking.

nondestructive cursor On a display device, a cursor that can be moved within a display surface without changing or destroying the data displayed on the screen. Contrast with destructive cursor.

nondestructive read Reading that does not erase the data in the source location. (T) Synonymous with nondestructive readout.

nondestructive readout (NDRO) Synonym for nondestructive read.

nondisjunction (1) The dyadic Boolean operation whose result has the Boolean value 1 if and only if each operand has the Boolean value 0. (I) (A) Synonymous with NEITHER-NOR operation, NOR operation. (2) Contrast with disjunction.

nondisplay A field attribute that prevents display of data.

non-display-based word processing equipment Word processing equipment that does not have an electronic display capability. Contrast with display-based word processing equipment.

nondisruptive installation The capability that allows the physical installation of additional units while normal operations continue without interruption. Contrast with nondisruptive removal. See also concurrent maintenance.

nondisruptive removal The capability that allows the physical removal of units while normal operations continue without interruption. Contrast with nondisruptive installation. See also concurrent maintenance.

nondrop time code Synonym for full-frame time code.

nonembedded command In text processing, a program instruction that causes an immediate change to the document being processed at the time the command is entered. (T) (A)

nonequivalence element A logic element whose action represents the Boolean connective exclusive OR.

nonequivalence operation (1) The dyadic Boolean operation whose result has the Boolean value 1 if and only if the operands have different Boolean values. (I) (A) Synonymous with exclusive-OR operation. (2) Contrast with equivalence operation.

nonerasable storage Deprecated term for read-only storage.

nonescaping key (1) A key that allows a character to be typed without changing the imprint position. (T) (2) A key that does not produce a character unless it is pressed in combination with another key.

nonexecutable program unit In XL FORTRAN, a block data subprogram.

nonexecutable statement (1) A statement used to supply information to a compiler but does not explicitly result in executable code; for example, a declaration. (T) (2) In the AIX operating system, a statement that describes the characteristics of a program unit, data, editing information, or statement functions, but does not cause any action to be taken. (3) Contrast with executable statement.

nongeneric alert (1) In the NetView program, encoded alert information that uses product-unique screens stored at the alert receiver, the NetView program. (2) In the NetView/PC program, an alert containing X'9F' in the alert network management vector transport.

nonidentity operation (1) The Boolean operation whose result has the Boolean value 1 if and only if all the operands do not have the same Boolean value. A nonidentity operation on two operands is a nonequivalence operation. (I) (A) (2) Contrast with identity operation.

nonimbedded command In word processing, a command that performs an immediate operation on a

document at the time it is entered. Contrast with embedded command.

nonimpact printer A printer in which printing is not the result of mechanically striking the printing medium. (T)

noninteractive A program or device that provides no interaction with the operator at execution time.

noninteractive program A running program that cannot receive input from the keyboard or other input device. Contrast with interactive program.

nonisolated amplifier An amplifier that has an electrical connection between the signal circuit and another circuit including ground. (T)

nonlabeled tape A tape that has no labels. Tape marks are used to indicate the end of the volume and the end of each data file.

nonlinear optimization Synonym for nonlinear programming.

nonlinear programming (1) In operations research, a procedure for locating the maximum or minimum of a function of variables that are subject to constraints when either the function, constraints, or both are nonlinear. (I) (A) Synonymous with nonlinear optimization. (2) Contrast with convex programming, dynamic programming, integer programming, linear programming, mathematical programming, quadratic programming.

nonloadable character set In the 3270 Information Display System, one or more character sets installed in the device that must be used as they are. These character sets cannot be extended or altered by the user. Contrast with loadable character set.

nonloaded lines Cable pairs or telecommunication lines with no added inductive loading. See also loading.

nonlocking A characteristic of code extension characters that applies any change in interpretation only to a specified number of the coded representations that follow, commonly only one. Contrast with locking.

nonmagnetic recording medium On dictation equipment, a recording medium, usually in the form of a disk or belt, on which mechanical recordings can be made. (I)

nonmerchandise Items other than actual merchandise; for example, alteration services or rentals.

non-message-driven program In IMS/VS with Fast Path, a type of program with access to online main storage databases and data entry databases. It is scheduled and executed in the same way as a batch-message program.

nonnative network (1) A subnetwork whose network identifier differs from the network identifier that a node uses for its own network-qualified resource names. (2) Any network attached to a gateway NCP that does not contain that NCP's resources.

nonnative network connection A connection in which an APPN or LEN node and the subarea to which it connects use different network identifiers.

non-NCP station In ACF/TCAM, a station attached to the host processor by a channel, an IBM 2701 Data Adapter Unit, an IBM 2702 or 2703 Transmission Control, or an IBM 3705 Communications Controller in EP mode.

nonnegative integer Synonym for natural number. (T) (A)

nonnegative number Synonym for natural number.

non-network control program station In ACF/TCAM, a station attached to the host processor by channel attachment, a 2701 Data Adapter Unit, a 2702 or 2703 Transmission Control, or a 3705 Communications Controller in EP mode.

nonnumeric item In COBOL, a data item whose description permits its contents to be composed of any combination of characters taken from the character set of the computer. Contrast with numeric item.

nonnumeric literal In COBOL, a literal bounded by quotation marks. The string of characters may include any character in the character set of the computer. Contrast with numeric literal.

nonoperational mode See asynchronous disconnected mode, initialization mode, normal disconnected mode.

nonpageable dynamic area In OS/VS, an area of virtual storage whose virtual addresses are identical to real addresses. It is used for programs or parts of programs that are not to be paged during execution. Synonymous with V=R dynamic area.

nonpageable partition In OS/VS1, a subdivision of the nonpageable dynamic area allocated to a job step or system task that is not to be paged during execution. In a nonpageable partition, each virtual address is identical to its real address. Synonymous with V=R partition.

nonpageable region In OS/VS2, a subdivision of the nonpageable dynamic area allocated to a job step or system task that is not to be paged during execution.

In a nonpageable region, each virtual address is identical to its real address. Synonymous with V=R region.

nonpaired data In the AS/400 Business Graphics Utility, GDDM, and System/38, data that is specified such that each X-value has a set of Y-values associated with it. Contrast with paired data.

nonpersistent session A session that is terminated if it remains inactive for a user-specified time.

non-physical-contact connector In an ESCON environment, an optical fiber connector type having an air gap between itself and its receptacle, thereby providing a junction point with a typically higher loss compared to a physical-contact connector.

nonpolarized return-to-zero recording Return-to-reference recording in which zeros are represented by the absence of magnetization, ones are represented by a specified condition of magnetization, and the reference condition is zero magnetization. The specified condition is usually saturation. Conversely, the absence of magnetization can be used to represent ones, and the magnetized condition to represent zeros. (A) Synonymous with dipole modulation.

nonprint On a calculator with a printing mechanism, disengagement of that mechanism. (T)

nonprinting calculating machine A calculating machine that can display one or more of the significant elements of a computation; the machine may be capable of direct processing of the elements as they are entered, or it may store the elements for later processing by the arithmetic unit. (A)

nonprinting character Synonym for control character.

nonprocedural language Synonym for non-procedure-oriented language.

non-procedure-oriented language A programming language that allows the user to express the solution to a problem in a form other than as an explicit algorithm. (T) Synonymous with nonprocedural language.

nonprocess runout (NPRO) An operation that moves paper through the paper line without printing.

nonproductive poll An indication from a tributary station that it has no data to send.

nonproductive task A task assigned the lowest network control program dispatching priority. This type of task is generally slower to free buffers and quicker to allocate them. It therefore is never executed during system slowdown. Contrast with productive task. See also appendage task, immediate task.

nonprogrammable Pertaining to a device whose functions cannot be changed by modifying instructions contained within it. (A)

nonprogrammable calculator A calculator whose program cannot be changed by the operator. (T) (A)

nonprogrammable terminal (NPT) (1) A user terminal having no processing capability. (T) (2) In SAA Basic Common User Access architecture, a terminal attached to a host processor in which all or most of the user-interface functions are controlled by the host processor. In SAA usage, this term is used only in the mainframe interactive (MFI) environment. The term used in other environments is nonprogrammable workstation (NWS). (3) Synonymous with fixed-function terminal.

nonprogrammable workstation (NWS) In SAA usage, a workstation that does not have processing capability and that does not allow the user to change its functions. Contrast with programmable workstation (PWS).

nonrecoverable error See irrecoverable error.

nonrecoverable transaction See unrecoverable transaction.

nonreflective ink An ink, usually black, with extremely low reflective characteristics to optical character or mark reading devices. This nonreflective ink contrasts greatly with the paper, and enables the scanner to form a recognition pattern to identify the character.

nonremovable disk Synonym for hard disk.

nonrequesting terminal program A program not associated with a requesting display station.

nonresident portion (of a control program) Control program routines that are loaded into main storage as they are needed and can be overlaid after their completion.

non-return-to-reference recording Synonym for non-return-to-zero recording (NRZ). (T)

non-return-to-zero change-on-ones recording (NRZ-1) (1) Non-return-to-reference recording in which the ones are represented by a change in the condition of magnetization, and zeros are represented by the absence of change. This method is called (mark) recording because only the one or mark signals are explicitly recorded. (I) (A) Synonymous with

non-return-to-zero (mark) recording. (2) Deprecated term for transition coding. See Figure 101.

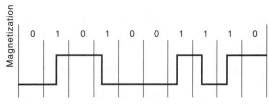

Figure 101. Non-Return-To-Zero Change-On-Ones Recording

non-return-to-zero change-on-zeros recording (NRZ-0) (1) Non-return-to-reference recording of binary digits in which the zeros are represented by a change in the condition of magnetization, and the ones are represented by the absence of a change. (2) Deprecated term for transition coding.

non-return-to-zero (change) recording NRZ[C]. Non-return-to-reference recording in which the zeros are represented by magnetization to a specified condition and ones by another condition; the magnetization changes only when the value to be represented changes. The two conditions may be saturation and zero magnetization, but are more commonly saturation in opposite senses. (T) See Figure 102.

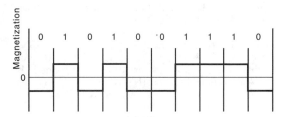

Figure 102. Non-Return-To-Zero (Change) Recording

non-return-to-zero (inverted) recording NRZI. Deprecated term for non-return-to-zero change-on-ones recording (NRZ-1).

non-return-to-zero (mark) recording NRZ(M). Synonym for non-return-to-zero change-on-ones recording.

non-return-to-zero recording (1) NRZ. Non-return-to-reference recording in which the reference condition is zero magnetization. (A) (2) Synonym for non-return-to-reference recording.

nonreusable An attribute indicating that the same copy of a routine cannot be used by another task.

nonreusable disk queuing In ACF/TCAM, the queuing scheme in which each record of a disk record message queues data set may be used only once. Contrast with reusable disk queuing.

nonsales mode An operating state in which a point of sale terminal is used for administrative support functions such as data maintenance or inquiry, or totals readout and reset. Contrast with sales mode.

nonscan field In an IBM 3886 Optical Character Reader, area of a line scanned without data transmission. A nonscan field must begin and end with address delimiters, not character delimiters.

nonsequenced display A display that is not part of a sequence. Contrast with primary display sequence, secondary display, sequenced display.

nonsimultaneous transmission Usually, transmission in which a device or facility can move data in only one direction at a time. Synonym for half-duplex. Contrast with duplex, simultaneous transmission.

Non-SNA Interconnection (NSI) An IBM licensed program that provides format identification (FID) support for selected non-SNA facilities. Thus, it allows SNA and non-SNA facilities to share SDLC links. It also allows the remote concentration of selected non-SNA devices along with SNA devices.

non-SNA station In ACF/TCAM, a channel-attached 2260 or 3270 Display Station or a station on a binary synchronous or start-stop line.

non-SNA terminal A terminal that supports non-SNA protocols; for example, channel-attached 3270 Information Display System or devices supported by Network Terminal Option (NTO) that use binary synchronous protocols. Contrast with SNA terminal.

nonspecific volume request In job control language (JCL), a request that allows the system to select suitable volumes.

nonstageable font In the 3800 Printing Subsystem, a font loaded from the host processor into raster pattern storage for immediate use. It remains there until deleted. Contrast with stageable font.

nonstaging drive In MSS, a drive attached to an IBM 3830 Storage Control Model 3 or an Integrated Storage Control with a Staging Adapter. The pack is formatted as a nonstaging pack. No staging is performed on this drive. Synonymous with real drive.

nonstandard labeled tape A tape that has labels that do not follow IBM labeling conventions.

nonstandard labels Labels that do not conform to American National Standard or IBM standard label conventions.

nonstore through cache A store operation in which data are immediately put into locations in cache storage. At some later time, the data are moved from the cache to main storage.

nonswappable storage The storage containing programs or data that must remain in storage.

nonswitched connection A connection that does not have to be established by dialing. Contrast with switched connection.

nonswitched data link A connection between a link-attached device and a communication controller that does not have to be established by dialing. Contrast with switched link. See also multipoint link, point-to-point link.

nonswitched line (1) A connection between systems or devices that does not have to be made by dialing. Contrast with switched line. (2) A telecommunication line on which connections do not have to be established by dialing. Synonymous with leased line.

nonswitched point-to-point line A telecommunication line that is permanently connected to a station.

nontemporary data set A data set that exists after termination of the job that created it. Contrast with temporary data set.

non-terminal-related main storage database In IMS/VS with Fast Path, a type of main storage database characterized by data used or updated frequently and by segments not owned by specific logical terminals. Direct update of segment fields is allowed, but not insertion or deletion of segments.

nontransparent mode A mode of binary synchronous transmission in which all transmission control characters are treated as transmission control characters, rather than as text. Contrast with transparent mode.

nonunique alternate key In VSAM, an alternate key that occurs in more than one data record in the base cluster. The alternate index record containing this key therefore has several pointers to the base cluster, one for each occurrence of the alternate key in the base cluster. Contrast with unique alternate key.

nonvolatile random access memory Random access memory that retains its contents after electrical power is shut off.

nonvolatile storage (1) A storage device whose contents are not lost when power is cut off. (T) (2) Contrast with volatile storage.

NO-OP No-operation instruction. (I) (A)

no operation (no op) instruction An instruction whose execution causes the computer to proceed to the next instruction to be executed, without performing an operation. (T)   Synonymous with do-nothing operation.

no-print key On a typewriter, a control that prevents a character from being typed. (T)

NOR A logic operator having the property that if P is a statement, Q is a statement, R is a statement,..., then the NOR of P, Q, R,... is true if all statements are false, false if at least one statement is true. P NOR Q is often represented by a combination of OR and NOT symbols, such as ~ ($P\forall Q$). P NOR Q is also called neither P nor Q. (A) Synonymous with NOT-OR.

NOR element Synonym for NOR gate.

no response In SNA, a protocol requested in the form-of-response-requested field of the request header that directs the receiver of the request not to return any response, regardless of whether or not the request is received and processed successfully. Contrast with definite response and exception response.

NOR gate A logic element that performs the Boolean operation of nondisjunction. (T)   Synonymous with NOR element, NOT-OR element.

normal direction flow A flow direction from left to right or top to bottom on a flowchart. (I)   (A)

normal disconnected mode (NDM) A nonoperational mode of an unbalanced data link in which the secondary station is logically disconnected from the data link and therefore cannot transmit or receive information.   See also asynchronous disconnected mode, initialization mode.

normal flow In SNA, a data flow designated in the transmission header (TH) that is used primarily to carry end-user data. The rate at which requests flow on the normal flow can be regulated by session-level pacing. Contrast with expedited flow.

Note: The normal and expedited flows move in both the primary-to-secondary and secondary-to-primary directions. Requests and responses on a given flow, whether normal or expedited, usually are processed sequentially within the path, but the expedited-flow traffic may be moved ahead of the normal-flow traffic within the path at queuing points in the half-sessions and for half-session support in boundary functions.

normal install In System/38, a process in which the Control Program Facility contained on diskettes is installed in auxiliary storage, replacing any CPF that is currently in the system.   Contrast with abbreviated install.

normal installation In the AS/400 system, a process in which the OS/400 operating system contained on tape is installed in auxiliary storage, replacing the operating system, if any, that is currently in the system. Contrast with abbreviated installation.

normalization (1) In databases, the process of restructuring a data model by reducing its relations to their simplest forms. (T)   (2) The process of restructuring a relation for the purpose of reducing it to its simplest form, so that each of its attributes is based on a simple domain that consists of single, noncomposite values. (A) (3) In video production, the process of stretching or compressing a signal vertically to fit into a range from 0 to 1.

normalize (1) In a floating-point representation system, to make an adjustment to the fixed-point part and the corresponding adjustment to the exponent in a floating-point representation to ensure that the fixed-point part lies within some prescribed range, the real number represented remaining unchanged.   For example, in order to bring the fixed-point part into the range 1 to 9.99..., the floating-point part representation 123.45×10^2 may be normalized to 1.2345×10^4. (I) (A) Synonymous with standardize. (2) Loosely, to scale. (A)   (3) Deprecated term for scale.

normalized device coordinates (NDC) (1) In computer graphics, coordinates in the range 0 to 1 commonly used to represent the display space of the device. (T)   (2) A coordinate specified in a device-independent intermediate coordinate system normalized to some range, typically 0 to 1. A display image expressed in normalized device coordinates lies in the same relative position when displayed on any device. (A)   (3) In AIX graphics, coordinates in the range from -1 to 1. All primitives that draw within the unit cube are visible on the screen unless masked by the screenmask. See also transformation, unit cube.

normalized form (1) The form taken by a floating-point representation when the mantissa lies within some prescribed standard range, so chosen that any given real number is represented by a unique pair of numerals. The number zero must have a prescribed characteristic, often "0." Synonymous with standard form. (T)   (2) One of the many floating-point representations of a real number that assumes a fixed position of the radix point in the mantissa, usually immediately before the first nonzero position.

normal mode rejection The capability of an amplifier to suppress the effect of the normal mode voltage. (T)

normal mode voltage The unwanted part of the voltage between the two input connection points of an amplifier that is added to the voltage of the original signal. (T)

normal priority In IMS/VS, the priority assigned to a transaction when the number of transactions enqueued and waiting to be processed is less than the limit count value. See also limit count, limit priority.

normal priority process In the OS/2 operating system, a process that can be completed in the time allotted.

normal queue In SNA distribution services (SNADS), a list of distribution items for a next system queue with a low priority for sending. There is one normal queue for each next system. When send times and queue depths are satisfied for both the priority and normal queues at the same time, the priority queue is sent first. Contrast with priority queue.

normal response Deprecated term for positive response.

normal response mode (NRM) An operational mode of an unbalanced data link in which the secondary station initiates transmission only as the result of receiving explicit permission from the primary station. See also asynchronous balanced mode, asynchronous response mode.

normal restart The restart of IMS/VS after a termination caused by a /checkpoint command.

NOR operation Synonym for nondisjunction.

no sale A function at a point of sale terminal that enables an operator to open the cash drawer electrically for a purpose other than a sales transaction.

NOT A logic operator having the property that if P is a statement, then the NOT of P is true if P is false, false if P is true. The NOT of P is often represented by $\overline{P}, \sim P, \neg P, P'$. (A)

NOT-AND Synonym for NAND.

NOT-AND element Synonym for NAND element.

NOT-AND operation Deprecated term for nonconjunction.

not-a-number (NaN) In binary floating-point computations, a value, not interpreted as a mathematical value, that contains a mask state and a sequence of binary digits.

notarization In cryptography security, a method of applying additional security to a key by utilizing the

identities of both the originator, and also the ultimate recipient.

notation (1) A set of symbols and the rules for their use for the representation of data. (I) (A) (2) A system of characters, symbols, or abbreviated expressions used to express technical facts or qualities. (3) See binary notation, decimal notation, infix notation, mixed-base notation, mixed-radix notation, parenthesis-free notation, positional notation, postfix notation, prefix notation.

NOT-BOTH operation Synonym for nonconjunction.

note Synonym for comment.

NOT element Synonym for NOT gate.

NOT gate A logic element that performs the Boolean operation of negation. (T) Synonymous with NOT element. See Figure 103.

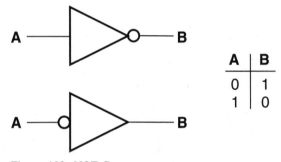

Figure 103. NOT Gate

notification message See notify message, reminder.

NOT-IF-THEN Synonym for exclusion.

NOT-IF-THEN element Synonym for NOT-IF-THEN gate.

NOT-IF-THEN gate A logic element that performs the Boolean operation of exclusion. (T) Synonymous with NOT-IF-THEN element.

NOT-IF-THEN operation Synonym for exclusion.

NOTIFY A network services request that is sent by a system services control point (SSCP) to a logical unit (LU) to inform the LU of the status of a procedure requested by the LU.

notify delivery In the AS/400 system and System/38, the method of delivering messages to a message queue in which the workstation user is notified that a message is on the queue. The notification is by means of an attention light or an audible alarm.

notify lock In DPCX, a system indication set for an indexed record by DPCX to indicate that the record is being read by a program without a lock and that the record cannot be deleted, lengthened, or shortened until the programs or system service using the record are finished with it.

notify message A message that describes a condition for which a program requires a reply from its caller, or a default reply is sent to the program.

notify object In System/38 and the AS/400 system, a message queue, a data area, or a database file that can be used to contain information identifying the last successful commitment operation. This information can be used by the programmer to establish a restarting point for an application following an abnormal system or routing step termination. See also commit identifier.

NOT operation Synonym for negation.

NOT-OR Synonym for NOR.

NOT-OR element Synonym for NOR element.

NOT-OR operation Deprecated term for nondisjunction.

noughts complement Synonym for radix complement.

NPA Network performance analyzer.

NPALU In NPM, the virtual logical unit generated in an NCP with which the network subsystem communicates.

NPDA (1) Network Problem Determination Application. (2) A command that starts the NetView hardware monitor. NPDA also identifies various panels and functions as part of the hardware monitor.

NPEL Noise power emission level.

n-plus-one address instruction An instruction that contains $n + 1$ addresses, "the plus-one" address being that of the instruction to be executed next. (T)

NPM NetView Performance Monitor.

NPR No print.

NPRO Nonprocess runout.

NPS Network product support.

NPSI X.25 NCP Packet Switching Interface.

NPT Nonprogrammable terminal.

NRF Network Routing Facility.

NRM (1) Normal response mode. (2) Network resource management.

NRZ Non-return-to-reference recording. (I) (A)

NRZ(C) Non-return-to-zero (change) recording. (A)

NRZI Non-return-to-zero (inverted) recording. Deprecated term for non-return-to-zero change-on-ones recording (NRZ-1).

NRZ(M) Non-return-to-zero (mark) change-on-ones recording. (A)

NRZ-0 Non-return-to-zero change-on-zeros recording.

NRZ-1 Non-return-to-zero change-on-ones recording. (I) (A)

NS Network services.

NSA (1) Network session accounting. (2) Nonsequenced acknowledgment.

N-select In VM/SP HPO, a page-slot selection algorithm that allocates a selected number of consecutive requests to the same allocation area of the same direct access storage device.

NSI Non-SNA Interconnection.

NSP Numeric space character.

NSPE Network Services Procedure Error.

NTF No trouble found.

NTN National terminal number.

NTO Network Terminal Option.

NTO device A non-SNA device that is supported through the Network Terminal Option in an SNA network as a PU type 1, LU type 1 device, such as an SDLC 3767 Communication Terminal.

NTRI NCP/Token-Ring interconnection.

NTSC National Television Standard Committee.

NTSC format The specifications for color television as defined by the NTSC committee, which include: (a) 525 scan lines, (b) broadcast bandwidth of 4 MHz, (c) line frequency of 15.75 KHz, (c) frame frequency of 30 frames per second, and (d) color subcarrier frequency of 3.58 MHz. See PAL format, SECAM format.

NTU Network terminating unit.

n-tuple length register N registers logically or physically connected to function as a single register. Each register may be individually accessed. (I) Synonymous with n-tuple register.

n-tuple register Synonym for n-tuple length register.

n-type semiconductor A semiconductor doped with donor impurities that when energized generates a predominance of negative charge carriers (free electrons). Contrast with p-type semiconductor. See also NMOS.

Note: N-type semiconductors have a higher level of conductivity than p-type semiconductors and have faster switching rates but allow lower-density packing of components. P-type and n-type semiconductor materials are often layered together to obtain a rectifying action between the two dissimilar materials (CMOS).

NUA Network user address.

nucleus That part of a control program resident in main storage. (I) Synonymous with resident control program.

nucleus initialization program (NIP) The program that initializes the resident control program; it allows the operator to request last minute changes to certain options specified during system generation.

NUI Network user identification.

NUL The null character. (A)

null (1) Empty. (2) Having no meaning. (3) Not usable.

NULL In XL C language, a pointer that does not point to a data object.

null address An address for a transmission frame not associated with any station. (T)

null character (NUL) (1) A control character that is used to accomplish media-fill or time-fill and that may be inserted into or removed from a sequence of characters without affecting the meaning of the sequence; however, the control of equipment or the format may be affected by this character. (I) (A) (2) The EBCDIC character that represents hex 00. (3) See also space character.

null character string (1) Two consecutive single quotation marks that specify a character constant of no characters. (2) Synonym for null string.

null line A logical line with a length of zero.

null name In 3800 Print Services Facility, a token name with X'FFFF' in first two bytes. A null name in an end structured field; for example end page, matches any name in a begin structured field.

null output message In IMS/VS, the message sent to a terminal when no other output is immediately available to satisfy terminal requirements.

null record (1) An empty record. (2) A record containing a null character string. (3) In binary synchronous communication, a record that contains no data; it contains only the data link control characters STX and ETX.

null resource In the NetView Graphic Monitor Facility, an object that is used only as an aid in formatting and drawing a view. A null resource always shows the status "unknown."

null set Synonym for empty set.

null statement A statement that contains only the delimiter symbol, but no characters.

null string (1) A string containing no element. (T) (2) The notion of a string depleted of its entities, or the notion of a string prior to establishing its entities. (A) (3) A character or bit string with a length of zero.

null suppression The bypassing of all null characters in order to reduce the amount of data to be transmitted.

null-terminated Having a zero byte at the end. In the C language, character strings are stored this way internally.

null value A parameter position for which no value is specified.

number (1) A mathematical entity that may indicate quantity or amount of units. (A) (2) Loosely, a numeral. (A) (3) See binary number, complex number, Fibonacci number, integral number, irrational number, level-number, natural number, random number, rational number, real number, record number, relative record number, segment number, serial number.

numbering plan A uniform numbering system wherein each telephone central office has unique designation similar in form to that of all other offices connected to the nationwide dialing network. In the USA and Canada, the first three of ten dialed digits denote area code; the next three, office code; and the remaining four, station number. See also area code.

number representation (1) A representation of a number in a numeration system. (I) (A) (2) Synonymous with numeration.

number representation system Synonym for numeration system.

number sequence See pseudo-random number sequence, random number sequence.

number system Deprecated term for numeration system.

numeral (1) A discrete representation of a number. The following are four different numerals that represent the same number, that is, a dozen, in the methods shown: twelve, by a word in the English language; 12, in the decimal numeration system; XII, by Roman numerals; 1100, in the pure binary numeration system. (I) (A) (2) See binary numeral, decimal numeral.

numeral row On a keyboard, a row of numeric keys in an ordered sequence. Synonymous with row E. See also letter row, lower letter row, middle letter row, upper row.

numeration Synonym for number representation.

numeration system (1) Any notation for the representation of numbers. (I) (A) Synonymous with number representation system. (2) See decimal numeration system, fixed-radix numeration system, mixed-base numeration system, mixed-radix numeration system, pure binary numeration system, radix numeration system.

numeric (1) Pertaining to data that consist of numerals. (T) (2) Pertaining to data or to physical quantities that consist of numerals. (A) Synonymous with numerical. (3) Pertaining to any of the digits 0 through 9.

numerical Synonym for numeric.

numerical accounting machine An accounting machine that does not have a means for entering unlimited alphabetic information. (A)

numerical analysis The study of methods of obtaining useful quantitative solutions to problems that have been expressed mathematically, including the study of the errors and bounds on errors in obtaining such solutions. (A)

numerical control (NC) A technique of operating machine tools or similar equipment in which motion responds to numerically coded commands.

Note: These commands may be generated by a CAD/CAM system on punched tapes or process involved in generating data or tapes necessary to guide a machine tool in manufacture of a part. (T)

numerical data Synonym for numeric data.

numeric array In BASIC, a named table of data items. BASIC allows up to seven dimensions in a numeric array.

numeric backspace character (NBS) A word processing formatting control that moves the printing or display point to the left by a fixed escapement value equal to the value for numbers in the pitch being used. Contrast with backspace character.

numeric bit data See binary picture data.

numeric character (1) Any one of the digits 0 through 9. (2) Synonym for digit *(1)*.

numeric character data See decimal picture data.

numeric character set A character set that contains digits and may contain control characters, special characters, but not letters. (T)

numeric character subset A character subset that contains digits and may contain control characters, special characters, and the space character, but not letters. (I) (A)

numeric code A code whose application results in a code element set whose elements are formed from a numeric character set. (T)

numeric coded character set A coded character set whose character set is a numeric character set. (I) (A)

numeric coded set A coded set whose elements are formed from a numeric character set. (T)

numeric constant (1) The actual numeric value to be used in processing, instead of the name of a field containing the data. A numeric constant can contain any of the numeric digits 0 through 9, a sign (plus or minus), and a decimal point. Contrast with character constant. (2) A constant that expresses an integer, real, or complex number. (3) See also bit constant, integer, fixed-point constant, floating-point constant, hexadecimal constant.

numeric data (1) Data represented by numerals. (I) (A) (2) Data in the form of numerals and some special characters; for example, a date represented as 81/01/01. Synonymous with numerical data.

numeric edited item In COBOL, a numeric item whose PICTURE character-string contains valid editing characters.

numeric expression A numeric constant, a simple numeric variable, a scalar reference to a numeric array, a numeric-valued function reference, or a sequence of the above, separated by numeric operators and parentheses.

numeric field (1) An area reserved for a particular unit of information and that can contain only the digits 0 through 9. Contrast with character field. (2) In the 3270 Information Display System, a display field that accepts only numeric (0-9), minus sign, decimal sign, and DUP keyboard entries.

numeric item (1) In COBOL, a data item that must be numeric. If signed, the item can also contain a representation of an operational sign. (2) Contrast with nonnumeric item.

numeric keypad On an IBM personal computer keyboard, the lighter-colored keys at the right-hand side that are labeled decimal point (.) and 0 through 9. When the keypad is deactivated by the Num Lock key, the same keys perform other functions: Home, PgUp, PgDn, Del, End, Ins, and cursor control.

numeric literal (1) A numeric character or string of characters whose value is implicit in the characters themselves; for example, 777 is the literal as well as the value of the number 777. A numeric literal can contain any of the numeric digits 0 through 9, a sign (plus or minus), and a decimal point. Contrast with character literal. (2) In COBOL, a literal composed of one or more numeric characters that may contain either a decimal point, an algebraic sign, or both. The decimal point must not be the rightmost character. The algebraic sign, if present, must be the leftmost character. (3) See literal.

numeric operator (1) A symbol representing an operation to be performed on numeric data, such as + or − to indicate addition or subtraction. (2) A symbol representing an operation to be performed on numeric data.

numeric optical disk Synonym for digital optical disk. (T) (A)

numeric pad A set of keys on a 3793 Keyboard-Printer, in normal operation used to enter letters or spaces, that can be used to enter numbers when the SRC KB field has been defined as numeric only. The keys are arranged like the numeric keys on an adding machine keyboard.

numeric punch A hole punched in one of the punch rows designated as zero through nine. A zero-punch, and sometimes an eight- or nine-punch, in combination with another numeric punch, is considered a zone punch. (A)

numeric representation A discrete representation of data by numerals. (I) (A)

numeric shift A control for selecting the numeric character set in an alphanumeric keyboard-printer.

numeric space character (NSP) A word processing formatting control used in proportionally spaced printing or display that causes the active position to move to the right a distance equal to the escapement value for numbers in the pitch being used. See also space character.

numeric variable The name of a numeric data item whose value is assigned or changed during program processing.

numeric word A word that consists of digits and possibly space characters and special characters; for example, in the Universal Decimal Classification, the numeric word 61(03)=20 is used as an identifier for any medical encyclopedia in English. (T)

Num Lock A key on a keyboard that a user presses to change the mode of the numeric keypad so that it produces a number for each key pressed.

NVRAM Nonvolatile random access memory.

NVT Network virtual terminal.

NWS Nonprogrammable workstation.

nybble Variant spelling for nibble. Deprecated term for a part of a byte, usually a halfbyte.

Nyquist limit In sampling, the highest frequency of input signal that can be correctly sampled. The Nyquist limit is equal to half of the sampling frequency.

O

OA Office automation. See automated office.

OACBRU Open ACB request/response unit.

OAF Origin address field.

OAF' Origin address field prime.

OAM Storage Management Component In the Object Access Method, the component that determines where objects should be stored, manages object movement within the object storage hierarchy, and manages expiration attributes based on the installation storage management policy.

OAR Operator authorization record.

object (1) In computer security, anything to which access is controlled; for example, a file, a program, an area of main storage. (2) A passive entity that contains or receives data; for example, bytes, blocks, clocks, fields, files, directories, displays, keyboards, network nodes, pages, printers, processors, programs, records, segments, words. Access to an object implies access to the information it contains. (3) In SAA Common User Access architecture, something that a user works with to perform a task. Text and graphics are examples of objects. (4) In AIX Enhanced X-Windows, a software abstraction consisting of private data and private and public routines that operate on the private data. Users can interact with an object only through calls to the public routines of the object. (5) In the AIX object data manager, an instance or member of an object class, conceptually similar to a structure that is a member or array of structures. See also object class. (6) In programming languages, a data object. (7) In AIX graphics, synonym for display list. (8) In the Network Computing System, an entity that is manipulated by well-defined operation; for example, a disk, a file, a printer. Every object has a type and is accessed through an interface. (9) In the IBM ImagePlus system, a collection of structured fields. The first structured field provides a begin-object function and the last structured field provides an end-object function. The object may contain one or more other structured fields whose content consists of one or more data elements of a particular data type. An object

may be assigned a name, which may be used to reference the object. Examples of objects are text, font, graphics, image, and formatted data objects. (10) In object-oriented design or programming, an abstraction consisting of data and the operations associated with that data. See also class. (11) In the AS/400 system, a named storage space that consists of a set of characteristics that describe itself and, in some cases, data. An object is anything that exists in and occupies space in storage and on which operations can be performed; for example, programs, files, libraries, and folders. (12) In SQL, anything that can be created or manipulated with SQL statements, such as databases, tables, views, or indexes. (13) See arithmetic object, compound object, data object, integral object.

Object Access Method (OAM) In the IBM ImagePlus system, a program that provides object storage, object retrieval, and object storage hierarchy management. The Object Access Method isolates applications from storage devices, storage management, and storage device hierarchy management.

object-action In SAA Common User Access architecture, a process sequence in which a user selects an object and then selects an action to apply to that object. Contrast with action-object.

object authority (1) In the AS/400 system, a specific authority that controls what a system user can do with an entire object; for example, object authority includes deleting, moving, or renaming an object. There are three types of object authorities: object existence, object management, and object operational. (2) The right to use or control an object. See also data rights, object rights.

object class A categorization or grouping of objects that share similar behaviors and circumstances.

object code Output from a compiler or assembler which is itself executable machine code or is suitable for processing to produce executable machine code. (A)

object code compatibility (1) Pertaining to object programs that can be run on two or more systems without recompilation or reassembly. (2) Contrast with source code compatibility.

OBJECT-COMPUTER In COBOL, the name of an Environment Division paragraph in which the computer environment, within which the object program is executed, is described.

object-computer entry In COBOL, an entry in the OBJECT-COMPUTER paragraph of the Environment Division that contains clauses that describe the computer environment in which the object program is to be executed.

object content architecture (OCA) In the IBM ImagePlus system, an architecture that defines the content of an image data stream.

object content envelope The beginning and end of information, in field content that is compatible with IBM data stream architecture conventions. It must be appended to the object, so that the object is self-described to the ImagePlus host components that must process the object.

object data manager (ODM) In the AIX operating system, a data manager intended for the storage of system data.

object decomposition In multimedia applications, the process of breaking an object into its component parts.

object definition (1) The set of information required to create and manage an object. (2) The creation of a control block for an object. It also defines the object as available to the user.

object definition table (ODT) (1) A part of the definition of a program that defines the program objects associated with the instructions in its instruction stream. Operands of an instruction refer to entries in this table. (2) In the AS/400 system, a table built at compile time by the system to keep track of objects declared in the program. The program objects in the table include variables, constants, labels, operand lists and exception descriptions. The table resides in the compiled program object.

object description The attributes, such as name, type, and owner name, that describe an object.

object distribution In the AS/400 system, a function that allows a user to send source and data files, save files, job streams, spooled files, and messages to another user, either locally or on an SNADS network.

Object Distribution Manager In the IBM ImagePlus system, the application that resides in the ImagePlus host and provides services to the front-end application hosts for the storage, retrieval, and routing of image objects and coded data.

Object Distribution Manager Vector table The table maintained in memory during operation of the Object Distribution Manager that points to the configuration information for the Object Distribution Manager.

object existence authority In the AS/400 system, an object authority that allows the user to delete the object, free storage of the object, save and restore the object, transfer ownership of the object, and create an object that was named by an authority holder. See also object operational authority, object management authority.

object existence rights The authority to delete, save, free the storage of, restore, and transfer ownership of an object.

object file A member file in an object library.

object handle In an AIX graphical file, the starting point of an arc or lines object.

object language (1) A target language for expressing object programs. (T) (2) A language that is specified by a metalanguage. (A) (3) Synonym for target language. (A)

object library An area on a direct access storage device used to store object programs and routines.

object management authority In the AS/400 system, an object authority that allows the user to specify the authority for the object, move or rename the object, and add members to database files. See also authorization list management authority, object existence authority, operational authority.

object management rights The authority to move, rename, grant authority to, revoke authority from, and change the attributes of an object.

object map In DPPX/DPS, a map that has been through the generate process and that can be used by DPPX/DPS at execution time.

object module (1) All or part of an object program sufficiently complete for linking. Assemblers and compilers usually produce object modules. (T) (2) A set of instructions in machine language produced by a compiler from a source program.

object module library A partitioned data set that is used to store and retrieve object modules. See also load module library, source module library.

object name (1) The name of an object. Contrast with qualified object name. (2) In the IBM ImagePlus system, the name that is provided to the Object Distribution Manager by the front-end application. The object name is used for both Copy and Store functions.

object of entry In COBOL, a set of operands and reserved words, within a Data Division entry of a COBOL Program, that immediately follows the subject of entry.

object operational authority In the AS/400 system, an object authority that allows the user to look at the description of an object and use the object as determined by the user's data authorities to the object. See also all authority, object existence authority, object management authority, use authority.

object orientation An orientation in a user interface in which the user works with objects, rather than applications, to perform tasks.

object-oriented language A programming language that reflects the concepts of object-oriented programming; for example, SMALLTALK. (T)

object-oriented programming A method for structuring programs as hierarchically organized classes describing the data and operations of objects that may interact with other objects. (T)

object owner A user who creates an object or an owner to whom the ownership of an object was reassigned. The object owner has complete control over the object.

object program (1) A target program suitable for execution. An object program may or may not require linking. (T) (2) In COBOL, a set or group of executable machine language instructions and other material designed to interact with data to provide problem solutions. In this context, an object program is generally the machine language result of the operation of a COBOL compiler on a source program. Where there is no danger of ambiguity, the word "program" alone may be used in place of the term "object program." (3) Synonym for target program. (4) Contrast with source program.

object reuse In computer security, the use of a data medium that once held one or more data objects to hold a new data object.

Note: For secure object reuse, scavenging must be prevented. To prevent scavenging, a system must either eliminate residue or prevent reading without writing.

object rights (1) The authority that controls what a system user can do to an object; for example, deleting, moving, or renaming an object. (2) See object existence rights, object management rights, operational rights.

object space The space in which a graphics object is defined. A convenient point is chosen as the origin and the object is defined relative to that point.

Object Storage and Retrieval (OSAR) A component of the Object Access Method that stores, retrieves, and deletes objects. OSAR stores objects in the storage hierarchy and maintains the information about these objects in DB2 databases.

object table See preexecution time table.

object time The time during which an object program is executed.

object type (1) The attributes that define the purpose of an object within a system. Each object type has associated with it a set of commands with which to process that type of object. (2) In AS/400 query management, the substring following the query command name that specifies the type of query object to be processed.

object universal unique identifier A universal unique identifier UUID that identifies a particular object. Both the remote procedure call runtime library and the Location Broker in the Network Computing System use object UUIDs to identify objects.

object user A user who has been authorized by the object owner, the security officer, or a user with object existence rights to perform certain functions on an object.

OBR (1) Outboard record. (2) Outboard recorder.

obscure (1) In AIX Enhanced X-Windows, pertaining to a window that is only partially visible because part of it is obstructed by another window. (2) In AIX Enhanced X-Windows, the action of a window that partially obstructs the viewing of another window.

obsolete element In COBOL, a language element in the current revision of Standard COBOL that is to be deleted from the next revision of Standard COBOL.

OCA Object content architecture.

OCC Operator control command.

OCCF Operator Communication Control Facility.

occlude (1) In AIX Enhanced X-Windows, pertaining to a window that is not visible because it is completely obstructed by another window. (2) In AIX Enhanced X-Windows, the action of a window that completely obstructs the viewing of another window.

OCDS Output command data set.

OCF Operator console facility.

OCL (1) Operation control language. (2) Operator control language.

OCL statement In office systems, a batch control statement used by an operator to control the printing of a document.

OCP Operator control panel.

OCR (1) Optical character recognition. (A) (2) Optical character reader.

OCR-A font size 1 Characters defined as OCR-A font, described in the USA standard character set for optical character recognition (USAS X3.17, 1966) and the OCR-A font size 1 described in the International Standards Organization recommendation R 1073, first edition, dated May 1969. (I)

OCR-B font size 1 Characters defined as OCR-B font, as revised by ECMA and published in the standard ECMA-11 for alphanumeric character set OCR-B for optical recognition, second edition, dated October 1971.

octal (1) Pertaining to a selection, choice, or condition that has eight possible different values or states. (I) (A) (2) Pertaining to a fixed-radix numeration having a radix of eight. (I) (A)

octal numeration system The fixed-radix-numeration system that uses the digits 0, 1, 2, 3, 4, 5, 6 and 7, and the radix eight and in which the lowest integral weight is 1. I the octal numeration system, the numeral "1750" represents the number one thousand, that is $1 \times 8^3 + 7 \times 8^2 + 5 \times 8^1 + 0 \times 8^0$. (T)

octave band In acoustics, the frequency interval between two frequencies having a ratio of 2 to 1.

octet (1) A byte that consists of 8 bits. (T) (2) A byte composed of eight binary elements. Synonymous with eight-bit byte. (A)

odd-even check Synonym for parity check.

odd field All of the odd-numbered scan lines on a video screen. See field, even field.

odd positive acknowledgment See ACK1.

ODM Object data manager.

ODP Open data path.

ODT Object definition table.

OEF Origin element field.

OEM Original equipment manufacturer.

OFB Output feedback.

off-hook (1) Pertaining to a telephone set that is activated. (2) Pertaining to a data set that answers automatically on a public switched system. (3) Contrast with on-hook. (4) See also switch hook.

office automation (OA) (1) The integration of office activities by means of an information processing system. This term includes in particular the processing and communication of text, images, and voice. (T) (2) The techniques and means used for the automation of office activities, in particular, the processing and communication of text, images, and voice. (A)

office automation system An information processing system used to integrate office activities. (T)

office products A group of programs supplied by IBM that work together to help you operate your office more efficiently. These products include WP/36, OFFICE/36, QUERY/36, and the interactive data definition utility (IDDU).

office profile A profile that contains information about an OFFICE/36 user.

office typewriter A typewriter designed for general office work, capable of constant use, that can produce originals with a large number of copies. Attachments can usually be fitted to the machine.

OFFICE/36 A licensed program used to work with lists of names and addresses, calendars, and electronic mail.

offline (1) Pertaining to the operation of a functional unit that takes place either independently of, or in parallel with, the main operation of a computer. (T) (2) Neither controlled by, nor communicating with, a computer. Contrast with online.

offline diagnostic program A special program the service representative uses to test operations of the printer; it is usually run when the printer is offline.

offline edit In multimedia applications, a preliminary or test edit usually done on a low-cost editing system using videocassette work tapes.

Note: An offline edit is done so that decisions can be made and approvals given prior to the final edit.

offline storage Storage not under control of a processing unit. (A)

offline system A system in which human operations are required between the original recording functions and the ultimate data processing function. This includes conversion operations as well as the necessary loading and unloading operations incident to the use of point-to-point or data-gathering systems. Contrast with online system.

offline terms code In PSS, a function that causes a terminal to prompt the operator for a terms code when the terminal is offline.

offset (1) The number of measuring units from an arbitrary starting point in a record, area, or control block, to some other point. (2) The distance from the beginning of an object to the beginning of a particular field. (3) In System/38 graphics and GDDM, the number of character grid units from a reference point. (4) The indentation of all lines of a block of text following the first line. (5) In the Overlay Generation Language, the coordinates of the corner of the overlay nearest to the paper origin. (6) In text processing, to indent all lines of a block of text, except the first line. (7) In XL Pascal, the selection mechanism in the SPACE data type; an element is selected by placing an integer value in brackets. The origin of SPACE is based on zero. (8) In the PenPM operating system extension, the distance between the location the pen touches and the location of the object that the user wants to select.

offset litho duplicating In a duplicator, a process in which the image is transferred from a master to the copy paper via an intermediate surface. The printing and nonprinting areas of the master are generally on the same plane; the former accepts the ink and the latter rejects it. (T) Contrast with direct litho duplicating. See also spirit duplicating, stencil duplicating.

offset litho duplicator A duplicator that uses the offset litho duplicating process to produce multiple copies from a master. (T)

offset pie slice In the AS/400 Business Graphics Utility, a slice that is slightly removed from a pie chart to emphasize it.

offset stacker A card stacker that can stack cards selectively under machine control so that they protrude from the balance of the deck to give physical identification.

offset stacking In AS/400 Advanced Function Printing (AFP) support, a function that allows the printed output pages to be offset for easy separation of the print jobs.

ohm A unit of measure of electrical resistance.

OIA Operator information area.

OIC Only-in-chain.

OK In SAA Advanced Common User Access architecture, a push button that accepts any changes made to information in a pop-up window, then closes it.

OLTEP Online test executive program. See also VSE/OLTEP.

OLTS Online test system.

OLTSEP Online stand-alone executive program.

OLTT Online terminal test.

OLU Origin logical unit.

OMC Optical mode conditioner.

omit function In the AS/400 system, a system function that determines which records from a physical file are to be omitted from a logical file. Contrast with select function.

on-demand system A system from which information or service is available at the time of request.

one-address Synonym for single-address.

one-address instruction An instruction that contains one address part. (I) (A)

one-ahead addressing A method of implied addressing in which the operation part of an instruction implicitly addresses the operands in the location following the location of the operands of the last instruction executed. (A)

one-core-per-bit storage A storage device in which each storage cell uses one magnetic core per binary character. (I) (A)

one-dimensional language (1) A language whose expressions are customarily represented as strings of characters; for example, FORTRAN. (A) (2) Contrast with multidimensional language.

one-for-one translation Conversion of one source language instruction to one machine language instruction.

one-inch videotape A videotape format used for professional or broadcast quality video recording and editing and which is sold in large, open reels.

one-level address Synonym for direct address.

one-plus-one address instruction An instruction that contains two addresses, "the plus-one" address being that of the instruction to be executed next. (I)

ones complement The diminished radix complement in the pure binary numeration system. Synonymous with complement-on-one. (T) (A) See Figure 104.

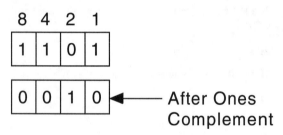

Figure 104. Ones Complement

one-way bracket A bracket in which data is sent from one NAU to another in a single chain with begin bracket, conditional end bracket, and exception response requested. When one-way brackets are used on CP-CP sessions, they are always sent on the contention-winner session.

one-way channel A logical channel that allows incoming calls only or outgoing calls only. Contrast with two-way channel.

one-way communication Data communication so that data is transferred in one preassigned direction. (I)

one-way conversation A conversation in which data is sent from one transaction program (the source) to another (the target) with no response requested and that is released after the data is sent. If the source TP terminates as soon as it releases the conversation, the data may still be in transit; thus, the source and target TPs are not necessarily active at the same time.

one-way encryption In computer security, encryption for which decryption is designed to be infeasible.

Note: One-way encryption is used for storage of values, such as passwords that never need to be recovered, but must be determined to equal a provided value.

one-way message delay The time elapsed from the moment that a message is sent from its origin until it reaches its destination.

one-way propagation time Synonym for transmission path delay. (T)

one-way transmission Synonym for simplex transmission.

one-way trunk A trunk between central exchanges where traffic can originate on only one end.

on-hook Deactivated (in regard to a telephone set). A telephone not in use is on-hook. See also switch hook. Contrast with off-hook.

online (1) Pertaining to the operation of a functional unit when under the direct control of the computer. (T) (2) Pertaining to a user's ability to interact with a computer. (A) (3) Pertaining to a user's access to a computer via a terminal. (A) (4) Controlled by, or communicating with, a computer. (5) Contrast with offline.

online backup (1) To copy all or part of a file while it is being created so that it can be recreated in the event that it is lost or damaged. (2) In System/38, use of the Copy File (CPYF) command to internally copy a database file to another database file for backup.

online batch processing The sharing of computer resources between one or more realtime programs and a batch program.

online edit In multimedia applications, the final edit, using the master tapes to produce a finished program.

online information Information stored in a computer system that can be displayed, used, and modified in an interactive manner without any need to obtain hard copy.

online retrieval SSP In ACF/TCAM, a system service program that allows operators at designated stations or logical units (LUs) to retrieve disk-queued messages, based upon origin or destination, time of entry, or input or output sequence number.

online storage Storage under the control of the processing unit. (A)

online system (1) A system in which the input data enters the computer directly from the point of origin or in which output data is transmitted directly to where it is used. (2) In telegraph usage, a system of transmitting directly into the system. See also line loop. Contrast with offline system.

online terminal test (OLTT) A diagnostic aid by which a terminal or console may request any of several kinds of tests to be performed upon either the same terminal or console or a different one.

online test In binary synchronous communication (BSC), a standardized set of tests used to ensure the proper operation and correct working of the data link portion of the total system.

online test executive program (OLTEP) An IBM program for managing the online tests that are available for device preventive maintenance and service. Normally, only IBM service personnel use this program.

online testing Testing of a remote terminal or station that is performed concurrently with execution of the user's programs – that is, while the terminal is still connected to the processing unit – with only minimal effect on the user's normal operation.

online test system (OLTS) A system that allows a user to test I/O devices concurrently with execution of programs. Tests may be run to diagnose I/O errors, verify repairs and engineering changes, or to periodically check devices. See also online test executive program.

online tutorial text Text presented to the online user when requesting help in an online function.

only element In SNA, deprecated term for only-in-chain (OIC).

only-element-of-chain In SNA, deprecated term for only-in-chain (OIC).

only field In the AS/400 system, a field that must contain only double-byte characters. See also either field, open field.

only-in-chain (OIC) A request unit for which the request header (RH) begin chain indicator and RH end chain indicator are both on. See also RU chain.

only-of-chain In SNA, deprecated term for only-in-chain (OIC).

only RU of chain In SNA, deprecated term for only-in-chain (OIC).

ON-statement action In PL/I, the specifically requested action built for a condition when the condition is raised. The ON-statement action overrides or suspends any previously established action unless it is overridden by a later ON statement for the same condition or until the block it was running in ends. Contrast with implicit action.

on-the-fly printer (1) An impact printer in which the type band or type slugs do not stop moving during the impression time. (T) (2) An impact printer whose type slugs do not stop moving during the impression time. (A) (3) Synonymous with hit-on-the-fly printer.

OPCE Operator control element.

op code See operation code.

open (1) The function that connects a file to a program for processing. (2) In the AS/400 system, a function that connects an object of type *FILE to a program for processing. (3) A break in an electrical circuit. (4) To prepare a file for processing. (5) In the IBM 3650 Retail Store System and the IBM 3660

Supermarket Store System, to perform the store and equipment procedures necessary to initiate operations at the point of sale terminal at the beginning of a sales period or at the beginning of a sales day. (6) Contrast with close. (7) In the IBM Token-Ring Network, to make an adapter ready for use.

Open In SAA Common User Access architecture, a choice in the File pull-down that users select to display an object.

open contact tone In telephony, an audible signal indicating that a contact is open.

open data path (ODP) (1) In System/38, the path through which all I/O operations for a file are performed. (2) In the AS/400 system, a control block created when a file is opened. An ODP contains information about the merged file attributes and information returned by input or output operations. The ODP only exists while the file is open.

open-ended Pertaining to a process or system that can be augmented. (A)

open field In the AS/400 system, a field that can contain a combination of alphanumeric and double-byte characters with shift-out and shift-in characters marking the transitions. See either field, only field.

open mode In COBOL, the state of a file after execution of an OPEN statement for that file and before the execution of a CLOSE statement without the REEL or UNIT phrase for that file. The particular OPEN mode is specified in the OPEN statement as either INPUT, OUTPUT, I-O, or EXTEND.

open numbering In telephony, a numbering system in which the number of digits is not known in advance.

open security environment In computer security, an environment in which authorizations, clearances, and configuration controls are insufficient to ensure that malicious logic cannot be introduced. Contrast with closed security environment. (T)

open shop (1) Pertaining to the operation of a computer facility in which most productive problem programming is performed by the problem originator rather than by a group of programming specialists. The use of the computer itself may also be described as open shop if the user/programmer also serves as the operator. (A) (2) Contrast with closed shop.

open subroutine (1) A subroutine, one copy of which must be inserted at each place the subroutine is used in a computer program. (I) (A) Synonymous with direct insert subroutine. (2) Contrast with closed subroutine.

open system (1) A system whose characteristics comply with standards made available throughout the industry and that therefore can be connected to other systems complying with the same standards. (T) (2) In computer security, a system in which resources that are not defined to the system are not protected. Contrast with closed system.

open systems architecture (OSA) A model that represents a network as a hierarchical structure of layers of functions; each layer provides a set of functions that can be accessed and that can be used by the layer above it.

Note: Layers are independent in the sense that implementation of a layer can be changed without affecting other layers.

Open Systems Interconnection (OSI) (1) The interconnection of open systems in accordance with standards of the International Organization for Standardization (ISO) for the exchange of information. (T) (A) (2) The use of standardized procedures to enable the interconnection of data processing systems.

Note: OSI architecture establishes a framework for coordinating the development of current and future standards for the interconnection of computer systems. Network functions are divided into seven layers. Each layer represents a group of related data processing and communication functions that can be carried out in a standard way to support different applications. See Figure 105.

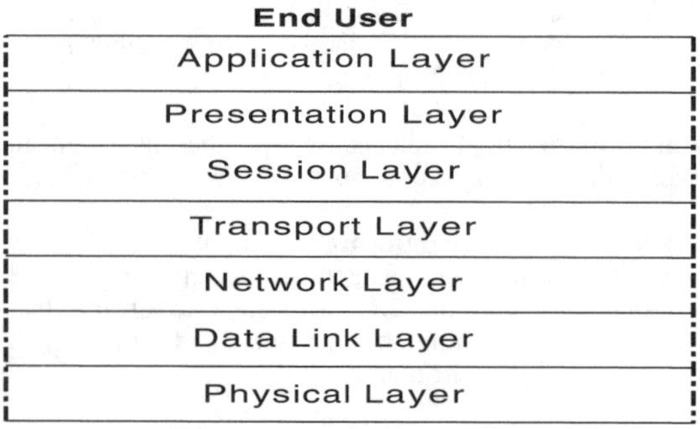

End User

| Application Layer |
| Presentation Layer |
| Session Layer |
| Transport Layer |
| Network Layer |
| Data Link Layer |
| Physical Layer |

Figure 105. Open Systems Interconnection

Open Systems Interconnection architecture Network architecture that adheres to that particular set of ISO standards that relates to open systems interconnection. (T)

Open Systems Interconnection reference model A model that describes the general principles of the open systems interconnection, as well as the purpose and the hierarchical arrangement of its seven layers. (T)

open wire (1) A conductor separately supported above the surface of the ground; that is, on insulators. (2) A broken wire.

open-wire line A pole line in which the conductors are principally in the form of bare, uninsulated wire. Ceramic, glass, or plastic insulators are used to physically attach the bare wire to the telephone poles. Short circuits between the individual conductors are avoided by appropriate spacing.

operable time The time during which a functional unit would yield correct results if it were operated. (I) (A) Synonymous with uptime.

operand (1) An entity on which an operation is performed. (I) (A) (2) That which is operated upon. An operand is usually identified by an address part of an instruction. (A) (3) Information entered with a command name to define the data on which a command processor operates and to control the execution of the command processor. (4) An expression to whose value an operator is applied. (5) In COBOL, any lowercase word or words that appears in a statement or entry format; as such, it is an implied reference to the data indicated. (6) See also keyword, keyword parameter, positional operand, positional parameter.

operate mode Synonym for compute mode. (I)

operating diskette (1) A diskette that contains the configuration image and other data relating to the operation of a controller. The operating diskette must be in the controller during its operation. (T) (2) In the 3790 Communication System, synonym for daily initialization diskette.

operating environment See operational environment.

operating space Synonym for display space.

operating system (OS) Software that controls the execution of programs and that may provide services such as resource allocation, scheduling, input/output control, and data management. Although operating systems are predominantly software, partial hardware implementations are possible. (T)

operating system files In the OS/2 operating system, files such as IBMBIO.COM and IBMDOS.COM that make up the operating system.

Operating System/Virtual Storage (OS/VS) A family of operating systems that control IBM System/360 and System/370 computing systems. OS/VS includes VS1, VS2, MVS/370, and MVS/XA.

operating time (1) That part of operable time during which a functional unit is operated. (A)   (2) Contrast with idle time.

operating voltage indicator On a calculator, a device giving a visual signal to indicate that the correct voltage is set for a main-powered machine or that the battery is insufficiently charged in a battery-powered machine. (T)

operation (1) A well-defined action that, when applied to any permissible combination of known entities, produces a new entity; for example, the process of addition in arithmetic; in adding five and three and obtaining eight, the numbers five and three are the operands, the number eight is the result, and the plus sign is the operator indicating that the operation performed is addition. (I) (A)   (2) A defined action, namely, the act of obtaining a result from one or more operands in accordance with a rule that completely specifies the result for any permissible combination of operands. (A)   (3) A program step undertaken or executed by a computer; for example, addition, multiplication, extraction, comparison, shift, transfer. The operation is usually specified by the operator part of an instruction. (A)   (4) The event or specific action performed by a logic element. (A)   (5) An action performed on one or more data items, such as adding, multiplying, comparing, or moving.   (6) In object-oriented design or programming, a service that can be requested at the boundary of an object. Operations include modifying an object or disclosing information about an object.

operational amplifier A high-gain amplifier connected to external elements to perform specific operations or functions. (I) (A)

Operational Assistant In the AS/400 system, a part of the operating system that provides a set of menus and displays for end users to do commonly performed tasks, such as working with printer output, messages, and batch jobs.

operational diskette Synonym for working diskette.

operational environment (1) The physical environment; for example, temperature, humidity, and layout. (2) All of the IBM-supplied basic functions and the user programs that can be executed by a store controller to enable the devices in the system to perform specific operations.   (3) The collection of IBM-supplied store controller data, user programs, lists, tables, control blocks, and files that reside in a subsystem store controller and control its operation. (4) See also configuration image.

operational expression In PL/I, an expression that consists of one or more operations.

operational key Synonym for session cryptography key.

operational mode See asynchronous balanced mode, asynchronous response mode, normal response mode.

operational rights The authority to use an object and to look at its description.

operational sign An algebraic sign associated with a numeric data item or a numeric literal that indicates whether the item is positive or negative.

operational unit (OU) number In System/36, the number that corresponds to the line connector, located on the back of the system unit, to which a line is attached.

operation code (1) A code for representing the operation parts of the machine instructions of a computer. (T)   (2) A code used to represent the operations of a computer.   (3) In SSP-ICF, a code used by a System/36 application program to request SSP-ICF data management or the subsystem to perform an action; for example, the operation $$SEND asks that data be sent.   (4) In RPG, a word or abbreviation, specified in the calculation specifications, that identifies an operation.

operation code trap A specific value that replaces the normal operation part of a machine instruction at a particular location to cause an interrupt when that machine instruction is executed. (T)

operation control language (OCL) A programming language used to code operation control statements.

operation control statement A statement in a job or job step that is used in identifying the job or describing its requirements to the operating system.

operation decoder A device that selects one or more control channels according to the operation part of a machine instruction. (A)

operation expression An expression containing one or more operators.

operation mode The normal working state of a product or system. See also maintenance mode.

operation part (1) The part of a machine instruction or microinstruction that specifies the operation to be performed. (T)   (2) The part of an instruction that specifies the operation to be performed. Synonymous with function part, operator part. (A)   (3) See also implied addressing.

operations analysis Synonym for operations research.

operations research (OR) The design of models for complex problems concerning the optimal allocation of available resources and the application of mathematical methods for solving those problems. (I) (A) Synonymous with operations analysis.

operation table (1) A table that defines an operation by listing all appropriate combinations of values of the operands and indicating the result for each of these combinations. (I) (A) (2) See Boolean operation table.

operator (1) A symbol that represents an operation to be done. (2) In a language statement, the lexical entity that indicates the action to be performed on operands. See also definition statement. (3) In the C, COBOL, and REXX languages, a token that specifies the type of action to be done on one or more terms. The four types of operators are concatenation, arithmetic, comparison, and logical. (4) In Pascal, a token that specifies the type of action to be done on one or more terms. The four types of operators are NOT, multiplication, addition, and relational. (5) In FORTRAN, a specification of a particular computation involving one or two operands. (6) A person or program responsible for managing activities controlled by a given piece of software such as MVS, the NetView program, or IMS. See also autotask, logged-on operator, network operator, operator station task. (7) A person who operates a device. (8) A person who keeps a system running.

operator's access code In the IBM 3790 Communication System, an 8-bit code, associated with a particular operator ID and stored in an internal 3791 table, that indicates the 3790 programs and controller functions the operator is allowed to use. Contrast with operator ID. See also password, program access code.

operator amplifier An amplifier which is connected to external elements to perform specific operations or functions. (T)

operator authorization record (OAR) A record referred to by a store controller when accepting or rejecting a request for signing on to a terminal, or for performing other procedures. The record also contains a list of procedures that each operator is allowed to perform.

operator command (1) A statement to a control program, issued via a console device or terminal, that causes the control program to provide requested information, alter normal operations, initiate new operations, or terminate existing operations. (2) See VTAM. operator command, operator control command.

Operator Communication Control Facility An IBM licensed program that allows communication with and the operation of remote MVS or VSE systems.

operator console (1) A functional unit containing devices that are used for communications between a computer operator and a computer. (T) (2) A display console used for communication between the operator and the system, used primarily to specify information concerning application programs and I/O operations and to monitor system operation.

operator console facility (OCF) A component of Subsystem Support Services that handles input and output on the host processor console printer.

operator control See basic operator control, extended operator control.

operator control address vector table In ACF/TCAM, a message control program area that contains parameters for the operator control module.

operator control command In ACF/TCAM, a command entered from an operator control station to examine or alter the status of the TCAM system during execution of ACF/TCAM.

operator control element (OPCE) In ACF/TCAM, a unit assigned to each ACF/TCAM operator control command that is used by operator control routines to process the command.

operator control function In the IMS/VS message format service, the means by which a terminal operator controls the display of output messages. Specific operator control functions are provided by IMS/VS, but their use must be defined by the user in an operator control table.

operator control panel (1) A functional unit that contains switches used to control all or part of a computer and possibly the indicators giving information about its functioning. An operator control panel may be part of an operator console or other operator-controlled device. (T) (2) A functional unit that contains switches used to control a computer or a part of it and that may contain indicators that provide information on the functioning of the system. (A)

operator control station See basic operator control station, extended operator control station, extended primary operator control station, extended secondary operator control station.

operator control table In the IMS/VS message format service, a user-defined table of operator control functions; a specific control function is invoked when the input device data or data length satisfies a predefined condition.

operator guidance code A code displayed on a display device that represents the system's response to certain operating conditions or operator actions.

operator guidance indicator In the 3790 Communication System, a light or other indication such as a message (on a console, keyboard, or other portion of a device) that shows the mode in which an operator is working, a particular action that has been taken, a particular condition that exists, or the next operator action that is required.

operator ID A number entered by an operator during logon that identifies the operator to the system. Contrast with operator's access code. See also password.

operator identification card (OIDCARD) A small card with a magnetic stripe encoded with unique characters and used to verify the identity of a terminal operator to RACF on an MVS system.

operator information area In the 3270 Information Display System, the area near the bottom of the display area where terminal or system status information is displayed.

operator logical paging An IMS/VS message format service facility that allows the device operator to request a specific logical page of an output message.

operator message A message from the operating system or a problem program directing the operator to perform a specific function, such as mounting a tape reel, or informing him of specific conditions within the system, such as an error condition.

operator part Synonym for operation part.

operator precedence In programming languages, an order relation defining the sequence of the application of operators within an expression. (I)

operator profile In the NetView program, the resources and activities a network operator has control over. The statements defining these resources and activities are stored in a file that is activated when the operator logs on.

operator/service panel In System/38, a panel located adjacent to the system console on the system unit that contains lights and switches that are used primarily when the system is started or serviced.

operator services See network operator services.

operator station In NCCF, a control point that links a terminal, an operator, and the control environment assigned to that operator (such as profile and span of control).

operator station task (OST) In NCCF, the subtask that establishes and maintains an online session with the network operator. There is one operator station task for each network operator who logs on to NCCF.

opm Operations per minute (equivalent to characters per minute when control functions are included).

OPNDST Open destination.

opportunity study A study to examine a problem and determine whether or not it requires being solved during the time period under consideration. (T)

opposite control field (1) Any control field that is specified by a 0 in column 7 of the field sequence specifications. (2) In System/36 SORT, a control field that is sorted in the opposite sequence of that specified in the header specification.

OPT Option.

optical cable A fiber, multiple fibers, or a fiber bundle in a structure built to meet optical, mechanical, and environmental specifications. (E) See also jumper cable, optical cable assembly, trunk cable.

optical cable assembly An optical cable that is connector-terminated. Generally, an optical cable that has been terminated by a manufacturer and is ready for installation. (E) See also jumper cable, optical cable.

optical character A graphic character printed or handwritten according to special rules in order to facilitate an automatic identification by optical means. (T)

optical character reader (1) An input unit that reads characters by optical character recognition. (T) (2) An optical scanner that recognizes only predefined characters. (A)

optical character recognition (OCR) (1) Character recognition that uses optical means to identify graphic characters. (I) (A) (2) Contrast with magnetic ink character recognition.

optical connector See optical fiber connector.

optical detector A transducer that generates an output signal when irradiated with optical power. (E) See also opto-electronic.

optical disc (1) A disc that contains data readable by optical techniques. (T) (A) (2) A disc with a plastic coating on which information, such as sound or visual images, is recorded digitally in the form of tiny pits and read using a laser.

optical drive A drive mechanism that rotates an optical disc.

optical fiber Any filament made of dielectric materials that guides light, regardless of its ability to send signals. (E) See also fiber optics, optical waveguide.

optical fiber cable Synonym for optical cable.

optical fiber connector A hardware component that transfers optical power between two optical fibers or bundles and is designed to be repeatedly connected and disconnected.

optical fiber splice A permanent joint that couples optical power between two fibers. See fusion splice, mechanical splice.

optical fiber waveguide Synonym for optical fiber.

optical form flash In the 3800 Printing Subsystem, a device that allows the use of form flash negative for the printing of overlays.

optical forms overlay See forms overlay.

optical link See link.

optical link loss See maximum allowable link loss.

optical link segment See link segment.

optical mark reading Synonym for mark scanning. (T)

optical memory A storage device that uses optical techniques. (T)

optical mode conditioner (OMC) A tool that, when inserted between an optical LED source and the ESCON link under test, provides a consistent method for measuring optical attenuation.

optical reader A device that reads hand written or machine printed symbols into a computing system.

optical receiver Hardware that converts an optical signal to an electrical logic signal. Contrast with optical transmitter.

optical reflective disc An optical videodisc that is read by means of the reflection of a laser beam from the shiny surface on the disc.

optical repeater In an optical fiber communication system, an opto-electronic device or module that receives a signal, amplifies it (or, for a digital signal, reshapes, retimes, or otherwise reconstructs it) and retransmits it. (E)

opticals In multimedia applications, visual effects produced optically by means of a device (an optical printer) that contains one camera head and several projectors. The projectors are precisely aligned so as to produce multiple exposures in exact registration on the film as in the camera head.

optical scanner (1) A scanner that uses light for examining patterns. (I) (A) (2) A device that scans optically and usually generates an analog or digital signal. (A)

optical spectrum Generally, the electromagnetic spectrum within the wavelength region extending from the vacuum ultraviolet at 40 nanometers to the far infrared, 1 millimeter. (E)

Optical Storage Subsystem Products (OSSP) High-capacity storage products, such as optical disks and optical disk drives, that support large-scale image processing.

optical time domain reflectometer (OTDR) A measurement device used to characterize a fiber wherein an optical pulse is transmitted through the fiber, and the resulting light is scattered and reflected back to the input and is measured as a function of time. Useful in estimating attenuation coefficient as a function of distance, and identifying defects and other localized losses. (E)

optical transmitter Hardware that converts an electrical logic signal to an optical signal. Contrast with optical receiver.

optical waveguide (1) A structure capable of guiding optical power. (E) (2) In optical communications, generally a fiber designed to send optical signals. (E) See optical fiber. See also cladding, core, fiber optics, multimode optical fiber, optical fiber, single-mode optical fiber.

optical wrap Signal transmission, used primarily for testing, that routes the signal from the optical output of a device directly to the optical input.

optimization See linear optimization, nonlinear optimization.

option (1) A specification in a statement that may be used to influence the execution of the statement. (2) See default option.

optional facilities In X.25 communications, facilities that may or may not be offered by the network provider to which customers choose whether or not to subscribe. See also closed user group, fast select, reverse charging, throughput-class negotiation.

optional file In COBOL, a file that is declared as being not necessarily present each time the object program is executed. The object program causes an interrogation for the presence or absence of the file.

optional network facilities Facilities that a user of a packet switching data network can request when establishing a virtual circuit. See also closed user group, reverse charging, throughput class negotiation.

optional pause instruction An instruction that allows manual suspension of the execution of a computer program. (I) (A) Synonymous with optional stop instruction.

optional stop instruction Synonym for optional pause instruction.

optional user facilities Facilities defined within the CCITT Recommendation X.25 that a user of a packet-switching data network can request when establishing a virtual circuit. See also closed user group, reverse charging, throughput class negotiation.

optional word In COBOL, a reserved word that is included in a specific format only to improve the readability of the language and whose presence is optional to the user when the format in which the word appears is used in a source program.

option field In ACF/TCAM, a storage area with data relating to a particular external logical unit (LU) or application program. Certain message-handler routines that need origin- or destination-related data to perform their functions have access to data in an option field. User-written message handler exit routines also have access to data in an option field.

option indicator In the AS/400 system, a 1-character field that is passed with an output data record from a program to the system that is used to control the output function, such as controlling the fields in the record that are to be displayed.

option list Synonym for menu.

Options In SAA Common User Access architecture, a choice in the action bar that can be used to customize objects or parts of objects in an application.

option set A set of functions that may be supported by products that implement a particular architecture. A product may support any number of option sets or none. For each option set supported, all functions in that set are supported. See also base set.

option table In ACF/TCAM, a table that contains option fields of user-provided information, using certain ACF/TCAM macroinstructions, related to external logical units (LUs) or application programs.

opto-electronic (1) Pertaining to a device that responds to optical power, emits or modifies optical radiation, or uses optical radiation for its internal operation. (E) (2) Any device that functions as an electrical-to-optical or optical-to-electrical transducer. (E)

OQL Outgoing quality level.

OR (1) A logic operator having the property that if P is a statement, Q is a statement, R is a statement,... then the OR of P, Q, R,..., is true if at least one statement is true, false if all statements are false. P OR Q is often represented by $P + Q, PvQ$. (A) Synonymous with Boolean ADD. (2) Operations research. (A) (3) Contrast with exclusive-OR.

Orange Book Synonym for Trusted Computing System Evaluation Criteria.

order (1) A specified arrangement used in ordering. (T) (2) To place items in an arrangement in accordance with specified rules. (I) (A) (3) Deprecated term for instruction, sequence. (4) A code used to format and define data for display or printing. See display command. (5) See merge order.

Note: In contrast to a sequence, an order need not be linear; for example, the ordering of a hierarchy of items.

order-by-merging To order by repeated splitting and merging. (I) (A)

order code Deprecated term for operation code.

ordered seek queuing In VM, a technique used by the CP I/O supervisor to minimize seek time by scheduling DASD I/O operations for nondedicated disks in a sequential progression of cylinder numbers.

ordering bias The manner and degree by which the order of a set of items departs from random distribution. An ordering bias will make the effort necessary to order a set of items more than or less than the effort that would be required for a similar set with random distribution. (I) (A)

orderly closedown The orderly deactivation of VTAM and its domain. See also cancel closedown, quick closedown.

Note: An orderly closedown does not complete until all application programs have closed their access method control blocks (ACBs). Until then, RPL-based operations continue; however, no new sessions can be established and no new ACBs can be opened. See also cancel closedown, quick closedown.

order sequence A string in the 3270 data stream that starts with an order and includes one or more characters associated with the order.

order set A group of records consisting of one header record followed by one or more detail records.

ordinal number One of the counting numbers, used to indicate position.

ordinal type In Pascal, a type whose members can be counted to indicate position.

ordinary identifier In SQL, a letter, which may be followed by zero or more characters, each of which is a letter (a-z and A-Z), a symbol ($, @, and #), a number, or the underscore character, used to form a name.

ordinary token In SQL, a numeric constant, an ordinary identifier, a host variable, or a keyword.

organization See file organization, indexed organization, relative organization, sequential organization.

OR gate (1) A gate that implements the logic OR operator. (A) (2) Synonymous with inclusive-OR gate. See Figure 106.

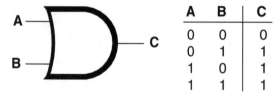

A	B	C
0	0	0
0	1	1
1	0	1
1	1	1

Figure 106. OR Gate

orientation (1) As applied to a teletypewriter, an adjustment of the time the receiving apparatus starts selection. The adjustment is made with respect to the start transition. See also range finder. (2) In the 3800 Printing Subsystem Models 3 and 8, the number of degrees an object is rotated relative to a reference; for example, the orientation of printing on a page, relative to the page coordinates. See also text orientation.

origin (1) The absolute storage address of the beginning of a program or block. (2) In relative coding, the absolute storage address to which addresses in a region are referenced. (3) An external logical unit (LU) or application program from which a message or other data originates. See also destination. (4) A picture element (pel) position from which placement and orientation of text, images, and page segments are specified. (5) See assembled origin, computer program origin, loaded origin.

origin address A code that identifies the location from which information is sent. Synonymous with source address. Contrast with destination address.

origin address field (OAF) (1) In SNA, a field in a FID0 or FID1 transmission header that contains the address of the originating network addressable unit (NAU). Contrast with destination address field. (2) See also format identification (FID) field, local session identification (LSID), origin address field prime (OAF'), origin element field (OEF), origin subarea field (OSAF).

origin address field prime (OAF') In SNA, a field in a FID2 transmission header that contains the local address of the originating network addressable unit (NAU). Contrast with destination address field prime (DAF'). See also format identification (FID) field, origin address field (OAF).

original In a document copying machine, the document to be copied. (T) See continuous-tone original, halftone original, line original, transparent original.

original equipment manufacturer (OEM) A manufacturer of equipment that may be marketed by another manufacturer.

original footage In multimedia applications, the footage from which a program is constructed. Synonymous with raw footage.

originator (1) The user who creates, addresses, and usually sends a message. (T) (2) Contrast with recipient.

origin element field (OEF) In SNA, a field in an FID4 transmission header that contains an element address, which combined with the subarea address in the origin subarea field (OSAF), gives the complete network address of the originating network addressable unit (NAU). Contrast with destination element field (DEF). See also format identification (FID) field.

origin logical unit (OLU) The logical unit from which data is sent. Contrast with destination logical unit (DLU).

origin subarea field (OSAF) In SNA, a field in an FID4 transmission header that contains a subarea address, which combined with the element address in the origin element field (OEF), gives the complete network address of the originating network addressable unit (NAU). Contrast with destination subarea field (DSAF). See also format identification (FID) field.

origin system Synonym for input system.

OR operation Synonym for disjunction.

orphan A first line of a paragraph or column of text that stands alone at the bottom of a page. Synonymous with orphan line. (T)

orphan line Synonym for orphan. (T)

OR relationship The specification of conditioning indicators so that the conditioned operation is done when any one of the conditions is met.

orthographic projection A graphical representation in which the lines of a projection are parallel. Orthographic projections lack perspective foreshortening and its accompanying sense of depth realism. Because they are simple to draw, orthographic projections are often used by draftsmen. See also perspective projection.

OS Operating system.

OSA Open systems architecture.

OSAF Origin subarea field.

OSAM Overflow sequential access method.

oscillating sort A merge sort in which the sorts and merges are performed alternately to form one sorted set. (A)

oscilloscope An instrument for displaying the changes in a varying current or voltage.

OSI Open systems interconnection.

OS/MVS hierarchical recovery Recovery or abnormal terminations at the lowest level task affected by the failure.

OSSP Optical Storage Subsystem Products.

OST Operator station task.

OS/VS Operating System/Virtual Storage.

OS/VS1 A virtual storage operating system that is an extension of OS/MFT.

OS/VS2 A virtual storage operating system that is an extension of OS/MVT.

OS/2 operating system IBM Operating System/2.

OS/2 mode A method of operation for running programs and applications that are designed to use the OS/2 operating system.

OS/400 CSP/AE OS/400 Cross System Product/Application Execution. In the AS/400 system, a function of the operating system that gives the user the capability to run CSP/AE applications, which have been defined and generated in one of the Cross System Product/Application Development (CSP/AD) environments. See also Cross System Product.

OTDR Optical time domain reflectometer.

other-domain resource A recommendation for a logical unit that is owned by another domain and is referenced by a symbolic name, which can be qualified by a network identifier.

OU number See operational unit number.

outage Synonym for disable state. (T)

out-basket A mailbox that contains only messages that have been sent. (T)

outboard LU Deprecated term for peripheral logical unit.

outboard record In VTAM, a record originated by I/O and communication components and supported by the access methods. The outboard record describes permanent errors or reports statistical data.

outboard recorder (OBR) In VSE, a feature that records pertinent data on the system recorder file when an unrecoverable I/O error occurs.

outbound (1) In the 3270 data stream, a transmission from the application program to a device. (2) In SNA, deprecated term for outgoing, sending.

outbound pacing Deprecated term for send pacing.

outbuffer subgroup The part of a message handler (MH) outgoing group that operates on each segment of an outgoing message.

outconnector (1) In flowcharting, a connector that indicates a point at which a flowline is broken for continuation at another point. (A) (2) Contrast with inconnector.

outgoing access In data communication, the ability of a user to communicate with a user in another network.

outgoing call In X.25 communications, a call being made to another data terminal equipment (DTE). Contrast with incoming call.

outgoing group In ACF/TCAM, that portion of the message handler that handles messages sent from the message control program (MCP) to any external logical units (LUs) or application programs. Contrast with incoming group.

outheader subgroup The part of a message handler (MH) outgoing group that operates on all or part of an outgoing message header.

OUTLIM Output limiting facility.

outline numbering Sequential numbering used to denote the organization of a document; for example, section 1.2.

outmessage subgroup Part of a message handler (MH) outgoing group noting actions to be taken after a whole message has been sent to an external logical unit (LU), or when special processing or error conditions are detected.

output (1) Pertaining to a device, process, or channel involved in an output process, or to the associated data or states. The word "output" may be used in place of "output data," "output signal," "output process," when such a usage is clear in a given context. (T) (2) Data that has been processed. (3) Data transferred from storage to an output device. (4) In XL Pascal, a predefined standard file definition. (5) See input/output real-time output. (6) Synonym for output data, output process.

output area An area of storage reserved for output. (A)

output blocking factor (Bo) In a tape sort, the number of data records in each record in the output file.

output channel A channel for conveying data from a device or logic element. (A)

output class In MFT, MVT, and OS/VS, one of up to 36 different categories, defined at an installation, to which output data produced during a job step can be assigned. When an output writer is started, it can be directed to process from one to eight different output data classes.

output data (1) Data that a data processing system or any of its parts transfers outside of that system or part. (T) (2) Data being produced or to be produced by a device or a computer program. (A) (3) Data delivered or to be delivered from a functional unit or from any part of a functional unit. (4) Synonymous with output.

output data set (1) A data set that contains data that is to be printed or displayed. (2) In ACF/TCAM, a data set that contains the messages or records returned from an application program to the message control program by a process entry in the terminal table. Contrast with input data set.

output device Synonym for output unit.

output display area On VM display devices, the upper portion of the display screen that contains a historical log of the most recent lines of console input to and output from the virtual machine and the control program. On the 3270, this area is protected, that is, the user is unable to key information into it.

output document In document processing, a machine-readable collection of lines of text or images that have been formatted or otherwise processed. An output document can be printed or it can be filed for future processing.

output feedback (OFB) A cryptographic operation that exclusively ORs plaintext with the output of a cryptographic algorithm and then transfers the output of the algorithm back to its input for the next operation. See also cipher feedback.

Note: Output feedback is used to achieve a stream cipher from a block cipher operation.

output field A field in a device file in which data can be modified by the program and sent to the device during an output operation.

output file (1) A file that contains the results of processing. (2) A file that has been opened in order to allow records to be written. (3) In RPG, a database or device file that has been opened to allow records to be written. Contrast with input file. (4) In COBOL, a file that is opened in either the output mode or the extend mode. (5) Contrast with input file.

output indicator In RPG, an indicator used to define the conditions under which an output record or an output field in the output specifications is written. An output indicator must be previously defined before it is used in the output specifications.

output/input field (1) A field in a display file that is used for both output and input operations. (2) In the AS/400 system, a field specified in a database, display, or ICF file that can be used for both the information supplied to the program and the information received from the program during processing. See also input field, output field.

output limiting facility (OUTLIM) Facility monitoring the number of logical records produced for SYSOUT data sets.

output line A line of text produced by a formatter.

output list A list of variables from which values are written to a file or device.

output message In IMS/VS, valid response mode conversational messages, exclusive mode messages,

IMS/VS system messages, and application program messages or message switches.

output mode (1) A mode in which records can be written to a file. (2) In COBOL, the state of a file after execution of an OPEN statement, with the OUTPUT or EXTEND phrase specified for that file and before the execution of a CLOSE statement without the REEL or UNIT phrase for that file. Contrast with input mode.

output primitive Synonym for display element.

output priority The priority used to determine the order in which spooled output files produced by the job are to be written. More than one file can have the same priority.

output procedure In COBOL, a set of statements to which control is given during execution of a SORT statement after the sort function is completed, or during execution of a MERGE statement after the merge function reaches a point at which it can select the next record in merged order when requested. Contrast with input procedure.

output process (1) The process that produces output data. (T) (2) The delivery of data from a functional unit or from any part of a functional unit. (3) In data processing, the return of information from a computer system to an end user, including the translation of data from a machine language to a language that the end user can understand. (4) Synonymous with output. (5) See also output data. (6) Contrast with input process.

output program A utility program that organizes the output process of a computer. (I) (A)

output queue (1) A list of output files to be printed or displayed. (2) In the AS/400 system, an object that contains a list of spooled files to be written to an output device, such as a printer or a diskette. (3) See output work queue.

output request In an 8100 BSC/SS transmit operation, a request by the control logic for another message from the processor. Contrast with input request.

output routine A utility routine that organizes the output process of a computer. (I) (A)

output specifications In RPG, the means by which the programmer describes the output records and their fields or adds RPG functions to an externally described output file.

output stream (1) Messages and other output data, printed or displayed on output devices by an operating system or a processing program. (2) In RJE, data received from the host system to the attached devices; for example, control characters, data files, and messages. Contrast with input stream.

output stream control Synonym for JES writer.

output subsystem That part of a process interface system that transfers data from the process computer system to a technical process. (T)

output unit A device in a data processing system by which data can be received from the system. (I) (A) Synonymous with output device.

output work queue A queue of control information describing system output data sets that specifies to an output writer the location and disposition of system output.

output writer A part of the job scheduler that transcribes specified output data sets onto a system output device independently of the program that produced the data sets.

overflow (1) That portion of the result of an operation that exceeds the capacity of the intended unit of storage. (2) In a register, loss of one or more of the leftmost whole-number digits because the result of an operation exceeded the size of the register. See also loss of significance. (3) The condition that occurs when the last line specified as the overflow line to be printed on a page has been passed. (4) See arithmetic overflow. (5) Contrast with underflow. See Figure 107.

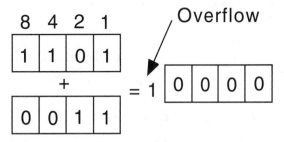

Figure 107. Overflow

overflow check A limit check to determine whether a representation of data exceeds a stipulated length. (T)

overflow condition (1) The condition that occurs when the overflow line on a page has been printed or passed. (2) A condition that occurs when a portion of the result of an operation exceeds the capacity of the intended unit of storage.

overflow exception A condition caused by the result of an arithmetic operation having a magnitude that exceeds the largest possible number.

overflow field In a summary tag-along sort, the field that allows for anticipated field expansion.

overflow handling The method of advancing from one printer page to the next.

overflow indicator (1) An indicator that is set on if the result of an arithmetic operation exceeds the capacity of the accumulator. The overflow indicator is often used in conjunction with a carry indicator to reflect an unusual or an error condition. (2) An indicator that signals when the overflow line on a page has been printed or passed. The indicator can be used to specify which lines are to be printed on the next page.

overflow line The line specified as the last line to be printed on a page.

overflow page The new page created when overflow occurs.

overflow position An extra position in the register in which the overflow digit is developed.

overflow record On an indirectly addressed file, a record whose key is randomized to the address of a full track or to the address of a home record.

overflow sequential access method (OSAM) In IMS/VS, a data management access method that combines selected characteristics of BSAM and BDAM for handling data overflow from ISAM. OSAM is used by HISAM, HIDAM, and by HDAM if VSAM is not used. OSAM is also used by some of the online pool management routines.

overhead (1) In a computer system, the time, operations, and resources used for operating system functions, rather than for application programs. (A) (2) The operating system activity required to perform a task.

overhead operation Synonym for housekeeping operation.

overlap To perform an operation at the same time that another operation is being performed; for example, to perform input/output operations while instructions are being executed by the processing unit.

overlapped span of control In NCCF, a condition that exists when the network resource name appears in one or more spans associated with more than one active network operator. Under such a condition, any

of the operators may control the resource. The status of the device depends on the cumulative effect of commands entered and the sequence in which the commands are received by the access method.

overlapping fields Fields in the same display or printer record that are defined to occupy the same positions on the display or the page. Option indicators can be used to select which of the overlapping fields is to be displayed or printed.

overlay (1) The technique of repeatedly using the same areas of internal storage during different stages of a program. (A) (2) In a document copying machine, a device for adding to or masking details from an original so that these are incorporated into or deleted from the copies. (T) (3) A program segment that is loaded into main storage and replaces all or part of a previously loaded program segment. (4) In AS/400 AFP support, an electronic overlay. (5) To load an overlay *(1)*. (T) (6) To write over existing data in storage. (7) A collection of predefined data such as lines, shading, text, boxes, or logos, that can be merged with variable data on a page while printing. Synonymous with medium overlay. See electronic overlay, forms overlay. See also preprinted form. (8) The ability to superimpose text or graphics onto motion or still video. Synonymous with graphic overlay. (9) See also overlay segment.

Overlay Generation Language A programming language used to create electronic overlays.

overlay image A document image (usually of a standard form) that is used with a coded data overlay.

overlay keyboard A keyboard with narrow keytops that allow an overlay panel to be installed to identify the key functions or fonts.

overlay linkage editor The part of the System Support Program Product that combines object programs to produce code that can be run and allows the user to determine overlays for programs.

overlay module A load module that has been divided into overlay segments, and has been provided by the linkage editor with information that enables the overlay supervisor to implement the desired loading of segments when requested.

overlay path All of the segments in an overlay tree between a particular segment and the root segment, inclusive.

overlay planes In computer graphics, one or more bit planes in a display buffer that are used to create visual data, such as text and graphics, that overlays the visual data in a nondestructive manner.

overlay program A program in which certain control sections can use the same storage locations at different times during execution.

overlay region A continuous area of main storage in which segments can be loaded independently of other regions.

overlay segment (1) One of several segments of a computer program that, one at a time, occupy the same area of main storage, when executed. (T) (2) A portion of a computer program that can be executed without loading the entire program into main storage at the same time.

overlay structure A graphic representation showing the relationships of segments of an overlay program and how the segments are arranged to use the same main storage area at different times.

overlay supervisor A routine that controls the proper sequencing and positioning of segments of computer programs in limited storage during their execution. (T) (A)

overlay tree See overlay structure.

overload For analog input, any absolute voltage value above which the analog-to-digital converter cannot distinguish a change. The overload value can be different for plus and minus inputs.

overpaint In System/38 graphics, the default result of the intersection of two or more colors, in which the first graphics primitive to appear is given the color of the graphics primitive that intersects it, at the point of intersection.

overpunch (1) To add holes in a card column or in a tape row that already contains holes. (I) (A) (2) Deprecated term for zone punch.

override (1) A parameter or value that replaces a previous parameter or value. (2) The attributes specified at run time that change the attributes specified in the file description or in the program. (3) To specify attributes at run time that change the attributes specified in the file description or in the program. (4) To replace a parameter or value.

overrun Loss of data because a receiving device is unable to accept data at the rate it is transmitted.

overstrike To place a character in a space occupied by another character.

overstriking The merging of two or more graphic characters on a sheet of paper.

over-the-shoulder (OS) In video and film production, a shot in which the camera is looking over one person's shoulder at another person or object.

overvoltage interruption (OVI) A signal indicating that a power supply has exceeded its voltage limits.

overwrite To write into an area of storage, thereby destroying the data previously stored in the same area. (T)

OVI Overvoltage interruption.

owned Supplied by and belonging to a customer, as opposed to private and public.

owner (1) The user or group who creates a profile or is named the owner of a profile. The owner can modify, list, or delete the profile. (2) The user who creates an entity or is named the owner of an entity. (3) See file owner.

owner record That record that is superordinate to all the other records in a set. (T)

P

Pa Pascal.

PAB (1) Primary application block. (2) Process anchor block.

PABX Private automatic branch exchange.

PAC Program authorized credentials.

pacing (1) A technique by which a receiving component controls the rate of transmission of a sending component to prevent overrun or congestion. See session-level pacing, send pacing, and virtual route (VR) pacing. See also flow control. (2) A file transfer protocol that controls data transfer by waiting for a specified character, or waiting a specified number of seconds between lines. This protocol prevents the loss of data when the block size is too large or when data is sent too quickly for the system to process.

pacing group Synonym for pacing window.

pacing response In SNA, an indicator that signifies the readiness of a receiving component to accept another pacing group. The indicator is carried in a response header (RH) for session-level pacing, and in a transmission header (TH) for virtual-route pacing. See also isolated pacing response.

pacing window (1) The path information units (PIUs) that can be transmitted on a virtual route before a virtual-route pacing response is received, indicating that the virtual route receiver is ready to receive more PIUs on the route. (2) The requests that can be transmitted on the normal flow in one direction on a session before a session-level pacing response is received, indicating that the receiver is ready to accept the next group of requests. (3) Synonymous with pacing group.

pack (1) To store data in a compact form in a storage medium by taking advantage of known characteristics of the data and of the storage medium, in such a way that the original form of the data can be recovered; for example, to make use of bit or byte locations that otherwise would go unused. (I) (A) (2) See disk pack.

packed decimal format A format in which each byte in a field except the rightmost byte represents two numeric digits. The rightmost byte contains one digit and the sign; for example, the decimal value +123 is represented as 0001 0010 0011 1100. Contrast with unpacked decimal format.

packed decimal item In COBOL, a numeric data item that is represented internally in packed decimal format.

packed decimal notation A binary-coded decimal notation in which two consecutive decimal digits, each having 4 bits, are represented by one byte. (T)

packed field A field that contains data in the packed decimal format.

packed format A data format in which a byte may contain two decimal digits or one decimal digit and a sign.

packed key A key in packed decimal format.

packed numeric A representation of numeric values that compresses each character representation in such a way that the original value can be recovered. (A)

packet (1) In data communication, a sequence of binary digits, including data and control signals, that is transmitted and switched as a composite whole. The data, control signals and, possibly, error control information are arranged in a specific format. (I) (2) Synonymous with data frame. (3) See also reset request. (4) In TCP/IP, the unit of data passed across the interface between the Internet layer and the link layer. A packet includes an IP header and data. A packet can be a complete IP datagram or a fragment of an IP datagram. See also datagram, segment. (5) In X.25, a data transmission information unit. A group of data and control characters, transferred as a unit, determined by the process of transmission. Commonly used data field lengths in packets are 128 or 256 bytes. (6) The field structure and format defined in the CCITT X.25 Recommendation.

packet assembler/disassembler (PAD) A functional unit that enables data terminal equipment not equipped for packet switching to access a packet switched network. (T) (A)

packet header In X.25 communications, control information at the start of the packet; the contents of the packet depend on the packet type.

packet level (1) The packet format and control procedures for exchange of packets containing control information and user data between data terminal equipment (DTE) and data circuit-terminating equipment (DCE).

See also data link level, higher level, physical level. (2) A part of Recommendation X.25 that defines the protocol for establishing logical connections between two DTEs and for transferring data on these connections.

packet level interface In packet mode operation, the level of the interface between data terminal equipment (DTE) and data circuit-terminating equipment (DCE) associated with the exchange of data and signals contained in packets. See also frame level interface.

packet major node In VTAM, a set of minor nodes representing resources, such as switched virtual circuits and permanent virtual circuits, attached through an X.25 port.

packet-mode host Any non-SNA, X.25 host system.

packet mode operation Synonym for packet switching.

packet mode terminal Data terminal equipment that can control, format, transmit, and receive packets. (I) (A)

packet modulo The highest sequence number the packet level uses before resetting the count and beginning the count again.

packet procedures See packet level.

packet sequence See complete packet sequence.

packet sequence number A number in the packet header by which the packet level protocol can determine whether packets have been lost. It also provides the count for the acknowledgment response.

packet sequencing A process of ensuring that packets are delivered to the receiving data terminal equipment (DTE) in the same sequence in which they were transmitted by the sending DTE. (I) (A)

packet size (1) In X.25 communications, the length of the user data in a data packet. (2) The maximum amount of user data in a packet.

packet switched data transmission service A user service that transmits and, if necessary, assembles and disassembles data in the form of packets.

packet switching (1) The process of routing and transferring data by means of addressed packets so that a channel is occupied only during transmission of a packet. On completion of the transmission, the channel is made available for transfer of other packets. (I) (2) Synonymous with packet mode operation. See also circuit switching.

packet switching data network (PSDN) A network that uses packet switching as a means of transmitting data.

packet window The maximum number of consecutive data packets that are allowed to flow between a data terminal equipment (DTE) and a data circuit-terminating equipment (DCE) before an acknowledgment is received for a given logical channel.

packing (1) The use of storage locations in a file. (2) In DPPX, the process by which data stored in the transaction data set are copied to the transmit data set. During packing, only fields flagged for transmission to the host are copied. (3) In the AIXwindows program and Enhanced X-Windows, the grouping of child objects within a parent container object. If the children are closely packed, the common distance between their borders is minimal; if they are loosely packed, the common distance border-to-border is maximized. (4) See also packing density.

packing density (1) Deprecated term for data density. (T) (2) The number of components on a given area of semiconductor material. (A)

packing factor The percentage of locations on a file that are actually used.

PAD Packet assembler/ disassembler.

pad (1) To fill unused portions of a field with dummy data, usually zeros or blanks. (2) A device that is used to introduce transmission loss into a circuit. It may be inserted to introduce loss or match impedances. (3) See also push-button dialing pad, switching pad. (4) See damping pad, key pad. See also damping pad holder.

pad character A character introduced to use up time or space while a function, usually mechanical, is being accomplished; for example, carriage return, form eject.

padding (1) Concatenating a string with one or more characters, called fillers, usually in order to achieve a specific length of the string. (T) (2) Deprecated term for filler.

padding character In COBOL, an alphanumeric character used to fill the unused character positions in a block.

paddle A device used in computer games to control the position of a cursor by moving a lever.

PAG Process access group.

page (1) In a virtual storage system, a fixed-length block that has a virtual address and is transferred as a unit between real storage and auxiliary storage. (I) (A) (2) A printed form. (3) The information displayed at the same time on the screen of a display device. (4) A defined unit of space on a storage medium. (5) In an IBM personal computer, the information displayed on a screen or printed on a single form, or the coded representation of that information that is contained in the screen buffer in memory. See active page, visual page. (6) A single side of one of the leaves of a book or the information that fills a screen or window. (7) In VSE, a fixed-length block of instructions, data, or both that can be located in processor storage or in the page data set on disk. (8) A screen in a LinkWay folder. (9) In word processing, a collection of information bound by the beginning page control and its associated page end control. (10) Each group of records in a subfile that are displayed at the same time. (11) In GDDM, a picture or chart. All specified graphics are added to the current page. An output statement always sends the current page to the device. (12) In COBOL, a vertical division of a report representing a physical separation of report data, the separation being based on internal reporting requirements, external characteristics of the reporting medium, or both. See logical page, physical page. (13) To replace the information displayed on the screen with prior or subsequent information from the same file. (14) See burst page, device page, logical page. (15) See also external page storage, page down, page up, paging, scroll.

pageable dynamic area In OS/VS, an area of virtual storage whose addresses are not identical to real addresses. It is used for programs that can be paged during execution. Synonymous with V=V dynamic area.

pageable nucleus In VM, infrequently used portions of the control program nucleus that are not normally resident in real storage.

pageable partition In OS/VS1, a subdivision of the pageable dynamic area that is allocated to a job step.

pageable region In OS/VS2, a subdivision of the pageable dynamic area that is allocated to a job step or a system task that can be paged during execution. Synonymous with V=V region.

page-at-a-time printer Synonym for page printer.

page body In COBOL, the part of a logical page in which lines can be written or spaced.

page break An embedded command that causes the end of printing on the current page and a printing restart procedure for the top of the next page. Synonymous with new page break. (T)

page buffer In the 3800 Printing Subsystem, writable control storage in which data to be printed are stored. The data are stored one line at a time until a page is complete and ready to print.

page capture The process of a data processing system receiving and storing a complete digitized image from a page scan.

page control A capability to operate one page at a time; for example, delete, skip, move, print. (T) (A)

page data The data that make up a page to be printed.

page data set (PDS) In System/370 virtual storage systems, a data set in external page storage in which pages are stored.

PAGEDEF Page definition.

page definition (PAGEDEF) (1) In AS/400 AFP support, a resource that contains the formatting controls for line data. A page definition can include controls for the number of lines per logical page, font selection, print direction, and mapping individual fields to positions on the logical page. (2) A resource, specified in the print data set JCL, that defines the rules for transforming the input to pages and text controls. (3) In the 3800 Print Management Facility, a member of a partitioned data set that contains the formatting instructions for a print data set, although it can be used for any compatible print data set. Synonymous with page map.

page depth (1) The number of lines to be printed on a page. Synonymous with page-end zone. (A) (2) Synonym for page length. (T)

page depth control (1) A control function for specifying page depth. (A) (2) Synonym for page length control. (T) (3) A control for specifying the maximum number of lines to be printed per page.

page description language A language used to specify the printed or displayed image of a document. (T)

Page Down, PgDn A key on a keyboard that a user presses to view information that is below the information that is currently visible on the screen or in a window.

page down (1) To display information below the information that is currently visible on the screen or in a window. (2) In SAA Advanced Common User Access architecture, a vertical scrolling action that displays information that follows the information that is visible in the window.

page editor An online function of SDF/CICS used to create, test, and edit SDF/CICS pages.

page end character (PE) A word processing formatting control that denotes the end of a page. Page end may be moved or ignored during text adjust mode operations. Synonymous with form feed character. See required page end character.

page-end zone Synonym for page depth. (T) (A)

page fault A program notification that occurs when an active page refers to a page that is marked as not in main storage. Synonymous with missing page interruption, page translation exception.

page fixing (1) Marking a page so that it is held in processor storage until it is explicitly released; until then, it cannot be paged out. (2) In System/370 virtual storage systems, marking a page as nonpageable so that it remains in real storage. Synonymous with page locking.

page flip A quick scroll between pages of a document or multiple one-page documents on an image display.

page footing In COBOL, a report group that is presented at the end of a report page as determined by the report writer control system.

page frame (1) In real storage, a storage location having the size of a page. (I) (A) (2) An area of main storage used to hold a page. (A)

page frame table In System/370 virtual storage systems, a table that contains an entry for each frame. Each frame table entry describes how the frame is being used.

page header Synonym for header. (T)

page heading In COBOL, a report group that is presented at the beginning of a report page as determined by the report writer control system.

page-in (1) In virtual storage systems, the process of transferring a page from external page storage to real storage. (2) The process of transferring a page from auxiliary storage to main storage. (3) In VSE, to read a page from the page data set into processor storage.

page image The electronic representation of a single-sided physical page. The bounds of a page image are determined by the electromechanical characteristics of the scanning equipment together with the image capture application specifications in the receiving data processing system.

page I/O Page-in and page-out operations.

page key In word processing, a control used to process text one page at a time. (T)

page left (1) To display information to the left of the information that is currently visible on the screen or in a window. (2) In SAA Advanced Common User Access architecture, a horizontal scrolling action that displays information preceding the information that is visible in a window.

page length The vertical dimension of the area available for printing or displaying on a screen or page. Page length is usually less than the actual paper size but it may exceed the usual paper size; for example, to create a foldout diagram. Synonymous with page depth. (T)

page length control In text processing, the capability to specify the page length. Synonymous with page depth control. (T)

page locking Synonym for page fixing.

page map Synonym for page definition.

page migration (1) In OS/VS2, the transfer of pages from a primary paging device to a secondary paging device to make more space available on the primary paging device. (2) In MVS/370, the transfer of pages from real storage to auxiliary storage. (3) In MVS/SP2 Release 1.3, the transfer of pages from real storage either to expanded storage or auxiliary storage.

page mode The mode of operation in which the 3800 Printing Subsystem can accept a page of data from a host processor to be printed on an all-points-addressable output medium. Printed data can consist of pages composed of text, images, overlays, and page segments. Contrast with compatibility mode.

page number In System/370 virtual storage systems, the part of a virtual storage address needed to refer to a page. See also frame number.

page-out (1) In virtual storage systems, transfer of a page from real storage to external page storage. (2) The transfer of a page from main storage to auxiliary storage. (3) In VSE, to write a page from processor storage into the page data set.

page pool In VSE, the set of page frames available for paging virtual mode programs.

page printer (1) A device that prints one page as a unit; for example, a COM printer, a laser printer. (I) (A) (2) In AS/400 AFP support, any of a class of printers that accepts composed pages, constructed of composed text and images, among other things. (3) Synonymous with page-at-a-time printer.

(4) Contrast with character printer, line printer. See Figure 108.

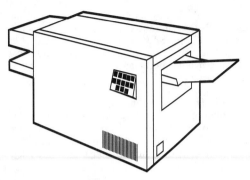

Figure 108. Page Printer

page reader A character reader whose input data is a printed text. (T)   (A)

page reclamation In OS/VS and VM, the process of making addressable the contents of a page in real storage that is waiting to be or has been paged out. Page reclamation can occur after a page fault or after a request to fix or load a page.

page right (1) To display information to the right of the information that is currently visible on the screen or in a window.   (2) In SAA Advanced Common User Access architecture, a horizontal scrolling action that displays information following the information that is visible in a window.

page scan The electromechanical process of scanning a physical page (paper) to create a bit image of the page.

page segment (1) An object that can contain text and images and be included on any addressable point on a page or electronic overlay.   It assumes the environment of an object it is included in.   (2) Library member that contains the definition of the page segment.   (3) In AS/400 AFP support, a resource object that can contain text and images and can be positioned on any addressable point on a page or an electronic overlay.   (4) Contrast with electronic overlay.

page stealing Taking away an assigned page frame from a user to make it available for another purpose.

page swapping The exchange of pages between main storage and auxiliary storage. (A)

page translation exception In MVS, a program interruption that occurs when the hardware cannot translate a virtual address because the invalid bit is set in the page table entry for that address.   Synonymous with page fault.   See also segment translation exception, translation specification exception.

page turning Synonym for paging (1).

Page Up, PgUp A key on a keyboard that a user presses to view information above the information that is currently visible on the screen or in a window.

page up (1) To display information above the information that is currently visible on the screen or in a window.   (2) In SAA Advanced Common User Access architecture, a vertical scrolling action that displays information preceding the information that is visible in a window.

page wait In OS/VS and VM, a condition in which a task or a virtual machine is placed in the wait state while a requested page is brought into real storage.

page zero In VM, storage locations zero to 4095.

paginate To number pages.

pagination In word processing, the automatic arrangement of text according to a preset number of page layout parameters. (T)

paging (1) The transfer of pages between real storage and auxiliary storage. (I) (A)   Synonymous with page turning.   (2) In System/370 virtual storage systems, the process of transferring pages between real storage and external page storage. Synonymous with page turning.   (3) In DPCX, the automatic transfer of storage blocks between the associative storage pool in processor storage and the virtual storage paging area in disk storage, and the reading of program blocks from disk or processor storage into the program area of a symbolic machine.   (4) See anticipatory paging, demand paging, logical paging.

paging activity indexes In VM/370, values that affect the algorithm used by CP in controlling the dispatching and scheduling of all active logged-on virtual machines.

paging area In VM, an area of direct access storage, and an associated area of real storage, that is used by CP for the temporary storage of pages when paging occurs.

paging device (1) An auxiliary storage device used primarily to hold pages. (A)   (2) A direct access storage device on which pages and, possibly, other data are stored.   (3) A small, pocket-size electronic device that emits an audible signal when it is energized to indicate that the owner is wanted on the phone.

paging rate In System/370 virtual storage systems, the average number of page-ins and page-outs per paging receiver.

paging supervisor In OS/VS and VM, a part of the supervisor that allocates and releases real storage space (page frames) for pages, selects the appropriate paging device, and initiates page-in and page-out operations.

paging technique A real storage allocation technique by which real storage is divided into page frames. (I) (A)

PAGTB Storage pool page table.

paint (1) In computer graphics, to shade an area of a display image; for example, with crosshatching or color. See overpaint. See Figure 109. (2) To assign colors or other forms of emphasis to display elements.

Figure 109. Paint

paired data In the AS/400 Business Graphics Utility, GDDM and System/38, data that is specified so that every X value has only one Y value associated with it. See also data group. Contrast with nonpaired data.

PA key Program access key.

PAL Phase Alternation Line.

palette In SAA Basic Common User Access architecture, a list of colors assigned to various areas on a panel. A user can change the color of these areas. See color palette, custom palette, standard palette. See also color map.

palette lookup In computer graphics, an encoding technique commonly used for color images. Instead of storing the color value of every pixel, the graphics software creates a palette that contains the colors used in the image.

palette shift In computer graphics, an undesired color change on an image caused by placing more colors on the screen than the current mode can handle; for example, more than 16 colors in VGA, or more than 256 colors in MCGA mode.

PAL format Phase alternation line format. The standard for color television in European countries except France and Russia. See NTSC format, SECAM format.

pan In multimedia applications: (1) A camera movement sideways on its stationary tripod. (2) In an audio system, left-to-right balance.

pane (1) In the AIX operating system, a display screen, a portion of a window used to present information to the user. A window can consist of one or more panes. (2) In AIX extended curses, an area of the display that shows all or part of the data contained in a presentation space associated with that pane. See active pane, fixed pane.

panel (1) In SAA Basic Common User Access architecture, a particular arrangement of information that is presented in a window or pop-up. If some of the information is not visible, a user can scroll through the information. (2) In an IBM 3791 Controller, a predefined display image contained in a panel data set. Synonymous with display panel. (3) In VSE/SP, the complete set of information shown in a single display on a display station screen. Each panel is like a manual page; scrolling back and forth through panels is like turning manual pages. See also data entry panel, selection panel. (4) A set of logically related information displayed on the screen for the purpose of communicating information to or from a computer user. (5) A formatted display of information that appears on a display screen. See help panel, task panel. (6) In computer graphics, a display image that defines the locations and characteristics of display fields on a display surface. (7) See control panel, display panel, maintenance panel, operator control panel, plasma panel.

panel area In SAA Basic Common User Access architecture, an area within a panel that contains related information. A panel area can be manipulated independently from the rest of the panel.

panel area separator In SAA Basic Common User Access architecture, a solid, dashed, or blank line that provides a visual distinction between two adjacent areas of a panel.

panel assembly The hardware parts making up an operator panel, control panel, or indicator panel.

panel body area In SAA usage, deprecated term for client area, work area.

panel data set A data set that contains predefined display images, called panels, to be displayed at display stations.

panel-definition program A program written to define one or more field-by-field panels to be stored in a panel data set.

panel element In SAA Basic Common User Access architecture, the smallest named part of a panel, such as an instruction, a selection field, an entry field, a panel title.

panel format In AS/400 query management, the format of the data in an externalized query or procedure file.

panel group In the AS/400 system, an object that contains display formats, print formats, or help information.

panel ID In SAA Basic Common User Access architecture, a panel identifier, located in the upper-left corner of a panel. A user can choose whether to display the panel ID.

panel interface A screen-oriented user interface designed to permit interactive processing. (A)

panel number A number assigned to the data record that will generate a particular display panel when the record is transmitted to a display station. The panel number is used in a program to retrieve the desired panel record from a panel data set.

panel services In DPCX, the part of application services that aids programs in creating, storing, and retrieving panels.

panel title In SAA Basic Common User Access architecture, an area at the top of a panel that identifies the information contained in the panel.

panning (1) Progressively translating an entire display image to give the visual impression of lateral movement of the image. (I) (A) (2) In computer graphics, the viewing of an image that is too large to fit on a single screen by moving from one part of the image to another.

Pantone Matching System (PMS) The system used universally for specifying colors in printing. A color defined by PMS is assigned a unique number and mixing formula, so that an artist specifying that number can be sure that the final printed product will match the chosen color.

paper bail A metal rod with a friction roller designed to hold the paper firmly against the platen above the typing position. (T)

paper break A separation of continuous form paper, usually at the perforations.

paper capacity The maximum number of sheets of paper of a specified weight that can be passed through the paper feed aperture. (T)

paper card See general-purpose paper card.

paper carrier An arrangement of components for holding and guiding paper in a machine. (T) See also moving paper carrier, stationary paper carrier.

paper cassette In a document copying machine, a container that holds a quantity of copy paper that can be fed directly into the machine. (T)

paper core In a document copying machine, the spool supporting copy. (T)

paper curl In a printer, the curve or bend of the paper. In the 3800 Printing Subsystem, some curl can be removed by using the decurl assembly on the burster-trimmer-stacker.

paper deflector A thin metal plate below the platen that guides the paper around that component. (T) See also delivery paper deflector.

paper delivery In a duplicator, the process of extracting finished copies from the machine. (T)

paper end stop In a duplicator, a device that contacts the back of the paper stack to maintain it in the proper position. (T)

paper extraction The release and removal of paper from the paper carrier on completion of a typing operation. (T) See also paper injection.

paper feed (1) On a calculator with a printing mechanism, the device for manually positioning paper according to the requirements of the operator. (T) (2) In a duplicator, the process of introducing copy paper into the machine. (T)

paper feed aperture The opening on a paper carrier through which paper is inserted and guided around the platen. (T)

paper feed mechanism An arrangement of components in the paper carrier for moving paper through the machine during the typing operation. (T)

paper feed rollers Spring-mounted rollers that hold paper tightly in contact with the platen. (T)

paper feed tray In a document copying machine, a tray that contains the paper stack. (T)

paper guide A device for setting paper in the desired position laterally on the platen. (T)

paper holder A device for holding paper close to the platen at the typing position. (T)

paper injection The insertion of paper into the paper carrier ready for typing. (T) See also paper extraction.

paper injector/extractor A control by means of which paper is fed rapidly around the platen to a pre-determined point and which may also be used to extract the paper rapidly from the machine. (T)

paper jam A condition in which paper forms have not fed properly during printing and have become wedged in the feeding or printing mechanism, thus preventing the correct forward movement of the forms. A paper jam usually causes one line to be printed over one or more other printed lines.

paper lift In a document copying machine or dupli-cator, the mechanism that automatically raises the paper stack to maintain the correct relationship between the feed mechanism and the top of the stack. (T)

paper line In the 3800 Printing Subsystem, the trans-port assembly. When the feature is installed and in use, it includes the burster-trimmer-stacker.

paper origin The left corner of the edge of a form that is fed through a printer.

paper path The path that paper is intended to take through a printer.

paper platform In a duplicator, the tray or platform on which the paper stack is supported. (T) Synony-mous with feedboard.

paper registration (1) In the 3800 Printing Sub-system, the position of the sheet-length perforations relative to reference points on the input ramp and the fuser station. (2) The relationship between printed output and the preprinted form of a forms overlay image.

paper release On a typewriter, a control permitting the paper to be moved freely in the paper carrier, independently of the paper feed mechanism. (T)

paper side guides In a document copying machine or duplicator, the components that contact the sides of the paper stack to maintain it in position. (T)

paper skip The movement of paper through a print mechanism at a speed effectively greater than that of individual single line spacing. Synonymous with paper throw, paper slew. (T)

paper slew Synonym for paper skip. (T) (A)

paper stack In a document copying machine or dupli-cator, a pile of paper on which copies will be produced and from which the paper feed mechanism is supplied. (T)

paper support A cover plate behind the platen that supports paper during insertion into the machine. (T)

paper tape Deprecated term for punch tape.

paper tape code (1) Deprecated term for punch tape code. (2) Synonym for perforated tape code.

paper tape reader A device that senses and translates the holes in perforated tape into electrical signals.

paper throw Synonym for paper skip. (T) (A)

paragraph (1) In word processing, one or more sen-tences that may be preceded by or followed by an appropriate indicator. (2) In the COBOL Procedure Division, a paragraph-name followed by a separator period and by zero, one, or more than one sentence. In the Identification and Environment Divisions, a par-agraph header followed by zero, one, or more than one entries. See file control, i-o-control, object-computer, source-computer, special-names.

paragraph control In text processing, a capability to process text one paragraph at a time; for example, skip, move, delete, print. (T) (A)

paragraph header In COBOL, a reserved word, fol-lowed by the separator period, that indicates the begin-ning of a paragraph in the Identification and Environment Divisions.

paragraph indent In text processing, a program instruction that indents one or more lines of a para-graph a preset number of characters or a preset dis-tance. (T) (A)

paragraph key In word processing, a control used to process text one paragraph at a time. (T)

paragraph-name (1) A programmer-defined word that identifies and precedes a paragraph. (2) In COBOL, a user-defined word that identifies and begins a paragraph in the Procedure Division.

parallax A condition that occurs when a gap exists between the locator position and the displayed trail resulting from writing with the pen. Parallax differs in both the horizontal and vertical views by how a user looks at the display.

parallel (1) Pertaining to a process in which all events occur within the same interval of time, each handled by a separate but similar functional unit; for example, the parallel transmission of the bits of a computer word along the lines of an internal bus. (T) (2) Pertaining to concurrent or simultaneous operation of two or more devices or to concurrent performance of two or more activities in a single device. (A) (3) Pertaining to concurrent or simultaneous occurrence of two or more related activities in multiple devices or channels. (A) (4) Pertaining to the simultaneity of two or more processes. (A) (5) Pertaining to the simultaneous processing of the individual parts of a whole, such as the bits of a character and the characters of a word, using separate facilities for the various parts. (A) (6) Contrast with serial.

parallel adder (1) An adder in which addition is performed simultaneously on all corresponding digit places of the operands. (T) (A) (2) Contrast with serial adder.

parallel addition Addition that is performed in parallel on digits in all corresponding digit places of the operands. (T)

parallel channel A channel having a System/360 and System/370 channel-to-control-unit I/O interface that uses bus-and-tag cables as a transmission medium. Contrast with ESCON channel.

parallel computer (1) A computer having multiple arithmetic or logic units that are used to accomplish parallel operations or parallel processing. (A) (2) Contrast with serial computer.

parallel data adapter A classification of transmission adapter used with the 2701 Data Adapter Unit in data acquisition and control. A circuit is provided for each bit in the code structure.

parallel device A device that can perform two or more concurrent activities. Contrast with serial device.

parallel DL/I In IMS/VS, a facility that permits all database calls to be processed in each message processing region or batch message processing region.

parallel extended routes In an ACF/TCAM extended network, multiple extended routes between a pair of host nodes. See also alternate extended route, extended route, primary extended route, route.

parallel links In SNA, two or more links between adjacent subarea nodes.

parallel operation (1) A processing mode in which operations are performed either concurrently in a single device, or concurrently or simultaneously in two or more devices. (I) (A) (2) Contrast with serial operation.

parallel port An access point through which a computer transmits or receives data that consists of several bits sent simultaneously on separate wires. Contrast with serial port.

parallel processing (1) The concurrent or simultaneous execution of two or more processes in a single unit. (A) (2) Contrast with serial processing. (3) See coarse-grain parallel processing, fine-grain parallel processing.

parallel processor architecture Computer architecture that uses many interconnected processors to access large amounts of data and to simultaneously process a large number of tasks at speeds far exceeding those of conventional computers. See also hypercube.

Note: "Fine-grain" parallel computers may use thousands of processors, usually in the range of 1024 to 256,000. "Medium-grain" parallel computers have about 32 to 1024 processors. "Coarse grain" parallel computers usually have 2 to 16 processors. Connectivity among processors varies considerably; many have connections only among neighboring processors.

parallel run (1) Operation of two information processing systems, a given one and its intended replacement, with the same application and source data, for comparison and confidence. (T) (2) A test run of a new or an altered data processing system with the same source data that is used in another system; the other system is considered as the standard of comparison. (A)

parallel search storage A storage device in which one or more parts of all storage locations are queried simultaneously. (A)

parallel-serial converter Synonym for serializer. (T)

parallel sessions Two or more concurrently active sessions between the same two network accessible units (NAUs) using different pairs of network addresses or local-form session identifiers. Each session can have independent session parameters.

parallel storage Storage device where digits, characters or words are accessed simultaneously or concurrently. (A)

parallel terminal A data terminal that transmits all components of a data character simultaneously. Contrast with serial terminal.

parallel-to-serial converter Synonym for serializer.

parallel transmission (1) The simultaneous transmission of the group representing a character or other entity of data. (I) (2) In data communication, the simultaneous transmission of a certain number of signal elements constituting the same telegraph or data signal; for example, use of a code according to which each signal is characterized by a combination of three out of twelve frequencies that are simultaneously transmitted over the channel. (A) (3) Contrast with serial transmission.

parallel transmission groups The multiple transmission groups (TGs) connecting two adjacent nodes.

parameter (1) A variable that is given a constant value for a specified application and that may denote the application. (I) (A) (2) In SAA Basic Common User Access architecture, a variable used in conjunction with a command to affect its result. (3) An item in a menu for which the user specifies a value or for which the system provides a value when the menu is interpreted. (4) Data passed between programs or procedures. (5) In Pascal, a value supplied to a command, program, or routine that is used either as input or to control the actions of the command, program, or routine. (6) In SQL, a keyword and value that further define an SQL precompiler command or an SQL statement. See also keyword. (7) See actual parameter, external program parameter, formal parameter, kernel parameter, keyword parameter, positional parameter, preset parameter, program-generated parameter, required parameter, symbolic parameter, type parameter.

parameter association In programming languages, the association of formal parameters with the corresponding actual parameters that are specified by a procedure call. (I)

parameter list A list of values that provides a means of associating addressability of data defined in a called program with data in the calling program. It contains parameter names and the order in which they are to be associated in the calling and called program.

parameter marker In SQL, a question mark (?) that appears in a statement string of a dynamic SQL statement in which a host variable could appear if the statement string were a static SQL statement. See also dynamic SQL, static SQL.

parameters In NETDA/2, the set of restrictions that affect only the output of a network design. A change in a parameter value does not change the input to the network design. Contrast with constraints.

parameter word A word that directly or indirectly provides or designates one or more parameters. (I) (A)

parent (1) In the AIX operating system, a process that has spawned a child process using the fork primitive. (2) In the AIXwindows program and Enhanced X-Windows, a graphical object that controls one or more smaller graphical objects attached to it. The smaller graphical objects are called children; they are automatically deleted when their parent is deleted.

parent class A class from which another class inherits.

parent device In the AIX operating system, the device to which another device is connected; for example, the parent device of a small computer systems interface (SCSI) disk may be an SCSI.

parent directory (1) In VM, the directory for a CMS disk that has a disk extension defined for it via the ACCESS command. (2) The directory one level above the current directory.

parent environment In DPPX, an environment whose resources can be shared or exclusively used by its sub-environments.

Note: Resources that are used exclusively by a sub-environment are no longer available to the parent environment.

parenthesis-free notation Synonym for prefix notation.

parent node A node to which one or more other nodes are subordinate.

parent of an alias In FORTRAN, the data object or subobject with which an alias appears in an IDENTIFY statement.

parent process In the OS/2 operating system, a process that creates other processes. Contrast with child process.

parent resource (1) In System/36, pertaining to a secured resource, either a file or library, whose user list is shared with one or more other files or libraries. Contrast with child resource. (2) In the NetView Graphic Monitor Facility, a resource that has one or more child resources below it in a hierarchy.

parent segment In a database, a segment that has one or more dependent segments below it in a hierarchy. See also child segment.

parent window In some operating systems, the window that controls the size and location of its children. If a window has children, it is a parent window.

parity A data transmission attribute used to ensure error-free transmission.

parity bit (1) A binary digit appended to a group of binary digits to make the sum of all the digits, including the appended binary digit, either odd or even as preestablished. (T) (2) A check bit appended to an array of binary digits to make the sum of all the binary digits, including the check bit, always odd or always even. (A) See Figure 110.

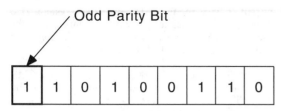

Figure 110. Parity Bit

parity check (1) A redundancy check by which a recalculated parity bit is compared to the pregiven parity bit. (T) (2) A check that tests whether the number of ones (or zeros) in an array of binary digits is odd or even. (A) (3) Synonymous with odd-even check. (4) See longitudinal parity check, transverse parity check.

parity error A transmission error that occurs when the received data does not have the parity expected by the receiving system. A parity error is usually caused by the sending and receiving systems having different parity settings.

parse (1) In systems with time sharing, to analyze the operands entered with a command and create a parameter list for the command processor from the information. (2) In REXX, to split a string into parts, using function calls or by using a parsing template on the ARG, PARSE, or PULL instructions.

parser (1) In personal computer games, software that interprets a player's responses and makes user input in the form of English language sentences understandable to the computer. (2) A program that interprets user input and determines what to do with the input.

partial carry (1) In parallel addition, a procedure in which some or all of the carries are stored temporarily instead of being transferred immediately. (I) (A) (2) Contrast with complete carry.

partial journal receiver In System/38, a journal receiver saved while it is attached to a journal. The

saved version of a partial journal receiver does not, therefore, contain all the journal entries in the attached journal receiver.

partially qualified name A qualified name that is incomplete, that is, one that includes the name of the member itself, as well as one or more, but not all, names in the hierarchical sequence above the structure member to which the partially qualified name refers.

partial page In the 3800 Printing Subsystem, a page that does not contain all the intended data. Partial pages can be printed after an error is sensed.

partial-write operation In DPCX, the process of automatically sending part of the data stream in the I/O blocks to its destination and releasing the I/O blocks.

partition (1) A fixed-size division of storage. See main storage partition, virtual partition. (2) In VSE, a division of the virtual address area that is available for program execution. (3) On an IBM personal computer hard disk, one of four possible storage areas of variable size; one may be accessed by DOS and each of the others may be assigned to another operating system. (4) Deprecated term for segment (1) and (2). (5) Synonymous with side.

partition balancing See dynamic partition balancing.

partitioned access method See basic partitioned access method.

partitioned data set (PDS) A data set in direct access storage that is divided into partitions, called members, each of which can contain a program, part of a program, or data. Synonymous with program library.

partitioned emulation programming extension A function of a network control program that enables a communication controller to operate some telecommunication lines in network control mode while simultaneously operating others in emulation mode.

partitioned mode An operating mode of the Model 65 Multiprocessing System in which main storage, control units, auxiliary storage units, and input/output devices are apportioned between the two processing units, which operate as separate and distinct systems. See also multisystem mode.

partition identifier In the 3270 data stream, a 1-byte code assigned to a partition by the Create Partition structured field to identify the partition. It identifies the presentation space, window, and viewport from which the partition is constructed.

partner In data communications, the remote application program or the remote computer.

partner-LU verification For logical unit (LU) 6.2, an exchange between two LUs with each LU using an LU-LU password and the Data Encryption Standard (DES) algorithm. See also end-user verification.

partner systems In an IMS/VS multisystem environment, two IMS/VS online systems that are connected by a multiple systems coupling (MSC) link.

party In telephony, an addressable end point of a telephone call. See also virtual party.

PASA Program automatic storage area.

Pascal (1) (Pa) The pressure of stress that results when a force of one newton (N) is applied evenly and perpendicularly to an area of one square meter (m^2). (2) A high-level, general-purpose programming language, related to ALGOL. Programs written in Pascal are block structured, consisting of independent routines. They can run on different computers with little or no modification.

Note: A Pascal program is compiled in two stages. The first stage compilation produces p-code, which is computer-independent. The second compilation translates p-code into machine instructions for the particular computer on which the program is to run.

pass (1) One cycle of processing a body of data. (A) (2) See sort pass.

pass-by-CONST In XL Pascal, the parameter-passing mechanism by which the address of a variable is passed to the called routine. The called routine is not permitted to modify the formal parameter. Synonymous with pass-by-read-only-reference.

pass-by-read-only-reference Synonym for pass-by-CONST.

pass-by-read/write-reference Synonym for pass-by-VAR.

pass-by-value In XL Pascal, the parameter-passing mechanism by which a copy of the value of the actual parameter is passed to the called routine. If the called routine modifies the formal parameter, the corresponding actual parameter is not affected.

pass-by-VAR In XL Pascal, the parameter-passing mechanism by which the address of a variable is passed to the called routine. If the called routine modifies the formal parameter, the corresponding actual parameter is also changed. Synonymous with pass-by-read/write-reference.

passed data set A data set allocated to a job step that is not deallocated at step termination but remains available to a subsequent step in the same job.

passive component In an ESCON environment, any link component that does not contain electronic logic; for example, a splice, connector, adapter, coupler, distribution panel, or optical cable. Contrast with active device.

passive gateway A gateway that does not exchange routing information. Contrast with active gateway. See also external gateway, interior gateway, neighbor gateway.

passive grab In Enhanced X-Windows, grabbing a key or button. The grab becomes an active grab when the key or button is pressed. Contrast with active grab. See also button grabbing, key grabbing, keyboard grabbing, pointer grabbing, server grabbing.

passive graphics A mode of operation of a display device that does not allow an online user to alter or interact with a display image. Contrast with interactive graphics.

passive mode In computer graphics, a mode of operation of a display device that does not allow an online user to alter or interact with a display image.

passive open In TCP/IP, the state of a connection that is prepared to provide a service on demand. Contrast with active open.

passive station (1) On a multipoint connection or a point-to-point connection using basic mode link control, any tributary station waiting to be polled or selected. (I) (2) A station that, at a given instant, cannot send messages to or receive messages from the control station. (3) A station in listening mode.

passive wiretapping In computer security, wiretapping to monitor or record data. Contrast with active wiretapping.

pass key Synonym for privacy key. (A)

pass-through (1) To gain access to another network. (2) See display station pass-through.

passthrough function The ability to pass data through a program transparently, without alteration.

passthrough simulation In TPNS, the role TPNS performs of a packet switching network, allowing communication between data terminal equipment (DTEs).

passthrough virtual circuit In TPNS, a virtual circuit on which TPNS performs the role of a packet switching network, and does not simulate either of the data terminal equipment (DTEs).

password (1) A value used in authentication or a value used to establish membership in a set of people having specific privileges. (2) A unique string of characters known to a computer system and to a user, who must specify the character string to gain access to a system and to the information stored within it. (3) In computer security, a string of characters known to the computer system and a user, who must specify it to gain full or limited access to a system and to the data stored within it. (4) See BIND password, communication authority password.

password change interval In computer security, the duration of a password's validity.

password security In computer security, the prevention of unauthorized use of a system, device, or program by checking user passwords. See also information security.

password-selection controls Restrictions on user's selection of their own passwords.

paste To copy a page, object, or picture into an existing folder or picture. See cut and paste.

Paste In SAA Common User Access architecture, a choice in the Edit pull-down that a user selects to move the contents of the clipboard into a preselected location.

patch (1) To modify an object module, a load module, or a loaded computer program. The modification is usually a temporary or expedient one. (T) (2) A temporary electrical connection. (A) (3) To modify a routine in a rough or expedient way. (I) (4) To modify an object program without recompiling the source program. (A) (5) In the 3800 Printing Subsystem, an irregular background or an area on a sheet where print is missing. (6) To change the contents of a file or library member.

patch cable In the IBM Cabling System, a length of type 6 cable with data connectors on both ends.

patch panel Synonym for distribution panel.

path (1) The route used to locate files; the storage location of a file. A fully qualified path lists the drive identifier, directory name, subdirectory name (if any), and file name with the associated extension. (2) In a network, any route between any two nodes. A path may include more than one branch. (T) (3) The series of transport network components (path control and data link control) that are traversed by the information exchanged between two network accessible units. See also explicit route (ER), route extension, and virtual route (VR). (4) In VTAM, when defining a switched major node, a potential dial-out port that

can be used to reach that node. (5) In the NetView/PC program, a complete line in a configuration that contains all of the resources in the service point command service (SPCS) query link configuration request list. (6) In a database, a sequence of segment occurrences from the root segment to an individual segment. (7) In VSAM, a named, logical entity providing access to the records of a base cluster either directly or through an alternate index. (8) In an online IMS/VS system, the route a message takes from the time it is originated through processing. In a multisystem environment, the route can include more than one IMS/VS system. (9) In the InfoExplorer program, the list of articles that were followed to get to the article that is currently displayed. (10) See access path, authorized path, logical link path, overlay path, read path.

path block In the NetView/PC program, a block of storage that contains the link connection component (LCC) information for all LCCs in one path.

path control (PC) The function that routes message units between network accessible units in the network and provides the paths between them. It converts the basic information units (BIUs) from transmission control (possibly segmenting them) into path information units (PIUs) and exchanges basic transmission units containing one or more PIUs with data link control. Path control differs by node type: some nodes (APPN nodes, for example) use locally generated session identifiers for routing, and others (subarea nodes) use network addresses for routing.

path control network Synonym for transport network.

path information unit (PIU) In SNA, a message unit consisting of a transmission header (TH) alone, or a TH followed by a basic information unit (BIU) or a BIU segment.

path name In the AIX operating system, a file name specifying all directories leading to the file. See full path name, relative path name.

path segment In the NetView/PC program, the portion of a path between two resources that are listed consecutively in the service point command service (SPCS) query link configuration request list.

path switch In ACF/TCAM, a field in the option table that determines whether a given subgroup is to be executed for a message.

path test A test provided by the NetView program that enables a network operator to determine whether a path is available between two LUs that are currently in session.

pattern (1) A recognizable shape, form, or configuration. (2) In computer graphics, a combination of toned and untoned picture elements (pels) that make up an image. (3) A regular expression or series of regular expressions that define a search pattern. (4) In AIX graphics, a 16x16, 32x32, or 64x64 array of bits defining the texturing of polygons on the system display.

pattern handling statement An executable statement that is used to specify a pattern to be found in text, and the action to be taken when it is found or not found; for example, replace all occurrences of "neither ... nor" with "either ... or." (T)

pattern matching The identifying of one of a predetermined set of items which has the closest resemblance to a given object, by comparing its coded representation against the representations of all the items. (T)

pattern-matching character A special character such as an asterisk (*) or a question mark (?) that can be used to represent one or more characters. Any character or set of characters can replace a pattern-matching character. Synonymous with global character, wildcard character.

pattern recognition The identification of shapes, forms, or configurations by automatic means. (I) (A)

pattern-sensitive fault (1) A fault that appears in response to a particular pattern of data. (A) (2) Contrast with data-sensitive fault, program-sensitive fault.

pattern strings In the AIX operating system, strings of regular expressions composed of special pattern-matching characters. The pattern strings can be used in addresses to specify lines and, in some subcommands, portions of a line.

pause (1) In multimedia applications, to temporarily halt the medium. Paused video remains displayed, but no audio is played. (2) In the PenPM operating system extension, an action where the pen remains motionless for an interval of time while it is in the proximity zone or touching a touch-sensitive surface. This interval of time starts a new action (for example, mouse-emulation mode).

Pause A key on a keyboard that a user presses to interrupt an operation temporarily.

pause instruction An instruction that specifies suspension of execution of a computer program. A pause instruction is usually not an exit. (I) (A) Synonymous with halt instruction. See optional pause instruction.

pause-retry A network control program option that allows a user to specify the number of times a program should try to retransmit data after a transmission error occurs, and how long the delay should be between successive attempts.

pause time An amount of time a user must pause with a pen before the system switches to a different input mode. See gesture mode, mouse-emulation mode. See also pause.

PAV Program activation vector.

PAX Private automatic exchange.

PBX Private branch exchange.

PC (1) Personal computer. (2) Path control. (3) Photoconductor. (4) Programming change.

PCB Pool control block.

PCB mask In IMS/VS, a data structure in an application program into which the IMS/VS DL/I puts the status of the application program's DL/I calls.

PC board A panel made of insulating material with semiconductor circuitry on one or both sides in the form of microchips. See also bubble board, daughterboard, expansion board, motherboard, multi-function board. See also short card.

PCD (1) Partition control descriptor. (2) Preconfigured definition.

PC-DOS See IBM Disk Operating System.

PCE (1) Processing and control element. (2) Procedure control expression.

PCF Primary control field.

PC gap In the 3800, an opening in the drum surface of about two inches through which the photoconductor is fed. See also gap seal.

PCI Program controlled interruption.

PCID Procedure-correlation identifier.

PCM (1) Pulse code modulation. (A) (2) Punched card machine. (A)

PC network A low-cost, broadband network that allows attached IBM personal computers to communicate and share resources.

PCS (1) Print contrast signal. (A) (2) Programmable character set.

PC session A session that uses PC-DOS, the OS/2 operating system, and other IBM programs on a personal computer attached to a mainframe.

PC Support asynchronous communications In the AS/400 system, the support that connects a personal computer to the ASCII Work Station Controller.

PC Support program diskettes In the AS/400 system, the diskettes that contain the support programs for a personal computer attached to an AS/400 system.

PCT (1) Partition control table. (2) Program Control table.

PDA Physical device address.

PDAID Problem determination aid.

PDB Pool descriptor block.

PDD Physical device driver.

PDF Parallel data field.

PDIR Peripheral data set information record.

PDN Public data network.

PDS (1) Partitioned data set. (2) Page data set.

PDU Protocol data unit.

PE Page end character.

peak In OCR, an extraneous mark extending outward from a character past the stroke edge of the character.

pedestal up/down In multimedia applications, a camera movement upward or downward on a boom.

peer (1) In network architecture, any functional unit that is in the same layer as another entity. (T) (2) A corresponding node or entity.

peer entities In Open Systems Interconnection architecture, entities in the same or different open systems that are in the same layer. (T)

peer-to-peer communication Pertaining to data communications between two nodes that have equal status in the interchange. Either node can begin the conversation. See also LU-LU session type 6.2.

peer-to-peer networking See Advanced Peer-to-Peer Networking (APPN).

pel Picture element.

pel density The number of picture elements per unit of linear measurement. See also resolution.

PEL matrix In computer graphics, a two-dimensional array of encoded points.

pel size The dimensions of a toned area at a picture element.

PEM Program execution monitor.

pen A pointing and input device used with a touch-sensitive device.

pen-aware programs Programs that are written or modified to use a pen or a finger as the standard input device rather than a keyboard or a mouse.

pending active session In VTAM, the state of an LU-LU session recorded by the system services control point (SSCP) when it finds both logical units (LUs) available and has sent a CINIT request to the primary logical unit (PLU) of the requested session.

Pending Modify table The Object Distribution Manager DB2 table that contains information concerning objects to be modified through the scanning process.

pending queue In DPPX, a forward-chained list of all threads added to a priority level since the scheduler for that level last referred to its queues.

penetration In computer security, unauthorized access to a system. See also attack.

Note: Penetration may be achieved by simple or inadvertent means.

pen-unaware programs Programs that are written to use a keyboard or a mouse and are not written to use a pen.

PEP Partitioned emulation programming.

PER Program event recording.

percentage function In a calculator, the function that automatically multiplies two entered numbers, one of which is understood to be a percentage, and divides the results by one hundred. (T)　(A)

percolation In error recovery, the passing along a preestablished path of control from a recovery routine to a higher-level recovery routine.

PERFM Performance.

perforated litho master In a duplicator, an offset litho master with a row of regularly spaced holes along its top and bottom edges. (T)

perforated tape (1) A tape on which a pattern of holes or cuts is used to represent data. (A) (2) Synonym for punched tape.

perforated tape code (1) A code used to represent data on perforated tape. (A)   (2) Synonymous with paper tape code.

perforated-tape reader (1) A device that converts holes or cuts in perforated tape into coded electrical pulse patterns. (A)   (2) Synonym for punched tape reader.

perforation A linear series of cuts that are unconnected in continuous forms paper. The perforation delineates either a fold or page boundary. See also cut-to-tie ratio, tie.

perforator (1) A device that punches holes or cuts in a recording medium such as paper tape. (2) See receiving perforator.

performance One of the two major factors, together with facility, on which the total productivity of a system depends. Performance is largely determined by a combination of throughput, response time, and availability.

performance class In the NetView program, a description of an objective or commitment of performance. It consists of a performance class name, boundary definitions, response time definition, response time ranges, and response time percentage objectives. Sessions may be assigned performance classes.

performance error Synonym for temporary error.

performance group A class, specified by an installation, that regulates the turnaround time of a user's jobs, job steps, and interactions.

performance monitor In the AS/400 system, a function of the operating system that observes system and device activity, and records these observations in a database file.

performance objective A category of information contained in an installation performance specification. Each performance objective specifies the service rate that an associated job is to receive for a number of different workload levels.

performance option In VM, one or more functions that can be assigned to a virtual machine to improve its performance, response time (if terminal-oriented), or throughput.

period definition In the system resources manager, a category of information contained in a performance group definition that indicates the performance objective that is to be followed, either during a real-time period or until a particular amount of service has been accumulated by an associated job.

peripheral Pertaining to an operation or to a device such as a stand-alone hard disk or a streaming tape drive that is used to support the primary operations of a computer.

peripheral border node A border node that interconnects adjacent APPN networks having different network identifiers in order to support LU-LU sessions that have one partner LU in its native network. Contrast with extended border node.

peripheral control unit Synonym for input/output controller.

peripheral data set information record In System/36 and System/38, a record that describes the format of printed output.

peripheral device Any device that can communicate with a particular computer; for example, input/output units, auxiliary storage. (T)

peripheral equipment (1) Any device that is controlled by and can communicate with a particular computer; for example, input/output units, auxiliary storage. (T)   (2) A functional unit that provides services external to a processing unit. Synonymous with peripheral device.

peripheral host node A node that provides an application program interface (API) for running application programs but does not provide SSCP functions and is not aware of the network configuration. The peripheral host node does not provide subarea node services. It has boundary function provided by its adjacent subarea. See also boundary function, boundary node, host node, node type, peripheral node, subarea host node, subarea node.

peripheral link In SNA, a link that connects a peripheral node to a subarea node. See also route extension (REX), subarea link.

peripheral logical unit (LU) In SNA, a logical unit in a peripheral node.

peripheral LU Peripheral logical unit.

peripheral node A node that uses local addresses for routing and therefore is not affected by changes in network addresses. A peripheral node requires boundary-function assistance from an adjacent subarea node. A peripheral node can be a type 1, 2.0, or 2.1 node connected to a subarea boundary node.

peripheral path control The function in a peripheral node that routes message units between units with local addresses and provides the paths between them. See also boundary function, path control, peripheral node, subarea node, subarea path control.

peripheral physical unit (PU) In SNA, a physical unit in a peripheral node.

peripheral PU Peripheral physical unit.

peripheral transfer The process of transmitting data between two peripheral units. (I)   (A)

peripheral unit (1) With respect to a particular processing unit, any equipment that can communicate directly with that unit. (A)   (2) Synonym for peripheral device.

permanent error (1) An error that cannot be eliminated by retrying an operation. (2) An error that can be corrected only by external intervention. (3) An error that cannot be resolved by error recovery programs. Contrast with temporary error.

permanent file A file retained from one initial program load until the next. Contrast with temporary file.

permanently resident volume A volume that cannot be physically demounted or that cannot be demounted until it is varied offline, that is, removed from control of the processing unit.

permanent memory See nonvolatile memory, read-only memory.

permanent object In the AS/400 system, an object, such as a database file or a program, that stays in the system until a user with the required authority deletes it.

permanent read/write error An error that cannot be eliminated by retrying a read/write operation.

permanent storage (1) A storage device that is non-erasable. (T)   (2) In a personal computer, storage on auxiliary storage devices such as diskettes and cassettes. (3) Contrast with erasable storage. (4) Synonym for read-only storage. (5) See also non-volatile storage.

permanent virtual circuit (PVC) In X.25 and frame-relay communications, a virtual circuit that has a logical channel permanently assigned to it at each

data terminal equipment (DTE). Call-establishment protocols are not required. Contrast with switched virtual circuit (SVC).

permissible action In a conceptual schema language, an action conforming to specified rules or constraints that changes a presumably consistent collection of sentences into a consistent one or makes known a consistent one present in the information base or conceptual schema. (T)

permission Synonym for access right. See access permission, base permission, extended permission.

permission code In the AIX operating system, a three-digit octal code or a nine-letter alphabetic code that indicates access permissions. The access permissions are read, write, and run. See also access permission.

permission field In the AIX operating system, one of the three-character fields within the permissions column of a directory list. The permission field indicates the read, write, and run permissions for the file or directory owner, for the group, and for all others.

permissions In the AIX operating system, codes that determine how a file can be used by any users who work on the system.

permit In packet switching, an authorization sent on a logical channel to transmit one or more data packets in the reverse direction.

permit count At the interface between a data terminal equipment (DTE) and a data circuit-terminating equipment (DCE), the difference between the number of data packets transmitted in a particular direction since establishment or last reset of a virtual circuit and the number of permits in the reverse direction.

permit packet At the interface between a data terminal equipment (DTE) and a data circuit-terminating equipment (DCE), a packet used to transmit permits over a virtual circuit.

permutation (1) An ordered arrangement of a given number of different elements selected from a set. (I)   (A)   (2) Contrast with combination.

perpendicular magnetic recording A technique of magnetic recording in which magnetic polarities representing data is aligned perpendicularly to the plane of recording surface. Synonymous with vertical magnetic recording. (T)

per-process data area In AIX kernel mode, a portion of the user process stack segment. This area is paged with the process and it contains process information such as the current directory of files opened by the process or input in I/O mode. This information occupies the top of the stack segment. See also user block.

persistence The length of time required for the light from a phosphor on a display screen to fade. See also phosphor.

persistent session In the NetView program, a network management session that remains active even though there is no activity on the session for a specified period of time.

personal code A code that identifies a user to a computer system. See also password.

personal computer (PC) (1) A microcomputer primarily intended for stand-alone use by an individual. (T) (2) A desk-top, floor-standing, or portable microcomputer that usually consists of a system unit, a display monitor, a keyboard, one or more diskette drives, internal fixed-disk storage, and an optional printer. PCs are designed primarily to give independent computing power to a single user and are inexpensively priced for purchase by individuals or small businesses. See also desktop computer, laptop computer, mainframe, microcomputer, minicomputer, portable computer, supermini.

personal document A document that is intended to be handled only by its owner or by someone who knows the personal document password specified by the owner.

perspective projection A graphical technique used to achieve realism when drawing primitives. In a perspective projection, the lines of projection meet at the viewpoint; thus, the size of a primitive varies inversely with its distance from the source projection. The farther a primitive or part of a primitive is from the viewer, the smaller it will be drawn. This effect, known as perspective foreshortening, is similar to the effect achieved by photography and by the human visual system. See also orthographic projection.

peta Two to the fiftieth power.

PF key Programmed function key.

PFM Program fault management.

PFT Page frame table.

PGB Presentation services global block.

PgDn See Page Down.

PGF Presentation graphics feature.

PG indicator See program-mode indicator.

PGR Presentation graphics routines.

PgUp See Page Up.

PH Phase. Also shown by the Greek letter omega (Ω).

phantom circuit A superimposed circuit derived from two side circuits, suitably arranged pairs of wires with each pair being a circuit that acts as one conductor of the phantom circuit.

phantom hyphen Synonym for soft hyphen. (T)

phase (1) A distinct part of a process in which related operations are performed. (2) A part of a sort/merge program; for example, sort phase, merge phase. (3) A part of a data call. See data transfer phase, network control phase. (4) In VSE, the smallest complete unit of executable code that can be loaded into virtual storage. (5) See assembly phase, compile phase, execute phase, translate phase.

Phase Alternation Line (PAL) The television broadcast standard for European video outside of France and the countries of the former Soviet Union.

phase coherent FSK Frequency shift keying where the two signaling frequencies are integrally related to the data rate and transitions between the signaling frequencies are made at zero crossings of the carrier waveform. (T)

phase continuous FSK Frequency shift keying where the transition between signaling frequencies is accomplished by a continuous change of frequency (as opposed to the discontinuous replacement of one frequency by another, such as might be accomplished by a switch); thus, it is also a form of frequency modulation. (T)

phase distortion See distortion.

phase encoding (1) Encoding in which the phase of the wave is used to encode digital data; for example, Manchester encoding. (T) (2) Synonym for phase modulation recording.

phase jitter A form of perturbation that causes intermittent variations of the phase of signals. (T)

phase modulation Modulation that varies the phase angle of a sinusoidal carrier from a reference carrier phase angle by an amount proportional to the instantaneous amplitude of the modulating signal.

phase modulation recording A magnetic recording in which each storage cell is divided into two regions that are magnetized in opposite senses. The sequence of these senses indicates whether the binary character represented is zero or one. (I) (A) Synonymous with phase encoding. See Figure 111.

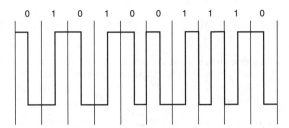

Figure 111. Phase Modulation Recording

phase shift keying (PSK) A form of phase modulation in which a digital modulating signal varies the output phase between a fixed number of predetermined values. (T)

PHIGS Programmers' Hierarchical Interactive Graphics System. An ANSI and ISO standard. PHIGS defines an application programming interface designed for interactive two-dimensional and three-dimensional graphics applications using retained data structures.

phone list A list of phone numbers to be called using a communication program and the autocall or X.25 feature.

phosphor On a display screen, one of the three colored dots—red, green, and blue, respectively—that make up each pixel. The intensity of the phosphors define the color of the pixel.

photocomposer A nonimpact printer that produces high quality text by means of a photographic process.

photoconductor (PC) A medium for transferring images to paper.

photoconductor gap In the 3800 Printing Subsystem, an opening on the drum surface through which the photoconductor is wrapped from the supply spool inside the drum, around the drum, and back through the opening on the drum surface to the takeup spool. The gap is sealed after the photoconductor is in place.

photographic document copying machine A document copying machine that uses the silver process. (T)

photoreceptor The element in an electrostatic document copying machine that is sensitive to light and on which the latent electrostatic image is formed. (T)

phototypesetter (1) A nonimpact printer that creates characters through photography. Synonymous with photocomposer. (T) (A) (2) A typesetting machine that operates by projecting light through film matrices

of the type characters upon light-sensitive paper or film.

phrase In COBOL, an ordered set of one or more consecutive COBOL character-strings that form a portion of a COBOL procedural statement or of a COBOL clause. See conditional phrase.

physical (1) Pertaining to actual implementation or location as opposed to conceptual content or meaning. (A) (2) Pertaining to the representation and storage of data on a medium such as magnetic disk, or to a description of data that depends on physical factors such as length of data elements, records, or pointers. (A) (3) Contrast with logical. (A)

physical access control In computer security, the use of physical mechanisms, rather than information-related mechanisms to provide access control. Contrast with logical access control.

physical access level Access to a data set by block, which may consist of one or more physical records.

physical block See block.

physical child In an IMS/VS database, a segment that is dependent on a segment at the next higher level in the database hierarchy. All segments except the root segment are physical child segments because each is dependent on at least the root. See also logical child.

physical circuit A circuit established without multiplexing. See also data circuit. Contrast with virtual circuit.

physical connection (1) A connection that establishes an electrical circuit. (2) In VTAM, a point-to-point connection or multipoint connection. (3) See also physical level (X.25).

physical-contact connector In an ESCON environment, an optical fiber connector type having a polished end face that aligns precisely with its receptacle, thereby providing an extremely low-loss junction point. Contrast with non-physical-contact connector.

physical control layer In SNA, the layer that provides a physical interface for any transmission medium to which it is attached. This layer defines the electrical and transmission (signaling) characteristics needed to establish, maintain, and terminate physical connections.

physical database In an IMS/VS database, an ordered set of physical database records.

physical database record In an IMS/VS database, a physical set of hierarchically related segments of one or more segment types.

physical database record occurrence In an IMS/VS database, an instance of a root segment and the hierarchical arrangement of all its dependent segment occurrences.

physical data block See block.

physical data structure (1) In a database, the form in which data is stored on storage media. (2) In IMS/VS, a hierarchy that represents segment types and the hierarchic arrangement of those segment types in a physical database. (3) Contrast with logical data structure.

physical device See device.

physical device address (PDA) An address or a set of addresses that identifies a particular device.

physical device driver (PDD) A system interface that handles hardware interrupts and supports a set of input and output functions.

physical file (1) In System/36, an indexed file containing data for which one or more alternative indexes have been created. (2) In System/38, a database file that describes how data are to be presented to or received from a program and how data are actually stored in the database. A physical file contains one record format and one or more members. Contrast with logical file.

physical file member In System/38, a named subset of the data records in a physical file. See also member.

physical interface The point at which discrete pieces of equipment are connected. (T)

physical I/O address In DPPX, an address assigned to an adapter.

physical IOCS (PIOCS) Supervisory routines that schedule and supervise the execution of channel programs. Physical IOCS controls the actual transfer of records between external storage and main storage, and provides I/O device error recovery.

physical layer In the Open Systems Interconnection reference model, the layer that provides the mechanical, electrical, functional, and procedural means to establish, maintain, and release physical connections over the transmission medium. (T)

physical level (1) All aspects dealing with the physical implementation of data structures in an information processing system. (T) (2) In X.25, the mechanical, electrical, functional, and procedural media used to activate, maintain, and deactivate the physical link between the data terminal equipment

(DTE) and the data circuit-terminating equipment (DCE). See also data link level, higher level, logical level, packet level.

physical link In an IMS/VS multisystem environment, the actual hardware connection between two systems. Contrast with logical link.

physical logging In IMS/VS, the process of writing log records from the log buffers to the system log. Contrast with logical logging.

physical main storage Deprecated term for processor storage.

physical map In SDF/CICS, a table of device-specific information about each constant and variable field in a map. A physical map also contains initial data. Physical maps can be generated from SDF/CICS source maps and held in the CICS/VS load library. There may be several physical maps, each for a different device type, corresponding to one source map.

physical medium attachment sublayer In a local area network, that portion of the physical layer implemented by the functional circuitry of the medium attachment unit. (T)

physical message In ACF/TCAM, the data entered on a link during a complete transmission sequence, from the first byte of data to the end of transmission character. Contrast with logical message.

physical network A network of devices linked by physical network cabling, modems, or other hardware. A physical network can contain one or several logical networks.

physical output device A physical device that stores, prints, or displays data, such as a terminal, disk file, line printer, or nonimpact printer.

physical page (1) In the IMS/VS message format service, all or part of a logical page that is to be entered or displayed at one time. See also logical page. (2) In COBOL, a device-dependent concept defined by the implementor. Contrast with logical page.

physical paging An IMS/VS message format service facility that permits data from a logical page to be displayed in several physical pages on a device.

physical parent In an IMS/VS database, a segment that has a dependent segment at the next lower level in the physical database hierarchy.

physical partition In the AIX operating system, the smallest unit of disk space allocation for a logical volume. The physical partition is contiguous space on a physical volume.

physical record (1) A record whose characteristics depend on the manner or form in which it is stored, retrieved, or moved. A physical record may contain all or part of one or more logical records. (2) The amount of data transferred to or from auxiliary storage. Synonymous with block.

Note: A physical record is a block, but a block may be composed of several contiguous physical records recorded together.

physical recording density The number of flux transitions recorded on a track per unit of length or of angle.

Note: Usually, the units used are flux transitions per millimeter (ftpmm) for length, and flux transitions per radian (ftprad) for angles. (T)

physical relationship In an IMS/VS database, the description of the relationship between two or more physical segments.

physical resource Any facility of a computer available to do work, such as the processor, main storage, or I/O device.

physical schema (1) A part of a database schema that pertains to the physical level. (T)   (2) In a database, a schema that describes a data structure. (3) See also logical schema.

physical security In computer security, protection of people or property by means such as barriers, locks, and guards.

physical segment In a database, the smallest unit of accessible data.

physical services header (PSH) (1) The protocol above the X.25 packet level used to provide adjacent node services for SNA-to-SNA communication to IBM 5973 Network Interface Adapters. (2) An X.25 protocol used by IBM Systems Network Architecture (SNA) data terminal equipment (DTE). Physical services header provides address services for physically connected systems or devices. Contrast with enhanced logical link control (ELLC), qualified logical link control (QLLC).

physical signaling sublayer (PLS sublayer) In a local area network, that portion of the physical layer that interfaces with the medium access control sublayer and performs bit symbol encoding and transmission, bit symbol reception and decoding, and optional isolation functions. (T)

physical structure The relationships among databases as they are actually stored. (T)

Note: Multiple logical structures may be derived from a single physical structure.

physical swapping In VM/SP HPO, the process of moving groups of virtual machine pages to or from specifically defined areas on direct access storage. Contrast with logical swapping.

physical terminal (PTERM) In IMS/VS, a hardware device attached to the computer and supported by the DC feature as a terminal. A physical terminal usually has one or more logical terminals associated with it.

physical twins In an IMS/VS database, all occurrences of a single physical child segment type that have the same physical parent segment type. See also logical twins, twin segments.

physical unit (PU) The component that manages and monitors the resources (such as attached links and adjacent link stations) associated with a node, as requested by an SSCP via an SSCP-PU session. An SSCP activates a session with the physical unit in order to indirectly manage, through the PU, resources of the node such as attached links. This term applies to type 2.0, type 4, and type 5 nodes only. See peripheral PU, subarea PU.

physical unit control point (PUCP) In SNA, a component that provides a subset of system services control point (SSCP) functions for activating the physical unit (PU) within its node and its local link resources. Each type 1, type 2, and type 4 node contains a PUCP; a type 5 node contains an SSCP.

physical unit (PU) services In SNA, components within a physical unit providing configuration and maintenance services for SSCP-PU sessions. See also logical unit (LU) services, SSCP services.

physical unit type (1) The type of physical unit in a node. (2) Deprecated term for node type.

physical volume Synonym for volume.

PI Program isolation.

pianola roll A roll of paper on which text and program instructions are represented by rows of punched holes.

PIB (1) Port information block. (2) Process information block.

pica A unit of about 1/6 inch used in measuring typographical material. It is similar to a cicero in the Didot point system.

pick device (1) An input device used to specify a particular display element or segment; for example, a light pen. (I) (A) (2) See also choice device, locator device, valuator device.

picking region In AIX graphics, a rectangular region around the cursor that is sensitive to picking events. If a drawing primitive draws within this region, a pick event is reported. The width and height of the region can be set by the user. If the z-buffer is enabled, the depth of the region is the entire z-buffer. See also picking, selecting region.

pick list Deprecated term for menu.

picosecond One trillionth of a second. One thousandth of a nanosecond.

pictogram Synonym for icon. (T)

pictorial character One of several predetermined patterns that are used to construct continuous lines, boxes, figures, logos, diagrams or other pictures. (T)

picture (1) In a programming language, a language construct that describes a data type by means of a model character string literal. (I) (2) The display image of an area on a document. (3) In a program, a string of characters used in editing to modify the individual characters in a field. There is a one-to-one relationship between the characters in a picture and the characters in its field.

picture cues In video production, the first set of nine pulses in the vertical blanking interval of the master videotape that identify the start of a complete frame. See chapter cues, still cues.

picture data (1) In the IBM 3886 Optical Character Reader with the picture processing feature, the image displayed on lines 9, 10, 11, and 12 of an IBM 3277 Display Station. (2) In PL/I, arithmetic data represented in character form.

picture element (pel, pixel) (1) In computer graphics, the smallest element of a display surface that can be independently assigned color and intensity. (T) . (2) The area of the finest detail that can be reproduced effectively on the recording medium. (3) An element of a raster pattern about which a toned area on a photoconductor can appear. See also raster pattern. (4) The addressable unit on a 3800 Printing Subsystem Model 3 or 8. See Figure 112.

picture-in-picture In multimedia applications, a video window within a larger video window.

picture object In the IBM LinkWay product, one of three types of objects in a folder.

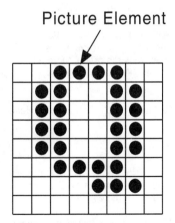

Figure 112. Picture Element

Picture Pop-up button A LinkWay button that "pops up" a picture in a window.

picture portion In the IBM 3886 Optical Character Reader with the picture processing feature, a portion of the output picture data equal in length to the output data record.

picture processing Synonym for image processing. (T)

picture record In the IBM 3886 Optical Character Reader with the picture processing feature, the data for one complete picture when written to the channel or to an IBM 3410 Magnetic Tape Unit.

picture space (1) In System/38 graphics, an area of the page that is located within the graphics field and defines the part of the graphics field in which graphics will be drawn. (2) In GDDM, the area of the page that contains the graphics.

picture specification In PL/I, a data item that has a numeric value but that can also be represented as a character value according to the editing characters specified in the item's declaration.

picture stop On a videodisc system, an instruction to the videodisc player to stop a motion sequence on a specific frame. Picture stops are encoded directly onto the videodisc and are used in Level One applications. See also Levels of Interactive Systems.

Piezoelectric Force Transducer A type of technology used to control the touch screen on the IBM InfoWindow display.

pilot project (1) A project designed to test a preliminary version of an information processing system under actual but limited operating conditions and which will then be used to test the definitive version of the system. (T) (A) (2) A project to develop a limited version of a system to be used under restricted, yet real, conditions to gain experience for the development of a full-scale system. (A) (3) See also prototype.

pin One of the conducting contacts of an electrical connector.

pinboard Synonym for plugboard.

pinfeed device On a typewriter, a device that guides and feeds paper provided with sprocket feed holes by means of pins engaging in these holes. (T)

pinfeed platen A cylindrical platen that drives paper by means of integral rings of pins engaging perforated holes, rather than by pressure.

pin pad A pad with twelve keys in a specific arrangement that display alphabetic and numeric characters that may be entered onto a financial transaction terminal. (T) (A)

PIO Programmed I/O.

PIOCS Physical IOCS.

PIP (1) Problem isolation procedure. (2) Program initialization parameters. (3) Picture-in-picture.

PIP data area In the AS/400 system, a 2000-byte data area that is associated with each prestart job. The PIP data area is used to hold program initialization parameters that are passed on the program start request to the prestart job.

pipe (1) To direct data so that the output from one process becomes the input to another process. The standard output of one command can be connected to the standard input of another with the pipe operator (|). Two commands connected in this way constitute a pipeline. (2) A one-way communication path between a sending process and a receiving process. See first-in first-out pipe, See also pipeline.

pipeline (1) A serial arrangement of processors or a serial arrangement of registers within a processor. Each processor or register performs part of a task and passes results to the next processor; several parts of different tasks can be performed at the same time. (2) A direct, one-way connection between two or more processes. See graphics pipeline. (3) In the NetView program, a message processing procedure that consists of one or more programs known as stages. (4) To perform processes in series. (5) To start execution of an instruction sequence before the previous instruction sequence is completed to increase processing speed.

pipeline options In AIX graphics, variables that control the flow of processing in the graphics pipeline. For instance, lighting is a pipeline option. If lighting is turned on, the color of a primitive is obtained by evaluating the lighting equations. If lighting is turned off, the last color specified is used.

pipeline processor A processor in which instruction execution takes place in a series of units, arranged so that several units can be simultaneously processing the appropriate parts of several instructions. (T)

piping In Advanced DOS, a feature that allows the output of a program as it is displayed on the screen to be used as input to another program without reentering the data on the keyboard.

piracy Illegal copying of software products or microchips.

PIRV Programmed interrupt request vector.

pit In optical recording, a microscopic hole in the information layer of a videodisc surface made by the recording laser beam. Recorded information is contained in the pits. See also land.

pitch (1) On a typewriter, the distance between corresponding points of two equal characters that are typed immediately adjacent to one another. (T) See typewriter with constant pitch, typewriter with proportional pitch. (2) A unit of width of type, based on the number of characters that can be placed in a linear inch; for example, 10-pitch type has ten characters per inch. (3) See feed pitch, row pitch, track pitch.

pitch selector On a typewriter, a control by means of which one of several pitch spacings can be set. (T)

PIU Path information unit.

pixel Picture element.

pixellation In a digital image, an undesirable condition in which pixels are large enough to become individually visible.

pixel map A three-dimensional array of bits. A pixel map can be thought of as a two-dimensional array of pixels, with each pixel being a value from zero to 2 to the power N -1, where N is the depth of the pixel map.

pixel operation The process of modifying a pixel value for a specific purpose.

pixel value In AIX Enhanced X-Windows, the number of bit planes used in a particular window or pixmap. For a window, a pixel value indexes a color map and derives an actual color to be displayed. A pixel is an N-bit value, where N is the number of bit planes (the depth) used in a particular window or pixmap.

pixmap (1) In the AIXwindows program and Enhanced X-Windows, a data type to which icons, originally created as bitmaps, are converted. After this conversion, the appropriate AIXwindows subroutines can generate pixmaps through references to a defaults file, by name, and through an argument list, by pixmap. See also drawable, image cache. (2) Synonym for pixel map.

PLA Programmable logic array. (A)

placeholder record In MSS, a temporary base-volume or copy-volume record that the mass storage volume control functions create and add to the inventory data set during operation of some of the Access Method Services commands of the IBM 3850 Mass Storage System.

plaintext (1) Nonencrypted data. Synonymous with cleartext. (2) Synonym for clear data.

planar A hardware part that has logic paths, low-voltage distribution paths, or grounding paths of a section of a machine.

plane See bit plane, clipping plane, overlay planes.

plane mask In AIX Enhanced X-Windows, a bit mask that restricts graphics operations to a subset of bit planes.

plasma panel A part of a display device that consists of a grid of electrodes in a flat, gas-filled panel. The image can persist for a long period of time without refresh. (T) Synonymous with gas panel.

plated wire storage A magnetic storage in which data are stored by magnetic recording in a film coated on the surface of wire. (I) (A)

platen (1) On a typewriter, a roller-type support around which the paper is guided and held during the typing operation. (T) (2) The part of a document copying machine, usually in the form of a glass plate, which may be curved, upon which the original is placed for copying. (T) (3) A backing, usually cylindrical, against which printing mechanisms strike or otherwise deposit ink to produce an image.

platen cover On a document copying machine, a cover made of some opaque material, usually with an inner light-reflective surface, which is placed over the platen during the copying process. (T) See also vacuum platen cover.

platen knob On a typewriter, the control by means of which the platen can be turned. (T)

platen machine See moving platen document copying machine, stationary platen document copying machine.

platen release lever On a typewriter, a control by means of which the detent for line spacing is released. (T)

platen variable knob On a typewriter, a control for operating the platen variable mechanism. (T)

platen variable mechanism On a typewriter, a device that permits adjustment of the platen independently of the line space ratchet. (T)

platform (1) The operating system environment in which a program runs. (2) In computer technology, the principles on which an operating system is based.

playback (1) On dictation equipment, the process of reproducing a recording by means of a playback head or a combined head. (I) (2) In word processing, to display or print out text from a recording medium. Synonymous with playout.

playback control (1) On dictation equipment, a device that enables a dictation machine to be made ready to reproduce information already recorded on the recording medium. (I) (2) In word processing, any means of enabling playback, such as a key or a command.

playback head On dictation equipment, a device that, when brought into contact or near contact with the recording medium, causes voice or other sound impulses already recorded to be reproduced. (I)

playout Synonym for playback. (T) (A)

PLB Presentation services local block.

PLC Program level change tape.

plenum A space used for environmental air; for example, the space above a suspended ceiling.

plenum cable A cable that is UL listed as having adequate fire resistance and low smoke producing characteristics for installation without conduit in ducts, plenums, and other spaces used for environmental air, as permitted by NEC Articles 725-2(b) and 800-3(d).

PL/I (1) Programming language one. A programming language designed for numeric scientific computations, business data processing, systems programming, and other applications. PL/I is capable of handling a large variety of data structures and easily allows variation of precision in numeric computation. (T) (2) A programming language that is designed for use in a wide range of commercial and scientific computer applications. (A)

PLM Program logic manual.

plot (1) To represent graphically on a medium. (2) To draw or diagram. (3) To connect point-by-point coordinate values.

plotter (1) An output unit that directly produces a hardcopy record of data on a removable medium, in the form of a two-dimensional graphic representation. (T) (2) See drum plotter, flatbed plotter. See Figure 113.

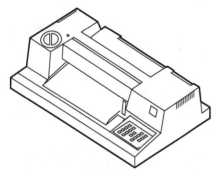

Figure 113. Plotter

plotter step size The increment size on a plotter. (I) (A)

plotting head The part of a plotter used to create marks on a display surface. (I) (A)

PLR Program library release.

PLU Primary logical unit.

plugboard A perforated board into which plugs or pins can be placed to control the operation of equipment. (I) (A) Synonymous with control panel, pinboard.

plugboard chart A chart that shows, for a given job, where plugs must be inserted into a plugboard. (I) (A) Synonymous with plugging chart.

plug-compatible Pertaining to devices provided by different manufacturers that can operate together.

plugging chart Synonym for plugboard chart.

plug-in tabulator On a typewriter, a tabulator stop that is set or changed directly by hand. (T)

PLV Production Level Video.

PM OS/2 Presentation Manager.

PMOS Positive-channel metal oxide semiconductor. A technology used in field effect transistors that utilizes the properties of a p-type semiconductor material, usually doped silicon, and that when energized produces a flow of positive charge carriers (holes).

PMS (1) Public Message Service. (2) Pantone Matching System.

PMX Programmable operator message exchange.

pocket A card stacker in a card sorter. (I) (A)

pocket calculator Synonym for hand-held calculator. (T) (A)

POF Point-of-failure restart.

POI Program operator interface.

point (1) In printing, a unit of about 1/72 of an inch used in measuring typographical material. There are twelve points to the pica. (2) In printing, in the Didot point system, a unit of 0.0147 inch. There are twelve Didot points to the cicero. (3) The second byte of a double-byte character set (DBCS) code, which uniquely identifies double-byte characters in the same ward. See also ward. (4) See addressable point, available point, branchpoint, breakpoint, checkpoint, decimal point, entry point, radix point, reentry point, rerun point, rescue point, restart point, view point.

pointer (1) A data element that indicates the location of another data element. (T) (2) In computer graphics, a manually operated functional unit used to specify an addressable point. A pointer may be used to conduct interactive graphic operations, such as selection of one member of a predetermined set of display elements, or indication of a position on a display space while generating coordinate data. (T) (3) An identifier that indicates the location of an item of data. (A) (4) In SAA Advanced Common User Access architecture, the symbol displayed on the screen that a user moves with a pointing device, such as a mouse. (5) A physical or symbolic identifier of a unique target. (6) In Pascal, a value used to define variables that contain the address of dynamic variables. (7) In the C language, a variable that holds the address of a data object or a function. (8) See current volume pointer, file pointer, horizontal pointer, instruction pointer, space pointer, space pointer machine object, system pointer, vertical pointer.

pointer grabbing In AIX Enhanced X-Windows, the action of a client taking control of the pointer so that button and motion events will be sent to that client, rather than the client to which the events normally would have been sent. See also active grab, button grabbing, key grabbing, keyboard grabbing, passive grab, pointer grabbing, server grabbing.

POINTER type In Pascal, a type used to define variables that contain the address of dynamic variables.

pointer value In PL/I, a value that identifies the location of data in storage.

pointing device (1) In SAA Advanced Common User Access architecture, an instrument, such as a mouse, trackball, or joystick, used to move a pointer on the screen. (2) In AIX Enhanced X-Windows, a device with effective dimensional motion, usually a mouse. One visible cursor is defined by the Core protocol; it tracks whatever pointing device is attached as the pointer.

point-of-failure (POF) restart In ACF/TCAM, a type of warm restart of the message control program that uses incident records to update an environment record when the system is restarted following closedown or system failure. Contrast with point-of-last-environment restart. See also cold restart, warm restart.

point-of-last-environment (POLE) restart In ACF/TCAM, a type of warm restart of the message control program that ignores incident records when the system is restarted following closedown or system failure. Contrast with point-of-failure restart. See also cold restart, warm restart.

point-of-sale device A device for recording sales data on machine-readable media at the time a sale is made. (A)

point of view (POV) In video and film production, the camera angle representing the view of a scene that would be held by a particular person, giving the illusion that the viewer is seeing what that person sees.

point size The height of a font in points.

point-to-point Pertaining to data transmission between two locations without the use of any intermediate display station or computer.

point-to-point channel-path configuration In an I/O interface, a configuration that consists of a single link between a channel and one control unit. Contrast with switched point-to-point channel-path configuration.

point-to-point connection A connection established between two data stations for data transmission. (I) (A)

Note: The connection may include switching facilities.

point-to-point line A switched or nonswitched telecommunication line that connects a single remote station to a computer. Contrast with multipoint line.

point-to-point network A network arrangement made up of point-to-point links. Contrast with multidrop network.

point-to-point topology A network topology that provides one communication path between a channel and a control unit and does not include switching facilities. Contrast with switched point-to-point topology. See also multidrop topology.

point-to-point transmission Transmission of data directly between two points without use of an intermediate terminal or computer.

polar coordinates A coordinate system in which positions are measured as a distance from the origin and an angle from some reference direction, usually, counterclockwise from the x-axis.

polarized dipole magnetization Deprecated term for polarized return-to-zero recording.

polarized return-to-zero recording (RZ(P)) Return to zero recording in which the zeros are represented by magnetization in one sense and the ones are represented by magnetization in the opposite sense. (T) See Figure 114.

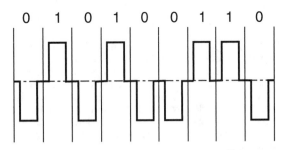

Figure 114. Polarized Return-to-Zero Recording

polar relay A relay containing a permanent magnet that centers the armature. The direction of movement of the armature is governed by the direction of current flow.

polar transmission A method of transmitting teletypewriter signals in which the marking signal is represented by direct current flowing in one direction, and the spacing signal is represented by an equal current flowing in the opposite direction. By extension to tone signaling, polar transmission is a method of transmission using three distinct states, two to represent a mark and a space, and one to represent the absence of a signal. Synonymous with bipolar transmission. See also neutral transmission, telegraph.

POLE Point-of-last-environment restart.

polish In multimedia applications, pertaining to the version of a script submitted for final approval.

Polish notation Synonym for prefix notation.

poll (1) To determine whether any remote device on a telecommunication line is ready to transmit data. (2) To execute a polling sequence.

polling (1) On a multipoint connection or a point-to-point connection, the process whereby data stations are invited one at a time to transmit. (I) (2) Interrogation of devices for such purposes as to avoid contention, to determine operational status, or to determine readiness to send or receive data. (A) (3) See also addressing, blind, lockout, selection, TSC.

polling characters A set of characters peculiar to a terminal and the polling operation. Response to these characters indicates to the computer whether the terminal has a message to enter.

polling delay In ACF/TCAM, a user-specified delay between polling passes through an invitation list for either a line or a line group. See also invitation delay, system interval.

polling ID The unique character or characters associated with a particular station.

polling list (1) A list that specifies the sequence in which stations are to be polled. (2) In the AS/400 system, a list of addresses that the host system uses to control the polling of control units or devices on a BSC or SDLC multipoint line. A general polling list contains the addresses of the control units only; a specific polling list contains the addresses of the devices, which include the addresses of the control units.

polygon (1) In GDDM, a sequence of adjoining straight lines that enclose an area. (2) See backfacing polygon.

polyline In computer graphics, a sequence of adjoining lines.

polymarker In computer graphics, a sequence of markers. The definition of the marker includes spe-

cific attributes such as color, style, width, height, pattern, and origin.

polyphase sort An unbalanced merge sort in which the distribution of sorted subsets is based on a Fibonacci series. (A)

pool A division of main or auxiliary storage. See also auxiliary storage pool, base pool, machine storage pool, main storage pool, shared storage pool, storage pool.

poor fusing A condition indicated by toner that can be easily rubbed off the printed sheet. See also ghost printing, toner migration, toner offset.

pop To remove an item from the top of a pushdown list. Contrast with push.

pop-down (1) In the AIXwindows program, the manner in which a type of MenuPane widget disappears suddenly from the display when a user action, usually clicking a mouse button, is completed. See also pull-down. (2) In Enhanced X-Windows, an action referring to a type of widget that closes when a pointer button is released.

pop-up (1) A box on the display screen that displays information or asks the user to make choices. (2) In the AIXwindows program, the manner in which a type of MenuPane widget appears suddenly (pops up) in the display as the result of a user action, usually clicking a mouse button. (3) In AIX Enhanced X-Windows, an action referring to a type of widget that opens automatically when a pointer button is held down within certain windows. (4) In SAA Basic Common User Access architecture, a bordered area of the screen containing information that supplements the interaction between a user and a computer. (5) See modal pop-up, modeless pop-up, spring-loaded pop-up.

pop-up cascade In AIX Enhanced X-Windows, several spring-loaded pop-ups emanating in succession from one modal pop-up.

pop-up child In AIX Enhanced X-Windows, a child on the pop-up list.

pop-up list In the AIX operating system, a list of pop-up children stored in a widget.

pop-up menu (1) On the display screen of a personal computer, a menu that emerges in an upward direction from a particular point or line on a display screen; for example, a secondary list of options that appears when the user selects an item in a menu. See also pull-down menu. See Figure 115. (2) In the AIXwindows program, a type of MenuPane widget that appears as the result of some user action, usually clicking a mouse button, and then disappears when the action is completed.

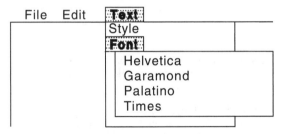

Figure 115. Pop-up Menu

pop-up widget In AIX Enhanced X-Windows, a window child of the root that is attached to its widget parent differently than the normal widget; a pop-up widget is not geometrically constrained by its parent widget.

pop-up window In SAA Advanced Common User Access architecture, a movable window, fixed in size, in which a user provides information required by an application so that it can continue to process a user request.

port (1) An access point for data entry or exit. (2) A connector on a device to which cables for other devices such as display stations and printers are attached. Synonymous with socket. See communication port, game port, I/O port, parallel port, serial port, terminal port. (3) A specific communications end point within a host. A port is identified by a port number. (4) The representation of a physical connection to the link hardware. A port is sometimes referred to as an adapter; however, there can be more than one port on an adapter. There may be one or more ports controlled by a single DLC process. (5) To make the programming changes necessary to allow a program that runs on one type of computer to run on another type of computer. (6) Deprecated term for adapter. (7) See delayed port, disabled port, protocol port, serial port, shared port, textport. (8) See also viewport.

portability (1) The capability of a program to be executed on various types of data processing systems without converting it to a different language and with little or no modification. (T) (2) The ability to transport equipment manually. (3) The ability to run a program on more than one computer without modifying it. (4) Synonymous with transportability. See data portability.

portable computer A microcomputer that can be hand carried for use in more than one location. (T)

portable dictation machine A dictation machine having a self-contained power supply and designed primarily for easy movement from one place to another. (I)

portable typewriter A typewriter designed primarily for easy movement from one place to another. It is usually supplied with a carrying case that also serves to protect the machine while it is being moved. (T)

port address In an ESCON Director, an address used to specify port connectivity parameters and to assign link addresses for attached channels and control units. See also link address.

port address name In an ESCON Director, a user-defined symbolic name of 24 characters or less that identifies a particular port.

Port-A-Punch equipment Portable punching equipment manufactured by IBM.

port card In an ESCON environment, a field-replaceable hardware component that provides the opto-mechanical attachment method for jumper cables and performs specific device-dependent logic functions.

port designation A 4-character identifier (such as LPT1 or COM1) assigned to a printer, plotter, or communications device so that the system has a unique way to refer to the resource.

portfolio In multimedia, a series of timed video stills, producing a "slide show" effect.

port group A group of ports identified by the common carrier with a single data terminal equipment (DTE) address. The network directs incoming calls to the first available port, using a sequential search technique.

port information block (PIB) In an ESCON Director, a data area that contains information relating to the connectivity of each available port.

port number (1) In an ESCON Director, a hexadecimal number that identifies a physical link connection point. This number is identical to its port address unless the service representative has reassigned the port associated with that address. (2) In TCP/IP, a 16-bit number used to communicate between TCP and a higher-level protocol or application. Some protocols, such as the File Transfer Protocol (FTP) and the Simple Mail Transfer Protocol (SMTP), use the same port number in all TCP/IP implementations. See well-known port.

portrait (1) The arrangement of text on a page so that it is oriented for normal reading when its length is greater than its width. Synonymous with portrait format, vertical format. (T) (2) Pertaining to a display or hardcopy with greater height than width. Contrast with landscape. (3) See upside-down portrait.

portrait format Synonym for portrait. (T)

portrait page In desktop publishing, a page that is designed and printed so that it can be read in a conventional manner without turning the page. Contrast with landscape page.

position (1) Any location in a string that may be occupied by an element and that is identified by a serial number. (T) (2) The location of a character in a series, as in a record, displayed message, or computer printout. (3) See bit position, character position, display position, punch position, sign position.

positional notation Synonym for positional representation system. (T)

positional operand An operand in a language statement that has a fixed position. See also definition statement. Contrast with keyword operand.

positional parameter A parameter that must appear in a specified location relative to other positional parameters. See also keyword parameter.

positional representation A representation of a real number in a positional representation system. (I) (A)

positional representation system Any numeration system in which a number is represented by an ordered set of characters in such a way that the value contributed by a character depends upon its position as well as its value. Synonymous with positional notation. (T)

position indicator (1) On dictation equipment, a device with a scale or counter that indicates a position on the recording medium. (I) (2) On a typewriter, a device indicating the imprint position. (T)

positioning In computer graphics, indicating in a display space the location at which a specified display group is to be placed. (T)

positioning time Synonym for seek time. (T) (A)

positive In a document copying machine, a copy having tonal arrangements as on the original. (T) Contrast with negative.

positive-channel metal oxide semiconductor See PMOS.

positive response (1) A response that indicates a message was received successfully. (2) In SNA, a response indicating that a request arrived and was successfully received and processed. Contrast with negative response. See also definite response, exception response.

POSIX Portable Operating System Interface For Computer Environments. An IEEE standard for computer operating systems.

POS registers Programmable Option Select registers. A set of registers that allow the software to automatically configure devices on the Micro Channel bus at the time the machine is turned on. These registers allow the setup software, which is run at the time the machine is turned on, to automatically identify the adapter and to set up various parameters on the adapter such as its starting address and interrupt level.

POST Power-on self-test.

post (1) In the AIX operating system, the action required to make a pop-up or pull-down menu appear. This action is normally a click or button press on one of the mouse buttons. (2) To enter a unit of information on a record. (3) To note the occurrence of an event. (4) To add information to a record in order to keep the record current.

postamble A sequence of bits recorded at the end of each block on a magnetic medium for the purpose of synchronization when reading backward. (A)

post code A code that indicates the status of an operation.

postcondition An assertion that pertains to a point immediately following, in the execution sequence, a specified portion of a program. (T)

post-development review Synonym for system follow-up.

postfix notation (1) A method of forming mathematical expressions in which each operator is preceded by its operands and indicates the operation to be performed on the operands or the intermediate results that precede it; for example: (a) A added to B and the sum multiplied by C is represented by the expression $AB + CX$. (b) P AND the result of Q AND R is represented by the expression PQR&&. (I) (A) (2) Synonymous with reverse Polish notation, suffix notation. (3) Contrast with infix notation, prefix notation.

post-implementation review Synonym for system follow-up.

posting See event posting.

postmortem Pertaining to the analysis of an operation after its completion.

postmortem dump A dump produced immediately after an abnormal termination of a run. (T)

postprocessor (1) A computer program that effects some final computation or organization. (I) (A) (2) In emulation, a program that converts data produced by an emulator to the format of the emulated system. (3) An SPPS II facility that assists the user by providing readable assembler listings and identifying certain unique SPPS II errors.

postproduction In multimedia applications, the online and offline editing process.

Post Telephone and Telegraph Administration (PTT) An organization, usually a government department, that provides communication common carrier services in countries other than the USA and Canada. An example of a PTT is the Bundespost in Germany.

potentiometer set mode The setup mode of an analog computer during which the coefficients of the problem are set. (I) (A)

POWER See VSE/POWER.

power cord The electrical connection between an AC power source and the computer.

power disconnect switch A device that makes and breaks the contact between the equipment and the main electricity supply. (T)

power down To turn the power off and bring an orderly end to system operation.

power factor The ratio of power consumed to apparent power.

power level The ratio of the power at a point to some arbitrary amount of power chosen as a reference. This ratio is usually expressed either in decibels based on 1 milliwatt (abbreviated dBm) or in decibels based on 1 watt (abbreviated dBw). See also decibel.

power-on self-test (POST) A series of diagnostic tests that are run automatically by a device when the power is turned on.

power sequence cables In the AS/400 system, signal cables that connect the secondary racks to each other and to the primary rack in a system with more than one rack, and allow complete control of the power from the primary rack.

power typing In word processing, high-speed entry of text that is to be proofread and corrected later.

PP Parallel print.

PPO Primary program operator application program.

PPT Primary program operator interface task.

PQA Protected queue area.

PR Print error.

pragmatics (1) The relationships of characters or groups of characters to their interpretation and use. (I) (A) (2) See also semantics, syntax.

PRC (1) Program required credentials. (2) Primary return code.

preamble (1) A sequence of bits recorded at the beginning of each block on a magnetic medium for the purpose of synchronization. (T) (2) A specified bit pattern transmitted by a data station that precedes a transmission frame in order to establish synchronization with other stations. (T) (3) See figure at transmission frame.

preassembly time The time at which an assembler processes macrodefinitions and performs conditional assembly operations.

precedence See operator precedence.

precedence prosign A group of characters that indicate how a message is to be handled.

precision (1) A measure of the ability to distinguish between nearly equal values; for example, four-place numerals are less precise than six-place numerals; nevertheless, a properly computed four-place numeral may be more accurate than an improperly computed six-place numeral. (I) (A) (2) The degree of discrimination with which a quantity is stated; for example, a three-digit numeral discriminates among 1000 possibilities. (A) (3) The number of digits that are printed or displayed. (4) Contrast with accuracy. (5) See double precision, multiple precision, single precision, triple precision.

precoded form A form on which certain items of invariant data have been entered prior to the entry of variable data. (T) Synonymous with prerecorded form.

precompile To process programs containing SQL statements before they are compiled. SQL statements are replaced with statements that will be recognized by the host language compiler. The output from this precompile includes source code that can be submitted to the compiler and used in the bind process.

precondition An assertion that pertains to a point immediately preceding, in the execution sequence, a specified portion of a program. (T)

preconfigured system definition (PCD) In the IBM 8100 Information System, a set of system parameters and corresponding command lists that define and activate a hardware arrangement, including terminals and storage units.

predefined Synonym for built-in.

Predefined Connection Object Class In the AIX operating system, a class that specifies the kind of connections that can be made to a device, and where.

predefined convention In XL FORTRAN, the implied type and length specification of a data item based on the initial character of its name, when no explicit specification is given. The initial characters I through N imply type integer of length 4; the initial characters A through H, O through Z, $, and _ imply type real of length 4.

predefined database In the AIX operating system, a database that contains configuration data for all possible devices supported by the system. See customized database, device configuration database.

Predefined Devices Object Class In the AIX operating system, a class that represents each device type, as determined by class, subclass, and type. The Predefined Devices Object Class contains basic information about the devices such as device method names and how to access the information contained in the other object classes.

predefined message A message whose description is created and stored in a message file before it is sent by the program. Contrast with immediate message.

predefined process In flowcharting, a process identified only by name and defined elsewhere. (A)

predefined specification In FORTRAN, the rule for defining a variable's type and length, which are based on the initial character of the variable name if no other specification is made. The characters I through N are INTEGER*4; the characters A through H, O through Z, and $ are REAL*4. Contrast with type declaration.

predefined value In the AS/400 system, a fixed value defined by IBM that has a special use in the control language (CL) and is reserved in the operating system. A predefined value usually has an asterisk (*) as the first character in the value.

predicate (1) A construct in a conceptual schema language, that qualifies one or more entities referred to in a sentence. (T) (2) A function that returns a truth value. (T) (3) In a conceptual schema language, a linguistic object, analogous to a verb, that may specify an attribute or action concerning one or more entities in the universe of discourse. (A) (4) In SQL, an element of a search value that expresses or implies a comparison operation.

preexecution-time table or array A table or array that is loaded with a program before execution of the program begins. Contrast with execution-time table or array.

preferential closed user group (CUG) In X.25 communications, the default closed user group.

preferential CUG Preferential closed user group.

preferred machine assist The hardware feature of the IBM 308X Processor Complex or the IBM 3033 Processor that improves MVS/SP (Release 1 enhancement, or later) V=R virtual machine performance. The MVS/SP guest virtual machine operates in supervisor state with direct control of its own I/O operations under VM/SP High Performance Option. Preferred machine assist is an extension of virtual machine assist, which eliminates control program simulation of certain instructions and interruptions.

preferred virtual machine (1) In VM/370, a particular virtual machine to which one or more of the performance options have been assigned. (2) In the VM/XA Migration Aid, a virtual machine that runs in the V=R (virtual=real) area. The control program gives this virtual machine preferred treatment in paging, processor assignment, I/O interrupt handling, and recovery.

prefill In the Folder Application Facility, to fill in a field or fields on a panel. This reduces data entry for the user and saves time by reducing the time normally spent to look up input values.

prefilled field A field that is filled in by the system before it is displayed to the user.

prefix (1) A code dialed by a caller before being connected. Contrast with suffix. (2) A code at the beginning of a message or record. (3) See buffer prefix.

prefix code See information file prefix code.

prefixing In System/370 Model 158/168 Multiprocessing, a technique in which two processing units sharing the same main storage do not use locations 0-4K for PSWs, CSWs, and CAW. Each processing unit has its own special 4K prefixed storage area of main storage addressed by the prefix register.

prefix notation (1) A method of forming mathematical expressions in which each operator precedes its operands and indicates the operation to be performed on the operands or the intermediate results that follow it. (I) (A) Synonymous with Lukasiewicz notation, parenthesis-free notation, Polish notation. (2) Contrast with infix notation, postfix notation.

pregenerated operating system An operating system such as VSE/SP that is shipped by IBM mainly in object code. IBM defines such key characteristics as the size of the main control program, the organization and size of libraries, and required system areas on disk. The customer does not have to generate an operating system.

P register Synonym for instruction address register. (T) (A)

preloaded system An AS/400 system that is shipped with the licensed programs and program temporary fixes (PTFs) already installed on the disk.

premastering In video production, the process of assembly, evaluation, revision, and coding of intermediate materials, resulting in a fully coded video tape used for the videodisc mastering process.

premix In a document copying machine, toner concentrate and dispersant used in some electrostatic processes to hold in suspension the toner particles and to act as a dilutant for the toner concentrate. (T)

pre-multiplication In AIX graphics, matrix multiplication on the left. If a matrix M is pre-multiplied by a matrix T, the result is TM.

prenegotiation phase An optional phase of link activation that occurs after physical connection of the link has been established. During this phase, polling may occur to determine if the adjacent link station is active, and prenegotiation XID3s are exchanged to allow each node to verify the identity of the adjacent node by examining the CP name in the Network Name control vector appended to the XID3 or the Node Identification field in the fixed part of the XID3. See connect phase, contact phase.

prepaging In VM/SP HPO, a physical swap-in that is initiated when a virtual machine is enqueued.

preparation function In CICS/VS, a synchronization processing function that is performed by a transaction processing system when more than two transaction programs are involved in performing a synchronized unit of work.

Prepare A PS header that flows as part of commit processing, indicating the partner has begun the first phase of the two-phase commit process.

prepared SQL statement In SQL, a named object that is in the form of an SQL statement that was processed by the PREPARE statement.

preprinted form A sheet of paper containing a preprinted design of constant data. Variable data can be merged on such a form. See also electronic overlay, forms overlay.

preprocessed display A display on which processing is done before the display is shown.

preprocessing Processing for a display that occurs before the display is shown.

preprocessor (1) A functional unit that effects preparatory computation or organization. (T) (2) A program that examines the source program for preprocessor statements which are then executed, resulting in the alteration of the source program. (3) In emulation, a program that converts data from the format of an emulated system to the format accepted by an emulator.

preprocessor statement In the C language, a statement that begins with the symbol # and is interpreted by the preprocessor during compilation.

preproduction In multimedia applications, the preparation stage for video production, when all logistics are planned and prepared.

preread head A read head adjacent to another read head and used to read data before the same data are read by the other read head. (T)

prerecorded data medium A data medium on which certain preliminary items of data are present, the remaining items of data being entered during subsequent operations. (T)

prerecorded form Synonym for precoded form.

pre-roll In video production, an editing procedure in which the videotape is rewound from the selected edit points before the master and source machines are started to give both machines sufficient time to reach the proper operating speed.

prerun-time array In RPG, an array that is loaded at the same time as the program, before the program actually begins to run. Contrast with compile-time array and run-time array.

prerun-time table In RPG, a table that is loaded at the same time as the source program, before the program actually begins to run. Contrast with compile-time table, run-time table.

preselected choice In SAA Advanced Common User Access architecture, a choice highlighted and selected by the application when a selection field first appears. A user can proceed immediately to the next field if the selected choice is acceptable. See also initial value.

preselector counter In a duplicator, a device that determines the number of copies to be produced. (T) See also total counter.

present In FORTRAN, pertaining to a dummy argument whose procedure has been invoked if there is a corresponding actual argument and the actual argument is a dummy argument that is present in the invoking procedure or is not a dummy argument of the invoking program unit.

presentation A completed interactive video program, ready for viewing and execution by a user.

presentation control In the AS/400 Business Graphics Utility, an option that allows parts of a chart to be included or excluded when produced.

presentation graphics Application software products that provide a library of predrawn images such as symbols, bar charts, and graphs, that can be combined with other artwork to create slides, overhead projection foils, videotape, hard copy printouts, or other graphics material for business presentations. See Figure 116.

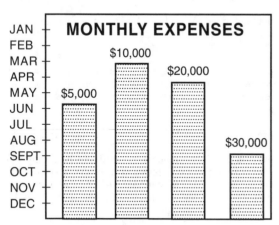

Figure 116. Presentation Graphics

presentation graphics feature (PGF) In NPM, a feature used in conjunction with the graphical data display manager (GDDM) to generate online graphs in the NPM graphic subsystem.

presentation graphics routines (PGR) In the AS/400 system and System/38, a group of routines within the operating system that allows business charts to be defined and displayed procedurally through function routines. Contrast with graphical data display manager (GDDM).

presentation layer In the Open Systems Interconnection reference model, the layer that provides for the selection of a common syntax for representing information and for transformation of application data into or from this common syntax. (T)

Presentation Manager The interface of the OS/2 operating system that presents, in windows, a graphics-based interface to applications and files installed and running under the OS/2 operating system.

presentation medium In SNA, a medium shared by the logical unit and the terminal operator. Examples of presentation media are the paper in a printer, the screen of a display, a magnetic card that is inserted into and removed from a terminal, and magnetic tapes or disks that can be mounted on and removed from the terminal. Keyboards and control panels are part of the presentation medium when they allow the operator to alter information on the medium or control operation.

presentation profile The file accompanying an interactive video presentation, which identifies and controls the author and user control options, special events, use of color, and touch and icon acknowledgments.

presentation services (PS) (1) A part of the DPPX/Base that adapts the data and control conventions of one end user of a session to the requirements of the other end user of the session. (2) In DPCX, a part of program services that provides the methods for programs to exchange data with both displays and with printers. (3) See session presentation services.

presentation services command processor In NCCF, a component that processes requests from a user terminal and formats displays to be presented at the user terminal.

presentation services layer In SNA, the layer that provides services for transaction programs, such as controlling conversation-level communication between them.

presentation space (1) The display space on a display device. (2) In the IBM 3270 Information Display System, a conceptual two-dimensional area on which data from the character buffer are mapped. See also window. Contrast with usable area, viewport. (3) In the AIX operating system, an array that contains the data and attributes associated with a window.

presentation surface Deprecated term for presentation medium.

Presentation Text Object Content Architecture In the IBM ImagePlus system, an architected collection of constructs used to interchange and present presentation text data. It defines the syntax and semantics for the text data content of a presentation text object.

preset To establish an initial condition, such as the control values of a loop, or the value to which a parameter is to be bound. (I)   (A)

preset destination mode In IMS/VS, an optional mode of terminal operation that allows the destination of terminal input to be fixed as a specific transaction code or logical terminal.

preset parameter A parameter that is bound when the computer program is constructed, flowcharted, coded, or compiled. (I)   (A)

presetting On a typewriter, the preparation of the machine for operation by setting function controls to the positions required for the work concerned. (T)

pressure See effective sound pressure, instantaneous sound pressure, static pressure.

pressure diazo In a document copying machine, a method of processing diazonium-sensitized material in which a very small quantity of coupler is applied under pressure to the exposed material so as to produce an almost dry print. (T)

pressure fixing In a document copying machine, the action in the copying process causing the image to be retained on the copy material by pressure. (T) Synonymous with pressure fusing.

pressure fusing Synonym for pressure fixing.

pressure roller In a duplicator, a roller that brings the paper into pressure contact with a master. (T)

pressure stencil In a duplicator, a master composed of fibrous tissue to which various types of ink-impervious coatings can be applied; the master is prepared by displacing the coating by means of typing or drawing with a stylus or by die-impressing. (T) See also electronic stencil, thermal stencil.

pressure-type spirit master In a duplicator, a master made by placing a sheet of suitable material in contact with the coated face of a transfer sheet and applying pressure on the face of the master by means of typing, writing, drawing, or die-impressing. (T)

prestart job In the AS/400 system, a job that starts running before the remote program sends a program start request.

prestore (1) To store, before a computer program, routine, or subroutine is entered, data that are required by the computer program, routine, or subroutine. (I)   (A)   (2) Contrast with initialize.

presumptive instruction An instruction that is not an effective instruction until it has been modified in a prescribed manner. (I)   (A)

preventive maintenance (1) Maintenance performed specifically to prevent faults from occurring. (A) (2) Contrast with corrective maintenance.

preventive maintenance time Time, usually scheduled, used to perform preventive maintenance. (A)

preventive service In VSE, the installation of one or more program temporary fixes (PTFs) to avoid the occurrence of anticipated problems.

previous release The last required release of a system, such as Release 1.0, prior to the current release, such as Release 2.0, including any modification levels, such as Release 1.0 Modification Level 1 or Modification Level 2, that were not required.

price change ticket A ticket attached to merchandise when the price of the merchandise is temporarily altered. The salesperson first wands the price change ticket. When the regular ticket is wanded for merchandise information, the terminal ignores the regular price.

price description record (PDR) In the IBM 3660 Supermarket Store System, a record referred to by the store controller to obtain information about the sale of an item. The record includes information such as the code, description, unit price, and tax status of the item.

primary (1) In high-level data link control (HDLC), the part of the data station that supports the primary control functions of the data link, generates commands for transmission, and interprets received responses. Specific responsibilities assigned to the primary include initialization of control signal interchange, organization of data flow, and actions regarding error control and error recovery functions.   (I)   (A) (2) In the AIX operating system, an irreducible unit of data; for example, a single constant, variable, or array element. See logical primary. (3) Contrast with secondary. (4) See arithmetic primary.

primary account number On an identification card for financial transactions, an identifier that consists of two parts; the first identifies the issuer of the card; the second identifies an individual. (T)   (A)

primary address space The address space whose segment table is used to fetch instructions. All data used by a VTAM macroinstruction request must be addressable in the primary address space.

primary application In DPPX/Base, an application that is responsible for control of the data link. Traffic over a data link is between a primary application and a secondary application.

primary application block (PAB) In DPCX, one 256-byte block of processor storage used as a system controlled collection of information to describe an active application program.

primary application program In VTAM, an application program acting as the primary half-session of an LU-LU session.

primary axis In GDDM, the axis used to plot data in a business chart. See also secondary axis.

primary center A control center connecting toll centers; a class 3 office. It can also serve as a toll center for its local end offices.

primary code page In the OS/2 operating system, the preferred code page that is selected at the time of initialization.

primary color In a tri-stimulus color video system, one of the three colors mixed to produce an image. See also additive color system, subtractive color system, tri-stimulus.

primary communication attachment buffer pool In DPCX, the part of the buffer pool in processor storage that contains data being transferred between DPCX and data link and loop devices.

primary communication attachment support In the IBM 8100 Information System, programming support provided for printer or display devices that are loop- or link-attached.

primary database The main database provided to the NetView user for recording error data. See also secondary database.

primary data set group In an IMS/VS database, the first or only data set group defined. The root segment type always resides in the primary data set group. See also secondary data set group.

primary device (1) The terminal with which a 3790 program is communicating. Contrast with secondary device. (2) In DPCX, a terminal that an operator uses to log on, and with which another terminal can communicate.

primary display sequence In System/36, the first set of displays coded in a workstation utility source program. See also secondary display sequence.

primary end of a session Deprecated term for primary half-session.

primary ESCON Manager In a system environment containing multiple ESCON Managers, the source of ESCM commands.

primary expression An identifier, parenthesized expression, function call, array element specification, structure member specification, or union member specification.

primary extended route In an ACF/TCAM extended network, the extended route between two host nodes that is used, when available, to route messages that belong to a particular transmission category. See also alternate extended route, extended route, parallel extended route, route.

primary file (1) In AS/400 data description specifications (DDS), for a join logical file, the first physical file specified on the JFILE keyword. Contrast with secondary file. (2) In RPG, if specified, the first file from which RPG reads a record. In multifile processing, the primary file is used to determine whether the matching record (MR) indicator is set on. Contrast with full procedural file.

primary focal point A network node that receives alerts from nodes that the user has defined in a sphere of control. Contrast with default focal point.

primary function The function that allows a data station to exert overall control of the data link in accordance with the link protocol.

primary half-session In SNA, the half-session that sends the session activation request. See also primary logical unit. Contrast with secondary half-session.

primary index An index for primary keys. (T)

primary key (1) A key that unambiguously identifies a record. (T) (2) A portion of the first block of each record in an indexed data set that can be used to find the record in the data set. See also secondary key.

primary key encrypting keys In the Programmed Cryptographic Facility, one of the three categories of cryptographic keys. It is used to encipher other cryptographic keys.

primary library In VSE, a library owned and directly accessible by a certain terminal user.

primary link station In SNA, the link station on a link responsible for control of the link. A link has only one primary link station. All traffic over the link is between the primary link station and a secondary link station. Contrast with secondary link station.

primary logical unit (PLU) In SNA, the logical unit (LU) that sends the BIND to activate a session with its partner LU. Contrast with secondary logical unit.

primary operator control station See basic primary operator control station, extended primary operator control.

primary paging device In OS/VS2 and VM, the direct access storage device with the highest effective data rate available for paging operations. Portions of a primary paging device can be used for purposes other than paging operations.

primary partition In the OS/2 operating system, the hard disk partition that contains the operating system that is active when the computer is started.

primary path (1) The channel an operation first uses. (2) In CCP, one of two paths defined for information flow to and from the physical units attached to the network by means of an IBM 3710 Network Controller. The primary path is the path that is normally used. See also alternate path.

primary POI task (PPT) Primary program operator interface task.

primary processing unit In MSS, the processing unit in a multiple processing unit configuration that processes unsolicited messages from the mass storage control.

primary program operator application program A program operator application program that is authorized to receive unsolicited messages. When the PPO is active, all unsolicited messages go to the PPO. Conversely, when the PPO is inactive, unsolicited messages go to the system console. There can be only one PPO in any domain.

primary program operator interface task In NCCF, a subtask that processes all unsolicited messages received from the VTAM program operator interface (POI) and delivers them to either the controlling operator or command processor. The primary POI task also processes the initial command specified to execute when NCCF is initialized, and timer request commands scheduled to execute under the PPT.

primary PSV In the IBM 8100 Information System, one of two program status vectors (PSVs) associated with each priority level; it is normally used to define a supervisory program. See also secondary PSV.

primary register set In DPPX/Base, one of two principal register sets assigned to a program for use as general registers. Contrast with secondary register set.

primary request In an IMS/VS multisystem environment, a message entered into a terminal before it is processed. See also response, secondary request.

primary return code (PRC) In DPPX, the rightmost four digits of the eight-digit return code; it identifies a specific error detected by a DPPX module.

primary session An extended recovery facility (XRF) session between the active application subsystem and a terminal user.

primary space allocation An area of direct access storage space initially allocated to a particular data set or file when the data set or file is defined. See also secondary space allocation.

primary station (1) In high-level data link control (HDLC), the part of a data station that supports the primary control functions of the data link, generates commands for transmission, and interprets received responses. (I) (2) In SNA, the station on an SDLC data link that is responsible for the control of the data link. There must be only one primary station on a data link. All traffic over the data link is between the primary station and a secondary station. (3) Contrast with secondary station. See also combined station.

Note: Specific responsibilities assigned to the primary station include initialization of control signal interchange, organization of data flow, and actions to perform error control and error recovery functions.

primary system control facility (PSCF) In the IBM 8100 Information System, system control facility circuitry associated with the processor.

primary system name In SNADS, the system name of an AS/400 system. Contrast with secondary system name.

primary system operator In VM, the first CP privilege class A user that is logged on after system initialization. Although class A may be assigned to more than one user, only one user at a time can use class A privileges.

primary system operator privilege class In VM, the CP privilege class A user; this operator has primary control over the VM system, and can enable and disable telecommunication lines, lock and unlock pages, force users off the VM system, issue warning messages, query, set (and reset) performance options for selected virtual machines, and invoke VM accounting. If the current primary system operator logs off, the next class A user to log on becomes the primary system operator.

primary task In DPCX, a task that can use a primary device. Contrast with subtask.

primary track On a direct access device, the original track on which data are stored. See also alternate track.

primary user disk Synonym for A-disk.

primary volume A volume under control of the Data Facility Hierarchical Storage Manager that contains data sets directly accessible to the user.

primary window In SAA Common User Access architecture, the window in which the main interaction between the user and the application takes place. See also message pop-up, pop-up window, secondary window.

prime compression character In SNA, the character selected to be represented, whenever it occurs in a string, by a single encoded control byte. Other compression characters require that each of the strings be represented by a control byte followed by the character itself. Therefore, a prime compression character string is represented by one byte, and other compression character strings are represented by two bytes

prime file In XL Pascal, a file containing precompiled declarations in the internal table format of the XL Pascal compiler. Prime files are used to initialize the internal tables of the compiler before compilation begins.

prime index In VSAM, the index component of a key-sequenced data set or file that has one or more alternate indexes. See also alternate index, index.

prime key In VSAM, the key of reference for a key-sequenced base cluster. See also alternate key.

prime record key In COBOL, a key whose contents uniquely identify a record within an indexed file.

prime subpool In VM/SP HPO, free storage used for control blocks that are aligned on cache lines.

priming control In a duplicator, a control for manually priming the damping system. (T) See also master priming control.

primitive (1) In computer graphics, one of several simple functions for drawing on the screen, including, for example, the rectangle, line, ellipse, polygon, and so on. (2) Synonym for service primitive. (T)

(3) See filter primitive, graphic primitive, input primitive. (4) See also display element,

Primitive class In AIX Enhanced X-Windows, a class that provides the resources and functionality for the low-level widgets that are managed by the manager class. Primitive class widgets cannot have normal widgets but they can have pop-up child widgets.

primitive coordinates In AIX graphics, the coordinates used to define a primitive. A convenient point is chosen as the origin and the primitive is defined relative to that point. Synonymous with primitive space. See also eye coordinates, screen coordinates, world coordinates.

primitive font A font in which characters are defined as primitives. Like all other primitives, primitive font characters can be scaled and rotated. See font, raster font.

primitive space Synonym for primitive coordinates.

primitive widget In AIX Enhanced X-Windows, a widget that instantiates its own children of a known class and does not expect external clients to do so. Primitive widgets do not have general geometry management methods. Primitive widgets that instantiate children are responsible for all operations requiring downward traversal below themselves.

print Synonym for copy.

Print In SAA Common User Access architecture, a choice in the File pull-down that a user selects to prepare something, such as a file, for a printer and schedule it to be printed.

printable area In printing, the area on a sheet of paper where a picture element (pel) can be located.

printable group In COBOL, a report group that contains at least one print line.

printable item In COBOL, a data item, the extent and contents of which are specified by an elementary report entry containing a COLUMN NUMBER clause, a PICTURE clause, and a SOURCE, SUM, or VALUE clause.

print band An interchangeable metal band that contains the print characters used by some printers.

print bar Synonym for type bar. (T)

print barrel Synonym for print drum.

print buffer In the 3270 Information Display System, an area of writable control storage where data to be printed are stored.

print chain A revolving carrier on which the type slugs of an impact printer are mounted on a chain. Synonymous with print train.

print contrast mark A standard mark printed in a specific area outside the printable area of a sheet. It is used by the printer to control the amount of toner fed during the developing process.

print contrast ratio (1) In optical character recognition, the ratio obtained by subtracting the reflectance at an inspection area from the maximum reflectance found within a specified distance from that area, and dividing the result by that maximum reflectance. (A)   (2) Contrast with print contrast signal.

print contrast signal (PCS) (1) In optical character recognition, a measure of the contrast between a printed character and the paper on which the character is printed. (A)   (2) Contrast with print contrast ratio.

print control character A control character for print operations such as line spacing, page ejection, or carriage return. (A)

print cup In word processing, an interchangeable printing element in the shape of a cup, used in some impact printers. (T)

print data set A data set in which programs store data to be printed.

print descriptor group In the AS/400 system, an object used to store print descriptors so they can be managed effectively on a system.

print device In the OS/2 operating system, a printer or plotter.

print direction Synonym for baseline direction.

print drum (1) A rotating cylinder that presents characters at each of the possible print positions. (T) (2) Synonymous with print barrel.

printed card form The layout or format of the printed matter on a card. The printed matter usually describes the purpose of the card and designates the precise locations of card fields. (A)

print entries See spool file entries.

printer (1) An output unit that produces a hard copy record of data mainly in the form of a sequence of discrete graphic characters that belong to one or more predetermined character sets. (T)   (2) A device that writes output data from a system on paper or other media.   (3) See bar printer, chain printer, character printer, drum printer, laser printer, line printer, matrix printer, on-the-fly printer, page printer, reader-printer.

Note: In many instances, printers may be used as plotters.

printer authorization matrix A matrix stored in the 3274 control unit that establishes printer assignment and classification.

printer/display layout A coding form on which the user can design the format for a report that is to be printed or displayed.

printer driver A file that describes the physical characteristics of a printer, plotter, or other peripheral device, and is used to convert graphics and text into device-specific data at the time of printing or plotting.

printer file (1) A device file created by the user to support a printer device. (2) A device file that determines what attributes printed output will have. A particular printer may or may not support all of the attributes specified in a printer file.

printer-independent file A file in a format that is independent of a particular printer type. See also printer-specific file.

printer operating speed The rate at which print-out occurs, in characters per second, or words of five recorded characters, including space, per minute.

printer-specific file A file that can be printed on only one type of printer. See also printer-independent file.

printer workstation An IBM ImagePlus workstation equipped with a printer.

printer writer In the AS/400 system, a system program that writes spooled files to a printer. See also diskette writer, spooling writer.

print file A file that is created for the purpose of printing data.

print function In the IBM ImagePlus system, the action of printing a document or a page at a workstation. The application is initiated using the front-end application or the ImagePlus workstation application.

print image (1) A character set that corresponds to the characters on a print belt. (2) In System/38, an object that contains a description of the print belt or train on a printer.

printing calculating machine A calculating machine that can print one or more of the significant elements of a computation. (A)

printing calculator A machine in which the data output is printed on paper or other suitable material. (T)

printing key On a typewriter, a control that, when actuated, causes a character to be typed on the paper and usually results in the paper carrier or type element being moved forward, ready for the next impression. (T)

printing line The writing line on a printer. (A)

printing position The imprint position on a printer. (A)

print inhibit A hardware feature on some typewriter terminals allowing a user to key in information via a keyboard without causing the data to be typed out on the terminal typewriter.

print intercept routine In System/36, the spooling routine that causes printer output to be placed in a spool file instead of being printed.

print line In a display image, a horizontal line at the top or bottom of a string of characters. See lower print line, upper print line.

Print Management Facility An interactive menu-driven program that can be used to create and modify fonts and to define output formatting for data printed on the IBM 3800 Printing Subsystem Models 3 and 8.

PrintManager A set of IBM programs or operating system functions that provide cross-system print management for an entire enterprise.

print-only ticket A ticket that contains only printed information and does not have a magnetic stripe.

print options Specifications for printing a document.

print-out In word processing, the printing or typing of recorded text. (T)

print position Any position on a medium where a character can be printed. See also display position.

print preview The display of an entire page of a document, closely reproducing the appearance the page will have when it is printed. The print preview function must be requested by the user, whereas WYSIWYG provides a continual display of pages as they will appear when printed. (T)

print quality The quality of printed output relative to existing standards and in comparisons with jobs printed earlier.

print quality standard patterns A set of print patterns used to evaluate print quality.

print queue (1) A list of items waiting to be printed. (2) In DPPX, a queue in the printer-sharing environment.

print record A record in a print data set. See also group *(2)*, group number *(2)*.

print record header Identification and control information at the beginning of the first block of a print record.

print record number A number assigned by the IBM 3791 Controller to a record in the print data set.

Print Screen, PrtSc A key on a keyboard that a user presses to print the information displayed on a screen.

print sequence number (PSN) In DPCX, a number assigned to each record in a print data set.

Print Services Facility (PSF) The access method that supports the 3800 Printing Subsystem Models 3 and 8. PSF can interface either directly to a user's application program or indirectly through the Job Entry Subsystems (JES) of MVS.

print speed The number of characters printed per unit of time. (T)

print spooler In the OS/2 operating system, a program that controls the printing of data from different applications. It temporarily stores information in separate files until they are printed.

print station In the IBM 3650 Retail Store System, one of three printing positions of the printer in the IBM 3653 Point of Sale Terminal. Each print position is for printing a different type of document: cash receipt, transaction journal, or sales check.

print text An option that allows the user to specify a line of text at the bottom of a list.

print through An undesired transfer of a recorded signal from one part of a magnetic medium to another part when both parts are brought into proximity. (T) (A)

print train Synonym for print chain.

print wheel (1) A rotating disk that presents all the characters of the set at a single print position. A daisy wheel is a type of print wheel. (T) Synonymous with type wheel. (2) In word processing, an interchangeable printing element, used in some impact printers. (T) (3) See also daisy wheel.

print zone In BASIC, the area within a given width on a display or printout in which characters are printed during unformatted printing. This area is 16 positions when single precision is specified and 26 positions when double precision is specified. The maximum is 80 and the minimum is 1.

priority (1) A rank assigned to a task that determines its precedence in receiving system resources. (2) The relative significance of one job to other jobs in competing for allocation of resources. See job priority. (3) See also dispatching priority, limit priority, time sharing priority.

priority indicator A group of characters that indicate the relative urgency of a message and thus its order of transmission.

priority interrupt (1) Temporary suspension of a computer program to permit execution of a program or part of a program of higher priority. (A)   (2) An event recognized by the system, and treated according to an assigned priority.

priority level In the IBM 8100 Information System, a number that designates relative precedence among interrupt requests so that processing on one level can be suspended temporarily when an interrupt request is generated for a level of higher priority.

priority number In the Folder Application Facility, the number assigned to documents that determines the order for distribution from the routing queue.

priority performance option In VM, a virtual machine parameter that influences the internal scheduling algorithm of the control program. The lower the priority value specified, the higher the priority of the virtual machine.

priority processing A method of operating a computer in which computer programs are processed in such a way that the order of operations to be performed is fully determined by a system of priorities. (A)

priority queue In SNADS, a queue that contains distribution queue entries for distributions with a service level of fast, status, or data high. When send times and queue depths are satisfied for both the priority and normal queues, the priority queue is serviced first. Contrast with normal queue.

priority scheduler A form of job scheduler that uses input and output work queues to improve system performance.

priority value In the ImagePlus system, a value assigned to an image object each day it remains on a work queue. The value is based on the base priority number and the aging priority number.

privacy The right of individuals and organizations to control collection and use of their data or data about themselves. (T)

privacy key In a database management system, a password, a data item, or a procedure defined to identify users and to verify their authority to access specific portions of a database and to perform specific operations on the stored data.   Synonymous with access control key, pass key. (A)

privacy lock (1) In a database management system, the facility specified to control access to a database in such a way that only authorized users may access specified portions of the database and perform only those operations on the stored data authorized specifically by the lock. (A)   (2) A facility specified as a literal, a data item, or a procedure used to prevent an operation from proceeding unless the matching privacy key is presented. (A)   (3) Synonymous with access lock, access control lock. (A)

privacy protection The establishment of appropriate administrative, technical, and physical safeguards to ensure the security and confidentiality of data records and to protect both security and confidentiality against any threat or hazard that could result in substantial harm, embarrassment, inconvenience, or unfairness to any individual about whom such information is maintained. (T)

private address space An address space assigned to a particular user.

private authority In the AS/400 system, the authority specifically given to a user for an object that overrides any other authorities, such as the authority of a user's group profile or an authorization list. Contrast with public authority.

private automatic branch exchange (PABX) A private automatic telephone exchange that provides for the transmission of calls to and from the public telephone network.

private automatic exchange (PAX) A dial telephone exchange that provides private telephone service to an organization and that does not allow calls to be transmitted to or from the public telephone network.

private branch exchange (PBX) (1) An automatic or manual private telephone exchange for transmission of calls to and from the public telephone network. (2) A switching system located on a customer's premises that consolidates the number of inside lines (extensions) into a smaller number of outside lines (trunks).

Many PBXs also provide advanced voice and data communication features.

private code An unnamed control section.

private key In computer security, a key that is known only to the owner. Synonymous with secret key. Contrast with public key. See also public key cryptography.

private library A user-owned library that is separate and distinct from the system library.

private line See nonswitched line.

private map specification library See multiple map specification libraries.

private note In the AIX operating system, one of two types of notes used in the InfoExplorer program, created by the user in a reading window. Only the user has access to read. See also public note.

private partition In VSE, a partition allocated for the execution of a specific program or application program. Storage in a private partition is not addressable by programs running in other virtual address spaces. See shared partition.

private storage In an IBM 3600 Finance Communication System, segments of programmable storage available only to the logical workstation for which the segments were defined. For each workstation, private storage consists of segments 0 through 12. See also global storage.

private volume A mounted volume that a system can allocate only to an output data set for which a specific volume request is made. A private volume is demounted after its last use in a job step. Contrast with public volume.

privilege In SQL, a capability given to a user by the processing of a GRANT statement.

privilege class In VM, one or more classes assigned to virtual machine user in the user's VM directory entry; each privilege class specified allows access to a logical subset of all the CP commands.

privileged instruction (1) An instruction that can be executed only in a specific mode. This mode is called the privileged mode and is usually reserved for the operating system. (T) (2) An instruction that can be executed only when the processing unit is in the supervisor state.

privileged instruction simulation In VM, the CP-incurred overhead to handle privileged instructions

for virtual machine operating systems that execute as if they were in supervisor state but which are executing in problem state under VM. See also virtual machine assist feature.

privileged state A state in which certain instructions can be used only by an operating system.

Note: A computer system may have several levels of privileged states.

privileged user In the AIX operating system, a user logged in to an account with root user authority.

privilege level A method of protection that allows only certain program instructions to be used by certain programs.

privilege mode In DPPX, the mode of program execution that determines the instructions a program may use. The four modes, from highest to lowest privilege, are master mode, supervisor mode, I/O mode, and application mode.

PRN Primary resource name.

problem analysis The process of finding the cause of a problem; for example, a program error, device error, or user error.

problem definition A statement of a problem, which may include a description of the data, the method, the procedures, and algorithms used to solve it. Synonymous with problem description. (T)

problem description Synonym for problem definition. (T)

problem determination The process of determining the source of a problem; for example, a program component, machine failure, telecommunication facilities, user or contractor-installed programs or equipment, environmental failure such as a power loss, or user error.

problem determination aid (PDAID) A program that traces a specified event when it occurs during operation of a program.

problem determination procedure A prescribed sequence of steps taken to identify the source of a problem.

problem diagnosis Analysis that results in identifying the precise cause of a hardware, software, or system failure.

problem isolation procedure (PIP) Written information used by service representatives to repair IBM equipment. A PIP contains yes/no questions and procedures that direct the user to the failing part of the equipment.

problem log A record of problems and of the status of the analysis of those problems.

problem management focal point In the AS/400 system, the management services responsible for the problem analysis and diagnosis for a sphere of control. An alert focal point is a subset of a problem management focal point. See alert focal point.

problem-oriented language A programming language that reflects the concepts of a particular application area; for example, SQL for database applications, COBOL for business applications. (T)

problem program Any program executed when the processing unit is in the problem state, that is, any program that does not contain privileged instructions. This includes IBM-distributed programs, such as language translators and service programs, as well as programs written by a user.

problem space A conceptual or formal area defined by all of the possible states that could occur as a result of interactions between elements and operators that are considered when a specific problem is studied. (T)

problem state A state during which the processing unit cannot execute input/output and other privileged instructions. Contrast with supervisor state.

problem throughput A measure of the average rate of processing a problem or batch of problems. (A)

problem time In simulation, the duration of a process or the length of time between two specified events of a process. (A)

PROC Command procedure.

procedural knowledge Immediately executable knowledge using declarative knowledge as data, but which may not be examined. (T)

procedural language A programming language in which computations are expressed in terms of statement sequences; for example, Pascal. (T) Synonym for procedure-oriented language.

procedural programming In RPG, a programming technique in which the input and output operations are controlled by programmer-specified operation codes instead of by the program cycle.

procedural security Synonym for administrative security.

procedural statement Synonym for instruction.

procedure (1) In a programming language, a block, with or without formal parameters, whose execution is invoked by means of a procedure call. (I) (2) The description of the course of action taken for the solution of a problem. (A) (3) A set of related control statements that cause one or more programs to be performed. (4) In COBOL, a paragraph or group of logically successive paragraphs, or a section or group of logically successive sections, within the Procedure Division. See input procedure, output procedure. (5) In BASIC, a set of commands, statements, input data, and comments that cause a specific set of functions to be performed. (6) In PL/I, a block of programming statements that can be started from various points within a program by use of a CALL statement and can process data passed to it from the block in which it was called. See also external procedure and internal procedure. (7) In Pascal, a routine, called by coding its name as a statement, that does not pass a result back to the calling program. (8) In AS/400 query management, a query object that consists of a related set of query commands. A procedure allows an application to run multiple query commands through one call to the callable interface. (9) In FORTRAN, a computation that may be invoked during program execution. It may be a function or a subroutine. A procedure subprogram may define more than one procedure if it contains ENTRY statements. See definition of a procedure or type, external procedure, internal procedure. (10) See access procedure, cataloged procedure, contingency procedure, shell procedure. (11) See also entry, return.

procedure branching statement In COBOL, a statement that causes the explicit transfer of control to a statement other than the next executable statement in the sequence in which the statements are written in the source program.

Note: The procedure branching statements are: ALTER, CALL, EXIT, EXIT PROGRAM, GO TO, MERGE (with the OUTPUT PROCEDURE phrase), PERFORM, and SORT (with the INPUT PROCEDURE or OUTPUT PROCEDURE phrase).

procedure call (1) In programming languages, a language construct for invoking execution of a procedure. (I) (2) See also parameter association.

Note: A procedure call usually includes an entry name and possible actual parameters.

procedure command A command that runs a procedure.

procedure control expression A set of statements and expressions that control how a procedure runs.

procedure-correlation identifier (PCID) In SNA, a value used to correlate all requests and replies associated with a given procedure.

Procedure Division One of the four main parts of a COBOL program. The Procedure Division contains instructions for solving a problem. The Procedure Division may contain imperative statements, conditional statements, paragraphs, procedures and sections.

procedure language statements In AS/400 query management, the query commands that are used in query procedures.

procedure level In BASIC, the relative position of a procedure within nested procedures; for example, if procedure A calls procedure B, and procedure B in turn calls procedure C, then procedure C is a third-level procedure.

procedure library A program library in direct access storage with job definitions. The reader/interpreter can be directed to read and interpret a particular job definition by an execute statement in the input stream.

procedure member A library member that contains statements, such as control language statements, necessary to perform one or more programs.

procedure-name In COBOL, a user-defined word that is used to name a paragraph or section in the Procedure Division. The procedure-name consists of a paragraph-name (which may be qualified), or a section-name.

procedure-oriented language A problem-oriented language that facilitates the expression of a procedure as an explicit algorithm; for example, FORTRAN, ALGOL, COBOL, PL/I. (I) (A) Synonymous with procedural language.

procedure recursion level In PL/I, the count that is increased when an internal procedure is called recursively. The procedure recursion level cannot be specified on the system debug commands, and only the last (most recent) procedure recursion level is available for debugging. Contrast with program recursion level.

Procedures Language The REXX language, extensions to the language, such as double-byte character set (DBCS) support, and environmental interfaces, such as exits.

procedure start request In System/36, a message from a remote system asking an SSP-ICF subsystem to start a procedure.

procedure statement A declaration used to assign a name to a procedure. (T) Synonymous with subroutine statement.

procedure step A unit of work associated with a processing program and related data within a cataloged or in-stream procedure. A cataloged procedure consists of one or more procedure steps.

procedure subprogram A function or subroutine subprogram.

process (1) A course of the events defined by its purpose or by its effect, achieved under given conditions. (2) In data processing, the course of events that occurs during the execution of all or part of a program. (T) (3) Any operation or combination of operations on data. (4) A function being performed or waiting to be performed. (5) To perform operations on data in a process. (I) (A)

processable scored card A scored card including at least one separable part that can be processed after separation. (A)

process access group (PAG) In the AS/400 system and System/38, a group of job-related objects that may be paged in and out of storage in a single operation when a job (a process) enters or leaves a long wait.

process anchor block (PAB) In VTAM, a process scheduling services dispatch point.

process assembly In the 3800 Printing Subsystem, the assembly that includes the air system, charge corona, cleaner, developer, drum, forms overlay, laser, operator panel, paper input ramp and splicer, and transfer station.

process check Synonym for program exception.

process computer system A computer system with a process interface system that monitors or controls a technical process. (T)

process control Automatic control of a process, in which a computer system is used to regulate usually continuous operations or processes. (I) (A)

process control equipment Equipment that measures the variables of a technical process, directs the process according to control signals from the process computer system, and provides appropriate signal transformation; for example, sensors, transducers, actuators. (T)

process control system A computer system, process control equipment, and, possibly, a process interface system.

Note: The process interface system may be part of a special-purpose computer.

process entry In ACF/TCAM, a terminal-table entry representing an application program. A process entry must be defined for each queue to which an application program can issue a GET or READ macroinstruction. At least one process entry must be defined for all PUT and WRITE macroinstructions from the same program. See also cascade entry, group entry, line entry, logtype entry, single entry, terminal-table entry.

process exception Synonym for program exception.

process group In the AIX operating system, a grouping of processes that permits the signaling of related groups of processes. A newly created process joins the process group of its creator.

processing (1) The performance of logical operations and calculations on data, including temporary retention of data in processor storage while the data is being operated on. (2) In a document copying machine, the treatment of sensitized material after exposure so as to reveal and retain the image. (T) (3) The action of performing operations on input data.

processing and control element (PCE) In the 8100 Information System, the part of the processor that contains sequencing and processing controls for instruction execution, interruption control, dynamic address translation, and other control and processing functions.

processing intent In IMS/VS, an application program attribute defined in the program communication block (PCB) that specifies the program's database access privileges, such as insert, delete, and replace.

processing level In System/36, a stage in the workstation utility program cycle.

processing limit In IMS/VS, a transaction attribute that defines how many messages the application program can process during one program execution.

processing program (1) A program that performs such functions as compiling, assembling, or translating for a particular programming language. (2) Any program capable of operating in the problem program state. This includes IBM-distributed language processors, application programs, service programs, and user-written programs.

processing services In DPCX, the part of program services that provides data processing capabilities.

processing system See data processing system. (A)

processing unit (1) A functional unit that consists of one or more processors and their internal storages. (I) (A) (2) See primary processing unit, processor. (3) See also mainframe, processor complex. See Figure 117.

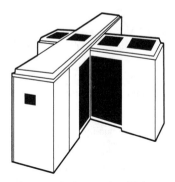

Figure 117. Processing Unit

process interface system A functional unit that adapts process control equipment to the computer system in a process computer system. (T)

process interrupt signal A signal that originates from a technical process and that causes an interrupt in the process computer system. (T)

process lock In the AIX operating system, a lock that allows the calling process to lock or unlock both its text and data segments into memory.

processor (1) In a computer, a functional unit that interprets and executes instructions. A processor consists of at least an instruction control unit and an arithmetic and logic unit. (T) (2) One or more integrated circuits that process coded instructions and perform a task. See also system processor, service processor, input/output processor. (3) Deprecated term for processing program.

processor address space In the IBM 8100 Information System, the set of relocated addresses numbered sequentially from zero to the maximum available address.

processor complex A configuration that consists of all the machines required for operation; for example, an IBM 3081 Processor Complex, consisting of a 3081 Processor Unit, 3082 Processor Controller, 3087 Coolant Distribution Unit, 3089 Power Unit, and a 3278 Display Console Model 2A.

processor configuration In the System/370 computing system, the ability to enable or disable storage elements for one or more processing units. In the multiprocessing mode, any storage element that is enabled for one processing unit can be accessed by another processing unit. Synonymous with cross-configuration. See processor complex.

processor storage (1) The storage provided by one or more processing units. (2) In virtual storage systems, synonymous with real storage.

process queue In ACF/TCAM, a destination queue for an application program. See also destination queue.

process table In the AIX operating system, a kernel data structure that contains relevant information about all processes in the system.

process uniformity Equal print quality in all portions of the printable area of a printed sheet.

PROC statement A job control statement used in cataloged or in-stream procedures. It can be used to assign default values for symbolic parameters contained in a procedure. For in-stream procedures, it is used to mark the beginning of the procedure.

producer In programming, an asynchronous procedure that provides data to be used by other asynchronous procedures. (T)

product The number or quantity that results from a multiplication. (I) (A)

product and support requirements request A mechanism by which customers and IBM personnel can provide feedback to the developers of a program, system, or System Control Program (SCP) indicating deficiencies that need correction, or major new functional or device support that should be added.

product data In an ESCON Director, information contained within an electrically erasable programmable read-only memory (EEPROM) module that defines specific hardware characteristics and can be displayed or modified.

production In videotaping, the actual shooting.

production control room The room or location where the monitoring and switching equipment is placed for the direction and control of a television production.

production-level video (PLV) In Digital Video Interactive (DVI) technology, the highest-quality video compression process, requiring the use of a large computer.

production library (1) A library that contains data needed for normal processing. Contrast with test library. (2) In a VSE pregenerated operating system

or product, the program library that contains the object code for the system or product.

production rule An if then-rule for representing knowledge in a production system. (T)

production system Synonym for rule-based system. (T)

production time See program production time, system production time.

productive poll An interrogation of a tributary station that results in receipt of data.

productive task A task assigned the third highest dispatching priority by the network control program. It initiates input/output either on the channel or a telecommunication line. Contrast with nonproductive task. See also appendage task, immediate task.

productivity See system productivity.

product-set identification (PSID) (1) In SNA, a technique for identifying the hardware and software products that implement a network component. (2) A management services common subvector that transports the information described in definition *(1)*.

profile (1) Data that describes the significant characteristics of a user, a group of users, or one or more computer resources. (2) In computer security, a description of the characteristics of an entity to which access is controlled. (3) A description of the control available to a particular network operator. See also authorized operator. (4) In word processing, a file that is used to control the formatting of one or more documents.

profile editor One of the online functions of SDF/CICS. It creates, displays, and edits SDF/CICS session profiles.

PROFILE EXEC In VM, a special EXEC procedure with a filename of PROFILE. The procedure is normally executed immediately after CMS is loaded into a virtual machine. It contains CP and CMS commands that are to be issued at the start of every terminal session.

profile list In RACF, a list of profiles indexed by class (for general resources) or by the high-level qualifier (for DATASET profiles) and built in storage by the RACF routines.

profile report In the IBM 3660 Supermarket Store System, a printed report generated after all definition statements have been edited textually and logically. The report reflects all the user-coded options specified in the definition statements. See also definition statement.

PROFS bridge See VM/MVS bridge.

PROGCK Program check.

program (1) A sequence of instructions suitable for processing by a computer. Processing may include the use of an assembler, a compiler, an interpreter, or a translator to prepare the program for execution, as well as to execute it. (I) (2) In programming languages, a logical assembly of one or more interrelated modules. (I) (3) In word processing, a set of instructions incorporated into the design of the equipment, read in from a recording medium, or entered by an operator, that enables the equipment to perform tasks without further intervention by the operator. (T) (4) A sequence of instructions that a computer can interpret and execute. (5) A syntactic unit that conforms to the rules of a particular programming language composed of declarations and statements or instructions needed to solve a certain function, task, or problem. Synonymous with computer program. (6) To design, write, and test computer programs. (I) (A) (7) Deprecated term for routine. (T)

program access (PA) key On a display device keyboard, a key that produces a call to a program that performs display operations. See also program function (PF) key.

program access to data sets (PADS) In MVS, a RACF function that allows an authorized user or group of users to access one or more data sets at a specified access authority only while running a specified RACF-controlled program. See also program control.

program activation vector (PAV) In the IBM 8100 Information System, the formatted information used to control which of two program status vectors (PSVs) is to be introduced when a new priority level is made active.

program area A conceptual area of 3791 Controller storage in which blocks of 3790 programs are executed.

program area block In DPCX, one of two 256-byte areas of a task's symbolic machine used to contain a part of a program being executed. Synonymous with program block.

program assertion A mathematical statement used in attempts to verify program corrections.

program attention key On a display device keyboard, a key that produces an interruption to solicit program action. See also program access (PA) key, program function (PF) key.

program authority An indication of the programs or program modules that can call a program, or an indication of the programs or program modules that can be called.

program authorized credentials (PAC) In DPPX, the value that determines the right of a load module to request execution of another load module.

program automatic storage area (PASA) In the AS/400 system, a system object that contains call level information for each program on the program stack. The PASA can also contain space for program variables, which is allocated when the program object is called.

program block (1) In program-oriented languages, a computer program subdivision that serves to group related statements, delimit routines, specify storage allocation, delineate the applicability of labels, or segment parts of the computer program for other purposes. (A) (2) The portion of a 3790 program stored in one sector of disk storage in a 3790 Controller. See also record block. (3) Synonym for program area block.

program check (1) A condition that occurs when programming errors are detected by an I/O channel. (2) In System/7, an error condition that occurs when the processor attempts to execute an invalid operation code or to access an address outside the capacity of the machine. This condition is signaled by a class interrupt.

program control In MVS, a RACF function that allows an installation to control who can run RACF-controlled programs. See also program access to data sets.

program control data In PL/I, a pointer, label, entry, and file data that is used to control a program.

program-controlled interruption (PCI) An interruption that occurs when an I/O channel fetches a channel control word (CCW) while the program-controlled interruption flag is on.

Program Control table (PCT) A CICS table defining all transactions that may be processed by the CICS system.

program counter (1) A register in the processing unit that steps the computer through the program. (A) (2) See also instruction address register, instruction counter.

program cycle In RPG, the series of operations performed by the computer for each record read.

program data The data associated with a program.

program date The date associated with a program or job step. See also creation date, session date, system date.

program-described data In System/38, data contained in fields that are described in the program that processes the file. Contrast with externally described data.

program-described file In the AS/400 system and System/38, a file for which the fields in the records are described only in the programs that process the file. To the operating system, the record appears as a character string. Contrast with externally described file.

program development time The part of operating time used for debugging. (A)

program device In the AS/400 system and System/38, a symbolic device that a program uses instead of a real device. When the program uses a program device, the system redirects the operation to the appropriate real device.

program device override In the AS/400 system, the attributes specified at run time that change the attributes of the program device.

program event recording (PER) A hardware feature used to assist in debugging programs by detecting and recording program events.

program exception The condition recognized by a processor that results from execution of a program that improperly specifies or uses instructions, operands, or control information. Synonymous with process check, process exception.

program execution monitor (PEM) In DPCX, a system service that allows a user to monitor execution of a program.

program execution services In DPCX, the part of program services that enables programs to control their own execution sequence or to transfer control to other programs or system services.

program execution time The interval during which the instructions of an object program are executed. (A)

program fault management (PFM) In the AIX operating system, a subsystem of the Network Computing System (NCS) that allows a user to set up cleanup routines when an application does not successfully complete.

program fetch time The time at which a program, in the form of load modules or phases, is loaded into main storage for execution.

program function (PF) key On a display device keyboard, a key that passes a signal to a program to call for a particular display operation. See also program access (PA) key.

program-generated parameter A parameter that is bound during execution of a computer program. (I) (A) Synonymous with dynamic parameter.

program generator A computer program that can produce other computer programs. (T)

program ID In the AS/400 system, a 1- to 8-character string entered from a finance device and associated with an AS/400 finance transaction program. Lists of valid program IDs and their associated application programs are maintained in program tables.

program identification entry In COBOL, an entry in the PROGRAM-ID paragraph of the Identification Division that contains clauses that specify the program-name and assign selected program attributes to the program.

program initialization parameters (PIP) (1) The initial parameter values passed to a target program as input or used to set up the process environment. (2) In the AIX operating system, data passed to a program when it starts running. This data modifies the actions taken by the program or the environment in which the program runs.

program instruction (1) In word processing, an instruction code that, when read, causes one or more functions to operate automatically. (T) (2) Control codes stored on the recording medium or in the processing device, causing the machine to respond as desired.

program interface See formatted program interface, unformatted program interface.

program interruption The suspension of execution of a program because of a program exception.

program isolation (PI) An IMS/VS facility that separates all activity of an application program from any other active application program until that application program indicates, by reaching a synchronization point, that the data it has modified are consistent and complete.

program isolation (PI) lock manager In IMS/VS, the facility that is used for local locking in systems for which no IMS/VS resource lock manager (IRLM) has been defined; otherwise, the IRLM is used for all lock management. Formally called PI enqueue-dequeue.

program level (1) Relating to an operation performed for a whole program. Contrast with command level. (2) In a network control program, an order of operational priorities set up by communication controller hardware. The five levels operate similar to that of subroutines, are responsible for certain phases of system operation, and become active by interruptions to individual levels. (3) The modification level, release, version, and fix level of a program. (4) In the AS/400 system, pertaining to an operation that is performed for an entire program; for example, a Monitor Message (MONMSG) command that immediately follows the last declare command in a control language CL program is a program-level MONMSG command. Contrast with command level.

program level change (PLC) tape In VM, a system update service that includes new functions as well as cumulative system changes.

program library (1) An organized collection of computer programs, or parts of computer programs, and possibly information pertaining to their use. A program library is often called according to the characteristic of its elements; for example, a procedure library, a source program library. (T) (2) Synonym for partitioned data set.

program loader See initial program loader, loader.

programmable Pertaining to a device that can accept instructions that alter its basic functions. (A)

programmable calculator A calculator whose program can be changed by the operator. (T) (A)

programmable character set (PCS) Synonym for geometric text.

programmable copier A copy machine that uses a microprocessor for self-diagnosis and function control and can be programmed to do complex copying and collating jobs. (T)

programmable logic array (PLA) An array of logic elements the interconnections of which can be programmed, usually mask programmable, sometimes field programmable, in order to perform a specific logical function. (A)

programmable operator facility (PROP) A VM facility that allows remote control of a virtual machine

by intercepting messages directed for that machine and taking preprogrammed action.

programmable operator message exchange The interface that gives the NetView operator the ability to communicate with the programmable operator facility.

programmable read-only memory (PROM) (1) A storage device that, after being written once, becomes a read-only memory. (T) (A) (2) Contrast with erasable programmable read-only memory (EPROM).

programmable storage (1) Storage that is able to be addressed by an application programmer. (2) That portion of the internal storage in a communication controller in which user-written programs are executed. Contrast with control storage.

programmable terminal Deprecated term for programmable workstation.

programmable workstation A workstation that has some degree of processing capability and that allows a user to change its functions. Contrast with nonprogrammable workstation (NWS).

program maintenance manual A document that provides the information necessary to maintain a program. (T)

program management The portion of a supervisory program that manages requests for execution of other programs.

programmed check (1) A check procedure that is part of a computer program. (A) (2) Contrast with automatic check.

Programmed Cryptographic Facility An IBM licensed program that provides facilities for enciphering and deciphering data and for creating, maintaining, and managing cryptographic keys.

programmed function (PF) key On a terminal, a key that can perform various functions selected by the user or determined by an application program.

programmed interrupt request vector (PIRV) In the IBM 8100 Information System, the formatted information used to indicate that an interrupt request has been generated by the program being executed.

programmed I/O (PIO) address In the IBM 8100 Information System, the information specified as an operand of an I/O instruction that identifies the I/O device to be selected for a programmed I/O (PIO) operation.

programmed I/O (PIO) operation In the IBM 8100 Information System, the transfer of data between the processor and an I/O device as part of the execution of an I/O instruction. The I/O instruction designates the address of the BSC/SS control logic, the command to be performed, and the processor register location into or from which the data is transferred.

programmed operator (1) In DPPX, the ability to provide system control through a program that simulates the operator's terminal. In DPPX, assembler users can code a programmed operator. (2) In VTAM, an application program that is authorized to issue VTAM operator commands and receive VTAM operator awareness messages. See also solicited messages, unsolicited messages.

programmed symbol set (PS) A set of fonts that can be system-defined or defined by the user and to which a code can be assigned.

programmed symbol set attribute An extended field attribute that can be used on several of the devices supported by SDF/CICS. Fields with a programmed symbol set attribute can be initialized with data on any SDF/CICS display device.

programmed symbols (PS) In the 3270 Information Display System, an optional feature that stores up to six user-definable, program-loadable character sets of 190 characters each in terminal read/write storage for display or printing by the terminal. See also loadable character set.

programmer A person who designs, writes, and tests computer programs. (A)

programmer logical unit In VSE, a logical unit available primarily for user-written programs. See also logical unit name.

programmer subsystem An interactive subsystem in which programmers can perform online programming through 5250 Display Stations.

programmer user profile In the AS/400 system and System/38, the system-supplied user profile that has the authority necessary for system and application programmers and the special authorities of save system authority and job control authority.

program message queue In the AS/400 system, an object used to hold messages that are sent between program calls of a routing step. The program message queue is part of the job message queue.

programming The design, writing, modifying, and testing of programs. (T)

programming change (PC) A modification to an IBM-supplied program.

programming change log A log of information about the application of program changes and patches to IBM products.

programming environment An integrated collection of software and hardware to support the development of computer programs. (T)

programming language An artificial language for expressing computer programs. (T)

programming module A discrete, identifiable set of instructions, usually handled as a unit, by an assembler, compiler, linkage editor, loading routine, or other type of routine or subroutine. (A)

programming request for price quotation PRPQ. A customer request for a price quotation on alterations or additions to the functional capabilities of system control programming or licensed programs. The PRPQ may be used in conjunction with computing system RPQs to solve unique data processing problems.

programming service rep. user profile In System/38, the user profile supplied by the Control Program Facility (CPF) that has the authority necessary for the programming service representative to service the system's programming and the special authorities of save system rights and job control rights.

programming statement One of a set of symbolic expressions used in writing programs.

programming system (1) In a programming environment, the software required for the development and use of computer programs. (T) (2) In a data processing system, the software needed to use one or more programming languages.

program mode In the AS/400 system and System/38, the entry mode in which the user can enter BASIC statements and commands into the system from the display station. The formats of the statements are checked as they are entered. Contrast with data mode.

program-name In the COBOL Identification Division and the end program header, a user-defined word that identifies a COBOL source program.

program name entry In COBOL, an entry in the PROGRAM-ID paragraph of the Identification Division that contains clauses that specify the program-name and assign selected program attributes to the program.

program object In the AS/400 system and System/38, one of two machine object classifications. It includes those objects used in programs that get their definition from an object definition table.

Program objects are used as the parameter or values of machine instructions. Contrast with system object.

program offering An unwarranted licensed program. See also vendor-logo product.

program operator An VTAM application program that is authorized to issue VTAM operator commands and receive VTAM operator awareness messages. See also solicited message, unsolicited message.

program operator interface (POI) A VTAM function that allows programs to perform VTAM operator functions.

program origin See computer program origin.

program parameter See external program parameter.

program patch (1) A temporary fix that is made to a program. (2) In System/38, a method of repairing a program at the machine interface program template level.

program product Deprecated term for licensed program.

program production time That part of system production time during which a user's computer program is successfully executed. (I) (A)

program recursion level In PL/I, a count that is increased when a program or external procedure is called repeatedly. The program recursion level can be specified on the system debug commands through the RCRLVL parameter. Contrast with procedure recursion level.

program register Synonym for instruction address register. (T) (A)

program required credentials (PRC) In DPPX, the value associated with a load module that determines whether a user must be authorized to request execution of the load module.

program run The performance of one or more programs. (T) (A)

program security See data processing system security.

program selection A function that identifies and actuates a program for operation.

program selector In word processing, a control that allows selection of a machine program for operation. (T)

program-sensitive fault (1) A fault that occurs as a result of the execution of some particular sequence of instructions. (I) (A) (2) Contrast with pattern-sensitive fault.

program services In DPCX, the logical layer that translates data manipulation requests from user programs and system services to resource manipulation requests to a resource manager.

program specification A document that describes the structure and functions of a program in sufficient detail to permit programming and to facilitate maintenance. (T)

program stack (1) In the AS/400 system, a list of programs linked together as a result of programs calling other programs with the CALL instruction, or implicitly from some other event, within the same job. (2) See invocation stack.

program static storage area (PSSA) In the AS/400 system, a system object that contains static variable data for programs on the program stack. The PSSA contains space for program variables that is activated when the program object is activated. The PSSA is contained in the process access group (PAG).

program status register A register that contains conditions that can be tested by branch or jump instructions.

program status vector (PSV) In the IBM 8100 Information System, the formatted information used to control the order in which instructions are executed by the associated program. See primary PSV, secondary PSV.

program status word (PSW) An area in storage used to indicate the order in which instructions are executed, and to hold and indicate the status of the computer system. Synonymous with processor status word.

program structure The manner in which the component parts of a computer program, such as identifiers, declarations, and statements are arranged. (T)

Program Support Representative (PSR) See IBM Program Support Representative.

program table In the AS/400 system, a list of the finance applications for use in an finance job. Each table entry consists of a program ID and the program name and library associated with that ID. Program IDs received in data streams from finance devices are located in the program table to determine the AS/400 application to be called.

program temporary fix (PTF) A temporary solution or by-pass of a problem diagnosed by IBM as resulting from a defect in a current unaltered release of the program.

program test time The part of system production time during which a user's computer program is tested. (I) (A)

program-to-program interface In the NetView program, a facility that allows user programs to send data buffers to or receive data buffers from other user programs. It also allows system and application programs to send alerts to the NetView hardware monitor.

program-to-program message switch An IMS/VS output message sent by one application program to another application program.

program unit (1) In Pascal, a name of a compilable block of code, known by the system, that gains control when the compiled program is called. See also unit, segment unit. (2) In FORTRAN, the fundamental component of a FORTRAN program; a sequence of statements and comment lines. It may be a main program or a subprogram. See external program unit, internal program unit. (3) See also compilation unit, module.

program validation services (PVS) A set of IBM-supplied programs that are executed in the host system to check the syntax of statements in programs, test the programs, and format the programs for later processing by subsystem support services. See batch PVS, interactive PVS.

program variable A named changeable value that can exist only within programs. Its value cannot be obtained or used when the program that contains it is no longer invoked.

program verification Proving that a program behaves according to its program specification. (T)

progress indicator In SAA Advanced Common User Access architecture, a window that informs a user about the progress of the user's request.

progressive overflow On a direct access storage device, the writing of the overflow records that are on the next consecutive track. Contrast with chaining overflow.

prohibited In an ESCON Director, the attribute that, when set, removes dynamic connectivity capability. Contrast with allowed.

project An undertaking with prescribed objectives, magnitude, and duration. (T) (A)

project control The activities concerned with monitoring the progress of a project, its direction, quality, and resource utilization, as compared with project plans. (T) (A)

projection An operation of relational algebra that forms a new relation by using a subset of the attributes of a given relation. (T)

projection copying In a document copying machine, a method of making a copy by using an image formed by an optical system. (T)

projection transformation In AIX graphics, transformation that defines the boundaries of the clipping region. Projection transformation maps viewer coordinates to normalized device coordinates; the clipping plane boundaries are at x equals plus or minus w, y equals plus or minus w, z equals plus or minus w. Projection transformations can be used to define what region of the world is visible on the screen.

project management The activities concerned with project planning and project control. (T)

project planning The activities concerned with the specification of the components, timing, resources, and procedures of a project. (T)

project specification A specification of the objectives, requirements, scope of a project and its relations to other projects. (T) (A)

Prolog Programmation Logique. A high-level applicative programming language for rule-based or logic programming, oriented to action when declared conditions are met; it is used for artificial intelligence applications, particularly expert systems, and is based on the first-order predicate calculus of mathematical logic. (A)

PROM Programmable read-only memory. (A)

prominent discrete tone In acoustics, a discrete tone whose sound pressure level is 10 decibels or more above the level of a discrete tone that is just audible in the presence of continuous wide-band noise.

prompt (1) A visual or audible message sent by a program to request the user's response. (T) (2) In SAA usage, a symbol or action that requests a user entry or selection. See command field prompt. (3) A displayed symbol or message that requests input from the user or gives operational information; for example, on the display screen of an IBM personal computer, the DOS A> prompt. The user must respond to the prompt in order to proceed. (4) See shell prompt.

Prompt In SAA Basic Common User Access architecture, an action assigned to a function key that a user presses while the cursor is in an entry field. Prompt produces a list of available choices for that entry field. A user can request a choice from the list and that choice will be inserted into the entry field.

prompt facility (1) A facility that displays messages describing required input or giving operational information. (2) In IMS/VS, an optional facility for notifying a terminal operator that a current page of output is the last page of a message.

prompting Issuing messages to a terminal user, requesting information necessary to continue processing.

prompt list pop-up In SAA Basic Common User Access architecture, a pop-up associated with the Prompt action that contains a selection list of valid choices for the entry field from which a user requested the Prompt action.

proof control In a duplicator, a device for obtaining single proof copies prior to automatic operation of the machine. (T)

PROP Programmable operator facility.

propagation delay The time needed for a signal to travel through a conductive medium from one point to another.

propagation time The time needed for a signal to travel from one point on a conductive medium to another. See round trip propagation time.

proper subset A subset that does not include all the elements of a particular set. (A)

property (1) In SAA Common User Access architecture, a unique characteristic of an object that can be changed or modified. The properties of an object describe the object. Type style is an example of a property. (2) In AIX Enhanced X-Windows, the name, type, data format, and data associated with a window. By using properties, clients and a window manager share information, such as resize hints, program names, and icon formats. It is a general-purpose naming mechanism for clients. The protocol does not interpret properties. (3) Public information associated with a window. (4) See entity-integrity property.

property list (1) A technique using lists of the properties, attributes, and values of objects for describing the state of the world. (T) (2) In AIX Enhanced X-Windows, the list of properties that are defined for a particular window.

proportionally spaced font A font with graphic characters contained in character cells varying with the size of each graphic character. This allows for even spacing between printed characters, and eliminates excess white space around narrow characters, such as the letter i. Contrast with uniformly spaced font. See Figure 118.

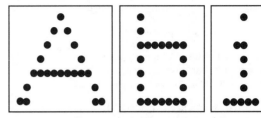

Figure 118. Proportionally Spaced Font

proportional space The distance moved between the paper carrier and the print or type element, parallel to the printing or typing line when the printing or typing position advances. This distance, which corresponds to the natural width of each character, is expressed in units of escapement.

proportional spacing Spacing of characters according to their natural width. Contrast with monospacing.

proportional spacing mechanism On a printer or typewriter, a device that moves the paper carrier or the print or type element in a step-by-step manner parallel to the printing or typing line. The distance moved corresponds to the natural width of each character. Contrast with constant-pitch spacing mechanism.

proposition (1) An assertion about entities. (T) (2) A conceivable state of affairs concerning entities about which it is possible to assert or deny that such a state of affairs holds for those entities. (3) See necessary proposition. (A)

proposition world In a conceptual schema language, a collection of propositions each of which holds for a given entity world. (A)

props In videotaping, the support material for the shoot; for example, equipment being promoted, auxiliary equipment, software, or supplies, or anything provided to make the set look realistic and attractive.

protected conversation An LU 6.2 conversation that is allocated using the sync point option and uses the two-phase commit and resync protocols.

protected dynamic storage Synonym for variable control block area.

protected field (1) In word processing, preset data or an area that can't be changed or overridden by an operator without altering the program. (T)   (2) On a display device, a display field in which a user can't enter, modify, or erase data.   Contrast with unprotected field.

protected file In the AS/400 system, a file that cannot be changed by an override file command.

protected free storage See free storage.

protected location A storage location whose contents are protected against accidental alteration, improper alteration, or unauthorized access. (I)   (A)

protected queue area In OS/VS1, an area located at the high address end of each virtual storage partition.

protected resource (1) Any resource to which access is controlled.   (2) In RACF, a resource that is defined for the purpose of controlling access to the resource. Some of the resources that can be protected by RACF include DASD and tape data sets, VM minidisks, DASD volumes, tape volumes, terminals, IMS/VS transactions, IMS/VS transaction groups, and any other resources defined in the class descriptor table. (3) In transaction processing, a local resource that can be modified only by the transaction program with which it is currently associated in a synchronized unit of work.   (4)   A resource, for example, a database, that can be modified only in accordance with sync point protocols.

protected-resource manager (PRM) See protection manager.

protected storage (1) Storage in which data cannot be modified except under specified conditions.   (2) In the AS/400 system, the part of the system auxiliary storage pool (ASP) that is reserved for the creation of permanent objects, such as libraries and files, when checksum protection is in effect.   The protection applies only to the system ASP.   (3) See also read-only storage, read/write protection.

protected text In SAA Basic Common User Access architecture, information in a panel that a user cannot interact with.

protection (1) An arrangement for restricting access to or use of all or part of a computer system. (I)   (A)   (2) Synonymous with lockout. (3) See privacy protection, storage protection.

protection key An indicator that appears in the current program status word whenever an associated task has control of the system.   This indicator must match the storage keys of all main storage blocks to be used by the task.   Synonymous with storage protection key.

protection manager A system component, associated with one or more protected resources, that interacts with sync point services to carry out two-phase commit protocols.   A protection manager implements the parts of the protocol that are specific to a particular resource type.   For example, the protection manager associated with a protected conversation builds and sends PS headers in response to instructions from sync point services.   Two types of protection managers are defined: conversational resource protection managers and local (nonconversational) resource protection managers.   Together, these resource protection managers are referred to as protected-resource managers.

protection master In multimedia applications, a copy of the edit master that is stored as a backup.

protective plug In an ESCON environment, a type of duplex connector that provides environmental and physical protection.   Contrast with wrap plug.

protect mode In the OS/2 operating system, a method of program operation that limits or prevents access to certain instructions or areas of storage.   Contrast with real mode.

protect notch See write-protect notch.

protect tab See write-protect tab.

protocol (1) A set of semantic and syntactic rules that determines the behavior of functional units in achieving communication. (I)   (2) In Open Systems Interconnection architecture, a set of semantic and syntactic rules that determine the behavior of entities in the same layer in performing communication functions.   (T)   (3) In SNA, the meanings of and the sequencing rules for requests and responses used for managing the network, transferring data, and synchronizing the states of network components.   See bracket protocol.   (4) Synonymous with line control discipline, line discipline.

protocol boundary The signals and rules governing interactions between two components within a node.

protocol control information (PCI) Information exchanged between entities of a given layer, using a connection at the next lower layer, to coordinate their joint operation. (T)

protocol converter A device that changes one type of coded data to another type of coded data for processing.   See also link protocol converter (LPC).

protocol converter non-SNA equipment A protocol converter that does not provide logical link control. The user provides any protocols above the X.25 packet level.

protocol data unit (PDU) A unit of data specified in a protocol of a given layer and consisting of protocol control information of this layer, and possibly user data of this layer. (T)

protocol family A set of related communications protocols that use a common addressing mechanism to identify end points; for example, the U.S. Department of Defense Internet Protocols. Synonymous with address family.

protocol port A unique host identifier used by transport protocols to specify a destination within a host.

prototype (1) A model or preliminary implementation suitable for evaluation of system design, performance, and production potential, or for better understanding or determination of the requirements. (T) (2) A model suitable for evaluation of system design, performance, and production potential. (A)

prototype statement Synonym for macro prototype statement.

proximity zone An area where action is sensed by a touch-sensitive device without the input device touching the touch-sensitive surface. The zone varies depending on the technology of the digitizer in the device, but it is usually no more than 6.35 mm (0.25 in.) from the surface.

PRPQ Programming Request for Price Quotation.

pruning (1) In an expert system, a process for cutting off or ignoring one or more branches of a search space in problem solving. Synonymous with cut-off. (T) (2) In AIX graphics, eliminating the drawing of parts of the display list because a bounding box test shows that the y axes are not visible. See also clipping, culling.

PS (1) Presentation services. (2) Programmed symbols. (3) Programmed symbol set.

P(S) In X.25 communications, the packet send sequence number.

PSCF Primary system control facility.

PSCP Presentation services command processor.

PSDN Packet switching data network.

pseudo Pertaining to an object or action that has the appearance or function of another object or action.

pseudobinary In MSP/7, a coding convention used to transmit binary data through the asynchronous communications control attachment.

pseudo-clock A main storage location used by timer supervision routines to calculate timer intervals and time of day.

pseudocode (1) An artificial language used to describe computer program algorithms without using the syntax of any particular programming language. Synonymous with structured English. (A) (2) A set of instructions that is logically structured but does not follow the syntax of any particular programming language.

pseudocolor In AIX Enhanced X-Windows, a class of colormap in which a pixel value indexes the colormap entry to produce independent red, green, and blue (RGB) values. The RGB values can be changed dynamically. See also background color, direct color, true color.

pseudocursor In computer graphics, a symbol that simulates the operation of a cursor on a display surface.

pseudocylinder In VM/SP HPO, a count-key-data (CKD) representation of a fixed-block-architecture (FBA) direct access storage address. A pseudocylinder is defined as pages per access position. It allows the same control block structure to be used for FBA and CKD devices.

pseudo-front-end system An IMS/VS system in a multisystem environment in which all terminals are handled and a small number of time-consuming transactions are routed to a transaction processing system. See also balanced system, front-end system, transaction processing system.

pseudo LU-LU session In ACF/TCAM, a session between a host primary logical unit (LU) and a binary synchronous or start/stop station.

pseudo page fault A facility available with the VM/VS handshaking feature that allows the VS1 virtual machine to dispatch another task while waiting for a page-in request to be completed for some other task. Without this facility, the virtual machine waits until the page request is satisfied, even if higher priority tasks are ready to execute.

pseudorandom number sequence An ordered set of numbers that has been determined by some defined arithmetic process but is effectively a random number sequence for the purpose for which it is required. (T) (A)

pseudo-text In COBOL, a sequence of text words, comment lines, or the separator space in a source program or COBOL library bounded by, but not including, pseudo-text delimiters.

pseudo-text delimiter In COBOL, two contiguous equal sign (=) characters used to delimit pseudo-text.

pseudo timer A special VM timing facility that provides date, time, virtual processing unit, and total processing unit time information to a virtual machine.

PSH Physical services header.

PSID Product-set identification.

PSM Proportional spacing machine.

PSN (1) Public switched network. (2) Print sequence number.

PSR IBM Program Support Representative.

PSRR Product and support requirements request.

PSS (1) Process scheduling services. (2) Programmable Store System.

PSSA Program static storage area.

PST Process scheduling table.

PSTN Public switched telephone network.

PSV Program status vector.

PSW (1) Program status word. (2) Processor status word.

PTE Storage pool page table entry.

PTERM Physical terminal.

PTF Program temporary fix.

PTF backup library A library that contains a copy of the load modules replaced by a PTF.

PTF library A library that contains the PTFs to be applied by the PTF procedure.

PTN Public telephone network.

PTOCA Presentation Text Object Content Architecture.

PTT Post Telephone and Telegraph Administration.

PTTC Paper tape transmission code.

p-type semiconductor A semiconductor doped with acceptor impurities that, when energized, generates a predominance of positive charge carriers (holes). Contrast with n-type semiconductor. See also PMOS.

Note: P-type semiconductors have a lower level of conductivity than n-type semiconductors and have slower switching rates, but allow higher-density packing of components. P-type and n-type semiconductor materials are often layered together to obtain a rectifying action between the two dissimilar materials.

PU Physical unit.

publication language A representation of a reference language using symbols that are particularly suitable for printing. (T)

public authority (1) The authority for an object granted to all users. (2) In the AS/400 system, the authority given to users who do not have any specific (private) authority to an object, who are not on the authorization list, if one is specified for the object, and whose group profile has no specific authority to the object. Contrast with private authority.

public data network (PDN) A communications common carrier network providing data communications services over switched or nonswitched lines. See public network.

public data transmission service In data communication, the circuit-switched, packet-switched, and non-switched services provided and operated by a telecommunication Administration over a public network.

public directory In basic network computing (BNU), the directory that is open to all BNU users. The public directory is used to transfer files and programs among systems linked by BNU or by other versions of the UNIX-to-UNIX Copy Program (UUCP).

public exchange See central exchange, central office.

public information In the AIX operating system, information that is available to any client.

public key In computer security, a key made available to anyone who wants to encrypt information Contrast with private key. See also public key cryptography.

public key cryptography In computer security, cryptography in which a public key is used for encryption and a private key is used for decryption. Contrast with symmetric cryptography. Synonymous with asymmetric cryptography.

Note: Bases for public key cryptography include discrete logarithms, factoring, and knapsack problem.

public library Synonym for alternate library.

public message service (PMS) The public telegram system offered by Western Union.

public network A network established and operated by a telecommunication administration or by a Recognized Private Operating Agency (RPOA) for the specific purpose of providing circuit-switched, packet-switched, and leased-circuit services to the public. Contrast with user-application network.

public note In the AIX operating system, one of two types of notes used in the InfoExplorer program. A public note is created for distribution to many users. Only a few users have write permission to create public notes. See also private note.

public switched network (PSN) Any switching system that provides a circuit switched to many customers. In the USA, there are four: Telex, TWX, telephone, and Broadband Exchange.

public-switched telephone network (PSTN) A communications common carrier network that provides voice and data communications services over switched lines.

public telephone network (PTN) A communications common carrier network that provides voice and data communications services over switched or non-switched lines.

public volume A mounted volume that a system can allocate to an output data set for which a nonspecific volume request is made. A public volume remains mounted until the device on which it is mounted is required for another volume. Contrast with private volume.

puck A device used to select a particular location on a tablet.

PUCP Physical unit control point.

pulldown In micrographics, the length of film advanced after each exposure.

pull-down (1) In SAA Common User Access architecture, pertaining to a choice in an action bar pull-down. (2) A shortened form of action bar pull-down. See action bar pull-down. (3) In the AIXwindows program, the manner in which a MenuPane widget gives the appearance of being "pulled down" from a MenuBar widget as the result of a user action, usually, clicking a mouse button. See also pop-down.

pull-down menu (1) On the display screen of a personal computer, a menu that emerges in a downward direction from a point or line at or near the top of the screen; for example, a menu that appears when the user selects a particular display element or points to a line in another menu by using a device such as a mouse. See also pop-up menu. See Figure 119.

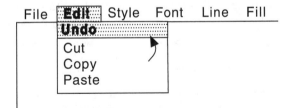

Figure 119. Pull-Down Menu

(2) In SAA Common User Access architecture, a list of choices extending from a selected menu-bar choice that gives users access to actions, routings, and settings related to an object. (3) In the AIXwindows program, a type of MenuPane widget that gives the appearance of being pulled down from a MenuBar widget as the result of a user action, usually, clicking a mouse button.

pulse (1) A variation in the value of a magnitude, short in relation to the time schedule of interest, the final value being the same as the initial value. (T) Synonymous with impulse. (2) In video systems, a signal recorded on every frame of a videotape to enable individual frames to be identified for editing and access. Synonymous with pulse code. See clock pulse, synchronization pulses.

pulse code Synonym for pulse.

pulse code modulation (PCM) In data communication, variation of a digital signal to represent information; for example, by means of pulse amplitude modulation (PAM), pulse duration modulation (PDM), or pulse position modulation (PPM).

pulse cross A television monitor mode used in testing; the display can be synchronized so that the synchronizing pulse portion of the video signal is shown in the center of the display.

pulse repetition rate The number of pulses per unit time. (A)

pulse string Synonym for pulse train.

pulse train A series of pulses having similar characteristics. (A) Synonymous with pulse string.

punch (1) A device for making holes in some kind of data medium. (I) (A) (2) A device that interprets coded electrical signals so as to produce holes in cards or tapes. (T) (3) A perforation, as in a punched card or paper tape. (A)

punch-and-crunch editing Synonym for assemble editing.

punch card (1) A card into which hole patterns can be punched. (A)   (2) See Hollerith card.

punch column (1) A line of punch positions parallel to the Y-datum line of a card. (A)   (2) A line of punch positions along a card column. (A)

punched card (1) A card punched with hole patterns. (A)   (2) In word processing, a card on which text and program instructions are represented by rows of punched holes. (T)   (3) See Hollerith card.

punched card reader Synonym for card reader.

punched tape (1) A tape punched with hole patterns. (I)   (A)   (2) Synonymous with perforated tape. (3) In word processing, a tape, usually of paper, on which text and program instructions are represented by rows of punched holes. (T)

punched tape code A code used to represent data on punched tape. (T) Synonymous with paper tape code, perforated tape code.

punched tape reader (1) A device that reads or senses hole patterns in a punched tape, transforming the data from the hole patterns to electrical signals. (I)   (A)   (2) Synonymous with perforated tape reader.

punching See interstage punching, multiple punching.

punching position Synonym for punch position.

punching station (1) The place in a card track where a punch card is punched. (A)   (2) Synonymous with punch station.

punch path In a punch, a card path that has a punch station. (I)   (A)

punch position A defined location on a data medium where a hole may be punched to record data. (I)   (A) Synonymous with code position, punching position.

punch row A line of punch positions along a card row. (A)

punch station Location in a punch where a data medium is punched. (I)   (A)

punch tape A tape in which hole patterns can be punched. (I)   (A)

punch tape code A code used to represent data on punch tape. (I)

punctuation On a calculator, the ability to divide displayed or printed numbers into groups of three digits to the left of the decimal marker. (T)

punctuation capability In a calculator, the ability to divide displayed or printed numbers into groups of three digits to the left of the decimal marker. (T)   (A)

punctuation character A character used to separate elements or to identify a particular type of element: a comma, semicolon, period, quotation mark, left or right parenthesis, space, or equal sign.

punctuation symbol Synonym for delimiter.

PUNS Physical unit services.

PU-PU flow In SNA, the exchange between physical units (PUs) of network control requests and responses.

PU-PU session Deprecated term for PU-PU flow.

pure binary numeration system The fixed-radix numeration system that uses the binary digits and the radix 2; for example, in this numeration system, the numeral 110.01 represents the number six and one quarter, that is,
$$1 \times 2^2 + 1 \times 2^1 + 0 \times 2^0 + 0 \times 2^{-1} + 1 \times 2^{-2}.$$
(I)   (A) Synonymous with binary numeration system.

purge To delete data from storage and remove all references to the data.

PUSCB Physical unit services control block.

PU services manager In SNA, a component that provides network services for all half-sessions within the physical unit (PU).

push To add an item to the top of a pushdown list. Contrast with pop.

push button In SAA Advanced Common User Access architecture, a rectangle with text inside. Push buttons are used in windows for actions that occur immediately when the push button is selected. See virtual push button.

push button dialing The use of keys or push buttons instead of a rotary dial to generate a sequence of digits that establish a circuit connection. The signal form is usually tones. Synonymous with key pulse, Touch-Call (gtE), Touch-Tone (AT&T). Contrast with rotary dial.

push button dialing pad A twelve-key device for starting tone keying signals. It usually is attached to rotary dial phones for starting data signals.

pushdown list (1) A list constructed and maintained so that the next data element to be retrieved is the most recently stored. (T) (2) Synonymous with push-down stack, stack.

Note: This method is characterized as last-in-first-out (LIFO).

pushdown stack Synonym for pushdown list.

pushdown storage A storage device in which data is ordered in such a way that the next item to be retrieved is the most recently stored item. This procedure is usually referred to as "last-in-first-out" (LIFO). Synonymous with stack. (T) (A)

pushup list Synonym for queue.

pushup storage A storage device in which data are ordered in such a way that the next data item to be retrieved is the item earliest stored; this method is characterized as first-in-first-out. (T) (A)

PUT Program update tape.

put To place a single data record into an output file.

PU type (1) Deprecated term for node type. (2) The type of physical unit in a node.

PU T2.1 Deprecated term for T2.1 node.

PU T5 Deprecated term for T5 node.

PVC Permanent virtual circuit.

PVI Primitive VTAM interface.

PVS Program validation services.

PXB Pool extension block.

Px64 A teleconferencing standard for low-bandwidth, wide-area transmissions, whose image quality is lower than that achieved with certain other standards, such as JPEG.

PZT Piezoelectric Force Transducer.

Q

Q Quadrature.

QAB Queue anchor block.

Q-bit In X.25 communications, the qualifier bit in a data packet that can be set by the sending data terminal equipment DTE to qualify the user data in some way that is meaningful to the receiving DTE. See D-bit, M-bit.

QCMD In the AS/400 system, the IBM-supplied control language processor that interprets and processes control language (CL) commands for the system.

qdaemon In the AIX operating system, the daemon process that maintains a list of outstanding jobs and sends them to the specified device at the appropriate time.

QGPL See general-purpose library.

QISAM Queued indexed sequential access method.

QLLC Qualified logical link control.

QOS Quality of service.

QSAM Queued sequential access method.

QSRV In the AS/400 system, the IBM-supplied user profile for a service representative.

QSYS See system library.

QTAM Queued telecommunications access method.

quad A structural unit employed in cable, consisting of four separately insulated conductors twisted together.

quadraplex A 2-inch video tape recorder using four rotating heads to record and play back video. Once the broadcast quality standard, quadraplex is being replaced with 1-inch and 3/4 inch formats.

quadratic programming (1) In operations research, a particular case of nonlinear programming in which the function to be maximized or minimized is a quadratic function and the constraints are linear functions. (I) (A) (2) Contrast with convex programming, dynamic programming, integer programming, linear programming, mathematical programming, minimum delay programming, nonlinear programming.

quadrature (Q) (1) The state of being at 90 degrees to a reference. (2) In NTSC video, the state of a color difference signal being 90 degrees out of phase with the color subcarrier. See also in-phase (I).

quadruple-length register Four registers that function as a single register. (I) (A) Synonymous with quadruple register.

quadruple register Synonym for quadruple-length register.

quad tabulation In text processing, a function that aligns a character or group of characters at any point within a column. (T) (A)

qualification See name qualification.

qualified call A DL/I call that contains at least one segment search argument.

qualified data-name In COBOL, an identifier that is composed of a data-name, followed by one or more sets of either of the connectives OF and IN followed by a data-name qualifier.

qualified job name A job name, a related user name, and system-assigned job number. Contrast with job name.

qualified logical link control (QLLC) An X.25 protocol that allows the transfer of data link control information between two adjoining SNA nodes that are connected through an X.25 packet-switching data network. The QLLC provides the qualifier "Q" bit in X.25 data packets to identify packets that carry logical link protocol information. Contrast with enhanced logical link control (ELLC), physical services header (PSH).

qualified name (1) A data name explicitly accompanied by a specification of the class to which it belongs in a specified classification system. (I) (A) (2) A name that has been made unique by the addition of one or more qualifiers. (3) In the AS/400 system, the name of the library containing an object and the name of the object. Contrast with object name.

qualified object name An object name and the name of the library containing the object. Contrast with object name.

qualified segment search argument (SSA) In IMS/VS, a segments search argument (SSA) that contains, in addition to the segment name, one or more qualification statements. A qualified SSA describes the segment type and occurrence that is to be accessed.

qualifier (1) A modifier that makes a name unique. (2) All names in a qualified name other than the right-most, which is called the simple name. (3) In COBOL, a data-name or a name associated with a level indicator that is used in a reference either together with another data-name which is the name of an item that is subordinate to the qualifier or together with a condition-name. (4) In COBOL, a section-name that is used in a reference together with a paragraph-name specified in that section. (5) In COBOL, a library-name that is used in a reference together with a text-name associated with that library.

qualifier bit See Q-bit.

quality assurance (QA) (1) The planned systematic activities necessary to ensure that a component or system conforms to established technical requirements. (T) (2) All actions that are taken to ensure that a development or organization delivers products that meet performance requirements and adhere to standards and procedures. (A) (3) The policy, procedures, and systematic actions established in an enterprise for the purpose of providing and maintaining some degree of confidence in data integrity and accuracy throughout the life cycle of the data, which includes input, update, manipulation, and output. (A)

quality of service (QOS) A set of communication characteristics required by an application. Each QOS defines a specific transmission priority, level of route reliability, and security level. Each QOS also defines whether the sessions are interactive. Contrast with class of service (COS).

quantization The subdivision of the range of values of a variable into a finite number of nonoverlapping, but not necessarily equal, subranges or intervals, each of which is represented by an assigned value within the subrange; for example, a person's age is quantized for most purposes with a quantum of one year. (A)

quantize To divide the range of a variable into a finite number of nonoverlapping intervals that are not necessarily of equal width, and to designate each interval by an assigned value within the interval; for example, a person's age is for many purposes quantized with a quantum (interval) of one year. (I) (A)

quantizing The second step in the three-step process of converting an analog signal to a digital signal. The

three steps are: sampling, quantizing, and encoding. In quantizing, a sample is converted from an analog value to a digital value having a limited number of bits, which is then ready for encoding. See also encoding, sampling.

quantizing noise The artifact caused by quantizing with too few levels.

quantum A subrange in quantization. (A)

quark In AIX Enhanced X-Windows, synonym for string.

quarter-speed One-fourth the rated speed of the associated equipment; in transoceanic telegraph, one-fourth of full speed, or 12.5 baud or 16+ wpm.

quarter-squares multiplier An analog multiplier whose operation is based on the identity:

$$xy = [(x + y)^2 - (x - y)^2]/4$$

incorporating inverters, analog adders, and square-law function generators. (I)

quartet A byte composed of four binary elements. (I) (A) Synonymous with four-bit byte.

quartz iodide light In video or film production, a very bright light source consisting of a thick glass or quartz bulb filled with a halogen gas, such as iodide, and containing an electrical filament that reaches a very high temperature during operation.

quasistable state Synonym for unstable state.

quaternary operator An operator that requires exactly four operands. (I) (A)

query (1) A request for data from a database, based on specified conditions; for example, a request for availability of a seat on a flight reservation system. (T) (2) The process by which a master station asks a slave station to identify itself and to give its status. (T) (3) In interactive systems, an operation at a terminal that elicits a response from the system. (4) A request for information from a file based on specific conditions; for example, a request for a list of all customers whose balance is greater than $1000. (5) In System/38, a utility that is part of the Interactive Data Base Utilities licensed program. (6) In the AS/400 system, the query management object that is used to define queries against relational data.

query application See application.

query command In the AS/400 system, the name of an action, and any associated parameters, that can be performed by query management. The query commands include ERASE, EXIT, EXPORT, GET, IMPORT, PRINT, RUN, SAVE, SET, and START.

query command procedure In AS/400 query management, a type of query procedure that contains a subset of the query commands allowed in a query procedure. The query command procedure can be used for initializing global variables.

query instance In AS/400 query management, a collection of system resources and a set of query commands within an application program.

query language (1) A data manipulation language for end users to retrieve or possibly modify data in a database. (T) (2) In database management systems, a language that enables an end user to interact directly with the database management system, and to retrieve and possibly modify data stored in a database. (A)

query management form In AS/400 query management, the type name of the OS/400 object on the AS/400 system that is comparable to the term form object as used for the Systems Application Architecture (SAA) solution.

query management object In AS/400 query management, any of the query management objects: query, form, or procedure.

query management query In AS/400 query management, the type name of the OS/400 object on the system that is comparable to the term query object, as used for the Systems Application Architecture (SAA) solution.

query mode In AS/400 query management, the processing mode associated with a query instance.

query reply In the 3270 data stream, an inbound structured field sent in response to a read partition query and used to define the characteristics of the terminal.

QUERY/36 In System/36, an IBM licensed program that produces files and reports of data from files that are defined through the use of the interactive data definition utility (IDDU).

queue (1) A list constructed and maintained so that the next data element to be retrieved is the one stored first. (T) (2) A line or list of items waiting to be processed; for example, work to be performed or messages to be displayed. (3) In COBOL, a logical collection of messages awaiting transmission or processing. See sub-queue. (4) To arrange in or form a queue. (5) See active page queue, double-ended

queue, event queue, hold page queue, hold queue, input work queue, read-ahead queue. (6) Synonymous with pushup list.

Note: This method is characterized as first-in-first-out (FIFO).

queue-back chain In ACF/TCAM, a time-sequential record of sending and receiving message traffic for the terminal or terminals of a specific destination queue control block (QCB).

queued access method Any access method that synchronizes the transfer of data between the computer program using the access method and input/output devices, thereby minimizing delays for input/output operations. (A)

queued BIND In VTAM, a BIND request sent from the primary logical unit (PLU) to the secondary logical unit (SLU) that has not yet been responded to by the SLU. This creates a pending active session at the SLU. When the SLU is a VTAM application program, it responds to a BIND by issuing an OPNSEC or SESSIONC macroinstruction.

queued call A telephone call that has been placed on hold and is waiting in the queue of telephone calls to be serviced by a system resource, such as an automatic call distribution (ACD) group.

queued CINIT In VTAM, a CINIT request sent from a system services control point (SSCP) to a logical unit (LU) that has not yet been responded to by the LU. This creates a pending active session at the LU. A VTAM application program responds to a CINIT by issuing an OPNDST ACCEPT or a CLSDST macroinstruction.

queue depth In SNADS, the number of distribution items on the distribution queue waiting to be sent. See also send depth, send time.

queued for connection In VTAM, the state of a terminal that has logged on to an application program but has not yet been accepted.

queued for logon In VTAM, the state of a terminal that has logged on to an application program but has not yet been accepted for connection. Contrast with connection.

queued indexed sequential access method QISAM. An extended version of the sequential form of the basic indexed sequential access method (BISAM). When this method is used, a queue is formed of input data blocks that are awaiting processing or of output data blocks that have been processed and are awaiting transfer to auxiliary storage or to an output device.

queued logon request In VTAM, a logon request that has been directed to a VTAM application program but not yet accepted.

queued printing services In DPCX, part of application services that helps a program store print data in record form. The data can be printed by a DPCX system service without user program intervention.

queue-driven task A task whose unit of work is represented by an element in a queue.

queued sequential access method (QSAM) An extended version of the basic sequential access method (BSAM). When this method is used, a queue is formed of input data blocks that are awaiting processing or of output data blocks that have been processed and are awaiting transfer to auxiliary storage or to an output device.

queued session In VTAM, pertaining to a requested LU-LU session that cannot be started because one of the logical units (LUs) is not available. If the session-initiation request specifies queuing, the SSCPs record the request and later continue with the session-establishment procedure when both LUs become available.

queued telecommunications access method A method used to transfer data between main storage and remote terminals. Application programs use GET and PUT macroinstructions to request transfer of data, which is performed by a message control program. The message control program synchronizes the transfer, thus eliminating delays for input/output operations.

queue element (1) A block of data in a queue. (2) An item in a queue.

queue file In VSE, a direct access file maintained by VSE/POWER that holds control information for the spooling of job input and job output.

queue management The network control program supervisor code controlling manipulation of block control units and queue control blocks. It manages input, pseudo-input, and work queues.

queue name In COBOL, a symbolic name that indicates to the message control system the logical path by which a message or a portion of a complete message may be accessible in a queue.

queue slice In VM, the maximum length of time that a virtual machine is allowed access to the processor before it is dropped from the user list.

queue stanza In the AIX operating system, a stanza that defines a queue for one or more devices to which jobs can be queued.

queue 1 In VM, a virtual machine that has just logged on or that finished its last turn in the run list before it exhausted its queue slice. It is interactive.

queue 2 In VM, a virtual machine that finished its last turn in the run list without completing its task. In VM/SP, it is noninteractive. In VM/SP HPO, a queue 2 virtual machine is not reclassified as noninteractive unless it remains queue 2 after its first queue 2 queue slice.

queue 3 In VM, virtual machines that have completed six or more queue slices or a queue 2 machine.

queuing The programming technique used to handle messages awaiting delivery. See also queue.

quick cell In OS/VS2, a reserved space in the system queue area or in a local system queue area that can be used to reduce the time required to allocate space for a control block.

quick cell facility A high-performance storage allocation technique using a fixed block size.

quick closedown (1) In VTAM, a closedown in which any RPL-based communication macroinstruction is terminated (posted complete with an error code), no new sessions can be established, and no new access method control blocks (ACBs) can be opened. See also cancel closedown, orderly closedown. (2) In ACF/TCAM, a closedown in which message traffic is stopped as soon as any messages are transmitted that are in the process of being sent or received at the time the request for closedown is received. Contrast with flush closedown. (3) See also closedown.

quick query A query that is run using only a file name and possibly some record selection specifications; an undefined query.

quick start Synonym for system restart (2).

quiesce (1) To end a process by allowing operations to complete normally. (2) In a VTAM application program, for one node to stop another node from sending synchronous-flow messages.

quiesce communication In VTAM, a method of communicating in one direction at a time. With this method, either node can assume the exclusive right to send synchronous-flow messages by getting the other node to agree not to send such messages. When the quiescing node wants to receive, it can release the other node from its quiesced state, allowing that node to send.

quiesce protocol In VTAM, a method of communicating in one direction at a time. Either the primary logical unit (PLU) or the secondary logical unit (SLU) assumes the exclusive right to send normal-flow requests, and the other node does not send such requests. When the sender wants to receive, it releases the other node from its quiesced state.

quiescing (1) The process of bringing a device or a system to a halt by rejection of new requests for work. (A)   (2) In a VTAM application program, a way for one node to stop another node from sending synchronous-flow messages.

quiet mode A mode that allows a process to be run unattended or from a remote workstation, which means that there is no user interaction required.

quiet recording mode In VM, a mode of operation in which transient processing unit and main storage errors that are corrected or circumvented by hardware retry or error correction code logic are not recorded on the VM error recording cylinders. This mode is entered via the SET MODE RETRY QUIET command or after 12 transient machine checks have occurred while in full recording mode.

quinary See biquinary code.

quintet A byte composed of five binary elements. (I)   (A)   Synonymous with 5-bit byte.

quit A key, command, or action that tells a system to return to a previous state or stop a process.

quotient (1) The number or quantity that is the value of the dividend divided by the value of the divisor and that is one of the results of a division operation. (I)   (A)   (2) The number or quantity that is the result of a division operation.   (3) See also remainder.

QWERTY The standard keyboard layout. The term is derived from the sequence of the first six keys in the first row of alphabetic keys. See also AZERTY, Dvorak. See Figure 120.

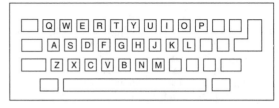

Figure 120. QWERTY Keyboard

R

RAB LU 6.2 resource allocation block.

RACDEF request In RACF, the issuing of the RACDEF macro or the RACROUTE macro with REQUEST=DEFINE specified. Also, using a RACF command to add or delete a resource profile causes a RACDEF request.

RACF Resource Access Control Facility.

RACF database A collection of interrelated or independent data items stored together without unnecessary redundancy, to serve Resource Access Control Facility (RACF).

RACF-indicated Pertaining to a data set that is RACF-protected.

Note: An indicator notifies the operating system that a data set is RACF-protected. For VSAM data sets, the indicator is in the catalog entry. For non-VSAM data sets, it is in the data set control block (DSCB) For data sets on tape, the indicator is in the tape volume profile of the volume that contains the data set.

RACF manager The routines within RACF that provide access to the RACF data base. Contrast with RACF storage manager.

RACF-protected (1) Pertaining to a resource that has either a discrete profile or an applicable generic profile. A data set that is RACF-protected by a discrete profile must also be RACF-indicated. (2) In RACF, a resource that has either a discrete profile or an applicable generic profile. A data set that is RACF-protected must also be RACF-indicated. (3) In MVS, pertaining to a data set for which the RACF indicator is set on.

RACF report writer A RACF function that produces reports on system use and resource use from information found in the RACF SMF records.

RACF segment The portion of a RACF profile that contains basic information needed to define a user, group, or resource to RACF. Synonymous with base

segment. See also DFP segment, DLFDATA segment, SESSION segment, TSO segment.

RACF storage manager In RACF, the routines that obtain and release system storage on behalf of RACF. Contrast with RACF manager.

RACINIT request In RACF, the issuing of the RACINIT macro or the RACROUTE macro with REQUEST=VERIFY or REQUEST=VERIFYX specified. A RACINIT request is used to verify the authority of a user to enter work into the system.

rack A free-standing framework that holds equipment.

rack configuration list In the AS/400 system, a list of all of the equipment within the rack and the logic cards within the card enclosure.

rack stabilizer In the AS/400 system, a plate that holds the rack stable or steady when a device is pulled out for service.

radial loop cable In the IBM 8100 Information System, a cable that connects a radial loop station connector (LSC) to a loop wiring concentrator (LWC).

radial transfer The process of transmitting data between a peripheral unit and a unit of equipment that is more central than that peripheral unit. (I)   (A)

radian A unit of angle measurement that can be converted into degrees of arc.

radiation The process of emitting energy consisting of electromagnetic waves.

radio button In SAA Advanced Common User Access architecture, a circle with text beside it. Radio buttons are combined to show a user a fixed set of choices from which only one can be selected. The circle is partially filled when a choice is selected.

radix (1) The positive integer by which the weight of the digit place is multiplied to obtain the weight of the digit place with the next higher weight; for example, in the decimal numeration system the radix of each digit place is 10, in a biquinary code the radix of each fives position is 2. (I)   (A)   (2) Deprecated term for base. (3) See floating-point radix, mixed radix notation.

radix complement (1) In a fixed radix numeration system, a complement that can be derived from a given number by subtracting it from a specified power of the radix. For example, "830" is the radix complement of "170" in the decimal numeration system using three digits, the power of the radix being "1000." (2) See diminished radix complement.

Note: The radix complement may be obtained by first deriving the diminished radix complement, then adding one to the least significant digit of the result and executing any carries required. (T)

radix-minus-one complement Synonym for diminished radix complement.

radix notation Synonym for radix numeration system.

radix numeration system A positional representation system in which the ratio of the weight of any one digit place to the weight of the digit place with the next lower weight is a positive integer. The permissible values of the character in any digit place range from zero to one less than the radix of that digit place. (I) (A) Synonymous with radix notation.

radix point In a representation of a number expressed in a radix numeration system, the location of the separation of the characters associated with the integral part from those associated with the fractional part. (I) (A)

ragged left Pertaining to text that is not aligned to the left margin. (T) Contrast with ragged right.

ragged right Pertaining to text that is not aligned to the right margin. (T) Contrast with ragged left.

ragged text Unjustified text.

rail Hardware attached inside a rack on which a device is installed.

rain barrel effect Sound on an overcompensated (equalized) line.

RAM Random access memory. (A)

RAMAC Random access memory. See direct access storage device.

RAM disk Synonym for virtual disk.

ramp See color ramp, gamma ramp.

random access (1) An access technique in which logical records are obtained from or placed in a storage device in a nonsequential manner. (2) In COBOL, an access mode in which the program-specified value of a key data item identifies the logical record that is obtained from, deleted from, or placed into a relative file or indexed file. Contrast with sequential access.

random access memory (RAM) (1) A storage device in which data can be written and read. (2) Deprecated term for direct access storage device. (T) (3) A storage device into which data is entered and

from which data is retrieved in a nonsequential manner. (4) See also direct access storage.

random access storage (RAS) Deprecated term for direct access storage.

random by key A processing method for files in which the value in the key field identifies the records to be processed.

random by relative record number A processing method for files in which relative record numbers identify the records to be processed.

random data set See direct data set.

randomizing A technique by which the range of keys for an indirectly addressed file is reduced to smaller ranges of addresses by some method of computation until the desired address is found.

random number (1) A number selected from a known set of numbers in such a way that each number in the set has the same probability of occurrence. (I) (A) (2) A number obtained by chance. (A) (3) One of a sequence of numbers considered appropriate for satisfying statistical tests or believed to be free from conditions that might bias the result of a calculation. (A)

random number sequence (1) A sequence of numbers each of which cannot be predicted only from a knowledge of its predecessors. (I) (A) (2) See pseudo-random number sequence.

random processing (1) The treatment of data without respect to its location in external storage, and in an arbitrary sequence governed by the input against which it is to be processed. (2) The processing of records in an order other than the order in which they exist in a file. See also consecutive processing, sequential processing. (3) In the AS/400 system, a method of processing in which records can be read from, written to, or deleted from a file order requested by the program that is using them. See also consecutive processing, sequential processing.

random scan Deprecated term for directed beam scan.

random-walk method In operations research, a variance-reducing method of problem analysis in which experimentation with probabilistic variables is traced to determine results of a significant nature. (A)

range (1) The set of values that a quantity or function may take. (I) (2) Synonym for span.

range check A limit check in which both high and low values are stipulated. (T)

range finder An adjustable mechanism on a teletypewriter receiver that allows the receiver-distributor face to be moved through an arc corresponding to the length of a unit segment. It is normally adjusted for best results under operating line conditions. See also orientation, receiving margin.

range specification The selection of the beginning and end of a character string of text. The range may be selected based on units such as word, line, paragraph, sentence, or page. (T)

rank (1) In FORTRAN, the number of dimensions of an array. It is zero for scalar. (2) Synonym for level number.

ranking Assigning weight factors to documents according to their relevance with respect to a query. (T)

RAR Route addition resistance.

RARP Reverse Address Resolution Protocol.

RAS (1) Random access storage. (2) Reliability, availability, serviceability.

raster (1) In computer graphics, a predetermined pattern of lines that provides uniform coverage of a display space. (T) (2) The coordinate grid that divides the display area of a display device. (A) (3) In the 3800 Printing Subsystem, an on/off pattern of electrostatic images produced by the laser print head under control of the character generator.

raster count In computer graphics, the number of lines in one dimension within a display space. (T)

raster display device A display device in which the display elements of a display image are generated on the display surface by raster graphics. (I) (A)

raster font A font in which the characters are defined directly by the raster bit map. See font, primitive font.

raster graphics (1) Computer graphics in which a display image is composed of an array of pixels arranged in rows and columns. (I) (A) (2) Contrast with coordinate graphics.

raster grid On a display device, the grid of addressable coordinates on the display surface.

raster overlay An overlay stored as raster patterns.

raster pattern (1) A series of picture elements (pels) arranged in scan lines to form an image. (2) In AS/400 advanced function printing (AFP) support, a series of pels arranged in scan lines. The toned or untoned status of each pel creates an image. A digitized raster pattern is an array of bits. The on or off status of each bit determines the toned or untoned status of each pel.

raster pattern generator (RPG) The electronic circuits that retrieve digitized raster patterns and convert them into a series of scan patterns.

raster pattern overlay An overlay loaded in the 3800 Printing Subsystem as a raster pattern.

raster pattern storage (RPS) An area of storage that holds raster patterns for fonts and images.

raster plotter A plotter that generates a display image on a display surface using a line-by-line scanning technique. (A)

raster scan (1) In computer graphics, a technique of generating or recording a display image by a line-by-line sweep across the entire display space; for example, the generation of a picture on a television screen. A raster scan may be directed by a program, in which case it may also be considered a directed-beam scan. (T) (2) In the 3800 Printing Subsystem, one horizontal sweep of the laser across the photoconductor. (3) See also directed beam scan.

raster unit In computer graphics, the distance between adjacent picture elements. (T)

rate See average information rate, average transinformation rate, data signaling rate, pulse repetition rate, refresh rate.

rate center A specified geographic location used by telephone companies to determine mileage measurements for the application of interexchange mileage rates.

rated speed Synonym for nominal speed.

ratio See error ratio, print contrast ratio, read-around ratio, residual error ratio.

rational number A real number that is the quotient of an integer divided by an integer other than zero. (I) (A)

raw data Data that have not been processed or reduced.

raw footage Synonym for original footage.

raw laser power The level of power, measured in milliwatts, of a laser beam measured at the laser.

ray-tracing In multimedia applications, a technique used by 3-D–rendering software programs that automatically determines the position of an object in three dimensions and calculates shadows, reflections, and hidden surfaces based on user-entered light locations and material characteristics; for example, if the user orders an object to be a mirror, the computer produces the mirror with all of its correct reflective properties.

RBA Relative byte address.

RCA Resident common area.

RCB Record control byte.

RCMS Remote change management server.

RCP Recognition and control processor.

RCR Required carrier return character.

RCS Revision Control System.

RCT Region control task.

RDT Resource definition table.

RDTE Resource definition table entry.

REA Request for Engineering Activity.

reaction shot In video or film production, a shot, usually a close-up, of a person intended to show the person's reaction to the immediately preceding events or actions.

read (1) To acquire or interpret data from a storage device, from a data medium, or from another source. (I) (A) (2) See destructive read, nondestructive read. (3) See CP read, VM read.

read access In computer security, permission to read information.

read-ahead queue In ACF/TCAM, an area of main storage from which an application program obtains work units in advance of a request from the application.

read-around ratio The number of times a specific spot, digit, or location in electrostatic storage may be consulted before spillover of electrons causes a loss of data stored in surrounding spots. The surrounding data must be restored before the deterioration results in any loss of data. (A)

read authority In the AS/400 system, a data authority that allows the user to look at the contents of an entry in an object or to run a program. See also add authority, delete authority, update authority.

read cycle time The minimum time interval between starts of successive read cycles of a storage device that has separate reading and writing cycles. (I) (A)

reader (1) In micrographics, a device that enlarges microimages for viewing. (A) (2) In word processing, a device that accesses coded information on recording media for further processing. (T) (3) A device that converts information in one form of storage to information in another form of storage. (4) A part of an operating system scheduler that reads an input stream into the system. (5) A program that reads jobs from an input device or database file and places them on a job queue. (6) In RJE, a program that reads jobs from a database file or interactive display station and sends them to the host system. (7) See card reader, character reader, microform reader, perforated-tape reader.

reader-copier See microform reader-copier.

reader/interpreter A part of job management that reads and interprets a series of job definitions from an input stream.

reader-printer In micrographics, a device that performs functions of a reader and a printer to produce hard copy enlargements of selected microimages. (A)

read-from-invited-program-devices operation In the AS/400 system, an input operation that waits for input from any one of the invited program devices for a user-specified time. Contrast with read-from-one-program-device operation.

read-from-one-program-device operation In the AS/400 system, an input operation that will not complete until the specified device has responded with input. Contrast with read-from-invited-program-devices operation.

read head A head that can only read.

reading Acquisition or interpretation of data from a storage device, from a data medium, or another source. (I) (A)

reading screen In the AIX operating system, one of two types of screens available when running the InfoExplorer program with an ASCII display. It contains procedural, conceptual, and information. One reading screen is available per InfoExplorer session. See navigation screen.

reading station Synonym for read station.

reading task In OS/VS, the job management task that controls reading and interpretation of job control statements, and reading and analysis of operator commands in an input stream.

reading window In the AIX operating system, one of three types of windows available when running the InfoExplorer program with a graphics display. It contains procedural, conceptual, and reference information. Multiple reading windows can be displayed in an InfoExplorer session. See artwork window, navigation window.

read intent In IMS/VS, one type of processing intent, defined for an application program, to process a database. IMS/VS schedules the program with any number of other programs except those with exclusive intent.

read lock In the AIX operating system, a lock that prevents any other process from setting a write lock on any part of the protected area. Contrast with write lock.

readme file A small file on a program diskette containing program and documentation updates.

read-modified operation In the 3270 Information Display System, an operation in which only display fields that have the modified data tag ON are transferred to the application program.

read-only A type of access to data that allows it to be read but not copied, printed, or modified. Synonymous with fixed.

read-only access See multiple map specification libraries, password protection.

read-only access mode In VM, an access mode associated with a virtual disk that allows a user to read, but not write or update, any file on the disk.

read-only intent In IMS/VS, the scheduling intent type that allows a program to be scheduled with any number of other programs except those with exclusive intent.

read-only memory (ROM) (1) A storage device in which data, under normal conditions, can only be read. (T) (2) Memory in which stored data cannot be modified by the user except under special conditions. Contrast with erasable storage. Synonymous with fixed storage. See control read-only memory, mask-program read-only memory, programmable read-only memory, reprogrammable read-only memory. See also CD-ROM, erasable programmable read-only memory (EPROM), programmable read-only memory (PROM), read-only storage (ROS).

read-only (RO) subpool In the IBM 8100 Information System, one of two subpools that make up the common address space section (CASS). The RO subpool does not let unauthorized users write into it,

but any process in any address space can read it. See also read-write (RW) subpool.

read-only storage (1) A storage device whose contents cannot be modified, except by a particular user, or when operating under particular conditions; for example, a storage device in which writing is prevented by a lock out. Synonymous with fixed storage. (I) (A) (2) See also read-only memory.

Note: The term read-only storage (ROS) is used primarily in large mainframes. The term read-only memory (ROM) is dominant in microcomputers and some minicomputers.

read-out device Synonym for character display device.

read path In a reader, a path that has a read station. (I) (A)

read protection Restriction of reading of the contents of a data set, file, or storage area by an unauthorized user or program.

read rights Authority to read the entries in an object. Contrast with add rights, delete rights, update rights.

read station The location in a reader where the data on a data medium are read. (I) (A) Synonymous with reading station, sensing station.

read/write access mode In VM, an access mode associated with a virtual disk that allows a user to read and write any file on the disk.

read/write head (1) A head capable of reading and writing. (I) (A) Synonymous with combined head. (2) The data sensing and recording unit of a diskette magazine drive or tape drive. See Figure 121.

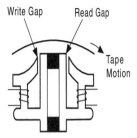

Figure 121. Read/Write Head

read/write opening Synonym for read/write slot. (I) (A)

read/write protection Restriction of access to a data set, file, or storage for reading and writing by authorized users or programs.

read-write (RW) subpool In the IBM 8100 Information System, one of two subpools that make up the common address space section (CASS). The RW subpool can be read or written into by any process in any address space. See also read-only (RO) subpool.

read/write slot Synonym for head slot.

ready condition The condition of a task that is in contention for the processing unit.

ready indicator On a document copying machine, an indicator that shows when the machine is ready to start. (T)

ready queue In ACF/TCAM, a chain of elements that represents the work to be performed.

ready state A state in which a task is ready to be activated and is contending for processor execution time.

real address (1) The address of a storage location in real storage. (I) (A) (2) In VM, the address of a location in real storage or the address of a real I/O device.

real address area In VSE, the area of virtual storage in which virtual addresses are equal to real addresses.

real address space In a VSE system operating in 370 mode, the address space whose addresses map one-to-one to the addresses in processor storage.

real constant A string of decimal digits that must have a decimal point, decimal exponent, or both.

real drive Synonym for nonstaging drive.

real estate In video systems, the space available for recording on a videodisc or videotape.

real image In multimedia, an image captured from nature, either through a still camera, a movie camera, or a television camera. Synonymous with realistic image.

realistic image Synonym for real image.

realm (1) A part of a database that can be opened and closed as a unit. (T) (2) In the CODASYL model, synonym for area *(2)*. (A)

real mode (1) In VSE, a mode in which a program may not be paged. See also virtual mode. (2) In the OS/2 operating system, a method of program operation that does not limit or prevent access to any instructions or areas of storage. The operating system loads the entire program into storage and gives the program access to all system resources.

real name The name by which a resource is identified in its native network.

real network address The address by which a logical unit (LU) is known within the SNA network in which it resides.

real number (1) A number that can be represented by a finite or infinite numeral in a fixed-radix numeration system. (I) (A) (2) A number containing a decimal point and stored in fixed-point or floating-point format.

real open system A real system that complies with the requirements of Open Systems Interconnection standards in its communication with other real systems. (T)

real resource (1) In VTAM, a resource identified by its real name and its real network identifier. (2) In the NetView Graphic Monitor Facility, an object that represents one resource. Contrast with aggregate resource.

real storage The main storage in a virtual storage system. Physically, real storage and main storage are identical. Conceptually however, real storage represents only part of the range of addresses available to the user of a virtual storage system. Traditionally, the total range of addresses available to the user was provided by the main storage. (I) (A)

real storage management (RSM) Routines that control allocation of pages in real storage.

real system In Open Systems Interconnection architecture, one or more computers, associated software, peripheral equipment, human operators, physical processes, and means of communication means that form an autonomous whole capable of performing information processing or information transfer. (T)

real system operator In the VM/XA Migration Aid, any user who loads and runs a VM/XA Migration Aid system in native mode. Contrast with virtual machine operator.

real table A physical file or a table created by SQL.

real time (1) In Open Systems Interconnection architecture, pertaining to the processing of data by a computer in connection with another process outside the computer according to time requirements imposed by the outside process. This term is also used to describe systems operating in conversational mode and processes that can be influenced by human intervention while they are in progress. (I) (A) (2) In Open Systems Interconnection architecture, pertaining to an application such as a process control system or a computer-assisted instruction system in which response to input is fast enough to affect subsequent input.

real-time control The control of a process by real-time processing. (I)   (A)

real-time input Input data received into a data processing system within time limits that are determined by the requirements of some other system or at instants that are so determined. (I)   (A)

real-time operation (1) In analog computing, operation in the computer mode, during which the time scale factor is one. (I)   (A)   (2) Synonym for real-time processing.

real-time output Output data delivered from a data processing system within time limits that are determined by the requirements of some other system or at instants that are so determined. (I)   (A)

real-time processing The manipulation of data that are required or generated by some process while the process is in operation; usually the results are used to influence the process, and perhaps related processes, while it is occurring. (I)   (A)   Synonymous with real-time operation.

real-time simulation The operation of a simulator so that the time scale factor is equal to one for a physical time specified by the system being simulated and by the corresponding computer time of the simulator. (A)

Real-Time Video (RTV) In Digital Video Interactive (DVI) technology, a video compression technique that operates in real time using the DVI system itself. It provides picture quality suitable for application development, but the final application is usually compressed using Production Level Video (PLV).

rear compression In VSAM, the elimination from a key of characters to the right of the first character that is unequal to the corresponding character in the following key.

reason code A code that identifies the reason for a detected error.

reasonableness check A check to determine whether a value conforms to specified criteria. (T)

reassign To mark a disk sector as damaged. The marked disk sector points to another sector location where the data from the damaged sector is moved.

reboot Synonym for system reset.

rebound distance On a typewriter, the distance between the face of the type element and the platen when the type element has engaged its stop. This dis-

tance influences the force of impression and depends on the thickness of the paper. (T)

rebuild maintenance A method of maintaining keyed access paths for database files. This method updates the access path only while the file is open. After the file is closed and reopened, the access path is rebuilt. Contrast with delay maintenance, immediate maintenance.

recall (1) In ACF/TCAM, a method of retrieving a message or a part of a message in order to process or redirect it.   (2) In the Data Facility Hierarchical Storage Manager, the process of moving a migrated data set from a level 1 or level 2 volume to a primary volume.

receive (1) To obtain and store data. (2) In systems with ACF/TCAM, to obtain a message transmitted from a terminal to the computer over a line. Contrast with send. See also accept, enter.

received line signal detector (RLSD) A signal defined in the EIA-232 standard that indicates to the data terminal equipment (DTE) that it is receiving a signal from the remote data circuit-terminating equipment (DCE).

receive interruption The interruption of a transmission to a terminal by a higher priority transmission from the terminal. Synonymous with break.

receive leg The side of a duplex line that is receiving. Contrast with transmit leg.

receive mode In the AS/400 system and System/38, a time during which the BSC adapter looks for synchronization characters, and stores the data characters in main storage.

receive not ready (RNR) In communications, a data link command or response that indicates a temporary condition of being unable to accept incoming frames.

receive not ready (RNR) packet See RNR packet.

receive-only typing reperforator A teletypewriter receiver producing perforated tape with characters along the tape edge. Synonymous with rotor.

receive pacing In SNA, the pacing of message units being received by a component. See also send pacing.

receiver (1) A person or thing that receives something. See also addressee. Contrast with sender. (2) See journal receiver.

receiver directory In the AS/400 system, summary information about the journal receivers that are or were attached to the specified journal and are still known to the system.

receive ready (RR) In communications, a data link command or response that indicates that a station is ready to receive protocol data units. Receive ready also acknowledges receipt of protocol data units.

receive ready packet See RR packet.

receiver-transmitter See universal receiver - transmitter.

receive state A state in which a transaction program can receive but not send data. Contrast with send state.

receive time-out In data communication, an indication that no data has been received in a specific period of time.

receiving In ACF/TCAM, the process by which the host processor obtains a message entered at a station. Contrast with sending.

receiving-end crossfire The crossfire in a telegraph channel introduced from one or more adjacent channels at the terminal end remote from the transmitter.

receiving margin In telegraph applications, the usable range over which a range finder may be adjusted. The normal range for a properly adjusted machine is approximately 75 points on a 120-point scale. Synonymous with operating range. See also range finder.

receiving perforator A punch that converts coded electrical pulse patterns into hole patterns or cuts in perforated tape. (A) Synonymous with tape punch.

receiving service user In Open Systems Interconnection architecture, a service user that acts as a data sink during the data transfer phase of a connection. (T)

receiving tray Synonym for delivery tray.

receptacle See lobe receptacle. See also port, EIA-232D.

reception congestion A network congestion condition occurring at a data switching exchange (DSE). (I) (A)

RECFMS Record formatted maintenance statistics.

recipient (1) The user to whom a message is addressed. (T) (2) In SAA usage, deprecated term for receiver. (3) Anyone or any location that receives data. (4) In data security, the person, institution, or other entity authorized to receive a message. (5) Contrast with originator.

RECMS Record maintenance statistics.

recognition See character recognition, magnetic ink character recognition, optical character recognition, pattern recognition.

recognition and control processor (RCP) In the IBM 3886 Optical Character Reader, a microprocessing unit that performs character recognition and controls operation of the machine.

recognition time In a digital input device, the time elapsed between the change of the value of a digital input signal and its recognition by the device. (T)

Recognized Private Operating Agency (RPOA) Any individual, company, or corporation, other than a government department or service, that operates a telecommunication service and is subject to the obligations undertaken in the Convention of the International Telecommunication Union and in the Regulations; for example, a communication common carrier. See also telecommunication Administration.

Recommendation X.3 See X.3.

Recommendation X.21 See X.21.

Recommendation X.25 See X.25.

Recommendation X.28 See X.28.

Recommendation X.29 See X.29.

recommended action Procedures suggested by the NetView program that can be used to determine the causes of network problems.

reconciliation procedure A control procedure that identifies and accounts for any difference between the values of a given balance and its associated control total. (T)

reconfiguration (1) A change made to a given configuration of a computer system; for example, isolating and bypassing a defective functional unit, connecting two functional units by an alternative path. Reconfiguration is effected automatically or manually and can be used to maintain system integrity. (T) (2) The process of placing a processing unit, main storage, and channels offline for maintenance, and adding or removing components. See I/O configuration, processor configuration.

reconstitution Synonym for reconstruction.

reconstruction The restoration of data to a previously known or defined state. (T)   Synonymous with reconstitution.

record (1) In programming languages, an aggregate that consists of data objects, possibly with different attributes, that usually have identifiers attached to them.   In some programming languages, records are called structures. (I)   (2) A set of data treated as a unit. (T)   (3) A set of one or more related data items grouped for processing. (4) In VTAM, the unit of data transmission for record mode.   A record represents whatever amount of data the transmitting node chooses to send. (5) In COBOL, synonym for logical record. See current record, fixed length record, next record, report writer logical record, variable length record.

record address file A file that indicates which records are to be read from another file, and the order in which the records are to be read.

record area In COBOL, a storage area allocated for the purpose of processing the record described in a record description entry in the File Section of the Data Division.   In the File Section, the current number of character positions in the record area is determined by the explicit or implicit RECORD

record block (1) In the 3790 Communication System, the basic storage and access unit of a record in a 3791 Controller. A relative data set record block contains one or more records (powers of 2), depending on the (fixed) record length.   An indexed data set record may consist of from one to eight record blocks and be variable in length within the data set. A buffer can contain only one record block at a time. (2) In DPCX, two or more records, a single record, or a portion of a record stored in one sector of disk storage. (3) See also program block.

record chain In DPCX, a series of blocks that make up a single indexed record.

record class In the query utility, one of the groups into which the query utility classifies records during preparation of a table.

record control byte (RCB) In the multi-leaving telecommunications access method (MTAM), a control character used to identify each record type within a transmission block.

record data transmission In PL/I, the transmission of data in the form of separate records.   Contrast with stream data transmission.

record description Synonym for record description entry.

record description entry In COBOL, the total set of record description entries associated with a particular record. Synonymous with record description.

recorded voice announcement (RVA) unit A device capable of continuous playback.

recorder file Synonym for system recorder file.

record file In BASIC, a file on disk in which the data is read and written in records.   Contrast with stream file.

record format The definition of how data are structured in the records contained in a file. The definition includes record name, field names, and field descriptions, such as length and data type. The record formats used in a file are contained in the file description. See Figure 122.

Fixed Length

| Record 1 | Record 2 | Record 3 | Record 4 |

Variable Length

| Record 1 | Rec 2 | Record 3 | Record 4 | Rec 5 | Rec 6 |

Unspecified Length

| Record 1 | |

Figure 122. Record Format

record format definition In IDDU, information that describes the arrangement or layout of fields in a record. A record format definition resides in a data dictionary. See also field definition, file definition.

record format description A description of the characteristics of the fields; for example, type and length, and the arrangement of the fields in a record created by the user.

record format descriptor A file in a store controller that can be used to describe the record layout of all keyed files.   These descriptors are used by the data maintenance/inquiry function to process records in the keyed files.

record format level identifier An identifier placed on a record format that uniquely identifies the record description. See also level checking.

record formatted maintenance statistics RECFMS. A statistical record built by an SNA controller and usually solicited by the host.

record gap Deprecated term for interblock gap, interrecord gap.

record ID code Record identification code.

record identification code Characters placed in a record to identify the record format.

record identifying indicator In the AS/400 system, an indicator that identifies the record just read.

recording density (1) Synonym for bit density. (2) The number of bits in a single linear track, measured per unit of length of the recording medium. (A)

recording filter In the NetView program, the function that determines which events, statistics, and alerts are stored on a database.

recording head On dictation equipment, a device that, when brought into contact or near contact with the recording medium, causes voice or other sound impulses to be recorded. (I)

recording level control On dictation equipment, a device used to control the strength of signals fed to the recording medium. (I)

recording level indicator On dictation equipment, a visual device that enables the operator to assess the strength of the recording signals. (I)

recording medium (1) A material on which program instructions and text are recorded. (T) (2) On dictation equipment, material on which voice or other sound impulses can be stored either in permanent or erasable form. (I) (3) See also data medium.

recording mode See full recording mode, intensive recording mode, quiet recording mode.

recording trunk A trunk from a local telephone central office or private branch exchange to a long distance office, used only for communication between operators.

record key (1) In word processing, a control key that places the equipment in record mode, that is, ready to receive text and program instructions on the recording medium or into storage. (T) (2) In the 3790 Communication System, a field within the first block of each record in an indexed data set that is used in storing and retrieving records in the data set. See also primary key, secondary key. (3) In RPG, all the key fields defined for the record type. (4) In COBOL, a key whose contents identify a record within an indexed file. Within an indexed file, a record key is either the prime record key or an alternate record key.

record layout The arrangement and structure of data or words in a record including the order and size of the components of the record. (I) (A)

record length Synonym for record size.

record level specifications In the AS/400 system and System/38, data description specifications coded on the same line as a record format name or on lines immediately following a record format name until the first field is specified.

record lock A lock that prevents some or all of a file from being written to or read.

record maintenance statistics (RECMS) An SNA error event record built from an NCP or line error and sent unsolicited to the host.

record mode (1) In VTAM, mode of data transfer in which the application program can communicate with logical units (LUs). Contrast with basic mode. (2) In IMS/VS message format service, the default input mode in which fields are defined as occurring in a specific record sent from the device. See also stream mode.

record-name In COBOL, a user-defined word that names a record described in a record description entry in the Data Division of a COBOL program.

record number (1) In COBOL, the ordinal number of a record in a file whose organization is sequential. (2) See print record number, relative record number, transaction record number. See also panel number.

record selection The process of selecting particular records from a file and including the information from the records; for example, in a report.

record separator A character used to indicate the end of one record and the beginning of another.

record separator character (RS) The information separator used to identify a logical boundary between records. (I) (A)

record size (1) The number of characters or bytes in a record. (T) (2) Synonymous with record length.

record type The classification of records in a file.

RECORD type In Pascal, the structured type that contains a series of fields. Each field may be of a type different from the other fields in the record.

recover After an execution failure, to establish a previous or new status from which execution can be resumed. (T)

recoverable abend An error condition in which control is passed to a specified routine that allows continued execution of the program. Contrast with unrecoverable abend. See also STAE, STAI.

recoverable catalog See VSAM recoverable catalog.

recoverable error An error condition that allows continued execution of a program.

recoverable resource See restorable resource.

recoverable transaction A transaction that can be restored in the event of a failure.

recovery (1) The reconstruction of a database; for example by means of backup files and after-images. (T)   (2) The resetting of system resources to a point at which computer programs can be restored without error in functional processing. (A)   (3) The act of resetting a system or data stored in a system to an operable state following damage.   (4) The process of restoring data from a backup file.   (5) See backward file recovery, error recovery, forward file recovery, inline recovery.

recovery and restart In a database management system, the procedures and capabilities available for reconstruction of the contents of a database to a state that prevailed before the detection of processing errors and before the occurrence of a hardware or software failure that resulted in the destruction of some or all of the stored data. (A)

recovery control (RECON) data sets Data sets in which database recovery control stores information about logging activity and events that might affect the recovery of data bases.

recovery function The capability of a functional unit to resume normal operation after a failure. (T)

recovery library A library containing information related to recovery of database operations after a system failure.

recovery management support (RMS) The facilities that gather information about hardware reliability and allow retry of operations that fail because of processing unit, I/O device, or channel errors. See also channel check handler, machine check handler.

recovery procedure (1) A process in which a specified data station attempts to resolve conflicting or erroneous conditions arising during the transfer of data. (T)   (2) An action performed by the operator when an error occurs to permit processing to continue.

recovery routine A routine entered when an error occurs during performance of an operation. It isolates the error, assesses its extent, indicates subsequent action, and attempts to correct the error and resume operation.

recovery termination manager A program that handles all normal and abnormal termination of tasks by passing control to a recovery routine associated with the terminated function.

recovery time When sending or receiving pulses, the time required between the end of a pulse and the beginning of the next pulse. (T)

recovery volume In systems with VSAM, the first volume of a prime index if the VSAM data set is key sequenced. Otherwise, the first volume of the data set.

recreatable database In DPPX/DTMS, database that is recoverable from a situation that would otherwise render the database unusable. Such a database can be reconstructed by using a previous copy in an unload data set, the audit file, and a DPPX/DTMS utility command. A recreatable database is also resettable and repairable. See also repairable database, resettable database.

recursion The performance of an operation in several steps, with each step using the output of the preceding step.

recursion level In the AS/400 system, the position of a program in a program stack; for example, the first occurrence of a program in a job has a recursion level of 1, the second occurrence of the same program has a recursion level of 2.

recursive (1) Pertaining to a process in which each step makes use of the results of earlier steps. (2) Pertaining to a program or routine that calls itself after each run until it is interrupted or until a specified condition is met.

recursive function A function whose values are natural numbers that are derived from natural numbers by substitution formula in which the function is an operand. (I)   (A)

recursively defined sequence (1) A series of terms in which each term after the first is determined by an operation in which the operands are some or all of the preceding terms. In a recursively defined sequence, there may exist a finite number of non-defined terms, possibly greater than one. (I)   (2) A series of terms in which each term after the first is determined by an operation in which earlier values of the function are operands. (A)

recursive procedure In the AS/400 system, an active procedure that can be called from within itself or from within another active procedure.

recursive program A program that can call itself, or be called by another program, and repeat indefinitely until a specified condition is met.

recursive routine A routine that can call itself or be called by another routine called by the recursive routine.

recursive subroutine A subroutine that may invoke itself. A recursive subroutine normally contains a call that invokes this subroutine directly or indirectly. (T)

recycle process A Data Facility Hierarchical Storage Manager process that, based on the percentage of valid data on a tape backup or migration level 2 volume, copies all valid data on the tape to a tape spill backup or migration level 2 volume.

Redbook audio In multimedia applications, the storage format of standard CDs and CD-ROMs formatted for use by computer systems. See also compact disc-digital audio (CD-DA).

REDUCE A programming language based on ALGOL and designed for nonnumeric manipulation of mathematical expressions.

reduced instruction-set computer (RISC) A computer that uses a small, simplified set of frequently used instructions for rapid execution.

reduction (1) In micrographics, a measure of the number of times the linear dimensions of an object are reduced when photographed. The reduction is generally expressed as 1:16, 1:24. (2) In a document copying machine, a copy on a scale smaller than 1:1 to the original. (T) (3) In a scanner, the action of reducing an image to a scale that is 1:1 smaller than the original size. (4) Contrast with enlargement. (5) See data reduction. (6) See also same size.

redundancy (1) In a functional unit, the existence of more than one means for performing a required function. (T) (2) In information theory, the amount R by which the decision content H_0 exceeds the entropy H; in mathematical notation:

$$R = H_0 - H$$

Usually, messages can be represented with fewer characters by using suitable codes; the redundancy may be considered as a measure of the decrease of the average length of the messages accomplished by

coding. (I) (A) (3) In the transmission of information, that fraction of the gross information content of a message that can be eliminated without loss of essential information. (4) See relative redundancy.

redundancy check (1) A check that uses one or more extra binary digits or characters attached to data for the detection of errors. (T) (2) See cyclic redundancy check.

redundancy check bit A check bit derived from a character and appended to the character. (A)

redundancy check character (1) A check character derived from a record and appended to the record. (A) (2) See cyclic redundancy check character.

reel (1) A cylinder with flanges on which tape or film can be wound. (I) (A) See -- Fig 'CN5R3' unknown --. (2) In COBOL, a discrete portion of a storage medium, the dimensions of which are determined by each implementor, that contains part of a file, all of a file, or any number of files. Synonymous with unit.

reel spindle On dictation equipment, a shaft that receives a supply reel. (I)

reenlargement In micrographics, a legible enlargement of a microimage. Synonymous with blow back.

reenterable Synonym for reentrant.

reenterable program Synonym for reentrant program.

reenterable routine Synonym for reentrant routine.

reenterable subroutine Synonym for reentrant subroutine.

reentrant The attribute of a program or routine that allows the same copy of a program or routine to be used concurrently by two or more tasks.

reentrant program (1) A computer program that may be entered at any time before any prior execution of the program has been completed. (T) (2) Synonymous with reenterable program.

reentrant routine (1) A routine that can be entered before completion of a prior execution of the same routine and execute correctly. (T) (2) Synonymous with reenterable routine.

reentrant subroutine (1) A subroutine that can be entered before completion of a prior execution of the same subroutine and execute correctly. (T) (2) Synonymous with reenterable subroutine.

reentry point The address or label of an instruction at which the computer program that called a subroutine is reentered from the subroutine. (I) (A)

reference (1) In programming languages, a language construct designating a declared language object. (I) (2) In FORTRAN, the appearance of a data object name or subobject designator in a context requiring the value at that point during execution, or the appearance of a procedure name, its operator symbol, or the assignment symbol in a context requiring execution of the procedure at that point.

Note: The act of defining a variable is not regarded as a reference.

reference bit In the System/370 system, a bit turned ON by hardware whenever the associated page in processor storage is referred to, that is, when it is read or stored into.

Note: In OS/VS1 and VSE, there is a reference bit in the storage key associated with each 2K storage block. In OS/VS2 and VM/370, there is a reference bit in each of two storage blocks associated with each page frame. In the MVS/XA system, there is one reference bit for each 4K of storage.

reference code (1) In text processing, an alphanumeric code at the beginning of a recorded document that identifies or describes the document; for example, a title line. (I) (A) (2) In the AS/400 system, the four-character name of a status or error condition.

reference code translation table An object that contains reference code and field-replaceable-unit (FRU) code records. These records are used to report hardware errors and for problem analysis and resolution.

reference edge (1) That edge of a data medium used to establish specifications or measurements in or on the medium. Synonymous with guide edge. (T) (2) See document reference edge.

reference format In COBOL, a format that provides a standard method for describing COBOL source programs.

reference language The set of characters and formation rules used to define a programming language. (I)

reference level See relative transmission level.

reference line In the AS/400 Business Graphics Utility, a straight line parallel to either the vertical or horizontal axis, relative to which data values are plotted on a chart. Synonymous with translated axis line.

reference modifier In COBOL, the leftmost character position and length used to establish and reference a data item.

reference noise The magnitude of circuit noise that will produce a circuit noise meter reading equal to that produced by ten micromicrowatts of electric power at 1000 cycles per second.

reference phrase In hypertext, text that is highlighted and preceded by a single-character input field used to signify the existence of a hypertext link.

reference phrase help In SAA Common User Access architecture, highlighted words or phrases within help information that a user selects to get additional information.

reference volume The magnitude of a complex electric wave, such as that on a standard volume indicator. The sensitivity of the volume indicator is adjusted so that reference volume, or zero VU, is read when the instrument is connected across a 600- ohm resistance to which is delivered a power of 1 milliwatt at 1000 cycles per second. See also voice unit.

refile The transmission of a message from a station on a leased line network to a station not serviced by the leased line network. This is usually accomplished by sending the message to a preselected telegraph office for retransmission as a telegram to the addressee.

reflectance (1) The ratio of reflected light to incident light. (2) The ratio of the intensity of a reflected beam relative to the source. (3) See also specular reflection.

reflected binary code Synonym for gray code.

reflective disc See optical reflective disc.

reflective marker See marker.

reflex copying In a document copying machine, a method of contact copying in which the sensitized material lies between the source of radiation and the master. (T)

refolder Synonym for continuous forms stacker.

reformat specification statement A single line of reformat specifications.

reformat specification statement set The reformat specification statements that make up a complete job.

refresh (1) In computer graphics, to repeatedly produce a display image on a display space so that the image remains visible. (T) (2) The process of repeatedly producing a display image on a display surface so that the image remains visible. (I) (A) (3) To recharge a memory location in volatile memory with an electric current so that it retains a state or binary value. (4) See system refresh.

Refresh In SAA Basic Common User Access architecture, an action that updates the information that a user is currently looking at.

refreshable The attribute of a load module that prevents it from being modified by itself or by any other module during execution. A refreshable load module can be replaced by a new copy during execution by a recovery management routine without changing either the sequence or results of processing.

refreshable program A program that can be replaced at any time with a new copy without changing either the sequence or results of processing.

refresh rate (1) The number of times per second that a display image is produced for refresh. (I) (A) (2) In word processing, the rate at which a displayed image is renewed in order to appear stable. (T)

regenerate (1) To restore information to its original state. (2) To recharge a dissipating storage device to its fully charged state.

regeneration (1) In computer graphics, the sequence of events needed to generate a display image from its representation in storage. (I) (A) (2) The restoration of stored information. (3) See signal regeneration.

regenerative track Part of a track on a magnetic drum or magnetic disk used in conjunction with a read head and a write head that are connected to function as a circulating storage. (A) Synonymous with revolver track.

region A variable-size subdivision of a dynamic area that is allocated to a job step or a system task.

regional center A control center (class 1 office) connecting sectional centers of the telephone system together. Every pair of regional centers in the United States has a direct circuit group running from one center to the other.

region class In IMS/VS, the class assigned to a message region to indicate the message classes that can be processed within the region. See also message class.

region control task (RCT) In TSO, the control program routine that handles quiesce/restore and LOGON/LOGOFF.

region job pack area (JPA) In OS/VS2, an area in a virtual region that contains modules that are not in the link pack area but are needed for the execution of jobs.

region size The amount of main storage available for a program to run. See also job region, step region.

register (1) A part of internal storage having a specified storage capacity and usually intended for a specific purpose. (T) (2) In DPCX, a field capable of containing 10 digits, a sign, and a decimal point, that can be used by a program for arithmetic calculations and for program control. (3) On a document copying machine, to accurately position the image of the original on the copy material. (T)

registered network ID An 8-byte name included in an IBM-maintained worldwide registry that has a structured format and is assigned to a particular IBM customer to uniquely identify a specific network.

register guides In a document copying machine, indicators on or near the platen that help position the original correctly. (T)

register insertion In a ring network configuration, a ring control scheme in which each station loads the frame it is transmitting into a shift register and, when the ring is idle, inserts the entire contents of the register into the ring. The sending station removes the register contents from the ring when it is returned by the receiving station. See also master node control, slotted-ring control, token-access control.

register length The storage capacity of a register. (I) (A)

registrable resource A logical unit that can be registered with a network node server, a central directory server, or both.

registration (1) The accurate positioning of an entity relative to a reference. (A) (2) On a document copying machine, the consistency of register on successive copies. (T) (3) In a duplicator, the consistency of the relative position of images printed on paper. (T) (4) In X.25, the process used between a data terminal equipment (DTE) and a data circuit-terminating equipment (DCE) to establish an agreement on which optional user facilities will be in effect; for example, the DTE can request that the DCE agree to or stop a previous agreement for an optional user facility. Also, a DCE can indicate the optional user facilities that are available or the optional user facilities that are currently in effect. The negotiation is accomplished through the exchange of registration packets. (5) In the ImagePlus system, the final step in the process of storing an object. Registration represents a positive identification of the object based on the temporary identifier. This results in the assignment of an object name and storage location committed to a permanent media through the Object Distribution Manager. The front-end application is notified after the object is stored.

registration mark In the 3800 Printing Subsystem, a standard mark printed above the print contrast mark for sensing by the printer to verify that the paper registration is correct.

REGS Registers.

regular command In the NetView program, any VTAM or NetView command that is not an immediate command and is processed by a regular command processor. Contrast with immediate command.

regulation Compensation for changes in loss as the temperature of a cable varies. Its purpose is to adjust equalization so that a flat frequency response is maintained as the temperature changes.

REJ Reject.

reject (REJ) (1) In communications, a data link command or response used to request the resending of information frames. (2) To cause portions of applied updates from becoming permanent parts of a data base. Contrast with commit.

reject character In the IBM 3886 Optical Character Reader, a character which cannot be recognized as a character in the font set specified for the field.

relation (1) In a relational database, a set of entity occurrences that have the same attributes. (T) (2) The comparison of two expressions to see if the value of one is equal to, less than, or greater than the value of the other. (3) In a relational database, a table that identifies entities and their attributes. Synonymous with flat file. (4) In COBOL, synonym for relational operator.

relational algebra An algebra for expressing and manipulating relations. Common operations in a relational algebra are projection, selection, join, cartesian product, union, intersection, and difference. (T)

relational calculus In a relational language, a means of generating new relations or subsets of existing relations by specifying characteristics of the desired tuples or their attributes. (A)

relational character In COBOL, one of the characters that express a relationship between two operands: = (equal to), > (greater than), < (less than).

relational checking (1) The evaluation of the operands in a relational expression, based on the relational

operator used. (2) In RPG, tests performed against two statements in a source program to ensure that the statements are valid; for example, a GOTO operation must have an associated TAG operation. This type of checking is done only by the compiler, as opposed to single-statement syntax checking that is done by the SEU function.

relational condition In BASIC and COBOL, a condition that relates two arithmetic expressions or data items.

relational database A database in which the data are organized and accessed according to relations. (T)

relational expression (1) An expression that consists of an arithmetic expression followed by a relational operator, followed by another arithmetic expression, and that can be reduced to a value that is true or false. (2) A logical statement that describes the relationship, such as greater than or equal to, of two arithmetic expressions or data items.

relational language In a database management system, a language for accessing, querying, and modifying a relation database. A relational language usually offers little computational capability. (T)

relational model (1) A data model whose pattern of organization is based on a set of relations defined in the form of tables whose rows of data items are ordered by the attributes of the associated data elements. (A) (2) A data model that provides for the expression of relationships among data elements as formal mathematical relations. (A)

relational operator (1) An operator that operates on at least two operands and yields a truth value; for example, ≤ (as in 5 ≤ 3, yielding false), "is initial word of" (as in XYZ is initial word of XYZU). (T) (2) The reserved words or symbols used to express a relational condition or a relational expression. (3) In COBOL, a reserved word, a relational character, a group of consecutive reserved words, or a group of consecutive reserved words and relational characters used to express a relational condition. (4) In FORTRAN, any of the set of operators that express an arithmetic condition that can be either true or false. The operators are: .gt., .GE., .LT., .LE., .EQ., and .NE.. They are defined as greater than, greater than or equal to, less than, less than or equal to, equal to, and not equal to, respectively.

relational structure A data structure whose data are arranged as tables of relations. (T)

relation character In COBOL, a character that belongs to the following set:

Character	Meaning
>	greater than
<	less than
=	equal to

relation condition In COBOL, the proposition, for which a truth value can be determined, that the value of an arithmetic expression, data item, nonnumeric literal, or index name has a specific relationship to the value of another arithmetic expression, data item, non-numeric literal, or index-name.

relationship In a relational database, an association, dependency, or link between two entities that is represented in the database.

relationship type A specified class of relationships, each of which is associated in the same way with a member of one class of entities. See also attribute type, entity type. (A)

relation type A specified set of relation having identical sets of attributes. A relation type can be characterized by a set of attribute names. (T)

relative address (1) A direct address that identifies a location by means of its displacement from a base address. (T) (2) See self-relative address. (3) Synonymous with displacement.

relative addressing (1) A method of addressing in which the address part of an instruction contains a relative address. (I) (A) (2) A means of addressing instructions and data areas by designating their locations in relation to the location counter or to some symbol.

relative block number A number identifying location of a block expressed as a difference with respect to a base address. The relative block number is used to retrieve a block from the data set.

relative byte address (RBA) (1) In RACF, the address of a profile in the RACF data base. (2) In systems with VSAM, the displacement of a data record or a control interval from the beginning of the storage space allocated to the data set or file to which it belongs.

relative coding Coding that uses machine instructions with relative addresses. (A)

relative command (1) In computer graphics, a display command that causes the display device to interpret the data following the command as relative coordinates. (I) (A) (2) Synonymous with relative instruction. Contrast with absolute command.

relative coordinate One of the coordinates that identify the position of an addressable point with respect to some other addressable point. (I) (A) See Figure 123.

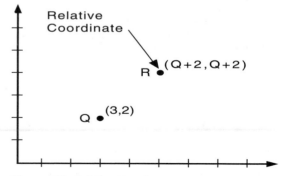

Figure 123. Relative Coordinate

relative data (1) In computer graphics, values in a computer program that specify displacements from the actual coordinates in a display space or in storage. Contrast with absolute data. (2) In the AS/400 Business Graphics Utility, values in a computer image that specify points relative to other points in the image.

relative data set A data set in which each record is assigned a record number according to its relative position within the data set storage space. The record number must be used to retrieve the record from the data set. See also indexed data set. See Figure 124.

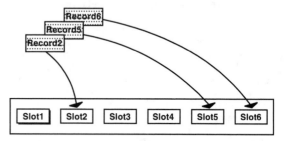

Figure 124. Relative Data Set

relative drawing commands Synonym for relative commend.

relative end position In RPG, an entry on the output specifications that indicates the number of blank positions that are to appear between a field or constant defined on one specification line and the field or constant defined on the preceding specification line. Contrast with exact end position.

relative entropy The ratio H_r of the entropy H to the decision content H_0; in mathematical notation:

$$H_r = H/H_0$$

(I) (A)

relative error The ratio of an absolute error to the true, specified, or theoretically correct value of the quantity that is in error. (I) (A)

relative file In COBOL, a file with relative organization.

relative file number In AS/400 data description specifications (DDS) for a join logical file, a sequential number assigned to a physical file based on the position of that file on the JFILE keyword specification.

relative instruction Synonym for relative command.

relative key In COBOL, a key whose contents identify a logical record in a relative file.

relative line number A number assigned by the user to a telecommunication line of a line group.

relative-name format In the AS/400 system, a print descriptor naming convention that uses group alias names instead of system-specific (actual) group names.

relative order Deprecated term for relative command.

relative organization In COBOL, the permanent logical file structure in which each record is uniquely identified by an integer value greater than zero, which specifies the logical ordinal position of the record in the file. Contrast with indexed organization, sequential organization.

relative path name In the AIX operating system, the name of a directory or file expressed as a sequence of directories followed by a file name, beginning from the current directory.

relative positioning In printing, the positioning of an element of an overlay with respect to the last position established by the last position command.

relative-record file A VSAM file whose records are loaded into fixed-length slots and are represented by the relative-record numbers of the slots they occupy.

relative-record number (RRN) (1) A number that indicates the location of a logical record, expressed as a difference with respect to a base address. The relative record number is used to retrieve the logical record from the data set. (2) A number that specifies the location of a record in relation to the beginning of a database file member or subfile; for example, the first record in a database file member or subfile has a relative record number of 1. (3) In VSAM, a number that identifies the slot, or data space, in a relative-record file and also the record occupying the slot. It is used as a key for keyed access to a relative-record

file. (4) A number assigned by a 3790 program to a record when that record is written to a relative data set. The record number must be used to retrieve the record from the data set. (5) In COBOL, the ordinal number of a record in a file whose organization is relative. This number is treated as a numeric literal which is an integer.

relative redundancy In information theory, the ratio r of the redundancy R to the decision content H_0; in mathematical notation:

$$r = \frac{R}{H_0} = \frac{H_0 - H}{H_0}$$

(I) (A)

relative sequential access method (RSAM) In DPPX, the access method that provides both sequential and direct processing of relative sequential data sets.

relative sequential data set (RSDS) In DPPX, a data set organized in terms of logical blocks. Each logical block may consist of records organized according to relative-record number.

relative-size pie In the AS/400 Business Graphics Utility, a piece in a pie chart drawn proportionally to another piece.

relative transmission level The ratio of the test-tone power at one point to the test-tone power at some other point in the system chosen as a reference point. The ratio is expressed in db. The transmission level at the transmitting switchboard is frequently taken as the zero level reference point. See also zero transmission level reference point.

relative vector Synonym for incremental vector.

relay center A central message switching center.

relay open system In Open Systems Interconnection Architecture, an open system that forwards data received from one open system to another open system. (T)

Note: A relay open system requires only the physical layer, data link layer, and network layer.

relay transaction A transaction program controlled by a CICS/VS transaction processing system that serves as an interface between a local terminal and a transaction program associated with another transaction processing system. The relay transaction routes message units back and forth between the local terminal and the remote transaction program.

release (1) A distribution of a new product or new function and APAR fixes for an existing product.

Normally, programming support for the prior release is discontinued after some specified period of time following availability of a new release. The first version of a product is announced as Release 1, Modification Level 0. See also modification level, version. (2) In VTAM, to relinquish control of resources (communication controllers or physical units). See also resource takeover. Contrast with acquire *(2)*

release-program-device operation In the AS/400 system and System/38, an operation that makes a program device not available for input/output operations. Contrast with acquire-program-device operation.

RELFILES In SMP/E, relative files. Files that contain modification text and JCL input data associated with SYSMOD.

reliability The ability of a functional unit to perform a required function under stated conditions for a stated period of time. (I) (A)

relief height The distance an embossed character is raised above the surface of a plastic identification card. (A)

relinquish In MSS, to free space on a staging drive; this may cause data to be destaged.

relocatable Attribute of a set of codes whose address constants can be altered to make up for a change in origin.

relocatable address An address that needs to be adjusted when the computer program containing it or data the address refers to is relocated. (T)

relocatable expression An expression whose value is affected by program relocation. A relocatable expression can represent a relocatable address.

relocatable load module A combination of object modules having cross references resolved and prepared for loading into storage for execution. Relocation dictionary (RLD) information is saved with the load module to allow it to be loaded at an address different from the one for which it was built.

relocatable module In VSE, a library member of the type "object module." It consists of one or more control sections cataloged as one member.

relocatable program An object program that is in such a form that it may be relocated. (T)

relocatable term A term whose value is affected by program relocation.

relocate (1) To move a computer program or part of the program in main storage and to make the necessary adjustment of address references so that the program can be executed after being moved. (A) (2) To move all or part of an object program in an address space and to make the necessary adjustment of addresses so that the object program can be executed in the new location. (T)

relocate hardware Synonym for dynamic address translation *(2)*.

relocating loader (1) A loader that adjusts addresses, relative to the assembled origin, by the relocation factor. (A) (2) In VSE, a function that modifies addresses of a phase, if necessary, and loads the phase into a partition selected by the user.

relocation (1) The modification of address constants to compensate for a change in origin of a module, program, or control section. (2) See dynamic relocation.

relocation dictionary The part of an object module or load module that identifies all addresses that must be adjusted when a relocation occurs. (A)

relocation factor The algebraic difference between the assembled origin and loaded origin of a computer program. (A)

relocation interrupt See page fault.

REM Ring error monitor.

remainder (1) In a division operation, the number or quantity that is the undivided part of the dividend, having an absolute value less than the absolute value of the divisor, and that is one of the results of a division operation. (I) (A) (2) See also quotient.

remark Synonym for comment.

remedial feedback In computer-aided instruction, an explanation issued by the application to a user of why a particular response was wrong.

reminder In System/36, a calendar item that includes a date but no start time or end time.

remote (1) Pertaining to a system, program, or device that is accessed through a telecommunication line. Contrast with local. (2) Synonym for link-attached.

remote access Pertaining to communication with a data processing facility through a data link. (A)

remote access data processing (1) Data processing in which some input/output functions are performed by devices that are connected to a computer system by data communication means. (T) (A) (2) Data processing in which certain portions of input/output functions are situated in different places and connected by transmission facilities. Synonymous with teleprocessing. See also distributed data processing (DDP).

remote access data processing network A network in which input/output devices are connected by data links to a central computer. See also distributed data processing network.

remote assistance Problem diagnosis and recovery, maintenance, and program help offered by IBM over a telecommunication line.

remote batch entry Submission of batches of data through an input unit that has access to a computer through a data link. (I) (A)

remote batch processing Batch processing in which input-output units have access to a computer through a data link. (I) (A)

remote change management server (RCMS) In the AS/400 retail communications and Point-of-Sale Communications Utility/400, a store controller program that communicates over an SNA/SDLC network that connects a host processor and a store controller. RCMS allows the NetView Distribution Manager to access point-of-sale controller files. It also provides error reporting and recovery for failures and data format conversion for files.

remote console function In the NetView/PC program, the function that allows one PC to control another.

remote controller (1) A device, attached to a telecommunication line, that controls the operation of one or more remote devices. (2) Contrast with local controller.

remote destination (1) Any location to which data is transmitted over a telecommunication line. (2) In an IMS/VS multisystem environment, a destination that is in a remote system. Contrast with local destination.

remote device A device that is connected to a computer over a telecommunication line.

remote entry services (RES) In OS/VS1, the set of functions added to the Job Entry Subsystem (JES) that allows jobs and their associated data to be entered from remote devices (System/38), processed at the central system, and then transmitted back to remote devices.

remote host Any host on a network except the one at which a particular operator is working. Synonymous with foreign host.

remote job entry (RJE) Submission of a job through an input unit that has access to a computer through a data link. (I) (A)

Remote Job Entry Facility (RJEF) A System/38 licensed program that allows transmission of jobs to a host system over a data link.

remote key In the Programmed Cryptographic Facility, a cryptographic key used to encipher or decipher the operational key used to encipher or decipher data on a portable medium; for example, magnetic tape.

remotely started session In System/36, a session started by an incoming procedure start request from the remote system. See also acquired session.

remote maintenance Maintenance of IBM rental or purchased products at other than the customer location; for example, at a branch office, regional center, or plant site.

remote modem self-test (RST) A check on hardware to identify a field-replaceable unit that is failing.

remote name server In TCP/IP, the function that allows a system to get an Internet address from a remote site rather than from its own host table.

remote network control program Synonym for link-attached network control program.

remote operations service element (ROSE) An application service element that provides generalized facility for initiating and controlling operations remotely. (T)

Remote Operation/Support Facility (ROSF) In System/36, a facility that allows an operator at a remote support group to use a remote display station and an optional remote printer to provide operational and technical assistance.

remote PC In the NetView/PC program, the PC that runs the local PC, which has had its keyboard locked by means of the remote control function. Contrast with local PC.

remote power off An optional, program-supported feature of a remote communication controller by means of which the controller power can be turned off on command from the host processor.

Remote PrintManager (RPM) In AS/400 Advanced Function Printing (AFP) support, a personal computer product that allows selected font data, overlays, and page segments that are present in Advanced Function Printing data streams to be available to a locally attached IBM page printer.

remote program loader A feature that includes a read-only storage unit and a small auxiliary-storage device installed in a remote controller to allow the controller to be loaded and dumped over a data link.

remote resource access capability A service provided by transaction processing systems that facilitates distribution of resources, such as files and queues, throughout a network and provides a means for transaction programs to access such resources easily.

Remote Spooling Communications Subsystem (RSCS) The licensed program that transfers spool files, commands, and messages between VM users, remote stations, and remote and local batch systems through HASP-compatible telecommunication facilities.

remote station (1) Data terminal equipment for communicating with a data processing system through a data link. (A)   (2) Synonym for link-attached station. See Figure 125.

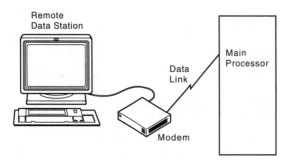

Figure 125. Remote Station

remote system Any other system in a network with which a system can communicate.

remote terminal Synonym for link-attached terminal.

remote terminal access method (RTAM) A facility that controls operations between remote terminals and the job entry subsystems, JES2 and JES3.

remote transaction In an IMS/VS multisystem environment, a transaction whose total processing is shared between two or more systems.   Contrast with local transaction.

remote transaction program The   transaction program at the other (remote) end of a conversation. Contrast with local transaction program.

remote workstation A workstation that is connected to a system by means of data transmission facilities. Contrast with local workstation.

remove (1) In journaling, to remove the after-images of records from a physical file member.   The file then contains the before-images of the records in the journal. Contrast with apply. (2) In the IBM Token-Ring Network, to take an attaching device off the ring.

Rename In SAA usage, a choice in the File pull-down that a user can select to change the name of a file.

render (1) In computer graphics, to create an image on a display screen from data that describes the scene. (2) In multimedia videotaping, to create a realistic image from objects and light data in a scene.

reorder Deprecated term for order *(2)*.

reorganization (1) A major change in the way a database is logically or physically structured. Synonymous with restructuring. (A)   (2) In a database management system, the rearrangement of the contents of a database that becomes necessary when the total storage space allocated to the database becomes exhausted, or when utilization of storage space becomes degraded and wasteful as a result of ongoing processing activity in database operations. Synonymous with restructuring. (A)   (3) A change of the physical arrangement of data to obtain a better correspondence of the physical and logical structures in order to speed up access and to utilize storage more efficiently. (T)

reorganize (1) To change the manner in which data is stored, printed, or displayed.   (2) To change the structure or contents of files.   (3) In System/36, to move folder members together at the front of the folder in order to reduce as much as possible the number of extents in the folder.

repagination (1) In text processing, a renumbering of pages that results from a change in the contents of a document. (A)   (2) In text processing, a recalculation of the page break points that result from a change in the contents of a document. (A)

repair See mean time to repair.

repeatability The measure of the difference between the mean value and some maximum expected value for a particular data reading.

repeatability measure In computer graphics, a measure of the spatial coincidence of each display image as it is produced repeatedly. (T)

repeat-action key A key that, when held fully depressed, causes an action, such as typing a character, to be repeated until the key is released;   for example, a typematic key.

repeat character (RPT) In word processing, a device control that causes a storage location pointer to reset to a designated buffer beginning point for the device. See also page end character, switch character.

repeated selection sort A selection sort in which the set of items is divided into subsets and one item that meets specified criteria from each subset is selected to form a second level subset. A selection sort is applied to this second level subset. The selected item in this second level subset is appended to the sorted set and is replaced by the next eligible item in the original subset. The process is repeated until all items are in the sorted set. (A)

repeater (1) A node of a local area network, a device that regenerates signals in order to extend the range of transmission between data stations or to interconnect two branches. (T) (2) A device used to amplify or reshape signals. See regenerative repeater, single-line repeater.

repeater coil A one-to-one ratio audio-frequency transformer for transferring energy from one electrical circuit to another and to permit, in wire telecommunication, the formulation of simplex and phantom circuits.

repeating key A key that continues to operate as long as it is held down. (I) (A)

repeat key (1) A control by means of which a function can be repeatedly performed as long as the key is kept depressed. (T) (2) A typematic key.

repeat key stroke On a typewriter, repeated actuation of the same key. (T)

reperforator See receiving perforator.

reperforator/transmitter (RT) A teletypewriter unit with a reperforator and tape transmitter, each independent of the other. It is used as a relaying device and is especially suitable for transforming incoming speed to a different outgoing speed, and for temporary queuing.

repertoire See instruction repertoire.

repetition instruction An instruction that causes one or more instructions to be executed an indicated number of times. (A)

repetitive addressing A method of implied addressing, applicable only to zero-address instructions, in which the operation part of an instruction implicitly addresses the operands of the last instruction executed. (I) (A)

repetitive operation The automatic repetition of the solution of a set of equations with fixed combinations of initial conditions and other parameters. Repetitive operation is often used to permit the display of an apparently steady solution. It is also used to permit manual adjustment or optimization of one or more parameters. (I) (A)

replace A function or mode that enables the user to substitute text for a specified part of previously entered text. (T)

replaceable parameter In the OS/2 operating system, a parameter whose value is supplied when a batch file is run.

replacement code point In alerts, a 2-byte code point in which the first byte indexes text providing a high-level description of a condition and the second byte indexes text providing a more specific description. The second byte is nonzero. See default code point.

replace mode In SAA Common User Access architecture, a method of text entry in which existing characters are replaced with the characters a user types. Contrast with insert mode.

replicate To copy all or a specified portion of data.

replication See index replication.

replicates Videodisc copies pressed from a stamper. See also stamper.

reply (1) A response to an inquiry. (2) In SNA, a request unit sent only in reaction to a received request unit. Synonymous with reply request. (3) In AIX Enhanced X-Windows, the manner in which information requested by a client program is sent back to the client. Both events and replies are multiplexed on the same connection. Most requests do not generate replies; some generate multiple replies.

reply message A message that is sent as a response to a received inquiry or notify message.

reply request Synonym for reply (2).

report In AS/400 query management, the formatted data that results from running a query and applying a form to it.

report clause In COBOL, a clause in the Report Section of the Data Division that appears in a report description entry or a report group description entry.

report description entry In COBOL, an entry in the Report Section of the Data Division that is composed of the level indicator RD, followed by the report-name, followed by a set of report clauses as required.

report file In COBOL, an output file whose file description entry contains a report clause. The contents of a report file consist of records that are written under control of the report writer control system.

report footing In COBOL, a report group that is presented only at the end of a report. Contrast with report heading.

report generation A technique for producing complete machine reports from information that describes the input file and the format and content of the output report. See RPG II.

report group In COBOL, a 01 level-number entry and its subordinate entries in the Report Section of the Data Division.

report group description entry In COBOL, an entry in the Report Section of the Data Division that is composed of the level-number 01, an optional data-name, a TYPE clause, and an optional set of report clauses.

report heading In COBOL, a report group that is presented only at the beginning of a report. Contrast with report footing.

report line In COBOL, a division of a page representing one row of horizontal character positions. Each character position of a report line is aligned vertically beneath the corresponding character position of the report line above it. Synonym for line.

Note: Report lines are numbered consecutively from 1, starting at the top of the page.

report-name In COBOL, a user-define word that names a report described in a report description entry within the Report Section of the Data Division.

Report Program Generator A programming language specifically designed for writing application programs that meet common business data processing requirements.

Report Section In COBOL, the section of the Data Division that contains zero, one, or more report description entries and their associated report group description entries.

report writer control system (RWCS) In COBOL, an object time control system, provided by the implementor, that accomplishes the construction of reports.

report writer logical record In COBOL, a record that consists of the report writer print line and associated control information necessary for its selection and vertical positioning.

reposition indicator On a typewriter, a device in typewriters with proportional pitch to relocate the typing position for a particular character. (T)

repositioning A process in which the 3800 Print Services Facility, following an indication from the printer of a potentially recoverable error, locates the proper spool record for recomposing one or more pages for printing.

reproduce Synonym for duplicate.

reproducer Synonym for reproducing punch.

reproducing punch A punched card device that prepares one punched card from another punched card, copying all or part of the data from the punched card that is read. (I) (A) Synonymous with reproducer.

reproduction scale In a document copying machine, the relative linear dimensions of the copy to the original. (T)

reprogrammable read-only memory Synonym for erasable programmable read-only memory. (T) (A)

repurposing The process of modifying the content of an existing computer program or video presentation to perform a function different from that for which it was originally intended.

REQMS Request for maintenance statistics.

request (1) A directive, by means of a basic transmission unit, from an access method that causes the network control program to perform a data-transfer operation or auxiliary operation. (2) In SNA, a message unit that signals initiation of an action or protocol; for example, INITIATE SELF is a request for activation of an LU-LU session. (3) In AIX Enhanced X-Windows, a command to the server to send a single block of data over a connection.

Request Commit A PS header that flows as part of commit processing, indicating that the sender is ready to commit or back out.

request data In System/38, data to be put in a job message queue that is used by a job, for example, a single command or group of commands.

request for maintenance statistics (REQMS) A host solicitation to an SNA controller for a statistical data record.

request for test (RFT) In BSC, a request to perform an online test function.

request functional transmission (RFT) In System/38 (RJEF) MTAM, a control character indicating a request for permission to send reader data or writer data. Contrast with grant functional transmission.

request header (RH) In SNA, a request unit (RU) header preceding a request unit.

request message A message that requests a function from the receiving program.

request parameter list (RPL) In VTAM, a control block that contains the parameters necessary for processing a request for data transfer, for establishing or terminating a session, or for some other operation.

request primitive In Open Systems Interconnection architecture, a primitive issued by a service user to invoke a procedure. (T)

request/response header (RH) In SNA, control information preceding a request/response unit (RU) that specifies the type of request/response unit and contains control information associated with the request/response unit.

request/response unit (RU) In SNA, a generic term for a request unit or a response unit.

request unit (RU) (1) A message unit that contains control information, end-user data, or both. (2) In DPCX, the smallest unit of data or control information that is sent to or received from a processor via a data link.

required carrier return A manually entered carrier return used after short lines or at end of a paragraph to ensure no more text is added to the line during automatic rearrangement of text.

required carrier return character (RCR) A word processing formatting control that moves the printing or display point to the first position of the next line and resets the indent tab mode. Required carrier return must be executed wherever it occurs in the character string. See also carrier return character. Synonymous with required new line character. Contrast with index return character.

required cryptographic session A cryptographic session in which all outbound data is enciphered and all inbound data is deciphered. Synonymous with mandatory cryptographic session. See also clear session, selective cryptographic session.

required hyphen (1) A hyphen that is normally used between two words rather than between syllables of a word. (2) Synonym for hard hyphen. (T)

required hyphen character (HYP) A word processing formatting graphic used whenever the graphic

hyphen must not be changed during formatting operations. Contrast with syllable hyphen character.

required list In AIX Enhanced X-Windows, an ordered list containing a subset of the installed color maps.

required new line character Synonym for required carrier return character.

required page break A function that enables the user to initiate the procedure for terminating a page. Synonymous with forced new page. (T)

required page end character (RPE) A word processing formatting control that initiates the procedure for terminating a page. Required page end must be honored as a page delimiter wherever it occurs in a character string. See also page end character.

required parameter A parameter for which no value is automatically supplied. The user must provide a value.

required space In word processing, a space or blank that must not be removed when adjusting a line or paragraph of text.

required space character (RSP) A word processing formatting graphic that causes the printing or display point to move to the right to the next active position. A required space is treated as a graphic character, not as an interword space or information separator, in implementing formatting operations; for example, to concatenate words in a phrase that is to be underscored using the word underscore character. See also space character.

requirement An essential condition that a system has to satisfy. (T)

requirements analysis A systematic investigation of user requirements to arrive at a definition of a system. (T)

rerun (1) A repeat of a machine run from its beginning, usually made desirable or necessary by a false start, interruption, or change. (I) (A) (2) To repeat a machine run. (A)

rerun mode A mode in which previously entered data are printed or displayed at the terminal. This mode allows the terminal operator to check the data, make a clean copy of the data, or correct the data. Contrast with enter/inquiry mode.

rerun point The location in the sequence of instructions in a computer program at which all information pertinent to the rerunning of the program is available. (A)

rerun time That part of operating time that is used for reruns due to faults or mistakes in operations. (T) (A)

RES Remote entry services.

rescale The process of changing characters of one point size to another point size; for example, in the Print Management Facility, the process of changing the picture element (pel) density of 3800 Printing Subsystem Model 1 character graphics so they can be printed on the 3800 Printing Subsystem Model 3 with its higher picture element (pel) density.

rescue point Synonym for restart point.

reserved filetypes (1) In VM, filetypes recognized by the CMS Editor as having specific default attributes that include record size, associated with that particular filetype. The Editor creates a file according to these attributes. (2) In VM, filetypes recognized by CMS commands, that is, commands that only search for and use particular filetypes, or create one or more files with a particular filetype.

reserved message codes Folder Application Facility message codes that are reserved for use by the application.

reserved page frame performance option In VM, a virtual machine option that reserves a specific number of page frames for use by one virtual machine. Generally, this option allows the most recently active pages of a virtual machine to remain allocated in real storage.

reserved page option In VM, a virtual machine option that allows the most active pages of a virtual machine to remain allocated in real storage.

reserved volume In OS/VS, a volume that remains mounted until the operator issues an UNLOAD command.

reserved word (1) In programming languages, a keyword that may not be used as an identifier. (I) (2) A word used in a source program to describe an action to be taken by the program or the compiler. It must not appear in the program as a user-defined name or a system name. (3) In COBOL, a COBOL word specified in the list of words that may be used in a COBOL source program, but that must not appear in the program as user-defined words or system-names.

reservoir See developer reservoir, toner reservoir.

reset (1) To cause a counter to take the state corresponding to a specified initial number. (I) (A) (2) To put all or part of a data processing device back into a prescribed state. (I) (A) (3) In SAA Advanced Common User Access architecture, a push button that resets changed fields to their initial values and displays them in the window. (4) On a virtual circuit, reinitialization of data flow control. At reset, all data in transit are eliminated. (5) To return a device or circuit to a clear state.

reset collision A condition that occurs when a data terminal equipment (DTE) and a data circuit-terminating equipment (DCE) simultaneously transmits a reset request packet and a reset indication packet over the same logical channel. See also call collision, carrier sense multiple access with collision detection (CSMA/CD), clear collision.

reset-confirmation packet In X.25 communications, a packet transmitted by the data terminal equipment (DTE) to inform the data circuit-terminating equipment (DCE) that a reset operation has been processed.

reset mode Synonym for initial condition mode.

reset packet A packet used to reset a virtual circuit at the interface between the data terminal equipment (DTE) and the data circuit-terminating equipment (DCE).

resident Pertaining to computer programs or data while they remain on a particular storage device. (T)

resident control executive area The area of main storage in which DPCX is stored.

resident control program Synonym for nucleus.

resident file A file that exists on disk until it is specifically deleted or changed to a scratch file.

resident program (1) A program that remains in a particular area of storage. (2) In DPCX, a program or system service that has been copied to processor storage so that disk paging is not needed for its execution.

resident program select list A list of programs in or scheduled to be copied into resident program storage.

resident program storage In DPCX, the part of the extended area in processor storage that contains resident programs, system services, or both. The size of resident program storage is specified as a part of system configuration.

residual error ratio The error ratio remaining after attempts at correction are made. (A)

residue In computer security, data remaining in a data medium but not associated with a data object.

residue check (1) A validation check in which an operand is divided by a number n to generate a remainder that is then used for checking. (A) (2) Synonym for modulo-N check.

resilience (1) Synonym for fault tolerance. (2) See system resilience.

resolution (1) In computer graphics, a measure of the sharpness of an image, expressed as the number of lines and columns on the display screen or the number of pels per unit of area. (2) See also definition. (3) A measure of the sharpness of an input or output device capability, as given by some measure relative to the distance between two points or lines that can just be distinguished. (4) The number of addressable pels per unit of length. (5) The number of lines in an image that an imaging system, such as a telescope, a camera, or the human eye, can resolve. A higher resolution makes text and graphics appear clearer.

resolve (1) In programming, to change a predefined, symbolic value to the actual value of the item being processed. For example, a symbolic value of LAST defined for the name of a file member is resolved to the name of the last member when the member is processed. (2) In WP/36, to prepare a document for printing.

resolver (1) A functional unit whose input analog variables are the polar coordinates of a point and whose output analog variables are the Cartesian coordinates of the same point, or vice versa. (I) (A) (2) A device whose input is a vector quantity and whose outputs are components of the vector. (A) See Figure 126. (3) In TCP/IP, a program or subroutine that obtains information from a domain name server or local table for use by a calling program.

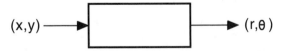

Figure 126. Resolver

resolver routine In the AIX operating system, a kernel process used to resolve symbolic host names into Internet addresses.

resource (1) Any of the data processing system elements needed to perform required operations, including storage, input/output units, one or more processing units, data, files, and programs. Synonymous with computer resource. (T) (2) Any facility of a computing system or operating system required by a job or task, and including main storage, input/output devices, processing unit, data sets, and control or processing programs. (3) A transaction

program controlled by a CICS/VS transaction processing system that serves as an interface between a local terminal and a transaction program associated with another transaction processing system. The relay transaction routes message units back and forth between the local terminal and the remote transaction program. (4) In AIX Enhanced X-Windows, an item such as a window, pixmap, cursor, font, graphics context, or colormap that has a unique identifier associated with it for naming purposes. The lifetime of a resource is bounded by the lifetime of the connection over which the resource was created. (5) In AIX Enhanced X-Windows, named data in a widget that can be set by a client, by an application, or by user defaults. (6) In the AIXwindows program and Enhanced X-Windows, a unique characteristic of appearance or behavior that is associated with one specific class of graphical object. Resources can be passed downward (inherited) by each subclass that is downstream from a higher-level class in the class hierarchy. (7) See child resource. (8) In COBOL, a facility or service, controlled by the operating system, that can be used by an executing program. (9) In the NetView program, any hardware or software that provides function to the network. (10) Synonym for resource object. (11) See network resource.

Resource Access Control Facility (RACF) An IBM-licensed program that provides for access control by identifying and by verifying the users to the system, authorizing access to protected resources, logging the detected unauthorized attempts to enter the system, and logging the detected accesses to protected resources.

resource access security In IMS/VS, the use of system definition macroinstructions and security maintenance utility control statements to limit the IMS/VS resources that can be used by application programs and utilities executing in dependent regions.

resource allocation (1) The assignment of the facilities of a computer system for the accomplishment of jobs; for example, assignment of main storage, input-output devices, or files. (I) (A) (2) See dynamic resource allocation.

resource-based access control In computer security, access control based on the subject's presentation of evidence of authorization, such as an object-related password, with a request for access to an object. Contrast with identity-based access control.

Resource Control table (RCT) The CICS table that contains customization information for a particular Object Distribution Manager installation.

resource definition A library member containing the set of records that collectively define a resource.

resource definition online (RDO) A CICS interactive facility to create and modify system resources.

resource definition table (RDT) In VTAM, a table that describes the characteristics of each node available to VTAM and associates each node with a network address. This is the main VTAM network configuration table.

resource group class In RACF, a class in which resource group profiles can be defined. A resource group class is related to another class, sometimes called a "member class"; for example, resource group class GTERMINL is related to class TERMINAL. See also resource group profile.

resource group profile In RACF, a general resource profile in a resource group class. A resource group profile can provide RACF protection for one or more resources with unlike names. See also resource group class.

resource hierarchy In VTAM, the relationship among network resources in which some resources are subordinate to others as a result of their position in the network structure and architecture; for example, the logical units (LUs) of a peripheral physical unit (PU) are subordinate to that PU, which, in turn, is subordinate to the link attaching it to its subarea node.

resource identifier (1) In ACF/TCAM, the portion of the TCAM network address of a resource that uniquely identifies the resource within the message control program (MCP) providing the message queuing for the resource. See also node identifier. (2) In AIX Enhanced X-Windows, an integer returned to an application program that identifies a resource that has been allocated for the program's use.

resource label In the NetView Graphic Monitor Facility, the textual information that identifies a particular aggregate or real resource. The resource label is displayed next to the resource symbol, and it cannot be changed by the network operator.

resource level In the NetView program, the hierarchical position of a device, and the software contained within it, in a data processing system; for example, a first-level resource could be the communication controller, and the second-level resource could be the line connected to it.

resource management (1) The function that protects serially accessed resources from concurrent access by competing tasks. (2) In DPCX, a logical layer of functions that accepts resource manipulation requests and controls 8100 hardware.

resource manager Any control program function responsible for allocation of a resource.

resource object In the 3800 Printing Subsystem, a collection of printing instructions, and sometimes data to be printed, that consists entirely of structured fields. A resource object is stored as a member of a library and can be called for by the Print Services Facility when needed. The different resource objects are: coded font, font character set, code page, page segment, overlay, FORMDEF, and PAGEDEF. Synonymous with external library member, external object, resource.

Resource Object Data Manager (RODM) A component of the NetView program that operates as a cache manager and that supports automation applications. RODM provides an in-memory cache for maintaining real-time data in an address space that is accessible by multiple applications.

resource pool See VSAM resource pool.

resource profile In RACF, a profile that provides protection for one or more resources. See discrete profile, generic profile, resource group profile.

Note: User, group, and connect profiles are not resource profiles. The information in a resource profile can include the data set profile name, profile owner, universal access authority, access list, and other data. Resource profiles can be discrete profiles or generic profiles.

resource registration The process of identifying names of resources, such as LUs, to a network node server or a central directory server.

resource resolution table (RRT) In NPM, this table contains the names of network resources for which data is to be collected. The NPM RRT corresponds with an NCP and is built by NPMGEN from an NCP Stage I and an NCP RRT.

resource security (1) In the AS/400 system, a security function of the operating system used to authorize users to any part of the system that is required by a job or task. (2) In System/36, a System Support Program Product option that restricts the use of information in files, libraries, folders, and folder members to specified operators.

resource security file A security file that contains information that restricts access to files, libraries, and folders.

resource sequence number (RSN) A value that identifies an update of a resource in a network topology database.

resource status collector A function of the NetView program that collects status information on monitored resources and forwards this information to the resource status manager.

resource status manager The part of the NetView Graphic Monitor Facility that maintains a database of SNA resource status information and that forwards this information to all attached server workstations.

resource symbol In the NetView Graphic Monitor Facility, a geometric shape (such as a line, square, or octagon) that represents a particular kind of resource and that indicates whether that resource is an aggregate resource. A square, for example, represents a host.

resource table In ACF/TCAM extended networking, a main-storage table that associates each resource identifier with an external logical unit (LU) or application program.

resource takeover In VTAM, an action initiated by a network operator to transfer control of resources from one domain to another without breaking the connections or disrupting existing LU-LU sessions on the connection. See also acquire, release.

resource types In the NetView program, a concept to describe the organization of panels. Resource types are defined as central processing unit, channel, control unit, and I/O device for one category; and communication controller, adapter, link, cluster controller, and terminal for another category. Resource types are combined with data types and display types to describe display organization. See also data types, display types.

responded output In VTAM, a type of output request that is completed when a response is returned. Contrast with scheduled output.

response (1) An answer to an inquiry. (2) In data communication, a reply represented in the control field of a response frame. It advises the primary or combined station of the action taken by the secondary or other combined station to one or more commands. See also command. (3) In SDLC, the control information, in the C-field of the link header, sent from the secondary station to the primary station. (4) In SNA, a message unit that acknowledges receipt of a request. A response consists of a response header (RH) and possibly a response unit (RU). See response header. (5) In IMS/VS, a message to a logical terminal destination specified by an I/O PCB, an alternate response PCB, or an application program. (6) In VTAM, synonym for reply. (7) See spectral response. (8) Contrast with command (2), reply.

response duration The time duration between the start of a pulse which influences a storage cell and the end of the response of that storage cell. (I) (A)

response frame A frame transmitted by a secondary station or a frame transmitted by a combined station that contains the address of the transmitting combined station.

response header (RH) In SNA, a header, optionally followed by a response unit (RU), that indicates whether a response is positive or negative and that may contain a pacing response. See also isolated pacing response, negative response, pacing response, positive response.

response indicator In the AS/400 system, a 1-character field passed with an input record from the system to a program to provide information about the data record or actions taken by the workstation user.

response mode (1) A mode in which a system can communicate with an end user. (2) In IMS/VS, a mode of terminal operation that synchronizes operations between the terminal operator and the application program. (3) See delayed response mode, immediate response mode.

response primitive In Open Systems Interconnection architecture, a primitive issued by a service user to indicate that it has completed a procedure previously invoked by an indication primitive at the same service access point. (T)

response/throughput bias (RTB) In the system resources manager, a category of information contained in a period definition that indicates how the workload manager is to weigh trade-offs between satisfying a system throughput objective and the IPS-specified service rate.

response time (1) The elapsed time between the end of an inquiry or demand on a computer system and the beginning of the response; for example, the length of time between an indication of the end of an inquiry and the display of the first character of the response at a user terminal. (I) (A) (2) For response time monitoring, the time from the activation of a transaction until a response is received, according to the response time definition coded in the performance class. (3) See also interaction time, turnaround time. (4) Contrast with access time.

response time monitor (RTM) A feature available with certain hardware devices to allow measurement of response times, which may be collected and displayed by the NetView program.

response time window In a token-bus network, a controlled interval of time, equal to a slot time, during which a data station, having transmitted a MAC frame, pauses and listens for a response. Synonymous with response window. (T)

response unit (RU) In SNA, a message unit that acknowledges a request unit. It may contain prefix information received in a request unit. If positive, the response unit may contain additional information such as session parameters in response to BIND SESSION. If negative, it contains sense data defining the exception condition.

response window Synonym for response time window. (T)

restart (1) The start of a database management system after a recovery from an error. (T)   (2) To resume the execution of a computer program using the data recorded at a checkpoint. (T)   (3) See checkpoint restart, emergency restart, normal restart, point-of-failure restart, point-of-last-environment restart. system restart.   (4) See also checkpoint entry, checkpoint record, checkpoint/restart facility, checkpoint routine.

restart condition In the execution of a computer program, a condition that can be reestablished and that permits restart of the computer program. (I)   (A)

restart-confirmation packet In X.25 communications, a call supervision packet transmitted by a data circuit-terminating equipment (DCE) to confirm to a data terminal equipment (DTE) that the link has been restarted.

restart data set In IMS/VS, the direct access data set used to contain the information necessary to restart IMS/VS.

restart-indication packet In X.25 communications, a call supervision packet transmitted by a data circuit-terminating equipment (DCE) to indicate to a data terminal equipment (DTE) that a restart-request has been received.

restart instruction An instruction in a computer program at which the computer program may be restarted. (I)   (A)

restart object name The name found in the parameter file used for a restart and recovery routine.

restart point (1) A place in a computer program at which execution may be restarted, in particular, the address of a restart instruction.   Synonymous with rescue point. (2) Deprecated term for restart condition.

restart-request packet In X.25 communications, a call supervision packet transmitted by a data terminal equipment (DTE) to request that a link be restarted.

restore (1) To return to an original value or image; for example, to restore data in main storage from aux-iliary storage.   See also save. (2) In VSE, to write back onto disk data that was previously written from disk onto an intermediate storage medium such as tape.   (3) To return a backup copy to the active storage location for use.

Restore In SAA Advanced Common User Access architecture, a choice in the system menu pull-down that returns a window to the size it was and the position it was in prior to a maximize or minimize action.

restore icon In SAA usage, an icon that a user can select to return a window to the size it was before a sizing action.   See also maximize icon, minimize icon.

restricted functions Functions that are normally available only to an operating system. In OS/VS, user programs may be authorized to use certain restricted functions via the authorized program facility.

restricted subnetwork In NETDA/2, a user-defined node or group of nodes that have a restricted set of routes.   Routes that are connected to a node in a restricted subnetwork must start or end with that subnetwork.   All other network traffic is routed around a restricted subnetwork.

restricted-use mass storage volume See restricted-use volume.

restricted-use volume In MSS, a mass storage volume assigned to a mass storage volume group and used only by requests that specify the mass storage volume identification.

Restructured Extended Executor (REXX) An interpretive language used to write command lists.

restructuring (1) A change of the logical structure of a database including a reorganization of the data already existing in the database. (T)   (2) Synonym for reorganization. (A)

result An entity produced by the performance of an operation. (I)   (A)

resultant identifier In COBOL, a user-defined data item that is to contain the result of an arithmetic operation.

resulting indicator In RPG, an indicator that signals the result of a calculation, such as whether the result is plus, minus, or zero;   whether a given field is greater than, less than, or equal to another field;   or whether an operation was successfully completed.

resync Recovery processing that is performed by sync point services when a failure of a session, transaction program, or LU occurs during sync point processing.

The purpose of resync is to return protected resources to consistent states.

retail communications In the AS/400 system, the data communications support that allows programs on an AS/400 system to communicate with programs on point-of-sale systems, using SNA LU session type 0 protocol.

retail exit routines In the IBM 3650 Retail Store System, routines called by Subsystem Support Services to format and print reports, dumps, and other data unique to the retail store system.

retail host program The program that tailors the IBM 3650 Retail Store System to installation needs. It consists of creation facilities program, the retail-unique control statement analyzer, and the retail exit routines.

retail passthrough An OS/400 system program that supports routing of user data between a System/370-type host processor and a retail controller using a single AS/400 system. Both the SNA upline facility and the retail communications support use separate intersystem communications function sessions.

retail sales receipt tape An itemized list of a retail sales transaction between a customer and a retail store. Contrast with customer receipt tape.

retail services One of two categories of fixed functions provided by IBM. Retail services are the sales, credit, and administrative support functions of the 3653 Point of Sale Terminal and the ticket-making and ticket-reading functions of the 3657 Ticket Unit. See also basic services.

retained data Data that is stored after completion of the process with which the data are associated and that can be used by subsequent processes. Contrast with temporary data.

retention cycle The length of time specified for data on a data medium to be preserved. Synonymous with retention period. (I) (A)

retention period (1) The length of time for which data on a data medium is to be preserved. (T) (2) Synonym for retention cycle. (A)

retention period check Synonym for expiration check.

retrace In video systems, the period of time that an electron beam is turned off while being repositioned by the deflection coils at the beginning of the next line or field.

retrieval See information retrieval.

retrieval code In micrographics, a code for manual or automatic retrieval of microimages. (A)

retrieval command A command that initiates selection that may be followed by some action on the selected data. (A)

retrieval engine A system consisting of software or hardware or both for accessing specific items of data from a large mass of data, such as a CD-ROM. See also TIFF (Tag Image File Format).

retrieval function In a data manipulation language, a capability to select and to locate stored records with specified characteristics and to transfer these records to a work area for any required further processing by an application program. (A)

retrieve To locate data in storage and read it so that it can be processed, printed, or displayed. Contrast with store.

Retrieve In SAA Basic Common User Access architecture, an action that displays again, one at a time, the previous commands that were issued. Each command is displayed in the command area entry field.

retrofit To modify an existing program or system by adding or replacing a section of code or a physical unit and making necessary modifications to related units.

retry To resend data a prescribed number of times or until the data are received correctly.

Retry In SAA Advanced Common User Access architecture, a push button in an action message that directs the computer to attempt again to complete the process that caused the message.

return (1) Within a subroutine, to effect a link to the computer program that called the subroutine. (I) (A) (2) In programming languages, a language construct within a procedure designating an end of an execution sequence in the procedure. (I) (3) See carriage return.

Note: The execution sequence usually continues from the point of the procedure call.

return character See carriage return character.

return code (1) A code used to influence the execution of succeeding instructions. (A) (2) A value returned to a program to indicate the results of an operation requested by that program.

return code register A register used to store a return code. (A)

return key/lever On a typewriter, a control effecting horizontal return. (T)

return-to-reference recording The magnetic recording of bits such that the patterns of magnetization used to represent zeros and ones occupy only part of the storage cell; the remainder of the cell is magnetized to a reference condition. (T)

return-to-zero recording Return-to-reference recording in which the reference condition is the absence of magnetization. (I) (A)

reusable The attribute of a routine that allows the same copy of the routine to be used by two or more tasks. See also reenterable, serially reusable.

reusable data set In VSAM, a data set that is not a base cluster and that can be defined to be reused as a work file regardless of its contents.

reusable disk queuing In ACF/TCAM, a queuing scheme in which messages are queued to a wrapped message queues data set; that is, serviced messages are overlaid by new messages entering the system. Contrast with nonreusable disk queuing.

reusable file A VSAM file that can be defined to be reused as a work file regardless of its contents.

reusable program A computer program that can be loaded once and executed repeatedly, subject to requirements that any instructions altered during execution are returned to their initial states and its external program parameters are preserved unchanged. (I) (A)

reusable routine A routine that can be loaded once and executed repeatedly, subject to the requirements that any instructions modified during its execution are returned to their initial states and its external program parameters are preserved unchanged. (I) (A)

Reverse Address Resolution Protocol (RARP) A protocol that maintains a database of mappings between physical hardware addresses and IP addresses.

reverse break Synonym for transmission interruption.

reverse channel A means of simultaneous communication from a receiver to a transmitter over half-duplex data transmission systems. The reverse channel is generally used only for transmission of control information.

reverse charging (1) An optional facility of a packet switching data network enabling a data terminal equip-

ment (DTE) to request the cost of a session it initiates be charged to the DTE that is called. See also optional network facilities. (2) In X.25, a packet-switching data network optional facility that allows the data terminal equipment (DTE) to request that the cost of a communications session be charged to the DTE that is called. See also optional user facilities.

reverse charging acceptance A facility that enables a data terminal equipment (DTE) to receive incoming packets that request reverse charging.

reverse clipping Synonym for shielding.

reverse direction flow In flowcharting, a flow in a direction other than left to right or top to bottom. (A)

reverse find Synonym for reverse search. (T)

reverse image Synonym for reverse video.

reverse indexing In word processing, the feature that causes the typing position or display pointer to be moved to the corresponding character position of the preceding typing line. (T)

reverse-interrupt character In binary synchronous communication (BCS), a transmission control character sent by a receiving station to request the sending station to stop sending and to receive a message.

reverse LAN channel Synonym for backward LAN channel. (T)

reverse Polish notation Synonym for postfix notation.

reverse printer Synonym for bidirectional printer. (A)

reverse search (1) In text processing, an automatic search from any position in a document toward the beginning of the document. (A) (2) A function or mode that enables automatic searching from any position within a document toward the beginning of the document. Synonymous with reverse find. (T)

reverse video (1) A form of highlighting a character, field, or cursor by reversing the color of the character, field, or cursor with its background; for example, changing a red character on a black background to a black character on a red background. Synonymous with reverse image. (2) In SAA Basic Common User Access architecture, a screen emphasis feature that interchanges the foreground and background colors of an item.

reversible counter A device with a finite number of states, each of which represents a number that can be increased or decreased by unity or by a given constant. Upon receipt of an appropriate signal, the device is usually capable of bringing the number represented to a specific value; for example, zero. (I) (A)

review file In NPM, a VSAM key-sequenced data set (KSDS) containing data collected and recorded as a result of a network start display command or start monitor command.

review mode In System/36, the workstation utility mode in which operators can selectively display transaction file records or move from one transaction file record to another.

Revision Control System (RCS) In the AIX operating system, a program that manages multiple revisions of text files. It controls frequently revised text, such as programs, form letters, and papers. It features automatic identification, storage, logging, retrieval, and merging of file revisions. See also Source Code Control System.

revision number In an information resource dictionary, a nonnegative integer that is a component of the version identifier of the access name of an entity and that is assigned consecutively to each change that affects the entity. (A)

revolver track Synonym for regenerative track.

rewind (1) To bring a magnetic tape or punched tape back to its starting position. (T) (2) To return a magnetic or paper tape to its beginning. (3) To move tape from the take-up hub to the supply hub.

rewind control In text processing, a control that causes magnetic tape to be rewound to the start position, normally at high speed. (T) (A)

rewind key In word processing, a control that causes magnetic tape to be rewound to the start position, normally at high speed. (T)

REX Route extension.

REXX Restructured Extended Executor. A general-purpose, procedural language for end-user personal programming, designed for ease by both casual general users and computer professionals. It is also useful for application macros. REXX includes the capability of issuing commands to the underlying operating system from these macros and procedures. Features include powerful character-string manipulation, automatic data typing, manipulation of objects familiar to people, such as words, numbers, and names, and built-in interactive debugging.

RFT (1) Request for test. (2) Request functional transmission.

RFT:DCA Revisable-Form Text: Document Content Architecture. In the AS/400 system, the architectural specification for the information interchange of documents whose text is in a revisable format. A Revisable-Form Text: Document Content Architecture document consists of structured fields, controls, and graphic characters that represent the format and meaning of the document.

RGB (1) Color coding in which the brightness of the additive primary colors of light, red, green, and blue, are specified as three distinct values of white light. (2) Pertaining to a color display that accepts signals representing red, green, and blue.

RGB display A red-green-blue color display.

RH Request/response header.

ribbon On a typewriter, a tape-like ink carrier with one or several different color zones. (T) See carbon ribbon, fabric ribbon.

ribbon carriage On a typewriter, a container holding the ribbon and ribbon spool in an enclosed unit for easy insertion into the machine. (T)

ribbon feed mechanism On a typewriter, an arrangement of components that advance the ribbon from the full spool to the empty one. (T)

ribbon guide On a typewriter, a device that guides the ribbon to the typing position. (T)

ribbon lift guide On a typewriter, the yoke-shaped part of the ribbon lift mechanism that guides the ribbon in the typing position. (T)

ribbon lift mechanism On a typewriter, a device that lifts the ribbon from its rest position to that required for impact of the type. This determines which zone of the ribbon is used for typing. (T)

ribbon reverse control On a typewriter, a control that reverses the normal ribbon feed direction. (T)

ribbon spool On a typewriter, a device for carrying the ribbon. During the typing operation, the ribbon is fed from a full spool to an empty one. (T)

ribbon zone selector On a typewriter, a control used to preselect the various zones of the inked ribbon or to disengage the ribbon lift mechanism for stencil cutting without ribbon. (T)

rid Resource identifier.

Right In SAA Basic Common User Access architecture, an action that shows the information that follows the visible information in a panel.

right-adjust Synonym for right-align.

right-adjusted Synonym for right-aligned. (T)

right-align (1) To control the display or printing position of characters on a page so that the right-hand margin but not the left-hand margin of the printing or display is regular. (A)   (2) To move the rightmost character of one or more items to a given position. Synonymous with right-adjust.   Contrast with left-align.   See also justify.

right-aligned Pertaining to text that is aligned to the right margin but need not be aligned to the left margin.   Synonymous with right-adjusted, flush right.   Contrast with left-aligned. (T)

right-hand indent In word processing, a function that allows the user to position lines or blocks of text at right-hand margin settings that are different from the settings for the remainder of the text.   Contrast with left-hand indent.

right-hand margin stop On a typewriter or word processor, a device limiting the length of the writing line on the right side of the paper. (T)   See also left-hand margin stop.

right-hand side The set of facts or statements in the "then" part of an if-then rule. (T)   Contrast with left-hand side.

right-justified Deprecated term for right-aligned. (T)

right-justify Deprecated term for right-align.

right margin The area between the rightmost character position and the right edge of the display or paper.

right-reading image In a document copying machine, an image that has its parts positioned as in the original. (T)   Contrast with mirror image.

ring See ring network.

ring attaching device In a ring network, any device equipped with an adapter that is physically attached to the ring.

ringback tone An audible signal indicating that the called party is being rung.

ring control scheme See master node control, register insertion, slot-access control.

ringdown A method of signaling subscribers and operators using either a 20-cycle AC signal, a 135-cycle AC signal, or a 1000-cycle AC signal interrupted 20 times per second.

ring error monitor (REM) In communications, a function of the token-ring manager that observes, collects, and analyzes recoverable and irrecoverable error reports sent by token-ring stations on a single token-ring network and assists in fault isolation and correction.

ring in In the IBM Token-Ring Network, the receive or input receptacle on an access unit.   See also ring out.

ring interface adapter A device that assumes the basic data transmission functions of node, such as frame recognition, address decoding, error checking, buffering of frames, fault detection, and, in token-ring networks, token generation.

ring latency In a token-ring network, the time, measured in bit times at the data transmission rate, required for a signal to propagate once around the ring.   Ring latency includes the signal propagation delay through the ring medium, including drop cables, plus the sum of propagation delays through each data station connected to the token-ring network. (T)

ring network (1) A network in which every node has exactly two branches connected to it and in which there are exactly two paths between any two nodes.   Synonymous with loop. (T)   (2) A network configuration in which devices are connected by unidirectional transmission links to form a closed path.   See also star/ring network, token-ring network.   See Figure 127.

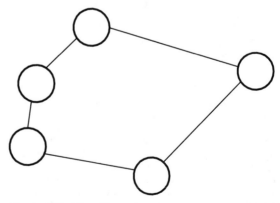

Figure 127. Ring Network

ring out In the IBM Token-Ring Network, the transmit or output receptacle on an access unit.   See also ring in.

ring station The functions necessary for connecting to the local area network and for operating with the token-ring protocols. These include token handling, transferring copied frames from the ring to the using node's storage, maintaining error counters, observing Medium Access Control (MAC) sublayer protocols (for address acquisition, error reporting, or other duties), and (in the full-function native mode) directing frames to the correct Data Link Control link station. A ring station is an instance of a MAC sublayer in a node attached to a ring.

ripple carry In parallel addition, a carry which is produced in one digit place as a result of addition for that digit place and which is propagated to the next high-order digit place. (T)

RISC Reduced instruction-set computer.

RISC System/6000 Graphics Processor Subsystem The high-function display adapter used on the IBM RISC System/6000 7016 POWERstation 730 workstation.

RISC System/6000 Graphics Processor Subsystem Adapter An interface card in the Graphics Subsystem that connects the IBM RISC System/6000 7016 POWERstation 730 Micro Channel to the Graphics Subsystem Bus Interface Card. It contains programmable option select (POS) registers for the Graphics Subsystem.

RISC System/6000 Graphics Processor Subsystem Bus The primary bus that connects the Graphics Subsystem graphics hardware to the Graphics Subsystem system interface cards.

RISC System/6000 Graphics Processor Subsystem DrP A graphics card (Drawing Processor) in the Graphics Subsystem that processes pixel data.

RISC System/6000 Graphics Processor Subsystem GCP A graphics card (Graphics Control Processor) in the Graphics Subsystem that processes FIFO elements.

RISC System/6000 Graphics Processor Subsystem Shp A graphics card (Shading Processor) in the Graphics Subsystem that provides hidden-line and hidden-surface removal.

RISC System/6000 Graphics Processor Subsystem GSBIC An interface card (Graphics System Bus Interface Card) in the Graphics Subsystem that performs most Graphics Subsystem system interface functions. It is connected to the Graphics Subsystem Adapter with a 64-pin ribbon cable.

rise time In the approximation of a step function, the time required for a signal to change from a specified low value to a specified high value. (T)

Note: These values usually are 10 percent and 90 percent of a specified value.

risk The probability that a particular threat will exploit a particular vulnerability of the system. See also countermeasure.

risk analysis In computer security, the identification and study of the vulnerability of a system and the possible threats to its security. See also risk management, threat analysis.

risk assessment In computer security, an evaluation, in terms of annualized loss expectancy, of assets, vulnerabilities of a system, and possible threats to its security. See also risk management, threat analysis.

risk index In computer security, in a multilevel device or in a multilevel secure system, a number that represents the security exposure that results when access is allowed to users whose clearance or authorization is the same or lower than the maximum classification of data in the system. When a user's classification or authorization is the same as the maximum classification of data, the risk index is zero.

risk management In computer security, risk analysis, risk assessment, and the responses to them, such as selection of countermeasures.

RJE Remote job entry.

RJE data set A system data set in which remote job entry files are stored.

RJEF Remote Job Entry Facility.

RJE message queue In DPCX, the message queue on disk storage in which remote job entry messages to or from the RJE operator are stored.

RJE operator In DPCX, a designated operator with a special operator ID who establishes RJE sessions and controls RJE data.

RJE system application In DPCX, a service that, with host RJE support, provides a means of initiating jobs at, transmitting job data to, and receiving job data from a host system.

RLD Relocation dictionary.

RLM Resident load module.

RLSD Received line signal detector.

RMS Recovery management support.

rms Root mean square.

RNAA Request network address assignment.

RNR Receive not ready.

RNR frame In X.25 communications, a receive-not-ready frame. Contrast with RR frame.

RNR packet A packet used by a data terminal equipment (DTE) or by a data circuit-terminating equipment (DCE) to indicate a temporary inability to accept additional packets for a virtual call or permanent virtual circuit.

RO (1) Read only. (2) Receive only. (3) A receive-only device, usually a page printer. A receive-only device can receive messages but cannot transmit.

robot (1) A mechanical device which can be programmed to perform some task of manipulation or locomotion under automatic control. (T)   (2) A device that performs programmed operations or that operates by remote control. A robot senses external feedback derived from ongoing operations and reacts to sensed data by modifying its actions accordingly. See also sensor, servomechanism.

robotics (1) The techniques used in designing, building, and using robots. (T)   (2) Computer-aided manufacturing in which robots are used to perform repetitive operations such as welding and assembly. See also AML/2, machine vision, vision system.

robot system A system including robot hardware and software consisting of the manipulator, the power supply, the control system, the end effectors and including any equipment the robot is interfacing with and any communications interface that is operating and monitoring the robot. (T)

RODM Resource Object Data Manager.

roll In computer graphics, to scroll in an upward or downward direction.

rollback (1) A programmed return to a prior checkpoint. (A)   (2) The process of restoring data changed by an application program or user to the state at its last commitment boundary. (3) In SQL, the process of restoring data changed by an application program or user to the state at its last commit point.

roll back To remove changes that were made to database files under commitment control since the last commitment boundary.

roller See conveying roller, damper applicator roller, damper vibrator roller, damping pressure roller, delivery rollers, ink distributor roller, ink duct roller, ink oscillating roller, ink vibrator roller, intake rollers, moistening pressure roller, moistening roller, pressure roller, squeegee rollers, trough roller.

roller ball The control ball inside a mouse that contacts a desktop or other hard surface.

roll in To restore to main storage the sets of data previously rolled out. (A)

rolling Scrolling restricted to an upward or downward direction.

roll out To transfer sets of data, such as files or computer programs of various sizes, from main storage to auxiliary storage for the purpose of freeing main storage for another use. (A)

rollout In the IBM LinkWay product, a procedure for managing memory in which LinkWay is temporarily taken out of memory and returned when an operation is complete.

rollout/rollin (1) A procedure for managing storage whereby certain programs are temporarily taken out of main storage, placed on disk storage, and returned when an operation is complete. (2) An optional feature of the MVT configuration of the control program that allows the temporary reassignment of one or more main storage regions from one job step to another. (3) See also roll in, roll out.

ROM Read-only memory. (A)

Roman numerals Roman letters used alone or in combinations to represent numbers; for example, I, II, III, IV, or i, ii, iii, iv. See also Arabic numerals.

ROM BIOS Read-Only Memory Basic Input/Output System. In an IBM personal computer, microcode in read-only memory that controls basic input/output operations such as interactions with cassettes, diskette drives, hard disk drives, and the keyboard. See also BIOS, NetBIOS.

Note: ROM BIOS allows the user to write programs and add or remove devices without concern for characteristics such as device addresses.

root (1) The highest level of a hierarchy. (A) (2) In the AIX operating system, the user name for the system user with the most authority. (3) In AIX Enhanced X-Windows, the screen on which the window is created. The root of a pixmap or graphics context is the same as the root of the drawable used when the pixmap or graphics context was created. The root of a window is the root window under which the window was created. (4) In the AIXwindows program and Enhanced X-Windows, the shell widget on the widget tree. (5) See root device, root directory, root file system, root record, root segment, root window.

root device In the AIX operating system, the device on which the root file system resides.

root directory (1) In IBM DOS, the directory on a disk or diskette that contains the list of files stored on that disk or diskette. If more than one directory is on a disk or diskette, the root directory is at the "top" of the hierarchy of directories. The root directory is created by DOS when the disk or diskette is formatted. (2) In the AIX operating system, the directory that contains all other directories in the system. See effective root directory.

root file system The basic AIX file system, onto which all other file systems can be mounted. The root file system contains the operating system files needed to run the system.

root node A node of a tree structure that has no parent nodes. (T)

root record In a hierarchical database or a network database, the record at the highest level of the hierarchy or at the first level of ownership. Synonymous with base node.

root segment (1) In an overlay operation, the part of a program that must remain in main storage when other overlay segments are executed: the first segment in an overlay program. (2) In a hierarchical database, the highest segment in the tree structure.

root window In the AIX operating system, a window that has no parent and that cannot be reconfigured or unmapped, but otherwise is like any other window.

ROS Read-only storage.

ROSF Remote Operation/Support Facility.

rotary dial In a switched system, the conventional dialing method that creates a series of pulses to identify the called station. Contrast with push button dialing, tone dialing.

rotated font A font whose graphic character representations are rotated 90 or 270 degrees to allow it to be printed at those orientations on a page.

rotating In computer graphics, turning all or part of a display image about an axis. See also tumbling. See Figure 128.

rotation (1) In printing, the number of degrees a graphic character representation is turned relative to the page coordinates. See also orientation. (2) In computer graphics, the number of degrees a display element or display image is turned about an axis.

rotational delay Synonym for search time. (T) (A)

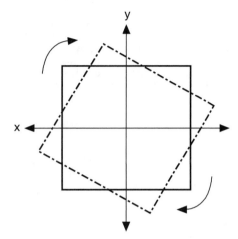

Figure 128. Rotating

rotational position sensing (1) A technique used to locate a given sector, a desired track, and a specific record by continuous comparison of the read/write head position with appropriate synchronization signals. (A) (2) A technique for continuously monitoring a disk position to indicate the position currently available for reading and writing. (T) (3) A feature that permits a disk storage device to disconnect from a block multiplexer channel or its equivalent, so that the channel can service other devices on the channel during positional delay.

rotor The rotating component of a sensor. See also stator.

rotoscope In multimedia applications, a camera setup that projects live-action film, one frame at a time, onto a surface so that an animator can trace complicated movements. When filmed, the completed animation exactly matches the motion of the original action.

ROTR Receive-only typing reperforator.

rough cut In multimedia applications: (1) The result of an offline edit. (2) A video program that includes the appropriate footage in the correct order but does not include special effects.

round (1) To delete or omit one or more of the least significant digits in a positional representation and to adjust the part retained in accordance with some specified rule. The purpose of rounding is usually to limit the precision of a numeral or to reduce the number of characters in the numeral, or both. The most common forms of rounding are rounding down, rounding up, and rounding off. (I)   (A)   (2) Contrast with truncation.

round down (1) To round, making no adjustment to the part of numeral retained. If a numeral is rounded down, its absolute value is not increased. Rounding down is a form of truncation; for example, numerals 12.6374 and 15.0625, when rounded down to two decimal places, become 12.63 and 15.06, respectively. (I) (A)   (2) On a calculator, elimination in result of a calculation of all digits beyond least significant digit. (T)

rounding error (1) An error due to rounding.   (I) (A)   (2) Contrast with truncation error.

round off (1) To round, adjusting part of numeral retained by adding 1 to the least significant of its digits and executing any necessary carries, if and only if the most significant of digits deleted is equal to or greater than half the radix of its digit place;   for example, numerals 12.6375 and 15.0625, when rounded off to two decimal places, become 12.64 and 15.06, respectively. (I) (A)   (2) On a calculator, increase of the least significant digit in result of a calculation to the next higher number where the subsequent digit in result is 5 or above.   Where the subsequent digit is 4 or below, the least significant digit remains unchanged. (T)

round-robin scheduling In the OS/2 operating system, a process that allows each thread to run for a specified amount of time.

round-trip message delay The sum of the one-way message delays from the origin to the destination and back, not including application processing time.

round-trip propagation time Twice the time required for a bit to travel between the two most distant data stations in a bus network.

Note: In a network using carrier sense, each transmission frame must be long enough so that a collision or jam signal may be detected by the transmitting station while this transmission frame is being transmitted. Its minimum length is therefore determined by the round-trip propagation time. (T)

round up (1) To round, adjusting the part of the numeral that is retained by adding 1 to the least significant of its digits and executing any necessary carries, if and only if one or more nonzero digits have been deleted. If a numeral is rounded up, its absolute value is not decreased;   for example, the numerals 12.6374 and 15.0625, when rounded up to two decimal places,

become 12.64 and 15.07, respectively.   (I)   (A) (2) On a calculator, the increase by one of the least significant digit in the result of a calculation if the highest decimal place dropped off has a value of more than zero. (T)

route An ordered sequence of nodes and transmission groups (TGs) that represent a path from an origin node to a destination node traversed by the traffic exchanged between them.

route addition resistance (RAR) A value that indicates a network node's capacity to perform intermediate session routing.

route extension (REX) In SNA, the path control network components, including a peripheral link, that make up the portion of a path between a subarea node and a network addressable unit (NAU) in an adjacent peripheral node.   See also explicit route (ER), path, virtual route (VR).

router (1)   A computer that determines the path of network traffic flow.   The path selection is made from several paths based on information obtained from specific protocols, algorithms that attempt to identify the shortest or best path, and other criteria such as metrics or protocol-specific destination addresses.   (2)   An attaching device that connects two LAN segments, which use similar or different architectures, at the reference model network layer.   Contrast with bridge, gateway.   (3)   In OSI terminology, a function that determines a path by which an entity can be reached. (4)   See Internet router.

Route Selection control vector (RSCV) A control vector that describes a route within an APPN network. The RSCV consists of an ordered sequence of control vectors that identify the TGs and nodes that make up the path from an origin node to a destination node.

route selection services (RSS) A subcomponent of the topology and routing services component that determines the preferred route between a specified pair of nodes for a given class of service.

Route Table Generator (RTG) IBM-supplied field developed program that assists the user in generating path tables for SNA networks.

route weight A value computed for the set of TGs and intermediate nodes interconnecting an origin and destination node; route weight determines which route is preferred during the route selection process.

routine (1) A program, or part of a program, that may have some general or frequent use. (T)   (2) In REXX, a series of instructions called with the CALL instruction or as a function.   A routine can be either internal or external to a user's program.   (3) See dump routine, input routine, library routine, output routine, recursive routine, reentrant routine, reusable routine, subroutine, supervisory routine, tracing routine, utility routine.

routine-name In COBOL, a user-defined word that identifies a procedure written in a language other than COBOL.

routing (1) The process of determining the path to be used for transmission of a message over a network. (T) (2) The assignment of the path by which a message is to reach its destination. (3) In SNA, the forwarding of a message unit along a particular path through a network, as determined by parameters carried in the message unit, such as the destination network address in a transmission header. (4) See affinity-based routing, invariant routing, message routing, routing by destination, routing by key, transaction-based routing.

routing affinity A temporary relationship between a source and a destination.

routing by destination In ACF/TCAM, message routing based on a destination name. Contrast with routing by key. See also affinity-based routing, invariant routing, transaction-based routing.

routing by key (1) In ACF/TCAM, message routing based on a key that matches a definition in the key table. The key identifies the destination of a message or special processing to be done on the message. Contrast with routing by destination. (2) See also affinity-based routing, invariant routing, transaction-based routing.

routing code (1) A combination of one or more digits used to route a call to a predetermined area. (2) A code assigned to an operator message and used, in systems with multiple console support (MCS), to route the message to the proper console. (3) In IMS/VS with expedited message handling (EMH), a user-defined code that allows transactions to be routed to programs within a load balancing group.

routing data In System/38, a character string that the Control Program Facility compares with character strings in the subsystem description routing entries in order to select the routing entry to be used to initiate a routing step. Routing data can be provided by a workstation user, specified in a command, or provided through the job description for the job.

routing entry In the AS/400 system and System/36, an entry in a subsystem description that specifies the program to be called to control a routing step that runs in the subsystem.

routing indicator An address or group of characters in the header of a message defining the final circuit or terminal to which the message has to be delivered.

routing information In the IBM ImagePlus system, information used by Workflow Management to ensure proper distribution of documents.

routing key See key.

routing key table See key table.

routing list (1) A list of users who are to receive an item when it is distributed, including all users specifically named and those users named on distribution lists by the sender. (2) In X.25 communications, a list that associates user names with network user addresses and other information, for the purpose of directing incoming calls.

routing path In an IMS/VS multisystem environment, the route through which IMS/VS passes a message from its origin through processing. One or more systems may be included in a routing path.

routing qualifier In the Network Communication Control Facility (NCCF), an explicit qualifier added to commands to accommodate cross-domain execution. NCCF removes the routing qualifier before the command is passed to the appropriate access method.

routing queue A list of documents waiting to be processed. See also document processing session.

routing step In the AS/400 system and System/38 the processing that results from running a program specified in a routing entry. Most jobs have only one routing step.

routing table (1) In the AIX operating system, a table that holds a list of valid paths through which hosts can communicate with other hosts. The routing table can hold static routes and dynamic routes. (2) In SNADS, a list of entries in a table that the system uses to route a message or electronic mail to a user on the system. Each entry is made up of a destination group name, such as a department or organization, and a destination element name (the user ID of each person in that department or organization).

row (1) A horizontal arrangement of characters or other expressions. (A) (2) Contrast with column. (3) See card row, mark-sense row, punch row.

row B Synonym for lower letter row.

row binary (1) Pertaining to the binary representation of data on cards in which the significances of punch positions are assigned along card rows. For example, each row in an 80-column card may be used to represent 80 consecutive binary digits. (A)   (2) Contrast with column binary.

row C Synonym for middle letter row.

row D Synonym for upper letter row.

row E Synonym for numeral row.

row pitch (1) The distance between adjacent tape rows measured along a track on a recorded data medium. (T)   (2) Synonymous with array pitch.

RPDS See VM/MVS bridge.

RPE Required page end character.

RPG (1) Report program generator.   (2) Raster pattern generator.

RPG II A commercially oriented programming language specifically designed for writing application programs intended for business data processing.

RPH Request parameter header.

RPL Request parameter list.

RPL-based macroinstruction In VTAM, a macroinstruction whose parameters are specified by the user in a request parameter list.

RPL exit routine In VTAM, an application program exit routine whose address has been placed in the EXIT field of a request parameter list (RPL). VTAM invokes the routine to indicate that an asynchronous request has been completed. See EXLST exit routine.

RPL string A set of chained request parameter lists (RPLs) used to gain access to a VSAM file by a single request macro, such as GET, PUT. Two or more RPLs or RPL strings may be used for concurrent direct or sequential requests made from a processing program or its subtasks.

RPM Remote PrintManager.

RPOA Recognized Private Operating Agency.

RPQ Request for price quotation.   See computing system RPQ, programming RPQ.

RPT Repeat character.

RQD Request discontact.

RQE Reply queue element.

RR Receive ready.

RRDS Relative record data set.

RR frame In X.25 communications, a receive-ready frame. Contrast with RNR frame.

RRN Relative-record number.

RRN response In VTAM, a response that indicates that the node sending the response has accepted recovery responsibility for the associated message.

RR packet A packet used by a data terminal equipment (DTE) or by a data circuit-terminating equipment (DCE) to indicate that it is ready to receive data packets within the window.

RRT Resource resolution table.

RS The record separator character. (A)

RSA Rivest-Shamir-Edelman.   A scheme for public-key cryptography.

RSAM Relative sequential access method.

RSCS Remote Spooling Communications Subsystem.

RSCS/PROFS bridge See VM/MVS bridge.

RSCS/PROFS distribution services (RPDS) See VM/MVS bridge.

RSCV Route Selection control vector.

RSHUTD An SNA command used to request an orderly session shutdown.

RSM Real storage management.

RSN Resource sequence number.

RSP (1) Required space character. (2) See response.

RSS Route selection services.

RST Remote modem self-test.

RS-232C See EIA 232D.

RS-310 An Electronic Industries Association (EIA) standard for designing racks to hold data processing equipment.

RS-422A See EIA 422A.

RT Reperforator/transmitter.

RTAM Remote terminal access method.

RTAM generation The process of assembling selected RTAM facilities and link editing them into VS1.

RTB Response/throughput bias.

RTG Route Table Generator.

RTM Realtime monitor.

RTTY Radio teletypewriter telecommunications.

RTV Real-Time Video.

RU Request/response unit.

rubber-banding In computer graphics, moving the common ends of a set of straight lines while the other ends remain fixed. (I) (A) See Figure 129.

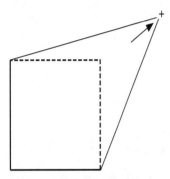

Figure 129. Rubber-Banding

rubber-band outline In the AIX operating system, a window with a moveable outline.

rub-out character Synonym for delete character.

RU chain In SNA, a set of related request/response units (RUs) consecutively transmitted on a particular normal or expedited data flow. The request RU chain is the unit of recovery. If one RU in the chain cannot be processed, the entire chain must be discarded.

Note: Each request unit belongs to only one chain, which has a beginning and an end indicated through control bits in request/response headers within the RU chain. Each RU can be designated as first-in-chain (FIC), last-in-chain (LIC), middle-in-chain (MIC), or only-in-chain (OIC). Response units and expedited-flow request units are always sent as only-in-chain.

rule A solid or patterned line of any weight, extending horizontally or vertically across a column or row.

rule-based system A computer system which performs inferences by applying a set of if then rules to a set of facts following given procedures. Synonymous with production system. (T)

rule interpreter Synonym for inference engine. (T)

ruler line A line that indicates where the left and right margins and any tab stops are set. (T)

run (1) A performance of one or more jobs. (I) (A) (2) A performance of one or more programs. (I) (A) (3) To cause a program, utility, or other machine function to be performed.

runaway task In CICS, a task that does not relinquish control within an interval of time defined by the user.

RUN disk The virtual disk that contains the VTAM, NetView, and VM/SNA console support (VSCS) load libraries, program temporary fixes (PTFs) and user-written modifications from the ZAP disk. See BASE disk, DELTA disk, MERGE disk, ZAP disk.

rundown In multimedia, an outline of the content of a video program for which a script is inappropriate or impossible, such as an interview.

run duration Synonym for running time.

run file In the AIX operating system, synonym for load module.

run-length coding A technique for compressing data that avoids having to code repeatedly data elements of the same value; instead, the value is coded once, along with the number of times for it to be repeated.

run list In VM/SP, a list of virtual machines that are receiving a queue slice on the processing unit. The virtual machine currently executing is called the runuser. When virtual machines are dropped from the run list, replacement is made from the eligible list. See also dispatch list, eligible list.

running foot (1) Synonym for footer. (T) (2) A footing that is repeated above the bottom margin area on consecutive pages or on consecutive odd-numbered or even-numbered pages in the text area of the page. Synonymous with footer.

running heading (1) Synonym for header. (T) (2) A heading that is repeated below the top margin area on consecutive pages or on consecutive odd-numbered or even-numbered pages in the text area of the page.

running open In telegraph applications, a term used to describe a machine connected to an open line or a line without battery (constant space condition). A telegraph receiver under such a condition appears to be running, as the type hammer continually strikes the type box but does not move across the page, because the open line is continually decoded as the baudot character BLANK, or ASCII character NULL.

RUNNING screen status For a display terminal used as a virtual console under VM, an indicator located in the lower right of the screen that displays that the user's virtual machine is in control (but not necessarily executing a program or command) and that the terminal is able to receive messages.

running time The elapsed time taken for the execution of a target program. (I) (A) Synonymous with run duration.

run stream Synonym for job stream.

run time Synonym for execution time. (T) (A)

run-time array In RPG, an array that is loaded or created by input or calculation specifications after the program starts to run. Contrast with compile-time array, prerun-time array.

run-time defaults In AS/400 query management, all of the formatting elements of a formatted report that were not explicitly specified in the form.

run-time environment (1) In the C, FORTRAN, and Pascal languages, a logical grouping of one or more program objects that must be connected at application run time to do some task. (2) In the AIX operating system, a collection of subroutines and shell variables that provide commonly used functions and information for system components.

run-time table In RPG, a table that is loaded or created by input or calculation specifications after the

program starts to run. Contrast with compile-time table, prerun-time table.

run unit (1) One or more object programs that are executed together. (2) In COBOL, one or more object programs that interact with each other and whose function at object time, is to act as an entity to provide problem solutions. (3) In PL/I, a set of programs, each of which is called by some other PL/I program within the set, except for the first program called, which is called from outside the set.

runuser In VM, the virtual machine in the dispatch list that is currently executing.

RUPE Request/response unit processing element.

RUPEDAP Request/response unit processing element work area address.

RVA Recorded voice announcement.

RVI (1) Reverse interrupt. (2) Reverse-interrupt character.

RW Read/write.

RWCS Report writer control system.

RWS Read/write storage.

RZ Return-to-zero recording. (I) (A)

RZ(NP) Nonpolarized return-to-zero recording. (I) (A)

RZ(P) Polarized return-to-zero recording. (I) (A)

S

SAA Systems Application Architecture.

SAA application An application that has some degree of conformance to one or more of the SAA architectures, and that runs in one or more SAA environments.

SAA architectures The Common User Access architecture, the Common Programming Interface, and the Common Communications Support.

SAA enabler Software that, while not necessarily having any SAA conformance itself, assists programmers in producing and running applications that do.

SAA environments Those environments in which IBM intends to provide full implementation of applicable SAA architectural elements.

SAA solution A large-scale application, set of applications, or set of tools that has some degree of conformance to one or more of the SAA architectures, and that is, or will be, available in multiple SAA environments.

SAB (1) Service application block. (2) Logical resource manager session allocation block.

SABM Set asynchronous balanced mode.

SABME Set asynchronous balanced mode extended.

SABME-UA Set asynchronous balanced mode-extended unnumbered acknowledgment.

SADP Serviceability aids and debugging procedures.

SAF Source address field.

safe area The area in the center of a video frame certain to be displayed on any television or monitor, regardless of make.

safety In multimedia applications, an extra shot of a scene that is taken as a backup after an acceptable shot (the "buy") has been acquired.

safety ring Synonym for file-protection ring. (A)

SAK Secure attention key.

salami technique In computer security, a method of stealing significant assets in small amounts, over time so that their loss is not noticed. See also attack.

sales mode An operating state of a point of sale terminal that is used for transactions involving a store's customers. Contrast with nonsales mode.

sales transaction The action of completing a sale by entering into a point of sale terminal the applicable information about merchandise being purchased. Also included is the method used by a customer to pay for the merchandise.

SAM Sequential access method.

same-domain Pertaining to communication between entities in the same SNA domain. Contrast with cross-domain. See also single-domain network.

same domain LU-LU session In SNA, an LU-LU session between logical units (LUs) in the same domain. Contrast with cross-domain LU-LU session.

same size In a document copying machine, a copy on the same nominal scale as the original. (T)

sample To obtain the values of a function for regularly or irregularly spaced distinct values from its domain. Other meanings of this term may be used in particular fields; for example in statistics. (I) (A)

sample-and-hold device A device that senses and stores the instantaneous value of an analog signal. (T)

sampler In multimedia applications, a device that converts real sound into digital information for storage on a computer.

sample rate Synonym for locator sample rate.

sampling (1) Obtaining the values of a function for regularly or irregularly spaced distinct values of an independent variable. (A) (2) In statistics, obtaining a sample from a population. (A) (3) The first step in the process of converting an analog signal into a digital signal. The three steps are: sampling, quantizing, and encoding. In sampling, the value of a signal is read at evenly spaced points in time. The sample obtained is then ready for quantizing and encoding. See also encoding, quantizing.

sampling rate In analog-to-digital conversion, the number of samples taken per second. Sampling errors can cause aliasing effects.

sanitizing In computer security, the degaussing or overwriting of all sensitive information in a magnetic or other recording medium so that the medium may be submitted to reclassification procedures. See also clearing.

SAP Service access point.

satellite computer (1) A computer that is under the control of another computer and performs subsidiary operations. (2) An offline auxiliary computer.

SATF Shared-access transport facility.

saturated colors In computer graphics, very bright colors (in particular, reds and oranges) that do not reproduce well on video but instead saturate the screen with color.

saturation The amounts of color and grayness in a hue that affect its vividness; that is, a hue with high saturation contains more color and less gray than a hue with low saturation. See also hue.

save (1) A function that enables a user to write into a file of a previously entered or modified text. (T) (2) To retain data by copying it from main storage to another storage device. See also restore.

Save In SAA Common User Access architecture, a choice in the File pull-down that users select to store what they are working on, such as a file, on the computer or a disk or diskette.

save area Area of main storage in which contents of registers are saved. (A)

Save as... In SAA Common User Access architecture, a choice in the File pull-down that users select to copy what they are working on, such as a file, into a new file without changing the original.

saved configuration In an ESCON environment, a stored set of connectivity attributes whose values determine a configuration that can be used to replace all or part of the ESCD's active configuration. Contrast with active configuration.

saved system In VM, a special nonrelocatable copy of a virtual machine's virtual storage and associated registers that is kept on a CP-owned disk and that can be loaded by name instead of by I/O device address. Loading a saved system by name substantially reduces the time it takes to IPL the system in a virtual machine. In addition, a saved system such as CMS can also share one or more 64K-byte segments of reenterable code in real storage between virtual machines. This reduces the cumulative real main storage requirements and paging demands of such virtual machines. See also shared read-only system residence disk.

save file In the AS/400 system, a file allocated in auxiliary storage that can be used to store saved data on disk (without requiring diskettes or tapes), to perform I/O operations from a high-level language program, or to receive objects sent through the network.

save/restore message queues (SMQ) SSP In ACF/TCAM, the function of a system services program that saves messages that have not been sent on a sequential storage device and restores them to an altered message control program (MCP) following a cold restart. This program also assists in recovery when the message queue data set on nonreusable disk becomes full. The program may be used to obtain an online dump of messages that have not been sent from one or more destination queues on disk.

saveset In the AIX operating system, a list of window clients that should not be destroyed when a connection is closed and should be remapped or unmapped. Usually, it is used by window managers to avoid losing windows if the manager is ended abnormally.

save storage In the AS/400 system, an operation that copies, sector by sector, all permanent data from configured disk units to tape.

save system authority In the AS/400 system, a special authority that allows the user to save and restore all objects on the system and free storage of all objects on the system. See also all object authority, job control authority, security administrator authority, service authority, spool control authority.

save system rights In System/38, the authority to save all objects.

SAW Session awareness.

SAW data Synonym for session awareness (SAW) data.

SBA Set buffer address.

SBConvert In the IBM LinkWay product, a program to convert pictures from StoryBoard Plus format to LinkWay format.

SBCS Single-byte character set.

SBS Subscript character.

SC Session control.

SCA System control area.

scalar (1) A quantity characterized by a single value. (I) (A) (2) A type of program object that contains either string or numeric data. It provides representation and operational characteristics to the byte string to which it is mapped. Contrast with pointer. (3) Pertaining to a single data item as opposed to an array of data items. (4) An arithmetic object or enumerated object. (5) In FORTRAN, a single datum that is not array-valued. (6) Contrast with vector.

scalar expression An expression that represents a single value rather than an array of values.

scalar function In SQL, an operation that produces a single value from another value and expresses it in the form of a function name followed by a list of arguments enclosed in parentheses.

scalar item A single data item. Contrast with array.

scalar type (1) In the AIX operating system, a type that defines a variable containing a single value at run time. Contrast with structured type. See base scalar type, enumerated scalar type, subrange scalar type. (2) In Pascal, a type that defines a variable containing a single value at run time. CHAR, BOOLEAN, INTEGER, SHORTINT, REAL, SHORTREAL, enumerated types, and subranges are scalar types. Contrast with structured type.

scalar variable In PL/I, a variable that represents a single data item. Contrast with array variable, structure variable.

scale (1) In GDDM, the number and progression of ticks along a vertical or horizontal axis. (2) A system of mathematical notation: fixed-point or floating-point scale of an arithmetic value. (3) To change the representation of a quantity, expressing it in other units, so that its range is brought within a specified range. (I) (A) (4) To adjust the representation of a quantity by a factor in order to bring its range within prescribed limits. (A) (5) In computer graphics, to enlarge all or part of a display image. (6) See reproduction scale.

scale factor (1) A number used as a multiplier in scaling; for example, a scale factor of 1/1000 would be suitable to scale the values 856, 432, -95, and -182 to lie in the range -1 to +1 inclusive. (I) (A) Synonymous with scaling factor. (2) A number that indicates the position of the decimal point in a real number. (3) See time scale factor.

scale line A line on a display showing margins, tabs, and character positions.

scale multiplier Synonym for coefficient unit. (T)

scaling (1) In computer graphics, enlarging or reducing all or part of a display image by multiplying the coordinates of the image by a constant value. (T) (2) In programming, indicating the number of digit positions in object code to be occupied by the fractional portion of a fixed-point or floating-point constant. (3) In AIX operating system graphics, uniform stretching of a primitive along an axis. See mouse scaling.

scaling factor Synonym for scale factor.

scan (1) To examine sequentially, part by part. (A) (2) In word processing, rapid review of displayed text by vertical scrolling. (T) (3) To briefly examine or read. See also browse, search. (4) To search records for a specified character string or syntax error. (5) See directed-beam scan, flying-spot scan, raster scan.

scan band In the IBM 3886 Optical Character Reader, the area on the document to be scanned by the read station. The scan band is centered about the top edge of the timing mark.

scan conversion In the AIX operating system, the process of generating pixel information in the frame buffer from an application program.

scan converter In multimedia applications, a device that converts digital signal to NTSC or PAL format.

scan head In the IBM 3886 Optical Character Reader, the electronic device used to scan a line. The scan head includes an infrared light source, a lens to focus this light on the document, and mirrors and photodiodes to receive the reflected light. When scanning a line, the scan head is moved across the document along the scan band to collect the character images. The output from the scan head is processed for character recognition in the recognition and control processor.

scan limit A type 2 communication scanner facility that allows the control program to limit the number of lines addressed by a scanner.

scan line (1) In a laser printer, one horizontal sweep of the laser beam across the photoconductor. (2) A sequence of pixels that are arranged in a line, typically horizontally, and are scanned sequentially.

scanner (1) A device that examines a spatial pattern one part after another, and generates analog or digital signals corresponding to the pattern. Scanners are often used in mark sensing, pattern recognition, or character recognition. (I) (A) (2) In DPCX, the part of application control code (ACC) that controls the identification and interpretive execution of DPCX instructions. (3) See flying spot scanner, optical scanner. See Figure 130. (4) For the 3725 communication controller, a processor dedicated to controlling a small number of telecommunication lines. It provides the connection between the line interface coupler hardware and the central control unit.

Figure 130. IBM 3118 Image Scanner

scanner interface trace (SIT) A record of the activity within the communication scanner processor (CSP) for a specified data link between an IBM 3725 Communication Controller and a resource.

scanner workstation An ImagePlus workstation equipped with a scanner that can digitize an image from a physical page.

scanning The systematic examination of data. (T) (A)

scanning control On dictation equipment, a device used to move the playback head rapidly from one part of the recording medium to another. (I)

scanning spot The beam of electrons generated by a cathode ray tube (CRT), which travels back and forth across the screen, laying down the information that makes up the picture on the monitor.

scan patterns In the 3800 Printing Subsystem, the bit patterns that make up the individual characters in each character cell (24 rows of 18-bit positions; not all bit positions are used).

scan pointer In ACF/TCAM, a pointer that refers to the proper header field when a macroinstruction that acts upon that field is given control. Some user-specified macroinstructions use this pointer to locate the field on which they act and automatically move the pointer to the next field before passing control to the next macroinstruction. The user must be aware of positioning of the scan pointer when designing the message handler.

scan resolution The distance between adjacent scan lines along a normal to the direction of the scan line.

scatter In input and output operations, to read data from a device and locate it in noncontiguous memory addresses. Contrast with gather.

scatter format A load module attribute that permits dynamic loading of control sections into noncontiguous areas of main storage.

scatter loading The placing of control sections of a load module into noncontiguous locations of main storage. Contrast with block loading.

scatter plot In GDDM, a type of line chart in which only the marked points, and not their joining lines, are drawn. See also line chart.

scavenge In computer security, to read data from a data medium before writing at the same location for the purpose of acquiring residue. See also attack.

SCB (1) Session control block. (2) String control byte.

SCCS Source Code Control System.

SCCS delta In the AIX operating system, a set of changes made to a Source Code Control System file. Creating a new delta saves only the changes made.

SCCS identification (SID) In the AIX Source Code Control System, a number assigned to each version of a program.

SCD System contents directory.

SCDR (1) Store controller definition record. (2) Subsystem controller definition record.

scene In multimedia applications, a portion of video captured by the camera in one continuous shot. The scene is shot repeatedly (each attempt is called a "take") until an acceptable version, called the "buy," is taken.

scene analysis The analysis of a scene by recognizing its constituent objects, their properties, and their spatial interrelations. (T)

SCF (1) Secondary control field. (2) System control facility.

schedule To select jobs or tasks that are to be dispatched. In some operating systems, other units of work such as input/output operations may also be scheduled. (I) (A)

scheduled maintenance Preventive maintenance carried out in accordance with an established time schedule. (T)

scheduled output In VTAM, a type of output request that is completed, as far as the application program is concerned, when the program's output data area is free. Contrast with responded output.

scheduler (1) A computer program designed to perform functions such as scheduling, initiation, and termination of jobs. (A)　(2) See job scheduler, master scheduler.

scheduler work area (SWA) An area in virtual storage that contains most of the job management control blocks, such as the JCT, JFCB, SCT, and SIOT. Each initiator has one scheduler work area.

scheduler work area data set (SWADS) In OS/VS1, a data set on auxiliary storage that contains most of the job management control blocks, such as the JCT, JFCB, SCT, and SIOT. Each initiator has one scheduler work area data set, unless the initiator has a scheduler work area associated with it.

scheduling intent In IMS/VS, an application program attribute defined in the program specification block (PSB) that specifies how the program should be scheduled if multiple programs are contending for scheduling.　See also exclusive intent, read-only intent, update intent.

scheduling priority (1) A specified sequence in which jobs, programs, or tasks are to be executed. (2) In IMS/VS, a transaction attribute that is used to calculate which transaction is selected for scheduling. Synonymous with selection priority.　See also limit priority, normal priority.

schema (1) Synonym for frame. (T)　(2) The set of statements, expressed in a data definition language, that completely describe the structure of a database. See conceptual schema, external schema, internal schema, logical schema, physical schema.

schematic capture Computer-assisted design (CAD) and layout of electronic circuits on screen of a personal computer.

Note: The stored code that represents the image can be "captured" and used as output to a plotter that can draw photographic-quality prints for the computer-assisted manufacture (CAM) of printed circuits.

SCIF Single console image facility.

SCIP exit Session control in-bound processing exit.

scissoring In computer graphics, removing parts of a display image that lie outside a window. (T)　Synonymous with clipping.　Contrast with shielding.　See Figure 131.

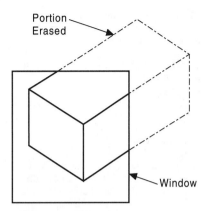

Figure 131. Scissoring

scope (1) The portion of an expression to which the operator is applied. (T)　(2) The portion of a computer program within which the definition of the variable remains unchanged. (T)　(3) See lexical scope.

scope check In the NetView program, the process of verifying that an operator is authorized to issue a particular command.

scope of commands In the NetView program, the facility that provides the ability to assign different responsibilities to various operators.

scope of commands facility In NCCF, a facility that allows restriction of NCCF commands and operands to a subset of all NCCF operators in the network.

scoping unit In FORTRAN, one of the following:

• A derived-type definition

• A procedure interface block, excluding any procedure interface blocks contained within it

• A program unit, excluding derived-type definitions, procedure interface blocks, and program units contained within it.

scored card (1) A special card that contains one or more scored lines to facilitate precise folding or separation of certain parts of the card. (A)　(2) See processible scored card.

scoring In video or film production, writing the musical accompaniment for a project.

SCP System control programming.

SCPF Start-control-program-function.

scratch (1) To erase data on a volume or delete its identification so that it can be used for another purpose.　(2) In MSS, to remove information about a mass storage volume from the mass storage volume inventory data set, and to put the identification of both cartridges on a list of scratch data cartridges.

scratch data cartridge In MSS, a data cartridge that is not part of a mass storage volume.

scratch diskette A diskette that has all of its data erased or its identification deleted.

scratch file A temporary work file.

scratchpad area (SPA) In IMS/VS conversational processing, a work area in main storage or on direct access storage used to retain information from the application program for executions of the application program from the same terminal.

scratch-pad memory A read/write storage device or register that can be used for temporary storage of intermediate data or pointers. (A)

scratch tape A reel of magnetic tape that has all of its data erased or its identification deleted.

screen (1) In document copying, a sheet of material, usually film, carrying a regular pattern of small dots. (T) (2) In SAA Basic Common User Access architecture, the physical surface of a display device upon which information is shown to a user. (3) In the AIX extended curses library, a window that is as large as the display screen of the workstation. See navigation screen, reading screen, standard screen. (4) See display screen, ink screen, touch-sensitive screen. (5) Deprecated term for display panel.

screen address In DPCX, an explicit address in a display image to which a program can refer in full-screen processing statements.

screen attribute byte A character position on the screen of a display terminal that defines the characteristics of the next field displayed on the screen such as protected, not protected, displayable, or nondisplayable.

screen buffer In IBM personal computers with the Color/Graphics Monitor Adapter, a buffer that can contain up to eight pages that can be displayed. See also active page, visual page.

screen coordinates The coordinate system that defines the display screen. Synonymous with screen space. See also eye coordinates, modeling coordinates, primitive coordinates, transformation, world coordinates.

screen design aid (SDA) (1) The utility of the Interactive Data Base Utilities licensed program that is used to interactively design, create, and maintain display record formats and menus. (2) In System/36, the part of the Utilities Program Product that helps the user design, create, and maintain displays and menus. SDA can also generate specifications for RPG and workstation utility programs. (3) A text editor that displays text and associated editing information on a display screen and allows editing of arbitrary strings using cursor position, without regard to line numbers. (T)

screen editor In text processing, a text editor that displays text and associated editing information on a display screen and allows editing of character strings indicated by positioning the cursor without regard for line numbers. (T) (A)

screen image In computer graphics, a pattern of points, lines, and characters displayed on the display surface of a video display terminal (VDT). See also display image.

Note: The term display image includes images drawn on hard copy, such as those drawn by a plotter. The term screen image is specific to VDTs.

screening In a document copying machine, a means of imposing a regular pattern of small dots onto the image of the original in order to produce an improved copy. (T)

screenmask In AIX operating system graphics, a rectangular area of the screen to which all drawing operations are clipped. It is normally set equal to the viewport.

screen space Synonym for screen coordinates.

screen status area On a display screen of a terminal used as a virtual console under VM, a field that indicates the current status of the screen. This field is located at the lower right of the display screen. See also CP READ screen status, HOLDING screen status, MORE screen status, NOT ACCEPTED screen status, RUNNING screen status, VM READ screen status.

screen symbol A representation of the status of a particular aspect of the ImagePlus Workstation Program; for example, the printer symbol indicates that a page is being printed.

scrim In video or film production, a wire mesh insert, usually circular, placed into a lighting instrument to diffuse the light or lower its intensity.

script (1) In artificial intelligence, a data structure pertaining to a particular area of knowledge and consisting of slots which represent a set of events which can occur under a given situation. (T) (2) A sequence of commands that performs a LinkWay button action.

Script button In the IBM LinkWay product, a type of LinkWay button object that activates a script.

script command A command used in a LinkWay script.

scripting In multimedia applications, the writing of dialog.

script intensity On a typewriter, the contrast between the typed character and the paper that is determined mainly by the force of impression, quality and color of the paper used, stroke thickness, and color and density of the inking used. (T)

scroll To move a display image vertically or horizontally to view data that otherwise cannot be observed within the boundaries of the display screen.

scrollable entry field In SAA Advanced Common User Access architecture, an entry field larger than the visible field.

scrollable partition In the 3270 Information Display System, a partition that has a presentation space larger than the viewport.

scroll bar (1) In the AIX operating system, a graphical device used to change a user's viewpoint of a list or data file. A scrollbar consists of a slider, scroll area, and scroll arrows. A user changes the view by sliding the slider up or down in the scroll area or by pressing one of the scroll arrows. This causes the view to scroll up or down in the window adjacent to the scroll bar. See also menu bar. (2) In SAA Advanced Common User Access architecture, a part of a window, associated with a scrollable area, that a user interacts with to see information that is not currently visible.

scroll box In SAA Common User Access architecture, a part of the scroll bar that shows the position of the visible information relative to the total amount of information available in the window. A user clicks on the scroll box with a pointing device and manipulates it to see information that is not currently visible.

scrolling (1) Moving a display image vertically or horizontally in order to view data not otherwise visible within the boundaries of the display screen. (2) Performing a scroll up, scroll down, scroll right, or scroll left operation. (3) See automatic scrolling. (4) See also rolling, translating.

scrolling action In SAA Basic Common User Access architecture, a function that enables a user to control the information visible in a window. The scrolling actions are Backward, Forward, Left, and Right.

scrolling arrows In SAA Basic Common User Access architecture, a type of scrolling information that consists of the word More, followed by a colon and arrows or symbols that indicate the direction in which more information is available by scrolling.

scrolling increment In SAA Basic Common User Access architecture, the fixed amount of information that scrolls.

scrolling information In SAA Basic Common User Access architecture, any of the three types of information that appear in a panel to indicate the directions in which additional information is available by scrolling. See scrolling arrows.

scroll region In the AIXwindows program, the rectangular portion of a ScrollBar widget that contains two arrows and a slider.

SCS SNA character string.

SCSI Small computer system interface.

SCSI adapter Small computer systems interface adapter.

SCT Section control table.

SDA (1) Screen design aid. (2) Sense data included.

SDB Storage descriptor block.

SDF (1) Screen definition facility. (2) Serial data field.

SDF/CICS Screen Definition Facility Customer Information Control System. An online application development tool used by application programmers to define or edit maps, map sets, and partitions for CICS/VS Basic Mapping Support.

SDF/CICS demo session Either of two demo sessions, one explaining the definition of a single map, the other explaining how a map can be converted to extended color display devices.

S-disk Synonym for CMS system disk.

SDLC Synchronous Data Link Control.

SDLC Communications Feature In the IBM 8100 Information System, a feature that allows system connection to a variety of devices that use Synchronous Data Link Control (SDLC) facilities and provides for attachment of loop facilities through the loop adapter.

SDLC link A data link over which communication is conducted using the synchronous data link control (SDLC) discipline.

SDLC primary station A station that has responsibility for the data link. It issues commands to secondary stations. See also SDLC secondary station.

SDLC secondary station A station that responds to requests from another station (the primary station) and has little control over data link operations. See also SDLC primary station.

SDR Statistical data recorder.

SDT (1) Start data traffic. (2) Static debugger trap. (3) In SNA, a command issued by the primary logical unit, which allows user data to be sent on the logical unit-to-logical unit (LU-to-LU) session.

SDVT Skeleton destination vector table.

SDWA System diagnostic work area.

sealing current A low-level current imposed on a data loop when the loop is in an idle state in order to reduce corrosion and improve reliability in areas where the atmosphere and operating environment are corrosive to electrical connections.

search (1) A function or mode that enables the user to locate occurrences of such things as particular character strings, embedded commands, or boldface letters in a document. Synonymous with find. (T) (2) The process of looking for a particular item. See also browse, scan. (3) To scan one or more data elements of a set in order to find elements that have a certain property. (4) See binary search, chaining search, dichotomizing search, Fibonacci search.

search and replace A function or mode that enables the user to locate occurrences of such things as particular character strings, embedded commands, or boldface letters within a document and to automatically replace all occurrences of one character string with another character string. This function may be performed partially or entirely in the whole text. Synonymous with find and replace. (T)

search argument (1) A string of characters used to find a match. Synonymous with search word. (2) In RPG, a literal or field name specified in factor 1 of certain file operations, such as CHAIN that identifies the record to be processed. (3) In RPG, data used to find a match or a greater than or less than quantity in a table or array. The search argument is specified in a lookup statement.

search chain In VSE, the order in which chained sublibraries are searched for the retrieval of a certain library member of a specified type.

search concentration A function, performed by network nodes and central directory servers, that mini-mizes the number of concurrent network searches that are sent for the same target resource.

search condition In SQL, a criterion for selecting rows from a table. A search condition consists of one or more predicates.

search cycle The part of a search that is repeated for each data element. (T)

search field A field that is referred to by one or more search arguments.

search index See index search.

search index database In the AS/400 system, the database files used by document library services for storing descriptive information about documents and folders, such as keywords, subjects, and dates. These database files are used when a search of the document library is requested on one or more document descriptors.

search key (1) In the conduct of a search, the data to be compared with specified parts of each item. (I) (A) (2) Synonym for seek key.

search time The time interval required for the read/write head of a direct access storage device to locate a particular record on a track corresponding to a given address or key. Synonymous with rotational delay. (T) (A)

search tree See binary search tree.

search value In the AS/400 system, user-defined information that is used either to make a list of filed documents with similar document details or find a directory entry.

search word A string of characters used to find a match.

SECAM Séquentiel Couleurs à Mémoire. The French standard for color television.

secondary In high level data link control (HDLC), the part of a data station that executes data link control functions as instructed by the primary. (I) (A)

secondary address space The address space whose segment table is used to access data in secondary address space control mode.

secondary application In DPPX/Base, an application that can deal only with a primary application. There is no data traffic between secondary applications. Contrast with primary application.

secondary application program An application program acting as the secondary half-session of an LU-LU session.

secondary axis In GDDM, a horizontal or vertical axis drawn parallel to the primary axis and capable of having a title, ticks, and labels different from those of the primary axis. See also primary axis.

secondary console In a system with multiple consoles, any console except the master console. The secondary console handles one or more assigned functions on the multiple console system.

secondary control point In high level data link control (HDLC), the location of a secondary in a network.

secondary data In the IBM 3886 Optical Character Reader with the picture processing feature, the data displayed on lines 1, 2, 4, and 7 when requested by the operator to obtain more detailed job-related information.

secondary database One of two databases provided by the NetView program for recording data. It provides backup or a temporary storage alternative to the primary database. See primary database.

secondary data set group In an IMS/VS database, one or more data set groups defined in addition to the primary data set. A secondary data set group is usually defined to improve utilization of auxiliary storage. See also primary data set group.

secondary destination Any of the destinations specified for a message except the first destination.

secondary device (1) In the 3790 Communication System, a line printer feature or a 3793 printer component that prints records contained in the print data set. Information can be sent to the print data set in addition to being sent to a primary device (a terminal). (2) In DPCX, an I/O device assigned to a DPCX task through the second of a set of device fields in the primary application block (PAB). A secondary device can be a tape unit or the transaction, transmit, or print data set. (3) Contrast with primary device.

secondary display sequence In System/36, the set of displays that follows the primary display sequence in a workstation utility source program.

secondary end of a session That end of a session that uses secondary protocols. For an LU-LU session, the secondary end of the session is the secondary logical unit (SLU). Contrast with primary end of a session. See also half-session, secondary logical unit (SLU).

secondary ESCON Manager In a system environment containing multiple ESCON Managers, an ESCM that receives a command from the primary ESCM through intersystem communication.

secondary file (1) In System/38 query, when file chaining is specified, the second database file referenced by a query application. The secondary file must be key accessed, and the name of the key fields may be floating-point fields. Contrast with primary file. (2) In RPG, any input file other than the primary file. (3) In the AS/400 data description specifications (DDS) for a join logical file, any physical file, other than the first physical file, that is specified on the JFILE keyword. Contrast with primary file.

secondary half-session In SNA, the half-session that receives the session-activation request. See also secondary logical unit. Contrast with primary half-session.

secondary index (1) An index for secondary keys. (T) (2) In IMS/VS, an index used to establish accessibility to a physical or logical database by a path different from the one provided by the database definition.

secondary key (1) A key that may identify more than one record. (T) (2) A portion of the first block of each record in an indexed data set that can be used to find the record in the data set. The secondary key is valid only when so defined in the data set control block (DSCB). See also primary key.

secondary key encrypting keys In the Programmed Cryptographic Facility, one of the three categories of cryptographic keys used to encipher data encrypting keys.

secondary link station In SNA, any link station on a link using a primary-secondary protocol that is not the primary link station. A secondary link station can exchange data only with the primary link station. No data traffic flows from one secondary link station to another. Contrast with primary link station.

secondary logical unit (SLU) In SNA, the logical unit (LU) that contains the secondary half-session for a particular LU-LU session. Contrast with primary logical unit. See also logical unit.

secondary logical unit (SLU) key A key encrypting key used to protect a session cryptography key during its transmission to the secondary half-session.

secondary operator control station See basic secondary operator control station, extended secondary operator control station.

secondary paging device In OS/VS2 and VM, an auxiliary storage device that is not used for paging operations until the available space on primary paging devices falls below a specified minimum. Portions of a secondary paging device can be used for purposes other than paging operations.

secondary processing sequence In an IMS/VS database, the hierarchic order of segment types in a physical or logical database that results automatically when a database is accessed through a secondary index.

secondary program operator (SPO) application A program operator application program that is not authorized to receive unsolicited messages. An SPO can receive only the messages generated by commands it issues. There can be more than one SPO in a domain, in addition to a primary program operator application program (PPO). Contrast with primary program operator application program.

secondary PSV In the IBM 8100 Information System, one of two program status vectors associated with each priority level and normally used to define an application program.

secondary recipient Synonym for copy recipient. (T)

secondary record format In query, when file chaining is specified, a record format in the secondary file. Contrast with primary record format.

secondary register set In DPPX/Base, one of two main register sets assigned to a program for use as general registers. Contrast with primary register set.

secondary request In an IMS/VS multisystem environment, a message sent to a transaction code destination by an application program. See also primary request, response.

secondary space allocation In systems with VSAM, area of direct access storage space allocated after primary space originally allocated is exhausted. See also primary space allocation.

secondary station (1) In high level data link control (HDLC), the part of a data station that executes data link control functions as instructed by the primary station and that interprets received commands and generates responses for transmission. (I)   (2) A data station that executes data link control functions as instructed by the primary station. A secondary station interprets received commands and generates responses for transmission. (3) See also combined station, secondary link station. (4) Contrast with primary station.

secondary storage Synonym for auxiliary storage.

secondary system control facility (SSCF) In the IBM 8100 Information System, system control facility circuitry associated with an I/O subsystem.

secondary system name In the AS/400 system, an alternative system name that can be used to identify an AS/400 system in a SNADS network. See also secondary system name table. Contrast with primary system name.

secondary system name table In SNADS, the table containing all the system names that can be used to identify the local system for distributions arriving on the system.

secondary window (1) In the AIX operating system, a window of short duration, such as a dialog box. Usually, the window is displayed only long enough to convey some information or to obtain some operational directions. (2) In SAA Advanced Common User Access architecture, a type of window that can be moved and sized and is always associated with a primary window. Help is an example of a secondary window. See also primary window, pop-up window.

second generation In multimedia applications, a direct copy from the master or original tape.

second-generation computer A computer utilizing solid state components.

second-level directory In VSE, a table located in the supervisor that contains the highest phase names found on the corresponding directory tracks of the system core image library.

second-level interrupt handler (SLIH) In the AIX operating system, a device-dependent routine that handles the processing of an interrupt from a specific adapter. An SLIH is called by the first-level interrupt handler (FLIH) associated with that interrupt level.

second-level message A message that provides additional information to that already given in a first-level message.

second-level message display A display containing the second-level message text and additional messages.

second-level statement In DPCX, a programming statement that assembles into more than one instruction. Contrast with first-level statement.

second-level storage In VM, the storage that appears to be real to a virtual machine. See also first-level storage, third-level storage.

secret key Synonym for private key.

section (1) In computer graphics, to construct the bounded or unbounded intersecting plane with respect to one or more displayed objects and then to display the intersection. (T) (2) In a VSAM index record, a group of consecutive index entries. The index entries in an index record are divided into approximately as many sections as the square root of the number of entries in order to speed up a search for an entry. (3) In COBOL, a set of zero, one, or more than one paragraphs or entries, called a section body, the first of which is preceded by a section header. See Communication Section, Configuration Section, Debugging Section, Input-Output Section, Linkage Section, Report Section, Working-Storage Section. Each section consists of the section header and the related section body. (4) In FORTRAN, see array section. (5) Deprecated term for segment. (6) See also control section.

sectional center A control center connecting primary centers. A class 1 office.

section header In COBOL, a combination of words followed by a separator period that indicates the beginning of a section in the Environment, Data, and Procedure Division. In the Environment and Data Divisions, a section header is composed of reserved words followed by a separator period. The permissible section headers in the Environment Division are Configuration Section and Input-Output Section.

The permissible headers in the Data Division are File Section, Working-Storage Section, Linkage Section, Communication Section, and Report Section.

Note: In the Procedure Division, a section header is composed of a section-name, followed by the reserved word SECTION, followed by an optional segment-number, followed by a separator period.

section-name In COBOL, a user-defined word that names a section in the Procedure Division.

sector (1) A predetermined angular part of a track or band on a magnetic drum or magnetic disk that can be addressed. (T) (2) On disk or diskette storage, an addressable subdivision of a track used to record one block of a program or data. (3) See hard sector, soft sector. See Figure 132.

sector label In System/38 graphics, the alphanumeric label that a user can assign to each sector on a pie chart.

secure Pertaining to the control of who can use an object and to the extent to which the object can be used by controlling the authority given to the user.

secure attention key (SAK) In the AIX operating system, a key sequence that ends all processes associ-

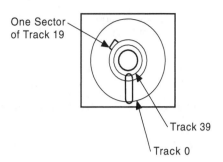

Figure 132. Sector

ated with a terminal in order to provide a trusted path for secure communication with the trusted computing base (TCB).

secure state In computer security, a system state in which subjects may access objects only in accordance with a particular security policy; for example, by comparing the clearance of a subject to the classification of an object to determine if the subject is authorized to access that object.

security See computer security, data processing system security, password security, resource access security, sign-on verification security, system security, transaction command security.

security administrator authority In the AS/400 system, a special authority that allows a user to add users to the system distribution directory, to create and change user profiles, to add and remove access codes, and to perform office tasks, such as delete documents, folders, and document lists, and change distribution lists for other users. See also all object authority, job control authority, save system authority, service authority, spool control authority.

security category In RACF, an installation-defined name corresponding to a department or area within an organization with similar security requirements.

security classification In RACF, the use of security categories, a security level, or both, to impose additional access controls on sensitive resources. An alternative way to provide security classifications is to use security labels.

security exit The point of departure from a module for entry to a user-supplied security verification process.

security feature In credit card processing, a visible or invisible feature of an identification card; it provides a means of authentication of a user and helps to deter counterfeiting. (T) (A)

security filter In computer security, a trusted subsystem that enforces a security policy on the data that pass through it.

security kernel In computer security, a relatively small, tamper-proof portion of an operating system that enforces security controls and mediates all accesses to programs and data. See also trusted computing base.

security keylock (1) In the 3790 Communication System, an optional feature that provides additional protection to prevent unauthorized access to terminals. (2) On the 3270, a feature that allows the device to disable all input functions and that blanks the display surface, except for the cursor and displayed indicators, except when the key is inserted in the lock and turned to the ON position.

security label In RACF, an installation-defined name that corresponds to a specific RACF security level with a set of (zero or more) security categories.

security level (1) The combination of a hierarchical classification and a set of nonhierarchical categories that represents the sensitivity of an object or the clearance of a subject. (2) In computer security, a classification of information defined by a sensitivity level and in some cases by the designation of one or more compartments. See also sensitivity level. (3) In RACF, an installation-defined name that corresponds to an numerical security level (the higher the number, the higher the security level).

security maintenance In IMS/VS, the process by which the control blocks that describe the user's data processing security requirements are created.

security number In the 3650 Retail Store System, a four-digit number that must be entered at the point of sale terminal as part of the terminal sign-on procedures. The security number is generated and printed (on the cash receipt) by the terminal during any final totals readout and reset procedure performed at the terminal.

security officer A person assigned to control all of the security authorizations provided with the system. A security officer can, for example, remove password or resource security or add, change, or remove security information about any system user.

security officer user profile In System/38, the user profile supplied by the Control Program Facility of the person who controls authorization of functions and data used in the installation.

security policy In computer security, the laws, rules, and practices that regulate how an organization manages, protects, and distributes sensitive information.

security policy model In computer security, an informal presentation of a formal security policy model.

security token In RACF, a collection of identifying and security information that represents data to be accessed, a user, or a job. This contains a userid, groupid, security label, node of origin, and other information.

seed fill In computer graphics, a paint technique that floods all connected regions with a specified color.

seek (1) To selectively position the access mechanism of a direct access device. (A)   (2) Deprecated term for search, search cycle.

seek key In word processing, a control used to locate an address on the recording medium. (T) Synonymous with search key.

seek time The time required for the access arm of a direct access storage device to be positioned on the appropriate track. Synonymous with positioning time. (T)   (A) See Figure 3.

SEG Special effects generator.

segment (1) A portion of a computer program that may be executed without the entire computer program being resident in main storage. (T)   See overlay segment. (2) A portion of a message that can be contained in a buffer. See message segment. (3) A group of display elements. See display segment. (4) A collection of composed text and images, prepared before formatting and included in a document when it is printed. See page segment. (5) In a video presentation, any material with a start and stop frame. (6) In VM, a contiguous 64K area of virtual storage that is not necessarily contiguous in real storage and that is allocated to a virtual machine or to CP. (7) In the IBM Token-Ring Network, a section of cable between components or devices. A segment may consist of a single patch cable, several patch cables that are connected, or a combination of building cable and patch cables that are connected. (8) In IMS/VS, the unit of access to a database; for the database system, the smallest amount of data that can be transferred by one DL/I operation. For input terminal operations using the DC feature, a segment is defined by the particular terminal type and is obtained by the application program with one call. (9) In AIX Enhanced X-Windows, one or more lines that are drawn but not necessarily connected at the end points. (10) For TCP/IP, the unit of end-to-end transmission in the TCP. A segment consists of a TCP header followed by application data. A segment is transmitted as an IP datagram. See also datagram, packet. (11) To divide a computer program into segments. (I) (A) (12) Synonym for BIU segment.

segment addressing In a 3600 assembler language program, a method of addressing a field in which the programmer sets the primary field pointer and field-length indicator in the segment header and then refers to the segment number in the instruction. See also fixed-field addressing.

segmentation A process by which path control (PC) divides basic information units (BIUs) into smaller units, called BIU segments, to accommodate smaller buffer sizes in adjacent nodes. Both segmentation and segment assembly are optional PC features. The support for either or both is indicated in the BIND request and response.

segmentation facility In VSE/POWER, a facility that breaks list or punch output into segments so printing or punching can be started before execution of the generating user program is ended.

segment file A file that contains all the path segments in a particular configuration segment.

segmenting of BIUs In SNA, an optional function of path control that divides a basic information unit (BIU) received from transmission control into two or more path information units (PIUs). The first PIU contains the request header (RH) of the BIU and usually part of the RU. The remaining PIU or PIUs contain the remaining parts of the RU.

Note: When segmenting is not done, a PIU contains a complete BIU.

segment number (1) The part of a virtual storage address needed to refer to a segment. (2) In COBOL, a user-defined word that classifies sections in the Procedure Division for the purpose of segmentation. Segment-numbers may contain only the characters "0," "1," "9." A segment number may be expressed either as a one or two digit number.

segment occurrence In an IMS/VS database, one instance of a set of similar segments.

segment protect A hardware feature available on the 308X Processor Complex that provides protection for shared segments at the hardware level.

segment search argument (SSA) In IMS/VS, the portion of a DL/I call that identifies a segment or group of segments to be processed. Each SSA contains a segment name and, optionally, one or more command codes and one or more qualification state-

ments. Multiple SSAs may be required to identify the desired segment.

segment sharing In MVS, the sharing of a storage segment for common system programs; for example, sharing of the supervisor between multiple virtual storage systems.

segment translation exception In System/370 virtual storage systems, a program interruption that occurs when a virtual address cannot be translated by the hardware because the invalid bit is set in the segment table entry for that address. See also page translation exception, translation specification exception.

segment type In an IMS/VS database, a user-defined category of data.

segment unit (1) In FORTRAN, a program object produced by the compilation of one or more program units, but excluding the program unit containing the main entry point. (2) In XL Pascal, an independently compilable piece of code containing routines linked with the program unit. See program unit.

segue In video or audio presentations, a transition from one program segment to another.

seion A Japanese syllable.

seize To gain control of a line in order to transmit data. Contrast with bid.

select (1) In SAA Common User Access architecture, to mark or choose an item. (2) In the AIX operating system, to choose a button on the display screen. (3) To place the cursor on an object (name or command) and press the Select (left) button on the mouse or the Select key on the keyboard.

selected emphasis (1) In SAA Advanced Common User Access architecture, a visual cue that shows a user that a choice is currently selected. Inverse color and marquee select are examples of selected emphasis. See also inverse color, marquee select. (2) In SAA Basic Common User Access architecture, a visual cue that shows a user that a choice is currently selected.

select function In the AS/400 system and System/38, a system function that determines the records in a physical file that are to be included in a logical file. Contrast with omit function.

selecting (1) On a multipoint connection or point-to-point connection, the process of requesting one or more data stations to receive data. (I) (2) In AIX operating system graphics, a method for finding what primitives are being drawn in a given volume in three-dimensional space. See also name stack, picking, picking region, selecting region.

selecting region In AIX operating system graphics, a rhomboid-shaped volume in world coordinates that is sensitive to selecting events. If a drawing primitive draws within this region, a select event is reported. See also picking region, selecting, transformation.

selection (1) An operation of relational algebra that forms a new relation which is a subset of the entity occurrences a given relation; for example, given a relation of books containing the attributes "author" and "title," the formation of the subset of the books written by particular author. (T) (2) In word processing, the choosing and assembling of blocks of recorded text for the purpose of constructing a new document. (T) (3) Addressing a terminal or a component on a selective calling circuit. (4) The process by which a computer requests a station to send it a message. (5) In AIX Enhanced X-Windows, an indirect property of a dynamic type maintained by the client (the owner) but belonging to the user. It is not private to a particular window subhierarchy or a particular set of clients. When a client asks for the contents of a selection, it specifies a target type. This target type can be used to control the transmitted representation of the contents. (6) The act of explicitly identifying one or more objects to which a subsequent choice will apply. (7) See also blind, lockout, option, polling.

selection check A check that verifies the choice of devices, such as registers, in the execution of an instruction. (A)

selection cursor In SAA Advanced Common User Access architecture, a visual indication that a user has selected a choice. It is represented by outlining the choice with a dotted box. See also text cursor.

selection field (1) A field tested for a condition to determine whether a record should be included in a sort. (2) In SAA Advanced Common User Access architecture, a set of related choices. See also entry field. (3) In SAA Basic Common User Access architecture, an area of a panel that cannot be scrolled and contains a fixed number of choices. See also entry field.

selection indicator In SAA Common User Access architecture, a visual cue that shows a user that a choice has been selected.

selection list (1) In SAA Advanced Common User Access architecture, choices that a user can scroll through to select one choice. (2) In SAA Basic Common User Access architecture, a set of choices that can be scrolled if there are more items in the list than can be seen at once.

selection menu Synonym for menu.

selection panel Synonym for menu.

selection priority Synonym for scheduling priority.

selection signal In a switched network, the sequence of characters that indicates all the information required to establish a call. (I) (A)

selection sort (1) A sort in which the items in a set are examined to find an item that fits specified criteria. This item is appended to the sorted set and removed from further consideration, and the process is repeated until all items are in the sorted set. (A) (2) See repeated selection sort.

selective calling The ability of a transmitting station to specify which of several stations on the same line is to receive a message. See also call directing code, station selection code.

selective cryptographic session A cryptographic session in which an application program can specify the request units to be enciphered. Contrast with mandatory cryptographic session. See also clear session.

selective dump The dumping of the contents of one or more specified storage areas. (I) (A) See also change dump.

selective prompting In the AS/400 system and System/38, a function of the operating system that allows the user to tailor command prompts at a parameter level. Contrast with conditional prompting.

select/omit field In the AS/400 system and System/38, a field in a logical file record format whose value is tested by the system to determine if records including that field are to be used. The test is a comparison with a constant, the contents of another field, a range of values, or a list of values; and the record is either selected or omitted as a result of the test. See also dynamic select/omit.

select/omit level specifications In the AS/400 system and System/38, data description specifications coded on the lines following the last key-field specification. These specifications are permitted only in a logical file. See also field level specifications, file level specifications, help level specifications, key field level specifications, record level specifications, join level specifications.

selector (1) In SAA usage, deprecated term for pointer, pointing device, selection cursor. (2) In Pascal, the term in a CASE statement that when evaluated determines which of the possible branches of the CASE statement will be processed. (3) A device for directing electrical input pulses onto one of two output lines, depending upon the presence or absence of a predetermined accompanying control pulse. See

Figure 133. (4) See copy length selector, copy selector, damping width selector, ink selector.

| Data | | Output 1 |
| Control Pulse | | Output 2 |

Figure 133. Selector

selector channel An I/O channel designed to operate with only one I/O device at a time. After the I/O device is selected, a complete record is transferred one byte at a time. Contrast with block multiplexer channel, multiplexer channel.

selector mode One of the two modes in which a block multiplexer channel can operate. See also block multiplexer mode.

selector pen (1) A pen-like instrument that can be attached to a display station. When a program using full-screen processing is assigned to the display station, the pen can be used to select items on the screen or to generate an attention. (2) Synonym for light pen.

selector pen attention Synonym for light pen attention.

self-adapting computer A computer that has the ability to change its performance characteristics in response to its environment. (I) (A)

self-adapting program A computer program that has the ability to change its performance characteristics in response to its environment. (I) (A)

self-check digit (1) A field, such as an account number, consisting of a base number and a check digit. (2) The far right digit of a self-check field. (3) In the 3790 Communication System, a digit that enables the controller to detect single-digit errors and single-transposition errors (for example, 2143 instead of 1234) in a numeric data field entry. (4) A digit generated by DPCX that enables DPCX to detect single-digit errors, single-transposition errors (for example, 1243 instead of 1234), and most double-transposition errors (for example, 2143 instead of 1234) in a numeric data field entry. If a numeric data field entry is detected when the program is self-checking an operator-entered field, the self-check message is displayed.

self-checking code Synonym for error-detecting code.

self-contained (1) Pertaining to the capability of being used on a stand-alone basis. (A) (2) Pertaining to a database management system that has a

complete programming language that has all the necessary facilities for control and processing of a database. (A)

self-contained database language A database language sufficient to write complete application programs using databases, and therefore not embedded in a host language. (T)

self-contained system A database management system whose capabilities and language are intended primarily for the nonprogrammer. (A)

self-defining delimiter Any character appearing in the first position of certain character strings in the TSO command language. A repetition of the character within the string is interpreted as a delimiter.

self-defining term A term whose value is implicit in the specification of the term itself.

self-monitoring system A system that includes a monitor used for its own control. (T)

self-relative address A relative address that uses as a base address the address of the instruction in which it appears. (I) (A)

self-relative addressing (1) A method of addressing in which the address part of an instruction contains a self-relative address. (I) (A) (2) See also absolute addressing, direct addressing, immediate addressing, indirect addressing, relative addressing, symbolic addressing.

self-relocating program A program that can be loaded into any area of main storage and that contains an initialization routine to adjust its address constants so it can be executed at that location.

self-test A test that runs automatically after a device is turned on.

semantic The relationships of characters or groups of characters to their meanings, independent of the manner of their interpretation and use. See also input semantics.

semantic error A compile-time error caused by incorrect definition of constants and identifiers. See also syntax error.

semantic network In artificial intelligence, a type of knowledge representation that formalizes objects and values as nodes and connects the nodes with arcs or links that indicate the relationships between the various nodes. (T)

semantics (1) The relationships of characters or groups of characters to their meanings, independent of

the manner of their interpretation and use. (I) (A)
(2) The relationships between symbols and their
meanings. (A)   (3) See also pragmatics, syntax.

semaphore (1) A variable that is used to enforce
mutual exclusion. (T)   (2) An indicator used to
control access to a file; for example, in a multiuser
application, a flag that prevents simultaneous access to
a file. (3) An entity used to control access to system
resources. Processes can be locked to a resource with
semaphores if the processes follow certain programming conventions.

semiautomatic message switching center A center at
which an operator routes messages according to information contained in them.

semiconductor A solid material, such as silicon or
germanium, whose electrical conductivity is between
that of a conductor and that of an insulator.

semi-dry process In a document copying machine, a
method of processing diazonium-sensitized material in
which the coupler is applied in liquid form to the
exposed material to produce the image on a copy that
may then need to be dried before being suitable for
use. (T)

send (1) In SAA usage, a choice in the File pull-
down that a user can select to move a file to another
computer or workstation.   (2) To transmit data.
(3) In systems with ACF/TCAM, to place a message
on a line for transmission from the computer to a terminal. Contrast with receive. See also accept, enter.

send depth In SNADS, the number of items that must
be on the distribution queue before any item is sent to
the next system.

sender A person or thing that sends something. Contrast with receiver.

sending In ACF/TCAM, the process by which the
host processor places a message on a line for transmission to a station. Contrast with receiving.

sending service user A service user that acts as a
data source during the data transfer phase of a connection. (T)

send pacing In SNA, pacing of message units that a
component is sending. See also receive pacing.

send state A state in which a transaction program can
send data but not receive data. Contrast with receive
state.

send time In SNADS, the values that specify the time
that distributions are sent to other locations in a

network. The from and to times inclusively specify
the range during which distributions can be sent; the
force time specifies the time at which distributions are
sent regardless of the number of items in the queue.

sense data (1) Data describing an I/O error. Sense
data are presented to a host system in response to a
Sense I/O command. (2) In SNA, the data sent with a
negative response, indicating the reason for the
response.

sense switch See alteration switch.

sensing See mark sensing.

sensing station Synonym for read station.

sensitive information In computer security, information that, as determined by a competent authority,
must be protected because its unauthorized alteration,
destruction, disclosure, or loss will cause perceivable
damage to someone or something.

sensitivity (1) A measure of the harm that could
result from the observation, modification, or
destruction of an object. (2) In computer security, the
level of confidentiality of information. (3) A DL/I
capability that ensures that only data segments or
fields predefined as sensitive are available for use in a
particular application.   Sensitivity also provides a
degree of control over data security, inasmuch as users
can be prevented from accessing particular segments
or fields by omission of those segments or fields from
the logical database.

sensitivity control On dictation equipment, a device
for changing the sensitivity of the input to the
recording medium. (I) Synonymous with conference
control.

sensitivity label In computer security, an item of
information that represents the security level of an
object and that describes the sensitivity of the information contained in the object.

sensitivity level In computer security, the level to
which an individual is given clearance to access information; for example, a sensitivity level of confidential
gives an individual access to unclassified, internal use
only, and confidential information but not to
registered-confidential information. See also security
level.

sensitized material In a document copying machine,
treated material used for document copying that reacts
to radiation, particularly light or heat. (T)

sensor A device that converts measurable elements of
a physical process into data meaningful to a computer.

sensor-based Pertaining to the use of sensing devices, such as transducers or sensors, to monitor a physical process.

sensor-based computer A computer designed and programmed to receive real-time analog or digital data from transducers, sensors, and other data sources that monitor a physical process. The computer can also generate signals to elements that control the process; for example, it might receive data from a gauge or flowmeter, compare the data with a predetermined standard, and then produce a signal that operates a relay, valve, or other control mechanism.

sensor-based system An organization of components, including a computer whose primary source of input is data from sensors and whose output can be used to control the related physical process.

sentence (1) A construct in a conceptual schema language that expresses a proposition. (T) (2) In word processing, a grammatically self-contained group of words. (3) In COBOL, a sequence of one or more statements, the last of which is terminated by a separator period.

sentence control In text processing, a control used to process text one sentence at a time; for example, skip, delete, move, print. (T) (A)

sentence key In word processing, a control used to process text one sentence at a time. (T)

sentinel Synonym for flag.

separate compilation Deprecated term for dependent compilation. (T)

separately compiled program In COBOL, a program that, together with its contained programs, is compiled separately from all other programs.

separating character Synonym for information separator.

separation of duties In computer security, assurance that one person does not control multiple tasks if that control could increase vulnerability.

separator (1) In COBOL, a character or two contiguous characters used to delimit character-strings. (2) In SAA Advanced Common User Access architecture, a line or color boundary that provides a visual distinction between two adjacent areas. (3) A punctuation character used to delimit character strings. See also file separator, job separator. (4) Synonym for delimiter. (5) See corner separator, data-item separator, information separator.

separator character (1) In data communication, the character used with some autocall units to separate the digits to be dialed. (2) See file separator character, group separator character, record separator character, unit separator character.

separator page A printed page used to show the end of output for one job and the start of output for another job.

septet A byte composed of seven binary elements. (I) (A) Synonymous with 7-bit byte.

sequence (1) A series of items that have been sequenced. (I) (A) (2) An arrangement of items according to a specified set of rules; for example, items arranged alphabetically, numerically, or chronologically. (A) (3) To place items in an arrangement in accordance with the order of the natural numbers. (T) (4) Deprecated term for order. (5) Synonym for collating sequence.

Note: Methods or procedures may be specified for mapping other natural linear orders onto the natural numbers. Sequencing for example, may be alphabetic or chronological.

sequence array In FORTRAN, an assumed-size array or an explicit-shape array without the RANGE attribute that is either a dummy array associated with a sequence array or is not a dummy argument.

sequence-by-merging To sequence by repeated splitting and merging. (I) (A)

sequence check A check to determine whether items follow one another in a prescribed manner. (T)

sequence checking In RPG, a function that checks the sequence of records in input, update, or combined files used as primary and secondary files.

sequence computer See arbitrary sequence computer, consecutive sequence computer.

sequence control register Deprecated term for instruction address register.

sequenced display A display within a sequence. See nonsequenced display.

sequenced frames Information segments arranged in numerical order for transmission-checking. See also frame, frame check sequence.

sequence error An error caused by trying to bypass required displays or end-of-sequence-set processing.

sequence field Synonym for key field.

sequence number (1) A numerical value assigned by VTAM to each message exchanged between two nodes. The value (one for messages sent from the application program to the logical unit, another for messages sent from the logical unit to the application program) increases by one for each successive message transmitted unless reset by the application program with an STSN indicator. (2) In the AS/400 system and System/38, the number of a record that identifies the record within the source member. (3) In the AS/400 system and System/38, a field in a journal entry that contains a number assigned by the system. This number is initially 1 and is increased by 1 until the journal is changed or the sequence number is reset by the user. See also line number. (4) See frame sequence number.

sequencer In multimedia applications, a digital tape recorder.

sequence set (1) In systems with VSAM, the lowest level of the index of a key-sequenced data set or file. It gives the locations of the control intervals in the data set or file. The sequence set and the index set together constitute the index. (2) In System/36, one or more related displays that appear in the order in which they occur in a source program.

sequence symbol A symbol that determines the sequence in which statements are processed.

sequencing Ordering in a series or according to rank or time.

sequencing key Synonym for sort key.

sequencing time In the 3800 Printing Subsystem, the amount of time it takes for the printer to become ready to print after being idle.

sequential (1) Pertaining to a process in which all events occur one after the other, without any time lapse between them. (T)   (2) Pertaining to the occurrence of events in time sequence with no simultaneity or overlap. (A)   (3) Contrast with consecutive. (4) See also concurrent, simultaneous.

sequential access (1) The capability to enter data into a storage device or a data medium in the same sequence as the data is ordered, or to obtain data in the same order as it has been entered. Synonymous with serial access. (T)   (2) An access method in which records are read from, written to, or removed from a file based on the logical order of the records in the file. (3) In systems with VSAM, the retrieval or storage of a data record in its entry sequence, key sequence, or relative-record sequence relative to the previously retrieved or stored record.   See also addressed sequential access, keyed sequential access. (4) In FORTRAN, a method of reading from, writing

to, or removing records from a file based on the way the records are arranged in the file. (5) In COBOL, an access mode in which logical records are obtained from or placed into a consecutive predecessor-to-successor logical record sequence determined by the order of records in the file. (6) Synonymous with serial access. (7) Contrast with direct access, random access.

sequential access method (SAM) See basic sequential access method, queued sequential access method.

sequential access storage A storage device in which the access time depends upon the location of the data and on a reference to data previously accessed. (I)

sequential batch processing A mode of operating a computer in which a run must be completed before another run can be started. (A)

sequential by key Method of indexed file processing where records are read or written in order of record keys.

sequential-by-key processing A method of processing indexed files in which records are read or written in the order of the key field in the record.

sequential circuit A logic device whose output values, at a given instant, depend on its input values and internal state at that instant, and whose internal state depends on the immediately preceding input values and the preceding internal state. (I)   (A)

Note: A sequential circuit can assume a finite number of internal states and may therefore be regarded abstractly as a finite automaton.

sequential computer A computer in which events occur in time sequence with little or no simultaneity or overlap of events. (A)

sequential data set A data set whose records are organized on the basis of their successive physical positions, such as on magnetic tape. Contrast with direct data set.

sequential dependent segment In an IMS data entry database, a segment chained off the root segment and inserted in a last-in, first-out manner into the last part of a data entry database area. After it is inserted by an online program, it may not be modified.

sequential file A file in which records are processed in the order in which they are entered and stored in the file. Contrast with direct file, indexed file.

sequential logic element (1) A device having at least one output channel and one or more input channels, all characterized by discrete states so that the state of each output channel is determined by the previous states of the input channels. (A)   (2) Contrast with combinational logic element.

sequential operation A mode of operation in which two or more operations are performed one after another. (I) (A) Synonymous with consecutive operation.

sequential organization (1) In COBOL, the permanent logical file structure in which a record is identified by a predecessor-successor relationship established when the record is placed into the file. Contrast with indexed organization, relative organization. (2) See consecutive data set organization.

sequential processing (1) The processing of logical records in the order in which they are accessed. (2) The processing of records in the order in which they exist in a file. Synonymous with consecutive processing. (3) See also random processing.

sequential scheduling system A form of the job scheduler that reads one input stream and executes only one job step at a time from that input stream.

sequential-within-limits processing A method of processing indexed files in which limits are specified for the beginning and ending values of the key field for the records to be read or written.

SERDES Serializer/deserializer. A device that serializes output from, and staticizes input to, a business machine. See also communication line adapter.

SEREP (1) System error record editing program. (2) System environmental recording, editing, and printing.

serial (1) Pertaining to a process in which all events occur one after the other; for example, serial transmission of the bits of a character according to V24 CCITT protocol. (T)   (2) Pertaining to the sequential or consecutive occurrence of two or more related activities in a single device or channel. (A)   (3) Pertaining to the sequential processing of the individual parts of a whole, such as the bits of a character or the characters of a word, using the same facilities for successive parts. (A)   (4) Contrast with parallel.

serial access Synonym for sequential access.

serial access storage A storage device in which access time depends on the location of the data and on a reference to data previously accessed. (I)   (A)

serial adder An adder in which addition is performed by adding, digit place after digit place, the corresponding digits of the operands. (T)   See Figure 134.

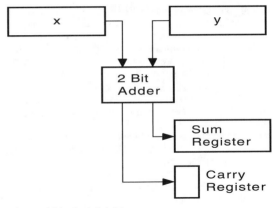

Figure 134. Serial Adder

serial addition Addition that is performed by adding, digit place after digit place, the corresponding digits of the operands. (I)   (A)

serial computer (1) A computer having a single arithmetic and logic unit. (A)   (2) A computer in which some specified characteristic is serial; for example, a computer that manipulates all bits of a word serially. (A)   (3) Contrast with parallel computer.

serial device A device that performs functions sequentially, such as a serial printer that prints one character at a time. Contrast with parallel device.

serial file A file in which records are ordered in sequence according to the values of one or more key fields in each record. (A)

serialization (1) The consecutive ordering of items. (2) In MVS, the process of controlling access to a resource to protect the integrity of the resource.

serialize To change from parallel-by-byte to serial-by-bit. Contrast with deserialize.

serializer (1) A functional unit that converts a set of simultaneous signals into a corresponding time sequence of signals. Synonymous with parallel-serial converter, dynamicizer. (T)   (2) Synonymous with dynamicizer, parallel-to-serial converter. (3) Contrast with staticizer.

serially reusable The attribute of a routine that allows the same copy of the routine to be used by another task after the end of the current use.

serially reusable load module A module that cannot be used by a second task until the first task has finished using it.

serially reusable resource (SRR) A logical resource or object that can be accessed by one task at a time.

serially shared resource In ACF/TCAM, a resource that is defined to more than one host node but can be owned by only one host node at a time. Serially shared resources can be binary synchronous or start-stop lines or stations, physical units (PUs), or logical units (LUs). See also concurrently shared resource.

serial interchange node search A search request for a specific target sent sequentially to each interchange node in an APPN network.

serial networks A group of SNA networks connected in series by gateways.

serial number An integer denoting the position of an item in a series. (I) (A)

serial operation (1) Pertaining to the sequential or consecutive execution of two or more operations in a single device such as an arithmetic and logic unit. (A) (2) Deprecated term for sequential operation. (3) Contrast with parallel operation.

serial-parallel converter Synonym for staticizer. (T)

serial port An access point through which a computer transmits or receives data, one bit at a time. Contrast with parallel port.

serial printer Synonym for character printer.

serial processing (1) Pertaining to sequential or consecutive execution of two or more processes in a single device, such as a channel or processing unit. (A) (2) Contrast with parallel processing.

serial search A search in which the members of a set are consecutively examined, beginning with the first member and ending with the last.

serial sort A sort that requires only sequential access to the items in a set. A serial sort can be performed using only serial access storage devices. (A)

serial terminal A terminal that transmits elements of a signal one after the other. Contrast with parallel terminal.

serial-to-parallel converter Synonym for deserializer.

serial transfer A transfer of data in which elements are transferred in succession over a single line.

serial transmission (1) The sequential transmission of the signal elements of a group representing a character or other entity of data. (I) (2) In data communication, transmission at successive intervals of signal

elements constituting the same telegraph or data signal. The sequential elements may be transmitted with or without interruption, provided that they are not transmitted simultaneously; for example, telegraph transmission by a time divided channel. (A) (3) Contrast with parallel transmission.

serveability The ability of a service to be obtained, within specified tolerances and other given conditions, when requested by the user and continue to be provided for a requested duration. (T)

server (1) A functional unit that provides shared services to workstations over a network; for example, a file server, a print server, a mail server. (T) (2) In a network, a data station that provides facilities to other stations; for example, a file server, a print server, a mail server. (A) (3) In the AIX operating system, an application program that usually runs in the background and is controlled by the system program controller. (4) In AIX Enhanced X-Windows, a program that provides the basic windowing mechanism. It handles interprocess communication (IPC) connections from clients, demultiplexes graphics requests onto screens, and multiplexes input back to clients. (5) See name server. (6) In TCP/IP, a system in a network that handles the requests of a system at another site, called a client-server.

server grabbing In the AIX operating system, the action of a client seizing the server for exclusive use to prevent processing requests from other client connections until the grab is complete. This is typically a transient state for such things as rubber-banding and pop-up menus or to run requests indivisibly. See button grabbing, key grabbing, keyboard grabbing, pointer grabbing. See also active grab, passive grab.

server workstation In the NetView Graphic Monitor Facility, a workstation with the graphic data server. This workstation uses the graphic monitor and the view administrator for administrative functions. The server workstation sends status information to client workstations over an LU 6.2 session.

service (1) In Open Systems Interconnection architecture, a capability of a given layer and the layers below it that is provided to the next higher layer. The service of a given layer is provided at the boundary between this layer and the next higher layer. (T) (2) A customer-related or product-related business function such as design/manufacturing error correction, installation planning, maintenance, customer education, or programming assistance. (3) The common-carrier facilities provided to meet customers' data transmission requirements; for example, telephone service.

serviceability The capability to perform effective problem determination, diagnosis, and repair on a data processing system.

service access point (SAP) (1) In Open Systems Interconnection architecture, the point at which the services of a layer are provided by an entity of that layer to an entity of the next higher layer. (T) (2) A logical point made available by an adapter where information can be received and transmitted. (3) The logical point at which an n+1-layer entity acquires the services of the n-layer. A single SAP can have many links terminating in it. (4) A logical address that allows a system to route data between a remote device and the appropriate communications support.

service adapter An EIA communication adapter that permits use of a control terminal with the network controller and can be set to receive remote assistance. The service adapter connects to the service modem.

service aids The group of procedures and programs used to determine and correct system problems.

service authority In the AS/400 system, a special authority that allows the user to perform the alter function in the service functions. See also all object authority, job control authority, save system authority, security administrator authority, spool control authority.

service class See user service class.

service clearance The minimum space required to allow working room for the person installing or servicing a unit.

service data unit (SDU) In Open Systems Interconnection architecture, a set of data sent by a user of the services of a given layer, and that must be transmitted to the user of these services at the other end of the connection. (T)

service facility In ACF/TCAM, an auxiliary routine that runs under control of the message control program (MCP) and is invoked by the user code in the MCP on an as-needed basis. See also system service program.

service hours The amount of time that is spent by one or more IBM service representatives in order to perform a service task; for example, three hours of service performed by two IBM service representatives amounts to a total of six service hours.

service level In SNADS, one of the four levels of service (fast, status, data high, or data low) that determines if a distribution is put on the normal or priority distribution queue. See also distribution service level.

Service Level Reporter (SLR) A licensed program that generates management reports from data sets such as System Management Facility (SMF) files.

service level update In DPPX, complete replacement of the basic machine readable material for a licensed program. It is the same as the previous service level of the licensed program with the latest fix package incorporated.

service library In the AS/400 system and System/38, the system library provided in the system that is used temporarily for loading IBM-supplied programming changes and creating APARs.

service log A file of information on errors that have been detected.

service meter A device activated by a service meter key that records the machine running time accumulated when the IBM service representative services the machine.

service meter key A special tool for deactivating a customer meter on a product or system and activating a service meter.

service mode State where a product or system can be serviced by a service representative. Synonymous with maintenance mode. See also operation mode.

service modem A machine element of a network controller that attaches to the service adapter and enables communication with the network controller over a telecommunication line.

service modem cable A short ribbon cable that connects the network controller service modem to the service adapter.

service mode switch A control that is used by a service representative to switch a product or system from an operation mode to a service mode. Synonymous with maintenance mode switch.

service/operator panel A panel in a product or system that is used by service representatives or operators for diagnostics or normal operations. Synonymous with maintenance/operator panel.

service order table (1) In the network control program, the list of devices on a multipoint line, or point-to-point line where the terminal has multiple components, in the order in which they are to be serviced by the network control program. (2) A sequence defined for an SNA multipoint line that specifies the order in which physical units are to be serviced.

service panel A panel in a product or system that is used by service representatives for diagnostic or test purposes. Synonymous with maintenance panel.

service point (SP) An entry point that supports applications that provide network management for resources not under the direct control of itself as an entry point. Each resource is either under the direct control of another entry point or not under the direct control of any entry point. A service point accessing these resources is not required to use SNA sessions (unlike a focal point). A service point is needed when entry point support is not yet available for some network management function.

service point command facility (SPCF) A program or function that exchanges data and control between the network operator, the link connection component manager (LCCM), and the link connection subsystem manager (LCSM).

service point command service (SPCS) An extension of the command facility in the NetView program that allows the host processor to communicate with a service point by using the communication network management (CNM) interface.

service primitive In Open Systems Interconnection architecture, an abstract description of an interaction between a service user and a service provider.

Note: A service user is usually an entity. A service provider, in a given layer, usually comprises entities of that layer and a lower layer service (except at the Physical Layer). Therefore, a service primitive is also an abstract description of an interaction between two adjacent entities. (T)

service processor In the AS/400 system, the logic that contains the processor function to start the system processor and handle error conditions. See also system processor.

service program (1) A computer program that performs utility functions in support of the system. (2) Synonym for utility program. (3) See service transaction program.

service provider In Open Systems Interconnection architecture, an abstract representation of all the entities that provide a service to peer service users.

Note: The behavior of a service provider is often described in terms of an abstract machine. (T)

service rate In the system resources manager, a measure of the rate at which system resources (services) are provided to individual jobs. It is used by the installation to specify performance objectives, and used by the workload manager to track the progress of individual jobs. Service is a linear combination of processing unit, I/O, and main storage measures that can be adjusted by the installation.

service reminder (SR) In the NetView/PC program, a notification set by the operator that is displayed on a panel and logs a specified message.

service representative An individual who performs maintenance services for products or systems. See IBM Customer Engineer (CE), IBM Customer Service Representative (CSR), IBM Program Support Representative, IBM service representative.

service representative basic user profile In the AS/400 system, a system-supplied user profile, named QSRVBAS, that provides limited authority for a service representative to use dedicated service tools (DST) and system service tools (SST). Contrast with service representative user profile.

service representative privilege class In VM, CP privilege class F users, usually IBM service representatives, who are permitted to set or change the level of detail of I/O device error recording to the level desired. See also full recording mode, intensive recording mode, quiet recording mode.

service representative user profile In the AS/400 system, a system-supplied user profile, named QSRV, that provides all the authority required by a service representative to use the dedicated service tools (DST) and system service tools (SST). Contrast with service representative basic user profile.

service routine Synonym for utility routine. (T) (A)

services display In System/38, the source entry services display from which scan/substitute, date, browse, and syntax checking operations are requested.

service-seeking The process by which the network control program interrogates devices on a start-stop or BSC multipoint line for requests to send data or for readiness to receive data.

service-seeking pause In the network control program, a user-specified interval between successive attempts at service-seeking on a line when all devices on the line are responding negatively to polling. The pause can be used to reduce the overhead associated with polling.

service transaction program Any IBM-supplied transaction program running in a network accessible unit. Contrast with application transaction program.

service update process The method for incorporating PTFs into system modification packages.

service user In Open Systems Interconnection architecture, an entity in a single open system that makes use of services through service access points. (T)

service virtual machine In the VM/XA Migration Aid, a virtual machine that provides system services. These services include accounting, error recording, and services provided by licensed programs.

servo See servomechanism.

servo mark A standard mark printed below the print contrast mark. It is used by the printer to position the optical-mark-sensor head over the print contrast mark.

servomechanism (1) An automatic device that uses feedback to govern the physical position of an element. (A)　　(2) A feedback control system in which at least one of the system signals represents mechanical motion. (A)

SESSEND Session ended.

SESSER Session serialization.

session (1) In network architecture, for the purpose of data communication between functional units, all the activities which take place during the establishment, maintenance, and release of the connection. (T) (2) A logical connection between two network accessible units (NAUs) that can be activated, tailored to provide various protocols, and deactivated, as requested. Each session is uniquely identified in a transmission header (TH) accompanying any transmissions exchanged during the session. (3) The period of time during which a user of a terminal can communicate with an interactive system, usually, elapsed time between logon and logoff. (4) The activity of all tasks within a single System/38 RJEF subsystem communicating with a single host system. (5) In remote communications, a period of communication with a remote system or host system. (6) In the AS/400 system, the length of time that starts when a user signs on at a display station and ends when the user signs off. (7) In the AS/400 system with finance communications, a logical connection by which an AS/400 system communicates with a finance controller. (8) In the AS/400 system with RJE, the activity of all tasks within a single AS/400 system communicating with a single host system. (9) In the AS/400 system with 3270 emulation, the activity that occurs on the communications line between the time that the user enters the command to start emulation and the time the user ends the emulation job.

session activation In SNA, the process of exchanging a session activation request and a positive response between network addressable units (NAUs). See also LU-LU session initiation. Contrast with session deactivation.

session activation request In SNA, a request that activates a session between two network addressable units (NAUs) and specifies session parameters that control various protocols during session activity; for example, BIND and ACTPU. Contrast with session deactivation request.

session address space In VTAM, an ACB address space or an associated address space in which an OPNDST or OPNSEC macroinstruction is issued to establish a session. See also ACB address space, associated address space.

session awareness (SAW) data Data collected by the NetView program about a session that includes the session type, the names of session partners, and information about the session activation status. It is collected for LU-LU, SSCP-LU, SSCP-PU, and SSCP-SSCP sessions and for non-SNA terminals not supported by NTO. It can be displayed in various forms, such as most recent sessions lists.

SESSIONC indicators In VTAM, indicators that can be sent from one node to another without using SEND or RECEIVE macroinstructions; for example, SDT, clear, and STSN.

session collection The NPM subsystem that collects, monitors, and displays data collected in the host for analysis.

session connector A session-layer component in an APPN network node or in a subarea node boundary or gateway function that connects two stages of a session. Session connectors swap addresses from one address space to another for session-level intermediate routing, segment session message units as needed, and (except for gateway function session connectors) adaptively pace the session traffic in each direction. See also half-session.

session control (SC) In SNA: (a) one of the components of transmission control. Session control is used to purge data flowing in a session after an unrecoverable error occurs, resynchronize the data flow after such an error, and perform cryptographic verification; and (b) an RU category used for requests and responses exchanged between the session control components of a session and for session activation/deactivation requests and responses.

session control block (SCB) In NPM, control blocks in common storage area for session collection.

session control in-bound processing exit A user exit that receives control when certain request units (RUs) are received by VTAM.

session control record The first record in the chain of records in the transaction file of each display station.

session count In SNA: (a) the number of currently active LU-LU sessions for a particular logical unit; and (b) the number of currently active sessions for a particular virtual route.

session cryptography key In SNA, a data encrypting key used to encipher and decipher function management data (FMD) requests transmitted in an LU-LU session that uses cryptography.

session cryptography seed In SNA, an 8-byte, nonzero, pseudo-random number used to verify that both half-sessions have the same session cryptography key. It is used thereafter as the initial chaining value.

session data Data about a session, collected by the NetView program, that consists of session awareness data, session trace data, and session response time data.

session date The date associated with a session. See also creation date, program date, system date.

session deactivation In SNA, the process of exchanging a session deactivation request and response between network addressable units (NAUs). Contrast with session activation.

session deactivation request In SNA, a request that deactivates a session between two network addressable units (NAUs); for example, UNBIND and DACTPU. Contrast with session activation request.

session default A session assumed by the system for temporary use.

session description In the AS/400 system and System/38, an object that contains a description of the operating characteristics of an RJE session.

session end Deprecated term for half-session.

session establishment See LU-LU session initiation, session activation.

session-establishment macroinstructions In VTAM, the set of RPL-based macroinstructions used to initiate, establish, or terminate LU-LU sessions.

session-establishment request In VTAM, a request to an LU to establish a session. For the primary logical unit (PLU) of the requested session, the session-establishment request is the CINIT sent from the system services control point (SSCP) to the PLU. For the secondary logical unit (SLU) of the requested session, the session-establishment request is the BIND sent from the PLU to the SLU.

session files library In the AS/400 system, the files library that will be in use when the current System/36 environment job ends.

session group In System/36 advanced program-to-program communication, a number of sessions managed as a unit.

session information block (SIB) A control block that contains information about a particular SNA session.

session information retrieval (SIR) The function that allows an operator to enable or disable session information retrieval for a particular gateway or for all gateway sessions. When a gateway session ends, trace information about the most recent sequence or FID0 numbers to cross the gateway is passed back to all system services control points (SSCPs) that have enabled SIR for that session or for all sessions. This information can also be passed back to the requesting host.

session initiation See LU-LU session initiation. See also LU-LU session termination.

session initiation request In SNA, an Initiate or logon request from a logical unit (LU) to a system services control point (SSCP) that an LU-LU session be activated.

session layer (1) In the Open Systems Interconnection reference model, the layer that provides the means necessary for two end users to organize and synchronize their dialogue and to manage their data exchange. These services establish, maintain, and terminate communication. (T) See Open Systems Interconnection reference model. (2) The composite layer consisting of the data flow control and transmission control layers forming the half-sessions and session connectors in the network.

session-layer component A half-session or session connector.

session-level field In System/36, a field that retains its value when the operating mode changes. Contrast with job-level field, mode-level field.

session-level LU-LU verification An LU 6.2 security service that is used to verify the identity of each logical unit when a session is established.

session-level pacing A flow control technique that permits a receiving half-session or session connector to control the data transfer rate (the rate at which it receives request units) on the normal flow. It is used to prevent overloading a receiver with unprocessed requests when the sender can generate requests faster than the receiver can process them. See pacing, virtual route (VR) pacing.

session-level security For logical unit (LU) 6.2, partner LU verification and session cryptography. See also conversation-level security.

session library The library specified or assigned as a default when signing on or while running a program.

session limit (1) The maximum number of concurrently active LU-LU sessions that a particular logical unit (LU) can support. (2) In NCP, the maximum number of concurrent line-scheduling sessions on a non-SDLC, multipoint line.

session management exit routine An installation-supplied VTAM exit routine that performs authorization, accounting, and gateway path selection functions.

session manager (SM) A product, such as NetView Access Services, that allows a user at a terminal to log on to multiple applications concurrently.

session monitor The component of the NetView program that collects and correlates session-related data and provides online access to this information.

session network services (1) In SNA, network services that are performed on a half-session by half-session basis, rather than for the network addressable unit (NAU) as a whole. (2) In DPCX, the protocols specified by the host that govern a particular host session.

session pacing Deprecated term for session-level pacing.

session parameters In SNA, the parameters that specify or constrain the protocols, such as bracket protocol and pacing, for a session between two network addressable units (NAUs).

session partner (1) In SNA, one of the two network addressable units (NAUs) having an active session. (2) In DPCX, either the DPCX program or the host program that communicates during a host session.

session path The half-sessions delimiting a given session and their interconnection (including any intermediate session connectors).

session presentation services In SNA, a component of the FMD services layer that provides within LU-LU sessions services for the application programmer or terminal operator, such as formatting data to be displayed or printed.

session profile For the 3270 Host Connect Program/6000, a profile describing the characteristics of a session between a RISC System/6000 system and an IBM System/370 host computer. See also 3270 Host Connect Program/6000.

session seed Synonym for initial chaining value.

session segment A synonym for session stage when the session components delimiting the stage are in physically adjacent nodes, as in an APPN network.

session sequence identifier In SNA, an identifier in the sequence number field that uniquely identifies a request unit, typically on the expedited flow, until that request unit receives a response. Unlike a session sequence number, the identifier is not necessarily updated sequentially.

session sequence number In SNA, a sequentially incremented identifier that is assigned by data flow control to each request unit on a particular normal flow of a session, typically an LU-LU session, and is checked by transmission control. The identifier is carried in the transmission header (TH) of the path information unit (PIU) and is returned in the TH of any associated response. Contrast with session sequence identifier, virtual route sequence number.

session services One of the types of network services in the control point (CP) and in the logical unit (LU). These services provide facilities for an LU or a network operator to request that a control point (an ENCP, NNCP, or SSCP) assist with initiating or terminating sessions between logical units. Assistance with session termination is needed only by SSCP-dependent LUs. See configuration services, maintenance services, management services.

session setup failure notification (SSFN) Session awareness data provided by the NetView program when there is a failure. It identifies the system services control point (SSCP) that detects the error, the SSCPs that are involved, and the names of the session partners affected.

session stage The portion of a session path consisting of two session-layer components that are logically adjacent (no other session-layer components between them), and their interconnection. An example is the paired session-layer components in adjacent type 2.1 nodes and their interconnection over the link between them. Examples include paired BF session connectors and their interconnection over a virtual route, and the paired session-layer components in adjacent type 2.1 nodes and their interconnection over the link between them. A session path may consist of one stage, as between LUs in two physically adjacent nodes; two stages, as in a session having one intermediate boundary function; or more than two stages, as in an APPN network where the number of stages equals one less than the number of nodes in the path.

session statistics file In NPM, an online VSAM key-sequenced data set (KSDS) used for storing session data.

session termination See LU-LU session termination.

session-termination request In VTAM, a request that an LU-LU session be terminated.

session trace In the NetView program, the function that collects session trace data for sessions involving specified resource types or involving a specific resource.

session trace data Data, relating to sessions, that is collected by the NetView program whenever a session trace is started and that consists of session activation parameters, VTAM path information unit (PIU) data, and NCP data.

SESSST Session started.

set (1) In NDL, a named set of records together with a hierarchical relationship between one record and the other records of this set. (T)   (2) A finite or infinite number of objects of any kind, of entities, or of concepts that have a given property or properties in common. (I) (A)   (3) In the AIX Network Control System (NCS), to associate an allocated remote procedure call (RPC) handle with a specific socket address. (4) In videotaping, the basic background or area for production.   (5) To cause a counter to take the state corresponding to a specified number. (I) (A) (6) To put all or part of a data processing device into a specified state. (I)   (7) Synonym for bind.

set asynchronous balanced mode (SABM) In communications, a data link control command used to establish a data link connection with the destination in asynchronous balanced mode. See also asynchronous balanced mode (ABM).

set asynchronous balanced mode extended SABME. In communications, a data link control command used to initiate data transfer in the extended asynchronous balanced mode of operation with a remote link station. The SABME command uses modulus 128 sequence numbers.   See also asynchronous balanced mode extended (ABME).

set normal response mode (SNRM) A data link control command that puts the link connection in normal response mode (NRM).

set occurrence In the CODASYL model, an occurrence of an owner record together with zero or more occurrences of its member records. (A)

set-off In a duplicator, the unwanted transfer of ink from one copy to another after completion of the duplicating process. (T)

settling time Following the initiation of a specified input signal to a system, the time required for the output signal to enter and remain within a specified narrow band centered on its steady-state value. (T)

Note: The input may be a step, impulse, ramp, parabola, or sinusoid. For a step or impulse, the band is often specified as ±2 percent of the final steady-state value.

set type In the CODASYL model, a specification of an association between two record types. (A)

SET type In Pascal, a type used to define a variable that represents all combinations of elements of some scalar type.

setup (1) In a computer that consists of an assembly of individual computing units, the arrangement of connections between the units, and the adjustments needed for the computer to operate on a problem. (I)   (2) The preparation of a computing system to perform a job or job step. Setup is usually performed by an operator and often involves performing routine functions, such as mounting tape reels and loading card decks. (3) See also customer setup.

setup tests Tests performed by the customer during and after customer setup to verify that a machine is ready for operation.

setup time The time required by an operator to prepare a computing system to perform a job or job step.

SEU Source entry utility.

seven-bit byte Synonym for septet.

seven-track compatibility A feature that enables a tape unit to write or read seven-track tape at 200, 556, or 800 characters per inch.

severity code A code that indicates how serious an error condition is.

severity filter In the Network Carrier Interconnect Agent program, a function that limits the status data that is sent to a carrier management system depending on the severity of the event received by the agent.

sexadecimal Synonym for hexadecimal.

sextet A byte composed of six binary elements. (I) (A) Synonymous with 6-bit byte.

SF order Start field order.

S frame Supervisory frame.

SFX (1) Sound effects. (2) Special effects.

SGP Statistics generation program.

shade (1) To darken, as if with a shadow. (2) To add shading to.

shading (1) In computer graphics, emphasizing a given display group by changing the attributes of all the other display groups in the same display field. (T) (2) See Gouraud shading.

shadow In the OS/2 operating system, a link between duplicate objects. The objects can be located in different folders. If a change is made in either the duplicate or the original, the change takes effect in the other as well.

shadow box In SAA usage, deprecated term for window border.

shadow log In the AS/400 system, a log of errors that occur from the time that an initial program load starts to the time storage management recovery ends. The log contains the latest occurring errors, and may contain errors not found in the error log.

shadow page table In VM, a table that maps real storage allocations (first-level storage) to the virtual storage of a virtual machine (third-level storage) for use by the real machine in its paging operations.

shadow resource In VTAM, an alternate representation of a network resource that is retained as a definition for possible future use.

shannon In information theory, a unit of logarithmic measures of information equal to the decision content of a set of two mutually exclusive events expressed by the logarithm to base two; for example, the decision content of a character set of eight characters equals three shannons ($\log_2 8 = 3$). (I) (A) Synonymous with information content binary unit.

shape In FORTRAN, the rank-one array whose elements are the extents in each dimension.

share To make a resource available to remote users or other processes.

share count Deprecated term for concurrent control count.

shared (1) Pertaining to the availability of a resource for more than one use at the same time. (2) In MSS, an attribute of a mass storage volume that allows more than one processing unit at a time to access the volume.

shared access path An access path used by more than one file to provide access to data common to the files.

shared-access transport facility (SATF) A transmission facility, such as a multipoint link connection, a public switched network, or a token-ring, on which multiple pairs of nodes can form concurrently active links.

shared control In SNA, sequential or concurrent control of network resources, such as physical units (PUs), logical units (LUs), links, link stations, and their associated resources, by two or more control points. See also concurrent control count, share limit.

shared-control gateway A gateway consisting of one gateway NCP that is controlled by more than one gateway system services control point (SSCP).

shared DASD option An option that enables independently operating computing systems to jointly use common data residing on shared direct access storage devices.

shared device (1) A device that is connected to more than one processor. (2) In MVS, a device that is both a JES3 device and a JES3-managed device.

shared environment A system in which ACF/TCAM and TSO tasks concurrently share all necessary system resources.

shared file (1) A file that can be used by two computers or two systems at the same time. A shared file can link two systems. (2) In the AS/400 system and System/38, a file whose open data path can be shared between two or more programs processing in the same job. See also open data path (ODP).

shared-for-read lock state In the AS/400 system and System/38, the lock state for a file in which the file can be shared with another program if the program does not request exclusive use of the file.

shared-for-update lock state In the AS/400 system and System/38, the lock state for a file in which the file can be shared either for update or for read operations with another program.

shared index database An IMS/VS secondary index database that contains more than one secondary index in the same physical operating system database.

shared lock In DPPX, data locking requested when a program connects to a database that allows the requesting program and other programs to access the database concurrently. As each program accesses a record in the database, the record is made unavailable to other programs as a protection against conflicting access. Once established, a connection to the database with a shared lock prevents connection to the database with an exclusive lock.

shared logic In word processing, an arrangement in which two or more proximate workstations share common facilities. (T)

shared logic word processing equipment Word processing equipment in which the resources of a processing unit and storage devices are shared between two or more workstations. (T) (A)

shared main storage multiprocessing A mode of operation in which two processing units have access to all of main storage.

shared memory In the OS/2 operating system, a segment that can be used by more than one program. Synonym for shared segment.

shared-no-update lock state In the AS/400 system and System/38, the lock state for a file in which the file can be shared with another program if the program requests either a shared-no-update lock state or a shared-for-read lock state.

shared partition In VSE, a partition allocated for a program such as VSE/POWER that provides services for and communicates with programs in other partitions of the system's virtual address spaces.

shared ports One of more communications ports on a single input/output processor using short-hold mode on a single SDLC line description.

shared read-only system residence disk In VM, a system residence disk that is tailored so that most of the system residence information is read-only and accessible to all relevant virtual machines, leaving a relatively smaller private read/write system disk that must be dedicated to each virtual machine. This technique can substantially reduce the disk requirements of an installation by avoiding needless duplication of disk packs by virtual machines that use the same operating system. See also saved system.

shared record format A record format used in more than one externally described file.

shared resource (1) In word processing, an arrangement in which two or more workstations share common facilities. (T) (2) Directories, data files, programs, printers, plotters, and serial devices, such as modems, made available to users on a network. The users access these resources from their own computer or workstation.

shared segment In VM, a feature of a saved system that allows one or more segments of reentrant code in real storage to be shared among many virtual machines; for example, if a saved CMS system is generated, segment 1 of the CMS nucleus is shared in real storage among all CMS virtual machines loaded by name, that is, every virtual storage segment of a CMS machine maps to the same 64K bytes of real storage. See also discontiguous segment, saved system.

shared session A feature of a saved system that can be shared by one or more segments of reentrant code in real storage in a virtual machine group.

shared spooling A function that permits the VSE/POWER account file, data file, and queue file to be shared among several computer systems with VSE/POWER.

shared storage pool In the AS/400 system, a storage pool that can be shared by more than one subsystem.

shared system See saved system, shared read-only system residence disk.

shared variable A variable that can be accessed by two or more asynchronous procedures or concurrently executed computer programs. (T)

shared virtual area (SVA) In VSE, a high address area of virtual storage that contains a system directory list (SDL) of frequently used phases, resident programs that can be shared between partitions, and an area for system support.

share limit In SNA, the maximum number of control points that can control a network resource concurrently. See concurrent control count, shared control.

sharing See time sharing.

shear In computer graphics, the forward or backward slant of a graphics symbol or string of such symbols relative to a line perpendicular to the baseline of the symbol. See Figure 135.

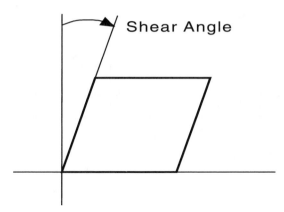

Figure 135. Shear

sheathing Synonym for jacket.

sheet In a continuous forms stacker, a rectangular sheet of paper usually bounded by tractor holes and perforations.

sheet detector In a document copying machine or a duplicator, a device that senses the presence of paper during the feeding process. (T)

sheet feeder In word processing, a device attached to a printer to automatically feed out sheets of paper or forms from one or more input drawers and to remove the finished printed sheets to an output drawer. (T)

Sheffer stroke Synonym for NAND.

shelf label A label printed by a supermarket terminal for use on the supermarket shelves. The label can include an item's name, number, price, or other user-defined information.

shelf life The period of time before deterioration renders a material unsuitable for use. (T)

shelf-resident optical volume In the Object Access Method, an optical volume that resides outside of an optical library.

shell (1) An empty expert system structure into which a particular field of expertise is built. Synonymous with expert system shell. (T) (2) A software interface between a user and the operating system of a computer. Shell programs interpret commands and user interactions on devices such as keyboards, pointing devices, and touch-sensitive screens and communicate them to the operating system. Shells simplify user interactions by eliminating the user's concern with operating system requirements. A computer may have several layers of shells for various levels of user interaction. (3) Software that allows a kernel program to run under different operating system environments. (4) In the AIX operating system, a command interpreter that acts as an interface between the user and the operating system. A shell can contain an other shell nested inside it; the outer shell is the parent shell and the inner shell is the child. See login shell, stand-alone shell, subshell. See also shell program.

shell document A document used during data/text merge that describes the format of the output, variable data to be inserted, and the location of the variable data to be inserted.

shell procedure In the AIX operating system, a series of commands, combined in a file, that carry out a particular function when the file is run or when the file is specified as a value to the SH command. Synonymous with shell script.

shell program A program that accepts and interprets commands for an operating system. See also shell, stand-alone shell.

shell prompt In the AIX operating system, the character string on the command line indicating that the system can accept a command (typically the $ character).

shell script Synonym for shell procedure.

shell variables In the AIX operating system, facilities of the shell program for assigning variable values to constant names.

shell widget In AIX Enhanced X-Windows, the widget that holds the top-level widgets that communicate directly with the window manager. These widgets do not have parents.

shielded twisted pair A transmission medium of two twisted conductors with a foil or braid shield.

shielding (1) In computer graphics, blanking of all portions of display elements falling within a specified region. (T) (2) Suppression of all or parts of display elements falling within a specified region. (A) (3) Synonymous with reverse clipping. (4) Contrast with scissoring.

shift (1) The concerted movement of some or all of the characters of a word each by the same number of character places in the direction of a specified end of the word. (I) (A) (2) On a typewriter, the movement of the type element to enable an alternate character or group of characters (a character set) to be typed. (T) (3) To move data to the right or left. (4) To adjust the contents of a line by moving information to the left or right of its original position. (5) See arithmetic shift, end-around shift, logical shift.

shift character A control character that determines the alphabetic/numeric shift of character codes in a message.

shift control character See shift-in character, shift-out character.

shift-in character (SI) (1) A code extension character used to terminate a sequence that has been introduced by the shift-out character to make effective the graphic characters of the standard character set. (I) (A)   (2) In the AS/400 system, a control character (hex 0F) that indicates the end of a string of double-byte characters. Contrast with shift-out character.

shift-in control character A character (hex 0F) that indicates the end of a string of ideographic characters. Contrast with shift-out control character.

Shift-Japanese Industrial Standard (SJIS) An encoding scheme consisting of single bytes and double bytes used for character encoding. Because of the large number of characters in the Japanese and other Asian languages, the 8-bit byte is not sufficient for character encoding.

shift key On a typewriter, a control for effecting a shift. (T)

shift lock On a typewriter, a latch-down key to hold the shift key in the shift position. (T)

shift motion On a typewriter, the distance between the two characters located on a type slug. (T)

shift-out character (SO) (1) A code extension character that substitutes for the graphic characters of the standard character set an alternative set of graphic characters upon which an agreement has been arrived at or that has been designated using code extension procedures. (I) (A)   (2) In the AS/400 system, a control character (hex 0E) that indicates the start of a string of double-byte characters. Contrast with shift-in character.

shift-out control character A character (hex 0E) that indicates the start of a string of ideographic characters. Contrast with shift-in control character.

shift register A register in which shifts are performed. (I) (A)

ship group Documents or material shipped with a product from a manufacturing location.

SHM Short-hold mode.

shoot In multimedia applications, to videotape the pictures needed for a production.

shooting ratio In video production, the amount of videotape recorded compared with the amount of tape actually used.

shooting script Synonym for final script.

short In the AIX object data manager (ODM), a terminal descriptor type used to define a variable as a signed 2-byte number. See also terminal descriptor.

short block A block of F-format data that contains fewer logical records than are specified for the block.

short card A special-purpose paper card that is shorter in length than a general-purpose paper card; for example, a 51-column card. (A)

short circuiting The evaluation of Boolean expressions with AND and OR such that the right operand is not evaluated if the result of the operation can be determined by evaluating the left operand. The evaluation of the expression is always from left to right.

short code dialing Synonym for short dialing.

short dialing Dialing by means of a one-digit code. Synonymous with short code dialing.

shortest-job-next (SJN) A method of queueing jobs where the shortest jobs are printed first. Contrast with first-come-first-serve.

short format In binary floating-point storage formats, the 32-bit representation of a binary floating-point number, not-a-number, or infinity. Contrast with long format.

short-hold mode (SHM) In SNA, a mode specified during configuration that allows the data terminal equipment (DTE) to connect or reconnect when no data is being transmitted over an X.21 circuit-switched line, while maintaining the logical connection of the SNA sessions across the circuit.

short interface In the AS/400 system, in query management, the set of language-specific interfaces that allow commands to run that do not require access to program variables. The short interface includes the communications area, command length, and command string.

short sign-on An abbreviated sign-on that can be used by a supermarket terminal that is already signed on for a store support procedure or for customer checkout. This procedure can be used to change the store support or customer checkout without signing the terminal off and then on again.

short status In the AIX operating system, status output in abbreviated form (short form) from the spooling subsystem.

short string In SQL, a string whose actual length, or a varying-length string whose maximum length, is 254 bytes.

shot In video or film production, a series of visual images and sounds recorded at one time.

shot list In multimedia applications, a list containing each shot needed to complete a production, usually broken down into a schedule.

shoulder tap A technique that enables one processing unit to communicate with another.

show cause In RECMS, the reason code that indicates to the VTAM or NetView program the threshold that was exceeded and whether or not the threshold has been dynamically altered.

ShP RISC System/6000 7016 POWERstation 730 Graphics Processor Subsystem Shading Processor.

SHUTC In SNA, a command used to complete a session.

SHUTD In SNA, a command used to begin an orderly end to a session.

shutdown The process of ending operation of a system or a subsystem, following a defined procedure.

shutdown time The interval of time that may be required by a document copying machine before it is isolated from the main electricity supply after completion of a copy production run. (T)

shutoff sequence (SO) In loop operation, eight consecutive zero bits sent around the loop to tell any transmitting station to stop transmitting immediately.

SHY Syllable hyphen character.

SI (1) The shift-in character. (I) (A) (2) Systeme International d'Unites, the international metric system.

SIB Session information block.

SIBIX Session information block initiation extension.

siblings In AIX Enhanced X-Windows, children of the same parent window.

sibling segments In an IMS/VS database, two or more segment types that have a common parent segment type.

sibling segment types In IMS/VS, two or more occurrences of different sibling segment types that have a common parent segment occurrence.

SIBRX Session information block resource extension.

SIBX Session information block cross-network extension.

side (1) The part of a sector address that indicates which surface of a double-sided diskette is to be accessed by the read/write head. (2) Synonym for partition.

sideband A frequency band above and below the carrier frequency, produced as a result of modulation.

side circuit A circuit arrangement for deriving a phantom circuit. In four wire circuits, the two wires associated with the GO channel form one side circuit, and those associated with the return channel form another. See also phantom circuit.

side circuit loading coil A loading coil for introducing a desired amount of inductance in a side circuit and a minimum amount of inductance in the associated phantom circuit.

side circuit repeating coil A repeating coil that operates simultaneously as a transformer at a terminal of a side circuit and as a device for superposing one side of a phantom circuit on that side circuit. Synonymous with side circuit repeat coil.

side effect In programming languages, any external effect caused by execution of a function procedure other than that of yielding the result value. (I)

side lay In a duplicator, a device against which the side of the paper is positioned relative to the position of the image on the master before the impression cycle is started. (T) See also front lay.

side lay adjuster In a duplicator, a control for adjusting the position of the image relative to the side edges of the paper. (T)

sift-down effect The copying of a value from a higher-level resource to a lower-level resource. The sift-down effect applies to many of the keywords and operands in NCP and VTAM definition statements. If an operand is coded on a macroinstruction or generation statement for a higher-level resource, it need not be coded for lower-level resources for which the same value is desired. The value becomes the default for all lower-level resources.

sifting sort Synonym for bubble sort.

sight check A check performed by sighting through the holes of two or more aligned punched cards toward a source of light to verify the punching; for example, to determine whether a hole has been punched in a corresponding punch position on all cards in a card deck. (A)

sigma memory (1) On a calculator, the facility for accumulating the results of a series of calculations. (T) (2) Synonymous with sigma storage.

sigma storage Synonym for sigma memory.

sign See currency sign, operational sign.

signal (1) A time-dependent variation of a physical quantity used to represent data. (T) (2) An SNA command used to request a break in data flow. (3) In AIX operating system operations, a method of inter-process communication that simulates software interrupts. See break signal, carrier signal, end signal. Contrast with exception, interrupt. (4) See enabling signal, inhibiting signal, jam signal, selection signal, start signal, stop signal. (5) See also carrier.

signal cable An electrical wire or set of wires, such as twinaxial, coaxial, or twisted pair cables used to attach devices to a computer.

signal distance The number of digit positions in which the corresponding digits of two binary words of the same length are different. (A) Synonymous with hamming distance.

signaling attention In VM, an indication that a user has pressed a key or keyed in a CP command to present an attention interrupt to CP or to the user's virtual machine.

signaling rate See data signaling rate.

signal mask A mask that defines the set of signals currently blocked from delivery to a process.

signal regeneration Signal transformation that restores a signal so that it conforms with its original characteristics. (T)

signal shaping Synonym for signal transformation.

signal-to-noise ratio (S/N) The relative power of the signal to the noise in a channel.

signal transformation The action of modifying one or more characteristics of a signal, such as its maximum value, shape, or timing. (I) (A) Synonymous with signal shaping.

signature In the OS/2 operating system, descriptive information about a file that is contained in a header and that specifies whether the file is executable.

sign bit A bit or binary element that occupies a sign position and indicates the algebraic sign of the number represented by the numeral with which it is associated. (I) (A) See Figure 136.

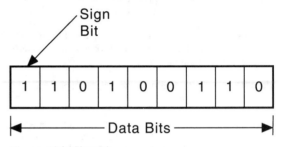

Figure 136. Sign Bit

sign change function In a calculator, the function that reverses the sign of a number. (T) (A)

sign character A character that occupies a sign position and indicates the algebraic sign of the number represented by the numeral with which it is associated. (I) (A)

sign condition In COBOL, the proposition, for which a truth value can be determined, that the algebraic value of a data item or an arithmetic expression is either less than, greater than, or equal to zero.

sign digit A digit that occupies a sign position and indicates the algebraic sign of the number represented by the numeral with which it is associated. (I) (A)

signed field A field that has a character in it to designate its algebraic sign.

signed packed decimal format The representation of a decimal value by two adjacent digits in a byte. The rightmost four bits of the field contain a sign. See also packed decimal format, unpacked decimal format.

significance Synonym for weight.

significand In binary floating-point format, the part of a number that contains the integer and fraction.

significant digit (1) In a numeral, a digit that is needed to preserve a given accuracy or a given precision. (T) (2) Any digit of a number that follows the leftmost digit which is not a zero and that is within the accuracy allowed.

significant digit arithmetic A method of making calculations by the use of a modified form of a floating-point representation system in which the number of significant digits in the result is determined with reference to the number of significant digits in the operands, the operation performed, and the degree of precision available. (T) (A)

significant figure Deprecated term for significant digit.

significant instant During modulation or demodulation of a signal, the point in time at which successive significant conditions of the signal begin. (T)

sign-off (1) To end a session at a display station. (2) To enter a command or to select an option from a menu at a workstation that instructs the system to end an interactive job. (3) See also log off.

sign-on (1) A procedure to be followed at a terminal or workstation to establish a link to a computer. (2) To begin a session at a workstation. (3) See also log on. (4) See also short sign-on.

sign-on command See fast sign-on.

sign-on option and parameters Option and parameter values that can be given on the sign-on screen and in the sign-on command. A specific function or subfunction can be directly selected with the option. Object identification values can be passed with the parameters.

sign-on verification security In IMS/VS, the use of system definition macroinstructions and security maintenance utility control statements to identify a particular user to IMS/VS.

sign position A position, normally located at one end of a numeral, that contains an indicator denoting the algebraic sign of the number represented by the numeral. (I) (A)

silver process In a document copying machine, a process in which copy results from the radiation effect, particularly light, on silver-sensitized material. (T) See also diffusion process, direct positive process, negative-positive process.

simple buffering (1) A technique for assigning buffering storage for the duration of the execution of a computer program. (I) (A) (2) A technique for controlling buffers in such a way that the buffers are assigned to a single data control block and remain so assigned until the data control block is closed.

simple checkpoint In IMS/VS, the periodic recording of control information and system status on the system log at user-specified intervals.

simple condition In COBOL, any single condition chosen from the set: relation condition, class condition, condition-name condition, switch-status condition, and sign condition. Contrast with negated simple condition.

simple gateway A gateway consisting of one gateway NCP and one gateway system services control point (SSCP).

simple HISAM In IMS/VS, the support for a HISAM database that contains only one segment type. See also hierarchic direct access method (HDAM), hierarchic indexed direct access method (HIDAM), hierarchic indexed sequential access method (HISAM), hierarchic sequential access method (HSAM).

simple image An image composed of a single raster pattern. Contrast with complex image.

simple list A list of like values; for example, a list of user names. Contrast with mixed list.

Simple Mail Transfer Protocol (SMTP) In TCP/IP, an application protocol for transferring mail among users in the Internet environment. SMTP specifies the mail exchange sequences and message format. It assumes that the Transmission Control Protocol is the underlying protocol.

simple object name Synonym for object name.

simplex Pertaining to printing on only one side of the paper. Contrast with duplex.

simplex circuit A one-way circuit.

simplex communication Synonym for one-way communication.

simplex copying Synonym for single-sided copying.

simplex transmission Data transmission in one preassigned path. (I) (A)

Simplified Chinese The Chinese character set that has been simplified by reducing the number of strokes in common characters and deleting complicated variants. Simplified Chinese characters are used primarily in the People's Republic of China.

Simplified Chinese double-byte character set An IBM-defined double-byte character set for Simplified Chinese. It consists of Simplified Chinese non-Chinese set, primary set, secondary set, and up to 1,880 user-definable characters.

Simplified Chinese non-Chinese character set A subset of the Simplified Chinese double-byte character set (DBCS), consisting of non-Chinese characters, such as Latin alphabet, Greek, Russian, Roman numeric, alphanumeric and related symbols, Katakana, Hiragana, Japanese, special symbols, and Chinese phonetic symbols. There are 712 characters in this set.

Simplified Chinese primary character set A subset of the Simplified Chinese double-byte character set (DBCS), consisting of commonly used Chinese characters. There are 3,755 characters in this set.

Simplified Chinese secondary character set A subset of the Simplified Chinese double-byte character set (DBCS), consisting of less commonly used Chinese characters. There are 3,008 characters in this set.

SIMSCRIPT A programming language used for discrete simulation. (T)

simulate (1) To represent certain features of the behavior of a physical or abstract system by the behavior of another system; for example, to represent a physical phenomenon by means of operations performed by a computer or to represent the operations of a computer by those of another computer. (I) (A) (2) To imitate one system with another, primarily by software, so that the imitating system accepts the same data, executes the same computer programs, and achieves the same results as the imitated system. (A) (3) Contrast with emulate.

simulated attention A function that allows terminals without attention keys to interrupt processing. The terminal is queried periodically for a specified character string. See also attention interruption.

simulated logon A session-initiation request generated when a VTAM application program issues a SIMLOGON macroinstruction. The request specifies a logical unit (LU) with which the application program wants a session in which the requesting application program will act as the primary logical unit (PLU).

simulation (1) The use of a data processing system to represent selected behavioral characteristics of a physical or abstract system; for example, the representation of air streams around airfoils at various velocities, temperatures, and air pressures. (T) (2) See real-time simulation. (3) Contrast with emulation.

simulator (1) A device, data processing system, or computer program that represents certain features of the behavior of a physical or abstract system. (I) (A)   (2) See computer simulator.

simultaneous (1) Pertaining to the occurrence of two or more events at the same instant of time. (A) (2) In a process, pertaining to two or more events that

occur within the same interval of time, each one handled by a separate functional unit; for example, in the execution of one or more programs, several input/output operations handled by input/output channels, input/output controllers, and associated peripherals may be simultaneous with one another and with other operations handled directly by the processing unit. (T) (A)   (3) Contrast with concurrent. (4) See also consecutive, sequential.

simultaneous computer A computer that contains a separate unit to perform each portion of the entire computation concurrently, the units being connected in a way determined by the computation. At different times in a run, a given connection carries signals representing different values of the same variable. (I) (A)

simultaneous operation A mode of operation in which two or more events occur at the same instant of time. (I) (A)

simultaneous processing The performance of two or more data processing tasks at the same instant of time. Contrast with concurrent processing.

simultaneous transmission Transmission of control characters or data in one direction while control characters or data are being received in the other direction. Contrast with nonsimultaneous transmission.

sine wave A waveform that represents periodic oscillations of a pure frequency.

singing Sound caused by unstable oscillations on a telecommunication line.

single-address Pertaining to an instruction format containing one address part. (A) Synonymous with one-address.

single-address message A message to be delivered to only one destination.

single buffer mode In AIX operating system graphics, a mode in which the frame buffer bitplanes are organized into a single large frame buffer. This frame buffer is the one currently displayed and is also the one in which all drawing occurs. See double buffer mode.

single-byte character set (SBCS) A character set in which each character is represented by a one-byte code. Contrast with double-byte character set.

single-byte coded font A font in which the characters are defined by one byte the code point. A single byte coded font has only one coded font section. Contrast with a double-byte coded font.

single-byte font Synonym for single-byte coded font.

single-cable broadband LAN A broadband LAN that uses one cable for both forward LAN channel and the backward LAN channel. (T)

single-choice selection field In SAA Basic Common User Access architecture, a selection field from which a user can select only one choice or make no selection. See selection field. See also multiple-choice selection field.

single-choice selection list In SAA Basic Common User Access architecture, a set of choices that can be scrolled. They can either be fixed or variable in content or number. A user can select only one choice or make no selection. See selection list. See also multiple-choice selection list.

single cluster feature In System/36, a hardware feature that allows up to four display stations and printers to be attached to a remote controller. See dual cluster feature.

single console image facility (SCIF) A VM facility that allows multiple consoles to be controlled from a single, virtual machine console.

single device file In System/38, a device file created with only one program device defined for it; for example, printer files, card files, diskette files, tape files, communication files, BSC files, display files, and mixed files created with only one defined device. Contrast with multiple device file.

single-domain network (1) A network that has only one host node. (T) (2) In SNA, a network with one system services control point (SSCP). Contrast with multiple-domain network.

single earpiece On dictation equipment, a lightweight listening device designed to be retained in or on the ear. (I)

single entry In ACF/TCAM, a terminal-table entry associated with a single external logical unit (LU) or application program. See also cascade entry, group entry, line entry, logtype entry, process entry, terminal-table entry. Contrast with distribution entry.

single file list In the OS/2 operating system, a list of directories and files on one drive.

single key stroke On a typewriter, the striking of a key only once to achieve the machine function required. (T)

single-level device In computer security, a device used to process data of a single security level at a particular time. Contrast with multilevel device.

single-level storage The technique of addressing multiple levels of storage through a single addressing structure.

single line communications adapter/attachment A feature that allows a single telecommunication line to be connected to System/36.

single-line entry field In SAA Advanced Common User Access architecture, a control into which a user types one line of information. See also multiple-line entry field.

single-line repeater A telegraph repeater utilizing a pair of cross-coupled polar relays that are inserted in series with a circuit to repower the signal.

single lock manager In IMS/VS, a function in which locks for database resources shared between programs or subsystems are handled by one control point. Either an IMS/VS resource lock manager (IRLM) or a program isolation locking function can be invoked for the subsystem.

single message mode In IMS/VS, a processing mode in which synchronization points occur as each message is read from the queue, as well as at application termination. See also multiple message mode, synchronization point.

single-mode optical fiber An optical fiber in which only the lowest-order bound mode (which can consist of a pair of orthogonally polarized fields) can propagate at the wavelength of interest. (E) Synonymous with monomode optical fiber. Contrast with multimode optical fiber.

single-office exchange An exchange served by a single central office.

single operation See half duplex.

single-picture segment In multimedia, a video picture that has no motion, but runs at a normal rate so that sound or voice-over can be used.

single plane In the 3270 Information Display System, a function that restricts the user to use of a single buffer when defining a symbol. Contrast with triple plane.

single ply Pertaining to forms that have only one layer.

single port sharing An arrangement for short-hold mode operation in which each port is shared by a set of data terminal equipments (DTEs), with the restriction that all reconnection calls (recalls) must use the same port as the first call for that logical connection.

single-precision (1) Pertaining to use of one computer word to represent a number in accordance with the required precision. (I) (A) (2) The specification that causes a floating-point value to be stored in the short format. See also precision. (3) In BASIC, the level of precision in which values printed in whole number and fixed-point format have a maximum of 6 significant digits, and values printed in floating-point format have a maximum of 7 significant digits. (4) Contrast with double-precision.

single requester terminal (SRT) program In System/36, a program that can process requests from only one display station or SSP-ICF session from each copy of the program. Contrast with multiple requester terminal program.

single selection In SAA Advanced Common User Access architecture, a selection technique that allows a user to select only one choice. See also extended selection.

single-sideband transmission Carrier transmission in which one sideband is transmitted and the other is suppressed. The carrier wave may be either transmitted or suppressed.

single-sided copying In a document copying machine, the making of one or more copies on only one side of the copy paper. (T) Synonymous with simplex copying. Contrast with double-sided copying.

single step Pertaining to a method of operating a computer in which each step is performed in response to a single manual operation. (A)

single-step operation A mode of operation of a computer in which a single computer instruction or part of a computer instruction is executed in response to an external signal. (I) (A) Synonymous with step-by-step operation.

single-thread application program A VTAM application program that processes requests for multiple sessions one at a time. Such a program usually requests synchronous operations from VTAM, waiting until each operation is completed before proceeding. Contrast with multithread application program.

single-wire line A telecommunication line that uses the ground as one side of the circuit.

sink See data sink, message sink.

SIO Start I/O.

SIR Session information retrieval.

SIT Scanner interface trace.

six-bit byte Synonym for sextet.

six sigma A very high level of quality, with only 3.4 defects, failures, or errors per million measurable units of product or service.

size In FORTRAN, for an array, the total number of elements. Its interface must conform with the core.

Size (1) In SAA Advanced Common User Access architecture, a selection technique that allows a user to select only one choice. See also extended selection. (2) In SAA Advanced Common User Access architecture, a choice in the system menu pull-down that a user selects to change the dimensions of a window.

size field In an AIX i-node, a field that indicates the size, in bytes, of the file associated with the i-node.

sizing The process of making paper resistant to liquids that may penetrate it.

SJIS Shift-Japanese Industrial Standard.

SJN Shortest-job-next.

skeletal code A set of instructions in which some parts, such as addresses, must be completed or specified in detail each time the set is used. (A)

skeleton In VSE/SP, a set of control statements, instructions, or both, that requires user-specific information to be inserted before it can be submitted for processing.

skew The angular or longitudinal deviation of a tape row from a specified reference. (T)

skip (1) In text processing, to pass over text such as a page or a paragraph. (T) (2) To ignore one or more instructions in a sequence of instructions. (A) (3) To pass over one or more positions on a data medium; for example, to perform one or more line feed operations. (A) (4) To cause a printer to move the printing medium to a specified line before or after it prints a line. (5) See also paper throw.

skip key In word processing, a control that initiates the skip process. (T) Synonymous with access button.

skipping On a typewriter, relative movement between the paper carrier and the typing position over an optional number of character spaces or line spaces without regard to preselected stops. (T) Synonymous with skip tabbing.

skip sequential access In systems with VSAM, keyed sequential retrieval or storage of records in ascending sequence with skips. VSAM scans the sequence set of the index to find a record or a collating position.

skip tabbing Synonym for skipping.

SKU Stockkeeping unit.

slate In video or film production, a chalkboard or other device with identifying information, used at the beginning of each shot for guidance during editing.

slave station In basic mode link control, the data station that is selected by a master station to receive data. (I) (A)

sleeping process In the AIX operating system, a process that is waiting for input or output to complete, time slices, an event to occur, or signals from other processes. When a process is sleeping, it can be paged out of memory.

sleep mode In VM, a mode in which the virtual machine is in a dormant state; that is, the virtual machine is not running, but connect time still accumulates and messages can be displayed at the terminal. The virtual machine is reactivated either at the end of a specified time interval or when the user signals attention to CP. See also signaling attention.

SLIB Subsystem library.

slice Those parts of a waveform lying inside two given amplitude limits on the same side of the zero axis. See also time slice.

slice label In GDDM, the alphanumeric label that a user can assign to each slice on a pie chart. See also spider label.

slicer A circuit that effectively amplifies a slice.

slide The hardware attached to a device on which the device moves and out of the rack in a drawer-like action. Contrast with rail.

slide imager In multimedia, a device that converts a 35mm color slide into a video signal for use as video input.

slider (1) In SAA Advanced Common User Access architecture, a graphical representation that represents a quantity and its relationship to the range of possible values for that quantity. A user can change the value of the quantity by using the slider. See slider arm. (2) In the AIXwindows program, a small interactive graphical object connected to an XmScrollBar bar widget. The slider controls the vertical or horizontal movement of text information or graphics across the display screen.

slider arm In SAA Advanced Common User Access architecture, the visual indicator in a slider that shows that the numerical value can be changed by manipulating it. See slider.

slider box In SAA Advanced Common User Access architecture: a part of the scroll bar that shows the position and size of the visible information in a window relative to the total amount of information available.

slide show presentation Synonym for storyboard.

SLIH Second level interrupt handler.

slip Loss or gain of digits caused by displacement of a sequence of digits. See also controlled slip.

slot (1) A subelement of a frame that contains features such as object names, attributes, values and pointers. (T) (2) In OS/VS, a continuous area on a paging device in which a page can be stored. (3) A portion of a transmission frame that is sent around a loop. (4) A position in a device used for removable storage media. See diskette slot, expansion slot, head slot. (5) In VSAM, a fixed-length, numbered space in a relative-record data set that accepts one data record. See also relative-record file, relative-record number. (6) See I/O slot.

slot group In OS/VS2, a set of slots on one or more tracks within a cylinder on a paging device.

slot number In OS/VS2, a part of an external page address that refers to a slot. Together with a device number and a group number, it identifies the location of a page in external page storage.

slot sorting In VM, a technique used by the CP paging supervisor to reduce the number of separate channel programs needed to read pages from or write pages on a paging device. This is accomplished by grouping in the same channel program the reading or writing of pages that occur in different relative record positions on the same track or within the same cylinder. See also ordered seek queuing.

slotted-ring control In a ring network configuration, a ring control scheme in which any station can place a data packet in one of several empty fixed-length data slots that flow continuously around the ring, along with appropriate address information. Each station examines the address information in each packet and copies the frames that are directed to that station. The sending station frees the slot by removing the packet from the slot after it has been copied by the receiving station. See also master node control, register insertion, token access control.

slotted-ring network A ring network that allows unidirectional data transmission between data stations by transferring data in predefined slots in the transmission stream over one transmission medium so that the data return to the originating station. (T) See Figure 137.

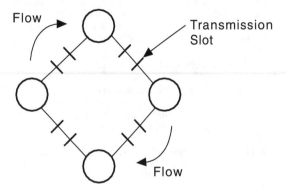

Figure 137. Slotted-Ring Network

slot time (1) In a CSMA/CD network, an implementation-dependent unit of time which, in case of collision, is used to determine the delay times after which data stations may attempt to retransmit. (T) (2) In carrier sense multiple access network with collision detection, a protocol that requires carrier sense and in which a transmitting data station that detects another signal while transmitting stops sending, sends a jam signal, and then waits for a variable length of time before trying again. (A)

slow motion In video systems, a mode in which a video sequence is played at an exaggeratedly slow speed.

slow time scale Synonym for extended time scale.

SLR Service Level Reporter.

SLSS Systems Library Subscription Service.

SLT (1) Section list table. (2) Solid logic technology.

SLU Secondary logical unit.

SLU key In ACF/TCAM, a key-encrypting key used to encipher the cryptographic session key contained in the BIND request unit sent to the secondary logical unit.

small caps (1) Capital letters in the same style as normal capital letters in a font, but approximately the size of lowercase letters. (2) See also caps.

small computer system interface (SCSI) An input and output bus that provides a standard interface between the OS/2 multimedia system and peripheral devices.

Small Computer Systems Interface Adapter An adapter that supports the attachment of various direct-access storage devices and tape drives to the RISC System/6000.

small data set packing In the Data Facility Hierarchical Storage Manager, the process used during migration of data sets that are equal to or fewer in number than a specified number of tracks of actual data. The data sets are written as one or more records into a VSAM data set on a migration level 1 volume.

small-data-set-packing data set In the Data Facility Hierarchical Storage Manager, a VSAM key-sequenced data set allocated on a migration level 1 volume and containing small data sets.

small integer In SQL, a data type indicating that the data is a binary number with a precision of 15 bits.

small programming enhancement (SPE) An addition to a software product or to a hardware/software product that has been released to customers. A single SPE can affect several products or several product components.

smart card In computer security, a credit-card-sized device containing an embedded microprocessor that stores information.

smear In multimedia, an analog artifact in which vertical edges in the picture are spread to the left or right.

SMF (1) System management facilities. (2) System measurement facility.

SMM System management monitor.

SMMF SSCP monitor mode function.

smooth (1) To apply procedures that decrease or eliminate rapid fluctuations in data. (A) (2) See also exponential smoothing.

smoothed data Statistical data, as in a curve or graph, freed from irregularities by ignoring random occurrences or by a process of continual averaging.

smoothline See nonloaded lines.

smoothness of curve (1) The manner in which plotted points are connected in a continuous curve. (2) See also curve fitting.

SMP System Modification Program.

SMP/E System Modification Program Extended.

SMPTE Society of Motion Picture and Television Engineers.

SMPTE time code A frame-numbering system developed by SMPTE that assigns a number to each frame of video. The 8-digit code is in the form HH:MM:SS:FF (hours, minutes, seconds, frame number). The numbers track elapsed hours, minutes, seconds, and frames from any chosen point.

SMQ Save/restore message queues.

SMS Storage Management Subsystem.

SMS complex A set of up to eight systems within an installation that are defined to MVS in the base configuration as SMS systems.

SMTP Simple Mail Transfer Protocol.

S/N Signal-to-noise ratio.

SNA Systems Network Architecture.

SNA backbone In an SNA network, the set of all interconnected nodes that consist of 37xx products running the Network Control Program.

SNA character string (SCS) In SNA, a character string composed of EBCDIC controls, optionally intermixed with end-user data, that is carried within a request/response unit.

SNA distribution services (SNADS) An IBM asynchronous distribution service that defines a set of rules to receive, route, and send electronic mail in a network of systems.

SNADS SNA distribution services.

SNADS receiver In the AS/400 system, a user-configured batch job that is started in the subsystem specified on the communications entry when the system receives SNADS distribution from a sending system in the SNADS network. Contrast with SNADS sender. See also SNADS router.

SNADS router In the AS/400 system, a system-provided batch job that runs in the QSNADS subsystem and routes distributions to the configured distribution queue. See also SNADS receiver, SNADS sender.

SNADS sender In the AS/400 system, a user-configured batch job that is started in the QSNADS subsystem, and sends distributions to another system in the SNADS network. Contrast with SNADS receiver. See also SNADS router.

SNA network The part of a user-application network that conforms to the formats and protocols of Systems Network Architecture. It enables reliable transfer of data among end users and provides protocols for controlling the resources of various network configurations. The SNA network consists of network accessible units (NAUs), boundary function, gateway function, and intermediate session routing function components; and the transport network.

SNA network interconnection The connection, by gateways, of two or more independent SNA networks to allow communication between logical units in those networks. The individual SNA networks retain their independence.

SNA Network Link (SNALINK) A function of the TCP/IP products for VM and MVS that allows the use of an SNA subarea routing network to transfer data using TCP/IP protocols. SNALINK provides the interface between TCP/IP and the SNA network. SNALINK must be defined as an application program to VTAM, which causes LU 0 sessions to be established between the SNALINK logical unit and other logical units in the SNA network.

SNALINK SNA Network Link.

SNA node A node that supports SNA protocols.

SNAP/SHOT System Network Analysis Program / Simulated Host Overview Technique.

snapshot dump (1) A dynamic dump of the contents of one or more specified storage areas. (I) (A) (2) A selective dump performed at various points in a machine run. (A)

snapshot program A trace program that produces output data only for selected instructions or for selected conditions. (I) (A)

SNA remote job entry In System/38, the portion of the remote job entry facility that allows the user to communicate with a host system in an SNA environment.

SNA station A station that supports SNA protocols.

SNASVCMG mode name SNA service manager mode name. This is the architecturally defined mode name identifying sessions on which CNOS is exchanged.

SNA terminal A terminal that supports SNA protocols.

SNA upline facility (SNUF) The communications support that allows an AS/400 system to communicate with CICS/VS and IMS/VS application programs on a host system.

SNA 3270 device emulation In the AS/400 system and System/38, a function of the operating system that allows an AS/400 system to appear to the host system as a 3274 Control Unit.

SNBU Switched network backup.

sneak current A leakage current that gets into telephone circuits from other circuits. It is too weak to cause immediate damage, but can produce harmful heating effects if allowed to continue.

SNI SNA network interconnection.

SNOBOL A programming language designed for string processing and pattern matching. (T)

SNRM Set normal response mode.

SNUF SNA upline facility.

SO (1) The shift-out character. (I) (A) (2) Shutoff sequence.

socket (1) In the AIX operating system: (a) A unique host identifier created by the concatenation of a port identifier with a transmission control protocol/Internet protocol (TCP/IP) address. (b) A port identifier. (c) A 16-bit port number. (d) A port on a specific host; a communications end point that is accessible through a protocol family's addressing mechanism. A socket is identified by a socket address. See also socket address. (2) The abstraction provided by the University of California's Berkeley Software Distribution (commonly called Berkeley UNIX or BSD UNIX) that serves as an endpoint for communication between processes or applications.

socket address In the AIX operating system, a data structure that uniquely identifies a specific communications end point. A socket address consists of a port number and a network address. It also specifies the protocol family. See also protocol family.

SOF Start-of-format control.

softcopy (1) A nonpermanent copy of the contents of storage in the form of a display image. (T) (2) One or more files that can be electronically distributed, manipulated, and printed by a user. Contrast with hardcopy. (3) Synonymous with machine-readable information (MRI), machine-sensible information.

soft error (1) An error that occurs sporadically and that may not appear on successive attempts to read data. Synonymous with transient error. (T) (2) An intermittent error on a network that requires retransmission. Contrast with hard error.

Note: A soft error by itself does not affect overall reliability of a network, but reliability may be affected if the number of soft errors reaches the ring error limit.

soft fault An intermittent error in transmission, usually caused by a degradation in the electrical signal or by electromagnetic interference. Contrast with hard fault. See also frame check sequence (FCS).

soft fonts In personal computing environments, optional fonts shipped as files. Soft fonts must be installed on a hard disk before they can be selected from programs. See also downloaded font.

soft hyphen A special character, inserted automatically or by the user in a word to mark where the word can be divided, and displayed as a hyphen when the word must be divided at the end of the line due to lack of space. Soft hyphens are subject to hyphen drop. Synonymous with discretionary hyphen, syllable hyphen, phantom hyphen. (T)

soft sector On a disk or diskette, a sector that is established electronically or by means of a software operation. See also hard sector.

soft sectoring (1) The identification of sector boundaries on a magnetic disk by using recorded information. (2) Contrast with hard sectoring. (T) (A)

soft wait See wait state *(2)*.

software (1) All or part of the programs, procedures, rules, and associated documentation of a data processing system. Software is an intellectual creation that is independent of the medium on which it is recorded. (T) (2) Contrast with hardware. (3) See application software, integrated software, system software.

software controls Programmed controls that monitor a computer system; for example, to detect and possibly to correct errors. (T)

software end-of-file In VSAM, a code that indicates that no data exist beyond it in the component. A software end-of-file is indicated by a zero value control interval definition field in conjunction with information in the VSAM catalog.

software engineering The systematic application of scientific and technological knowledge, methods, and experience to the design, implementation, and testing of software to optimize its production and support. (T)

software package A complete and documented set of programs supplied to several users for a generic application or function. Some software packages are alterable for a specific application. (T)

software piracy Illegal use or copying of software products. (T)

software recording facility (SRF) A facility used by functional recovery routines to write system error records.

SOH (1) The start-of-heading character. (I) (A) (2) Start-of-header character.

solicited message (1) In MSS, a message from the mass storage control to the processing unit that is expected by that processing unit. (2) A response from VTAM to a command entered by a program operator. Contrast with unsolicited message.

solicit operation In VTAM, the process of obtaining or attempting to obtain data from a local BSC or start-stop terminal or from a 3270 Information Display System and moving the data into VTAM buffers.

solicit request Any request that causes VTAM to perform a solicit operation.

solid logic technology (SLT) Miniaturized modules used in computers that result in faster circuitry because of reduced distance for current to travel.

solid modeling In computer-integrated manufacturing, three-dimensional modeling in which the solid characteristics of an object under design are built into the database, so complex internal structures and external shapes can be realistically represented. (T)

solid state component A component whose operation depends on control of electric or magnetic phenomena in solids; for example, a transistor, a crystal diode. (A)

solid state computer A computer that uses solid state, or semiconductor, components. Synonymous with second generation computer.

SOM Start-of-message code.

Some... In SAA usage, a choice in the View pull-down that a user can select to specify particular items to be displayed. See also All, By....

sonic delay line Synonym for acoustic delay line.

sort (1) The operation of sorting. (A) (2) In word processing, rearrangement of blocks of text according to specific instructions. (3) To segregate items into groups according to specified criteria. (I) (A) (4) To arrange a set of items according to keys used as a basis for determining the sequence of the items; for example, to arrange the records of a personnel file in alphabetical sequence by using the employee names as sort keys. (A) (5) Synonym for order.

Note: Sorting involves ordering but need not involve sequencing, for the groups may be arranged in an arbitrary order.

sort blocking factor In sorting, the number of data records to be placed in each block.

sorter (1) A device that deposits punched cards in pockets selected according to the hole patterns in the cards. (I) (A) (2) A person, device, or computer routine that sorts. (A) (3) In a document copying machine, a device that sorts copies from an original set into sets of copies, or sorts copies from a single original into a number of sets. (T) See Figure 138.

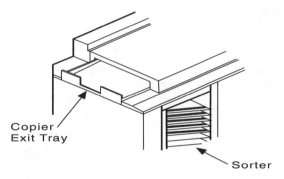

Copier Exit Tray

Sorter

Figure 138. Sorter

sort file In COBOL, a collection of records to be sorted by a SORT statement. The sort file is created by and can be used by only the sort function.

sort key (1) A key used as a basis for determining the sequence of items in a set. (A) (2) One or more keys within an item, used as a basis for determining the sequencing of items in a set. (A) Synonymous with sequencing key.

sort-merge file description entry In COBOL, an entry in the File Section of the Data Division that is composed of the level indicator (SD), followed by a file-name, and then followed by a set of file clauses as required.

sort/merge program A processing program that can be used to sort or merge records in a prescribed sequence.

sort pass The phase of a sort-merge program that consists of reading a set of unsorted data items, ordering them, and placing the ordered set (string) on a data medium. This process is repeated until all input data are placed in a string. The merge phase is then begun to merge the strings into one ordered set. (A)

sort program (1) A computer program that sorts items of data. (I) (A) (2) See also sort pass.

sort selection In word processing, selection of storage addresses by means of predetermined codes. (T)

sort sequence specifications Source statements that specify the sequence of a sort.

sort utility A function of an operating system used to arrange records in a sequence determined by data contained in one or more fields in the record.

SOS Silicon on sapphire.

SOTUS Sequentially Operated Teletypewriter Universal Selector. In the 81D1 Automatic Teletypewriter Systems, a station control device located at each Model 19 type station on a multistation line. SOTUS is the selecting device at each station.

sound card In multimedia, an add-on adapter card that incorporates a synthesizer without a musical keyboard and has audio output jacks for the sound created.

sound effects (SFX) In multimedia, any sound, other than voices and music, intentionally included in an audio track.

sounder A telegraph receiving instrument in which an electromagnet attracts an armature each time a pulse arrives. The armature makes an audible sound as it hits against its stops at the beginning and end of each current impulse, and the intervals between these sounds are translated by the operator from code into the received message.

sound level meter In acoustics, an instrument that includes a microphone, amplifier, output circuit, and frequency weighting networks (A, B, and C) for measuring noise and sound pressure levels in a specified manner. The meter can be set for the dynamic characteristics impulse, fast, and slow.

sound power level (Lw) In acoustics, a level that in decibels is 10 times the logarithm to the base 10 of the ratio of the sound power to the reference sound power (1 picowatt).

sound pressure level (Lp) In acoustics, a level that in decibels is 20 times the logarithm to the base 10 of the ratio of a given sound pressure to the reference sound pressure (20 micropascals). Synonymous with noise level.

sound track Synonym for audio track.

source (1) In advanced program-to-program communications, the system or program that starts jobs on another system. (2) A system, a program within a system, or a device that makes a request to a target. Contrast with target. (3) In COBOL, the symbolic identification of the originator of a transmission to a queue. (4) See data source, message source.

source address Synonym for origin address.

source area (1) A work area for holding information read from a source or information to be written to a destination. (2) In DPCX, 200 bytes of processor storage assigned to each task for data movement. Data are put into this area, edited, or taken out of this area while executing the task.

source area block In DPCX, one 256-byte block of an address space that contains the source area.

source book In VSE, a group of source statements written in any of the languages supported by VSE and cataloged in one of the system sublibraries.

source code The input to a compiler or assembler, written in a source language. Contrast with object code.

source code compatibility (1) Relating to source programs that can be run on two or more systems but may need recompilation or reassembly. (2) Contrast with object code compatibility.

Source Code Control System (SCCS) In the AIX operating system, a program for maintaining version control for the source files of a developing program. It stores the changes made to a file instead of the changed file, thus allowing several versions of the same file to exist in the system.

SOURCE-COMPUTER In COBOL, the name of an Environment Division paragraph in which the computer environment, within which the source program is compiled, is described.

source computer entry In COBOL, an entry in the SOURCE-COMPUTER paragraph of the Environment Division that contains clauses which describe the computer environment in which the source program is to be compiled.

source data (1) The data provided by the user of a data processing system. (2) The data contained in a source program or source module. (3) In a 3790 program, the data in the source area at a given time.

source data card A card that contains manually or mechanically recorded data that are subsequently to be punched into the same card. (A)

source deck In video editing, the video recorder or player used to play back the unedited tape from which an edited master is being assembled.

source directory The directory from which information is read. Contrast with target directory.

source diskette In a diskette-copying procedure, the diskette from which information is read. Contrast with target diskette.

source document A machine-readable collection of lines of text or images that is used for input to a computer program.

source drive The drive from which information is read. Contrast with target drive.

source entry utility (SEU) In System/36 and System/38, the utility used to enter and update source members.

source file (1) A file that contains source statements for such items as high-level language programs and data description specifications. (2) A file of programming code that has not been compiled into machine language.

source item In COBOL, an identifier designated by a source clause that provides the value of a printable item.

source language (1) A language from which statements are translated. (A) (2) The programming language for expressing source programs that a particular translator can accept. (T)

source listing (1) A portion of a compiler listing that contains source statements and, optionally, diagnostics. See also compiler listing. (2) In the 3800 Printing Subsystem, a listing of the overlay definition and messages after the Overlay Generation Language has processed the definition.

source macrodefinition A macrodefinition included in a source module. When entered into a program library, it becomes a library macrodefinition.

source map In SDF/CICS, a map in internal form, that is, the form in which it is held before the generate process. It contains, among other things, descriptions of constant fields, variable fields, the application struc-

ture, and constant data. In SDF/CICS, all editing is done on the source map.

source map set An object kept in the map specification library and defined by the SDF/CICS user, identifying the source map or maps for use by an application program at one time.

source member A library member that contains information in the form in which it was entered, such as RPG specifications. Contrast with load member.

source module (1) All or part of a source program sufficiently complete for compilation. Synonymous with compilation unit. (T) (2) The source statements that constitute the input to a language translator for a particular translation.

source module library A partitioned data set that is used to store and retrieve source modules. See also load module library, object module library.

source program (1) A program that a particular translator can accept. (T) (2) A set of instructions written in a programming language that must be translated to machine language before the program can be run. (3) In communications, the program that starts a session with a remote system. Contrast with target program. (4) In COBOL, a syntactically correct set of COBOL statements. A COBOL source program commences with the Identification Division, a COPY statement, or a REPLACE statement. It is terminated by the end program header, if specified, or by the absence of additional source program lines. (5) Contrast with object program.

source program maintenance online (SPM) A CICS program that provides a means of manipulating and submitting source programs for compilation without requiring the programmer to handle decks of cards.

source recording The recording of data in machine-readable documents, such as punched cards, punched paper tape, or magnetic tape. Once in this form, the data can be transmitted, processed, or reused without manual processing.

source segment In IMS/VS, a database segment that contains the data used to construct the secondary index pointer segment.

source service access point (SSAP) In SNA and TCP/IP, a logical address that allows a system to send data to a remote device from the appropriate communications support. See also destination service access point (DSAP).

source/sink See data sink, data source.

source statement (1) A statement written in symbols of a programming language; for example, RPG, COBOL, BASIC, and PL/I specifications are source statements. (2) A statement written in a programming language.

source system (1) In communications, the system that issues a request to establish communications with another system. (2) In distributed data management (DDM), the system on which an application program issues a request to use a remote file. Contrast with target system.

source table In a program, a table containing predefined data elements from which the program can select an element to be moved automatically into the source area.

SP (1) Service point. (2) Space character. (I) (A)

SPA Scratchpad area.

space (1) A site intended for storage of data; for example, a site on a printed page or a location in a storage medium. (A) (2) A basic unit of area, usually the size of a single character. (A) (3) One or more space characters. (A) (4) On a typewriter, escapement that occurs in the writing direction without a character being typed on the paper. (T) (5) In a neutral circuit, an impulse that causes the loop to open or causes absence of signal. In a polar circuit it causes the loop current to flow in a direction opposite to that for a mark impulse. A space impulse is equivalent to a binary zero. (6) A blank area separating words or lines. (7) To advance the reading or display position according to a prescribed format; for example, to advance the printing or display position horizontally to the right or vertically downward. (A) (8) To cause a printer to move the paper a specified number of lines either before or after it prints a line. (9) See address space, display space, image storage space, virtual space, working space. (10) Contrast with backspace.

spacebar On a typewriter, a control for the space function. (T)

space character (SP) (1) A character that causes the print or display position to advance one position along the line without producing any graphic character. (T) (2) See also null character, numeric space character, required space character.

Note: The space character is a control character, but it may be used as a graphic character.

space expand key On a typewriter, a control for expand escapement. (T)

space-hold The normal no-traffic line condition in which a steady space is transmitted. It may be a user-selectable option.

space management In the Data Facility Hierarchical Storage Manager, the process of managing data sets on primary and migration volumes. The three types of space management are migration, data set deletion, and data set retirement.

space manager (1) In MSS, the person responsible for managing space on mass storage volumes. (2) In the Data Facility Hierarchical Storage Manager, a person authorized to issue system programmer and space manager commands and responsible for managing direct access storage device space.

space pointer In System/38, a pointer that provides addressability to a byte string in the space part of machine interface object.

space pointer machine object A space pointer that has no defined storage form (representational characteristic). It is contained in internal machine storage rather than in a space. It exists only within the invocation of the program that defines it. Synonymous with machine space pointer.

spacer In SDF/CICS, a character used in the field definition function of the map editor to indicate that two adjacent fields should be separated according to the number of trailing blank characters in the line.

space-to-mark transition The switching from a spacing impulse to a marking impulse.

SPACE type In Pascal, a type used to define a variable whose components may be positioned at any byte in the total space of the variable.

spacing bias See distortion.

span (1) The difference between highest and lowest values a quantity or function may take. (I) (A) Synonymous with range. (2) In NCCF, a user-defined group of network resources within a single domain. Each major or minor node is defined as belonging to one or more spans. See also span of control. (3) In the NetView program, a user-defined group of network resources within a single domain. Each major or minor node is defined as belonging to one or more spans. See also span of control. (4) See error span.

SPANC Storage pool anchor block.

spanned record A logical record contained in more than one block.

span of control The total network resources over which a particular network operator has control. All the network resources listed in spans associated through profile definition with a particular network operator are within that operator's span of control.

sparse file In the AIX operating system, a file that is created with a length greater than the data it contains, leaving empty spaces for future addition of data. See hole in a file.

spatial resolution In computer graphics, horizontal and vertical resolutions caused by subdividing and quantizing a screen into individual pixels.

SPC System program controller.

SPCF Service point command facility.

SPCS Service point command service.

SPE Small programming enhancement.

special authority (1) In the AS/400 system, the types of authority a user can have to perform system functions, including all object authority, save system authority, job control authority, security administrator authority, spool control authority, and service authority. Contrast with specific authority. (2) The right to perform certain system control operations, such as save system and job control.

special character (1) A graphic character that is not a letter, digit, or blank character, and usually not an ideogram; for example, a punctuation mark, general currency symbol, percent sign. (T) (2) A character other than a digit, letter, or #, $, or @; for example, *, +, and % are special characters. (3) A character other than a digit, a letter, or $, #, @, ., or _; for example, *, +, and % are special characters. (4) In BASIC and COBOL, a character that is neither numeric nor alphabetic. (5) In REXX, a token that acts as a delimiter when found outside a literal string. Special characters include the comma (,), semicolon (;), colon (:), right parenthesis ()), left parenthesis ((), and the individual characters from the operators. (6) In COBOL, a character that belongs to the following set:

Character	Meaning
+	plus sign
–	minus sign
*	asterisk
/	slant (solidus)
=	equal sign
$	currency sign
,	comma (decimal point)
;	semicolon
.	period (decimal point, full stop)
,,	quotation mark
(	left parenthesis
)	right parenthesis
>	greater than symbol
<	less than symbol
:	colon

special character word In COBOL, a reserved word that is an arithmetic operator or a relation character.

special effects In videotaping, any activity that is not live footage, such as digital effects, computer manipulation of the picture, and nonbackground music.

special effects generator (SEG) In video production, a device capable of producing electronic special effects such as dissolves, fades, wipes, and keys and of combining two or more video signals into a single signal using such effects. See also switcher.

special feature A feature that can be ordered to enhance the capability, storage capacity, or performance of an IBM product, but is not essential for its basic work; for example, a feature that enables a modem to be connected to a public switched network as well as to a nonswitched line. See also diskette-only feature, specify feature.

special file In the AIX operating system, a file that provides an interface to input/output devices. There is at least one special file for each device connected to the computer. Contrast with directory. See also block file, character special file.

specialized application language Synonym for special purpose language.

SPECIAL-NAMES In COBOL, the name of an Environment Division paragraph in which implementor-names are related to user-specified mnemonic-names.

special names entry In COBOL, an entry in the SPECIAL-NAMES paragraph of the Environment Division that provides a means for specifying the currency sign, choosing the decimal point, specifying symbolic characters, relating implementor-names to user-specified mnemonic names, relating alphabet-names to character sets or collating sequences, and relating class-names to sets of characters.

special purpose computer A computer designed to operate on a restricted class of problems. (I) (A)

special purpose language A programming language designed for use in relatively narrow aspects of broader application areas; for example, COGO for civil engineering, CDL for logical design, GPSS for simulation. (T) Synonymous with specialized application language.

special register In COBOL, a compiler-generated storage area whose primary use is to store information produced in conjunction with the use of specific COBOL feature. See linage counter.

special variable (1) In CMS, a reserved variable name that is assigned a value by the EXEC interpreter. The values of EXEC special variables can be tested in an EXEC procedure. (2) In REXX, a variable set automatically by the language processor during execution. Special variables are RC, RESULT, and SIGL.

specific address (1) An SDLC address that is unique to one secondary station. (2) Synonym for absolute address.

specification (1) A detailed formulation, in document form, which provides a definitive description of a system for the purpose of developing or validating the system. (T) (2) In system development, a description of how the design of a system, device, or program is to be implemented. (3) In SDF/CICS, a description of how a map will be presented on a certain device type or group of device types. This description includes map characteristics, such as width and depth, placement of variable and constant fields, field attributes and constant or initial data, and a list of devices for which the specification applies. (4) See file specification.

specification check A synchronous indication of a condition, caused by data that are incorrect or invalid, that was transmitted as the result of a channel command. The specification check condition appears in the status information sent to the channel.

specification display In the source entry utility, the display that guides an operator through the entry of a particular type of statement.

specification statement In FORTRAN, one of the set of statements that provide the compiler with information about the data used in the source program. In addition, the statement supplies information required to reserve storage for this data.

specific authority In the AS/400 system, the types of authority a user can be given to use the system resources, including object authorities and data authorities. See also object authority, data authority. Contrast with special authority.

specific coding Synonym for absolute coding.

specific mode (1) In VTAM, the form of a RECEIVE request that obtains input from one specific session. (2) In VTAM, the form of an accept request that completes establishment of a session by accepting a specific queued CINIT request. (3) Contrast with any-mode. (4) See continue-specific mode.

specific poll One of the locations on a polling list. See polling list.

specific polling A polling technique that sends invitation characters to a device to find out whether the device is ready to enter data. See also general polling.

specific volume request A request for volumes that informs the system of the volume serial numbers.

specify feature One of a group of similar features for an IBM product that is needed and therefore must be specified so that the product can do its basic work; for example, one of ten features for keyboard languages that the customer must order for a terminal.

specify task abnormal exit (STAE) See STAE.

spectral response The variation in sensitivity of a device to light of different wavelengths. (A)

spectrum In acoustics: (a) the amplitude distribution of the components of a sound wave as a function of frequency, and (b) a continuous range of frequencies, usually wide in extent; for example, the audible spectrum.

spectrum level In acoustics, the sound pressure level in a band that is one hertz wide.

specular reflection The percentage of a ray of incident light that is reflected from a surface at an angle equal to that of the incident ray of light.

speech recognition The recognition of voice communication as a series of words or sentences. (T)

speech transmission index (STI) A system of rating the understandability of a spoken message; on a scale of 0 to 1.0, 1.0 represents the best possible understanding of a given message.

speed In a document copying machine, a measure of the light sensitivity of the coating of sensitized materials. (T)

speed change control On dictation equipment, a device that makes it possible to choose between several predetermined speeds of the recording medium. (I)

speed control In a duplicator, a device for controlling the speed of operation of the machine. (T)

spell aid A document proofreading function that replaces a misspelled word when the correct spelling is chosen from a list of similarly spelled words provided by the system from one or more dictionaries.

spelling checker A computer program in a text processing system that verifies the spelling of words in text by means of a stored dictionary. Checking may be performed on words as they are being entered, or in subsequent processing. (T)

spelling dictionary A list of words used to automatically check spelling in machine readable documents.

spell mode The method of operation that uses spell aid and spell check functions to proofread and replace words in a document.

SPF Structured programming facility.

sphere of control (SOC) The set of control point domains served by a single management services focal point.

spherical type head In word processing, an interchangeable printing element in the shape of a sphere, used in some impact printers. (T)

spider label In GDDM, a label used to add a comment or a note for a pie-chart slice. Each label is joined to its associated slice by a line.

spike A sudden, temporary rise in voltage on a power line that can damage data and computer components. See Figure 139.

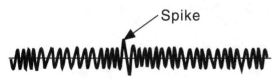

Figure 139. Spike

spill area In the AIX operating system, a storage area used to save the contents of registers.

spill backup volume A Data Facility Hierarchical Storage Manager volume to which all but the latest backup version of a data set are moved when more space is needed on a DASD daily backup volume or to which all valid versions are moved when a tape backup volume is recycled.

spill process A Data Facility Hierarchical Storage Manager process that moves all but the latest backup version of a data set from a direct access storage device daily backup volume to a spill backup volume. More space is needed on a daily backup volume.

spin button In SAA Advanced Common User Access architecture, a type of entry field that shows a scrollable ring of choices from which a user can select a choice. After the last choice is displayed, the first choice is displayed again. A user can also type a choice from the scrollable ring into the entry field without interacting with the spin button.

spirit (or other fluid) duplicator A duplicator that uses the spirit (or other fluid) duplicating process to produce multiple copies from a master. (T)

spirit (or other fluid) master In a duplicator, a master that carries the mirror image of the original material to be copied in the form of spirit-soluble pigments. (T)

SPL Station polling list.

splice See optical fiber splice.

splice loss Synonym for insertion loss.

splicer In the 3800 Printing Subsystem, a flat surface located ahead of the transfer carriage tractors. The splicer has a vacuum plate and tractor drive pins that can be used to correctly align and put together the last sheet in an old box and the first sheet in a new box.

spline curve In computer graphics, a shape created when a user specifies a series of points and the computer software draws a curve that smoothly approaches those points.

Split In SAA Advanced Common User Access architecture, a choice in the system menu pull-down that shows different views of the same thing. See split window.

split-browse display The source entry utility display that has records from a member being browsed at the top of the display and records from another browse member or from a spooled output file at the bottom of the display.

split display In SAA usage, deprecated term for split screen, split window.

split-edit display The source entry utility display that has records from the member being edited on the top part of the display and records from the browse member or spooled output file on the bottom part of the display.

split key A key for an indexed file, defined from more than one field within each record.

split screen (1) The facility for dividing a display into two or more independent areas. (T) (2) In SAA usage, a display screen that contains two or more display images that can be manipulated independently. (3) A display screen that can be used by two or more programs to display images concurrently. See also window, windowing.

splitter In a local area network, a passive device used at a node to connect more than two branches. (T)

Note: A splitter does not amplify or regenerate data signals.

splitting (1) The partitioning of the capacity of a storage device into independent sections. (T) (2) The division of a display image into sections so that different images can be viewed at the same time. (3) In a network, the use of a splitter to divide a branch into two branches. (4) The division of a power system into balanced subsystems.

split window In SAA Advanced Common User Access architecture, an interface style that displays something divided into several parts that scroll independently.

SPM (1) Source program maintenance online. (2) CICS/VS Source Program Maintenance.

SPO Secondary program operator application program.

spoof In computer security, to act as part of a trusted system to gain information that one is not authorized to receive. See also attack.

spool (1) Simultaneous peripheral operations online. (2) See tape spool. See also spooling.

spool access support A function of VSE/POWER that allows user programs or subsystems running on a VSE system to access the spool files of VSE/POWER.

spool control authority In the AS/400 system, a special authority that allows the user to perform spooling functions, such as display, delete, hold, and release spooled files on the output queue for himself and other users. This authority also allows the user to change the spooled file attributes, such as the printer used to print the file. See also all object authority, job control authority, save system authority, security administrator authority, service authority.

spooled input file See inline data file.

spooled output file See spool file.

spooler A program that intercepts data going to a device driver and writes it to a disk. The data is later printed or plotted when the required device is available. A spooler prevents output from different sources from being intermixed.

spool file (1) A file that contains output data that has been saved for later processing. (2) One of three VSE/POWER files on disk: queue file, data file, and account file.

spool file class In VM, a one-character class associated with each virtual unit record device that allows the user to control which input spool files are to be read next, and allows the spooling operator to better control or reorder the printing or punching of output spool files having similar characteristics or priorities. The spool file class value can be A-Z, 0-9, or *.

spool file tag In VM, a 136-character data field associated with each output spool file generated. The use, content, and format of this field are decided by the originator and receiver of the file. In RSCS, the spool file tag contains the location identifier of the link on which the file is to be transmitted, the user ID of the virtual machine that is to receive the file, and a transmission priority value.

spooling (1) The use of auxiliary storage as buffer storage to reduce processing delays when transferring data between peripheral equipment and the processors of a computer. The term is derived from the expression Simultaneous Peripheral Operation On Line. (T) (A) (2) Reading and writing input and output streams on an intermediate device in a format convenient for later processing or output. (3) Performing a peripheral operation such as printing while the computer is busy with other work. (4) Synonymous with concurrent peripheral operations.

spooling operator privilege class In VM, the CP privilege class D user who controls the real unit record equipment and all closed spool files.

spooling subsystem In the AS/400 system and System/38, a part of the system that provides the operating environment for the programs that read jobs onto job queues to wait for processing and write files from an output queue to an output device.

spooling unit record I/O See spooling, virtual spooling device.

spool intercept buffer In System/36, an area of main storage containing printer data to be written in the spool file.

spool job In DPCX, data in the RJE data set received from the host system and stored in DPCX for printing.

spool spindle On dictation equipment, a shaft that receives a take-up spool. (I)

spool writer The part of the System Support Program Product that prints output saved in the spool file.

spot A circular area on a printed sheet that is either darker or lighter than desired. See also background, gray bar.

spot carbon Paper from which carbon is omitted in certain areas to suppress printing of data on specified copies.

spot punch A device for punching one hole at a time in a data medium. (I)   (A)

SPPS Subsystem Program Preparation Support.

SPPS II Subsystem Program Preparation Support II. An IBM program product that consists of programming languages, macroinstructions, and the 3275 terminal display language. SPPS II enables the user to write programs for execution in the programmable store system store controllers and programmable terminals. See Subsystem Program Preparation Support.

SPR System parameter record.

spray tube In a duplicator, a tube with suitably spaced holes used to apply a fine spray of fluid to the damping pad. (T)

spread Synonym for irrelevance.

spreadsheet A worksheet arranged in rows and columns, in which a change in the contents of one cell can cause electronic recomputation of one or more cells, based on user defined relations among the cells. (A)

spreadsheet application (1) A program that displays a worksheet in which a table of cells is arranged in rows and columns, and in which the change of the contents of one cell can cause recomputation of one or more cells based on user defined relations among the cells. (T)   (2) Personal computer application software that allows a user to define mathematical or other logical relationships between columns and rows of cells and to determine the effect of a change in the value of one cell on the values in other cells on a trial-and-error basis. When a cell value is changed, the values of other affected cells are immediately recalculated.

spreadsheet program A program that displays a table of cells arranged in rows and columns, in which the change of the contents of one cell can cause recomputation of one or more cells based on user-defined relations among the cells. (T)

spring-loaded pop-up In the AIX operating system, a kind of widget, such as a menu, that is not visible to the window manager. A spring-loaded pop-up disables user-event processing except for events that occur in the menu.

sprite graphics In multimedia applications, a small graphics picture, or series of pictures, that can be moved independently around the screen, producing animated effects.

sprocket hole Synonym for feed hole.

sprocket track Synonym for feed track.

SPS (1) Superscript character.   (2) Sync point services.

SPT System parameter table.

SPX circuit Simplex circuit.

SQA System queue area.

SQL Structured query language.

SQLCA SQL communication area.

SQL communication area (SQLCA) In the AS/400 system, a set of variables that are used by SQL to provide an application program with information about the processing of SQL statements within the program.

SQLDA SQL descriptor area.

SQL descriptor area (SQLDA) In the AS/400 system, a set of variables that are used in the processing of certain SQL statements. The SQLDA is intended for dynamic SQL programs.

SQL query In AS/400 query management, a type of query that is created by running an IMPORT command against a file containing an SQL statement.

square On a calculator, the facility that directly multiplies a number by itself. (T)

square function The function that multiplies a number by itself directly. (T)   (A)

square root On a calculator, the facility that directly provides a factor that, when multiplied by itself, produces the original number. (T)

square root function The function that directly provides a number that, when multiplied by itself, produces the original number. (T)   (A)

squeegee rollers In a document copying machine, rollers through which the copy material is passed to remove surplus fluid following wet development. (T)

squeeze-zoom In multimedia applications, a digital video effect in which one picture is reduced in size and displayed with a full-screen picture.

SR Service reminder.

SRC System reference code.

SRCB Subrecord control byte.

SRF Software recovery facility.

SRJE SNA remote job entry.

SRM System resources manager.

SRR Serially reusable resource.

SRT (1) Segmentation register table. (2) Symbol resolution table.

SRTD Symbol resolution table directory.

SRTE Symbol resolution table entry.

SRT program Single requester terminal program.

S/S Source/sink. See data sink, data source.

SS (1) Start-stop. (2) Session services.

SSA Segment search argument.

SSAP Source service access point.

SSCF Secondary system control facility.

SSCP System services control point.

SSCP backup A facility that allows a system services control point (SSCP) located in one domain to assume ownership of resources located in another domain, either as a result of host node failure in the other domain or as a means of processor load balancing in the host processor.

SSCP-dependent LU An LU that requires assistance from a system services control point (SSCP) in order to initiate an LU-LU session. It requires an SSCP-LU session.

SSCP ID In SNA, a number that uniquely identifies a system services control point. The SSCP ID is used in session activation requests which are sent to physical units and other system services control points.

SSCP-independent LU An LU that is able to activate an LU-LU session (that is, send a BIND request) without assistance from an SSCP. It does not have an

SSCP-LU session. Currently, only an LU 6.2 can be an independent LU.

SSCP-LU session In SNA, a session between a system services control point (SSCP) and a logical unit (LU). The session enables the LU to request the SSCP to help initiate LU-LU sessions.

SSCP monitor mode function (SMMF) A function within NCP that keeps NCP resources active when an external SSCP has not established ownership of NCP.

SSCP-PU session In SNA, a session between a system services control point (SSCP) and a physical unit (PU); SSCP-PU sessions allow SSCPs to send requests to and receive status information from individual nodes in order to control the network configuration.

SSCP rerouting In SNA network interconnection, the technique used by the gateway system services control point (SSCP) to send session-initiation request units (RUs), by way of a series of SSCP-SSCP sessions, from one SSCP to another, until the owning SSCP is reached.

SSCP services In SNA, the components within a system services control point (SSCP) that provide configuration, maintenance, management, network, and session services for SSCP-LU, SSCP-PU, and SSCP-SSCP sessions. See also logical unit (LU) services, physical unit (PU) services.

SSCP services manager An SNA component that provides network services for all the half-sessions of the system services control point (SSCP).

SSCP-SSCP session In SNA, a session between the system services control point (SSCP) in one domain and the SSCP in another domain. An SSCP-SSCP session is used to initiate and terminate cross-domain LU-LU sessions.

SSCP takeover See resource takeover.

SSDR Supermarket subsystem definition record.

SSFN Session setup failure notification.

SSID Subsystem identification.

SSP (1) System service program. (2) System Support Programs. See Advanced Communications Function for System Support Programs.

SSP-ICF System Support Program – Interactive Communications Feature.

SSS Subsystem support services.

SST (1) System scheduler table. (2) System service tools.

ST Session configuration screen abbreviation.

stability See computational stability, light stability.

stabilizing In a document copying machine, the action in some silver processes of rendering inert any silver salts not acted upon by the exposure and development, making the copy relatively insensitive to light. (T)

stable state (1) In a circuit, a state in which the circuit remains until application of a suitable pulse. (T) (2) Synonymous with state.

stack (1) An area in storage that stores temporary register information and return addresses of subroutines. (2) In AIX kernel mode, an area that is paged with the user process. The kernel maintains a stack for each process. It saves the process information such as the call chain and local variables used by the kernel for the user process. See invocation stack, name stack, program stack. (3) Synonym for pushdown list, pushdown storage. (4) See console stack, paper stack.

stack buffer A storage area that stores retrievable data in sequence. The last data item stored is the first data item removed.

stacked job Synonym for batched job (2).

stacked job processing A technique that permits multiple job definitions to be grouped (stacked) for presentation to the system, which automatically recognizes the jobs, one after the other. More advanced systems allow job definitions to be added to the group (stack) at any time and from any source, and also honor priorities. See also batch processing.

stacked tape An IBM-supplied product-shipment tape containing the code of two or more licensed programs.

stacker See burster-trimmer-stacker, card stacker.

stack indicator Synonym for stack pointer.

stacking order In AIX Enhanced X-Windows, the relationship between sibling windows that are stacked on top of each other.

stack pointer The address of the main storage location that contains the data item most recently stored in pushdown storage. Synonymous with stack indicator. (T) (A)

stack segment In the OS/2 operating system, a segment that holds return addresses, dynamic data, temporary data, and parameters; these items are used

in the opposite order in which they were pushed onto the stack, last-in, first-out.

stack storage Synonym for pushdown storage. (A)

STAE (specify task abnormal exit) A macroinstruction that specifies a routine to receive control in the event of abnormal termination of the issuing task. See also ESTAE.

stage (1) A program that processes messages in a NetView pipeline. Stages send messages to each other serially. (2) In MSS, to move data from a data cartridge to a staging drive.

stageable font In the 3800 Printing Subsystem, a font that can be loaded from the host processor into printer diskette font storage for use when printing selected graphic characters. Contrast with nonstageable font.

stage 1 system definition The first part of the process of defining an IMS/VS system. Stage 1 checks input specifications and generates a series of OS/VS job steps that are the input to stage 2.

stage 2 system definition The second part of the process of defining an IMS/VS system. Stage 2 builds IMS/VS system libraries, execution procedures, and the IMS/VS online control program tailored to support the desired set of IMS/VS functions. Stage 2 then stores these in an IMS/VS library.

staging (1) The moving of data from an offline or low-priority device back to an online or higher-priority device, usually on demand of the system or on request of the user. Contrast with data migration. (2) See also data staging.

staging adapter (1) An addition to a System/370 Model 158 or 168 Integrated Storage Control (ISC) feature that enables the integrated storage control to operate in a 3850 Mass Storage System. (2) An IBM 3830 Model 3 Storage Control, which is a 3830 Model 2 Storage Control that has been modified to operate in a 3850 Mass Storage System.

staging drive A direct access storage device that is designated by the mass storage control table create program to receive data from a 3851 Mass Storage Facility.

staging drive group In MSS, a collection of staging drives for space management and recovery that is created by the user by means of the mass storage control table create program.

staging effective data rate In MSS, the amount of data transferred in one second between the data recording devices and the staging drives, normally averaged over an hour.

staging error In MSS, the result of a permanent reading error during an attempt to read a particular stripe of a data cartridge.

staging libraries Those libraries that are modified by offline functions in a system using online change. Changes are first applied to the staging libraries, which are then copied to the inactive libraries.

staging pack A 3336 Disk Pack that has been initialized to receive data from a 3851 Mass Storage Facility.

STAIRS Storage and Information Retrieval System.

STAI (subtask ABEND intercept) A keyword of the ATTACH macroinstruction that specifies a routine to receive control after the abnormal termination of a subtask.

stamper In replication of optical disks, a negative copy of the original master, with which copies are pressed for distribution.

stand-alone Pertaining to operation that is independent of any other device, program, or system.

stand-alone data processing system A data processing system that is not served by telecommunication facilities.

stand-alone dump A dump performed separately from normal system operations that does not require the system to be in a condition for normal operations.

stand-alone emulator An emulator whose execution is not controlled by a control program. It does not share system resources with other programs and excludes all other jobs from the computing system while it is being executed.

stand-alone modem A modem that is separate from the unit with which it operates. Synonymous with external modem.

stand-alone shell In the AIX operating system, a limited version of the shell program used for system maintenance.

stand-alone system A system that runs application programs independently of another system. The exchange of data files or applications with another system is done manually, through portable media, such as disk or tape.

stand-alone word processing equipment Word processing equipment for use by one operator at a time that does not depend on the resources of other equipment for its normal operation. (T)

stand-alone workstation In AIX operating system for the RISC System/6000, a workstation that can perform tasks without being connected to other resources such as servers or host systems. Contrast with dependent workstation.

standard access list In RACF, a list within a profile of all authorized users and their access authorities. See also conditional access list.

standard action bar choices In SAA Advanced Common User Access architecture, the choices File, Edit, View, Options, and Help.

standard data format In COBOL, the concept used in describing data in a COBOL Data Division under which the characteristics or properties of the data are expressed in a form oriented to the appearance of the data on a printed page of infinite length and breadth, rather than a form oriented to the manner in which the data are stored internally in the computer or on a particular medium.

standard form Synonym for normalized form.

standard information In word processing, text or format instructions entered for later use in documents. (T)

standard input (STDIN) In the AIX operating system, the primary source of data entered into a command. Standard input comes from the keyboard unless redirection or piping is used, in which case standard input can be from a file or the output from another command.

standard input device In IBM personal computers with Advanced DOS, a keyboard.

Note: In Advanced DOS, input and output can be redirected to or from files or devices other than the standard input and standard output devices.

standardize Synonym for normalize.

standard label A fixed-format record that identifies a volume of data such as a tape reel or a file that is part of a volume of data.

standard NCCF mode In NCCF, a form of screen presentation where a message area of a terminal screen consists of 69 bytes for each message and an 11-byte prefix. Contrast with full-line mode.

standard output (STDOUT) In the AIX operating system, the primary destination of data coming from a command. Standard output goes to the display unless redirection or piping is used, in which case standard output can go to a file or to another command.

standard output device In IBM personal computers with Advanced DOS, a display screen.

Note: In Advanced DOS, input and output can be redirected to or from files or devices other than the standard input and standard output devices.

standard palette A set of colors that is common among applications or images. See also color palette, custom palette.

standard screen In the AIX extended curses library, a memory image of the screen to which the routines can make changes.

standard test-tone power One milliwatt (0 dBm) at 1000 cycles per second.

standby (1) A condition of equipment that permits complete resumption of stable operation within a short span of time. (2) A duplicate set of equipment to be used if a primary unit becomes unusable because of malfunction. (3) The condition of low electrical power in which a document copying machine may need to remain in order to eliminate startup time between copy production runs. (T)

standby display In System/36, a display that allows an operator to enter data but not commands. When a standby display appears, the display station can be acquired by a program. Contrast with command display.

standby line A modem feature that allows a point-to-point nonswitched line modem to function also on a point-to-point switched line.

standing-on-nines carry In the parallel addition of numbers represented by decimal numerals, a procedure in which a carry to a given digit place is bypassed to the next digit place if the current sum in the given digit place is 9, and the 9 is changed to 0. (I) (A)

stanza In the AIX operating system, a group of lines in a file that together have a common function or define a part of the system. Stanzas are usually separated by blank lines or colons, and each stanza has a name. See device stanza, queue stanza.

star network (1) A radial, or star-like, configuration of nodes connected to a central controller or computer in which each node exchanges data directly with the central node. (2) See also star/ring network. (3) Synonymous with centralized network.

Note: Examples are the network topologies used in computerized branch exchanges (CBXs) and in private branch exchanges (PBXs). See Figure 140.

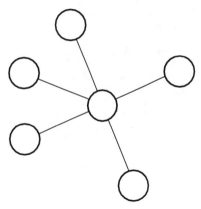

Figure 140. Star Network

star/ring network A ring network with unidirectional transmission, laid out in such a way that several data stations are grouped and interconnected to the network by means of lobe attaching units. This configuration allows attachment and removal of data stations without disrupting network operations. (A) See Figure 141.

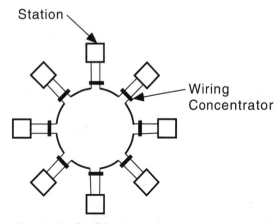

Figure 141. Star/Ring Network

start (1) To begin operation; for example, by pressing a start button on a console. (2) In TCAM; for external logical units (LUs), the state in which an LU is able to enter an LU-LU session.

start bit Synonym for start signal.

start control On a document copying machine or a duplicator, a device that initiates operation of the machine. (T)

start-control-program-function (SCPF) job In the AS/400 system, a job used during a portion of the initial program load process that starts the operating system.

start element (1) In SNA, deprecated term for first-in-chain (FIC). (2) Synonym for start signal.

starter diskette A diskette used in a controller to initiate communication with the host computer and to prepare the controller for reception and recording of the configuration image. See also operating diskette.

start field order In System/38, an instruction in the data stream of a write operation that indicates that the next byte is an attribute character.

start frame In multimedia, the first frame of a video or audio segment.

start frame delimiter Synonym for starting-frame delimiter. (T)

starting-frame delimiter (1) A specified bit pattern that indicates the start of a transmission frame. Synonymous with start frame delimiter, frame start delimiter. (T) (2) Contrast with ending frame delimiter. (3) See figure at transmission frame.

starting point On a CRT display device, same as current beam position.

start key In word processing, the control used to initiate certain preset functions of the equipment. (T) Synonymous with enter key, execute key.

Note: On some equipment, this control may also be used to locate the beginning of the recorded text prior to printout.

start-of-chain In SNA, deprecated term for first-in-chain (FIC).

start-of-format control (SOF) A unique word processing control grouping of characters used as a leading delimiter for a format parameter list embedded in a character string. Start-of-format delimits parameters that control tab stop settings, right margin, choice of single or double index, and text adjust mode operation.

start-of-heading character (SOH) A transmission control character that is used as the first character of a message heading. (T) (A)

start of line On a typewriter, the predetermined position on the paper carrier at which the writing line starts. (T)

start-of-message (SOM) code A character or group of characters transmitted by the polled terminal and indicating to other stations on the line that what follows are addresses of stations to receive the answering message.

start-of-text character (STX) (1) A transmission control character that precedes a text and can be used to terminate the message heading. (I) (A) (2) In BSC, a transmission control character used to begin a logical set of records that is ended by the end-of-text character or end-of-transmission-block character.

start of track control On dictation equipment, a device for setting the recording head, playback head, or combined head at the beginning of the required track on the recording medium. (I)

start option In VTAM, a user-specified or IBM-supplied option that determines certain conditions that are to exist during the time a VTAM system is operating. Start options can be predefined or specified when VTAM is started.

start signal (1) In a start-stop transmission, a signal at the beginning of a character that prepares the receiving device for reception of the code elements. (I) (2) A signal to a receiving mechanism to get ready to receive data or perform a function. (A) (3) Synonymous with start bit, start element.

Note: A start signal is limited to one signal element that generally has the same duration as a unit interval.

start-stop character A character including one start signal at the beginning and one or two stop signals at the end. (I)

start-stop devices Terminal devices that indicate the beginning and end of each character they send with start and stop bits.

start-stop (SS) transmission (1) Asynchronous transmission such that each group of signals representing a character is preceded by a start signal and is followed by a stop signal. (T) (A) (2) Asynchronous transmission in which a group of bits is (a) preceded by a start bit that prepares the receiving mechanism for the reception and registration of a character, and (b) followed by at least one stop bit that enables the receiving mechanism to come to an idle condition pending reception of the next character. See also binary synchronous transmission, synchronous data link control.

start-stop system A data transmission system in which each character is preceded by a start signal and followed by a stop signal. (T)

start-stop tape drive A magnetic tape unit that stops at each interblock gap when reading or writing data. Contrast with streaming tape drive.

startup See system startup.

startup drive The drive that contains the OS/2 operating system.

startup/restart message generation facility In ACF/TCAM, a facility that generates and sends tailored messages to external logical units (LUs) when the message control program (MCP) is started or restarted.

startup sequence In personal-computer systems, the order that the computer uses to search the direct-access storage devices for an operating system.

startup time The interval of time that may be required by a document copying machine before it is ready for use after switching on the main power. (T)

starvation A situation in which an activation of an asynchronous procedure is incapable of proceeding within any predictable period of time because other concurrent activations permanently retain required resources. (T)   See also deadlock.

state (1) Synonym for stable state.   (2) See input state, output state, unstable state.

state information In the AIX operating system, information about the current state of the appearance and behavior of a widget or gadget. This information is recorded within each individual widget and gadget and updated as necessary.

statement (1) In programming languages, a language construct that represents a step in a sequence of actions or a set of declarations. (I)   (2) In computer programming, a symbol string or other arrangement of symbols. (A)   (3) An instruction in a program or procedure. (4) In COBOL, a syntactically valid combination of words, literals, and separators, beginning with a verb, written in a COBOL source program. See arithmetic statement, compiler directing statement, conditional statement, delimited scope statement, inoperative statement, input-output statement, procedure branching statement. (5) A language syntactic unit consisting of an operator, or other statement identifier, followed by one or more operands. See definition statement.

statement entity In FORTRAN, an entity identical from a lexical element

statement function (1) In FORTRAN, a user-written function that is defined and referred to within the same program. The user-written function is defined in a statement function definition statement. See also function subprogram, subroutine.   (2) In XL FORTRAN, a name, followed by a list of dummy arguments, that is equated to an arithmetic, logical, or character expression, and that can be substituted for the expression throughout the program.   See also macro instruction.

statement function definition In XL FORTRAN, a statement that defines a statement function. Its form is a statement function, followed by an equal sign (=), followed by an arithmetic, logical, or character expression.

statement identifier The lexical entity in a language statement that indicates the purpose of the statement, such as the action to be performed or the resource being defined.   See also definition statement, definition statement identifier, operator.

statement keyword In FORTRAN, a word that is part of the syntax of a statement and that may be used to identify the statement.

statement label In FORTRAN, a number of from 1 through 5 decimal digits that is used to identify a statement. Statement labels can be used to transfer control, to define the range of a DO loop, or to refer to a FORMAT statement.

statement verb The keyword that describes the function to be performed when a statement is presented to a computer program.

static (1) In programming languages, pertaining to properties that can be established before execution of a program; for example, the length of a fixed length variable is static. (I)   (2) Pertaining to an operation that occurs at a predetermined or fixed time. (3) Contrast with dynamic.

statically defined peer-to-peer session In a LEN or APPN end node, a session that is set up without assistance from an SSCP and without invoking any APPN Locate functions. Routing information is provided during system definition of the local directory.

static buffer allocation Synonym for static buffering.

static buffering (1) The assignment of a buffer to a job, program, or routing at the beginning of execution, rather than at the time it is needed. (2) Synonymous with static buffer allocation.   (3) Contrast with dynamic buffering.

static CP area In VS1 and VM, the portions of virtual storage allocated to CP during system generation and initial program load.

static debugger trap (SDT) In the AIX operating system, a trap instruction placed in a predefined point in code that calls the debug program. The trap instruction causes a program check when run and, as a result of the program check, the debug program is activated.

static display image Synonym for background image.

static dump Dumping that is performed at a particular point in time with respect to a machine run, often at the end of a run, and usually under control of the computer operator or a supervisory program. (I) (A)

static image Synonym for background image.

staticize (1) To convert serial or time-dependent parallel data into static form. (A) (2) Loosely, to retrieve an instruction and its operands from storage prior to its execution. (A)

staticizer (1) A functional unit that converts a time sequence of signals into a corresponding set of simultaneous signals. Synonymous with serial-parallel converter. (T) (2) Synonymous with deserializer, serial-to-parallel converter. (3) Contrast with serializer.

static magnetic cell Synonym for magnetic cell.

static pressure In acoustics, the pressure that would exist at a point in a medium in the absence of sound waves. See also effective sound pressure, instantaneous sound pressure.

static routing In the AIX operating system, a method of setting paths between hosts, networks, or both, by manually entering routes into the routing table. Static routes are not affected by routing daemons and must be updated manually. See also dynamic routing, routing table.

static SQL SQL statements that are embedded within a program, and are prepared during the program preparation process before the program is run. After being prepared, the statement itself does not change, although values of host variables specified by the statement may change.

static storage (1) A storage device that does not require periodic refreshment. (T) (2) A read/write storage unit in which data are retained in the absence of control signals. Static storage may use dynamic addressing or sensing circuits. (A) (3) Storage other than dynamic storage. (A)

static storage allocation The allocation of storage for static variables.

static test mode A setup mode of an analog computer during which special initial conditions are set in order to check the patching, and consequently, the proper operation of all computing devices except the integrators. (I) (A)

static variable A variable that is allocated before execution of a program begins and remains allocated during program execution. Contrast with automatic variable.

station (1) An input or output point of a system that uses telecommunication facilities; for example, one or more systems, computers, terminals, devices, and associated programs at a particular location that can send or receive data over a telecommunication line. (2) A location in a device at which an operation is performed; for example, a read station. (3) In SAA usage, deprecated term for workstation. (4) In SNA, a link station.

station arrangement A tariff term for a device such as a modem required on certain subvoice-grade leased channels. See also data loop transceiver.

stationary information source Synonym for stationary message source.

stationary message source A message source from which each message has a probability of occurrence independent of the time of its occurrence. (I) (A) Synonymous with stationary information source.

stationary paper carrier On a typewriter, a paper carrier that moves the paper only in a direction perpendicular to the typing line. (T)

stationary platen document copying machine A document copying machine in which the original is laid flat on the platen, which is stationary during exposure. Contrast with moving platen document copying machine. (T)

station battery The electric power source for signaling at a station.

station lock In ACF/TCAM, a facility that maintains a connection between a station and an application program to ensure that the next message received by the station, after it enters an inquiry message, is a reply to that inquiry. During station lock, the line is available to other stations. See also extended lock mode, line lock, lock mode, message lock mode.

station protector A device attached to the system cable to protect workstations attached in different buildings from lightning.

station selection code An identifying call that is transmitted to an outlying telegraph receiver and automatically turns its printer on. See also call directing code, selective calling.

statistic In the NetView program, a resource-generated database record that contains recoverable error counts, traffic, and other significant data about a resource.

statistical coding In video compression, a coding technique based on the principle that all pixel values are not equally probable.

statistical data recorder (SDR) In VSE, a feature that records the cumulative error status of an I/O device on the system recorder file.

stator The stationary part of a sensor. See also rotor.

status The condition or state of hardware or software, usually represented by a status code.

status analysis In ACF/TCAM, the function provided by a user-written routine to determine on the basis of previous output to a concentrator whether output is to continue or be delayed.

status area In SAA Advanced Common User Access architecture, a part of a window that displays information indicating the state of the current view of an object.

status code (1) In IMS/VS, a two-character code in the program communication block (PCB) mask that indicates the results of a DL/I call. (2) In the 3800 Printing Subsystem, two hexadecimal numbers associated with printer conditions. A status code displayed in the status indicators on the operator panel shows when these conditions occur. (3) In VTAM, information on the status of a resource as shown in a 10-character state code; for example, STATEACTIV for active.

status filter file In the Network Carrier Interconnect Agent program, a host file that contains a list of resources to be reported to a carrier management system. This file determines what configuration and status data is sent to a carrier management system.

status line (1) In display-based word processing equipment, a line reserved for display of information to the operator concerning the processing of the text. (T) (2) In the AS/400 system, a line at the top of a display that contains information about a document and current operations, including an audit window, the document name, and page and line number.

status modifier (1) In a System/370 status code, an indicator of the input/output (I/O) status. (2) In VTAM, a specific character appearing in specific positions of the status code; for example, B in the 10th position indicates a backup.

status monitor A component of the NetView program that collects and summarizes information on the status of resources defined in a VTAM domain.

STD Set control vector time and date.

STDERR Standard error.

STDIN Standard input.

STDOUT Standard output.

steady state The stable state of a system or process after it passes the transient phase. See also transient response.

steering assembly In the 3800 Printing Subsystem, a device that causes the paper to move straight through the fuser station.

stencil See electronic stencil, pressure stencil, thermal stencil. See also stencil duplicating, stencil duplicator, stencil master.

stencil duplicating In a duplicator, a process in which ink passes through perforations in a stencil master to form an image on the copy paper. (T)

stencil duplicator A duplicator having one or more revolving cylinders that uses the stencil duplicating process for production of multiple copies from a master. (T) See also direct litho duplicator, offset litho duplicator, spiriti duplicator.

stencil master In a duplicator, a sheet of material that carries the image of the original material to be copied in the form of perforations. (T)

step (1) One operation in a computer routine. (A) (2) To cause a computer to execute operation. (A) (3) See job step, single step.

step backward In multimedia applications, to move the medium backward one frame or segment at a time.

step-by-step operation Synonym for single-step operation.

step-by-step switch A switch that moves in synchronism with a pulse device, such as a rotary telephone dial. Each digit dialed causes the movement of successive selector switches to carry the connection forward until the desired line is reached. Synonymous with stepper switch. See also crossbar switch, line switching.

step-by-step system A type of line-switching system that uses step-by-step switches.

step forward In multimedia applications, to move the medium forward one frame or segment at a time.

step frame A function of videodisc players that enables a user to move frame-by-frame in either direction.

step-index fiber An optical fiber having a uniform refractive index in the core. (E) Contrast with graded-index fiber.

stepper switch Synonym for step-by-step switch.

step region In System/36, the main storage space reserved by the System Support Program Product for use by a program.

step restart A restart that begins at the beginning of a job step. The restart may be automatic or deferred, where deferral involves resubmitting the job. See also checkpoint restart.

step selection In SDF/CICS, user selection of the next function from a step selection menu.

stepwise refinement A method for constructing programs in successive steps such that at each step an action is expressed in terms of more primitive actions. (T)

stethophone On dictation equipment, a unit consisting of a listening device connected to one or more tubes with earpieces. (I)

sticky bit In the AIX operating system, an access permission bit that causes an executable program to remain on the swap area of the disk. Only someone with root authority can set the sticky bit. This bit is also used on directories to indicate that only file owners can link or unlink files in that directory.

still A static image.

still cues In video production, a set of nine pulses in the vertical blanking interval of a master videotape; these pulses tell the disc-mastering equipment to place a code on the disc to switch the disc player automatically to freeze-frame mode. See chapter cues, picture cues.

still frame In multimedia, a single film or video frame presented as a single, unmoving image.

still-frame audio Synonym for compressed audio.

still-video camera In video systems, a camera that records still pictures on a video floppy disc.

still-video capture adapter In multimedia applications, an adapter that, when attached to a computer, enables a video camera to become an input device. See also motion video capture adapter.

stipple In the AIX operating system, a bitmap used to tile a region.

stockkeeping unit (SKU) An identifier for each item of merchandise. It is the lowest level of numeric identification of merchandise, which is usually identified by department, class, vendor, style, color, size, and location.

Stop In SAA Advanced Common User Access architecture: (1) A push button that cancels any processing the computer is currently performing. It appears in a pop-up window that shows the status of complex and time-consuming user requests that are being performed. (2) A push button used in a progress indicator to cancel the current operation at the next non-destructive breaking point.

stop bit (1) In start-stop transmission, a signal at the end of a character that prepares the receiving device for reception of a subsequent character. (I) (2) A signal to a receiving mechanism to xait for the next signal. (A)

Note: A stop bit is usually limited to one signal element having any duration equal to or greater than a specified minimum value. (3) Synonymous with stop signal. (4) See also stop element.

stop character (STP) A word processing control that interrupts the sequence of output processing and provides a means for the operator or machine to make changes in text processing parameters or data. See also repeat character, switch character.

stop code In word processing, a program instruction that causes the reader to stop. If the device is interactive, it is generally used as an index for a stop list for operator changes or corrections. (T)

stop control On a document copying machine or a duplicator, a device that stops the operation of the machine. (T)

stop element (1) The last element of a character in asynchronous serial transmission, used to ensure recognition of the next start element. In baudot teletypewriter operation, it is 1.42 mark bits; in an IBM 1050 Data Communication System, it is 1.0 mark bit. (2) See also stop bit. (3) See also start-stop transmission.

stop instruction An exit that specifies the termination of the execution of a computer program. (I) (A)

stop key In word processing, a control that terminates or interrupts an operation. (T) Synonymous with break key, cancel key.

stopped state In the AIX operating system, a state in which a device is not available, but still has its device driver loaded and bound in the kernel and is still known by the device driver.

stop signal Synonym for stop bit.

stop/start control On dictation equipment, the means of stopping and starting the forward movement of the recording medium. (I)

stop word A word which, in a certain description procedure, is excluded as a descriptor. (T)

storage (1) A functional unit into which data can be placed, in which they can be retained and from which they can be retrieved. (T)   (2) The action of placing data into a storage device. (I) (A)   (3) A storage device. (A)

Note: The terms storage and memory are sometimes used loosely as synonyms. In a more precise and useful sense, the term memory pertains to the part of storage in which instructions are executed (main storage or execution space) and excludes auxiliary storage devices such as disks, diskettes, mass storage devices, and magnetic tape. The term memory is used primarily in microcomputers and calculators, whereas the term main storage is used primarily in large and intermediate systems.

storage allocation (1) The assignment of storage areas to specified data. (I) (A)   (2) See dynamic storage allocation.

Storage Authorization Control table (SCT) The Object Distribution Manager DB2 table that contains information concerning objects that are to be stored.

storage block (1) A continuous area of main storage, consisting of 2048 bytes, to which a storage key can be assigned.   (2) In OS/VS1, a 2K block of real storage to which a storage key can be assigned. See also page frame.

storage capacity The amount of data that can be contained in a storage device measured in binary characters, bytes, words, or other units. For registers, the term "register length" is used with the same meaning. Synonymous with storage size. (T) (A)

storage cell (1) The smallest unit that can be addressed in storage. Synonymous with storage element.   (T)   (2) The smallest subdivision of storage into which a unit of data has been or can be entered, in which it is or can be stored, and from which it can be retrieved. (A)

storage class (SC) A named list of storage attributes. The list of attributes identifies a storage service level provided for data associated with the storage class. No physical storage is directly implied or associated with a given storage class name.

storage compaction In the OS/2 operating system, the process of relocating allocated storage segments into contiguous locations.

storage control In an IBM 3830 Storage Control Model 3, direct-access-storage-device control unit in the 3850 Mass Storage System controlling data transfer during staging and destaging.

storage cycle The periodic sequence of events that occurs when information is transferred to or from main storage.

storage descriptor In VSE/POWER, a 16-byte alpha-numeric character string that identifies important areas in a storage dump.

storage device (1) A functional unit into which data can be placed, in which they can be retained, and from which they can be retrieved. (I) (A)   (2) A facility in which data can be retained. (T)   (3) Synonym for storage cell. (T)

storage device controller See magnetic storage device controller.

storage device subsystem In the AS/400 system, a part of the computer consisting of the controller and one or more attached storage devices.

storage dump A printout of system storage at a given time.

storage element Synonym for storage cell. (A)

storage expansion blank In a network controller, a machine element that maintains proper airflow in the control unit in the absence of the storage expansion unit.

storage expansion unit A machine element that is installed in a device to provide additional storage capacity.

storage fragmentation (1) A condition in which there are many scattered areas of storage that are too small to be used productively.   (2) In virtual system, inability to assign real storage locations to virtual addresses because the available spaces are smaller than the page size. See Figure 142.

storage group (SG) A named collection of physical devices to be managed as a single object storage area. It consists of an object directory (DB2 table space), and object storage on DASD (DB2 table spaces) with optional library-resident optical volumes. See also table space.

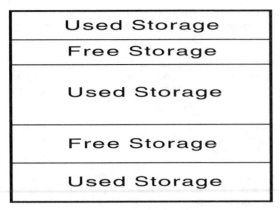

Figure 142. Storage Fragmentation

storage hierarchy An arrangement in which data can be stored in several types of storage devices that have different characteristics, such as capacity and speed of access.

storage image The representation of a computer program and its related data as they exist at the time they reside in main storage. (I) (A)

storage indicator On a calculator, a visual indication that a number is being held in storage. (T)

storage interference In a system with shared storage, the referencing of the same block of storage by two or more processing units.

storage key An indicator associated with one or more storage blocks that requires that tasks have a matching protection key in order to use the blocks.

storage levels See first level storage, second level storage, third level storage.

storage location A position in a storage device that is uniquely specified by means of an address. (T)

storage location selection In word processing, selection of a group or groups of text by preselecting a particular storage address or addresses. (T)

storage management cycle In the Object Access Method, the procedure that ensures that every object scheduled for processing is placed in the proper level of the object storage hierarchy (as specified by its storage class), is expired or backed up (as specified by its management class or by an explicit application request), and, if necessary, is flagged for action during a subsequent storage management cycle.

storage management recovery In the AS/400 system, a function that prepares the system to access data from all disk units configured to the system.

Storage Management Subsystem (SMS) A component of MVS/DFP that is used to automate and centralize the management of storage by providing the storage administrator with control over data class, storage class, management class, storage group, and ACS routine definitions.

storage map A compiler printout that shows the names and storage locations of variables and statement numbers in the object program.

storage object In computer security, an object that supports both read access and write access.

storage overlay See overlay segment.

storage overlay area See overlay area.

storage partitioning Synonym for memory partitioning. (A)

storage pool A logical division of storage reserved for processing a job or group of jobs.

storage protection (1) The limitation of access to a storage device, or to one or more storage locations, by preventing writing, reading, or both. (I) (A) (2) See also fetch protection, store protection. (3) Synonymous with memory protection.

storage protection key See protection key, storage key.

storage queue Contrast with disk queue.

storage reconfiguration See processor configuration.

storage region See main storage region, overlay region, virtual storage region.

storage register A device for holding a unit of information.

storage schema In the CODASYL model, the statements of the data storage definition language that describe storage areas, stored records, and any associated indexes and access paths that support the records and sets defined by a given schema. (A)

storage size Synonym for storage capacity. (T)

storage stack Synonym for pushdown list.

storage structure A stored representation of a data structure that preserves its relationships. The logical elements of the data structure are mapped into their stored physical counterparts; for example, the records of a record type are mapped into stored records of a file; data items are mapped into fields. (T)

storage structure language Synonym for data storage description language. (T)

storage tab setting In word processing, the feature of a machine that enables tabulator settings to be entered on the recording medium or into storage so that these settings can be used in subsequent operations. (T)

storage tube (1) A type of cathode ray tube (CRT) that retains a display image without requiring refresh. (I) (A)   (2) Contrast with electrostatic storage.

storage unit subassembly In ImagePlus, that part of the OSAR Library that contains the drives and storage cells for the data cartridges.

storage usage map An overlay linkage editor printout that shows the names and storage locations of routines that make up the load member.

store (1) To place data into a storage device. (I) (A) (2) To retain data in a storage device. (I) (A) (3) Deprecated term for storage.

store and forward Pertaining to the operation of a data network in which packets, messages, or frames are temporarily stored before they are retransmitted toward the destination. (T)

store and forward mode (1) A manner of operating a data network in which packets or messages are stored before transmission to the ultimate destination. (T)   (2) See also message switching.

store controller (1) A programmable unit in a network used to collect data, direct inquiries, and control communication within a system. (2) In PSS, the primary link between the host processor and the terminals attached to it. Synonymous with subsystem controller. See Figure 143.

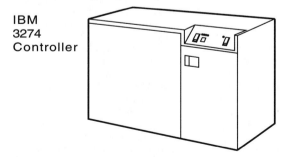

IBM 3274 Controller

Figure 143. Store Controller

store controller data IBM-provided modules, tables, lists, and control blocks that are used by the programmable store system host support at the host processor

in order to create an operational environment for a store controller.

store controller definition record (SCDR) (1) In PSS, a control record residing in the subsystem library that specifies part of the configuration and options for an individual subsystem controller. (2) Synonymous with subsystem controller definition record.

store controller disk An integral part of a programmable store system controller that is used for auxiliary storage of store controller data, user files, and application programs.

store controller storage (1) The auxiliary disk storage and active monolithic storage in an IBM 3651 or 7480 Store Controller or the control segment of an IBM 3684 Point of Sale – Control Unit. (2) In SPPS II, the portion of store controller working storage available to the user for executing application programs.

store controller storage save The automatic writing of the critical areas of store controller storage onto the integrated disk when power is turned off or when a power failure is detected.

stored format instruction In word processing, a pre-recorded instruction that determines the layout of textual or other information. (T)

stored paragraph Synonym for boilerplate.

stored program computer A computer controlled by internally stored instructions that can synthesize and store instructions and that can subsequently execute these instructions. (I) (A)

stored record (1) A physical record that represents an entry. Synonymous with internal record. (T) (2) In systems with VSAM, a data record together with its control information, as stored in auxiliary storage.

store function The action of storing a document or object at a workstation using the Object Distribution Manager, the front-end application, and the Object Access Method.

store indicator Synonym for memory indicator. (A)

store loop A cable over which data are transmitted between the store controller and the terminals of the programmable store system.

store loop driver A hardware component used to connect a store controller to the store loop.

store protection A storage protection feature that determines right of access to main storage by matching a protection key associated with a store reference to main storage with a storage key associated with each block of main storage. See also fetch protection.

store support procedure A procedure that assists personnel in administrative, operational, and managerial operations apart from customer checkout.

store through cache In a processing unit, a store (write) operation, in which data are immediately put into both cache and main storage locations.

storing (1) The action of placing data into a storage device. (2) To place data into a storage device. (3) To retain data in a storage device. (T)

storyboard In multimedia applications, a visual representation of the script, showing a picture of each scene and describing its corresponding audio. Synonymous with slide show presentation.

storyboarding In multimedia applications, producing a sequence of still images, such as titles, graphics, and images, to work out the visual details of a script.

STP Stop character.

STR Synchronous transmitter receiver.

straight line coding (1) A set of instructions without loops. (I) (A) (2) Programming technique in which loops are avoided by unwinding. (I) (A)

stratified language (1) A language that cannot be used as its own metalanguage; for example, FORTRAN. (I) (A) (2) Contrast with unstratified language.

streak A narrow area on a printed sheet that is either darker or lighter than desired. Contrast with gray bar, spot.

stream (1) To send data from one device to another. (2) See data stream.

stream data transmission In PL/I, the transmission of data in which the organization of the data into records is ignored and the data is treated as though it were a continuous stream of individual data values in character form. Contrast with record data transmission.

stream editor In text processing, a text editor that treats the entire text as a single string, even when the string is broken into lines for viewing purposes. (T) (A)

streamer Synonym for streaming tape drive.

stream file In BASIC, a file on disk in which data is read and written in consecutive fields without record boundaries. Contrast with record file.

streaming (1) A condition in which a device remains in a transmit state for an abnormal length of time. (2) A method of writing and reading data on magnetic tape as continuous fields without record boundaries.

streaming tape drive A magnetic tape unit especially designed to make a nonstop dump or restore of magnetic disks without stopping at interblock gaps. Synonymous with streamer. (T) Contrast with start-stop tape drive.

streaming tape recording A method of recording on magnetic tape that maintains continuous tape motion without the requirement to start and stop within the interrecord gap. (A)

stream mode A method of sending and receiving data in which records are defined as a stream of data without boundaries.

strength member In an optical cable, material that can be located either centrally or peripherally and that functions as a strain relief.

stress patterns In printing, severe print-quality standard patterns used to test print quality.

strict type checking In C language, checking data types for compliance with the rules of C language more strictly than C compiler checking.

strike In videotaping, to clear away, remove, or dismantle anything on the set.

strikeover A character entered in a space currently occupied by another character.

string (1) A sequence of elements of the same nature, such as characters considered as a whole. (T) (2) In programming languages, the form of data used for storing and manipulating text. (3) In XL Pascal, an object of the predefined type STRING. (4) In the AS/400 system, a group of auxiliary storage devices connected in a series on the system. The order and location in which each device is connected to the system determines the physical address of the device. (5) In PL/I, a sequence of characters or bits that is treated as a single data item. (6) In SQL, a character string. (7) See alphabetic string, binary element string, bit string, character string, compound string, conformant string, literal string, mixed string, null string, pattern string, symbol string, text string, unit string.

string constant In Pascal, a string whose value is fixed by the compiler.

string control byte In SNA, an optional control byte in the SNA character string (SCS) data stream that identifies how end-user data are compressed or compacted. See also compaction, compression.

STRING type In Pascal, a type consisting of a series of like elements, such as a specific sequence of characters, whose size may vary up to a maximum at run time.

stringy floppy Deprecated term for streaming tape. See also backup storage, magnetic tape cartridge.

Note: In personal computers, "stringy floppies" are inexpensive magnetic tapes such as audio cartridges that are used to back up hard disk drives.

strip buffer In the 3800 Printing Subsystem, a buffer containing 128 scan lines, part of the data to be printed, that accepts input from the character generator while the serializer is removing data.

stripe (1) In MSS, the portion of the data cartridge magnetic tape that is accessible to a head position. (2) See also magnetic stripe.

striping In flowcharting, the use of a line across the upper part of a flowchart symbol to signify that a detailed representation of a function is located elsewhere in the same set of flowcharts. (A) See Figure 144.

stripper In a duplicator, a device that separates the paper from the printing mechanism. (T)

stripping An action taken by an originating data station to remove its transmission frames from the network after a successful revolution on the ring. (T)

stroke (1) In character recognition, a straight line or arc used as a segment of a graphic character. (A) (2) In computer graphics, a straight line or arc used as a segment of a display element. (T)   (3) See Sheffer stroke.

stroke centerline In character recognition, a line midway between the two stroke edges. (A)

stroke character generator A character generator that generates character images composed of line segments. (I)   (A)

stroke device An input device providing a set of coordinates that record the path of the device. (A)

stroke edge In character recognition, the line of discontinuity between a side of a stroke and the background, obtained by averaging over the length of the stroke the irregularities resulting from printing and detecting. (A)

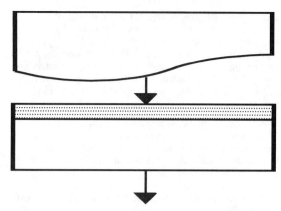

Figure 144. Striping

stroke generator See stroke character generator.

stroke text Synonym for geometric text.

stroke width In character recognition, the distance measured perpendicularly to the stroke centerline between the two stroke edges. (A)

strong typing Typing in which each object may take on only those values that are allowed for its type and in which the only operations that may be performed on objects are those that are defined for their types. The type of each object must be known at compile time. (A)

structure (1) A variable that contains an ordered group of data objects.   Unlike an array, the data objects within a structure can have varied data types. See user structure.   (2) In PL/I, a collection of data items that need not have identical attributes. Contrast with array.   (3) In FORTRAN, an object of derived type.   (4) See block structure, intra-record data structure.   (5) See also record.

structured English Synonym for pseudocode.

structured field (1) A mechanism that permits variable-length data or non-3270 data to be encoded for transmission in the 3270 data stream.   (2) In the 3800 Print Services Facility, a self-identifying string of bytes and its data or parameters.   (3) In the AS/400 AFP support, a self-identifying string of bytes and its data or parameters.

structured field syntax A syntax that permits variable-length data to be encoded for transmission in such a way that the device processing the data sequentially can translate a sequence of fields into its component fields without having to examine every byte.

structured programming (1) A method for constructing programs using only hierarchically nested constructs each having a single entry and a single exit point. Three types of control flow are used in structured programming: sequential, conditional, and iterative. (T)   (2) A technique for organizing and coding programs that makes them easier to debug, modify, and replace.

Note: Typically, a structured program is a hierarchy of modules that all have a single entry point and a single exit point. Control is passed downward through the structure without unconditional branches to higher levels of the structure.

structured programming facility (SPF) An IBM product that is a full-screen editor.

Structured Query Language Communication Area A structure used to provide an application program with information about the execution of its SQL statements.

structured type (1) In Pascal, any of several data types that define variables having multiple values; for example, records and arrays. See also component. Contrast with scalar type. (2) In the AIX operating system, any of several data types that define variables having multiple values; for example, records and arrays. Each value is a component of the structured type. Contrast with scalar type.

structured walk-through A systematic examination of the requirements, design, or implementation of a system, or any part of it, by qualified personnel. (T)

structure variable In PL/I, a variable that represents a collection of data items that might not have identical attributes. Contrast with array variable, scalar variable.

STSN Set and test sequence numbers.

stub (1) In the AIX Network Computing System (NCS), a program module that transfers remote procedure calls and responses between a client and a server. Stubs perform marshalling, unmarshalling, and data format conversion. Both clients and servers have stubs. The Network Interface Definition Language (NIDL) compiler generates client and server stub code from an interface definition. (2) Hooking functions used as extensions to the protocol to generate protocol requests for AIX Enhanced X-Windows. Synonym for hooking routine.

stub cable Synonym for drop cable. (T)

stub card A special-purpose paper card that has a separable stub attached to a general-purpose paper card. A stub card may be a scored card. (A)

stunt box A device that controls the nonprinting functions of a teletypewriter terminal, such as carriage return or line feed, and recognizes line control characters; for example, call directing code.

STX The start-of-text character. (I)   (A)

stylus (1) In computer graphics, a pointer that is operated by placing it in a display space or a tablet; for example, a light pen, sonic pen, or voltage pencil. (I)   (A)   (2) In SAA usage, deprecated term for pointing device.

stylus printer A matrix printer that uses a stylus to produce patterns of dots.

SUB The substitute character. (I)   (A)

subaddress In X.25 communications, the unallocated digits at the end of the national terminal number (NTN). If the network provider allocates all digits to the NTN, there can be no subaddress.

suballocated file In VSE, a VSAM file that occupies a portion of an already defined data space. The data space may contain other files. Contrast with unique file.

suballocation In VSAM, the allocation of a part of one extent for occupancy by elements of a component other than the one occupying the remainder of the extent.

subarea A portion of the SNA network consisting of a subarea node, attached peripheral nodes, and associated resources. Within a subarea node, all network addressable units (NAUs), links, and adjacent link stations in attached peripheral or subarea nodes that are addressable within the subarea share a common subarea address and have distinct element addresses.

subarea address In SNA, a value in the subarea field of the network address that identifies a subarea. See also element address.

subarea/element address split The division of a 16-bit network address into a subarea address and an element address.

subarea host node A host node that provides both subarea function and an application program interface (API) for running application programs. It provides system services control point (SSCP) functions, subarea node services, and is aware of the network configuration. See also boundary function, boundary node, communication management configuration host node, data host node, host node, node type, peripheral node, subarea node.

subarea ID Deprecated term for subarea address.

subarea link In SNA, a link that connects two subarea nodes. See also peripheral link. Synonymous with cross-subarea link.

subarea LU In SNA, a logical unit in a subarea node. Contrast with peripheral LU.

subarea network Interconnected subareas, their directly attached peripheral nodes, and the transmission groups that connect them.

subarea node (SN) A node that uses network addresses for routing and maintains routing tables that reflect the configuration of the network. Subarea nodes can provide gateway function to connect multiple subarea networks, intermediate routing function, and boundary function support for peripheral nodes. Type 4 and type 5 nodes can be subarea nodes. See boundary node, host node, intermediate routing node, node, peripheral node, subarea host node. See also boundary function, node type, peripheral node, subarea link.

subarea path control The function in a subarea node that routes message units between network addressable units (NAUs) and provides the paths between them. See also boundary function, path control, peripheral path control, subarea node.

subarea physical unit (PU) In SNA, a physical unit in a subarea node.

subarea routing function In SNA, a path control capability in a subarea node that receives and routes path information units (PIUs) that originate in or are destined for units in the subarea. See also boundary function.

subarea subnetwork In NETDA/2, a group of subarea nodes that are connected through subarea protocols and have the same network ID.

subblock (1) The portion of a BSC message terminated by an ITB line-control character. (2) To handle large blocks of data in small segments, where a subblock is a user-defined number of buffers.

subcarrier In a television system, a high-frequency carrier on which the chrominance (color) information is modulated, before being combined with the luminance (brightness) signal.

subchannel (1) A division of a channel data path. (2) The channel facility required for sustaining a single I/O operation.

subclass (1) A class that is derived from another class. The subclass inherits the data and methods of the parent class and can define new methods or override existing methods to define new behavior not inherited from the parent class. See inheritance. (2) In the AIX operating system, a class of widgets that inherits resources from a higher class. See device subclass. See also superclass.

subcommand A request for an operation that is within the scope of work requested by a previously issued command.

subconsole In System/36, a display station that controls one or more printers.

subconsole display In System/36, a display that can be requested only from a command display that appears on a subconsole. From a subconsole display an operator can display and send messages, and enter all control commands except those that can be entered only at the system console. See also console display.

subdirectory (1) In an IBM personal computer, a file referred to in a root directory that contains the names of other files stored on the diskette. (2) In the AIX file system hierarchy, a directory contained within another directory.

subenvironment In DPPX, a subordinate environment in a hierarchy of environments.

subfield (1) A subdivision of a field, that is, a field within a field. (2) In RPG, the layout of a field within a data structure.

subfile In the AS/400 system and System/38, a group of records of the same record format that can be displayed at the same time at a display station. The system sends the entire group of records to the display in a single operation and receives the group from the display in another operation.

subfile control record format In the AS/400 system and System/38, one of two record formats required to define a subfile in data description specifications (DDS). The subfile control record format describes the size of the subfile and the size of the subfile page, and is used by the program to write the subfile to and read the subfile from the display. See also subfile record format.

subfile record format In the AS/400 system and System/38, one of two record formats required to define a subfile in data description specifications (DDS). The subfile record format defines the fields in a subfile record and is used by the program to perform input, output, and update operations to the subfile. See also subfile control record format.

subgroup (1) In ACF/TCAM, a subdivision of either an incoming or outgoing group. An incoming group is made up of inheader, inblock, inbuffer, and inmessage subgroups. An outgoing group is made up of outheader, outbuffer, and outmessage subgroups. (2) In the 3800 Print Services Facility, a set of modifications within a copy group that applies to a certain number of copies of a form. A copy group can contain more than one subgroup.

subheap In XL Pascal, part of a heap that is treated in a stack-like manner within a heap.

subject In computer security, an active entity that can access objects, for example, a process that involves execution of a program, a person about whom data are collected and maintained.

Note: A subject causes information to flow among objects or changes the state of the system. In a time sharing system, several subjects or processes may run on the same computer system concurrently.

subject of entry In COBOL, an operand or reserved word that appears immediately following the level indicator or the level-number in a Data Division entry.

sublayer (1) In the Open Systems Interconnection reference model, a conceptually complete group of services, functions, and protocols that may extend across all open systems and that is included in a layer. (T) (2) See also logical link control (LLC) sublayer, medium access control (MAC) sublayer.

sublibrary In VSE, a subdivision of a library. See also library.

sublibrary directory In VSE, an index which enables the system to locate a certain member in the accessed sublibrary.

sublock In DPPX, one of the locks that make up a particular class lock.

subloop A loop that emanates from a terminal or other unit that is itself part of a loop. When the subloop involves telecommunication lines, it is sometimes referred to as a remote subloop.

submenu A menu related to and reached from a main menu.

submit In VSE, a function that passes a job to the system for processing.

submodular phase A phase made up of selected control sections from one or more modules as compared with a phase made up of all control sections from one or more modules.

subnet (1) In TCP/IP, a part of a network that is identified by a portion of the Internet address. (2) In the AIX operating system, synonym for subnetwork.

subnet address (1) In the AIX operating system, a part of the local host address reserved to indicate the subnetwork. Subnet addressing allows an autonomous system made up of multiple networks to share the same Internet network address. (2) An extension of the Internet addressing scheme by which a single Internet address can be used for multiple physical networks.

subnet address mask In the AIX operating system, a bit mask used by a local system to determine whether a destination is on the same network as the source or if the destination can be reached directly through one of the local interfaces.

subnet mask A bit template that identifies to the TCP/IP protocol code the bits of the host address that are to be used for routing to specific subnets.

subnet value The bit template that identifies to the TCP/IP protocol code the host or hosts that are defined by this route. This bit template must be a subset of the subnet mask.

subnetwork (1) Any group of nodes that have a set of common characteristics, such as the same network ID. (2) In the AIX operating system, one of a group of multiple logical network divisions of another network, such as can be created by the Transmission Control Protocol/Internet Protocol (TCP/IP) interface program.

subobject In FORTRAN, part of a data object. It may be an array element, an array section, a structure component, or a substring.

suboperand One of multiple elements in a list comprising an operand. See also definition statement.

subparameter One of the variable items of information that follow a keyword parameter and can be either positional or identified by a keyword.

subpool All of the storage blocks allocated under a subpool number for a particular task.

subport (1) An access point for data entry or exit over a logical connection. The relationship between the physical line and the port is analogous to the relationship between the logical connection and the subport. (2) In a frame-relay network, the representation of a logical connection on a frame-relay physical line and the point where the logical connection attaches to the frame-relay frame handler (FRFH). Each subport on a physical line has a unique data link connection identifier (DLCI) and can represent an

FRTE, FRFH, or LMI connection. See frame handler subport (FHSP), terminal equipment subport (TESP).

subprogram (1) A program invoked by another program. Contrast with main program. (2) In FORTRAN, a function subprogram, a subroutine subprogram, a module subprogram, or a block data subprogram. See function subprogram, instance of a subprogram, subroutine subprogram. (3) In COBOL, synonym for called program.

subquery In SQL, a subselect within a search condition that refers to a value or set of values needed for the first query to be answered. A subquery can include search conditions of its own, and these search conditions can, in turn, include subqueries.

sub-queue In COBOL, a logical hierarchy division of a queue.

subrange scalar type In Pascal, a type used to define a variable whose value is restricted to some subset of values of a base scalar type.

subrecord control byte (SRCB) In MTAM and RJE, a control character used to provide additional information about a record.

subroutine (1) A sequence of instructions whose execution is invoked by a call. (T)   (2) A sequenced set of instructions or statements that may be used in one or more computer programs and at one or more points in a computer program. (T)   (3) A group of instructions that can be part of another routine or can be called by another program or routine.   (4) In BASIC, a group of statements in a program of statements in a program started by a GOSUB statement, or a separately compiled program started by the CALL statement.   (5) In PL/I, a procedure that has no RETURNS option in the PROCEDURE statement. Contrast with function. (6) In RPG, a group of calculation specification statements in a program that can be run several times in that program.   (7) In FORTRAN, a procedure that is invoked by a CALL statement or an assignment statement. (8) See closed subroutine, dynamic subroutine, open subroutine, recursive subroutine, reentrant subroutine.

subroutine call (1) The subroutine in object coding that performs the call function. (A)   (2) In a source program, a language construct that invokes a subroutine. (3) In PL/I, an entry reference that must represent a subroutine, followed by an optional and possibly empty argument list that appears in a CALL statement. Contrast with function reference.

subroutine member A library member that contains information that must be combined with one or more members before being run by a system.

subroutine statement Synonym for procedure statement.

subsampling In video systems, a technique used to manage the overflow of data when fast-motion video sequences overfill buffer memory.

subschema A subset of the schema that provides a complete description of a database from the perspective of a specific application. Synonymous with view. See conceptual subschema. (A)

subscriber A user who is authorized to use one or more services of an office automation system. (T)

subscriber's drop The line from a telephone cable to a subscriber's building.

subscriber's loop See local loop.

subscript (1) A symbol associated with the name of a set to identify a particular subset or element. (I) (A)   (2) One or more characters printed one-half line below the normal printing line. Contrast with superscript. (3) An integer or variable whose value selects a particular element in a table or array. (4) In BASIC, a number or variable whose value refers to a particular element in an array. Contrast with superscript. (5) In COBOL, an occurrence number represented by either an integer, a data-name optionally followed by an integer with the operator + or -, or an index-name optionally followed by an integer with the operator + or -, which identifies a particular element in a table. (6) In FORTRAN, an item of a list of subscripts that selects an element of a named array or an array-valued structure component. See many-to-one vector subscript, vector subscript.

subscript character (SBS) A word processing formatting control that causes the display position or printing position to move down approximately one-half the normal single line space increment with no horizontal motion. The subscript character is a latching control that requires a superscript character to cause the printing or display point to return to the previous horizontal alignment. Contrast with superscript character.

subscripted data-name In COBOL, an identifier that is composed of a data-name, followed by one or more subscripts enclosed in parentheses.

subscripting In programming languages, a mechanism for referencing an array element by means of an array reference and one or more expressions that, when evaluated, denote the position of the element. (I) See Figure 145.

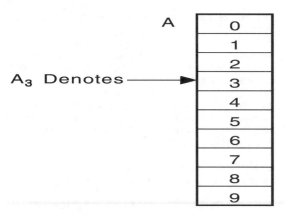

A₃ Denotes ──────→

Figure 145. Subscripting

subscript quantity In XL FORTRAN, a component of a subscript. A subscript quantity is an integer or real constant, a variable, or an expression.

subselect In SQL, that form of the SELECT statement that does not include ORDER BY or UNION operators.

subsequence field In an IMS/VS secondary index, a field added to the index segment key data to make the pointer segment key unique.

subserver In the AIX operating system, a system resource that is directly controlled by a server program running under control of the system program controller (SPC).

subset (1) A set each element of which is an element of a specified other set. (I)　(A)　(2) A variant form of a programming language with fewer features or more restrictions than the original language. (T) (3) A set contained within a set. (4) In telecommunication, a subscriber set such as a telephone. (5) See alphabetic character subset, alphanumeric character subset, character subset, numeric character subset.

subshell In the AIX operating system, an instance of the shell program started from an existing shell program.

substitute The source entry utility operation in which a specified string of characters replaces a string of characters located by a scan operation.

substitute character (SUB) A control character used in place of a character recognized to be invalid or in error, or that cannot be represented on a given device. (I)　(A)

substitute mode A transmittal mode used with exchange buffering in which segments are pointed to and exchanged with user work areas. See also locate mode, move mode.

substitution string A specified string of characters that replaces a string of characters that were located by a scan operation.

substitution variable A variable used to pass information such as a file name for use in a message.

substrate (1) The molded plastic portion of a videodisc or compact disc. (2) In a microcircuit, the supporting material upon which or within which an integrated circuit is fabricated, or to which an integrated circuit is attached. (3) Synonym for base *(5)*.

substring (1) A part of a character string. See character substring.　(2) In FORTRAN, a contiguous portion of a scalar character string.

Note: An array section can include a substring-range; the result is called a section and not a substring.

subsystem (1) A secondary or subordinate system, usually capable of operating independently of, or asynchronously with, a controlling system. (T)　(2) In Open Systems Interconnection architecture, an element in a hierarchical division of an open system that directly interacts only with elements in the next higher division or the next lower division of that open system. A hierarchical division of an open system may be either a layer or a sublayer. (T)　(3) In the AS/400 system, an operating environment, defined by a subsystem description, in which the system coordinates processing and resources. (4) See IMS/VS subsystem.

subsystem attributes In System/38, specifications in a subsystem description that specify the amount of main storage available to the subsystem and the number of jobs that can execute concurrently in the subsystem.

subsystem component In Subsystem Support Services, a programmable communication controller or a programmable terminal that is a remote unit in a network.

subsystem controller Synonym for store controller.

subsystem controller definition record (SCDR) (1) In DPCX, a subsystem support services record, maintained in the subsystem library, that contains information about programs and DSCBs in the DPCX library and at the processor. (2) Synonym for store controller definition record.

subsystem definition statement One of the statements used to define either the configuration of terminals attached to a subsystem controller or the processing options for data within the subsystem. See also definition statement, supermarket subsystem definition record.

subsystem description In the AS/400 system and System/38, a system object that contains information defining the characteristics of an operating environment controlled by the system.

subsystem identification (SSID) An identification on each device in the 3850 Mass Storage System. The devices include staging adapters, staging drives, mass storage facilities, data recording devices, and data recording controls.

subsystem information retrieval facility In DPCX, a facility that provides centralized support to aid in problem determination and servicing of the 8100/DPCX system.

subsystem interface In ACF/TCAM, a function that enables users who are already using the facilities of ACF/TCAM to also use ACF/TCAM as the single access method for certain IBM subsystems.

subsystem library (SLIB) (1) A VSAM key-sequenced data set at the host processor, used to contain all of the IBM-supplied subsystem controller data, certain control records, and user programs for subsystem controllers connected to the host processor. It also contains the control records (SCDRs) that specify the configuration and options for individual store controllers. (2) In DPCX, a library at the host system, created and maintained by subsystem support services, that provides services for subsystems such as creating and updating subsystem libraries, processing programs and data to be used by the subsystems, and transmitting the programs and data to communication controllers and program-controlled terminals.

Subsystem Program Preparation Support (SPPS) A set of macroinstructions, IBM System/370 Assembler language statements, and transformation definition language (TDL) statements used to write application programs for execution in the store controller. See SPPS II.

subsystem store controller See store controller.

subsystem support program Any program that is part of the subsystem support services. A subsystem support program is executed in the host system.

subsystem support services (SSS) A set of IBM-supplied programs, executed in the host system, that provide services for subsystems such as creating and updating subsystem libraries at the host system, processing programs and data to be used by the subsystems, and transmitting the programs and data to communication controllers and program-controlled terminals. See also subsystem support program.

subtask (1) A task initiated and terminated by a higher order task. (2) In DPCX, a task restricted from communication with an operator device.

subtotal On a calculator, the display or printing of an interim result of a calculation. (T)

subtotal function In a calculator, a function that allows the display or printing of an interim result of a calculation. (T) (A)

subtracter (1) A functional unit whose output data are a representation of the difference between the numbers represented by its input data. (T) (2) See adder-subtracter, full-subtracter, half-subtracter.

subtractive color system A system that reproduces colors by mixing appropriate amounts of color paints on white paper. These paints reflect certain colors and absorb—or subtract—others. The primary subtractive colors are red, blue, and yellow. "Red" as used in painting is technically a magenta color, and "blue" is technically a cyan color. See also primary color. Contrast with additive color system.

subtrahend In a subtraction operation, the number or quantity subtracted from the minuend. (I) (A)

subtype See library member subtype.

subvector A subcomponent of the NMVT major vector.

subvoice-grade channel A channel of bandwidth narrower than that of voice-grade channels. Such channels are usually subchannels of a voice-grade line.

Note: Common usage excludes telegraph channels from this definition.

subwidget In the AIXwindows program and Enhanced X-Windows, a widget class directly beneath a higher widget class in a widget-gadget hierarchy.

suction feeder In a duplicator, a device for lifting successive sheets of paper by suction from the paper stack and feeding them into the machine. (T)

suffix A code dialed by a caller who is already engaged in a call. Contrast with prefix.

suffix notation Synonym for postfix notation.

sum (1) The number or quantity that is the result of the addition of two or more numbers or quantities. (I) (A) (2) See also checksum.

Note: Augend + addend = sum.

sum check Synonym for summation check.

sum counter In COBOL, a signed numeric item established by a SUM clause in the Report Section of the Data Division. The sum counter is used by the report writer control system to contain the result of designated summing operations that take place during production of a report.

summary data field In a summary tag-along sort, a data field designated for accumulated totals.

summary journal A record of operational activity at a supermarket terminal that is printed at the terminal.

summary punch A card punch used to record data that were calculated or summarized by another device. (T) (A)

summation check (1) A comparison of checksums computed on the same data on different occasions or on different representations of the data in order to verify data integrity. (T) Synonymous with sum check. (2) A check based on the formation of the sum of the digits of a numeral. The sum of the individual digits is usually compared with a previously computed value. (A)

summer (1) A functional unit whose output analog variable is equal to the sum, or a weighted sum, of two or more input analog variables. (I) (A) (2) Synonymous with analog adder.

summing integrator A functional unit whose output analog variable is the integral of a weighted sum of the input analog variables with respect to time or with respect to another input analog variable. (I) (A)

super In multimedia applications, pertaining to titles or graphics overlaid on a picture electronically. See superimpose.

superblock In an AIX file system layout, block 1, which is used to keep track of the file system and is the most critical part of the file system. It contains information about every allocation or deallocation of blocks in the file system. See also i-list, i-node.

superclass In the AIXwindows program and Enhanced X-Windows, a class of widgets that passes inheritable resources down the hierarchy to a lower subclass. See also core.

supercomputer Any of the class of computers that have the highest processing speeds available at a given time for solving scientific and engineering problems. (T) See also fifth generation computer, supermini.

Note: Processing capability of supercomputers is measured in megaflops: millions of basic floating-point operations per second. The next generation of supercomputers will have processing capabilities measured in gigaflops: billions of basic floating-point operations per second.

superimpose In multimedia, to place two images on the screen simultaneously so that one appears to overlay the other.

superlattice A microchip that consists of several layers of different semiconductive materials.

supermarket subsystem definition record In the 3660 Supermarket Store System, one of 42 records built from subsystem definition statements and that make up the operational environment of a supermarket.

supermini Any of the group of minicomputers that have the fastest processing speeds available at a given time.

superposed circuit An additional channel obtained from one or more circuits and normally provided for other channels to enable all channels to be used simultaneously without mutual interference.

superposed (superimposed) ringing Party-line telephone ringing in which a combination of alternating and direct currents is utilized; the direct currents of both polarities are provided for selective ringing.

superscript In word processing, one or more characters printed one-half line above the normal printing line. Contrast with subscript.

superscript character (SPS) A word processing formatting control that causes the printing or display point to move up approximately one-half the normal single line space increment with no horizontal motion. The superscript character is a latching control that requires a subscript character to cause the printing or display point to return to the previous horizontal alignment. Contrast with subscript character.

super storyboard In multimedia, a description of all the audio, video, graphic, and logical control elements for multimedia presentation.

superuser authority In the AIX operating system, the unrestricted authority to access and modify any part of the operating system, usually associated with the user who manages the system.

Super-VHS An enhanced VHS tape format in which the luminance (brightness) information is separated from the chrominance (color) information, not combined into one signal, thus producing a higher-quality picture.

supervisor (1) The part of a control program that coordinates the use of resources and maintains the flow of processing unit operations. See also system supervisor. (2) Synonym for supervisory program, supervisory routine. (3) See overlay supervisor.

supervisor authority In the Folder Application Facility, authorization to add or delete system users, modify user profiles, redirect and suspend document assignments, and monitor all work in the routing queue.

supervisor call (SVC) A request that serves as the interface into operating system functions, such as allocating storage. The SVC protects the operating system from inappropriate user entry. All operating system requests must be handled by SVCs.

supervisor call instruction An instruction that interrupts a program being executed and passes control to the supervisor so that it can perform a specific service indicated by the instruction.

supervisor lock In OS/VS and VM, an indicator used to inhibit entry to disabled code while a disabled page fault is being resolved.

supervisor mode In DPPX, the privilege mode that allows processing of all instructions. See also application mode, I/O mode, master mode.

supervisor-privileged instruction In the IBM 8100 Information System, an instruction that can be executed in supervisor or master modes but not in application or I/O modes.

supervisor services The part of DPCX that provides the environment for one or more DPCX tasks to execute in the 8100 system.

supervisor state A state during which a processing unit can execute input/output and other privileged instructions. Contrast with problem state.

supervisory Pertaining to a frame format that performs data link control functions such as acknowledging information frames, requesting retransmission, and requesting temporary suspension of transmission. Receive ready (RR), receive not ready (RNR), and reject (REJ) are examples of supervisory frame formats.

supervisory program A computer program, usually part of an operating system, that controls execution of other computer programs and regulates the flow of work in a data processing system. (I) (A) Synonymous with executive program, supervisor.

supervisory relay A relay that, during a telephone call, is controlled by the transmitter current supplied to a subscriber line to receive from the associated stations the signals that control the actions of operators or switching mechanisms.

supervisory routine A routine, usually part of an operating system, that controls the execution of other routines and regulates the flow of work in a data processing system. (I) (A) Synonymous with executive routine, supervisor.

supervisory services (1) A general term for all functions in the supervisor that are available to the user. (2) The network control program supervisor code that provides miscellaneous services, such as the communication adapter interface, starting channel output, controlling timer operations, and data manipulation and utility services.

supervisory (S) format A format used to perform data link supervisory control functions, such as acknowledge I frames, request retransmission of I frames, and request temporary suspension of transmission of I frames. See also information format, unnumbered format.

supervisory (S) frame A frame in supervisory format used to transfer supervisory control functions. See also information format, unnumbered format.

supervisory signals Signals used to indicate the various operating states of circuit combinations.

supplemental windows In SAA Advanced Common User Access architecture, windows that enable applications to extend the dialog with a user. The two supplemental windows are secondary windows and dialog boxes. See secondary window, dialog box.

supply reel A spool from which magnetic tape unwinds during operation of a cartridge or cassette. See also take-up reel.

supply voltage indicator On dictation equipment, a device giving an audible or visible indication that the correct voltage is set for a main-powered machine or that the battery is sufficiently active in a battery-powered machine. (I)

support In system development, to provide the necessary resources for the correct operation of a functional unit. (T) See also system support.

suppressible text Text that is to be ignored in certain copy operations.

suppression (1) In AS/400 AFP support, the electronic equivalent of the "spot carbon," which prevents selected data from being printed on certain copies. (2) See zero suppression. (3) Synonym for text suppression.

suppression character In the NetView program, a user-defined character that is coded at the beginning of a command list statement or a command to prevent the statement or command from appearing on the operator's terminal screen or in the network log.

surface chart In GDDM, a chart similar to a line chart, except that no markers appear and the areas between successive lines are shaded.

surge resistance (1) The capability of a device to remain functionally intact after exposure to overvoltages. (T)   (2) Synonymous with surge withstand capability.

surge withstand capability Synonym for surge resistance. (A)

surge withstand resistance Synonym for surge resistance.

surveyor See Data Base Surveyor utility feature.

suspended state A software state in which a task is not dispatched by the system and is not contending for the processor.

SUW Synchronized unit of work.

SUW error In CICS/VS, an error condition that relates to the end-user interpretation of data in a message unit. Correction of an SUW error generally involves resynchronization of the transaction programs involved in processing the transaction. See also SUW restart, SUW retry. Contrast with chain error.

SUW restart In CICS/VS, an attempt to correct an SUW error by re-executing the failing synchronized unit of work following resynchronization. An SUW restart is performed as part of the same conversation in which the error took place. Contrast with SUW retry.

SUW retry In CICS/VS, an attempt to correct an SUW error by re-executing the failing synchronized unit of work following resynchronization. An SUW retry is performed within a new conversation, not within the same conversation in which the error took place. Contrast with SUW restart.

SVA Shared virtual area.

SVC (1) Supervisor call. (2) Switched virtual circuit.

SVC interruption An interruption caused by the execution of a supervisor call instruction, causing control to be passed to the supervisor.

SVC routine A control program routine that performs or begins a control program service specified by a supervisor call instruction.

SVC 76 Error Recording Interface In VM/370, a means for VM/370 to record error incidents encountered by certain operating systems running in virtual machines. When a virtual operating system issues an SVC 76, the VM translates the virtual storage and I/O device addresses to real addresses, records the information, and returns control to the issuing virtual machine. This interface bypasses the error recording routine of the virtual machine and avoids duplicate error recording.

S-video (1) Separated video or super video. (2) A signal system using a Y/C format. (3) See also component video, composite video, Y/C.

SVS Single virtual storage system.

SW Switch character.

SWADS Scheduler work area data set.

swap (1) In systems with virtual storage, to write the main storage image of a job to auxiliary storage and read the image of another job into processor storage. (2) In OS/VS2 with TSO, to write the active pages of a job to external page storage and read pages of another job from external page storage into real storage.

swap allocation unit In TSO, an arbitrary unit of auxiliary storage space into which a swap data set is divided, and by which it is allocated.

swap data set In TSO, a data set dedicated to swapping.

swap fault In VM/SP HPO, an address translation exception that occurs when reference is made to a page physically swapped to a swap area.

swap-in (1) In systems with virtual storage, the process of reading the real storage image of a job from auxiliary storage into real storage. (2) In OS/VS2 with TSO, the process of reading pages of a terminal job from auxiliary storage into real storage.

swap-out (1) In systems with virtual storage, the process of writing the real storage image of a job from real storage to auxiliary storage. (2) In OS/VS2 with TSO, the process of writing the active pages of a terminal job from real storage to auxiliary storage.

swapping (1) A process that interchanges the contents of an area of real storage with the contents of an area in auxiliary storage. (I) (A) (2) In a system with virtual storage, a paging technique that writes the active pages of a job to auxiliary storage and reads pages of another job from auxiliary storage into real storage. (3) In System/36, the process of temporarily removing an active job from main storage, saving it on disk, and processing another job in the area of main storage formerly occupied by the first job. (4) See logical swapping, page swapping, physical swapping.

swap set (1) The pages that are to be swapped in or swapped out for a job or for system programs. (2) In VM/SP HPO, a group of pages belonging to a specific virtual machine to be written to or read from direct access storage as a group. The maximum number of pages contained in a swap-set is a system generation variable.

SWB Save/work block.

sweep In computer graphics, movement along an arc around a given center point. See Figure 146.

sweetening In multimedia applications: (1) The equalization of audio to eliminate noise and obtain the cleanest and most level sound possible. (2) The addition of laughter to an audio track.

swim In computer graphics, undesired movement of display elements about their normal positions. (T)

swinging delivery tray In a duplicator, a delivery tray that pivots laterally during paper delivery for presorting copies. (T)

SWINN Switched intermediate network node.

switch (1) A choice of one jump from a selection of jumps, controlled by a flag. (T) (2) A device or programming technique for making a selection; for example, a toggle, a conditional jump. (A) (3) In SAA usage, to move the cursor from one point of interest to another; for example, to move from one screen or window to another or from a place within a displayed image to another place on the same displayed image. (4) See external switch, main switch. (5) Synonymous with switchpoint.

switchable-mode line See line mode switching, switched connection.

switchback In an IBM 3745 Communication Controller with twin central control units (CCUs) in backup mode, the process by which, after fallback, buses are moved back to the central control unit (CCU) that originally operated them.

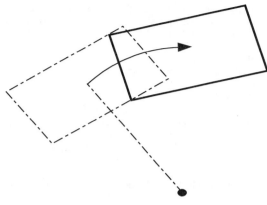

Figure 146. Sweep

switch block In an IBM personal computer, a group of slide switches or rocker switches on an expansion board.

switch character (SW) A word processing device control that causes reading of a character string to switch from one character string source to another without operator intervention. See also repeat character, stop character.

switch code In word processing, a program instruction for switching between different elements of recording media on the same machine or between different sections of storage. (T)

switch control statement A control transfer statement that causes control to transfer to one of a number of possible statements, depending on existing or prior conditions; for example, the switch in ALGOL 60, the computed GOTO in FORTRAN. (T)

switch core A core in which the magnetic material generally has a high residual flux density and a high ratio of residual to saturated flux density, with a threshold value of magnetizing force below which switching does not occur. (T) (A)

switched connection (1) A mode of operating a data link in which a circuit or channel is established to switching facilities as; for example, in a public switched network. (T) (2) A connection established by dialing. (3) Contrast with nonswitched connection.

switched intermediate network node (SWINN) Deprecated term for intermediate routing node.

switched line A telecommunication line in which the connection is established by dialing. Contrast with nonswitched line.

switched major node In VTAM, a major node whose minor nodes are physical units and logical units attached by switched SDLC links.

switched network Any network in which connections are established by closing switches; for example, by dialing.

switched network backup (SNBU) An optional facility that allows a user to specify, for certain types of physical units, a switched line to be used as an alternate path if the primary line becomes unavailable or unusable.

switched point-to-point channel-path config. In an I/O interface, a configuration that consists of a link between a channel and an ESCON Director and one or more links from the ESCD, each of which attaches to a control unit. This configuration depends on the capabilities of the ESCD for establishing and removing connections between channels and control units. Contrast with point-to-point channel-path configuration.

switched point-to-point topology A network topology that uses switching facilities to provide multiple communication paths between channels and control units. See also multidrop topology. Contrast with point-to-point topology.

switched SNA major node In VTAM, a major node whose minor nodes are physical units (PUs) and logical units (LUs) attached by switched SDLC links.

switched telecommunication network A switched network furnished by communication common carriers or telecommunication Administrations.

switched virtual circuit (SVC) (1) An X.25 circuit that is dynamically established when needed. The X.25 equivalent of a switched line. (2) A virtual circuit that is requested by a virtual call. It is released when the virtual circuit is cleared. Contrast with permanent virtual circuit (PVC).

switcher In video systems, a device that can be used to select from various signal sources (such as cameras or video recorders).

switch hook A switch on a telephone set, associated with the structure supporting the receiver or handset. It is operated by removal or replacement of the receiver or handset on the support. See also off-hook, on-hook.

switch indicator Synonym for flag.

switching (1) Pertaining to a connection established by closing switches between a remote terminal and a computer. (2) See automatic volume switching, circuit switching, line switching, message switching, packet switching. (3) In multimedia applications, electronically designating, from between two or more video sources, the source's pictures that are to be recorded on tape. Switching can occur during a shoot or during an edit.

switching center A location that terminates multiple circuits, and is capable of interconnecting circuits or transferring traffic between circuits. See automatic switching center, semiautomatic switching center, torn-tape switching center.

switching element Deprecated term for logic element.

switching function A function that has only a finite number of possible values and whose independent variables each have only a finite number of possible values. (I) (A)

switching pad A transmission loss pad automatically cut in and out of a toll circuit for different operating conditions.

switching variable A variable that can take only a finite number of possible values or states. (I) (A)

switch instruction In word processing, a program instruction for switching between different elements of recording media on the same machine or between different sections of storage. (T)

switch room The part of a telephone central office building that houses switching mechanisms and associated apparatus.

switch split window In SAA Advanced Common User Access architecture, an action that moves the cursor in a clockwise direction from one window pane to the next in a split window.

switch-status condition In COBOL, the proposition, for which a truth value can be determined that an implementor-defined switch, capable of being set to an "on" or "off" status, has been set to a specific status.

switch table The table used by the AIX file system to locate the entry points of a character device.

Switch to... In SAA Advanced Common User Access architecture, a choice in the system menu pull-down that shows a list of the active applications.

Switch to action bar (1) In SAA Advanced Common User Access architecture, an action that moves the cursor to the action bar. (2) In SAA Basic Common User Access architecture, an action that moves the cursor to and from the action bar. It is listed as Actions in the function key area.

switch train A sequence of switches through which connection must be made to establish a circuit between a calling telephone and a called telephone. See also train.

switch window In SAA Advanced Common User Access architecture, an action that changes the active window within an application.

switch window in multiple-document interface In SAA Advanced Common User Access architecture, an action that changes the active secondary window within a multiple-document interface application.

syllable A character string or a binary element string in a word. (I)   (A)

syllable hyphen Synonym for soft hyphen. (T)   (A)

syllable hyphen character (SHY) A word processing formatting graphic that prints only at syllable boundaries at line endings to indicate continuation of a word on the next line. A syllable hyphen may be ignored or dropped if words are repositioned during text adjust mode operations. Contrast with required hyphen character.

symbol (1) A graphic representation of a concept that has meaning in a specific context. (T)   (2) A representation of something by reason of relationship, association, or convention. (A)   (3) A name in a source document that can be replaced with something else, for example, a character string. (4) In OS/VS, any group of eight or less alphanumeric and national characters that begins with an alphabetic character or the characters (@, #, $). (5) See abstract symbol, aiming symbol, currency symbol, flowchart symbol, logic symbol, mnemonic symbol, sequence symbols, tracking symbol, variable symbol.

symbolic address An identifier that represents an address. (T)

symbolic addressing A method of addressing in which the address part of an instruction contains a symbolic address. (I)   (A)

symbolic-character In COBOL, a user-defined word that specifies a user-defined figurative constant.

symbolic coding The preparation of routines and computer programs in a symbolic language. (A)

symbolic constant In FORTRAN, a named data object whose value must not change during execution of an executable program.

symbolic debugger A tool that aids in the debugging of programs written in certain high-level languages.

symbolic description map A set of source statements in a particular programming language, such as Assembler, COBOL, PL/I, or RPGII, that name and describe the variable fields of a map.

symbolic I/O assignment A means by which a problem program can refer to an I/O device by a specific I/O symbolic name. Before the program is executed, a device is assigned to the symbolic name.

symbolic language A programming language that expresses addresses and operation codes of instructions in symbols convenient to humans rather than in machine language. (A)

symbolic logic The discipline in which valid argument and operations are dealt with using an artificial language designed to avoid the ambiguities and logical inadequacies of natural languages. (I)   (A)   Synonymous with mathematical logic.

symbolic machine In DPCX, a set of resources, including control and data storage blocks, allocated by DPCX for execution of user programs or system services.

symbolic name (1) In a programming language, a unique name used to represent an entity such as a field, file, data structure, or label. (2) In FORTRAN, an alphanumeric name for an entity.

symbolic parameter In job control language, a symbol preceded by an ampersand that represents a parameter or the value assigned to a parameter or subparameter in a cataloged or in-stream procedure. Values are assigned to symbolic parameters when the procedure in which they appear is called.

symbolic placeholder A symbol in a command list that is replaced by an actual value when the command list is executed.

symbolic pointer In IMS/VS, the concatenation of the keys in the sequence fields of all segments that must be retrieved to reach the desired segment, including the sequence field key of the desired segment.

symbol manipulation The processing of symbols without regard for their numerical values. (A)

symbol rank Synonym for digit place.

symbols See editing symbols.

symbol set In the AS/400 Business Graphics Utility, a supplied character set used for text strings on charts, such as headings, legend text, labels, and notes.

symbol string A string consisting solely of symbols. (I)   (A)

symbol substitution The replacement of a symbol with a character string.

symmetrical channel A channel pair in which the send and receive directions of transmission have the same data signaling rate. (T) See also binary symmetric channel.

symmetrical I/O unit In multiprocessing, a unit attached to two processors. It appears as the same I/O unit to each processor, and can be accessed in the same manner by each processor.

symmetrical list A chained list in which each data element also contains information for locating the preceding one. (T)

symmetric binary channel See binary symmetric channel.

symmetric channel See binary symmetric channel.

symmetric cryptography In computer security, cryptography in which the same key is used for encryption and decryption. Contrast with public key cryptography.

symmetric processors Processors with identical configurations.

symmetric storage configurations Machine configurations with identical storage units.

symmetric video compression A technology in which the personal computer can be used to create, as well as play back, full-motion, full-color video.

symptom string A structured character string written to a file when VTAM detects certain error conditions.

SYN The synchronous idle character. (I) (A)

SYNAD exit routine A synchronous EXLST exit routine that is entered when a physical error is detected.

sync Synchronization.

sync bits Synonym for framing bits.

sync information In video systems, the part of the video signal that ensures the display scanning is synchronized with the camera scanning.

synch point An intermediate or end point during processing of a transaction at which an update or modification to one or more of the transaction's protected resources is logically complete and error free. Synonymous with synchronization point.

synchronization (1) The action of forcing certain points in the execution sequences of two or more asynchronous procedures to coincide in time. (T) (2) In video systems, the timing pulses that control the TV scanning system.

synchronization character See synchronous idle character (SYN).

synchronization point Synonym for sync point.

synchronization processing In CICS/VS, processing that is performed by transaction processing systems at a synchronization point in order to ensure that the transaction processing systems can perform a resynchronization if a synchronized unit of work fails.

Note: Synchronization processing permits coordination of changes being made to protected resources by conversing transaction programs. It always involves the commitment function and may also involve the preparation function or the resynchronization function.

synchronization pulses Pulses introduced by transmission equipment into the receiving equipment to keep the two equipments operating in step. (A)

synchronized unit of work The portion of a transaction that occurs between two synchronization points.

synchronizer Deprecated term for input/output controller.

synchronous (1) Pertaining to two or more processes that depend upon the occurrence of specific events such as common timing signals. (T) (2) Occurring with a regular or predictable time relationship.

Synchronous Data Link Control (SDLC) A discipline conforming to subsets of the Advanced Data Communication Control Procedures (ADCCP) of the American National Standards Institute (ANSI) and High-level Data Link Control (HDLC) of the International Organization for Standardization, for managing synchronous, code-transparent, serial-by-bit information transfer over a link connection. Transmission exchanges may be duplex or half-duplex over switched or nonswitched links. The configuration of the link connection may be point-to-point, multipoint, or loop. (I) See also binary synchronous communications.

synchronous data network A data network that uses a method of synchronization between data circuit-terminating equipment (DCE) and the data switching exchange (DSE), and between DSEs. The data signaling rates are controlled by timing equipment within the network. (T)

synchronous data transfer A physical transfer of data to or from a device that has a predictable time relationship with the execution of an I/O request.

synchronous data transmission See synchronous transmission.

synchronous flow See normal flow.

synchronous idle character (SYN) A transmission control character used in synchronous transmission systems to provide a signal from which synchronism or synchronous correction may be achieved between data terminal equipment, particularly when no other character is being transmitted. (T) (A)

synchronous I/O In VTAM, suspension of processing of a request sent by the system services control point (SSCP) until the response is received. A variable work area remains allocated while the SSCP waits for the response. When the response is received, the suspended process resumes at the next sequential instruction.

synchronous level In AS/400 finance communications, a level at which a logical unit (LU) determines if it can allocate and deallocate system resources.

synchronous line control A scheme of operating procedures and control signals for controlling telecommunication lines.

synchronous operation (1) An operation that occurs regularly or predictably with respect to the occurrence of a specified event in another process; for example, the calling of an input/output routine that receives control at a precoded location in a computer program. (I) (A) (2) A mode of operation in which each action is started by a clock. (A) (3) In VTAM, a communication, or other operation in which VTAM, after receiving the request for the operation, does not return control to the program until the operation is completed. Contrast with asynchronous operation.

synchronous processing In the AS/400 system and System/38, a series of operations that are done as part of the job in which they were requested; for example, calling a program in an interactive job at a workstation. Contrast with asynchronous processing.

synchronous request In VTAM, a request for a synchronous operation. Contrast with asynchronous request.

synchronous transmission (1) Data transmission in which the time of occurrence of each signal representing a bit is related to a fixed time base. (I) (2) In data communication, a method of transmission in which the sending and receiving of characters are controlled by timing signals. Contrast with asynchronous transmission. (3) Synonymous with isochronous transmission.

Note: The sending and receiving devices are operated at substantially the same frequency and are kept in an appropriate phase relationship.

synchronous transmitter receiver (STR) The transmission unit of the class of IBM terminals employing synchronous transmission and a unique 4-out-of-8-bit coding. The STR unit maintains line synchronization, transmits and receives characters, and transmits and receives checking and control information.

sync point (1) An intermediate or end point during processing of a transaction at which an update or modification to one or more of the transaction's protected resources is logically complete and error free. (2) Synonymous with synchronization point.

sync point manager (SPM) The component of the node that implements two-phase commit and resynchronization processing. The subcomponents of the SPM are sync point services (SPS) and the protection managers (the conversation resource protection managers and the local resource protection managers).

sync point services (SPS) The component of the sync point manager that is responsible for coordinating the managers of protected resources during sync point processing. SPS coordinates two-phase commit protocols, resync protocols, and logging.

sync signal Video signal used to synchronize video equipment.

synonym (1) In an indirectly addressed file, a record whose key randomizes to the address of a home record. (2) In CMS, an alternative command name defined by the user as equivalent to an existing CMS command name. Synonyms are entries in a CMS file with a filetype of SYNONYM. Issuing the SYNONYM command allows use of those synonyms until the terminal session ends or until the use of synonyms is revoked by issuing the SYNONYM command without operands.

synonym aid A document proofreading function that replaces a given word with one having a similar meaning that the user chooses from a list of synonyms provided by a dictionary.

synonym chain In DPCX, a method of storing indexed records whose key fields are transformed to the same value after hashing. The first record in the synonym chain is pointed to by an entry in the data set index. Each subsequent record in the chain contains a field that points to the next record.

synonyms Different terms that refer to the same entity. (T)

syntactic analysis An analysis of a program to determine the structure of the program and whether it conforms with the syntax of a particular programming language.

syntax (1) The relationship among characters or groups of characters, independent of their meanings or the manner of their interpretation and use. (I) (A) (2) The structure of expressions in a language. (A) (3) The rules governing the structure of a language. (A) (4) The relationship among symbols. (A) (5) The rules for the construction of a statement. (6) See also pragmatics, semantics.

syntax checker A program that tests source statements in a programming language for violations of syntax.

syntax-directed editor A text editor that is designed for a particular programming language and that preserves the syntactical integrity of the text. (T)

syntax error A compile-time error caused by incorrect syntax. See also semantic error.

syntax language A metalanguage used to specify or describe the syntax of another language. (A)

synthesizer See audio synthesizer.

synthetic address Synonym for generated address.

SYSDEF System definition.

SYSGEN System generation. (A)

SYSIN A system input stream, also the name used as the data definition name of a data set in the input stream.

SYSLOG System log.

SYSMOD System modification.

SYSOUT A system output stream, also an indicator used in data definition statements to signify that a data set is to be written on a system output unit.

SYSOUT class A category of output with specific characteristics and written on a specific output device.

sysplex A multiple-MVS system environment that allows MCS consoles or extended MCS consoles to receive messages and send commands across systems.

SYSREC System error file.

SYSRES System residence disk.

system (1) In data processing, a collection of people, machines, and methods organized to accomplish a set of specific functions. (I) (A) (2) A computer and its associated devices and programs.

system activity measurement facility (MF/1) A facility that collects information such as paging activity and use of the processing unit, channels, and I/O devices to produce trace records and reports.

system address list In the AIX system, the address list, controlled by the system manager, that all users on the system can use to make outgoing X.25 calls. See also address list, user address list.

system administrator The person at a computer installation who designs, controls, and manages the use of the computer system.

system analysis A systematic investigation of a real or planned system to determine the information requirements and processes of the system and how these relate to each other and to any other system. Synonymous with systems analysis. (T) (A)

system analyst privilege class In VM/370, the CP privilege class E user, normally a system analyst, who can query, examine, and print or display, but not modify, certain areas of the CP nucleus, and can create saved systems. See also saved system.

system arbiter In System/38, a system job that provides overall control of the work being done on the system.

system ASP In the AS/400 system, the auxiliary storage pool where system programs and data reside. It is the storage pool used if a storage pool is not defined by the user. See also auxiliary storage pool, user ASP

system-assisted linkage In DPPX, a linkage from a program in one load module to a program in another load module.

system authentication key In the Programmed Cryptographic Facility, a value that is directly related to the value of the host master key. The system authentication key is used to derive cryptographic key test patterns.

system board In a system unit, the main circuit board that supports a variety of basic system devices, such as a keyboard or a mouse, and provides other basic system functions.

system checkpoint A point at which a system records its operating status and control information so that it can restore the same operating environment at a later time if recovery is necessary.

system complex See sysplex.

system configuration A process that specifies the devices and programs that form a particular data processing system.

system configuration list In the AS/400 system, a list of devices that are provided with the system.

system console A console, usually equipped with a keyboard and display screen, that is used by an operator to control and communicate with a system.

system contents directory In IMS/VS, a data area whose primary function is to contain major entry pointers for all IMS/VS facilities. Its secondary function is to contain system data and the status of the log functions and commands.

system control area An area on the screen of a display component providing 3790 system communication and instructions for the control operator. It is normally positioned at the bottom of the screen and is composed of four areas: command, communication, message pending, and mode.

system control facility (SCF) In the IBM 8100 Information System, a system component that consists of one primary system control facility and one or more secondary system control facilities.

system control file In CP, the file that consists of macros that describe the CP system residence disk, real main storage size, CP-owned DASD volumes, VM system operator's user ID, and system timer value.

system control programming (SCP) IBM-supplied programming that is fundamental to the operation and maintenance of the system. It serves as an interface with licensed programs and user programs and is available without additional charge.

system customization The process of specifying the devices, programs, and users for a particular information processing installation. See also configuration.

system data analyzer A program that analyzes collected data about hardware errors in the 3850 Mass Storage System.

system data set In DPCX, a data set generally used only by DPCX and not by users that is stored in system disk space and is accessible only through DPCX system services.

system date (1) The date established for the system when it is started. (2) The date assigned by the system operator during the initial program load procedure. See also creation date, program date, session date.

system default A default value defined in the system profile.

system-defined category In DPCX, a category used to define all user disk space.

system definition The process, completed before a system is put into use, by which desired functions and operations of the system are selected from various available options. Synonymous with system generation.

system description Documentation that results from system design defining the organization, essential characteristics and the hardware and software requirements of the system. (T)

system design A process of defining the hardware and software architecture, components, modules, interfaces, and data for a system to satisfy specified requirements. (T) See also conceptual system design.

system development A process that usually includes requirements analysis, system design, implementation, documentation and quality assurance. (T)

system directory Synonym for root directory.

system distribution directory A list of user IDs and identifying information, such as network addresses, used to send distributions.

system documentation The collection of documents that describe the requirements, capabilities, limitations, design, operation, and maintenance of an information processing system. (T)

system dump (1) A dump of all or part of storage. (2) In AIX for RISC System/6000, a copy from storage of selected data areas. Synonymous with kernel dump.

system effective data rate In MSS, an amount of data transferred in one second between the staging drives and the processing unit, normally averaged over an hour.

system error log A collection of records about errors that is maintained by a transaction processing system. Depending on the transaction processing system, the system error log may be located on a disk file, tape file, printer, buffer, or on another medium.

system error record editing program (SEREP) A stand-alone program used to edit and print hardware error condition logout data from main storage.

system file In VSE, a file used by the operating system, for example, the hardcopy file, recorder file, page data set.

system follow-up The study of the effects of a system after it has reached a stabilized state of operational use. Synonymous with post-implementation review, post-development review. (T)　　See also evaluation report.

system font One of the fonts available for screen display and printing. The font can support any language. The user can specify any size for this font. Contrast with device font.

system generation (SYSGEN) The process of selecting optional parts of an operating system and of creating a particular operating system tailored to the requirements of a data processing installation. (I) (A)　Synonym for system definition.

system group In SNADS, the second part of a system name in the system distribution directory.

system help support The part of the System Support Program Product that uses menus, prompts, and descriptive text to aid an operator.

system high The highest level of security label in a system. It is defined as the highest security level in the system and includes all security categories.

system hold status In the VM/XA Migration Aid, a spool file status that prevents a file from being printed, punched, or read until the real system operator releases it. Contrast with user hold status.

system identification In an IMS/VS multisystem environment, the means of identifying a system that is part of a logical link path.

system image The representation of a program and its related data as it exists in main storage.

system image buffer In DPCX, an area of processor storage through which all I/O data between a DPCX task and a directly attached display or printer must pass.

System Initialization table (SIT) A CICS table containing user-specified data that will control a system initialization process.　This table contains startup parameters.

system-initiated scratch function In MSS, a part of space management that scratches and uncatalogs non-VSAM data sets to manage space on mass storage volumes.

system input device A device specified as a source of an input stream.

system integration The progressive assembling of system components into the whole system. (T)

system integrity (1) In computer security, the quality of a system that can perform its intended function in an unimpaired manner, free from deliberate or inadvertent unauthorized manipulation of the system. (2) The condition that exists as long as a computing system remains available and operates properly.　See also application integrity, data integrity.

system interval In ACF/TCAM, a user-specified time interval during which polling and addressing are suspended on multipoint lines to polled stations.　The system interval minimizes unproductive polling and processing unit meter time, and synchronizes polling on the polled lines in the system.　See also invitation delay.

System IPO/E System Installation Productivity Option/Extended.　In VSE, a set of products and a series of optional features designed to aid in system installation and system service.

system key A key that protects system data against damage or modification by unauthorized users.

system library (1) A collection of data sets or files in which the parts of an operating system are stored. (2) In the AS/400 system, the library shipped with a system that contains objects, such as authorization lists and device descriptions created by a user, and the licensed programs, system commands, and any other system objects shipped with the system.　(3) In System/38, the library provided by the Control Program Facility to contain system-oriented objects provided as part of CPF. (4) In System/36, the library that contains the System Support Program Product. (5) In VSE, one of a set of libraries in which the various parts of the operating system are stored.

system life cycle The course of developmental changes through which a system passes from its conception to the termination of its use; for example, the phases and activities associated with the analysis, acquisition, design, development, test, integration, operation, maintenance, and modification of a system. (T)　(A) See Figure 147.

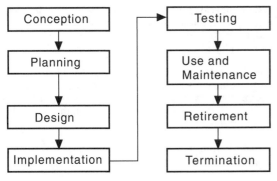

Figure 147. System Life Cycle

system list device The device that receives output for most System Support Program Product utility programs and service aids.

system literal In IMS/VS, a literal field provided by the message format service and defined by the user for inclusion in an output message.

system loader See loader *(2)*.

system lock In OS/VS1, an indicator in the communications vector table, used to inhibit the dispatching of any task except paging supervisor tasks.

system log device In System/36, a device designated to record messages and OCL statements.

system log message queue In System/38, a message queue used for sending from any job in the system information to the system history log, service log, or programming change log.

system log (SYSLOG) (1) A data set or file in which job-related information, operational data, descriptions of unusual occurrences, commands, and messages to or from the operator may be stored. (2) In IMS/VS, the data set on which a record of all significant system and database activity is maintained. The system log is required for IMS/VS recovery purposes and is also a source for obtaining statistics about system operation.

system low The lowest level of security label in a system. It is the lowest security level and has no security categories associated with it.

system macrodefinition A library macrodefinition supplied by IBM.

system macroinstruction A macroinstruction that calls for processing of IBM-supplied library macrodefinitions, for example, the ATTACH macro.

system maintenance The modification of a system to correct faults, to improve performance, or to adapt the system to a changed environment or changed requirements. (T)

system management The tasks involved in maintaining the system in good working order and modifying the system to meet changing requirements.

system management facilities (SMF) An optional control program feature of OS/VS that provides the means for gathering and recording information that can be used to evaluate system usage.

system management monitor (SMM) The part of DPCX that handles special supervisor services, such as program checks and certain types of addressing changes.

system measurement facility (SMF) System Support Program Product (SSP) routines that, in conjunction with control storage routines, observe system and device activity and SSP work area usage and record the data in a disk file.

system menu (1) In SAA Advanced Common User Access architecture, the pull-down available from the system menu icon. From it a user can restore, move, size, minimize, and maximize the window. A user can also exit the application, close a window, or interact with a list of active applications. (2) In the AIXwindows program, the pull-down in the top left-hand corner of a window that allows users to restore, move, size, minimize, and maximize the window; to exit the application or close a window; and to cause the appearance of a dialog box that contains a list of the active applications. With the optional split window technique, it also allows users to view many parts of the same object at one time.

system menu icon In SAA Advanced Common User Access architecture, the leftmost icon in a window's title bar. When a user selects the system menu icon, the system menu pull-down appears.

system message field In the IMS/VS message format service, an output device field on 3270 display devices that can be defined to receive system messages, thereby preventing unsolicited IMS/VS messages from destroying a screen format.

system modification (SYSMOD) The input data to SMP or SMP/E that define the introduction, replacement, or update of elements in the operating system and associated distribution libraries to be installed under control of SMP or SMP/E. A system modification is defined by a set of modification control statements.

System Modification Program (SMP) A program used to install software and software changes on MVS systems.

System Modification Program Extended An IBM-licensed program used to install software and software changes on MVS systems. In addition to providing the services of SMP, SMP/E consolidates installation data, allows more flexibility in selecting changes to be installed, provides a dialog interface, and supports dynamic allocation of data sets.

system monitor (1) The portion of the configuration image in a 3601 Finance Communication Controller that handles communications with control operators and records error statistics and other operational data. (2) In the AS/400 finance communications, a 4700 controller program used to perform service, configuration, and debugging functions on that controller.

system monitor session In SSP-ICF, a session started by the finance subsystem to load the applications into a finance controller.

system name (1) An IBM-supplied name that uniquely identifies a system. It is used as a network value for certain communications applications such as APPC. (2) In COBOL, a word that is used to communicate with the operating environment.

system name table In the VM control program the table that contains the name and location of saved systems, including discontiguous shared and nonshared segments.

system node In the AIX operating system, the highest node in the hierarchy of device locations. The connection path from every hardware device leads to the system node; for example, a small computer systems interface (SCSI) disk is connected to an SCSI adapter, that is connected to a bus, that is connected to the system node.

system nucleus See nucleus.

system object (1) The system profile, system maps, and system JCL masks used by SDF/CICS for communication with users. System objects are kept in the map specification library and can be maintained by the SDF/CICS master operator. (2) In the AS/400 system, a machine object classification. Any of the machine objects shipped with the system or any of the operating system objects created by the system.

System Object Model (SOM) A mechanism for language-neutral, object-oriented programming in the OS/2 environment.

system operator (1) An operator responsible for performing system-oriented procedures. (2) In System/38, the person who operates the system and looks after the peripheral equipment necessary to initiate computer runs or finalize computer output in the form of completed reports and documents.

system operator message queue In System/38, the message queue used by the system operator to receive and reply to messages from the system, workstation users, and application programs.

system operator user profile In System/38, the user profile supplied by the Control Program Facility that has the authority necessary for the system operator and the special authorities of save system rights and job control rights.

system output device A device assigned to record output data for a series of jobs.

system output writer A job scheduler function that transcribes specified output data sets onto a system output unit, independently of the program that produced the data sets.

system parameter Synonym for kernel parameter.

system parameter record (SPR) A user-built record in the 3660 Supermarket Store System that selects the operation sequence of a store controller and terminals.

system parameter table (SPT) A Subsystem Support Services table containing information needed by all Subsystem Support Services functions. It contains counters used to control Subsystem Support Services processing, flags to indicate Subsystem Support Services system status, buffer addresses, work file pointers, and FCB pointers used by the various functions within Subsystem Support Services.

system pointer In the AS/400 system and System/38, a pointer that contains addressability to a machine interface system object.

system prefix The first three characters of the message code that identifies the system or environment for the Folder Application Facility.

system printer The printer used for any printed output that is not specifically directed to another printer.

system processor In the AS/400 system, the logic that contains the processor function to translate and process the OS/400 control language commands and programming language statements. See also service processor.

system production time That part of operating time which is actually used by a user. (T)

system productivity A measure of the work performed by a system. System productivity largely depends on a combination of two other factors: the facility (ease of use) of the system and the performance (throughput, response time, and availability) of the system.

system profile (1) A file containing the default values used in system operations. (2) See profile.

system program controller (SPC) In the AIX operating system, a system program that controls the operation of other application programs (daemons) that run in the background.

system programmer (1) A programmer who plans, generates, maintains, extends, and controls the use of an operating system with the aim of improving overall productivity of an installation. (2) A programmer who designs programming systems and other applications.

system programmer privilege class In VM, the CP privilege class C user, normally the system programmer, who can modify any real storage locations in the machine.

system queue area (SQA) In OS/VS, an area of virtual storage reserved for system-related control blocks. It contains fixed pages and is assigned protection key zero.

system quiesce A procedure that allows an authorized operator to start an orderly shutdown of store system activity before changing from one application program to another, turning power off to the store controller, or using terminal resources to perform additional jobs.

system record Information that the NetView/PC program uses to identify itself to a network.

system recorder file In VSE, the file used to record hardware reliability data. Synonymous with recorder file.

system reference code (SRC) (1) A code that contains information, such as a failing field-replaceable unit, for a service representative. (2) In the AS/400 system, the characters that identify the name of the unit that detected a condition and the reference code that describes the condition.

system refresh In VSE/SP, to upgrade a VSE/SP system with the latest level of corrective service.

system reset To reinitialize the execution of a program by repeating the initial program load (IPL) operation. Synonymous with reboot.

system residence volume (1) The volume on which the nucleus of the operating system and the highest-level index of the catalog are located. (2) In VSE, the

volume on which the system library is stored and from which the hardware retrieves the initial program load routine for system start-up.

system resident file In DPCX, the disk storage file that contains the DPCX operating system as defined during installation.

system resilience The ability of a computer system to continue to function correctly despite the existence of a fault or faults in one or more of its component parts. (T)

Note: The speed of performance, throughput, or both, of the computer system may be diminished from normal until faults are corrected.

system resource operator privilege class In VM, a CP privilege class B user who controls all the other real resources of the machine, such as real storage, disk drives, and tape drives, that are not controlled by the primary system or spooling operators.

system resources Those resources controlled by the system, such as programs, devices, and storage areas that are assigned for use in jobs.

system resources manager (SRM) A group of programs that controls the use of system resources in order to satisfy the performance objectives of the installation.

system response field The portion of a basic transmission unit (BTU) containing the network control program status response to a request issued by the host.

system restart (1) A restart that allows reuse of previously initialized input and output work queues. Synonymous with warm start. (2) A restart that allows reuse of a previously initialized link pack area. Synonymous with quick start. (3) Synonym for initial program load.

systems analysis Synonym for system analysis. (T)

Systems Application Architecture solution A set of IBM software interfaces, conventions, and protocols that provide a framework for designing and developing applications that are consistent across systems.

system scheduled checkpoint In IMS/VS, a simple checkpoint that the system log automatically initiates after a user-defined quantity of log records are written.

system security (1) A system function that restricts the use of objects to certain users. (2) In the AS/400 system, a system function that restricts the use of files, libraries, folders, and devices to certain users.

system service display station A display station that can use all the procedures, programs, and commands needed to service the system.

system service program (SSP) In ACF/TCAM, an IBM-supplied or user-supplied program that performs system-oriented auxiliary functions in support of the message control program. System service programs run under control of the initiator as attached subtasks. See also basic operator control SSP, extended operator control SSP, online retrieval SSP, save/restore message queues SSP.

system services In DPCX, executable service routines provided to perform everyday operations such as printing or packing data. These system services are similar to system utilities provided with other systems.

system services control point (SSCP) A component within a subarea network for managing the configuration, coordinating network operator and problem determination requests, and providing directory services and other session services for end users of the network. Multiple SSCPs, cooperating as peers with one another, can divide the network into domains of control, with each SSCP having a hierarchical control relationship to the physical units and logical units within its own domain.

system services control point identifier See SSCP ID.

system service tools (SST) In the AS/400 system, the part of the service function used to service the system while the operating system is running.

system service tool user profile In the AS/400 system, the system-supplied user profile that has the authority necessary to service the system programming and the special save system authorities and job control authorities.

system slowdown A network control program mode of reduced operation invoked when buffer availability drops below a threshold level. The network control program limits the amount of new data the system accepts while continuing normal output activity.

systems management Functions in the application layer related to the management of Open Systems Interconnection resources and their status across all layers of the OSI architecture. (T)

Systems Network Architecture (SNA) The description of the logical structure, formats, protocols, and operational sequences for transmitting information units through, and controlling the configuration and operation of, networks.

Note: The layered structure of SNA allows the ultimate origins and destinations of information, that is, the end users, to be independent of and unaffected by the specific SNA network services and facilities used for information exchange. See Figure 148.

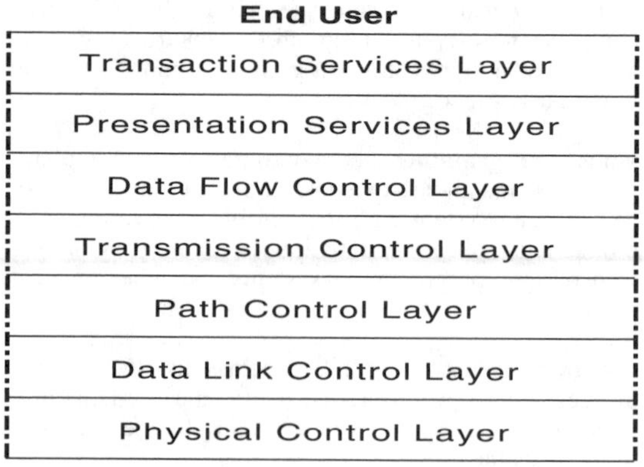

End User

| Transaction Services Layer |
| Presentation Services Layer |
| Data Flow Control Layer |
| Transmission Control Layer |
| Path Control Layer |
| Data Link Control Layer |
| Physical Control Layer |

Figure 148. Systems Network Architecture

system software (1) Application-independent software that supports the running of application software. (T) (2) Software that is part of or made available with a computer system and that determines how application programs are run; for example, an operating system. Contrast with application software.

system space In DPCX, the part of disk storage not available to the user for storing user data.

system-specific format In the AS/400 system, a print descriptor naming convention required to store a print descriptor in a print descriptor group.

system startup Synonym for initial program load.

system supervisor The network control program code that provides the functional interface between the line scheduler and message processing tasks in the background, and the I/O interrupt handlers. It is composed of four services: task, queue, and buffer management, and supervisor services.

system-supplied formats In the AS/400 system, the communications record formats provided as part of the intersystem communications function (ICF) support that allows a user's program to control data communications with a remote system. System-supplied formats perform such communications functions as starting remote programs, sending and receiving data, ending communications transactions, and ending sessions.

system support The continued provision of services and material necessary for the use and improvement of an implemented system. (T) (A)

System Support Program Product (SSP) A group of IBM-licensed programs that manage the running of other programs and the operation of associated devices, such as the display station and printer. The SSP also contains utility programs that perform common tasks, such as copying information from diskette to disk.

system task A control program function performed under control of a task control block.

system termination The state in which all processing on a system is stopped. See also abnormal termination.

system test and evaluation plan Synonym for test plan. (T)

system test time The part of operating time during which the functional unit is tested for proper operation. Since a functional unit may consist of a computer and its operating system, system test time in some cases includes the time for testing computer programs belonging to the operating system. (T) (A)

system time The elapsed time from the point at which a system was started to the current time. If system time is changed to local time when the system is started, the current system time is the local time of day.

system trace A chronological record of specific operating system events. The record is usually produced for debugging purposes.

system unit (1) A part of a computer that contains the processing unit and devices, such as disk and diskette drives. (2) In an IBM personal computer, the unit that contains the processor circuitry, read-only memory (ROM), random access memory (RAM), and the I/O channel. It may have one or two diskette drives. See also expansion unit. See Figure 149.

system user (1) A person, device, or system that uses the facilities of a system. (2) In SDF/CICS, a user with the system user privilege who maintains system objects and is authorized to inspect the passwords of password-protected objects.

system utility device A device assigned for temporary storage of intermediate data for a series of job steps.

system utility programs A collection of problem state programs designed for use by a system programmer in performing such functions as changing or extending the indexing structure of the catalog.

system value In the AS/400 system and System/38, control information for the operation of certain parts

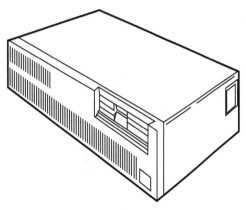

Figure 149. System Unit

of the system; for example, system date and library list. A user can change the system value to define the working environment.

system VM event profile A resource profile that can be used to define the settings for audit and control of VM events for all users. Contrast with individual VM event profile.

Note: On VM/SP, the profile is in the VMEVENT class. On VM/XA, the profile is in the VMXEVENT class.

System/36 environment In the AS/400 system, a function of the operating system that processes most of the System/36 operator control language (OCL) statements and procedure statements to run System/36 application programs and allows the user to process the control language (CL) commands. Contrast with System/38 environment.

System/36 object In the AS/400 system, a configuration description in System/36 terms that defines the System/36 environment.

System/370 mode In VM, a virtual machine operating mode in which System/370 functions are simulated. Contrast with 370-XA mode.

System/38 A general purpose data processing system for interactive and batch processing. The system has several models that vary in the size of main storage and auxiliary storage within the system unit, depending on the model. It also contains a diskette magazine drive and an optional tape drive for offline storage. System/38 allows both local and remote attachment of display stations and printers and supports several communications protocols. See Figure 150.

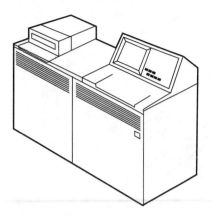

Figure 150. System/38

System/38 environment A function of the operating system that processes most of the System/38 control language (CL) statements and programs to run System/38 application programs. Contrast with System/36 environment.

S/3 System/3.

T

T Tera; ten to the twelfth power, 1,000,000,000,000 in decimal notation. When referring to storage capacity, two to the fortieth power, 1,009,511,627,776 in decimal notation.

tab (1) A preset point in the typing line at which typing or printing stops. A preset point in an output line. (2) In SAA Advanced Common User Access architecture, a typing action that moves the cursor to the beginning of the next entry field or the next selection field if no choice is selected. If the next selection field contains a selected choice, the cursor moves to that choice. Contrast with backtab. (3) In SAA Basic Common User Access architecture, a typing action that moves the cursor to the next entry field. The cursor moves from left to right and top to bottom. At the bottom, right field, the cursor moves to the top, left field. Contrast with backtab. (4) A tab character. (5) To move the imprint position of a printer or typewriter to a preset location. (6) To move a cursor to a preset location on a display screen. (7) See tabulator. (8) See also write-protect tab.

TAB Terminal anchor block.

tabbing The positioning of a cursor to predefined tab positions by means of tabbing function keys. Tabbing can be horizontal or vertical depending on device characteristics.

tab group In AIXwindows, a means of organizing XmPrimitive widgets into groups for more efficient traversal within and between groups.

tab interval A value that determines the number of positions that are to be skipped when the Tab key is pressed.

table (1) An array of data each item of which can be unambiguously identified by means of one or more arguments. (I) (A) (2) A two-dimensional array in which each item and its position with respect to other items is identified. (3) An orderly arrangement of data in rows and columns that can contain numbers, text, or a combination of both. See also translation table. (4) In COBOL, a set of logically consecutive items of data that are defined in the Data Division of a COBOL program by means of the OCCURS clause. (5) In the AS/400 CSP/AE, a collection of related data items arranged as a two-dimensional array of columns and rows that can be used in verifying map inputs or identifying related factors for standard calculations. (6) In RPG, a series of elements with like characteristics. A table can be searched for a uniquely identified element, but elements in a table cannot be accessed by their position relative to other elements. Contrast with array. (7) In SQL, a named data object consisting of a specific number of columns and some unordered rows. (8) A repository for data that NETDA/2 uses to design a network. Each table contains information related to the network. (9) See Boolean operation table, decision table, function table, operation table, translate table, truth table.

table element In COBOL, a data item that belongs to the set of repeated items comprising a table.

table file In RPG, an input file that contains a table.

table lookup A procedure for obtaining the value corresponding to an argument from a table of values. (I) (A)

table lookup instruction An instruction that initiates a table lookup. (I) (A)

table reference character (TRC) In the 3800 Printing Subsystem, a numeric character (0, 1, 2, or 3) corresponding to the order in which the character arrangement table names have been specified with the CHARS keyword. It is used for selection of a character arrangement table during printing.

table space A page set used to store the records of one or more tables in the DB2 program.

tables pack See mass storage control tables pack.

tablet (1) A special flat surface with a mechanism for indicating positions thereon, normally used as a locator. (I) (A) See Figure 151. See also puck.

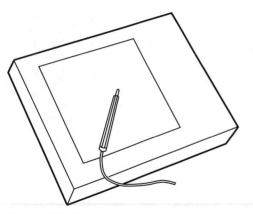

Figure 151. Tablet

table-top word processing equipment Word processing equipment designed as a stand-alone unit for operation on a desk or table. If not integrated word processing equipment, its control unit may be designed also to stand on a desk, table, or elsewhere. (T)

tablet origin A point on a tablet to which all other locations on the tablet correspond. The origin is either the lower-left corner or the center of the tablet.

tabulate (1) To format data into a table. (A) (2) To print totals. (A)

tabulation (1) On a printer, typewriter, or display screen, movement of the writing position to a predetermined location on the same writing line or to a different writing line. (2) See horizontal tabulation, vertical tabulation.

tabulation character See horizontal tabulation character, vertical tabulation character.

tabulator (1) A device that reads data from a data medium such as punched cards or punched tape, and produces lists, tables, or totals. (I) (A) (2) See key-set tabulator, plug-in tabulator. (3) See also tabbing.

tabulator clear key On a typewriter, a control on the keyboard for disengaging individual tabulator stops set in the working position. (T)

tabulator gang clear key On a typewriter, a control for canceling simultaneously all tabulator stops set in the working position. (T)

tabulator key On a typewriter, a control that effects tabulation. (T) See decimal tabulator key, hold-down tabulator key, horizontal tabulator key, latch-out tabulator key, vertical tabulator key. See also

tabulator clear key, tabulator gang clear key, tabulator set key.

tabulator mechanism On a typewriter, an arrangement of components that enables the paper carrier or type element to be moved rapidly to predetermined positions for tabular work. (T)

tabulator set key On a typewriter, a control on the keyboard for setting the tabulator stops in the working position. (T)

tabulator setting In word processing, the feature of a machine that enables tabulator settings to be entered on to the recording medium or into storage so that these settings may be used in subsequent operations. (T)

tabulator stop On a typewriter, that part of the tabulator mechanism that determines the position at which the paper carrier or type element shall stop. (T)

TADAC Tracking analog to digital and comparator.

TAF Terminal access facility.

tag (1) One or more characters attached to a set of data that contain information about the set, including its identification. (I) (A) (2) In Generalized Markup Language markup, a name for a type of document or document element that is entered in the source document to identify it. (3) In AIX graphics, a marker in the display list used as a location for display list editing. (4) Synonym for label.

tag-along sort A sort that arranges records by a specified control field and includes other specified data fields in the output.

tag field In Pascal, the field of a record that defines the structure of a variant part. See also variant part.

tag slot In RSCS, the area in storage that contains status and attribute information pertaining to a spool file that has been accepted and enqueued for transmission by RSCS.

tag sort A sort in which addresses of records (tags), but not the records themselves, are moved during the comparison procedures.

tail frame Synonym for end frame.

tailing A feature on a multichannel modem that allows another modem link to be attached to one of the channels. See also fanout, multitailed, twin-tailed.

tailor In VSE, a process that defines or modifies the characteristics of the system.

take In multimedia applications, one of several attempts to shoot a scene; for example, Scene 1, Take 1; Scene 1, Take 2.

take-grant model See computer security model.

takeoff zone Synonym for landing zone.

takeover The process by which the failing active subsystem is released from its extended recovery facility (XRF) sessions with terminal users and replaced by an alternate subsystem. See resource takeover.

take-up reel A spool on which magnetic tape is wound during the operation of a cartridge or cassette. See also supply reel.

talent In multimedia applications, an on-screen person (a professional or an amateur) who appears before the camera or does voice-over narration.

tally light In video production, a lamp on a camera that indicates that recording is in process.

TAM Telephone answering machine.

tandem data circuit A data circuit that contains more than two data circuit-terminating equipments (DCEs) in series. (I) (A)

tangent point The single point at which a straight line (a tangent line) meets a curve or surface.

tap To briefly touch a touch-sensitive surface with a pointing device and then quickly remove it.

TAP Trace analysis program.

tape See carriage control tape, chadless tape, magnetic tape, perforated tape.

tape cartridge A case containing a reel of magnetic tape that can be put into a tape unit without stringing the tape between reels.

tape code See perforated tape code.

tape deck Deprecated term for magnetic tape unit.

tape drive (1) A device for moving magnetic tape and controlling its movement. Synonymous with tape transport. (T) (2) See magnetic tape drive.

tape frame Synonym for tape row. (T)

tape mark A mark on tape that indicates the beginning or end of a file or tape.

tape punch (1) A punch that automatically produces on a punch tape, a record of data in the form of hole patterns. (T) (2) Synonym for receiving perforator.

tape reader Synonym for punched tape reader.

tape reel See reel.

tape relay A method of relaying messages between transmitting and receiving stations using perforated tape as intermediate storage.

tape reproducer A device that prepares one tape from another tape by copying all or part of the data from the tape that is read. (I) (A)

tape request word See I/O request word.

tape resident system An operating system that uses magnetic tape for online storage of system routines.

tape row A group of binary characters recorded or sensed in parallel on a line perpendicular to the reference edge of a tape. Synonymous with tape frame. (T)

tape spool A cylinder on which tape may be wound. Synonymous with hub.

tape stand-alone dump/restore In DPCX, the stand-alone facility that dumps disk data to tape and restores data from tape to disk.

tape station Deprecated term for magnetic tape unit.

tape storage See magnetic tape storage.

tape-to-card Pertaining to equipment or methods that transmit data from either magnetic tape or punched tape to punched cards.

tape transport (1) The mechanism in a videotape recorder that moves the videotape. (2) Synonym for tape drive. (T) (3) Deprecated term for magnetic tape unit.

tape transport mechanism Synonym for magnetic tape drive.

tape unit (1) A device containing a magnetic tape drive, magnetic heads, and associated controls. (T) (2) See incremental tape unit, magnetic tape unit.

tape volume A reel of magnetic tape.

tape volume table of contents In MVS, information about a tape data set that RACF stores in the TAPEVOL profile for the volume on which the data set resides.

Note: The TVTOC includes the data set name, data set sequence number, creation date, and an indicator as to whether a discrete tape data set profile exists.

target (1) In micrographics, an aid to technical or bibliographic control that is photographed on the film preceding or following an associated document. (T) (2) Pertaining to a storage device to which information is written. (3) The program or system to which a request is sent. (4) The location to which the information is destined. (5) A system, program, or device that interprets, rejects or satisfies, and replies to requests received from a source. (6) Contrast with source.

target data set In DPPX, a relative sequential data set containing user data and imbedded keys that correspond to keys in an index data set and that can be used to access the data.

target directory The directory to which information is written. Contrast with source directory.

target diskette In a diskette or storage copying procedure, the diskette onto which information is written. Contrast with source diskette.

target drive The drive to which information is written.

target language (1) The output language of a translator. (T) (2) Synonymous with object language.

target libraries In SMP/E, a collection of data sets in which the various parts of an operating system are stored. These data sets are sometimes called system libraries.

target path A directory description that indicates where a file is to be stored on a particular drive.

target program (1) In communications, the program that is started on the remote system at the request of the source system. Contrast with source program. (2) In AS/400 display station passthrough, a program that runs on the remote system. (3) Synonym for object program. (A)

target segment In IMS/VS secondary indexing, the segment to be retrieved.

target system (1) The system that receives a request from another system to establish communications. (2) In a distributed data management (DDM) network, the system that receives a request from an application program on another system to use one or more files located on the target system. Contrast with source system.

target zone In SMP/E, a collection of VSAM records describing the target system macros, modules, assemblies, load modules, source modules, and libraries copied from DLIBs during system generation, and the SYSMODs applied to the target system.

tariff (1) The published rate for a specific unit of equipment, facility, or type of service provided by a telecommunication facility. Also, the vehicle by which regulating agencies, such as the FCC in the US, approve or disapprove such facilities or services. (2) In a packet-switching data network, the fee charged to a user for sending data. The tariff is usually based on the number of packets sent over the network.

task (1) In a multiprogramming or multiprocessing environment, one or more sequences of instructions treated by a control program as an element of work to be accomplished by a computer. (I) (A) (2) In DPCX, a unit of work for the processor that is used for the execution of a program or a system function. A task is represented by a series of 256-byte blocks called the symbolic machine. (3) In VSE, the basic unit of synchronous program execution. A task competes with other tasks for computer system resources such as processing time and I/O channels. (4) See data services task, hardcopy task, logger task, operator station task, TCAM control task.

task dispatcher In OS/VS, the control program function that selects from the task queue the task that is to have control of the processing unit and gives control to that task.

task dump In System/36, a dump of a program that has failed along with its associated data. Contrast with system dump.

task execution area In DPCX, an area of processor storage in which the symbolic machines of active tasks reside during execution.

task identification (task ID) In the 3660 Supermarket Store System, Subsystem Support Services, and SPPS, any of nine IDs (SA through SI) coded in columns 73 – 74 of subsystem definition statements. Each task ID corresponds to a function that the supermarket host program performs. Subsystem Support Services uses the task ID to call the supermarket-unique modules needed to process the definition statement. See also subsystem definition statement.

tasking See multitasking.

task management The functions of the control program that regulate use by tasks of the processing unit and other resources, except for input/output devices.

task panel Online display from which you communicate with the program in order to accomplish the program's function, either by selecting an option provided on the panel or by entering an explicit command. See help panel.

task queue A queue of all task control blocks present in a system at the same time.

task-scheduling priorities A network control program method of ordering the sequence of task execution according to changing network conditions. Tasks are dispatched in this order: appendage tasks, immediate tasks, productive tasks, and nonproductive tasks.

task start The creation of a new task in a system.

task state (1) The state of execution status of a task relative to the processor: active state, ready state, suspended state, and wait state. (2) In the network control program, the active state, ready state, pending state, and disconnect state.

task switch (1) Allocation of a processor to another task; for example, a ready or active task of higher priority than task currently in execution. (2) A change in a task in control of the processor. State of the task changes from ready to active, and current task is placed in a state other than active.

task virtual storage In DPCX, up to 32 kilobytes assigned to a task for a specific use. Task virtual storage is paged between an associative storage pool in processor storage and a virtual storage paging area on disk.

TB Terabyte.

TC (1) Transmission control. (2) Test control.

TCAM Telecommunications Access Method. See Advanced Communications Function for the Telecommunications Access Method.

TCAM application program A user-written program that interfaces with the message control program (MCP) using READ, WRITE, CHECK, GET, or PUT macroinstructions.

TCAM control task (TCT) In NCCF, the subtask that controls communication between NCCF and ACF/TCAM.

TCAM host logical unit (LU) A TCAM-generated logical unit (LU) that is the access method control block (ACB) interface to VTAM; for example, PROGID. External LUs must establish a session with a TCAM host LU in order to use TCAM services. See host logical unit (LU).

TCAM network address (1) In an ACF/TCAM extended network, a unique identifier for an application program or an external logical unit (LU). A TCAM network address consists of a node identifier and a resource identifier. See also node identifier, resource identifier. (2) The TCAM origin address field (TOAF) and TCAM destination address field (TDAF) in the fixed header prefix associated with a message. Contrast with SNA network address.

TCAM node A message control program (MCP) to which a node identifier has been assigned. See also node identifier.

TCAM system A subsystem controlled by a single message control program (MCP) with a collection of external logical units (LUs) and application programs.

TCAS Terminal control address space.

TCB Trusted computing base.

TCF Terminal configuration facility.

TCP Transmission Control Protocol.

TCP/IP Transmission Control Protocol/Internet Protocol. A set of communication protocols that support peer-to-peer connectivity functions for both local and wide area networks.

TCT (1) TCAM control task. (2) Terminal control table.

TCU Transmission control unit.

T-disk See temporary disk.

TDL (1) Transformation definition language. (2) Terminal display language.

TDLC Twinaxial data link control.

TDM Time-division multiplexing.

TDU Topology database update.

technical information exchange (TIE) A part of the electronic customer support function that allows a user to send files to and receive files from an IBM support system, and to search for information on an IBM support system. The files are sent and received through an IBM Information Network.

technical process A set of operations performed by equipment in which physical variables must be monitored or controlled; for example, in a refinery, distillation and condensation; in an aircraft, autopiloting and automatic landing. (T)

technique See paging technique. (A)

TECT Temporary error counter.

tele-autograph A writing telegraph instrument, in which movement of a pen in the transmitting apparatus varies the current in two circuits in such a way as to cause corresponding movement of a pen at the remote receiving instrument. Synonymous with telewriter.

telecine Synonym for film chain.

telecommunication (1) The transmission of control signals and information between two or more locations, such as by telegraph, radio, or television. (2) The transmission of data between computer systems over telecommunication lines and between a computer system and remote devices.

telecommunication administration Any governmental department or service responsible for discharging the obligations undertaken in the Convention of the International Telecommunication Union and in the Regulations. See also Recognized Private Operating Agency.

telecommunication control unit See communication control unit.

telecommunication facility Transmission capabilities, or the means for providing such capabilities, made available by a communication common carrier or by a telecommunication Administration.

telecommunication line (1) The portion of a data circuit external to a data-circuit terminating equipment (DCE) that connects the DCE to a data-switching exchange (DSE), that connects a DCE to one or more other DCEs, or that connects a DSE to another DSE. (T) (2) Any physical medium, such as a wire or microwave beam, that is used to transmit data. (3) Synonymous with data transmission line, transmission line. (4) Contrast with data link.

Note: A telecommunication line is the physical medium; for example, a telephone wire, a microwave beam. A data link includes the physical medium of transmission, the protocol, and associated devices and programs; it is both logical and physical.

Telecommunications Access Method (TCAM) An access method used to transfer data between main storage and remote or local terminals.

teleconferencing Interactive communication among participants at different locations, conference calls and videoconferencing with still or moving images. (T) See also conference call, videoconferencing.

telecopier Synonym for facsimile machine.

telecopy Synonym for fax.

telefax Synonym for facsimile. (T)

telegraph A system employing the interruption or change in polarity of direct current for the transmission of signals. See also polar transmission.

telegraph grade circuit A circuit suitable for transmission by teletypewriter equipment. Normally, the circuit is considered to use DC signaling at a maximum speed of 75 bauds.

telemeter To transmit digital or analog metering data by telecommunication facilities; for example, data can be telemetered from a satellite and recorded at a ground station. See Figure 152.

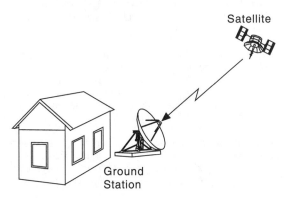

Figure 152. Telemeter

Telepak A leased channel offering of telephone companies and Western Union providing specific-size bundles of voice-grade, telegraph-grade, subvoice-grade, and broadband channels between two points; also just the broadband channels. Mileage charges are constant for each mile rather than regressive as in conventional single-leased lines.

telephone call state In telephony, the condition of a telephone call that reflects what the past action on that call has been and what the next set of actions may be.

telephone recording attachment A device that enables telephone conversations to be recorded on a dictation machine. (I)

telephone recording control On dictation equipment, a control for switching on or off the telephone recording attachment. (I)

telephony The use or operation of systems for the transmission of voice or data communications between separate points.

teleprocessing (1) Synonym for remote access data processing. Deprecated term for distributed data processing. (2) See also distributed function.

teleprocessing network Synonym for remote access data processing network.

teleprocessing network simulator (TPNS) A testing package that enables a user to test and evaluate teleprocessing systems before actual terminal installation.

teleprocessing online test executive (TOTE) In ACF/TCAM, a facility that allows a system console operator or a remote control station user to test communication controllers, transmission control units, and stations not attached through the network control program.

teleprocessing request block (TPRB) A function used by NPM to control input/output requests to or from terminals to files.

teletex An international electronic mail service that provides letter-quality communications among subscribers. Teletex is an enhanced version of telex. It provides both uppercase and lowercase transmission at higher speeds than telex. (T)   See also videotex.

teletext A broadcasting service that provides selectable text material such as news, weather reports, and advertisements, directly to a subscriber's television set. The subscriber must have a special decoder to receive teletext signals.   Synonymous with broadcast videography.   (T)

Teletype Trademark of Teletype Corporation, usually referring to a series of different types of teleprinter equipment such as tape punches, reperforators, and page printers, utilized for telecommunication.

teletypewriter exchange service (TWX) Teletypewriter service in which suitably arranged teletypewriter stations are provided with lines to a central office for access to other such stations throughout the US and Canada. Both baudot- and ASCII-coded machines are used. Business machines may also be used, with certain restrictions.

teletypewriter switching systems Total message switching systems where the terminals are teletypewriter equipment.

telewriter Synonym for teleautograph.

telex An international public switched service for text transmission between teleprinters or compatible devices. (T)

Telnet In TCP/IP, an application protocol that allows a user at one site to access a remote system as if the user's display station were locally attached.   Telnet uses the Transmission Control Protocol as the underlying protocol.

temperature coefficient The measure of a change in mean error resulting from temperature variations.

TEMPID Temporary identifier.

template (1) A pattern to help the user identify the location of keys on a keyboard, functions assigned to keys on a keyboard, or switches and lights on a control panel. (2) A line entered from a keyboard and stored in memory from which it can be retrieved, used again, or modified. See also keyboard overlay. (3) In System/38, a contiguous string of bytes that defines the attributes or values of a machine interface object. (4) See error record template.

temporary data Data that are retained only for the duration of the process with which they are associated. Contrast with retained data.

temporary data set A data set that is created and deleted in the same job. Contrast with nontemporary data set.

temporary disk In VM, an area on a direct access storage device allocated to the user at logon time or allocated via the CP DEFINE command on which newly created or stored files are retained until logoff, at which time the area is released.

temporary error A resource failure that can be resolved by error recovery programs.   Synonymous with performance error.   Contrast with permanent error.

temporary file A file that can be erased or overwritten when it is no longer needed.   Contrast with permanent file.

temporary group In the AS/400 system, a list of existing calendars used to schedule items for a group of users in one step.   The list can be used in the current session only, after which the list is deleted.

temporary identifier (TEMPID) In the ImagePlus system, the temporary identification of a document, generated by the front-end application, when it is scanned into the system.

temporary library In the AS/400 system, a library that is automatically created for each job to contain temporary objects that are created by the system for that job.   The objects in the temporary library are deleted when the job ends.

temporary memory In an IBM personal computer, synonym for user memory.

temporary objects In the AS/400 system, objects, such as data paths or compiler work areas, that are automatically deleted by the system when the operating system is loaded.

temporary read/write error An error that is eliminated by retrying a read/write operation.

temporary storage In computer programming, storage locations reserved for intermediate results. (A) Synonymous with working storage.

temporary text delay (TTD) A control character sequence sent by a transmitting station either to indicate a delay in transmission or to initiate an abort of the transmission in progress.

temporary-text-delay (TTD) character In BSC, a transmission control character that is used to maintain the data link when no text is being transmitted. TTD indicates to the receiving station that there is a temporary delay in transmission of data.

tens complement The radix complement in the decimal numeration system. (I) (A) Synonymous with complement-on-ten.

tensile strength A measure of the tension that a material such as continuous forms can accept without tearing.

tensioning In the 3800 Printing Subsystem, stretching or causing extension of continuous forms while they are threaded in the printer.

tera (1) Ten to the twelfth power; 1,000,000,000,000 in decimal notation. When referring to storage capacity, two to the fortieth power; 1,099,511,627,776 in decimal notation. (2) A unit of measure equal to 10^{12} bytes; 1 000 000 000 000 in decimal notation.

term (1) A construct in a conceptual schema language that refers to an entity. (T) (2) The smallest part of an expression that can be assigned a value. (3) See absolute term, arithmetic term, logical term, relocatable term.

terminal (1) A functional unit in a system or communication network at which data may enter or leave. (T) (2) A point in a system or communication network at which data can either enter or leave. (A) (3) A device, usually equipped with a keyboard and display device, capable of sending and receiving information. (4) In COBOL, the originator of a transmission to a queue, or the receiver of a transmission from a queue.

Note: The terms terminal and workstation are often used interchangeably. However, a terminal may not have a human operator. A workstation is a terminal at which a human operator performs an application.

terminal access facility (TAF) In the NetView program, a facility that allows a network operator to control a number of subsystems. In a full-screen or operator control session, operators can control any combination of such subsystems simultaneously.

terminal address card In a 3600 Finance Communication System, an addressable logic element that connects a terminal to a local loop or to a subloop, and that handles signals passing through the terminal. Synonymous with terminal loop adapter.

terminal component A separately addressable part of a terminal that performs an input or output function, such as the display component of a keyboard-display device or a printer component of a keyboard-printer device.

terminal configuration facility (TCF) A set of macrostatements to be coded by the user and modules in programmable store system host support that are used to define and create the terminal operational environment.

terminal control address space (TCAS) The part of TSO/VTAM that provides logon services for TSO/VTAM users.

Terminal Control table (TCT) A table describing a configuration of terminals, logical units, or other CICS systems in a CICS network with which the CICS system communicates.

terminal descriptor In the AIX object data manager (ODM), a named variable of the type short, long, binary, char, or vchar used to define the basic data types in an ODM object class definition. See also binary, char, long, object class, short, vchar.

terminal display language (TDL) A set of SPPS II statements coded by the application programmer to control the IBM 3275 Display Station screen. These statements define the formats of data to be transferred between a keyboard/display and an application program buffer. They require translation by the terminal definition language translator. See also transformation definition language.

terminal emulation The capability of a microcomputer or personal computer to operate as if it were a particular type of terminal linked to a processing unit and to access data. See also download, upload.

terminal emulator A program that allows a device such as a microcomputer or personal computer to enter and receive data from a computer system as if it were a particular type of attached terminal. See also download, upload.

terminal entry (1) Any input operation on a terminal. (2) See terminal-table entry.

terminal equipment See data terminal equipment.

terminal equipment subport (TESP) A subport that serves as a termination point on a virtual circuit. Contrast with frame handler subport (FHSP).

terminal input buffer Synonym for console stack.

terminal input/output task (TIOT) In the 3680 Programmable Store System, an execution of a program that provides communication between an I/O device in a terminal; for example, a display, cash drawer, or printer, and the control segment of a 3684 Model 2 Point of Sale Control Unit associated with the terminal. There must be a TIOT task in a 3683 Point of Sale Terminal, and there may be one in a 3684 Model 1.

terminal I/O wait The condition of a task in which the task cannot continue processing until a message is received from a terminal.

terminal job In systems with time sharing, the processing performed on behalf of one terminal user from logon to logoff.

terminal loop adapter Synonym for terminal address card.

terminal monitor program (TMP) In TSO, a program that accepts and interprets commands from the terminal and causes the appropriate command processors to be scheduled and executed.

terminal node (1) In a hierarchical database, a node that has no subordinate records or segments. (2) In SNA products, a peripheral node that is not user-programmable and has less processing capability than a cluster controller node. Examples are nodes consisting of the IBM 3277 Data Station, 3767 Communication Terminal, 3614 Consumer Transaction Facility, and 3624 Consumer Transaction Facility.

terminal port (1) In a network, the functional unit of a node through which data can enter or leave the network. (T) (2) The part of a processor that is dedicated to a single data channel for the purpose of receiving data from or transferring data to one or more external or remote devices.

terminal quiesce An orderly shutdown of all terminal activity.

terminal-related main storage database In IMS/VS, a type of main storage database (MSDB) in which: (1) each segment is assigned to and owned by one logical terminal (LTERM), (2) the owner with terminal security may alter or update that segment, and (3) a segment may be referred to by someone other than the owner.

Note: Terminal-related MSDBs may be fixed, allowing changes; or dynamic, permitting segment insertion and deletion.

terminal repeater A repeater for use at the end of a trunk line.

terminal response mode In IMS/VS, a type of response mode that suspends all input operations from the terminal until the application program generates the output message. See also line response mode, response mode.

terminal room A room associated with a telephone central office, private branch exchange, or private exchange that contains distributing frames, relays, and similar apparatus except for the apparatus mounted in the switchboard sections.

terminal screen Synonym for display screen.

terminal security In IMS/VS, the use of system definition macros and security maintenance utility control statements to authorize a particular logical or physical terminal to issue some or all of the operator commands and to send or receive some or all of the defined transactions.

terminal session (1) The period of time during which a user of a terminal can communicate with an interactive system. Usually, it is the elapsed time from when a terminal user logs on the system until the user logs off. (2) In VM, the period of time from logon to final logoff when a user and the virtual machine can utilize the facilities of CP, CMS, RSCS, IPCS, or the operating system. This includes any time when the virtual machine is running in disconnect mode. See also disconnect mode. (3) See session.

terminal table In ACF/TCAM, an ordered collection of information about each origin or destination of messages in the network. See also terminal-table entry.

terminal-table entry (TTE) In ACF/TCAM, information in a terminal table identifying each origin or destination of messages in a network. See cascade entry, group entry, line entry, logtype entry, process entry, single entry.

terminal transaction facility (TTF) A program that handles terminal control functions for VSE/ICCF when CICS/VS is not being used. TTF, an integral part of

VSE/ICCF, is the minimal terminal control program required for the product.

terminal user In systems with time sharing, anyone who is eligible to log on.

terminate (1) In SNA products, a request unit that is sent by a logical unit (LU) to its system services control point (SSCP) to cause the SSCP to start a procedure for ending one or more designated LU-LU sessions. (2) To stop the operation of a system or device. (3) To stop execution of a program. See also abnormal termination.

TERMINATE In SNA, a request unit that is sent by a logical unit (LU) to its system services control point (SSCP) to cause the SSCP to start a procedure to end one or more designated LU-LU sessions.

terminated line A telecommunication line with a resistance attached across its far end equal to the characteristic impedance of the line, so that no reflection and no standing waves are present when a signal is placed on it at the near end. Contrast with bridge tap.

terminate graphics In System/38 graphics, to end the state in which calls to GDDM and PGR routines can occur. Contrast with initialize graphics.

terminating plug A part that ends the cable path on a computer system. The terminating plug is attached to the last disk, diskette, or tape unit in a series.

terminating room See wiring closet.

termination (1) The act of putting a system or an element of a system in a state in which it no longer performs its normal function. See also system termination. (2) Cessation of the execution of a task. See also closedown. (3) See abnormal termination, LU-LU session termination.

terminator (1) The part of a program that performs the action necessary to end a job or program. (2) In System/36, the part of the System Support Program Product that performs the action necessary to end a job or program. (3) See explicit scope terminator, implicit scope terminator.

ternary (1) Pertaining to a selection, choice, or condition that has three possible different values or states. (I) (A) (2) Pertaining to a fixed-radix numeration system having a radix of three. (I) (A)

ternary incremental representation Incremental representation in which the value of an increment is rounded to one of three values, plus or minus one quantum or zero. (I) (A)

tertiary device In DPCX, an I/O device assigned to a DPCX task through the third of a set of device fields in the primary application block (PAB). A tertiary device can be a 3277 Display Station, printer, diskette, or tape unit; or transaction, print, or transmit data sets. See also primary device, secondary device.

TESP Terminal equipment subport.

test (1) The operation of a functional unit and comparison of its achieved result with the defined result to establish acceptability; for example, a device test or program test. (T) (2) See marginal test, usability test, validation test, verification test.

test condition A statement that, when taken as a whole, may be either true or false, depending on the circumstances existing at the time the expression is evaluated.

test control (TC) A signal sent by the data terminal equipment (DTE) to the attached data circuit-terminating equipment (DCE) to signal a testing mode.

test data The data used for a check problem. (T)

testing The running of a system or a program against a predetermined series of data to arrive at a predictable result for the purpose of establishing the acceptability of the system or program. (T)

test instruction An instruction that checks the condition of data and that sets status or overflow flag bits for a subsequent branch instruction. In some instances, test and branch are considered a dual operation within a single instruction. (A)

test library (1) A library used for diagnostic operations. It does not contain the data needed for normal processing. Contrast with production library. (2) In the AS/400 system, a user-defined library used for debugging operations that does not contain objects needed for normal processing. Contrast with production library.

test plan A plan that establishes detailed requirements, criteria, general methodology, responsibilities, and general planning for test and evaluation of a system. (T)

test request message (TRM) In the network control program, a message entered from a station or console requesting that a specified online terminal test be performed on that station or console or on another station or console. The network control program passes the test request message to ACF/TCAM in the host.

test task In DPCX with the program execution monitor, the task in which the program or subtask to be monitored is executed.

test terminal In DPCX with the program execution monitor, the terminal at which a test task is initiated to execute a program to be monitored. The test terminal serves as the primary device of the test task.

test time See program test time, system test time.

test tone A tone used in identifying circuits for trouble location or for circuit adjustment. See also standard test tone power.

test value A value used to compare for a specified condition.

text (1) In text processing, a sequence of elements intended to convey a meaning, whose interpretation is essentially based upon the reader's knowledge of some natural language or artificial language; for example, a business letter printed on paper or displayed on a screen. The elements may consist of characters, symbols, words, phrases, paragraphs, sentences, or tables. (T) Synonymous with word processing. (2) In the ASCII and data communication, a sequence of characters treated as an entity if preceded and terminated by one STX and one ETX communication control character, respectively. (A) (3) The part of a message that is not the header or control information. See message text. (4) Contrast with heading. (5) In AIX kernel mode, kernel program code that is run. It is read only by a user process. (6) See geometric text, library text, pseudo-text.

text area The area of a single page or screen in which graphic elements may normally appear. Synonymous with type area. (T)

text attribute In GDDM, characteristics of chart information, such as color or type style.

text body The main body of printed or written matter, excluding headers and footers on a page.

text box In System/38 graphics, the imaginary rectangle that encloses a string of mode-2 or mode-3 graphics symbols.

text buffer In ACF/TCAM, a buffer containing any segment of a message other than the first segment, which is contained in a header buffer. Contrast with header buffer.

text compression See compression.

text control In the 3800 Printing Subsystem, structured field data that control the printing of text. Text controls appear in composed-text data structured fields.

text control chaining In the 3800 Printing Subsystem, two or more text controls that are started with a single set of control characters.

text control sequence In the 3800 Printing Subsystem, a text control and its associated data.

text-coordinate origin The origin of a composed-text block.

text cursor In SAA Advanced Common User Access architecture, a symbol displayed in an entry field that shows a user where typed or pasted input will appear. See also selection cursor.

text editing (1) The process of manipulating text, such as rearranging or changing text, including additions and deletions or reformatting. Synonymous with editing, text revision. (T) (2) In word processing, the process of making additions, deletions, and changes in a stored document.

text editor (1) A computer program that enables a user to create and revise text. (T) (2) A program used to create, modify, and print or display text files.

text formatting program A program that determines the manner in which data will be placed on a page.

text library (1) In VM, a CMS file that contains relocatable object modules and a directory that indicates the location of each of the modules within the library. (2) In System/36, a library of documents created and maintained using WP/36.

text line A line that contains only text.

text lock In AIX, a lock that allows the calling process to lock or unlock its text segments into memory.

text-name In COBOL, a user-defined word that identifies library text.

text orientation A description of the appearance of text as a combination of print direction and character rotation.

textport In AIX graphics, a region on the display screen used to present textual output from graphical or nongraphical programs.

Text Pop-up button In the IBM LinkWay product, a type of LinkWay button object that displays a "window" containing text. The window "pops up" on the screen when the user clicks on this type of button.

text processing (1) Performing operations on text, such as entering, editing, sorting, merging, or printing, using hardware and software. Synonymous with word processing. (T) (2) Pertaining to computer systems, stand-alone devices, and application software products that allow a user to enter, modify, rearrange, format, display, and print out text. Synonymous with word processing.

Note: The term text processing is often used to describe entry, modification, formatting, display, and printing of text on mainframe computers. The term word processing is frequently used to describe the performance of the same functions on personal computers, microprocessors, and stand-alone word processors.

text processor A device with associated software or a computer program that allows a user to do text processing. Synonymous with word processor. (T)

text revision (1) The process of changing the information content of a document. (A) (2) Synonym for text editing. (T)

text segment A portion of a message that contains no part of the message header.

text stream In the C and Pascal languages, an ordered sequence of characters where each sequence or line is ended with a new line control sequence and consists of zero or more characters. characters sent in the data are treated as specific bit patterns, unless they are preceded by the DLE control character.

text string search In word processing, a function that enables a point or points to be found within the recorded text by entering a set of unique characters identifying the desired point. (T)

text suppression The intentional omission of portions of text.

text transmission Electronic transfer of text from one point to another over a network. (T)

text transparency A provision that allows BSC to send and receive messages containing any or all of the 256 character combinations in EBCDIC, including transmission control characters. Transmission control characters sent in a message are treated as data unless they are preceded by the DLE control character.

textual edit In the 3660 Supermarket Store System, the verification of parameters coded in the subsystem definition statements. This edit makes punctuation and syntactical checks of the definition statements. Contrast with logical edit. See also subsystem definition statement.

textual scrolling information In SAA Basic Common User Access architecture, a type of scrolling information that can be used with scrolling arrows. Textual

scrolling information uses the words Bottom and More... to tell a user the relative position of the cursor within scrollable information.

textual scrolling location information In SAA Basic Common User Access architecture, a type of scrolling information that gives a user optional information about the relative position of the cursor within scrollable information; for example:

```
Lines 5 to 18 of 180
```

texture In computer graphics, a pattern used to fill display objects.

text word In COBOL, a character or a sequence of contiguous characters between margin A and margin R in a COBOL library, source program, or in pseudo-text that is:

1. A separator, except for: space, a pseudo-text delimiter, and the opening and closing delimiters for nonnumeric literals. The right parenthesis and left parenthesis characters, regardless of context within the library, source program, or pseudo-text, are always considered text words.

2. A literal including, in the case of nonnumeric literals, the opening quotation mark and the closing quotation mark that bound the literal.

3. Any other sequence of contiguous COBOL characters except comment lines and the word "COPY," bounded by separators, which is neither a separator nor a literal.

text wrap See word wrap.

TG Transmission group.

TGID Transmission group identifier.

TG vector See transmission group vector.

TG weight A quantitative measure of how well the values of a transmission group's (TG's) characteristics satisfy the criteria specified by the class-of-service definition, as computed during route selection for a session. If the TG does not satisfy the criteria specified by the class-of-service definition, it is assigned an infinite weight.

TH Transmission header.

thermal printer A nonimpact printer in which the characters are produced by applying heated elements to heat-sensitive paper directly or by melting ink from a ribbon onto plain paper. (T)

thermal stencil In a duplicator, a specially coated fibrous tissue master on which an image is produced by heat reflection. (T) See also electronic stencil, pressure stencil.

thermal-type spirit master In a duplicator, a master made by placing a sheet of suitable material in contact with the coated face of a transfer sheet and applying, pressure on the face of the master by means of typing, writing, drawing, or die-impressing. (T)

thermal-type spirit transfer sheet In a duplicator, a sheet of material specially coated with a compound that is transferred to a master by heat reflection from an original document. (T)

thermographic document copying machine A document copying machine that uses the thermographic process. (T)

thermographic process In a document copying machine, a process in which the copy results from the effect of infrared radiation on specially prepared material. (T)

thin film Loosely, magnetic thin film. (A)

thin film storage Loosely, magnetic thin film storage. (A)

think time Synonym for intermessage delay.

third-generation computer A computer that uses logic technology components.

third-level storage The virtual storage created and controlled by an OS/VS, or VM virtual machine. See also first-level storage, second-level storage.

thousands separator The character (a comma in the United States) placed every third number starting left of the decimal point; for example, three thousands separators are used in the number: 641,322,974,821.

thrashing (1) In a virtual storage system, a condition in which the system can do little useful work because of excessive paging. (2) In the Data Facility Hierarchical Storage Manager, a condition in which the system can do little useful work because of excessive data movement between primary and migration volumes.

thread (1) In the OS/2 operating system, the smallest unit of operation to be performed within a process. (2) A link between an IMS/VS subsystem and a Database 2 (DB2) subsystem; resources in the external DB2 subsystem are allocated to that link or thread. (3) In DPPX, a collection of processes whose order determines the process eligible for execution. A thread is the element that is scheduled, and to which resources such as execution time, locks, and queues may be assigned.

threading Passing paper by hand through the paper line.

threat In computer security, any circumstance or event with the potential to cause harm to a system in the form of destruction, disclosure, modification of data, or denial of service. See also attack.

threat agent In computer security, a method used to exploit a vulnerability in a system, operation, or facility.

threat analysis In computer security, the examination of all actions and events that might adversely affect a system, operation, or facility. See also risk analysis.

threat monitoring In computer security, the analysis, assessment, and review of audit trails and other data collected for the purpose of searching out system events that may constitute violations or attempted violations of system security.

three-address instruction An instruction that contains three address parts. (I) (A)

three-bit byte Synonym for triplet.

three-input adder Synonym for full adder.

three-plus-one address instruction An instruction that contains three address parts. The plus-one address is the address of the next instruction to be executed unless otherwise specified. (I) (A)

three-point curve In computer graphics, a shape in which two points anchor the ends of a curve and the third selects the apex.

three-quarter-inch videotape A videotape format used for most industrial video applications. It is sold in inch-thick cassettes.

three-schema architecture A database architecture comprising three schemas: the conceptual schema, the internal schema, and the subschemas. (T)

threshold (1) A logic operator having the property that if P is a statement, Q is a statement, R is a statement, ..., then the threshold of P, Q, R, ... is true if at least N statements are true, false if less than N statements are true, where N is a specified nonnegative integer called the threshold condition. (A) (2) The threshold condition as in *(1)*. (A) (3) In computer graphics, a level above which all gray-scale image data can be represented as white and below which all gray-scale image data can be represented as black. (4) In the AS/400 system, a level set in the system at which a message is sent or an error-handling program is called; for example, in a user auxiliary storage pool, the user can set the threshold level in the system values, and the system notifies the system operator when that level is reached. (5) In the NetView program, a percentage value, set for a resource and compared to a calculated error-to-traffic ratio. (6) In NPM, high or low values supplied by the user to monitor data and statistics being collected. (7) See fault-rate threshold, fault threshold, mouse threshold.

threshold analysis and remote access (1) A component of the NetView program that can notify a central operator about network problems and errors. It provides remote control of IBM 3600 and 4700 controllers and can record, analyze, and display performance and status data on IBM 3600 and 4700 Finance Communications Systems. (2) The feature of the back-level NPDA licensed program that performs some of these functions.

threshold element Synonym for threshold gate.

threshold function A two-value switching function of one or more not necessarily Boolean arguments that take the value one if a specified mathematical function of the arguments exceeds a given threshold value, and zero otherwise. For example, the threshold function:

$$f(a_1,...., a_n) = 0 \text{ if } g \leq T$$
$$f(a_1,...., a_n) = 1 \text{ if } g > T$$
$$\text{with } g = W_1 a_1 + ... + W_n a_n$$

where W_1, ..., W_n are positive weights for the real arguments a_1, ..., a_n and T is the threshold. (I) (A)

threshold gate (1) A logic element that performs a threshold operation. Synonymous with threshold element. (T) (2) A device that performs the logic threshold operation but in which the truth of each input statement contributes to the output determination a weight associated with that statement.

thresholding In computer graphics, converting gray-scale image data to binary image data by representing all gray-scale image data above a certain level as 1, indicating white, and all gray-scale data below that level as 0, indicating black.

threshold operation An operation that evaluates the threshold function of its operands. (I) (A)

threshold quantity The number of items that must be purchased to qualify for a reduced price.

throughput (1) A measure of the amount of work performed by a computer system over a period of time, for example, number of jobs per day. (I) (A) (2) In data communication, the total traffic between stations per unit of time. (3) See problem throughput.

throughput class negotiation A packet switching data network optional facility that allows a data terminal equipment (DTE) to negotiate the speed at which its packets travel through the packet switching data network.

thumb wheel In computer graphics, a wheel, movable about its axis, that provides a scalar value. A pair of thumb wheels can be used as a locator. (I) (A)

TIB Task information block.

TIC Token-ring interface coupler.

tick In the AS/400 Business Graphics Utility, a reference point on either the vertical or horizontal axis of some chart types that represents the location of specified data values. See also major tick, minor tick.

ticket In computer security, a representation of one or more access rights that any processor has to an object. See also capability.

ticket-based access control In computer security, access control in which access rights occur in ticket lists. See also list-based access control.

ticket list In computer security, a collection of all tickets for one subject's access rights

ticking In OCR, the marks caused by the bottom of the upper case character while typing in lower case, or vice versa.

TID Task identifier.

tie In perforated continuous forms paper, the interval between cuts.

TIE Technical information exchange.

tie line A private-line communication channel of the type provided by communication common carriers for linking two or more points together.

tie trunk A telephone line or channel directly connecting two branch exchanges.

TIFF (Tag Image File Format) In computer graphics, a graphic file format used to store and exchange scanned images; compatible with a number of personal computing platforms.

tightly coupled multiprocessing In the System/370 system, multiprocessing in which two or more processing units share real storage, are controlled by the same control program, and can communicate directly with each other. See also loosely coupled multiprocessing.

TIK Task identification key.

tile (1) One of several nonoverlapping, rectangular divisions of a display screen. (2) In the AIX operating system: (a) To fill a region with a pixmap. (b) To replicate a pixmap in two dimensions.

Tile In SAA Advanced Common User Access architecture, a choice in the Window pull-down of some applications. It modifies the size of each secondary window and icon and arranges the windows so that they appear side-by-side and top-to-bottom.

till A tray in the cash drawer or the point of sale terminal, used to keep the different denominations of bills and coins separated and easily accessible.

tilt In multimedia applications, a camera movement in which the camera pivots up or down on its stationary tripod.

time See access time, assembly time, available time, compilation time, down time, environmental loss time, external loss time, incidental time, inoperable time, makeup time, miscellaneous time, operable time, operating time, program production time, program test time, read cycle time, real time, recovery time, rerun time, response time, system production time, system test time, turnaround time, unavailable time, uptime, write cycle time. (A)

time base In video systems, the timing of a portion of the video signal, particularly the horizontal and vertical sync pulses.

time base corrector (TBC) In video systems, a device that corrects for time base errors in video tape recorders.

time base errors In video tape recorders, analog artifacts caused by the tape or tape head drum not moving in a consistent speed.

time bomb In computer security, a Trojan horse that is inserted to be triggered later.

time code See SMPTE time code.

time-critical process In the OS/2 operating system, a process that must be performed within a specified time after an event has occurred.

time-division multiplexing (TDM) Division of a transmission facility into two or more channels by allotting the common channel to several different information channels, one at a time. See also frequency-division multiplexing.

time frame A defined structure, based on two or more events, using time as a basis of measurement. (T)

time-line processor A type of authoring facility that displays an event as elements that represent time from the start of the event.

time-of-day (TOD) clock A System/370 hardware feature that is incremented once every microsecond, and provides a consistent measure of elapsed time suitable for indicating date and time. The TOD clock runs regardless of whether the processing unit is in a running, wait, or stopped state.

timeout (1) An event that occurs at the end of a predetermined period of time that began at the occurrence of another specified event. (I) (2) A time interval allotted for certain operations to occur; for example, response to polling or addressing before system operation is interrupted and must be restarted. (3) A terminal feature that logs off a user if an entry is not made within a specified period of time. (4) See acknowledge timeout, receive timeout.

Note: Timeout can be prevented by an appropriate signal.

time-out control A network control program function that presents an interruption to indicate that a predetermined period of time has elapsed without occurrence of an expected event.

timeout recovery Restarting system operations after they have been interrupted by failure of a certain event to occur.

timer A register whose contents are changed at regular intervals in such a manner as to measure time. (T) Synonymous with clock register, time register.

time register Synonym for timer.

timer initiation facility In NCCF, a facility that allows the operator to schedule a command or command list to be executed either at a specific time or repetitively at specified time intervals.

timer supervision In MVS/370, routines that provide the date and time of day, measure time intervals, schedule activities, and set the interval timer.

time scale (1) A number used as a multiplier to transform the real time of the problem into computer time. (T) (2) See extended time scale, fast time scale, variable time scale.

time scale factor A number used as a multiplier to transform the real time of the problem into computer time. (I) (A)

time share To use a device for two or more interleaved purposes. (A)

time sharing (1) An operating technique of a data processing system that provides for the interleaving in time of two or more processes in one processor. (T) (2) A method of using a computing system that allows a number of users to execute programs concurrently and to interact with the programs during execution. (3) Deprecated term for conversational mode, time slicing. See Figure 153.

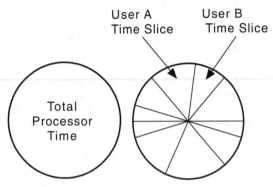

Figure 153. Time Sharing

time sharing control task (TSC) In TSO, a system task that handles system initialization, allocation of time shared regions, swapping, and general control of the time sharing operation.

time sharing driver In TSO, an addition to the dispatcher that determines which task is to be executed next.

time sharing input QCB (TSID) In ACF/TCAM, an area of main storage that contains the addresses of the time sharing routines.

Time Sharing Option (TSO) An operating system option; for the System/370 system, the option provides interactive time sharing from remote terminals.

Time Sharing Option Extensions (TSO/E) The base for all TSO enhancements. It provides MVS users with additional functions, improved usability, and better performance. In the MVS/ESA environment, TSO/E also provides virtual storage constraint relief.

Time Sharing Option for VTAM (TSO/VTAM) An optional configuration of the operating system that provides conversational time sharing from remote stations in a network using VTAM.

time sharing priority In systems with time sharing, a ranking within the group of tasks associated with a single user, used to determine their precedence in receiving system resources.

Time Sharing System (TSS) A programming system that provides users with conversational online access to a computing system with one or more processing units and simultaneously processes batched jobs.

time slice (1) The period of processing time allocated for running a program. (2) An interval of time on the processing unit allocated for use in performing a task. After the interval has expired, processing unit time is allocated to another task, so a task cannot monopolize processing unit time beyond a fixed limit. (3) In systems with time sharing, a segment of time allocated to a terminal job. (4) In the AS/400 system and System/38, the amount of processor time, specified in milliseconds, allowed for a job before other waiting jobs of equal priority are allowed to process data. (5) See major time slice, minor time slice. (6) See also work slice.

time slicing (1) A feature that can be used to prevent a task from monopolizing the processing unit and thereby delaying the assignment of processing unit time to other tasks. (2) In systems with time sharing, the allocation of time slices to terminal jobs. (3) Deprecated term for time sharing. (T)

time stamp (1) To apply the current system time. (2) The value on an object that is an indication of the system time at some critical point in the history of the object. (3) In query, the identification of the day and time when a query report was created that query automatically provides on each report.

time to repair See mean time to repair. (A)

TIOT Terminal input/output task.

tip The end of a plug used to make circuit connections in a manual switchboard. The tip is the connector attached to the positive side of the common battery that powers the station equipment. It is the positive battery side of a telecommunication line. Synonymous with tip side. See also common battery central office.

tip side Synonym for tip.

title See panel title, window title.

title bar In SAA Advanced Common User Access architecture, the area at the top of each window that contains the window title and system menu icon. When appropriate, it also contains the minimize, maximize, and restore icons.

TL Test loop.

TLB Translation lookaside buffer.

TML Tutorial and message library.

TMP Terminal monitor program.

TNSTAT Tuning statistics.

TOD Time of day. See time-of-day clock.

toggle (1) A switching device such as a toggle key on a keyboard. (2) Pertaining to any device having two stable states. (A) (3) Pertaining to a switching device, such as a toggle key on a keyboard, that allows a user to switch between two types of operations. (4) To switch between two modes; for example, on a personal computer connected to a network, to switch between the data entry and command entry modes or between stand-alone operation and terminal emulation. (5) Synonym for flip-flop.

toggle button In AIXwindows and Enhanced X-Windows, a graphical object that simulates a toggle switch; it switches sequentially from one optional state to another.

token (1) In a local area network, the symbol of authority passed successively from one data station to another to indicate the station temporarily in control of the transmission medium. Each data station has an opportunity to acquire and use the token to control the medium. A token is a particular message or bit pattern that signifies permission to transmit. (T) (2) A sequence of bits passed from one device to another along the token ring. When the token has data appended to it, it becomes a frame. (3) In a programming language, a character string, in a particular format, that has some defined significance. (4) The smallest independent unit of meaning of a program as defined by either a parser or the lexical analyzer. A token can contain data, a language keyword, an identifier, or other parts of a language syntax. (5) In the AS/400 system, a predefined message or character pattern that gives the receiver of the token the permission to transmit information. (6) In SQL, any single keyword, user-supplied word, or arithmetic or comparison operator. See delimiter token, ordinary token. (7) In the 3800 Print Services Facility, a string of characters treated as a single entity. (8) See also lexical token, token passing procedure, transmission frame.

token access control In a ring network configuration, a ring control scheme in which a node that is ready to transmit inserts data into a unique bit pattern called a token, which is passed from node to node. The receiving node removes the data from the token, and a new token is generated. See also master node control, register insertion, slotted ring control.

token-bus network A bus network in which a token passing procedure is used. (T)

token monitor Synonym for active monitor.

token name In the 3800 Print Services Facility, an 8-byte name that can be given to all internal objects and resource objects.

token passing In a token-ring network, the process by which a node captures a token; inserts a message, addresses, and control information; changes the bit pattern of the token to the bit pattern of a frame; transmits the frame; removes the frame from the ring when it has made a complete circuit; generates another token; and transmits the token on the ring where it can be captured by the next node that is ready to transmit.

token passing procedure In a local area network using a token, the set of rules that governs how a data station acquires, uses, and transfers the token. (T)

token ring A network with a ring topology that passes tokens from one attaching device to another; for example, the IBM Token-Ring Network.

token-ring adapter type 1 A token-ring interface coupler (TIC) that operates at 4-Mbps (megabits per second) token-ring speed.

token-ring adapter type 2 A token-ring interface coupler (TIC) supported only on an IBM 3745 Communication Controller. The adapter can be configured to support 4-Mbps (megabits per second) or 16-Mbps token-ring speed and to support subarea and peripheral nodes on the same adapter. When configured for 16-Mbps, the token-ring adapter type 2 provides the capability for early token release.

token-ring adapter type 3 A token-ring interface coupler (TIC) supported only on an IBM 3745 Communication Controller 3746 Model 900 expansion frame. The adapter can be configured to support 4-Mbps (megabits per second) or 16-Mbps token-ring speed and to support subarea and peripheral nodes on the same adapter. When configured for 16-Mbps, the token-ring adapter type 3 supports early token release.

token-ring interface coupler (TIC) An adapter that can connect a 3720, 3725, or 3745 Communication Controller to an IBM Token-Ring Network.

token-ring network (1) A ring network that allows unidirectional data transmission between data stations, by a token passing procedure, such that the transmitted data return to the transmitting station. (T) (2) A network that uses a ring topology, in which tokens are passed in a circuit from node to node. A node that is ready to send can capture the token and insert data for transmission.

tolerance The allowable range of deviation from the nominal value of an attribute.

toll In public switched systems, a charge based on time and distance for a connection beyond an exchange boundary.

toll center A central office in which channels and toll message circuits terminate. While this is usually one central office in a city, larger cities may have several central offices in which toll message circuits terminate. A class 4 office.

toll-free number Synonym for enterprise number.

tone (1) On a document copying machine, the intensity of light reflected from integral parts of the subject matter on the original or its image. (T)   (2) See discrete tone, prominent discrete tone.

tone control On dictation equipment, a device used to vary the relative intensity of bass sounds and treble sounds during playback. (I)

tone dialing Synonym for push button dialing.

toner (1) In a document copying machine, image-forming material used in electrostatic processes. (T) (2) A thermoplastic material impregnated with lampblack. Toner adheres to the exposed areas on the photoconductor during the developing process and is then transferred to the paper to form the developed image on the paper.   (3) In the 3800 Printing Subsystem, the material that forms the image on the paper.

toner carrier In a document copying machine, solid elements that carry and disperse the toner when it is used in a dry powder form. (T)

toner concentrate In a document copying machine, a concentrated solution used in some electrostatic processes containing the toner particles. (T)

toner concentration The ratio of toner weight to carrier-bead weight in the developer mix.

toner container In a document copying machine, a receptacle that contains the toner material in a dry process development electrostatic machine. (T)

toner migration Unwanted movement of toner on paper before the toner is fused into the paper, causing blurs.   See also ghost printing, poor fusing, toner offset.

toner offset Unwanted movement of toner caused by the fuser, which results in ghost printing.   See also ghost printing, poor fusing, toner migration.

toner reservoir In a document copying machine, a receptacle containing toner, which may or may not be in concentrated form, used in a wet process development electrostatic machine. (T)

toning control See automatic toning control, manual toning control.

tool Software that permits the development of an application program without using a traditional programming language.

Toolkit In AIXwindows and Enhanced X-Windows, a collection of C language data structures and subroutines that expedite the development of graphical user interfaces for compatible applications written in C language.   See AIXwindows Toolkit.

tool palette In SAA Advanced Common User Access architecture, a set of choices that provide a limited range of function within a window.   When a user selects a choice from the tool palette, the pointer changes to reflect the task or tasks that a user can perform.

toolpath A path followed by a tool in a numerical control machine. (T)

TOPAS Topology Overview Pricing Analysis System.

topdown Pertaining to a method or procedure that starts at the highest level of abstraction and proceeds towards the lowest level. (T)   Contrast with bottom-up.

topdown programming The design and coding of computer programs using a hierarchical structure in which related functions are performed at each level of the structure.

top-level specification A nonprocedural description of system behavior at the most abstract level;   for example, a functional specification that omits all implementation details.

top-level widget In AIXwindows and Enhanced X-Windows, widget classes that are at or near the top level of the object class hierarchy, known as the Core class.

top-level window In AIXwindows and Enhanced X-Windows, the main window that contains all other windows associated with a client application.

top margin (1) On a page, the space between the body or running heading and the top edge of the page. (2) In COBOL, an empty area that precedes the page body.

topological sort A sorting file that sorts an unordered list of ordered pairs.

topology and routing services (TRS) An APPN control point component that manages the topology database, computes routes, and provides a Route Selection control vector (RSCV) that specifies the best route through the network for a given session based on its requested class of service.

topology database update (TDU) A message about a new or changed link or node that is broadcast among APPN network nodes to maintain the network topology database, which is fully replicated in each network node. A TDU contains information that identifies the following:

- The sending node

- The node and link characteristics of various resources in the network

- The sequence number of the most recent update for each of the resources described.

topology layout utility A GraphicsView/2 utility that calculates the coordinates, or x and y values, for the resource symbols in a view.

Topology Overview Pricing Analysis System A system that provides link tariff data in response to online user requests that use a specified table format.

top shadow In AIXwindows, a narrow band of lighter color across the top of a rectangular graphical object (a widget or gadget) that creates a three-dimensional appearance when the object is manipulated. See also bottom shadow.

total On a calculator, the result of a calculation that may be displayed or printed and cannot be reused without manual re-entry. (T)

total counter In a duplicator, a device that indicates the number of copies that have been produced. (T) See also preselector counter.

total function In a calculator, the function that provides the result of a calculation that may be displayed or printed and that cannot be reused without manual reentry. (I) (A)

TOTE Teleprocessing online test executive.

touch On a typewriter, the force required for actuation of the keys. (T)

touch acknowledgment On a touchscreen, the visual or aural feedback a user receives upon touching an active touch area.

touch area Synonym for hot spot.

touch-down point Location, plotted by a digitizer, where contact is made with a touch-sensitive surface.

touch screen (1) A display device, that allows the user to interact with a computer system by touching an area on its screen. Synonymous with touch-sensitive screen. (T) (2) A touch-sensitive display screen on a visual display unit. See Figure 154.

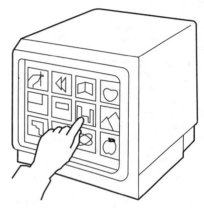

Figure 154. Touch Screen

touch-sensitive Pertaining to a device such as a keypad or screen that generates coordinate data when a pointing device approaches or contacts the surface, thereby allowing a user to interact directly with a computer without entering commands from a keyboard.

touch-sensitive screen Synonym for touch screen. (T)

touch tabulator key Synonym for latch-out tabulator key.

tournament sort A repeated selection sort in which each subset consists of no more than two items. (A)

TP (1) Transaction program. (2) Transmission priority.

TPF Transaction processing facility.

TPIOS A facility that supports programmable telecommunication control units (TCUs) and generates channel programs for the channel scheduler.

TPLIB Transient program library.

TPNS Teleprocessing network simulator.

TPNS network The set of statements defining resources to be simulated by TPNS. Should not be confused with a packet switching network.

TPRB Teleprocessing request block.

TPRINT Trace print.

TR Trace.

TRAC Trace record.

trace (1) A record of the execution of a computer program. It exhibits the sequences in which the instructions were executed. (A)   (2) In MSS, a monitor in the mass storage control that records data about the activity of the system, staging, and destaging. The data describe completed 3850 Mass Storage System functions from the activity schedule queues plus time stamps.   (3) The process of recording the sequence in which the statements in a program are executed and, optionally, the values of the program variables used in the statements.   (4) To record a series of events as they occur.   (5) See address trace, fault trace, line trace, link trace.

trace analysis program (TAP) A program service aid that assists in analyzing trace data produced by VTAM, TCAM, and NCP and provides network data traffic and network error reports. Synonymous with ACF/TAP.

trace daemon In the AIX operating system, a daemon that reads from the trace device driver and writes to the trace log file.

trace file A file that contains a record of events that occur in a system.

trace function A function used for problem determination.

trace log A file in which trace events are recorded.

trace program A computer program that performs a check on another computer program by exhibiting the sequence in which the instructions are executed and, usually, the results of executing the instructions. (I) (A)

trace table A storage area into which trace information is placed. See also CP trace table.

tracing facility In a programming or knowledge engineering language, a means of displaying the subroutines or rules executed along with the values of the variables used. (T)

tracing routine A routine that provides an historical record of specified events in the execution of a computer program. (A)

track (1) A path associated with a single read/write head as the data medium moves past it. (T)   (2) A circular path on the surface of a disk or diskette on which information is recorded and from which recorded information is read. (3) See address track, card track, clock track, feed track, magnetic track, regenerative track. See Figure 155.

Track

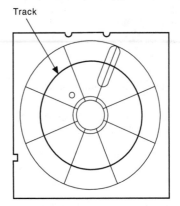

Figure 155. Track

track advance In multimedia applications, to advance the medium to the beginning of the next track.

track and hold unit A functional unit whose output analog variable is equal to either the input analog variable or a sample of this variable selected by the action of an external Boolean signal. When tracking, the device follows the input analog variable. When holding, the device holds the value of the input analog variable at the instant of switching. (I) (A) Synonymous with track and store unit.

track and store unit Synonym for track and hold unit.

trackball In computer graphics, a ball, rotatable about its center, that is used as an input device, normally as a locator. (I) (A)   Synonymous with control ball.

track change control On dictation equipment, a device that selects one of several tracks on a magnetic recording medium, thus enabling more than one recording to be made along the length of the medium or played back from it. (I)

track density The number of tracks per unit of length, measured in a direction perpendicular to the tracks.

Note: The track density is inversely related to the track pitch. (T)

tracker In computer security, a query that enables a user of a database to obtain indirectly information without authorization. See also attack.

track group In VSE/POWER, the basic organizational unit of the data file for count-key-data (CKD) devices. Each track group consists of a certain number of tracks.

track hold In VSE, a function that protects a track that is being updated by one program from being accessed by another program.

tracking In computer graphics, a technique of echoing a locator, using a cursor. (T)

tracking analog to digital and comparator A part of DSS that tracks the voltage and current output of a power supply. The output is converted from analog to digital and is compared with a high and low limit set by the power/thermal microcode. If the high or low limits are exceeded, a unique bit is set in the analog event register.

tracking symbol A symbol on the display surface that indicates the position corresponding to the coordinate data produced by a locator. (I) (A)

track pitch The distance between adjacent tracks, measured in a direction perpendicular to the tracks.

Note: The track pitch is inversely related to the track density. (T)

track recovery In IMS/VS, an option for recovery from permanent read/write errors on VSAM data sets. Track recovery permits database reconstruction at the track level, rather than at the database level.

track reverse In multimedia applications, to rewind the medium to the beginning of the current track. If it is already at the beginning of the track, it will jump to the beginning of the previous track.

track selector A device that enables selection of a particular track on a recording medium. (T)

tractor A mechanism that controls movement of continuous forms paper by means of the carrier holes.

tractor feeder A device attached to a printer to automatically feed edge-perforated roll paper or forms. (T)

tractor holes Synonym for carrier holes.

Traditional Chinese The Chinese character set expressed in traditional form. Traditional Chinese

characters are used in Taiwan, Hong Kong and other parts of the world.

Traditional Chinese double-byte character set An IBM-defined double-byte character set (DBCS) for Traditional Chinese, consisting of Traditional Chinese non-Chinese set, primary set, secondary set, and up to 2,632 user-definable characters.

Traditional Chinese non-Chinese character set A subset of the Traditional Chinese double-byte character set (DBCS), consisting of non-Chinese characters, such as Greek, Russian, Roman numeric, alphanumeric and related symbols, Katakana, Hiragana, special symbols and Chinese phonetic symbols. There are 675 characters in this set.

Traditional Chinese primary character set A subset of the Traditional Chinese DBCS, consisting of commonly used Chinese characters. There are 5,401 characters in this set.

Traditional Chinese secondary character set A subset of the Traditional Chinese DBCS, consisting of less commonly used Chinese characters. There are 7,652 characters in this set.

traffic See data traffic.

traffic requirement In NETDA/2, the bidirectional stream of messages required between a pair of communicating nodes (an origin node and a destination node) by one or more sessions and one or more application programs.

trail See audit trail. (A)

trailer (1) The portion of magnetic tape that follows the end-of-tape marker. (T) (2) Control information added to the end of a record. See also trailer label.

trailer card (1) A card that contains information related to data on preceding cards. (A) (2) Synonymous with detail card.

trailer label (1) A file or data set label that follows the data records on a unit of recording medium. (2) Synonym for end-of-file label.

trailer record A record that follows one or more records and contains data related to those records.

trailing decision (1) A loop control that is executed after the loop body. (A) (2) Contrast with leading decision.

trailing edge litho master In a duplicator, a litho master that is attached to the master cylinder by its leading edge only. (T)

trailing end The end of a perforated tape that last enters a perforated-tape reader. (A)

trailing zero In positional notation, a zero in a less significant digit place than the digit place of the least significant nonzero digit of a numeral. (A)

trail printer In word processing, a printer that is not uniquely associated with a particular keyboard or display-based workstation and that is used for automatic printout of text already recorded on a recording medium or in electronic storage within associated word processing equipment. Printing follows or trails the text generation. (T) See also attended trail printer, unattended trail printer.

train (1) A sequence of pieces of apparatus joined together to forward or complete a call. See also switch train. (2) See pulse train.

tranquility Keeping the security classification of an object constant while it is in use; keeping the security classification of a subject constant while it is active.

transaction (1) In a batch or remote batch entry, a job or job step. (2) An exchange between a workstation and another device that accomplishes a particular action or result; for example, the entry of a customer's deposit and the updating of the customer's balance. (3) An item of business; for example, the handling of customer orders and customer billing. (4) A specific set of input data that triggers execution of a specific process or job; a message destined for an application program. (5) In communications, an exchange between a program on a local system and a program on a remote system that accomplishes a particular action or result. See also conversation, session. (6) In SQL, the work that occurs between begin a unit of work and a commit or rollback. A transaction defines the set of operations that are part of an integral set. (7) In PSS, the process of recording item sales, processing refunds, recording coupons, handling voids, verifying checks before accepting them as tender, and arriving at the amount to be paid by or to a customer. The receiving of payment for merchandise of service is also included in a transaction. (8) In IMS/VS, a specific set of input data that triggers execution of a specific processor job; a message destined for an application program. (9) In CICS/DOS/VS, one or more application programs that can be used by a display station operator. A given transaction can be used concurrently from one or more display stations. The execution of a transaction for a certain operator is also referred to as a task: a task can relate to only one operator. (10) In System/38 commitment control, a group of changes made to database files that appear to the workstation user to be a single change but that require multiple operations by the application program.

transaction-based routing In ACF/TCAM, message routing in which messages are routed to their destinations individually, according to one or more destination names or routing keys entered in the message header by the originator. See also affinity-based routing, invariant routing, routing by destination, routing by key.

transaction code In the AS/400 IMS subsystem, the first of one-to-eight characters of the first segment of a message sent to IMS/VS. The transaction code identifies the application program for which the message is intended.

transaction command security In IMS/VS, the use of system definition macroinstructions and security maintenance utility control statements to permit specific application programs to issue some of the IMS/VS operator commands.

transaction display On the 3653 Point of Sale Terminal, an electronic panel that visually presents current transaction details for viewing by an operator and a customer.

transaction file (1) A file containing relatively transient data that, for a given application, is processed together with the appropriate master file. (I) Synonymous with detail file. (2) In COBOL, an input-output file used to communicate with display stations and ICF sessions.

transaction journal (1) A record of changes in files of data that result from transactions. (2) In PSS, a printed record of all transactions that have taken place at a point of sale terminal. Within programmable store system host support, a record kept of all functions performed that have gained access to the subsystem library or that have affected the information in it. Contrast with summary journal. (3) In DPCX, a log maintained by subsystem support services of all operations that have altered data in the subsystem library or transmitted data to DPCX.

transaction load balancing In IMS/VS, an optional facility that enables a transaction to be scheduled into more than one message region or batch message region at the same time.

transaction log In the programmable store system, a record of transactions performed at the point of sale terminal. This log is magnetically recorded and stored on the store controller integrated disk.

transaction processing A sequence of operations on a database that is viewed by the user as a single, individual operation. (A)

transaction processing facility (TPF) A high-availability, high-performance system, designed to support real-time, transaction driven applications. The specialized architecture of TPF is intended to optimize system efficiency, reliability, and responsiveness for data communication and database processing. TPF provides real-time inquiry and update to a large, centralized database, where message length is relatively short in both directions, and response time is generally less than three seconds. Formerly known as the Airline Control Program/Transaction Processing Facility (ACP/TPF).

transaction processing system (1) A system that supervises the sharing of resources for processing multiple transactions concurrently. Transaction processing systems are designed to support interactive applications in which requests submitted by people at terminals are processed as soon as they are received. Results are returned to the requester in a relatively short period of time. (2) An IMS/VS system in a multisystem environment accepting transactions from a front-end system, calls application programs for transaction processing, and routes all replies back to front-end system for response to terminal. See also balanced system, front-end system, pseudo-front-end system.

transaction program (1) In DPPX, an application program executed in response to a transaction request. (2) A program that processes transactions in an SNA network. There are two kinds of transaction programs: application transaction programs and service transaction programs. See also conversation. (3) In VTAM, a program that performs services related to the processing of a transaction. One or more transaction programs may operate within a VTAM application program that is using the VTAM application program interface (API). In that situation, the transaction program would request services from the application program, using protocols defined by that application program. The application program, in turn, could request services from the VTAM program by issuing the APPCCMD macroinstruction. (4) In the AS/400 system, a user-supplied application program for processing data received by the AS/400 system from a finance device.

transaction record A record in a transaction data set created by one or more executions of a program that is coded to generate transaction records.

transaction record header Identification and control information at the beginning of the first block of a transaction record.

transaction routing In CICS/VS, a facility that allows operators of terminals controlled by a CICS/VS transaction processing system to initiate transactions involving transaction programs controlled by other transaction processing systems. The CICS/VS trans-

action routing facility utilizes the SNA transaction program conversational capability to facilitate a conversation between the transaction program and a relay transaction controlled by the transaction processing system at which the initiating terminal is located.

transaction services In DPCX, the part of application services that aids a program in creating and storing the results of operator transactions.

transaction services layer The layer that includes service transaction programs and provides configuration services, directory services, management services, session services, and topology and routing services.

transaction type A value that identifies the work to be performed on a document.

transceiver (1) Any terminal that can transmit and receive traffic. (2) In AS/400 communications, the device that connects the transceiver cable to the Ethernet coaxial cable. The transceiver is used to transmit and receive data.

transceiver cable In communications, the cable and its connectors that connects the input/output adapter to the transceiver.

transcribe To copy data from one data medium to another, converting them as necessary for acceptance by the receiving medium. (T)

transcript In AIX remote communications, a file that contains a record of commands entered on the remote system and the response of the remote system to those commands.

transcription machine A machine designed solely to reproduce speech recorded by a dictation machine so that a written record can be produced. (I)

transducer A device for converting energy from one form to another. (A)

transfer (1) To send data from one place and receive the data at another place. (I) (A) Synonymous with move. (2) In word processing, the movement of selected recorded text from one element of a recording medium to another. (T) (3) To read data from auxiliary storage or from an input device into processor storage or from processor storage to auxiliary storage or to an output device. (4) Deprecated term for jump. (5) See binary-image transfer, block transfer, peripheral transfer, radial transfer.

Note: A transfer usually does not erase data from the original location.

transfer check A check on the accuracy of a data transfer. (A)

transfer corona The unit that electrically charges paper to attract photoconductor toner and onto the paper. It has a thin, electrically charged wire inside a metal tube with a narrow opening.

transfer instruction Deprecated term for jump instruction.

transfer interpreter A device that prints on a punched card the characters corresponding to hole patterns punched in another card. (I) (A)

transfer key In word processing, a control initiating a transfer process. (T)

transfer option An option for transferring control between specific subfunction steps, eliminating the need to return to step selection after completion of each subfunction.

transfer rate See data transfer rate.

transferred information Synonym for transinformation content.

transfer sheet In a duplicator, a coated piece of material, the coated side of which is placed in contact with the reverse side of the master used in spirit (or other fluid) duplicators to transfer the mirror image by means of pressure or heat. (T)

transfer station In the 3800 Printing Subsystem, the assembly where a toned image on the photoconductor is transferred to the paper.

transfer time The time interval between the instant at which a transfer of data starts and the instant at which the process is completed. (T)

transfer vector In an overlay, a linkage to an entry point that allows the overlay to be loaded into storage before control is passed to the entry point.

transform To change the form of data according to specified rules without significantly changing the meaning of the data. (I) (A)

transformation In AIX graphics, a four-by-four matrix that helps determine the location at which three-dimensional drawing occurs, the position of the viewpoint (the viewer's "eye"), and the amount of the scene encompassed and visible. Transformations occur at four points within the graphics pipeline. See key transformation, modeling transformation, projection transformation, signal transformation, viewing transformation, viewport transformation.

transformation definition language (TDL) A set of SPPS statements that are coded by an application pro-

grammer to control the IBM 3275 Display Station screen. These statements define the formats of data to be transferred between a keyboard/display and an application-program buffer. They require translation by the transformation definition language translator. See also terminal display language.

transformer A device that converts power from one circuit to another at the same frequency, but at a changed voltage and current.

transform layer In DPPX, an I/O layer that acts as an interface between a terminal device and the DPPX/Base, which sends and expects to receive SNA-formatted data.

transient Pertaining to a program or subroutine that does not reside in main storage or to a temporary storage area for such a program.

transient analysis The investigation of the behavior of a system, process, or device before it reaches the steady state.

transient area (1) A storage area used for temporary storage of transient programs or routines. (2) In VSE, an area within the control program used to provide high-priority system services on demand.

transient control executive area The area of processor storage used by parts of DPCX that reside on disk storage and are read into the processor only when needed.

transient data queue A sequential data set used by the Folder Application Facility in CICS/MVS to log system messages.

transient error (1) Synonym for soft error. (T) (2) An error that occurs once or at unpredictable intervals. (3) In the System/370 system, any processing unit or main storage condition that is detected and corrected or circumvented by retry or error correction code logic.

transient program area In CMS, the virtual storage area occupying locations X'E000' to X'10000'. Some CMS commands and user programs can be executed in this area of CMS storage.

transient response The behavior of a system or process before it reaches the steady state.

transient routine (1) A routine permanently stored on a system residence device and loaded into the transient area of main storage when it is needed for execution. (2) In DPCX, an instruction processing routine that resides on disk storage and is read into control storage when needed.

transient state The condition of a station when it is setting up to transmit.

transinformation content (1) In information theory, the difference between the information content conveyed by the occurrence of an event and the conditional information content conveyed by the occurrence of the same event, given the occurrence of another event; in mathematical notation: x_i, y_j be a pair of events, such as an input message x_i and an output message y_j, $p(x_i,y_j)$ the joint probability of the occurrence of both events, $p(x_i|y_j)$ the conditional probability of the occurrence of the event x_i, given the occurrence of the event y_j, $p(y_j|x_i)$ the conditional probability of the occurrence of the event y_j, given the occurrence of the event x_i, $p(x_i)$ the probability of the occurrence of event x_i, $p(y_j)$ the probability of the occurrence of event y_j, then this difference $T(x_i|y_j)$ for the pair of events x_i, y_j is expressed as:

$$T(x_i|y_j) = \log \frac{1}{p(x_i)} - \log \frac{1}{p(x_i|y_j)}$$

$$= \log \frac{p(x_i|y_j)}{p(x_i)} = \log \frac{p(x_i, y_j)}{p(x_i)p(y_j)}$$

$$= \log \frac{p(y_j|x_i)}{p(y_j)} = T(y_j|x_i)$$

(I) (A) Synonymous with mutual information, transferred information, transmitted information. (2) See average transinformation content, character mean transinformation content, mean transinformation content.

transinformation rate See average transinformation rate.

transistor A small solid-state semiconducting device that can perform nearly all the functions of an electronic tube, including amplification and rectification. See Figure 156.

transistor-transistor logic (TTL) A circuit in which the multiple-diode cluster of the diode-transistor logic circuit has been replaced by a multiple-emitter transistor.

transit delay In X.25 communications, the time it takes a packet to travel from one data terminal equipment (DTE) to the other. See end-to-end transit delay.

transition The switching from one state (for example, positive voltage) to another (negative voltage) in a serial transmission.

transition effects In video and film production, special effects occurring between shots.

transit time In NPM, transit time is the same as response time. See response time.

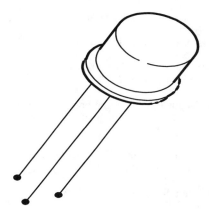

Figure 156. Transistor

translate (1) In programming languages, to transform all or part of a program expressed in one programming language, into another programming language or into a machine language suitable for execution. (T) (2) In computer graphics, to move a display image on the display space in a straight line from one location to another without rotating the image. (T)

translated axis line In System/38 graphics, a straight reference line parallel to either axis relative to which data values are plotted on a chart. Synonymous with reference line, translated line.

translated line Synonym for translated axis line.

translate duration Synonym for translating time.

translate phase The logical subdivision of a run that includes execution of the translator. (I) (A) Synonymous with translating phase.

translating In computer graphics, moving all or part of a display image on a display space from one location to another without rotating the image. (T) See Figure 157.

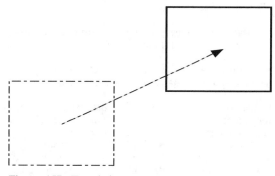

Figure 157. Translating

translating phase Synonym for translate phase.

translating program Synonym for translator.

translating time The elapsed time taken for the execution of a translator. (I) (A)

translation In computer graphics, the application of a constant displacement to the position of one or more display elements. (I) (A)

translation look-aside buffer (TLB) Hardware that contains the virtual-to-real address mapping.

translation program Synonym for translator. (T)

translation specification exception In System/370 virtual storage systems, a program interruption that occurs when a page table entry, segment table entry, or the control register pointing to the segment table contains information in an invalid format. See also page translation exception, segment translation exception.

translation table A table used to replace one or more characters with alternative characters; for example, to translate characters representing a virtual address to those representing a real address, characters representing an event to those representing a procedure call, characters of a national character set to those of another national language, or characters representing a relocated address to those representing an absolute address.

translation time (1) Any instant at which translation takes place. (T)   (2) The amount of time needed to translate a program. (T) Synonymous with translate duration.

translator (1) A computer program that can translate. (T)   Synonymous with translation program. (T) (2) In telephone equipment, the device that converts dialed digits into call-routine information. (3) Synonymous with translating program, translation program. (4) See address translator.

translator directive A language construct for controlling the translation of a program. (T)

transliterate To convert characters of one alphabet to the corresponding characters of another alphabet. (A)

transmission (1) The sending of data from one place for reception elsewhere. (A)   (2) In the ASCII and data communication, a series of characters including headings and texts. (A)   (3) The dispatching of a signal, message, or other form of intelligence by wire, radio, telegraphy, telephony, facsimile, or other means. (T)   (4) One or more blocks or messages. For BSC and start-stop devices, a transmission is ter-minated by an EOT character. See also block, message. (5) See asynchronous transmission, burst transmission, duplex transmission, half-duplex transmission, one-way transmission, parallel transmission, serial transmission, start-stop transmission, synchronous transmission. (6) See also data communication.

Notes:

1. *Transmission implies only the sending of data; the data may or may not be received.*

2. *The term transmit is used to describe the sending of data in telecommunication operations. The terms move and transfer are used to describe movement of data in data processing operations.*

transmission block (1) In data communication, a group of records recorded, processed, or sent as a unit. (2) The portion of a message terminated by an EOB or ETB line-control character or, if it is the last block in the message, by an EOT or ETX line-control character. (3) In VTAM, the unit of data that is transmitted between an application program and a terminal that is connected in basic mode.

transmission-block character See end-of-transmission-block character. (A)

transmission category In an ACF/TCAM extended network, utility session messages that have similar characteristics and are handled similarly; for example, messages flowing in an inquiry/reply application and messages flowing in a high-volume, low-priority data collection application are placed in different transmission categories.

Note: Different versions of the following TCAM techniques and capabilities may be applied to messages in different transmission categories: queuing medium, message priority, sequence checking, error handling, load balancing, and data staging.

transmission code A code for sending information over telecommunication lines.

transmission control character (1) A control character used to control or facilitate transmission of data between data terminal equipments. (I) (A)   (2) In data communications, special characters that are included in a message to control communications over a data link. For example, the sending station and the receiving station use transmission control characters to exchange information; the receiving station uses transmission control characters to indicate errors in data it receives. (3) Characters transmitted over a line that are not message data but cause certain control operations to be performed when encountered. Among such operations are addressing, polling, message delimiting and blocking, transmission error checking, and carriage return. (4) Synonymous with communication control character.

transmission control (TC) layer The layer within a half-session or session connector that synchronizes and paces session-level data traffic, checks session sequence numbers of requests, and enciphers and deciphers end-user data. See also half-session.

Transmission Control Protocol (TCP) A communications protocol used in Internet and in any network that follows the U.S. Department of Defense standards for inter-network protocol. TCP provides a reliable host-to-host protocol between hosts in packet-switched communications networks and in interconnected systems of such networks. It assumes that the Internet protocol is the underlying protocol.

transmission control unit (TCU) A communication control unit whose operations are controlled solely by programmed instructions from the computing system to which the unit is attached. No program is stored or executed in the unit, for example, the IBM 2702 and 2703 Transmission Controls. Contrast with communication controller. Synonymous with telecommunication control unit.

transmission copying In a document copying machine, a method of contact copying in which the master lies between the source of radiation and the sensitized material so that the radiation has to pass through the master. (T)

transmission extension A simplified nonringing extension to which a local serial data terminal is attached.

transmission frame (1) In data transmission, data transported from one node to another in a particular format that can be recognized by the receiving node. In addition to a data or information field, a frame has some kind of delimiter that marks its beginning and end and usually control fields, address information that identifies the source and destination, and one or more check bits that allow the receiver to detect errors that may occur after the sender has transmitted the frame. (2) In synchronous data link control (SDLC), the vehicle for every command, every response, and all information that is transmitted using SDLC procedures. Each frame begins and ends with a flag. See sequenced frame. See also frame check sequence. (3) In SDLC under SNA, synonym for basic link unit (BLU). (4) In high level data link control (HDLC), the sequence of contiguous bits bracketed by and including opening and closing flag (01111110) sequences. (5) In a token-ring network, a bit pattern containing data that a station has inserted for transmission after capturing a token. (6) In a time-division multiplex (TDM) system, a repetitive group of signals resulting from a signal sampling of all channels, including any additional signals for synchronizing and

other required system information. (7) Synonym for frame. (T)   See Figure 158.

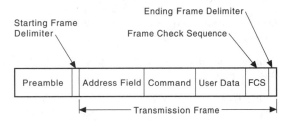

Figure 158. Transmission Frame

transmission group In SNA, a group of links between adjacent subarea nodes appearing as a single logical link for routing of messages.

Note: A transmission group may consist of one or more SDLC links (parallel links) or of a single System/370 channel.

transmission group identifier (TGID) In SNA, a set of three values, unique for each transmission group, consisting of the subarea addresses of the two adjacent nodes connected by the transmission group, and the transmission group number (1-255).

transmission group (TG) profile In VTAM, a named set of characteristics (such as cost per byte, cost per unit of time, and capacity) that is used for APPN links.

transmission group (TG) vector A representation of an endpoint TG in a T2.1 network, consisting of two control vectors: the TG Descriptor ($X'46'$) control vector and the TG Characteristics ($X'47'$) control vector.

transmission header (TH) In SNA, control information, optionally followed by a basic information unit (BIU) or a BIU segment, that is created and used by path control to route message units and to control their flow within the network. See also path information unit.

transmission interface A shared boundary defined by functional characteristics, common physical interconnection characteristics, signal characteristics, and other characteristics as appropriate.

Note: The interface involves specification of the connection of two devices having different functions.

transmission interruption The interruption of a transmission from a terminal by a higher priority transmission to the terminal. Synonymous with reverse break.

transmission level See relative transmission level.

transmission limit In the network control program, the maximum number of transmissions that can be sent to or received from a start-stop or BSC device during a session on a multipoint line before the network control program suspends the session to service other devices on the line.

transmission line Synonym for telecommunication line.

transmission medium The physical medium that conveys signals between data stations; for example, twisted-pair wire, optical fiber, coaxial cable. (T)

Note: Free space is a transmission medium for electromagnetic waves.

transmission number In the 3800 Printing Subsystem, the number designating the number of transmissions of a particular print data set. It is used by Print Services Facility to select the appropriate form environment group.

transmission path delay The time required for a bit to travel between the two most distant data stations in a bus network. Synonymous with one-way propagation time. (T)

transmission priority A rank assigned to a message unit that determines its precedence for being selected by the path control component in each node along a route for forwarding to the next node in the route.

transmission security Protection against wiretapping.

transmission service A circuit switched, packet switched, or a leased circuit is service that is provided by a communication common carrier, a recognized private operating agency (RPOA), or a telecommunication Administration. See circuit-switched data transmission service, leased circuit data transmission service, packet-switched transmission service, public data transmission service.

transmission services (TS) profile In SNA, a specification in a session activation request (and optionally, in the responses) of transmission control (TC) protocols, such as session-level pacing and the usage of session-level requests, to be supported by a particular session. Each defined transmission services profile is identified by a number.

transmission subsystem component (TSC) The component of VTAM program that comprises the transmission control, path control, and data link control layers of SNA.

transmit (1) To send data from one place for reception elsewhere. (A) (2) To move an entity from one place to another; for example, to broadcast radio waves, to dispatch data via a transmission medium, or to transfer data from one data station to another via a line. (T) (3) See also transfer.

transmit burst In data communications, a group of transmit packets that are sent without an intervening receive or time-out operation.

transmit flow control A transmission procedure that controls the rate at which data can be transmitted from one point so that it is equal to the rate at which it can be received by a remote point. (T)

Notes:

1. *This procedure may apply between a data terminal equipment (DTE) and the adjacent data switching exchange (DSE) or between two DTEs. In the latter case, the data signaling rate may be controlled due to network or remote DTE requirements.*

2. *This procedure operates independently in the two directions of data transfer, thus permitting different data signaling rates in both directions of transmission.*

transmit leg The side of a duplex line that is transmitting. Contrast with receive leg.

transmittal mode The method by which the contents of an input buffer are made available to the program, and by which a program makes records available for output.

transmitted information Synonym for transinformation content.

transmitter See optical transmitter, universal receiver-transmitter.

transmitter-receiver subassembly (TRS) In an ESCON environment, the electronic component that contains an optical transmitter and an optical receiver. See also fiber optic subassembly.

transparency (1) An acetate sheet containing information to be shown by means of an overhead projector. Synonymous with foil. (2) On a document copying machine, a master or copy on material that transmits light without diffusion. (T) (3) See also transparent, transparent mode.

transparency mode See transparent mode.

transparent (1) Pertaining to operations or data that are of no significance to the user. (2) In data transmission, pertaining to information not recognized by the receiving program or device as transmission control characters. (3) See code transparent, code transparent data transmission, inherent transparency.

transparent data (1) Data that is of no significance to the receiver. (2) Data that can contain any hexadecimal value.

transparent original On a document copying machine, an original through which sufficient light or other radiation can pass to produce an acceptable copy. (T)

transparent mode A method of binary synchronous text transmission in which transmission control characters are treated as text unless they are preceded by the DLE control character. Contrast with nontransparent mode.

transportability Synonym for portability.

transport assembly The unit that contains the transfer station, fuser station, continuous forms input station, and continuous forms stacker.

transport layer (1) In the Open Systems Interconnection reference model, the layer that provides a reliable end-to-end data transfer service. There may be relay open systems in the path. (T) (2) See also Open Systems Interconnection reference model.

transport mechanism subassembly In the IBM ImagePlus system, the part of the OSAR Library that contains the mechanical units for moving the data cartridges to and from the drives and cells.

transport network The part of the SNA network that includes the data link control and path control layers. Synonymous with path control network.

transposed file A file in which fields of one record type are stored contiguously, in contrast to the usual practice of storing entire records contiguously. (T)

transposition Interchanging the position of open-wire conductors relative to each other to reduce induced signals.

transverse crosstalk coupling Between a disturbing and a disturbed circuit in any given section, the vector summation of the direct couplings between adjacent short lengths of the two circuits, without dependence on intermediate flow in other nearby circuits.

transverse parity check (1) A parity check on a column of binary digits that are members of a set forming a matrix; for example, a parity check on the set of bits on a tape row. (T) (2) Synonymous with transverse redundancy check.

transverse redundancy check (TRC) Synonym for transverse parity check.

trap (1) An unprogrammed conditional jump to a specified address that is automatically activated by hardware. A recording is made of the location from which the jump occurred. (I) (2) In REXX, to recognize that a currently enabled condition occurred and to perform the CALL or SIGNAL instruction specified when the condition trap is enabled. (3) See static debugger trap.

trap door In computer security, an intentionally hidden hardware or software mechanism that permits system protection mechanisms to be circumvented or disabled. See also attack.

trap handler A trap routine used when a trap occurs. See also exception.

trap number In the OS/2 operating system, a diagnostic code that identifies a condition that caused an interrupt or trap.

tray delivery mechanism In a duplicator, a delivery system in which paper is ejected from the machine and falls into the delivery tray. (T)

TRC (1) Table reference character. (2) Traverse redundancy check.

TRCPL Trace parameter list.

treatment A detailed design document of the video.

tree See file tree, widget tree.

tree network A network in which there is exactly one path between any two nodes. (T) See Figure 159.

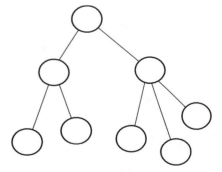

Figure 159. Tree Network

tree search In a tree structure, a search in which it is possible to make a decision at each step which part of the tree may be rejected without a further search. (T)

tree structure (1) A data structure that represents entities in nodes, with at most one parent node for each node, and with only one root node. (T) (2) A hierarchical calling sequence, that consists of both a root segment and also one or more levels of the segments called via the root segment.

TRFILE Trace file.

triboelectricity An electric charge created by friction.

tributary station (1) On a multipoint connection or a point-to-point connection using basic mode link control, any data station other than the control station. (I) (2) A secondary device on a multipoint line.

trigger (1) Synonym for hot spot. (2) To cause immediate execution of a computer program, often by intervention from the external environment; for example, by means of a manually controlled jump to an entry point. (I) (A)

trigger circuit (1) A circuit that possesses a number of unstable states and at least one stable state. The circuit is designed so that a desired transition can be initiated by the application of a suitable pulse. (T) (2) See also bistable trigger circuit, monostable trigger circuit.

trimmer assembly In a burster-trimmer-stacker, a device that removes margin carrier strips.

trimming In VM/SP HPO, the process of adding unreferenced pages of a virtual machine to the trim set.

trimming loops In the AIX system, a set of oriented closed curves used to set the boundaries of a non-uniform rational B-spline surface NURBS.

trim set In VM/SP HPO, the set of unreferenced virtual machine pages that are prepared to replenish the list of pages available in order to satisfy the page requests.

triple-length register Three registers that function as a single register. (I) (A) Synonymous with triple register.

triple plane In the 3270 Information Display System, a function that allows the user to define a whole symbol or portions of a symbol in the same address location in three different buffers. Contrast with single plane. See also triple plane symbol set.

triple plane symbol set In the 3270 Information Display System, a programmed symbol set that possesses a portion of a symbol or the whole symbol defined in each of the primary color planes (red, blue, and green), allowing the user to display or to print a whole symbol in one color, multiple colors, or else a blend of colors.

triple precision Pertaining to the use of three computer words to represent a number in accordance with the required precision. (I) (A)

triple register Synonym for triple-length register.

triplet A byte composed of three binary elements. (I) (A) Synonymous with three-bit byte.

tri-stimulus In video systems, a method of color reproduction that uses three primary colors or three signals for image transmission and reproduction.

trivial response In TSO, a response from the system to a request for processing that should require only one time slice; for example, a syntax check of one FORTRAN statement.

TRM Test request message.

troff A phototypesetting utility originally designed to support a Graphics Systems phototypesetting machine, but now capable of supporting a variety of phototypesetters.

Trojan horse In computer security, a program with an actual function or an apparently useful function that contains hidden functions that surreptitiously exploit the legitimate authorizations of an invoking process to the detriment of security measures; for example, a program that makes a blind copy of a sensitive file. See also attack, logic bomb, time bomb, virus.

Note: The term is often misused to mean hidden functions.

troubleshoot (1) To detect, locate, and eliminate errors in computer programs or faults in hardware. (2) Synonym for debug.

trouble unit A weighting figure that is applied to telephone circuits in order to indicate the expected performance in a given period.

trough roller In a duplicator, a roller that rotates in the reservoir to feed fluid into the damping system. (T)

TRS (1) Transmitter-receiver subassembly. (2) Topology and routing services.

truck In videotaping, a sideways camera movement of the tripod on which the camera is mounted.

true color (1) In AIX Enhanced X-Windows, a degenerate case of direct color in which the subfields in the pixel value directly encode the corresponding red, green, blue RGB values; that is, the colormap has predefined read-only RGB values. The values are typically near-linearly-increasing ramps. (2) Pertaining to the use of 24-bits per pixel direct red, green, blue RGB, in which there are 8 bits (256 levels) of red, 8 bits (256 levels) of green, and 8 bits (256 levels) of blue, for a total of 256*256*256 or 16 777 216 different combinations of red, green, and blue intensities. The number of different colored pixels that can then be simultaneously displayed is only limited by the number of pixels displayable from the frame buffer. (3) See also background color, direct color, pseudocolor.

true complement Deprecated term for radix complement.

true run list Synonym for dispatch list.

truncate (1) To terminate a computational process in accordance with some rule; for example, to end the evaluation of a power series at a specified term. (A) (2) To remove the beginning or ending elements of a string. (3) To drop data that cannot be printed or displayed in the line width specified or available. Contrast with fold *(3)*. (4) To shorten a field or statement to a specified length.

truncated binary exponential backoff In a local area network, the algorithm used to schedule retransmission after a collision such that the retransmission is delayed by an amount of time derived from the slot time and the number of attempts to retransmit. (T)

truncation (1) The deletion or omission of a leading or of a trailing portion of a string in accordance with specified criteria. (I) (A) (2) The termination of a computation process, before its final conclusion or natural termination, if any, in accordance with specified rules. (I) (A) (3) Contrast with round.

truncation error An error due to truncation. (I) (A)

trunk (1) In telephony, circuits that connect two switching systems, as opposed to connecting a customer line to a switching system. (2) A telephone channel between two central offices or switching devices that is used in providing a telephone connection between subscribers. (3) See tie trunk. (4) See also line, link, path, route.

trunk cable (1) A cable connecting trunk coupling units for the purpose of allowing communication among data stations. (T) (2) In an ESCON environment, a cable consisting of multiple fiber pairs that do not directly attach to an active device. This cable usually exists between distribution panels and can be located within, or external to, a building. Contrast with jumper cable.

trunk coupling unit A physical device that connects a data station to a trunk cable by means of a drop cable. The trunk coupling unit contains the means for inserting the station into the network or having it bypassed. (T)

trunk exchange An exchange devoted primarily to interconnecting trunks.

trunk group Those trunks between two points, both of which are switching centers, individual message distribution points, or both, and that use the same multiplex terminal equipments.

trunk hunting A method of switching incoming calls to the next consecutive or next available number if the first called number is busy.

trunk line A telecommunication line that links a private telecommunication system to a public switched network.

trusted computer system In computer security, a system that employs sufficient hardware and software data integrity measures to allow simultaneous processing of a range of sensitive or classified information.

trusted computing base (TCB) In computer security, all of the protection mechanisms within a computer system, including hardware, software, and firmware, the combination of which enforces a security policy. It creates a basic protection environment and provides additional user services required for a trusted computer system.

Trusted Computing System Evaluation Criteria In computer security, a standard of the U.S. Government for the evaluation of trusted computer systems. Synonymous with Orange Book.

trusted path In computer security, a mechanism by which a person at a terminal can communicate directly with the trusted computing base. This mechanism can be activated only by the person or the trusted computing base and cannot be imitated by untrusted software.

trusted software In computer security, the software portion of a trusted computing base.

truth table (1) An operation table for a logic operation. (I) (A) (2) A table that describes a logic function by listing all possible combinations of input values and indicating for each combination the output value. (A)

truth value In COBOL, the representation of the result of the evaluation of a condition in terms of one of two values: true, false.

TS Transmission services.

TSC (1) Telecommunications subsystem controller. (2) Time sharing control task. (3) Transmission subsystem component.

TSCB Transmission subsystem control block.

TSID Time sharing input QCB.

TSO Time Sharing Option.

TSO command language The set of commands, subcommands, and operands recognized under the time sharing option (TSO).

TSO/E Time Sharing Option Extensions.

TSO segment The portion of a RACF profile containing TSO/E logon information.

TSO/VTAM Time Sharing Option for the Virtual Telecommunications Access Method.

TSPL Transmission subsystem parameter list.

TSS Time Sharing System.

TT Test terminal.

TTD Temporary text delay.

TTE Terminal-table entry.

TTF Terminal transaction facility.

TTL Transistor-transistor logic.

TTY Teletypewriter.

tty In the AIX operating system, any device that uses the standard terminal device interface. Tty devices typically perform input and output on a character-by-character basis.

tty device See tty.

tumbling In computer graphics, turning all or part of a display image about an axis that is continually changing its position. See also rotating.

Note: Tumbling can be used to obtain a better understanding of the shape of a displayed three-dimensional object.

tuning The process of adjusting an application or a system to operate in a more efficient manner in the work environment of a particular installation.

tuning control On dictation equipment, a device for accurate alignment of the playback head, or combined head, to the track on the recording medium. (I)

tuple (1) In a relational database, a part of a relation that uniquely describes an entity and its attribute. A tuple can be represented by one row of a relation table. (T) (2) See also n-tuple length register.

Turing machine (1) A mathematical model of a device that changes its internal state and reads from, writes on, and moves, a potentially infinite tape, all in accordance with its present state, thereby constituting a model for computer-like behavior. (A) (2) See universal Turing machine. (3) See also finite state machine.

turnaround See line turnaround. See also turnaround time.

turnaround sequence In loop operation, a unique 16-bit sequence transmitted by the primary station to indicate to the secondary stations that the primary station is changing from a transmitter to a receiver. The turnaround sequence is: 01111110 00000000.

turnaround time (1) Elapsed time between submission of a job and return of the complete output. (I) (A) (2) Actual time needed to reverse direction of transmission from send to receive or vice versa when using a half-duplex circuit. For most telecommunication facilities, time is needed for line propagation and line effects, modem timing, and machine reaction. A typical time is 200 milliseconds on a half-duplex telephone connection. (3) See also response time.

turnkey system A data processing system that is ready to use when installed, and supplied to the user in a ready-to-run condition possibly customized to a specific user or application. Delivery does not necessarily include preparatory work on the user's data. (T)

turn-on stability time The time interval between the instant power is applied to a device and the instant at which the device performs according to its operating specifications. (T)

turn page Synonym for landscape page.

tutorial Information presented in a teaching format.

Tutorial In SAA Common User Access architecture, a help action that gives a user access to a tutorial.

tutorial and message library (TML) A VSAM file in which the tutorial topics and messages of SDF/CICS are kept. The TML may hold messages, topics, or both in more than one national language.

tutorial sample In SDF/CICS, online tutorial sample screens for the map editor functions and associated editing commands presented to the online user when requesting help in the tutorial sample mode.

tutorial sample mode The SDF/CICS mode established with the SAMPLE command, where online tutorial sample topics are displayed when requesting help in the map editor function.

Tutorial System Support In the AS/400 system, an education course, supplied with the operating system licensed program, that provides introductory education for a variety of computer users, including system operators and business and data processing professionals. Tutorial System Support is part of the total IBM curriculum for the AS/400 system, which consists of classroom training and other methods of self-study.

tutorial text mode The SDF/CICS mode established with the SAMPLE command, where online tutorial text topics are displayed when requesting help in online functions.

TVTOC Tape volume table of contents

twelve-punch A punch in the top row of a Hollerith card. (A) Synonymous with y-punch.

twinaxial cable (1) A cable consisting of two conductors, usually small copper tubes or wires insulated from each other, within and insulated from another conductor of larger diameter, usually copper tubing or copper braid. (2) A cable made of two twisted wires inside a shield.

twinaxial data link control (TDLC) A communications function that allows personal computers, which are attached to the workstation controller by twinaxial cable, to use Advanced Program-to-Program Communication (APPC) or Advanced Peer-to-Peer Networking (APPN).

twin port See mass storage control twin port.

twin segments In an IMS/VS database, all child segments of the same segment type that have a particular instance of the same parent segment type. Root segments are also considered twins. See also sibling segments.

twin-tailed In NCP, pertaining to the attachment of a communication controller to two host processors. See also fanout, multitailed, tailing.

twisted pair (1) A transmission medium that consists of two insulated electrical conductors twisted together to reduce noise. (T) (2) See shielded twisted pair.

two-address instruction An instruction that contains two address parts. (I) (A)

two-bit byte Synonym for doublet.

two-channel switch (1) A hardware feature that allows an input/output device to be attached to two channels. (2) An optional feature for attaching the 3800 Printing Subsystem via two separate channels. The switching is done manually using the Enable/Disable switches on the 3800 usage meter panel. Only one interface can be enabled at a time. A dynamic switch feature can be added which allows both interfaces to be enabled at the same time with selection determined by programming.

two-input adder Synonym for half-adder.

two-level address An indirect address that specifies two levels of addressing. (A)

two-out-of-five code (1) A binary-coded decimal notation in which each decimal digit is represented by a binary numeral consisting of 5 bits of which 2 are of one kind, conventionally ones, and 3 are of the other kind, conventionally zeros. The usual weights are 0-1-2-3-6 except for the representation of zero, which is then 01100. (I) (A) (2) A positional notation in which each decimal digit is represented by five binary digits of which two are one kind (for example, ones) and three are the other kind (for example, zeros). (A)

two-phase commit In an IMS/VS system, a two-step process by which recoverable resources and an external subsystem are committed. During the first step, the subsystems are polled to ensure that they are ready to commit. If all subsystems respond positively, they are then told to execute commit processing.

two-phase commit protocol The protocol that permits updates to one or more protected resources to be committed or backed out as a unit. In the first phase, the initiator sends Prepare, requesting that all agents receiving it vote by responding Request Commit or Backout, indicating whether the logical unit of work should be committed or backed out. All agents must vote to commit if the transaction is to be committed. When all the votes are collected, the second phase begins. In this phase, the initiator informs the agents to commit or back out. At various times, the sync point participants write state information to nonvolatile storage so that the protected resources can be resynchronized if any failures occur during the two-phase commit processing.

two-plus-one address instruction An instruction that contains three addresses, the "plus-one" address being that of the instruction to be executed next. (T)

twos complement The radix complement in the binary numeration system. (T) Synonymous with complement-on-two. See Figure 160.

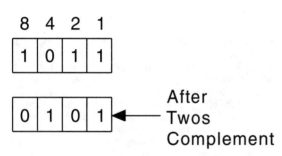

Figure 160. Twos Complement

two-shot (2S) In video and film production, a camera shot of two persons giving equal emphasis to both.

two-tone keying See frequency-shift keying.

two-way alternate communication (1) Data communication so that data are transferred in both directions, one direction at a time. (I) (A) (2) Synonymous with either-way communication.

two-way channel In X.25 communications, a logical channel that allows both incoming and outgoing calls. Contrast with one-way channel.

two-way simultaneous communication (1) Data communication in which data are transferred in both directions at the same time. (I) (A) (2) Synonym for duplex operation.

two-wire circuit A metallic circuit formed by two conductors insulated from each other. It is possible to use the two conductors as a one-way transmission path, a half-duplex path, or a duplex path.

TWX Teletypewriter exchange service.

type (1) A raised character on a type element used to make an imprint. (T) (2) In AIX Enhanced X-Windows, an arbitrary atom used to identify the data. A type is solely for the benefit of clients and is not interpreted by the server. Enhanced X-Windows predefines type atoms for many frequently used types. Clients also can define new types. (3) In FORTRAN, see data type, definition of a procedure or type, derived type. (4) In Pascal, one of several data classes that define the permissible values that can be assigned to a variable. (5) A class of objects. All objects of a specific type can be accessed through one or more of the same interfaces.

type (of an entity) In a conceptual schema language, the proposition establishing that an entity is a member of a particular class of entities, implying as well that there is such a class of entities. (A)

type area Synonym for text area. (T)

type ball A spherically shaped type element with types arranged on its surface. (T)

type ball typewriter A typewriter in which characters are situated on a type ball. (T)

type bar (1) A bar, mounted on an impact printer, that holds type slugs. (I) (A) (2) A pivoted type carrier having a type slug at its free end. (T) (3) Synonymous with print bar.

type bar fulcrum A rod in the type-bar segment on which the type bars are pivoted. (T)

type bar guide A device for guiding a type bar immediately before it reaches the typing position. (T)

type bar rest pad A device on which a type bar is supported in the rest position. (T)

type bar segment A structural unit holding and guiding type bars. (T)

type bar typewriter A typewriter in which characters in the form of type slugs are carried on type bars. (T)

type carrier A component carrying one or several type elements. (T)

type compatibility See compatible types.

type cylinder A cylindrical type element with types arranged on its surface. (T)

type cylinder typewriter A typewriter in which the characters are situated on a type cylinder. (T)

type declaration (1) The specification of the type and, optionally, the length of a variable or function in a specification statement. (2) In FORTRAN, the specification of the type and, optionally, the length of a variable or function in a specification statement. Contrast with predefined specification. (3) In Pascal, the specification of a data type. The declaration can be explicit or can appear within a variable declaration. Synonymous with type definition.

type definition A definition of a name for a data type.

type disk A disk-shaped type element with types arranged on its face. (T)

type disk typewriter A typewriter in which characters are situated on a type disk. (T)

type element (1) A device carrying one or more types. (T) (2) A typing ball used on an IBM

SELECTRIC typewriter. On printing devices, it is called a print element.

typeface (1) A specific type style, such as Universe or Press Roman. (2) One of the many attributes of a font, others, for example, being size and weight. (3) A collection of fonts, each having a different height or size of character sets.

type font Type of a given size and style, for example, 10-point Bodoni Modern. (A)

type identifier (1) The name given to a declared type. See also type specifier. (2) In Pascal, the name given to a declared type.

type impression control A control for varying the force of impression. (T)

typematic key A key that repeats its function when pressed and held down.

typematic key stroke Actuation of a repeat key. (T)

Type over In SAA Basic Common User Access architecture, a choice in action lists that a user selects to change the characteristics of something by typing over its currently displayed attributes.

type parameter In FORTRAN, a parameter of a parameterized data type.

type parameter values In FORTRAN, the values of the type parameters of a data entity of parameterized data type.

type plate A rectangular plate-shaped type element with types arranged on its surface. (T)

type plate typewriter A typewriter in which characters are situated on a type plate. (T)

type posture A typeface style variation indicating whether a typeface is upright as in Roman or slanted to the right as in italic or cursive.

type rod A movable rod carrying one or several types. (T)

type rod typewriter A typewriter in which characters are situated on type rods. (T)

type segment A curved type element with types arranged on its face. (T)

type segment typewriter A typewriter in which characters are situated on a type segment. (T)

typeset (1) To arrange the type on a page for printing. (2) Pertaining to material that has been set in type.

type size (1) A measurement in pitch or points of the height and width of a graphic character in a font. (2) One of the many attributes of a font, others; for example, being weight and typeface.

type slug A type element, usually having two types arranged one above the other for mounting on a type bar. (T)

type specifier A name of a data type.

type style The form of characters within a set of the same font; for example, elite, pica. (T)

Note: Attributes such as posture, weight, and width may vary in a type style.

type UUID In the AIX system, a universal unique identifier UUID that permanently identifies a particular type. Both the remote procedure call RPC runtime library and the Location Broker use type UUIDs to specify types.

type weight (1) The degree of boldness of a typeface series, caused by different thicknesses of the strokes that form a graphic character. (2) One of the many attributes of a font, others, for example, being size and typeface.

type wheel (1) On a typewriter, a wheel-shaped type element with types arranged in rows on its circumference. (T) (2) Synonym for print wheel.

type wheel typewriter A typewriter in which characters are situated on a type wheel. (T)

type width The horizontal size (set size) of a given typeface. The width may be given in units of measurement, such as set 9 point, or it may be descriptive: ultra condensed or expanded.

typewriter A machine designed to produce print-like text on paper or similar material as a result of an operator manually depressing keys consecutively on a keyboard. (T)

typewriter key On the keyboard of an IBM personal computer, any key that is normally found on standard typewriter keyboards. See also function key.

type 1 batch A group of procedures for transferring data over a data link between the host system and the 8100/DPCX system by using 8100/DPCX-defined batch protocols.

type 2 batch A group of procedures for transferring data over a data link between the host system and the 8100/DPCX system by using SNA-defined protocols.

type 2.0 node A node that attaches to a subarea network as a peripheral node and provides a range of end-user services but no intermediate routing services.

type 2.1 node A node that can be an APPN network node, an APPN end node, or an LEN node. It can also attach as a peripheral node to a subarea boundary node in the same way as a type 2.0 node.

type 4 node A node that contains a PUCP rather than an SSCP and that is controlled by one or more type 5 nodes. It can be a subarea node, or, together with other type 4 nodes and their owning type 5 node, it can be included in a group of nodes forming a composite LEN node or a composite network node.

type 5 node A node that can be any one of the following:

- APPN end node
- APPN network node
- LEN node
- Interchange node
- Migration data host (a node that acts as both an APPN end node and a subarea node)
- Subarea node (with an SSCP)

Together with its subordinate type 4 nodes, it can also form a composite LEN node or a composite network node.

typing In programming languages, assigning a specific type to each object; for example, integer, real, logical. See strong typing, weak typing. (A)

typing key A numeric or letter key such as those used on conventional typewriters. Synonymous with typewriter key. (A)

typing line (1) An imaginary line on paper upon which the bottom part of capital and small letters without descenders rests. (T) (2) See also writing line.

typing position The position on a typewriter where types impact the paper. (T)

typing reperforator A reperforator which types on chadless tape about one-half inch beyond where corresponding characters are punched. Some units type on the edge of special-width tape.

typing speed On a typewriter, the number of machine functions required for typing within a specified time, usually expressed in terms of words of five single key strokes per minute. (T)

typist's remote control On dictation equipment, a device connected to but separate from a machine that permits a typist to control certain functions of the machine during transcription. The device may be designed for either foot or hand operation. (I)

U

UA Unnumbered acknowledgment.

UACC Universal access authority.

ublock User block.

UBS Unit backspace character.

UCF Utility control facility.

UCLIN In SMP/E, the command used to initiate changes to SMP/E data sets. Actual changes are made by subsequent UCL statements.

UCS Universal character set.

UDDS User-defined data stream.

UDP User Datagram Protocol.

UDS Utility definition specifications.

UECB User exit control block.

U format (1) A data set format in which blocks are of unknown length. (2) Unnumbered format.

UFP Utility facilities program.

U frame Unnumbered frame.

UGB Utilities services task global block.

UI Unnumbered information frame.

UID User number.

ultrafiche In micrographics, microfiche with images reduced more than ninety times. (A)

ultraviolet Invisible radiation having a wavelength less than 400 nm. (T) See also infrared.

umask Synonym for user number.

unary expression An expression that contains one operand.

unary operation Synonym for monadic operation.

unary operator (1) An arithmetic operator having only one term. The unary operators that can be used in absolute, relocatable, and arithmetic expressions are: positive (+) and negative (−). (2) In COBOL, a plus (+) or a minus (−) sign that precedes a variable or a left parenthesis in an arithmetic expression and that has the effect of multiplying the expression by +1 or -1 respectively. (3) In Pascal, an operator that represents an operation on one operand only; for example, 'NOT' is a unary operator. Contrast with binary operator.

unassign In remote-resource applications, to release a local device name from a shared resource on a network.

unattended mode A mode in which no operator is present or in which no operator station is included at system generation.

unattended operation The automatic transmission and reception of messages on an unattended basis. Contrast with attended operation.

unattended trail printer In word processing, a trail printer to which is attached a sheet feeder, tractor feeder, or other paper handling device, and that therefore can print a number of pages without operator intervention. (T) Contrast with attended trail printer.

unauthorized APPN end node An APPN end node that is not authorized to supply information about itself to its network node server. The authorization status of an end node is system-defined in its network node server. If an end node is unauthorized, then the network node server must verify the correctness of all information coming from that end node before allowing it to penetrate the APPN network; in this way, the network node server protects the APPN network from potential harm by unauthorized end nodes. Contrast with authorized APPN end node.

unauthorized end node Synonym for unauthorized APPN end node.

unavailable choice In SAA Common User Access architecture, an item that an application does not allow a user to select because of some condition in the application. Contrast with available choice.

unavailable emphasis In SAA Common User Access architecture, a visual cue that shows a user which items in a list of choices cannot be selected. See also graying.

unavailable time From the point of view of a user, the time during which a functional unit cannot be used. (I) (A)

unbalanced (to ground) The state of impedance on a two-wire line when the impedance to ground as measured from one wire is different from the impedance to ground as measured from the other wire. Contrast with balanced to ground.

unbalanced data link A data link between a primary station and one or more participating secondary stations. The primary station organizes data flow, performs data link level error recovery operations, and transmits command frames to the secondary stations. The secondary stations transmit response frames. Contrast with balanced data link.

unbalanced merge sort (1) A merge sort, which is an external sort, such that the sorted subsets created by the internal sorts are unequally distributed among some of the available auxiliary storage devices. The subsets are merged onto the remaining auxiliary storage devices and the process repeated until all items are in one sorted set. (A) (2) Contrast with balanced merge sort.

unbind In SNA, to deactivate a session between logical units.

UNBIND In SNA, a request to deactivate a session between two logical units (LUs). See also session deactivation request. Contrast with BIND.

UNBIND command In SNA, a command used to reset the protocols for a session. Contrast with BIND command.

unblank In computer graphics, to turn the beam on.

unblock Deprecated term for deblock.

unblocked In an ESCON Director, the attribute that, when set, establishes communication capability for a specific port. Contrast with blocked.

unbounded geometry An object as defined by the intersection of a series of infinite surfaces. (T)

unconditional branch A control transfer that never requires a decision. (I) (A)

unconditional branch instruction Deprecated term for unconditional jump instruction.

unconditional control transfer instruction Deprecated term for unconditional jump instruction.

unconditional force In System/36 SORT, a specification that always results in a character being forced into a control field before the records are sorted.

unconditional jump (1) A jump that takes place whenever the instruction that specified it is executed. (I) (A) (2) Contrast with conditional jump.

unconditional jump instruction (1) A jump instruction that specifies a mandatory jump. (T) (2) Contrast with conditional jump instruction.

unconditional statement In programming languages, a statement that specifies only one possible execution sequence. (I)

unconditional transfer instruction Deprecated term for unconditional jump instruction.

unconfigure In the AIX operating system: (a) To take a device from the available (configured) state to the defined state. This is accomplished by running the unconfigure method for a device. The device status field in the Customized Devices Object Class reflects this action. (b) To take out of use by the current computer system.

undefine In the AIX operating system: (a) To take a device instance out of the system. This is accomplished by running the undefine method for the device. All information for the device in the Customized Database is purged by this operation. (b) To cause a command to be no longer recognized by the current computer system.

undefined record A record having an unspecified or unknown length. See also U format.

undelete In SAA usage, deprecated term for restore.

underflow (1) On a calculator, a condition in which the result shown is the most significant part of a number that exceeds the output capacity of the machine to the right of the decimal marker. (T) (2) In BASIC, a condition that occurs when a numeric value is so small that accuracy is lost during calculation, or it takes more numbers than will fit in the field to write the decimal positions. (3) Synonym for arithmetic underflow, monadic operation.

underflow exception A condition caused by the result of an arithmetic operation having a magnitude less than the smallest possible nonzero number.

underflow indicator On a calculator, a visual indication that the machine is in the underflow condition. (T)

underline To print or display a line directly under a character, or group of characters. Synonymous with underscore. (T)

underrun Loss of data caused by inability of a transmitting device or channel to provide data to the communication control logic (SDLC or BSC/SS) at a rate that is fast enough for the attached data link or loop.

underscanned In video systems, scanning in which the edges of the raster are visible.

underscore (1) A line printed under a character. (2) To place a line under one or more characters; to underline. (3) Synonym for underline. (T)

underscore attribute In SAA Basic Common User Access architecture, a display device function that displays an underscore beneath each character position in an entry field to indicate the length of that entry field.

under-the-cover modem Deprecated term for integrated modem.

undo A function that enables a user to cancel the effects of the most recently executed command or commands.

Note: Some commands are irreversible. (I) (A)

Undo In SAA Common User Access architecture, a choice in the Edit pull-down that can be used to reverse the action of the most recently entered user action.

unerase In SAA usage, deprecated term for restore.

unformatted (1) Pertaining to that which is not defined, organized, or arranged in a required manner. (2) In VTAM, pertaining to commands, such as LOGON or LOGOFF, entered by an end user and sent by a logical unit in character form. The character-coded command must be in the syntax defined in the user's unformatted system services definition table. Synonymous with character-coded. Contrast with field-formatted.

unformatted data In FORTRAN, data that is transferred between main storage and an input/output device with a one-to-one relationship between bytes in main storage and positions in the record. See also formatted data, list-directed data.

unformatted diskette A diskette that contains no data and no track or sector format information. Contrast with formatted diskette. See also daily initialization diskette, diagnostic diskette, installation diskette.

unformatted display A display screen on which the user has not defined a display field. Contrast with formatted display. See also protected field.

unformatted file A file displayed with data that is not arranged with particular characters.

unformatted image In DPCX, a display image in which attribute bytes are not defined. The screen is treated as if it is one continuous, unprotected field into which the operator can enter data and on which the program can display data. Contrast with formatted image.

unformatted mode (1) In document formatting, the state in which each input line is processed and printed without formatting. Other SCRIPT/VS control words remain in effect and are recognized. (2) In document printing using the UNFORMAT option, the state in which each input line (control words as well as text) is printed as it exists in the input, in the order in which it is processed. No formatting is done.

unformatted program interface The part of 3270 emulation support that allows user-written programs to access the 3270 data stream in the form in which it is sent from the host system. Contrast with formatted program interface.

unformatted record (1) A record transmitted with a one-to-one relationship between storage locations and positions in the record. (2) In BASIC, a record without a FORM or IMAGE statement that is transferred with a one-to-one relationship between bytes in storage and positions in the record. (3) In FORTRAN, a record without a FORMAT statement, that is transferred with a one-to-one relationship between storage locations and positions in the record.

unformatted request Synonym for character-coded request.

unformatted system services (USS) In SNA products, a system services control point (SSCP) facility that translates a character-coded request, such as a LOGON or LOGOFF request, into a field-formatted request for processing by formatted system services and translates field-formatted replies and responses into character-coded requests for processing by a logical unit.

unidirectional microphone A microphone that responds to sound from only one direction and is not subject to change of direction. Unidirectional microphones are used with computers capable of voice recognition.

unidirectional printing A printing method in which the print head on the printer prints only while it moves in one direction, instead of also printing while it moves in the opposite direction. This method of printing usually produces higher-quality print output.

unidirectional transmission A transmission that occurs always in one direction, along a transmission medium. (T)

uniform baseline offset The distance from the top left corner of a character box to the picture element (pel) position that appears to rest on the baseline. This value is the same for all the characters in a font.

uniformly spaced font A font with graphic characters contained in character cells of uniform size. The distance between reference points of adjacent graphic characters is constant in the inline progression. The white space between the graphic characters may vary. Synonymous with fixed-space font. Contrast with proportionally spaced font.

uniform referencing In a programming language use of two or more language constructs for referencing are of the same form; for example, language constructs for name qualification and indirect references, language constructs for subscripting and actual parameters. (I)

uninterpreted name In SNA, a character string that a system services control point (SSCP) can convert into the network name of a logical unit (LU).

uninterruptible power supply (UPS) A buffer between utility power or other power source and a load that requires uninterrupted, precise power.

union (1) In C language, a variable that can hold any one of several data types, but only one data type at a time. See discriminated union. (2) In SQL, an operation that combines the results of two subselects. Union is often used to merge lists of values obtained from several tables.

union tag The identifier that names a union data type.

unipolar See neutral transmission.

uniprocessing Sequential execution of instructions by a processing unit or independent use of a processing unit in a multiprocessing system.

unique alternate key In systems with VSAM, an alternate key that occurs in only one data record in the base cluster. The alternate index record containing this key has only one pointer to the base cluster. Contrast with nonunique alternate key.

unique file A VSAM file that occupies a data space of its own. The data space is defined at the same time as the file and cannot contain any other file. Contrast with suballocated file.

unique index In SQL, an index that assures that no identical key values are stored in a table.

unit (1) A device having a special function. (A) (2) A basic element. (A) (3) In XL FORTRAN, a

means of referring to a file in order to use input/output statements. A unit can be connected or not connected to a file. If connected, it refers to the file. The connection is symmetric; that is, if a unit is connected to a file, the file is connected to the unit. (4) In the AS/400 system, the defined space within disk units that is referred to by the system. (5) In Pascal, an independently compilable piece of code. The two types of units are segment units and program units. See also segment unit, program unit. (6) Synonym for reel, volume. (7) See arithmetic and logic unit, arithmetic unit, buffer unit, compilable unit, control unit, corona unit, delay unit, functional unit, information content natural unit, input-output unit, input unit, instruction control unit, lexical unit, logic unit, magnetic tape unit, main control unit, main storage unit, output unit, peripheral control unit, processing unit, program unit, raster unit, scoping unit, tape unit, work unit.

unit address The three-character address of a device, specified at the time a system is installed; for example, 191 or 293. See also device type, group name.

unit backspace character (UBS) A word processing formatting control that moves the printing or display point to the left one escapement unit as defined to provide character alignment in proportionally spaced text. See also backspace character.

unit cube In AIX graphics, a volume defined by the following planes: x = -1, x = 1, y = -1, y = 1, z = -1, and z = 1. See also normalized device coordinates.

unit identifier (1) In a FORTRAN input/output statement, a constant or variable that specifies the file that is to be read from or written to. (2) In XL FORTRAN, the number that specifies an external unit or internal file. The number can be one of the following:

- An integer expression whose value must be zero or positive

- An asterisk (*) that corresponds to unit 5 for input or unit 6 for output

- The name of a character array, character array element, or character substring for an internal file.

unit interval In a system using synchronous transmission, an interval of time such that the nominal directions of the significant intervals of a modulation signal are all whole multiples of that interval. (T)

unit number In the AS/400 system, the unique identifier of an actuator within the system.

unit of display A body of information that must be displayed as a single unit. The exact format of the display is left to the discretion of the focal-point product.

unit of escapement The minimum escapement used in typewriters with proportional pitch. (T)

unit of recovery A sequence of operations within a unit of work between commit points.

unit of transfer (1) In VSE, the amount of data that can be transferred between virtual storage and an I/O device in response to a read or write request. (2) In VSE/POWER, the amount of virtual storage containing a sufficient number of fixed-block architecture (FBA) blocks to make up a data block.

unit of work (1) In advanced program-to-program communications, the amount of processing that is started directly or indirectly by a program on the source system. (2) In IMS/VS Fast Path, a number of contiguous control intervals in the root-addressable part of a data entry database area. (3) See synchronized unit of work.

unit-of-work identifier In the AS/400 advanced program-to-program and System/38 communications, a unique label assigned to a unit of work. The ID is established when the program on the source system is started and is associated with each job started by that source system on the target system. The unit-of-work identifier provides a beginning-to-end audit trail within an APPC network.

unit record (1) A card containing one complete record, a punched card. (2) Pertaining to card I/O or printer output.

unit reference code In the AS/400 system, a group of numbers displayed on the console or control panel that identifies failing parts, system or device states, or system or device status conditions.

unit space The minimum amount of additional spacing acceptable for purposes of horizontal justification, as specified by the font designer.

unit string A string that contains one element. (T)

unit test A test of individual programs or modules in order to ensure that there are no analysis or programming errors. (T)

universal access authority (UACC) In RACF, the default access authority that applies to a resource if the user or group is not specifically permitted access to the resource. The universal access authority can be any of the access authorities.

universal address Synonym for master address.

universally administered address In a local area network, the address permanently encoded in an adapter at the time of manufacture. All universally administered addresses are unique. Contrast with locally administered address.

universal administration Address administration in which all LAN individual addresses are unique within the same or other local area networks. Synonymous with global administration. (T)

universal character set (UCS) A printer feature that permits the use of a variety of character arrays.

universal controller See basic controller.

universal instruction set A set of instructions that includes those for floating-point arithmetic, fixed-point binary arithmetic and logic, decimal arithmetic, and protection feature.

universal product code (UPC) A standard bar code, commonly used to mark the price of items in stores, that can be read and interpreted by a computer.

universal receiver-transmitter A circuit used in asynchronous, synchronous, or combined synchronous and asynchronous data communication applications to provide all the necessary logic to receive data serial-in parallel-out and to transmit parallel-in serial-out; usually it transmits by means of duplex transmission, and can accommodate various word lengths. (A)

universal set A set that includes all of the elements of concern in a given study. (I) (A)

universal Turing machine A Turing machine that can simulate any other Turing machine. (A)

Universal Unique Identifier (UUID) A 128-bit value used for identification. The Network Computing System NCS uses UUIDs to identify interfaces, objects and types. See also object UUID, type UUID.

universe of discourse In a database, all entities in a particular context, that exist, did exist, or might exist. A universe of discourse may include many entity worlds, possibly including entities that are not yet perceived. (T)

UNIX operating system An operating system developed by Bell Laboratories that features multiprogramming in a multi-user environment. The UNIX operating system was originally developed for use on minicomputers but has been adapted for mainframes and microcomputers. (Trademark of AT&T Bell Laboratories)

Note: The AIX operating system is IBM's implementation of the UNIX operating system. See AIX operating system.

UNIX-to-UNIX Copy Program (UUCP) In the AIX operating system, a group of commands, programs, and files, on most UNIX systems, that allows the user to communicate with another UNIX system over a dedicated line or a telephone line. See also Basic Networking Utilities.

unjustified text Text that has uneven line endings.

unlink In IDDU and the System/36 interactive data definition utility, to remove the association between a database file on disk and a file definition in a data dictionary. Contrast with link.

unload data set In DPPX/DTMS, a data set that contains a copy of the target data set records of a database. The copy can be used as a primary source of input for recreating the database.

unlock In the AS/400 system, to release an object or system resource that was previously locked, and return it to general availability.

unlocked resource In CICS/VS, a protected resource that is not associated with a transaction program as part of a synchronized unit of work. An unlocked resource is available for such an association. It cannot be modified until after such an association takes place.

unmanaged widget In the AIX operating system, a widget whose size cannot be changed.

unmapped conversation In System/38 advanced program-to-program communications, a temporary connection between an application program and an APPC session in which the user must provide all the information on how the data is formatted. Contrast with mapped conversation.

unmapped physical storage Synonym for unaddressable storage.

unmapped window In the AIX operating system, a window that is not visible on the screen.

Unmark In SAA Common User Access architecture, a choice in the Edit pull-down that users select to unmark something they had previously marked for selection.

unmarshall In the Network Computing System NCS, to copy data from a remote procedure call packet. Stubs perform unmarshalling. Contrast with marshall.

unmodified instruction Deprecated term for presumptive instruction.

unnumbered In communications, pertaining to a frame format that provides additional control functions, such as XID, DISC, DM, SABM, SABME, UA, and FRMR.

unnumbered acknowledge (UA) A link control frame.

unnumbered acknowledgment (UA) In the AS/400 system, a data link command or response that acknowledges the receipt and acceptance of the SABM, SABME, and DISC command protocol data units.

unnumbered information (UI) frame A transmission frame in unnumbered format, used to transfer unnumbered control functions.

unnumbered (U) format A format used to provide additional data link control functions and unnumbered information transfer. See also information format, supervisory format.

unnumbered (U) frame A frame in unnumbered format, used to transfer unnumbered control functions. See also information frame, supervisory frame.

unnumbered (U) response A response that does not contain sequence numbers in the control field.

unordered In binary floating-point, pertaining to a relationship existing between two values that indicates they cannot be ordered according to relative value. The relationship between two values is unordered when a not-a-number is compared to any value or when infinity is compared to any value other than infinity.

unpack To recover the original form of the data from packed data. (I) (A)

unpacked decimal format (1) A binary-coded decimal notation in which each decimal digit is represented by one byte. (T) (2) A format for representing numbers in which the digit is contained in bits 4 through 7 and the sign is contained in bits 0 through 3 of the rightmost byte. Bits 0 through 3 of all other bytes contain 1s (hex F); for example, in zoned decimal format, the decimal value of +123 is represented as 1111 0001 1111 0010 1100 0011. Contrast with packed decimal format. Synonymous with zoned decimal format. See also signed packed decimal format.

unprivileged state A hardware protection state in which the processor can run only unprivileged instructions. The unprivileged state supports the virtual machine's operating system state and problem state. Contrast with privileged state.

unprotected dynamic storage Synonym for dynamic storage.

unprotected field A displayed field in which a user can enter, modify, or delete data. Contrast with protected field.

unprotected storage (1) In the AS/400 system, the part of the system auxiliary storage pool that is not protected by the checksum option. (2) In the AS/400 system, the storage reserved for temporary objects and internal machine data while a job is running.

unpunched litho master In a duplicator, a litho master with unperforated edges. (T)

unqualified call In IMS/VS, a DL/I call that does not contain a segment search argument.

unqualified segment search argument In IMS/VS, a segment search argument (SSA) that contains only a segment name specifying the segment type to be accessed.

unrecoverable abend An error condition that results in abnormal termination of a program. Contrast with recoverable abend.

unrecoverable error Synonym for irrecoverable error.

unrecoverable transaction In IMS/VS, an inquiry transaction that is not recovered in the event of a failure.

unsolicited interrupt In the AIX operating system, an interrupt that is sent to a virtual machine when its last virtual terminal is closed. See interrupt.

unsolicited message (1) In MSS, a message from the mass storage control to the primary processing unit that is not requested or expected by the processing unit. (2) A message from VTAM to a program operator that is unrelated to any command entered by the program operator. Contrast with solicited message.

unstable state (1) In a circuit, a state in which the circuit remains for a finite period of time at the end of which it returns to a stable state without the application of a pulse. (T) (2) Synonymous with metastable state, quasistable state.

unstratified language (1) A language that can be used as its own metalanguage; for example, most natural languages. (I) (A) (2) Contrast with stratified language.

unsuccessful execution In COBOL, the attempted execution of a statement that does not result in the execution of all the operations specified by that statement. The unsuccessful execution of a statement does not affect any data referenced by that statement, but may affect status indicators.

unviewable In AIX graphics, pertaining to a mapped window with an unmapped ancestor. Contrast with viewable.

unwind To state explicitly and in full, without the use of modifiers, all the instructions involved in the execution of a loop. (I) (A)

UP Unnumbered poll (SDLC).

UPC Universal product code.

update (1) To add, change, or delete items. (2) To modify a master file with current information according to a specified procedure.

update authority (1) The ability to add, change, or cancel items. (2) In the AS/400 system, a data authority that allows the user to change the data in an object, such as a journal, a message queue, or a data area. See also add authority, delete authority, read authority.

updated-record mark In the IBM 3790 Communication System, an indication, set in the control information for an index record, that the record has been changed. See also mark function.

update file A file from which a program reads a record, updates fields in the record, and writes the record back into the location from which it came.

update install The process of modifying an 8100/DPCX system. Contrast with full install.

update intent In IMS/VS, the scheduling intent type that permits application programs to be scheduled with any number of other programs except those with exclusive intent.

update mark In DPCX, a byte in the control record for an indexed record that can be written by a user program to indicate access or change to the record.

update-only recovery An IMS/VS facility that allows the user to define inquiry transactions as unrecoverable.

update operation An I/O operation that modifies the information in a file.

update rights The authority to change the entries in an object. Contrast with add rights, delete rights, read rights.

update script In the AIX operating system, a shell procedure or executable file created by the developer of an application program to update a program. The script file must follow specific guidelines in order to be compatible with the program update tools that are provided in the operating system.

update transaction In IMS/VS, a transaction in a system with the DC feature with capabilities for updating a database. Update transactions are recoverable.

upgrade set In VSAM, all of the alternate indexes that are to be updated whenever there is a change to the data component of the related base cluster.

upline Pertaining to the direction opposite to the direction of transmission. Contrast with downline.

uplink Pertaining to data transmission from a data station to the headend. (T)　Contrast with downlink.

upload (1) To transfer programs or data from a connected device, typically a personal computer, to a computer with greater resources. (T)　(2) To transfer data from a device, such as a workstation or a microcomputer, to a computer. Contrast with download. See also terminal emulation.

uppercase Pertaining to the capital letters, as distinguished from the small letters; for example, A, B, G, rather than a, b, g.

upper curtate The adjacent card rows at the top of a punch card. (A)

upper letter row On a keyboard, the top letter row. Synonymous with row D.　See lower letter row, middle letter row. See also numeric row.

upper print line On a display screen, the line through the upper 50-percent luminance contour of the highest row of pels of the uppercase character matrix. Contrast with lower print line.

UPS Uninterruptible power supply.

upside-down portrait A page orientation such that the top of the printed image is at the trailing edge of the paper as it emerges from the printer.

upstop (1) A mechanical device limiting upward motion of a movable part.　(2) A physical part, usually nonmovable, used to limit or stop the upward travel of the armature in an electromechanical device such as a relay.

upstream (1) In the direction opposite to data flow or toward the source of transmission.　(2) Toward the

processor from an attached unit or end user.　(3) In the direction toward a host computer or toward a host system.　(4) Contrast with downstream.

upstream device For the IBM 3710 Network Controller, a device located in a network so that the device is positioned between the 3710 and a host. A communication controller upstream from the 3710 is an example of an upstream device. Contrast with downstream device.

uptime (1) Synonym for operable time. (T)　(2) Deprecated term for available time.　(3) Synonym for operating time.

upward compatibility The capability of a computer to execute programs written for another computer without major alteration, but not vice versa.

upward reference In overlay, a reference made from a segment to another segment higher in the same path, that is, closer to the root segment.

URC Unit reference code.

US The unit separator character. (A)

usability The quality of a system, program, or device that enables it to be easily understood and conveniently employed by a user. See also utility.

usability test A test to determine whether an implemented system fulfills its functional purpose as determined by its users. Synonymous with fitness-for-use test. (T)

usable area (1) In the 3270 Information Display System, the area on a display surface that can be used to display data, (2) In the 3270 Information Display System, data in a query reply structured field that defines the size and characteristics of the screen available for defining viewports.

use authority In the AS/400 system, an object authority that allows the user to run a program or to display the contents of a file. Use authority combines object operational authority, read authority.

user (1) A person who requires the services of a computing system.　(2) Any person or any thing that may issue or receive commands and messages to or from the information processing system. (T)　(3) Anyone who requires the services of a computing system. See also end user, multiuser, terminal user. (4) In the AIX operating system, the name associated with an account. See privileged user. (5) Contrast with customer.

user account See account.

user address list In the AIX operating system, the address list that an individual can use to make outgoing X.25 calls. See also address list, system address list.

user-application network A configuration of data processing products, such as processors, controllers, and terminals, established and operated by users for the purpose of data processing or information exchange, which may use services offered by communication common carriers or telecommunication Administrations. (T)   Contrast with public network.

user application record In the NetView/PC program, a record that defines the communication path between the NetView/PC program and the device it is communicating with.

user area (1) The parts of main storage and auxiliary storage that are available to the user.   (2) In SDF/CICS, an area of a split screen that can contain a window over a scrollable list, a window over an editing area, or a complete editing area. See also menu area.

user ASP In the AS/400 system, one or more auxiliary storage pools used to isolate some system objects from the other system objects stored in the system auxiliary storage pool (ASP).   See also auxiliary storage pool (ASP), system (ASP).

user attribute (1) The extraordinary privileges, restrictions, and processing environments assigned to a user.   In RACF, the user attributes are SPECIAL, AUDITOR, CLAUTH, OPERATIONS, GRPACC, ADSP, and REVOKE.   (2) A characteristic of a user that defines the type of functions that a user can perform.

user attribute data set (UADS) In TSO, a partitioned data set with a member for each authorized user. Each member contains the appropriate passwords, user identifications, account numbers, LOGON procedure names, and user characteristics that define the user.

user block In the AIX operating system, a data structure maintained by the AIX kernel that contains system information about a user process, such as its real and effective user IDs, the list of open file descriptors, and signal-handling settings. The user structure specifies the exact information that is kept in the user block.

user catalog See VSAM user catalog.

user class In the AS/400 system, the classification of a user by the system task, such as security officer, security administrator, programmer, system operator, and user. Each user class has a set of special authorities depending on the security level of the system.

The user class determines which options are shown on the IBM-supplied menus.

user class of service A category of data transmission service provided by a data network in which the data signaling rate, the data terminal equipment operating mode, and the code structure, if any, are standardized. (T)

user contact-hour In interactive video, a unit of "length" of an interactive presentation, assuming all the material provided is accessed. It is based on such factors as the length of the video, the number of graphics and still frames, and the logical complexity of the application.

user coordinate (1) A coordinate specified by a user and expressed in a coordinate system that is device independent. (I) (A)   (2) See also world coordinates.

user correlator A 4-byte value supplied to VTAM by an application program when certain macroinstructions, such as REQSESS, are issued. It is returned to the application program when subsequent events occur, such as entry to a SCIP exit routine upon receipt of BIND, that result from the procedure started by the original macroinstruction.

user data Data transferred between entities in a layer on behalf of the entities in the next higher layer for which the former entities are providing services. (T)

User Datagram Protocol (UDP) In TCP/IP, a packet-level protocol built directly on the Internet protocol layer. UDP is used for application-to-application programs between TCP/IP host systems.

user data segment In AIX kernel mode, the virtual memory segment that contains user data, which consists of initialized data variables.

user data set (1) In MVS, a data set defined to RACF where either the high-level qualifier of the data set name or the qualifier supplied by an installation exit routine is a RACF userid. (2) A data set defined to RACF with a RACF user ID as the high-level qualifier.

user-defined data stream (UDDS) In the AS/400 system, a data stream in which the user has defined and embedded all device control characters.

user-defined edit code In the AS/400 system and System/38 a number (5 through 9) indicating that editing should be done on a numeric output field according to a pattern predefined to the system program. User-defined edit codes can take the place of edit words, so that repetitive coding of the same edit word is not necessary.

user-defined function In BASIC, a function defined by the user in the DEF of a function definition. Contrast with intrinsic function.

user-defined word In COBOL, a word that must be supplied by the user to satisfy the format of a clause or statement.

user disk See CMS user disk.

user environment In SDF/CICS, an object that defines user identification and sign-on passwords and other user- and session-oriented parameters.

user exit (1) A point in an IBM-supplied program at which a user exit routine may be given control. (2) A programming service provided by an IBM software product that may be requested during the execution of an application program for the service of transferring control back to the application program upon the later occurrence of a user-specified event.

user exit queue A structure built by VTAM that is used to serialize the execution of application program exit routines. Only one exit routine on each user exit queue can run at a time.

user exit routine A user-written routine that receives control at predefined user exit points. User exit routines can be written in assembler or a high-level language.

user facility (1) A set of functions available on demand to a user, and provided as a part of a data network transmission service. (I) (A) (2) Synonymous with user service.

Note: Some facilities may be available on a per-call basis, and others may be assigned for an agreed period at the request of the user. On certain assigned facilities, per-call options may also be available.

user-friendly (1) Pertaining to the ease and convenience of use by humans. (T) (2) See usability.

Note: The term user-friendly describes a program, system, or device that can be easily used by a person who has little or no experience with computers.

user hold status In the VM/XA Migration Aid, a spool file status that prevents a file from being printed, punched, or read until the file owner releases it. Contrast with system hold status.

user ID User identification.

userid A string of characters that uniquely identifies a user to a system.

user ID/address In the AS/400 system, the two-part network name used in the system distribution directory and in the office applications to uniquely identify a user and send electronic mail.

user identification (user ID) (1) A string of characters that uniquely identifies a user to a system. (2) The name used to associate the user profile with a user when a user signs on the system. See also user profile name. (3) In the AS/400 system, the first part of a two-part network name used in the system distribution directory and in the office applications to uniquely identify a user. The network name is usually the same as the user profile name, but does not need to be.

user identification and verification (1) In RACF, the actions of identifying and verifying a RACF-defined user to the system during logon or batch job processing. RACF identifies the user by the userid and verifies the user by the password or operator identification card (MVS only) supplied during logon processing or the password supplied on a batch JOB statement. (2) A system action that identifies and verifies a user at logon or when a batch job is received for processing.

user input area On a display device, the lines of the screen where the user is required to key in command or data lines. See Figure 161.

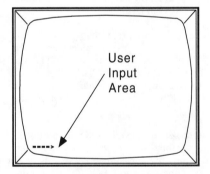

Figure 161. User Input Area

user interface (1) Hardware, software, or both that allows a user to interact with and perform operations on a system, program, or device. (2) In SAA usage, any of the actions or items defined by Common User Access (CUA) architecture that allow a user to interact with and perform operations on a computer.

user main storage map In TSO, a map of the allocated storage in a user region, built by the region control task, and used to determine how much of the region needs to be swapped.

user manual Documentation that describes how to use a functional unit, and that may include description of the rights and responsibilities of the user, the owner, and the supplier of the unit. Synonymous with user's guide. (T)

user memory In an IBM personal computer, random access memory (RAM) inside the system unit or in an expansion unit that is available to the user for doing work. User memory is volatile, meaning that its contents are lost when the power is turned off. Synonymous with temporary memory.

Note: Although the system unit also contains read-only memory (ROM), in IBM PC documentation the term memory usually refers to user memory.

user message queue In the AS/400 system, a user-created object used to receive messages sent from the system, other users, and application programs.

user mode In the AIX operating system, a mode in which a process is carried out in the user's program rather than in the kernel. Contrast with kernel mode.

user name In RACF, one to twenty alphanumeric characters that represent a RACF-defined user.

user number (UID) In the AIX operating system, a number that uniquely identifies a user to the system. It is the internal number associated with a user ID. Synonymous with umask.

user object In SAA Advanced Common User Access architecture, the information created by a user within an application. Contrast with application object.

user option In SAA Common User Access architecture, a choice of appearance or interaction characteristics that programmers give a user during the operation of an application. See also application option.

user password A unique string of characters entered to identify a user to the system.

user profile (1) In computer security, a description of a user that includes such information as user ID, user name, password, access authority, and other attributes obtained at logon. (2) In the AS/400 system, an object with a unique name that contains the user's password, the list of special authorities assigned to a user, and the objects the user owns. (3) In the AIX operating system, a file in the user's home directory that contains shell commands that set initial user-defined characteristics and defaults for the login session.

user profile name (1) The name or code that the system associates with a user when that user signs on the system. See also user identification (user ID). (2) See also authorization ID.

user program A user-written program.

user program area In CMS, the virtual storage area occupying location X'20000' to the end of the user's virtual machine. The beginning of the user program area is the default loading point for user programs and for many CMS commands.

user service (1) Any set of data processing functions made available to the user. (2) Synonym for user facility.

user service class A category of data transmission service provided by a data network in which the data signaling rate, data terminal equipment (DTE) operating mode, and code structure, if any, are standardized. (I) (A)

user's guide Synonym for user manual.

user space (1) Storage space that is not system space. (2) The area of storage used for execution of user programs. (3) In the AIX operating system, the address space seen by a process in user mode. See also user structure.

user's set An apparatus located on the premises of a user of a telecommunication or signaling service and designed to function with other parts of a system.

user structure In AIX kernel mode, the data area that contains information that must be accessible while a process runs. One user structure is allocated for each active process. See also per-process data area. user block.

user table (1) In the AS/400 system, a list of user IDs authorized to a finance job. (2) In TPNS, one or more text data entries contained in a table format, which may be referred to for logic testing and message generation.

user terminal A terminal that enables a user to communicate with a computer. (T)

USERVAR A variable whose value is the name of the logical unit to which VTAM routes session-establishment requests.

user variable See USERVAR.

user view A collection of data in a form appropriate to a specific user or user group and representing information about a universe of discourse relevant to that user or user group. (T)

user-written generation application A user-written program that runs with the NCP/EP definition facility (NDF) during NCP generation. It processes definition statements and operands.

using node (1) In NCP, the NCP in the host's domain that reports a link error condition. (2) For the command facility of the NetView program and for NCCF, the ID parameter of certain network control commands.

USS Unformatted system services.

Utilities Program Product An IBM-licensed program that contains the data file utility (DFU), the source entry utility (SEU), the workstation utility (WSU), and the screen design aid (SDA).

utility (1) The capability of a system, program, or device to perform the functions for which it is designed. Synonymous with functionality, functional performance. See also usability, user interface. (2) See utility program, utility routine.

utility control facility (UCF) An optional IMS/VS facility that provides a method of performing most database utility and maintenance operations in preparation for recovery and reorganization.

utility control statement A statement that gives a utility program information about the way the program is to perform or the output it is to produce.

utility definition specification (UDS) In System/38, a group of source statements that have the same syntax as control language commands, and from which a data file utility or query application is created.

utility facilities program (UFP) A function-level routine of Subsystem Support Services used for system maintenance of the subsystem library, and for formatting command buffers for other functions.

utility program (1) A computer program in general support of computer processes; for example, a diagnostic program, a trace program, a sort program. (T) Synonymous with service program. (2) A program designed to perform an everyday task such as copying data from one storage device to another. (A)

utility routine A routine in general support of the processes of a computer; for example, an input routine. Synonymous with service routine. (I) (A)

utility session In ACF/TCAM extended networking, a pair of LU-LU sessions between TCAM nodes. One utility session is established between each pair of TCAM nodes for each transmission category defined for the pair. Data messages routed between TCAM nodes flow on the utility session corresponding to their transmission category.

UTS Unbound task set.

UUCP Unix-to-Unix Copy Program.

UUCP login ID In the AIX operating system, a login name, provided with the Basic Networking Utilities (BNU), that has complete access to all BNU files and directories. See also Basic Network Utilities.

UUID Universal Unique Identifier.

V

V Volt.

V.24 In data communications, a specification of the CCITT that defines the list of definitions for interchange circuits between data terminal equipment (DTE) and data circuit-terminating equipment (DCE).

V.25 In data communications, a specification of the CCITT that defines the automatic answering equipment and parallel automatic calling equipment on the General Switched Telephone Network, including procedures for disabling of echo controlled devices for both manually and automatically established calls.

V.35 In data communications, a specification of the CCITT that defines the list of definitions for interchange circuits between data terminal equipment (DTE) and data circuit-terminating equipment (DCE) at data rates of 48 kilobits per second.

V AC Volts alternating current.

vaccine program In computer security, a program that watches for typical things that viruses do, halts them, and warns the computer operator.

vacuum bed In a document copying machine, a type of exposure area fitted to some machines that uses a vacuum to hold copy material during exposure. (T)

vacuum column In a magnetic tape drive, a cavity in which a lower air pressure is maintained so as to attract a tape loop between the spool and the driving mechanism. (T)

vacuum control In a duplicator, a means of adjusting the vacuum pressure in the suction feed mechanism. (T)

vacuum platen cover In a document copying machine, a type of platen cover that permits creation of a vacuum to achieve high contact pressure between the original and the platen. (T)

validation (1) The checking of data for correctness or for compliance with applicable standards, rules, and conventions. (A)　(2) In X.25 communications, the process by which the receiving data terminal equip-

ment (DTE) accepts the packet size, packet window size, and throughput class of the sending (DTE), on condition that they are valid. Contrast with negotiation. (3) See input data validation.

validation test (1) A test to determine whether an implemented system fulfills its specified requirements. (T)　(2) A test to check hardware for error-free operation following repair, replacement, or engineering changes. (3) See also verification test.

valid exclusive reference In an overlay program, an exclusive reference in which a common segment contains a reference to the symbol used in the exclusive reference.

validity check A check to determine if a code group is actually a character of the particular code in use.

validity checker In System/38, a user-written program that tests commands for errors in parameter values. Validity checking is done in addition to the checking done by the command analyzer.

valley In OCR, an indentation in a stroke.

valuator (1) An input unit that provides a scalar value; for example, a thumb wheel, a potentiometer. (I) (A)　(2) In AIX graphics, an input/output device that returns a value in a range; for example, a mouse logically has two valuators: the x position and the y position.

valuator device (1) An input device that provides a scalar value; for example, a thumb wheel, a potentiometer. (I) (A)　(2) See also choice device, locator device, pick device.

value (1) A specific occurrence of an attribute; for example, "blue" for the attribute "color." (T)　(2) A quantity assigned to a constant, a variable, parameter or a symbol. See also argument. (3) In the AS/400 system, data (numbers or character strings) entered in any entry field, and data supplied in parameters of control language (CL) commands. (4) In the AS/400 system, the smallest unit of data manipulated by the Structured Query Language.　(5) In the AS/400 system, in query management, a quantity assigned to a keyword or variable associated with a query command. If the keyword is part of the command string, its value is separated from it with an equal sign (=). If the keyword is an argument on the extended interface, its value is also an argument. (6) See truth value.

value added tax function A selectable function that allows a user to produce a cash receipt that indicates the amount of value-added tax included in a sales transaction.

value attribute In FORTRAN, an attribute that describes whether a data object is constant or variable and whether it has a defined initial value.

value set In SAA Advanced Common User Access architecture, a group of choices, usually graphical, from which a user can select one.

value type In AS/400 query management, one of the arguments passed to the extended interface. The value type specifies the data type of the value associated with the keyword.

variable (1) In programming languages, a language object that may take different values, one at a time. The values of a variable are usually restricted to a certain data type. (I) (2) A quantity that can assume any of a given set of values. (A) (3) A name used to represent a data item whose value can be changed while the program is running. (4) A name used to represent data whose value can be changed while the program is running by referring to the name of the variable. (5) In FORTRAN, a named storage location whose value can be changed while the program is running by referring to the name of the variable. (6) In COBOL, a data item whose value may be changed by execution of the object program. A variable used in an arithmetic expression must be a numeric elementary item. (7) In FORTRAN, a data object or subobject that is not a constant. It may be a symbolic variable, an array element, an array section, a structure component, or a substring. (8) In the NetView command list language, a character string beginning with "&" that is coded in a command list and is assigned a value during execution of the command list. (9) Contrast with constant. (10) See analog automatic variable, character variable, DO variable, dynamic variable, environment variable, external variable, static variable, switching variable. See also shell variables.

variable field marks User-defined characters which are used in the field definition function of the SDF/CICS map editor to mark the beginning of variable fields.

variable-format messages Messages in which line control characters are not to be deleted upon arrival nor inserted upon departure. Variable-format messages are intended for terminals with similar characteristics. Contrast with fixed-format messages.

variable function generator A function generator in which the function it generates may be set by the user before or during computation. (I)

variable information In word processing, information or text that is entered or altered by the operator for each document. (T)

variable-length record (1) A record having a length independent of the length of other records with which it is logically or physically associated. Contrast with fixed-length record. See also V format. (2) Pertaining to a file in which the records need not be uniform in length. (A) (3) In COBOL, a record associated with a file whose file description entry or sort-merge description entry permits records to contain a varying number of character positions.

variable occurrence data item In COBOL, a table element that is repeated a variable number of times. Such an item must contain an OCCURS DEPENDING ON clause in its data description entry, or be subordinate to such an item.

variable pitch Deprecated term for proportional spacing. (A)

variable-pitch spacing See proportional spacing.

variable-pitch spacing mechanism See proportional spacing mechanism.

variable-point representation (1) A positional representation in which the position of the radix point is explicitly indicated by a special character at that position. (A) (2) Contrast with floating-point representation.

variable-point representation system (1) A radix numeration system in which the radix point is explicitly indicated by a special character at that position. (T) (2) A numeration system in which a real number is represented by a single series of digits but in which the radix point is explicitly indicated by a special character. Contrast with fixed-point representation system. See also floating-point representation system.

variable space font Synonym for proportionally spaced font.

variable speed control On dictation equipment, a device used to vary the speed of the recording medium. (I)

variable substitution The ability to change and display the values of variables in a string, replacing a name of a variable with the value it represents.

variable symbol In a CMS EXEC procedure, a symbol beginning with an ampersand (&) that is assigned a value by the user, or in some cases by the EXEC interpreter. The value of variable symbols may be tested and changed using EXEC control statements. See also special variable.

variable time scale In simulation, the time scale used in data processing when the time scale factor is not constant during a run. (A)

variant part (1) A part of a record whose data objects are defined in alternative ways. Both the number and composition of data objects can vary. (I) (2) In Pascal, that portion of a record that may vary from one occurrence of the record to another. The variant portion consists of a series of variable data that may share the same physical storage.

variation name (1) In an information resource dictionary, a character string used to identify each of several logically related entities with the same assigned access name or descriptive name. (A) (2) A component of the version identifier of an entity in an information resource dictionary. (A)

varying-length string In SQL, a character string whose length is not fixed, but variable within limits. Contrast with fixed-length string.

vary off To make a device, control unit, or line unavailable for its normal intended use.

vary offline (1) To change the status of a device from online to offline. When a device is offline, no data set may be opened on that device. (2) To place a device in a state where it is not available for use by the system; however, it is still available for executing I/O. (3) In the ImagePlus Object Access Method, to change the status of an optical library or an optical drive from online to offline. Varying a library offline does not affect the online/offline status of the drives it contains. When a library or drive is offline, no data may be accessed on optical discs through the offline drive or the drives in the offline library.

vary on To make a device, control unit, or line available for its normal intended use.

vary online (1) To restore a device to a state where it is available for use by the system. (2) In the ImagePlus Object Access Method, to change the status of an optical library or an optical drive from offline to online. This makes the drive or drives in the library being varied online available for the optical disc access.

V.25 bis In data communications, an interim specification of the CCITT that defines the connection of data terminal equipment to a serial-dial interface of a public switched telephone network.

V.25 bis protocol A procedure defined by CCITT that allows call establishment and data transfer to take place over the same link. The support eliminates the need for two physical lines or ports when automatic call units (ACUs) are employed in a switched connection.

VC Virtual circuit.

vchar In the AIX object data manager (ODM), a terminal descriptor type used to define a variable as a variable-length, null-terminated string. See also terminal descriptor.

V.35 communication adapter A communication adapter that can combine and send information on one line at speeds up to 64 kbps, and conforms to the CCITT V.35 standard.

VCR Videocassette recorder.

VDC Volts direct current.

VDD Virtual device driver.

VDT (1) Video display terminal. (2) Visual display terminal.

VDU (1) Video display unit. (2) Visual display unit.

vector (1) A quantity usually characterized by an ordered set of numbers. (I) (A) (2) In computer graphics, a directed line segment. (3) In the IBM 8100 Information System, one or more related fields of data, in a specified format, associated with the control of the processor, channel, or floating-point facility. (4) A one-dimensional array. (5) In GDDM, a directed line segment; a straight line between two points. (6) In SNA, a data structure containing three fields: a length field that specifies the length of the vector in which it is contained, an identifier or type field, and a value field. The value field may contain subvectors. (7) The MAC frame information field. (8) See absolute vector, relative vector. (9) Contrast with scalar.

vector array In System/38 graphics, an array used by a GDDM routine to construct a vector line.

vectored interrupt An interrupt system in which each interrupt can be immediately serviced without having to determine which interrupt has occurred by polling. (A)

vector facility An attachment to a processor that enables the processor to run programs that issue vector instructions. Vector instructions are particularly useful in scientific calculations.

vector generator A functional unit that generates directed line segments. (I) (A)

vector graphics See coordinate graphics.

vector line In System/38 graphics, a series of lines constructed by one GDDM routine.

vector processor Synonym for array processor.

vectorscope In video systems, a device that displays information about the color part of a video signal.

vector subscript In FORTRAN, a section subscript that is a rank-one integer expression.

vector symbol set (VSS) In computer graphics, a graphics symbol set in which each character is treated as a small picture and is described by a sequence of lines and arcs. Characters in a vector symbol set can be drawn to scale, rotated, and positioned precisely. Contrast with image symbol set. See also graphics symbol set.

VEIB Virtual external interrupt block.

Veitch diagram A means of representing Boolean functions in which the number of variables determines the number of squares in the diagram. The number of squares needed is the number of possible states, that is, two raised to a power determined by the number of variables. (I) (A) See also Venn diagram.

vendor-logo product A product sold by IBM but licensed by the original supplier.

Note: A vendor-logo product is handled by IBM in the same manner as a program offering, but it is not an IBM-licensed program. Vendor-logo products are licensed to customers under individual vendor agreements, not under the Agreement for IBM-Licensed Programs or the IBM Program License Agreement.

Venn diagram (1) A graphic image consisting of overlapping circles that represent the logical relationship of two sets of information. (I) (A) (2) See also Veitch diagram. See Figure 162.

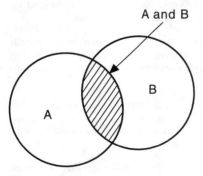

Figure 162. Venn Diagram

verb (1) See LU 6.2 verb. (2) In COBOL, a word that expresses an action to be taken by a COBOL compiler or object program.

verge-punched card Synonym for edge-punched card.

verification (1) In computer security, the process of comparing two levels of system specification for proper correspondence; for example, the comparison of a security policy model with a top-level specification, the comparison of source code with object code. See formal verification. (2) The act of determining whether an operation has been accomplished correctly. (T) See key stroke verification, user identification and verification. (3) See node verification, write verification.

verification test (1) A test of a system to prove that it meets all its specified requirements at a particular stage of its development. (T) (2) A test to confirm whether a device is functioning correctly. (3) See also validation test.

verifier A device that checks the correctness of transcribed data, usually by comparing it with a second transcription of the same data or by comparing a retranscription with the original data. (I) (A)

verify (1) To determine whether a transcription of data or other operation has been accomplished accurately. (A) (2) To check results of keypunching. (A) (3) To confirm correctness of something. (4) To check accuracy of entered data by entering data again and comparing the second entry with the first.

Versatile Message Transfer Protocol (VMTP) In the AIX operating system, a protocol that provides datagram communication service at the user level. Unlike most programs that use the User Datagram Protocol/Internet Protocol (UDP/IP), programs using VMTP do not have to implement time out, retransmission, or estimation of network delays, because VMTP provides end-to-end datagram delivery.

version A separate IBM-licensed program, based on an existing IBM-licensed program, that usually has significant new code or new function. Each version has its own license, terms, conditions, product type number, monthly charge, documentation, test allowance (if applicable), and programming support category. See also fix level, modification level, release.

Note: Numbering of versions starts with version 2. The first release of an IBM-licensed program is referred to as Release 1 with no indication of version number.

vertical blanking interval In a video system, certain lines on a display screen, in which frame numbers, picture stops, chapter stops, full-frame IDs, closed captions, and so on, may be encoded. These lines do not appear on the display screen, but maintain image stability and enhance image access. See horizontal blanking interval.

vertical drop distance In the IBM Cabling System, the vertical distance from the faceplate to the raceway, which is either the ceiling or floor.

vertical feed Pertaining to the entry of a punch card into a card feed with a short edge first. (A)

vertical format Synonym for portrait. (T)

vertical format information In TCP/IP, information, such as tab markers, that automatically positions lines of text with respect to other lines of text, according to defined rules. Vertical format information is usually associated with word processing.

vertical formatting (1) In word processing, automatic positioning of lines of text with respect to other lines according to defined rules. (2) Synonym for vertical tabulation.(T)

vertical form skip control Synonym for first line find. (A)

vertical justification Redistribution of the extra vertical white space at the end of a column between lines of text, so as to make the columns appear to be the same length.

vertical licensed internal code (VLIC) Programming that defines logical operations on data. The vertical licensed internal code translates the machine interface (MI) instructions.

vertical lines of resolution In video systems, the number of horizontal lines a camera can distinguish.

vertically displayed records Subfile records that are grouped so that each record is displayed on one or more lines. Each record begins a new line.

vertical magnetic recording Synonym for perpendicular magnetic recording. (T)

vertical microcode (VMC) In System/38, microcode that defines logical operations on data. The microcode is primarily sequential in execution and supports the System/38 machine instruction set.

vertical pointer In systems with VSAM, a pointer in an index record of a given level that gives the location of a record in the next lower level or the location of a control interval in the data set or file controlled by the index.

vertical positions See addressable vertical positions.

vertical redundancy check (VRC) (1) An odd parity check performed on each character of a block as the block is received. See also cyclic redundancy check, longitudinal redundancy check. (2) Deprecated term for transverse redundancy check.

vertical retrace The action of moving the electron beam from the bottom to the top of a display screen. See also refresh rate.

vertical tabulation (1) The capability of a text editor to position text vertically within limits defined by the user. Synonymous with vertical formatting. (T) (2) On a printer or typewriter, movement of the imprint position to another writing line. (3) On a display device, movement of the cursor to another display line. (4) See also horizontal tabulation.

vertical tabulation character (VT) A format effector that causes the print or display position to move to the corresponding position on the next of a series of predetermined lines. (I)   (A)

vertical tabulator key On a typewriter, a control that effects vertical tabulation. (T)

vertical wraparound On a display device, the continuation of cursor movement from the bottom character position in a vertical column to the top character position in the next column, or from the top position in a column to the bottom position in the preceding column. Contrast with horizontal wraparound.

V format A data set format in which logical records are of varying length and include a length indicator, and in which V-format logical records may be blocked, with each block containing a block length indicator.

VGA mode A mode of a video display that provides 640 x 480 resolution with 16 colors and is supported on VGA systems. See also video graphics adapter (VGA).

VGB VTAM services global block.

VHS (1) Very high speed. A consumer and industrial tape format (VHS format). (2) Very-high-speed integrated circuit.

very large scale integrated (VLSI) circuit A circuit technology that makes it possible to integrate large and complex mainframe computing features on a chip.

video Pertaining to the portion of recorded information that can be seen.

video black In video presentations, the absence of pictures and sound, usually at the beginning and end of a program and between segments.

video board Synonym for graphics adapter.

videocassette recorder (VCR) A device for recording or playing back videocassettes.

video clip A section of filmed or videotaped material.

videoconferencing Teleconferencing that provides transmission of still or moving images, in addition to voice, text, and graphics. (T) See also conference call, teleconferencing.

video digitizer Any system for converting analog video material to digital representation.

videodisc A disc on which programs have been recorded for playback on a computer or a television set; a recording on a videodisc. The most common format in the United States and Japan is an NTSC signal recorded on the optical reflective format.

videodisc player In multimedia, a device that provides video playback for prerecorded videodiscs.

video display terminal (VDT) (1) A user terminal with a display screen, and usually equipped with an input device such as a keyboard. Synonymous with visual display unit (VDU). (T) (2) In SAA usage, deprecated term for display device.

video display unit (VDU) (1) Synonym for visual display unit. (2) In SAA usage, deprecated term for display device.

video encoder A device that transforms a high-resolution digital image from a computer into a standard television signal, thereby allowing the computer to create graphics for use in video production.

video gain The strength of a video signal.

video graphics adapter (VGA) A computer adapter that provides high-resolution graphics and a total of 256 colors. See enhanced graphics adapter (EGA).

video head The mechanism inside a videotape player that reads the video information recorded on the tape.

video lookup table (VLT) A color map implemented in hardware.

video monitor A display device capable of accepting a video signal that is not modulated for broadcast either on cable or over the air. In videotaping, a television screen on which the footage can be viewed as it is being recorded.

video scan converter A device that emits a video signal in one standard into another device of different resolution or scan rate.

video segment A contiguous set of recorded data from a video track. A video segment may or may not be associated with an audio segment.

videotape (1) A tape used to record visual images and sound. (2) In multimedia applications, a recording of visual images and sound on magnetic tape. All shooting is done in this format, even if the results are later transferred to videodisc or film. (3) To make a videotape.

videotape formats See one-inch videotape, three-quarter-inch videotape, half-inch videotape, eight-millimeter (8mm) videotape.

videotape recorder (VTR) A device for recording and playing back videotapes.

video terminal paging An IMS/VS facility that allows the application programmer to send multiple screens of information to a display device. The screens may then be viewed by the terminal operator either in or out of sequence and as many times as desired.

videotex (1) A service that provides interactive exchange of alphanumeric and graphic information, over common carrier facilities to the general public. The user must have a special display terminal or adapted television set. Synonymous with interactive videography, viewdata. (T) (2) A system that provides two-way interactive information services, including the exchange of alphanumeric and graphic information, over common carrier facilities to a mass consumer market using modified TV displays with special decoders and modems. See also teletext.

Note: Several versions of videotex have been developed outside the US; for example, in Canada Telidon, in Germany Bildschirmtext, in Japan Captain, and in the U.K. Prestel.

view (1) In an information resource dictionary, the combination of a variation name and revision number that is used as a component of an access name or of a descriptive name. (A) (2) In SQL, an alternative representation of data from one or more tables. A view can include all or some of the columns contained in the table or tables on which it is defined. (3) In the OS/2 operating system, the appearance of the contents of an open object. (4) In IBM network management products, a graphical representation of a network or a part of a network. A view consists of resource symbols and resource labels; it may also include a background picture or text that a network operator has placed within it. (5) Synonym for subschema.

View In SAA Common User Access architecture, an action bar choice that enables the user to display different perspectives of an application structure diagram.

viewable In AIX graphics, pertaining to a mapped window whose ancestors are all mapped, but not necessarily visible. Graphics requests can be performed on a window when it is not viewable, but output will not be retained unless the server is maintaining backup storage. Contrast with unviewable. See also visible.

view administrator The part of the NetView Graphic Monitor Facility that downloads the views created by the view preprocessor and that provides these views to the graphic data server.

viewdata Synonym for videotex.

viewer coordinates Synonym for eye coordinates.

viewing coordinates Synonym for eye coordinates.

viewing filter In the NetView program, the function that allows a user to select the alert data to be displayed on a terminal. All other stored data is blocked.

viewing matrix In AIX graphics, a matrix used to describe the location of the viewer. See also transformation, world coordinates.

viewing transformation (1) In AIX graphics, transformation that maps from world coordinates to viewer coordinates. The origin of the viewer coordinate system can be thought of as the location of the viewer's "eye." Viewing transformations can be used to move the "eye" around in world coordinates. (2) Synonym for window/viewport transformation.

view manager In the NetView Graphic Monitor Facility, a facility that generates views according to Resource Object Data Manager (RODM) definitions and that provides status changes to the graphic data server.

viewpoint (1) In computer graphics, the origin from which angles and scales are used to map virtual space into display space. (T) (2) In System/38 graphics, a rectangular area within the picture space that defines where the output of the current page will appear on the display device.

viewport (1) A predefined part of the display space. (I) (A) (2) In AIX graphics, a mapping from normalized device coordinates to device coordinates. The

viewport maps the unit cube x/w = (+/-)1, y/w = (+/-)1, z/w = (+/-)1 to the screen space, as measured in pixels. The viewport is the last transformation in the graphics pipeline. The viewport can be smaller or larger than the window or smaller or larger than the screenmask, although in most applications, it is the same size. (3) In GDDM, a rectangular area within the picture space that defines where the output of the current page appears on the workstation. (4) In the 3270 Information Display System, an area on the usable area of the display surface through which an operator views all or a portion of the data outlined by the window on the presentation plane. (5) In SAA usage, deprecated term for window.

viewport transformation In AIX graphics, transformation that maps normalized device coordinates to device coordinates. A viewport is usually the same size as the window, but its size can be adjusted. Synonymous with normalized device coordinate (NDC) to device coordinate (DC) transformation.

view preprocessor A part of the IBM NetView Graphic Monitor Facility that creates unformatted views of SNA resources from the VTAM definition library (VTAMLST).

VIO Virtual I/O.

virgin medium Synonym for blank medium. (T)

virtual Pertaining to a functional unit that appears to be real, but whose functions are accomplished by other means. (T)

virtual address The address of a location in virtual storage. A virtual address must be translated into a real address in order to process the data in processor storage.

virtual address area The area available as a program address range.

virtual address space (1) In virtual storage systems, the virtual storage assigned to a batched or terminal job, a system task, or a task initiated by a command. (2) In VSE, a subdivision of the virtual address area available to the user for the allocation of private, non-shared partitions.

virtual address translation The conversion of virtual storage addresses to real storage addresses.

virtual block multiplexer mode In VM/370, a virtual machine option that allows the interleaving of data to different virtual devices on the same virtual channel path.

virtual call facility In data communication, a user facility in which a call setup procedure and a call clearing procedure determine a period of communication between two data terminal equipments (DTEs) in which user data is transferred in the network in the packet mode of operation. All user data is delivered from the network in the order it is received by the network.

virtual card reader In VM, a simulation on disk by CP of a real card reader having the ability to read card, punch, or printer records of up to 151 characters in length. The default spool file class is asterisk (*). The virtual device type and I/O device address are normally defined in the VM user directory. See also spool file class, universal card reader.

virtual circuit (1) In packet switching, the facilities provided by a network that give the appearance to the user of an actual connection. (T) See also data circuit. Contrast with physical circuit. (2) A logical connection established between two DTEs. (3) In a packet-switching data network, a logical end-to-end transmission channel—as opposed to a physical connection—that connects X.25 users. Virtual circuits allow physical transmission facilities to be shared by many users simultaneously. A virtual circuit is a logical connection established between two data terminal equipments (DTEs). See also permanent virtual circuit (PVC), switched virtual circuit (SVC). (4) See switched virtual circuit, permanent virtual circuit.

virtual computing system Synonym for virtual machine.

virtual connection See virtual circuit.

virtual console In VM, a console simulated by CP on a terminal such as a 3270. The virtual device type and I/O address are defined in the VM directory entry for that virtual machine.

virtual console function In VM, a CP command executed via the diagnose interface.

virtual console spooling In VM, the writing of console input/output on disk as a printer spool file instead of, or in addition to, having it typed or displayed at the virtual machine console.

Note: The console data includes messages, responses, commands, or data from or to CP and the virtual machine operating system. The user can invoke or terminate console spooling at any time. When the console spool file is closed, it becomes a printer spool file.

virtual device (1) A device that appears to the user as a separate entity, but is actually a shared portion of a real device; for example, several virtual terminals can exist simultaneously, but only one is active at any given time. (2) In the AS/400 system, a device

description that does not have hardware associated with it. It is used to form a connection between a user and a physical work station attached to a remote system. A virtual device can be a virtual display station or a virtual printer. See also virtual work-station controller.

virtual device driver (VDD) Synonym for device handler.

virtual disk (1) Main storage used as if it were a disk device. (2) In VM, a physical disk storage device, or a logical subdivision of a physical disk storage device, that has its own address, consecutive storage space for data, and index or description of stored data so that the data can be accessed. (3) Synonym for minidisk. (T)

virtual disk initialization program In VM, the program that can initialize virtual as well as real disks for use by VSE, OS, and OS/VS virtual machines executing under VM.

virtual drive In MSS, a direct access storage device that does not physically exist. It exists logically on one or more staging drives.

virtual=real area In VM, the part of real storage, starting with the real page 1, where the virtual=real machine can execute. The CP maintains control of real page zero; only page 0 (zero) of the virtual=real machine is relocated.

Note: Only one virtual machine at a time can occupy the virtual=real area. The area must be defined during VM system generation to contain the largest virtual=real machine that is likely to run.

virtual=real option A VM performance option that allows a virtual machine to run in the virtual=real area of VM. This option eliminates CP paging and optionally, CCW translation for the virtual machine.

virtual-equals-real (V=R) storage Synonym for nonpageable dynamic area.

virtual file system In the AIX operating system, a remote file system that has been mounted so that it is accessible to the local user.

virtual image In computer graphics, the complete visual representation of an encoded image that could be displayed if a display surface of sufficient size were available.

virtual I/O (VIO) (1) A facility that pages data into and out of external page storage. (2) To a problem program, the data to be read from or written to direct access storage devices.

virtual I/O (VIO) area In VSE, an extension of the page data set used by the system as intermediate storage, primarily for control data.

virtual machine (VM) (1) A virtual data processing system that appears to be at the exclusive disposal of a particular user, but whose functions are accomplished by sharing the resources of a real data processing system. (T) (2) A system in which each user appears to have his own computer and input/output devices. (3) A functional simulation of a computer and its associated devices. Each virtual machine is controlled by a suitable operating system; for example, the conversational monitor system. VM/370 controls concurrent execution of multiple virtual machines on a single System/370 computing system. (4) In VM, a functional equivalent of a computing system. On the 370 Feature of VM, a virtual machine operates in System/370 mode. On the ESA Feature of VM, a virtual machine operates in System/370, 370-XA, ESA/370, or ESA/390 mode. Each virtual machine is controlled by an operating system. VM controls the concurrent execution of multiple virtual machines on an actual processor complex.

virtual machine assist feature In VM, a hardware feature available on certain VM-supported System/370 Models, that causes a significant reduction in the real supervisor state time used by VM to control operation of virtual storage systems such as VSE and OS/VS and, to a lesser extent, CMS, VSE, and OS when running under VM. VM supervisor state time is reduced because the Virtual Machine Assist feature, instead of VM, intercepts and handles interruptions caused by SVCs, other than SVC76, and certain privileged instructions.

Virtual Machine/Extended Architecture (VM/XA) An operating system that facilitates conversion to MVS/XA by allowing several operating systems (a production system and one or more test systems) to run simultaneously on a single 370-XA processor. The VM/XA Migration Aid has three components: the control program (CP), the conversational monitor system (CMS), and the dump viewing facility.

Virtual Machine Facility (VM/370) A time sharing system control program that consists of: (a) a control program (CP) managing resources of an IBM System/370 computing system so that multiple remote terminal users have a functional simulation of a computing system (a virtual machine) at their disposal, and (b) the conversational monitor system (CMS), which provides general time sharing, program development, and problem solving facilities.

virtual machine group One or more virtual machines that have been loaded in the same group control system (GCS).

virtual machine operator In the VM/XA Migration Aid, any user who loads and runs an operating system in a virtual machine. Contrast with real system operator.

Virtual Machine/System Product (VM/SP) An IBM-licensed program that manages the resources of a single computer so that multiple computing systems appear to exist. Each virtual machine is the functional equivalent of a "real" machine.

virtual memory Synonym for virtual storage.

virtual mode In VSE, the mode in which a program may be paged.

virtual mount point In the AIX operating system, the directory or file in the file tree where another file system is mounted.

virtual node Synonym for virtual routing node.

virtual partition (1) In OS/VS1, a division of the dynamic area of virtual storage, established at system generation. (2) In VSE, a division of the dynamic area of virtual storage.

virtual party In telephony, a party that does not actually take part in a telephone call. A virtual party is represented by a special directory number or numbers.

virtual printer In the AIX operating system, a view of a printer that refers only to the high-level data stream, such as an ASCII data stream, that the printer can accept. It does not include any information about how the printer hardware is attached to the host computer or the protocol used to transfer bytes of data to and from the printer.

virtual printer (or punch) In VM, a printer (or card punch) simulated on disk by CP for a virtual machine. The virtual device type and virtual I/O address are normally defined in the VM directory entry for the virtual machine.

virtual processing time The time required to execute the instructions of a virtual machine.

virtual push button (1) In computer graphics, a display element that can be selected by an input device and that is programmed to operate as a function key. (T) (2) In computer graphics, a display group used to simulate a choice device by means of a pick device. (3) Synonymous with light button.

virtual reality A computer-generated simulation of reality with which users can interact using specialized peripherals such as data gloves and head-mounted computer graphic displays. Synonymous with artificial reality.

virtual region In OS/VS2, a subdivision of the dynamic area that is allocated in segment-size blocks to a job step or a system task.

virtual route (VR) (1) A path between a data source and a data sink that may be created by various circuit configurations during the transmission of packets or messages. (T) (2) In SNA, a logical connection: (a) between two subarea nodes that is physically realized as a particular explicit route, or (b) that is contained wholly within a subarea node for intra-node sessions. A virtual route between distinct subarea nodes imposes a transmission priority on the underlying explicit route, provides flow control through virtual route pacing, and provides data integrity through sequence numbering of path information units (PIUs). See also explicit route (ER), path, route extension (REX).

virtual route identifier (VRID) In SNA, a virtual route number and a transmission priority number that, when combined with the subarea addresses for the subareas at each end of a route, identify the virtual route.

virtual route (VR) pacing In SNA, a flow control technique used by the virtual route control component of path control at each end of a virtual route to control the rate at which path information units (PIUs) flow over the virtual route. VR pacing can be adjusted according to traffic congestion in any of the nodes along the route. See also pacing, session-level pacing.

virtual route pacing response (VRPRS) A nonsequenced, supervisory path information unit (PIU) that flows at network priority. It may overtake VR-sequenced PIUs and consists of a transmission header with no basic information unit (BIU) data.

virtual route selection exit routine In VTAM, an optional installation exit routine that modifies the list of virtual routes associated with a particular class of service before a route is selected for a requested LU-LU session.

virtual route sequence number In SNA, a sequential identifier assigned by the virtual route control component of path control to each path information unit (PIU) that flows over a virtual route. It is stored in the transmission header of the PIU. Contrast with session sequence number.

virtual routing node A representation of a node's connectivity to a connection network defined on a shared-access transport facility, such as a token ring. Synonymous with virtual node.

virtual slot On a personal computer, a high-speed port to which a user can attach devices that are usually installed by means of expansion boards.

virtual space In computer graphics, a space in which the coordinates of the display elements are expressed in a device-independent manner. (I) (A)

virtual spooling device In VM, a unit record device simulated on disk by CP.

Note: The machine type and virtual I/O device addresses are defined in the VM directory or else by means of the CP DEFINE command.

virtual storage (1) The storage space that may be regarded as addressable main storage by the user of a computer system in which virtual addresses are mapped into real addresses. The size of virtual storage is limited by the addressing scheme of the computer system and by the amount of auxiliary storage available, not by the actual number of main storage locations. (I) (A) (2) Addressable space that is apparent to the user as the processor storage space, from which the instructions and the data are mapped into the processor storage locations. (3) Synonymous with virtual memory. See Figure 163.

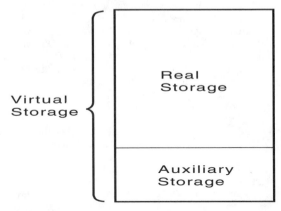

Figure 163. Virtual Storage

Virtual Storage Access Method (VSAM) An IBM licensed program that controls communication and the flow of data in an SNA network. It provides single-domain, multiple-domain, and interconnected network capability.

Virtual Storage Extended (VSE) An IBM licensed program whose full name is the Virtual Storage Extended/Advanced Function. It is a software operating system controlling the execution of programs. Synonymous with VSE/Advanced Functions.

virtual storage management (VSM) Routines that allocate address spaces and virtual storage areas within address spaces and keep a record of free and allocated storage within each address space.

virtual storage paging area In DPCX, a predefined area of disk storage on which blocks of task virtual storage can be paged.

virtual storage partition See virtual partition.

virtual storage region See virtual region.

virtual supervisor state In the VM/XA Migration Aid, a state, controlled by the current PSW of a virtual machine, during which the control program allows the virtual machine to issue input/output and other privileged instructions. The control program intercepts these instructions and simulates the functions of these instructions for the virtual machine.

Virtual Telecommunications Access Method VTAM. A set of programs that maintain control of the communication between terminals and application programs running under DOS/VS, OS/VS1, and OS/VS2 operating systems.

Virtual Telecommunications Access Method Entry VTAME. A licensed program that provides single-domain and multiple-domain network capability for 4300 systems using VSE.

virtual terminal (1) A generalized logical model of different terminals of a certain class, describing how terminals of that class will perform in the OSI environment. (T) (2) In the AIX operating system, any of several logical equivalents of a display station. A virtual terminal supports the illusion that more devices exist than are physically present. Virtual terminals are logically independent of each other, but share physical resources over time. See active virtual terminal, command virtual terminal. See also high function terminal. (3) In TCP/IP, a system object, created and controlled by an application program that provides a functional representation or simulation of a physical display station.

virtual terminal data (VTD) In the AIX operating system, a prefix attached to a virtual terminal control structure.

virtual terminal manager (VTM) In the AS/400 system, a vertical licensed internal code (VLIC) component that provides an interface to handle input/output to virtual devices on the system.

virtual terminal manager/function manager In the AS/400 system, the function that provides an application program interface to terminal handling components residing below the machine interface on the system.

virtual terminal subsystem In the AIX operating system, a collection of services that implement multiple virtual user interface devices, including displays, keyboards, locators, valuators, lighted programmable function keys, and sound generators.

virtual unit address In MSS, an address for a virtual drive. The virtual unit address can be assigned to any staging drive group. Each staging drive can have more than one virtual unit address, but only one real unit address.

virtual volume The concept of a volume that may be regarded as residing on an addressable unit of auxiliary storage by the user of a computer system in which virtual-device addresses correspond to real-device addresses. The attributes of a virtual volume are predefined and do not change as the implementation of that volume changes.

Note: In MSS, a virtual volume is called from a mass storage volume.

virtual wait time In the VM/XA Migration Aid, the amount of time the control program suspends the processing of a program while a required resource is unavailable.

virtual workstation controller In the AS/400 system, a workstation controller description that has the characteristics of a locally attached workstation controller but does not exist as hardware. See also virtual device.

virus In computer security, a self-propagating program that infects and may damage another program. See also attack.

visible Pertaining to a region of a window that is mapped and not occluded on the screen by another window. See also viewable.

vision processor In robotics, a processor that makes a comparison of image data with computer-aided design data for purposes such as automatic inspection and robot guidance in manufacturing operations.

vision system In robotics, a system that make use of machine vision for applications such as robot guidance as well as automated inspection and quality control.

visual display In word processing, a device for electronically displaying text. Depending on the equipment, the display may be full page, partial page, single, or partial line. (T)

visual display terminal Synonym for video display terminal.

visual display unit (VDU) Synonym for video display terminal (VDT). (T)

visual page In IBM personal computers with the Color/Graphics Monitor Adapter, one of the eight pages which are in the screen. See also active page, screen buffer.

Note: The user can display a visual page while working on a different active page in the screen buffer.

visual scanner Deprecated term for optical scanner.

VIT VTAM internal trace.

vital product data (VPD) (1) In the AIX operating system, information that uniquely defines system, hardware, software, and microcode elements of a processing system. (2) In the AS/400 system, a structured description of a device or program. It is recorded in a device at manufacture and includes at least the type, model, serial number, and installed features. It may include the manufacturer's ID and other fields. For programs, it is compiled as a data area accompanying the program and includes the name of the licensed program or licensed internal code group, the release and modification, the program module names, the national language or languages selected, and possibly other fields. Vital product data is transferred from the device to the system and stored for display. Vital product data is also visible on the device name plate or a similar tag.

VLB VTAM services local block.

VLIC Vertical licensed internal code.

VLIC log In the AS/400 system, a list of problem analysis information created by vertical licensed internal code.

VLSI circuit Very large scale integrated circuit.

VLT Video lookup table.

VM Virtual machine.

VMC Vertical microcode.

VM/ESA Virtual Machine/Enterprise Systems Architecture.

VM event The use of a CP command, DIAGNOSE function, or a user request related to communication among virtual machines, such as "spool file open."

VM/MVS bridge A function of the AS/400 Communications Utilities licensed program that provides distribution services between an AS/400 SNADS network

and both a VM/370 Remote Spooling Communications Subsystem (RSCS) network and a Multiple Virtual Storage/Job Entry Subsystem (MVS/JES) network. Formerly known as RSCS/PROFS bridge. See also bridge, Remote Spooling Communications Subsystem (RSCS).

VM read In VM, the mode in which a user's virtual machine is not executing, but is waiting for a response or a request for work from the user. On a typewriter terminal, the keyboard is unlocked. On a display terminal, the screen status area indicates VM READ.

VM READ screen status For a display terminal used as a virtual console under VM, an indicator located in the lower right of the screen. It indicates that the user's virtual machine is not executing, but is waiting for a response or a request for work from the user.

VM/SNA console support (VSCS) A VTAM component for the VM environment that provides Systems Network Architecture (SNA) support. It allows SNA terminals to be virtual machine consoles.

VM/SP Virtual Machine/System Product.

VM/SP directory A CP disk file that defines the normal configuration of a virtual machine: the user ID, password, normal and maximum allowable virtual storage, CP command privilege class or classes allowed, dispatching priority, logical editing characters to be used, account number, and CP options desired. The directory exists in two forms: card image and control blocks.

VM/SP HPO Virtual Machine/System Product High Performance Option. An IBM-licensed program that can be installed and executed in conjunction with VM/System Product to extend the capabilities of the VM/System Product with programming enhancements, support for microcode assists, and additional functions. The VM/SP High Performance Option program package is not executable by itself. It requires installation of VM System Product or an equivalent IBM-licensed program.

VM/SP user directory See VM/SP directory.

VMTP Versatile Message Transaction Protocol.

VM/VCNA VM/VTAM Communications Network Application.

VM/VS handshaking feature A communication interface between VM and OS/VS1 that makes each system control program aware of certain capabilities and requirements of the other.

VM/VTAM Commun. Network Application An IBM licensed program that provides SNA support for

VM. It allows SNA terminals to be used as virtual machine consoles. See also VM/SNA console support.

VM/XA Virtual Machine/Extended Architecture.

VM/XA Migration Aid (1) IBM Virtual Machine Facility Extended Architecture Migration Aid. (2) Virtual Machine/Extended Architecture Migration Aid.

VM/XA Migration Aid control program (CP) The component of the VM/XA Migration Aid that manages the resources of a single System/370-Extended Architecture system so that multiple computing systems appear to exist. Each virtual machine is the functional equivalent of either a System/370 computing system or a System/370-Extended Architecture computing system.

VM/XA Migration Aid directory A control program disk file that includes an entry for each user in the system. The entry defines the characteristics of the user's normal virtual machine configuration. These characteristics include the user ID, the password, normal and maximum allowable virtual storage, the privilege class, the dispatching priority, logical editing characters, and the account number.

VM/370 IBM Virtual Machine Facility/370.

VM/370 control program (CP) The component of VM/370 that manages the resources of a single computer with the result that multiple computing systems appear to exist. Each virtual machine is the functional equivalent of an IBM System/370 computing system.

VM/370 directory See VM/SP directory.

VM/370 user directory See VM/SP directory.

v-node Virtual i-node. In the AIX operating system, an object in a file system that represents a file. Unlike an i-node, there is no one-to-one correspondence between a v-node and the file system; multiple v-nodes can refer to a single file. V-nodes are used to communicate between the upper half of the file system and file system representations. See also i-node, intermediate node, system node.

VO Voice-over.

VOGAD Voice-Operated Gain-Adjusting Device. A voice-operated device somewhat similar to a compandor and used on some radio systems. It removes fluctuation from input speech and transmits at a constant level. No restoring device is needed at the receiving end.

voice-band The frequency band, from about 300 Hz to 3000 Hz, used on telephone equipment for the transmission of voice and data.

voice chip A computer chip that synthesizes speech.

voice-frequency carrier telegraphy That form of carrier telegraphy in which the carrier currents have frequencies such that the modulated currents may be transmitted over a voice-frequency telephone channel.

voice-frequency telegraph system A telegraph system permitting use of up to 20 channels on a single circuit by frequency division multiplexing.

voice-grade channel A data communication channel suitable for transmission of speech, digital data, or analog data, or for facsimile telegraphy, usually with a frequency range of about 300 to 3000 Hz.

voice-grade telephone line A telephone line that is normally used for transmission of voice communication. The line requires a modem for data communication.

voicegram A spoken message recorded and transmitted to one or more recipients. (T)

voice mail The use of computers to alert recipients that recorded telephone messages are waiting. See also electronic mail.

voice-operated device A device used on a telephone circuit to permit the presence of telephone currents to effect a desired control. Such devices are used in most echo suppressors. See also VOGAD.

voice-over (VO) (1) In multimedia applications, the voice of an unseen narrator in a video presentation. (2) In multimedia applications, a voice indicating the thoughts of a visible character without the character's lips moving.

voice response unit (VRU) In telephony, hardware or software that receives incoming calls by playing one or more prerecorded messages. The messages may require the caller to give additional information by touching buttons on a Touch-Tone keypad. The sequence of messages planned may be determined dynamically by this additional input.

voice synthesizer A device that simulates a human voice by producing a sequence of sounds that represent letters or syllables rather than complete words. See also audio response unit.

voice unit A measure of the gross amplitude of volume of an electrical speech or program wave. See also reference volume.

void (1) In character recognition, the inadvertent absence of ink within a character outline. (A)   (2) In OCR, a light spot in a character surrounded by ink. (3) A missing part of printing, or a missing part of the continuous forms. Contrast with background and spot.

void item Function at a point of sale terminal that allowing an operator to delete a single line entry previously entered during current transaction. The line entry is deleted electronically from the terminal but remains on printout at the terminal. See also void transaction.

void transaction A function at a point of sale terminal that enables an operator to delete the entire transaction in progress. See also void item.

void-transaction log A record of void transactions performed at a point of sale terminal. This log is recorded and stored on the store controller integrated disk.

VOL Beginning-of-volume label.

volatile attribute In XL C, the keyword "volatile," used in a definition, declaration, or cast. It causes the C language compiler to place the value of the data object in storage and to reload this value at each reference to the data object.

volatile register In a C language program, a register whose value on entry need not be preserved when the called routine returns.

volatile storage A storage device whose contents are lost when power is cut off. Contrast with nonvolatile storage. (T)

volatility The percentage of records on a file that are added or deleted in a run. See also activity.

voltage pencil Synonym for stylus.

volume (1) Sound level. (2) A certain portion of data, together with its data carrier, that can be handled conveniently as a unit. (I)   (3) A data carrier mounted and demounted as a unit; for example, a reel of magnetic tape, a disk pack. (I)   (4) The portion of a single unit of storage accessible to a single read/write mechanism, for example, a drum, a disk pack, or part of a disk storage module. (5) In COBOL, a discrete portion of a storage medium, the dimensions of which are determined by each implementor, that contains part of a file, all of a file, or any number of files. Synonymous with unit.

volume control On dictation equipment, a device used to vary the intensity of sound signals during playback. (I)

volume group See mass storage volume group, default mass storage volume group.

volume header Synonym for beginning-of-volume label.

volume label (1) An area on a standard label tape used to identify the tape volume and its owner. This area is the first 80 bytes and contains VOL 1 in the first four positions. (2) Synonym for beginning-of-volume label.

volume serial number A number in a volume label assigned when a volume is prepared for use in a system.

volume set The collection of volumes on which a multivolume data set resides. In RACF, a volume set is represented in one RACF profile.

volume switch procedures Standard procedures executed automatically when the end of a unit or reel has been reached before end-of-file has been reached.

volume table of contents (VTOC) (1) A table on a direct access volume that describes each data set on the volume. (2) An area on a disk or diskette that describes the location, size, and other characteristics of each file and library on the disk or diskette. (3) In the AS/400 system, an area on a disk or diskette that describes the location, size, and other characteristics of each file, library, and folder on the disk or diskette.

VP (1) Variable pageable. (2) Vital product data.

VPD Vital product data.

VR Virtual route.

VRC Vertical redundancy check.

V=R dynamic area Synonym for nonpageable dynamic area.

V response An answer or response of a teletypewriter terminal to a poll or address selection. Synonymous with M response.

VRID Virtual route identifier.

V=R partition Synonym for nonpageable partition.

VRPRS Virtual route pacing response.

V=R storage Synonym for nonpageable dynamic area.

VRU Voice response unit.

VS Virtual storage. See OS/VS, OS/VS1, OS/VS2, VSE.

VSAM Virtual Storage Access Method.

VSAM managed space A user-defined space on disk that is under the control of VSAM.

VSAM master catalog A key-sequenced data set or file with an index containing extensive data set and volume information that VSAM requires to locate data sets or files, allocate and deallocate storage space, verify the authorization of a program or operator to gain access to a data set or file, and accumulate usage statistics for data sets or files.

VSAM recoverable catalog A VSAM catalog defined with the recoverable attribute, causing duplicate catalog entries to be placed into catalog recovery for recovery in the event of a catalog failure. See also catalog recovery area.

VSAM resource pool A virtual storage area used to share I/O buffers, I/O-related control blocks, and channel programs among VSAM data sets. A resource pool is local or global (MVS only), that is, it serves tasks in one partition or address space or tasks in all address spaces in the system.

VSAM user catalog An optional VSAM catalog used in the same way as the master catalog and pointed to by the master catalog. Use of user catalogs lessens the contention for the master catalog and facilitates volume portability.

VSCS VM/SNA console support.

VSE Virtual Storage Extended. Synonym for VSE/Advanced Functions.

VSE/Advanced Functions Synonymous with VSE.

VSE/DITTO VSE/Data Interfile Transfer, Testing and Operations Utility. An IBM-licensed program that provides file-to-file services for card I/O, magnetic tape, and disk devices.

VSE/ESA Virtual Storage Extended/Enterprise Systems Architecture.

VSE/FCOPY VSE/Fast Copy Data Set Program. A program for fast copy data operations from disk to disk and dump/restore operations via an intermediate dump file on magnetic tape or disk.

VSE/ICCF VSE/Interactive Computing and Control Facility. An IBM-licensed program that makes the services of a VSE-controlled computing system available to authorized display station users. Availability

of services is on a time-shared basis, and display stations must be linked to the central processor of a system.

VSE/OCCF Virtual Storage Extended/Operator Communication Control Facility. A facility that intercepts messages from the VSE supervisor. NCCF and VSE/OCCF help an NCCF operator control multiple VSE systems from a central site.

VSE/OLTEP VSE Online Test Executive Program. An IBM program for managing the online tests available for device preventive maintenance and service. Normally, only IBM service representatives use this program.

VSE/POWER An IBM-licensed program primarily used to spool input and output. The networking functions of the program enable a VSE/SP system to exchange files with or run jobs on another remote processor.

VSE/SP Virtual Storage Extended/System Package.

VSE/VSAM See virtual storage access method.

VSM (1) VTAM service machine. (2) A program that has opened an ACB to identify itself to VTAM and can now issue VTAM macroinstructions. (3) Virtual storage management.

VSS Vector symbol set.

VT (1) The vertical tabulation character. (A) (2) Validation test. (3) Virtual terminal.

VTAM Virtual Telecommunications Access Method.

VTAM application program A program that has opened an access method control block (ACB) to identify itself to VTAM and can issue VTAM macroinstructions. See also TCAM application program.

VTAM definition The process of defining the user application network to VTAM and modifying IBM-defined characteristics to suit the needs of the user.

VTAM definition library The operating system files or data sets that contain the definition statements and start options filed during VTAM program definition.

VTAME Virtual Telecommunications Access Method Entry. Synonymous with ACF/VTAME.

VTAM internal trace (VIT) A trace used in VTAM to collect data on channel I/O, use of locks, and storage management services.

VTAM load module library The library containing the VTAM load modules in OS/VS or containing a VTAM phase in VSE.

VTAM operator A person or program authorized to issue VTAM operator commands. See domain operator, network operator *(2)*, program operator.

VTAM operator command A command used to monitor or control a VTAM domain. See also definition statement.

VTAM terminal I/O coordinator (VTIOC) The part of TSO/VTAM that converts TSO TGET, TPUT, TPG, and terminal control macroinstructions into SNA request units.

VTD Virtual terminal data.

VTIOC VTAM terminal I/O coordinator.

VTM Virtual terminal manager.

VTM/FM Virtual terminal manager/function manager.

VTOC Volume table of contents.

VTR Videotape recorder.

VU (1) Voice unit. (2) Volume unit.

VU (volume unit) meter A device, often part of an audio mixer, that measures the sound level on an audio channel.

vulnerability In computer security, a weakness in security policy, procedures, personnel, management, administration, hardware, software, physical layout, organization, or other factors affecting security that may allow harm to an information processing system. See also countermeasure, exposure, risk.

Note: The presence of a vulnerability does not in itself cause harm; a vulnerability is merely a condition or set of conditions that may allow the information processing system to be harmed by an attack.

V=V dynamic area Synonym for pageable dynamic area.

W

W Watt.

WACK Wait before transmitting positive acknowledgment character. A character sequence sent by a receiving station as a positive response and to indicate that it is temporarily not ready to receive.

wafer A sheet of semiconductive material from which microchips are manufactured.

waiting time (1) The condition of a task that depends on one or more events in order to enter the ready condition. (2) The condition of a processing unit when all operations are suspended. (3) Synonym for latency.

Note: The wait state may be a hard wait or a soft wait. The difference between the two wait states is that system recovery from a hard wait is impossible without performing a new initial program load (IPL) procedure, whereas recovery from a soft wait may be accomplished without impairing program or system operation.

wait state Synonym for latency.

walk-through In multimedia applications, a type of animated presentation that simulates a walking tour of a three-dimensional scene.

WAN Wide area network.

wand A device used to read information encoded on merchandise tickets, credit cards, and employee badges.

wanding Passing the tip of a wand reader over a magnetically encoded stripe; for example, on a merchandise ticket, credit card, or employee badge.

wand reader In the 3650 Retail Store System, a special feature available for the 3653 Point of Sale Terminal, used to read magnetically encoded information on merchandise tickets, credit cards, and employee badges.

ward A section of a double-byte character set (DBCS) where the first byte of the (DBCS) codes belonging to that section are the same value. According to IBM standards for DBCS codes, there are 190 wards, and each ward has up to 190 points on which DBCS characters can be assigned. Contrast with point.

warm restart Restart of ACF/TCAM following either a quick or a flush closedown. The ACF/TCAM checkpoint/restart facility restores the ACF/TCAM environment as nearly as possible to its condition before closedown or failure. Contrast with cold restart. See also point-of-failure restart, point-of-last-environment restart.

warm start (1) The start of a database management system with preprocessing of before-images. (T) (2) A restart that allows reuse of previously initialized input and output work queues. (3) In VM, the result of an initial program load (IPL) that does not erase previous system data. (4) In VM, the automatic reinitialization of the VM control program that occurs if the control program cannot continue processing. Closed spool files and the VM accounting information are not lost. Contrast with checkpoint start, cold start, force start. (5) Synonym for system restart *(1)*. (6) See also warm restart.

warning message (1) An indication that a possible error has been detected. Contrast with error message. (2) In SAA Common User Access architecture, a message that tells a user that a requested action has been suspended because something undesirable could occur. A user can continue the requested action, withdraw the requested action, or get help. See also action message, information message.

WATS Wide Area Telephone Service. A service that provides a special line on which the subscriber may make unlimited calls to certain zones on a direct-distance-dialing basis for a flat monthly charge.

wave file A file used for audio sounds on a waveform device.

waveform (1) A graphic representation of the shape of a wave that indicates its characteristics, such as frequency and amplitude. (2) A digital method of storing and manipulating audio data.

waveform monitor In video systems, a device that measures the characteristics of a video signal.

wavelength The distance from one point of a periodic waveform to the same point in the next cycle. See Figure 164

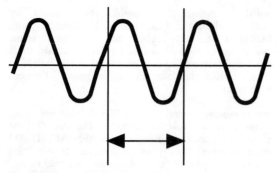

Figure 164. Wavelength

way station A station on a multipoint circuit.

WCC Write control character.

weak external reference (WXTRN) An external reference that does not have to be resolved during linkage editing. If it is not resolved, it appears as though its value were resolved to zero.

weak typing In programming languages, typing that is not strongly enforced. Weak typing allows objects to take on values not normally allowed for their type. Types of all objects may not be known at compile time. (A)

WEB Work element block.

weight In a positional representation system, the factor by which the value represented by a character in a digit place is multiplied to obtain its additive contribution in the representation of a number. (T) Synonymous with significance.

weighted moving average A moving average in which recent data are given greater emphasis than older data. See also exponential smoothing.

weighting See A-weighting.

well-behaved application program (1) An application program that runs without disruption to the network. (2) An application program that runs in the Disk Operating System (DOS) partition without disrupting NetView/PC functions.

well-known host name A conventional name associated with an Internet Protocol address on a particular network.

well-known port (1) In the AIX operating system, a conventional port assignment used by hosts that support the same protocols, whether or not the hosts are on the same network. Synonymous with contact port. (2) In TCP/IP, a port that is assigned the same port number in all TCP/IP implementations.

wet process development In a document copying machine, a developing process using a liquid developer. (T) Contrast with dry process development.

whetstone A measure of a computer's performance of arithmetic operations.

WHILE statement A C language looping statement that contains the keyword "while," followed by an expression in parentheses (the condition) and a statement (the action).

white balance The process of adjusting a video camera to establish which light frequencies are to be rendered as "white" and thereby to ensure that colors are accurately rendered.

white flag Synonym for full-frame ID.

who-are-you (WRU) See inquiry character.

whole array In FORTRAN, a named array.

wide area network (WAN) (1) A network that provides communication services to a geographic area larger than that served by a local area network or a metropolitan area network, and that may use or provide public communication facilities. (T) (2) A data communications network designed to serve an area of hundreds or thousands of miles; for example, public and private packet-switching networks, and national telephone networks. Contrast with local area network (LAN).

wideband Synonym for broadband. (T)

wide shot Synonym for long shot.

widget (1) In the AIX operating system, a graphic device that can receive input from the keyboard or mouse and communicate with an application or with another widget by means of a callback. Every widget is a member of only one class and always has a window associated with it. (2) The fundamental data type of the AIX Enhanced X-WindowsToolkit. (3) An object that provides a user-interface abstraction; for example, a Scrollbar widget. It is the combination of an AIX Enhanced X-Windows window (or subwindow) and its associated semantics. A widget implements procedures through its widget class structure.

widget class In the AIX operating system, the general group to which a specific widget belongs. It is a pointer to a structure. Synonymous with widget type.

widget gravity Synonym for window gravity.

widget ID In the AIX operating system, a unique identification number associated with each widget instantiated in an interface.

widget instance In the AIX operating system, a specific widget object, as opposed to a general widget class. It is composed of a data structure containing instance-specific values and another data structure containing information applicable to all widgets of that class.

widget tree (1) In the AIX operating system, the symbolic structure for Enhanced X-Windows Toolkit code. The basic element is a widget class. See also leaves, intermediate nodes, root. (2) A hierarchy of widgets within a specific client application. The Shell widget is the root of the widget tree. Widgets with no children of any kind are leaves of the tree.

widget type Synonym for widget class.

widow (1) A last line of a paragraph that is carried over to the top of the next column or page, where it stands alone. Synonymous with widow line. (T) (2) In word processing and desktop publishing, a heading, a line, or a few lines of text beginning a paragraph that are printed or displayed at the end of a page. See also orphan.

widow line Synonym for widow. (T)

width slots In the 3800 Printing Subsystem, the openings that mechanically lock the paper width lever in the continuous forms stacker. A specific opening is associated with each of the paper widths.

wildcard character Synonym for pattern-matching character.

wild footage Synonym for original footage.

willful intercept The act of intercepting messages intended for stations having equipment or line trouble. See also miscellaneous intercept.

Winchester Pertaining to a technology used in hard disk drives in which a movable read/write head floats above a rotating disk on a cushion of air produced by the rotating surface. When rotation stops, the air cushion is lost and the head comes to rest on the surface of the disk in a landing zone where no data recorded. See also Bernoulli, landing zone, loading zone.

Note: Winchester drives are sealed to prevent contamination that can cause head crashes.

window (1) A portion of a display surface in which display images pertaining to a particular application can be presented. Different applications can be dis-

played simultaneously in different windows. (A) (2) An area of the screen with visible boundaries within which information is displayed. A window can be smaller than or the same size as the screen. Windows can appear to overlap on the screen. (3) A division of a screen in which one of several programs being executed concurrently can display information. (4) In data communication, the number of data packets a DTE or DCE can send across a logical channel before waiting for authorization to send another data packet. The window is the main mechanism of pacing, or flow control, of packets. (5) In MSS, the portion of a sequential data set on a virtual volume that can be staged for processing. A window is a multiple of a page (8 cylinders) and can range from 2 to 25 pages. (6) In the AIX operating system, a rectangular area of the screen that a user can move about, place on top of another window, pull under another window, or iconize. (7) In AIX curses and extended curses, the internal representation of what a portion of the display may look like at some point in time. Windows can be any size, from the entire display screen to a single character.

Window (1) In SAA Advanced Common User Access architecture, a choice in the action bar of some applications. Users select it to arrange the display of several windows or to change the active window. (2) In SAA Advanced Common User Access architecture, a choice in the action bar of multiple-document interface applications. (3) In SAA Advanced Common User Access architecture, an icon that represents a general window in a user's work or parts box.

window class The grouping of windows whose processing requirements conform to the services provided by one window procedure.

window class style The set of properties that apply to every window in a window class.

window component In SAA Advanced Common User Access architecture, the smallest named visual part of a window, such as the title bar, system menu icon, action bar, and scroll bar.

window coordinates In System/38 graphics, the user-defined set of coordinates mapped on the viewport from which the scale is drawn.

window edge The sequence number of the last data packet in a window *(2)*.

window gravity In the AIX operating system, the attraction of a subwindow to some part of its parent. Window gravity causes subwindows to be automatically repositioned, relative to an edge, corner, or center of a window when resized. Synonymous with widget gravity.

window ID In the AIX operating system, a unique identification number associated with each newly opened window in an AIXwindows or Enhanced X-Windows environment.

windowing (1) The technique for partitioning a display surface into two or more distinct areas in which different texts can be displayed concurrently and manipulated separately or together. (T) (2) Dividing a display screen into distinct areas in which different display images can be viewed at the same time; for example, in order to simultaneously display different parts of a spreadsheet. See Figure 165.

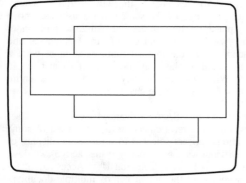

Figure 165. Windowing

window manager (1) In AIX graphics, the client that manipulates windows on a screen and provides much of the user interface. (2) In AIX graphics, software that manages the multiple windows associated with AIXwindows and Enhanced X-Windows.

window operation In System/38, the source entry utility (SEU) operation that controls the horizontal positioning of data displayed on a screen.

window size (1) The specified number of frames of information that can be sent before receiving an acknowledgment response. (2) In SNA, synonym for pacing group size.

window title In SAA Advanced Common User Access architecture, the area in the title bar that contains the name of the application and the OS/2 operating system file name, if applicable.

window/viewport transformation A mapping of the boundary and contents of a window into the boundary and interior of a viewport. Synonymous with viewing transformation. (I) (A) See Figure 166.

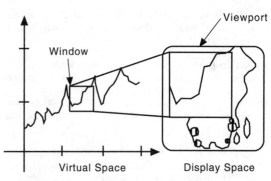

Figure 166. Window/Viewport Transformation

WIN-OS/2 session A session, created by the OS/2 operating system, that supports the independent processing of programs that are compatible with the Microsoft Windows (trademark of Microsoft Corporation) program.

wipe In multimedia applications, to fade away a display image in order to reveal another.

wipe pattern The shape, placement, and direction of a wipe.

wiper In a document copying machine, a blade or pad of flexible material that removes residues during the developing process. (T)

wire fault An error condition caused by a break in a wire or a short circuit between the wires or shield in a cable.

wire frame In computer graphics, a mode of display showing all lines, including hidden lines. (T)

wire-frame graphics A computer-aided design technique for displaying a three-dimensional object on a screen as a series of lines outlining its surface. Synonym for wire-frame representation. (I) (A) See Figure 167.

wire-frame representation Synonym for wire-frame graphics. (T)

wire printer A matrix printer that uses wires to produce patterns of dots.

wiretapping In computer security, surreptitious access to a line to obtain information. See active wiretapping, passive wiretapping. See also attack.

wiring closet A room that contains one or more equipment racks and distribution panels that are used to connect cables.

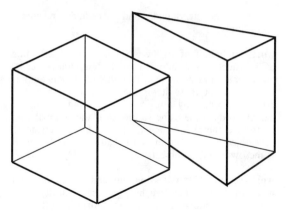

Figure 167. Wire-Frame Graphics

wiring concentrator In a star/ring network, a lobe concentrator that allows attaching devices to gain access to the ring at a central point, such as a wiring closet or an open work area. See also lobe, lobe bypass.

Note: In the event of a fault in a cable or at a station on the lobe, the wiring concentrator can bypass the fault by disconnecting the lobe from the rest of the ring. Wiring concentrators also simplify reconfiguration and network maintenance.

word (1) A character string considered as a unit for a given purpose. (T) (2) A character string or a bit string considered as an entity. (A) (3) In COBOL, a character-string of not more than 30 characters that forms a user-defined word, a system-name, or a reserved word. See COBOL word, keyword, optional word, reserved word, special character word, text word, user-defined word. (4) Synonymous with fullword. (5) See alphabetic word, computer word, doubleword, halfword, index word, instruction word, machine word, numeric word, parameter word, reserved word.

word boundary Any storage position at which data must be aligned for certain processing operations in the System/370 computing system. The halfword boundary must be divisible by 2; the fullword boundary by 4; the doubleword boundary by 8.

word control In text processing, the capability to operate one word at a time; for example, skip, move, delete, print. (I) (A)

word counter In text processing, a function of the system that allows for counting the number of words printed on each page of text. (T)

word key In word processing, a control used to process text one word at a time. (T)

word length Synonym for word size.

word locator On dictation equipment, an indicator that permits accurate location of words or syllables on the recording medium. (I)

word-organized storage A storage device into which data can be stored or from which data can be retrieved in units of a computer word, or, with the same duration, in parts of a computer word. (T)

word processing Synonym for text processing.

Note: The term word processing is often used to describe entry, modification, formatting, display, and printing of text on personal computers, microprocessors, and stand-alone word processors whereas the term text processing is frequently used to describe the performance of the same functions on mainframe computers.

word processing control function character One of several unique characters used to format text for correspondence and communications. (T)

word processor A desktop or portable device into which text can be entered and stored along with format control characters. Stored text can be moved, copied, deleted, altered, added to, displayed, and printed, usually in various formats and fonts.

Note: Word processors usually perform other operations such as checking spelling against a stored dictionary.

word size (1) The number of characters in a word. (T) (2) Synonymous with word length.

word space The space placed between words in a line. Synonymous with interword blank, interword space.

word time In a storage device that provides serial access to storage locations, the time interval between the appearance of corresponding parts of successive words. (A)

word underscore character (WUS) A word processing control that causes the word immediately preceding it to be underscored.

word wrap (1) A function that enables text entered after the last character position on a line to be placed automatically on the next line. (T) (A) (2) Synonymous with wraparound *(2)*.

work area (1) An area reserved for temporary storage of data that are to be operated on. (2) An area in which devices such as displays, keyboards, and printers are located. (3) In SAA Basic Common User Access architecture, the main part of a panel located between the panel title and the message area. (4) In ACF/TCAM, an area of storage associated with an application program that receives messages or records transferred to the application program from ACF/TCAM by GET or READ macroinstructions, and from which messages or records are transferred to ACF/TCAM by PUT or WRITE macroinstructions. (5) See also working space.

work entry An entry in a subsystem description that specifies a source from which jobs can be accepted for execution in the subsystem.

work factor In computer security, an estimate of the resources required to defeat a security measure.

work file (1) A file used for temporary storage of data being processed. (2) In sorting, an intermediate file used for temporary storage of data between phases. (3) See also work volume.

Workflow Management A feature of the Folder Application Facility that automatically distributes documents needing processing to system users.

working area (1) On a screen, area where a user can enter data other than commands. See also command area. (2) Synonym for work space. (T)

working directory Synonym for current directory.

working diskette A diskette to which files are copied from another diskette for use in everyday operation. Synonymous with operational diskette.

working display See basic working display.

working set (1) The set of a user's pages that must be active in order to avoid excessive paging. (2) The amount of real storage required for paging in order to avoid a thrashing condition. (3) In the ImagePlus system, all the pages in the workstation at any given time.

working space (1) A portion of storage used by a computer program to hold data temporarily. Synonymous with working area. (T) (2) Synonym for work space. (A)

working storage Synonym for temporary storage, working space.

Working-Storage Section In COBOL, the section of the Data Division that describes working storage data items, composed either of noncontiguous items or working storage records or of both.

work load manager A part of the system resources manager that allows an installation to determine the performance that any group of users will receive,

monitors the workload, and schedules resources accordingly.

work on behalf of In the AS/400 system, pertaining to the function that allows users to temporarily access documents, folders, or mail that another user is authorized to except those items that are marked personal. Tasks performed by a user working on another user's behalf produce the same results as if the original user performed the task; for example, if user A creates a new object while working on behalf of user B, user B is the owner of the object.

work session (1) A session initiated by an operator when the logon sequence has been successfully completed and ending when the operator logs off. An inquiry session may be included as part of the work session. See also inquiry session, session. (2) The time during which an operator uses a workstation utility program.

work session control record The first record in the chain of records of each work session in the transaction file.

work-session-initiation indicator (IW) The indicator that is set when an operator starts a WSU program.

work-session-initiation processing level The processing level that occurs once when an operator starts a workstation utility program. For the first display station operator, the work session begins when the job has been started.

work slice In DPCX, a specific amount of processing time, determined by a maximum number of instructions, that is allocated to a task before the task is suspended and another is dispatched.

work space (1) That portion of main storage that is used by a computer program for temporary storage of data. Synonymous with working space. (I) (A) (2) In the AS/400 system, an area of the disk storage used temporarily by licensed programs to hold work data while the licensed programs are running.

work stack (1) A list constructed and maintained so that the next information to be retrieved is the most recently stored information in the list, that is, a last-in-first-out (LIFO) or pushdown list. (2) An area of unprotected main storage allocated to each task and used by the programs executed by that task.

workstation (1) A functional unit at which a user works. A workstation often has some processing capability. (T) (2) One or more programmable or nonprogrammable devices that allow a user to do work. See also programmable workstation, nonprogrammable workstation. (3) A terminal or microcomputer, usually one that is connected to a mainframe or to a network, at which a user can perform applications. (4) See dependent workstation, stand-alone workstation. (5) See also data processing station, programmable workstation. See Figure 168.

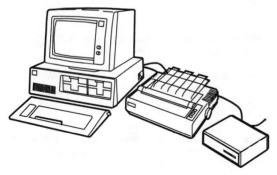

Figure 168. Workstation

workstation address (1) In the AS/400 system, a number used in a configuration file to identify a workstation attached to a computer port. (2) In the AS/400 system, the address to which the switches on a workstation are set, or the internal address assumed by the system, if no address is specified.

workstation controller (WSC) (1) A device that provides for a direct connection of local workstations to the system. (2) In the AS/400 system, an I/O controller card in the card enclosure that provides the direct connection of local workstations to the system.

workstation data management The part of the System Support Program Product that enables a program to present data on a display screen by providing a string of data fields and a format name.

workstation entry In the AS/400 and System/38, an entry in a subsystem description that specifies the workstations from which users can sign on to the subsystem or from which interactive jobs can transfer to the subsystem.

workstation message queue In System/38, a message queue associated with a particular workstation and that is used for sending and receiving messages sent to the workstation.

workstation user profile In the AS/400 and System/38, the system-supplied user profile that has the authority required by workstation operators.

workstation utility (WSU) The part of the Utilities Program Product that helps in writing programs for data entry, editing, and inquiry.

work unit The amount of data transferred from ACF/TCAM to an application program by a single

GET or READ macroinstruction or transferred from an application program to the MCP by a single PUT or WRITE macroinstruction. A work unit may be a message or a record.

work volume A volume made available to the system to provide storage space for temporary files or data sets at peak loads.

world coordinates (1) A device-independent Cartesian coordinate system used by the application program for specifying graphical input and output. (I) (A) (2) In System/38 graphics, the coordinates, used as reference points, of which a window forms a part. (3) In GDDM, the user-defined set of coordinates that define the graphics window, and that serve as the horizontal and vertical range for all graphics primitives within the graphics window. (4) In AIX graphics, the user-defined coordinate system in which an image is described. Modeling commands are used to position primitives in world space. Viewing and projection transformations define the mapping of the world space to screen space. See also modeling coordinates, primitive coordinates, screen coordinates, transformation. Synonymous with world space. (5) See also user coordinate.

world knowledge Knowledge about a domain of interest. (T)

world space Synonym for world coordinates.

worm (1) In computer security, a program that places copies of itself into connected systems and that may do damage or waste resources. (2) In computer security, malicious logic that consumes storage. (3) See also attack. (4) A copy protection program that destroys stored data when it detects an illegally copied program.

WORM Write-once-read-many; usually in the context of optical discs. (A)

WPM Words per minute. A common measure of speed in telegraph systems.

WP/36 A System/36 licensed program that can be used for creating, revising, browsing, and printing documents that are produced in an office environment.

wrap In general, to go from the maximum to the minimum in computer storage; for example, the continuation of an operation from the maximum value in storage to the first minimal value.

wraparound (1) In display-based word processing equipment, the automatic disposition of a printable line of text onto two or more display lines, necessitated by the horizontal limits of the display. (T) (2) The continuation of an operation from the maximum addressable location in storage to the first addressable location. (3) The continuation of register addresses from the highest register address to the lowest. (4) The movement of the point of reference in a file from the end of one line to the beginning of the next, or from one end of a file to the other. (5) See horizontal wraparound, vertical wraparound.

wrap capability The ability to directly connect the input and output lines of a modem.

wrap connector A test connector that connects the output of a controller or cable to the input of the controller or cable. A wrap test then verifies that the controller or cable output and input circuits are working correctly.

wrap count In the NetView program, the number of events that can be retained on the database for a specific resource or the number of alerts that are retained on the database.

wrapping (1) In the IBM 8100 Information System, a manual operation at a loop wiring concentrator (LWC) or a loop station connector (LSC) at two points on a loop, performed in order to isolate a faulty section of the main loop cable. (2) In a star/ring network, the configuring of wiring concentrators to bypass a fault in such a way that the logical order of nodes on the ring is not changed.

wrap plug In an ESCON environment, a type of duplex connector used to wrap the optical output signal of a device directly to the optical input. Contrast with protective plug.

wrap test (1) A test that checks attachment or control unit circuitry without checking the mechanism itself by returning the output of the mechanism as input; for example, when unrecoverable communication adapter or machine errors occur, a wrap test can transmit a specific character pattern to or through the modem in a loop and then compare the character pattern received with the pattern transmitted. (2) A diagnostic test that returns the output of a device as input.

WRE Waiting request element.

writable character generation module (WCGM) In the 3800 Printing Subsystem, a 64-position portion of character generation storage that holds the scan elements of a single character set. There are two WCGMs in the basic 3800. Optional added storage provides two more WCGMs.

writable control storage (WCS) In the 3800 Printing Subsystem, printer storage into which data can be entered, held, and retrieved. Writable control storage

contains microcode instructions and other control information; for example, the print buffer.

write To make a permanent or transient recording of data in a storage device or on a data medium. (I) (A)

write access In computer security, permission to write to an object.

write back cache In AIX Enhanced X-Windows, graphics contexts cached by the library to allow updating the cache locations only during a write operation.

write control character reset In the 3270 Information Display System, the resetting of the characteristics of a device to its defined default values.

write control character (WCC) (1) A control character that follows a write command in the 3270 data stream and provides control information for executing display and printer functions. (2) A character used in conjunction with a write-type command to specify that a particular operation, or combination of operations, is to be performed at a display station or printer.

write cycle time The minimum time interval between starts of successive write cycles of a storage device that has separate reading and writing cycles. (I) (A)

write enable To install a write-enable ring in a tape reel. Such a reel is write enabled. A reel with the ring removed is protected.

write-enable ring A device installed in a tape reel to permit writing on the tape. A tape mounted on a tape unit without the ring in position is protected; writing to the tape cannot occur.

write-enable sensor A device that detects if the write-enable ring is present in the bottom of the tape reel.

write head A head that can only write.

write inhibit In MSS, an attribute of a mass storage volume that prevents writing on the mass storage volume. Synonymous with read-only.

write lock In the AIX operating system, a lock that prevents any other process from setting a read lock or a write lock on any part of the protected area. Contrast with read lock.

write mask In the AIX operating system, a bit mask that controls write access to the bitplanes, one bit for each bitplane of the frame buffer. During any drawing operation, only those planes enabled by a 1 (one) in the bit mask can be altered. Planes set to 0 (zero) are marked read only.

write once/read many (WORM) Pertaining to an optical disc that once written to, cannot be over-written. Storage capacity ranges from 400MB to 3.2GB. Present technology allows only one side to be read at a time; to access the other side, the disc must be flipped over.

write operation An output operation that sends a processed record to an output device or output file.

write protection Restriction of writing into a data set, file, or storage area by a user or program not author-ized to do so.

write-protection label A removable label that by its presence or absence on a diskette prevents writing on the diskette.

Note: Some diskettes cannot be written on when the label is attached; other diskettes cannot be written on when the label is removed.

write-protect notch A device that allows the recording of data on a diskette; prerecorded data is erased.

write-protect tab A device that is placed over the write-protect notch on a diskette to prevent the recording of data so that prerecorded data will not be erased. See Figure 169.

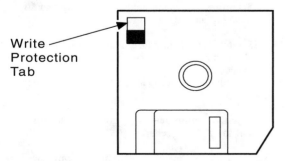

Figure 169. Write-Protect Tab

writer (1) In the AS/400 and System/38, the part of the operating system spooling support that writes spooled files to an output device independently of the program that produced the output. (2) In remote job

entry (RJEF), a program that receives output data from the host system. (3) See output writer.

write-to-operator (WTO) An optional user-coded service that allows a message to be written to the system console operator informing the operator of errors and unusual system conditions that may need to be corrected.

write verification A mode in which the system auto-matically performs a read operation after performing a write operation. It then compares the data to ensure they are the same.

writing The action of making a permanent or tran-sient recording of data in a storage device or on a data medium. (I) (A)

writing line An imaginary line along which characters can be displayed, printed, or typed.

writing position The location at which the next char-acter can be displayed, printed, or typed.

writing task In OS/VS, a job management task con-trolling transfer to a specified output device of system messages and SYSOUT data sets from a direct access volume on which they were first written. Contrast with reading task.

WS Wide shot.

WSC Workstation controller.

WSU Work station utility.

WSU display A display selected by the workstation utility display command key that allows operators to select a display, review a record, or end a work session.

WTO Write-to-operator.

WUS Word underscore character.

WXTRN Weak external reference.

WYSIWYG (1) What-you-see-is-what-you-get. A capability of a text editor to continually display pages exactly as they will be printed. (2) In word proc-essing and desktop publishing, a capability that allows a user to display page characteristics such as fonts, type size, and format as they will appear when they are printed.

X

XA Extended architecture.

X-address In MSS, the coordinate of a unique physical cell address that indicates the position of a particular cartridge cell to the right of the left accessor garage. See also Y-address, Z-address.

X axis (1) In a system of coordinates, the axis of the first component used to locate points in space. See also Y axis, Z axis. (2) In printing, an axis perpendicular to the direction in which the paper moves through the printer. See also Y axis.

XCA External communication adapter.

X-datum line An imaginary line used as a reference edge along the top edge of a punch card, that is, a line along the edge nearest the twelve-punch row of a Hollerith card.

XENIX (Trademark of Microsoft Corporation with enhancements by the University of California at Berkeley) An operating system based on UNIX (Trademark of AT&T Bell Laboratories) that provides multitasking of concurrent background and foreground application programs. See also IBM XENIX.

XI X.25 SNA Interconnection.

XID (1) Exchange station ID. (2) Exchange identification.

XMIT Transmit.

X-off Transmitter off.

X-on Transmitter on.

XOR In the IBM LinkWay product, a method of placing objects on the screen that mixes the object's color pixels with the background color pixels, resulting in different colors. When a color is "XORed" onto an identical color, the two cancel out each other and the color disappears.

Xp orientation In printing, the orientation of a font along the X-axis.

XPT External page table.

x-punch Synonym for eleven-punch.

XRF Extended recovery facility.

X.21 An International Telegraph and Telephone Consultative Committee (CCITT) recommendation for a general-purpose interface between data terminal equipment and data circuit-terminating equipment for synchronous operations on a public data network.

X.21 bis An International Telegraph and Telephone Consultative Committee (CCITT) interim recommendation that defines the connection of data terminal equipment (DTE) to an X.21 (public data) network using V-series interchange circuits such as those defined by CCITT V.24 and CCITT V.35.

X.21 communication adapter A communication adapter that can combine and send information on one line at speeds up to 64 kbps, and that conforms to CCITT X.21 standards.

X.21 feature A feature that allows a system to be connected to an X.21 network.

X.25 An International Telegraph and Telephone Consultative Committee (CCITT) recommendation for the interface between data terminal equipment and packet-switched data networks. See also packet switching.

X.25 feature A feature that allows a system to be connected to an X.25 network.

X.25 interface An interface consisting of a data terminal equipment (DTE) and a data circuit-terminating equipment (DCE) in communication over a link using the procedures described in the CCITT Recommendation X.25.

X.25 native equipment The non-SNA devices that support the X.25 procedures.

X.25 NCP Packet Switching Interface An IBM-licensed program that allows SNA users to communicate over packet switched data networks that have interfaces complying with Recommendation X.25 (Geneva 1980) of the International Telegraph and Telephone Consultative Committee (CCITT). It allows SNA programs to communicate with SNA equipment or with non-SNA equipment over such networks.

X.25 protocol The connection-mode network service that the CCITT specifies in Recommendation X.25.

X.25_1980 CCITT Recommendation X.25 (Geneva, 1980)

X.25_1984 CCITT Recommendation X.25 (Malaga-Torremolinos, 1984)

X.75 A standard that defines ways of connecting two X.25 networks.

Y

Y-address In MSS, the coordinate of a unique physical cell address that indicates the position of a particular cartridge cell above the bottom row of cells. See also X-address, Z-address.

Y axis (1) In a system of coordinates, the second component that is utilized to locate points in space. See also X axis, Z axis. (2) In printing, an axis parallel with the direction in which the paper moves through the printer. See also X axis.

Y/C Color image encoding scheme that separates luminance (Y) from phase encoded chroma (C). Synonymous with S-video.

Y-datum line An imaginary line used as a reference edge passing along the right edge of a punch card at right angles to the X-datum line. (A)

Y-disk An extension of the CMS system disk.

Yellow Book standards See compact disc-read-only memory (CD-ROM).

Yes In SAA Advanced Common User Access architecture, a push button used in messages to provide a positive response to a question.

YIQ Image encoding scheme similar to YUV that selects the direction of the two color axes, I and Q, to align with natural images. As an average, the I signal bears much more information than the Q signal. YIQ is used in the NTSC video standard.

Yp orientation In printing, the orientation of a font along the Y axis.

y-punch Synonym for twelve-punch.

YUV A color image encoding scheme that separates luminance (Y) and two color signals: red minus Y (U), and blue minus Y (V). Transmission of YUV can take advantage of the eye's greater sensitivity to luminance detail than color detail.

Z

Z Characteristic impedance.

Z-address In MSS, the coordinate of a unique physical cell address that indicates the wall on which a particular cartridge cell is located. See also X-address, Y-address.

ZAP disk The virtual disk in the VM operating system that contains the user-written modifications to VTAM code. See also BASE disk, DELTA disk, MERGE disk, RUN disk.

Z axis In a system of coordinates, the third component used to locate points in space. See also X axis, Y axis.

z-buffer In the AIX operating system, the region of memory that stores z-values, which represent the depth, or distance from the viewer's eye to the pixel.

z-buffering In AIX 3D computer graphics, removing hidden lines and hidden surfaces. If z-buffering is enabled, each pixel stores a depth value and a color value. Whenever a drawing routine tries to update a pixel, it first checks the current pixel's "depth" or "z-value" and only updates that pixel with new values if the new pixel is closer than the current pixel.

Z-disk An extension of the CMS system disk.

zero (1) In data processing, the number that, when added to or subtracted from any other number, does not alter the value of the other number. Zero may have different representations in computers, such as positively or negatively signed zero (which may result from subtracting a signed number from itself) and floating-point zero (in which the fixed point part is zero while the exponent in the floating-point representation may vary). (I) (A) (2) See leading zero, trailing zero.

zero address instruction A machine instruction that has no address part; for example, certain instructions for a stack machine. (T)

zerofill (1) To fill unused storage locations with the representation of the character denoting zero. (T) (2) Synonymous with zeroize.

zeroize Synonym for zerofill.

zero-length buffer In ACF/TCAM, a buffer that is sent to the message handler to indicate that there is an error on the line. If user code is not executed correctly with a zero-length buffer, the programmer must check for zero length and branch around the code that does not execute correctly.

zero-level address Synonym for immediate address.

zero punch A punch in the third row from the top of a Hollerith card. (A)

zeros-complemented transition coding A method of coding data by reversing the state of the transmitted signal for each 0 bit in the data stream.

zero suppression (1) The elimination from a numeral of zeros that have no significance in the numeral. Zeros that have no significance include those to the left of the nonzero digits in the integral part of a numeral and those to the right of the nonzero digits in the fractional part. (I) (A) (2) On a calculator, the process by which unwanted zeros are omitted from the printed or displayed result of a calculation. (T) (3) The substitution of blanks for leading zeros in a number; for example, 00057 becomes 57 when using zero suppression.

zero transmission level reference point An arbitrarily chosen point in a circuit to which all relative transmission levels are referred. The transmission level at the transmitting switchboard is frequently taken as the zero transmission level reference point. See also relative transmission level.

z-fold paper Synonym for fanfold paper. (T)

Z force The pressure sensitivity of a touch screen.

Z format In the AIX operating system, the format of a pixmap organized as a set of pixel values in scanline order. See XY format.

zig-zag fold paper Synonym for fanfold paper. (A)

zombie process In the AIX system, an ended process whose entry remains in the process table, but to which a user or kernel space is not allocated.

zone (1) In ACF/TCAM, a portion of disk records that resides in an algebraic quarter of a reusable disk message queues data set. (2) See landing zone, loading zone.

zone boundary In ACF/TCAM, any of four disk records, one at each of the following positions in a reusable disk message queues data set: the first, the

1/4, the 1/2, and the 3/4 records through the entire data set.

zoned decimal format A format for representing numbers in which the digit is contained in bits 4 through 7 and the sign is contained in bits 0 through 3 of the least significant byte; bits 0 through 3 of all other bytes contain 1's (hex F); for example, in zoned decimal format, the decimal value of +123 is represented as 1111 0001 1111 0010 1100 0011. Synonymous with unpacked decimal format. Contrast with packed decimal format.

zoned field A field that contains data in the zoned decimal format.

zone of authority In the AIX operating system, the set of names managed by a single name server.

zone punch (1) A hole punched in one of the upper three card rows of a twelve-row punch card. (I) (A) (2) Contrast with digit punch. See Figure 170.

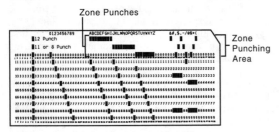

Figure 170. Zone Punches

zone-setting In the CMS Editor, the specification of a number range to indicate the positions that can be scanned and edited within each data line.

zone width The number of positions to the left of the right margin in which to end words.

zoom In SAA usage, to progressively increase or decrease the size of a part of an image on a screen or in a window. See also Maximize, Minimize, Size.

zoom factor A multiplier to determine the amount of enlargement of a specified rectangle on the screen. The x zoom factor determines the enlargement in the x direction; the y zoom factor determines the enlargement in the y direction.

zoom in An optical camera change whereby the camera appears to approach the subject it is shooting.

zooming (1) The progressive scaling of an entire display image in order to give the visual impression of movement of all or part of a display group toward or away from an observer. (I) (A) (2) In the IBM ImagePlus system, the action of magnifying a selected portion of the displayed image area for enhanced viewing.

zoom out In multimedia applications, an optical camera change whereby the camera appears to back up from the subject it is shooting.

Numerics

100% principle In a conceptual schema language, all general, static, and dynamic rules of the universe of discourse that are described in the conceptual schema.

12-hour clock A clock that keeps time from 12:00 a.m. (midnight) to 12:00 p.m. (noon), and from 12:00 p.m. (noon) to 12:00 a.m. (midnight). Compare with 24-hour clock.

1024-byte format A format for diskette 2D diskettes with 1024 bytes per sector and 8 sectors per track.

1255 Magnetic Character Reader A device that reads documents printed with magnetic ink characters.

128-byte format A format for diskette 1 diskettes with 128 bytes per sector and 26 sectors per track.

1/3 octave band In acoustics, the frequency interval between two frequencies having a ratio of $(2/1)^{1/3}$.

2-wire coupler A type of coupler that has two wires attached to it. The two wires connect to one telephone line.

24-hour clock A clock that keeps time from 0000 (midnight) to 1200 (noon), and from 1200 (noon) to 2400 (midnight). Compare with 12-hour clock.

256-byte format A format for diskette 2D diskettes with 256 bytes per sector and 26 sectors per track.

3D modeling Presenting material in a three-dimensional format.

31-bit storage addressing The storage address structure available in an MVS/XA* operating system.

3164 ASCII Color Display Station A general purpose asynchronous ASCII/ISO display station that is designed to attach to both IBM and non-IBM systems.

3180 display station A display station that uses the 5250 data stream.

3:2 pulldown A method for overcoming the incompatibility of film and video frame rates when con-

verting or transferring film to video. It involves displaying 24 frames/second motion picture film on a 30 frames/second (interlaced) television system. One film frame is shown for three television fields and the next frame is shown for two television fields. Thus, two of every five video frames consist of fields that contain information from two different film frames. Those video frames are called interfield frames. See also interfield frame.

3270 attention field A field on a display screen that contains a null, a space, or an ampersand in the first position. The field can be selected using the Cursor Select key, which causes data to be sent to the host system.

3270 BSC Support Subsystem The subsystem that provides program-to-program communication with IMS/VS, CICS/VS, TSO, VM, or system application programs using 3270 BSC protocols, and provides support for the BSC portion of the 3270 Device Emulation feature.

3270 data stream Data being transferred from or to an allocated primary or tertiary device, or to the host system, as a continuous stream of data and 3270 Information Display System control elements in character form.

3270 data stream compatibility (DSC) In the IBM 8100 Information System, the facility that provides access to System/370 applications that communicate with 3270 Information Display System terminals.

3270 device emulation In the AS/400 system and System/36, the operating system support that allows an AS/400 system to appear as a 3274 Control Unit in a BSC multipoint network or an SNA network. See also 3270 display emulation, 3270 printer emulation.

3270 display emulation In the AS/400 system, the function of the operating system 3270 device emulation support that converts 3270 data streams intended for a 3278 display station into data streams that can be recognized by a display station attached to the AS/400 system.

3270 emulation The use of a program that allows a device or system such as a personal computer or a System/38 to operate in conjunction with a host system as if it were a 3270-series display station or control unit. See device emulation, display emulation, printer emulation. See also terminal emulator.

3270 printer emulation In the AS/400 system, the function of the operating system IBM 3270 device emulation support that converts 3270, DSC, and SCS data streams intended for a 328X printer into data streams that can be recognized by a printer attached to the AS/400 system.

3270 SNA Support Subsystem The subsystem that provides support for the SNA portion of the 3270 Device Emulation feature.

3276 cluster The IBM 3276 Control Unit Display Station and any IBM 3278 Display Stations and 3287 Printers attached to it.

3600 Finance Communication System The financial transaction products and other data processing products that together form a data processing subsystem with the 3601 Finance Communication Controllers and their attached terminals and the application programs that execute in the 3601 Finance Communication Controllers.

3650 Retail Store System A complex of retail-store transaction products and other processing products that together form a data processing subsystem with the 3651 Store Controllers, their attached terminals, and the application programs that execute in the 3651 Store Controllers.

370 mode See System/370 mode.

370-XA mode A virtual machine operating mode in which System/370-Extended Architecture functions are simulated. Contrast with System/370 mode.

3850 Mass Storage System (MSS) A system that extends virtual storage capacity to direct access storage and extends a user's online data-storage capacity to as much as 472 billion characters of information.

3851 Mass Storage Facility (MSF) The component of a 3850 Mass Storage System that contains the data cartridges and facilities for accessing the magnetic tape contained on them.

4-wire coupler A type of coupler that has four wires attached to it. The four wires connect to two telephone lines.

4700 Support Facility The function of the NetView hardware monitor that provides support for the IBM 3600 and 4700 Finance Communication Systems.

512-byte format A format for diskette 1 diskettes with 512 bytes per sector and 8 sectors per track.

5208 Link Protocol Converter In the AS/400 system, a device that attaches asynchronous-attached workstations using ASCII encoding to the system as if they were 5250 workstations. Compare with 5209 Link Protocol Converter.

5209 Link Protocol Converter In the AS/400 system, a device that attaches 327x workstations to the system as if they were 5250 workstations. Compare with 5208 Link Protocol Converter.

5250 emulation In the AS/400 system, any one of many licensed programs that allow a personal computer to perform like a 5250 display station or printer, and use the functions of an AS/400 system.

5394 Remote Control Unit A control unit that attaches up to sixteen 5250 display stations and printers.

77-level-description entry In COBOL, a data description entry that describes a noncontiguous data item with the level-number 77.

8100/DPCX system The combination of the 8100 Information System hardware with the DPCX operating system.

8100 Information System A collection of processors and devices that can be connected to form a system for general use. 8100 Information Systems can be used stand-alone, connected to other 8100 Information Systems, and connected to a System/370 computing system.